Fodor's

GERMANY

26th Edition

Fodor's Travel Publications   New York, Toronto, London, Sydney, Auckland

www.fodors.com

FODOR'S GERMANY

Editors: Salwa Jabado, *lead editor;* Rachel Klein

Editorial Contributors: Bethany Beckerlegge, Andrew Collins
Writers: Leonie Adeane, Kimberly Bradley, Lee A. Evans, Sarah Harman, Jeff Kavanagh, Ben Knight, David Levitz, Monica McCollum, Catherine C. Moser, Giulia Pines, Dominika Polatin, Tania Ralli, Paul Wheatley

Production Editor: Jennifer DePrima
Maps & Illustrations: Mark Stroud and David Lindroth, *cartographers;* Bob Blake, Rebecca Baer, *map editors;* William Wu, *information graphics*
Design: Fabrizio La Rocca, *creative director;* Guido Caroti, *art director;* Tina Malaney, Nora Rosansky, Chie Ushio, Jessica Walsh, *designers;* Melanie Marin, *associate director of photography*
Cover Photo: (Vineyard, Mosel): Sodapix/F1Online/photolibrary.com
Production Manager: Angela L. McLean

COPYRIGHT

26th Edition

ISBN 978–0–679–00959–7

ISSN 1525–5034

SPECIAL SALES

This book is available at special discounts for bulk purchases for sales promotions or premiums. Special editions, including personalized covers, excerpts of existing books, and corporate imprints, can be created in large quantities for special needs. For more information, write to Special Markets/Premium Sales, 1745 Broadway, MD 3-2, New York, NY 10019, or e-mail specialmarkets@randomhouse.com.

AN IMPORTANT TIP & AN INVITATION

Although all prices, opening times, and other details in this book are based on information supplied to us at press time, changes occur all the time in the travel world, and Fodor's cannot accept responsibility for facts that become outdated or for inadvertent errors or omissions. So **always confirm information when it matters**, especially if you're making a detour to visit a specific place. Your experiences—positive and negative— matter to us. If we have missed or misstated something, **please write to us.** Share your opinion instantly through our online feedback center at fodors.com/contact-us.

PRINTED IN COLOMBIA

10 9 8 7 6 5 4 3

CONTENTS

Fodor's Features

MAPS

ABOUT
THIS BOOK

Our Ratings

At Fodor's, we spend considerable time choosing the best places in a destination so you don't have to. By default, anything we recommend in this book is worth visiting. But some sights, properties, and experiences are so great that we've recognized them with additional accolades. Orange **Fodor's Choice** stars indicate our top recommendations; black stars highlight places we deem **Highly Recommended**; and **Best Bets** call attention to top properties in various categories. Disagree with any of our choices? Care to nominate a new place? Visit our feedback center at www.fodors.com/feedback.

> For expanded hotel reviews, visit **Fodors.com**

Hotels

Hotels have private bath, phone, and TV, and do not offer meals unless we specify that in the review. We always list facilities but not whether you'll be charged an extra fee to use them.

Restaurants

Unless we state otherwise, restaurants are open for lunch and dinner daily. We mention dress only when there's a specific requirement and reservations only when they're essential or not accepted—it's always best to book ahead.

Credit Cards

We assume that restaurants and hotels accept credit cards. If not, we'll note it in the review.

Budget Well

Hotel and restaurant price categories from ¢ to $$$$ are defined in the opening pages of the respective chapters. For attractions, we always give standard adult admission fees; reductions are usually available for children, students, and senior citizens.

Listings
- ★ Fodor's Choice
- ★ Highly recommended
- ⊠ Physical address
- ✛ Directions or Map coordinates
- ⌂ Mailing address
- ☎ Telephone
- 🖶 Fax
- ⊕ On the Web

- ✎ E-mail
- 🎫 Admission fee
- ☉ Open/closed times
- Ⓜ Metro stations
- ⊟ No credit cards

Hotels & Restaurants
- ⊡ Hotel
- ⇱ Number of rooms
- ⚲ Facilities
- ⏐⊙⏐ Meal plans
- ✕ Restaurant
- ⚲ Reservations
- ⚲ Dress code
- ⤷ Smoking

Outdoors
- ⚑ Golf
- ⚠ Camping

Other
- ☺ Family-friendly
- ⇨ See also
- ⊠ Branch address
- ☞ Take note

Experience
Germany

GERMANY TODAY

About the size of Montana but home to Western Europe's largest population, Germany is in many ways a land of contradictions. The land of "Dichter und Denker" ("poets and thinkers") is also one of the world's leading export countries, specializing in mechanical equipment, vehicles, chemicals, and household goods. It's a country that is both deeply conservative, valuing tradition, hard work, precision, and fiscal responsibility, and one of the world's most liberal countries, with a generous social welfare state, a strongly held commitment to environmentalism, and a postwar determination to combat xenophobia. But Germany, which reunited 22 years ago after 45 years of division, is also a country in transition. The longstanding, unwritten taboo against displaying German flags lifted during the 2006 World Cup, and as the horrors of World War II, though not forgotten, recede, the country is in the process of working out a new relationship with itself and its neighbors.

Integration

During the "Wirtschaftswunder," the postwar economic boom of the 1950s and 1960s, West Germany invited "guest workers" from Italy, Greece, and above all Turkey to help in the rebuilding of the country. Because the Germans assumed these guest workers would return home, they provided little in the way of cultural integration policies. But the guest workers, usually manual workers from the countryside with little formal education, often did not return to the economically depressed regions they had come from. Instead, they brought wives and family members to join them and settled in Germany, often forming parallel societies cut off from mainstream German life. Unlike the United States, Germany is historically a land of emigrants, not immigrants, and the country has fumbled when it comes to successful integration. Today, Germany's largest immigrant group is Turkish. In fact, Berlin is the largest Turkish city after Istanbul. The Germans are now trying to redress the lack of a coherent integration policy that has led to a situation in which Turkish communities live in cultural isolation, and third- or fourth-generation German Turks sometimes do not speak German. These Turkish communities are now an indelible part of the German society—one blond-hair, blue-eyed German soldier deployed to Afghanistan famously said that the thing he missed most about home was the *döner* kebab, the ubiquitous Turkish-German fast-food dish. But young Turkish-Germans face incommensurate hurdles to professional and scholastic success. As the German population ages, the country is facing a population crisis, and a more inclusive, functional approach to immigration will be increasingly important.

Worldwide Recession

Germany, the world's fourth-largest economy, was the world's largest exporter until 2009, when China overtook it. The recession hit Germany hard, though thanks to a strong social network, the unemployed and underemployed did not suffer on the level we are used to in the United States. In Germany, losing your job does not mean you lose your health insurance, and the unemployed receive financial help from the state to meet housing payments and other basic expenses. Germany is particularly strong when it comes to high-tech engineering and automotive exports, with 60% of their goods going to other European countries, though debt incurred by the extensive and expensive rebuilding of the former East after reunification is a

source of concern to many in this traditional, don't-spend-more-than-you-earn culture. By far the most important economy in the European Union, Germany has a strong voice in setting the EU's economic agenda and has traditionally acted as a kind of rich uncle that other countries turn to when they need an economic bailout. With the Greek financial crisis in early 2010, Chancellor Angela Merkel made waves by being the first German chancellor to insist on putting Germany's economic interests first, though in the end Germany and France came up with measures to rescue the Greek economy from collapse.

Privacy, Please!

The Germans are not big fans of Facebook. With good reason: with recent experiences of life in a police state under both the Nazi regime and the East German regime, they don't like the idea of anyone collecting personal information about them. Germany has some of the most extensive data privacy laws in the world, with everything from credit card numbers to medical histories strictly protected.

To the Left, to the Left

By American standards, German politics are distinctly left-leaning. Germany's foreign minister, Guido Westerwelle, and the mayor of Berlin are both openly gay. As Klaus Wowereit, Berlin's mayor, famously said in his public coming-out speech, "I'm gay, and it's good that way." The Green Party is a powerful player in the country's coalition government, and has enacted wide-reaching environmental reform in the past 30 years. One thing that's important to know is that the Germans don't have a two-party system; rather they have several important parties, and these must form alliances after elections to pass initiatives. Thus, there's an emphasis on cooperation and deal making, sometimes (but not always) pairing odd bedfellows. A "Red-Green" (or "stoplight") coalition between the Green Party and the socialist SPD held power from 1998 to 2002; since then, there has been a steady move to the center-right in Germany, with recent reforms curtailing some social welfare benefits and ecological reforms. In 2005, Germany elected the first female chancellor, center-right Christian Democratic party member Angela Merkel. A politician from the former East Germany who speaks Russian, Merkel has enjoyed consistent if not overwhelming popularity and easily won reelection in 2009.

Renew, Recycle, Reuse

The Green Party, founded in 1980, is an established and important player in the German government. This makes sense for an extremely environmentally conscious country, 60% of whose citizens are against nuclear energy. But that's not all. Thanks to aggressive government legislation initiated by the Greens in the past decades, Germany today is a leader in green energy technology and use—in 2010, 10% of all energy used in Germany came from renewable sources. Importantly, the move to renewable electricity sources is paid for entirely by electricity consumers. Germans pay a hugely popular across-the-board renewable energy surcharge to fund these initiatives, which adds about 1% to the average customer's bill. Thanks to these initiatives, more than 15% of the electricity you use in your hotel room (and everywhere else in the country) comes from renewable resources.

WHAT'S WHERE

The following numbers refer to chapter numbers.

2 Munich. Beautiful Munich boasts wonderful opera, theater, museums, and churches—and the city's chic residents dress their best to visit them. This city also has lovely outdoor spaces, from parks, beer gardens, and cafés, to the famous Oktoberfest grounds.

3 The Bavarian Alps. Majestic peaks, lush green pastures, and frescoed houses brightened by flowers make for one of Germany's most photogenic regions. Quaint villages like Mittenwald, Garmisch-Partenkirchen, Oberammergau, and Berchtesgaden have preserved their charming historic architecture. Nature is the prime attraction here, with the country's finest hiking and skiing.

4 The Romantic Road. The Romantische Strasse is more than 355 km (220 mi) of soaring castles, medieval villages, *fachwerk* (half-timber) houses, and imposing churches, all set against a pastoral backdrop. Winding its way from Würzburg to Füssen, it features such top destinations as Rothenburg-ob-der-Tauber and Schloss Neuschwanstein, King Ludwig II's fantastical castle.

5 Franconia and the German Danube. Thanks to the centuries-old success of craftsmanship and trade, Franconia is a proud, independent-minded region in northern Bavaria. Franconia is home to historic Nürnberg, the well-preserved medieval jewel-box town of Bamberg, and Bayreuth, where Wagner lived and composed.

6 The Bodensee. The sunniest region in the country, the Bodensee (Lake Constance) itself is the highlight. The region is surrounded by beautiful mountains, and the dense natural surroundings offer an enchanting contrast to the picture-perfect towns and manicured gardens.

7 The Black Forest. Synonymous with cuckoo clocks and primeval woodland that is great for hiking, the Black Forest includes the historic university town of Freiburg—one of the most colorful and hippest student cities in Germany—and proud and elegant Baden-Baden, with its long tradition of spas and casinos.

8 Heidelberg and the Neckar Valley. This medieval town is quintessential Germany, full of cobblestone alleys, half-timber houses, vineyards, castles, wine pubs, and Germany's oldest university.

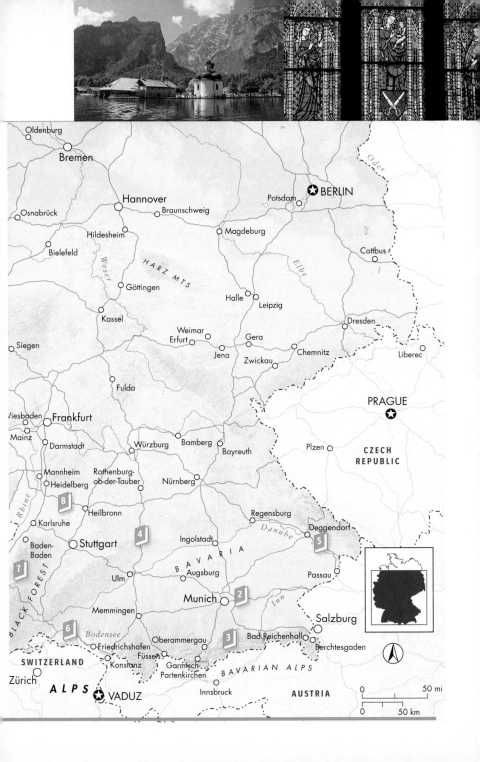

WHAT'S WHERE

9 Frankfurt. Nicknamed "Mainhattan" because it is the only German city with appreciable skyscrapers, Frankfurt is Germany's financial center and transportation hub.

10 The Pfalz and Rhine Terrace. Wine reigns supreme here. Bacchanalian festivals pepper the calendar between May and October, and wineries welcome drop-ins for tastings year-round. Three great cathedrals are found in Worms, Speyer, and Mainz.

11 The Rhineland. The region along the mighty Rhine River is one of the most dynamic in all of Europe. Fascinating cities such as Köln (Cologne), steeped in Roman and medieval history, offer stunning symbols of Gothic architecture, such as the Kölner Dom. Visit during Karneval for boisterous celebrations.

12 The Fairy-Tale Road. The Märchenstrasse, stretching 600 km (370 mi) between Hanau and Bremen, is definitely the Brothers Grimm country. They nourished their dark and magical imaginations as children in Steinau an der Strasse, a beautiful medieval town in this region of misty woodlands and ancient castles.

13 Hamburg. Hamburg, with its long tradition as a powerful and wealthy Hanseatic port city, is quintessentially elegant. World-class museums of modern art; the wild red-light district along the Reeperbahn; and HafenCity, a new supermodern, environmentally, and architecturally avant-garde quarter currently under construction, make Hamburg well worth a visit.

14 Schleswig-Holstein and the Baltic Coast. Off the beaten path, this region is scattered with medieval towns, fishing villages, unspoiled beaches, and summer resorts like Sylt, where Germany's jet set go to get away.

15 Berlin. No trip to Germany is complete without a visit to Berlin—the German capital is Europe's hippest urban destination. Gritty, creative, and broke, cheap rents draw artists from all over the world. Cutting-edge art exhibits, stage dramas, musicals, and bands compete for your attention with two cities' worth of world-class museums, three opera houses, eight state theaters, and two zoos.

16 Saxony, Saxony-Anhalt, and Thuringia. The southeast is a secret treasure trove of German high culture. Friendly, vibrant cities like Dresden, Leipzig, Weimar, and Eisenach are linked to Schiller, Goethe, Bach, Luther, and the like.

North Se

Groningen

NETHERLANDS

AMSTERDAM

Arnhem

Münster

Rhine

Dortmund

Duisburg

Düsseldorf   Hagen

Köln

Aachen   Bonn

Liège

Koblenz

BELGIUM

11

Mosel

LUX   Trier

M

LUXEMBOURG   Kaiserslautern

Metz   Saarbrücken

GERMANY PLANNER

When to Go

A year-round destination, Germany is particularly wonderful May through September for the long warm days that stretch sightseeing hours and are perfect for relaxing in beer gardens.

In the north, January can be dark, cold, and moody, with wind that cuts to the bone. Southern Germany, on the other hand, is a great winter destination, with world-class skiing, spas, and wellness options.

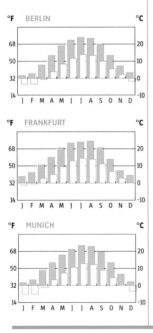

Getting Here

Most flights into Germany arrive at Frankfurt's Flughafen Frankfurt Main (FRA) or Munich's Flughafen München (MUC), but beginning in June 2012 the new Berlin Brandenburg International Airport (BBI) will open. Flying time to Frankfurt is 1½ hours from London, 7½ hours from New York, 10 hours from Chicago, and 12 hours from Los Angeles. Some international carriers serve Köln (Cologne), Hamburg, and Berlin. Germany has a fantastic train system, and is well connected to all overland European destinations. Hamburg, followed by Bremen, is Germany's most important harbor, and cruise ships and ferries connect the German north coast to England, Scandinavia, Russia, and the Baltics.

Getting Around

Once in Germany you can travel by train, car, bus, or air. Keep in mind that tickets with flexible schedules cost more but may be well worth it.

Travel by train is the most relaxing and often fastest way to go. The Deutsche Bahn (German Railroad) serves most destinations with relative frequency, speed, and comfort. Train stations are in the city center, and served by extensive intercity public transportation networks. Domestic air travel can be cheaper than the train, especially between bigger cities. Air Berlin and Germanwings offer very low fares on inter-German routes.

All major car-rental companies are represented in Germany. Gasoline is expensive (about €5.96 per gallon), and parking in major cities can be difficult. Nevertheless, Germany has one of the world's best maintained and most extensive highway systems, and a car gives you the flexibility to explore on your own, particularly in less densely populated areas. Most cars in Germany have manual transmission. A few rules of the road to remember: Large German cities like Berlin require all cars to meet environmental standards before entering the city center—rental cars and foreign visitors are not exempt. Always obey speed limits—although some stretches of the autobahn have no speed limit, speeds are restricted approaching towns.

Dining: The Basics

Lunch specials, or *Tageskarten*, offer meals at lower rates. Seasonal menus, or *Saisonkarten*, feature seasonal dishes, like white asparagus or red cabbage.

In most restaurants it is not customary to wait to be seated. Simply walk in and take any unreserved space.

German restaurants do not automatically serve water. If you order water, you will be served mineral water and be expected to pay for it. The concept of free refills or the bottomless cup of coffee is also completely foreign.

Tipping: When you get the check for something small, like a cup of coffee, round up to the next even euro. For larger amounts, tip 10%. Also, instead of leaving the tip on the table, add it to the total amount when you pay. For example, if the bill is €2.70, tell the waitress "€3, please" when she comes to collect the money. The waiter will often wear a fanny pack with change they will dole out if you pay in cash, so be sure to know the amount you want back including the tip.

German waitstaff are more than happy to split the check so that everyone can pay individually. Remember to pay the waiter directly; do not place the money on the table and leave.

Credit cards are increasing in popularity, but are not accepted in many places.

Money

Most Germans still make most of—if not all—their purchases the old-fashioned way: with cash. The use of credit cards in Germany is among the lowest in Europe. That said, you'll easily be able to pay your hotel bill, train tickets, or car rental with a credit card.

But if you're picking up a snack at a bakery, a little souvenir, or having a cup of coffee, it's easiest to pay cash. The same goes for buying tickets on public transportation or paying for a taxi.

Exchange services and banks are plentiful in cities and towns. However keep in mind that you'll generally get the best exchange rate at a *Geldautomat* (ATM), not to mention the convenience of 24-hour access. Before starting your trip, check on the fees your bank charges for international ATM transactions. You may find that these are less than the commissions charged at currency exchange booths and banks.

Social Mores

When addressing someone always use the formal *sie* until you are begged by them to switch to the informal *du*. When in doubt, shake hands; both as a greeting and at parting.

It's polite to ask if someone speaks English (*Sprechen sie Englisch?*) before addressing them in English.

Germans have done a lot of soul searching as a nation as to their role in and responsibility for the atrocities of World War II. They tend to be very well informed about world affairs—and often know more about the minute workings of the American political process than Americans do. Discussions about history and politics will almost always make for an interesting evening.

Dress and Undress

Casual clothes and jeans can be worn just about anywhere as long as they're neat. When visiting churches, dress conservatively—shorts and halter tops are not appropriate.

Don't be surprised to find nude sunbathers, even in the most public parks. It's also normal to see children running around without clothes on in parks, at swimming pools, or at the beach.

GERMANY
TOP ATTRACTIONS

Berlin, Capital City

(A) Berlin was the capital of Prussia, the German Empire, the Weimar Republic, and the Third Reich before being divided after World War II. The must-visit Reichstag (parliament building) was reconstructed with a special glass dome after reunification. From the dome, you can see directly down into the parliament chambers below—a symbol of government transparency. The iconic East German TV tower, a symbol of political power, also makes a great stop. The Checkpoint Charlie museum details accounts of people escaping the GDR. The new Topography of Terror exhibit hall, another must-see, is a rich source of information on the Nazi regime.

Frauenkirche, Dresden

(B) Dresden's Church of Our Lady is a masterpiece of baroque architecture. Completed in 1743, the magnificent domed church was destroyed as a result of Allied bombing in February 1945. In 2005, the church was rebuilt from the original rubble, thanks entirely to private donations.

Heidelberg Castle

(C) Heidelberg's immense ruined fortress is a prime example of Gothic and Renaissance styles. It inspired the 19th-century Romantic writers, especially the poet Goethe, who admired its decay amidst the beauty of the Neckar Valley.

Jüdisches Museum, Berlin

(D) Under the Nazis, at least 6 million Jews, along with homosexuals, the disabled, Gypsies, and political and religious dissidents, were rounded up and sent to slave labor and death camps. Berlin's Jewish Museum, a riveting, angular building designed by Daniel Libeskind, documents Jewish life in Germany and confronts the scars of World War II.

Kölner Dom

(E) Köln's breathtaking cathedral, one of Germany's best-known monuments, is the first thing that greets you when you step out of the train station. The Gothic marvel took more than 600 years to build.

Munich's Oktoberfest

(F) For 12 days at the end of September and into early October, Munich hosts the world's largest beer bonanza. Originally, the festival celebrated the marriage of Therese von Sachsen to Ludwig I in 1810. It soon morphed into a yearly festival, one that now welcomes more than 6 million visitors and serves more than 5 million liters of beer.

Neuschwanstein Castle

(G) Walt Disney modeled the castle in *Sleeping Beauty* and later the Disneyland castle itself on Neuschwanstein. "Mad" King Ludwig II's creation is best admired from the heights of the Marienbrücke, a delicate-looking bridge over a deep, narrow gorge.

Roman Ruins, Trier

(H) Founded in 16 BC as Augusta Treverorum, Trier is home to impressive, well-preserved Roman ruins. Visit the Porta Nigra (*Black Gate*), thermal baths, and the amphitheater, where you can still see gladiators battle it out.

Weimar: Goethe, Schiller, Bauhaus

(I) In the 18th and 19th centuries, Weimar was home to such German luminaries as Goethe and Schiller, whose homes are now museums. The Bauhaus movement, which gave rise to much of modern architecture and design, was also born here—as you'll learn on a visit to the Bauhaus Museum Weimar.

TOP EXPERIENCES

Imbibe in a Beer Garden

As soon as the sun comes out, beer gardens sprout all over Germany. With as much sunshine per year as Anchorage, Alaska, the Germans know a good thing when they see it, and are quick to set up tables and chairs under the open skies as soon as temperatures allow. Bavaria is the "home" of the beer garden, but you can sample local variations of beer and bratwurst outdoors wherever you happen to be. If the sun's out and you don't see a beer garden, take a beer to the park: Germany has no open-container laws.

Hike a Mountain

The Germans are a fiercely outdoor folk, and if you are anywhere near the mountains (or a hill, or even a relatively flat open space), you'll likely see plenty of people out walking. Pack a bag lunch and some extra bandages and join the crowd—it's a great way to get a feel for the real Germany.

Eat White Asparagus

If you visit between April and June, you're in luck: it's asparagus season. Not just any asparagus, either. Germans are crazy for their very own white asparagus, which is only available during this season. Thicker and larger than green asparagus, the white stuff has to be peeled of its hard sheath (done before cooking). Enjoy it with a slice of ham and potatoes with butter or hollandaise sauce.

Go to a Museum

No matter where you are in Germany, chances are you're close to a museum. Every big city has major, world-class art museums. Technical museums, like Munich's Deutsches Museum, are also impressive and informative. *Freiluft*, or open-air museums, offer collections of buildings from previous epochs that visitors can walk through to get a sense of daily life in the past. Even sparsely populated areas have their own quirky museums that depict the history of everything from marzipan to beds.

Take a Bike Tour through the City

Whether you're discovering Munich, Dresden, Cologne, Hamburg, Berlin, or one of Germany's many smaller cities, a bike tour is the way to do it. Tour companies offer guided tours (and bikes and helmets, though Germans often don't wear them), or you can rent a bike and set out on your own. Wind your way through Munich's English Garden or along Hamburg's harbor and you'll find that you see much more than you would from a tour bus.

Eat a German Breakfast

The German breakfast is a major affair, involving several types of bread rolls, a salami and dry sausage spread, hard cheeses, butter, chocolate spread, honey, jam, sliced tomatoes, sliced cucumber, liver pate, other meats, hard-boiled eggs eaten in the shell, and coffee. Show up hungry.

Visit the Baker

Germany has an incredible *brotkultur*, or bread culture. Bread is a historically important part of the German diet, and there are many, many types of bread to sample. Breads vary greatly from region to region, but they are without exception delicious. Go to a good artisanal bakery and you will be astounded by what you find.

Take a Curative Bath

With more than 300 *Kurorte* (health spas) and *Heilbaeder* (spas with healing waters), Germany has a long tradition of spa destinations. Located by the sea, near mineral-rich mud sources, near salt

deposits, or natural springs, these spas date back to the time of the Kaisers. Visit, and you'll be treated to salt baths, mud baths, saunas, thermal hot springs, and mineral-rich air, depending on the special attributes of the region you're visiting.

Cruise along the Rhine

No trip to Germany is complete without a boat tour of the Rhine. Board in Rudesheim and follow the river to Bingen (or do the reverse). Along the way, you'll see an unparalleled number of castles rising up from the banks along the river. Keep a look out for the rock of the Loreley, the beautiful river maiden of legend who lures sailors to their deaths with her song.

Visit a Christmas Market

Just about every city, town, and village has a Christmas market (and larger cities have more than one—in Berlin, for example, there are as many as 60 small markets each year). The most famous are the markets in Dresden and Nuremburg, both of which have long traditions. Christmas markets, which are held outdoors, open the last week of November and run through Christmas. Bundle up and head to one with money in your pocket to buy handmade gifts like the famous wooden figures carved in the Erzgebirge region as you sip traditional, hot-spiced "Gluehwein" wine to stay warm.

Find a Volksfest

Nearly every city, town, and village hosts an annual Volksfest, or folk festival. These can be very traditional and lots of fun. A cross between a carnival and county fair, these are great places to sample local food specialties, have a home-brewed beer, and generally join in the fun.

Take a Spin in a Fine German Automobile

Germany is the spiritual home of precision auto engineering, and Germans love their cars. You can rent a Porsche, Mercedes, or BMW for a day to see what it's like to drive like the Germans. Take your car-for-a-day to the Nürburgring, a world-famous racetrack built in the 1920s. There, you can get a day pass to drive your car around the track. Visit the on-site auto museum afterward. Both BMW and Mercedes-Benz have recently opened fantastic new museums, as well.

Swim in a Lake

Germany is dotted with lakes, and when the weather is warm, locals strip down and go swimming. Don't worry if you don't have your suit with you: it's usually fine (even normal) to skinny-dip.

Rent a Paddleboat

If swimming's not your thing, most lakes have paddleboat rentals in summer. While away the afternoon in the company of the ducks. This is what summer is all about.

Go to a Soccer Game

Soccer is the national sport and it provokes even the most stoic German man's passion (some women follow eagerly, as well). Even if you aren't a soccer fan, going to a live game is exciting. There's a palpable energy and it's easy to follow the action. You can catch a soccer game just about anywhere, anytime except for June and July, and over the Christmas break.

Go Sledding

In winter, children and adults alike head for the nearest incline, sleds in hand. If you don't have a sled, just stand back and enjoy the spectacle. The children's old-fashioned wooden sleds are truly charming.

QUINTESSENTIAL GERMANY

Culture Vultures

With more theaters, concert halls, and opera houses per capita than any other country in the world, high culture is an important part of German life. Before the formation of the German state, regional courts competed to see who had the best artists, actors, musicians, and stages, resulting in the development of a network of strong cultural centers that exists to this day. For Germans, high culture is not just for the elite, and they consider it so important to provide their communities with a rich cultural life that they use their tax money to do it. One of the results, aside from a flourishing, world-class cultural scene, is that tickets to these publicly funded operas, classical music concerts, ballet, and plays are quite inexpensive, with tickets readily available in the €10 to €40 range. Drop in on a performance or concert—it's one of the best travel bargains around.

Another Beer, Bitte

The German *Kneipekultur*, or pub culture, is an important and long-standing tradition. *Stammgäste*, or regulars, stop by their local pub as often as every evening to drink beer and catch up. In summer, *Kneipe* life moves outdoors to beer gardens. Some, such as the famous Chinese Pavilion in Munich's English Garden, are institutions, and might seat hundreds. Others are more casual, consisting of a café's graveled back garden under soaring chestnut trees. Most beer gardens offer some sort of food: self-serve areas might sell pastas or lamb in addition to grilled sausages and pretzels. Although beer gardens are found all over Germany, the smoky beer-hall experience—with dirndls and oompah bands—is traditionally Bavarian. You'll discover how different the combination of four key ingredients— malt, hops, yeast, and water—can taste.

1

If you want to get a sense of contemporary German culture and indulge in some of its pleasures, start by familiarizing yourself with the rituals of daily life.

Easy Being Green

Germany has one of the world's most environmentally conscious societies. Conserving resources, whether electricity or food, is second nature for this country where postwar deprivation has not yet faded from memory. Recycling is practically a national sport, with separate garbage bins for regular trash, clear glass, green glass, plastics and cans, and organic garbage. Keep your eyes out for the giant brown, green, and yellow pods on the streets—these are used for neighborhood recycling in cities. Particularly in cities, there are well-defined bike lanes and many people ride their bikes to work (even in high heels or business suits) much of the year. Drivers know to look for them, and as a visitor you'll need to be careful not to walk in the bike lanes, or you'll hear a bell chiming to let you know a biker is nearby. Great public transportation is also part of this environmental commitment.

Kaffe und Kuchen

The tradition of afternoon coffee and cake, usually around 3 pm, is a serious matter. If you can, finagle an invitation to someone's house to get the real experience, which might involve a simple homemade *Quarkkuchen* (cheese cake), or a spread of several decadent creamy cakes, topped with apples, rhubarb, strawberries, or cherries and lots of whipped cream. Otherwise, find an old-fashioned *Konditorei*, or pastry shop and choose from their amazing selection. Germans bake more than a thousand different kinds of cakes, with infinite regional variations. Among the most famous is the *Schwarzwälder Kirschtorte* (Black Forest cake), a chocolate layer cake soaked in *Kirsch* schnapps, with cherries, whipped cream, and chocolate shavings. Another favorite is the *Bienenstich* (bee sting), a layered sponge cake filled with cream and topped with a layer of crunchy honey-caramelized almonds.

IF YOU LIKE

Being Outdoors

The Germans have a long-standing love affair with Mother Nature. The woods, as well as the mountains, rivers, and oceans, surface repeatedly in the works of the renowned German poets and thinkers. That nature is the key to the mysteries of the soul can be seen in works as different as those of naturalist Romantic painter Caspar David Friedrich and the 20th-century philosopher Martin Heidegger. Today, Germany has designated large tracts of land as national recreation areas, and cities boast extensive urban parks and gardens.

A particularly lovely mountain landscape of twisting gorges and sheer cliffs can be found about 30 km (19 mi) south of Dresden, in the **Sächsische Schweiz** park. Rock climbers fascinate those driving up the steep switchbacks to reach bald mesas. At a much higher altitude are the Bavarian Alps, where the Winter Olympics town **Garmisch-Partenkirchen** offers cable cars to ascend Germany's highest mountain. This is one of the country's best spots for skiing in winter and hiking in summer.

Lakes such as **Chiemsee** and **Bodensee** dot the area between the Alps and Munich and many hikers and bikers enjoy circling them. Boat rentals are possible, but you'll often need a German-recognized license. On the island of **Rügen,** the turn-of-the-20th-century resort town **Binz** fronts the gentle (and cold) waters of the Baltic Sea. Even on windy days you can warm up on the beach in a sheltered beach chair for two. Among the Baltic Coast's most dramatic features are Rügen's white chalk cliffs in **Jasmund National Park,** where you can hike, bike, or sign up for nature seminars and tours.

Medieval Towns

The trail of walled towns and half-timber houses known as the **Romantic Road** is a route long marketed by German tourism, and therefore the road more traveled. The towns, particularly Rothenburg-ob-der-Tauber, are lovely, but if you'd prefer fewer tour groups spilling into your photographs, venture into the **Harz Mountains** in the center of Germany.

Goslar, the unofficial capital of the Harz region, is one of Germany's oldest cities, and is renowned for its Romanesque Kaiserpfalz, an imperial palace. Goslar has been declared a UNESCO World Heritage site, as has the town of **Quedlinburg,** 48 km (30 mi) to the southeast. With 1,600 half-timber houses, Quedlinburg has more of these historic, typically northern German buildings than any other town in the country.

A mighty fortress south of the Harz Mountains is the **Wartburg,** in the ancient, half-timber town of **Eisenach.** Frederick the Wise protected Martin Luther from papal proscription within these stout walls in the 16th century.

Options for exploring closer to Munich include **Regensburg** and **Nürnberg.** The former is a beautiful medieval city, relatively unknown even to Germans, and has a soaring French Gothic cathedral that can hold 6,000 people. Nürnberg dates to 1050, and is among the most historic cities in the country. Not only emperors but artists convened here, including the Renaissance genius Albrecht Dürer.

The Arts

With as many as 600 galleries, world-class private collections, and ateliers in every *Hinterhof* (back courtyard), **Berlin** is one of Europe's contemporary art capitals. For not-so-modern art, Berlin's **Museumsinsel** (Museum Island), a UNESCO World Heritage site, is the absolute must-see. A complex of five state museums packed onto one tiny island, these include the **Altes Museum**, with a permanent collection of classical antiquities; the **Alte Nationalgalerie**, with 18th- to early-20th-century paintings and sculptures from the likes of Cézanne, Rodin, Degas, and Germany's own Max Liebermann; the **Bode-Museum**, containing German and Italian sculptures, Byzantine art, and coins; and the **Pergamonmuseum**, whose highlight is the world-famous Pergamon Altar, a Greek temple dating from 180 BC.

Leipzig is a "new" star in the European art world. The **Museum der Bildenden Künste** (Museum of Fine Arts) is the city's leading gallery, followed closely by the **Grassimuseum** complex. The **Spinnerei** (a former cotton mill) has become Leipzig's prime location for contemporary art, and houses more than 80 artists and galleries, especially those of the New Leipzig School.

Fans of old master painters must haunt the halls of the **Zwinger** in Dresden, where most works were collected in the first half of the 18th century, and the **Alte Pinakothek** in Munich, which has one of the world's largest collections of Rubens.

Castles and Palaces

Watching over nearly any town whose name ends in "-burg" is a medieval fortress or Renaissance palace, often now serving the populace as a museum, restaurant, or hotel.

The **Wartburg** in Eisenach is considered "the mother of all castles" and broods over the foothills of the Thuringian Forest. Abundant vineyards surround **Schloss Neuenburg**, which dominates the landscape around the sleepy village of Freyburg (Unstrut). The castle ruins overlooking the Rhine River are the result of ceaseless fighting with the French, but even their remains were picturesque enough to inspire 19th-century Romantics. **Burg Rheinstein** is rich with Gobelin tapestries, stained glass, and frescoes.

Schloss Heidelberg mesmerizes with its Gothic turrets, Renaissance walls, and abandoned gardens. Other fortresses lord over the **Burgenstrasse** (Castle Road) in the neighboring **Neckar Valley**. You can stay the night (or just enjoy an excellent meal) at the castles of **Hirschhorn** or **Burg Hornberg,** or at any of a number of other castle-hotels in the area.

The medieval **Burg Eltz** in the Mosel Valley looms imposingly, and with its high turrets looks like it's straight out of a Grimm fairy tale. The castle has been perfectly preserved and has been owned by the same family for almost a thousand years.

Louis XIV's Versailles inspired Germany's greatest castle-builder, King Ludwig II, to construct the opulent **Schloss Herrenchiemsee**. One of Ludwig's palaces in turn inspired a latter-day visionary—his **Schloss Neuschwanstein** is the model for Walt Disney's Sleeping Beauty Castle. **Schloss Linderhof**, also in the Bavarian Alps, was Ludwig's favorite retreat.

FLAVORS OF GERMANY

Traditional German cuisine fell out of fashion several decades ago, and was replaced by Italian and Mediterranean food, Asian food, and Middle Eastern food. But there's a growing movement to go back to those roots, and even high-class German chefs are rediscovering old classics, from sauerkraut (pickled cabbage) to *Sauerbraten* (traditional German pot roast). Traditional fruits and vegetables, from parsnips and pumpkins to black salsify, sunchoke, cabbage, yellow carrots, and little-known strawberry and apple varietals, are all making a comeback. That said, "German food" is a bit of a misnomer, as traditional cooking varies greatly from region to region. Look for the "typical" dish, wherever you are, to get the best sense of German cooking in that region.

Generally speaking, regions in the south, like Baden-Wuerttemberg and Bavaria, have held onto their culinary traditions more than regions in the North. But with a little effort, you can find good German food just about anywhere you go.

Bavaria: White Sausage and Beer (for Breakfast)

In Bavaria, a traditional farmer's *Zweites Fruehstueck* (second breakfast) found at any beer hall consists of fat white sausages, called *Weisswurst* made of veal and eaten with sweet mustard, pretzels, and, yes, a big glass of *Helles* or *Wiessbier* (light or wheat beer). Other Bavarian specialties include *Leberkäse* (literally, "liver cheese"), a meat loaf of pork and beef that can be eaten sliced on bread and tastes a lot better than it sounds. *Knödelgerichte*, or noodle dishes are also popular.

Swabia: The Sausage Salad

Swabia (the area surrounding Stuttgart) is generally thought to have some of the best traditional food in Germany, having held on to its culinary heritage better than other areas. *Schwäbische Wurstsalat* (Swabian sausage salad), a salad of sliced sausage dressed with onions, vinegar, and oil, is a typical dish, as is *Kässpätzle* (Swabian pasta with cheese), a noodle-like dish made from flour, egg, and water topped with cheese. *Linsen mit Spätzle* (lentils and spätzle) could be considered the Swabian national dish: it consists of egg noodles topped with lentils and, often, a sausage.

Franconia: Nürnberger Bratwürste

Perhaps the most beloved of all *bratwürste* (sausages) in a country that loves sausages is the small, thin sausage from the city of Nürnberg. Grilled over a beechwood fire, this sausage is served 6 or 12 at a time with horseradish and sauerkraut or potato salad. Fresh marjoram and ground caraway seeds give the pork-based sausage its distinctive flavor.

Hessen: Apfelwein in Frankfurt

Apfelwein (apple wine) is a specialty in and around Frankfurt. Look for an *Apfelweinkneipe* (cider bar), where you can spend a pleasant evening sipping this tasty alcoholic drink. Order *Handkäse*, traditional Hessian curdled milk cheese, to go with it. If you order *Handkäse mit Musik* (Handkäse with music), you'll get it with onions. Another winner is *Frankfurter Rippchen*, spareribs served with sauerkraut.

Rhineland: Horse Meat and Kölsch

In Köln, influenced by nearby Belgium and Holland, there's a traditional taste for horse meat, which they use in their local version of the pot roast, *Rheinische*

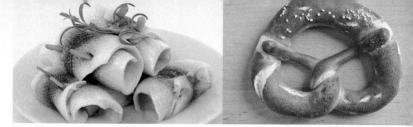

Sauerbraten. Wash this down with the local beer, *Kölsch.* Or try the *Kölsche Kaviar*—blood sausage with onions.

Northwest Germany: Herring with That?

States on the north coast, like Bremen, Hamburg, Westphalia, and Schleswig-Holstein, all have cuisines that are oriented toward the sea. Cod, crab, herring, and flatfish are all common traditional foods. *Labskaus,* a meat stew, is also a traditional northern German dish that might be served with a fried egg, pickle, and red beets. Potatoes, cabbage, and rutabagas are all important vegetables, and are served stewed or pickled. *Rote Grütze,* a traditional dessert, is a berry pudding often served with whipped cream.

Northeast Germany: Currywurst and More

Berlin is known for its *Eisbein* (pork knuckle), *Kasseler* (smoked pork chop), *Bockwurst* (large sausage), and *Boulette* (a kind of hamburger made of beef and pork), though its most famous dish might be its *Currywurst,* a Berlin-born dish that consists of sausage cut in pieces and covered in ketchup with curry. Idyllic Spreewald is famous for its pickles.

The East: Da, Soljanka

In former GDR states like Saxony, Saxony-Anhalt, and Thuringia, the Soviet influence can be felt in the popularity of traditionally Russian dishes like *Soljanka* (meat soup). *Rotkäppchen* sparkling wines come from Saxony-Anhalt, Germany's northernmost wine growing region (named for the company's bottles with red tops, Rotkäppchen is also the German name for Little Red Riding Hood). Another local treat is *Baumkuchen,* or tree cake, so named because it is formed by adding layer upon layer of batter on a spit and rotating this around a heat source, such that when you cut into it, it looks like the rings of a tree.

The Döner: It's for Dinner

Although not a traditional German dish, the Turkish döner kebab is ubiquitous in Germany and it would be hard to spend much time here without trying one. Made from some combination of lamb, chicken, pork, or beef roasted on a spit then sliced into pita pockets with cabbage, lettuce, and yogurt sauce, döners are one of the most popular fast foods around. A spicy, inexpensive alternative to German fare, they're good for a meal or a pick-me-up.

Seasonal Favorites

Germans are still very much attuned to seasonal fruits and vegetables. Traditional German produce like white asparagus, strawberries, plums, cherries, blueberries, and apples are available in supermarkets, farmers' markets, and sidewalk sellers in abundance, and are eagerly snapped up by locals. When in season, these are delicious items to add to your diet and a healthy way to keep your blood sugar up as you set off to explore Germany.

BEERS OF GERMANY

Beer, or "liquid bread" as it was described by medieval monks who wanted to avoid God's anger, is not just a vital element of German cuisine, but of German culture. The stats say Germans are second only to the Czechs when it comes to per capita beer consumption, though they have been losing their thirst recently—from a peak of 145 liters (38.3 gallons) per head in 1980, each German now only manages 102 liters (26.9 gallons) every year. And yet the range of beers has never been wider.

Reinheitsgebot (Purity Law)

There are precisely 1,327 breweries in Germany, offering more than 5,000 types of beer. This might strike you as odd. What about Germany's legendary "Beer Purity Law," or *Reinheitsgebot*, which allegedly allows only three ingredients: water, malt, and hops? How many different recipes can there be?

The truth is that the Purity Law has now become more of a marketing tool, though it was once real enough. It has its origins in medieval times, when various towns imposed restrictions on local brewers—not to guarantee beer purity, but to protect the bread supply. By restricting the ingredients of beer, it ensured wheat would be used to make bread.

It was the Bavarians who took the law most seriously, officially enshrining their *Reinheitsgebot* in 1516, and the rest of Germany adopted the law in 1906. But while the law survived several centuries and a number of wars, it was no match for European Union food regulations—in 1987, the European Court of Justice ruled that the *Reinheitsgebot* was a form of protectionism, and forced Germany to repeal it.

Germany's Major Beer Varieties

Pils: One effect of the Beer Purity Law was that Germany became dominated by one kind of beer: *Pils*. Invented in Bohemia (now the Czech Republic) in 1842, and aided by Bavarian refrigeration techniques, Pils was the first beer to be chilled and stored thus allowing bottom fermentation, better clarity, and a longer shelf-life. Today, the majority of German beers are brewed in the Pils, or Pilsner, style. German Pils tends to have a drier, bitterer taste than what you might be used to, but a trip to Germany is hardly complete without the grand tour along these lines: Augustiner in Bavaria, Bitburger in the Rhineland, Flensburger in the North.

Helles: *Hell* is German for "light," but when it comes to beer, that refers to the color rather than the alcohol content. Helles is a crisp and clear Bavarian pale lager with between 4.5% and 6% alcohol. It was developed in the mid-19th century by a German brewer named Gabriel Sedlmayr, who adopted and adapted some British techniques to create the new beer for his famous Spaten Brewery in Bavaria. Another brewer, Josef Groll, used the same methods to produce one of the first German Pils, Pilsner Urquell. Spaten is still one the best brands for a good Helles, as are Löwenbräu, Weihenstephaner, and Hacker-Pschorr—all classic Bavarian beers.

Dunkelbier: At the other side of the beer rainbow from Helles is dark beer, or *Dunkelbier*. The dark, reddish color is a consequence of the darker malt that is used in the brewing. Despite suspicions aroused by the stronger, maltier taste, Dunkelbier actually contains no more alcohol than Helles. Dunkelbier was common in rural Bavaria in the early 19th century. All the

major Bavarian breweries produce a Dunkelbier to complement their Helles.

Bock: Dunkelbier should not be confused with *Bock*, which also has a dark color and a malty taste but is a little stronger. It was first created in the middle ages in the northern German town of Einbeck, before it was later adopted by the Bavarian breweries, which had come to regard themselves as the natural home of German beer. In fact, the name Bock comes from the Bavarian interpretation of the word "Einbeck." Bock often has a sweeter flavor, and is traditionally drunk on public holidays. There are also subcategories, like *Eisbock* and *Doppelbock*, which have been refined to make an even stronger beverage.

Kölsch: If you're looking for lighter refreshment, then *Kölsch* is ideal. The traditional beer of Cologne, Kölsch is a mild, carbonated beer that goes down easily. It is usually served in a small, straight glass, called a *Stange*, which is much easier to wrangle than the immense Bavarian *Mass* (liter) glasses. If you're part of a big party, you're likely to get Kölsch served in a *Kranz*, or wreath—a circular wooden rack that holds up to 18 *Stangen*. Kölsch is very specific to Cologne and its immediate environs, so there's little point in asking for it anywhere else. Consequently, the major Kölsch brands are all relatively small; they include Reissdorf, Gaffel, and Früh.

Hefeweizen: Also known as *Weissbier* or *Weizenbier*, *Hefeweizen* is essentially wheat beer, and it was originally brewed in southern Bavaria. It has a very distinctive taste and cloudy color. It's much stronger than standard Pils or Helles, with an alcohol content of more than 8%. On the other hand, that content is slightly compensated for by the fact that wheat beer can be very filling. For a twist, try the clear variety called *Kristallweizen*, which tastes crisper, and is often served with half a slice of lemon. Hefeweizen is available throughout Germany, and the major Bavarian breweries all brew it as part of their range.

Top Brews by Region

Bavaria: Helles, Dunkelbier, Hefeweizen.

The six most famous brands, and the only ones allowed to be sold at the Oktoberfest are: Löwenbräu, Augustiner, Paulaner, Hacker-Pschorr, Spaten-Franziskanerbräu and Hofbräu. Tegernseer Hell is also very good.

Rhineland: Kölsch, Pils.

Apart from Kölsch, which is impossible to avoid, look out for Krombacher and Bitburger.

Eastern Germany: Pils.

Radeberger and Hasseröder, are two of the few beers in the region to have survived the fall of communism in the former East Germany.

Berlin: Pils.

The most famous brands are Berliner Kindl, Schultheiss, and Berliner Pilsner, which are all worth trying.

Hamburg: Pils.

Astra—with its anchor-heart logo—is a cult Pils that is very much identified with Germany's biggest port city.

Northern Germany: Pils, Bock.

The best brands include Flensburger, Jever, and, of course, Beck's, which comes from the northern city of Bremen.

WINES OF GERMANY

Germany produces some of the finest white wines in the world. Although more and more quality red wine is being produced, the majority of German wines are white due to the northern continental German climate. Nearly all wine production in Germany takes place by the River Rhine in the southwest. As a result, a single trip to this lovely and relatively compact wine region can give you a good overview of German wines.

German Wines: Then and Now
A Brief History

The Romans first introduced viticulture to the southernmost area of what is present-day Germany about 2,000 years ago. By the time of Charlemagne, wine making centered around monasteries. A 19th-century grape blight necessitated a complete reconstitution of German grape stock, grafted with pest-resistant American vines, and formed the basis for today's German wines. With cold winters, a relatively northern climate, and less sun than other wine regions, the Germans have developed a reputation for technical and innovative panache. The result has traditionally been top-quality sweet Rieslings, though Germany has been making excellent dry and off-dry white wines and Rieslings in the past 30 years.

Today's Wine Scene

For years, German wines were known by their lowest common denominator, the cheap, sweet wine that was exported en masse to the United States, England, and other markets. However, more recently there has been a push to introduce the world to the best of German wines. Exports to the United States, Germany's largest export market, have grown steadily, followed by England, The Netherlands, Sweden, and Russia. Eighty-three percent of its exports are white wines. The export of *Liebfraumilch*, the sugary, low-quality stuff that gave German wine a bad name, has been steadily declining, and now 66% of exports are so-called *Qualitätswein*, or quality wines. Only 15% of exports are destined to be wine-in-a-box. This is a more accurate representation of German wine as it exists in Germany.

Germany's Dominant Varietals
Whites

Müller-Thurgau: Created in the 1880s, this grape is a cross between a Riesling and a Madeleine Royale. Ripening early, it's prone to rot and, as the grape used in most Liebfraumilch, has a less than golden reputation.

Riesling: The most widely planted (and widely famous) of German grapes, the Riesling ripens late. A hardy grape, it's ideal for late-harvest wines. High levels of acidity help wines age well. When young, grapes have a crisp, floral character.

Silvaner: This grape is dying out in most places, with the exception of Franconia, where it is traditionally grown. With low acidity and neutral fruit, it can be crossed with other grapes to produce sweet wines like Kerner, Pinot Gris, Pinot Blanc, Bacchus, and others.

Reds

Dornfelder: A relatively young varietal. Dornfelder produces wines with a deep color, which distinguishes them from other German reds, which tend to be pale, light, and off-dry.

Spätburgunder (Pinot Noir): This grape is responsible for Germany's full-bodied, fruity wines, and is grown in more southerly vineyards.

Terminology

German wine is a complex topic, even though the wine region is relatively small. Wines are ranked according to the ripeness of the grapes when picked, and instead of harvesting a vineyard all at once, German vineyards are harvested up to five times. The finest wines result from the latest harvests of the season, due to increased sugar content. Under the category of "table wine" fall *Deutscher Tafelwein* (German table wine) and *Landwein* (like the French Vin de Pays). Quality wines are ranked according to when they are harvested. *Kabinett* wines are delicate, light, and fruity. *Spätlese* ("late-harvest" wine) has more-concentrated flavors, sweetness, and body. *Auslese* wines are made from extra-ripe grapes, and are even richer, even sweeter, and even riper. *Beerenauslese* are rare and expensive, made from grapes whose flavor and acid has been enhanced by noble rot. *Eiswein* ("ice" wine) is made of grapes that have been left on the vine to freeze and may be harvested as late as January. They produce a sugary syrup that creates an intense, fruity wine. Finally, *Trockenbeerenauslese* ("dry ice" wine) is made in tiny amounts using grapes that have frozen and shriveled into raisins. These can rank amongst the world's most expensive wines. Other terms to keep in mind include *Trocken* (dry) and *Halbtrocken* ("half-dry," or off-dry).

Wine Regions

Mosel: The Mosel's steep, mineral-rich hillsides produce excellent Rieslings. With flowery rather than fruity top-quality wines, the Mosel is a must-stop for any wine lover. The terraced hillsides rising up along the banks of the River Mosel are as pleasing to the eye as the light-bodied Rieslings are to the palate.

Nahe: Agreeable and uncomplicated: this describes the wines made from Müller-Thurgau and Silvaner grapes of the Nahe region. The earth here is rich not just in grapes, but also in semiprecious stones and minerals, and you might just detect a hint of pineapple in your wine's bouquet.

Rheinhessen: The largest wine-growing region of Germany, Rheinhessen's once grand reputation was tarnished in the mid-20th century, when large, substandard vineyards were cultivated and low-quality wine produced. Nonetheless, there's plenty of the very good stuff to be found, still. Stick to the red sandy slopes over the river for the most full-bodied of Germany's Rieslings.

Rheingau: The dark, slatey soil of the Rheingau is particularly suited to the German Riesling, which is the major wine produced in this lovely hill country along the River Rhine. Spicy wines come from the hillsides, while the valley yields wines with body, richness, and concentration.

Pfalz: The second-largest wine region in Germany, the Pfalz stretches north from the French border. Mild winters and warm summers make for some of Germany's best Pinot Noirs and most opulent Rieslings. Wine is served here in a special dimpled glass called the *Dubbeglas*.

Baden: Farther to the south, Baden's warmer climate helps produce ripe, full-bodied wines that may not be well known but certainly taste delicious. The best ones, both red and white, come from Kaiserstuhl-Tuniberg, between Freiburg and the Rhine. But be forewarned: the best things in life do tend to cost a little extra.

GREAT ITINERARIES

GRAND TOUR OF GERMANY

Coming to Germany for the first time? Consider a journey of the best the country has to offer: stunning landscapes, charming medieval towns, and cosmopolitan capital cities. Make the most of your time by taking the train between stops. You'll eliminate the hassles of parking and the high cost of gasoline. Best of all, you'll take in the views—in complete relaxation—as they roll by your window.

Days 1 and 2: Munich

Kick off your circle tour of quintessential Germany in Bavaria's capital city. Get your bearings by standing in the center of Munich's Marienplatz, and watch the charming, twirling figures of the Glockenspiel in the tower of the *Rathaus* (city hall). Visit the world-class art museums, then wander through the *Englischer Garten* (English Garden) to the beer garden for a cool beer and pretzel. ⇨ *See Chapter 2, Munich.*

Day 3: Garmisch-Partenkirchen

Take a day trip to visit Germany's highest mountain peak (9,731 feet), the Zugspitze. You'll take in astounding views of the mountains and breathe the bracing Alpine air. Have lunch at one of two restaurants on the peak, then bask in the sun like the Germans on the expansive terrace. If you're feeling sporty, hundreds of kilometers of trails offer some of Germany's best hiking across blooming mountain meadows and along steep mountain gorges. Otherwise take the cable car up and down and savor the dramatic vistas. ⇨ *See Chapter 3, The Bavarian Alps.*

Days 4 and 5: Freiburg

In the late morning, arrive in Freiburg, one of Germany's most beautiful historic cities. Damaged during the war, it's been meticulously rebuilt to preserve its delightful medieval character. Residents love to boast that Freiburg is the country's sunniest city, which is true according to meteorological reports. Freiburg's cathedral is a masterpiece of Gothic architecture, built over three centuries. Explore on foot, or by bike, and look out for the *Bächle*, or little brooks, that run for kilometers through Freiburg. ⇨ *See Chapter 7, The Black Forest.*

Day 6: The Black Forest

Freiburg puts you at the perfect point from which to explore the spruce-covered low-lying mountains of the Black Forest. Set out for Titisee, a placid glacial lake, visiting dramatic gorges along the way. Or, head toward the northern Black Forest to visit tony Baden-Baden. Then spend the afternoon relaxing in the curative waters at one of the famous spas. ⇨ *See Chapter 7, The Black Forest.*

Day 7: Würzburg

This gorgeous city sits on the Main River, and as you look out onto the hills that surround the city, you'll see that lush vineyards encircle the valley. Würzburg's two must-see attractions are the massive *Festung Marienburg* (Marienburg Fortress) and the Residenz an awe-inspiring baroque palace. The palace is considered to be one of Europe's most luxurious. The best way to sample the local wine is to go straight to the source: the vineyards. In the afternoon, follow the Stein-Wein-Pfad, a pathway that takes you straight to the local vintners, and try their wines while also drinking in incredible views

of the city below. ⇨ *See Chapter 4, The Romantic Road.*

Day 8: Bamberg

In the morning, arrive in Bamberg, which is on UNESCO's World Heritage Site list. The town is remarkable for not having sustained damage during World War II, and for looking much as it has for hundreds of years. Narrow cobblestone streets lead you to Bamberg's heart, a small island ringed by the Regnitz River. Bamberg has almost a dozen breweries—try the *Rauchbier*, a dark beer with a smoky flavor. ⇨ *See Chapter 5, Franconia and the German Danube.*

Days 9 and 10: Hamburg

Hamburg is one of Germany's wealthiest cities. It's also an important port, and served as a leader of the medieval Hanseatic League. If you're in Hamburg on Sunday, visit the open-air *Fischmarkt* (fish market) early in the morning. Then, take a cruise through the city's canals to see the historic warehouse district. Exploring the harbor you'll see the enormous ocean liners that stop in Hamburg before crossing the Atlantic. The city offers exclusive shopping along the Junfernstieg, a lakeside promenade. ⇨ *See Chapter 13, Hamburg.*

Days 11 and 12: Berlin and Potsdam

Berlin is Germany's dynamic capital, a sprawling and green city. No matter where you go, it's hard to escape Berlin's recent history as a divided city. You're brought face-to-face with the legacy of World War II, and contrast of East and West. Walk from the Brandenburg Gate to the famous Museum Island and visit the Pergamon Alter. In the afternoon, visit KaDeWe, Europe's largest department store, and walk along the *Kurfürstendamm*, the posh shopping boulevard. Spend the next morning in Potsdam, touring the opulent palaces and manicured gardens. Return to the city to explore its neighborhoods, like Turkish Kreuzberg or hip Prenzlauer Berg. ⇨ *See Chapter 15, Berlin.*

GERMAN ABCS: ARCHITECTURE, BEER, AND CAPITAL CITIES

Day 1: Arrival Munich

Though it is a wealthy city with Wittelsbach palaces, great art collections, and a technology museum holding trains, planes, and even an imitation coal mine, what really distinguishes Munich from other state capitals are its beer halls, beer gardens, and proud identity: even designer-conscious Müncheners wear traditional dirndls and hunter-green jackets for special occasions. Stroll the streets of the Altstadt (Old City), visit the Frauenkirche, choose a museum (the best ones will occupy you for at least three hours), and save the Hofbräuhaus or any other teeming brew house for last. Munich might be touristy, but hordes of German tourists love it as well. ⇨ *See Chapter 2, Munich.*

Day 2: Neuschwanstein

From Munich it's an easy day trip to Germany's fairy-tale castle in Schwangau. Though the 19th-century castle's fantastic silhouette has made it famous, this creation of King Ludwig II is more opera set than piece of history—the interior was never even completed. A tour reveals why the romantic king earned the nickname "Mad" King Ludwig. Across the narrow wooded valley from Schloss Neuschwanstein is the ancient castle of the Bavarian Wittelsbach dynasty, Schloss

Hohenschwangau, also open for tours. ⇨ *See Chapter 4, The Romantic Road.*

Day 3: Munich to Dresden

That Saxony's capital, Dresden, is the pinnacle of European baroque is obvious in its courtyards, newly rebuilt Frauenkirche, and terrace over the Elbe River. The city was largely shaped by Augustus the Strong, who in 1730 kindly invited the public to view the works crafted from precious stones in his Green Vault. Many of Dresden's art treasures lie within the Zwinger, a baroque showpiece. Spend the evening at the neo-Renaissance Semper Opera, where Wagner premiered his works, and drink Radeberger Pilsner at intermission. It's the country's oldest pilsner. ⇨ *See Chapter 16, Saxony, Saxony-Anhalt, and Thuringia.*

Day 4: Dresden and Berlin

Spend the morning touring some of Dresden's rich museums before boarding a train to Berlin. Germany's capital is not only unique for its division between 1949 and 1989, but is unlike any other German city in its physical expanse and diversity. Attractions that don't close until 10 pm or later are Sir Norman Foster's glass dome on the Reichstag, the TV tower at Alexanderplatz, and the Checkpoint Charlie Museum. ⇨ *See Chapters 15 and 16, Berlin and Saxony, Saxony-Anhalt, and Thuringia.*

Days 5 and 6: Berlin

Begin your first Berlin morning on a walk with one of the city's excellent tour companies. They'll connect the broadly spaced dots for you and make the events of Berlin's turbulent 20th century clear. Berlin is a fascinating city in and of itself, so you don't have to feel guilty if you don't get to many museums. Since the mid-1990s, world-renowned architects have changed

the city's face. You'll find the best nightlife in residential areas such as Prenzlauer Berg, Kreuzberg, Friedrichshain, or Mitte. Berlin is a surprisingly inexpensive city, so you can treat yourself to more here than in Munich. ⇨ *See Chapter 15, Berlin.*

Day 7: Munich

On your last day, have breakfast with the morning shoppers at the open-air Viktualienmarkt. Try to find *Weisswurst* (white sausage), a mild, boiled sausage normally eaten before noon with sweet mustard, a pretzel—and beer! ⇨ *See Chapter 2, Munich.*

CASTLES IN WINE COUNTRY

Day 1: Arrival Koblenz

Start your tour in Koblenz, at the confluence of the Rhine and Mosel rivers. Once you have arrived in the historic downtown area, head straight for the charming little Hotel Zum weissen Schwanen, a half-timber inn and mill since 1693. Explore the city on the west bank of the Rhine River and then head to Europe's biggest fortress, the impressive Festung Ehrenbreitstein on the opposite riverbank. ⇨ *See Chapter 11, The Rhineland.*

Day 2: Koblenz and Surrounding Castles

Get up early and drive along the most spectacular and historic section of "Vater Rhein." Stay on the left riverbank and you'll pass many mysterious landmarks on the way, including Burg Stolzenfels, and later the Loreley rock, a 430-foot slate cliff named after a legendary, beautiful, blonde nymph. Stay the night at St. Goar or St. Goarshausen, both lovely river villages. ⇨ *See Chapter 11, The Rhineland.*

Day 3: Eltville and the Eberbach Monastery

The former Cistercian monastery Kloster Eberbach, in Eltville, is one of Europe's best-preserved medieval cloisters. Parts of the film *The Name of the Rose*, based on Umberto Eco's novel and starring Sean Connery, were filmed here. If you're interested in wine, spend the night at the historic wine estate Schloss Reinhartshausen. This is a great opportunity to sample the fantastic wines of the region. ⇨ *See Chapter 11, The Rhineland.*

Day 4: Heidelberg

On Day 4, start driving early so you can spend a full day in Heidelberg (the drive from Eltville takes about an hour). No other city symbolizes German spirit and history better than this meticulously restored, historic town. Do not miss the impressive Schloss, one of Europe's greatest Gothic-Renaissance fortresses. Most of the many pubs and restaurants here are touristy, overpriced, and of poor quality—so don't waste your time at them. Instead, head for the Romantik Hotel zum Ritter St. Georg, a charming 16th-century inn with a great traditional German restaurant. ⇨ *See Chapter 8, Heidelberg and the Neckar Valley.*

Days 5 and 6: The Burgenstrasse and the Neckar Valley

Superb food and wine can be enjoyed in the quaint little villages in the Neckar Valley just east of Heidelberg—the predominant grapes here are Riesling (white) and Spätburgunder (red). Try to sample wines from small, private wineries—they tend to have higher-quality vintages. Sightseeing is equally stunning, with a string of castles and ruins along the famous Burgenstrasse (Castle Road). Since you have two days for this area, take your time and follow B-37 to Eberbach and its romantic Zwingenberg castle, tucked away in the deep forest just outside the village. In the afternoon, continue on to Burg Hornberg at Neckarzimmern, the home to the legendary German knight Götz von Berlichingen. Stay the night here, in the former castle stables.

The next morning, continue farther to Bad Wimpfen, the most charming valley town at the confluence of the Neckar and Jagst rivers. Spend half a day in the historic city center and tour the Staufer Pfalz (royal palace). Soaring high above the city, the palace was built in 1182, and emperor Barbarossa liked to stay here. ⇨ *See Chapter 8, Heidelberg and the Neckar Valley.*

Day 7: German Wine Route

Devote your last day to the German Wine Route, which winds its way through one of the most pleasant German landscapes, the gentle slopes and vineyards of the Pfalz. The starting point for the route is Bad Dürkheim, a spa town proud to have the world's largest wine cask, holding 1.7 million liters (450,000 gallons). You can enjoy wine with some lunch in the many Weinstuben here or wait until you reach Neustadt farther south, Germany's largest wine-growing community. Thirty of the vintages grown here can be sampled (and purchased) at the downtown Haus des Weines. If time permits, try to visit one of the three major castles along the route in the afternoon: Burg Trifels near Annweiler is a magnificent Hohenzollern residence, perched dramatically on three sandstone cliffs, the very image of a medieval castle in wine country. ⇨ *See Chapter 10, The Pfalz and the Rhine Terrace.*

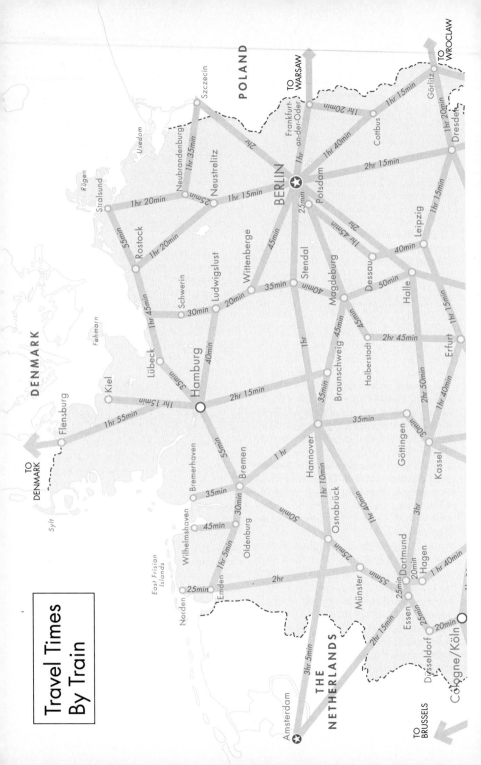

Travel Times
By Train

DENMARK

POLAND

THE NETHERLANDS

TO DENMARK

TO BRUSSELS

TO WARSAW

TO WROCLAW

Amsterdam

Cologne/Köln

BERLIN

Hamburg

Flensburg — 1hr 55min
Kiel — 1hr 15min
Lübeck — 35min
Lübeck — 40min Hamburg
Stralsund — 55min
Rostock — 1hr 20min
Rostock — 1hr 20min
Schwerin — 1hr 45min
Schwerin — 30min
Ludwigslust — 20min
Ludwigslust — 35min
Wittenberge — 40min
Stendal — 1hr
Neubrandenburg — 1hr 35min
Neustrelitz — 25min
Neustrelitz — 1hr 15min BERLIN
Szczecin — 2hr
Frankfurt-an-der-Oder — 1hr
Frankfurt-an-der-Oder — 1hr 20min
Cottbus — 1hr 40min
Cottbus — 1hr 15min Görlitz
Görlitz — 1hr 20min Dresden
Dresden — 2hr 15min
Potsdam — 25min
Potsdam — 45min
Leipzig — 1hr 15min
Leipzig — 40min Halle
Dessau — 2hr
Dessau — 50min Halle
Magdeburg — 1hr 45min
Magdeburg — 40min Stendal
Magdeburg — 45min
Braunschweig — 45min
Halberstadt — 2hr 45min
Erfurt — 1hr 15min
Erfurt — 1hr 40min
Erfurt — 2hr 50min
Kassel — 30min
Göttingen — 3hr
Göttingen — 2hr 45min
Göttingen — 35min
Hannover — 1hr
Hannover — 35min
Hannover — 1hr 10min
Osnabrück — 1hr 40min
Osnabrück — 25min
Münster — 55min
Dortmund — 25min
Hagen — 20min
Hagen — 1hr 40min
Essen — 25min
Düsseldorf — 20min
Düsseldorf — 2hr 15min
Bremen — 55min
Bremen — 30min
Bremen — 1hr
Bremerhaven — 35min
Wilhelmshaven — 45min
Oldenburg — 1hr 5min
Emden — 25min Norden
Emden — 2hr
Amsterdam — 3hr 5min
Hannover — 50min
Osnabrück — 50min

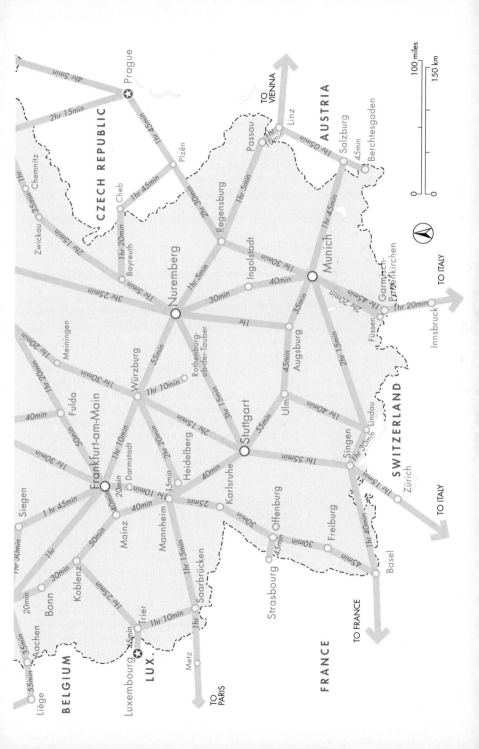

LODGING PRIMER

Whether budget and spare, or luxurious and opulent, you'll find top-quality accommodations throughout Germany to rest your travel-weary bones at the end of the day. And more often than not, you can count on sinking into a featherbed since Germans prize down-filled duvets over blankets. Whatever your pleasure, from a cozy *Gasthof* to life on the *Bauernhof*, there's a broad spectrum of choices wherever your journey takes you.

Hotels

German hotels adhere to a high standard, and you'll find that even the most basic offerings are scrupulously clean and comfortable. Of course as the number of stars goes up, so do the amenities, and you can count on the largest and best city hotels to offer concierge services and fine dining. If you prefer something more intimate, *Gasthöfe* (country inns that also serve food) offer a great value. You can also opt to stay at a winery's *Winzerhof* or at an historic castle (*Schloss*). Families can consider a *Familienhotel*, which cater to children with special menus, activities, pools, and play areas. Depending on the hotel, rates are calculated by room or by person. Prices are generally higher in summer, so consider visiting during the off-season. Most resorts offer between-season (*Zwischensaison*) and edge-of-season (*Nebensaison*) rates, and tourist offices can provide lists of hotels that offer low-price weekly packages (*Pauschalangebote*). It's wise to avoid cities during major trade fairs as rates skyrocket. Consider staying in nearby towns and commuting in.

Bed-and-Breakfasts

If you're looking for a more personal—and less expensive—alternative to a hotel, B&Bs are a good choice. Often called *Pensions*, they offer simple rooms and friendly, helpful staff. Keep in mind that not all rooms will have a private bathroom, but your stay will, of course, include breakfast. Another option is a *Fremdenzimmer*, meaning simply "rooms," normally in private houses. These are found most often in resort towns. And although it's not nearly as private as staying in a hotel or inn, it will give you a peek at how the locals live. For a taste of rural life, try an *Urlaub auf dem Bauernhof,* a farm that rents rooms.

Apartment and House Rentals

To really get a sense of how the natives live, rent a house or apartment. Known as *Ferienwohnung* or *Ferien-Appartements,* it's a popular option in Germany. In a city, you'll feel the pulse of a neighborhood, or in the country you might step out onto your balcony to take in a mountain view. When traveling with family or a group, a private home may be a better deal than booking multiple hotel rooms. Not to mention that you're likely to end up with more space.

Hostels

The country's hundreds of *Jugendherbergen* (youth hostels) are among the most efficient and up-to-date in Europe. In fact, the first youth hostel opened in Germany a hundred years ago. Hostels now cater to budget travelers of all ages, and it's not just dorm living; these days, many hostels offer rooms for families and couples.

⇨ *For resources and booking information, see Travel Smart Germany.*

TRACING YOUR GERMAN ROOTS

More than 51 million Americans claim German ancestry, and many of these Americans have a strong desire to trace their long-lost roots. The first significant waves of immigration from Germany came after the failed democratic revolutions of 1848, a time period coupled with potato blight in parts of Germany. The numbers of German immigrants did not let up until the early 20th century. If you've ever dreamed of wandering your family's ancestral village, standing in the church where your great-grandmother was baptized, or meeting the cousins who share your name, it's become easier than ever to make it happen.

Before You Go

The more you can learn about your ancestors before you go, the more fruitful your search will be once you're on German soil. The first place to seek information is directly from members of your family. Even relatives who don't know any family history may have documents stored away that can help with your sleuthing—old letters, wills, diaries, photo albums, birth and death certificates, and Bibles can be great sources of information. The first crucial facts you'll need are the name of your ancestor; his or her date of birth, marriage, or death; town or city of origin in Germany; date of emigration; ship on which he or she emigrated; and where in America he or she settled.

If family resources aren't leading you anywhere, try turning to the **Mormon Church.** The Mormon Church has made it its mission to collect mountains of genealogical information, much of which it makes available free of charge at ⊕ *www. familysearch.org.* The **National Archives** (⊕ *www.nara.gov*) keeps census records,

and anyone can, for a fee, get information from the censuses of 1940 and earlier.

Keep in mind that the spelling of your family name may not be consistent through time. Over the course of history varying rates of literacy in Germany meant that the spelling of names evolved through recent centuries. And on arrival in the States many names changed again to make them more familiar to American ears.

Once you've established some basic facts about your ancestor it's possible to start searching some German resources. Germans are excellent record keepers, but because Germany as we know it today didn't unify until 1871, records are scattered. Lists of German ship passengers—many of which are now available online—are a good next step since they often included a person's "last residence." So if you can target your ancestor's hometown, you'll open the door to a potential trove of records. Many parish registers, or church books, go back to the 15th century and documented births, baptisms, marriages, deaths, and burials.

Be sure to check out the **German National Tourist Office's** Web sites ⊕ *germanoriginality.com, www.germany.travel,* both of which provide an abundance of useful links. If you're tracking down living cousins, don't forget to try the German phonebook ⊕ *DasTelefonbuch.de.*

On the Ground in Germany

Once you arrive in Germany, you can use the computerized facilities of Bremerhaven's **German Emigration Center** (⊕ *www. dah-bremerhaven.de*) or enlist the help of an assistant to search the complete passenger lists of the HAPAG shipping line, at the **Family Research Center** in BallinStadt, Hamburg (⊕ *www.BallinStadt.de*).

WORLD WAR II SITES

When it comes to World War II, Germany has a grim past to reckon with. The country's darkest days began with Adolph Hitler's rise to power in 1933. Hitler led Germany into war in 1939 and perpetrated the darkest crimes against humanity, murdering 6 million Jews in the Holocaust. To gain perspective on the extent of the horror, it's possible to visit sites around Germany that document the atrocities.

Upon his election, Hitler set about turning **Obersalzburg** into the southern headquarters for the Nazi party and as a mountain retreat for its elite. Located in the Bavarian Alps near the German-Austrian border, the enormous compound included luxurious homes for party officials. Today you can walk through the extensive bunker system while learning about the Nazi's takeover of the area. Not far from Obersalzburg you'll find the **Kehlsteinhaus**, Hitler's private home. Designed as a 50th birthday gift for Hilter by the Nazi party, the house is also known as *Adlerhorst* (Eagle's Nest). It's perched on a cliff, seemingly at the top of the world. The house's precarious location probably saved it from British bombing raids. ⇨ *See Chapter 3, The Bavarian Alps.*

The Nazi organized nationwide bookburnings, one of which took place in Berlin on **Bebelplatz**. On an evening in May 1933, Nazis and Hitler Youth gathered here to burn 20,000 books considered offensive to the party. Today there is a ghostly memorial of empty library shelves sunken in the center of the square. ⇨ *See Chapter 15, Berlin.*

Masters of propaganda, the Nazis staged colossal rallies intended to impress the German people. Hitler considered Nürnberg so quintessentially German he developed an enormous complex here, the **Nazi Party Rally Grounds**, to host massive parades, military exercises, and major assemblies of the Nazi party. The Congress Hall, meant to outshine Rome's Colosseum, is the largest remaining building from the Nazi era. It houses a **Documentation Center** that explores the Nazi's tyranny. At the **Nürnberg Trials Memorial** you'll see where the war crimes trials took place between November 1945 and October 1946. In this courthouse Nazi officials stood before an international military tribunal to answer for their crimes. The Allied victors chose Nürnberg on purpose—it's the place Germany's first anti-Semitic laws passed, decreeing the boycott of Jewish businesses. ⇨ *See Chapter 5, Franconia and the German Danube.*

The **KZ-Gedenkstätte Dachau** is a memorial and site of the former notorious death camp. Hitler created Dachau soon after taking power. It was the first concentration camp to be built and became the model for all other camps. Tens of thousands of prisoners perished here. Today you'll see a few remaining cell blocks and the crematorium, along with moving shrines and memorials to the dead. ⇨ *See Chapter 2, Munich.*

Bergen-Belsen, the most infamous of the concentration camps, is the place Anne Frank perished along with more than 80,000 other prisoners. Starving and sick prisoners lived in abject squalor, deliberately neglected by their captors. A meadow is all that remains of the camp, but it is still a chilling place to visit. The documentation center offers a detailed history of concentration camps and shows wrenching photos of unburied bodies and emaciated prisoners. ⇨ *See Chapter 12, The Fairy Tale Road.*

Munich

WORD OF MOUTH

"Who wouldn't love Munich? The transportation system zips you everywhere you need to go, the city is lively and interesting, and has a good mix of locals and tourists."

—jahlie

WELCOME TO MUNICH

TOP REASONS TO GO

★ **Deutsches Museum:** The museum has an impressive collection of science and technology exhibits, and its location on the Isar River is perfect for a relaxing afternoon stroll.

★ **Englischer Garten:** With expansive greens, beautiful lakes, and beer gardens, the English Garden is a great place for a bike ride or a long walk.

★ **Gärtnerplatz:** Gärtnerplatz and the adjoining Glockenbach-viertel are the hip hoods of the moment, with trendy bars, restaurants, cafés, and shops.

★ **Views from the Frauenkirche:** This 14th-century church tower gives you a panorama of downtown Munich that can't be beat. There are 86 steps in a circular shaft to get to the elevator, but the view is worth it.

★ **Viktualienmarkt:** Experience farmers'-market-style shopping, where there's fresh produce, finger food, and a beer garden; it's not to be missed.

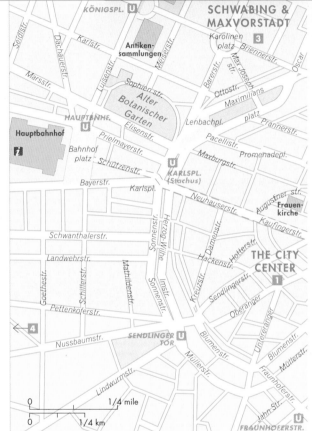

1 The City Center. Marienplatz, the Rathaus, and the surrounding streets are a hub for locals and tourists alike. Here you'll find the soaring towers of the Frauenkirche, Munich's landmark church. East of Marienplatz, down toward the Isar River, is the maze of Old Town's smaller streets.

2 Royal Munich. The Residenz, or royal palace, is the focus here. Bordering the Residenz to the north is the Hofgarten, or Court Garden. Farther northeast is the Englischer Garten, great for sunbathing or something sportier.

3 Schwabing and Maxvorstadt. On one side of Maxvorstadt is Ludwigstrasse,

2

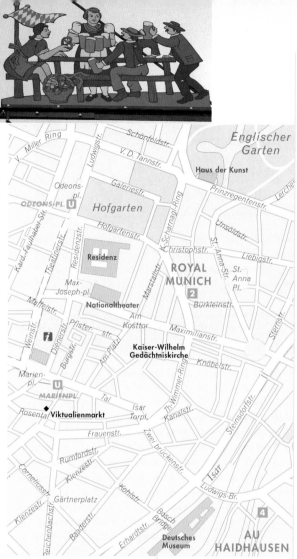

GETTING ORIENTED

In the relaxed and sunnier southern part of Germany, Munich (München) is the proud capital of the state of Bavaria. Even Germans come here to vacation, mixing the city's pleasures with the nearby natural surroundings—on clear days, from downtown the Alps appear to be much closer than around 40 mi away. The city bills itself *"Die Weltstadt mit Herz"* ("the cosmopolitan city with heart"), but in rare bouts of self-deprecatory humor, friendly Bavarians will remind you that it isn't much more than a country town with a million people. Münchners will also tell visitors that the city is special because of its *Gemütlichkeit*—loosely translated as "conviviality." This can be overdone, but with open-air markets, numerous parks, the lovely Isar River, and loads of beer halls, Munich has a certain charm that few cities can match.

a wide avenue flanked by impressive buildings, running from the Feldherrnhalle and Odeonsplatz to the Victory Arch. A block farther west are Maxvorstadt's smaller streets, lined with shops and restaurants frequented by students. The big museums lie another two blocks west. Schwabing starts north of the Victory

Arch, where Ludwigstrasse becomes Leopoldstrasse.

4 Outside the Center. Ludwigvorstadt is southwest of the City Center and includes the Oktoberfest grounds. The western part of the city is dominated by Nymphenburg Castle and its glorious grounds. Across the Isar is fashionable Lehel, and Au-Haidhausen areas.

VIKTUALIENMARKT
MUNICH'S FARMERS' MARKET

It's not just the fascinating array of fruit, vegetables, olives, breads, cheeses, meats, pickles, and honey that make *Viktualienmarkt* (victuals market) so attractive. The towering maypole, small *Wirtshäuser* (pub-restaurants), and beer gardens also set the scene for a fascinating trek through Munich's most famous market.

Vegetables, fruits, and jarred and prepared foods are available at Munich's biggest farmers' market.

The Viktualienmarkt's history can be traced to the early 19th century, when King Max I Joseph decreed that Marienplatz was too small to house the major city market. In 1807, a bigger version was created a few hundred meters to the south, where it stands today. You are just as likely to find a Münchner buying something here as you are a visitor. Indeed, a number of City Center restaurants proudly proclaim that they get their ingredients "fresh from the market." This is the place to pick up a *Brotzeit*: bread, olives, cheeses, gherkins, and whatever else strikes your fancy, then retreat to a favorite *Biergarten* to enjoy the bounty.

—Paul Wheatley

MARKET ETIQUETTE

All stalls are open weekdays 10–6 and Saturday 10–3, though some stalls open earlier or close later. It's not kosher to touch the fresh produce but it is to ask to taste a few different olives or cheeses before buying. The quality of the various produce is invariably good; competition is fierce, so it has to be. Therefore, buy the best of what you fancy from a number of stalls, not just one or two.

VIKTUALIENMARKT BEST BUYS

BEER AND PREPARED FOOD

If it's just a beer you're after, there are a number of beer stalls not far from the towering maypole. **Biergarten am Viktualienmarkt** is the main location, but there are also small *Imbissstände* (snack bars) where you can pick up roast pork and beer. **Kleiner Ochsenbrater** sells delicious organic roast dishes. **Poseidon** and the nearby **Fisch Witte** rustle up a fine selection of fish dishes, including very good soups and stews. **Luigino's Bio Feinkost,** an organic deli that also has fine cheeses and wines, is the spot for a quick grilled sandwich. And the modest-looking **Münchner Suppenküche** dishes out delightful helpings of soup, including oxtail, chicken, and spicy lentil.

FRUITS AND VEGETABLES

The mainstay of the market is fruit and vegetables, and there are a number of top-quality stalls to choose from. The centrally located **Frutique** has some of the freshest, most attractive-looking, and ripest produce on display. For something a little more exotic, try out **Exoten Müller,** which specializes in unusual fruits and vegetables from around the world.

HONIGHÄUSEL AM MÜNCHNER VIKTUALIENMARKT

Honighäusel means "small honey house" and is an apt description of this petite

honey wonderland. Much of the produce comes from Bavaria, but there's also a selection of honeys from farther afield: Italy, France, even New Zealand. This is also the place to buy honey marmalades and soaps, and beeswax candles. For a chilly evening, pick up a bottle of Bavarian honey schnapps.

LUDWIG FREISINGER'S "SAURE ECKE"

This is the place to create the perfect *Biergarten Brotzeit* (beer garden snack). Ask for a mixture of green and black olives with different fillings. You can also pick up the traditional biergarten cheese spread, *Obatzter*, which is made of Camembert and other white cheeses, butter, paprika, and onions. There's a huge selection of peppers filled with cheese, plus feta salad, hummus, and the enormous *Essiggurke* (gherkins). The best are crunchy when you bite into them but tender inside, with a light tanginess. A *Fladenbrot*, a circular, flat white bread, is enough for two people, and the perfect accompaniment.

SCHENK'S

There are numerous stalls at the market that serve mouthwatering, freshly pressed fruit drinks, so no matter where you buy, you won't be disappointed. Schenk's is a favorite because the drinks are top-notch and the staff is engaging, speaks English, and takes the time to explain the ingredients in each drink.

MUNICH'S BEER GARDENS

With a bit of sunshine, a handful of picnic tables, and a few of the finest beers around, you have yourself a *Biergarten* (beer garden). There are beer gardens throughout Germany, and many imitations across the world but the most traditional, and the best, are still found in and around Munich. The elixir that transforms the traditional Munich beer garden into something special is the unbeatable atmosphere.

(above and lower right) It's easy to make new friends in the convivial atmosphere of a beer garden. (upper right) The Chinese Tower within the Englisher Garten is one of the most famous beer gardens in Munich.

Beer gardens formed out of necessity. Brewers in the 18th and 19th centuries struggled to keep beer cool to prevent it from spoiling in warm weather. As early as 1724, Munich brewers dug cellars and began to store beer next to the shady shores of the river Isar. Local residents promptly took along their beer glasses for a cool drink and before long the odd table and bench appeared, and the beer garden tradition was born.
—Paul Wheatley

BIERGARTEN ETIQUETTE

Often, a beer garden is separated between where guests can bring food and where they must buy it. Simply ask to avoid confusion or look for tablecloths—generally these are table-service only. The basis of a beer garden *Brotzeit* (snack) is delicious black bread, Obatzter, sausage, gherkin, and radish. As tradition dictates, remember to also order *Ein Mass Bier bitte! (A liter of beer please!)*

MUNICH'S BEST BEER GARDENS

AUGUSTINER KELLER BIERGARTEN

This is perhaps the most popular beer garden in Munich and certainly one of the largest. It is part of the **Augustiner Keller** restaurant, a few hundred meters from Hackerbrücke S-bahn station, or 5–6 minutes from the Hauptbahnhof. The main garden is separated half between where you can bring your own food and half where you buy food from the beer garden. The leaves from countless horse chestnut trees provide a canopy covering, which adds to the dreamy atmosphere.

HOFBRÄUKELLER AM WIENER PLATZ

Some of the best beer gardens are found away from the City Center. This one is a 15-minute walk (or take Tram 18 or 19 from the Hauptbahnhof) over the Isar River, past the Maximilianeum, to Wiener Platz, a delightful square well worth visiting. The beer garden attracts Münchners, as well as groups of British, Australian, and American expats. The staple beer garden chicken, fries, roast pork, and spare ribs are better here than most.

KÖNIGLICHER HIRSCHGARTEN

With seating for 8,000, this is the biggest and most family-friendly beer garden in Munich. In a former royal hunting area outside the City Center, it takes a little time and effort to reach.

Your best bet is to rent a bike and cycle there. The rewards are clear: surrounded by trees and green parkland, the tables and benches seem to go on forever. The food and beer is good and there is even a small deer sanctuary, lending the "Deer Park" its name.

PARK CAFÉ

This is where trendsetters head for a more modern and sunny—there isn't much shade here—take on the traditional beer garden. Set in Munich's old botanical garden, five minutes from the Hauptbahnhof, this medium-size beer garden regularly has DJs and other musical events in the evenings. It also has a good selection of cakes and a hip indoor bar.

SEEHAUS IM ENGLISCHEN GARTEN

Within Munich's very own oasis, the **Englisher Garten**, it was an inspired decision to build this beer garden next to a boating lake. A leisurely stroll through the garden to the Seehaus takes about an hour, but go early because it's popular after 11:30. Lots of people visit the Englischer Garten to play soccer and other sports, and if you want to join in you might want to pass on the roast dinner and instead snack on a *Brezn* (pretzels), Obatzter, and salad.

Updated by
Paul Wheatley

Known today as the city of laptops and lederhosen, modern Munich is a cosmopolitan playground that nevertheless represents what the rest of the world incorrectly sees as "typically German": world-famous Oktoberfest, traditional *lederhosen* (leather pants), busty Bavarian waitresses in *dirndls* (traditional dresses), beer steins, and sausages.

Munich's cleanliness, safety, and Mediterranean pace give it a slightly rustic feel. The broad sidewalks, fashionable boutiques and eateries, views of the Alps, a sizable river running through town, and a huge green park make Munich one of Germany's most visited cities. When the first rays of spring sun begin warming the air, follow the locals to their beloved beer gardens, shaded by massive chestnut trees.

The number of electronics and computer firms—Siemens, Microsoft, and SAP, for starters—makes Munich a sort of mini–Silicon Valley of Germany, but for all its business drive, this is still a city with roots in the 12th century, when it began as a market town on the "salt road" between mighty Salzburg and Augsburg.

That Munich was the birthplace of the Nazi movement is a difficult truth that those living here continue to grapple with. To distance the city from its Nazi past, city leaders looked to Munich's long pre-Nazi history to highlight what they decreed was the real Munich: a city of great architecture, high art, and fine music. Many of the Altstadt's architectural gems were rebuilt post-war, including the lavish Cuvilliés-Theater, the Altes Rathaus, and the Frauenkirche.

The city's appreciation of the arts began under the kings and dukes of the Wittelsbach Dynasty, which ruled Bavaria for eight centuries, until 1918. The Wittelsbach legacy is alive and well in many of the city's museums and exhibition centers, the Opera House, the philharmonic, and, of course, the Residenz, the city's royal palace. Any walk in the City Center will take you past ravishing baroque decoration and grand 19th-century neoclassical architecture.

PLANNING

WHEN TO GO

Munich is a year-round city, but it's nicer to walk through the Englischer Garten and have your beer under a shady chestnut tree when the weather's fine in summer. If fate takes you to Munich through its long, cold winter, though, there are world-class museums and good restaurants to keep you entertained. Theater and opera fans will especially enjoy the winter season, when the tour buses and the camera-toting crowds are gone. Munich comes alive during Fasching, the German Mardi Gras, in the pre-Easter season. The festival of festivals, Oktoberfest, takes place from the end of September to early October. A few post-summer sunny days are usual, but the Oktoberfest is also an indication that fall is here, and the short march to winter has arrived.

GETTING HERE AND AROUND

AIR TRAVEL

Munich's International Airport is 28 km (17 mi) northeast of the City Center and has excellent air service from all corners of the world. An excellent train service links the airport with downtown. The S-1 and S-8 lines operate from a terminal directly beneath the airport's arrival and departure halls. S-bahn trains leave at 20-minute intervals on both lines, and the journey takes around 40 minutes. The easiest way is to buy a *Tageskarte* (day card) for the Gesamtnetz, costing €10.80, which allows you to travel anywhere on the system for the rest of the day until 6 am the next morning. The similarly priced bus service is slower than the S-bahn link and not recommended. A taxi from the airport costs around €50. During rush hours (7 am–10 am and 4 pm–7 pm), allow up to an hour of driving time. If you're driving from the airport to the city yourself, take the A-9 and follow the signs for "München Stadtmitte" (downtown). If you're driving from the City Center, head north through Schwabing, join the A-9 autobahn at the Frankfurter Ring intersection, and follow the signs for the airport ("Flughafen").

Airport Information Flughafen München ☎ *089/97500* ⊕ *www.munich-airport.de.*

BUS TRAVEL

With its futuristic architecture, Munich's 2009-finished Central Bus Terminal (ZOB) means that many excursions and longer trips are now centralized five minutes from the main train station. As well as numerous shops and banks, travel firms offer bus tickets and destination advice at the ZOB.

Touring Eurolines buses arrive at and depart from the ZOB. Check their excellent Web site for trips to Neuschwanstein and the Romantic Road.

Bus Information Central Bus Station Munich (*ZOB*). ✉ *Hackerbrücke, Ludwigvorstadt, Munich* ⊕ *ZOB is about 800 m from the main station along Arnulfstrasse; if traveling by S-bahn, it's adjacent to Hackerbrücke S-bahn station* ☎ *089/4520–9890* ⊕ *www.muenchen-zob.de.*

CAR TRAVEL

If you're driving to Munich from the north (Nürnberg or Frankfurt), leave the autobahn at the Schwabing exit. From Stuttgart and the west, the autobahn ends at Obermenzing, one of Munich's most westerly suburbs. The autobahns from Salzburg and the east, Garmisch and the south, and Lindau and the southwest all join the Mittlerer Ring (city beltway). When leaving any autobahn, follow the signs reading "Stadtmitte" for downtown Munich.

PUBLIC TRANSIT

Munich has one of the most efficient and comprehensive public-transportation systems in Europe, consisting of the U-bahn (subway), the S-bahn (suburban railway), the Strassenbahn (also called "Tram," streetcars), and buses. Marienplatz forms the heart of the U-bahn and S-bahn network, which operates regularly from around 5 am to 1 am (intermittently otherwise, so check times if you're expecting a long night or early start). The main service counter under Marienplatz sells tickets and gives out information, also in English. The Web site ⊕ *www. muenchen.de* has an excellent and extensive transportation section, also in English.

A basic *Einzelfahrkarte* (one-way ticket) costs €1.20 for a journey of up to four stops, €2.50 for a longer ride in the inner zone. If you're taking a number of trips around the city, save money by buying a *Streifenkarte*, or multiple 10-strip ticket for €12. On a journey of up to four stops validate one ticket, for the inner zone, two. If you plan to do several trips during one day, buy a *Tageskarte* (day card) for €10.80, which allows you to travel anywhere until 6 am the next morning. For a family of up to five (two adults and three children under age 15) the *Tageskarte* costs €19.60. A three-day card costs €13.30 for a single and €22.80 for the partner version. All tickets must be validated at one of the blue time-stamping machines at the station, or on buses and trams as soon as you board (wait till you've found a seat, and if an inspector's around you'll get a spot fine). Spot checks for validated tickets are common, and you'll be fined €40 if you're caught without a valid ticket. All tickets are sold at the blue dispensers at U- and S-bahn stations and at some bus and streetcar stops. Bus drivers have only single tickets (the most expensive kind). ■TIP➡ Holders of a EurailPass, a Youth Pass, or an Inter-Rail card can travel free on all suburban railway trains (S-bahn). Be forewarned: If caught on anything but the S-bahn without a normal public transport ticket, you will be fined €40, with no exceptions.

Public Transportation Information Munich Transport Company (MVG). 🕾 089/4142–4344 ⊕ www.mvg-mobil.de.

TAXI TRAVEL

Munich's cream-color taxis are numerous. Hail them in the street or phone for one (there's an extra charge of €1.20 if you call). Rates start at €3.30. Expect to pay €8–€10 for a short trip within the city. There's a €0.60 charge for each piece of luggage.

Taxi Information Taxi München 🕾 089/21610, 089/19410 ⊕ www.taxi-muenchen.com.

2

TRAIN TRAVEL

All long-distance rail services arrive at and depart from the Hauptbahnhof; trains to and from some destinations in Bavaria use the adjoining Starnberger Bahnhof, which is under the same roof. The high-speed InterCity Express (ICE) trains connect Munich, Augsburg, Frankfurt, and Hamburg on one line, Munich, Nürnberg, Würzburg, and Hamburg on another. Regensburg can be reached from Munich on Regio trains. You can purchase tickets by credit card at vending machines. For travel information at the main train station, go to one of the four Deutsche Bahn (German Rail) counters at the center of the main arrival and departures hall with German- and English-speaking personnel or contact ⊕ *www.bahn.de.* With more complex questions, go to the EurAide office, which also serves English-speaking train travelers.

Train Information Deutsche Bahn ☎ *0800/150–7090* ⊕ *www.bahn.de.*

TOURS

The tourist office offers individual guided tours for fees ranging between €100 and €250. Bookings must be made at least 10 days in advance. ⇨ *See Sports and the Outdoors for information on bike tours.*

A novel way of seeing the city is to hop on one of the bike-rickshaws. The bike-powered two-seater cabs operate between Marienplatz and the Chinesischer Turm in the Englischer Garten. Just hail one; the cost is €37 per hour.

BUS TOURS

The best way to get a feel of Munich is to board one of the double-decker sightseeing buses with big signs that read "Stadtrundfahrten" (city sightseeing). They leave from across the main railway station. There are the blue ones run by Autobus Oberbayern and, 80 meters to the left, yellow and red ones run by Yellow Cab Muenchen. Tours cost €13 per person (cheaper if booked online) and offer hop-on, hop-off service throughout the City Center with commentary via headphones available in eight languages. There are five stops and the full tour takes about an hour. Both bus lines run about every 20 to 30 minutes, between 9 am and 5 pm. The only difference is that the blue line has—in addition to the headphones for other languages—a live host who offers running commentary in English and German, so seamlessly that after five minutes you're sure you speak both languages. On the bus ask for a brochure with many other suggestions for bus trips.

WALKING TOURS

Radius Tours & Bikes has theme walks of Munich highlights, Third Reich Munich, and the Dachau concentration camp. Third Reich tours depart from the Radius offices, in the Hauptbahnhof, just across from platform 31, daily at 3 pm between early April and mid-October (Monday, Tuesday, Friday, and Sunday at 11:30 am the rest of the year). The Dachau tour is daily at 9:15 and 12.30 early April to mid-October and daily at 11 for the rest of the year. Advance booking is not necessary for individuals.

Tour Information Munich Tourist Office ☎ *089/2339–6500* ⊕ *www.munich-tourist.de.* **Radius Tours & Bike Rental** ✉ *Hauptbahnhof, Arnulfstr. 3, Ludwigvorstadt* ☎ *089/5502–9374* ⊕ *www.radius-tours.de.*

VISITOR INFORMATION

The Munich Tourist office has two locations. The Hauptbahnhof (main train station) tourist office is open Monday–Saturday 9–8 (in winter 10–6) and Sunday 10–6. The Tourist office in the Rathaus (city hall) is open weekdays 10–8 and Saturday 10–4.

For information on the Bavarian mountain region south of Munich, contact the Tourismusverband München-Oberbayern.

As well as tourist offices, a great way to start your Munich visit is to go to infopoint, in the Alterhof's Kaiserburg, an information center for castles across Bavaria. Here, in a superbly atmospheric vaulted cellar, there are two films (ask for English versions), which combined make a great introduction to any Munich visit. One film is about the city's history, the other about the Alterhof. From Marienplatz, walk 170 meters down the attractive Burgstrasse, through the Alterhof tower. On the right is infopoint. Around 100 meters farther, you'll pass the Münzhof entrance, and another 50 meters is the Residenz Theater, next to the Residenz. Along with the films, this walk is an incredible 350-meter introduction to 1,000 years of Munich history.

Visitor Information Munich Tourist Office—Hauptbahnhof ⊠ *Hauptbahnhofpf, Bahnhofpl. 2, Ludwigvorstadt* ☎ *089/2339–6500* ⊕ *www.munich-tourist. de.* **Munich Tourist Office—Rathaus** ⊠ *Marienpl., Neues Rathaus, City Center* ☎ *089/2339–6500.* **Tourismusverband München-Oberbayern (**Upper Bavarian Regional Tourist Office**).** ⊠ *Radolfzeller Str. 15, Westkreuz, Aubing* ☎ *089/829–2180* ⊕ *www.bavarian-alps.travel.*

PLANNING YOUR TIME

Set aside at least a whole day for the Old Town, hitting Marienplatz when the glockenspiel plays at 11 am or noon before a crowd of spectators. There's a reason why Munich's Kaufingerstrasse has Germany's most expensive shop rents. Munich is Germany's most affluent city and Münchners like to spend. The pedestrian zone can get maddeningly full between noon and 2, when everyone in town seems to be taking a quick shopping break, though it's hardly any better up until around 5. If you've already seen the glockenspiel, try to avoid the area at that time. Avoid the museum crowds in Schwabing and Maxvorstadt by visiting as early in the day as possible. All Munich seems to discover an interest in art on Sunday, when most municipal and state-funded museums are free; you might want to take this day off from culture and have a late breakfast or brunch at the Elisabethmarkt. Some beer gardens and taverns have Sunday-morning jazz concerts. Many Schwabing bars have happy hours between 6 and 8—a relaxing way to end your day.

EXPLORING MUNICH

Munich is a wealthy city—and it shows. At times this affluence may come across as conservatism. But what makes Munich so unique is that it's a new city superimposed on the old. Hip neighborhoods are riddled with traditional locales, and flashy materialism thrives together with a love of the outdoors.

The Aeronautics Hall of the Deutsches Musuem displays aircraft from the early days of flight to jets and helicopters.

THE CITY CENTER

Munich's Old Town (Altstadt) has been rebuilt so often over the centuries that it no longer has the homogeneous look of so many other German towns. World War II leveled a good portion of the center, but an amazing job has been done to restore a bit of the fairy-tale feel that once prevailed here.

TOP ATTRACTIONS

Fodor's Choice ★

Deutsches Museum (*German Museum*). Aircraft, vehicles, cutting-edge technology, historic machinery, and even a mine fill a monumental building on an island in the Isar River, which comprises one of the best science and technology museums in the world. The collection is spread out over 47,000 square meters, six floors of exhibits, and about 50 exhibition areas. The Centre for New Technologies includes interactive exhibitions, including nanotechnology, biotechnology, and robotics. It could change the way you think about science forever. Children have their own area, the Kinderreich, where they can learn about modern technology and science through numerous interactive displays (parents must accompany their children). One of the most technically advanced planetariums in Europe has four shows daily. The Internet café on the third floor is open daily 9–3, other cafés until 4. ■ TIP→ To arrange for a two-hour tour in English, call at least six weeks in advance. The **Verkehrszentrum** (Center for Transportation), on the former trade-fair grounds at the Theresienhöhe, has been completely renovated and houses an amazing collection of the museum's transportation exhibits. ✉ *Museumsinsel 1, Ludwigvorstadt* ☎ *089/21791* ⊕ *www.deutsches-museum.de* ⊠ *Museum €8.50* ⊗ *Daily 9–5* Ⓜ *Isartor (S-bahn).*

★ **Frauenkirche** (*Church of Our Lady*). Munich's *Dom* (cathedral) is a distinctive late-Gothic brick structure with two huge towers. Each is 99 meters high, an important figure today because, in a nonbinding referendum, Münchners narrowly voted to restrict all new buildings to below this height within the city's middle ring road. The main body of the cathedral was completed in 20 years (1468–88)—a record time in those days, and the distinctive onion-dome-like cupolas were added by 1525. Shortly after the original work was completed in 1688, Jörg von Halspach, the Frauenkirche's architect, died, but he became celebrated for the unique achievement of seeing a project on such a scale from start to finish. The twin towers are easily the most recognized feature of the city skyline and a Munich trademark. In 1944–45, the building suffered severe damage during Allied bombing raids, and was restored between 1947 and 1957. Inside, the church combines most of von Halspach's plans, with a stark, clean modernity and simplicity of line, emphasized by slender, white octagonal pillars that sweep up through the nave to the tracery ceiling. As you enter the church, look on the stone floor for the dark imprint of a large foot—the *Teufelstritt* (Devil's Footprint). According to lore, the devil challenged von Halspach to build a church without windows. The architect accepted the challenge. When he completed the job, he led the devil to a spot in the bright church from which the 66-foot-high windows could not be seen. The devil triumphantly stomped his foot and left the *Teufelstritt*, only to be enraged when he ventured further inside and realized that windows had been included. The cathedral houses an elaborate 15th-century black-marble tomb guarded by four 16th-century armored knights. It's the final resting place of Duke Ludwig IV (1302–47), who became Holy Roman Emperor Ludwig the Bavarian in 1328. One of the Frauenkirche's great treasures is the collection of numerous wooden busts of the apostles, saints, and prophets above the choir, carved by the 15th-century Munich sculptor Erasmus Grasser. The observation platform high up in the south tower offers a splendid view of the city and the Alps. But beware, you must climb 86 steps to reach the tower elevator. ✉ *Frauenpl., City Center* ☎ 089/290–0820 ✍ *Cathedral free, tower €3* ⊙ *Tower elevator Apr.–Oct., Mon.–Sat. 10–5* Ⓜ *Marienplatz (U-bahn and S-bahn).*

★ **Marienplatz.** Bordered by the Neues Rathaus, shops, and cafés, this square is named after the gilded statue of the Virgin Mary that has watched over it for more than three centuries. It was erected in 1638 at the behest of Elector Maximilian I as an act of thanksgiving for the city's survival of the Thirty Years' War, the cataclysmic, partly religious struggle that devastated vast regions of Germany. When the statue was taken down from its marble column for cleaning in 1960, workmen found a small casket in the base containing a splinter of wood said to be from the cross of Christ. ■TIP➜ On the fifth floor of a building facing the Neues Rathaus is the Café Glockenspiel. It overlooks the entire square and provides a perfect view of the glockenspiel from the front and St. Peter's Church from the back terrace. Entrance is around the back. ✉ *Bounded by Kaufingerstr., Rosenstr., Weinstr., and Dienerstr., City Center* Ⓜ *Marienplatz (U-bahn and S-bahn).*

2

Michaelskirche. A curious story explains why this hugely impressive Renaissance church, adjoining a former extensive Jesuit college, has no tower. Seven years after the start of construction, in 1583, the main tower collapsed. Its patron, pious Duke Wilhelm V, regarded the disaster as a heavenly sign that the church wasn't big enough, so he ordered a change in the plans—this time without a tower. Completed in 1597, the barrel vaulting of St. Michael's is second in size only to that of St. Peter's in Rome. The duke is buried in the crypt, along with 40 other Wittelsbach family members, including the eccentric King Ludwig II. A severe neoclassical monument in the north transept contains the tomb of Napoleon's stepson, Eugène de Beauharnais, who married a daughter of King Maximilian I and died in Munich in 1824. Once again a Jesuit church, it is the venue for free performances of church music. A poster to the right of the front portal gives the dates. ⊠ *Neuhauser Str. 6, City Center* ☎ *089/231–7060* ⊠ *€2 crypt* ☉ *Mon. and Fri. 10–7, Tues.–Thurs. and Sat. 8–7, Sun. 7–10:15; all except during services* Ⓜ *Karlsplatz (U-bahn and S-bahn).*

Neues Rathaus (*New Town Hall*). Munich's present neo-Gothic town hall was built in three sections and two phases between 1867 and 1908. It was a necessary enlargement on the nearby Old Town Hall, but city fathers also saw it as presenting Munich as a modern city, independent from the waning powers of the Bavarian Wittelsbach royal house. Architectural historians are divided over its merits, although its dramatic scale and lavish detailing are impressive. Perhaps the most serious criticism is that the Dutch and Flemish styles of the building seem out of place amid the baroque and rococo styles of parts of the Altstadt. The main tower's 1908-finished **glockenspiel** (a chiming clock with mechanical figures), the largest in Germany, plays daily at 11 am, noon, and 9 pm, with an additional performance at 5 pm March–October. As chimes peal out over the square, the clock's doors flip open and brightly colored dancers and jousting knights act out two events from Munich's past: a tournament held in Marienplatz in 1568 and the *Schäfflertanz* (Dance of the Coopers), which commemorated the end of the plague of 1515–17. ■TIP➔ You, too, can travel up there, by elevator, to an observation point near the top of one of the towers. On a clear day the view across the city and the Alps behind is spectacular. ⊠ *Neues Rathaus, Marienpl. 8, City Center* ⊠ *Tower €2* ☉ *Nov.–Apr., Mon.–Thurs. 9–4, Fri. 9–1; May–Oct., weekdays 9–7, weekends 10–7* Ⓜ *Marienplatz (U-bahn and S-bahn).*

Peterskirche (*St. Peter's Church*). The Altstadt's oldest parish church (called locally Alter Peter, Old Peter) traces its origins to the 12th century, and has been restored in various architectural styles, including Gothic, baroque, and rococo. The rich baroque interior has a magnificent high altar and aisle pillars decorated with exquisite 18th-century figures of the apostles. In clear weather it's well worth the long climb up the 300-foot-high tower, with a panoramic view of the Alps. ⊠ *Rindermarkt, City Center* ☎ *089/260–4828* ⊠ *Tower €1.50* ☉ *Mon.–Sat. 9–6, Sun. 10–6* Ⓜ *Marienplatz (U-bahn and S-bahn).*

★ **Viktualienmarkt** (*Victuals Market*). The city's open-air market really is the beating heart of downtown Munich. It has just about every fresh fruit or vegetable you can imagine, as well as German and international specialties. All kinds of people come here for a quick bite, from well-heeled businesspeople and casual tourists to mortar- and paint-covered workers. It's also the realm of the garrulous, sturdy market women who run the stalls with dictatorial authority. ■TIP➔ Whether here, or at a bakery, do not try to select your pickings by hand. Ask, and let it be served to you. Try Poseidon's for quality fish treats, Mercado Latino on the south side of the market for an empanada and fine wines from South America, or Freisinger for Mediterranean delights. There's also a great beer garden (open pretty much whenever the sun is shining), where you can enjoy your snacks with cold local beer. A sign above the counter tells you what's on tap. The choice rotates throughout the year among the six major Munich breweries, which are displayed on the maypole. These are also the only six breweries officially allowed to serve their wares at the Oktoberfest. ☯ *Mon.–Fri. 10–6; Sat. 10–3* Ⓜ *Marienplatz (U-bahn and S-bahn).*

WORTH NOTING

Alter Hof (*Münchner Kaiserburg*). The Alter Hof was the original medieval residence of the Wittelsbachs, the ruling dynasty of Bavaria, established in 1180. The palace now serves various functions. Its **info-point** serves as a tourist information center for Bavaria's many castles. Beneath this, in the atmospheric late-Gothic vaulted hall of the **Münchenner Kaiserburg**, there is a multimedia presentation about the palace's history. The west wing is home to the **Vinorant Alter Hof,** a fine restaurant and wine cellar with decent prices. For the more adventurous, try out the restaurant's "dinner in the dark" four-course menu, during which you'll be served and eat your meal in pitch black. All of your senses—from taste to touch—will seem to be on red alert, leading to a unique culinary experience. ✉ *Alter Hof 1, City Center* ☎ *089/2101–4050* ⊕ *infopoint: www.infopoint-museen-bayern.de; Kaiserburg: www.muenchner-kaiserburg.de; Vinorant Alter Hof: www.alter-hof-muenchen.de* ☯ *Kaiserburg: Mon.–Sat. 10–6; Vinorant Alter Hof: restaurant, Mon.–Sat. 11–1, wine cellar, daily 3–1* Ⓜ *Marienplatz (U-bahn and S-bahn).*

☾ **Altes Rathaus** (*Old Town Hall*). Much of the work on Munich's first town hall was done in the 15th century, though it had various alterations through the centuries. Its great hall—destroyed in 1943–45 but now fully restored—was the work of great architect Jörg von Halspach. Postwar the tower was rebuilt as it looked in the 15th century and now it's used for official receptions and is not usually open to the public. The tower provides a fairy-tale-like setting for the **Spielzeugmuseum** (Toy Museum), accessible via a winding staircase. Its toys, dolls, and teddy bears are on display, with a collection of Barbies from the United States. ✉ *Marienpl. 15, City Center* ☎ *089/294–001 Spielzeugmuseum* ☞ *Museum €3* ☯ *Daily 10–5:30* Ⓜ *Marienplatz (U-bahn and S-bahn).*

★ **Asamkirche** (*St.-Johann-Nepomuk-Kirche*). Perhaps Munich's most ostentatious church, it has a suitably extraordinary entrance, framed by raw-rock foundations. The insignificant door, crammed between its craggy shoulders, gives little idea of the opulence and lavish detailing within the small 18th-century church (there are only 12 rows of pews). Above the doorway St. Nepomuk, the 14th-century Bohemian monk and patron saint of Bavaria, who drowned in the Danube, is being led by angels from a rocky riverbank to heaven. The church's official name is Church of St. Johann Nepomuk, but it's known as the Asamkirche for its architects, the brothers Cosmas Damian and Egid Quirin Asam. The interior of the church is a prime example of true southern German late-baroque architecture. Frescoes by Cosmas Damian Asam and rosy marble cover the walls. The sheer wealth of statues and gilding is stunning—there's even a gilt skeleton at the sanctuary's portal. ✉ *Sendlinger Str. 32, City Center* ☼ *Daily 9–5:30* Ⓜ *Sendlingertor (U-bahn).*

Hauptbahnhof (*Central Station*). The train station isn't a cultural site, but it's a particularly handy starting point for exploring. The city tourist office here has maps and helpful information on events around town. On the underground level are all sorts of shops that remain open even on Sunday and holidays. There are also a number of places to get a late-night snack in and around the station. ✉ *Bahnhofpl., Hauptbahnhof* ☎ *089/130810555* ⊕ *www.hauptbahnhof-muenchen.de* Ⓜ *Hauptbahnhof (U-bahn and S-bahn).*

Jewish Center Munich. The striking new Jewish Center at St.-Jakobs-Platz has transformed a formerly sleepy area into an elegant, busy modern square. The buildings signify the return of the Jewish community to Munich's City Center, six decades after the end of the Third Reich. The center includes a museum focusing on Jewish history in Munich (plus kosher cafe), and the impressive Ohel Jakob Synagogue, with its rough slabs topped by a latticelike cover, manifesting a thought-provoking sense of permanence. The third building is a community center, which includes the kosher Einstein restaurant (⊕ *www.einstein-restaurant.de*). Guided tours of the synagogue are in great demand, so to see it, arrange a time weeks in advance (*089/202400–100*). ✉ *St.-Jakobspl. 16, City Center* ☎ *089/233–989–96096* ⊕ *www.juedisches-museum-muenchen. de* 🖃 *Museum €6; synagogue tour €5* ☼ *Museum Tues.–Sun. 10–6; synagogue by prior arrangement* Ⓜ *Marienplatz (U-bahn and S-bahn).*

Karlsplatz. In 1728 Eustachius Föderl opened an inn and beer garden here, which, according to one theory, is why it became known as Stachus. The beer garden is long gone, but the name has remained—locals still refer to this busy intersection as Stachus. One of Munich's most popular fountains is here—it acts as a magnet on hot summer days, when city shoppers and office workers seek a cool place to relax. ■ TIP→ In winter it makes way for an ice-skating rink. It's a bustling meeting point, more so since the complete renovation and extension of the underground shopping center in 2010–11. ⊕ *www.stachus-passagen. com* Ⓜ *Karlsplatz (U-bahn and S-bahn).*

Münchner Stadtmuseum (*City Museum*). On St.-Jakobs-Platz, this museum is as eclectic inside as the architecture is outside. The buildings, facing St.-Jakobs-Platz, originally date to the 15th century, though were destroyed by Allied bombs in 1944–45 and subsequently rebuilt. Recent extensive renovation has revitalized the City Museum, exemplified by its fabulous **Typical Munich!** exhibition, charting a riotous history few other city's can match: royal capital, brewery center, capital of art and classical music, and now wealthy, high-tech and cultural center par

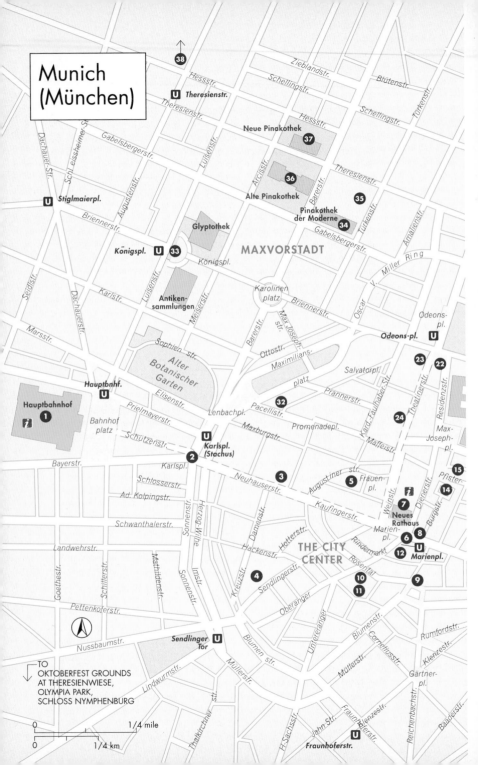

excellence. There is also a separate, permanent exhibition dealing with the city's Nazi past. The museum is home to a film museum showing rarely screened movies, a puppet theater, while there are numerous photo and other temporary exhibitions. Check out the museum shop, servus.heimat, with the great and good of Munich kitsch, and some pretty good Munich souvenirs. ■TIP→ **Even the threat of sunshine makes it difficult to get a table outside the lively museum café on St.-Jakobs-Platz. Try the inner courtyard, which still catches the sun but can be less packed.** ✉ *St.-Jakobspl. 1, City Center* ☎ *089/2332–2370* ⊕ *www.stadtmuseum-online.de/* 🎫 *€4 (€6 special exhibitions), €1 Sun.* ⊙ *Tues.–Sun. 10–6* Ⓜ *Marienplatz (U-bahn and S-bahn).*

ROYAL MUNICH

From the modest palace of the Alter Hof, the Wittelsbachs expanded their quarters northward, away from the jumble of narrow streets in the old quarter. Three splendid avenues radiated outward from their new palace and garden grounds, and fine homes arose along them. One of them—Prinzregentenstrasse—marks the southern edge of Munich's huge public park, the Englischer Garten, a present from the royal family to the locals. Lehel, an upmarket residential neighborhood that straddles Prinzregentenstrasse, plays host to one of Munich's most famous museums, the Haus der Kunst, as well as to some lesser-known but architecturally stunning museums.

TOP ATTRACTIONS

Fodor's Choice
★

Englischer Garten (*English Garden*). Bigger than New York's Central Park and London's Hyde Park, this seemingly endless green space blends into the open countryside at the north of the city. It was a former favorite royal hunting ground until partly opened to the public by Benjamin Thompson, later Count Rumford, a great American-British reformer and scientist. Born in Massachusetts, he left after siding with the British during the Revolutionary War. Thompson's Munich garden plans were expanded on and the park became a gift from Elector Karl Theodor to the people of Munich. Today's park covers more than 1,000 acres and has 78 km (48 mi) of paths, 8.5 km (5.2 mi) of streams, and more than 100 foot- and other bridges. The open, informal landscaping—reminiscent of the rolling parklands with which English aristocrats of the 18th century liked to surround their country homes—gave the park its name. It has a boating lake, four beer gardens, and a series of curious decorative and monumental constructions, including the Monopteros, a Greek temple designed by Leo von Klenze for King Ludwig I, and built in 1837 on an artificial hill in the southern section of the park. There are great sunset views of Munich from the Monopteros hill. In the center of the park's most popular beer garden is a Chinese pagoda, erected in 1790. It was destroyed during the war and then reconstructed. ■TIP→ **The Chinese Tower beer garden is hugely popular, but the park has prettier places for sipping a beer: the Aumeister, for example, along the northern perimeter, is in an early-19th-century hunting lodge.** At the Seehaus, on the shore of the Kleinhesseloher *See* (lake), choose between a smart restaurant or a cozy *Bierstube* (beer tavern) in addition to the beer garden right on the lake.

The Englischer Garten is a paradise for joggers, cyclists, musicians, soccer players, sunbathers, and, in winter, cross-country skiers. The park has semiofficial areas for nude sunbathing—the Germans have a positively pagan attitude toward the sun—so in some areas don't be surprised to see naked bodies bordering the flower beds and paths. ⊠ *Main entrances at various points on Prinzregentenstr. and Königinstr., City Center/Schwabing.*

Feldherrnhalle (*Field Marshals' Hall*). Erected in 1841–44, this open pavilion, fronted with three huge arches, was modeled on the 14th-century Loggia dei Lanzi in Florence. It opens the grand Ludwigstrasse (closed by Siegestor) on Odeonsplatz, and was built to honor Bavarian military leaders and the Bavarian army. Two huge Bavarian lions are flanked by the larger-than-life statues of Count Johann Tserclaes Tilly, who led Catholic forces in the Thirty Years' War, and Prince Karl Philipp Wrede, hero of the 19th-century Napoleonic Wars.

There's an astonishing photograph of a 25-year-old Adolf Hitler standing in front of the Feldherrnhalle on August 2, 1914, amid a huge crowd gathered to celebrate the beginning of World War I. The imposing structure was turned into a militaristic shrine in the 1930s and '40s by the Nazis, to whom it was significant because it marked the site of Hitler's abortive coup, or putsch, in 1923 (today, there's a plaque on the ground, 20 meters from the lion on the left, commemorating the four policemen who were killed in the putsch attempt). During the Third Reich, all who passed it had to give the Nazi salute. Viscardigasse, a tiny alley behind the Feldherrnhalle, linking Residenzstrasse and Theatinerstrasse, and now lined with exclusive boutiques, was used by those who wanted to dodge the routine. Its nickname was *Drückebergergasse*, or Dodgers' Alley. ⊠ *South end of Odeonspl., Residenzstr. 1, City Center* Ⓜ *Odeonsplatz (U-bahn).*

Haus der Kunst (*House of Art*). This colonnaded, classical-style building is one of Munich's most significant examples of Hitler-era architecture, and was officially opened as Haus der deustchen Kunst (House of German Art) by the Führer himself. During the Third Reich it showed only work deemed to reflect the Nazi aesthetic. One of its most successful postwar exhibitions was devoted to works banned by the Nazis. It now hosts cutting-edge exhibitions on art, photography, and sculpture, as well as theatrical and musical happenings. With the departure to London's prestigious Tate Modern in October 2011 of the gallery's hugely successful director Chris Derkon, Nigerian-born (but U.S.-based) Okwui Enwezor has large shoes to fill. The survival-of-the-chicest disco, P1, is in the building's west wing. ⊠ *Prinzregentenstr. 1, Lehel* ☎ *089/2112–7113* ⊕ *www.hausderkunst.de* ☜ *Varies €5–€10* ☼ *Mon.-Sun. 10–8, Thurs. 10–10* Ⓜ *Odeonsplatz (U-bahn).*

Hofbräuhaus. Duke Wilhelm V founded Munich's most famous brewery in 1589; it's been at its present location since 1808. As beer and restaurants became major players in the city's economy, it needed to be completely rebuilt and modernized in 1897. The last major work was its reconstruction in 1950 after its destruction in the war. *Hofbräu* means "court brewery," and the golden beer is poured in pitcher-size liter mugs. If the cavernous ground-floor hall is too noisy for you, there is a quieter restaurant upstairs. In this legendary establishment Americans, Australians, and Italians often far outnumber locals, who regard it as too much of a tourist trap. The brass band that performs here most days adds modern pop and American folk music to the traditional German numbers. ⊠ *Platzl 9, City Center* ☎ *089/2913–6100* ☉ *Daily 9–11:30* Ⓜ *Marienplatz (U-bahn and S-bahn).*

Hofgarten (*Court Garden*). The formal court garden was once part of the royal palace grounds, dating back to at least the early 15th century. It's now bordered on two sides by arcades designed in the 19th century by court architect Leo von Klenze. On the east side of the garden is the state chancellery (office of the Bavarian Minister President), built in 1990–93 around the ruins of the 19th-century Army Museum and incorporating the remains of a Renaissance arcade. Bombed during World War II air raids, the museum stood untouched for almost 40 years as a reminder of the war. Critics were horrified that a former army museum building could be used to represent modern, democratic Bavaria, not to mention about the immense cost. In front of the chancellery stands one of Europe's most unusual—some say most effective—war memorials. Instead of looking up at a monument, you are led down to a **sunken crypt** covered by a massive granite block. In the crypt lies a German soldier from World War I. The crypt is a stark contrast to the **memorial** that stands unobtrusively in front of the northern wing of the chancellery: a simple cube of black marble bearing facsimiles of handwritten wartime manifestos by anti-Nazi leaders, including the youthful members of the White Rose resistance movement. ∎TIP➡ As you enter the garden from Odeonsplatz, take a look at the frescoes (drawn by art students 1826–29 and of varying degrees of quality) in the passage of the Hofgartentor with depictions from Bavarian history. ⊠ *Hofgartenstr., north of Residenz, City Center* Ⓜ *Odeonsplatz (U-bahn).*

★ **Residenz** (*Royal Palace*). One of Germany's true treasures, Munich's royal Residenz (Residence) began in 1363 as the modest **Neuveste** (New Fortress) on the northeastern city boundary. By the time the Bavarian monarchy fell, in 1918, the palace could compare favorably with the best in Europe. The Wittelsbach dukes moved here when the tenements of an expanding Munich encroached on their Alter Hof. In succeeding centuries the royal residence developed according to the importance, requirements, and whims of its occupants. It came to include, for example, the Königsbau (on Max-Joseph-Platz); the Festsaal (Banquet Hall); the newly renovated Cuvilliés-Theater (Altes Residenztheater); the Allerheiligen-Hofkirche (All Saints' Church); and the adjoining Nationaltheater (Bavarian State Opera).

Fire was one of the biggest fears for all citizens for centuries: in 1674, fire destroyed large parts of the palace on Residenzstrasse, while most of the Neuevest complex burned to the ground in 1750, including the theater. This meant a new court theater was needed, and the result was the incomparable rococo Cuvilliés-Theater.

With the Residenz's central location, it was pretty much inevitable that the Allied bombing of 1944–45 would cause immense damage, and susbequent reconstruction took decades. For tourists today, however, it really is a treasure chamber of delight. To wander around the Residenz can last anywhere from three hours to all day. The 16th-century, 70-meter-long arched **Antiquarium**, built for Duke Albrecht V's collection of antiques and library, is recognized as one of the most impressive Renaissance creations outside Italy (today it's used chiefly for state receptions). There are a number of halls and courtyards that show concerts, from the postwar **Neuer Herkulessaal** to the outdoor **Brunnenhof**. And particular favorites for visitors are the re-creation of many private royal chambers and apartments. The accumulated Wittelsbach treasures are on view in several museums that comprise the Residenz. ■ TIP→ All the different rooms, halls, galleries, chapels, and museums within the Residenzmuseum, as well as the Cuvilliés-Theater and Treasury, can be visited with a combination ticket that costs €13.

Schatzkammer (*Treasury*). The Schatzkammer comprises around 1,250 masterworks, including a host of treasures from the Wittelsbach royal crown jewels. A highlight is the crown belonging to Bavaria's first king, Maximilian I, created in Paris in 1806–07. The Schatzkammer collection has a staggering centerpiece—a renowned 50-cm-high Renaissance statue of St. George studded with diamonds, pearls, and rubies. ⊠ *€7, combined ticket with Residenzmuseum €11* ⊙ *Apr.–Oct. 15, daily 9–6; Oct. 16–Mar., daily 10–4.*

Residenzmuseum. The Residenzmuseum comprises everything in the Residenz apart from the Schatzkammer (Treasury) and the Cuvilliés-Theater. Paintings, tapestries, furniture, and porcelain are housed in various rooms and halls. Look out for the **Grüne Galerie** (**Green Gallery**), named after its green silk decoration, and the great and the good of the Wittelsbach royal family in the Ahnengalerie (Ancestral Gallery). ⊠ *€7* ⊙ *Apr. 1–Oct. 17, daily 9–6; Oct. 18–Mar. 31, daily 10–5.*

Staatliche Münzsammlung. More than 300,000 coins, bank notes, medals and stones, some 5,000 years old, star in the Staatliche Münzsammlung. ✚ *Entrance via Residenzstr.* ☏ *089/227–221* ⊠ *€2.50, €1 Sun.* ⊙ *Tues.–Sun. 10–5*

Staatliche Sammlung Ägyptischer Kunst. Various Bavarian rulers were fascinated with the ancient world and in the 19th century accumulated huge quantities of significant Egyptian treasures, part of which make up the Staatliche Sammlung Ägyptischer Kunst. In 2013 the collection will move from its current location in the Residenz to an impressive new building in Munich's superb Kunstareal (Art Quarter). ⊠ *Hofgarten entrance, Hofgartenstr., Residenz, City Center* ☏ *089/298–546* ⊠ *€5, Sun. €1* ⊙ *Tues. 9–9, Wed.–Fri. 9–5, weekends 10–5* Ⓜ *Odeonsplatz (U-bahn).*

Cuvilliés-Theater. In summer, chamber-music concerts take place in the inner courtyard. Also in the center of the complex is the small, rococo Altes Residenztheater/Cuvilliés-Theater. It was built by François Cuvilliés between 1751 and 1755, and performances are still held here. The French-born Cuvilliés was a dwarf who was admitted to the

Bavarian court as a decorative "bauble." Prince Max Emanuel recognized his innate artistic ability and had him trained as an architect. The prince's eye for talent gave Germany some of its richest rococo treasures. ⊠ *Max-Joseph-Pl. 3, for tickets, enter from Max-Joseph-Platz, City Center* ☎ *089/290–671* ⊕ *www.residenz-muenchen.de* ⊙ *Residenz Museum and Treasury Apr. 1–Oct. 17, daily 9–6; Oct. 18–Mar. 31, daily 10–5* Ⓜ *Odeonsplatz (U-bahn).*

Theatinerkirche (St. Kajetan) (*Theatine Church*). This glorious baroque church owes its Italian appearance to its founder, Princess Henriette Adelaide of Savoy, who commissioned it in gratitude for the birth of her son and heir, Max Emanuel, in 1662. A native of Turin, the princess distrusted Bavarian architects and builders and thus summoned Agostino Barelli, a master builder from Bologna, to construct her church. It is modeled on Rome's Sant'Andrea della Valle. Barelli worked on the building for 12 years, but he was dismissed as too quarrelsome. It was another 100 years before the building was finished in a style similar to today's. Its striking yellow facade stands out, and its two lofty towers, topped by delightful cupolas, frame the entrance, with the central dome at the back. The superb stuccowork on the inside has a remarkably light feeling owing to its brilliant white color. ■ TIP➔ The expansive Odeonsplatz in front of the Feldherrnhalle and Theatinerkirche is often used for outdoor stage events. ⊠ *Theatinerstr. 22, City Center* ☎ *089/210–6960* Ⓜ *Odeonsplatz (U-bahn).*

┌ QUICK
BITES

Tambosi. Open since 1775, Tambosi is Munich's longest-running café. As well as an impressive provenance, its location is superb, partly sitting in full view of Theatinerkirche on Odeonsplatz and partly in the Hofgarten. Watch the hustle and bustle of Munich's street life from an outdoor table in the city side, or retreat through a gate in the Hofgarten's western wall to the café's tree-shaded beer garden. If the weather is cool or rainy, find a corner in the cozy, eclectically furnished interior. ⊠ *Odeonspl. 18, City Center* ☎ *089/298–322.*

WORTH NOTING

Archäologische Staatssammlung (*Bavarian State Archaeological Collection*). This is Bavaria's fascinating record of its prehistoric, Roman, and Celtic past. The perfectly preserved body of a ritually sacrificed young girl, recovered from a Bavarian peat moor, is among the more spine-chilling exhibits. Head down to the basement to see the fine Roman mosaic floor. ⊠ *Lerchenfeldstr. 2, Lehel* ☎ *089/211–2402* ⊕ *www.archaeologie-bayern.de* ⊠ *€3, €1 on Sun.* ⊙ *Tues.–Sun. 9:30–5* Ⓜ *Lehel (U-bahn); Nationalmuseum (tram).*

Bayerisches Nationalmuseum (*Bavarian National Museum*). Although the museum places emphasis on Bavarian cultural history, it has art and artifacts of international importance and regular exhibitions that attract worldwide attention. The museum is a journey through time, principally from the early Middle Ages to the 20th century, with medieval and Renaissance wood carvings, works by the great Renaissance sculptor Tilman Riemenschneider, tapestries, arms and armor, a unique collection of Christmas crèches (the *Krippenschau*), Bavarian and German folk art and a significant Jugendstil collection. ⊠ *Prinzregentenstr. 3, Lehel* ☏ *089/2112–4216* ⊕ *www.bayerisches-nationalmuseum.de* 🎫 *€5 recommended combined ticket for museum and Bollert collection, €1 Sun.* ⊙ *Tues.–Sun. 10–5, Thurs. 10–8* Ⓜ *Lehel (U-bahn).*

Kunsthalle der Hypo-Kulturstiftung (*Hall of the Hypobank's Cultural Foundation*). Chagall, Giacometti, Picasso, and Gauguin are among the artists featured in the past at this highly regarded exhibition hall in the middle of the commercial pedestrian zone, within the upscale Fünf Höfe shopping mall, designed by the Swiss architect team Herzog and de Meuron, who also designed London's Tate Modern. Exhibitions at the Kunsthalle rarely disappoint, making it one Germany's most interesting exhibition venues. It often works in cooperation with international institutes of the highest repute, such as in its 2010 version of London's Victoria & Albert Museum Maharaja exhibition. ■ TIP→ The accompanying Cafe Kunsthalle is a destination for exhibition visitors and general public alike. The very good main menu changes weekly, though it's worth a visit just for the cakes. ⊠ *Theatinerstr. 8, City Center* ☏ *089/224–412* ⊕ *www.hypo-kunsthalle.de* 🎫 *Varies but usually around €10* ⊙ *Daily 10–8; Cafe Kunsthalle weekdays 8–8, Sat. 9–8, Sun. 10–8* Ⓜ *Odeonsplatz (U-bahn).*

Ludwigskirche (*Ludwig's Church*). Planted halfway along the stark, neoclassical Ludwigstrasse is this superb twin-towered Byzantine- and Italian-influenced church, built between 1829 and 1838 at the behest of King Ludwig I to provide his newly completed suburb with a parish church. From across the other side of the road, look up to see the splendidly colored, 2009-finished mosaic on the church's roof. Inside, see one of the great modern frescoes, the *Last Judgment* by Peter von Cornelius, in the choir. At 60 feet by 37 feet, it's also one of the world's largest. ⊠ *Ludwigstr. 22, Maxvorstadt* ☏ *089/287–7990* ⊙ *Daily 7–7* Ⓜ *Universität (U-bahn).*

Maximilianstrasse. Munich's most expensive and exclusive shopping street was named after King Maximilian II, who wanted to break away from the Greek-influenced classical architecture favored by his father, Ludwig I. He thus created this broad boulevard lined with majestic buildings culminating on a rise above the river Isar at the stately **Maximilianeum.** Finished in 1874, this building was conceived as an elite education foundation for the most talented young people across Bavaria, regardless of status or wealth. It is still home to an education foundation, but its principle role is as the grand, if slightly confined, home to the Bavarian state parliament. ■ TIP→ Rather than take the tram to see the Maximilianeum, the whole walk along Maximilianstrasse (from Max-Joesph-Platz) is rewarding. You'll pass various boutiques, plus the five-star Hotel Vier Jahreszeiten, the Upper Bavarian Parliament, the Museum für Völkerkunde (State Museum of Ethnology) and cross the picturesque river Isar. Five minutes past the Maximilianeum, on the charming Wiener Platz, is the Hofbräukeller and its excellent beer garden. Ⓜ *Maximilianeum (Tram).*

Museum Villa Stuck. This dramatic neoclassical villa is the former home of one of Germany's leading avant-garde artists at the turn of the 20th century, Franz von Stuck (1863–1928). His work, at times haunting, frequently erotic, and occasionally humorous, covers the walls of the ground-floor rooms. Stuck was prominent in the Munich art Secession (1892), though the museum is today famous for its fabulous Jugendstil (art nouveau) collections. The museum also features the artist's former quarters as well as special exhibits. ⊠ *Prinzregentenstr. 60, Haidhausen* ☎ *089/455–5510* ⊕ *www.villastuck.de* ☖ *€9* ⊙ *Tues.–Sun. 11–6* Ⓜ *Prinzregentenplatz (U-bahn).*

Nationaltheater (*National Theater*). Bavaria's original National Theater at Max-Joseph-Platz didn't last long. Though opened in 1818, in 1823, before it was completely finished, it burned to the ground. It had been rebuilt by 1825 with its eight-column portico, and went on to premiere Richard Wagner's world-famous *Tristan und Isolde* (1865), *Meistersinger von Nürnberg* (1868), *Rheingold* (1869), and *Walküre* (1870). Allied bombs destroyed much of the interior in 1943, and its facade and elements of its interior were rebuilt as it was prewar. It finally reopened in 1963. Today, it is one of Europe's largest opera houses and contains some of the world's most advanced stage technologies. Moreover, as the principle home to the Bavarian State Opera, it is considered one of the world's outstanding opera houses. ⇨ *See also Cuvilliès Theatre and Prinzregententheater, which are also home to the Bavarian State Opera.* ⊠ *Max-Joseph-Pl. 2, City Center* ☎ *089/218–501 for tickets* Ⓜ *Odeonsplatz (U-bahn).*

Sammlung Schack (*Schack-Galerie*). Around 180 German 19th-century paintings from the Romantic era up to the periods of Realism and Symbolism make up the collections of the Sammlung Schack, originally the private collection of Count Adolf Friedrich von Schack. ■TIP➔ A day ticket to the state museums of the three Pinakotheks, Brandhorst, and Sammlung Schack costs €12. ⊠ *Prinzregentenstr. 9, Lehel* ☎ *089/2380–5224* ☖ *€4, €1 Sun.* ⊙ *Wed.–Sun. 10–6* Ⓜ *Lehel (U-bahn).*

Siegestor (*Victory Arch*). Built to bookend the Feldherrnhalle and mark the end of Ludwigstrasse, Siegestor nowadays also marks the beginning of Leopoldstrasse. Unsurprisingly, it has Italian origins and was modeled on the Arch of Constantine in Rome, and was built (1849) to honor the achievements of the Bavarian army during the Wars of Liberation (1813–15) against Napoléon. It received heavy bomb damage in 1944, and at the end of the war Munich authorities decided it should be torn down for safety reasons. Major Eugene Keller, the head of the U.S. military government in the postwar city intervened and saved it. Its postwar inscription on the side facing the inner city is best translated as: "dedicated to victory, destroyed by war, a monument to peace." ⊠ *Siegestor, Schwabing* Ⓜ *Universität (U-bahn).*

Bavaria: A Country Within a Country

For most visitors, Bavaria, with its own sense of Gemütlichkeit, beer gardens, quaint little villages, and culturally rich cities, is often seen as the quintessence of Germany. In fact, nothing could be further from the truth. Of the 16 German Länder, as the German federal states are called, none is more fiercely independent than Bavaria. In fact, it was an autonomous dukedom and later kingdom until 1871, when it was incorporated into the German nation state.

For Bavarians, anything beyond the state's borders remains foreign territory. The state has its own anthem and its own flag, part of which—the blue-and-white lozenges in the center—has virtually become a regional trademark symbolizing quality and tradition. Bavarian politicians discussing the issue of Europe in speeches will often refer to Bavaria almost as if it were a national state. They inevitably

call it by its full official name: Freistaat Bayern, or simply der Freistaat, meaning "the Free State." The term was coined by Kurt Eisner, Minister President of the Socialist government that rid the land of the Wittelsbach dynasty in 1918. It is simply a German way of saying republic—a land governed by the people. Bavaria's status as a republic is mentioned in the first line of the separate Bavarian constitution that was signed under the aegis of the American occupation forces in 1946.

Bavaria is not the only Freistaat in Germany, a fact not too many Germans are aware of. Thuringia and Saxony also boast that title. But the Bavarians are the only ones who make such a public point of it. As they say, clocks in Bavaria run differently. Now you know why.

—Marton Radkai

SCHWABING AND MAXVORSTADT: ART MUSEUMS AND GALLERIES

Some of the finest museums in Europe are in lower Schwabing and Maxvorstadt, particularly the *Kunstareal* (Art Quarter), crossing Barer Strasse and Theresienstrasse. Schwabing, the former artists' neighborhood, is no longer quite the bohemian area where such diverse residents as Lenin and Kandinsky were once neighbors, but the cultural foundations of Maxvorstadt are immutable. Where the two areas meet, in the streets behind the university, life hums with a creative vibrancy that is difficult to detect elsewhere in Munich. The difficult part is having time to see it all.

Head east or west of Leopoldstrasse to explore the side streets: around Wedekindplatz near Münchner Freiheit, a few hundred yards from the Englischer Garten, or enjoy the shops and cafés in the student quarter to the west of Leopoldstrasse. On Sunday, one euro gets you admission to all three of the fantastic Pinakothek museums. As for snacks along the way as you explore, Elisabethmarkt is the place to pick up a quick bite to eat or to relax with a beer in the small beer garden.

TOP ATTRACTIONS

Fodor's Choice
★ **Alte Pinakothek.** With numerous Old Master paintings from the Netherlands, Italy, France, and Germany, the long redbrick Alte Pinakothek holds one of the most significant art collections in the world. It was originally constructed by Leo von Klenze between 1826 and 1836 to exhibit the collection of 14th- to 18th-century works (started by Duke Wilhelm IV in the 16th century). Wittelsbach rulers through the centuries were avid collectors and today the collection comprises about 700 pieces. Among the European masterpieces on view are paintings by Dürer, Titian, Rembrandt, da Vinci, Rubens (the museum has one of the world's largest Rubens collections), and two celebrated Murillos. Most of the picture captions are in German only, so it is best to rent an English audio guide, although the audio tour does not cover every painting. Nevertheless, this museum is not to be missed. Along with the Pinakothek der Moderne, Neue Pinakothek, and Museum Brandhorst, the Alter Pinakothek forms a central part of Munich's world-class *Kunstareal* (Art Quarter). Museums and collections here are of the highest quality, and are a few hundred meters apart. ■ TIP➔ To save money, get a Tageskarte (day ticket), which provides entry to all these museums (plus the Schack Gallery, in Lehel) for just €12. ✉ *(Entrance facing Theresienstr.), Barerstr. 27, Maxvorstadt* ☎ *089/2380–5216* ⊕ *www. alte-pinakothek.de* 💷*€7, €1 Sun.* ⊙ *Wed.–Sun. 10–6, Tues. 10–8* Ⓜ *Königsplatz (U-bahn).*

Königsplatz. Munich's greatest monarch, Ludwig I, was responsible for Munich in the 19th century becoming known as Athens on the Isar, and the impressive buildings designed by Leo von Klenze that line this elegant and expansive square bear testament to his obsession with antiquity. The two templelike structures facing one another are now the **Antikensammlungen** (an acclaimed collection of Greek and Roman antiquities) and the **Glyptothek** (a fine collection of Greek and Roman statues) museums. During the Third Reich, this was a favorite parade ground for the Nazis, and it was paved over for that purpose in the 1930s. Although today a busy road passes through it, Munich authorities ensured the square returned to the more dignified appearance intended by Ludwig I. Today, the broad green lawns in front of the museums attract students and tourists in the warmer months, who gather for concerts, films, and other events. ■ TIP➔ The area around here, focused on Briennerstrasse, became the national center of the Nazi Party in the 1930s and '40s, with various buildings taken over or built by Nazi authorities. Nazi HQ, the Brown House, was between Königsplatz and the obelisk at Karolinenplatz. Destroyed in the war, the empty space is to be filled with the new Munich Documentation Centre for the History of National Socialism. On Arcisstrasse 12 is the Nazi-era building (now a music school) where in 1938 Britain's Prime Minister, Neville Chamberlain, infamously thought he had negotiated "peace in our time" with Hitler. ☎ *089/5998–8830 Antikensammlungen, 089/286100 Glyptothek* 💷 *Both €3.50* ⊙ *Antikensammlungen: Tues. and Thurs.– Sun. 10–5, Wed. 10–8. Glyptothek: Fri.–Sun. and Tues. 10–5; Thurs. 10–8* Ⓜ *Königsplatz (U-bahn).*

Museum Brandhorst. This multicolor abstract box is filled with videos, painting, sculptures, and installations by artists such as Andy Warhol, Damien Hirst, Gerhard Richter, and Joseph Beuys, and is a real treat for contemporary art fans. The location in the middle of the historic Kunstareal art district, although shocking to some less progressive art aficionados, highlighted that the city has broken out of the shackles of its postwar conservatism. ■TIP➔ Königsplatz U-Bahn is a simple way to get to the Kunstareal, though it involves a pleasant 15-minute walk. Tram 27 takes you directly from Karlsplatz to the Pinakothek stop, in the heart of the Kunstareal. ⊠ *Theresienstr. 35a, Maxvorstadt, Munich* ☎ *089/ 2380–52286* ⊕ *www.museum-brandhorst.de* ⊡ *€7, €1 Sun.* ☉ *Tues., Wed., and Fri.–Sun. 10–6, Thurs. 10–8* Ⓜ *Königsplatz (U-bahn); Pinakotheken (Tram 27).*

Fodor's Choice   **Neue Pinakothek.** Another museum packed with masters, the fabulous
★   Neue Pinakothek reopened in 1981 to house the royal collection of modern art left homeless and scattered after its original building was destroyed in the war. The exterior of the modern building mimics an older one with Italianate influences. The interior offers a magnificent environment for picture gazing, partly owing to the natural light flooding in from skylights. French impressionists—Monet, Degas, Manet— are all well represented, while the comprehensive collection also includes great Romantic landscape painters Turner and Caspar David Friedrich, and other artists of the caliber of Van Gogh, Cezanne, and Monet. This is another must-see. ⊠ *Barerstr. 29, Maxvorstadt* ☎ *089/2380–5195* ⊕ *www.neue-pinakothek.de* ⊡ *€7, €1 Sun.* ☉ *Wed. 10–8, Thurs.–Mon. 10–6* Ⓜ *Königsplatz (U-bahn); Pinakotheken (Tram 27).*

Pinakothek der Moderne. Opened to much fanfare in 2002, this fascinating, light-filled building is home to four outstanding museums under one cupola-topped roof: art, graphic art, architecture, and design. The striking 12,000-meter-square glass-and-concrete complex by Stefan Braunfels has permanent and temporary exhibitions throughout the year in each of the four categories. The design museum is particularly popular, showing permanent exhibitions in vehicle design, computer culture, and design ideas. ⊠ *Barerstr. 40, Maxvorstadt* ☎ *089/2380–5360* ⊕ *www. pinakothek.de* ⊡ *€10, €1 Sun.* ☉ *Tues., Wed., Fri.–Sun. 10–6, Thurs. 10–8* Ⓜ *Königsplatz (U-bahn); Pinakotheken (Tram).*

QUICK BITES   **Brasserie Tresznjewski.** A good spot, especially if you're visiting the neighboring Pinakothek museums, the ever-popular Brasserie Tresznjewski serves an eclectic menu, well into the wee hours. ⊠ *Theresienstr. 72, corner of Barerstr., Maxvorstadt* ☎ *089/282–349* ⊕ *www.tresznjewski.com* ☉ *Mon.–Thurs. 8–1, Fri. and Sat. 8–2.*

Dreifaltigkeitskirche. Take a quick look at this fanciful church near Maximiliansplatz. After a local woman prophesied doom for the city unless a new church was erected, its striking baroque exterior was promptly built between 1711 and 1718. It has frescoes by Cosmas Damian Asam depicting various heroic scenes.

Elisabethmarkt. Schwabing's permanent outdoor market is smaller than the popular Viktualienmarkt, but hardly less colorful. It has a pocket-size beer garden, where a jazz band performs on Saturday in summer.

The Glyptothek museum on Königsplatz houses Greek and Roman statues.

OUTSIDE THE CENTER

TOP ATTRACTIONS

Oktoberfest Grounds at Theresienwiese. The site of Munich's famous **Oktoberfest** and the winter version of the city's **Tollwood music, art, and food festival** (it's at the Olympic area in summer) is a 10-minute walk from the Hauptbahnhof, or one stop on the subway (U-4 or U-5). The enormous exhibition ground is named after Princess Therese von Sachsen-Hildburghausen, who celebrated her marriage to future King Ludwig I here in 1810 with thousands of Münchners. The event was such a success that it became an annual celebration that has now grown into a 16-day international beer and fair-ride bonanza attracting more than 6 million people each year (it is the *October*fest because it always ends on the first Sunday in October).

Bavaria. Overlooking the Theresienwiese, home of the Oktoberfest, is a 19th-century hall of fame (Ruhmeshalle) featuring busts of famous Bavarian scientists, artists, engineers, generals, and philosophers, and a monumental bronze statue of the maiden Bavaria. Unsurprisingly, it was commissioned by the art- and architecture-obsessed King Ludwig I, though not finished before his abdication in 1848. The Bavaria is more than 60 feet high and at the time was the largest bronze figure since antiquity. The statue is hollow, and an initial 48 steps take you up to its base. Once inside, there are 66 steps to her knee, and a further 52 all the way into the braided head, the reward being a view of Munich through Bavaria's eyes. 🖼 *€3 🕑 Apr.–Oct. 15, daily 9–6 (open till 8 during Oktoberfest)* Ⓜ *Theresienhöhe (U-bahn).*

Continued on page 80

CELEBRATING OKTOBERFEST

By Ben Knight

Oktoberfests are found around the world, but the original Munich Oktoberfest has never been equaled. Six million participants over 17 days make this one of Europe's largest and best-attended festivals. It's a glorious celebration of beer, Bavarian culture, beer, folk traditions, and still more beer. So tap a barrel, grab a *Mass*, and join the party with the immortal cry: *O'zapft is!* ("It's tapped!").

You could be forgiven for reducing the world's most famous beer festival to a string of clichés—drunken revelers, deafening brass bands, and red-faced men in leather shorts and feathered hunting hats singing uproariously. But Oktoberfest appeals to a broad range of people—it can be a great day out for families, a fun night for couples, or the scene of a spectacular party for larger groups—and provides enough entertainment to exhaust kids of all ages. Party aside, Oktoberfest is a cultural institution that the people of Munich are extremely proud of. The costumes, parades, and traditions play an important role in Oktoberfest and are an integral part of local identity.

OKTOBERFEST BY THE NUMBERS

More than 7 million liters (1.85 million gallons) of beer are put away, along with 650,000 sausages, 530,000 roast chickens, and around 120 oxen all on the 103-acre Theresienwiese.

Left, Theresienwiese fairground. Top, Festival procession band.

OKTOBERFEST 101

HISTORY

The original Oktoberfest was a royal wedding party conceived in 1810 by Major Andreas Michael Dall'Armi, an officer in the Bavarian national guard. In those days, Bavaria was a pictur-esque, rural, independent monarchy. The major suggested a horse race to celebrate the wedding of Crown Prince Ludwig I (the future king) and Princess Therese of Saxony-Hildburghausen. The sports event proved popular, and was repeated every year, but it was not as popular as the barrels of beer and wagons of roasted meat that came from the countryside to feed the onlookers. Out of these catering departments, the Oktoberfest was born.

The Oktoberfest grounds were named *Theresienwiese* after Princess Therese (literally "Therese meadow"), which gave rise to the popular nickname *Wiesn* now used to denote the grounds.

Above, Opening ceremony.
Opposite. Top, Muenchner Kindl. Below, Bavarian couple dancing at Oktoberfest. Far right, Brat-wurst sausage with beer and mustard.

TOP EVENTS

Three not-to-miss Oktoberfest events are worth planning your trip around. First, there's the **ceremonial arrival of the brewers and landlords**, which starts at about 10:50 am on the first day of the festival. Setting off from Josephspital-strasse approximately a mile east of the Theresienwiese, the brewers and beer-tent landlords arrive at the Oktoberfest grounds on horse-drawn carriages fes-tooned with flowers.

This is followed at noon by the **tapping of the first barrel**, performed by the mayor of Munich with a cry of *"O'zapft is!"* in the Schottenhamel tent.

The next day, the first Sunday of the festival, sees the **Costume and Rifleman's Procession** (*Trachten- und Schützenzug*). This is Europe's biggest folk parade, consisting of some 9,000 people prom-enading through Munich on horse-drawn wagons, in marching bands, or in formation, all in their full folk rega-lia. It begins between 9 and 10 am at the Maximilianeum and follows a four-mile route to the Oktoberfest grounds.

○

COSTUMES

Walking to the Theresienwiese, you'll see more and more people wearing the traditional Oktoberfest costumes—*dirndls* (traditional dresses with a fitted bodice, blouse, skirt, and apron) for the ladies, and *lederhosen* (leather breeches) and leather waistcoats for the gentlemen. As a first-time visitor, you might be surprised by how many people of all ages actually wear the traditional Bavarian garb, also known as *Trachten*. Plenty of visitors wear it too; you can buy your Trachten from **Angermaier, Moser,** and department stores like **C&A** and **Galeria Kaufhof. Kostümverleih Breuer** (⊕ *www.kostuemverleih.com*) is a good place to rent, but call ahead to check availability.

NOSTALGIA ZONE

The introduction of a nostalgia area in 2010, to mark the 200th anniversary of the first Oktoberfest, showed how well-loved the old sights and sounds remain. It recreated the Oktoberfests of simpler eras, complete with horse-racing, wooden fairground rides, and beer brewed using traditional recipes. It has now become a regular feature of the fest, the **Oide Wiesn** (Old Wiesn).

FOOD

The full range of hearty and surprisingly excellent Bavarian cuisine is available by table service in the tents. Tents that specialize in food, rather than beer (although they sell beer too), include sausage-centered **Zur Bratwurst;** fish emporium **Fischer-Vroni; Able's Kalbs-Kuchl,** where you can try veal in myriad forms, among them the famous *Wiener Schnitzel;* and the **Ochsen-braterei,** which features ox meat.

The wide avenues between the tents are lined with stalls selling roast chicken, sugared almonds, *Lebkuchen* (decorated Bavarian gingerbread), and plenty of other baked or deep-fried treats for those who don't get a seat in a tent.

A main course in a tent can easily cost €20, while half a chicken from a stall can cost €10–12. Purchases are made in cash only, but there are ATMs near the main entrance, at the Theresienwiese U-bahn station, and throughout the Oktoberfest grounds.

GUIDE TO MAJOR BEER TENTS

The spectacular vista inside a beer tent is really what a trip to Oktoberfest is all about. There is something awe-inspiring about the sight of up to 10,000 people raising immense glasses of beer above their heads while a band leads a robust sing-along. This is a setting where the often reserved Germans let their inhibitions go, and since most of the seats are at long, communal tables, it's easy to make new friends. Below are descriptions of five of the 14 major tents. There are also 21 smaller beer tents, which together provide 105,000 seats.

SCHOTTENHAMEL

Scene: This is arguably the center of the Oktoberfest, because the mayor of Munich officially opens the festival here by tapping the first barrel. There's room for 10,000 people and it's considered the central party tent, where the young, single people of Munich gather.

Pros: Extremely lively, uninhibited atmosphere.
Cons: The emphasis is on drinking and dancing. This is not the place for a quiet, cozy chat.
Beer: Spaten-Franziskaner-Bräu has a fresh, malty taste with a clear amber color.

HIPPODROM

Scene: The ornate, Ringling Brothers–style red-and-gold facade suits the Hippodrom, which often plays host to the Oktoberfest's media circus. This is the unofficial red carpet area for celebrity guests. In the past few years, these have included Kim Kardashian, Salma Hayek, and *True Blood* star Alexander Skarsgaard. German glitterati like Boris Becker are also regulars.
Pros: The very popular champagne bar is a great place to chat with the beautiful people.
Cons: With room for only 4,200 people, this is one of the smallest of the big beer tents, making it fairly hard to get a seat. Still, it's worth wandering around.
Beer: Spaten-Franziskaner-Bräu

ABOUT THE BEER

Only the six Munich breweries (Spaten-Franziskaner-Bräu, Augustiner, Paulaner, Hacker-Pschorr, Hofbräu, and Löwenbräu) are allowed to sell beer at Oktoberfest. Each brews a special beer for the Oktoberfest with a higher alcohol percentage (6%, as opposed to 5%), and runs a major beer tent. Beer costs between €8.70 and €9.20 per *Mass* (liter).

HOFBRÄU-FESTZELT

Scene: This is the official Oktoberfest presence of the Hofbräuhaus, the immense beer hall in central Munich that has become one of the city's main tourist attractions. The proprietors take special pride in their international guests, and the tent has become an Oktoberfest launchpad for many U.S. and Australian revelers, with close to 10,000 seats.

Pros: This is the only main tent with a dance floor in front of the band. So you're spared precariously getting your groove on atop a wooden bench.

Cons: Since it's connected to the Hofbräuhaus, it can feel pretty touristy.

Beer: Hofbräu München has a sweet, yeasty flavor with a good frothy head.

LÖWENBRÄU-FESTZELT

Scene: The traditional home tent of Munich's soccer club TSV 1860 München, this 8,500-seat tent is the closest the Oktoberfest comes to a real, working-class Munich feel. Patrons are regaled at the entrance by a giant, beer-swilling plastic lion, who occasionally roars the name of his favorite beer—Löwenbräu—at new arrivals.

Pros: This tent has an unpretentious, what-you-see-is-what-you-get atmosphere.

Cons: Although the food here is good, it is pretty basic fare.

Beer: Löwenbräu is a strong beer with a slightly spicy flavor.

HACKER-FESTZELT

Scene: This tent is often nicknamed the "Bavarian heaven," mainly because of the painted clouds and other sky-related decor that hang from the ceiling (installed by Oscar-winning designer Rolf Zehetbauer). It has also become a favorite tent for native Bavarians.

Pros: This tent offers unique features including a rotating bandstand and a partially retractable roof for sunny days.

Cons: Because it's generally considered the most attractive of the tents, it fills up particularly quickly—so get a seat early.

Beer: Copper-colored **Hacker-Pschorr** has a bready taste and is one of the best of the Oktoberfest beers.

PLANNING FOR OKTOBERFEST

ADVANCE PLANNING Oktoberfest is one of Germany's biggest tourist events—it's estimated to contribute one billion euros ($1.4 billion) to Munich's economy—so you should plan everything at least six months in advance.

WHERE TO STAY Booking in advance is advisable for hotels, although you're unlikely to get a cheap deal anywhere in the immediate vicinity of Oktoberfest. For cheaper city-center options, especially if you're part of a bigger group, check out **Jaeger's Hotel** (⊕ *www.jaegershotel.de*) or **Easy Palace** (⊕ *www.easypalace.de*). Otherwise book a hotel in Munich's outskirts and take public transit in.

RESERVATIONS The tents are free to enter, but if you want to sit and carouse into the evening, you need to reserve a seat at least six months in advance. Reservations are free, but the beer tents require you to buy food and drink vouchers with the reservation. Two liters of beer and half a chicken per seat is the usual standard minimum, and the cost ranges from €20 to €80 per person, depending on the tent and

the time of day (evenings and weekends are more expensive). The vouchers can either be sent to you by mail, or picked up from special offices in Munich up to two weeks in advance. Reservations are only available through the individual beer tents, not through the Oktoberfest organizers. You can find the websites of the tents, plus addresses of the ticket offices on ⊕ *www.oktoberfest.de*.

WITHOUT RESERVATIONS There is only table service at the major tents, so in order to get served you must have a seat. If you don't have a reservation, come as early as you can; by mid-morning at the latest. One section of the central area of each tent (known as the *Mittelschiff*, or "mid-ship") is always reservation-free and you can snag a seat if you get there early. You can also sit in a reserved seat until its owner arrives.

HOURS Oktoberfest takes place September 22–October 7, 2012 and September 21–October 6, 2013. It is open from 10 am to 11:30 pm every day, although the tents open at 9 am on weekends and public holidays. Last call is 10:30 pm.

Above, interior of Hippodrom tent. Opposite, chain carousel at Oktoberfest fairground.

RESTROOMS You can use the restrooms in any tent even if you're not drinking there. They are generally clean, well lit, and easy to find.

FAMILY DAYS Tuesdays are designated family days when there are discounts on all the fairground rides. Rides range from old-fashioned carousels to vertiginous modern rollercoasters and cost between €3 and €8. There are also haunted houses, halls of mirrors, a flea circus, and many carnival games. Children are allowed in the beer tents, but kids under 6 years old must exit the tents after 8 pm.

PUBLIC TRANSIT The **Theresienwiese U-Bahn** (subway) stop is right outside Oktoberfest. However, this stop gets extremely crowded, particularly at closing time, so it might be worth walking to either the nearby **Goetheplatz** or **Poccistrasse** stations. The **Hauptbahnhof**, where virtually all public transit lines converge, is just a 10- to 15-minute walk away.

TAXIS There is one taxi stand at the southern end of the Oktoberfest area, and taxis are easy to flag down in the city. Fares start at €1.70 per km (roughly $2.50 per 0.6 mi), although the per-km price drops the farther the distance traveled.

SAFETY Oktoberfest is generally very safe. There are plenty of security personnel in the tents and at the doors, and fights are rare. There is an information center, first aid, and police station behind the Schottenhammel tent. Sexual assault is not unknown at the Oktoberfest, but facilities have been revamped to increase safety, and a security point has been added near the police and first aid stations by the *Sichere Wiesn für Mädchen und Frauen* (Safe Oktoberfest for Women and Girls). See ⊕ *www.sicherewiesn.de* for more safety information for women.

FOR MORE INFORMATION The official Oktoberfest website is ⊕ *www.oktoberfest.de*, which includes a useful English guide. The official "Oktoberfest.de" iPhone app offers news on upcoming events and a location feature in case you get lost.

Ⓒ **Olympiapark** (*Olympic Park*). Built for the 1972 Olympic Games on the staggering quantities of rubble delivered from the war-time destruction of Munich, the Olympiapark was—and still is—considered an architectural and landscape wonder. The jewel in the crown is the Olympic Stadium, former home of Bayern Munich soccer team. With its truly avant-garde sweeping canopy roof, winding its way across various parts of the complex, it was an inspired design for the big events of the 1972 Olympic Games. Tragically, a bigger event relegated what was heading to be the most successful Games to date to the sidelines. It was from the adjacent accommodation area that a terrorist attack on the Israeli team began, eventually leaving 17 people dead.

Unlike many former Olympic sites around the world, today the area is heavily used and is home to numerous events, such as the **summer Tollwood** festival, concerts, sporting events, and it is a haven for joggers and people just wishing to relax. Tours of the park are conducted on a Disneyland-style train throughout the day. For the more adventurous, how about climbing the roof of the Olympic Stadium and rappelling down? For the best view of the whole city and the Alps, take the elevator up the 955-foot **Olympiaturm** (Olympic Tower) or try out the revolving Michelin-starred **Restaurant 181** on the same level. ☎ *089/350948181 restaurant* ⊕ *Olympiapark: www.olympiaparkmuenchen.de; Restaurant 181: www.restaurant181.com* 🚆 *Train tour €3, stadium tour €6, prices vary for other tours, tower €4.50* ⊙ *Tour schedules vary; call ahead for departure times* Ⓜ *Olympiazentrum (U-bahn 3).*

★ **Schloss Nymphenburg.** This glorious baroque and rococo palace, the largest of its kind in Germany, draws around 560,000 visitors a year; only the Deustches Museum is more popular in Munich. The palace grew in size and scope over more than 200 years, beginning as a summer residence built on land given by Prince Ferdinand Maria to his beloved wife, Henriette Adelaide, on the occasion of the birth of their son and heir, Max Emanuel, in 1663. The princess hired the Italian architect Agostino Barelli to build both the Theatinerkirche and the palace, which was completed in 1675 by his successor, Enrico Zuccalli. It represents a tremendous high point of Italian cultural influence, in what is undoubtedly Germany's most Italian city. Within the original building, now the central axis of the palace complex, is the magnificent **Steinerner Saal** (Great hall). It extends over two floors and is richly decorated with stucco and grandiose frescoes by masters such as Francois Cuvilliés the Elder and Johann Baptist Zimmermann. In summer, chamber-music concerts are given here. One of the surrounding royal chambers houses Ludwig I's famous **Schönheitsgalerie** (Gallery of Beauties). The walls are hung from floor to ceiling with portraits of women who caught the roving eye of Ludwig, among them a shoemaker's daughter and Lady Jane Ellenborough, the scandal-thriving English aristocrat. Lady Jane's affair with Ludwig, however, was a minor dalliance compared with the adventures in Munich of the most famous female on the walls here. Lola Montez was born in Ireland and passed herself off as a Spanish dancer during a tour of Europe's major cities, during which time she became the mistress of Franz Liszt and later Alexandre Dumas. Montez arrived in Munich in 1846 and so enchanted King Ludwig I that she became his closest advisor, much to the chagrin of his ministers and many Münchners. With revolution in the air across France and the German lands in 1848, Bavaria's greatest monarch abdicated rather than be told whom he could and could not appoint as his advisor. And Lola? She left Munich and left the king for adventures in the U.S., where she eventually died.

Amalienburg hunting lodge is a rococo gem built by François Cuvilliés. The detailed stuccowork of the little Amalienburg creates an atmosphere of courtly high life, making clear that the pleasures of the chase did not always take place outdoors. Of the lodges, only Amalienburg is open in winter. In the lavishly appointed kennels you'll see that even the dogs lived in luxury. The **Pagodenburg** was built for slightly informal royal tea parties. Its elegant French exterior disguises an Asian-influenced interior, in which exotic teas from India and China were served. Swimming parties were held in the **Badenburg,** Europe's first post-Roman heated pool. Take Tram 17 or Bus 51 from the City Center to the Schloss Nymphenburg stop.

Marstallmuseum & Porzellan Manufaktur Nymphenburg (*Museum of Royal Carriages & Porcelain Manufacturer Nymphenburg*). Nymphenburg contains so much of interest that a day hardly provides enough time. Don't leave without visiting the former royal stables, now the Marstallmuseum. It houses a fleet of vehicles, including an elaborately decorated sleigh in which King Ludwig II once glided through the Bavarian twilight, flaming torches lighting the way. Also exhibited in the Marstallmuseum are examples of the world-renowned Nymphenburg porcelain, which has been produced on the palace grounds since 1761. ■TIP→ Nymphenburg porcelain has dedicated stores at Odeonsplatz and the luxury Bayerische Hof hotel (Promenadeplatz), while it is also available in numerous other shops around the city. ☎ 089/179–080 *Schloss Nymphenburg* ☝ *€4.50* ⊙ *Apr. 1–Oct. 15 daily 9–6; Oct. 16–Mar. 31 daily 10–4.*

Museum Mensch und Natur (*Museum of Man and Nature*). This popular museum in the north wing of Schloss Nymphenburg has nothing to do with the Wittelsbachs but is one of the palace's major attractions. The Museum Mensch und Natur concentrates on three areas of interest: the variety of life on Earth, the history of humankind, and our place in the environment. Main exhibits include a huge representation of the human brain and a chunk of Alpine crystal weighing half a ton. ☎ *089/1795890* ☝ *€3, Sun. €1* ⊙ *Tues., Wed., Fri. 9–5, Thurs. 9–8, weekends 10–6* ⊠ *Schloss Nymphenburg, Nymphenburg* ☎ *089/179–080* ⊕ *www.schloesser.bayern.de* ☝ *Schloss Nymphenburg complex, combined ticket including Marstallmuseum (including Museum Nymphenburger Porzellan) but not Museum Mensch und Natur, €11.50 (Apr.–mid-Oct.) or €9.50 (mid-Oct.–Apr.)* ⊙ *Apr.–Oct. 15, daily 9–6; Oct. 16–Mar. 31, daily 10–4.*

Wander the extensive grounds of Schloss Nymphenburg.

WORTH NOTING

BMW Museum. Munich is the home of the famous BMW car company. The circular tower of its museum is one of the defining images of Munich's modern cityscape. It contains not only a dazzling collection of BMWs old and new but also items and exhibitions relating to the company's social history and its technical developments. It's a great place to stop in if you're at the Olympiapark already.

BMW Welt. The BMW factory is also nearby and can be toured on weekdays. However, registration for plant tours (which last a maximum of 2½ hours) is only possible in advance using the electronic registration form or via phone. ■TIP→ Reserve weeks in advance. ⊠ *Am Olympiapark 2, Milbertshofen* ☎ *0180/211–8822* ⊕ *www.bmw-welt. com* ☎ *€12; tour €15* ☉ *Tues.–Sun. 10–6* Ⓜ *Olympiazentrum (U-bahn).*

Botanischer Garten (*Botanical Garden*). On the northern edge of Schloss Nymphenburg, this collection of 14,000 plants, including orchids, cacti, cycads, Alpine flowers, and rhododendrons, makes up one of the most extensive botanical gardens in Europe. Take Tram 17 from the City Center. ⊠ *Menzingerstr. 67, Nymphenburg* ☎ *089/1786–1350* ⊕ *www. botmuc.de* ☎ *€4* ☉ *Garden Jan., Nov., and Dec., daily 9–4:30; Feb., Mar., Oct., daily 9–5; Apr. and Sept., daily 9–6; May–Aug., daily 9–7. Hothouses close 30 mins earlier and during lunch 11:45–1 in summer.*

☺ **Tierpark Hellabrunn.** On the Isar, just upstream from the city, this attractive zoo has many parklike enclosures but a minimum of cages. This zoo is slightly different from most others in that it's a self-styled nature reserve, and it follows a concept called Geo-Zoo, which means care has been taken to group animals according to their natural and geographical habitats. Critics of the concept of zoos won't agree, but supporters appreciate the extra attention to detail. As well as the usual tours, there are also nighttime guided tours with special night-vision equipment (call ahead of time). The huge zoo area also includes restaurants and children's areas, and some of the older buildings are in typical *Jugendstil* (Art Nouveau) style. From Marieneplatz, take Bus 52 from U-bahn 3 to Thalkirchen, at the southern edge of the city. ☒ *Tierparkstr. 30, Thalkirchen* ☏ *089/625–080* ⊕ *www.tierpark-hellabrunn.de* ✉ *€11* ⊙ *Apr.–Sept., daily 8–6; Oct.–Mar., daily 9–5* Ⓜ *Thalkirchen (U-bahn).*

WHERE TO EAT

Munich claims to be Germany's gourmet capital. It certainly has an inordinate number of fine restaurants, but you won't have trouble finding a vast range of options in both price and style.

Typical, more substantial dishes in Munich include *Tellerfleisch*, boiled beef with freshly grated horseradish and boiled potatoes on the side, served on wooden plates. Among roasts, sauerbraten (beef) and *Schweinebraten* (roast pork) are accompanied by dumplings and sauerkraut. *Hax'n* (ham hocks) are roasted until they're crisp on the outside and juicy on the inside. They are served with sauerkraut and potato puree. Game in season (venison or boar, for instance) and duck are served with potato dumplings and red cabbage. As for fish, the region has not only excellent trout, served either smoked as an hors d'oeuvre or fried or boiled as an entrée, but also the perchlike *Rencke* from Lake Starnberg.

You'll also find soups, salads, casseroles, hearty stews, and a variety of baked goods—including pretzels. For dessert, indulge in a bowl of Bavarian cream, apple strudel, or *Dampfnudel*, a fluffy leavened-dough dumpling usually served with vanilla sauce.

The generic term for a snack is *Imbiss*, and thanks to growing internationalism you'll find a huge variety, from the generic *Wiener* (hot dogs) to the Turkish *Döner Kebab* sandwich (pressed and roasted lamb, beef, or chicken). Almost all butcher shops and bakeries offer some sort of *Brotzeit* snack, which can range from a modest sandwich to a steaming plate of goulash with potatoes and salad.

Some edibles come with social etiquette attached. The *Weisswurst,* a tender minced-veal sausage—made fresh daily, steamed, and served with sweet mustard and a crisp roll or a pretzel—is a Munich institution and, theoretically, should be eaten before noon with a *Weissbier* (wheat beer), supposedly to counteract the effects of a hangover. Some people use a knife and fork to remove the inside from the skin, while others might indulge in *auszuzeln*, sucking the sausage out of the Weisswurst.

Another favorite Bavarian specialty is *Leberkäs*—literally "liver cheese," though neither liver nor cheese is among its ingredients. Rather, it's a sort of meatloaf baked to a crust each morning and served in succulent slabs throughout the day. A *Leberkäs Semmel*—a wedge of the meat loaf between two halves of a bread roll slathered with a slightly spicy mustard—is the favorite Munich on-the-go snack.

Use the coordinate (✛ B3) at the end of each listing to locate a site on the corresponding map.

WHAT IT COSTS IN EUROS				
	¢	$	$$	$$$	$$$$
AT DINNER	under €9	€9–€15	€16–€20	€21–€25	over €25

Price per person for a main course or equivalent combination of smaller dishes at dinner.

CITY CENTER

$
GERMAN
✕**Andechser am Dom.** At this Munich mainstay, the vaulted, frescoed ceiling and the old stone floor recall the nearby Andechs monastery. As with many smaller Bavarian *Wirtshäuser* (pub-restaurant), it's invariably pretty full, so be prepared to find seats on a table already half full, though this is part of the lively charm of the place. The boldly Bavarian food—blood sausage with potatoes or roast duck—and fine selection of delectable Andechs beers will quickly put you at ease. The covered terrace, steps from the Frauenkirche, is a favorite meeting place, rain or shine, for shoppers, local businesspeople, and even the occasional VIP. ✉ *Weinstr. 7a, City Center* ☏ *089/298–481* ⊕ *www.andechser-am-dom. de* Ⓜ *Marienplatz (U-bahn and S-bahn)* ✛ *D4.*

¢
GERMAN
✕**Bier-und Oktoberfest Museum.** In one of the oldest buildings in Munich, dating to the 14th century, the museum takes an imaginative look at the history of this popular elixir, the monasteries that produced it, the purity laws that govern it, and Munich's own long tradition with it. The rustic Museumsstüberl restaurant, consisting of a few heavy wooden tables, accompanies the museum. It serves traditional *Brotzeit* (breads, cheeses, and cold meats) during the day and hot Bavarian dishes from 6 pm. ■ TIP→ You can visit the Museumsstüberl restaurant without paying the museum's admission fee and try beer from one of Munich's oldest breweries, the Augustiner Bräu. The museum is open Tuesday–Saturday 1–6, but you can visit the restaurant Monday and 1–midnight Tuesday–Saturday. ✉ *Sterneckerstr. 2, City Center* ☏ *089/2424–3941* ⊕ *www.bier-und-oktoberfestmuseum.de* 🍴 *Museum €4* ✇ *Closed Sun.* Ⓜ *Isartor (U-bahn and S-bahn)* ✛ *F5.*

$$
CONTINENTAL
★
✕**Brasserie OskarMaria.** After New York, Munich has more publishing houses than any other city in the world. Literaturhaus is a converted Renaissance-style schoolhouse that, as the name suggests, is now a "literature" center, for authors, publishers, and book fans. The front side of the building is a stylish brasserie, named after Munich writer Oskar Maria Graf, an exile after the Nazis took power in Germany in 1933, and who eventually settled in New York. The brasserie's vaulted high ceiling and plate-glass windows create a light and spacious atmosphere. The range of dishes here is pretty eclectic, from beef tartare and lobster risotto to beef Stroganoff and fish burgers. It has a sprawling terrace, and it's one of the city's best outdoor eating locations, whether for a main meal or cappuccino and *Kuchen* (cake). ■ TIP→ About 100 meters away, on Jungfernturmstrasse, is one of the oldest remaining remnants of the city wall. Opposite the brasserie is the Hugendubel English bookshop. ✉ *Salvatorpl. 1, City Center* ☏ *089/2919–6029* ⊕ *www.oskarmaria. com* Ⓜ *Odeonsplatz (U-bahn)* ✛ *D4.*

BEST BETS FOR MUNICH DINING

Fodor's Choice★	$$	BAVARIAN
Limoni, $$, p. 94	Brasserie Oskar Maria, p. 84	Alter Simpl, $, p. 94
Mark's, $$$$, p. 90	Buffet Kull, p. 85	Gasthaus Isarthor, $, p. 94
Restaurant Dallmayr, $$$$, p. 91	Limoni, p. 94	Wirtshaus in der Au, $, p. 96
Tantris, $$$$, p. 95	**$$$**	
	Dukatz, p. 88	ITALIAN
Best By Price		Due passi, ¢, p. 88
	$$$$	Limoni, $$, p. 94
¢	Restaurant Dallmayr, p. 91	
Bier-und Oktoberfest	Mark's, p. 90	CONTINENTAL
Museum, p. 84	Tantris, p. 95	Mark's, $$$$, p. 90
Bratwurstherzl, p. 85		
Due passi, p. 88	**Best By Cuisine**	FRENCH
		Dukatz, $$$, p. 88
$	GERMAN	Brasserie Oskar Maria, $$, p. 84
Andechser am Dom, p. 84	Halali, $$$, p. 88	L'Atelier Art & Vin, $, p. 90
L'Atelier Art & Vin, p. 90	Weinhaus Neuner, $$$, p. 93	

¢
GERMAN
✕ **Bratwurstherzl.** Tucked into a quaint little square off the Viktualien-markt, this delightful Bratwurst joint cooks up specialty sausages right in the main room over an open grill. For those looking for a bit less meat, there is also a hearty farmer's salad with turkey strips and tasty oyster mushrooms. They have outdoor seating, perfect for people-watching when the weather is good. ⊠ *Dreifaltigkeitspl. 1, City Center* ☎ *089/295–113* ⊕ *www.bratwurstherzl.de* ☉ *Closed Sun. and public holidays* Ⓜ *Marienplatz (U-bahn and S-bahn)* ✛ *E5.*

$$
CONTINENTAL
★
✕ **Buffet Kull.** This simple yet comfortable international bistro delivers a high-quality dining experience accompanied by a good variety of wines and friendly service. Dishes range from Bohemian pheasant soup to the excellent New York steak. The daily specials are creative, portions are generous, and the prices are good value for the quality. Reservations are recommended (dinner service starts at 6 pm). ⊠ *Marienstr. 4, City Center* ☎ *089/221–509* ⊕ *www.buffet-kull.de* Ⓜ *Marienplatz (U-bahn and S-bahn)* ✛ *F5.*

$
CAFÉ
✕ **Daylesford Organic.** There are far too few organic restaurants in Munich, so it's great news for the eco-conscious that the 2009-opened Daylesford Organic has firmly established itself in the culinary life of the city. All ingredients are locally sourced in Bavaria, and the carefully

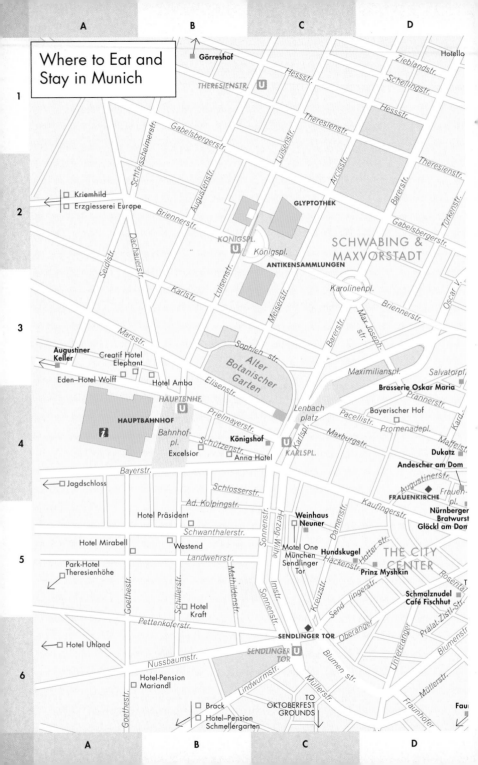

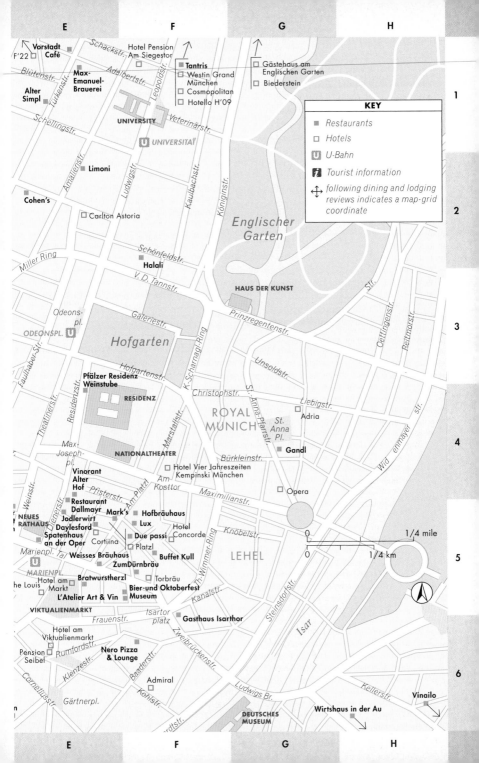

chosen building, dating from 1264, with vaulted ceilings and white-washed walls, is the perfect City Center location. The atmosphere is barlike informal, and it's possible to mix and match from a selection of starters and salads. The food is not overcomplicated, exemplified by the good Daylesford steak sandwich main meal, with delicious balsamic onions, ghurkin, and tomato, in a light sauce. The restaurant also serves as a shop, selling a range of broadly artisanal, independent-produced goods, from foods to hand lotions, all adhering to the environmental strictures the company promotes. ⊠ *Ledererstr. 3, City Center, Munich* ☎ *089/4520–9833* ✚ *E5.*

¢ ✕ **Due passi.** So small it's easy to miss, this former dairy shop, now an
ITALIAN Italian specialty shop, offers Italian meals for a quick lunch. There's a small but fine selection of fresh antipasti and pasta. You can eat at the high wooden tables and counters or have your food to go. Menus change daily. ⊠ *Ledererstr. 11, City Center* ☎ *089/224–271* ⊕ *www. duepassi.de* ⊟ *No credit cards* ⊘ *Closed weekends* Ⓜ *Marienplatz (S-bahn, U-bahn)* ✚ *F5.*

$$$ ✕ **Dukatz.** Even in a medium-size city such as Munich, it's not difficult
FRENCH to escape the hustle and bustle of the tourist hotspots. A short four-or five-minute walk from Marienplatz can take you to Dukatz, where you can enjoy a drink at the well-stocked bar or in the pleasant courtyard of the Schäfflerhof, part of the Fünf Höfe, the upscale shopping mall in the center of Munich between Schäfflerstrasse, Weinstrasse and Maffeistrasse. Move one floor up from the bistro for dinner at the upscale restaurant, where starters might include mussels with orange and rocket, and you may be tempted with a Bavarian entrecôte with glazed cherry tomatoes and young spinach as a main. The fish menu changes daily. ⊠ *Schäfflerhof (in the Fünf Höfe), Maffeistr. 3a, City Center* ☎ *089/7104–07373* ⊕ *www.dukatz.de* ⊘ *Restaurant closed Sun. (bar-bistro open daily)* Ⓜ *Marienplatz (U-bahn and S-bahn)* ✚ *D4.*

$ ✕ **Faun.** Not quite City Center, but still central to the action, the beloved
ECLECTIC Faun is off Klenzestrasse, past Gärtnerplatz. It's a happy combination
★ of Munich tavern and international bistro, with great outdoor seating on a small square where five streets meet and five trees are planted. The Thai curries are wonderful, and their juicy Schweinebraten will satisfy any meat cravings. The dishes on the daily changing menu are tasty, filling, and easy on your wallet. The beer served is Augustiner, so you can't go wrong there. Build up your appetite by browsing your way through the neighborhood shops and boutiques, or walk off your meal along the river back toward Isartor and the City Center. ⊠ *Hans-Sachs-Str. 17, Isarvorstadt* ☎ *089/263–798* ⊕ *www.faun.mycosmos.biz* ⊟ *No credit cards* ✚ *D6.*

$$$ ✕ **Halali.** With nearly 100 years of history to its credit, polished wood
GERMAN paneling, and antlers on the walls, the Halali is an old-style Munich restaurant that is *the* place to try traditional dishes of venison, pheasant, partridge, and other game in a quiet and elegant atmosphere. Save room for the crème brûlée with potted nectarine and mocha bean ice cream. ⊠ *Schönfeldstr. 22, City Center* ☎ *089/285–909* ⊕ *www.restaurant-halali. de* ⌣ *Reservations essential* ⌂ *Jacket and tie* ⊘ *Closed Sun. and public holidays. No lunch Sat.* Ⓜ *Odeonsplatz (U-bahn and S-bahn)* ✚ *F2.*

$ ✕ **Hofbräuhaus.** The Hofbräuhaus is the most famous beer hall not just
GERMAN in Munich but in the world. Regulars aside, many Bavarians see it as the
biggest tourist trap ever created, and few go more than once, but they
are still proud that it attracts so many visitors. Yes, it's a little kitschy,
but the pounding oompah band draws the curious, and the singing and
shouting drinkers contribute to the festive atmosphere. This, then, is no
place for the fainthearted, and a trip to Munich would be incomplete
without at least having a look. Upstairs is a quieter restaurant, where
the food is fine, although there are better places for Bavarian cuisine.
In March, May, and September ask for one of the special, extra-strong
seasonal beers (Starkbier, Maibock, Märzen), which complement the
traditional Bavarian fare. ⊠ *Platzl 9, City Center* ☎ *089/2901–36100*
⊕ *www.hofbraeuhaus.de* ⚞ *Reservations not accepted* Ⓜ *Marienplatz
(U-bahn and S-bahn)* ✛ *F5.*

$$$ ✕ **Hotel Lux Restaurant.** The chef here learned his trade at Munich's much-
GERMAN vaunted Königshof. Much of the meat here is organic; ask the ever-
charming staff for information. The creamy asparagus risotto is a real
treat for lunch, while the duck with ratatouille and potato-celery gratin
is a highlight of the evening menu. The small bar is also terrific. Hotel
Lux is also a hotel with 17 rooms (€149), free Wi-Fi, and simply fur-
nished rooms, except for the top-floor Ponyhof room, designed by Hans
Langner, who is famous for his bird depictions. This extraordinary blue,
bird-filled room is not to everyone's taste, but good fun for a night or
two. ⊠ *Ledererstr. 13, City Center, Munich* ☎ *089/4520–7300* ⊕ *www.
hotel-lux-muenchen.de* ✛ *E5.*

$$ ✕ **Hundskugel.** Dating from at least 1440, this has good claim to be
GERMAN Munich's oldest tavern, and also one of the city's smallest. You'll be
asked to squeeze together and make room for latecomers looking for a
spot at one of the few tables clustered in the handkerchief-size dining
room. This provides a good atmosphere to match the honest Bavarian
food served. ⊠ *Hotterstr. 18, City Center* ☎ *089/264–272* Ⓜ *Marienplatz (U-bahn and S-bahn)* ✛ *C5.*

$ ✕ **Jodlerwirt.** This cozy Alpine lodge–style restaurant in a small street
GERMAN behind the Rathaus is a treat for those craving an Old World tavern,
complete with live accordion playing. As its name suggests, yodelers
perform most nights, telling jokes and poking fun at their adoring
guests in unintelligible Bavarian slang. The food is traditional, including
Käsespätzle (a hearty German version of macaroni and cheese), goulash,
and meal-size salads. The tasty beer is from the Ayinger brewery. The
place is small and fills up fast. ⊠ *Altenhofstr. 4, City Center* ☎ *089/221–
249* ⊕ *www.jodlerwirt-muenchen.net* ⊟ *No credit cards* ☉ *Closed Sun.
and Mon. No lunch* Ⓜ *Marienplatz (U-bahn and S-bahn)* ✛ *E5.*

$$$$ ✕ **Königshof.** Don't be fooled as you cross the threshold of the dour and
GERMAN unremarkable-looking postwar Hotel Königshof. The contrast with the
★ opulent interior is remarkable. From a window table in this elegant
and luxurious restaurant in one of Munich's grand hotels, you can
watch the hustle and bustle of the Karlsplatz below. You'll forget the
outside world, however, when you taste the outstanding French- and
Japanese-influenced dishes created by Michelin-starred chef Martin
Fauster, former sous-chef at Tantris. Ingredients are fresh and menus

change often, but you might see lobster with fennel and candied ginger, or venison with goose liver and celery, and for dessert, flambéed peach with champagne ice cream. Let the sommelier help you choose from the fantastic wine selection. ⊠ *Karlspl. 25, City Center* ☏ *089/551–360* ⊕ *www.koenigshof-hotel.de* ⚄ *Reservations essential* 🎩 *Jacket and tie* ☼ *Closed 1st wk in Jan., Aug., Sun., and Mon.* Ⓜ *Karlsplatz (U-bahn and S-bahn)* ✛ *C4.*

$ ✕ **L'Atelier Art & Vin.** Take a seat by the wall of windows, or at the
FRENCH   long blond-wood bar, in this airy, casual brasserie, which specializes in French food and wine. On nice days, tables are also set outside on the sidewalk of the pleasant, relatively quiet street. The light, crisp quiches, in particular, are a delight, and the wine list is a curated list of French wines. The Bier & Oktoberfest Museum is a few doors away, highlighting the wonderful contrasts that are so typical of this city. ⊠ *Westenriederstr. 43, City Center* ☏ *089/2126–6782* ⊕ *www.atelier-artetvin.de* ⊟ *No credit cards* ☼ *Closed Sun. and public holidays* Ⓜ *Marienplatz (U-bahn and S-bahn)* ✛ *F5.*

$$$$ ✕ **Mark's.** A wonderful culinary experience is reached on three literal
CONTINENTAL   levels at Mark's in the Hotel Mandarin Oriental. You can enjoy lunch
Fodor's Choice   either in the hotel lobby or—weather permitting—eight floors up on the
★   magnificent roof terrace, which has 360-degree views of the city. And at dinnertime, Mark's is set on the balcony of the luxurious lobby, with a wide white marble staircase leading up to it. The 2011-appointed head chef, Simon Larese, creates decadent dishes like a starter of tartare of Scottish wild salmon, light sour cream and St. James caviar plus walnut blinis. Equally impressive is the light saffron soup, bouillabaisse vegetables, panfried king prawn, and then roast-beef fillet, panfried potatoes with baby vegetables, and red wine sauce. For dessert try the pistachio soufflé, balsamico strawberries and pistachio cream with a light strawberry sorbet. ⊠ *Neuturmstr. 1, City Center* ☏ *089/290–980* ⊕ *www.mandarinoriental.com* ✛ *E5.*

$ ✕ **Nero Pizza & Lounge.** The pizzas are great at this independent restau-
ITALIAN   rant: try the diavolo, with spicy Neopolitan salami. On a side street between Gärtnerplatz and Isartor, Nero has high ceilings and large windows that give it an open, spacious feel; you can sit upstairs in the lounge for a cozier experience. ⊠ *Rumfordstr. 34, City Center* ☏ *089/2101–9060* ⊕ *www.nero-muenchen.de* Ⓜ *Marienplatz (U-bahn)* ✛ *F6.*

$ ✕ **Nürnberger Bratwurst Glöckl am Dom.** One of Munich's most popular
GERMAN   beer taverns is dedicated to the delicious *Nürnberger Bratwürste* (finger-size sausages), a specialty from the rival Bavarian city of Nüremberg. They're served by a busy team of friendly waitresses dressed in Bavarian dirndls who flit between the crowded tables with remarkable agility. In warmer months, tables are placed outside, partly under a large awning, beneath the towering Frauenkirche. In winter the mellow dark-panel dining rooms provide relief from the cold. ■TIP➡ For a quick beer go to the side door where, just inside, there is a little window serving fresh Augustiner from a wooden barrel. You can stand around with the regulars or enjoy the small courtyard if the weather is nice. ⊠ *Frauenpl. 9, City Center* ☏ *089/291–9450* ⊕ *www.bratwurst-gloeckl.de* Ⓜ *Marienplatz (U-bahn and S-bahn)* ✛ *D5.*

For a romantic meal, reserve a table at Mark's at the Mandarin Oriental.

¢

GERMAN

✗ **Pfälzer Residenz Weinstube.** A huge stone-vaulted room, a few smaller rooms on the side, wooden tables, flickering candles, dirndl-clad waitresses, and a long list of wines add up to a storybook image of a timeless Germany. The wines are mostly from the *Pfalz* (Palatinate), as are many of the specialties on the limited menu. Beer drinkers, take note—beer is not served here. ⊠ *Residenzstr. 1, City Center* ☎ *089/225–628* ⊕ *www. bayernpfalz.de* Ⓜ *Odeonsplatz (U-bahn)* ✛ *E4.*

$

VEGETARIAN

★

✗ **Prinz Myshkin.** Traditional Bavarian dishes can sometimes be heavy affairs, and after a meal or three they can become a bit much. This restaurant is one of the finest in the city, and it's vegetarian to boot, with a selection of vegan dishes. The delightful holiday from meat here provides an eclectic choice of skillfully prepared antipasti, quiche, pizza, gnocchi, tofu, crepes, stir-fried dishes, plus excellent wines. The airy room has a high, vaulted ceiling, and there's always some art exhibited to feed the eye and mind. ⊠ *Hackenstr. 2, City Center* ☎ *089/265–596* ⊕ *www.prinzmyshkin.com* Ⓜ *Sendlinger Tor (U-bahn)* ✛ *D5.*

$$$$

CONTINENTAL

Fodor's Choice

★

✗ **Restaurant Dallmayr.** Enter one of Munich's premier delicatessens, where rows of specialties tempt your nose. If you can tear yourself away from the mesmerizing displays of foods, take a carpeted flight of stairs either to the much-vaunted **Restaurant Dallmayr** or the adjoining elegant-yet-casual **Café-Bistro.** Whether your choice is restaurant or café, this place is a sheer delight, showcasing delicacies from the delicatessen, while the service is friendly and attentive. Few were surprised when Diethard Urbansky, head chef at Restaurant Dallmayr, won two Michelin stars in 2009 and 2010. Standout Urbansky starters include rolled veal on tuna carpaccio with avocado. For mains, there might be roast rack of lamb filled with bell pepper or sea bass with

Within the grand Hotel Königshof is this elegant restaurant.

tomato vinaigrette and saffron gnocchi. ⊠ *Dienerstr. 14–15, City Center* ☎ *089/21350* ⊕ *www.dallmayr.de* ⊗ *Restaurant closed Sun. and Mon., and first 3 wks of Aug.* ✢ *E4*.

¢ ✕ **Schmalznudel Café Frischhut.** From the deep Bavarian accent to the
GERMAN food on offer, this is as Bavarian as one could get, though it serves neither typical great slabs of meat nor *Knödel*. The fryers are turned on each day and by midday lines of people are waiting for helpings of freshly cooked *Schmalznudel*, a selection of doughnut-type creations, from apple to sugar-coated to plain. It's really no more than a narrow passage-kind-of café, located on a busy street between the Stadtmuseum and Viktualienmarkt, and easily missed by those not in the know. Regulars are equally happy whether they manage to find a seat inside or at the handful of tables outside. And there's always the option to take away and eat as you wind your way through the ever-colorful market. ⊠ *Prälat-Zistl-Str. 8, City Center, Munich* ☎ *089/268–237* ▭ *No credit cards* ✢ *D5*.

$$$$ ✕ **Spatenhaus an der Oper.** The best seats are the window tables on the
GERMAN second floor. The quiet dining room walls and ceiling are paneled with old hand-painted wood and have a wonderful view of the square and the opera house. Make a reservation if you want to come after a performance. The outdoor tables are a favorite for people-watching. There are few better places for roasted fillet of brook trout, lamb with ratatouille, or duck with apple and red cabbage. And they do the best Wiener schnitzel in the city. Leave room for one of the wonderful desserts featuring fresh fruit. ⊠ *Residenzstr. 12, City Center* ☎ *089/290–7060* ⊕ *www.kuffler-gastronomie.de/de/muenchen/spatenhaus* Ⓜ *Odeonsplatz (U-bahn)* ✢ *E5*.

$ ✕ **Vinorant Alter Hof.** If you don't make it to Franconia, then you can at
GERMAN least get a taste of the region's food and wine in this simply decorated
restaurant nestled in the old vaulted cellar and first floor of Munich's
first residence castle, the Alter Hof. The wine bar in the cellar serves
hearty Franconian snacks along with Franconian wines, which can
be ordered in small amounts, allowing your taste buds to travel the
region's vineyards. ■ TIP→ This is a good place to end the evening after a
concert at the nearby National Theater or the Residenz. It's also the location for a fine "Dinner in the Dark" experience ⊠ *Alter Hof 3, City Center* ☎ *089/2424–3733* ⊕ *www.alter-hof-muenchen.de* Ⓜ *Marienplatz
(U-bahn and S-bahn)* ✛ *E4.*

$$$ ✕ **Weinhaus Neuner.** Munich's oldest wine tavern serves good food as
GERMAN well as superior wines in its two nooks: the wood-panel restaurant and
the Weinstube. The choice of food is remarkable, from roast duck to fish
to traditional Bavarian. ⊠ *Herzogspitalstr.8, City Center* ☎ *089/260–
3954* ⊕ *www.weinhaus-neuner.de* ☽ *Closed Sun. and holidays* Ⓜ *Ma-
rienplatz (U-bahn and S-bahn)* ✛ *C5.*

$ ✕ **Weisses Bräuhaus.** If you've developed a taste for Weissbier, this insti-
GERMAN tution in downtown Munich is the place to indulge. The tasty brew
from Schneider, a Bavarian brewery in existence since 1872, is served
with hearty Bavarian dishes, mostly variations of pork and dumplings
or cabbage. The restaurant itself was beautifully restored in 1993 to
something approaching how it would have looked when first opened
in the 1870s. The waitresses here are famous in Munich for being a
little more straight-talking than visitors might be used to in restaurants
back home. But if you're good-natured, the whole thing can be quite
funny. Credit cards are accepted for totals over 20 euros, but with the
good beer and food, this shouldn't be difficult to reach. ⊠ *Tal 7, City
Center* ☎ *089/290–1380* ⊕ *www.weisses-brauhaus.de* Ⓜ *Marienplatz
(S-bahn and U-bahn)* ✛ *E5.*

$ ✕ **Zum Dürnbräu.** In existence in one form or another since 1487, this
GERMAN is easily one of the oldest establishments serving food in Munich, and
there's little surprise that the food is resolutely traditional: lots of roast
meat, potato and bread dumplings, fish, and equally hearty desserts. As
the *Bräu* in the name suggests, this was also a brewery centuries ago. The
front biergarten is small so get there early in good weather. Inside, the
central 21-foot table is a favorite spot and fills up first. It's popular and
attracts everyone from business people to students. ⊠ *Dürnbräugasse 2,
City Center* ☎ *089/222–195* Ⓜ *Marienplatz (U-bahn and S-bahn)* ✛ *F5.*

LEHEL

$$$ ✕ **Gandl.** This Italian specialty shop, where you can buy various staples
ITALIAN from vinegar to coffee, doubles as a comfortable, relaxed restaurant.
Their extensive Saturday buffet breakfast is popular in the neighborhood.
Seating can become a little crowded inside, but the excellent service will
make up for it and you'll feel right at home. For lunch it's just the place
for a quick pastry or excellent antipasto misto before proceeding with the
day's adventures. Dinner is more relaxed, with Mediterranean-influenced
cuisine. ⊠ *St.-Anna-Pl. 1, Lehel* ☎ *089/2916–2525* ⊕ *www.gandl.de*
🚭 *No credit cards* ☽ *Closed Sun.* Ⓜ *Lehel (U-bahn)* ✛ *G4.*

$ ✕ **Gasthaus Isarthor.** This old-fashioned *Wirtshaus* is one of the few
GERMAN places that serve Augustiner beer exclusively from wooden kegs, freshly
★ tapped on a daily basis. Beer simply doesn't get any better than this.
The traditional Bavarian fare is good, and the midday menu changes
daily. All kinds are drawn to the simple wooden tables of this unspectacular establishment. Antlers and a wild boar look down on actors,
government officials, apprentice craftspersons, journalists, and retirees,
all sitting side by side. ⊠ *Kanalstr. 2, Lehel* ☎ *089/227–753* ⊕ *www.
gasthaus-isarthor.de* ▭ *No credit cards* Ⓜ *Isartor (S-bahn)* ✛ *F5.*

SCHWABING AND MAXVORSTADT

$ ✕ **Alter Simpl.** Named after Germany's most famous satirical magazine,
GERMAN *Simplicissimus*, this pub-restaurant has been a Munich institution since
1903, when it was a meeting place center for leading writers, come-
dians, and artists. Today the pictures of those days hang on the dark
wood-panel walls. It's quite small and far from salubrious, but the beer's
good and the equally good food is served until 2 am (beer until 3 am).
The menu includes filling options like roast pork, Munich schnitzel, and
a bacon-cheeseburger with french fries. ⊠ *Türkenstr. 57, Maxvorstadt*
☎ *089/272–3083* ⊕ *www.altersimpl.com* ▭ *No credit cards* ✛ *E1.*

$ ✕ **Cohen's.** There is little overly fancy at Cohen's. There doesn't need to
ISRAELI be. Reviving the old Jewish central European tradition of good, healthy
cooking combined with hospitality and good cheer seems to be the
underlying principle. Dig into a few hearty latkes, a steaming plate of
Chulend stew, or standard gefilte fish doused with excellent Golan wine
from Israel. The kitchen is open from 12:30 pm to about 10:30 pm, and
if the atmosphere is good, patrons sometimes hang out chattering until
the wee hours. ■ TIP➜ **Klezmer singers perform on some Friday evenings.**
⊠ *Theresienstr. 31, Maxvorstadt* ☎ *089/280–9545* ⊕ *www.cohens.de*
Ⓜ *Theresienstrasse (U-bahn)* ✛ *E2.*

$ ✕ **Görrreshof.** In 1893 Augustiner, the oldest brewery in Munich, built
GERMAN this sturdy *Wirtshaus* to sustain travelers on the 12-km trek from
Munich to the castles at Schleissheim. This pub-restaurant has been
renovated over the years and is today as much a forum for good eating
and drinking as it was more than 100 years ago. You'll get hearty food
in a dining room festooned with antlers. If you want to relax further,
retire to the small Bibliothek (library), or head outside to sit on the covered terrace. ⊠ *Görresstr. 38, Maxvorstadt* ☎ *089/2020–9550* ⊕ *www.
goerreshof.de* Ⓜ *Josephsplatz (U-bahn)* ✛ *B1.*

$$ ✕ **Limoni.** It's not just Munich's neoclassical architecture that underpins
ITALIAN its playful, centuries' old moniker as Italy's most northern city. There are
Fodor'sChoice a number of fine Italian restaurants around the city, and this is certainly
★ one of the best. There is a Bavarian professionalism combined with Ital-
ian grace and elegance in how the delicacies are served: pea and ginger
cream soup, fusilli and calf ragout, artichokes and grated horseradish
to name just a few, and then the fantastic chocolate cake with mascar-
pone cream. Be sure to reserve your table in good weather so you can
sit on the charming patio out the back. ⊠ *Amalienstr. 38, Maxvorstadt*
☎ *089/2880–6029* ⊕ *www.limoni-ristorante.com* ☾ *Closed Sun., and
public holidays. Sat. no lunch* ✛ *E2.*

$ ✕ **Max-Emanuel-Brauerei.** This historic old brewery tavern is a great
GERMAN value, with great value Bavarian dishes. The best part about this place,
however, is the cozy, secluded little beer garden with huge chestnut
trees, tucked in the back amid the apartment blocks. ☒ *Adalbertstr. 33,
Schwabing* ☎ *089/271–5158* ⊕ *www.max-emanuel-brauerei.de* Ⓜ *Universität (U-bahn)* ✛ *E1.*

$$$$ ✕ **Tantris.** Despite the slightly dramatic exterior, which is adorned by
CONTINENTAL three concrete animals, few restaurants in Germany can match Tantris.
Fodor's Choice Select the menu of the day and accept the suggestions of the somme-
★ lier or choose from the à la carte options and you'll be in for a treat,
for example: variation of char with marinated white asparagus and
orange hollandaise, followed by roast lamb fillets with spinach, beans
and fennel-curry puree, superbly complemented by stuffed semolina
dumpling with raspberries and curd cheese ice cream. It surprises few
that head chef Hans Haas has kept his restaurant at the top of the critics' charts in Munich for so long. ☒ *Johann-Fichte-Str. 7, Schwabing*
☎ *089/361–9590* ⊕ *www.tantris.de* ⟐ *Reservations essential* ⟐ *Jacket
and tie* ⊙ *Closed Sun., Mon., and bank holidays* Ⓜ *Münchner Freiheit
(U-bahn)* ✛ *F1.*

$ ✕ **Vorstadt Café.** Young professionals mix with students at this lively
GERMAN restaurant on the corner of Adalbert and Türkenstrasse. The 13 different breakfasts are a big draw: the Vorstadt Classic includes ham and
eggs, rolls and several kinds of bread, with a plate of salami and home
made jam; the Miami Beach has ham and eggs with potatoes, pancakes
with maple syrup, fresh fruit salad, bread, jam and peanut butter. Their
daily lunch specials, served quickly, are good value. The atmosphere at
dinner is relaxed, complete with candlelight. Reservations are advised
at weekends. ☒ *Türkenstr. 83, Maxvorstadt* ☎ *089/272–0699* ⊕ *www.
vorstadtcafe.de* ▭ *No credit cards* Ⓜ *Universität (U-bahn)* ✛ *E1.*

LEOPOLDVORSTADT

$ ✕ **Augustiner Keller.** This flagship beer restaurant of one of Munich's
GERMAN oldest breweries originated about 1812. It is also the location of the
unbeatable Augustiner beer garden, which should be at the top of any
visitor's beer garden list. The menu offers Bavarian specialties, including
half a duck with a good slab of roast suckling pig, dumpling, and blue
cabbage. If you're up for it, end your meal with a *Dampfnudel* (yeast
dumpling served with custard), though you probably won't feel hungry
again for quite a while. ☒ *Arnulfstr. 52, Maxvorstadt* ☎ *089/594–393*
⊕ *www.augustinerkeller.de* Ⓜ *Hauptbahnhof (U-bahn and S-bahn)*
✛ *A3.*

HAIDHAUSEN

$$ ✕ **Vinaiolo.** Munich is sometimes referred to as Italy's northernmost
ITALIAN city, and this bright, busy place is the proof. In the setting of an old
apothecary, diners can enjoy specialties from Venice and other north-
ern Italian regions, such as spaghetti with sardines or roast goat, pre-
pared to perfection by chef Marco Pizzolato. Service is good-humored

and conscientious and the menu changes every 14 days. ⊠ *Steinstr. 42, Haidhausen* ☎ *089/4895–0356* Ⓜ *Rosenheimer Platz (S-bahn)* ✛ *H6.*

$
GERMAN
★
✕ **Wirtshaus in der Au.** *Wirtshaus* is a kind of bar-restaurant serving traditional Bavarian food and beer. This has been serving since 1901 and it's one of the best. A stone's throw from the Deutsches Museum, it has a great vaulted room and collections of beer steins, providing one of the best atmospheres around. It has a combination of fantastic service and outstanding local dishes, from *Hofente* (roast duck) to *Schweinsbraten* (roast pork). But the real specialty, and for which it is renowned, is *Knödel* (dumplings), which, in addition to traditional *Semmel* (bread) and *Kartoffel* (potato) varieties, come in spinach, cheese, and even red-beet flavors. Weather permitting, you can sit in the small beer garden under, of course, chestnut trees. A day in the Deutsches Museum followed by an evening here, and Munich doesn't get much better. ⊠ *Lilienstr. 51, Haidhausen* ☎ *089/448–1400* ⊕ *www.wirtshausinderau.de* Ⓜ *Isartor (S-bahn and Tram)* ✛ *H6.*

WHERE TO STAY

For expanded hotel reviews, visit Fodors.com.

Though Munich has a vast number of hotels in all price ranges, booking one can be a challenge, as this is a trade-show city as well as a prime tourist destination. If you're visiting during any of the major trade fairs such as the ispo (sports, fashion) in February or the IHM (crafts) in mid-March, or during Oktoberfest at the end of September, try to make reservations at least a few months in advance. It is acceptable practice in Europe to request to see a room before committing to it, so feel free to ask the concierge.

Some of the large, upscale hotels that cater to expense-account business travelers have attractive weekend discount rates—sometimes as much as 50% below normal prices. Conversely, most hotels raise their regular rates by at least 30% during big trade fairs and Oktoberfest. Online booking sites like Hotel Reservation Service (⊕ *www.hrs.com*) often have prices well below the hotel's published prices (i.e., price ranges in this book) in slow periods and on short notice. Look for the names we suggest here and search online for potential deals.

■ TIP➡ Munich's tourist-information office has two outlets that can help you with hotel bookings if you haven't reserved in advance. One is at the central station and the other is on Marienplatz, in the Rathaus. Your best bet is to visit in person.

A technical note: A few years ago, some hotels in Munich chose to farm out their wireless Internet services to third parties—meaning that you could get online with their Wi-Fi hotspot, but you had to log in with a credit card and pay with a separate service provider. Thankfully, this is changing, and most of the newer hotels, plus some forward-thinking older establishments, offer Wi-Fi for free throughout.

Use the coordinate (✛ B3) at the end of each listing to locate a site on the corresponding map.

BEST BETS FOR MUNICH LODGING

Fodor's Choice★

Admiral, $$$, p. 101
Bayerischer Hof, $$$$, p. 98
Hotel Uhland, $, p. 104
The Louis Hotel, $$, p. 98
Pension am Siegestor, $, p. 101

Best by Price

$
Hotel Am Markt, p. 98
Hotel Uhland, p. 104
Pension am Siegestor, p. 101

$$
The Louis Hotel, p. 98

$$$
Cortiina, p. 98
Platzl Hotel, p. 99

$$$$
Bayerischer Hof, p. 98
Hotel Vier Jahreszeiten München Kempinski, p. 98

Best by Experience

BEST HOTEL BARS
Admiral, $$$, p. 101
Bayerischer Hof, $$$$, p. 98

BEST LOBBY
Hotel Vier Jahreszeiten München Kempinski, $$$$, p. 98

BUSINESS TRAVEL
Anna Hotel, $$$, p. 97
Cosmopolitan, $$, p. 101

BEST VIEWS
Anna Hotel, $$$, p. 97

BIGGEST HOTELS
Bayerischer Hof, $$$$, p. 98
Westin Grand München, $$, p. 104

BEST LOCATION
Eden-Hotel Wolff, $$$, p. 99
Hotel Amba, $$, p. 100

BEST FOR JOGGERS
Biederstein, $$, p. 101
Gästehaus am Englischen Garten, $, p. 103

BEST FOR OKTOBERFEST
Brack, $, p. 103
Hotel Uhland, $, p. 104

WHAT IT COSTS IN EUROS				
	¢	$	$$	$$$	$$$$
FOR TWO PEOPLE	under €50	€50–€100	€101–€175	€176–€225	over €225

Prices reflect the rack rate of a standard double room for two people in high season, including tax. Check online for off-season rates and special deals or discounts.

CITY CENTER

$$$ **Anna Hotel.** Modern, slightly minimalist decor and features are the characteristic of this design hotel. **Pros:** terrific location; fabulous views from the top floor; beds are huge; free Wi-Fi throughout. **Cons:** bar and restaurant get hectic from passersby on the busy street; no single rooms. ⊠ *Schützenstr. 1, City Center* ☎ *089/599–940* ⊕ *www.annahotel.de* ↗ *73 rooms* ⚭ *In-room: a/c, Wi-Fi. In-hotel: restaurant, bar, business center, parking, some pets allowed* ❏ *Breakfast* ✛ *B4.*

$$$$
Fodor's Choice
★

⊡ **Bayerischer Hof.** There's the Michelin-starred restaurant, the swanky suites, the rooftop Blue Spa and Lounge with panoramic city views, fitness studio, pool, private cinema, and to top it all suites in Palais Montgelas, the adjoining early 19th-century palace. **Pros:** superb public rooms with valuable oil paintings; the roof garden restaurant has an impressive view of the Frauenkirche two blocks away; Atelier restaurant has been awarded a Michelin star. **Cons:** expensive; Wi-Fi is extra. ⊠ *Promenadepl. 2–6, City Center* ☎ *089/21200* ⊕ *www.bayerischerhof. de* ↪ *350 rooms, 60 suites* ⟲ *In-room: a/c, Internet, Wi-Fi. In-hotel: restaurant, bar, pool, spa, business center, parking, some pets allowed* ⫼*Breakfast* Ⓜ *Karlsplatz (U-bahn and S-bahn), Marienplatz (U-bahn and S-bahn)* ⊹ *D4.*

$$$
⊡ **Cortiina.** One of Munich's design hotels, Cortiina follows the minimalist gospel. **Pros:** welcoming modern reception and bar; nice, comfortable rooms; personalized service. **Cons:** Hotel's Bar Central is over the road. ⊠ *Ledererstr. 8, City Center* ☎ *089/242–2490* ⊕ *www. cortiina.com* ↪ *75 rooms* ⟲ *In-room: Internet, Wi-Fi. In-hotel: bar, parking, some pets allowed* ⫼*Breakfast* Ⓜ *Marienplatz (U-bahn and S-bahn)* ⊹ *E5.*

$
⊡ **Hotel am Markt.** You can literally stumble out the door of this hotel onto the Viktualienmarkt. **Pros:** excellent location; friendly and helpful staff; free Wi-Fi; decent restaurant. **Cons:** rooms are simple; some spots could use fresh paint; no credit cards. ⊠ *Heiliggeiststr. 6, City Center* ☎ *089/225–014* ⊕ *www.hotel-am-markt.eu* ↪ *22 rooms* ⟲ *In-room: no a/c* ⊟ *No credit cards* ⫼*Breakfast* Ⓜ *Marienplatz (U-bahn and S-bahn)* ⊹ *E5.*

$
⊡ **Hotel Kraft.** Conveniently located between the City Center and the Oktoberfest grounds, the lobby of this basic hotel is inviting with wood paneled walls and comfortable armchairs. **Pros:** privately owned; hotel and rooms well cared for; quiet neighborhood. **Cons:** quiet neighborhood, no nightlife. ⊠ *Schillerstr. 49, City Center* ☎ *089/550–5940* ⊕ *www.hotel-kraft.com* ↪ *33 rooms* ⟲ *In-room: Wi-Fi. In-hotel: business center, parking, some pets allowed* ⫼*Breakfast* Ⓜ *Marienplatz (U-bahn and S-bahn)* ⊹ *B5.*

$$$$
⊡ **Hotel Vier Jahreszeiten Kempinski München.** It likes to call its lobby the "most beautiful living room in Munich," and just as the world's wealthy and titled have felt for more than 150 years, you'll feel at home enjoying a drink and a bite in this "lived-in" spacious and luxurious room with glass dome and with dark-wood paneling. **Pros:** great location; occasional special packages that are a good value. **Cons:** Wi-Fi (free) in lobby only (via cable in rooms). ⊠ *Maximilianstr. 17, City Center* ☎ *089/2125–2799* ⊕ *www.Kempinski-Vierjahreszeiten.de* ↪ *303 rooms, 65 suites* ⟲ *In-room: Internet. In-hotel: restaurant, bar, pool, gym, business center, parking, some pets allowed* ⫼*Breakfast* Ⓜ *Tram 19 Kammerspiele (Tram)* ⊹ *F4.*

$$
Fodor's Choice
★

⊡ **The Louis Hotel.** No other hotel in Munich manages to combine the subdued elegance of a design hotel, first-rate service, and perhaps the best City Center location, overlooking Viktualienmarkt, as this hotel. **Pros:** brilliant location; attentive service; modern designs; very good restaurant. **Cons:** some rooms pricey; the bustle of the Viktualienmarkt is not for everyone; parking costs €24 a day. ⊠ *Viktualienmarkt 6, City Center, Munich* ☎ *089/4111–9080* ⊕ *www.louis-hotel.com* ⤶ *72* ♿ *In-room: a/c, Internet, Wi-Fi. In-hotel: restaurant, bar, gym, spa, laundry facilities, business center* ⏲ *Breakfast* ✛ *E5.*

$ 🛏 **Motel One München Sendlinger Tor.** With well-thought-out designs and free Wi-Fi, the Motel One chain has jumped ahead of the game with its simple but classy concept. **Pros:** great prices and location; decent designs; amiable, attentive service; kids ages 1–6 get a free breakfast. **Cons:** staying in one is like staying in all of them; no restaurant or room service; breakfast costs €7.50 extra. ⊠ *Herzog-Wilhelm-Str. 28, City Center, Munich* ☎ *089/5177–7250* ⊕ *www.motel-one.com/de* ⤶ *241 rooms* ♿ *In-room: Wi-Fi. In-hotel: bar, parking, some pets allowed* ⏲ *Breakfast* ✛ *C5.*

$$$ 🛏 **Platzl Hotel.** The privately owned Platzl has won awards and wide recognition for its ecologically aware management, which uses heat recyclers in the kitchen, environmentally friendly detergents, recyclable materials, waste separation, and other eco-friendly practices. **Pros:** good restaurant; progressive environmental credentials; around the corner from the Hofbräuhaus. **Cons:** rooms facing the Hofbräuhaus get more noise; some rooms are on the small side; Wi-Fi is expensive, and is only available in lobby and first floor. ⊠ *Sparkassenstr. 10, City Center* ☎ *089/237–030* ⊕ *www.platzl.de* ⤶ *167 rooms* ♿ *In-room: no a/c, Internet, Wi-Fi. In-hotel: restaurant, bar, gym, parking, some pets allowed* ⏲ *Breakfast* Ⓜ *Marienplatz (U-bahn and S-bahn)* ✛ *E5.*

$$$ 🛏 **Torbräu.** The welcoming Torbräu has been looking after guests in one form or another since 1490, making it the oldest hotel in Munich, and it has been run by the same family for more than a century. **Pros:** nice rooms; central location; good restaurant; very attentive service. **Cons:** underground parking difficult; front rooms a little noisy. ⊠ *Tal 41, City Center* ☎ *089/242–340* ⊕ *www.torbraeu.de* ⤶ *91 rooms* ♿ *In-room: a/c, Internet, Wi-Fi. In-hotel: restaurant, business center, some pets allowed* ⏲ *Breakfast* Ⓜ *Isartor (S-bahn)* ✛ *F5.*

HAUPTBAHNHOF

$ 🛏 **Creatif Hotel Elephant.** Tucked away on a quiet street near the train station, this hotel appeals to a wide range of travelers, from businesspeople to tourists on a budget. **Pros:** close to main station. **Cons:** no restaurant; modest furnishings. ⊠ *Lämmerstr. 6, Maxvorstadt* ☎ *089/555–785* ⊕ *www.creatifelephanthotel.com* ⤶ *40 rooms* ♿ *In-room: no a/c, Wi-Fi. In-hotel: some pets allowed* ⏲ *Breakfast* Ⓜ *Hauptbahnhof (U-bahn and S-bahn)* ✛ *A3.*

$$$ 🛏 **Eden-Hotel Wolff.** Beyond a light-filled lobby, a spacious bar with dark-wood paneling beckons, contributing to the old-fashioned elegance of this downtown favorite. **Pros:** great location; all rooms have air-conditioning. **Cons:** rooms with windows toward main station çan get noisy. ⊠ *Arnulfstr. 4, Hauptbahnhof* ☎ *089/551–150* ⊕ *www.ehw.de* ⤶ *209 rooms, 2 suites* ♿ *In-room: Internet, Wi-Fi. In-hotel: restaurant, bar, gym, spa, parking, some pets allowed* ⏲ *Breakfast* Ⓜ *Hauptbahnhof (U-bahn and S-bahn)* ✛ *A3.*

$$$ ⊡ **Hotel Excelsior.** Just a short walk along an underpass from the Haupt-bahnhof station, the Excelsior welcomes you with smiles after the hustle and bustle of the busy train station. **Pros:** welcoming reception; spacious rooms; excellent breakfast; free Wi-Fi throughout. **Cons:** some parts of the decor are ready for updating (the overstuffed armchairs in the lobby are starting to look scuffed). ⊠ *Schützenstr. 11, Hauptbahnhof* ☏ *089/551–370* ⊕ *www.excelsior-hotel.de* ⤳ *112 rooms* ⚕ *In-room: a/c, Wi-Fi. In-hotel: restaurant, bar* ☉ *No lunch Sun. in restaurant* †○┤ *Breakfast* ✛ *B4.*

$$ ⊡ **Hotel Amba.** Right across the street from the main train station, Amba provides clean, bright rooms, good service, no expensive frills, and everything you need to plug and play. **Pros:** convenient to train station and sights. **Cons:** no restaurant; rooms that face the main street and the station are noisy. ⊠ *Arnulfstr. 20, Hauptbahnhof* ☏ *089/545–140* ⊕ *www.hotel-amba.de* ⤳ *86 rooms* ⚕ *In-room: no a/c, Wi-Fi. In-hotel: business center, some pets allowed* †○┤ *Breakfast* Ⓜ *Hauptbahnhof (U-bahn and S-bahn)* ✛ *B3.*

$ ⊡ **Hotel Mirabell.** This family-run hotel is used to American tourists
★   who appreciate the friendly service, central location (between the main railway station and the Oktoberfest fairgrounds), and reasonable room rates. **Pros:** Wi-Fi free throughout; family run; personalized service. **Cons:** no restaurant; this area of the Hauptbahnhof is not the most salubrious. ⊠ *Landwehrstr. 42, entrance on Goethestr., Hauptbahnhof* ☏ *089/549–1740* ⊕ *www.hotelmirabell.de* ⤳ *65 rooms, 3 apartments* ⚕ *In-room: no a/c, Wi-Fi. In-hotel: bar, some pets allowed* †○┤ *Breakfast* Ⓜ *Hauptbahnhof (U-bahn and S-bahn)* ✛ *A5.*

$ ⊡ **Hotel Präsident.** The location—just a block from the main train station—is the biggest draw of this hotel. **Pros:** central location. **Cons:** rooms toward the street are noisy; streets around the hotel are somewhat shady; parking 100 yards away costs €5. ⊠ *Schwanthalerstr. 20, Ludwigvorstadt* ☏ *089/549–0060* ⊕ *www.hotel-praesident.de* ⤳ *42 rooms* ⚕ *In-room: no a/c, Wi-Fi. In-hotel: parking, some pets allowed* †○┤ *Breakfast* Ⓜ *Hauptbahnhof (U-bahn and S-bahn)* ✛ *B5.*

LEHEL

$$ ⊡ **Adria.** This modern hotel is near a number of great museums and the English Garden. **Pros:** good location; nice lobby. **Cons:** no bar or restaurant. ⊠ *Liebigstr. 8a, Lehel* ☏ *089/242–1170* ⊕ *www.adria-muenchen.de* ⤳ *45 rooms* ⚕ *In-room: no a/c, Internet, Wi-Fi. In-hotel: some pets allowed* †○┤ *Breakfast* Ⓜ *Lehel (U-bahn)* ✛ *G4.*

$$ ⊡ **Hotel Concorde.** The privately owned Concorde is in the middle of Munich and yet peaceful owing to its location on a narrow side street. **Pros:** quiet; functional; good location. **Cons:** no restaurant or bar. ⊠ *Herrnstr. 38–40, Lehel* ☏ *089/224–515* ⊕ *www.concorde-muenchen.de* ⤳ *72 rooms* ⚕ *In-room: no a/c, Wi-Fi. In-hotel: parking, some pets allowed* †○┤ *Breakfast* Ⓜ *Isartor (S-bahn)* ✛ *F5.*

$$$ ⊡ **Hotel Opera.** In the quiet residential district of Lehel, Hotel Opera offers rooms decorated in an elegant style—lots of Empire, some art deco. **Pros:** free Wi-Fi throughout; elegant; pleasant courtyard; quiet location; special service. **Cons:** not enough parking close to the hotel; no restaurant. ⊠ *St.-Anna-Str. 10, Lehel* ☎ *089/210–4940* ⊕ *www.hotel-opera.de* ⇦ *25 rooms* ⑁ *In-room: no a/c, Wi-Fi. In-hotel: bar, some pets allowed* ⑪ *Breakfast* Ⓜ *Lehel (U-bahn)* ✛ *G4.*

ISARVORSTADT

$$$

Fodor'sChoice

★

⛭**Admiral.** The small, privately owned, tradition-rich Admiral enjoys a quiet side-street location and its own garden, close to the river Isar, minutes from the Deutsches Museum. **Pros:** attention to detail; quiet; excellent service. **Cons:** no restaurant. ⊠ *Kohlstr. 9, Isarvorstadt* ☎ *089/216–350* ⊕ *www.hotel-admiral.de* ⇦ *33 rooms* ⑁ *In-room: no a/c, Internet, Wi-Fi. In-hotel: bar, business center, parking, some pets allowed* ⑪ *Breakfast* Ⓜ *Isartor (S-bahn)* ✛ *F6.*

$ ⛭**Pension Seibel.** If you're looking for an affordable little "pension" a stone's throw from the Viktualienmarkt, this is the place. **Pros:** great location at a great price. **Cons:** tiny breakfast room; no elevator; Wi-Fi, but the price is oddly determined after you use it. ⊠ *Reichenbachstr. 8, Isarvorstadt* ☎ *089/231–9180* ⊕ *www.seibel-hotels-munich.de* ⇦ *15 rooms* ⑪ *Breakfast* Ⓜ *Marienplatz (U-bahn and S-bahn)* ✛ *E6.*

MAXVORSTADT

$$ ⛭**Carlton Astoria.** Downtown, near the art museums and the university you can reach many places on foot. **Pros:** centrally located; fairly priced. **Cons:** rooms on main street can be noisy; no Wi-Fi; parking is a short walk away. ⊠ *Fürstenstr. 12, Maxvorstadt* ☎ *089/383–9630* ⊕ *www.carlton-astoria.de* ⇦ *48 rooms* ⑁ *In-room: no a/c* ⑪ *Breakfast* Ⓜ *Between Universität and Odeonsplatz (U-bahn)* ✛ *E2.*

$

Fodor'sChoice

★

⛭**Hotel Pension Am Siegestor.** Modest but appealing, this is a great deal in Germany's most expensive city. **Pros:** a delightful and homey place to stay. **Cons:** if elevators make you nervous, don't use this old one; no restaurant or bar. ⊠ *Akademiestr. 5, Maxvorstadt* ☎ *089/399–550* ⊕ *www.siegestor.com* ⇦ *20 rooms* ⑁ *In-room: no a/c, no TV. In-hotel: business center* ⊟ *No credit cards* ⑪ *Breakfast* Ⓜ *Universität (U-bahn)* ✛ *F1.*

SCHWABING

$$ ⛭**Biederstein.** A modern, block of a building, but covered with geraniums in summer, the Biederstein seems to want to fit into its old Schwabing surroundings at the edge of the English Garden. **Pros:** wonderfully quiet location; all rooms have balconies; exemplary service; U-bahn is four blocks away. **Cons:** no restaurant. ⊠ *Keferstr. 18, Schwabing* ☎ *089/3302–9390* ⊕ *www.hotelbiederstein.de* ⇦ *34 rooms, 7 suites* ⑁ *In-room: no a/c, Wi-Fi. In-hotel: bar, business center, parking, some pets allowed* Ⓜ *Münchner Freiheit (U-bahn)* ✛ *G1.*

$$ ⛭**Cosmopolitan.** The entrance to this inviting hotel is on the lively Hohenzollernstrasse, but once you pass through what looks rather like a garage opening, you'll find yourself in a quiet courtyard. **Pros:** right in the middle of Schwabing, Münchner Freiheit a city block away; quiet courtyard rooms. **Cons:** no restaurant; street-side rooms are noisy. ⊠ *Hohenzollernstr. 5, Schwabing* ☎ *089/383–810* ⊕ *www.*

Bayerischer-Hof

Bayerischer-Hof

The Louis Hotel

The Louis Hotel

Pension Am Siegestor

Pension Am Siegestor

cosmopolitanhotel.de ⇆ *71 rooms; 8 suites* ♿ *In-room: no a/c, Wi-Fi. In-hotel: bar, parking, some pets allowed* 🍽 *Breakfast* Ⓜ *Münchner Freiheit (U-bahn)* ✥ *F1.*

$ ★ **Gästehaus am Englischen Garten.** Reserve well in advance for a room at this popular converted water mill, more than 300 years old, adjoining the English Garden. **Pros:** quiet location; ideal for walking or cycling; wonderfully cozy rooms. **Cons:** no elevator; no restaurant. ✉ *Liebergesellstr. 8, Schwabing* ☎ *089/383–9410* 🌐 *www.hotelenglischergarten.de* ⇆ *12 rooms, 6 with bath or shower; 13 apartments* ♿ *In-room: no a/c. In-hotel: parking, some pets allowed* 🍽 *Breakfast* Ⓜ *Münchner Freiheit (U-bahn)* ✥ *G1.*

$$ **H'otello F'22.** This is a high-caliber example of the design- and style-driven nature of the new Munich hotel scene. **Pros:** great location; well-thought-out design; some rooms have balconies. **Cons:** no Wi-Fi. ✉ *Fallmerayerstr. 22, Schwabing, Munich* ☎ *089/4583–1200* 🌐 *www.hotello.de* ⇆ *74* ♿ *In-room: a/c, Internet. In-hotel: parking* 🍽 *Breakfast* ✥ *E1.*

$$ **H'otello H'09.** The second in the H'otello chain to open in Munich, this high-design hotel is a five-minute walk to the Englischer Garden. **Pros:** great location; well-thought-out design; uncomplicated rooms. **Cons:** no Wi-Fi. ✉ *Hohenzollernstr. 9, Schwabing, Munich* ☎ *089/4583–1200* 🌐 *www.hotello.de* ⇆ *71* ♿ *In-room: a/c, Internet. In-hotel: parking* 🍽 *Breakfast* ✥ *F1.*

LUDWIGVORSTADT

$ **Brack.** A nice, light-filled lobby makes the first good impression here. **Pros:** good location for accessing Oktoberfest and city; late breakfast; free use of bikes. **Con:** noisy front rooms. ✉ *Lindwurmstr. 153, Ludwigvorstadt* ☎ *089/747–2550* 🌐 *www.hotel-brack.de* ⇆ *50 rooms* ♿ *In-room: no a/c, Wi-Fi. In-hotel: parking, some pets allowed* 🍽 *Breakfast* Ⓜ *Poccistrasse (U-bahn)* ✥ *B6.*

$ **Hotel am Viktualienmarkt.** What was once a dour, old-fashioned, and not particularly enjoyable hotel was transformed in 2010 into a highly recommendable middle-market design-led hotel. **Pros:** refreshing atmosphere; service attentive but not overbearing; great location; lovely courtyard for breakfast; competitive prices. **Cons:** no air-conditioning; no restaurant; parking around the corner. ✉ *Utzschneiderstr. 14, Ludwigvorstadt, Munich* ☎ *089/231–1090* 🌐 *www.hotel-am-viktualienmarkt.de* ⇆ *27 rooms* ♿ *In-room: no a/c, Internet, Wi-Fi. In-hotel: some pets allowed* 🍽 *Breakfast* ✥ *E6.*

$ **Hotel-Pension Mariandl.** The American armed forces commandeered this turn-of-the-20th-century neo-Gothic mansion in May 1945 and established Munich's first postwar nightclub, the Femina, on the ground floor. **Pros:** hotel and café are a charmingly worn and a bit bohemian. **Cons:** hotel and café are charmingly worn and a bit bohemian; no elevator. ✉ *Goethestr. 51, Ludwigvorstadt* ☎ *089/552–9100* 🌐 *www.hotelmariandl.com* ⇆ *28 rooms* ♿ *In-room: no a/c, no TV, Wi-Fi. In-hotel: restaurant, business center, some pets allowed* 🍽 *Breakfast* Ⓜ *Hauptbahnhof (U-bahn and S-bahn)* ✥ *A6.*

$ ☂ **Hotel-Pension Schmellergarten.** Popular with young budget travelers, this genuine family business tries to make everyone feel at home. **Pros:** good location; good price. **Cons:** no elevator; no hotel services. ✉ *Schmellerstr. 20, Ludwigvorstadt* ☎ *089/773–157* ⊕ *www.schmellergarten.de* ↝ *14 rooms* ♨ *In-room: no a/c, no TV. In-hotel: some pets allowed* ❑ *Breakfast* Ⓜ *Poccistrasse (U-bahn)* ✛ *B6.*

$ ☂ **Hotel Uhland.** This stately villa is a landmark building and is additionally special in that the owner and host was born here and will make you feel at home, too. **Pros:** a real family atmosphere; care is given to details. **Cons:** no restaurant or bar. ✉ *Uhlandstr. 1, Ludwigvorstadt* ☎ *089/543–350* ⊕ *www.hotel-uhland.de* ↝ *27 rooms* ♨ *In-room: no a/c, Wi-Fi. In-hotel: business center, some pets allowed* ✛ *A6.*

Fodor'sChoice
★

THERESIENHÖHE

$ ☂ **Park-Hotel Theresienhöhe.** The Park-Hotel claims that none of its rooms is less than 400 square feet. **Pros:** spacious rooms; good quiet location. **Cons:** no restaurant; modern but not great charm; Wi-Fi costs €14 for 24 hours. ✉ *Parkstr. 31a, Theresienhöhe* ☎ *089/519–950* ⊕ *www.parkhoteltheresienhoehe.de* ↝ *40 rooms* ♨ *In-room: no a/c, Wi-Fi. In-hotel: bar, some pets allowed* ❑ *Breakfast* Ⓜ *Theresienwiese (U-bahn)* ✛ *A5.*

$ ☂ **Westend.** Visitors have praised the friendly welcome and service they receive at this well-maintained and affordable lodging above the Oktoberfest grounds. **Pros:** good location; good prices. **Cons:** no restaurant; rooms are simple; it's best to confirm your reservation. ✉ *Schwantalerstr. 121, Theresienhöhe* ☎ *089/5409860* ⊕ *www.kurpfalz-hotel.de* ↝ *44 rooms* ♨ *In-room: no a/c, Internet. In-hotel: bar, some pets allowed* ❑ *Breakfast* Ⓜ *Hackerbrücke (S-bahn)* ✛ *B5.*

NYMPHENBURG

$ ☂ **Erzgiesserei Europe.** Rooms in this modern hotel are bright, decorated in soft pastels with good reproductions on the walls. **Pros:** relatively quiet location; nice courtyard; air-conditioning in all rooms. **Cons:** charm of a business hotel; Wi-Fi costs €6.50 for 24 hours. ✉ *Erzgiessereistr. 15, Nymphenburg* ☎ *089/126–820* ⊕ *www.topinternational.com* ↝ *105 rooms, 1 suite* ♨ *In-room: no a/c, Wi-Fi. In-hotel: restaurant, bar, parking, some pets allowed* ❑ *Breakfast* Ⓜ *Stiglmaierplatz (U-bahn)* ✛ *A2.*

$ ☂ **Kriemhild.** This welcoming, family-run pension is in a quiet western suburb. **Pros:** quiet location; family run. **Cons:** far from the city sights; no elevator. ✉ *Guntherstr. 16, Nymphenburg* ☎ *089/171–1170* ⊕ *www.kriemhild.de* ↝ *18 rooms* ♨ *In-room: no a/c, Wi-Fi. In-hotel: bar, parking, some pets allowed* ❑ *Breakfast* Ⓜ *Kriemhildstrasse (Tram-bahn 16/17)* ✛ *A2.*
☾

BOGENHAUSEN

$$ ☂ **Westin Grand München.** The building itself, with 22 floors, may raise a few eyebrows. **Pros:** luxurious lobby and restaurant; rooms facing west toward the city have a fabulous view. **Cons:** it's not possible to
★

reserve west-facing rooms; hotel is difficult to reach via public transportation; at €29, breakfast is expensive; high-speed Wi-Fi limited to certain areas. ✉ *Arabellastr. 6, Bogenhausen* ☎ *089/92640* ⊕ *www.westin. com/munich* ➳ *627 rooms, 28 suites* ♿ *In-room: Internet, Wi-Fi. In-hotel: restaurant, bar, pool, business center, parking, some pets allowed* ⍔ *Breakfast* Ⓜ *Arabellapark (U-bahn)* ✛ *F1.*

OUTSIDE THE CENTER

$$ ⍤ **Jagdschloss.** This century-old hunting lodge in Munich's leafy Obermenzing suburb is a delightful hotel. **Pros:** peaceful location; beer garden; easy parking. **Cons:** out in the middle of nowhere; convenient only with a car; no elevator. ✉ *Alte Allee 21, München-Obermenzing* ☎ *089/820–820* ⊕ *www.jagd-schloss.com* ➳ *22 rooms, 1 suite* ♿ *In-room: no a/c, Internet. In-hotel: restaurant, bar, parking, some pets allowed* ⍔ *Breakfast* ✛ *A4.*

NIGHTLIFE AND THE ARTS

THE ARTS

Bavaria's capital has an enviable reputation as an artistic hot spot. Details of concerts and theater performances are listed in *Vorschau* and *Monatsprogramm,* booklets available at most hotel reception desks, newsstands, and tourist offices. *Prinz* magazine lists almost everything happening in the city, as do a host of other city magazines, while the superb and official city Web site (⊕ *www.muenchen.de*) has listings. Otherwise, just keep your eye open for advertising pillars and posters.

Box Office of the Bavarian State Theaters. Tickets for performances at the Bavarian State Theater, Nationaltheater, Staatstheater am Gärtnerplatz, plus many other locations, are sold at the central box office. It's open Monday to Saturday 10–7. ✉ *Marstallpl. 5, City Center* ☎ *089/2185– 1920* ⊕ *www.staatstheater-tickets.bayern.de/willkommen.html.*

München Ticket. One ticket agency, München Ticket, has a German-language Web site where tickets for most Munich theaters can be booked. ☎ *089/5481–8181* ⊕ *www.muenchenticket.de.*

Zentraler Kartenverkauf. Two Zentraler Kartenverkauf ticket kiosks are in the underground concourse at Marienplatz, and one at Stachus. ✉ *City Center* ☎ *089/292540 Marienplatz, 089/5450–6060 Stachus* ⊕ *www. zkv-muenchen.de.*

CONCERTS

Munich and music go together. The city has two world-renowned orchestras. The Philharmonic is now directed by Christian Thielemann (though due to be replaced by Lorin Maazel for the 2012 season), formerly of the Deutsche Oper in Berlin; the Bavarian State Opera Company is managed by Japanese-American director Kent Nagano. The leading choral ensembles are the Munich Bach Choir, the Munich Motettenchor, and Musica Viva, the last specializing in contemporary music. The choirs perform mostly in city churches.

Gasteig Culture Center. This world-class concert hall is in the Gasteig Culture Center, a hugely expensive, not particularly beautiful brick complex standing high above the Isar River, east of downtown. Its Philharmonic Hall is the permanent home of the Munich Philharmonic Orchestra and the largest concert hall in Munich. Gasteig also hosts the occasional English-language work. It hosts the annual book fair and numerous other events and celebrations. ■TIP→ The sizeable open kitchen Gast (⊕ *www.gast-muenchen.de*), part of the Gasteig complex, is a good option for a range of quick foods, from Thai curries to pizzas. ✉ *Rosenheimerstr. 5, Haidhausen* ☎ *089/480–980* ⊕ *www.gasteig.de* Ⓜ *Rosenheimerplatz (S-bahn).*

Herkulessaal in der Residenz. This highly regarded orchestral and recital venue is in the former throne room of King Ludwig I. ✉ *Residenzstraße 1, City Center* ☎ *0180/5481–8181 München Ticket* ⊕ *www. muenchenticket.de.*

Hochschule für Musik. Free concerts featuring conservatory students are given at the Hochschule für Musik. ✉ *Arcisstr. 12, Maxvorstadt* ☎ *089/ 28903* ⊕ *www.musikhochschule-muenchen.de.*

Nationaltheater (*Bayerische Staatsoper*). The Bavarian State Orchestra is based at the Nationaltheater. ✉ *Max-Joseph-Platz 2, City Center* ☎ *089/ 218–501* ⊕ *www.staatsorchester.de.*

Olympiahalle. One of Munich's major pop-rock concert venues is the Olympiahalle, and the official ticket seller is München Ticket.

München Ticket. You can also book by calling München Ticket. ☎ *089/5481–8181* ✉ *U-3 Olympiazentrum stop, Milbertshofen* ⊕ *www. olympiapark-muenchen.de; www.muenchenticket.de for tickets.*

Staatstheater am Gärtnerplatz. The romantic art nouveau Staatstheater am Gärtnerplatz has a variety of performances including operas, ballet, and musicals. Tickets from the theater weekdays 10–6, Saturday 10–1 or Zentraler Kartenvorverkauf in Marienplatz, and Stachus. ✉ *Gärtnerpl. 3, Isarvorstadt* ☎ *089/2185–1960* ⊕ *www.staatstheater-am-gaertnerplatz.de.*

FESTIVALS   **Long Night of Music.** In late May the Long Night of Music is devoted to live performances through the night by untold numbers of groups, from heavy-metal bands to medieval choirs, at more than 100 locations throughout the city. One ticket covers everything, including transportation on special buses between locations. ☎ *089/3061–0041* ⊕ *www. muenchner.de/musiknacht* ▱ *€15.*

OPERA, BALLET, AND MUSICALS
Nationaltheater. Munich's Bavarian State Opera Company and its ballet ensemble perform at the Nationaltheater. ✉ *Max-Joseph-Platz 2, City Center* ☎ *089/218–501.*

THEATER
Munich has scores of theaters and variety-show venues, although most productions will be largely impenetrable if your German is shaky. Listed here are all the better-known theaters, as well as some of the smaller and more progressive spots. Note that most theaters are closed during July and August.

Amerika Haus (*America House*). Amerika Haus is the venue for the very active American Drama Group Europe, which presents regular English-language productions. ✉ *Karolinenpl. 3, Maxvorstadt* ☎ *089/552–5370* ⊕ *www.amerikahaus.de.*

Bayerisches Staatsschauspiel (*Bavarian State Theater*). Bayerisches Staatsschauspiel is Munich's leading ensemble for classic playwrights such as Goethe, Schiller, Lessing, Shakespeare, and Chekhov. Its main home is the Residenz Theater, but it also plays at the Cuvilliés-Theater and at Marstall. ✉ *Max-Joseph-Pl., City Center* ☎ *089/2185–1920* ⊕ *www.bayerischesstaatsschauspiel.de; www.staatstheater-tickets.bayern.de for tickets.*

Münchner Kammerspiele. A city-funded rival to the nearby state-backed Bayerisches Staatschauspiel, Münchner Kammerspiele-Schauspielhaus presents the classics as well as new works by contemporary playwrights. ✉ *Maximilianstr. 26–28, City Center* ☎ *089/2339–6600* ⊕ *www.muenchner-kammerspiele.de.*

NIGHTLIFE

Munich has a lively night scene ranging from beer halls to bars to chic clubs. The fun areas for a night out are the City Center, Isarvorstadt (Gärtnerplatz and Glockenbachviertel are arguably the best in the city), and Schwabing around Schellingstrasse and Münchner Freiheit. Regardless of their size or style, many bars, especially around Gärtnerplatz, have DJs spinning either mellow background sounds or funky beats.

However many fingers you want to hold up, just remember the easy-to-pronounce *Bier* (beer) *Bit-te* (please) when ordering a beer. The tricky part is, Germans don't just produce *one* beverage called beer; they brew more than 5,000 varieties. Germany has about 1,300 breweries, 40% of the world's total.

In Munich you'll find the most famous breweries, the largest beer halls and beer gardens, the biggest and most indulgent beer festival, and the widest selection of brews. Even the beer glasses are bigger: a *Mass* is a 1-liter (almost 2-pint) serving; a *Halbe* is half liter and the standard size. The Hofbräuhaus is Munich's best-known beer hall, but you'll find locals in one of the English Garden's four beer gardens or in a *Wirtshaus* (tavern).

In summer, last call at the beer gardens is around 11 pm. Most of the traditional places stay open until 1 am or so and are great for a few hours of wining and dining before heading out on the town. Most bars stay open until at least 3 am on weekends; some don't close until 5 or 6 am.

BARS

CITY CENTER **Bar Centrale.** Around the corner from the Hofbräuhaus, Bar Centrale is very Italian—the waiters don't seem to speak any other language. The coffee is excellent; small fine meals are served as well. They have a retro-looking back room with leather sofas. ✉ *Ledererstr. 23, City Center* ☎ *089/223–762.*

Atomic Café. Also near the Hofbräuhaus is the Atomic Café. This club/lounge has excellent DJs nightly, playing everything from '60s Brit pop to '60s/'70s funk and soul. Atomic also has great live acts on a regular basis. ⊠ *Neuturmstr. 5, City Center* ☎ *089/228–3053* ⊕ *www.atomic.de.*

Kilian's Irish Pub and Ned Kelly's Australian Bar. Just behind the Frauenkirche, Kilian's Irish Pub and Ned Kelly's Australian Bar offers an escape from the German tavern scene. Naturally, they have Guinness and Foster's, but they also serve Munich's lager, Augustiner, and regularly televise international soccer, rugby, and sports in general. ⊠ *Frauenpl. 11, City Center* ☎ *089/2421–9899 Both bars.*

Schumann's. At Schumann's, Munich's most famous bar, the bartenders are busy shaking cocktails after the curtain comes down at the nearby opera house. ⊠ *Odeonspl. 6–7, City Center* ☎ *089/229–060* ⊕ *www.schumanns.de.*

Trader Vic's. Exotic cocktails are the specialty at Trader Vic's, a smart cellar bar in the Hotel Bayerischer Hof that's as popular among out-of-town visitors as it is locals. ⊠ *Promenadenpl. 2–6, City Center* ☎ *089/212–0995* ⊕ *www.bayerischerhof.de/en/bars.*

Night Club Bar. The Bayerischer Hof's Night Club Bar has live music, most famously international stars from the jazz scene, but also reggae to hip-hop and everything in between. ⊠ *Promenadepl. 2–6, City Center* ☎ *089/212–0994 Table reservation* ⊕ *www.bayerischerhof.de/en/bars.*

Eisbach. Eisbach occupies a corner of the Max Planck Institute building opposite the Bavarian Parliament. The bar is among Munich's biggest and is overlooked by a mezzanine restaurant area where you can choose from a limited but ambitious menu. Outdoor tables nestle in the expansive shade of huge parasols. The nearby Eisbach brook, which gives the bar its name, tinkles away, lending a relaxed air. ⊠ *Marstallpl. 3, City Center* ☎ *089/2280–1680* ⊕ *www.eisbach.eu.*

Hotel Vier Jahreszeiten Kempinski. The Hotel Vier Jahreszeiten Kempinski offers piano music until 9 pm, and then dancing to recorded music or a small combo. ⊠ *Maximilianstr. 17, City Center* ☎ *089/2125–2799* ⊕ *www.kempinski.com/de/munich.*

Around Gärtnerplatz and Glockenbachviertel are a number of cool bars and clubs for a somewhat younger, hipper crowd.

Cafe Trachtenvogl. Take a seat on Grandma's retro couches at Cafe Trachtenvogl. Trachtenvogl serves good toasties and Tegernseer beer, a favorite in Munich. ⊠ *Reichenbachstr. 47, Isarvorstadt* ☎ *089/201–5160* ⊕ *www.trachtenvogl.de.*

Holy Home. For a New York City–corner-bar type experience, check out Holy Home. A hip local crowd frequents this smoky hole-in-the-wall that books great low-key DJs. ⊠ *Reichenbachstr. 21, Isarvorstadt* ☎ *089/201–4546.*

Café am Hochhaus. If you're looking for a bit more action, check out the Café am Hochhaus. The glass-fronted former coffee shop is now a scene bar with funky DJs playing music to shake a leg to (if it's not too crowded). ⊠ *Blumenstr. 29, Isarvorstadt* ☎ *089/8905–8152* ⊕ *www.cafeamhochhaus.de.*

SCHWABING **Alter Simpl.** Media types drink Weissbier, Helles, as well as Guinness and Kilkenny, at the square bar at Alter Simpl. More than 100 years old, this establishment serves German food until 2 am. ⊠ *Türkenstr. 57, Schwabing* ☎ *089/272–3083* ⊕ *www.eggerlokale.de.*

Türkenhof. Across the street is the Türkenhof, another solid local joint that serves Augustiner and good food. ⊠ *Türkenstr. 78, Schwabing* ☎ *089/280–0235* ⊕ *www.augustiner-braeu.de.*

Schall und Rauch. Up on Schellingstrasse is Schall und Rauch. This legendary student hangout, whose name literally means "Noise and Smoke," has great music and food. ⊠ *Schellingstr. 22, Schwabing* ☎ *089/2880–9577.*

Schelling Salon. Another absolute cornerstone in the neighborhood is the Schelling Salon. On the corner of Barerstrasse, the bar has several pool tables and even a secret ping-pong room in the basement with an intercom for placing beer orders. The food's good and pretty inexpensive. It's closed Tuesday and Wednesday. ⊠ *Schellingstr. 54, Schwabing* ☎ *089/272–0788* ⊕ *www.schelling-salon.de.*

BEER GARDENS

Everybody in Munich has at least one favorite beer garden, so you're usually in good hands if you ask someone to point you in the right direction. You do not need to reserve. No need to phone either: if the weather says yes, then go. Some—but not all—allow you to bring your own food, but if you do, don't defile this hallowed territory with something so foreign as pizza or a burger. Note that Munich has very strict noise laws, so beer gardens tend to close around 11.

CITY CENTER **Biergarten am Viktualienmarkt.** The only true beer garden in the City Center, and therefore the easiest to find, is the one at the Viktualienmarkt. The beer on tap rotates every six weeks among the six Munich breweries to keep everyone happy throughout the year. ☎ *089/2916–5993* ⊕ *www.biergarten-viktualienmarkt.com.*

Park Café. This is one of Munich's hippest cafés, restaurants, nightclubs, and beer gardens. It often draws a younger crowd, attracted by a thriving music scene in the café itself, which ranges from DJs to live bands, and the occasional celebrity spotting. There's a great atmosphere to go with the good food and drinks, even better when the sun is shining and the beer garden is open. ⊠ *Sophienstr. 7, City Center, Munich* ☎ *089/5161–7980* ⊕ *www.parkcafe089.de.*

The rest of the beer gardens are a bit farther afield and can be reached handily by bike or S- and U-bahn.

AROUND TOWN **Biergarten am Chinesischen Turm.** The famous Biergarten am Chinesischen Turm is at the five-story Chinese Tower in the Englischer Garten. Enjoy your beer to the strains of oompah music played by traditionally dressed musicians. ⊠ *Englischer Garten 3* ☎ *089/383–8730* ⊕ *www.chinaturm.de.*

Hirschau. The Hirschau, pleasantly located in the Englischer Garten, has room for 2,500 guests, and it's about 10 minutes north of the Kleinhesselohersee. ⊠ *Gysslingstr. 15, Englischer Garten* ☎ *089/322–1080* ⊕ *www.hirschau-muenchen.de.*

Seehaus im Englischen Garten. The Seehaus im Englischen Garten is on the banks of the artificial lake Kleinhesseloher See, where all of Munich converges on hot summer days. Take Bus 44 and exit at Osterwaldstrasse or U-bahn 3/6 and stroll through the park. ⊠ *Kleinhesselohe 3* ☎ *089/381–6130* ⊕ *www.kuffler-gastronomie.de/de/muenchen/seehaus.*

Augustiner Keller Biergarten. The Augustiner Keller is one of the more authentic of the beer gardens, with excellent food, beautiful chestnut shade trees, a mixed local crowd, and Munich Augustiner beer. It's a few minutes from the Hauptbahnhof and Hackerbrucke. ⊠ *Arnulfstr. 52, Hauptbahnhof* ☎ *089/594–393* ⊕ *www.augustinerkeller.de.*

Königlicher Hirschgarten. Out in the district of Nymphenburg is the huge Königlicher Hirschgarten, a great family-oriented beer garden. To get there, rent bikes and make a day of it in the park and beer garden, or take Bus 151 or 51 to Hirschgarten, then walk for 10 to 15 minutes. Bike or bus, use a map, it'll be worth it. ⊠ *Hirschgarten 1, Nymphenburg* ☎ *089/1799–9119* ⊕ *www.hirschgarten.de.*

Taxisgarten. The crowd at the Taxisgarten in the Gern district (U-bahn Gern, Line 1 toward Olympia Einkaufszentrum) is more white-collar and tame, but the food is excellent, and while parents refresh themselves, children exhaust themselves on the playground. ⊠ *Taxisstr. 12, Neuhausen-Nymphenburg* ☎ *089/156–827* ⊕ *www.taxisgarten.de.*

Munich has more than 100 beer gardens, ranging from huge establishments that seat several hundred to small terraces tucked behind neighborhood pubs. Beer gardens are such an integral part of Munich life that a council proposal to cut down their hours provoked a storm of protest in 1995, culminating in one of the largest demonstrations in the city's history. They open whenever the thermometer creeps above 10°C (50°F) and the sun filters through the chestnut trees that are a necessary part of the scenery.

DANCE CLUBS

There are a few dance clubs in town worth mentioning, but be warned: the larger the venue, the more difficult the entry. In general, big nightclubs are giving way to smaller, more laid-back lounge types of places scattered all over town. If you're really hankering for a big club, go to Optimolwerke in the Ostbahnhof section. Otherwise, enjoy the handful of places around the City Center.

Optimolwerke. A former factory premises hosts the city's largest latenight party scene: the Optimolwerke has no fewer than 10 clubs (the number changes) including a Brazil bar, the self-styled "party bar" Optimal, and the female-only Candy Club. ⊠ *Friedenstr. 10, Ostbahnhof* ☎ *089/450–6920* ⊕ *www.optimolwerke.de* Ⓜ *Ostbahnhof S-bahn.*

P1. Bordering the Englischer Garten, in a wing of Haus der Kunst, P1 is definitely one of the most popular clubs in town for the see-and-be-seen crowd. It is chockablock with the rich and the wannabe rich and can be fun if you're in the mood. The bouncers can be choosy about whom they let in, so if you don't get lucky, head across the street to Edmoses at Prinzregentenstrasse 2 (⊕ *www.edmosesbar.com*). ⊠ *Prinzregentenstr.1, on west side of Haus der Kunst, Altstadt-Lehel* ☎ *089/294–252* ⊕ *www.p1-club.de.*

GAY AND LESBIAN BARS

Munich's well-established gay scene stretches between Sendlingertorplatz and Isartorplatz in the Glockenbach neighborhood. For an overview, check ⊕ *www.munich-cruising.de.*

Morizz. The upscale Morizz fills with a somewhat moneyed crowd. ⊠ *Klenzestr. 43, Isarvorstadt* ☎ *089/201–6776.*

Ochsengarten. The Ochsengarten is Munich's leather bar. ⊠ *Müllerstr. 47, Isarvorstadt* ☎ *089/266–446.*

Selig. The laid-back Selig has a bit of outdoor seating, diverse cuisine, and good breakfasts. ⊠ *Hans-Sachs-Str. 3, Isarvorstadt* ☎ *089/2388–8878* ⊕ *www.einfachselig.de.*

JAZZ

Munich has a decent jazz scene, and some beer gardens have even taken to replacing their brass oompah bands with funky combos. Jazz musicians sometimes accompany Sunday brunch, too.

Alfonso's Live Music Club. At tiny Alfonso's the nightly live music redefines the concept of intimacy. ⊠ *Franzstr. 5, Schwabing* ☎ *089/338–835* ⊕ *www.alfonsos.de.*

The Big Easy. This classy restaurant features jazz-accompanied Sunday brunch for €19, not including drinks. Pricey, but good. ⊠ *Frundsbergstr. 46, Nymphenburg* ☎ *089/1589–0253* ⊕ *www.thebigeasy.de.*

Jazzbar Vogler. The Jazzbar Vogler is a nice bar with jam sessions on Monday nights and regular jazz concerts. ⊠ *Rumfordstr. 17, City Center/Isarvorstadt* ☎ *089/294–662* ⊕ *www.jazzbar-vogler.com.*

Mr. B's. The tiny Mr. B's is a treat. It's run by New Yorker Alex Best, who also mixes great cocktails and, unlike so many other barkeeps, usually wears a welcoming smile. ⊠ *Herzog-Heinrich-Str. 38, Ludwigvorstadt* ☎ *089/534–901* ⊕ *www.misterbs.de.*

Unterfahrt. The Unterfahrt is the place for the serious jazzologist, though hip-hop is making heavy inroads into the scene. ⊠ *Einsteinstr. 42, Haidhausen* ☎ *089/448–2794* ⊕ *www.unterfahrt.de.*

SPORTS AND THE OUTDOORS

Olympiapark. The Olympiapark, built for the 1972 Olympics, is one of the largest sports and recreation centers in Europe. The Olympic-size pool is open for swimming. ⊠ *Olympiapark, Spiridon-Louis-Ring 21, Milbertshofen* ☎ *089/30670* ⊕ *www.olympiapark.de* Ⓜ *Olympiazentrum (U-bahn).*

Sporthaus Schuster. The focus here is on adventure sports, so if it's climbing, trekking, biking, or walking you're into, this huge store, meters off Marienplatz, is the place. ⊠ *Rosenstr. 1–5, City Center, Munich* ☎ *089/237–070* ⊕ *www.sport-schuster.de.*

SportScheck. For general information about sports in and around Munich, contact the sports emporium SportScheck. The big store not only sells every kind of equipment but is very handy with advice. ⊠ *Sendlingerstr. 6, City Center* ☎ *089/21660* ⊕ *www.sportscheck.com.*

Skier at Olympiapark.

BICYCLING

A bike is hands-down the best way to experience this flat, pedal-friendly city. There are loads of bike lanes and paths that wind through its parks and along the Isar River. The rental shop will give you maps and tips, or you can get a map at any city tourist office.

Weather permitting, here is a route to try: Go through Isartor to the river and head north to the Englischer Garten. Ride around the park and have lunch at a beer garden. Exit the park and go across Leopoldstrasse into Schwabing, making your way back down toward the museum quarter via the adorable Elisabethmarkt. Check out one or two of the galleries then head back to town passing Königsplatz.

You can also take your bike on the S-bahns (except during rush hours from 6 am to 9 am and from 4 pm to 6 pm), which take you out to the many lakes and attractions outside town. Bicycles on public transportation cost either one strip on a multiple ticket or €2.50 for a day ticket, €0.90 for a single ticket.

TOURS **Mike's Bike Tours.** The oldest bike tour operation in Munich, Mike's tours last 3½ hours, with a 45-minute break at a beer garden, and cover approximately 6 km (4 mi). Tours start daily at the Altes Rathaus at the end of Marienplatz at 11:30 and 4 (April 15–August 31) and at 12:30 (March 1–April 14 and September 1–November 10). There are tours at 12:30 on Saturday in November and February if weather permits. The cost is €24, including the bike. No reservations required. Bus Bavaria (part of Mike's Bikes) also offers a more active day trip to Neuschwanstein castle. You travel to the area via coach in high season

(€49), via train in the shoulder season (€39). ✉ *Bräuhausstr. 10, City Center* ☎ *089/2554–3988* ⊕ *www.mikesbiketours.com.*

RENTALS **Mike's Bike Tours.** Mike's Bike Tours also rents bikes, Mike's is around the corner from the rear entrance of the Hofbräuhaus. Day rental is €15 for the first day, €12 for subsequent days, €70 for a week. Return time is 8 pm May–August, earlier in other seasons. ✉ *Bräuhausstr. 10, City Center* ☎ *089/2554–3988* ⊕ *www.mikesbiketours.com.*

Radius Tours and Bikes. Based at the central station, Radius Tours and Bikes rents bikes. A three- to eight-gear bike costs €14.50 a day. A 24-gear bike costs €22. Hourly rates are €3 and €5, respectively. ✉ *Opposite platform 32, Hauptbahnhof* ☎ *089/5434877730* ⊕ *www. radiustours.com.*

ICE-SKATING

Global warming permitting, there's outdoor skating on the lake in the Englischer Garten and on the Nymphenburger Canal in winter. Watch out for signs reading "gefahr" (danger), warning you of thin ice.

Karlsplatz. In winter the fountain on Karlsplatz is turned into a public rink with music and an outdoor bar.

SHOPPING

Munich has three of Germany's most exclusive shopping streets as well as flea markets to rival those of any other European city. In between are department stores, where acute German-style competition assures reasonable prices and often produces outstanding bargains. Artisans bring their wares of beauty and originality to the Christmas markets. Collect their business cards—in summer you're sure to want to order another of those little gold baubles that were on sale in December.

SHOPPING DISTRICTS

Munich has an immense central shopping area, a 2-km (1-mi) *Fussgängerzone* (pedestrian zone) stretching from the train station to Marienplatz and then north to Odeonsplatz. The two main streets here are Neuhauser Strasse and Kaufingerstrasse, the sites of most major department stores. For upscale shopping, Maximilianstrasse, Residenzstrasse, and Theatinerstrasse are unbeatable. Schwabing, north of the university, has more offbeat shopping streets—Schellingstrasse and Hohenzollernstrasse are two to try. ■TIP➔ The neighborhood around Gärtnerplatz also has lots of new boutiques.

DEPARTMENT STORES AND MALLS

The main pedestrian area has two mall-type locations.

Arcade. The aptly named Arcade is where the young find the best designer jeans and accessories. ✉ *Neuhauser Str. 5, City Center.*

Fünf Höfe. For a more upscale shopping experience, visit the many stores, boutiques, galleries, and cafés of the Fünf Höfe, a modern arcade carved into the block of houses between Theatinerstrasse and

Kardinal-Faulhaber-Strasse. The architecture of the passages and court-yards is cool and elegant, in sharp contrast to the facades of the buildings. There's a decent Thai restaurant in there as well.

Hirmer. Hirmer has Munich's most comprehensive collection of German-made men's clothes, with a markedly friendly and knowledgeable staff. International brands are also here. ✉ *Kaufingerstr. 28, City Center* ☎ *089/236–830.*

★ **Karstadt.** Karstadt commands an entire city block between the train station and Karlsplatz. It is the largest and one of the best department stores in the city. On the fourth floor is a cafeteria with a great selection of excellent and inexpensive dishes. ✉ *Bahnhofpl. 7, City Center* ☎ *089/55120.*

Kaufinger Tor. Kaufinger Tor has several floors of boutiques and cafés packed neatly together under a high glass roof. ✉ *Kaufingerstr. 117, City Center.*

Ludwig Beck. Ludwig Beck is considered a step above other department stores by Münchners. It's packed from top to bottom with highly original wares and satisfies even the pickiest of shoppers. ✉ *Marienpl. 11, City Center* ☎ *089/236–910.*

Oberpollinger. This upscale department store in the 100-year-old Haus Oberpollinger, at the start of the Kaufingerstrasse shopping mall, is a good source for Bavarian arts and crafts. ✉ *Neuhauser Str. 18, City Center* ☎ *089/290–230* ✉ *Schleissheimerstr. 93, Schwabing* ☎ *089/13020.*

Pool. Pool is a hip shop on the upscale Maximilianstrasse, with fashion, music, and accessories for house and home. A shopping experience for the senses. ✉ *Maximilianstr. 11, City Center* ☎ *089/266–035.*

Slips. Slips, a beautiful shop on Gärtnerplatz, has a wide range of dresses, jeans, shoes, and accessories. Prices are a bit outrageous, but it's a successful store, so they must be doing something right. ✉ *Gärtnerplatz. 2, Isarvorstadt* ☎ *089/202–2500.*

When departing from Munich for home, you can claim your V.A.T. refund (for purchases made during your stay). If the items are packed in your check-in luggage, tell the check-in agent who will give you a destination sticker for your bags, which you then take to German customs at Terminal 1/B. Present your receipts, which will be stamped, and customs will forward your luggage to your flight (it's simpler to pack the items in your carry-on bag, and follow the same procedure). With your stamped receipts in hand, go to the Global Refund office, 54 yards from the customs office to receive your V.A.T. refund.

GIFT IDEAS

Munich is a city of beer, and items related to its consumption are obvious choices for souvenirs and gifts. Munich is also the home of the famous Nymphenburg Porcelain factory. Between Karlsplatz and the Viktualienmarkt there are loads of shops for memorabilia and trinkets.

Shops line Marienplatz in Munich's City Center.

CRAFTS

Bayerischer Kunstgewerbe–Verein. Bavarian craftspeople have a showplace of their own, the Bayerischer Kunstgewerbe–Verein; here you'll find every kind of handicraft, from glass and pottery to textiles. ⊠ *Pacellistr. 6–8, City Center* ☎ *089/290–1470.*

Max Krug. If you've been to the Black Forest and forgot to acquire a clock, or if you need a good Bavarian souvenir, try Max Krug in the pedestrian zone. ⊠ *Neuhauser Str. 2, City Center* ☎ *089/224–501.*

FOOD AND BEER

Chocolate & More. Stock up here for all things chocolate. ⊠ *Westenrieder Str. 15, City Center* ☎ *089/2554–4905.*

Dallmayr. This elegant gourmet food store sells treats ranging from the most exotic fruits to English jams, served by efficient Munich matrons in smart blue-and-white-linen costumes. The store's famous specialty is coffee, with more than 50 varieties to blend as you wish. This is also the place to prepare yourself a high-class—if pricey—picnic. ⊠ *Dienerstr. 14–15, City Center* ☎ *089/21350.*

Götterspeise. The name of this delectable chocolate shop across the street from the restaurant Faun means "ambrosia," a fitting name for their gifts, delights, and hot drinks. ⊠ *Jahnstr. 30, Isarvorstadt* ☎ *089/ 2388-7374.*

PORCELAIN

Kunstring. For Dresden and Meissen porcelain wares, go to Kunstring, near Odeonsplatz. ⊠ *Briennerstr. 4, City Center* ☎ *089/281–532.*

Porzellan Nymphenburg. This shop resembles a drawing room in the Munich palace of the same name and has delicate, expensive porcelain safely locked away in bowfront cabinets.

Schloss Nymphenburg. You can buy directly from the factory called Porzellanmanufaktur Nymphenburg (open weekdays 10–5, Saturday 11–4) on the grounds of Schloss Nymphenburg ⊠ *Nördliches Schloss-rondell 8, Nymphenburg* ☎ *089/179–1970* ⊠ *Odeonspl. 1, City Center* ☎ *089/282–428.*

MISCELLANEOUS

Lehmkuhl. Munich's oldest and one of its finest bookshops, Lehmkuhl also sells beautiful cards. ⊠ *Leopoldstr. 45, Schwabing* ☎ *089/380–1500.*

Sebastian Wesely. Check out Sebastian Wesely for beer-related vessels and schnapps glasses (*Stampferl*), walking sticks, scarves, and napkins with the famous Bavarian blue-and-white lozenges. ⊠ *Rindermarkt 1, at Peterspl., City Center* ☎ *089/264–519.*

Spielwaren Obletters. Browse two extensive floors of toys, many of them handmade playthings of great charm and quality. ⊠ *Karlspl. 11–12, City Center* ☎ *089/5508–9510.*

SPECIALTY STORES

ANTIQUES

A few small shops around the Viktualienmarkt sell Bavarian antiques, though their numbers are dwindling under the pressure of high rents. Also try the area north of the university—Türkenstrasse, Theresien-strasse, and Barerstrasse are all filled with antiques stores.

Strictly for window-shopping—unless you're looking for something really rare and special and money's no object—are the exclusive shops lining Prannerstrasse, at the rear of the Hotel Bayerischer Hof. Interesting and inexpensive antiques and assorted junk from all over Eastern Europe are laid out at the weekend flea markets beneath the Donnersberger railway bridge on Arnulfstrasse (along the northern side of the Hauptbahnhof).

Antike Uhren Eder. In Antike Uhren Eder, the silence is broken only by the ticking of dozens of highly valuable antique German clocks and by discreet negotiation over the high prices. ⊠ *Opposite Hotel Bayerischer Hof, Prannerstr. 4, City Center* ☎ *089/220–305.*

Die Puppenstube. For Munich's largest selection of dolls and mario-nettes, head to Die Puppenstube. ⊠ *Luisenstr. 68, Maxvorstadt* ☎ *089/ 272–3267.*

Roman Odesser. Antique German silver is the specialty at Roman Odesser. ⊠ *Westenriederstr. 21, City Center* ☎ *089/226–388.*

FOLK COSTUMES

If you want to deck yourself out in lederhosen or a dirndl, or acquire a green loden coat and little pointed hat with feathers, you have a wide choice in the Bavarian capital. ■ TIP→ There are a couple of other shops along Tal Street that have new and used lederhosen and dirndls at good prices in case you want to spontaneously get into the spirit of the 'Fest.

C&A. For a more affordable option on loden clothing, try the department store C&A in the pedestrian zone. ⊠ *Kaufingerstr. 13, City Center* ☎ *089/231–930.*

Lederhosen Wagner. The tiny Lederhosen Wagner, right up against the Heiliggeist Church, carries lederhosen, woolen sweaters called *Walk* (not loden), and children's clothing. ⊠ *Tal 2, City Center* ☎ *089/225–697.*

Loden-Frey. Much of the fine loden clothing on sale at Loden-Frey is made at the company's own factory, on the edge of the Englischer Garten. ⊠ *Maffeistr. 7, City Center* ☎ *089/210–390.*

MARKETS

Christkindlmarkt. From late November until December 24, the open-air Christkindlmarkt is a great place to find gifts and warm up with mulled wine. Two other perennial Christmas-market favorites are those in Schwabing (Münchner-Freiheit Square) and at the Chinese Tower, in the middle of the Englischer Garten. ⊠ *Marienpl., City Center.*

Elisabethplatz. If you're in the Schwabing area, the daily market at Elisabethplatz is worth a visit—it's much smaller than the Victualienmarkt but the range and quality of produce are comparable. Whereas at the Viktualienmarkt you have visitors from many lands pushing past the stands, here life is more peaceful and local. There is a beer garden here as well. The Elisabethplatz, like the Viktualienmarkt, is open daily from 8 to 6.

Farmers' markets. In addition to Elisabethplatz and Viktualienmarkt, there are about 40 other weekly farmers' markets in Munich. Some are just a few fruit and vegetable stands on a side street, and some are also the weekly meeting point for the neighborhood. There's a farmers' market out near the zoo on Wednesday and Saturday, from 8 am to 1 pm: Take Bus 52, which leaves every 10 minutes from central Marienplatz to the Tiergarten (zoo). Get off at Mariahilfplatz, stroll the farmers' market at the foot of the church, grab a bite, and take the next bus to the zoo. Also on Saturday from 8 am to 1 pm is the farmers' market near the university: take Subway 3 or 6 to Universität and walk through the university to the corner of Gabersbergerstrasse/Türkenstrasse, where the market stalls are erected on the eastern wall of the museum Pinakothek der Moderne. You can get a good glass of wine from the Franconia wine grower and a made-to-order sandwich from the butcher at the next stall then grab a place at one of the stand-up tables and you're set. Thursday afternoon is the time to visit the farmers' market with the prettiest and most historic site—and it's the closest to the City Center. Take the number 4 or 5 subway from Odeonsplatz to the Lehel stop at St. Anna Platz.

Viktualienmarkt. Munich's Viktualienmarkt is *the* place to shop and to eat. Just south of Marienplatz, it's home to an array of colorful stands that sell everything from cheese to sausages, flowers to wine. A visit here is more than just an opportunity to find picnic makings; it's a key part of understanding the Münchners' easy-come-easy-go nature, especially at the Viktualienmarkt's shady Bavarian Biergärten (beer garden). ⊗ *Mon.–Fri. 10–6, Sat. 10–3.*

SIDE TRIPS FROM MUNICH

Munich's excellent suburban railway network, the S-bahn, brings several quaint towns and attractive rural areas within easy reach for a day's excursion. Dachau attracts overseas visitors, mostly because of its concentration-camp memorial site, but it's a picturesque and historic town in its own right.

■ TIP➔ Keep in mind that there are quite a few options for day trips to the famous castles built by King Ludwig, which are only a couple of hours away. Mike's Bike Tours organizes trips, or ask at your hotel for bus-tour excursions. A train out to Füssen and Schloss Neuschwanstein takes 2½ hours. ⇨ *For more information on this fairy-tale castle and others, see Chapter 4, The Romantic Road.*

DACHAU

20 km (12 mi) northwest of Munich.

Dachau predates Munich, with records going back to the time of Charlemagne. It's a handsome town, too, built on a hilltop with views of Munich and the Alps, which was why it became such a favorite for numerous artists. A guided tour of the town, including the castle and church, leaves from the Rathaus on Saturday at 10:30, from May through mid-October. Dachau is infamous worldwide as the site of the first Nazi concentration camp, which was built just outside it. Dachau preserves the memory of the camp and the horrors perpetrated there with deep contrition while trying, with commendable discretion, to signal that the town has other points of interest.

GETTING HERE AND AROUND

Take the B-12 country road or the Stuttgart autobahn to the Dachau exit from Munich. Dachau is also on the S-bahn 2 suburban line, a 20-minute ride from Munich's Marienplatz.

ESSENTIALS

Visitor Information **Tourist-Information Dachau** ✉ *Konrad-Adenauer-Str. 1* ☎ *08131/75286* ⊕ *www.dachau.de.*

EXPLORING

Bezirksmuseum. To get a sense of the town's history, visit the Bezirksmuseum, the district museum, which displays historical artifacts, furniture, and traditional costumes from Dachau and its surroundings. ✉ *Augsburgerstr. 3* ☎ *08131/56750* 💶 *€3.50* ⊙ *Tues.–Fri. 11–5, weekends 1–5.*

Dachau Concentration Camp Memorial Site. The site of the infamous camp, officially called KZ-Gedenkstätte Dachau, is just outside town. Photographs, contemporary documents, the few remaining cell blocks, and the grim crematorium create a somber and moving picture of the camp, where more than 30,000 of the 200,000-plus prisoners lost their lives. A documentary film in English is shown daily at 11:30 and 3:30. The former camp has become more than just a grisly memorial: it's now a place where people of all nations meet to reflect upon the past and on the present. Several religious shrines and memorials have been built to honor the dead, who came from Germany and all occupied nations. By public transport take the S-2 from Marienplatz or Hauptbahnhof in the direction of Petershausen, and get off at Dachau. From there, take the clearly marked bus from right outside the Dachau S-bahn station (it leaves about every 20 minutes). If you are driving from Munich, take the autobahn toward Stuttgart, get off at Dachau, and follow the signs.

Schloss Dachau. This hilltop castle dominates the town. What you'll see is the one remaining wing of a palace built by the Munich architect Josef Effner for the Wittelsbach ruler Max Emanuel in 1715. During the Napoleonic Wars the palace served as a field hospital and then was partially destroyed. King Max Joseph lacked the money to rebuild it, so all that's left is a handsome cream-and-white building, with an elegant pillared and lantern-hung café on the ground floor and a former ballroom above. About once a month the grand Renaissance hall, with a richly decorated and carved ceiling, covered with painted panels depicting figures from ancient mythology, is used for chamber concerts. The east terrace affords panoramic views of Munich and, on fine days, the distant Alps. There's also a 250-year-old *Schlossbrauerei* (castle brewery), which hosts the town's beer and music festival each year in the first two weeks of August. ⊠ *Schlossstr. 2* ☎ *08131/87923* ✉ *€2* ⊘ *Apr.–Sept., Tues.–Sun. 9–6; Oct.–Mar., Tues.–Sun. 10–4.*

St. Jacob. Dachau's parish church was built in the early 16th century in late-Renaissance style on the foundations of a 14th-century Gothic structure. Baroque features and a characteristic onion dome were added in the late 17th century. On the south wall you can admire a very fine 17th-century sundial. ⊠ *Konrad-Adenauer-Str. 7* ⊘ *Daily 7–7.*

Gemäldegalerie. An artists' colony formed here during the 19th century, and the tradition lives on. Picturesque houses line Hermann-Stockmann-Strasse and part of Münchner Strasse, and many of them are still the homes of successful artists. The Gemäldegalerie displays the works of many of the town's 19th-century artists. ⊠ *Konrad-Adenauer-Str. 3* ☎ *08131/56750* ✉ *€3.50* ⊘ *Tues.–Fri. 11–5, weekends 1–5.*

WHERE TO STAY

For expanded hotel reviews, visit Fodors.com.

$ 🛏 **Hotel Fischer.** You can see this hotel across the square from the S-bahn station. The family atmosphere is welcoming, the rooms are pleasantly modern, and good traditional Bavarian meals are served in the restaurant. Order the "Weisswurst" special with a drop of Weissbier and you'll get a good laugh at how the "drop" is served. **Pros:** prime location; good restaurant. **Cons:** on nice evenings, noise from the patio may filter up to your room. ⊠ *Bahnhofstr. 4, City Center* ☎ *08131/612–200* ⊕ *www.hotelfischer-dachau.de* ⟿ *29 rooms* ⌂ *In-room: no a/c, Wi-Fi. In-hotel: restaurant, some pets allowed.*

The Bavarian Alps

WORD OF MOUTH

"My favorite area in Bavaria is Berchtesgaden, less than two hours from Munich. The scenery is beyond gorgeous."

—tcreath

WELCOME TO THE BAVARIAN ALPS

TOP REASONS TO GO

★ **Herrenchiemsee:** Take the old steam-driven ferry to the island in Chiemsee to visit the last and most glorious castle of Mad King Ludwig.

★ **Great nature:** From the crystalline Königsee lake and grandiose Karwendel Mountains, to Garmisch's powdery snow, and the magical forests, it's everything a nature lover needs.

★ **Meditating in Ettal monastery:** If it isn't the sheer complexity of the baroque ornamentation and the riot of frescoes, then it might be the fluid sound of the ancient organ that puts you in a deep, relaxing trance. A great brewery and distillery round out the deeply religious experience.

★ **Rejuvenation in Reichenhall:** The new Rupertus spa in Bad Reichenhall has the applications you need to turn back your body's clock, from saltwater baths to mudpacks.

★ **Confronting History in Berchtesgaden:** Explore the darkest chapter of German history at Obersalzberg, Hitler's mountain retreat.

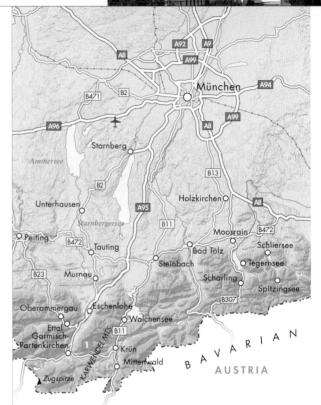

1 **Werdenfelser Land and Wetterstein Mountains.** Like a village lost in time, Mittenwald and Oberammergau are both famous for their half-timber houses covered in *Lüftlmalerei* frescoes. The entire region sits serenely in the shadow of Germany's highest point: the Zugspitze. The Wetterstein Mountains offer fantastic skiing and hiking.

2 **Chiemgau.** Bavaria's Lake District is almost undiscovered by Westerners but has long been a secret destination for Germans. Several fine, hidden lakes dot the area. The Chiemsee dominates the Chiemgau, with one of the most impressive German palaces and great water sports. Residents, or Chiemgauer, especially in Bad Tölz, often wear

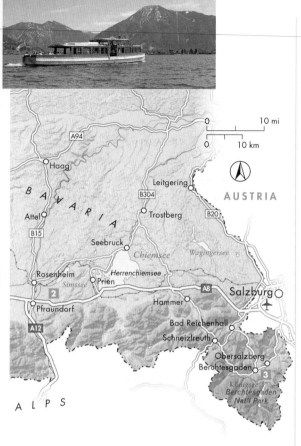

GETTING ORIENTED

Ask a Bavarian about the "Bavarian Alps" and he'll probably shake his head in confusion. To Bavarians "the Alps" consist of several adjoining mountain ranges spanning the Ammergau, Wetterstein, and Karwendel Alps in the West to the Chiemgauer and Berchtesgadener Alpen in the East. Each region has its die-hard fans. The constants, however, are the incredible scenery, clean air, and a sense of Bavarian *Gemütlichkeit* (coziness) omnipresent in every *Hütte* (cottage), *Gasthof* (guesthouse), and beer garden. The area is an outdoor recreation paradise, and almost completely lacks the high-culture institutions that dominate German urban life.

traditional Trachten, elaborate lederhosen and dirndl dresses, as an expression of their proud cultural heritage.

3 Berchtesgadener Land. The Berchtesgadener Land is not the highest point in the country, but is certainly one of the most ruggedly beautiful regions. Hundreds of miles of hiking trails with serene Alpine cottages and the odd cow make the area

a hiking and mountaineering paradise. Berchtesgaden and Bad Reichenhall are famous for the salt trade, and the salt mines provide the visitor with a unique and entertaining insight into the history and wealth of the region. The Königsee is the most photographed place in the country, and for good reason.

OUTDOORS IN THE BAVARIAN ALPS

Bursting up from the lowlands of southern Germany like a row of enormous, craggy teeth, the Bavarian Alps form both an awe-inspiring border with Austria and a superb natural playground for outdoor enthusiasts.

(above) Mountain bikers in the Bavarian foothills. (upper right) Bavarian Alps. (lower right) Backcountry skiers.

Visible from Munich on a clear day, this thin strip of the Alps stretches over 300 km (186 mi) from Lake Constance in the west to Berchtesgaden in the east, and acts as a threshold to the towering mountain ranges that lie further south. Lower in altitude than their Austrian, Swiss, and French cousins, the Bavarian Alps have the advantage of shorter distances between their summits and the valleys below, forming an ideal environment for casual walkers and serious mountaineers alike.

In spring and summer cowbells tinkle and wild flowers blanket meadows beside trails that course up and down the mountainsides. In winter snow engulfs the region, turning trails into paths for cross-country skiers and the mountainsides into pistes for snowboarders and downhill skiers to carve their way down.

—Jeff Kavanagh

LEDERHOSEN

Along with sausages and enormous mugs of frothy beer, lederhosen form the holy trinity of what many foreigners believe to be stereotypically "German." The reality, however, is that the embroidered leather breeches are traditionally worn in the south of the country, particularly in Alpine areas, where the durability and protection of leather have their advantages. Nowadays they are worn at special events.

BEST WAYS TO EXPLORE

BY FOOT

It's not without good reason that wanderlust is a German word. The desire to travel and explore has been strong for hundreds of years in Germany, especially in places like the Alps where strenuous strolls are rewarded with breathtaking vistas. There are over 7000 km (4350 mi) of walking trails in the Allgäu region alone to wander, conveniently divided into valley walks, midaltitude trails, and summit hikes reflecting the varying altitude and difficulty. Hikes can be undertaken as day trips or as weeks-long endeavors, and there are campsites, mountain huts, farmhouses, and hotels to overnight in along the way, as well as a decent infrastructure of buses, trains and cable cars to get you to your starting point. The Bavaria Tourism Office ⊕ www.bavaria.by has more information on hiking trails.

BY BIKE

You don't actually need to venture onto their slopes to appreciate the Alps' beauty, and cycling through the foothills at their base affords stunning views of the mountains combined with the luxury of refreshing stop-offs in beer gardens and dips in beautiful lakes like the Tegernsee. There's plenty of accommodation tailored to cyclists throughout the region and local trains are normally equipped with a cycle carriage or two to transport you to more remote locations. The Alps also have thousands of miles of mountain-bike-friendly trails and a number of special bike parks serviced by cable cars.

BY SKIS

Neither as high or famous as their neighbors, the Bavarian Alps are frequently overlooked as a winter sport destination. Resorts on the German side of the border may have shorter seasons than places like Zermatt and Chamonix, but they're also generally cheaper in terms of food and accommodation, and many, including Zugspitze, are easily accessed from Munich for day trips.

3

BEST PHOTO OPS

No matter where you are around the Alps you'll be inundated with sights worth snapping. Here are a few:

■ More Disney than Disney, **Neuschwanstein Castle** sits theatrically atop a mountain, its grand towers set against a background of tree- and snow-covered peaks.

■ The panoramic view from close to 10,000 feet at the peak of Germany's highest mountain, the **Zugspitze** takes in 400 peaks in four countries.

■ Reputedly the cleanest lake in Germany, **Königsee** is also endowed with steep rock formations which soar thousands of meters up above the lake, beautifully framing its crystalline waters.

■ If sitting outside **Tegernsee's** lovely Benedictine monastery with a liter of the local beer in one hand and a bratwurst in the other isn't the shot you're after, you can wander down to the lake for spectacular vistas of its glittering surface and the Alps beyond.

Updated by
Lee A. Evans

Fir-clad mountains, rocky peaks, lederhosen, and geranium-covered houses: the Bavarian Alps come closest to what many of us envision as "Germany." Quaint towns full of frescoed half-timber houses covered in snow pop up among the mountain peaks and shimmering hidden lakes, as do the creations of "Mad" King Ludwig II. The entire area has sporting opportunities galore, regardless of the season.

Upper Bavaria (Oberbayern) fans south from Munich to the Austrian border, and as you follow this direction, you'll soon find yourself on a gently rolling plain leading to lakes surrounded by ancient forests. In time the plain merges into foothills, which suddenly give way to jagged Alpine peaks. In places such as Königsee, near Berchtesgaden, snow-capped mountains rise straight up from the gemlike lakes.

Continuing south, you'll encounter cheerful villages with richly painted houses, churches and monasteries filled with the especially sensuous Bavarian baroque and rococo styles, and several spas where you can "take the waters" and tune up your system. Sports possibilities are legion: downhill and cross-country skiing, snowboarding, and ice-skating in winter; tennis, swimming, sailing, golf, and, above all (sometimes literally), hiking, paragliding, and ballooning in summer.

PLANNING

WHEN TO GO
This mountainous region is a year-round holiday destination. Snow is promised by most resorts from December through March, although there's year-round skiing on the glacier slopes at the top of the Zugspitze. Spring and autumn are ideal times for leisurely hikes on the many mountain trails. November is a between-seasons time, when many hotels and restaurants close down or attend to renovations. Note, too, that many locals take a vacation after January 6, and businesses may be

closed for anywhere up to a month. The area is extremely popular with European visitors, who flood the Alps in July and August.

GETTING HERE AND AROUND

AIR TRAVEL

Munich, 95 km (59 mi) northwest of Garmisch-Partenkirchen, is the gateway to the Bavarian Alps. If you're staying in Berchtesgaden, consider the closer airport in Salzburg, Austria—it has fewer international flights, but it is a budget-airline and charter hub.

Airport Information Salzburg Airport (*SZG*). ☎ *0662/8580* ⊕ *www.salzburg-airport.com.*

CAR TRAVEL

The Bavarian Alps are well connected to Munich by train, and an extensive network of buses links even the most remote villages. Since bus schedules can be unreliable and are timed for commuters, the best way to visit the area is by car. Three autobahns reach into the Bavarian Alps: A-7 comes in from the northwest (Frankfurt, Stuttgart, Ulm) and ends near Füssen in the western Bavarian Alps; A-95 runs from Munich to Garmisch-Partenkirchen; take A-8 from Munich for Tegernsee, Chiemsee, and Berchtesgaden. ⚠ The A-8 is statistically the most dangerous autobahn in the country, partially due to it simultaneously being the most heavily traveled highway and the road most in need of repair. The driving style is fast, and tailgating is common, though it is illegal. The "guideline speed" (Richtgeschwindigkeit) on the A-8 is 110 kph (68 mph); if an accident occurs at higher speeds, your insurance will not necessarily cover it. It is a good idea to pick a town like Garmisch-Partenkirchen, Bad Tölz, or Berchtesgaden as a base and explore the area from there. The Bavarian Alps are furnished with cable cars, steam trains, and cog railroads that whisk you to the tops of Alpine peaks allowing you to see the spectacular views without hours of mountain climbing.

TRAIN TRAVEL

Most Alpine resorts are connected with Munich by regular express and slower service trains. Due to the rugged terrain, train travel in the region can be challenging, but with some careful planning—see ⊕ *www.bahn.de* for schedules and to buy tickets—you can visit this region without a car.

RESTAURANTS

Restaurants in Bavaria run the gamut from the casual and gemütlich (cozy) Gasthof to formal gourmet offerings. More-upscale establishments try to maintain a feeling of casual familiarity, but you will probably feel more comfortable at the truly upscale restaurants if you dress up a bit. Note that many restaurants take a break between 2:30 and 6 pm. If you want to eat during these hours, look for the magic words *Durchgehend warme Küche,* meaning warm food served throughout the day, possibly snacks during the off-hours. Many restaurants in the region still don't accept credit cards.

HOTELS

With few exceptions, a hotel or *Gasthof* in the Bavarian Alps and lower Alpine regions has high standards and is traditional in style, with balconies, pine woodwork, and gently angled roofs upon which the snow sits and insulates. Many in the larger resort towns offer special packages online. Private homes all through the region offer Germany's own version of bed-and-breakfasts, indicated by signs reading "zimmer frei" (rooms available). Their rates may be less than €25 per person. As a general rule, the farther from the popular and sophisticated Alpine resorts you go, the lower the rates. Note, too, that many places offer a small discount if you stay more than one night. By the same token, some places frown on staying only one night, especially during the high seasons, in summer, at Christmas, and on winter weekends. In spas and many mountain resorts a "spa tax," or Kurtaxe, is added to the hotel bill. It amounts to no more than €3 per person per day and allows free use of spa facilities, entry to local attractions and concerts, and use of local transportation at times. Breakfast is included, unless indicated otherwise.

WHAT IT COSTS IN EUROS				
	¢	$	$$	$$$	$$$$
Restaurants	under €9	€9–€15	€16–€20	€21–€25	over €25
Hotels	under €50	€50–€100	€101–€175	€176–€225	over €225

Restaurant prices are per person for a main course at dinner. Hotel prices are for two people in a standard double room, including tax and service.

PLANNING YOUR TIME

The Alps are spread along Germany's southern border, but are fairly compact and easy to explore. Choose a central base and fan out from there. Garmisch-Partenkirchen and Berchtesgaden are the largest towns with the most convenient transportation connections.

Although the area is a popular tourist destination, the smaller communities like Mittenwald and Ettal are quieter and make for pleasant overnight stays. For an unforgettable experience, try spending the night in an Alpine hut, feasting on a simple but hearty meal and sleeping in the cool night air.

DISCOUNTS AND DEALS

One of the best deals in the area is the German Railroad's Bayern Ticket. The Bayern Ticket allows up to five people to travel on any regional train—and almost all buses in the Alps—for €29, and is valid from 9 am until 3 am that night. There is a "single" version for €21. Ticket holders receive discounts on a large number of attractions in the area, including the Zugspitzbahn, a cog railroad and cable car that takes you up to the top of the Zugspitze. The ZugspitzCard (three days €44) offers discounts in almost every city near the Zugspitze. Visitors to spas or spa towns receive a Kurkarte, an ID that proves payment of the spa tax. The document allows discounts and often free access to sights in the town or area. If you've paid the tax, be sure to show the card everywhere you go.

The Zugspitze is the highest mountain in Germany and is reachable from Garmisch-Partenkirchen.

VISITOR INFORMATION
Tourismusverband München Oberbayern ⊠ *Bodenseestr. 113, Munich*
☎ *089/829–2180* ⊕ *www.oberbayern-tourismus.de.*

WERDENFELSER LAND AND
WETTERSTEIN MOUNTAINS

With Germany's highest peak and picture-perfect Bavarian villages, the Werdenfelser Land offers a splendid mix of natural beauty combined with Bavarian art and culture. The region spreads out around the base of the Zugspitze, where the views from the top reach from Garmisch-Partenkirchen to the frescoed houses of Oberammergau, and to the serene Cloister Ettal.

GARMISCH-PARTENKIRCHEN

90 km (55 mi) southwest of Munich.

Garmisch, as it's more commonly known, is a bustling, year-round resort and spa town and is the undisputed capital of Alpine Bavaria. Once two separate communities, Garmisch and Partenkirchen fused in 1936 to accommodate the Winter Olympics. Today, with a population of 28,000, the area is the center of the Werdenfelser Land and large enough to offer every facility expected from a major Alpine resort. Garmisch is a spread-out mess of wide car-friendly streets, hordes of tourists, and little charm. The narrow streets and quaint architecture

Maibaum: Bavaria's Maypole

The center of every town in Bavaria is the Maibaum or Maypole. The blue-and-white striped pole is decorated with the symbol of every trade and guild represented in the town, and is designed to help visitors determine what services are available there. The effort and skill required to build one is a source of community pride.

The tradition dates back to the 16th century, and is governed by a strict set of rules. Great care is taken in selecting and cutting the tree, which must be at least 98 feet tall. Once completed, it cannot be erected before May 1. In the meantime, tradition and honor dictate that men from surrounding towns attempt to steal the pole and ransom it for beer and food, so it must be guarded 24 hours a day. Once the pole goes up, with quite a bit of leveraging and manual labor, it cannot be stolen and may only stand for three years.

of smaller Partenkirchen make it a slightly better choice. In both parts of town pastel frescoes of biblical and bucolic scenes decorate facades.

Winter sports rank high on the agenda here. There are more than 99 km (62 mi) of downhill ski runs, 40 ski lifts and cable cars, and 180 km (112 mi) of *Loipen* (cross-country ski trails). One of the principal stops on the international winter-sports circuit, the area hosts a week of races every January. You can usually count on good skiing from December through April (and into May on the Zugspitze).

GETTING HERE AND AROUND

Garmisch-Partenkirchen is the cultural and transportation hub of the Werdenfelser Land. The autobahn A-95 links Garmisch directly to Munich. Regional German Rail trains head directly to Munich (90 minutes), Innsbruck (90 minutes), and Mittenwald (20 minutes). German Rail operates buses that connect Garmsich with Oberammergau, Ettal, and the Wieskirche. Garmisch is a walkable city, and you probably won't need to use its frequent city-bus services.

Partenkirchen was founded by the Romans, and you can still follow the Via Claudia they built between Partenkirchen and neighboring Mittenwald, which was part of a major route between Rome and Germany well into the 17th century.

Bus tours to King Ludwig II's castles at Neuschwanstein and Linderhof and to the Ettal Monastery, near Oberammergau, are offered by DER travel agencies. Local agencies in Garmisch also run tours to Neuschwanstein, Linderhof, and Ettal, and into the neighboring Austrian Tyrol.

The Garmisch mountain railway company, the Bayerische Zugspitzbahn, offers special excursions to the top of the Zugspitze, Germany's highest mountain, by cog rail and cable car.

ESSENTIALS

Bus Tours DER ☎ *08821/55125*. **Dominikus Kümmerle** ☎ *08821/72455*. **Hans Biersack** ☎ *08821/4920*. **Hilmar Röser** ☎ *08821/2926*. **Weiss-Blau-Reisen** ☎ *08821/3766*.

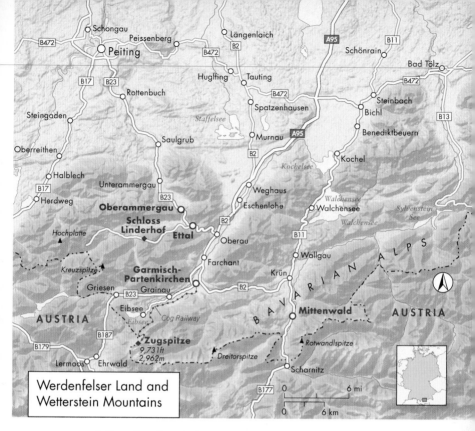

Werdenfelser Land and
Wetterstein Mountains

Railway Tour Bayerische Zugspitzbahn ☎ 08821/7970.

Visitor Information Garmisch-Partenkirchen ✉ Verkehrsamt der Kurverwaltung, Richard-Strauss-Pl. 2 ☎ 08821/180–420 ⊕ www.gapa.de.

EXPLORING

Richard Strauss Villa. On the eastern edge of Garmisch, at the end of Zöppritzstrasse, stands the home of composer Richard Strauss, who lived here until his death in 1949. It's the center of activity during the *Richard-Strauss-Tage,* an annual music festival held in mid-June that features concerts and lectures on the town's most famous son. Displays are audiovisual, and each day at 10, noon, 2, and 4 samples of Strauss's works are played in the concert hall.

St. Martin Church. In Garmisch, some beautiful examples of Upper Bavarian houses line Frühlingstrasse, and a pedestrian zone begins at Richard-Strauss-Platz. Off Marienplatz, at one end of the car-free zone, is the 18th-century parish church. It contains some significant stuccowork by the Wessobrunn artists Schmutzer, Schmidt, and Bader. The chancel is by another fine 18th-century artist from Austria, Franz Hosp.

St. Martin Church. Across the Loisach River, on Pfarrerhausweg, stands another St. Martin church, dating from 1280, whose Gothic wall paintings include a larger-than-life-size figure of St. Christopher.

Werdenfelser Museum. Objects and exhibitions on the region's history can be found in this excellent museum, which is itself housed in a building dating back to around 1200. The museum is spread over five floors, and explores every aspect of life in the Werdenfelser region, which was an independent county for more than 700 years (until 1802). ⊠ *Ludwigstr. 47, Partenkirchen* ☎ *08821/2134* ⊡ *€2.50* ☉ *Tues.–Sun. 10–5.*

Fodor's Choice **Zugspitze.** The highest mountain (9,731 feet) in Germany, this is the
★ number one attraction in Garmisch. There are two ways up the mountain: a leisurely 75-minute ride on a cog railway from the train station in the town center, combined with a cable-car ride up the last stretch; or a 10-minute hoist by cable car, which begins its giddy ascent from the Eibsee, 10 km (6 mi) outside town on the road to Austria. There are two restaurants with sunny terraces at the summit and another at the top of the cog railway. ■TIP➡ A round-trip combination ticket allows you to mix your modes of travel up and down the mountain. Prices are lower in winter than in summer, even though winter rates include use of all the ski lifts on the mountain. You can rent skis at the top. ■TIP➡ Ascending the Zugspitze from the Austrian side is cheaper and more scenic. The *Tiroler Zugspitzbahn* departs three times per hour from near the village of Ehrwald. The round-trip ticket costs €35.50 and buses connect the gondolas to the Ehrwald train station. There are also a number of other peaks in the area with gondolas, but the views from the Zugspitze are the best. A four-seat cable car goes to the top of one of the lesser peaks: the **Wank** or the **Alpspitze,** some 2,000 feet lower than the Zugspitze. You can tackle both mountains on foot, provided you're properly shod and physically fit. ⊠ *Zugspitze: Cog railway leaves from Olympiastr. 27 (approximately 100 meters from the Garmisch train station)* ☎ *08821/7970* ⊕ *www.zugspitze.de* ⊡ *Funicular or cable car €48 in summer, €39 in winter, round-trip; parking €3* ☉ *Daily 8–4:45.*

WHERE TO EAT

$ ✕**See-Hotel Riessersee.** On the shore of a small, blue-green, tranquil
GERMAN lake—a leisurely 3-km (2-mi) walk from town—this café-restaurant is an ideal spot for lunch or afternoon tea (on summer weekends there's live zither music from 3 to 5). House specialties are fresh trout and seasonal local game (which fetches the higher prices on the menu). ⊠ *Riess 6* ☎ *08821/95440* ⊕ *www.riessersee.de* ☉ *Closed Mon. and Dec. 1–15.*

WHERE TO STAY

For expanded hotel reviews, visit Fodors.com.

For information about accommodation packages with ski passes, call the Zugspitze or get in touch with the tourist office in Garmisch (☎ *08821/7970* ⊕ *www.zugspitze.de*).

$ ⌂**Edelweiss.** Like its namesake, the "nobly white" Alpine flower of *The Sound of Music* fame, this small downtown hotel has plenty of

EATING WELL IN THE BAVARIAN ALPS

Bavarian cooking originally fed a farming people, who spent their days out of doors doing heavy manual labor. *Semmelknödel* (dumplings of old bread), pork dishes, sauerkraut, bread, and hearty soups were felt necessary to sustain a person facing the elements. The natural surroundings provided further sustenance, in the form of fresh trout from brooks, *Renke* (pike-perch) from the lakes, venison, and mushrooms. This substantial fare was often washed down with beer, which was nourishment in itself, especially during the Lenten season, when the dark and powerful "Doppelbock" was on the market. Today this regimen will suit sporty types who have spent a day hiking in the mountains, skiing in the bracing air, or swimming or windsurfing in chilly lakes.

Bavaria is not immune to eclectic culinary trends, however: minimalist Asian daubs here, a touch of French sophistication and Italian elegance there, a little Tex-Mex to brighten a winter evening, even some sprinklings of curry. Menus often include large sections devoted to salads, and there are tasty vegetarian dishes even in the most traditional regions. Schnapps, which customarily ended meals, has gone from being a step above moonshine to a true delicacy extracted from local fruit by virtuoso distillers. Yes, Bavarian cooking—hearty, homey, and down-to-earth—is actually becoming lighter.

One area remains an exception: desserts. The selection of sinfully creamy cakes in the Konditorei (cake shop), often enjoyed with whipped-cream-topped hot chocolate, continues to grow. These are irresistible, of course, especially when homemade. A heavenly experience might be a large portion of warm *Apfelstrudel* (apple-and-nut-filled pastry) fresh from the oven in some remote mountain refuge.

mountain charm. **Pros:** small; comfortable; homey; great for families with children. **Cons:** small hotel; lacking in many services. ⊠ *Martinswinkelstr. 15–17* ☏ *08821/2454* ⊕ *www.hoteledelweiss.de* ⌁ *31 rooms* ⚭ *In-room: no a/c. In-hotel: some pets allowed* ⏐⊙⏐ *Breakfast.*

$ ⊡ **Gasthof Fraundorfer.** You can ride to dreamland in this beautiful old Bavarian Gasthof—some of the bed frames are carved like antique automobiles and sleighs. **Pros:** great location and dining experience. **Cons:** a musty "old" feeling; in need of renovation; kitchen smell and noise a problem for the rooms in the back of hotel. ⊠ *Ludwigstr. 24* ☏ *08821/9270* ⊕ *www.gasthof-fraundorfer.de* ⌁ *20 rooms, 7 suites* ⚭ *In-room: no a/c, Internet. In-hotel: restaurant, some pets allowed* ⊙ *Closed late Nov.–early Dec.* ⏐⊙⏐ *Breakfast.*

$ ⊡ **Hotel-Gasthof Drei Mohren.** All the simple, homey comforts you'd expect can be found in this 150-year-old Bavarian inn tucked into Partenkirchen village. **Pros:** perfect setting in a quaint corner of the town center. **Cons:** restaurant noise on the first floor; some double rooms too small. ⊠ *Ludwigstr. 65* ☏ *08821/9130* ⊕ *www.dreimohren.de* ⌁ *21 rooms, 2 apartments* ⚭ *In-room: no a/c. In-hotel: restaurant, bar, business center, some pets allowed* ⏐⊙⏐ *Breakfast.*

$$ ⌃ **Hotel Waxenstein.** It's worth the 7-km (4½-mi) drive eastward to Grainau just to spend a night or a few at the delightful Waxenstein. **Pros:** great service; beautiful views of the Zugspitze from the north-facing rooms. **Cons:** only accessible by car; rooms somewhat small; no views of the Zugspitze from the south-facing rooms. ✉ *Höhenrainweg 3* ☎ *08821/9840* ⊕ *www.waxenstein.de* ⌥ *35 rooms, 6 suites* ⌂ *In-room: no a/c, Internet. In-hotel: restaurant, bar, pool, spa, some pets allowed* ⌘ *Breakfast.*

$$
★ ⌃ **Reindl's Partenkirchner Hof.** Owner Karl Reindl ranks among the world's top hoteliers. **Pros:** ample-size rooms; great views. **Cons:** front rooms are on a busy street. ✉ *Bahnhofstr. 15* ☎ *08821/943–870* ⊕ *www.reindls.de* ⌥ *35 rooms, 17 suites* ⌂ *In-room: no a/c, Wi-Fi. In-hotel: restaurant, bar, pool, gym, spa* ⌘ *Breakfast.*

NIGHTLIFE AND THE ARTS

In season there's a busy après-ski scene. Many hotels have dance floors, and some have basement discos that pound away until the early hours. Bavarian folk dancing and zither music are regular features of nightlife.

Bayernhalle. In summer there's entertainment every Saturday evening at the Bayernhalle. ☎ *08821/55199.*

Garmisch-Partenkirchen-Ticket. Concerts are presented from Saturday to Thursday, mid-May through September, in the park bandstand in Garmisch, and on Friday in the Partenkirchen park. Tickets are available at Garmisch-Partenkirchen-Ticket. ✉ *Richard-Strauss-Pl. 2* ☎ *08821/752–545* ⊕ *www.ticketshop-gap.de* ⊗ *Weekdays 9–1 and 2–7, Sat. 9–1.*

Gasthof Fraundorfer. Wednesday through Monday the cozy tavern-restaurant Gasthof Fraundorfer hosts yodeling and folk dancing. ✉ *Ludwigstr. 24* ☎ *08821/9270.*

Spielbank Garmisch. The casino, Spielbank Garmisch, is open weekdays 3 pm–2 am and Saturday 3 pm–3 am, with more than 100 slot machines and roulette, blackjack, and poker tables. ✉ *Am Kurpark 10* ☎ *08821/95990.*

SPORTS AND THE OUTDOORS

HIKING AND WALKING   There are innumerable spectacular walks on 300 km (186 mi) of marked trails through the lower slopes' pinewoods and upland meadows. If you have the time and good walking shoes, try one of the two trails that lead to striking gorges (called Klammen).

Deutscher Alpenverein (*German Alpine Association*). Call here for details on hiking and on staying in the mountain huts. ✉ *Von-Kahr-Str. 2–4, Munich* ☎ *089/140–030* ⊕ *www.alpenverein.de.*

Höllentalklamm. The Höllentalklamm route starts at the Zugspitze Mountain railway terminal in town and ends at the mountaintop (you'll want to turn back before reaching the summit unless you have mountaineering experience). ⊠ *Olympiastr. 27.*

Partnachklamm. The Partnachklamm route is quite challenging, and takes you through a spectacular, tunneled water gorge (entrance fee), past a pretty little mountain lake, and far up the Zugspitze; to do all of it, you'll have to stay overnight in one of the huts along the way. Ride part of the way up in the **Eckbauer cable car** (€9 one-way, €12 round-trip), which sets out from the Skistadion off Mittenwalderstrasse. The older, more scenic, **Graseckbahn** takes you right over the dramatic gorges (€43.50 one-way, €6 round-trip). There's a handy inn at the top, where you can gather strength for the hour-long walk back down to the Graseckbahn station.

Lohnkutschevereinigung. Horse-drawn carriages also cover the first section of the route in summer; in winter you can skim along it in a sleigh. The carriages wait near the Skistadion. Or you can call the local coaching society, the Lohnkutschevereinigung, for information. ☎ *08821/942–920.*

SKIING AND SNOWBOARDING Garmisch-Partenkirchen was the site of the 1936 Winter Olympics, and remains Germany's premier winter-sports resort. The upper slopes of the Zugspitze and surrounding mountains challenge the best ski buffs and snowboarders, and there are also plenty of runs for intermediate skiers and families. The area is divided into two basic regions. The **Riffelriss** with the **Zugspitzplatt** is Germany's highest skiing area, with snow guaranteed from November to May. Access is via the **Zugspitzbahn** funicular. Cost for a day pass is €35; for a 2½-day pass €80 (valid from noon on the first day). The **CLASSIC-Gebiet**, or classical area, has 17 lifts in the **Alpspitz, Kreuzeck,** and **Hausberg** regions. Day passes cost €29.50, a two-day pass €53. The town has a number of ski schools and tour organizers.

Alpine Auskunftstelle. The best place for information for all your snow-sports needs is the Alpine office at the tourist-information office, Alpine Auskunftstelle. ⊠ *Richard-Strauss-Pl. 2, Garmisch* ☎ *08821/180–744* ☉ *Mon.–Thurs. 4–6.*

Erste Skilanglaufschule Garmisch-Partenkirchen. Cross-country skiers should check with the Erste Skilanglaufschule Garmisch-Partenkirchen at the eastern entrance of the Olympic stadium in Garmisch. ☎ *08821/1516.*

Skischule Alpin. Skiers looking for instruction can try the Skischule Alpin. ⊠ *Reintalstr. 8, Garmisch* ☎ *08821/945–676.*

Snowboardschule Erwin Gruber. For snowboarders, there's the Snowboardschule Erwin Gruber. ⊠ *Mittenwalderstr. 47d, Garmisch* ☎ *08821/76490.*

Telemark Schule Leismüller. Telemark skiing is also popular in these rugged mountains. For information, contact the Telemark Schule Leismüller. ⊠ *Waldeckstr. 7, Garmisch* ☎ *08821/752–696.*

ETTAL

16 km (10 mi) north of Garmisch-Partenkirchen, 85 km (53 mi) south of Munich.

★ The village of Ettal is presided over by the massive bulk of Kloster Ettal, a great monastery and centuries-old distillery.

GETTING HERE AND AROUND

Ettal is easily reached by bus and car from Garmisch and Oberammergau. Consider staying in Oberammergau and renting a bike. The 4-km (2½-mi) ride along the river is clearly marked, relatively easy, and a great way to meet locals.

ESSENTIALS

Visitor Information Ettal ⊠ *Verkehrsamt, Kaiser-Ludwig-Pl.* ☎ *08822/3534.*

EXPLORING

Fodor's Choice
★

Kloster Ettal. The great monastery was founded in 1330 by Holy Roman Emperor Ludwig the Bavarian for a group of knights and a community of Benedictine monks. This is the largest Benedictine monastery in Germany; approximately 55 monks live here. The abbey was replaced with new buildings in the 18th century and now serves as a school. The original 10-sided church was brilliantly redecorated in 1744–53, becoming one of the foremost examples of Bavarian rococo. The church's chief treasure is its enormous dome fresco (83 feet wide), painted by Jacob Zeiller circa 1751–52. The mass of swirling clouds and the pink-and-blue vision of heaven are typical of the rococo fondness for elaborate ceiling painting.

Today, the Kloster owns most of the surrounding land and directly operates the Hotel Ludwig der Bayer, the Kloster-Laden, and the Kloster-markt. All of the Kloster's activities, from beer production to running the hotel serve one singular purpose: to fund the famous college-prep and boarding schools, which are tuition-free.

Ettaler liqueurs, made from a centuries-old recipe, are still distilled at the monastery. The monks make seven different liqueurs, some with more than 70 mountain herbs. Originally the liqueurs were made as medicines, and they have legendary health-giving properties. The ad tells it best: "Two monks know how it's made, 2 million Germans know how it tastes." ■ TIP➜ You can visit the distillery right next to the church and buy bottles of the libation from the gift shop and bookstore. The honey-saffron schnapps is the best.

It's possible to tour the distillery, but not the brewery, since they still use open fermentation tanks. Tours must be arranged prior to arrival with Frau Steffl (☎ *08822/74217*). The tour includes samples of the seven different kinds of herbal liqueurs and a visit to the beer museum. ☎ *08822/740 for guided tour of church* ☑ *Free* ☉ *Daily 8–6.*

Schaukäserei. Besides its spirit and spirits, Ettal has made another local industry into an attraction: namely cheese, yogurt, and other milk derivatives. You can see cheese, butter, cream, and other dairy products in the

The dome fresco at Kloster Ettal (Ettal Monastery) was painted by Jacob Zeiller and is an excellent example of Bavarian rococo.

making at this public cheese-making plant. There is even a little buffet for a cheesy break. ✉ *Mandlweg 1* ☎ *08822/923–926* 🌐 *www.milch-und-kas.de* 🎫 *Free, €2.50 with tour* ⏲ *Tues.–Sat. 10–6, Sun. noon–5.*

WHERE TO EAT AND STAY

For expanded hotel reviews, visit Fodors.com.

¢ GERMAN ✕ **Edelweiss.** This friendly café and restaurant next to the monastery is an ideal spot for a light lunch or coffee and homemade cakes. ✉ *Kaiser-Ludwig-Pl. 3* ☎ *08822/92920* ▭ *No credit cards.*

$ 🏨 **Hotel Ludwig der Bayer.** Backed by mountains, this fine old hotel is run by the Benedictine order. **Pros:** good value; close to Kloster; indoor pool. **Cons:** expensive; slightly disorganized management; breakfast often not included in price. ✉ *Kaiser-Ludwig-Pl. 10* ☎ *08822/9150* 🌐 *www.ludwig-der-bayer.de* *70 rooms, 30 apartments* *In-room: no a/c. In-hotel: restaurant, bar, pool, tennis court, gym, some pets allowed* *No meals.*

SCHLOSS LINDERHOF

Fodor's Choice ★ **Schloss Linderhof.**

⇨ *See "The Fairy-tale Castles of King Ludwig II" in Chapter 4.*

OBERAMMERGAU

20 km (12 mi) northwest of Garmisch-Partenkirchen, 4 km (2½ mi) northwest of Ettal, 90 km (56 mi) south of Munich.

Its location alone, in an Alpine valley beneath a sentinel-like peak, makes this small town a major attraction (allow a half hour for the drive from Garmisch). Its main streets are lined with painted houses (such as the 1784 Pilatushaus on Ludwig-Thoma-Strasse), and in summer the village bursts with color. Many of these lovely houses are occupied by families whose men are highly skilled in the art of wood carving, a craft that has flourished here since the early 12th century. Oberammergau is completely overrun by tourists during the day, but at night you'll feel like you have a charming Bavarian village all to yourself.

GETTING HERE AND AROUND

The B-23 links Oberammergau to Garmsich-Partenkirchen and to the A-23 to Munich. Frequent bus services connect to Garmisch, Ettal, the Wieskirche, and Füssen. No long-distance trains serve Oberammergau, but a short ride on the Regional-Bahn to Murnau will connect you to the long-distance train network.

ESSENTIALS

Visitor Information Oberammergau ⊠ *Verkehrsamt, Eugen-Papst-Str. 9a* ☎ *08822/92310* ⊕ *www.oberammergau.de.*

EXPLORING

Passion Play. Oberammergau is best known for its Passion Play, first presented in 1634 as an offering of thanks after the Black Death stopped just short of the village. In faithful accordance with a solemn vow, it will next be performed in the year 2020, as it has every 10 years since 1680. Its 16 acts, which take 5½ hours, depict the final days of Christ, from the Last Supper through the Crucifixion and Resurrection. It's presented daily on a partly open-air stage against a mountain backdrop from late May to late September. The entire village is swept up in the production, with some 1,500 residents directly involved in its preparation and presentation. Men grow beards in the hope of capturing a key role; young women have been known to put off their weddings—the role of Mary went only to unmarried girls until 1990, when, amid much local controversy, a 31-year-old mother of two was given the part. ⊕ *www.passionstheater.de.*

Pilatushaus. You'll find many wood-carvers at work in town, and shop windows are crammed with their creations. From June through October a workshop is open free to the public here at Pilatushaus; working potters and painters can also be seen. Pilatushaus was completed in 1775, and the frescoes—considered among the most beautiful in town—were done by Franz Seraph Zwinck, one of the greatest Lüftlmalerei painters. The house is named for the fresco over the front door depicting Christ before Pilate. A collection of reverse glass paintings depicting religious and secular scenes has been moved here from the Heimatmuseum. Contact the tourist office to sign up for a weeklong course in wood carving (classes are in German), which costs from about €450 to €600, depending on whether you stay in a Gasthof or a hotel. ⊠ *Ludwig-Thoma-Str. 10* ☎ *08822/92310 tourist office* ⊠ *€6.*

Oberammergau Museum. Here you'll find historic examples of the wood craftsman's art and an outstanding collection of Christmas crèches, which date from the mid-18th century. Numerous exhibits also document the wax and wax-embossing art, which also flourishes in Oberammergau. A notable piece is that of a German soldier carved by Georg

Korntheuer on the Eastern Front in 1943: the artist was later killed in 1944. ⊠ *Dorfstr. 8* ☏ *08822/94136* ▣ *€6, includes Pilatushaus* ⊙ *Apr.–Oct. and Dec.–Feb., Tues.–Sun. 10–5.*

Oberammergau Passionsspielhaus. This immense theater is where the Passion Play is performed. Visitors are given a glimpse of the costumes, the sceneries, the stage, and even the auditorium. ■TIP→ **The Combi-ticket for the Oberammergau Museum, Pilatushaus, and the Passionsmuseum** costs €6. ⊠ *Passionstheater, Passionswiese* ☏ *08822/945–8833* ▣ *€4* ⊙ *Summer daily 10–5, winter irregular.*

St. Peter and St. Paul Church. The 18th-century church is regarded as the finest work of rococo architect Josef Schmutzer, and has striking frescoes by Matthäus Günther and Franz Seraph Zwinck (in the organ loft). Schmutzer's son, Franz Xaver Schmutzer, did a lot of the stuccowork. ⊠ *Pfarrpl. 1* ☏ *No phone* ⊙ *Daily 9 am–dusk.*

> ### LÜFTLMALEREI
>
> The *Lüftlmalerei* style of fresco painting is unique to Bavaria and the Tirol where the opulently painted facades were used as a display of wealth. Commonly known as trompe l'œil, the detailed frescoes give the illusion of three dimensions. They are painted directly onto fresh plaster, which preserves the painting for centuries.
>
> The term "Lüftlmalerei" originated in Oberammergau after the famous fresco artist Franz Seraph Zwinck painted a fresco on his house, the Zum Lüftl. Zwinck became the Lüftlmaler, or the painter of the Lüftl.

WHERE TO EAT

$
GERMAN
✕ **Alte Post.** You can enjoy carefully prepared local cuisine, including several venison and boar dishes, at the original pine tables in this 350-year-old inn. There's a special children's menu, and, in summer, meals are also served in the beer garden. The front terrace of this delightful old building is a great place to watch traffic, both pedestrian and automotive. A part of the café has been reserved for Web surfing. ⊠ *Dorfstr. 19* ☏ *08822/9100* ⊙ *Closed Nov.–mid-Dec.*

$
GERMAN
✕ **Ammergauer Stubn.** A homey restaurant with pink tablecloths and a lot of wood, the Stubn has a comprehensive menu that serves both Bavarian specialties and international dishes. You can expect nice roasts and some Swabian dishes, such as *Maultaschen*, a large, meat-filled ravioli. ⊠ *Wittelsbach Hotel, Dorfstr. 21* ☏ *08822/92800* ⊙ *Closed Tues. and Nov.–mid-Dec. No lunch.*

$
GERMAN
✕ **Gasthaus zum Stern.** This is a traditional place (around 500 years old), with coffered ceilings, thick walls, an old Kachelofen (enclosed, tiled, wood-burning stove) that heats the dining room beyond endurance on cold winter days, and smiling waitresses in dirndls. The food is hearty, traditional Bavarian. For a quieter dinner or lunch, reserve a space in the Bäckerstube (Baker's Parlor). ⊠ *Dorfstr. 33* ☏ *08822/867* ⊙ *Closed Wed.*

WHERE TO STAY

For expanded hotel reviews, visit Fodors.com.

$ ⛪ **Gasthof zur Rose.** The eight members of the Frank family offer basic rooms in a spacious remodeled barn. **Pros:** quiet; affordable; right off the city center; friendly service. **Cons:** rustic and worn; few amenities. ✉ *Dedlerstr. 9* ☎ *08822/4706* ⊕ *www.hotel-oberammergau.de* ⇱ *21 rooms* ⚲ *In-room: no a/c, Wi-Fi. In-hotel: restaurant* ▭ *No credit cards.*

$ ⛪ **Hotel Landhaus Feldmeier.** This quiet family-run hotel, idyllically set just outside the village, has mostly spacious rooms with modern pine-wood furniture. **Pros:** small and distinguished; quiet. **Cons:** outside the city center. ✉ *Ettalerstr. 29* ☎ *08822/3011* ⊕ *www.hotel-feldmeier. de* ⇱ *22 rooms, 4 apartments* ⚲ *In-room: no a/c, Internet, Wi-Fi. In-hotel: restaurant, gym, business center, some pets allowed* ⊙ *Closed mid-Nov.–mid-Dec.* ⎪◯⎪ *Breakfast.*

$ ⛪ **Hotel Turmwirt.** Rich wood paneling reaches from floor to ceiling in
★ this transformed 18th-century inn, set in the shadow of Oberammergau's mountain, the Kofel. **Pros:** great for families with children. **Cons:** service can be brusque; nearby church bells ring every 15 minutes. ✉ *Ettalerstr. 2* ☎ *08822/92600* ⊕ *www.turmwirt.de* ⇱ *44 rooms* ⚲ *In-room: no a/c, Internet, Wi-Fi. In-hotel: restaurant, business center, some pets allowed* ⊙ *Closed Jan. 7–21* ⎪◯⎪ *Breakfast.*

THE ARTS

Though the Passion Play theater was traditionally not used for anything other than the Passion Play (next performance, 2020), Oberammergau-ers decided that using it for opera or other theatrical events during the 10-year pause between the religious performances might be a good idea. The first performances of Verdi's *Nabucco* and Mozart's *Magic Flute* in 2002 established a new tradition. Other passion plays are also performed here. Ticket prices are between €20 and €52. For reservations, call ☎ *08822/923–158.*

SPORTS AND THE OUTDOORS

BIKING It's easy to bike to Schloss Linderhof (14 km) and to Ettal (4 km) along the scenic paths along the river, where there are several good places to go swimming and have a picnic. The trail to Ettal branches off in the direction of Linderhof (marked as Graswang) where it becomes part of an old forestry road. Take the branch of the Ettal path that goes via the Ettaler-Mühle (Ettal Mill); it's quieter, the river is filled with trout, and the people you meet along the way give a friendly *Grüss Gott* (Greet God)! The path opens up at a local-heavy restaurant with fantastic views of the Kloster.

Sport-Zentrale Papistock. Stop in here to rent bikes for €10 per day. They are located across the street from the train station, directly at the trailhead to Ettal and Linderhof. ✉ *Bahnhofstr. 6a* ☎ *08822/4178* ⊕ *www. sportzentrale-papistock.de* ⊙ *Closed Sun.*

MITTENWALD

20 km (12 mi) southeast of Garmisch, 105 km (66 mi) south of Munich.

Many regard Mittenwald as the most beautiful town in the Bavarian Alps. It has somehow avoided the architectural sins found in other Alpine villages by maintaining a balance between conservation and the needs of tourism. Its medieval prosperity is reflected on its main street, **Obermarkt,** which has splendid houses with ornately carved gables and brilliantly painted facades. Goethe called it "a picture book come alive," and it still is. The town has even re-created the stream that once flowed through the market square. In the Middle Ages Mittenwald was the staging point for goods shipped from the wealthy city-state of Venice by way of the Brenner Pass and Innsbruck. From Mittenwald, goods were transferred to rafts, which carried them down the Isar River to Munich. By the mid-17th century the international trade routes shifted to a different pass, and the fortunes of Mittenwald evaporated.

In 1684 Matthias Klotz, a farmer's son turned master violin maker, returned from a 20-year stay in Cremona, Italy. There, along with Antonio Stradivari, he studied under Nicolo Amati, who developed the modern violin. Klotz taught the art of violin making to his brothers and friends and before long, half the men in the village were crafting the instruments, using woods from neighboring forests. Mittenwald became known as the Village of a Thousand Violins and the locally crafted instruments are still treasured around the world. In the right weather—sunny, dry—you may even catch the odd sight of laundry lines hung with new violins out to receive their natural dark hue. The violin has made Mittenwald a small cultural oasis in the middle of the Alps. Not only is there an annual violin- (and viola-, cello-, and bow-) building contest each year in June, with concerts and lectures, but also an organ festival in the church of St. Peter and St. Paul held from the end of July to the end of September. The town also boasts a violin-making school.

GETTING HERE AND AROUND

The B-11 connects Mittenwald with Garmisch. Mittenwald is last stop on the Munich-Garmisch train line.

ESSENTIALS

Visitor Information **Mittenwald** ⊠ *Kurverwaltung, Dammkarstr. 3* ☎ *08823/33981* ⊕ *www.mittenwald.de.*

EXPLORING

The Geigenbau und Heimatmuseum. The violin-building and local museum describes in fascinating detail the history of violin making in Mittenwald. Ask the museum curator to direct you to the nearest of several violin makers—they'll be happy to demonstrate the skills handed down to them. ⊠ *Ballenhausg. 3* ☎ *08823/2511* ◖ *€4.50* ⊙ *Mid-May–Oct., Tues.–Sun. 10–5; Nov.–mid-May, Tues.–Sun. 11–4.*

St. Peter and St. Paul Church. On the back of the altar in this 18th-century church (as in Oberammergau, built by Josef Schmutzer and decorated by Matthäus Günther), you'll find Matthias Klotz's name, carved there by the violin maker himself. ■TIP➜ Note that on some of the ceiling frescoes, the angels are playing violins, violas da gamba, and lutes. In front of the church, Klotz is memorialized as an artist at work in vivid bronze sculpted by Ferdinand von Miller (1813–79), creator of the mighty Bavaria Monument in Munich. The church, with its elaborate and joyful stuccowork coiling and curling its way around the interior, is one of the most important rococo structures in Bavaria. Note its Gothic choir loft, added in the 18th century. The bold frescoes on its exterior are characteristic of Lüftlmalerei, where images, usually religious motifs, were painted on the wet stucco exteriors of houses and churches. On nearby streets you can see other fine examples on the facades of three famous houses: the Goethehaus, the Pilgerhaus, and the Pichlerhaus. Among the artists working here was the great Franz Seraph Zwinck. ⊠ *Ballenhausg., next to Geigenbau und Heimatmuseum.*

WHERE TO EAT

$$
CONTINENTAL
★
✕ **Arnspitze.** Get a table at the large picture window and soak in the views of the towering Karwendel mountain range as you ponder a menu that combines the best traditional ingredients with international touches. Chef and owner Herbert Wipfelder looks beyond the edge of his plate all the way to Asia, if need be, to find inspiration. The fish pot-au-feu has a Mediterranean flair; the jugged hare in red wine is truly Bavarian. The restaurant also offers accommodations in a separate house. ⊠ *Innsbrucker Str. 68* ☎ *08823/2425* ⊘ *Closed Nov.–mid-Dec. and Tues. and Wed.*

WHERE TO STAY

For expanded hotel reviews, visit Fodors.com.

$
⛱ **Alpenrose.** Once part of a monastery and later given one of the town's most beautiful painted baroque facades, the Alpenrose is one of the area's handsomest hotels. **Pros:** great German decor; friendly staff. **Cons:** some rooms are cramped; accommodations can get warm in summer. ⊠ *Obermarkt 1* ☎ *08823/92700* ⊕ *www.hotel-alpenrose-mittenwald.de* 🛏 *16 rooms, 2 apartments* ⅏ *In-room: no a/c. In-hotel: restaurant, bar, business center, some pets allowed* ◯ *Breakfast.*

$
⛱ **Bichlerhof.** Carved oak furniture gives the rooms of this Alpine-style hotel a solid German feel. **Pros:** amazing views; well-kept spa area. **Cons:** disorganized reservation system; built to look traditionally Bavarian, but is actually only 30 years old. ⊠ *Adolf-Baader-Str. 5* ☎ *08823/9190* ⊕ *www.bichlerhof-mittenwald.de* 🛏 *30 rooms* ⅏ *In-room: no a/c, Internet. In-hotel: pool, gym, some pets allowed* ◯ *Breakfast.*

$
⛱ **Gasthof Stern.** This white house with brilliant blue shutters is right in the middle of Mittenwald. **Pros:** friendly service; clean, basic hotel with a great beer garden. **Cons:** needs a renovation; upper rooms warm in summer; credit cards not accepted. ⊠ *Fritz-Plössl-Pl. 2* ☎ *08823/8358* ⊕ *www.stern-mittenwald.de* 🛏 *5 rooms* ⅏ *In-room: no a/c. In-hotel: restaurant, bar, some pets allowed* ▭ *No credit cards* ◯ *Breakfast.*

$$
⛱ **Post.** Stagecoaches carrying travelers and mail across the Alps stopped here as far back as the 17th century. **Pros:** art nouveau rooms in the back. **Cons:** no elevator; street noise in the evening. ⊠ *Obermarkt 9* ☎ *08823/938–2333* ⊕ *www.posthotel-mittenwald.de* 🛏 *74 rooms, 7 suites* ⅏ *In-room: no a/c, Internet. In-hotel: restaurant, bar, pool, some pets allowed* ◯ *Breakfast.*

SPORTS AND THE OUTDOORS

Mittenwald lies literally in the shadow of the mighty **Karwendel** Alpine range, which rises to a height of nearly 8,000 feet. There are a number of small lakes in the hills surrounding Mittenwald. You can either walk to the closer ones or rent bikes and adventure farther afield. The information center across the street from the train station has maps, and they can help you select a route.

The **Dammkar** run is nearly 8 km (5 mi) long and offers some of the best free-riding skiing, telemarking, and snowboarding in the German Alps.

Bergerlebnis und Wanderschule Oberes Isartal. You can book a guide with Bergerlebnis und Wanderschule Oberes Isartal. ☎ 08651/5835.

Erste Schischule Mittenwald. Skiers, cross-country and downhill, and snowboarders can find all they need, including equipment and instruction, at the Erste Schischule Mittenwald. ✉ *Bahnhofsparkpl (parking next to train station)* ☎ 08823/3582, 08823/8548.

Karwendelbahn cable car. The Karwendelbahn cable car carries hikers and skiers to a height of 7,180 feet, the beginning of numerous trails down, or farther up into the Karwendel range. ☎ 08823/8480 ⌨ €14 *one-way, €22 round-trip* ☉ *Dec.–Oct., daily 8:30–5.*

SHOPPING

It's not the kind of gift every visitor wants to take home, but if you'd like a violin, a cello, or even a double bass, the Alpine resort of Mittenwald can oblige. There are more than 30 craftspeople whose work is coveted by musicians throughout the world.

Anton Maller. If you're buying or even just feeling curious, call on Anton Maller. He's been making violins and other stringed instruments for more than 25 years. ✉ *Obermarkt 2* ☎ 08823/5865.

Gabriele Schneider's SchokoLaden. Find out where all the milk from the local cows goes with a visit to Gabriele Schneider's SchokoLaden, a homemade-chocolate shop. ✉ *Dekan-Karl-Pl. 15* ☎ 08823/938–939 ⊕ *www.schokoladen-mittenwald.de.*

Trachten Werner. For traditional Bavarian costumes—dirndls, embroidered shirts and blouses, and lederhosen—try Trachten Werner. ✉ *Hochstr. 1* ☎ 08823/3785.

CHIEMGAU

With its rolling hills with serene lakes in the shadow of the Alpine peaks, the Chiemgau is a natural paradise and a good transition to the Alps. The main attraction is, without a doubt, the Chiemsee with the amazing palace on the Herreninsel, the biggest of the islands on the Chiemsee. The area is dotted with clear blue lakes and, although tourism is fairly well established, you'll feel that you have much of the area all to yourself. Beer lovers flock to the Tegernsee and relax afterward in the iodine spa in Bad Tölz.

BAD TÖLZ

14 km (8 mi) north of Sylvenstein Lake, 48 km (30 mi) south of Munich.

Bad Tölz's new town, dating from the mid-19th century, sprang up with the discovery of iodine-laden springs, which allowed the locals to call their town *Bad* (bath or spa) Tölz. You can take the waters, either by drinking a cupful from the local springs or going all the way with a full

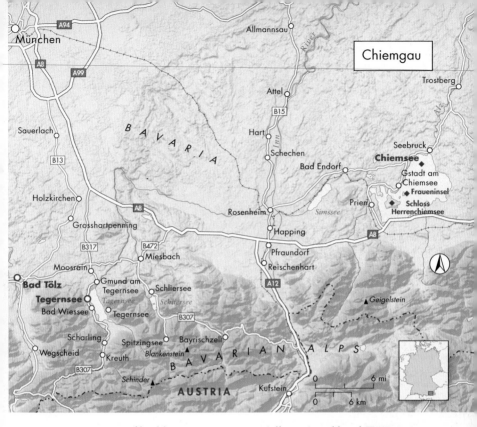

course of health treatments at a specially equipped hotel. ■ TIP→ If you can, visit on a Friday morning when a farmers' market stretches along the main street to the Isar River and on the Jungmayr-Fritzplatz.

This town clings to its ancient customs more tightly than any other Bavarian community. It is not uncommon to see people wearing traditional clothing as their daily dress. If you're in Bad Tölz on November 6, you'll witness one of the most colorful traditions of the Bavarian Alpine area: the Leonhardiritt equestrian procession, which marks the anniversary of the death in 559 of St. Leonhard of Noblac, the patron saint of animals, specifically horses. The procession ends north of town at an 18th-century chapel on the Kalvarienberg, above the Isar River.

GETTING HERE AND AROUND
Bad Tölz is on the B-472, which connects to the A-8 to Munich. Hourly trains link Bad Tölz with Munich. Bad Tölz is easily walkable and has frequent city-bus services.

ESSENTIALS
Visitor Information Bad Tölz ✉ Tourist-Information, Max-Höfler-Pl. 1
☎ 08041/78670 ⊕ www.bad-toelz.de.

EXPLORING

★ **The Alpamare.** Bad Tölz's very attractive spa complex pumps spa water into its pools, one of which is disguised as a South Sea beach complete with surf. Its five waterslides include a 1,082-foot-long adventure run. Another—the Alpa-Canyon—has 90-degree drops, and only the hardiest swimmers are advised to try it. A nightmarish dark tunnel is aptly named the Thriller. There is a complex price structure, depending on time spent in the spa and other wellness activities for the various individual attractions, or combo tickets for more than one. ✉ *Ludwigstr. 13* ☎ *08041/509–999* ⊕ *www.alpamare.de* 🎫 *4-hr ticket €28; €22 after 5 pm* ⊙ *Daily 9:30 am–10 pm.*

> **SPAS**
>
> *Bad* is the German word for bath or spa. You can take the waters at several towns in the Bavarian Alps region, from the Bad Tölz *Jodquellen*, iodine springs, to the Bad Reichenhall saline spring. Most Alpine towns have some sort of wellness offering. Ask at information centers for details.

The Stadtmuseum. Located in the Altes Rathaus (Old Town Hall), you'll find many fine examples of *Bauernmöbel* (farmhouse furniture), as well as a fascinating exhibit on the history of the town and its environs. ✉ *Marktstr. 48* ☎ *08041/504–688* 🎫 *€3* ⊙ *Mar.–Jan., Tues.–Sun. 10–4.*

WHERE TO STAY

For expanded hotel reviews, visit Fodors.com.

$$$ 📺 **Hotel Jodquellenhof-Alpamare.** The *Jodquellen* are the iodine springs
★ that have made Bad Tölz wealthy. **Pros:** elegant hotel; free access to the spa. **Cons:** busy during local school holidays. ✉ *Ludwigstr. 13–15* ☎ *08041/5090* ⊕ *www.jodquellenhof.com* 🛏 *71 rooms* ⚹ *In-room: no a/c, Internet. In-hotel: restaurant, pool, spa* ⧉ *Breakfast.*

$ 📺 **Hotel Kolbergarten.** Located right near the Old Town and surrounded by a quiet garden with old trees, this hotel offers comfortable rooms, each carefully done in a particular style such as baroque or Biedermeier. **Pros:** large clean rooms; staff is great with children. **Cons:** often fully booked. ✉ *Fröhlichg. 5* ☎ *08041/78920* ⊕ *www.hotel-kolbergarten.de* 🛏 *12 rooms, 2 suites* ⚹ *In-room: no a/c, Internet. In-hotel: business center, some pets allowed* ⧉ *Breakfast.*

NIGHTLIFE AND THE ARTS

Boys' choir. Bad Tölz is world renowned for its outstanding boys' choir. When not on tour, the choir gives regular concerts in the Kurhaus. ☎ *08041/78670 for program details from Städtische Kurverwaltung.*

Kult/Advokatenhaus. The Kult/Advokatenhaus has a rather wide range of themes, and it features live music in the terrific setting of an old brewery, with barrel vaults and painted brick walls. ✉ *Wachterstr. 19* ⊕ *www.kult-toelz.de.*

Tom's Bar. This nightspot has '60s furnishings with modern music (DJs, theme nights), reasonable prices, and plenty of space. ✉ *Demmeljochstr. 42.*

The brine pool at Alpamare spa has green water due to the mineral iodine; it is meant to stimulate circulation.

SPORTS AND THE OUTDOORS

Blomberg. Bad Tölz's local mountain, the Blomberg, 3 km (2 mi) west of town, has moderately difficult ski runs and can also be tackled on a toboggan in winter and on a luge in summer. The winter run of 5 km (3 mi) is the longest in Bavaria. The concrete summer luge-run snakes 3,938 feet down the mountain and is great fun; you'll want the three-ride ticket. A ski-lift ride to the start of the run and toboggan or roller luge are included in the price. ☎ 08041/3726 ⊕ www.blombergbahn. de 🖾 €4 per toboggan ride; 3 rides for €11 ⊗ Jan.–Oct., daily 9–4; Nov.–Dec., summer toboggan run hrs depend on weather conditions.

SHOPPING

Bad Tölz is famous for its painted furniture, particularly farmhouse cupboards and chests. Several local shops specialize in this type of Bauernmöbel (farmhouse furniture, usually hand carved from pine) and will usually handle export formalities. Ask at your hotel or tourist-information center for a recommendation on where to shop.

Antiquitäten Schwarzwälder. For traditional Bauernmöbel furniture, try Antiquitäten Schwarzwälder. ⊠ Badstr. 2 ☎ 08041/41222.

TEGERNSEE

16 km (10 mi) east of Bad Tölz, 50 km (31 mi) south of Munich.

★ The beautiful shores of the Tegernsee are among the most expensive property in all of Germany. The interest in the region shown by King Maximilian I of Bavaria at the beginning of the 19th century attracted VIPs and artists, which led to a boom that has never really faded.

Horses pull a sleigh through the snow in Rottach-Egern, one of the three main towns on Lake Tegernsee.

Most accommodations and restaurants, however, still have reasonable prices, and there are plenty of activities for everyone. Tegernsee's wooded shores, rising gently to scalable mountain peaks of no more than 6,300 feet, invite hikers, walkers, and picnicking families. The lake itself draws swimmers and yachters. In fall the russet-clad trees provide a colorful contrast to the snowcapped mountains. Beer lovers are drawn to Tegernsee by one of the best breweries in Europe. There are three main towns on the lake: Tegernsee, Rottach-Egern, and Bad Wiessee.

GETTING HERE AND AROUND

The best way to reach all three towns is to take the BOB train from Munich to Tegernsee (hourly) and then take a boat ride on one of the eight boats that circle the lake year-round. The boats dock near the Tegernsee train station and make frequent stops, including stops at the Benedictine monastery in Tegernsee, in Rottach-Egern, and in Bad Wiessee. The monastery is a pleasant half-mile walk from the train station. Buses connect Tegernsee to Bad Tölz.

ESSENTIALS

Visitor Information **Rottach-Egern/Tegernsee** ⊠ *Kuramt, Hauptstr. 2* ☎ *08022/180–140* ⊕ *www.tegernsee.de.*

EXPLORING

★ **Benedictine monastery.** On the eastern shore of the lake, the laid-back town of Tegernsee is home to this large Benedictine monastary. Founded in the 8th century, this was one of the most productive cultural centers in southern Germany; the Minnesänger (wandering lyrical poets) Walther von der Vogelweide (1170–1230) was a welcome guest. Not so welcome were Magyar invaders, who laid waste to the monastery in the 10th century. During the Middle Ages the monastery made a lively business producing stained-glass windows, thanks to a nearby quartz quarry, and in the 16th century it became a major center of printing. The late-Gothic **church** was refurbished in Italian baroque style in the 18th century. The frescoes are by Hans Georg Asam, whose work also graces the Benediktbeuren monastery in Bavaria. Secularization sealed the monastery's fate at the beginning of the 19th century: almost half the buildings were torn down. Maximilian I bought the surviving ones and had Leo von Klenze redo them for use as a summer retreat.

Today there is a high school on the property, and students write their exams beneath inspiring baroque frescoes in what was the monastery. The **Herzogliches Bräustüberl**, a brewery and beer hall, is also on-site. ■ TIP➔ Try a Mass (a liter-size mug) of their legendary Tergernseer Helles or Spezial beer. ⊠ *Schlosspl.*

The Grosses Paraplui. Maximilian showed off this corner of his kingdom to Czar Alexander I of Russia and Emperor Franz I of Austria during their journey to the Congress of Verona in October 1821. You can follow their steps through the woods to the Grosses Paraplui, one of the loveliest lookout points in Bavaria. A plaque marks the spot where they admired the open expanse of the Tegernsee and the mountains beyond. The path starts opposite Schlossplatz in Tegernsee town and is well marked.

The Olaf Gulbransson Museum. This museum is devoted to the Norwegian painter Olaf Gulbrannson, who went to Munich in 1902 and worked as a caricaturist for the satirical magazine *Simplicissimus*. His poignant caricatures and numerous works of satire depict noisy politicians and snooty social upper-crusters as well as other subjects. The museum is housed in a discreet modern building set back from the main lakeside road of Tegernsee. ⊠ *Im Kurgarten* ☎ *08022/3338* ⊕ *www.olaf-gulbransson-museum.de* ⊠ *€6* ⊗ *Tues.–Sun. 10–5.*

WHERE TO EAT

$$ ✕ **Freihaus Brenner.** Proprietor Josef Brenner has brought a taste of nouvelle cuisine to the Tegernsee. His attractive restaurant commands fine views from high above Bad Wiessee. Try any of his suggested dishes, ranging from roast pheasant in wine sauce to fresh lake fish. There are flexible portion sizes for smaller appetites. ⊠ *Freihaus 4, Bad Wiessee* ☎ *08022/82004* ⊕ *www.freihaus-brenner.de* ⊗ *Closed Tues.*

CONTINENTAL

$ ✕ **Herzogliches Bräustüberl.** Once part of Tegernsee's Benedictine monastery, then a royal retreat, the Bräustüberl is now an immensely popular beer hall and brewery. The tasty Bavarian snacks (sausages, pretzels, all the way up to steak tartare), all for under €10, can't be beat. More-substantial fare can be had in the adjoining **Schlossgaststätte** ($–$$). In summer, quaff your beer beneath the huge chestnut trees and admire the delightful view of the lake and mountains. ⊠ *Schlosspl. 1* ☎ *08022/4141* ♙ *Reservations not accepted* 🚫 *No credit cards.*

GERMAN

¢ ✕ **Landhaus Wilhelmy.** Although everything is modern, this inn in Bad Wiessee takes you back to a less-frantic era, and the Ziegelbauers, who restored the buildings, know how to make you feel at home. Classical music accompanies unpretentious yet tasty meals. Try the fish specialties

GERMAN

or the light guinea fowl with herb rice and enjoy tea and cake in the little garden. ⊠ *Freihausstr. 15, Bad Wiessee* ☎ *08022/98680.*

WHERE TO STAY

For expanded hotel reviews, visit Fodors.com.

$$$ ⊞ **Das Tegernsee Hotel & Spa.** The elegant, turreted Hotel Tegernsee and its two spacious annexes sit high above the Tegernsee, backed by the wooded slopes of Neureuth Mountain. **Pros:** hotel in almost mint condition due to renovations completed in 2009; historical elegance; Czar Nicholas I was a frequent guest; great views. **Cons:** very expensive; difficult to reach. ⊠ *Neureuthstr. 23* ☎ *08022/1820* ⊕ *www.dastegernsee.de* ⤳ *63 rooms, 10 suites* ⅄ *In-room: no a/c, Internet. In-hotel: restaurant, bar, pool, spa, some pets allowed* �"⊙⎸ *Breakfast.*

$ ⊞ **Seehotel Zur Post.** The lake views from most rooms are somewhat compromised by the main road outside, but a central location, a winter garden, a terrace, and a little beer garden are pluses. **Pros:** great views; friendly service; excellent breakfast. **Cons:** the property is past its prime and could stand some renovation. ⊠ *Seestr. 3* ☎ *08022/66550* ⊕ *www. seehotel-zur-post.de* ⤳ *43 rooms* ⅄ *In-room: no a/c. In-hotel: restaurant, business center, some pets allowed* ⎸⊙⎸ *Breakfast.*

NIGHTLIFE AND THE ARTS

Every resort has its **spa orchestra**—in summer they play daily in the music-box-style bandstands that dot the lakeside promenades. A strong Tegernsee tradition is the summer-long program of **festivals**, some set deep in the forest. Tegernsee's lake festival in August, when sailing clubs deck their boats with garlands and lanterns, is an unforgettable experience.

Bischoff am See. The Bischoff am See, on the lakeshore in Tegernsee, has a sensational terrace bar with prices to match one of Bavaria's finest views. ⊠ *Schweighoferstr. 53* ☎ *08022/3966.*

Casino. Bad Wiessee's casino lies near the entrance of town coming from Gmund. It's open Sunday–Thursday 3 pm–3 am and Friday and Saturday 3 pm–4 am, and is the biggest and liveliest venue in town for the after-dark scene. ☎ *08022/98350.*

SPORTS AND THE OUTDOORS

Tourist office. Contact the tourist office in the town of Tegernsee for hiking maps. ☎ *08022/180–140* ⊕ *www.tegernsee.de.*

Wallberg. For the best vista in the area, climb the Wallberg, the 5,700-foot mountain at the south end of the Tegernsee. It's a hard four-hour hike or a short 15-minute cable-car ride up (€9 one-way, €14 round-trip). At the summit are a restaurant and sun terrace and several trailheads; in winter the skiing is excellent.

GOLF **Tegernseer Golfclub e.V.** Besides swimming, hiking, and skiing, the Tegernsee area has become a fine place for golfing. The Tegernseer Golfclub e.V. has an 18-hole course overlooking the lake with a clubhouse and excellent restaurant. It also has fine apartments for rent. ⊠ *Bad Wiessee* ☎ *08022/8769* ⊕ *www.tegernseer-golf-club.de).*

CHIEMSEE

80 km (50 mi) southeast of Munich, 120 km (75 mi) northeast of Garmisch-Partenkirchen.

Chiemsee is north of the Deutsche Alpenstrasse, but it demands a detour, if only to visit King Ludwig's huge palace on one of its idyllic islands. It's the largest Bavarian lake, and although it's surrounded by reedy flatlands, the nearby mountains provide a majestic backdrop. The town of **Prien** is the lake's principal resort. ■TIP➜ The tourist offices of Prien and Aschau offer a €24 transportation package covering a boat trip, a round-trip rail ticket between the two resorts, and a round-trip ride by cable car to the top of Kampen Mountain, above Aschau.

GETTING HERE AND AROUND

Prien is the best jumping-off point for exploring the Chiemsee. Frequent trains connect Prien with Munich and Salzburg. The regional trains are met by a narrow-gauge steam train for the short trip to Prien-Stock, the boat dock. The only way to reach the Herreninsel and the Fraueninsel is by boat.

ESSENTIALS

Visitor Information Chiemsee ✉ *Kur- und Tourismusbüro Chiemsee, Alte Rathausstr. 11* 🕾 *08051/69050* ⊕ *www.chiemsee.de.*

EXPLORING

Fraueninsel. Boats going between Stock and Herrenchiemsee Island also call at this small retreat known as Ladies' Island. The **Benedictine convent** there, founded 1,200 years ago, now serves as a school. One of its earliest abbesses, Irmengard, daughter of King Ludwig der Deutsche, died here in the 9th century. Her grave in the convent chapel was discovered in 1961, the same year that early frescoes there were brought to light. The chapel is open daily from dawn to dusk. Otherwise, the island has just a few private houses, a couple of shops, and a hotel. ■TIP➜ The Benedictine Sisters make delicious fruit liqueurs and marzipan.

Fodor's Choice
★

Schloss Herrenchiemsee.

⇨ *See "The Fairy-tale Castles of King Ludwig II" in Chapter 4.*

WHERE TO STAY

For expanded hotel reviews, visit Fodors.com.

$ ⊡ **Hotel Luitpold am See.** Boats to the Chiemsee islands tie up right outside your window at this handsome old Prien hotel, which organizes shipboard disco evenings as part of its entertainment program. **Pros:** directly on the lake. **Cons:** near a busy boat dock. ✉ *Seestr. 110, Prien am Chiemsee* 🕾 *08051/609–100* ⊕ *www.luitpold-am-see.de* ⌨79

BOATING AND SAILING

All the Bavarian Alpine lakes have sailing schools that rent sailboards as well as various other types of boats. At Tegernsee you can hire motorboats at the pier in front of the Schloss Cafe, in the Tegernsee town center. Chiemsee, with its wide stretch of water whipped by Alpine winds, is a favorite for both sailing enthusiasts and windsurfers. There are boatyards all around the lake and the very good windsurfing school, Surf-schule Chiemsee, at Bernau.

Schloss Herrenchiemsee, King Ludwig II's last building project, lies in the middle of Lake Chiemsee on the Herreninsel.

rooms ☺ In-room: no a/c. In-hotel: restaurant, business center, some pets allowed ⎜○⎜ Breakfast.

$$ 🖵 **Inselhotel zur Linde.** Catch a boat to this enchanting inn on the car-free Fraueninsel for dinner: but remember, if you miss the last connection to the mainland (at 9 pm), you'll have to stay the night. **Pros:** set in lush gardens; nice beer garden. **Cons:** the Fraueninsel isn't exactly famous for its nightlife. ✉ Fraueninsel im Chiemsee 1 ☎ 08054/90366 ⊕ www. inselhotel-zurlinde.de ⤺ 14 rooms ☺ In-room: no a/c. In-hotel: restaurant, bar, business center ⊘ Closed mid-Jan.–mid-Mar. ⎜○⎜ Breakfast.

SPORTS AND THE OUTDOORS

Chiemsee Golf-Club Prien e.V. The gentle hills of the region are ideal for golf. Chiemsee Golf-Club Prien e.V., in Prien, has a year-round 9-hole course. ☎ 08051/62215.

Mistral-Windsurfing-Center. There are boatyards all around the lake and several windsurfing schools. The Mistral-Windsurfing-Center, at Gstadt am Chiemsee, has been in operation for decades. From its boatyard the average windsurfer can make it with ease to the next island. ✉ Waldstr. 20 ☎ 08054/909–906.

SportLukas. SportLukas provides equipment for any kind of sport imaginable, from skiing to kayaking, climbing to curling, and it organizes tours. ✉ Hauptstr. 3, Schleching ☎ 08649/243.

Surfschule Chiemsee. For those wanting to learn windsurfing or to extend their skills, the Surfschule Chiemsee provides lessons and offers a package deal including board and bike rentals. ✉ Ludwig-Thoma-Str. 15a, Bernau ☎ 08051/8877.

BERCHTESGADENER LAND

Berchtesgadener Land is the Alps at their most dramatic and most notorious. Although some points are higher, the steep cliffs, hidden mountain lakes, and protected biospheres make the area uniquely beautiful. The salt trade brought medieval Berchtesgaden and Bad Reichenhall incredible wealth, which is still apparent in the large collection of antique houses and quaint streets. Bad Reichenhall is an impressive center of German spa culture. Berchtesgaden's image is a bit tarnished by its most infamous historical resident, Adolf Hitler. Berchtesgaden National Park is a hiker's dream, and the resounding echo of the trumpet on the Königssee shouldn't be missed.

BAD REICHENHALL

60 km (30 mi) east of Prien, 20 km (12 mi) west of Salzburg.

Bad Reichenhall is remarkably well located, near the mountains for hiking and skiing, and near Salzburg in Austria for a lively cultural scene. The town shares a remote corner of Bavaria with another prominent resort, Berchtesgaden. Although the latter is more famous, Bad Reichenhall is older, with saline springs that made the town rich. Salt is so much a part of the town that you can practically taste it in the air. Europe's largest source of brine was first tapped here in pre-Christian times; salt mining during the Middle Ages supported the economies of cities as far away as Munich and Passau. The town prospered from a spa in the early 20th century. Lately, it has successfully recycled itself from a somewhat sleepy and stodgy "cure town" to a modern, attractive center of wellness.

GETTING HERE AND AROUND

Bad Reichenhall is well connected to Berchtesgaden and Salzburg Hauptbahnhof once every hour. The hourly trains to Munich require a change in Freilassing. To reach the Bürgerbräu and the Predigtstuhl cable car, take Bus 180 and Bus 841 to Königssee.

ESSENTIALS

Visitor Information Bad Reichenhall ⊠ *Kur-und-Verkehrsverein, im Kurgastzentrum, Wittelsbacherstr. 15* ☎ *08651/606–303* ⊕ *www.bad-reichenhall.de.*

EXPLORING

The Alte Saline und Quellenhaus. In the early 19th century King Ludwig I built this elaborate saltworks and spa house, in vaulted, pseudomedieval style. The pump installations, which still run, are astonishing examples of 19th-century engineering. A "saline" **chapel** is part of the spa's facilities, and was built in exotic Byzantine style. An interesting museum in the same complex looks at the history of the salt trade. ⊠ *Salinen Str.* ☎ *08651/700–2146* ⊕ *www.alte-saline-bad-reichenhall.de* 🖃 *€6.90, combined ticket with Berchtesgaden's salt mine €18* ⊙ *May–Oct., daily 10–11:30 and 2–4; Nov.–Apr., Tues., Fri., and 1st Sat. in the month 2–4.*

Predigtstuhl. The pride and joy of the Reichenhallers is the steep, craggy mountain appropriately named the Preacher's Pulpit, which stands at 5,164 feet, southeast of town. A ride to the top offers a splendid view

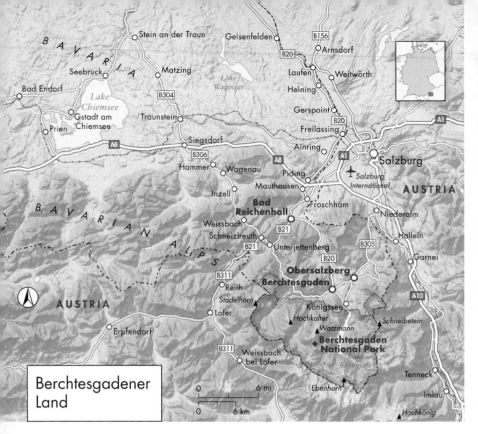

Berchtesgadener
Land

of the area. You can hike, ski in winter, or just enjoy a meal at the **Berghotel Predigtdstuhl** ($–$$). The cable-car ride costs €11 one-way, €18 round-trip. Departures begin at 9:30 am and continue (as needed) until the last person is off the mountain. The hotel is closed in winter. ⊠ *Südtiroler Pl. 1* ☏ *08651/2127* ⊕ *www.predigtstuhl-bahn.de.*

Fodor's Choice ★ **Rupertus Therme.** Part of Bad Reichenhall's revival included building this new spa facility, the brand-new "spa and fitness resort." Pools, saunas, and steam rooms are rounded off with a host of special applications using salt, essential oils, mud packs, and massages. The therme can be popular, especially in winter, so online reservations are a good idea. ⊠ *Friedrich-Ebert-Allee 21* ☏ *01805/606–706* ⊕ *www.rupertustherme. de* ☏ *€24, includes sauna area for the day; €19 without the sauna* ☉ *Daily 9 am–10 pm.*

St. Zeno. This ancient church is dedicated to the patron saint of those imperiled by floods and the dangers of the deep, an ironic note in a town that flourishes on the riches of its underground springs. This 12th-century basilica, the largest in Bavaria, was remodeled in the 16th and 17th centuries, but some of the original Romanesque cloisters remain, although these can be seen only during services and from 11 to noon on Sunday and holidays. ⊠ *Kirchpl. 1.*

Wandelhalle. Hotels here base spa treatments on the health-giving properties of the saline springs and the black mud from the area's waterlogged moors. The waters can also be taken in this elegant, pillared pavilion of the attractive spa gardens throughout the year. Breathing salt-laden air is a remedy for various lung conditions. All you need to do is walk along the 540-foot Gradierwerk, a massive wood-and-concrete construction that produces a fine salty mist by trickling brine down a 40-foot wall of dense blackthorn bundles. ⊠ *Salzburgerstr.* ⊙ *Mon.–Sat.* 8–12:30 *and* 3–5, *Sun.* 10–12:30.

WHITE GOLD

Salt, or white gold as it was known in medieval times, has played a key role in the history of both Bad Reichenhall and Berchtesgaden. Organized salt production in the region began around 450 BC, and even included a 30-km (20-mi) wooden pipeline for salt built in the early 1600s. It wasn't until the early 19th century, however, that the town began utilizing its position and geological advantages to attract tourists. The production of salt continues to this day, as does the flow of travelers on the search for the healing saline pools.

WHERE TO EAT

$
GERMAN
★ ✕ **Bürgerbräu.** Each dining area in this old brewery inn reflects the social class that once met here: politicos, peasants, burghers, and salt miners. Reichenhallers from all walks of life still meet here to enjoy good conversation, hearty local beer, and excellent food. Rooms at the inn are simple, but airy and modern, and centrally located. ⊠ *Am Rathauspl.* ☎ *08651/6089* ❢❂ *Breakfast.*

$
GERMAN ✕ **Obermühle.** Tucked away off the main road leading from Bad Reichenhall to the autobahn, this 16th-century mill is a well-kept secret. Fish is the specialty here, though meats (the game in season is noteworthy) are also on the menu. The terrace is an inviting place for a few helpings of excellent homemade pastries. ⊠ *Tumpenstr. 11* ☎ *08651/2193* ▭ *No credit cards* ⊙ *Closed Mon. and Tues.*

WHERE TO STAY

For expanded hotel reviews, visit Fodors.com.

$ 🏨 **Hotel-Pension Erika.** This four-story pink villa, highlighted with a staid red, has been family-run since 1898, and it shows in the best sense. **Pros:** large, spacious rooms; near the pedestrian zone. **Cons:** no elevator or air-conditioning; upper rooms are warm in summer. ⊠ *Adolf-Schmid-Str. 3* ☎ *08651/95360* ⊕ *www.hotel-pension-erika.de* ⇆ *32 rooms, 1 suite* ⚷ *In-room: no a/c, Internet. In-hotel: restaurant, some pets allowed* ⊙ *Closed Nov.–Feb. Restaurant closed Sun.*

$$ 🏨 **Parkhotel Luisenbad.** If you fancy spoiling yourself in a typical German fin de siècle spa hotel, consider staying here. **Pros:** quiet; centrally located. **Cons:** in dire need of renovation and staff attitude adjustment. ⊠ *Ludwigstr. 33* ☎ *08651/6040* ⊕ *www.parkhotel.de* ⇆ *70 rooms, 8 suites* ⚷ *In-room: no a/c, Wi-Fi. In-hotel: restaurant, bar, pool, gym, business center, some pets allowed* ❢❂ *Breakfast.*

$
★ 🏨 **Pension Hubertus.** This delightfully traditional family-run lodging stands on the shore of the tiny Thumsee, 5 km (3 mi) from the town

center. **Pros:** incredible views; private guests-only sunbathing area. **Cons:** far from city center; no elevator. ⊠ *Am Thumsee 5* ☎ *08651/2252* ⊕ *www.hubertus-thumsee.de* ⇱ *18 rooms* ♿ *In-room: no a/c. In-hotel: gym, some pets allowed* ¶⊚ *Breakfast.*

NIGHTLIFE AND THE ARTS

Casino. As a spa town and winter resort, Bad Reichenhall is a natural for night haunts. The big draw is the elegant casino, open daily 3 pm–1 or 2 am depending on business. ⊠ *Wittelsbacherstr. 17* ☎ *08651/95800* ⊠ *€2.50, free with a Kurkarte; ask for one at your hotel* 👔 *Jacket and tie.*

Orchesterbüro. Bad Reichenhall is proud of its long musical tradition and of its orchestra, founded more than a century ago. It performs six days a week throughout the year in the chandelier-hung Kurgastzentrum Theater or, when weather permits, in the open-air pavilion, and at a special Mozart Week in March. Call the Orchesterbüro for program details. ☎ *08651/8661.*

Tanzcafe am Kurgarten. For some traditional ballroom dancing to live music in the evenings, head for the Tanzcafe am Kurgarten. Occasionally they also show soccer games. ⊠ *Salzburger Str. 7* ☎ *08651/1691.*

SPORTS AND THE OUTDOORS

Though Berchtesgaden definitely has the pull for skiers, Bad Reichenhall is proud of its Predigtstuhl, which towers over the town to the south. Besides fresh air and great views, it offers some skiing, lots of hiking, biking, and even rock climbing. The tourist-information office on Wittelsbacherstrasse, just a couple of hundred yards from the train station, has all the necessary information regarding the numerous sporting activities possible in Bad Reichenhall and its surrounding area.

SHOPPING

Josef Mack Company. Using flowers and herbs grown in the Bavarian Alps, the Josef Mack Company has made medicinal herbal preparations since 1856. ⊠ *Ludwigstr. 36* ☎ *08651/78280.*

Kerzenwelt Donabauer. Candle making is a local specialty, and Kerzenwelt Donabauer, just outside Bad Reichenhall, has a selection of more than 1,000 decorative items in wax. It also has a free wax museum depicting fairy-tale characters. ⊠ *Reichenhaller Str. 15, Piding* ☎ *08651/8143.*

Leuthenmayr. Leuthenmayr is a youngster in the business, selling its "cure-all" dwarf-pine oil since 1908. ⊠ *Ludwigstr. 27* ☎ *08651/2869.*

Paul Reber. Your sweet tooth will be fully satisfied at the confection emporium of Paul Reber, makers of the famous chocolate, nougat, and marzipan *Mozartkugel* and many other caloric depth-charges. ⊠ *Ludwigstr. 10–12* ☎ *08651/60030.*

BERCHTESGADEN

18 km (11 mi) south of Bad Reichenhall, 20 km (12 mi) south of Salzburg.

Berchtesgaden's reputation is unjustly rooted in its brief association with Adolf Hitler, who dreamed of his "1,000-year Reich" from the mountaintop where millions of tourists before and after him drank in

Rupertus Therme, in Bad Reichenhall offers spa treatments such as the full-body salt scrub.

only the superb beauty of the Alpine panorama. The historic old market town and mountain resort has great charm. In winter it's a fine place for skiing and snowboarding; in summer it becomes one of the region's most popular (and crowded) resorts. An ornate palace and working salt mine make up some of the diversions in this heavenly setting.

Salt was once the basis of Berchtesgaden's wealth. In the 12th century Emperor Barbarossa gave mining rights to a Benedictine abbey that had been founded here a century earlier. The abbey was secularized early in the 19th century, when it was taken over by the Wittelsbach rulers. Salt is still important today because of all the local wellness centers. The entire area has been declared a "health resort region" (*Kurgebiet*) and was put on the UNESCO biosphere list.

GETTING HERE AND AROUND

The easiest way to reach Berchtesgaden is with the hourly train connection via Freilassing, or with the bus from Salzburg Hauptbanhof. Keep in mind that there is no long-distance train service to or from Berchtesgaden, and travel from here requires a change in Freilassing. Salzburg's main train station is undergoing renovation through 2013, and the frequent train connection to and from Berchtesgaden is unavailable until then. Bus 840 runs once per hour (45 minutes, €4.90) from Salzburg to Berchtesgaden, making this the fastest connection from Munich. Frequent local bus service makes it easy to explore the town and to reach Berchtesgaden National Park and the Königssee. Local bus services, except from Documentation center to the Eagle's Nest, are included when you pay the Kurtaxe. The Schwaiger bus company runs tours of the area and across the Austrian border as far as Salzburg. An

American couple runs Berchtesgaden Mini-bus Tours out of the local tourist office, opposite the railroad station.

ESSENTIALS

Visitor and Tour Information Berchtesgaden ⊠ *Kurdirektion* ☎ *08652/9670* ⊕ *www.berchtesgadener-land.com.* **Berchtesgaden Mini-bus Tours** 🖷 *08652/64971.* Schwaiger ☎ *08652/2525.*

EXPLORING

The Heimatmuseum. This museum located in the Schloss Adelsheim displays examples of wood carving and other local crafts. Wood carving in Berchtesgaden dates to long before Oberammergau established itself as the premier wood-carving center of the Alps. ⊠ *Schroffenbergallee 6* 🖷 *08652/4410* ⊕ *www.heimatmuseum-berchtesgaden.de* 🖾 *€2.50* ۞ *Dec.–Oct., Tues.–Sun. 10–4.*

Königliches Schloss Berchtesgaden Museum. The last royal resident of the Berchtesgaden abbey, Crown Prince Rupprecht (who died here in 1955), furnished it with rare family treasures that now form the basis of this permanent collection. Fine Renaissance rooms exhibit the prince's sacred art, which is particularly rich in wood sculptures by such great late-Gothic artists as Tilman Riemenschneider and Veit Stoss. You can also visit the abbey's original, cavernous 13th-century dormitory and cool cloisters. ⊠ *Schlosspl. 2* 🖷 *08652/947–980* ⊕ *www.haus-bayern. com* 🖾 *€7 with tour* ۞ *Mid-May–mid-Oct., Sun.–Fri. 10–noon and 2–4; mid-Oct.–mid-May, weekdays 11–2.*

The Obersalzberg. The site of Hitler's luxurious mountain retreat, is part of the north slope of the Hoher Goll, high above Berchtesgaden. It was a remote mountain community of farmers and foresters before Hitler's deputy, Martin Bormann, selected the site for a complex of Alpine homes for top Nazi leaders. Hitler's chalet, the Berghof, and all the others were destroyed in 1945, with the exception of a hotel that had been taken over by the Nazis, the Hotel zum Türken. The round-trip from Berchtesgaden's post office by bus and elevator costs €15 per person. The bus runs mid-May through September, daily from 9 to 4:50. By car you can travel only as far as the Obersalzberg bus station. From there the round-trip fare is €14.50. The full round-trip takes one hour. ■ TIP→ To get the most out of your visit to the Kehlsteinhaus, consider taking one of the informative tours offered by David Harper. Reserve in advance at ☎ *08652/64971* or ⊕ *www.eagles-nest-historical-tours.com.* Tours meet across from the train station and cost €50.

Bunkers. Beneath the hotel is a section of the labyrinth of tunnels built as a last retreat for Hitler and his cronies; the macabre, murky bunkers can be visited. 🖾 *€3* ۞ *May–Oct., Tues.–Sun. 9–5; Nov.–Apr., daily 10–3.*

Dokumentation Obersalzberg. Nearby, the Dokumentation Obersalzberg documents the notorious history of the Third Reich with some surprisingly rare archive material. ⊠ *Salzbergstr. 41* 🖷 *08652/947–960* ⊕ *www.obersalzberg.de* 🖾 *€3* ۞ *Apr.–Oct., Tues.–Sun. 9–5; Nov.–Mar., Tues.–Sun. 10–3.*

Kehlsteinhaus. Beyond Obersalzberg, the hairpin bends of Germany's highest road come to the base of the 6,000-foot peak on which sits the Kehlsteinhaus, also known as the Adlerhorst (Eagle's Nest), Hitler's personal retreat and his official guesthouse. It was Martin Bormann's gift to the führer on Hitler's 50th birthday. The road leading to it, built in 1937–39, climbs more than 2,000 dizzying feet in less than 6 km (4 mi). A tunnel in the mountain will bring you to an elevator that whisks you up to what appears to be the top of the world (you can walk up in about half an hour). There are refreshment rooms and a restaurant. ☎ *08652/2969* 🌐 *www.kehlsteinhaus.de.*

3

★ **The Salzbergwerk.** This salt mine is one of the chief attractions of the region. In the days when the mine was owned by Berchtesgaden's princely rulers, only select guests were allowed to see how the source of the city's wealth was extracted from the earth. Today, during a 90-minute tour, you can sit astride a miniature train that transports you nearly 1 km (½ mi) into the mountain to an enormous chamber where the salt is mined. Included in the tour are rides down the wooden chutes used by miners to get from one level to another and a boat ride on an underground saline lake the size of a football field. Although the tours take about an hour, plan an extra 45–60 minutes for purchasing the tickets and changing into and out of miners clothing. You may wish to partake in the special four-hour **brine dinners** down in the mines (€75). These are very popular, so be sure to book early. ✉ *2 km (1 mi) from center of Berchtesgaden on B–305 Salzburg Rd.* ☎ *08652/600–220* 🌐 *www.salzzeitreise.de* 🎫 *€14.90, combined ticket with Bad Reichenhall's saline museum €18* ⏲ *May–mid-Oct., daily 9–5; mid-Oct.–Apr., Mon.–Sat. 11:30–3.*

Watzmann Therme. Here you'll find fragrant steam rooms, saunas with infrared cabins for sore muscles, an elegant pool, whirlpools, and more. If you happen to be staying a few days, you might catch a tai chi course, enjoy a bio-release facial massage, or partake in an evening of relaxing underwater exercises. ✉ *Bergwerkstr. 54* ☎ *08652/94640* 🌐 *www.watzmann-therme.de* 🎫 *2 hrs €9.70, 4 hrs €12.20, day pass including sauna €17.90* ⏲ *Daily 10–10.*

WHERE TO STAY

For expanded hotel reviews, visit Fodors.com.

$ **Alpenhotel Denninglehen.** The house was built in 1981 in Alpine style, with lots of wood paneling, heavy beams, and wide balconies with cascades of geraniums in summer. **Pros:** heated pool with views of the Alps; great hotel for kids. **Cons:** narrow and steep access road difficult to find. ✉ *Am Priesterstein 7, Berchtesgaden-Oberau* ☎ *08652/97890* 🌐 *www.denninglehen.de* *In-room: no a/c. In-hotel: restaurant, pool, some pets allowed* ⏲ *Closed last 2 wks in Jan.* 🍽 *Breakfast.*

$ **Hotel Grünberger.** Only a few strides from the train station in the town center, the Grünberger overlooks the River Ache—it even has a private terrace beside the river you can relax on. **Pros:** quaintly situated on the river; close to the train station. **Cons:** quite far from skiing and outdoor activities. ✉ *Hansererweg 1* ☎ *08652/976–590* 🌐 *www.*

hotel-gruenberger.de ⇄ *65 rooms* ♿ *In-room: no a/c, no TV. In-hotel: restaurant, bar, pool* ☾ *Closed Nov.–mid-Dec.* ⵙ *Breakfast.*

$ ⚏ **Hotel Wittelsbach.** This is one of the oldest (built in 1892) and most traditional lodgings in the area, so it is wise to reserve well ahead of time. Pros: nice, comfortable rooms; exceptional staff; daily pamphlets show local events and weather. Cons: horrible parking; streetside rooms can get noisy. ⊠ *Maximilianstr. 16* ☎ *08652/96380* ⊕ *www. hotel-wittelsbach.com* ⇄ *26 rooms, 3 apartments* ♿ *In-room: no a/c, Wi-Fi. In-hotel: some pets allowed* ⵙ *Breakfast.*

$$ ⚏ **Hotel zum Türken.** The view alone is worth the 10-minute journey from Berchtesgaden to this hotel. Pros: great location; sense of history; Frau Schafenberg can cook! Cons: not all rooms have attached bathrooms. ⊠ *Hintereck 2, Obersalzberg-Berchtesgaden* ☎ *08652/2428* ⊕ *www.hotel-zum-tuerken.de* ⇄ *17 rooms, 12 with bath or shower* ♿ *In-room: no a/c. In-hotel: some pets allowed* ☾ *Closed Nov.–Dec. 20* ⵙ *Breakfast.*

$ ⚏ **Stoll's Hotel Alpina.** Set above the Königsee in the delightful little village of Schönau, the Alpina offers rural solitude and easy access to Berchtesgaden. Pros: bedrooms are large and comfortable; good for families with children; great view of the Adlershorst. Cons: service can be brusque. ⊠ *Ulmenweg 14, Schönau* ☎ *08652/65090* ⊕ *www.stolls-hotel-alpina.de* ⇄ *52 rooms, 8 apartments* ♿ *In-room: no a/c, Internet. In-hotel: restaurant, pool, some pets allowed* ☾ *Closed early Nov.–mid-Dec.* ⵙ *Breakfast.*

SPORTS AND THE OUTDOORS

Buried as it is in the Alps, Berchtesgaden is a place for the active. The Rossfeld ski area is one of the favorites, thanks to almost guaranteed natural snow. The piste down to Oberau is nearly 6 km (4 mi) long (with bus service at the end to take you back to Berchtesgaden). There is a separate snowboarding piste as well. Berchtesgaden also has many cross-country trails and telemark opportunities. The other popular area is on the slopes of the Götschenkopf, which is used for World Cup races. Snow is usually artificial, but the floodlit slopes at night and a lively après-ski scene make up for the lesser quality.

In summer, hikers, power-walkers, and paragliders take over the region. The Obersalzberg even has a summer luge track. Avid hikers should ask for a map featuring the refuges (Berghütten) in the mountains, where one can spend the night either in a separate room or a bunk. Simple, solid meals are offered. In some of the smaller refuges you will have to bring your own food. For more information, check out ⊕ *www. berchtesgaden.de.* And though the Königsee is beautiful to look at, only cold-water swimmers will appreciate its frigid waters.

Consider walking along the pleasant mountain path from the Eagle's Nest back to Berchtesgaden.

Berchtesgaden Golf Club. Germany's highest course, the Berchtesgaden Golf Club, is on a 3,300-foot plateau of the Obersalzberg. Only fit players should attempt the demanding 9-hole course. Seven Berchtesgaden hotels offer their guests a 30% reduction on the €25 greens

The gemlike Königsee Lake is the most photographed panorama in Germany.

fee—contact the tourist office or the club for details. ✉ *Salzbergstr. 33* ☎ *08652/2100.*

Erste Bergschule Berchtesgadenerland. Whatever your mountain-related needs, whether it's climbing and hiking in summer or cross-country tours in winter, you'll find it at the Erste Bergschule Berchtesgadenerland. ✉ *Silbergstr. 25, Strub* ☎ *08652/2420 May–Oct., 08652/5371 Nov.–Apr.*

SHOPPING

Berchtesgadener Handwerkskunst. The Berchtesgadener Handwerkskunst offers handicrafts—such as wooden boxes, woven tablecloths, wood carvings, and Christmas-tree decorations—from Berchtesgaden, the surrounding region, and other parts of Bavaria. ✉ *Schlosspl. 1½* ☎ *08652/ 979–790.*

BERCHTESGADEN NATIONAL PARK

5 km (3 mi) south of Berchtesgaden.

Berchtesgaden National Park. The deep, mysterious, and fabled Königsee is the most photographed panorama in Germany. Together with its much smaller sister, the Obersee, it's nestled within the Berchtesgaden National Park, 210 square km (82 square mi) of wild mountain country where flora and fauna have been left to develop as nature intended. No roads penetrate the area, and even the mountain paths are difficult to follow. The park administration organizes guided tours of the area from June through September. ✉ *Nationalparkhaus, Franziskanerpl. 7* ☎ *08652/64343* ⊕ *www.nationalpark-berchtesgaden.de.*

Fodor's Choice ★   **Königsee.** One less strenuous way into the Berchtesgaden National Park is by boat. A fleet of 21 excursion boats, electrically driven so that no noise disturbs the peace, operates on the Königsee (King Lake). Only the skipper of the boat is allowed to shatter the silence—his trumpet fanfare demonstrates a remarkable echo as notes reverberate between the almost vertical cliffs that plunge into the dark green water. A cross on a rocky promontory marks the spot where a boatload of pilgrims hit the cliffs and sank more than 100 years ago. The voyagers were on their way to the tiny, twin-tower baroque chapel of St. Bartholomä, built in the 17th century on a peninsula where an early-Gothic church once stood. The princely rulers of Berchtesgaden built a hunting lodge at the side of the chapel; a tavern and restaurant now occupy its rooms.

Smaller than the Königsee but equally beautiful, the **Obersee** can be reached by a 15-minute walk from the second stop (Salet) on the boat tour. The lake's backdrop of jagged mountains and precipitous cliffs is broken by a waterfall, the Rothbachfall, which plunges more than 1,000 feet to the valley floor.

Boat service. Boat service on the Königsee runs year-round, except when the lake freezes. A round-trip to St. Bartholomä and Salet, the landing stage for the Obersee, lasts almost two hours, without stops, and costs €16. A round-trip to St. Bartholomä lasts a little over an hour and costs €13. In summer the Berchtesgaden tourist office organizes evening cruises on the Königsee, which include a concert in St. Bartholomä Church and a four-course dinner in the neighboring hunting lodge. ☎ 08652/96360 ⊕ www.bayerische-seenschifffahrt.de.

The Romantic Road

WORD OF MOUTH

"You can visit Neuschwanstein and Hohenschwangau castles in the same day. We loved them. If I remember well, you can buy a combined ticket for both. Another beautiful castle is not far from Munich, it is Herrenchiemsee, on Chiemsee Lake. It has a copy of Mirror Hall in Versailles."

—valtor

WELCOME TO
THE ROMANTIC ROAD

TOP REASONS
TO GO

★ **Neuschwanstein:**
Walt Disney may have
spread the word about
this castle, but the sight
of the original, rising
up against its theatrical
backdrop of green moun-
tainside, speaks for itself.

★ **Rothenburg-ob-
der-Tauber:** Patrol the
city walls with the night
watchman, explore the
streets in the morning light
(perfect for photos), then
get out of town before
the tour buses arrive.

★ **Wieskirche:** A slight
detour off the Romantic
Road, this "Church
of the Meadow" is
a rococo jewel.

★ **Ulm's Münster:** It
takes 768 steps to reach
the top of the highest
church steeple in the
world, but the incredible
view is worth the effort.

★ **Wurzburg's Residenz:**
The best artists of the
18th century, including
Neumann and Tiepolo,
helped create the lavishly
ostentatious palace.

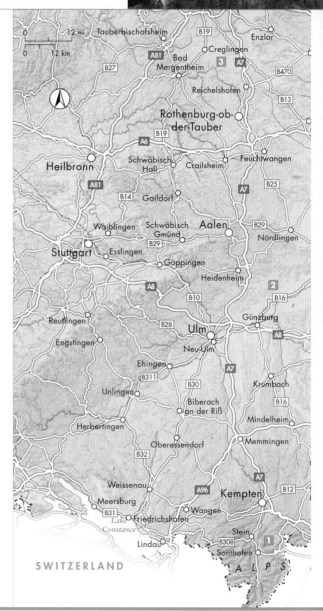

1 **Toward the Alps.** In this region, vineyards are replaced by Alpine meadows and beer beats out wine in the small inns of towns like Landsberg and Schongau. The marvelous Wieskirche (Church of the Meadow) is here, just a bit off the Romantic Road, and finally mountains give way to the plain and the fairy-tale Neuschwanstein and Hohenschwangau castles come into view.

2 **Central Romantic Road.** After crossing the Danube from the south, the route takes you through the affluent city of Augsburg and its surrounding diverse countryside, before continuing on through the lovely Tauber valley. It passes through charming old towns like well-known Rothenburg-ob-der-Tauber, with vineyards visible on the northern slopes of the small valley.

3 **Northern Romantic Road.** Wine lovers should plan an extra day for Würzburg, where they can sample good local wines at reasonable prices. Bad Mergentheim and Creglingen are also worth a look for the home of the Teutonic Knights and the Tilman Riemenschneider altar in the Herrgottskirche.

GETTING ORIENTED

The Romantic Road is not limited to one area of Germany—it is Germany in a nutshell. From the famous King Ludwig II's fantastical castle Neuschwanstein in the south, to the best-preserved medieval town on the continent, Rothenburg-ob-der-Tauber, farther north, the route runs from Füssen on the Austrian border, crisscrossing between the states of Bavaria and Baden-Württemberg, through the handsome Renaissance city of Augsburg, all the way up to Würzburg, in central Germany, an hour from Frankfurt.

4

Updated by
Nicki Polatin

Of all the tourist routes that crisscross Germany, none rivals the aptly named Romantische Strasse, or Romantic Road. The scenery is more pastoral than spectacular, but the route is memorable for the medieval towns, villages, castles, and churches that anchor its 355-km (220-mi) length. Many of these are tucked away beyond low hills, their spires and towers just visible through the greenery.

The Romantic Road concept developed as West Germany rebuilt its tourist industry after World War II. A public-relations wizard coined the catchy title for a historic passage through Bavaria and Baden-Württemberg that could be advertised as a unit. In 1950 the Romantic Road was born. The name itself isn't meant to attract lovebirds, but rather uses the word *romantic* as meaning wonderful, fabulous, and imaginative. And, of course, the Romantic Road started as a road on which the Romans traveled.

Along the way, the road crosses centuries-old battlefields. The most cataclysmic conflict, the Thirty Years' War, destroyed the region's economic base in the 17th century. The depletion of resources prevented improvements that would have modernized the area—thereby assuring the survival of the historic towns' now charmingly quaint infrastructures.

PLANNING

WHEN TO GO

Late summer and early autumn are the best times to travel the Romantic Road, when the grapes ripen on the vines around Würzburg and the geraniums run riot on the medieval walls of towns such as Rothenburg and Dinkelsbühl. You'll also miss the high-season summer crush of tourists. Otherwise, consider visiting the region in the depths of December, when Christmas markets pack the ancient squares of the Romantic Road towns and snow gives turreted Schloss Neuschwanstein a final magic touch.

GETTING HERE AND AROUND

AIR TRAVEL

The major international airports serving the Romantic Road are Frankfurt and Munich. Regional airports include Nürnberg and Augsburg.

Airport Contacts Nürnberg Airport ⊠ *Flughafenstr.* ☎ *0911/93700* ⊕ *www. airport-nuernberg.de.*

BUS TRAVEL

If you prefer not to rent a car, daily bus service covers the northern stretch of the Romantic Road, between Frankfurt and Munich, from April through October. A second bus covers the section of the route between Dinkelsbühl and Füssen. All buses stop at the major sights along the road. Deutsche Touring also operates six more-extensive tours along the Romantic Road for which reservations are essential.

Bus Contacts Deutsche Touring ⊠ *Am Römerhof 17, Frankfurt am Main* ☎ *069/790–3501* ⊕ *www.touring.de.*

CAR TRAVEL

The Romantic Road is most easily traveled by car. If you're coming up from the south and using Munich as a gateway, Augsburg is 70 km (43 mi) from Munich via A-8. The roads are busy and have only two lanes, so figure on covering no more than 70 km (40 mi) each hour, particularly in summer. From there, you will continue north and end in Würzburg, the northernmost city 124 km (77 mi) from Frankfurt. If you're traveling from the north, you'll begin in Würzburg and follow country highway B-27 south to meet roads B-290, B-19, B-292, and B-25 along the Wörnitz River. It's on the Frankfurt–Nürnberg autobahn, A-3, and is 115 km (71 mi) from Frankfurt. For route maps, with roads and sights highlighted, contact the Romantische Strasse Touristik-Arbeitsgemeinschaft (Romantic Road Central Tourist-Information) based in Dinkelsbühl.

TRAIN TRAVEL

Infrequent trains link most major towns of the Romantic Road, but both Würzburg and Augsburg are on the InterCity and high-speed InterCity Express routes, and have fast, frequent service to and from Munich, Stuttgart, and Frankfurt.

BIKE TOURS

From April through September, Velotours offers a five-day bike trip from Würzburg to Rothenburg for €365 per person and a five-day trip from Rothenburg to Donauwörth for €365 per person. These two trips can be combined for an eight-day tour for €583. The tour operator Alpenland-Touristik offers several guided six- to eight-day bike tours starting from Landsberg am Lech into the Alpine foothills.

Bike Tour Contacts Alpenlandtouristik ⊠ *Postfach 101313, Landsberg* ☎ *08191/308–620* ⊕ *www.alpenlandtouristik.de.* **Velotours** ⊠ *Bücklestr. 13, Konstanz* ☎ *07531/98280* ⊕ *www.velotours.de.*

RESTAURANTS

During peak season, restaurants along the Romantic Road tend to be crowded, especially in the larger towns. ■TIP→ You may want to plan your mealtimes around visits to smaller villages, where there are fewer people and the restaurants are pleasant. The food will be more basic Franconian or Swabian, but it will also be generally less expensive than in the well-known towns. You may find that some of the small, family-run restaurants close around 2 pm, or whenever the last lunch guests have left, and open again at 5 or 5:30 pm. Some serve cold cuts or coffee and cake during that time, but no hot food.

HOTELS

With a few exceptions, the Romantic Road hotels are quiet and rustic, and you'll find high standards of comfort and cleanliness. If you plan to stay in one of the bigger hotels in the off-season, do ask for weekend rates. Make reservations as far in advance as possible if you plan to visit in summer. Hotels in Würzburg, Rothenburg, and Füssen are often full year-round. Augsburg hotels are in great demand during trade fairs in nearby Munich. Tourist-information offices can usually help with accommodations, especially if you arrive early in the day.

WHAT IT COSTS IN EUROS					
	¢	$	$$	$$$	$$$$
Restaurants	under €9	€9–€15	€16–€20	€21–€25	over €25
Hotels	under €50	€50–€100	€101–€175	€176–€225	over €225

Restaurant prices are per person for a main course at dinner. Hotel prices are for two people in a standard double room, including tax and service.

PLANNING YOUR TIME

The two bigger cities on the Romantic Road, Augsburg and Würzburg, can handle large influxes of visitors at any time. But at the two best-known and therefore most visited places, Rothenburg-ob-der-Tauber and Neuschwanstein, it pays to arrive by night in order to get up early to tour the next morning. You can follow the night watchman in Rothenburg as he makes his rounds, and then see the town in the early morning. Have a late but leisurely breakfast as you watch the bus-tour groups push through the streets around 11. For Neuschwanstein an early start is even more important to beat the crowds.

VISITOR INFORMATION

Visitor Information **Romantische Strasse Touristik-Arbeitsgemeinschaft** (*Romantic Road Central Tourist-Information*). ⊠ *Segringerstr. 19, Dinkelsbühl* 🕾 *09851/551–387* ⊕ *www.romantischestrasse.de.*

TOWARD THE ALPS

An hour west of Munich, the Romantic Road climbs gradually into the foothills of the Bavarian Alps, which burst into view between Landsberg and Schongau. The route's most southern tip can be found at the northern wall of the Alps at Füssen, on the Austrian border. Landsberg was

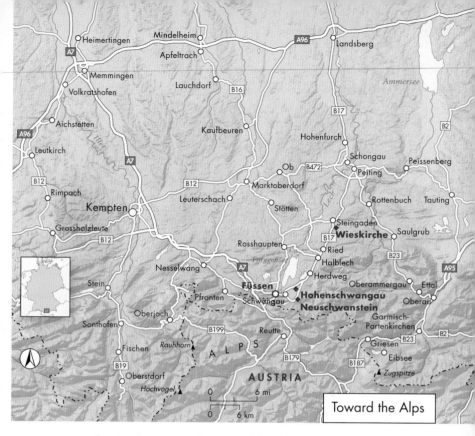

Toward the Alps

founded by the Bavarian ruler Heinrich der Löwe (Henry the Lion) in the 12th century, and grew wealthy from the salt trade. Solid old houses are packed within its turreted walls; the early-18th-century Rathaus is one of the finest in the region.

Schongau has virtually intact wall fortifications, complete with towers and gates. In medieval and Renaissance times the town was an important trading post on the route from Italy to Augsburg. The steeply gabled 16th-century Ballenhaus was a warehouse before it was elevated to the rank of Rathaus. A popular Märchenwald ("fairy-tale forest") lies 1½ km (1 mi) outside Schongau, suitably set in a clearing in the woods. It comes complete with mechanical models of fairy-tale scenes, deer enclosures, and an old-time miniature railway.

HOHENSCHWANGAU AND NEUSCHWANSTEIN

103 km (64 mi) south of Augsburg, 121 km (75 mi) southwest of Munich.

These two famous castles belonging to the Wittelbachs, one historic and the other nearly "make-believe," are 1 km (½ mi) across a valley from each other, near the town of Schwangau. Bavaria's King Ludwig II (1845–86) spent much of his youth at Schloss Hohenschwangau

(Hohenschwangau Castle). It's said that its neo-Gothic atmosphere provided the primary influences that shaped his wildly romantic Schloss Neuschwanstein (Neuschwanstein Castle), the fairy-tale castle he built after he became king, which has since become one of Germany's most recognized sights.

GETTING HERE AND AROUND

From Schwangau (5 km [3 mi] north of Füssen, 103 km [64 mi] south of Augsburg, 121 km [75 mi] southwest of Munich), follow the road signs marked "Königschlösser" (King's Castles). After 3 km (2 mi) you come to Hohenschwangau, a small village consisting of a few houses, some good hotels, and five spacious parking lots (parking €4.50). You have to park in one of them and then walk to the ticket center serving both castles. If you are staying in Füssen, take the bus to Hohenschwangau. The clearly marked bus leaves from the train station in Füssen every hour from morning to night, and the cost is €1.60 per person one-way. Tickets are for timed entry, and the average wait to enter Neuschwanstein is one hour. With a deposit or credit-card number you can book your tickets in advance for either castle through the ticket center. You can change entrance times or cancel up to two hours before the confirmed entrance time. The main street of the small village Hohenschwangau is lined with restaurants and quick eateries of all categories.

WORD OF MOUTH

"The castles [Neuschwanstein and Hohenschwangau] have a 'wow' factor that gets to just about anyone, along with a mystery about the young king. Not to mention, it makes fabulous pics to show to your friends and family. You can get an authentic German meal at some of the restaurants as the base of the castle." —Rei_n_hubs

TIMING

The best time to see either castle without waiting a long time is a weekday between January and April. The prettiest time, however, is in fall.

■ TIP➜ Bear in mind that more than 1 million people pass through one or both castles every year. If you visit in summer, get there early.

ESSENTIALS

Ticket Center ⊠ Alpseestr. 12, Hohenschwangau ☎ 08362/930–830 ⊕ www. hohenschwangau.de.

EXPLORING

★ **Schloss Hohenschwangau.** Built by the knights of Schwangau in the 12th century, this castle was remodeled later by King Ludwig II's father, the Bavarian crown prince (and later king) Maximilian, between 1832 and 1836. Unlike Ludwig's more famous castle across the valley, Neuschwanstein, the somewhat garishly yellow Schloss Hohenschwangau has the feeling of a noble home, where comforts would be valued as much as outward splendor. It was here that the young Ludwig met the composer Richard Wagner. Their friendship shaped and deepened the future king's interest in theater, music, and German mythology—the mythology Wagner drew upon for his *Ring* cycle of operas.

After obtaining your ticket at the ticket center in the village, you can take a 25-minute walk up either of two clearly marked paths to the castle, or board one of the horse-drawn carriages that leave from the ticket center (uphill €4, downhill €2) or the Hotel Müller (uphill €6, downhill €3). ⊠ *Alpseestr. 12, Hohenschwangau* ☎ *08362/930–830* ⊕ *www.hohenschwangau.de* 🎫 *€10.50, including guided tour; combined ticket for Hohenschwangau and Neuschwanstein €21.50* ☽ *Apr.– Sept., daily 8–5:30; Oct.–Mar., daily 9–3:30.*

Fodor's Choice ★ **Schloss Neuschwanstein.**
⇨ *See "The Fairy-tale Castles of King Ludwig II" in this chapter.*

WHERE TO STAY
For expanded hotel reviews, visit Fodors.com.

$$ 🏨 **Hotel Müller.** Between the two Schwangau castles, the Müller fits beautifully into the stunning landscape, its creamy Bavarian baroque facade complemented by the green mountain forest. **Pros:** view of the castles; personalized service; variety of rooms. **Cons:** crowds during the day; expensive in season. ⊠ *Alpseestr. 16, Hohenschwangau* ☎ *08362/81990* ⊕ *www.hotel-mueller.de* 🛏 *39 rooms, 4 suites* ⚬ *In-room: no a/c, Wi-Fi. In-hotel: restaurant, bar, parking, some pets allowed* ☽ *Closed beginning of Jan. through Apr. 1* ❙◯❙ *Breakfast.*

$$ 🏨 **Schlosshotel Lisl und Jägerhaus.** These jointly run 19th-century properties are across the street from one another, and share views of the nearby castles. **Pros:** elegant rooms in the Jägerhaus; varied rooms and prices; view of the castles. **Cons:** no breakfast in the Jägerhaus; small lobby. ⊠ *Neuschwansteinstr. 1–3, Hohenschwangau* ☎ *08362/8870* ⊕ *www. lisl.de* 🛏 *43 rooms, 4 suites* ⚬ *In-room: no a/c. In-hotel: restaurant, bar, parking, some pets allowed* ☽ *Closed Jan.–mid-Feb.*

FÜSSEN

5 km (3 mi) southwest of Schwangau, 129 km (08 mi) south of Munich.

Füssen is beautifully located at the foot of the mountains that separate Bavaria from the Austrian Tyrol. The Lech River, which accompanies much of this section of the Romantic Road, embraces the town as it rushes northward.

ESSENTIALS
Visitor Information Füssen ⊠ *Tourismus und Marketing, Kaiser-Maximilian-Pl. 1* ☎ *08362/93850* ⊕ *www.tourismus-fuessen.de.*

EXPLORING
Hohes Schloss (*High Castle*). The town's Hohes Schloss is one of the best-preserved late-Gothic castles in Germany. It was built on the site of the Roman fortress that once guarded this Alpine section of the Via Claudia, the trade route from Rome to the Danube. Evidence of Roman occupation of the area has been uncovered at the foot of the nearby Tegelberg Mountain, and the **excavations** next to the Tegelberg cable-car station are open for visits daily. The Hohes Schloss was the seat of Bavarian rulers before Emperor Heinrich VII mortgaged it and the rest of the town to the bishop of Augsburg for 400 pieces of silver. The mortgage was never redeemed, and Füssen remained the property of the Augsburg episcopate until secularization in the early 19th century. The bishops of Augsburg used the castle as their summer Alpine

Continued on page 180

FAIRY-TALE CASTLES OF KING LUDWIG II

By Catherine Moser

King Ludwig II's image permeates Bavarian culture—the picture of the raven-haired king with soulful eyes adorns everything from beer steins to the local autobahn. The fairy-tale palaces he built have drawn millions of visitors, but who was Ludwig II? Adopting the words of his favorite poet, Friedrich Schiller, he wrote: "I wish to remain an eternal enigma to myself and to others." A tour of his castles reveals a glimpse of the man behind the story of the "Dreamer King."

Born on August 25, 1845, in Nymphenburg Palace, Ludwig II became king at 18 after his father's, King Maximilian II's, sudden death in 1864. He would become the most famous king in the 900-year Wittelsbach dynasty, known not for his rule—he had little power, as Bavaria was governed by a constitutional monarchy—but for his eccentricities.

Ludwig attended Richard Wagner's *Lohengrin* at age 15. Identifying with the Swan Knight, he yearned for the heroic medieval world Wagner portrayed. As king, Ludwig became Wagner's greatest patron and funded the creation of his opera festival in Bayreuth. Wagner was so influential, and Ludwig's love for him so unabashed, that concerned Munich officials sent the composer away in 1865.

Seeking solace in the isolated, idealized world of his own creation, Ludwig embarked on three palace-building projects beginning in 1868. By 1885, he had amassed a personal debt of 14 million marks, putting a massive strain on the Wittelsbach fortune. A commission of doctors, enthralled with the emerging studies of psychology, was assembled to analyze the behavior of the recluse king. Led by Dr. von Gudden, the commission diagnosed the king with paranoia and declared him insane without ever examining Ludwig himself. Ludwig was arrested in the early-morning hours of June 12, 1886, and taken from Schloss Neuschwanstein to Castle Berg on the shores of Lake Starnberg. Just before midnight the following day, the bodies of Ludwig and Dr. von Gudden were found floating in the lake. Theories abound to this day about their deaths, but the truth of Ludwig's demise is unknown.

Opposite, Schloss Neuschwanstein. Above left, King Ludwig II. Above right, Golden angel fountain, Schloss Linderhof.

SCHLOSS LINDERHOF

Set in sylvan seclusion in Graswang Valley, high in the Alps, lies the royal palace of Linderhof. Built on the site of his father's hunting lodge, this was the first of Ludwig's building projects and the only one completed during his lifetime. Begun in 1868, the small villa based on the Petit Trianon of Versailles took six years to complete.

ENTRANCE HALL

Two lifesize Sèvres **peacocks** were placed outside the entry doors to signify when Ludwig was in residence. Upon entering the castle, there is a large bronze **statue of King Louis XIV**, Ludwig's idol. On the ceiling above the statue is a gold sun, symbolizing the "Sun King" of France, inscribed with his motto: *Nec Pluribus Impar* ("I stand above others").

Above, Schloss Linderhof. Opposite (top) Venus grotto, (bottom) Hall of Mirrors.

THRONE ROOM AND BEDCHAMBER

With paintings of Louis XIV and XV watching over him, Ludwig spent hours meticulously overseeing the architectural plans of his other projects from the green and gold **throne room**. The **bedchamber**, with its three-dimensional golden tapestries set against his favorite color, royal blue, look out to a waterfall cascading down the hill to the **Neptune fountain**, with its 100-foot water jet.

DINING ROOM

Ludwig would eat alone in the adjoining **dining room**. His extreme sweet tooth had wreaked havoc on his mouth so that by the time he was 30, most of his teeth were missing and dining was a messy affair. For his privacy, the dining table could be lowered down through the floor by cables and pulleys to the kitchen below. It would then reappear

with Ludwig's meal so that he never had to dine with servants in the room.

HALL OF MIRRORS
The reclusive king spent his time reading and literally reflecting in the **hall of mirrors,** with its optical illusion infinitely reflecting his image and vast collection of vases lining the walls.

LINDERHOF'S GROUNDS
In the **Venus grotto,** Ludwig spent many evenings being paddled around in a scallop-shaped boat imagining he was in the world of Wagner's *Tannhäuser.* Ludwig would gather his equerries for decadent evenings spent in the **Moorish kiosk,** which was purchased wholesale from the 1867 Paris Universal Exposition, imagining himself as an Arabian knight lounging on his magnificent **peacock throne.** Deeper into the park is the **Hunding's hut,** a medieval-style lodge based on the set designs for the opening act of Wagner's *Die Walküre.* Ludwig took moonlit rides in winter to the original Hut, set deeply in the Alpine forest, in his gilt **gala sleigh.**

GETTING HERE AND AROUND

✉ Linderhof 12, Ettal-Linderhof
☎ 08822/92030 or -21
🌐 www.schlosslinderhof.de
🎫 €8.50, €7.50 winter
🕐 Open April–Oct. 15, daily 9-6; Oct. 16–March, daily 10-4; park buildings (grotto, Moorish kiosk, etc.) closed in winter

Car Travel: Take the A–95 motorway and the B–2 to Oberau. Follow the signs in Oberau to the B–23 (Ettaler Strasse). Outside Ettal turn left onto ST–2060. In Linderhof turn right to reach the palace.

Train Travel: Take the regional Deutsche Bahn train from Munich Hauptbahnhof to Oberammergau. Buy the Bayern Ticket, which allows for a full day of travel, including bus fare, for €25 for up to five people. From there, take bus 9622 to Linderhof.

Bus Tours: There are several tours combining both Linderhof and Neuschwanstein castles, but none that go just to Linderhof. Gray Line Tours (☎ 8954/907–560 🌐 www.grayline.com) offers a day trip, including Linderhof, Neuschwanstein, and a short stop to shop in Oberammergau. It leaves daily at 8:30 am from the Karstadt Department store in front of the Munich Hauptbahnhof. Tickets are €72 for adults and €35 for children, not including admission.

SCHLOSS NEUSCHWANSTEIN

Neuschwanstein, the most famous of the three castles, was King Ludwig's crowning achievement. The castle soars from its mountainside like a stage creation—it should hardly come as a surprise that Walt Disney took it as the model for his castle in the movie *Sleeping Beauty* and later for the Disneyland castle itself.

Prince Ludwig spent idyllic childhood summers at **Hohenschwangau**, the neighboring medieval-style palace. The young prince was undoubtedly influenced by the vast murals of the legends of *Lohengrin* and romantic vision of these ancient times. Perhaps he envisioning his own, mightier palace when looking north to the mountains and the old ruins of a fortress of the Knights

of Schwangau. Upon commencing construction in 1868, Ludwig wrote to Wagner, "The Gods will come to live with us on the lofty heights, breathing the air of heaven."

THRONE ROOM

Wagner's *Tannhäuser* inspired the Byzantine-style **throne room**, drawn from plans for the original stage set for the opera; however, the actual throne was never constructed. The massive chandelier is styled after a Byzantine crown and surrounded by images of angels, apostles, and six kings of history who were canonized as saints. Look closely at the image of St. George, the patron saint of the Wittelsbachs, slaying a dragon in front of another medieval castle. That castle, Falkenstein, was set to be the next, even grander castle of Ludwig II. The elaborate mosaic floor contains two million stones.

Above, Schloss Neuschwanstein. Opposite (top) Singers' Hall, (bottom) Ludwig II's bedchamber.

BEDCHAMBER

The king spent his last days as ruler huddled in his late-Gothic-style **bedchamber** modeled after the nuptial chamber of *Lohengrin*. It took fourteen craftsman more than four years to carve this room alone. The symbol of the swan occurs throughout Neuschwanstein, appearing here in the fixtures of the sink.

GROTTO

Reminiscent of the larger one at Linderhof, but stranger for its placement inside the palace, the **grotto** overlooking the Schwangau Valley once had a running waterfall lit by tinted lights.

SINGERS' HALL

Ludwig's favorite room, the **Singers' Hall**, was modeled after the stage design for the Forest of the Holy Grail from *Parsifal* and designed for the best acoustics. On moonless nights, the king would hike out to the Marienbrücke, over the rocky gorge, to watch the candlelit splendor of this hall. Ludwig never saw a performance here, but concerts are now held every September.

GETTING HERE AND AROUND

✉ Alpseestrasse 12, Hohenschwangau

☎ 8362/930–830

⊕ www.neuschwanstein.de

🎫 €12 tickets are for a set tour time, reserve ahead online. English tours every 15 minutes.

🕙 Open April–Sept. daily 8–5; Oct.–March daily 9–3

Car Travel: Take the A–7 (direction Ulm-Kempten-Füssen) to the end. From Füssen, take B–17 to Schwangau, then follow signs to Hohenschwangau.

Train Travel: Take the regional Deutsche Bahn train from Munich Hauptbahnhof to Füssen (buy the Bayern Ticket). From Füssen, take either bus 73 toward Steingaden/Garmisch-Partenkirchen or bus 78 toward Schwangau until the Hohenschwangau/Alpseestrasse stop.

Getting to the Castle: Allow 30–40 minutes for the uphill walk from the ticket center to the castle. In summer, you can take a a bus (€1.80 uphill, €1 downhill) or horse-drawn carriage (€6 uphill, €3 downhill) up to the castle.

Bus Tours: Bus Bavaria (☎ 89255/43987 or -988 ⊕ mikesbiketours.com) leaves from central Munich daily from mid-April through mid-October. Tours cost €39–€49, not including admission.

SCHLOSS HERRENCHIEMSEE

The third and what would be the last of King Ludwig II's building projects, Herrenchiemsee, modeled after Louis XIV's Versailles, stands as a monument to the institution of the monarchy and the Bourbon kings he idolized. Ludwig never intended to use this palace as a place to live but rather a place to visit to transport himself to the days when the Sun King ruled the glorious court of Versailles. Ludwig stayed at this palace only once, for a brief ten-day visit in September 1885.

CONSTRUCTION OF HERRENCHIEMSEE

Ludwig purchased the Herreninsel, the biggest of the three islands on Lake Chiemsee in 1873. Work soon began on gardens to rival the ones at Versailles.

Above, Schloss Herrenchiemsee. Opposite (top) Hall of Mirrors, (bottom) fountain.

By the time the foundation stone of the palace was laid in 1878, the soaring fountains were already in use. Although 300 local craftsmen worked day and night to replicate the Sun King's palace, only 20 of the planned 70 rooms saw completion during the following eight years of construction. They abound with marble, gilt, and paintings of the Bourbon court, the French style replicated by skilled Bavarian artists.

PARADE BEDCHAMBER

The sumptuous red brocade bedspread and wall hangings in the **parade bedchamber**, which is twice the size of the original in Versailles, took 30 women seven years to embroider. Red silk curtains can be pulled over the bay windows to give the room a glow of regal red, the symbolic color of the Bourbon court. Ludwig never slept in this room; it was created in memory of Louis XIV. Instead, Ludwig slept in the **king's bed-**

chamber, softly lit by blue candlelight from the large blue orb over his bed.

HALL OF MIRRORS
In the **hall of mirrors,** longer than the original in Versailles, Ludwig held private concerts during his short stay here. A team of 35 servants took a half-hour to light the 2,000 candles of the chandeliers and candelabra lining the golden room.

LUDWIG II MUSEUM
Ludwig gave strict orders that no image of the Wittelsbach rulers or of himself should be found in his French palace. Today, however, this is the only one of his three palaces to have a museum devoted to the king. You can see his christening gown, uniforms, architectural plans for future building projects, and even sample his favorite cologne in the castle's **Ludwig II Museum.**

GETTING HERE AND AROUND

✉ Herrenchiemsee
☎ 8051/68870
⊕ www.herrenchiemsee.de
💶 €8
🕐 Open April–Oct. 15, daily 9-6; Oct. 16–March, daily 9:40-4:15

Boat Travel: Herrenchiemsee lies on the island of Herreninsel in Lake Chiemsee. **Chiemsee Schifffahrt's** (✉ *Seestrasse 108, Prien am Chiemsee* ☎ *8051/6090* ⊕ *www.chiemsee-schifffahrt.de*) ferries leave regularly from Prien/Stock daily from 7 am–6:30 pm. Tickets cost €6.90.

Car Travel: Take the A-8 motorway (Salzburg-Munich), leaving at the Bernau exit to continue to Prien am Chiemsee. At the roundabout outside Prien follow the signs to Chiemsee or Königsschloss.

Train Travel: Take the regional Deutsche Bahn train to Prien am Chiemsee, about an hour's ride from Munich (buy the Bayern Ticket). From the station, take the quaint **Chiemsee Bahn,** which winds through the town to the boats. It runs from April–October. Train and boat combination tickets cost €9.

Bus Tours: Gray Line Tours (☎ *8954/907-560* ⊕ *www.grayline.com*) offers a day trip, including the boat trip out to the castle (but not admission) and a visit to the Fraueninsel on Chiemsee for €47.

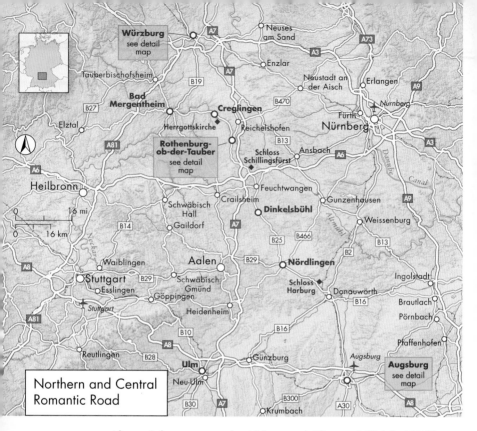

Northern and Central Romantic Road

residence. It has a spectacular 16th-century **Rittersaal** (Knights' Hall) with a carved ceiling, and a princes' chamber with a Gothic tile stove. ✉ *Magnuspl. 10* ☎ *08362/903–146* 💶 *€6* ⏱ *Apr.–Oct., Tues.–Sun. 11–5, Nov. –March. Fri. –Sun. 1–4.*

Rathaus. The summer presence of the bishops of Augsburg ensured that Füssen received an impressive number of baroque and rococo churches. Füssen's Rathaus was once a Benedictine abbey, built in the 9th century at the site of the grave of St. Magnus, who spent most of his life ministering in the area. A Romanesque crypt beneath the baroque abbey church has a partially preserved 10th-century fresco, the oldest in Bavaria. In summer, chamber concerts are held in the high-ceiling baroque splendor of the former abbey's **Fürstensaal** (Princes' Hall). Program details are available from the tourist office. ✉ *Lechalde 3.*

Reichenstrasse. Füssen's main shopping street, called Reichenstrasse, was, like Augsburg's Maximilianstrasse, once part of the Roman Via Claudia. This cobblestone walkway is lined with high-gabled medieval houses and backed by the bulwarks of the castle and the easternmost buttresses of the Allgäu Alps.

WHERE TO EAT AND STAY
For expanded hotel reviews, visit Fodors.com.

EATING WELL ON THE ROMANTIC ROAD

To sample the authentic food of this area, venture off the beaten track of the official Romantic Road into any small town with a nice-looking Gasthof. Order *Rinderbraten* (roast beef) with *Spaetzle* (small boiled ribbons of rolled dough), or try *Maultaschen* (oversize Swabian ravioli), another typical regional dish.

Franconia (including Würzburg) is the sixth-largest wine-producing area of Germany. Franconian wines—half of which are Müller-Thurgau, a blending of Riesling and Sylvaner—are served in distinctive green, flagon-shape wine bottles. Riesling and red wines account for only about 5% of the total production of Franconian wine.

Before you travel north on the Romantic Road, be sure to enjoy the beer country in the south. There is a wide range of Franconian and Bavarian brews available from *Räucherbier* (literally, "smoked beer") to the lighter ales of Augsburg. If this is your first time in Germany, beware of the potency of German beer. Even the regular ones are much stronger than the normal American brew. If you want a light beer, in most parts of Germany you ask for "Export"; a small one will be 0.3 liters, a big one 0.5 liters. In most beer tents you will be only served a stein with 1 liter.

¢ ✕**Markthalle.** This is a farmers' market where you can grab a quick bite GERMAN and drink at reasonable prices. Try the fish soup. The building started in 1483 as the *Kornhaus* (grain storage) and then became the *Feuerhaus* (fire station). ⊠ *Schranneg. 12* ⊟ *No credit cards* ☉ *Weekdays 10–6, Sat. 10–2 pm. Closed Sun.*

$ ⌂ **Altstadthotel Zum Hechten.** Geraniums flower most of the year on this comfortable inn's balconies. **Pros:** in the center of town; good value with breakfast included in the rates; nice restaurant. **Cons:** difficult stairs to climb; some rooms noisy. ⊠ *Ritterstr. 6* ☎ *08362/91600* ⊕ *www.hotel-hechten.com* ↯ *35 rooms* ⚘ *In-room: no a/c, Wi-Fi. In-hotel: restaurant, parking, some pets allowed* ❚⊘❙ *Breakfast.*

$$ ⌂ **Hotel Hirsch.** A mother-and-daughter team provides friendly service at this traditional Füssen hotel. **Pros:** in the center of town; eclectic rooms; good restaurant. **Cons:** front rooms noisy; modern lobby. ⊠ *Kaiser-Maximilian-Pl. 7* ☎ *08362/93980* ⊕ *www.hotelhirsch.de* ↯ *53 rooms* ⚘ *In-room: no a/c, Wi-Fi. In-hotel: restaurant, bar, parking, some pets allowed* ☉ *Closed 3 wks in Jan.* ❚⊘❙ *Breakfast.*

■ OFF THE BEATEN PATH
Wieskirche. This church—a glorious example of German rococo architecture—stands in an Alpine meadow just off the Romantic Road. In the village of Steingaden (22 km [14 mi] north of Füssen on the B-17), turn east and follow the signs to Wieskirche. Its yellow-and-white walls and steep red roof are set off by the dark backdrop of the Trauchgauer Mountains. The architect Dominicus Zimmermann, former mayor of Landsberg and creator of much of that town's rococo architecture, built the church in 1745 on the spot where six years earlier a local woman claimed to have seen tears running down the face of a picture of Christ. Although the church was dedicated as the Pilgrimage Church of the Scourged Christ, it's now known simply as the Wieskirche (Church of

the Meadow). ■ TIP→ Visit it on a bright day if you can, when light streaming through its high windows displays the full glory of the glittering interior. A complex oval plan is animated by brilliantly colored stuccowork, statues, and gilt. A luminous ceiling fresco completes the decoration. Concerts are presented in the church from the end of June through the beginning of August. ⊠ *Wies 12, Steingaden* ☎ *8862/932–930* ⊕ *www.wieskirche.de* ▨ *Free* ☉ *Summer months, 8–7; winter months, 8–5.*

CENTRAL ROMANTIC ROAD

Picturesque Rothenburg-ob-der-Tauber is the highlight of this region, though certainly not the road less traveled. For a more intimate experience check out the medieval towns of Dinkelsbühl or Nördlingen, or go off the beaten track and off the Romantic Road to see Ulm's famous Münster (church).

AUGSBURG

70 km (43 mi) west of Munich.

Augsburg is Bavaria's third-largest city, after Munich and Nürnberg. It dates to 15 years before the birth of Christ, when a son of the Roman emperor Augustus set up a military camp here on the banks of the Lech River. The settlement that grew up around it was known as Augusta, a name Italian visitors to the city still call it. It was granted city rights in 1156, and 200 years later was first mentioned in municipal records of the Fugger family, who were to Augsburg what the Medici were to Florence.

GETTING HERE AND AROUND

Augsburg is on a main line of the superfast ICE trains, which run every hour—about 45 minutes from Munich. The center of town with the main attractions can be visited on foot. To continue on the Romantic Road, take a regional train from the main train station to Ulm, Donauwörth, or Nördlingen.

Walking tours (€7) set out from the Rathaus daily at 2. All tours are conducted in German and English.

TIMING

A walking tour of Augsburg is easy, because signs on almost every street corner point the way to the chief sights. The signs are integrated into three-color, charted tours devised by the tourist board. You'll need a complete day to see Augsburg if you linger in any of the museums.

ESSENTIALS

Visitor Information **Augsburg** ⊠ *Tourist-Information, Rathauspl. 1* ☎ *0821/324-9410* ⊕ *www.augsburg.de.*

EXPLORING

TOP ATTRACTIONS

Dom St. Maria (*Cathedral of St. Mary*). Augsburg's cathedral, which was built in the 9th century, stands out within the city's panorama because of its square Gothic towers, the product of a 14th-century update. A

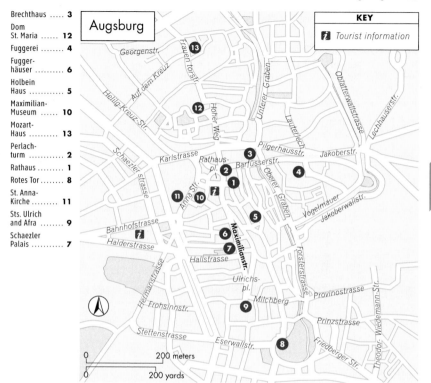

10th-century Romanesque crypt, built in the time of Bishop Ulrich, also remains from the cathedral's early years. The 11th-century windows on the south side of the nave, depicting the prophets Jonah, Daniel, Hosea, Moses, and David, form the oldest cycle of stained glass in central Europe. Five important paintings by Hans Holbein the Elder adorn the altar.

A short walk from the cathedral will take you to the quiet courtyards and small raised garden of the former episcopal residence, a series of 18th-century buildings in baroque and rococo styles that now serve as the Swabian regional government offices.

Diözesanmuseum St. Afra. The cathedral's treasures are on display at this museum. ⊠ *Kornhausg. 3–5* 🖾 *€4* ⊙ *Tues.–Sat. 10–5, Sun. noon–6* ⊠ *Dompl., Johannisg. 8* ⊙ *Daily 9–dusk.*

Fuggerei. This neat little settlement is the world's oldest social housing project. It was established by the Fugger family in 1516 to accommodate the city's deserving poor. The 67 homes with 140 apartments still serve the same purpose and house about 150 people today, financed almost exclusively from the assets of the foundation as the annual rent of "one Rhenish guilder" (€1) hasn't changed, either. Residents must be Augsburg citizens, Catholic, and destitute through no fault of their own—and they must pray daily for their original benefactors, the Fugger family. The most famous resident was Mozart's great-grandfather. ✉ *Main entrance is located at Jakoberstr., Fuggerei 56* ☎ *0821/3198–8114* ⌂ *€4* ☉ *Apr.–Sept. 8–8; Oct.–Mar. 9–6.*

Maximilian-Museum. Augsburg's main museum houses a permanent exhibition of Augsburg arts and crafts in a 16th-century merchant's mansion. ✉ *Fuggerpl. 1, Philippine-Welser-Str. 24* ⌂ *€7* ☉ *Tues.10–8, Wed.–Sun. 10–5.*

Perlachturm (*Perlach Tower*). This 258-foot-high plastered brick bell tower has foundations dating to the 11th century. Although it's a long climb to the top of the tower, the view over Augsburg and the countryside is worth the effort. ✉ *Rathauspl.* ☎ *No phone* ⌂ *€1* ☉ *May–Oct., daily 10–6.*

Rathaus. Augsburg's town hall was Germany's largest when it was built in the early 17th century; it's now regarded as the finest Renaissance secular structure north of the Alps. Its **Goldener Saal** (Golden Hall) was given its name because of its rich decoration—a gold-based harmony of wall frescoes, carved pillars, and coffered ceiling. ✉ *Rathauspl. 2* ⌂ *€2* ☉ *Daily 10–6 (when no official functions take place).*

Sts. Ulrich and Afra. Standing at the highest point of the city, this basilica was built on the site of a Roman cemetery where St. Afra was martyred in AD 304. The original structure was begun in the late-Gothic style in 1467; a baroque preaching hall was added in 1710 as the Protestant church of St. Ulrich. St. Afra is buried in the crypt, near the tomb of St. Ulrich, a 10th-century bishop who helped stop a Hungarian army at the gates of Augsburg in the Battle of the Lech River. The remains of a third patron of the church, St. Simpert, are preserved in one of the church's most elaborate side chapels. From the steps of the magnificent altar, look back along the high nave to the finely carved baroque wrought-iron and wood railing that borders the entrance. As you leave, look into the separate but adjacent church of St. Ulrich, the former chapter house that was reconstructed by the Lutherans after the Reformation. ✉ *Ulrichspl. 19* ☉ *Daily 9–dusk.*

Schaezlerpalais. This elegant 18th-century city palace was built by the von Liebenhofens, a family of wealthy bankers. Schaezler was the name of a baron who married into the family. Today the palace rooms contain the **Deutsche Barockgalerie** (German Baroque Gallery), a major art collection that features works of the 17th and 18th centuries. The palace adjoins the former church of a Dominican monastery. A steel door behind the banquet hall leads into another world of high-vaulted ceilings, where the **Staatsgalerie Altdeutsche Meister,** a Bavarian state collection, highlights old-master paintings, among them a Dürer portrait of one of the Fuggers. ✉ *Maximilianstr. 46* ⌂ *€7* ☉ *Tues. 10–8, Wed.–Sun. 10–5.*

> **TOURING TIPS**
>
> **Scenic spot:** There's an excellent view over the center of the city from the spot where Maximilianstrasse joins Rathausplatz (Town Hall Square).
>
> **Snacks:** Recuperate from the climb at the cafés and restaurants on Rathausplatz and Maximilianstrasse.

Climb the 258 steps of the Perlachturm (Perlach Tower) beside the Rathaus for a spectacular vantage point over Augsburg.

WORTH NOTING

Brechthaus. This modest artisan's house was the birthplace of the renowned playwright Bertolt Brecht (1898–1956), author of *Mother Courage* and *The Threepenny Opera*. ☒ *Auf dem Rain 7* 🎫 *€2* ☉ *Tues.– Sun. 10–5*.

Fuggerhäuser. The 16th-century former home and business quarters of the Fugger family now house a restaurant in their cellar and offices on the upper floors. In the ground-floor entrance are busts of two of Augsburg's most industrious Fuggers, Raymund and Anton. Beyond a modern glass door is the *Damenhof* (Ladies' Courtyard), originally reserved for the Fugger women. The three courtyards are accessible to the public, while the rest of the buildings are reserved for staff. ☒ *Maximilianstr. 36–38* ☉ *Courtyards are open in summer 11–3 and 6–midnight*.

Holbein Haus. The rebuilt 16th-century home of painter Hans Holbein the Elder, one of Augsburg's most famous residents, is now a city art gallery, with changing exhibitions. ☒ *Vorderer Lech 20* 🎫 *Admission varies* ☉ *May–Oct., Tues., Wed., and Fri.–Sun. 10–5, Thurs. 10–8; Nov.–Apr., Tues., Wed., and Fri.–Sun. 10–4, Thurs. 10–8*.

Maximilianstrasse. This main shopping street was once a medieval wine market. Most of the city's sights are on this thoroughfare or a short walk away. Two monumental and elaborate fountains punctuate the long street. At the north end is the **Merkur,** designed in 1599 by the Dutch master Adrian de Vries (after a Florentine sculpture by Giovanni da Bologna), which shows winged Mercury in his classic pose. Farther up Maximilianstrasse is another de Vries fountain: a bronze **Hercules** struggling to subdue the many-headed Hydra.

Mozart-Haus (*Mozart House*). Leopold Mozart, the father of Wolfgang Amadeus Mozart, was born in this bourgeois 17th-century residence; he was an accomplished composer and musician in his own right. The house was renovated in 2006 and now serves as a Mozart memorial and museum, with some fascinating contemporary documents on the Mozart family. ✉ *Frauentorstr. 30* ☎ *0821/518–588* 💷 *€3.50* ⊙ *Tues.– Sun. 10–5.*

Rotes Tor (*Red Gate*). The city's most important medieval gate once straddled the main trading road to Italy. It provides the backdrop to an open-air opera and operetta festival in June and July. ✉ *Rote-Torwall-Str..*

St. Anna-Kirche (*St. Anna's Church*). This site was formerly part of a Carmelite monastery, where Martin Luther stayed in 1518 during his meetings with Cardinal Cajetanus, the papal legate sent from Rome to persuade the reformer to renounce his heretical views. Luther refused, and the place where he publicly declared his rejection of papal pressure is marked with a plaque on Maximilianstrasse. ■TIP➔ **You can wander through the quiet cloisters, dating from the 14th century, and view the chapel used by the Fugger family until the Reformation.** ✉ *Anna-Str., west of Rathauspl.* ⊙ *Mon. noon–5, Tues.–Sat. 10–12:30 and 3–6, Sun. 10-12:30 (services) and 3–4.*

WHERE TO EAT

$$$
CONTINENTAL
Fodor's Choice
★

✕ **Die Ecke.** On an *Ecke* (corner) of the small square right behind Augsburg's town hall, the Ecke is valued for the imaginative variety of its cuisine and the scope of its wine list. In season, the venison dishes are among Bavaria's best. The fish, in particular the *Zander* (green pike) or the trout sautéed in butter and lightly dressed with herbs and lemon, is magnificent, and complemented nicely by the Riesling Gimmeldinger Meersspinne, the house wine for 40 years. In summer ask for a table on the patio. ✉ *Elias-Holl-Pl. 2* ☎ *0821/510–600* ⊕ *www.restaurant-die-ecke.de* ⌖ *Reservations essential.*

WHERE TO STAY

For expanded hotel reviews, visit Fodors.com.

$
★

🛏 **Dom Hotel.** Just around the corner from Augsburg's cathedral, this snug establishment has personality. **Pros:** family-run; attention paid to details; nice view from upper rooms, complimentary parking. **Cons:** stairs to entrance and some rooms; no restaurant or bar. ✉ *Frauentorstr. 8* ☎ *0821/343–930* ⊕ *www.domhotel-augsburg.de* ⌸ *44 rooms, 8 suites* ⌕ *In-room: no a/c, Wi-Fi. In-hotel: pool, gym, parking* ⊙ *Closed late Dec.–mid-Jan.* ⎢○⎢ *Breakfast.*

$ 🛏 **Hotel-Garni Schlössle.** From the main railroad station, a 10-minute ride on tram Number 3 to the end of the line at Stadtbergen brings you to this friendly, family-run hotel. **Pros:** good value, friendly; family-run. **Cons:** no restaurant or bar; small rooms. ✉ *Bauernstr. 37, Stadtbergen* ☎ *0821/243–930* ⌸ *14 rooms* ⌕ *In-room: no a/c* ⎢○⎢ *Breakfast.*

$$ 🛏 **Privat Hotel Riegele.** The hotel is just opposite the main railway station. **Pros:** good restaurant; cheaper weekend rates. **Cons:** chintzy; some parts need refurbishing. ✉ *Viktoriastr. 4* ☎ *0821/509–000* ⊕ *www.hotel-riegele.de* ⌸ *28 rooms* ⌕ *In-room: no a/c, Wi-Fi. In-hotel: restaurant, some pets allowed* ⊙ *No dinner Sun.* ⎢○⎢ *Breakfast.*

$ ★ ☐ **Romantikhotel Augsburger Hof.** A preservation order protects the beautiful Renaissance facade of this charming old Augsburg mansion but rather than remake an old-world atmosphere inside, the owners opted for a cheerful but classic look with natural wood finishes and flowered curtains. **Pros:** welcoming lobby; rooms with a personal touch; good food. **Cons:** noisy front rooms; must book far in advance. ⊠ *Auf dem Kreuz 2* ☎ *0821/343–050* ⊕ *www. augsburger-hof.de* ⤳ *36 rooms* ⌂ *In-room: no a/c, Wi-Fi. In-hotel: restaurant, bar, parking, some pets allowed* ⊙ *Breakfast.*

> ### WORD OF MOUTH
>
> "You can't 'do' the Romantic Road as a day excursion. It is a long route connecting a number of interesting towns. My family spent 5 days touring it by car and that was only the tip of the iceberg. Given that you will be without a car, your best bet is to choose one town to visit and spend the day there." —hausfrau

THE ARTS

Augsburg has chamber and symphony orchestras, as well as ballet and opera companies. The city stages a Mozart Festival of international stature in September.

☾ **Augsburger Puppenkiste** (*Puppet theater*). This children's puppet theater has been an institution in Germany since its inception in 1948 and is loved by kids and parents alike. ⊠ *Spitalg. 15, next to Rotes Tor* ☎ *0821/450–3450* ⊕ *www.augsburger-puppenkiste.de.*

Freilichtbühne. One of Germany's most beautiful open-air theaters, Augsburg's Freilichtbühne is the setting for a number of operas, operettas and musicals from mid-June through July. The stunning backdrop of the Freilichtbühne is worth a visit and has featured guest performances by many famous actors and directors. ⊠ *Am Roten Tor* ☎ *0821/324–4900 tourist office* ⊕ *www.theater.augsburg.de.*

Kongresshalle. The Kongresshalle presents music and dance performances and can be rented for events. ⊠ *Gögginger Str. 10* ☎ *0821/324–2348.*

ULM

80 km (49 mi) west of Augsburg.

Ulm isn't considered part of the Romantic Road, but it's definitely worth visiting, if only for one reason: its mighty Münster, which has the world's tallest church tower (536 feet). Ulm grew as a medieval trading city thanks to its location on the Danube River. Today the proximity of the Old Town to the river adds to Ulm's charm. In the Fishermen's and Tanners' quarters the cobblestone alleys and stone-and-wood bridges over the Blau (a small Danube tributary) are especially picturesque.

GETTING HERE AND AROUND

To get to Ulm from Augsburg, take Highway A-8 west or take a 40-minute ride on one of the superfast ICE (Intercity Express) trains that run to Ulm every hour.

The tourist office's 90-minute tour includes a visit to the Münster, the Old Town Hall, the Fischerviertel (Fishermen's Quarter), and the

DID YOU KNOW?

Ulm's Münster has the world's highest church spire at 161 meters. You can climb the 768 steps to the top of the tower for views of Ulm and the Alps.

Danube riverbank. The departure point is the tourist office (Stadthaus) on Münsterplatz; the cost is €6. From May to mid-October you can view Ulm from aboard the motor cruiser *Ulmer Spatz*. There are 50-minute cruises at 2 and 3 daily (€8). The boats tie up at the Metzgerturm, a two-minute walk from the town hall.

ESSENTIALS

Visitor Information Ulm ⊠ *Tourist-Information, Münsterpl. 50* ☎ *0731/161–2830* ⊕ *www.tourismus.ulm.de.*

EXPLORING

Marktplatz. The central Marktplatz is bordered by medieval houses with stepped gables. Every Wednesday and Saturday farmers from the surrounding area arrive by 6 am to erect their stands and unload their produce. Potatoes, vegetables, apples, pears, berries, honey, fresh eggs, poultry, homemade bread, and all kinds of other edible things are carefully displayed. ■TIP➜ Be sure to get here early; the market packs up around noon.

Fodor'sChoice
★

Münster. Ulm's Münster, which was unscathed by wartime bombing, is the largest evangelical church in Germany and boasts the world's highest church tower. It stands over the huddled medieval gables of Old Ulm, visible long before you hit the ugly suburbs encroaching on the Swabian countryside. Its single, filigree tower challenges the physically fit to plod 536 feet up the 768 steps of a giddily twisting spiral stone staircase to a spectacular observation point below the spire. On clear days the steeple will reward you with views of the Swiss and Bavarian Alps, 160 km (100 mi) to the south. The Münster was begun in the late-Gothic age (1377) and took five centuries to build, with completion in the neo-Gothic years of the late 19th century. It contains some notable treasures, including late-Gothic choir stalls and a Renaissance altar. ■TIP➜ The mighty organ can be heard in special recitals every Sunday at 11:15 from Easter until November. ⊠ *Münsterpl. 21* ☎ *Tower €4* ☉ *Church daily 9–5; tower 9–3:45; organ recitals May–Oct., daily at 11:30.*

Museum der Brotkultur (*German Bread Museum*). German bread is world renowned, so it's not surprising that a national museum is devoted to bread making. The Museum der Brotkultur is housed in a former salt warehouse, just north of the Münster. It's by no means as crusty or dry as some might fear, with some often-amusing tableaux illustrating how bread has been baked over the centuries. ⊠ *Salzstadelg. 10* ☎ *0731/69955* ⊕ *www.museum-brotkultur.de* ☎ *€3.50* ☉ *Daily 10–5.*

Old city wall. Complete your visit to Ulm with a walk down to the banks of the Danube, where you'll find long sections of the old city wall and fortifications intact.

Rathaus. A reproduction of local tailor Ludwig Berblinger's flying machine hangs inside the elaborately painted Rathaus. In 1811 Berblinger, a tailor and local eccentric, cobbled together a pair of wings and made a big splash by trying to fly across the river. He didn't make it, but he grabbed a place in German history books for his efforts. ⊠ *Marktpl. 1.*

WHERE TO EAT AND STAY
For expanded hotel reviews, visit Fodors.com.

$ ✕ **Zunfthaus der Schiffleute.** The sturdy half-timber Zunfthaus (Guildhall)
GERMAN   has stood here for more than 500 years, first as a fishermen's pub and
now as a charming tavern-restaurant. Ulm's fishermen had their guild
headquarters here, and when the nearby Danube flooded, the fish swam
right up to the door. Today they land on the menu. One of the "foreign" intruders on the menu is Bavarian white sausage, *Weisswurst*. The
local beer is an excellent accompaniment. ⊠ *Fischerg. 31* ☎ *0731/64411*
⊕ *www.zunfthaus-ulm.de.*

$ ✕ **Zur Forelle.** For more than 350 years the aptly named Forelle, which
GERMAN   means "trout," has stood over the small, clear River Blau, which flows
★   through a large trout basin right under the restaurant. If you're not a
trout fan, there are five other fish dishes available, as well as excellent
venison in season. ■TIP➔ On a nice summer evening, try to get a table
on the small terrace. You'll literally sit over the small river, with a weeping willow on one side, half-timber houses all around you, and the towering cathedral in the background. ⊠ *Fischerg. 25* ☎ *0731/63924* ⊕ *www.
zurforelle.com.*

$ ☷ **Hotel am Rathaus/Reblaus.** The owner's love of antique paintings, fur-
niture, and dolls is evident throughout this hotel. **Pros:** center of the
city; artistic touches; good value. **Cons:** no elevator; not enough parking; no breakfast in annex. ⊠ *Kroneng. 8–10* ☎ *0731/968–490* ⊕ *www.
rathausulm.de* ⤳ *34 rooms* ⟨ *In-room: no a/c, Wi-Fi. In-hotel: parking*
☺ *Closed late Dec.–mid-Jan.* ⏧ *Breakfast.*

$$ ☷ **Maritim.** Whether you come here to eat or stay, be prepared for incred-
ible views. **Pros:** spacious lobby and rooms; romantic views; nice bar.
Cons: rooms expensive on weekdays; impersonal atmosphere. ⊠ *Bas-
teistr. 40* ☎ *0731/9230* ⊕ *www.maritim.de* ⤳ *287 rooms* ⟨ *In-room:
no a/c, Internet, Wi-Fi. In-hotel: restaurant, bar, pool, gym, parking.*

NÖRDLINGEN

*28 km (17 mi) southeast of Donauwörth, 72 km (44 mi) northwest
of Augsburg.*

In Nördlingen the cry "*So G'sell so*"—"All's well"—still rings out every
night across the ancient walls and turrets.

ESSENTIALS
Visitor Information Nördlingen ⊠ *Tourist-Information, Marktpl. 2*
☎ *09081/84116* ⊕ *www.noerdlingen.de.*

EXPLORING
Ries. Nördlingen lies in the center of a huge, basinlike depression, the
Ries, which until the beginning of this century was believed to be the
remains of an extinct volcano. In 1960 it was proven by two Americans
that the 24-km-wide (15-mi-wide) crater was caused by an asteroid at
least 1 km (½ mi) in diameter. ■TIP➔ The compressed rock, or Suevit,
formed by the explosive impact of the meteorite was used to construct many
of the town's buildings, including St. Georg's tower.

St. Georg. Sentries sound out the traditional "*So G'sell so*" message from the 300-foot tower of the central parish church of St. Georg at half-hour intervals between 10 pm and midnight. The tradition goes back to an incident during the Thirty Years' War, when an enemy attempted to slip into the town and was detected by a resident. You can climb the 365 steps up the tower—known locally as the Daniel—for an unsurpassed view of the town and countryside, including, on clear days, 99 villages. The ground plan of the town is two concentric circles. The inner circle of streets, whose central point is St. Georg, marks the earliest medieval boundary. A few hundred yards beyond it is the outer boundary, a wall built to accommodate expansion. Fortified with 11 towers and punctuated by five massive gates, it's one of the best-preserved town walls in Germany. ⊠ *Marktpl.* 🕾 *Tower €2.50* ⊙ *Apr.–Oct., weekdays 9:30–12:30 and 2–5; weekends 9:30–5; winter months, Tues.–Sat. 10:30–12:30. Tower Apr.–June, Sept. and Oct., 9–6; July and Aug., 9–7; Nov., Jan., Feb.–Mar., 1–5; Dec. 9–5; and on weekends 9–5 year-round.*

BIKING THE ROMANTIC ROAD

There are three ways to explore the Romantic Road by bicycle and the path (all 420 km [260 mi] of it) is well marked. You can either venture out with as little baggage as possible, finding places to stay along the way. Or, have a tour operator book rooms for you and your group and transport your luggage. Or, you can do day trips. In any town on the Romantic Road you can board the Deutsche Touring bus (with a trailer for bicycles), which travels the length of the Romantic Road daily.

4

WHERE TO STAY
For expanded hotel reviews, visit Fodors.com.

$ 🏨 **Gasthof Kirchenwirt.** This Gasthaus in the central square, directly opposite the city tower, was first mentioned in city archives in 1481 as "a place to eat and drink." **Pros:** good value; center of town. **Cons:** rooms on the lower floors toward the street are noisy; not enough parking. ⊠ *Marktpl. 12* 🕾 *09081/290–120* ⊕ *www.gasthof-kirchenwirt.eu* ➥ *14 rooms* ⚹ *In-room: no a/c, Wi-Fi. In-hotel: restaurant, some pets allowed* ⦿*Breakfast.*

$ 🏨 **Hotel Goldene Rose.** This small, modern hotel just inside the town
☆   wall is ideal for those wishing to explore Nördlingen on foot. **Pros:** family-friendly vibe; parking in courtyard. **Cons:** front rooms noisy; restaurant closed Sunday. ⊠ *Baldingerstr. 42* 🕾 *09081/86019* ⊕ *www.goldene-rose-noerdlingen.de* ➥ *17 rooms, 1 apartment* ⚹ *In-room: no a/c. In-hotel: restaurant, parking* ⦿*Breakfast.*

SPORTS AND THE OUTDOORS
Nördlingen Ries. Ever cycled around a huge meteor crater? You can do just that in the Nördlingen Ries, the basinlike depression left by an asteroid that hit the area 14.5 million years ago and is referred to as "The Ries event." This impact crater is a designated national geopark and the best preserved impact crater in all of Europe.

Nördlingen tourist office. The Nördlingen tourist office has a list of 10 recommended bike routes, including one 47-km (29-mi) trail around the northern part of the meteor crater. ⊠ *Marktplatz 2* ☎ *09081/84116*

Donauwörth. At the old walled town of Donauwörth, 28 km (17 mi) southeast of Nördlingen, the Wörnitz River meets the Danube. If you're driving, pull off into the clearly marked lot on B-25, just north of town. Below you sprawls a striking natural relief map of Donauwörth and its two rivers.

Käthe-Kruse-Puppen-Museum. The town is the home of the famous Käthe Kruse dolls, beloved for their sweet looks and frilly, floral outfits. You can buy them at several outlets in town, and they have their own museum, where more than 130 examples dating from 1912 are displayed in a specially renovated monastery building, the Käthe-Kruse-Puppen-Museum. ⊠ *Pflegstr. 21a* ☎ *0906/789–170* ⊠ *€2.50* ☺ *May and Sept., Tues.–Sun. 11–5; June, July, and Aug., Tues.–Sun. 10–5; Apr. and Oct., Tues.–Sun. 2–5; Nov.–Mar., Wed. and weekends 2–5; Dec. 25–Jan. 9, 2–5 daily.*

DINKELSBÜHL

32 km (20 mi) south of Nördlingen.

★ Within the walls of Dinkelsbühl, a beautifully preserved medieval town, the rush of traffic seems a lifetime away. There's less to see here than in Rothenburg, and the mood is much less tourist-oriented. Like Rothenburg, Dinkelsbühl was caught up in the Thirty Years' War, and it also preserves a fanciful episode from those bloody times. An annual open-air-theater festival takes place from mid-June until mid-August. You can patrol the illuminated Old Town with the night watchman at 9 pm free of charge, starting from the Münster St. Georg.

ESSENTIALS

Visitor Information Romantische Strasse Touristik-Arbeitsgemeinschaft (*Romantic Road Central Tourist-Information*). ⊠ *Segringerstr. 19* ☎ *09851/551–387* ⊕ *www.romantischestrasse.de.* **Dinkelsbühl** ⊠ *Tourist-Information, Marktpl., Altrathauspl. 14* ☎ *09851/902–440* ⊕ *www.dinkelsbuehl.de.*

EXPLORING

Münster St. Georg (*Cathedral St. George*). This is the standout sight in town. At 235 feet long it's large enough to be a cathedral, and it's among the best examples in Bavaria of the late-Gothic style. Note the complex fan vaulting that spreads sinuously across the ceiling. If you can face the climb, head up the 200-foot tower for amazing views over the jumble of rooftops. ⊠ *Marktpl., Kirchhöflein 6* ☎ *09851/2245* ⊠ *Tower €1.50* ☺ *Church: summer months 9–noon and 2–7 daily; winter months 9–noon and 2–5 daily; tower: May–Sept., Fri.–Sun. 2–5.*

WHERE TO STAY

For expanded hotel reviews, visit Fodors.com.

$ ☷ **Goldene Rose.** Since 1450 the inhabitants of Dinkelsbühl and their guests—among them Queen Victoria in 1891—have enjoyed a good night's sleep, great food, and refreshing drinks in this half-timber house. **Pros:** family-friendly atmosphere; good food; parking lot. **Cons:** some rooms need renovating; front rooms are noisy. ⊠ *Marktpl. 4* ☎ *09851/57750* ⊕ *www.hotel-goldene-rose.com* ⌇ *34 rooms* ⟳ *In-room: no a/c, Wi-Fi. In-hotel: restaurant, bar, parking, some pets allowed* ❛◯❜ *Breakfast.*

$$ ⊡ **Hotel Deutsches Haus.** As you step into this medieval inn with a facade of half-timber gables and flower boxes, an old sturdy bar gives you a chance to register while sitting down and enjoying a drink. **Pros:** modern touches like free Wi-Fi. **Cons:** some rooms noisy; pricey; steps to climb. ⊠ *Weinmarkt 3* ☎ *09851/6058* ⊕ *www.deutsches-haus-dkb.de* ⌇ *16 rooms, 2 suites* ⟳ *In-room: no a/c, Internet. In-hotel: restaurant, bar, parking* ⊙ *Closed Jan. and Feb.* ❛◯❜ *Breakfast.*

> **LOCAL LEGEND**
>
> When Dinkelsbühl was under siege by Swedish forces and in imminent danger of destruction, a young girl led the children of the town to the enemy commander and implored him in their name for mercy. The commander of the Swedish army is said to have been so moved by the plea that he spared the town. Whether or not it's true, the story is retold every year during the Kinderzech Festival, a pageant by the children of Dinkelsbühl during a 10-day festival in July.

SHOPPING

Deleika. This store makes barrel organs to order, although it won't deliver the monkey! The firm also has a museum of barrel organs and other mechanical instruments. It's just outside Dinkelsbühl. Call ahead. ⊠ *Waldeck 33* ☎ *09857/97990.*

ROTHENBURG-OB-DER-TAUBER

50 km (31 mi) north of Dinkelsbühl, 90 km (56 mi) west of Nürnberg.

Fodor's Choice ★ Rothenburg-ob-der-Tauber (literally, "red castle on the Tauber") is the kind of medieval town that even Walt Disney might have thought too picturesque to be true, with half-timber architecture galore and a wealth of fountains and flowers against a backdrop of towers and turrets. As late as the 17th century, it was a small but thriving market town that had grown up around the ruins of two 12th-century churches destroyed by an earthquake. Then it was laid low economically by the havoc of the Thirty Years' War, and with its economic base devastated, the town slumbered until modern tourism rediscovered it. It's undoubtedly something of a tourist trap, but genuine enough for all the hype.

GETTING HERE AND AROUND

The easiest way to get here is by car. There are large parking lots just outside the town wall. You can also come by the Romantic Road bus from Augsburg via Donauwörth, Nördlingen, and Dinkelsbühl with a layover if you want. By local train it takes about 2½ hours from Augsburg with two train changes. All attractions within the walled town can easily be reached on foot. The costumed night watchman conducts a nightly tour of the town, leading the way with a lantern. From Easter to December a one-hour tour in English begins at 8 pm and costs €6 (a 90-minute daytime tour begins at 2 pm). All tours start at the Marktplatz (Market Square). Private group tours with the night watchman can be arranged through ⊕ *www.nightwatchman.de.*

TIMING

Sights are dotted around town, and the streets don't lend themselves to a particular route. Be aware that crowds will affect the pace at which you can tour the town. Early morning is the only time to appreciate the place in relative calm. The best times to see the mechanical figures on the Rathaus wall are in the evening, at 8, 9, or 10.

ESSENTIALS

Visitor Information Rothenburg-ob-der-Tauber ⊠ *Tourist-Information, Rathaus, Marktpl. 1* ☎ *09861/4040* ⊕ *www.rothenburg.de.*

EXPLORING

TOP ATTRACTIONS

Herterichbrunnen (*Herterich Fountain*). A *Schäfertanz* (Shepherds' Dance) was performed around the ornate Renaissance fountain on the central Marktplatz whenever Rothenburg celebrated a major event. The dance is still done, though it's now for the benefit of tourists. It takes place in front of the Rathaus several times a year, chiefly at Easter, on Whitsunday, and in September. ⊠ *Marktpl.*

Mittelalterliches Kriminalmuseum (*Medieval Criminal Museum*). The gruesome medieval implements of torture on display here are not for the fainthearted. The only museum in Europe that provides an overview of the history of law, also soberly documents the history of German legal processes in the Middle Ages. ⊠ *Burgg. 3* ☎ *09861/5359* ⊕ *www. kriminalmuseum.rothenburg.de* ⌨ *€4* ☉ *Apr., daily 1–5; May–Oct., daily 10–6; Nov., Jan., and Feb., daily 2–4; Dec. and Mar., daily 1–4.*

Stadtmauer (*City Wall*). Rothenburg's city walls are more than 2 km (1 mi) long and provide an excellent way of circumnavigating the town from above. The walls' wooden walkway is covered by eaves. Stairs every 200 or 300 yards provide ready access. There are superb views of the tangle of pointed and tiled red roofs and of the rolling country beyond.

WORTH NOTING

Meistertrunkuhr. Tales of the Meistertrunk (Master Drink) and a mighty civil servant are still told in Rothenburg. The story originates from 1631, when the Protestant town was captured by Catholic forces during the Thirty Years' War. During the victory celebrations, the conquering general was embarrassed to find himself unable to drink a great tankard of wine in one go, as his manhood demanded. He volunteered to spare the town further destruction if any of the city councilors could drain the mighty six-pint draft. The mayor took up the challenge and succeeded, and Rothenburg was preserved. The tankard itself is on display at the Reichsstadtmuseum. On the north side of the main square is a fine

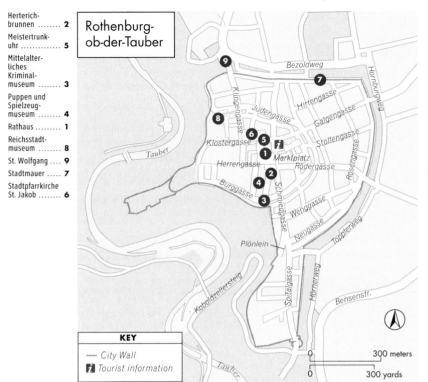

4

KEY

—— *City Wall*

🛈 *Tourist information*

0 _____ 300 meters

0 _____ 300 yards

clock, placed there 50 years after the mayor's feat. A mechanical figure acts out the epic Master Drink daily on the hour from 11 to 3 and in the evening at 8, 9, and 10. The feat is also celebrated at two annual pageants, when townsfolk parade through the streets in 17th-century garb. ⊠ *Marktpl. 1, undefined, Rothenburg-ob-der-Tauber.*

Puppen und Spielzeugmuseum (*Doll and Toy Museum*). This complex of medieval and baroque buildings houses more than 1,000 dolls, the oldest dating from 1780, the newest from 1940, as well as a collection of dollhouses, model shops, and theaters guaranteed to charm the kids. ⊠ *Hofbronneng. 13* ☎ *09861/7330* 💰 *€4* ⊘ *Jan. and Feb., daily 11–5; Mar.–Dec., daily 9:30–6.*

Rathaus. Half of the town hall is Gothic, begun in 1240; the other half is neoclassical, started in 1572, and renovated after its original facade was destroyed by a fire 500 years ago. ■ TIP➡ The Rathaus tower offers a good view of the medieval town.

Historiengewölbe (*Historic Vaults*). Below the Rathaus building are the historic vaults, which house a museum that provides information on the Thirty Years' War. ⊠ *Rathaus, Lichthof* 💰 *€2.50* ⊘ *Mar. 6–21, weekdays noon–4; Apr., weekdays 10–4; May–Nov. 1, weekdays 9:30–5:30; Nov. 2–26, weekdays 1–4 and weekends 10–4; Nov. 27–Dec. 23, weekdays 1–4 and weekends 10–7* ⊠ *Rathauspl., Marktpl. 1.*

Reichsstadtmuseum (*Imperial City Museum*). This city museum is two attractions in one. Its artifacts illustrate Rothenburg and its history. Among them is the great tankard, or *Pokal,* of the *Meistertrunk* (Master Drink). The setting of the museum is the other attraction; it's in a former Dominican convent, the oldest parts of which date from the 13th century. Tour the building to see the cloisters, the kitchens, and the dormitory; then see the collections. ⊠ *Klosterhof 5* ☏ *09861/939–043* ⌨ *€4* ☉ *Apr.–Oct., daily 10–5; Nov.–Mar., daily 1–4.*

St. Wolfgang. A historic parish church of Gothic origins with a baroque interior, St. Wolfgang's is most notable for the way it blends into the forbidding city wall. ⊠ *Klingeng.* ⌨ *€1.50* ☉ *Apr.–Oct., Mon., Wed.–Sun., 10–1 and 2:30–5.*

Stadtpfarrkirche St. Jakob (*Parish Church of St. Jacob*). The church has some notable Riemenschneider sculptures, including the famous *Heiliges Blut* (Holy Blood) altar. Above the altar a crystal capsule is said to contain drops of Christ's blood. There are three 14th- and 15th-century stained-glass windows in the choir, and the Herlin-Altar is famous for its 15th-century painted panels. ⊠ *Klosterg. 15* ☏ *09861/700–620* ⌨ *€2* ☉ *Church tours weekends at 11 and 2:30; English tour Sat. at 3.*

WHERE TO STAY

For expanded hotel reviews, visit Fodors.com.

$$
Fodor's Choice
★
Burg-Hotel. This exquisite little hotel abuts the town wall and was once part of a Rothenburg monastery. **Pros:** no crowds; terrific view from most rooms; nice touches throughout; expanded parking. **Cons:** no restaurant; too quiet for kids. ⊠ *Klosterg. 1–3* ☏ *09861/94890* ⊕ *www.burghotel.eu* ⟿ *15 rooms, 2 apartments* ⌂ *In-room: no a/c, Wi-Fi. In-hotel: spa, parking* ⫧*Breakfast.*

$
Gasthof Klingentor. This sturdy old staging post is outside the city walls but still within a 10-minute walk of Rothenburg's historic center. **Pros:** good value; restaurant liked by locals and guests. **Cons:** front rooms noisy; no elevator. ⊠ *Mergentheimerstr. 14* ☏ *09861/3468* ⊕ *www.hotel-klingentor.de* ⟿ *20 rooms, 16 with bath* ⌂ *In-room: no a/c, no TV. In-hotel: restaurant, bar* ⫧*Breakfast.*

$
★
Hotel Eisenhut. It's fitting that the prettiest small town in Germany should have one of the prettiest small hotels. **Pros:** elegant lobby; exceptional service; good food. **Cons:** expensive; nothing for kids. ⊠ *Herrng. 3–5/7* ☏ *09861/7050* ⊕ *www.eisenhut.com* ⟿ *78 rooms, 2 suites* ⌂ *In-room: no a/c, Wi-Fi. In-hotel: restaurant, bar, parking.*

$
Hotel-Gasthof Post. This small family-run hotel, two minutes on foot from the eastern city gate, must be one of the friendliest in town. **Pros:** good value; friendly family atmosphere. **Cons:** front rooms noisy; no elevator. ⊠ *Ansbacherstr. 27* ☏ *09861/938–880* ⊕ *www.post-rothenburg. com* ⟿ *23 rooms* ⌂ *In-room: no a/c. In-hotel: restaurant* ⫧*Breakfast.*

$
Hotel Reichs-Küchenmeister. Master chefs in the service of the Holy Roman Emperor were the inspiration for the name of this historic hotel-restaurant, one of the oldest trader's houses in Rothenburg. **Pros:** in the middle of town. **Cons:** small reception area. ⊠ *Kirchpl.8* ☏ *09861/9700* ⊕ *www.reichskuechenmeister.com* ⟿ *45 rooms, 2 suites, 5 apartments* ⌂ *In-room: no a/c, Wi-Fi. In-hotel: restaurant, bar* ⫧*Breakfast.*

With its half-timber houses, fountains, statues, and flowers, Rothenburg-ob-der-Tauber makes a great photo-op.

$ ⌂ **Hotel-Restaurant Burg Colmberg.** East of Rothenburg in Colmberg, this
★ castle-turned-hotel maintains a high standard of comfort within its original medieval walls. **Pros:** romantic; kids love staying in a real castle. **Cons:** lonely location; quite a few stairs to climb. ⊠ *An der Burgenstr., 18 km (11 mi) east of Rothenburg, Colmberg* ☎ *09803/91920* ⊕ *www. burg-colmberg.de* ⊸ *24 rooms, 2 suites* ⚒ *In-room: no a/c. In-hotel: restaurant, bar, golf course* ☉ *Closed Feb.* †○l *Breakfast.*

$$ ⌂ **Romantik-Hotel Markusturm.** The Markusturm began as a 13th-century
★ customs house, an integral part of the city defense wall, and has since developed over the centuries into an inn and staging post and finally into a luxurious small hotel. **Pros:** tasteful decor; elegant atmosphere; responsive owner. **Cons:** no bar; steps to climb. ⊠ *Röderg. 1* ☎ *09861/ 94280* ⊕ *www.markusturm.de* ⊸ *23 rooms, 2 suites* ⚒ *In-room: no a/c, Wi-Fi. In-hotel: restaurant, parking* †○l *Breakfast.*

FESTIVALS

Highlights of Rothenburg's annual calendar are the **Meistertrunk Festival,** over the Whitsun weekend, celebrating the famous wager said to have saved the town from destruction in the Thirty Years' War, and the **Reichstadt-Festtage,** on the first weekend of September, commemorating Rothenburg's attainment of Free Imperial City status in 1274. Both are spectacular festivals, when thousands of townspeople and local horsemen reenact the events in period costume.

SHOPPING

Anneliese Friese. You'll find everything from cuckoo clocks and beer tankards to porcelain and glassware at this old and atmospheric shop. ⊠ *Grüner Markt 7–8, near Rathaus* ☎ *09861/7166.*

Haus der 1000 Geschenke. If you are looking specifically for Hummel figurines, you've found the right place. ⊠ *Obere Schmiedeg. 13* ☏ *09861/4801*.

Käthe Wohlfahrt. The Christmas Village part of the store is a wonderland of mostly German-made toys and decorations, particularly traditional ornaments. ⊠ *Herrng. 1* ☏ *09861/4090*.

☾ **Teddyland.** Germany's largest teddy-bear population, numbering more than 5,000, is housed here. ■TIP→ Children adore the place, but be prepared: these are pedigree teddies, and they don't come cheap. ⊠ *Herrng. 10* ☏ *09861/8904* ⊕ *www.teddyland.de* ☾ *Mon.–Sat., 9–6; Sun., Apr.–Dec. 10–6.*

■ EN
ROUTE

Schloss Schillingsfürst. This baroque castle of the Princes of Hohenlohe-Schillingsfürst, is 20 km (12 mi) south of Rothenburg-ob-der-Tauber. Standing on an outcrop, it can be seen from miles away. You can watch eagles and falcons shoot down from the sky to catch their prey on a single command during the falconry deomonstration. ■TIP→ Try to arrive in time for one of the Bavarian falconry demonstrations held in the courtyard at 11 and 3 from March to October. ⊠ *Am Wall 14, Schillingsfürst* ☏ *09868/812* ⊕ *www.schloss-schillingsfuerst.de* ☒ *€4, €7 with falconry demonstration* ☾ *Mar.–Oct. daily 10–5; tours at 10, noon, 2, and 4 or by appointment.*

NORTHERN ROMANTIC ROAD

After heading through the plains of Swabia in the south, your tour of the Romantic Road skirts the wild, open countryside of the Spessart uplands. It's worth spending a night in Würzburg, but Creglingen and Bad Mergentheim can be quick stops along the road.

CREGLINGEN

18 km (11 mi) northwest of Rothenburg-ob-der-Tauber, 40 km (25 mi) south of Würzburg.

The village of Creglingen has been an important pilgrimage site since the 14th century, when a farmer plowing his field had a vision of a heavenly host.

Fingerhutmuseum. The only museum of its kind worldwide, the privately run Fingerhutmuseum features a large selection of thimbles and sewing tools from antiquity to modern times. ⊠ *Kohlesmühle 6* ☏ *07933/370* ⊕ *www.fingerhutmuseum.de* ☒ *€2* ☾ *Apr.–Oct., daily 10–12:30 and 2–5; Nov.–Mar., Tues.–Sun. 1–4.*

Herrgottskirche (*Chapel of Our Lord*). The Herrgottskirche was recently renovated and is located in the Herrgottstal (Valley of the Lord), 3 km (2 mi) south of Creglingen; the way there is well signposted. The chapel was built by the counts of Hohenlohe on the exact spot where the farmer had his vision, and in the early 16th century Riemenschneider carved an altarpiece for it. This enormous work, 33 feet high, depicts in minute detail the life and ascension of the Virgin Mary. Riemenschneider entrusted much of the background detail to the craftsmen of his Würzburg workshop, but he allowed no one but himself to attempt its life-size figures. Its intricate detail and attenuated figures are a high point of late-Gothic sculpture. ⊠ *Herrgottskirche* ☎ *07933/338* ⊕ *www. lucakilkenny.com* 🖼*€2* ⊙ *Feb.–Mar., Tues.–Sun. 1–4pm; Apr.–Aug. 14, 9:15–6 daily; Aug. 15–31, 9:15–6:30 daily; Sept.–Oct. 9:15–6 daily; Nov.–Dec. 23, Tues.–Sun. 1–4pm; Dec. 26–30, Tues. –Sun. 1–4pm* ⊙ *Closed Dec. 31–Jan. 31.*

WHERE TO STAY

For expanded hotel reviews, visit Fodors.com.

¢ 🖼 **Heuhotel Ferienbauernhof.** For a truly off-the-beaten-track experience, ⟳ book a space in the hayloft of the Stahl family's farm in a suburb of Creglingen. **Pros:** kids love it; easy on the wallet. **Cons:** in the middle of nowhere; nearly impossible to find without GPS. ⊠ *Weidenhof 1* ☎ *07933/378* ⊕ *www.ferienpension-heuhotel.de* ⟿ *Granary accommodates 20 people, 1 cottage, 1 apartment, 3 rooms* ⟳ *In-room: no a/c, no TV* ⟼ *No credit cards* ⟦◯⟧ *Breakfast.*

BAD MERGENTHEIM

24 km (15 mi) west of Creglingen.

Between 1525 and 1809, Bad Mergentheim was the home of the Teutonic Knights, one of the most successful medieval orders of chivalry. In 1809, Napoléon expelled them as he marched toward his ultimately disastrous Russian campaign. The expulsion seemed to sound the death knell of the little town, but in 1826 a shepherd discovered mineral springs on the north bank of the river. They proved to be the strongest sodium sulfate and bitter saltwaters in Europe, with health-giving properties that ensured the town's future prosperity.

ESSENTIALS

Visitor Information Bad Mergentheim ⊠ *Tourist-Information, Marktplatz 1* ☎ *07931/57135* ⊕ *www.bad-mergentheim.de.*

EXPLORING

Deutschordensschloss. The Deutschordensschloss, the Teutonic Knights' former castle, at the eastern end of the town, has a museum that follows the history of the order. The castle also hosts classical concerts, lectures, and events that cater to families and children. ⊠ *Schloss 16* ☎ *07931/52212* ⊕ *www.deutschordensmuseum.de* 🖼*€5, €2 for tours* ⊙ *Apr.–Oct., Tues.–Sun. 10:30–5.*

⟳ **Wildpark Bad Mergentheim.** Located a few miles outside of Bad Mergentheim, this wildlife park has the Continent's largest selection of European species, including wolves and bears. ■**TIP**➔ You can help feed the animals twice a day, at 9:45 and 1:30. ⊠ *Wildpark 1* ✛ *Off the B-290, 1 km south of town* ☎ *07931/41344* ⊕ *www.wildtierpark.de* 🖼*€8.50* ⊙ *Mid-Mar.–Oct., daily 9–6.*

WHERE TO STAY

For expanded hotel reviews, visit Fodors.com.

$ 🖼 **Hotel Victoria.** The hotel management changed hands in 2011 and now only has 40 rooms, all of which were renovated during that time. **Pros:**

good food with excellent service; guest rooms are spacious. **Cons:** some guest rooms are not well ventilated; reception understaffed. ⊠ *Post-str. 2–4* ☎ *07931/5930* ⊕ *www.victoria-hotel.de* ➘ *40 rooms, 6 junior suites, 1 suite* ⟐ *In-room: no a/c, Wi-Fi. In-hotel: restaurant, bar, parking* ☺ *Zirbelstube closed Jan., Aug., and Sun. and Mon.* ⦿ *Breakfast.*

WÜRZBURG

200 km (124 mi) north of Ulm, 115 km (71 mi) east of Frankfurt.

The baroque city of Würzburg, the pearl of the Romantic Road, is a heady example of what happens when great genius teams up with great wealth. Beginning in the 10th century, Würzburg was ruled by powerful (and rich) prince-bishops, who created the city with all the remarkable attributes you see today.

The city is at the junction of two age-old trade routes, in a calm valley backed by vineyard-covered hills. Festung Marienberg, a fortified castle on the steep hill across the Main River, overlooks the town. Constructed between 1200 and 1600, the fortress was the residence of the prince-bishops for 450 years.

Present-day Würzburg is by no means completely original. On March 16, 1945, seven weeks before Germany capitulated, Würzburg was all but obliterated by Allied saturation bombing. The 20-minute raid destroyed 87% of the city and killed at least 4,000 people. Reconstruction has returned most of the city's famous sights to their former splendor. Except for some buildings with modern shops, it remains a largely authentic restoration.

GETTING HERE AND AROUND

Würzburg is on a main line of the superfast ICE Intercity Express trains, two hours from Munich and a bit more than an hour from Frankfurt. Most attractions in the old part of town are easily reached on foot. There's a bus to take you to Marienberg Castle up on the hill across the river. A car is the best means of transport if you want to continue your journey, but you can also use regional trains and buses.

One-hour guided strolls (in English) through the Old Town start at the Haus zum Falken tourist office and take place from mid-June to mid-September, daily at 6:30 pm. Tickets (€5) can be purchased from the guide. If you'd rather guide yourself, pick up a map from the same tourist office and follow the extremely helpful directions marked throughout the city by distinctive signposts.

The Würzburger Schiffstouristik Kurth & Schiebe operates excursions. A wine tasting (€8) is offered as you glide past the vineyards.

TIMING

You need two days to do full justice to Würzburg. The Residenz alone demands several hours of attention. If time is short, head for the Residenz as the doors open in the morning, before the first crowds assemble, and aim to complete your tour by lunchtime. Then continue to the nearby Juliusspital Weinstuben or one of the many traditional taverns in the area for lunch. In the afternoon, explore central Würzburg. The

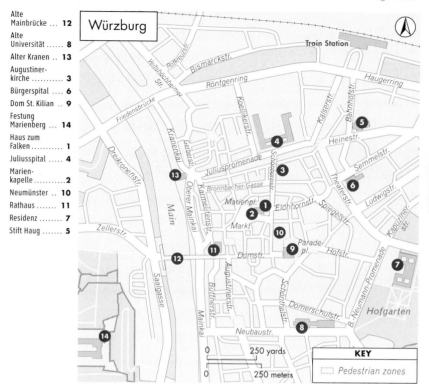

next morning cross the Main River to visit the Festung Marienberg along with the Mainfränkisches Museum and the Fürstenbaumuseum.

ESSENTIALS

Visitor Information Stadt Würzburg ⊠ *Rückermainstra. 2* ☎ *0931/370* ⊕ *www.wuerzburg.de.* **Würzburger Schiffstouristik Kurth & Schiebe** ⊠ *St.-Norbert-Str. 1, Zell* ☎ *0931/58573* ⊕ *www.schiffstouristik.de.*

EXPLORING

TOP ATTRACTIONS

Alte Mainbrücke (*Old Main Bridge*). The site of Germany's first stone bridge of 1120, this ancient structure over the Main River was restored beginning in 1476. Twin rows of infinitely graceful statues of saints line the bridge. They were placed here in 1730, at the height of Würzburg's baroque period, and were largely destroyed in 1945, but have been lovingly restored since then. Note the *Patronna Franconiae* (commonly known as the Weeping Madonna). There's a beautiful view of the Marienberg Fortress from the bridge.

★ **Festung Marienberg** (*Marienberg Fortress*). This complex was the original home of the prince-bishops, beginning in the 13th century. The oldest buildings—note especially the **Marienkirche** (Church of the Virgin Mary)—date from around 700, although excavations have disclosed evidence that there was a settlement here in the Iron Age, 3,000 years

The baroque Würzburg Residenz is a UNESCO World Heritage Site.

ago. In addition to the rough-hewn medieval fortifications, there are a number of Renaissance and baroque apartments. ■ TIP→ To reach the hilltop Marienberg, make the fairly steep climb on foot through vineyards or take bus Number 9, starting at the Residenz, with several stops in the city. It runs about every 40 minutes from April to October.

Mainfränkisches Museum (*Main-Franconian Museum*). The highlight is the remarkable collection of art treasures in the Mainfränkisches Museum, which traces the city's rich and varied history. Be sure to visit the gallery devoted to Würzburg-born sculptor Tilman Riemenschneider, who lived from the late 15th to the early 16th century. Also on view are paintings by Tiepolo and Cranach the Elder, as well as exhibits of porcelain, firearms, antique toys, and ancient Greek and Roman art. Other exhibits include enormous old winepresses and exhibits about the history of Franconian wine making. From April through October, tours around the fortress are offered for €2 per person, starting from the Scherenberg Tor. 🕾 *0931/205–940* ⊕ *www.mainfraenkisches-museum. de* 💳 *€4* 🕓 *Apr.–Oct., Tues.–Sun. 10–5; Nov.–Mar., Tues.–Sun. 10–4*

Fürstenbaumuseum (*Princes' Quarters Museum*). The Marienberg collections are so vast that they spill over into another outstanding museum that is part of the fortress, the Fürstenbaumuseum, which traces 1,200 years of Würzburg's history. The holdings include breathtaking exhibits of local goldsmiths' art ⊠ *Festung Marienberg, Oberer Burgweg* 💳 *Combined ticket for Mainfränkisches and Fürstenbau museums €6* 🕓 *mid-March.–Oct., Tues.–Sun. 9–6* ⊠ *Oberer Burgweg* 🕓 *The museum is closed from November through mid-March.*

Juliusspital. Founded in 1576 by Prince-Bishop Julius Echter as a home for the poor, the elderly, and the sick, this enormous edifice now houses an impressive restaurant serving wine from the institution's own vineyards. It also sells wineglasses. All profits from the restaurant are used to run the adjacent home for the elderly. ■ TIP➔ Three glasses of wine are already included in the tours. ✉ *Juliuspromenade 19* ☎ *0931/3930* 🎫 *Tour €11* ⊙ *Fri. and Sat. at 5pm, Sun. at 10:30 am.*

Fodor'sChoice
★

Residenz (*Residence*). The line of Würzburg's prince-bishops lived in this glorious baroque palace after moving down from the hilltop Festung Marienberg. Construction started in 1719 under the brilliant direction of Balthasar Neumann. Most of the interior decoration was entrusted to the Italian stuccoist Antonio Bossi and the Venetian painter Giovanni Battista Tiepolo. It's the spirit of the pleasure-loving prince-bishop Johann Philipp Franz von Schönborn, however, that infuses the Residenz. Now considered one of Europe's most sumptuous palaces, this dazzling structure is a 10-minute walk from the railway station, along pedestrian-only Kaiserstrasse and then Theaterstrasse.

As you enter the building, the largest baroque staircase in the country, the **Treppenhaus,** greets you. Halfway up, the stairway splits and peels away 180 degrees to the left and to the right. Soaring above on the vaulting is Tiepolo's giant fresco *The Four Continents,* a gorgeous exercise in blue and pink, with allegorical figures at the corners representing the four continents known at the time (take a careful look at the elephant's trunk). Tiepolo immortalized himself and Balthasar Neumann as two of the figures—they're not too difficult to spot. ■ TIP➔ The fresco, which survived a devastating wartime bombing raid, is being restored bit by bit, so don't be surprised to find a small section covered by scaffolding.

Next, make your way to the **Weissersaal** (White Room) and then beyond to the grandest of the state rooms, the **Kaisersaal** (Throne Room). Tiepolo's frescoes show the 12th-century visit of Emperor Frederick Barbarossa, when he came to Würzburg to claim his bride. If you take part in the guided tour, you'll also see private chambers of the various former residents (guided tours in English are given daily at 11 and 3).

Finally, tour the **Hofgarten** (Court Gardens). The 18th-century formal garden has stately gushing fountains and trim ankle-high shrubs outlining geometric flower beds and gravel walks. ✉ *Residenzplatz 2* ☎ *0931/355–170* ⊕ *www.residenz-wuerzburg.de* 🎫 *€7.50, including guided tour* ⊙ *Apr.–Oct., daily 9–6; Nov.–Mar., daily 10–4:30.*

WORTH NOTING

Alte Universität (*Old University*). Founded by Prince-bishop Julius Echter and built in 1582, this rambling institution is one of Würzburg's most interesting Renaissance structures. ✉ *Sanderring 2.*

Alter Kranen (*Old Crane*). Near the Main River and north of the Old Main Bridge, the crane was erected in 1772–73 by Balthasar Neumann's son, Franz Ignaz Michael. It was used to unload boats; beside it is the old customs building.

Augustinerkirche (*Church of St. Augustine*). This baroque church, a work by Balthasar Neumann, was a 13th-century Dominican chapel. Neumann retained the soaring, graceful choir and commissioned Antonio

Bossi to add colorful stuccowork to the rest of the church. ⊠ *Domini-kanerpl. 2* ☎ *0931/30970* ⊘ *Daily 7–7.*

Bürgerspital (*Almshouse*). Wealthy burghers founded this refuge for the city's poor and needy in 1319. The buildings also house a winery, which produces highly respected wines and sales are used to support the refuge facility. The arcade courtyard is baroque in style. ■**TIP**→ **The winery offers tours of the facilities with wine tastings on select Fridays.** ⊠ *Theaterstr. 19* ☎ *0931/35030* ⊕ *www.buergerspital.de* ☜ *Tour €6.*

Haus zum Falken. The city's most splendid baroque mansion, formerly a humble inn, now houses the city tourist office. Its colorful rococo facade was added in 1751. ⊠ *Am Marktpl. 9* ☎ *0931/372–398* ⊘ *Jan.–Mar., weekdays 10–4, Sat. 10–2; Apr.–Dec., weekdays 10–6, Sat. 10–2; May–Oct., also Sun. and holidays 10–2.*

Marienkapelle (*St. Mary's Chapel*). This tranquil Gothic church (1377–1480) tucked modestly away at one end of Würzburg's market square is almost lost amid the historic old facades. Balthasar Neumann lies buried here. ⊠ *Marktpl.* ☎ *0931/3861–1150* ⊘ *Daily 9–6.*

Neumünster (*New Minster*). Next to the Dom St. Kilian, this 11th-century Romanesque basilica was completed in 1716. The original church was built above the grave of the early Irish martyr St. Kilian, who brought Christianity to Würzburg and, with two companions, was put to death here in 689. Their missionary zeal bore fruit, however—17 years after their death a church was consecrated in their memory. By 742 Würzburg had become a diocese, and over the following centuries 39 flourishing churches were established throughout the city. ⊠ *Domerpfarrg. 10* ☎ *0931/3866–2800* ⊘ *Mon.–Sat. 6–6:30, Sun. 8–6:30.*

Rathaus. The Gothic town hall, once headquarters of the bishop's administrator, has been the center of municipal government since 1316. A permanent exhibition in the tower documents Würzburg's destruction by Allied bombs, some examples of which are on display. ⊠ *Marktpl., Rückermainstr. 2* ☎ *0931/370* ☜ *Free* ⊘ *Weekdays 9–6, information only; tours May–Oct., Sat. at 11.*

Stift Haug. Franconia's first baroque church, designed by the Italian architect Antonio Petrini, was built between 1670 and 1691. Its elegant twin spires and central cupola make an impressive exterior. The altarpiece is a 1583 Crucifixion scene by Tintoretto. ⊠ *Bahnhofstr. at Heinestr.* ☎ *0931/54102* ⊘ *Daily 8–7.*

WHERE TO EAT

$ ✕ **Backöfele.** More than 400 years of tradition are sustained by this old
GERMAN tavern. Hidden away behind huge wooden doors on a backstreet, the
★ Backöfele's cavelike interior is a popular meeting and eating place for regulars and newcomers alike. The surprisingly varied menu includes local favorites such as suckling pig and marinated pot roast, as well as good fish entrées and classic desserts, all at reasonable prices. ⊠ *Ursulinerg. 2* ☎ *0931/59059* ⊕ *www.backoefele.de.*

$ ✕ **Juliusspital Weinstuben.** This tavern serves wine from its own vine-
GERMAN yard and good portions of basic Franconian fare. ■**TIP**→ **In summer you can enjoy your food and drinks on a quiet terrace in the courtyard.**

✉ *Juliuspromenade 19, Ecke Barbarossaplatz* ☎ *0931/54080* ⊕ *www.juliusspital.de.*

$ ✕ **Ratskeller.** The vaulted cellars of Würzburg's Rathaus shelter one
GERMAN of the city's most popular restaurants. Beer is served, but Franconian
wine is what the regulars drink. The food is staunch Franconian fare.
✉ *Beim Grafeneckart, Langg. 1* ☎ *0931/13021* ⊕ *www.wuerzburger-ratskeller.de.*

$$ ✕ **Wein- und Speisehaus zum Stachel.** On a warm spring or summer day,
GERMAN have a seat in the ancient courtyard of the Stachel, which is shaded by
★ a canopy of vine leaves and enclosed by tall, ivy-covered walls. The
entrées are satisfyingly Franconian, from lightly baked onion cake to
hearty roast pork. The specialty is fish, and—as the name suggests—
there are a variety of excellent wines to sample, mainly from the region.
The atmosphere is satisfyingly unstuffy. ✉ *Gresseng. 1* ☎ *0931/52770*
⊕ *www.weinhaus-stachel.de* ⊙ *Closed Sun. and Mon.*

WHERE TO STAY

For expanded hotel reviews, visit Fodors.com.

$$ ⊡ **Hotel Greifensteiner Hof.** The modern Greifensteiner offers comfort-
★ able, individually furnished rooms in a quiet corner of the city, just
off the market square. **Pros:** center of town; excellent restaurants; nice
bar packed with locals. **Cons:** no spectacular views or grand lobby.
✉ *Dettelbacherg. 2* ☎ *0931/35170* ⊕ *www.greifensteiner-hof.de* ⌖ *49
rooms* ⌂ *In-room: no a/c, Wi-Fi. In-hotel: restaurant, bar, parking,
some pets allowed.*

$$ ⊡ **Hotel Rebstock zu Würzburg.** This hotel's rococo facade has welcomed
guests for centuries. **Pros:** historical building with modern amenities
and quick access to all of the town's sights. **Cons:** popular hotel for
conferences and large groups. ✉ *Neubaustr. 7* ☎ *0931/30930* ⊕ *www.rebstock.com* ⌖ *63 rooms, 9 suites* ⌂ *In-room: no a/c, Wi-Fi. In-hotel:
restaurant, bar* ⍟ *Breakfast.*

$$ ⊡ **Hotel Walfisch.** Guest rooms are furnished in solid Franconian style
with farmhouse cupboards, bright fabrics, and heavy drapes. **Pros:** nice
view from front rooms; good restaurant. **Cons:** difficult parking; small
improvements needed. ✉ *Am Pleidenturm 5* ☎ *0931/35200* ⊕ *www.hotel-walfisch.com* ⌖ *40 rooms* ⌂ *In-room: no a/c, Wi-Fi. In-hotel:
restaurant, parking.*

$ ⊡ **Ringhotel Wittelsbacher Höh.** Most of the cozy rooms in this historic
redbrick mansion offer views of Würzburg and the vineyards. **Pros:**
nice view from rooms and terrace; good food. **Cons:** 3 km (2 mi)
from town; parking difficult. ✉ *Hexenbruchweg 10* ☎ *0931/453–040*
⊕ *www.wuerzburg-hotel.de* ⌖ *73 rooms, 1 suite* ⌂ *In-room: no a/c,
Wi-Fi. In-hotel: restaurant, parking, some pets allowed* ⍟ *Breakfast.*

$ ⊡ **Strauss.** Close to the river and the pedestrians-only center, the pink-
stucco Strauss has been in the same family for more than 100 years.
Pros: close to main station and Old Town; decent restaurant. **Cons:** small
lobby; some rooms need updating. ✉ *Juliuspromenade 5* ☎ *0931/30570*
⊕ *www.hotel-strauss.de* ⌖ *75 rooms, 3 suites* ⌂ *In-room: no a/c, Wi-Fi.
In-hotel: restaurant, parking, some pets allowed* ⊙ *Restaurant closed
Tues. and late Dec.–late Jan.*

4

FESTIVALS

Würzburg's cultural year starts with the International Film Weekend in January and ends with a Johann Sebastian Bach Festival in November. The annual jazz festival is also in November.

Hofkeller Würzburg. This cellar is one of the city's famous underground wine bars and the host of a series of wine festivals throughout the year. ⊠ *Residenzpl. 3* ☎ *0931/305–0923* ⊕ *www.hofkeller.de.*

Mainfranken Theater Würzburg. Founded in 1804, the Mainfranken Theater Würzburg puts on a variety of plays for adults, as well as for children. It also houses the city's orchestra. ⊠ *Theaterstr. 21* ☎ *0931/ 390–8124* ⊕ *www.theaterwuerzburg.de.*

Mozartfest. The city of Würzburg hosts the annual Mozart Festival or "Mozartfest" between May and July, attracting visitors from all over the world. Most concerts are held in the magnificent setting of the Residenz and feature world-class performers intepreting Mozart's works. ⊠ *Rückermainstr. 2* ☎ *0931/372–336* ⊕ *www.mozartfest.de.*

SPORTS AND THE OUTDOORS

Stein-Wein-Pfad. Wine lovers and hikers should visit the Stein-Wein-Pfad, a signposted trail through the vineyards that rises up from the northwest edge of Würzburg. A two-hour round-trip affords stunning views of the city as well as the chance to try the excellent local wines directly at the source. ■ TIP→ From May through mid-October, join the guided tour of the wineries every other Saturday for €7, which includes a glass of the local wine.

Weingut am Stein, Ludwig Knoll. The starting point for the Stein-Wein-Pfad walk is the vineyard of Weingut am Stein, Ludwig Knoll, 10 minutes on foot from the main railway station. ⊠ *Mittlerer Steinbergweg 5* ☎ *0931/25808* ⊕ *www.weingut-am-stein.de*

SHOPPING

Würzburg is the true wine center of the Romantic Road. Visit any of the vineyards that rise from the Main River and choose a *Bocksbeutel,* the distinctive green, flagon-shape wine bottle of Franconia. It's claimed that the shape came about because wine-guzzling monks found it the easiest to hide under their robes.

Die Murmel. This is the place to go if you enjoy browsing through large selections of unique and hand-picked toys to find the one that's right for you. ⊠ *Augustinerstr. 7* ☎ *0931/59349.*

Ebinger. Fine antique jewelry, clocks, watches, and silver are on sale here. ⊠ *Karmelitenstr. 23* ☎ *0931/59449.*

Eckhaus. In summer the selection consists mostly of garden and terrace decorations; from October through December the store is filled with delightful Christmas ornaments and candles. This is the place to go for high-quality gifts. ⊠ *Langg. 8, off Marktpl.* ☎ *0931/12001.*

Franconia and the German Danube

WORD OF MOUTH

"Bamberg is another very pleasant option and can be a base or a great day trip from Würzburg. Regensburg is a lovely small city within easy access by train. We like small to midsize cities so these work for us."

—kfusto

WELCOME TO FRANCONIA AND THE GERMAN DANUBE

TOP REASONS TO GO

★ **Bamberg's Altstadt:** This one isn't just for the tourists. Bamberg may be a UNESCO World Heritage Site, but it's also a vibrant town living very much in the present.

★ **Vierzehnheiligen:** Just north of Bamberg, this church's swirling rococo decoration earned it the nickname "God's Ballroom."

★ **Nürnberg's Kaiserburg:** Holy Roman emperors once resided in the vast complex of this imperial castle, which has fabulous views over the entire city.

★ **Steinerne Brücke in Regensburg:** This 12th-century Stone Bridge was considered an amazing feat of engineering in its time.

★ **An organ concert in Passau:** You can listen to the mighty sound the 17,774 pipes of Dom St. Stephan's organ create at weekday concerts.

1 Northern Franconia. As one of the few towns not destroyed by World War II, Bamberg lives and breathes German history. Wagner fans flock to Bayreuth in July and August for the classical music festival. The beer produced in Kulmbach is famous all over the country.

2 Nürnberg (Nuremberg). It may not be as well known as Munich, Heidelberg, or Berlin, but when you visit Nuremberg you feel the wealth, power, and sway this city has had through the centuries. Standing on the ramparts of the Kaiserburg (Imperial Castle) and looking down on the city, you'll begin to understand why emperors made Nuremberg their home.

3 The German Danube. Regensburg and Passau are two relatively forgotten cities tucked away in the southeast corner of Germany in an area bordered by Austria and the Czech Republic. Passau is one of the oldest cities on German soil, built by the Celts and then ruled by the Romans 2,000 years ago. Regensburg is a bit younger; about a thousand years ago it was one of the largest and most affluent cities in Germany.

GETTING ORIENTED

Franconia's northern border is marked by the Main River, which is seen as the dividing line between northern and southern Germany. Its southern border is the Danube, where Lower Bavaria (Niederbayern) begins. Despite its size, Franconia is a homogeneous region of rolling agricultural landscapes and thick forests climbing the mountains of the Fichtelgebirge. Nürnberg is a major destination in the area, and the towns of Bayreuth, Coburg, and Bamberg are an easy day trip from one another. The Danube River defines the region as it passes through the Bavarian Forest on its way from Germany to Austria. West of Regensburg, river cruises and cyclists follow its path.

5

CZECH REPUBLIC

Roding · Janahof

Patersdorf

B22

B8

Aiterhofen
Rottenmann

Pilsting

A92

B20

Deggendorf

B85

A3

B8

Preying

Danube

Passau

AUSTRIA

CRUISING THE DANUBE

Rising from the depths of the Black Forest and emptying into the Black Sea, the Danube is the queen of rivers; cloaked in myth and legend, it cuts through the heart of Europe.

(above and lower right) Cruise ship passengers relaxing on the Danube. (upper right) Enjoy views of Passau from various river cruises.

The name Dānuvius, borrowed from the Celts, means swift or rapid, but along the Danube, there is no hurry. Boats go with the flow and a river journey is a relaxed affair with plenty of time to drink in the history.

Whether you choose a one-hour, one-week, or the complete Danube experience, cruising Europe's historical waterway is a never-to-be-forgotten experience. Of the Danube's 1,770-mi length, almost 1,500 mi is navigable and the river flows through some of Europe's most important cities. You can head to major boating hubs, like Passau, Vienna, and Budapest or through historical stretches from Ulm to Regensburg. The Main-Donau Canal connects Nürnberg.

—Lee A. Evans

WHEN TO GO

Between May and July the Danube is busy with passenger and commercial traffic; this is the best time of year for a cruise. Fall is also good, when the changing leaves bathe the river in a sea of color. The Danube rarely freezes in the winter and several companies offer Christmas market tours from Nuremberg to Regensburg, Passau, and Vienna. Spring is the least optimal time to go.

A DAY ON THE DANUBE

On the map, the sheer length of the Danube is daunting at best. A great option is to choose an idyllic daylong excursion.

One of the best day cruises leaves from **Regensburg** and reaches the imposing temple **Walhalla**, a copy of the Parthenon erected by Ludwig I. **Personenschifffahrt Klinger** boats depart from the Steinerne Brücke daily at 10:30 and 2. Each departure gives you about an hour to explore the temple and the whole trip lasts three hours.

Donauschiffahrt Wurm + Köck offers a variety of Danube day trips. Their most popular is a daily excursion from **Passau** to the Austrian city of **Linz**, which departs at 9 am. If you don't have all day, they also offer a three-river tour that explores Passau at the convergence of the Ilz, Inn, and Danube that lasts about 45 minutes.

CRUISING ALL OF THE DANUBE

Although Passau is the natural gateway to the cruising destinations of Eastern Europe on the Danube, it is by no means the only starting point. You can board a deluxe river cruise ship in Nürnberg, landlocked but for the very small Pegnitz River, then cruise "overland" through Franconia on the Main-Danube canal across the Continental Divide until you join the Danube at Kelheim, a few

miles west of Regensburg. After Passau you enter Austria, where you come to the city that most people automatically associate with the Blue Danube, **Vienna**. The next border crossing brings you into Slovakia and to your second capital, **Bratislava. Budapest**, Hungary is next, and capital number four is **Belgrade**, Serbia. Some of the Danube cruises begin in Amsterdam, making them five-capital cruises.

Amadeus Waterways (☎ 800/626–0126 ⊕ *www.amadeuswaterways.com*) offers half a dozen cruises through Franconia and the German Danube, including a Christmastime cruise, which stops at the fascinating Christmas markets between Nürnberg and Budapest. The reverse direction is also available.

Viking River Cruises (☎ 800/304–9616 ⊕ *www.vikingrivercruises.com*) has a Grand European Tour from Amsterdam to Budapest. The two-week Eastern European Odyssey starts in Nürnberg and ends at Bucharest. The reverse direction is also available on both cruises.

The British **Blue Water Holidays** (☎ 01756/706–500 ⊕ *www.cruisingholidays.co.uk*) has nine cruises starting on the Rhine, some from Basel in Switzerland, which follow the Main-Danube Canal to the Danube and four cruises from Nürnberg or Passau to Vienna or Budapest.

5

GERMANY'S CHRISTMAS MARKETS

Few places in the world do Christmas as well as Germany, and the country's Christmas markets, sparkling with white fairy lights and rich with the smells of gingerbread and mulled wine, are marvelous expressions of yuletide cheer.

(above and lower right) You can purchase handmade ornaments at the atmospheric Nuremberg Christkindlesmarkt. (upper right) The Spandau Christmas market is one of 60 in Berlin.

Following a centuries-old tradition, more than 2,000 *Weihnachtsmärkte* spring up outside town halls and in village squares across the country each year, their stalls brimming with ornate tree decorations and handmade pralines. Elegant rather than kitsch, the markets last the duration of Advent—the four weeks leading up to Christmas Eve—and draw festive crowds to their bustling lanes, where charcoal grills sizzle with sausages and cinnamon and spices waft from warm ovens. Among the handcrafted angels and fairies, kids munch on candy apples and ride old-fashioned carousels while their parents shop for stocking stuffers and toast the season with steaming mugs of *Glühwein* and hot chocolate.

—Jeff Kavanagh

GLÜHWEIN

Glühwein, or mulled wine, literally translated, means "glowing wine" and a few cups of it will definitely add some color to your cheeks. Made with red wine, it can be fortified with a "schuss" or shot of schnapps, often rum or amaretto. *Feuerzangen-bowle*, a supercharged version, is made by dripping burning, rum-soaked sugar into the wine. The nonalcoholic version is known as *Kinderpunsch*, or children's punch.

BEST CHRISTMAS MARKETS

Perhaps the most famous Christmas Market in Germany, the **Nuremberg Christkindlesmarkt** (✉ *Hauptmarkt, Nuremberg* ⊘ *Nov. 25–Dec. 24, Mon.–Thurs. 9:30–8, Fri. and Sat. 9:30–10, Sun. 10:30–8, Christmas Eve 9:30–2* ⊕ *www.christkindlesmarkt.de*) sits on the town's cobble-stoned main square beneath the wonderful Frauenkirche. Renowned for its food, particularly *Nürnberger Bratwurstchen*, tasty little pork and marjoram sausages, and *Lebkuchen*, gingerbread made with cinnamon and honey, the market is also famed for its little figures made out of prunes called *Nürnberger Zwetschgenmännla* or "Nuremberg Plum People."

Dresden's Striezelmarkt (✉ *Altmarkt, Dresden* ⊘ *Nov. 24–Dec. 24, daily 10–9, Christmas Eve 10–2* ⊕ *www.dresden-striezelmarkt.de*) dates back to 1434. Named after the city's famous Stollen, a buttery Christmas fruitcake often made with marzipan and sprinkled with powdered sugar, the market hosts a festival in its honor on the Saturday of the second weekend of Advent, complete with an enormous, 9,000-pound cake. Traditional wooden toys produced in the nearby Erzgebirge mountains are the other major draw.

Of **Cologne's** four main Christmas markets the **Weihnachtsmarkt am Kölner Dom** (✉ *Roncalliplatz, Cologne* ⊘ *Nov.*

21–Dec. 23, Sun.–Thurs. 11–9 ⊕ *www.koelnerweihnachtsmarkt.com*), in the shadow of the city's UNESCO-listed cathedral, is the most impressive. Set against the backdrop of the church's magnificent twin spires, a giant Christmas tree stands proudly in the middle of the market's 160 festively adorned stalls, which offer mulled wine, roasted chestnuts, and many other German yuletide treats.

Hamburg's Historischer Weihnachtsmarkt (✉ *Rathausmarkt 1, Hamburg* ⊘ *Nov. 21–Dec. 23, Sun.–Thurs. 10–9, Fri. and Sat. 10–10* ⊕ *www.hamburger-weihnachtsmarkt.com*) enjoys a spectacular backdrop—the city's Gothic town hall. The market's stalls are filled with rows of candy apples, chocolates, and doughnuts. Woodcarvers from Tyrol, bakers from Aachen, and gingerbread makers from Nuremburg come to ply their wares. Designed by the circus company Roncalli, every evening at 4, 6, and 8, Santa Claus ho-ho-hos his way along a tight-wire high above the market.

The most popular of **Berlin's** 60 Weihnachtsmärkte is in front of the **Kaiser Wilhelm Gedächtniskirche** (✉ *Breitscheidplatz, Berlin* ⊘ *Nov. 22–Jan. 1, Sun.–Thurs. 11–9, Fri. and Sat. 11–10*), which was only partially rebuilt after World War II. The capital's modernity is reflected in the funky knickknacks and artwork on offer in the stalls.

Updated by
Lee A. Evans

All that is left of the huge, ancient kingdom of the Franks is the region known today as Franken (Franconia), stretching from the Bohemian Forest on the Czech border to the outskirts of Frankfurt. The Franks were not only tough warriors but also hard workers, sharp tradespeople, and burghers with a good political nose. The name *frank* means bold, wild, and courageous in the old Frankish tongue. It was only in the early 19th century, following Napoléon's conquest of what is now southern Germany, that the area was incorporated into northern Bavaria.

Although more closely related to Thuringia, this historic homeland of the Franks, one of the oldest Germanic peoples, is now begrudgingly part of Bavaria. Franconian towns such as Bayreuth, Coburg, and Bamberg are practically places of cultural pilgrimage. Rebuilt Nürnberg (Nuremberg in English) is the epitome of German medieval beauty, though its name recalls both the Third Reich's huge rallies at the Zeppelin Field and its henchmen's trials held in the city between 1945 and 1950.

Franconia is hardly an overrun tourist destination, yet its long and rich history, its landscapes and leisure activities (including skiing, golfing, hiking, and cycling), and its gastronomic specialties place it high on the enjoyment scale.

PLANNING

WHEN TO GO

Summer is the best time to explore Franconia, though spring and fall are also fine when the weather cooperates. Avoid the cold and wet months from November to March; many hotels and restaurants close, and no matter how pretty, many towns do seem quite dreary. If you're in Nürnberg in December, you're in time for one of Germany's largest and loveliest Christmas markets. Unless you plan on attending the Wagner Festival in Bayreuth, it's best to avoid this city in July and August.

GETTING HERE AND AROUND

AIR TRAVEL The major international airport serving Franconia and the German Danube is Munich. Nürnberg's airport is served mainly by regional carriers.

Airport Information Airport Nürnberg ⌧ *Flughafenstr. 100* ☎ *0911/93700* ⊕ *www.airport-nuernberg.de.*

CAR TRAVEL Franconia is served by five main autobahns: A-7 from Hamburg, A-3 from Köln and Frankfurt, A-81 from Stuttgart, A-6 from Heilbronn, and A-9 from Munich. Nürnberg is 167 km (104 mi) north of Munich and 222 km (138 mi) southeast of Frankfurt. Regensburg and Passau are reached by way of the A-3 from Nürnberg.

Franconia boasts one of southern Germany's most extensive train networks and almost every town is connected by train. Nürnberg is a stop on the high-speed InterCity Express north–south routes, and there are hourly trains from Munich direct to Nürnberg. Regular InterCity services connect Nürnberg and Regensburg with Frankfurt and other major German cities. Trains run hourly from Frankfurt to Munich, with a stop at Nürnberg. The trip takes about three hours to Munich, two hours to Nürnberg. There are hourly trains from Munich to Regensburg.

Some InterCityExpress trains stop in Bamberg, which is most speedily reached from Munich. Local trains from Nürnberg connect with Bayreuth and areas of southern Franconia. Regensburg and Passau are on the ICE line from Nürnberg to Vienna.

RESTAURANTS

Many restaurants in the rural parts of this region serve hot meals only between 11:30 am and 2 pm, and 6 pm and 9 pm. ■TIP→ "Durchgehend warme Küche" means that hot meals are also served between lunch and dinner.

HOTELS

Make reservations well in advance for hotels in all the larger towns and cities if you plan to visit anytime between June and September. During the Nürnberg Toy Fair at the beginning of February, rooms are at a premium. If you're visiting Bayreuth during the annual Wagner Festival in July and August, consider making reservations up to a year in advance. Remember, too, that during the festival prices can be double the normal rates.

WHAT IT COSTS IN EUROS				
¢	$	$$	$$$	$$$$
Restaurants	under €9	€9–€15	€16–€20	€21–€25	over €25
Hotels	under €50	€50–€100	€101–€175	€176–€225	over €225

Restaurant prices are per person for a main course at dinner. Hotel prices are for two people in a standard double room, including tax and service.

PLANNING YOUR TIME

Nürnberg warrants at least a day of your time. It's best to base yourself in one city and take day trips to others. Bamberg is the most central of the northern Franconia cities and makes a good base. It is also a good idea to leave your car at your hotel and make the trip downstream to Regensburg or Passau by boat, returning by train.

VISITOR INFORMATION

Franconia Tourist Board. ⊠ *Tourismusverband Franken e.V., Wilhelminenstr. 6, Nürnberg* ☎ *0911/941–510* ⊕ *www.frankentourismus.de.*

NORTHERN FRANCONIA

Three major German cultural centers lie within easy reach of one another: Coburg, a town with blood links to royal dynasties throughout Europe; Bamberg, with its own claim to German royal history and an Old Town area designated a UNESCO World Heritage Site; and Bayreuth, where composer Richard Wagner finally settled, making it a place of musical pilgrimage for Wagner fans from all over the world.

COBURG

105 km (65 mi) north of Nürnberg.

Coburg is a surprisingly little-known treasure that was founded in the 11th century and remained in the possession of the dukes of Saxe-Coburg-Gotha until 1918; the current duke still lives here. The remarkable Saxe-Coburg dynasty established itself as something of a royal stud farm, providing a seemingly inexhaustible supply of blue-blood marriage partners to ruling houses the length and breadth of Europe. The most famous of these royal mates was Prince Albert (1819–61), who married the English Queen Victoria, after which she gained special renown in Coburg. Their numerous children, married off to other kings, queens, and emperors, helped to spread the tried-and-tested Saxe-Coburg influence even farther afield. Despite all the history that sweats from each sandstone ashlar, Coburg is a modern and bustling town.

ESSENTIALS

Visitor Information Coburg ⊠ *Tourismus Coburg, Herrng. 4* ☎ *09561/898–000* ⊕ *www.coburg-tourist.de.*

EXPLORING

Marktplatz (*Market Square*). Coburg's Marktplatz has a statue of Prince Albert, Victoria's high-minded consort, standing proudly surrounded by gracious Renaissance and baroque buildings. The **Stadhaus,** former seat of the local dukes, begun in 1500, is the most imposing structure here. A forest of ornate gables and spires projects from its well-proportioned facade. Opposite is the **Rathaus** (Town Hall). ■ TIP➜ Look on the building's tympanum for the statue of the Bratwurstmännla (it's actually St. Mauritius in armor); the staff he carries is said to be the official length against which the town's famous bratwursts are measured. These tasty sausages, roasted on pinecone fires, are available on the market square.

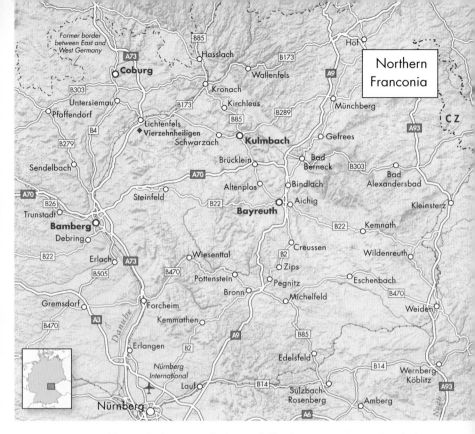

Former border
between East and
West Germany

Coburg

Hasslach

B85

Wallenfels

B173

Hof

Northern Franconia

Kronach

Untersiemau

B303

Pfaffendorf

Kirchleus

B173

B85

B289

Münchberg

A9

A93

C Z

B4

Lichtenfels
♦ Vierzehnheiligen

Schwarzach

Kulmbach

Gefrees

B279

Sendelbach

Brücklein

Bad
Berneck

B303

Bad
Alexandersbad

Kleinsterz

A70

Altenplos

Bindlach

A70

B26

Trunstadt

Steinfeld

B22

Bayreuth

Aichig

Kemnath

B22

Bamberg

Debring

B22

Erlach

A73

B505

B470

Wiesenttal

Pottenstein

Bronn

Creussen

B2

Zips

Pegnitz

Michelfeld

Wildenreuth

Eschenbach

B470

Weiden

Gremsdorf

B470

A3

Forcheim

Kemmathen

Danube

Erlangen

B2

Nürnberg
International

Lauf

A9

B85

Edelsfeld

B14

Sulzbach
Rosenberg

Amberg

Wernberg
Köblitz

A93

Nürnberg

A6

Schloss Callenberg. Perched on a hill 5 km (3 mi) west of Coburg is Schloss Callenberg, until 1231 the main castle of the Knights of Callenberg. In the 16th century it was taken over by the Coburgs. From 1842 on it served as the summer residence of the hereditary Coburg prince and later Duke Ernst II. It holds a number of important collections, including that of the Windsor gallery; arts and crafts from Holland, Germany, and Italy from the Renaissance to the 19th century; precious baroque, Empire, and Biedermeier furniture; table and standing clocks from three centuries; a selection of weapons; and various handicrafts. The best way to reach the castle is by car via Baiersdorf. City Bus 5 from Coburg's Marktplatz stops at the castle only on Sunday; on other days you need to get off at the Beirsdorf stop and walk 25 minutes. ⊠ *Callenberg 1* ☎ *09561/55150* ⊕ *www.schloss-callenberg.de* ☑ *€5* ☉ *Daily 11–5.*

Schloss Ehrenburg. Prince Albert spent much of his childhood in Schloss Ehrenburg, the ducal palace. Built in the mid-16th century, it has been greatly altered over the years, principally following a fire in the early 19th century. Duke Ernst I invited Karl Friedrich Schinkel from Berlin to redo the palace in the then-popular neo-Gothic style. Some of the original Renaissance features were kept. The rooms of the castle are quite special, especially those upstairs, where the ceilings are heavily decorated with stucco and the floors have wonderful patterns of various woods. The Hall of Giants is named for the larger-than-life caryatids that support the ceiling; the favorite sight downstairs is Queen Victoria's flush toilet, which was the first one installed in Germany. Here, too, the ceiling is worth noting for its playful, gentle stuccowork. The baroque chapel attached to Ehrenburg is often used for weddings. ⊠ *Schlosspl. 1* ☎ *09561/80880* ⊕ *www.sgvcoburg.de* ⌑ *€4.50* ☉ *Tour Tues.–Sun. 10–3 on the hr.*

QUICK BITES

Burgschänke. Relax and soak up centuries of history while sampling a Coburg beer at this tavern. The basic menu has traditional dishes. ⊠ Veste Coburg ☎ 09561/80980 ☉ Closed Mon. and Jan.–mid-Feb.

Veste Coburg. This fortress, one of the largest and most impressive in the country, is Coburg's main attraction. The brooding bulk of the castle guards the town from a 1,484-foot hill. Construction began around 1055, but with progressive rebuilding and remodeling today's predominantly late-Gothic–early-Renaissance edifice bears little resemblance to the original crude fortress. One part of the castle harbors the **Kunstsammlungen,** a grand set of collections including art, with works by Dürer, Cranach, and Hans Holbein, among others; sculpture from the school of the great Tilman Riemenschneider (1460–1531); furniture and textiles; magnificent weapons, armor, and tournament garb spanning four centuries (in the so-called **Herzoginbau,** or Duchess's Building); carriages and ornate sleighs; and more. The room where Martin Luther lived for six months in 1530 while he observed the goings-on of the Augsburg Diet has an especially dignified atmosphere. The **Jagdintarsien-Zimmer** (Hunting Marquetry Room), an elaborately decorated room that dates back to the early 17th century, has some of the finest woodwork in southern Germany. Finally, there's the **Carl-Eduard-Bau** (Carl-Eduard Building), which contains a valuable antique glass collection, mostly from the baroque age. Inquire at the ticket office for tours and reduced family tickets. ☎ *09561/8790* ⊕ *www.kunstsammlungen-coburg.de* ⌑ *€5, combination ticket with with Schloss Ehrenburg €10* ☉ *Museums Apr.–Oct., daily 10–5; Nov.– Mar., Tues.–Sun. 1–4.*

WHERE TO EAT AND STAY

For expanded hotel reviews, visit Fodors.com.

$ ✕ **Ratskeller.** The basic local specialties taste better here beneath the old
GERMAN vaults and within earshot of the Coburg marketplace. Try the *Tafelspitz* (boiled beef with creamed horseradish), along with a glass of crisp Franconian white wine. The prices become a little higher in the evening, when the menu adds a few more dishes. ⊠ *Markt 1* ☎ *09561/92400* ⊕ *www.ratskeller-coburg.de* ⊟ *No credit cards.*

¢ ▥ **Goldene Rose.** One of the region's oldest, this agreeable inn is located about 5 km (3 mi) southeast of Coburg. **Pros:** friendly; family run; very good value; large parking lot behind the hotel. **Cons:** in a small village; front rooms noisy. ⊠ *Coburgerstr. 31, Grub am Forst* ☎ *09560/92250* ⊕ *www.goldene-rose.de* ⇱ *14 rooms* ⌕ *In-room: no a/c. In-hotel: restaurant, parking* ☉ *Restaurant closed Mon.* ⎮⊙⎮ *Breakfast.*

$ 🛏 **Romantic Hotel Goldene Traube.** Rooms are individually decorated in this fine historical hotel (1756), and for dining you can choose between the elegant restaurant Esszimmer or the more casual Meer und Mehr (Sea and More), which serves fine seafood and regional specialties. **Pros:** welcoming spacious lobby; two good restaurants; center of town; nice small wineshop. **Cons:** traffic noise in front rooms; stairs up to the lobby. ⊠ *Am Viktoriabrunnen 2* 🕾 *09561/8760* ⊕ *www.goldenetraube. com* ᔐ *72 rooms, 1 suite* ⌗ *In-room: no a/c. In-hotel: restaurant, bar, gym, parking, some pets allowed* ❢⊘❙ *Breakfast.*

FESTIVALS

Coburg's **Brazilian Samba Festival** is a three-day bacchanal held in mid-July. Check the Coburg tourist office's Web site for this and other events.

SHOPPING

■TIP➔ Coburg is full of culinary delights; its Schmätzen (gingerbread) and Elizenkuchen (almond cake) are famous. You'll find home-baked versions in any of the many excellent **patisseries** or at a Grossman store (there are three in Coburg).

Hummel Museum. Rödental, northeast of Coburg, is the home of the world-famous M. I. Hummel figurines, made by the Göbel porcelain manufacturer. There's a Hummel Museum devoted to them, and 18th- and 19th-century porcelain from other manufacturers. The museum is open weekdays 9–5 and Saturday 9–noon. Besides the museum's store, there are several retail outlets in the village. ⊠ *Coburgerstr. 7, Rödental* 🕾 *09563/92303* ⊕ *www.goebel.de.*

KULMBACH

19 km (12 mi) southeast of Kronach.

A quarter of Kulmbachers earn their living directly or indirectly from beer. Kulmbach celebrates its brewing traditions every year in a nine-day festival that starts on the last Saturday in July. The main festival site, a mammoth tent, is called the *Festspulhaus*—literally, "festival swill house"—a none-too-subtle dig at nearby Bayreuth and its tony Festspielhaus, where Wagner's operas are performed. If you're here in winter, be sure to try the seasonal *Eisbock*, a special dark beer that is frozen as part of the brewing process; making it stronger.

ESSENTIALS

Visitor Information Kulmbach ⊠ *Tourismusservice, Stadthalle, Sutte 2* 🕾 *09221/958–820* ⊕ *www.kulmbach.de.*

EXPLORING

Kulmbacher Brewery. This brewery, which merged four Kulmbach breweries into one, produces, among others, the *Doppelbock Kulminator 28*, which takes nine months to brew and has an alcohol content of 12%.

Bayerisches Brauereimuseum Kulmbach (*Bavarian Brewery Museum*). The Kulmbacher Brewery runs this musuem jointly with the nearby Mönchshof-Bräu brewery and inn. ■TIP➔ The price of admission includes a "taste" from the museum's own brewer. ⊠ *Hoferstr. 20* 🕾 *09221/80514* ⊕ *www.bayerisches-brauereimuseum.de* ᔐ *€4.50* ⊘ *Tues.–Sun. 10–5*

⊠ *Lichtenfelserstr. 9* ☎ *09221/7050*
⊕ *www.kulmbacher.de.*

↻ **Neuenmarkt.** In this "railway village" near Kulmbach, more than
25 beautifully preserved gleam-
ing locomotives huff and puff in
a living railroad museum. Every
now and then a nostalgic train will
take you to the Brewery Museum
in Kulmbach, or you can enjoy a
round-trip to Marktschorgast; both
trips take you up the very steep
"schiefe Ebene" stretch (literally,

> ### KULMBACH BREWS
>
> In a country where brewing and
> beer drinking break all records,
> Kulmbach produces more beer
> per capita than anywhere else:
> 9,000 pints for each man, woman,
> and child. The locals claim it's the
> sparkling-clear spring water from
> the nearby Fichtelgebirge hills
> that makes their beer so special.

slanting level). The museum also has model trains set up in incredibly
detailed replicas of landscapes. ⊠ *Birkenstr. 5* ☎ *09227/5700* ⊕ *www.
dampflokmuseum.de* 🎫 *€5* ☉ *Tues.–Sun. 10–5.*

↻ **Plassenburg.** The most important Renaissance castle in the country, it
stands on a rise overlooking Kulmbach, a 20-minute hike from the
Old Town. The first building here, begun in the mid-12th century, was
torched by marauding Bavarians who were eager to put a stop to the
ambitions of Duke Albrecht Alcibiades—a man who spent several years
murdering, plundering, and pillaging his way through Franconia. His
successors built today's castle, starting in about 1560. Externally, there's
little to suggest the graceful Renaissance interior, but as you enter the
main courtyard the scene changes abruptly. The tiered space of the
courtyard is covered with precisely carved figures, medallions, and other
intricate ornaments, the whole comprising one of the most remarkable
and delicate architectural ensembles in Europe. Inside, the **Deutsches
Zinnfigurenmuseum** (Tin Figures Museum), with more than 300,000
miniature statuettes and tin soldiers, holds the largest collection of its
kind in the world. The figures are arranged in scenes from all periods
of history. During the day you cannot drive up to the castle. There's a
shuttle bus that leaves from the main square every half hour from 9 to
6; cost is €2.20. ☎ *09221/947–505* 🎫 *€4.50* ☉ *Apr.–Oct., daily 9–6;
Nov.–Mar., daily 10–4.*

WHERE TO STAY
For expanded hotel reviews, visit Fodors.com.

$ ⬚ **Hotel Kronprinz.** This old hotel tucked away in the middle of Kulm-
bach's Old Town, right in the shadow of Plassenburg Castle, covers all
basic needs, with the help of an extraordinary breakfast buffet. **Pros:**
center of town; excellent cakes in café; 3 nice rooms in annex. **Cons:**
plain rooms above café; no elevator. ⊠ *Fischerg. 4–6* ☎ *09221/92180*
⊕ *www.kronprinz-kulmbach.de* ⟅ *22 rooms* ⬧ *In-room: no a/c. In-
hotel: restaurant, bar* ☉ *Closed Dec. 24–29* � *Breakfast.*

The torch-bearing figure of Apollo on his chariot adorns the Sonnentempel (Sun Temple) of Bayreuth's Neues Schloss.

BAYREUTH

24 km (15 mi) south of Kulmbach, 80 km (50 mi) northeast of Nürnberg.

The small town of Bayreuth, pronounced "bye-*roit*," owes its fame to the music giant Richard Wagner (1813–83). The 19th-century composer, musical revolutionary, and Nazi poster-child finally settled here after a lifetime of rootless shifting through Europe. Here he built his great theater, the Festspielhaus, as a suitable setting for his grand operas on Germanic mythological themes. The annual Wagner Festival dates to 1876, and brings droves of Wagner fans who push prices sky-high, fill hotels to bursting, and earn themselves much-sought-after social kudos in the process. The festival is held from late July until late August, so unless you plan to visit the town specifically for it, this is the time to stay away.

GETTING HERE AND AROUND

To reach Bayreuth, take the Bayreuth exit off the Nürnberg–Berlin autobahn. It's 1½ hours north of Nürnberg. The train trip is an hour from Nürnberg. In town you can reach most points on foot.

ESSENTIALS

Visitor Information Bayreuth ⊠ *Kongress- und Tourismuszentrale, Luitpoldpl. 9* ☎ *0921/88588* ⊕ *www.bayreuth.de.*

EXPLORING

Altes Schloss Eremitage. This palace, 5 km (3 mi) north of Bayreuth on B–85, makes an appealing departure from the sonorous and austere Wagnerian mood of much of the town. It's an early-18th-century palace, built as a summer retreat and remodeled in 1740 by the Margravine

Wilhelmine. Although her taste is not much in evidence in the drab exterior, the interior, alive with light and color, displays her guiding hand in every elegant line. The extraordinary **Japanischer Saal** (Japanese Room), filled with Asian treasures and chinoiserie furniture, is the finest room. The park and gardens, partly formal, partly natural, are enjoyable for idle strolling. Fountain displays take place at the two fake grottoes at the top of the hour 10–5 daily. ☎ *0921/759–6937* ✉ *Schloss €4.50, park free* ☉ *Schloss Apr.–Sept., daily 9–6.*

Brauerei und Büttnerei-Museum (*Brewery and Coopers Museum*). Near the center of town, in the 1887 Maisel Brewery building, this museum reveals the tradition of the brewing trade over the past two centuries with a focus on the Maisel's trade, of course. The brewery operated here until 1981, when its much bigger home was completed next door. ■ TIP➔ After the 90-minute tour you can quaff a cool, freshly tapped traditional Bavarian Weissbier (wheat beer) in the museum's pub. The pub is also one of a handful of places to try Maisel's Dampfbier; a delicious steam-brewed ale. ✉ *Kulmbacherstr. 40* ☎ *0921/401–234* ⊕ *www.maisel.com* ✉ *€4* ☉ *Tour daily at 2 pm; individual tours by prior arrangement.*

Markgräfliches Opernhaus (*Margravial Opera House*). In 1745 Margravine Wilhelmine commissioned the Italian architects Guiseppe and Carlo Bibiena to build this rococo jewel, sumptuously decorated in red, gold, and blue. Apollo and the nine Muses cavort across the frescoed ceiling. It was this delicate 500-seat theater that originally drew Wagner to Bayreuth; he felt that it might prove a suitable setting for his own operas. It's a wonderful setting for the concerts and operas of Bayreuth's "other" musical festivals, which go on virtually throughout the year. ✉ *Opernstr.* ☎ *0921/759–6922* ✉ *€5* ☉ *Apr.–Sept., daily 9–6; Oct.–Mar., daily 10–4. Closed during performances and on rehearsal days.*

★ **Neues Schloss** (*New Palace*). This glamorous 18th-century palace was built by the Margravine Wilhelmine, sister of Frederick the Great of Prussia and a woman of enormous energy and decided tastes. Though Wagner is the man most closely associated with Bayreuth, his choice of this setting is largely due to the work of this woman, who lived 100 years before him. Wilhelmine devoured books, wrote plays and operas (which she directed and, of course, acted in), and had buildings constructed, transforming much of the town and bringing it near bankruptcy. Her distinctive touch is evident at the palace, built when a mysterious fire conveniently destroyed parts of the original one. Anyone with a taste for the wilder flights of rococo decoration will love it. Some rooms have been given over to one of Europe's finest collections of faience. ✉ *Ludwigstr. 21* ☎ *0921/759–6921* ✉ *€5.50* ☉ *Apr.–Sept., daily 9–6; Oct.–Mar., Tues.–Sun. 10–4.*

WAGNER IN BAYREUTH

Festspielhaus (*Festival Theater*). This high temple of the Wagner cult—where performances take place only during the annual Wagner Festival—is surprisingly plain. The spartan look is explained partly by Wagner's desire to achieve perfect acoustics. The wood seats have no upholstering, for example, and the walls are bare. The stage is enormous, capable of holding the huge casts required for Wagner's largest operas. The festival is still meticulously controlled by descendants of the composer. ⊠ *Festspielhügel 1* ☏ *0921/78780* 🗗 *€5* ⊙ *Tours Dec.–Oct., Tues.–Sun. at 10, 2, and 3. Closed during rehearsals and on performance days during festival.*

Richard-Wagner-Museum. "Wahnfried," built by Wagner in 1874 and the only house he ever owned, is now the Richard-Wagner-Museum. It's a simple, austere neoclassical building whose name, "peace from madness," was well earned. Wagner lived here with his wife Cosima, daughter of pianist Franz Liszt, and they were both laid to rest here. King Ludwig II of Bavaria, the young and impressionable "Fairy-Tale King" who gave Wagner so much financial support, is remembered in a bust before the entrance. The exhibits, arranged along a well-marked tour through the house, require a great deal of German-language reading, but it's a must for Wagner fans. The original scores of such masterpieces as *Parsifal, Tristan und Isolde, Lohengrin, Der Fliegende Holländer,* and *Götterdämmerung* are on display. You can also see designs for productions of his operas, as well as his piano and huge library. A multimedia display lets you watch and listen to various productions of his operas. The little house where Franz Liszt lived and died is right next door and can be visited with your Richard-Wagner-Museum ticket, but be sure to express your interest in advance. It, too, is heavy on the paper, but the last rooms—with pictures, photos, and silhouettes of the master, his students, acolytes, and friends—are well worth the detour. ■ TIP➜ **The museum will be closed until 2013, but true loyalists will still want to come to see the outside of the house.** ⊠ *Richard-Wagner-Str. 48* ☏ *0921/757–2816* ⊕ *www.wagnermuseum.de* ⊙ *Closed until 2013.*

WHERE TO EAT

$ ✕ **Oskar.** A huge glass ceiling gives the large dining room a light atmo-
GERMAN   sphere even in winter. In summer, try for a table in the beer garden to
★   enjoy fine Franconian specialties and Continental dishes. The kitchen uses the freshest produce. The room fills up at night and during Sunday brunch, especially if a jazz band is playing in one of the alcoves. ⊠ *Maximilianstr. 33* ☏ *0921/516–0553* ⊕ *www.oskar-bayreuth.de* 🖃 *No credit cards.*

$ ✕ **Wolffenzacher.** This self-described "Franconian nostalgic inn" harks
GERMAN   back to the days when the local *Wirtshaus* (inn-pub) was the meeting place for everyone from the mayor's scribes to the local carpenters. Beer and hearty food are shared at wooden tables either in the rustic interior or out in the shady beer garden (in the middle of town), weather permitting. The hearty Franconian specialties are counterbalanced by a few lighter Mediterranean dishes. ⊠ *Sternenpl. 5* ☏ *0921/64552.*

WHERE TO STAY
For expanded hotel reviews, visit Fodors.com.

$$ 🛏 **Goldener Anker.** No question about it, this is *the* place to stay in
Fodor's Choice   Bayreuth; the hotel is right next to the Markgräfliches Opernhaus and
★   has been entertaining composers, singers, conductors, and instrumentalists for hundreds of years. **Pros:** authentic historic setting with all modern amenities; exemplary service; excellent restaurant. **Cons:** no elevator; some rooms are on the small side; restaurant closed Monday

5

EATING WELL IN FRANCONIA

Franconia is known for its good and filling food and for its simple and atmospheric *Gasthäuser*. Pork is a staple, served either as *Schweinsbraten* (a plain roast) or with *Knödel* (dumplings made from either bread or potatoes). The specialties in Nürnberg, Coburg, and Regensburg are the Bratwürste—short, spiced sausages. The Nürnberg variety is known all over Germany; they are even on the menu on the ICE trains. You can have them grilled or heated in a stock of onions and wine (*saurer Zipfel*). Bratwürste are traditionally served in denominations of 3, 6, or 8 with sauerkraut and potato salad or dark bread.

On the sweet side, try the *Dampfnudel*, a kind of sweet yeast-dough dumpling that is tasty and filling. *Nürnberger Lebkuchen*, a sort of gingerbread eaten at Christmastime, is loved all over Germany. A true purist swears by Elisen Lebkuchen,

which are made with no flour. Both Lebkuchen and Bratwürste are protected under German law and are only "legal" when made in or around Nürnberg.

Not to be missed are Franconia's liquid refreshments from both the grape and the grain. Franconian wines, usually white and sold in distinctive flat bottles called *Bocksbeutel*, are renowned for their special bouquet. (Silvaner is the traditional grape.) The region has the largest concentration of local breweries in the world (Bamberg alone has 9, Bayreuth 7), producing a wide range of brews, the most distinctive of which is the dark, smoky *Rauchbier* and the even darker and stronger *Schwärzla*. Then, of course, there is Kulmbach, with the *Doppelbock Kulminator 28*, which takes nine months to brew and has an alcohol content of 12%.

and Tuesday. ⊠ *Opernstr. 6* ☎ *0921/65051* ⊕ *www.anker-bayreuth.de* ⟿ *38 rooms, 2 suites* ⟡ *In-room: no a/c, Internet. In-hotel: restaurant, parking, some pets allowed* ⊙ *Restaurant closed Mon. and Tues., except during the festival* ⦿| *Breakfast.*

$$ 🏨 **Hotel Lohmühle.** The old part of this hotel is in Bayreuth's only half-timber house, a former sawmill by a stream. **Pros:** nice setting with reasonable prices; good food. **Cons:** stairs between hotel and restaurant; front rooms let in traffic noise. ⊠ *Badstr. 37* ☎ *0921/53060* ⊕ *www.hotel-lohmuehle.de* ⟿ *42 rooms* ⟡ *In-room: no a/c, Wi-Fi. In-hotel: restaurant, some pets allowed* ⊙ *No dinner Sun.* ⦿| *Breakfast.*

NIGHTLIFE AND THE ARTS

Markgräfliches Opernhaus. If you don't get Wagner Festival tickets, console yourself with visits to the exquisite 18th-century Markgräfliches Opernhaus. In May the *Fränkische Festwochen* (Franconian Festival Weeks) take the stage with works of Wagner, of course, but also Paganini and Mozart. ⊠ *Opernstr.* ☎ *0921/759–6922.*

Wagner Festival. Opera lovers swear that there are few more intense operatic experiences than the annual Wagner Festival in Bayreuth, held July and August. You'll do best if you plan your visit a couple of years in advance. ■ TIP→ It is nearly impossible to find a hotel room during the festival: try finding a room in Kronach instead of Bayreuth.

Bayreuther Festspiele Kartenbüro. For tickets to the Wagner Festival, write to the Bayreuther Festspiele Kartenbüro by the end of September the year before, at the latest. Be warned: The waiting list is years long, and they don't respond to email or fax inquiries. ⊠ *Postfach 100262* ☎ *0921/78780.*

SHOPPING

Hofgarten Passage. Off Richard-Wagner-Strasse, this is one of the fanciest shopping arcades in the region; it's full of smart boutiques selling everything from German high fashion to simple local craftwork. ⊠ *Richard-Wagner-Str. 22.*

BAMBERG

65 km (40 mi) west of Bayreuth, 80 km (50 mi) north of Nürnberg.

Fodor's Choice
★

Few towns in Germany survived the war with as little damage as Bamberg, which is on the Regnitz River. ■ TIP→ This former residence of one of Germany's most powerful imperial dynasties is on UNESCO's World Heritage Site list. Bamberg, originally nothing more than a fortress in the hands of the Babenberg dynasty (later contracted to Bamberg), rose to prominence in the 11th century thanks to the political and economic drive of its most famous offspring, Holy Roman Emperor Heinrich II. He transformed the imperial residence into a flourishing Episcopal city. His cathedral, consecrated in 1237, still dominates the city center. For a short period Heinrich II proclaimed Bamberg the capital of the Holy Roman Empire of the German Nation. Moreover, Bamberg earned fame as the second city to introduce book printing, in 1460.

GETTING HERE AND AROUND

Traveling to Bamberg by train will take about 45 minutes from Nürnberg; from Munich it takes about two hours. Bamberg is a worthwhile five-hour train trip from Berlin. Bamberg's train station is a 30-minute walk from the Altstadt (Old Town). On the A-73 autobahn, Bamberg is two hours from Munich. Everything in town can be reached on foot.

TOURS

In Bamberg, Personenschiffahrt Kropf boats leave daily from March through October beginning at 11 am for short cruises on the Regnitz River and the Main-Donau Canal; the cost is €7.

The Bamberg Tourist Information center offers an audio tour in English for €8.50 for four hours. It also offers brewery and beer-tasting tours of the nine Bamberg breweries.

ESSENTIALS

Boat Tours Personenschiffahrt Kropf. ⊠ *Kapuzinerstr. 5* ☎ *0951/26679* ⊕ *www.personenschiffahrt-bamberg.de.*

Visitor Information Bamberg. ⊠ *Tourismus und Congresservice, Geyerswörthstr. 5* ☎ *0951/297–6200* ⊕ *www.bamberg.info.*

5

EXPLORING

Altes Rathaus (*Old Town Hall*). At Bamberg's historic core, the Altes Rathaus, is tucked snugly on a small island in the Regnitz. To the west of the river is the so-called Bishops' Town; to the east, Burghers' Town. The citizens of Bamberg built this rickety, extravagantly decorated building on an artificial island when the Bishop of Bamberg refused to give the city the land for a town hall. The excellent collection of porcelain here is a vast sampling of 18th-century styles, from almost sober Meissens with bucolic Watteau scenes to simple but rare Haguenau pieces from Alsace and faience from Strasbourg. ⊠ *Obere Brücke 1* ☎ *0951/871–871* ⌫ *€3.50* ⊙ *Tues.–Sun. 9:30–4:30.*

QUICK BITES

Rathaus-Schänke. Before heading up the hill to the main sights in the Bishops' Town, take a break with coffee, cake, small meals, or cocktails in the half-timber Rathaus-Schänke. It overlooks the river on the Burghers' Town side of the Town Hall. ⊠ *Obere Brücke 3* ☎ *0951/208–0890.*

Diözesanmuseum (*Cathedral Museum*). Directly adjacent to the Bamberg Dom, this museum contains one of many nails and splinters of wood reputed to be from the cross of Jesus. The "star-spangled" cloak stitched with gold that was given to Emperor Heinrich II by an Italian prince is among the finest items displayed. More macabre exhibits in this rich ecclesiastical collection are the elaborately mounted skulls of Heinrich and Kunigunde. The building itself was designed by Balthasar Neumann (1687–1753), the architect of Vierzehnheiligen, and constructed between 1730 and 1733. ⊠ *Dompl. 5* ☎ *0951/502–325* ⌫ *€4* ⊙ *Tues.–Sun. 10–5; tour in English by prior arrangement.*

★ **Dom** (*Cathedral*). Bamberg's great cathedral is a unique building that tells not only the town's story but that of Germany as well. The first building here was begun by Heinrich II in 1003, and it was in this partially completed cathedral that he was crowned Holy Roman Emperor in 1012. In 1237 it was destroyed by fire, and the present late-Romanesque–early-Gothic building was begun. The dominant features are the massive towers at each corner. Heading into the dark interior, you'll find a striking collection of monuments and art treasures. The most famous piece is the **Bamberger Reiter** (Bamberg Horseman), an equestrian statue carved— no one knows by whom—around 1230 and thought to be an allegory of chivalrous virtue or a representation of King Stephen of Hungary. Compare it with the mass of carved figures huddled in the tympana above the church portals. In the center of the nave you'll find another masterpiece, the massive tomb of Heinrich and his wife, Kunigunde. It's the work of Tilman Riemenschneider. Pope Clement II is also buried in the cathedral, in an imposing tomb beneath the high altar; he's the only pope to have been buried north of the Alps. ⊠ *Dompl.* ☎ *0951/502–330* ⊙ *Nov.–Mar., daily 10–5; Apr.–Oct., daily 10–6. No visits during services.*

Kloster St. Michael (*Monastery of St. Michael*). A former Benedictine monastery, this structure has been gazing over Bamberg since about 1015. After being overwhelmed by so much baroque elsewhere, entering this haven of simplicity can be a relief. The entire choir is intricately carved, but the ceiling is gently decorated with very exact depictions of 578 flowers and healing herbs. The tomb of St. Otto is in a little chapel off the transept, and the stained-glass windows hold symbols of death and transfiguration. The monastery is now used as a home for the aged. One tract, however, was taken over by the **Franconian Brewery Museum,** which exhibits everything that has to do with beer, from the making of malt to recipes. ✉ *Michelsberg 10f* ☎ *0951/53016* 🖼 *Museum €4* ☉ *Apr.–Oct., Wed.–Sun. 1–5.*

Neue Residenz (*New Residence*). This glittering baroque palace was once the home of the prince-electors. Their plan to extend the immense palace even further is evident at the corner on Obere Karolinenstrasse, where the ashlar bonding was left open to accept another wing. The most memorable room in the palace is the **Kaisersaal** (Throne Room), complete with impressive ceiling frescoes and elaborate stuccowork. The rose garden behind the Neue Residenz provides an aromatic and romantic spot for a stroll with a view of Bamberg's roof landscape. You have to take a tour to see the Residenz itself, but you can visit the library free of charge at any time during its open hours.

Staatsbibliothek (*State Library*). The Neue Residenz is also home to the Staatsbibliothek. Among the thousands of books and illuminated manuscripts here are the original prayer books belonging to Heinrich II and his wife, a 5th century codex of the Roman historian Livy, and manuscripts by the 16th-century painters Dürer and Cranach. ☎ *0951/955–030* ⊕ *www.Staatsbibliothek-bamberg.de* 🖼 *Free* ☉ *Weekdays 9–5, Sat. 9–noon* ✉ *Neue Residenz, Dompl. 8* ☎ *0951/955–030* 🖼 *€4.50* ☉ *Neue Residenz by tour only, Apr.–Sept., daily 9–6; Oct.–Mar., daily 10–4.*

Obere Pfarre (*Upper Parish*). Bamberg's wealthy burghers built no fewer than 50 churches. The Church of Our Lady, known simply as the Obere Pfarre, dates back to around 1325, and is unusual because the exterior remains entirely Gothic, while the interior is heavily baroque. The grand choir, which lacks any windows, was added much later. An odd squarish box tops the church tower; this watchman's post was placed there to keep the tower smaller than the neighboring cathedral, thus avoiding a medieval scandal. Note the slanted floor, which allowed crowds of pilgrims to see the object of their veneration, a 14th-century Madonna. Don't miss the *Ascension of Mary* by Tintoretto at the rear of the church. Around Christmas, the Obere Pfarre is the site of the city's greatest Nativity scene. Avoid the church during services, unless you're worshipping. ✉ *Untere Seelg.* ☉ *Daily 7–7.*

NEAR BAMBERG

Kloster Banz (*Banz Abbey*). This abbey, which some call the "holy mountain of Bavaria," proudly crowns the west bank of the Main north of Bamberg. There had been a monastery here since 1069, but the present buildings—now a political-seminar center and think tank—date from the end of the 17th century. The highlight of the complex is the **Klosterkirche** (Abbey Church), the work of architect Leonard Dientzenhofer and his brother, the stuccoist Johann Dientzenhofer (1663–1726). Balthasar Neumann later contributed a good deal of work. Concerts are occasionally held in the church, including some by members of the

Bamberg's Altes Rathaus is perched precariously on an artificial island in the middle of the Regnitz River.

renowned Bamberger Symphoniker. To get to Banz from Vierzehnheiligen, drive south to Unnersdorf, where you can cross the river. ⊠ *Bad Staffelstein* ☎ *09573/7311* ☉ *May–Oct., daily 9–5; Nov.–Apr., daily 9–noon; call to request a tour.*

Fodor's Choice **Vierzehnheiligen.** In Bad Staffelstein, on the east side of the Main north
★ of Bamberg, is a tall, elegant yellow-sandstone edifice whose interior represents one of the great examples of rococo decoration. The church was built by Balthasar Neumann (architect of the Residenz at Würzburg) between 1743 and 1772 to commemorate a vision of Christ and 14 saints—*vierzehn Heiligen*—that appeared to a shepherd in 1445. The interior, known as "God's Ballroom," is supported by 14 columns. In the middle of the church is the Gnadenaltar (Mercy Altar) featuring the 14 saints. Thanks to clever play with light, light colors, and fanciful gold-and-blue trimmings, the interior seems to be in perpetual motion. Guided tours of the church are given on request; a donation is expected. On Saturday afternoon and all day Sunday the road leading to the church is closed and you have to walk the last half mile. ⊠ *36 km (22 mi) north of Bamberg via Hwy. 173, Bad Staffelstein* ☎ *09571/95080* ⊕ *www.vierzehnheiligen.de* ☉ *Mar.–Oct., daily 7–6; Nov.–Feb., daily 8–5.*

WHERE TO EAT

$ ✕ **Bischofsmühle.** It doesn't always have to be beer in Bamberg. The old
GERMAN mill, its grinding wheel providing a sonorous backdrop for patrons, specializes in wines from Franconia and elsewhere. The menu offers Franconian specialties such as the French-derived *Böfflamott*, or beef stew.

✉ *Geyerswörthstr. 4* ☎ *0951/27570* ⊕ *www.bischofsmuehle-mueller.de* ▬ *No credit cards* ⊗ *Closed Wed.*

¢ ✕**Klosterbräu.** This massive old stone-and-half-timber house has been
GERMAN standing since 1533, making it Bamberg's oldest brewpub. Regulars nurse a dark, smoky beer called Schwärzla near the big stove—though the best beer is the Klosterbraun. If you like the brew, you can buy a 5-liter bottle (called a *Siphon*) as well as other bottled beers and the requisite beer steins at the counter. The cuisine is basic, robust, filling, and tasty, with such items as a bowl of beans with a slab of smoked pork, or marinated pork kidneys with boiled potatoes. ✉ *Obere Mühlbrücke* ☎ *0951/52265* ⊕ *www.klosterbraeu.de* ▬ *No credit cards.*

$ ✕**Schlenkerla.** Set in the middle of the old town, this tavern has been
GERMAN serving beer inside an ancient half-timbered house since 1405. The fare, atmosphere, and partons are the definition of traditional Bamberg. Be sure to try the *Bamberger Zwiebel*, a local onion stuffed with pork. The real reason to come here is to try the *Aecht Schenkerla Rauchbier*, a beer brewed with smoked malt. This *Rauchbier* (smoked beer) is served from huge wooden barrels and tastes like liquid ham—it's an aquired taste, but one worth sampling. ✉ *Dominikanerstr. 6, Bamberg* ☎ *951/56050* ⊕ *www.schlenkerla.de.*

WHERE TO STAY

For expanded hotel reviews, visit Fodors.com.

$$ ⌂**Hotel-Restaurant St. Nepomuk.** This half-timber house seems to float
Fodor's Choice over the river Regnitz; many of the comfortable rooms have quite a
★ view of the water and the Old Town Hall on its island. **Pros:** nice view; an elegant dining room with excellent food. **Cons:** hotel on a pedestrian-only street; public garage 200 meters away. ✉ *Obere Mühlbrücke 9* ☎ *0951/98420* ⊕ *www.hotel-nepomuk.de* ⟿ *47 rooms* ♿ *In-room: no a/c, Wi-Fi. In-hotel: restaurant, parking, some pets allowed* ℺ *Breakfast.*

$$ ⌂**Romantik Hotel Weinhaus Messerschmitt.** This comfortable hotel has
★ spacious and luxurious rooms, some with exposed beams and many of them lighted by chandeliers. **Pros:** elegant dining room with good food; variety of rooms to choose from. **Cons:** older property; front rooms are noisy; expensive. ✉ *Langestr. 41* ☎ *0951/297–800* ⊕ *www.hotel-messerschmitt.de* ⟿ *67 rooms* ♿ *In-room: no a/c. In-hotel: restaurant, bar* ℺ *Breakfast.*

THE ARTS

Capella Antiqua Bambergensis. The city's first-class choir, Capella Antiqua Bambergensis, concentrates on ancient music.

Dom. Throughout summer organ concerts are given Saturday at noon in the Dom. Call for program details and tickets to all cultural events. ✉ *Dompl.* ☎ *0951/297–6200.*

Hoffmann Theater. Opera and operettas are performed here from September through July. ✉ *E.-T.-A.-Hoffmann-Pl. 1* ☎ *0951/873–030.*

Sinfonie an der Regnitz. This fine riverside concert hall, is home to Bamberg's world-class resident symphony orchestra. ✉ *Muss-Str. 1* ☎ *0951/964–7200.*

SHOPPING

■TIP➜ If you happen to be traveling around Christmastime, make sure you keep an eye out for crèches, a Bamberg specialty. Check the tourism website (⊕ *www.bamberg.info*) for the locations of nativity scenes and descriptions.

Café am Dom. For an edible souvenir, take home handmade chocolates like the only-in-Bamberg Rauchbier truffles made with Schlenkerla smoked beer. This café also has a roomy seating area to take a load off while you nibble a delicious pastry. ✉ *Ringleinsg. 2, Bamberg* ☎ *0951/519–290* ⊕ *www.cafeamdom.de*.

Magnus Klee. This shop sells nativity scenes of all different shapes and sizes, including wood-carved and with fabric clothes. ✉ *Obstmarkt 2* ☎ *0951/26037*.

Vinothek im Sand. Head to this wine store for Franconian wine as well as a sampling of Bamberg's specialty beers. ✉ *Obere Sandstr. 8, Bamberg* ☎ *0151/5473–8779*.

APFELWEIBLA

As you puruse the shops in Bamberg's Altstadt, you may notice an applelike face that adorns jewelry and housewares, the Apfelweibla. A replica of the Apfelweibla, a whimsical doorknob depicting an elderly woman's face, can be found at Eisgrube 14. The original doorknob is on display at the Museum of History at Domplatz. The doorknob inspired E.T.A. Hoffmann's novella *The Golden Pot*. It's said that rubbing the Apfelweibla will bring you good luck.

EN ROUTE

From Bamberg you can take either the fast autobahn (A-73) south to Nürnberg or the parallel country road (B-4) that follows the Main-Donau Canal (running parallel to the Regnitz River at this point) and joins A-73 just under 25 km (15 mi) later at Forchheim-Nord.

Levi-Strauss Museum. Eighteen kilometers (11 mi) south of Bamberg in the village of Buttenheim is a little blue-and-white half-timber house where Löb Strauss was born—in great poverty—in 1829. Take the audio tour of the Levi-Strauss Museum and learn how Löb emigrated to the United States, changed his name to Levi, and became the first name in denim. The stonewashed color of the house's beams, by the way, is the original 17th-century color. ✉ *Marktstr. 33, Buttenheim* ☎ *09545/442–602* ⊕ *www.levi-strauss-museum.de* 💶 *€2.60* ⊗ *Tues. and Thurs. 2–6, weekends 11–5 and by appointment*.

NÜRNBERG (NUREMBERG)

Nürnberg (Nuremberg in English) is the principal city of Franconia and the second-largest city in Bavaria. With a recorded history stretching back to 1050, it's among the most historic of Germany's cities; the core of the Old Town, through which the Pegnitz River flows, is still surrounded by its original medieval walls. Nürnberg has always taken a leading role in German affairs. It was here, for example, that the Holy Roman emperors traditionally held the first Diet, or convention of the estates, of their incumbency. And it was here, too, that Hitler staged the most grandiose Nazi rallies; later, this was the site of the Allies' war trials, where top-ranking Nazis were charged with—and almost without

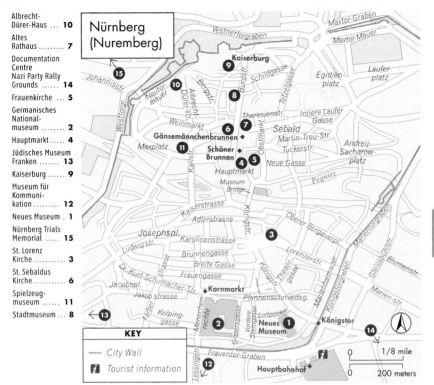

exception convicted of—crimes against humanity. The rebuilding of Nürnberg after the war was virtually a miracle, considering the 90% destruction of the Old Town. Nürnberg, in 2001, became the world's first city to receive the UNESCO prize for Human Rights Education.

As a major intersection on the medieval trade routes, Nürnberg became a wealthy town where the arts and sciences flowered. Albrecht Dürer (1471–1528), the first indisputable genius of the Renaissance in Germany, was born here. He married in 1509 and bought a house in the city where he lived and worked for the rest of his life. Other leading Nürnberg artists of the Renaissance include painter Michael Wolgemut (a teacher of Dürer), stonecutter Adam Kraft, and the brass founder Peter Vischer. The tradition of the Meistersinger also flourished here in the 16th century, thanks to the high standard set by the local cobbler Hans Sachs (1494–1576). The Meistersinger were poets and musicians who turned songwriting into a special craft, with a wealth of rules and regulations. They were celebrated three centuries later by Wagner in his *Meistersinger von Nürnberg*.

The Thirty Years' War and the shift to sea routes for transportation led to the city's long decline, which ended only in the early 19th century when the first railroad opened in Nürnberg. Among a great host of inventions associated with the city, the most significant are the pocket watch, gun casting, the clarinet, and the geographic globe (the first of which was made before Columbus discovered the Americas). Among Nürnberg's famous products are *Lebkuchen* (gingerbread of sorts) and Faber-Castell pencils.

GETTING HERE AND AROUND

Nuremberg is centrally located and well connected, an hour north of Munich and two hours east of Frankfurt by train. Five autobahns meet here: A-3 Düsseldorf–Passau, A-6 Mannheim–Nürnberg, A-9 Potzdam–München, A-73 Coburg–Feucht, and B-8 (four lane near Nürnberg) Würzburg–Regensburg. Most places in the Old Town may be reached on foot.

> **UNDERGROUND NUREMBERG**
>
> Beer aficionados can get a deeper look at Nuremberg's brewing history with a tour into the cellars where beer was made and stored since the 1300s. The tour, offered by Underground Nuremberg, costs €7, which includes a beer tasting, but is only offered in German. English-language group tours are available by appointment, see ⊕ *www.felsengaenge-nuernberg.de.*

English-language bus tours of the city are conducted April–October and in December, daily at 9:30, starting at the Mauthalle, Hallplatz 2. The 2½-hour tour costs €15. For more information, call ☎ *0911/202–290.* An English-language tour on foot through the Old Town is conducted daily May–October at 1; it departs from the tourist-information office on the Hauptmarkt. The tour costs €9 (plus entrance to the Kaiserburg €2). City tours are also conducted in brightly painted trolley buses April–October, daily at one-hour intervals beginning at 10 at the Schöner Brunnen. The cost is €6. For more information call the Nürnberg tourist office.

TIMING

You'll need a full day to walk around Nürnberg's Old Town, two if you wish to take more time at its fascinating museums and churches. Most of the major sights are within a few minutes' walk of each other. The Kaiserburg is a must-visit on any trip to Nürnberg. Plan at least half a day for the Germanisches Nationalmuseum, which is just inside the city walls near the main station. Add another half a day to visit the Nazi Party Rally Grounds.

ESSENTIALS

Visitor Information **Nürnberg** ⊠ *Congress- und Tourismus-Zentrale, Frauentorgraben 3* ☎ *0911/23360* ⊕ *www.nuernberg.de.*

EXPLORING NÜRNBERG'S OLD TOWN

Walls, finished in 1452, surround Nürnberg's Old Town. Year-round floodlighting adds to the brooding romance of their moats, sturdy gateways, and watchtowers.

TOP ATTRACTIONS

★ **Albrecht-Dürer-Haus** (*Albrecht Dürer House*). The great painter Albrecht Dürer lived here from 1509 until his death in 1528. This beautifully preserved late-medieval house is typical of the prosperous merchants'

Outside the Germanisches Nationalmuseum is the "Way of Human Rights," an outdoor sculpture consisting of thirty columns inscribed with the articles from the Universal Declaration of Human Rights.

homes that once filled Nürnberg. Dürer, who enriched German art with Italianate elements, was more than a painter. He raised the woodcut, a notoriously difficult medium, to new heights of technical sophistication, combining great skill with a haunting, immensely detailed drawing style and complex, allegorical subject matter, while earning a good living at the same time. A number of original prints adorn the walls, and printing techniques using the old press are demonstrated in the studio. An excellent opportunity to find out about life in the house of Dürer is the Saturday 2 pm tour with a guide role-playing Agnes Dürer, the artist's wife. ⊠ *Albrecht-Dürer-Str. 39* ☎ *0911/231–2568* ⊠ *€5, with tour €7.50* ⏱ *Tues., Wed., and Fri.–Sun. 10–5; Thurs. 10–8; guided tour in English Sat. at 2.*

Fodor'sChoice
★
Germanisches Nationalmuseum (*German National Museum*). You could spend days visiting this vast museum, which showcases the country's cultural and scientific achievements, ethnic background, and history. It's the largest of its kind in Germany, and perhaps the best arranged. The museum is in what was once a Carthusian monastery, complete with cloisters and monastic outbuildings. The extensions, however, are modern. The exhibition begins outside, with the tall, sleek pillars of the Strasse der Menschenrechte (Street of Human Rights), designed by Israeli artist Dani Karavan. Thirty columns are inscribed with the articles from the Universal Declaration of Human Rights. There are few aspects of German culture, from the Stone Age to the 19th century, that are not covered by the museum, and quantity and quality are evenly matched. One highlight is the superb collection of Renaissance German paintings (with Dürer, Cranach, and Altdorfer well represented).

Climb to the top of Nürnberg's Kaiserburg (Imperial Castle) for wonderful views of the city.

Others may prefer the exquisite medieval ecclesiastical exhibits—manuscripts, altarpieces, statuary, stained glass, jewel-encrusted reliquaries—the collections of arms and armor, the scientific instruments, or the toys. ⊠ *Kartäuserg 1* ☎ *0911/13310* ⊕ *www.gnm.de* 🎫 *€6* ⊙ *Tues. and Thurs.–Sun. 10–6, Wed. 10–9.*

QUICK BITES

Vivere. Opposite the Germanisches Nationalmuseum is Vivere. Al dente pasta or meat and fish dishes with excellent wines will revive you after the long hours spent in the museum. ⊠ *Kartäuserg. 12* ☎ *0911/244-9774* ⊙ *Closed Mon.*

Fodor'sChoice ★ **Kaiserburg** (*Imperial Castle*). The city's main attraction is a grand yet playful collection of buildings standing just inside the city walls; it was once the residence of the Holy Roman emperors. The complex comprises three separate groups. The oldest, dating from around 1050, is the **Burggrafenburg** (Castellan's Castle), with a craggy old pentagonal tower and the bailiff's house. It stands in the center of the complex. To the east is the **Kaiserstallung** (Imperial Stables), built in the 15th century as a granary and now serving as a youth hostel. The real interest of this vast complex of ancient buildings, however, centers on the westernmost part of the fortress, which begins at the **Sinwell Turm** (Sinwell Tower). The **Kaiserburg Museum** is here, a subsidiary of the Germanisches Nationalmuseum that displays ancient armors and has exhibits relating to horsemanship in the imperial era and to the history of the fortress. This section of the castle also has a wonderful Romanesque **Doppelkappelle** (Double Chapel). The upper part—richer, larger, and more ornate than the lower chapel—was where the emperor and his family worshipped. Also visit the **Rittersaal** (Knights' Hall) and the **Kaisersaal** (Throne Room). Their heavy oak beams, painted ceilings, and sparse interiors have changed little since they were built in the 15th century. ⊠ *Burgstr.* ☎ *0911/2446–59115* 🎫 *€5.50* ⏰ *Apr.–Sept., daily 9–6; Oct.–Mar., daily 10–4.*

★ **Neues Museum** (*New Museum*). Anything but medieval, this museum is devoted to international design since 1945. The collection, supplemented by changing exhibitions, is in a slick, modern edifice that achieves the perfect synthesis between old and new. It's mostly built of traditional pink-sandstone ashlars, while the facade is a flowing, transparent composition of glass. The interior is a work of art in itself—cool stone, with a ramp that slowly spirals up to the gallery. Extraordinary things await, including a Joseph Beuys installation (*Ausfegen,* or *Sweep-out*) and *Avalanche* by François Morellet, a striking collection of violet, argon-gas-filled fluorescent tubes. The café-restaurant adjoining the museum contains modern art, silver-wrapped candies, and video projections. ⊠ *Luitpoldstr. 5* ☎ *0911/240–200* 🎫 *€4* ⏰ *Tues.–Fri. 10–8, weekends 10–6.*

WORTH NOTING

Altes Rathaus (*Old Town Hall*). This ancient building on Rathausplatz abuts the rear of St. Sebaldus Kirche; it was erected in 1332, destroyed in World War II, and subsequently restored. Its intact medieval dungeons, consisting of 12 small rooms and one large torture chamber called the **Lochgefängnis** (or the Hole), provide insight into the gruesome applications of medieval law. **Gänsemännchenbrunnen** (Gooseman's Fountain) faces the Altes Rathaus. This lovely Renaissance bronze fountain, cast in 1550, is a work of rare elegance and great technical sophistication. ⊠ *Rathauspl. 2* ☎ *0911/231–2690* 🎫 *€3.50, minimum of 5 people for tours* ⏰ *Tues.–Sun. 10–4.*

Frauenkirche (*Church of Our Lady*). The fine late-Gothic Frauenkirche was built in 1350, with the approval of Holy Roman Emperor Charles IV, on the site of a synagogue that was burned down during the1349 pogrom. The modern tabernacle beneath the main altar was designed to look like a Torah scroll as a memorial to that despicable act. The church's main attraction is the **Männleinlaufen**, a clock dating from 1509, which is set in its facade. It's one of those colorful mechanical marvels at which Germans have long excelled. ■TIP→ Every day at noon the seven electors of the Holy Roman Empire glide out of the clock to bow to Emperor Charles IV before sliding back under cover. It's worth scheduling your morning to catch the display. ⊠ *Hauptmarkt* ⏰ *Mon.–Sat. 9–6, Sun. 12:30–6.*

Hauptmarkt (*Main Market*). Nürnberg's central market square was once the city's Jewish Quarter. When the people of Nürnberg petitioned their emperor, Charles IV, for a big central market, the emperor was in desperate need of money and, above all, political support. The Jewish Quarter was the preferred site, but as the official protector of the Jewish people, the emperor could not just openly take away their property. Instead, in 1349 he instigated a pogrom that left the Jewish Quarter in flames and more than 500 dead. He then razed the ruins and resettled the remaining Jews.

Towering over the northwestern corner of the Hauptmarkt, **Schöner Brunnen** (Beautiful Fountain) looks as though it should be on the summit of some lofty cathedral. Carved around the year 1400, the elegant 60-foot-high Gothic fountain is adorned with 40 figures arranged in tiers—prophets, saints, local noblemen, sundry electors of the Holy Roman Empire, and one or two strays such as Julius Caesar and Alexander the Great. ■ TIP→ A gold ring is set into the railing surrounding the fountain, reportedly placed there by an apprentice carver. Touching it is said to bring good luck. A market still operates in the Hauptmarkt. Its colorful stands are piled high with produce, fruit, bread, homemade cheeses and sausages, sweets, and anything else you might need for a snack or picnic. It's here that the Christkindlemarkt is held. ⊠ *Hauptmarkt.*

Jüdisches Museum Franken. The everyday life of the Jewish community in Franconia and Fürth is examined in this Jewish museum: books, seder plates, old statutes, and children's toys are among the exhibits. Among the most famous members of the Fürth community was Henry Kissinger, born here in 1923. Changing exhibitions relate to contemporary Jewish life in Germany, and in the basement is the *mikwe*, the ritual bath, which was used by the family who lived here centuries ago. In the museum you will also find a good Jewish bookshop as well as a nice small café. A subsidiary to the museum, which houses special exhibitions, is in the former synagogue in nearby Schnaittach. To get to the museum from Nürnberg, you can take the U-1 U-bahn to the Rathaus stop. ⊠ *König-str. 89, 10 km (6 mi) west of Nürnberg, Fürth* ☎ *0911/770–577* ⊕ *www.juedisches-museum.org* ≊ *€3* ⊙ *Wed.–Sun. 10–5, Tues. 10–8.*

Museum für Kommunikation (*Communication Museum*). Two museums have been amalgamated under a single roof here: the German Railway Museum and the Museum of Communication—in short, museums about how people get in touch. The first train to run in Germany did so on December 7, 1835, from Nürnberg to nearby Fürth. A model of the epochal train is here, along with a series of original 19th- and early-20th-century trains and stagecoaches. Philatelists will want to check out some of the 40,000-odd stamps in the extensive exhibits on the German postal system. You can also find out about the history of sending messages—from old coaches to optical fiber networks. ⊠ *Lessingstr. 6* ☎ *0911/219–2428* ⊕ *www.mfk-nuernberg.de* ≊ *€4* ⊙ *Tues.–Sun. 10–5.*

St. Lorenz Kirche (*St. Laurence Church*). In a city with several striking churches, St. Lorenz is considered by many to be the most beautiful. It was begun around 1250 and completed in about 1477; it later became a Lutheran church. Two towers flank the main entrance, which is covered with a forest of carvings. In the lofty interior, note the works by sculptors Adam Kraft and Veit Stoss: Kraft's great stone tabernacle, to the left of the altar, and Stoss's *Annunciation,* at the east end of the nave, are their finest works. There are many other carvings throughout the building, testimony to the artistic wealth of late-medieval Nürnberg. ⊠ *Lorenzer Pl.* ⊘ *Mon.–Sat. 9–5, Sun. noon–4.*

St. Sebaldus Kirche (*St. Sebaldus Church*). Although St. Sebaldus lacks the quantity of art treasures found in its rival St. Lorenz, its nave and choir are among the purest examples of Gothic ecclesiastical architecture in Germany: elegant, tall, and airy. Veit Stoss carved the crucifixion group at the east end of the nave, while the elaborate bronze shrine containing the remains of St. Sebaldus himself was cast by Peter Vischer and his five sons around 1520. Not to be missed is the **Sebaldus Chörlein,** an ornate Gothic oriel that was added to the Sebaldus parish house in 1361 (the original is in the Germanisches Nationalmuseum). ⊠ *Albrecht-Dürer-Pl. 1* ☎ *0911/214–2500* ⊘ *Daily 10–5.*

🐾 **Spielzeugmuseum** (*Toy Museum*). Young and old are captivated by this playful museum, which has a few exhibits dating from the Renaissance; most, however, are from the 19th century. Simple dolls vie with mechanical toys of extraordinary complexity, such as a wooden Ferris wheel from the Erz Mountains adorned with little colored lights. The top floor displays Barbies and intricate Lego constructions. ⊠ *Karlstr. 13–15* ☎ *0911/231–3164* 🔊 *€5* ⊘ *Tues.–Sun. 10–5.*

Stadtmuseum (*City Museum*). This city history museum is in the Fembohaus, a dignified patrician dwelling completed in 1598. It's one of the finest Renaissance mansions in Nürnberg. Each room explores another aspect of Nürnberg history, from crafts to gastronomy. The 50-minute multivision show provides a comprehensive look at the city's long history. ⊠ *Burgstr. 15* ☎ *0911/231–2595* 🔊 *€5* ⊘ *Tues.–Sun. 10–5.*

EXPLORING NÜRNBERG'S NAZI SIGHTS

Documentation Centre Nazi Party Rally Grounds. On the eastern outskirts of the city, the **Ausstellung Faszination und Gewalt** (Fascination and Terror Exhibition) documents the political, social, and architectural history of the Nazi Party. The sobering museum helps illuminate the whys and hows of Hitler's rise to power during the unstable period after World War I and the end of the democratic Weimar Republic. This is one of the few museums that documents how the Third Reich's propaganda machine influenced the masses. The 19-room exhibition is within a horseshoe-shape Congressional Hall that was intended to harbor a crowd of 50,000; the Nazis never completed it. The Nazis did make famous use of the nearby Zeppelin Field, the enormous parade ground where Hitler addressed his largest Nazi rallies. Today it sometimes shakes to the amplified beat of pop concerts. ■ TIP→ To get to the Documentation Center, take Tram 9 from the Hauptbahnhof to the Doku-Zentrum stop. If you are driving, follow Regensburger Strasse in the direction of Regensburg until you reach Bayernstrasse. ⊠ *Bayernstr. 110* ☎ *0911/231–5666* ⊕ *www.museen.nuernberg.de* 🔊 *€5* ⊘ *Museum daily 9–6, weekends 10–6.*

Nürnberg Trials Memorial. Nazi leaders and German organizations were put on trial here in 1945 and 1946 during the first international war-crimes trials, conducted by the Allied victors of World War II. The trials were held in the Landgericht (Regional Court) in courtroom No. 600 and resulted in 11 death sentences, among other convictions. The guided tours are in German, but English-language material is available. ■ TIP→ Take the U-1 subway line to Bärenschanze. ⊠ *Bärenschanzstr. 72* ☎ *0911/231–8411* ⊕ *www.memorium-nuremberg.de* ⊡ *€5* ⊙ *Wed.– Mon. 10–6.*

WHERE TO EAT

$$$$
GERMAN
Fodor'sChoice
★

✕ **Essigbrätlein.** The oldest restaurant in Nürnberg is also the top restaurant in the city and among the best in Germany. Built in 1550, it was originally used as a meeting place for wine merchants. Today its tiny but elegant period interior caters to the distinguishing gourmet with a taste for special spice mixes (owner Andrée Köthe's hobby). The menu changes daily, but the four-course menu can't be beat. Don't be put off if the restaurant looks closed, just ring the bell and a friendly receptionist will help you. ⊠ *Weinmarkt 3* ☎ *0911/225–131* ⚑ *Reservations essential* ⊙ *Closed Sun., Mon., and late Aug.*

$
GERMAN

✕ **Hausbrauerei Altstadthof.** For traditional regional food, such as Nürnberg bratwurst, head to this atmospheric brewery. You can see the copper kettles where the brewery's organic *Rotbier* (red beer) is made. For a bit of shopping after lunch, the brewery store sells a multitude of beer-related products such as beer vinegar, brandy, and soap. Located above a network of deep, dark cellars where beer was once brewed and stored, this brewery is the meeting point for cellar tours (⊕ *historische-felsengaenge.de*), which are offered in English on Sunday at 11:30 am and cost €5. ⊠ *Bergstrasse 19–21, Nürnberg* ☎ *911/244–9859* ⊕ *www. hausbrauerei-altstadthof.de.*

$
GERMAN
★

✕ **Heilig-Geist-Spital.** Heavy wood furnishings and a choice of more than 100 wines make this huge, 650-year-old wine tavern—built as the refectory of the city hospital—a popular spot. Try for a table in one of the alcoves, where you can see the river below you as you eat your seasonal fresh fish. The menu also includes grilled pork chops, panfried potatoes, and other Franconian dishes. ⊠ *Spitalg. 16* ☎ *0911/221–761* ⊕ *www. heilig-geist-spital.de.*

$
GERMAN
☾
★

✕ **Historische Bratwurst-Küche Zum Gulden Stern.** The city council meets here occasionally to decide upon the official size and weight of the Nürnberg bratwurst. (They have to be small enough to fit through a medieval keyhole, which in earlier days enabled pub owners to sell them after hours.) It's a fitting venue for such a decision, given that this house, built in 1375, holds the oldest bratwurst restaurant in the world. The famous Nürnberg bratwursts are always freshly roasted on a beech-wood fire; the boiled variation is prepared in a tasty stock of Franconian wine and onions. ⊠ *Zirkelschmiedg. 26* ☎ *0911/205–9288* ⊕ *www.bratwurstkueche.de.*

WHERE TO STAY

For expanded hotel reviews, visit Fodors.com.

$ ⬚ **Agneshof.** This comfortable hotel is north of the Old Town between the fortress and St. Sebaldus Church. **Pros:** many rooms have great views of the castle; warm yet professional welcome; lobby and rooms modern yet tasteful. **Cons:** deluxe rooms overpriced; parking and hotel access difficult; no restaurant. ⊠ *Agnesg. 10* ☎ *0911/214–440* ⊕ *www.agneshof-nuernberg.de* ⭲ *72 rooms* ⬦ *In-room: no a/c, Wi-Fi. In-hotel: bar, parking, some pets allowed* ⦿ *Breakfast.*

$ ⬚ **Burghotel Stammhaus.** The service is familial and friendly at this quaint hotel where accommodations are small but cozy. **Pros:** great location in the city center; comfortable; pool; good value. **Cons:** small rooms; tiny lobby; parking not easy; service sometimes too casual. ⊠ *Schildg. 14* ☎ *0911/203–040* ⊕ *www.invite-hotels.de* ⭲ *22 rooms* ⬦ *In-room: no a/c, Wi-Fi. In-hotel: pool, parking, some pets allowed* ⦿ *Breakfast.*

$ ⬚ **Hotel Drei Raben.** Legends and tales of Nürnberg form the leitmotif
★ running through the designer rooms at this hotel. **Pros:** free drink at the reception desk; designer rooms; valet parking; Wi-Fi. **Cons:** neon-lighted bar isn't relaxing; no restaurant. ⊠ *Königstr. 63* ☎ *0911/274–380* ⊕ *www.hotel-drei-raben.de* ⭲ *25 rooms* ⬦ *In-room: no a/c, Wi-Fi. In-hotel: bar, some pets allowed* ⦿ *Breakfast.*

$$ ⬚ **Hotel-Weinhaus Steichele.** An 18th-century bakery has been skillfully converted into this hotel, which has been managed by the same family for four generations. **Pros:** comfortable; good location; good restaurants. **Cons:** small rooms and lobby; some rooms show their age. ⊠ *Knorrstr. 2–8* ☎ *0911/202–280* ⊕ *www.steichele.de* ⭲ *56 rooms* ⬦ *In-room: no a/c. In-hotel: restaurant, bar, some pets allowed* ⦿ *Breakfast.*

$$ ⬚ **Le Meridien Grand Hotel.** Across the square from the central railway
★ station is this stately building with the calling card "Grand Hotel" arching over its entranceway. **Pros:** luxury property; impressive lobby; excellent food; valet parking. **Cons:** expensive, with additional fees for every possible contingency; Germanic efficiency at reception desk; difficult to reach the hotel with big bags from the main station as you have to go through an underpass with stairs. ⊠ *Bahnhofstr. 1* ☎ *0911/23220* ⊕ *www.nuremberg.lemeridien.com* ⭲ *186 rooms, 5 suites* ⬦ *In-room: Internet. In-hotel: restaurant, bar, business center, parking, some pets allowed.*

FESTIVALS

Nürnberg is rich in festivals and celebrations. By far the most famous is the **Christkindlesmarkt** (Christmas Market), an enormous pre-Christmas fair that runs from the Friday before Advent to Christmas Eve. One of the highlights is the candle procession, held every second Thursday of the market season, during which thousands of children parade through the city streets.

Kaiserburg. From May through July classical music concerts are given in the Rittersaal of the Kaiserburg. ☎ *0911/244–6590.*

Sommer in Nürnberg. Nürnberg has an annual summer festival, Sommer in Nürnberg, from May through July, with more than 200 events. Its international organ festival in June and July is regarded as Europe's finest.

SHOPPING

Handwerkerhof. Step into this "medieval mall," in the tower at the Old Town gate (Am Königstor) opposite the main railway station, and you'll think you're back in the Middle Ages. Craftspeople are busy at work turning out the kind of handiwork that has been produced in Nürnberg for centuries: pewter, glassware, basketwork, wood carvings, and, of course, toys. The Lebkuchen specialist **Lebkuchen-Schmidt** has a shop here as well. ☉ *Mid-March–Dec. 24, weekdays 10–6:30, Sat. 10–4; Dec. 1–24 also open Sun. 10–6:30.*

THE GERMAN DANUBE

For many people, the sound of the Danube River (Donau in German) is the melody of *The Blue Danube,* the waltz written by Austrian Johann Strauss. The famous 2,988-km-long (1,800-mi-long) river originates in Germany's Black Forest and flows through 10 countries. In Germany it's mostly a rather unremarkable stream as it passes through cities such as Ulm on its southeasterly route. However, that changes at Kelheim, just west of Regensburg, where the Main-Donau Canal (completed in 1992) brings big river barges all the way from the North Sea. The river becomes sizable in Regensburg, where the ancient Steinerne Brücke (Stone Bridge) needs 15 spans of 30 to 48 feet each to bridge the water. Here everything from small pleasure boats to cruise liners joins the commercial traffic. In the university town of Passau, two more rivers join the waters of the Danube before Europe's longest river continues into Austria.

REGENSBURG

85 km (52 mi) southeast of Nürnberg, 120 km (74 mi) northwest of Munich.

Few visitors to Bavaria venture this far off the well-trodden tourist trails, and even Germans are surprised when they discover medieval Regensburg. ■TIP➔ The town escaped World War II with no major damage, and it is one of the best-preserved medieval cities in Germany.

Regensburg's story begins with the Celts around 500 BC. In AD 179, as an original marble inscription in the Historisches Museum proclaims, it became a Roman military post called Castra Regina. The Porta Praetoria, or gateway, built by the Romans, remains in the Old Town, and whenever you see huge ashlars incorporated into buildings, you are looking at bits of the old Roman settlement. When Bavarian tribes migrated to the area in the 6th century, they occupied what remained of the Roman town and, apparently on the basis of its Latin name, called it Regensburg. Anglo-Saxon missionaries led by St. Boniface in 739 made the town a bishopric before heading down the Danube to convert the heathen in even more far-flung lands. Charlemagne, first of

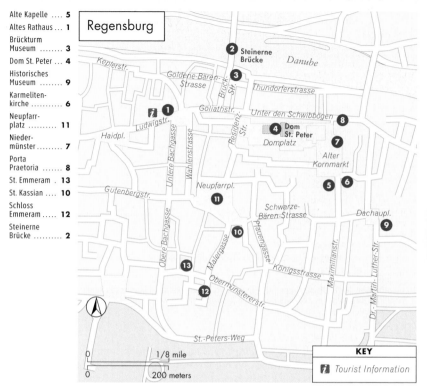

the Holy Roman emperors, arrived at the end of the 8th century and incorporated Regensburg into his burgeoning domain. Regensburg benefited from the fact that the Danube wasn't navigable to the west, and thus it was able to control trade as goods traveled between Germany and Central Europe.

By the Middle Ages Regensburg had become a political, economic, and intellectual center. For many centuries it was the most important city in southeast Germany, serving as the seat of the Perpetual Imperial Diet from 1663 until 1806, when Napoléon ordered the dismantling of the Holy Roman Empire.

Today the ancient and hallowed walls of Regensburg continue to buzz with life. Students from the university fill the restaurants and pubs, and locals do their daily shopping and errand running in the inner city, where small shops and stores have managed to keep international consumer chains out.

GETTING HERE AND AROUND

Regensburg is at the intersection of the autobahns 3 and 93. It is an hour away from Nürnberg and two hours from Munich by train. Regensburg is compact; its Old Town center is about 1 square mi. All of its attractions lie on the south side of the Danube, so you won't have to cross it more than once—and then only to admire the city from the north bank.

English-language guided walking tours are conducted May–September and during the Christmas markets, Wednesday and Saturday at 1:30. They cost €6 and begin at the tourist office.

In Regensburg all boats depart from the Steinerne Brücke. The most popular excursions are boat trips to Ludwig I's imposing Greek-style Doric temple of Walhalla. There are daily sailings to Walhalla from Easter through October. The round-trip costs €10.50 and takes three hours. Don't bother with the trip upriver from Regensburg to Kelheim.

TIMING
Although the Old Town is quite small, you can easily spend half a day strolling through its narrow streets. Any serious tour of Regensburg includes an unusually large number of places of worship. If your spirits wilt at the thought of inspecting them all, you should at least see the Dom (cathedral), famous for its Domspatzen (boys' choir—the literal translation is "cathedral sparrows"). You'll need about another two hours or more to explore Schloss Emmeram and St. Emmeram church.

ESSENTIALS
Boat Tours Personenschifffahrt Klinger ⊠ *Thundorfstr. 1* ☎ *0941/55359* ⊕ *www.schifffahrtklinger.de.*

Visitor Information Regensburg ⊠ *Regensburg Tourismus Altes Rathaus* ☎ *0941/507–4410* ⊕ *www.regensburg.de.*

EXPLORING
TOP ATTRACTIONS
Altes Rathaus (*Old Town Hall*). The picture-book complex of medieval half-timber buildings, with windows large and small and flowers in tubs, is one of the best-preserved town halls in the country, as well as one of the most historically important. It was here, in the imposing Gothic **Reichssaal** (Imperial Hall), that the Perpetual Imperial Diet met from 1663 to 1806. This parliament of sorts consisted of the emperor, the electors (seven or eight), the princes (about 50), and the burghers, who assembled to discuss and determine the affairs of the far-reaching German lands. The hall is sumptuously appointed with tapestries, flags, and heraldic designs. Note the wood ceiling, built in 1408, and the different elevations for the various estates. The Reichssaal is occasionally used for concerts. The neighboring **Ratssaal** (Council Room) is where the electors met for their consultations. The cellar holds the city's torture chamber; the **Fragstatt** (Questioning Room); and the execution room, called the **Armesünderstübchen** (Poor Sinners' Room). Any prisoner who withstood three degrees of questioning without confessing was considered innocent and released—which tells you something about medieval notions of justice. ⊠ *Rathauspl.* ☎ *0941/507–4411* ⊠ *€8* ☺ *Guided tours in English Apr.–Oct., daily at 3.*

QUICK BITES

Prinzess Confiserie Café. Just across the square from the Altes Rathaus is the Prinzess Confiserie Café, Germany's oldest coffeehouse, which first opened its doors to the general public in 1686. The homemade chocolates are highly recommended, as are the rich cakes. ⊠ *Rathauspl. 2* ☎ *0941/595–310.*

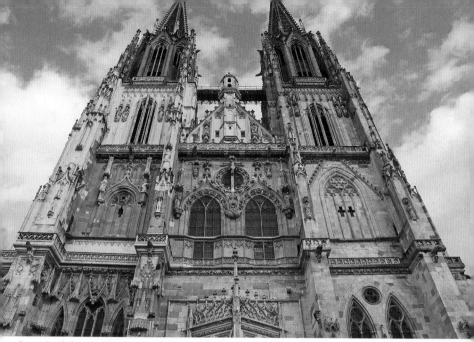

Regensburg's Dom St. Peter is an excellent example of the French Gothic style.

Brückturm Museum (*Bridge Tower Museum*). With its tiny windows, weathered tiles, and pink plaster, this 17th-century tower stands at the south end of the Steinerne Brücke. The tower displays a host of items relating to the construction and history of the old bridge. It also offers a gorgeous view of the Regensburg roof landscape. The brooding building with a massive roof to the left of the Brückturm is an old salt warehouse. ✉ *Steinerne Brücke* ☎ *0941/507–5888* 🖂 *€2* 🕙 *Apr.–Oct., daily 10–5; call ahead to ask about tours in English.*

Fodor'sChoice ★ **Dom St. Peter** (*St. Peter's Cathedral*). Regensburg's transcendent cathedral, modeled on the airy, vertical lines of French Gothic architecture, is something of a rarity this far south in Germany. Begun in the 13th century, it stands on the site of a much earlier Carolingian church. Remarkably, the cathedral can hold 6,000 people, three times the population of Regensburg when building began. Construction dragged on for almost 600 years, until Ludwig I of Bavaria, then ruler of Regensburg, finally had the towers built. These had to be replaced in the mid-1950s. Behind the Dom is a little workshop where a team of 15 stonecutters is busy full-time in summer recutting and restoring parts of the cathedral.

Before heading into the Dom, take time to admire the intricate and frothy carvings of its facade. Inside, the glowing 14th-century stained glass in the choir and the exquisitely detailed statues of the Archangel Gabriel and the Virgin in the crossing (the intersection of the nave and the transepts) are among the church's outstanding features.

Be sure to visit the **Kreuzgang** (Cloisters), reached via the garden. There you'll find a small octagonal chapel, the Allerheiligenkapelle (All Saints' Chapel), a Romanesque building that is all sturdy grace and massive walls, a work by Italian masons from the mid-12th century. You can barely make out the faded remains of stylized 11th-century frescoes on its ancient walls. The equally ancient shell of St. Stephan's Church, the cloisters, the chapel, and the Alter Dom (Old Cathedral), are included in the Cathedral tour.

Domschatzmuseum (*Cathedral Museum*). This museum contains valuable treasures going back to the 11th century. Some of the vestments and the monstrances, which are fine examples of eight centuries' worth of the goldsmith's trade, are still used during special services. The entrance is in the nave. ⊠ *Dompl.* ☎ *0941/597–2530* 🕮 *€2* ⊘ *Apr.–Oct., Tues.– Sat. 10–5, Sun. noon–5; Dec.–Mar., Fri. and Sat. 10–4, Sun. noon–4* ⊠ *Dompl.* ☎ *0941/586–5500* 🕮 *Tour, only in German (for tours in English call ahead), €3* ⊘ *Cathedral tour daily at 2.*

NEED A BREAK? **Haus Heuport.** The restaurant Haus Heuport, opposite the entrance to the Dom, was once one of the old and grand private ballrooms of the city. The service is excellent, and the tables at the windows have a wonderful view of the Dom. In summer, head for the bistro area in the courtyard for sandwiches and salads. ⊠ *Dompl. 7* ☎ *0941/599–9297.*

★ **Historisches Museum** (*Historical Museum*). The municipal museum vividly relates the cultural history of Regensburg. It's one of the highlights of the city, both for its unusual and beautiful setting—a former Gothic monastery—and for its wide-ranging collections, from Roman artifacts to Renaissance tapestries and remains from Regensburg's 16th-century Jewish ghetto. The most significant exhibits are the paintings by Albrecht Altdorfer (1480–1538), a native of Regensburg and, along with Cranach, Grünewald, and Dürer, one of the leading painters of the German Renaissance. Altdorfer's work has the same sense of heightened reality found in that of his contemporaries, in which the lessons of Italian painting are used to produce an emotional rather than a rational effect. His paintings would not have seemed out of place among those of 19th-century Romantics. Far from seeing the world around him as essentially hostile, or at least alien, he saw it as something intrinsically beautiful, whether wild or domesticated. Altdorfer made two drawings of the old synagogue of Regensburg, priceless documents that are on exhibit here. ⊠ *Dachaupl. 2–4* ☎ *0941/507–2448* ⊕ *www.museen-Regensburg.de* 🕮 *€2.20* ⊘ *Tues.–Sun. noon–4.*

Schloss Emmeram (*Emmeram Palace*). Formerly a Benedictine monastery, this is the ancestral home of the princely Thurn und Taxis family, which made its fame and fortune after being granted the right to carry official and private mail throughout the empire and Spain by Emperor Maximilian I (1493–1519) and by Philip I, king of Spain, who ruled during the same period. Their business extended over the centuries into the Low Countries (Holland, Belgium, and Luxembourg), Hungary, and Italy. The horn that still symbolizes the post office in several European countries comes from the Thurn und Taxis coat of arms. In its heyday Schloss Emmeram was heavily featured in the gossip columns thanks to the wild parties and somewhat extravagant lifestyle of the young

The Golden Gate Bridge may be better known today, but the 12th-century Steinerne Brücke (Stone Bridge) was its match in terms of engineering ingenuity and importance in its day.

dowager Princess Gloria von Thurn und Taxis. After the death of her husband, Prince Johannes, in 1990, she had to auction off belongings in order to pay inheritance taxes. Ultimately a deal was cut, allowing her to keep many of the palace's treasures as long they were put on display.

The **Thurn und Taxis Palace,** with its splendid ballroom and throne room, allows you to witness the setting of courtly life in the 19th century. A visit usually includes the fine **Kreuzgang** (cloister) of the former Benedictine abbey of St. Emmeram. The items in the **Thurn und Taxis Museum,** which is part of the Bavarian National Museum in Munich, have been carefully selected for their fine craftsmanship—be it dueling pistols, a plain marshal's staff, a boudoir, or a snuffbox. The palace's **Marstallmuseum** (former royal stables) holds the family's coaches and carriages as well as related items. ☎ 0941/504–8133 ✉ *Museum €4.50, palace and cloisters €11.50* ✆ *Museum Apr.–Oct., daily 1–5. Tours of palace and cloisters Apr.–Oct., weekdays at 11, 2, 3, and 4; weekends at 10, 11, 1, 2, 3, 4.*

Fodor's Choice ★ **Steinerne Brücke** (*Stone Bridge*). This impressive old bridge resting on massive pontoons is Regensburg's most celebrated sight. It was completed in 1146 and was rightfully considered a miraculous piece of engineering at the time. As the only crossing point over the Danube for miles, it effectively cemented Regensburg's control over trade. The significance of the little statue on the bridge is a mystery, but the figure seems to be a witness to the legendary rivalry between the master builders of the bridge and those of the Dom.

WORTH NOTING

Alte Kapelle (*Old Chapel*). Erected by the Calolingian order in the 9th century, the Old Chapel's dowdy exterior hides joyous rococo treasures within—extravagant concoctions of sinuous gilt stucco, rich marble, and giddy frescoes, the whole illuminated by light pouring in from the upper windows. ⊠ *Alter Kornmarkt 8* ⊘ *Daily 9–dusk.*

Karmelitenkirche (*Church of the Carmelites*). This lovely church, in the baroque style from crypt to cupola, stands next to the Alte Kapelle. It has a finely decorated facade designed by the 17th-century Italian master Carlo Lurago. ⊠ *Alter Kornmarkt.*

Neupfarrplatz. This oversize square was once the heart of the Jewish ghetto. Hard economic times and superstition led to their eviction by decree in 1519. While the synagogue was being torn down, one worker survived a very bad fall. A church was promptly built to celebrate the miracle, and before long a pilgrimage began. The **Neupfarrkirche** (New Parish Church) was built as well to accommodate the flow of pilgrims. During the Reformation, the Parish Church was given to the Protestants, hence its bare-bones interior. In the late 1990s, excavation work (for the power company) on the square uncovered well-kept cellars and, to the west of the church, the old synagogue, including the foundations of its Romanesque predecessor. Archaeologists salvaged the few items they could from the old stones (including a stash of 684 gold coins) and, not knowing what to do with the sea of foundations, ultimately carefully reburied them. Recovered items were carefully restored and are on exhibit in the Historisches Museum. Only one small underground area to the south of the church, the **Document,** accommodates viewing of the foundations. In a former cellar, surrounded by the original walls, visitors can watch a short video reconstructing life in the old Jewish ghetto. Over the old synagogue, the Israeli artist Dani Karavan designed a stylized plaza where people can sit and meet. Call the educational institution VHS for a tour of the Document (reservations are requested). For spontaneous visits, tickets are available at Tabak Götz on the western side of the square, at Neupfarrplatz 3. ⊠ *Neupfarrpl.* ☎ *0941/507–2433 for tours led by VHS* ⊕ *www.vhs-regensburg.de* 🖃 *Document €5* ⊘ *Church daily 9–dusk, document tour Thurs.–Sat. at 2:30.*

■ NEED A BREAK? **Dampfnudel Uli.** A Dampfnudel is a steamed often sweet, but sometimes savory, yeast-dough dumpling that is tasty and filling. The best in Bavaria can be had at this small establishment in a former chapel. The decoration is incredibly eclectic, from Bavarian crafts to an autographed portrait of Ronald Reagan. ⊠ *Watmarkt 4* ☎ *0941/53297* ⊘ *Tues.–Fri. 10–6, Sat. 10–4.*

Niedermünster. This 12th-century building with a baroque interior was originally the church of a community of nuns, all of them from noble families. ⊠ *Alter Kornmarkt 5* ☎ *0941/586–5500.*

Porta Praetoria. The rough-hewn former gate to the old Roman camp, built in AD 179, is one of the most interesting relics of Roman Regensburg. Look through the grille on its east side to see a section of the original Roman road, about 10 feet below today's street level. ⊠ *North side of Alter Kornmarkt.*

St. Emmeram. The family church of the Thurn und Taxis family stands across from their ancestral palace, the Schloss Emmeram. The foundations of the church date to the 7th and 8th centuries. A richly decorated baroque interior was added in 1730 by the Asam brothers. St. Emmeram contains the graves of the 7th-century martyred Regensburg bishop Emmeram and the 10th-century saint Wolfgang. ⊠ *Emmeramspl. 3* ☎ *0941/51030* ⊗ *Mon.–Thurs. and Sat. 10–4:30, Fri. 1–4:30, Sun. noon–4:30.*

St. Kassian. Regensburg's oldest church was founded in the 8th century. Don't be fooled by its plain exterior; inside, it's filled with delicate rococo decoration. ⊠ *St. Kassianpl. 1* ⊗ *Daily 9–5:30.*

NEAR REGENSBURG

Stiftskirche Sts. Georg und Martin (*Abbey Church of Sts. George and Martin*). In Weltenburg (25 km [15 mi] southwest of Regensburg) you'll find the great Stiftskirche Sts. Georg und Martin, on the bank of the Danube River. The most dramatic approach to the abbey is by boat from Kelheim, 10 km (6 mi) downstream. On the stunning ride the boat winds between towering limestone cliffs that rise straight up from the tree-lined riverbanks. The abbey, constructed between 1716 and 1718, is commonly regarded as the masterpiece of the brothers Cosmas Damian and Egid Quirin Asam, two leading baroque architects and decorators of Bavaria. Their extraordinary composition of painted figures whirling on the ceiling, lavish and brilliantly polished marble, highly wrought statuary, and stucco figures dancing in rhythmic arabesques across the curving walls is the epitome of Bavarian baroque. Note especially the bronze equestrian statue of St. George above the high altar, reaching down imperiously with his flamelike, twisted gilt sword to dispatch the winged dragon at his feet. In Kelheim there are two boat companies that offer trips to Kloster Weltenburg every 30 minutes in summer. You cannot miss the landing stages and the huge parking lot. ■ TIP→ No Bavarian monastery is complete without a brewery and Kloster Weltenburg's is well worth visiting. ⊗ *Daily 9–dusk.*

★ **Walhalla.** Walhalla (11 km [7 mi] east of Regensburg) is an excursion you won't want to miss, especially if you have an interest in the wilder expressions of 19th-century German nationalism. Walhalla—a name resonant with Nordic mythology—was where the god Odin received the souls of dead heroes. Ludwig I erected this monumental temple in 1840 to honor important Germans from ages past. In keeping with the neoclassic style of the time, the Greek-style Doric temple is actually a copy of the Parthenon in Athens. The expanses of costly marble are evidence of both the financial resources and the craftsmanship at Ludwig's command. Walhalla may be kitschy, but the fantastic view it affords over the Danube and the wide countryside is definitely worth a look.

A boat ride from the Steinerne Brücke in Regensburg is the best way to go. On the return trip, you can steer the huge boat about half a mile, and, for €5 extra, you can earn an "Honorary Danube Boat Captain" certificate. Kids and grown-ups love it (*see Getting Here and Around, above*). To get to the temple from the river, you'll have to climb 358 marble steps.

To drive to it, take the Danube Valley country road (unnumbered) east from Regensburg 8 km (5 mi) to Donaustauf. The Walhalla temple is 1 km (½ mi) outside the village and well signposted.

WHERE TO EAT

$ ╳**Café Felix.** A modern bilevel café and bar, Felix offers everything
ECLECTIC from sandwiches to steaks, and buzzes with activity from breakfast until the early hours. Light from an arty chandelier and torchlike fixtures bounces off the many large framed mirrors. The crowd tends to be young. ⊠ *Fröhliche-Türkenstr. 6* ☏ *0941/59059* ⊟ *No credit cards.*

¢ ╳**Historische Wurstküche.** At the world's oldest, and possibly smallest,
GERMAN bratwurst grill, succulent Regensburger sausages—the best in town—are prepared right before your eyes on an open beech-wood charcoal grill. If you want to eat them inside in the tiny dining room, you'll have to squeeze past the cook to get there. On the walls—outside and in—are plaques recording the levels the river reached in over a century of floods that temporarily interrupted service. ⊠ *Thundorferstr. 3, just by stone bridge* ☏ *0941/466–210* ⊟ *No credit cards.*

$ ╳**Leerer Beutel.** The "Empty Sack" serves excellent international cui-
ECLECTIC sine—from antipasti to solid pork roast—is served in a pleasant vaulted room supported by massive rough-hewn beams. The restaurant is in a huge warehouse that's also a venue for concerts, exhibitions, and film screenings, making it a good place to start or end an evening. ⊠ *Bertoldstr. 9* ☏ *0941/58997.*

WHERE TO STAY

For expanded hotel reviews, visit Fodors.com.

¢ ▦ **Am Peterstor.** The clean and basic rooms of this popular hotel in the heart of the Old Town are a solid value. **Pros:** low prices; good location. **Cons:** spartan rooms; no restaurant or bar; no phones in rooms; breakfast extra. ⊠ *Fröhliche-Türken-Str. 12* ☏ *0941/54545* ⊕ *www. hotel-am-peterstor.de* ⇱ *36 rooms* ⌂ *In-room: no a/c.*

$ ▦ **Hotel Münchner Hof.** This little hotel provides top service at a good price with Regensburg at your feet. **Pros:** some rooms with historic touch; center of town; nice little lobby. **Cons:** entrance on narrow street; difficult parking. ⊠ *Tändlerg. 9* ☏ *0941/58440* ⊕ *www.muenchner-hof. de* ⇱ *53 rooms* ⌂ *In-room: no a/c, Wi-Fi. In-hotel: restaurant, some pets allowed.*

$ ▦ **Hôtel Orphée.** It's difficult to choose from among the very spacious
Fodor'sChoice rooms at the three different properties of this establishment—the Grand
★ Hotel Orphée; the Petit Hotel Orphée on the next street; and the Country Manor Orphée on the other side of the river about 2 km (1 mi) away. **Pros:** very tastefully renovated; excellent restaurant; center of town. **Cons:** difficult parking; front rooms are noisy. ⊠ *Grand Hôtel Orphee: Untere Bachg. 8; Petit Hotel Orphee: Wahleng. 1; Country Manor Orphée: Andreasstr. 26* ☏ *0941/596–020* ⊕ *www.hotel-orphee. de* ⇱ *56 rooms* ⌂ *In-room: no a/c, Wi-Fi. In-hotel: restaurant, bar, parking, some pets allowed.*

$$ ▦ **Hotel-Restaurant Bischofshof am Dom.** This is one of Germany's most historic hostelries, a former bishop's palace where you can sleep in an apartment that includes part of a Roman gateway. **Pros:** historic

building; no-smoking rooms only; nice courtyard beer garden. **Cons:** no-smoking rooms only; restaurant not up to hotel's standards. ⊠ *Krauterermarkt 3* ☏ *0941/58460* ⊕ *www.hotel-bischofshof.de* ↰ *55 rooms, 4 suites* ⏶ *In-room: no a/c. In-hotel: restaurant, bar, parking, some pets allowed.*

$ ⟦T⟧ **Kaiserhof am Dom.** Renaissance windows punctuate the green facade of this historic city mansion, but the rooms are 20th-century modern. **Pros:** front rooms have a terrific view; historic breakfast room. **Cons:** front rooms are noisy; no restaurant or bar. ⊠ *Kramg. 10–12* ☏ *0941/585–350* ⊕ *www.kaiserhof-am-dom.de* ↰ *30 rooms* ⏶ *In-room: no a/c, Wi-Fi. In-hotel: some pets allowed* ⊘ *Closed Dec. 21– Jan. 8.*

SHOPPING

The winding alleyways of the Altstadt are packed with boutiques, ateliers, jewelers, and other small shops offering a vast array of arts and crafts. You may also want to visit the Neupfarrplatz market (Monday through Saturday 9–4), where you can buy regional specialties such as *Radi* (juicy radish roots), which locals wash down with a glass of wheat beer.

NIGHTLIFE AND THE ARTS

Regensburg offers a range of musical experiences, though none so moving as a choral performance at the cathedral. ■ TIP→ Listening to the Regensburger Domspatzen, the boys' choir at the cathedral, can be a remarkable experience, and it's worth scheduling your visit to the city to hear them. The best sung Mass is held on Sunday at 9 am. If you're around in summer, look out for the Citizens Festival (Bürgerfest) and the Bavarian Jazz Festival (Bayreisches Jazzfest ⊕ *www.bayernjazz.de*) in July, both in the Old Town.

The kind of friendly, mixed nightlife that has become hard to find in some cities is alive and well in this small university city in the many *Kneipen*, bar-cum-pub-cum-bistros or -restaurants, such as the Leerer Beutel. Ask around to discover the latest in-spot.

PASSAU

137 km (86 mi) southeast of Regensburg, 179 km (111 mi) northeast of Munich.

Flanking the borders of Austria and the Czech Republic, Passau dates back more than 2,500 years. Originally settled by the Celts, then by the Romans, Passau later passed into the possession of prince-bishops whose domains stretched into present-day Hungary. At its height, the Passau episcopate was the largest in the entire Holy Roman Empire.

Passau's location is truly unique. Nowhere else in the world do three rivers—the Ilz from the north, the Danube from the west, and the Inn from the south—meet. Wedged between the Inn and the Danube, the Old Town is a maze of narrow cobblestone streets lined with beautifully preserved burgher and patrician houses and riddled with churches. Many streets have been closed to traffic making the Old Town a fun and mysterious place to explore.

GETTING HERE AND AROUND

Passau is on the A-3 autobahn from Regensburg to Vienna. It's an hour from Regensburg and about four hours from Vienna by train.

TOURS

The Passau tourist office leads tours from May through October at 10:30 and 2:30 on weekdays and at 2:30 on Sunday; November through April the tours are held weekdays at noon. Tours start at the entrance to the cathedral. A one-hour tour costs €4.

In Passau cruises on the three rivers begin and end at the Danube jetties on Fritz-Schäffer Promenade. Donauschiffahrt Wurm + Köck runs eight ships.

TIMING

Passau can be toured leisurely in the course of one day. Try to visit the Dom at noon to hear a recital on the world's largest organ. Early morning is the best time to catch the light falling from the east on the Old Town walls and the confluence of the three rivers.

ESSENTIALS

Boat Tours **Donauschiffahrt Wurm + Köck** ☎ *0851/929–292* ⊕ *www. donauschiffahrt.de.*

Visitor Information **Passau** ⊠ *Tourist-Information Passau, Rathauspl. 3* ☎ *0851/955–980* ⊕ *www.passau.de.*

EXPLORING

TOP ATTRACTIONS

Fodor's Choice ★ **Dom St. Stephan** (*St. Stephan's Cathedral*). The cathedral rises majestically on the highest point of the earliest-settled part of the city. A baptismal church stood here in the 6th century. Two hundred years later, when Passau became a bishop's seat, the first basilica was built. It was dedicated to St. Stephan and became the original mother church of St. Stephan's Cathedral in Vienna. A fire reduced the medieval basilica to ruins in 1662; it was then rebuilt by Italian master architect Carlo Lurago. What you see today is the largest baroque basilica north of the Alps, complete with an octagonal dome and flanking towers. Little in its marble- and stucco-encrusted interior reminds you of Germany, and much proclaims the exuberance of Rome. Beneath the dome is the largest church organ assembly in the world. Built between 1924 and 1928 and enlarged in 1979–80, it claims no fewer than 17,774 pipes and 233 stops. The church also houses the most powerful bell chimes in southern Germany. ⊠ *Dompl.* ☎ *0851/3930* 🖃 *Concerts midday €4, evening €8* ⊙ *Daily 6:30–10:45 and 11:30–6; tours May–Oct., weekdays at 12:30; Nov.–Apr., weekdays at noon.*

Domplatz (*Cathedral Square*). This large square in front of the Dom is bordered by sturdy 17th- and 18th-century buildings, including the **Alte Residenz,** the former bishop's palace and now a courthouse. The neoclassical statue at the center is Bavarian king Maximilian I, who watches over the Christmas Market in December. ⊠ *Domplatz.*

Domschatz- und Diözesanmuseum (*Cathedral Treasury and Diocesan Museum*). The cathedral museum houses one of Bavaria's largest collections of religious treasures, the legacy of Passau's rich episcopal history.

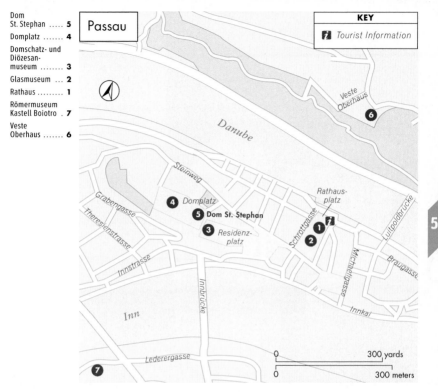

Passau

KEY

🛈 Tourist Information

The museum is part of the **Neue Residenz,** which has a stately baroque entrance opening onto a magnificent staircase—a scintillating study in marble, fresco, and stucco. ⊠ *Residenzpl.* 💶 *€1.50* ⊘ *May–Oct., Mon.–Sat. 10–4.*

Veste Oberhaus (*Upper House Stronghold*). The powerful fortress and summer castle commissioned by Bishop Ulrich II in 1219 looks over Passau from an impregnable site on the other side of the river, opposite the Rathaus. Today the Veste Oberhaus is Passau's most important museum, containing exhibits that illustrate the city's 2,000-year history. ▪TIP➔ From the terrace of its café-restaurant (open Easter–October), there's a magnificent view of Passau and the convergence of the three rivers. ⊠ *Oberhaus 125* ☎ *0851/493–3512* 💶 *Museum €5* ⊘ *May–Oct., weekdays 9–5, weekends 10–6* ☞ *Bus (€5) from Rathauspl. to museum Apr.–Nov. daily every ½ hr 10:30–5.*

WORTH NOTING

Glasmuseum (*Glass Museum*). The world's most comprehensive collection of European glass is housed in the lovely Hotel Wilder Mann. The history of Central Europe's glassmaking is captured in 30,000 items, from baroque to art deco, spread over 35 rooms. ⊠ *Am Rathauspl.* ☎ *0851/35071* 💶 *€5* ⊘ *Daily 1–5.*

Rathaus. Passau's 14th-century town hall sits like a Venetian merchant's house on a small square fronting the Danube. It was the home of a wealthy German merchant before being declared the seat of city government after a 1298 uprising. Two assembly rooms have wall paintings depicting scenes from local history and lore, including the (fictional) arrival in the city of Siegfried's fair Kriemhild, from the Nibelungen fable. ■ TIP➜ The Rathaus tower has Bavaria's largest glockenspiel, which plays daily at 10:30 am, 2 pm, and 7:25 pm, with an additional performance at 3:30 pm on Saturday. ⊠ *Rathauspl.* ☎ *0851/3960* 🖃 *€1.50* ☼ *Apr.– Oct. and late Dec.–early Jan., daily 10–4.*

Römermuseum Kastell Boiotro (*Roman Museum*). While excavating a 17th-century pilgrimage church, archaeologists uncovered a stout Roman fortress with five defense towers and walls more than 12 feet thick. The Roman citadel Boiotro was discovered on a hill known as the Mariahilfberg on the south bank of the river Inn, with its Roman well still plentiful and fresh. Pottery, lead figures, and other artifacts from the area are housed in this museum at the edge of the site. ⊠ *Ledererg. 43* ☎ *0851/34769* 🖃 *€2* ☼ *Mar.–Nov., Tues.–Sun. 10–4.*

WHERE TO EAT

$ ╳ **Blauer Bock.** This is one of Passau's oldest houses (first mentioned in
GERMAN   city records in 1257) and has been welcoming travelers since 1875. The Danube flows by the tavern windows, and in summer you can watch the river traffic from a beer garden. The food is traditional; you'll find pork and potatoes in every variety. The tavern also offers accommodation in tastefully fitted rooms. ⊠ *Höllg. 20* ☎ *0851/34637.*

$ ╳ **Gasthaus zur blauen Donau.** Passau's esteemed chef Richard Kerscher
CONTINENTAL   turned this old house with thick walls and recessed windows into a simple but stylish restaurant. The first-floor dining room has a commanding view of the Danube. His delicacies are all based on traditional German recipes. ⊠ *Höllg. 14* ☎ *0851/490–8660* 🖃 *No credit cards.*

$ ╳ **Hacklberger Bräustüberl.** Shaded by magnificent old trees, locals sit
GERMAN   in this famous brewery's enormous beer garden (seating more than 1,000), sipping a Hacklberger and tucking into a plate of sausages. In winter they simply move to the wood-panel interior, where beer has been on tap from the brewery next door since 1618. ⊠ *Bräuhauspl. 7* ☎ *0851/58382* ⊕ *www.hacklbergers.de.*

$ ╳ **Heilig-Geist-Stiftsschenke.** For atmospheric dining this 14th-century
GERMAN   monastery–turned–wine cellar is a must. In summer eat beneath chestnut trees; in winter seek out the warmth of the vaulted, dark-paneled dining rooms. The wines—made in Austria from grapes from the Spitalkirche Heiliger Geist vineyards—are excellent and suit all seasons. The fish comes from the Stift's own ponds. ⊠ *Heilig-Geist-G. 4* ☎ *0851/2607* ☼ *Closed Wed. and last 3 wks in Jan.*

$ ╳ **Peschl Terrasse.** The beer you sip on the high, sunny terrace overlook-
GERMAN   ing the Danube is brought fresh from Peschl's own brewery below, which, along with this traditional Bavarian restaurant, has been in the same family since 1855. ⊠ *Rosstränke 4* ☎ *0851/2489.*

WHERE TO STAY

For expanded hotel reviews, visit Fodors.com.

$ ⊡ **Hotel König.** Though built in 1984, the König blends successfully with the graceful Italian-style buildings alongside the elegant Danube waterfront. **Pros:** some rooms with an impressive view of the Danube; spacious rooms. **Cons:** no restaurant; uninspired bathrooms; some small rooms. ⊠ *Untere Donaulände 1* ☎ *0851/3850* ⊕ *www.hotel-koenig.de* ⤺ *61 rooms* ᗱ *In-room: no a/c, Wi-Fi. In-hotel: bar, parking, some pets allowed.*

$ ⊡ **Hotel Wilder Mann.** Passau's most historic hotel dates from the 11th century and shares prominence with the ancient town hall on the waterfront market square. **Pros:** historic hotel with some luxurious suites; center of town; some rooms with nice view of the river; others are a good value. **Cons:** some rooms in need of updating; some face bell tower; no restaurant or bar. ⊠ *Am Rathauspl. 1* ☎ *0851/35071* ⊕ *www. wilder-mann.com* ⤺ *49 rooms, 5 suites* ᗱ *In-room: no a/c, Wi-Fi. In-hotel: parking.*

¢ ⊡ **Rotel Inn.** The first permanent Rotel Inn is on the bank of the Danube in central Passau and resembles an ocean liner ("Rotels" are usually hotels on wheels, an idea developed by a local entrepreneur to accommodate tour groups in North Africa and Asia.) **Pros:** very easy on the wallet. **Cons:** very, very small rooms; bathrooms down the hall; no restaurant, breakfast €6. ⊠ *Am Hauptbahnhof/Donauufer* ☎ *0851/95160* ⊕ *www.rotel-inn.de* ⤺ *100 rooms with shared bath* ᗱ *In-room: no a/c* ▭ *No credit cards* ⊗ *Closed Oct.–late Apr.*

$ ⊡ **Schloss Ort.** This 13th-century castle's large rooms have views of the Inn River, which flows beneath the hotel's stout walls. **Pros:** wonderful view of the river; nice garden; good restaurant. **Cons:** old linens; thin walls; not in the center of town. ⊠ *Ort 11* ☎ *0851/34072* ⊕ *www. schlosshotel-passau.de* ⤺ *18 rooms* ᗱ *In-room: no a/c. In-hotel: restaurant, parking, some pets allowed.*

FESTIVALS

Christkindlmarkt. Passau's Christmas fair is the biggest and most spectacular of the Bavarian Forest. It's held in front of Dom St. Stephan from late November until just before Christmas. ⊠ *Dompl.*

Europäische Wochen (*European Weeks*). Passau is the cultural center of Lower Bavaria. Its Europäische Wochen festival—featuring everything from opera to pantomime—is a major event on the European music calendar. The festival runs from June to July.

Kartenzentrale der Europäischen Wochen Passau. For program details and tickets for the Europäische Wochen, register on this Web site. ⊠ *Dr.- Hans-Kapfinger-Str. 22* ☎ *0851/752–020* ⊕ *www.ew-passau.de* .

The Bodensee

WORD OF MOUTH

"We spent three days in Uberlingen last September. It's very close to Meersburg so you could spend time there also. It has a very long lovely lake promenade with a nice park adjacent. We were very impressed with this town and have also spent time in Meersburg and Lindau. Lindau is charming . . ."

—bettyk

WELCOME TO THE BODENSEE

TOP REASONS TO GO

★ **Zeppelin Museum, Friedrichshafen:** Step inside the gracious passenger rooms of the airship, and you may question whether the air transport of today, though undeniably bigger and faster, is a real improvement.

★ **Altes Schloss in Meersburg:** Explore the oldest continuously inhabited castle in Germany, from the sinister dungeons to the imposing knights' hall.

★ **Schloss Salem, near Überlingen:** The castle itself has plenty to see, what with furnished rooms, stables, gardens, and museums.

★ **Wallfahrtskirche Birnau, near Überlingen:** A vineyard slopes down from this pilgrimage church to Schloss Maurach on the lakeshore. The scene behind the church's pink exterior is a riot of color and embellishment.

★ **Mainau Island:** More than 1 million tulips and narcissi grace the flower island in spring—later they're followed by rhododendrons and azaleas, roses, and dahlias.

1 The Northern Shore. A dozen charming little villages and towns line the northern shore of the lake. In good weather there's a wonderful view across the water to the Swiss mountains.

2 The Upper Swabian Baroque Road. Nearly every village has its own baroque treasure, from the small village church to the mighty Basilica Weingarten. The more miles between you and the Bodensee, the easier it is on your wallet, which may be reason enough to venture to this region.

3 Around the Bodanrück Peninsula. Konstanz is the biggest city on the international lakeshore, situated on the Bodanrück Peninsula and separated from the northern shore by a few miles of water. Konstanz survived WWII unscathed by leaving its lights burning every night, so the Allied bomber

GETTING ORIENTED

The Bodensee (Lake Constance) is off the beaten path for visitors from overseas and from other parts of Europe. If you venture here, you can be pretty sure you won't meet your countrypeople. Even the Swiss and the Austrians, who own part of the shore of the Bodensee, tend to vacation elsewhere. For Germans, however, it is a favorite summer vacation spot, so it's wise to reserve rooms in advance.

6

pilots could not distinguish it from the neighboring Swiss city of Kreuzlingen. The small towns of the "Untersee" (Lower Lake), as this part of the Bodensee is called, have a more rural atmosphere than those of the northern shore.

BIKING THE BODENSEE

The best way to experience the Bodensee area is by bike. In as little as three days, you can cross the borders of three nations, and the only burn your thighs will suffer on the flat landscape is from the sun.

(above and upper right) Cyclists on the banks of the Bodensee. (lower right) You can take in the sights from the seat of your bike.

You could start anywhere, but this short Lindau-to-Lindau tour begins at the southeastern corner of the lake. Book a room in Meersburg or Konstanz for the first night; in Romanshorn, Switzerland, for the second night; and in Lindau for the third. Leave your baggage at your Lindau hotel, bringing with you only what you can comfortably carry on your back or in panniers (don't forget your bathing suit). For an easier pace, add more overnight stays and cover less distance per day. A sign displaying a bicyclist with a blue back wheel will be your guide for the bike paths through all three countries. Even without the signs or map, the water is an easy point of reference.

—Leonie Adeane

BIKING ESSENTIALS

You can rent a bike as a guest at many hotels, at some tourist offices, from bike shops, and from bicycle tour operators. Biking maps are available from newspaper stands, bookshops, and tourist offices, and you can leave your baggage in the long-term storage available at the train stations in Konstanz, Überlingen, Friedrichshafen, and Lindau. You can cut across the lake on a ferry at numerous points.

Departing **Lindau**, head west along the lake toward Wasserburg, 5 km (3 mi) away. Continue on through meadows and marshland, passing charming villages like Nonnenhorn and Langenargen—9 km (5½ mi) from Wasserburg. **Friedrichshafen** is another 10 km (6 mi) northwest from Langenargen. Pay a visit to the **Zeppelin Museum** there. After Friedrichshafen the path runs along the main road; follow the sign to Immenstaad (10 km [6 mi]) to get away from the traffic. Pass through the village and continue to Hagnau. After another 5 km (3 mi), stay overnight in lovely **Meersburg**, rising early to catch the ferry to Konstanz.

When you come off the ferry, head to the flower island of **Mainau** to enjoy the blooms. Onward to **Konstanz**, pass the ferry dock again, and keep as close as you can to the water, which will bring you into Konstanz through the scenic "back entrance." Cross the bridge over the Rhine. Take in the old town, and the buzzing small harbor. When you set off again, you'll be in the Swiss city of Kreuzlingen in a few minutes. After 23 km (14 mi) you'll arrive in **Romanshorn** for your second overnight.

Leave Romanshorn early in the morning, passing Arbon (after 9 km [5½ mi]), Rorschach (another 7 km [4½ mi]) and Rheineck, on the Austrian border (another 9 km [5½ mi]). After the border there are several paths to follow—keep as close to the lake as possible. Twenty kilometers (12 mi) beyond the border is **Bregenz**, Austria. Ascend the Pfänder cablecar 3,870 feet (5½ mi) for a marvelous view. If you're too tired to bike the 9 km (5½ mi) back to Lindau, you can board a train or ferry with your bicycle in Bregenz.

REFUELING

Copious amounts of fresh lake air and pedalling is bound to trigger your appetite. If the weather is ripe for a picnic, be on the lookout for supermarket chains such as **Aldi**, **Edeka** and **Lidl**, where you can fill your picnic basket.

For **Brot** (bread), a fresh **Brezel** (prezel) or a piece of **Kuchen** (cake), even the smallest village center will contain a **Bäckerei** (bakery). Don't be shy about venturing into the village **Metzgerei** (butcher) either, if you want some meat for between your bread, or lunch-to-go. Most meat markets offer delicious **Leberkäse** or **Fleischkäse Brotchen** (the name differs between Bavaria and Baden Württemburg), a slice of warm sausage-meatloaf in a bread roll; **Wurst Brotchen**, cold sliced sausage in a bread roll, and tangy **Fleischsalat**, sliced sausage-meat salad and pickles with salad dressing.

Updated by
Leonie Adeane

Lapping the shores of Germany, Switzerland, and Austria, the Bodensee (Lake Constance), at 65 km (40 mi) long and 15 km (9 mi) wide, is the largest lake in the German-speaking world.

Though called a lake, it's actually a vast swelling of the Rhine, gouged out by a massive glacier in the Ice Age and flooded by the river as the ice receded. The Rhine flows into its southeast corner, where Switzerland and Austria meet, and flows out at its west end. On the German side, the Bodensee is bordered almost entirely by the state of Baden-Württemberg (a small portion of the eastern tip, from Lindau to Nonnenhorn, belongs to Bavaria).

A natural summer playground, the Bodensee is ringed with little towns and busy resorts. It's one of the warmest areas of the country, not just because of its southern latitude but also owing to the warming influence of the water, which gathers heat in summer and releases it in winter. The lake itself practically never freezes over—it has done so only once in the past two centuries. The climate is excellent for growing fruit, and along the roads you'll find stands and shops selling apples, peaches, strawberries, jams, juices, wines, and schnapps, much of it homemade.

PLANNING

WHEN TO GO

The Bodensee's temperate climate makes for pleasant weather from April to October. In spring, orchard blossoms explode everywhere, and on Mainau, the "island of flowers," more than a million tulips, hyacinths, and narcissi burst into bloom. Holiday crowds come in summer, and autumn can be warm and mellow. Several hotels and restaurants as well as many tourist attractions close for winter.

GETTING HERE AND AROUND

AIR TRAVEL

The closest major international airport is in Zürich, Switzerland, 60 km (37 mi) from Konstanz, connected by the autobahn. There are also direct trains from the Zürich airport to Konstanz. There are several domestic and international (primarily of U.K. and European origin) flights to the regional airport at Friedrichshafen—these are mostly operated by budget airlines.

Airport Contacts **Flughafen Friedrichshafen (FDH)** ☎ *07541/284–01* ⊕ *www.fly-away.de.* **Zürich Airport (ZRH)** ☎ *410/4381–62211* ⊕ *www.zurich-airport.com.*

BOAT AND FERRY TRAVEL

■TIP→ Note that the English pronunciation of "ferry" sounds a lot like the German word fähre, which means car ferry. Schiffe is the term used for passenger ferries. Car and passenger ferries have different docking points in the various towns. The car ferries run all year; in summer you may have to wait in line. The passenger routes, especially the small ones, often do not run from November to March.

The Weisse Flotte line of boats, which is run by the BSB, or Bodensee-Schiffsbetriebe, links most of the larger towns and resorts. One of the nicest trips is from Konstanz to Meersburg and then on to the island of Mainau. The trip takes about an hour and costs about €14. Excursions around the lake last from one hour to a full day. Many cross to Austria and Switzerland; some head west along the Rhine to Schaffhausen and the Rheinfall, the largest waterfall in Europe. Information on lake excursions is available from all local tourist offices and travel agencies.

Boat and Ferry Contacts **Bodensee-Schiffsbetriebe** ✉ *Hafenstr. 6, Konstanz* ☎ *07531/364–0389* ⊕ *www.bsb-online.com.*

BUS TRAVEL

Buses serve most smaller communities that have no train links, but service is infrequent. Along the shore there are buses that run regularly throughout the day from Überlingen to Friedrichshafen, stopping in towns such as Meersburg, Hagnau, and Immenstaad.

CAR TRAVEL

The A-96 autobahn provides the most direct route between Munich and Lindau. For a more scenic, slower route, take B-12 via Landsberg and Kempten. For another scenic and slower route from Frankfurt, take B-311 at Ulm and follow the Oberschwäbische Barockstrasse (Upper Swabian Baroque Road) to Friedrichshafen. From Stuttgart, follow the A-81 autobahn south. At Exit 40 take B-33 to Konstanz, or take the A-98 autobahn and B-31 for the northern shore. Lindau is also a terminus of the picturesque Deutsche Alpenstrasse (German Alpine Road), running east–west from Salzburg to Lindau.

Lakeside roads, particularly those on the northern shore, boast wonderful vistas but experience occasional heavy traffic in summer, and on weekends and holidays, year-round. Stick to the speed limits in spite of tailgaters—speed traps are frequent, especially in built-up areas. Formalities at border-crossing points are few. However, in addition to your passport you'll need insurance and registration papers for your car. For rental cars, check with the rental company to make sure you are allowed to take the car into other countries. Crossing into Switzerland, you're required to have an autobahn tax sticker (CHF40, but purchasable in €) if you plan to drive on the Swiss autobahn. These are available from border customs offices, and from petrol stations and post offices in Switzerland. This sticker is not necessary if you plan to stick to non-autobahn roads. Car ferries link Romanshorn, in Switzerland, with Friedrichshafen, as well as Konstanz with Meersburg. Taking either ferry saves substantial mileage. The fare depends on the size of the car.

TRAIN TRAVEL

From Frankfurt to Friedrichshafen and Lindau, take the ICE (InterCity Express) to Ulm and then transfer (total time 3½ hours). There are direct trains to Konstanz from Frankfurt every 2 hours (travel takes 4½ hours), which pass through the beautiful scenery of the Black Forest. From Stuttgart to Konstanz, take the IC (InterCity) to Singen, and transfer to an RE or IRE (Regional/Inter Regio Express) for the brief last leg to Konstanz (total time 2½ hours). From Munich to Lindau, the EC (Europe Express) train takes 2½ hours. From Zürich to Konstanz, the trip lasts 1½ hours. Local trains encircle the Bodensee, stopping at most towns and villages.

TOURS

Most of the larger tourist centers have city tours with English-speaking guides. The Bodensee is a paradise for bike travelers, with hundreds of miles of well-signposted paths that keep riders safe from cars. You can go on your own or enjoy the comfort of a customized tour with accommodations and baggage transport (including rental bike, if need be). Wine-tasting tours are available in Überlingen, Konstanz, and Meersburg. Call the local tourist offices for information. Zeppelin tours operated by the DZR (Deutsche Zeppelin Reederei) are not cheap (sightseeing trips cost €200–€745), but they do offer a special feel and a reminder of the grand old days of flight. The zeppelins depart from the airport in Friedrichshafen.

Tour Contacts **Bodensee-Radweg-Service GmbH** ⊠ *Fritz-Arnold-Str. 16a, Konstanz* ☎ *07531/819–930* ⊕ *www.bodensee-radweg.com.* **Deutsche Zeppelin Reederei** ⊠ *Allmannsweilerstr. 132, Friedrichshafen* ☎ *07541/59000* ⊕ *www.zeppelinflug.de.* **Velotours Touristik GmbH** ⊠ *Bücklestr. 13, Konstanz* ☎ *07531/98280* ⊕ *www.velotours.de.*

RESTAURANTS

In this area, international dishes are not only on the menu but on the map—you have to drive only a few miles to try the Swiss or Austrian dish you're craving in its own land. *Seeweine* (lake wines) from vineyards in the area include Müller-Thurgau, Spätburgunder, Ruländer, and Kerner.

HOTELS

The towns and resorts around the lake have a wide range of hotels, from venerable wedding-cake-style, fin de siècle palaces to more-modest *Gasthöfe.* If you're visiting in July and August, make reservations in advance. For lower rates in a more rural atmosphere, consider staying a few miles away from the lake.

WHAT IT COSTS IN EUROS				
	¢	$	$$	$$$	$$$$
Restaurants	under €9	€9–€15	€16–€20	€21–€25	over €25
Hotels	under €50	€50–€100	€101–€175	€176–€225	over €225

Restaurant prices are per person for a main course at dinner. Hotel prices are for two people in a standard double room, including tax and service.

PLANNING YOUR TIME

Choosing a place to stay is a question of finance and interest. The closer you stay to the water, the more expensive and lively it becomes. Many visitors pass by on their way from one country to another, so during the middle of the day, key hubs like Konstanz, Mainau, Meersburg, and Lindau tend to be crowded. Try to visit these places either in the morning or in the late afternoon, and make your day trips to the lesser-known destinations, the baroque churches in upper Swabia, the Swiss towns along the southern shore, or the nearby mountains.

VISITOR INFORMATION

Visitor Information **Internationale Bodensee Tourismus** ✉ *Hafenstr. 6, Konstanz* ☎ *07531/90940* ⊕ *www.bodensee.eu.*

6

THE NORTHERN SHORE

There's a feeling here, in the midst of a peaceful Alpine landscape, that the Bodensee is part of Germany and yet separated from it—which is literally the case for Lindau, which sits in the lake tethered to land by a causeway. Überlingen, a beautiful resort at the northwestern finger of the lake, attracts many vacationers and spa goers. Clear days reveal the snowcapped mountains of Switzerland to the south and the peaks of the Austrian Vorarlberg to the east.

LINDAU

180 km (112 mi) southwest of Munich.

By far the best way to get to know this charming old island town is on foot. Lose yourself in the maze of small streets and passageways flanked by centuries-old houses. Wander down to the harbor for magnificent views, with the Austrian shoreline and mountains close by to the east. Just 13 km (8 mi) away, they are nearer than the Swiss mountains visible to the southwest.

Lindau was made a Free Imperial City within the Holy Roman Empire in 1275. It had developed as a fishing settlement and then spent hundreds of years as a trading center along the route between the rich lands of Swabia and Italy. The Lindauer Bote, an important stagecoach service between Germany and Italy in the 18th and 19th centuries, was based here; Goethe traveled via this service on his first visit to Italy in 1788. The stagecoach was revived a few years ago, and every June it sets off on its 13-day journey to Italy. You can book a seat through the Lindau tourist office.

As the German empire crumbled toward the end of the 18th century, battered by Napoléon's revolutionary armies, Lindau fell victim to competing political groups. It was ruled by the Austrian Empire before passing into Bavarian control in 1805. Lindau's harbor was rebuilt in 1856.

GETTING HERE AND AROUND
Lindau is halfway between Munich and Zurich, and about two hours from both on the EC (European Express) train. From Frankfurt it takes about four hours—change from the ICE (Inter City Express) train in Ulm to the IRE (Inter Regio Express) train. You can also reach Lindau by boat: it takes about 25 minutes from Bregenz across the bay. Once in Lindau, you can reach everything on foot.

ESSENTIALS
Visitor Information Lindau Tourist-Information ⊠ *Alfred-Nobel-Pl. 1* ☎ *08382/260–030* ⊕ *www.lindau-tourismus.de.*

EXPLORING
TOP ATTRACTIONS
Altes Rathaus (*Old Town Hall*). The Old Town Hall is the finest of Lindau's handsome historic buildings. It was constructed between 1422 and 1436 in the midst of a vineyard and given a Renaissance face-lift 150 years later, though the original stepped gables remain. Emperor Maximilian I held an imperial diet here in 1496; a fresco on the south facade depicts the scene. The building houses offices and cannot be visited. ⊠ *Bismarckpl. 4.*

Altstadt. The old town is a maze of ancient streets with half-timber and gable houses making up for most of the island. The center is main street, pedestrian-only Maximilianstrasse.

Bavarian Lion (*Der Bayerische Löwe*). A proud symbol of Bavaria, Der Bayerische Löwe (the Bavarian Lion) is Lindau's most striking landmark. Carved from Bavarian marble and standing 20 feet high, the lion stares out across the lake from a massive plinth.

Mangenturm (*Mangturm*). This former lighthouse at the end of the former city walls dates to the 13th century, making it one of the lake's older lighthouses. Although the structure is indeed old, its vibrantly colored rooftop is not so—following a lightning strike in the 1970s, the roof tiles were replaced, giving the tower the bright top it now bears.

Neuer Leuchtturm (*New Lighthouse; Neuer Lindauer Leuchtturm*). Germany's southernmost lighthouse stands sentinel with the Bavarian Lion across the inner harbor's passageway.

WORTH NOTING
Barfüsserkirche (*Stadttheater Lindau; Church of the Barefoot Pilgrims*). This church, built from 1241 to 1270, is now Lindau's principal theater, and the Gothic choir is a memorable setting for concerts. ⊠ *Barfüsserpl. 1a.*

Haus zum Cavazzen. Dating to 1728, this house belonged to a wealthy merchant and is now considered one of the most beautiful in the Bodensee region, owing to its rich decor of frescoes. Today it serves as a local history museum, with collections of glass and pewter items, paintings, and furniture from the past five centuries, alongside touring exhibitions of an international standard. ⊠ *Marktpl. 6* ☎ *08382/944–073* ☒ *€3* ⊗ *Apr.– Oct., daily 11–5.*

Marktplatz. Lindau's market square is lined by a series of sturdy and attractive old buildings. The Gothic **Stephanskirche** (St. Stephen's Church) is simple and sparsely decorated, as befits a Lutheran place of worship. It dates to the late 12th century but went through numerous transformations. One of its special features is the green-hue stucco ornamentation on the ceiling, which immediately attracts the eye

BREGENZ, AUSTRIA

Bregenz is a mere 13 km (8 mi) from Lindau, on the other side of the bay. It's a 20-minute boat ride to get there, which makes for a great side trip. Wander around the lakeshore and the lovely, romantic remains of the once-fortified medieval town. An enormous floating stage is the site for performances of grand opera and orchestral works under the stars. Ascend Pfänder Mountain, in Bregenz's backyard, via the Pfänderbahn cable tramway for views that stretch as far as the Black Forest and the Swiss Alps.

toward the heavens. In contrast, the Catholic **Münster Unserer Lieben Frau** (St. Mary's Church), which stands right next to the Stephanskirche, is exuberantly baroque.

Peterskirche (*St. Peter's Church*). This solid 10th-century Romanesque building is reputedly the oldest church in the Bodensee region. On the inside of the northern wall, frescoes by Hans Holbein the Elder (1465–1524) depict scenes from the life of St. Peter, the patron saint of fishermen. Peterskirche houses a memorial to fallen German soldiers from World Wars I and II, and a memorial plaque for victims of Auschwitz. Attached to the church is the 16th-century bell foundry, now a pottery works. Also of note is the adjacent fairy-tale-like **Diebsturm.** Look closely and you might see Rapunzel's golden hair hanging from this 13th-century tower, awaiting a princely rescuer. Follow the old city wall behind the tower and church to the adjoining Unterer Schrannenplatz, where the bell-makers used to live. A 1989 fountain depicts five of the *Narren* (Fools) that make up the VIPs of *Fastnacht*, the annual Alemannic Carnival celebrations. ⊠ *Oberer Schrannenpl.*

Stadtgarten (*City Park*). Ludwigstrasse and Fischergasse lead to a watchtower, once part of the original city walls with a little park behind it. If it's early evening, you'll see the first gamblers of the night making for the neighboring casino. .

WHERE TO EAT

$
GERMAN
✕ **Gasthaus zum Sünfzen.** This ancient inn was serving warm meals to the patricians, officials, merchants, and other good burghers of Lindau back in the 14th century. The current chef insists on using fresh ingredients preferably from the region, such as fish from the lake in season, venison from the mountains, and apples—pressed to juice or distilled to schnapps—from his own orchard. Try the herb-flavored *Maultaschen* (large ravioli), the excellent *Felchen* (whitefish) fillet in wine sauce,

EATING WELL BY THE BODENSEE

On a nice day you could sit on the terrace of a Bodensee restaurant forever, looking across the sparkling waters to the imposing heights of the Alps in the distance. The fish on your plate, caught that very morning in the lake perhaps, is another reason to linger. Fish predominates on the menus of the region; 35 varieties swim in the lake, with *Felchen* (whitefish) the most highly prized. Felchen belongs to the salmon family and is best eaten *blau* (poached in a mixture of water and vinegar with spices called *Essigsud*) or *Müllerin* (baked in almonds). A white *Seewein* (lake wine) from one of the vineyards around the lake provides the perfect wine match. Sample a German and a Swiss version. Both use the same grape, and yet they produce wines with very different tastes, despite the fact that the vineyards are only a few miles apart. The Swiss like their wines very dry, whereas the Germans prefer them slightly sweeter.

One of the best-known Swabian dishes is *Maultaschen*, a kind of ravioli, usually served floating in a broth strewn with chives. Another specialty is *Pfannkuchen* (pancakes), generally filled with meat, or chopped into fine strips and scattered in a clear consommé known as *Flädlesuppe*. Hearty *Zwiebelrostbraten* (beef steak with lots of fried onions) is often served with a side of *Spätzle* (hand-cut or pressed, golden soft-textured egg noodles) and accompanied by a good strong Swabian beer.

or the peppery Schübling sausage. ⊠ *Maximilianstr. 1* ☎ *08382/5865* ⊕ *www.suenfzen.de.*

$$$$ ✗ **Restaurant Hoyerberg Schlössle.** A commanding terrace view across
CONTINENTAL   the lake to Bregenz and the Alps combined with excellent nouvelle
★   cuisine makes this one of the best dining experiences in Lindau. The specialties, which change seasonally, are fish and game, and there are prix-fixe menus of four and six courses (€64–88.50); one offers tuna carpaccio, monkfish medallion, and Thai coconut soup with scampi. Brick-trim arched windows, fresh flowers, and elegant high-back chairs complete the experience. ⊠ *Hoyerbergstr. 64* ☎ *08382/25295* ⊕ *www. hoyerbergschloessle.de* ⚖ *Reservations essential* ⊗ *Closed Mon. No lunch Tues.*

WHERE TO STAY

For expanded hotel reviews, visit Fodors.com.

$ ⊞ **Gasthof Engel.** Tucked into one of the Old Town's ancient, narrow streets, this ancient property with a pedigree dating back to 1390, positively exudes history. **Pros:** quaint rooms; historic building; in the center of town. **Cons:** no elevator; room furnishings basic. ⊠ *Schafg. 4* ☎ *08382/5240* ⊕ *www.engel-lindau.de* ⇆ *9 rooms, 7 with shower* ⚘ *In-room: no a/c, no TV. In-hotel: restaurant* ⊚ *Breakfast.*

$$$ ⊞ **Hotel Bayerischer Hof.** This is *the* address in town, a stately hotel
★   directly on the edge of the lake, its terrace lush with semitropical, long-flowering plants, trees, and shrubs. **Pros:** pretty lake view from many rooms; elegant dining room with good food. **Cons:** not all rooms have a lake view; on weekends in summer parking is difficult. ⊠ *Seepromenade*

☎ 08382/9150 ⊕ www.bayerischerhof-lindau.de ⬎ 97 rooms, 2 suites ♨ In-room: a/c, Internet, Wi-Fi. In-hotel: restaurant, bar, pool, spa, laundry facilities, business center, parking, some pets allowed ⭐Breakfast.

$$ 🏨 **Hotel Garni Brugger.** This small, family-run hotel stands on the site occupied by the city wall in the Middle Ages. **Pros:** center of town; family-run atmosphere; good value for families. **Cons:** caters to families; no elevator. ✉ Bei der Heidenmauer 11 ☎ 08382/93410 ⊕ www.hotel-garni-brugger.de ⬎ 23 rooms ♨ In-room: no a/c, Internet, Wi-Fi. In-hotel: parking, some pets allowed ⊗ Closed 2 wks in Dec. ⭐Breakfast.

$$ 🏨 **Insel-Hotel.** In fine weather, enjoy breakfast al fresco as you watch the town come alive at this friendly central hotel on pedestrian-only Maximilianstrasse. **Pros:** center of town; family run. **Cons:** some rooms need some new furnishings and paint; parking is difficult. ✉ Maximilianstr. 42 ☎ 08382/5017 ⊕ www.insel-hotel-lindau.de ⬎ 24 rooms ♨ In-room: no a/c, Wi-Fi. In-hotel: restaurant, some pets allowed ⭐Breakfast.

NIGHTLIFE AND THE ARTS

Bregenzer Festspiele (*Bregenz Music Festival*). A dramatic floating stage supports orchestras and opera stars during the famous Bregenz Festspiele from mid-July to the end of August. Make reservations well in advance. The Austrian town of Bregenz is 13 km (8 mi) from Lindau, on the other side of the bay. ✉ Bregenz ☎ 0043/5574–4076 ⊕ www.bregenzerfestspiele.com.

Lindauer Marionettenoper. Enjoy opera in an intimate setting at the Lindauer Marionettenoper, where puppets do the singing.

Stadttheater. Tickets to the Lindauer Marionettenoper are available at the Stadttheater. ✉ Barfüsserpl. 1a ☎ 08382/944–650 ⊕ www.lindauer-mt.de ⊗ Mon.–Thurs. 10–1:30 and 3–6 ✉ Barfüsserpl. 1a ☎ 08382/944 650 ⊕ www.marionettenoper.de.

Spielbank Lindau Casino. You can play roulette, blackjack, poker, and slot machines at Lindau's modern and elegant casino, which is open noon–2 am. ✉ Chelles Allee 1 ☎ 08382/27740 ⊕ www.spielbanken-bayern.de.

SPORTS AND THE OUTDOORS

Bodensee Yachtschule. The Bodensee Yachtschule, in Lindau, charters yachts and has one-week camp sessions for children. ✉ Christoph Eychmüller Schiffswerfte 2 ☎ 08382/944–588 ⊕ www.bodensee-yachtschule.de.

Windsurfschule Kreitmeir. You can rent windsurfing boards at Windsurfschule Kreitmeir. ✉ Strandbad Eichwald ☎ 08382/23330 ⊕ www.hermanno.de.

SHOPPING

Biedermann en Vogue. Biedermann carries the expensive Collections Femmes et Hommes from Italy, as well as custom-made clothing, cashmere sweaters, and Italian shoes. ✉ Maximilianstr. 2 ☎ 08382/944–913.

Böhm (*Böhm - Die Einrichtungen GmbH & Co KG*). A find for interior decorators, Böhm consists of three old houses full of lamps, mirrors, precious porcelain, and elegant furniture. ✉ Maximilianstr. 21 ☎ 08382/94880 ⊕ www.boehm-dieeinrichtungen.de.

6

Internationale Bodensee-Kunstauktion (*Auktionshaus Michael Zeller*). Michael Zeller organizes the celebrated Internationale Bodensee-Kunstauktion (International Bodensee Art Auction), held four times yearly. Visit the Web site for the catalogue and dates of upcoming auctions. ⊠ *Binderg. 7* ☎ *08382/93020* ⊕ *www.zeller.de.*

EN ROUTE

Wasserburg. Six kilometers (4 mi) west of Lindau lies Wasserburg, whose name means "water castle," an exact description of what this enchanting island town once was—a fortress. It was built by the St. Gallen monastery in 924, and the owners, the counts of Montfort zu Tettnang, sold it to the Fugger family of Augsburg. The Fuggers couldn't afford to maintain the drawbridge that connected the castle with the shore and instead built a causeway. In the 18th century the castle passed into the hands of the Habsburgs, and in 1805 the Bavarian government took it over. ■**TIP→** Wasserburg has some of the most photographed sights of the Bodensee: the yellow, stair-gabled presbytery; the fishermen's St. Georg Kirche, with its onion dome; and the little Malhaus museum, with the castle, Schloss Wasserburg, in the background. ⊕ *www.wasserburg-bodensee.de.*

FRIEDRICHSHAFEN

24 km (15 mi) west of Lindau.

Named for its founder, King Friedrich I of Württemberg, Friedrichshafen is a young town (dating to 1811). In an area otherwise given over to resort towns and agriculture, Friedrichshafen played a central role in Germany's aeronautics tradition, which saw the development of the zeppelin airship before World War I and the Dornier seaplanes in the 1920s and '30s. The zeppelins were once launched from a floating hangar on the lake, and the Dornier water planes were tested here. The World War II raids on its factories virtually wiped the city off the map. The current layout of the streets is the same, but the buildings are all new and not necessarily pretty. The atmosphere, however, is good and lively, and occasionally you'll find a plaque with a picture of the old building that stood at the respective spot. The factories are back, too. Friedrichshafen is home to such international firms as EADS (airplanes, rockets, and helicopters) and ZF (gear wheels).

GETTING HERE AND AROUND

It takes about one hour from Ulm on the ICE (Inter City Express) train. Most trains stop at Friedrichshafen airport. The car ferry takes you on a 40-minute run across the lake to Romanshorn in Switzerland, where you have direct express trains to the airport and Zürich. In town you can reach most places on foot.

A fascinating way to view the lake is from a three-passenger Cessna operated by Slansky/Dussmann from Friedrichshafen's airport. They will also take you into the Alps, if you wish.

SWISS STOPS

There are two towns on the Swiss shores of the Bodensee that are convenient for quick trips from Germany. Ferries travel between Friedrichshafen in Germany and **Romanshorn**, a yachting and sportfishing center, in Switzerland. You can catch trains in Romanshorn to eastern Switzerland and to Zürich. **Kreuzlingen** is the small Swiss city across the border from Konstanz. There's little to see here, but you can catch a train to Zürich.

The Zeppelin Museum houses a collection of fascinating artifacts from the days of the airship. You can also tour a reproduction of the *Hindenburg*.

ESSENTIALS

Airplane Tours Konair. Konair provide scenic flights, flight lessons, and an air taxi service around the Bodensee region. ⊠ *Riedstr. 82, Konstanz* ☏ *07531/361 6905* ⊕ *www.konair.de.*

Visitor Information Friedrichshafen ⊠ *Tourist-Information, Bahnhofpl. 2* ☏ *07541/30010* ⊕ *www.friedrichshafen.de.*

EXPLORING

Deutsche Zeppelin Reederei GmbH. The Deutsche Zeppelin Reederei GmbH operates zeppelins at the Friedrichshafen airport. You can board the *Zeppelin NT* (New Technology) for an aerial tour, or from April through November you can tour the zeppelin in its hangar. ⊠ *Allmannsweilerstr. 132* ☏ *07541/59000* ⊕ *www.zeppelinflug.de.*

Fodor's Choice
★

Zeppelin Museum. Graf Zeppelin (Ferdinand Graf von Zeppelin) was born across the lake in Konstanz, but Friedrichshafen was where, on July 2, 1900, his first "airship"—the LZ 1—was launched. The fascinating story is told in the Zeppelin Museum, which holds the world's most significant collection of artifacts pertaining to airship history. In a wing of the restored Bauhaus **Friedrichshafen Hafenbahnhof** (harbor railway station), the main attraction is the reconstruction of a 108-foot-long section of the legendary *Hindenburg*, the LZ 129 that exploded at its berth in Lakehurst, New Jersey, on May 6, 1937. (The airships were filled with hydrogen, because the United States refused to sell the Germans helium, for political reasons.) Climb aboard the airship via a retractable stairway and stroll past the authentically furnished passenger room, the original lounges, and the dining room. The illusion of traveling in a zeppelin is followed by exhibits on the history and technology of airship aviation: propellers, engines, dining-room menus, and films of the airships traveling or at war. Car fans will appreciate the great Maybach standing on the ground floor; passengers once enjoyed being transported to the zeppelins in it. The museum's restaurant is a good place to take a break and enjoy lunch or dinner. ⊠ *Seestr. 22* ☏ *07541/38010* ⊕ *www.zeppelin-museum.de* 🎫 *€7.50* ☼ *May–Oct., daily 9–5 (last entry at 4:30); Nov.–Apr., Tues.–Sun. 10–5.*

WHERE TO EAT

$$

GERMAN

✕ **Lukullum.** Students, businesspeople, and guests from the nearby hotels rub elbows at this lively, novel restaurant. The friendly service keeps up with the pace of the socializing. The restaurant is divided into eight *Stuben* (rooms), all themed: sit in a beer barrel, dine in Tirol, or relax under the image of an airship in the Zeppelin Bräu Stüble. There's also a beer garden. The dishes are good and basic, with surprising international touches—everything from Balkan kebabs to New Orleans jambalaya. ⊠ *Friedrichstr. 21* ☏ *07541/6818* ⊕ *www.lukullum.de* ☼ *Closed Mon. No lunch Tues.–Fri.*

$

GERMAN

✕ **Zeppelin-Museumrestaurant.** The grand view of the harbor and the lake is only one of the attractions of this café and restaurant in the Zeppelin Museum. You can enjoy cakes and drinks, a wide range of Swabian specialties, and several Italian dishes. ⊠ *Seestr. 22* ☏ *07541/953–0088.*

WHERE TO STAY

For expanded hotel reviews, visit Fodors.com.

$

🏨 **Buchhorner Hof.** This traditional family-run hotel near the train station is decorated with hunting trophies, leather armchairs, and Turkish rugs; bedrooms are large and comfortable. **Pros:** business floor; cozy and big lobby; excellent restaurant; many rooms have nice views. **Cons:** many rooms look onto a busy main street; parking is difficult. ⊠ *Friedrichstr. 33* ☏ *07541/2050* ⊕ *www.buchhorn.de* 📞 *92 rooms, 4 suites, 2 apartments* ⚘ *In-room: no a/c, Internet, Wi-Fi. In-hotel: restaurant, bar, gym, parking, some pets allowed* �"O�" *Breakfast.*

$$

🏨 **Flair Hotel Gerbe.** A farm with a tannery in Friedrichshafen Ailingen, about 5 km (3 mi) from the city center, is now a pleasant, spacious hotel whose rooms (many with balconies) overlook the gardens, the countryside, and—on a clear day—the Swiss mountains. **Pros:** new rooms in a historic building; spacious rooms with good views; ample parking. **Cons:** 5 km (3 mi) from center of town; some rooms have street noise. ⊠ *Hirschlatterstr. 14, Ailingen* ☏ *07541/5090* ⊕ *www.hotel-gerbe.de* 📞 *59 rooms* ⚘ *In-room: no a/c, Wi-Fi. In-hotel: restaurant, bar, pool, gym, business center, parking* �"O�" *Breakfast.*

$$

★

🏨 **Ringhotel Krone.** This large Bavarian-theme hotel in the Schnetzenhausen district's semirural surroundings, 6 km (4 mi) from the center of town, has a lot to offer active guests, including tennis, minigolf, rental bicycles, a gym, saunas, and an indoor pool. **Pros:** great variety of rooms; good food; lots of parking. **Cons:** 6 km (4 mi) from the center of town; a few rooms have street noise. ⊠ *Untere Mühlbachstr. 1* ☏ *07541/4080* ⊕ *www.ringhotel-krone.de* 📞 *135 rooms* ⚘ *In-room:*

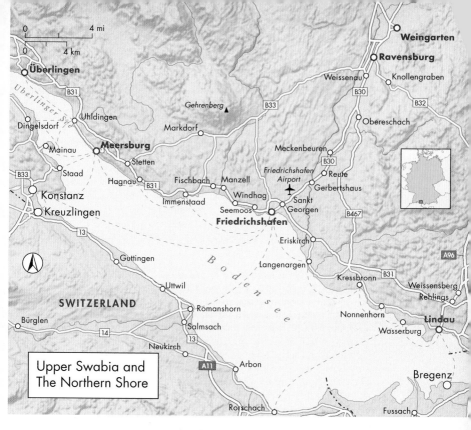

Upper Swabia and
The Northern Shore

*no a/c, Wi-Fi. In-hotel: restaurant, bar, pool, tennis court, gym, spa,
business center, parking, some pets allowed* ⃝ *Breakfast.*

NIGHTLIFE AND THE ARTS

Cafebar Belushi. College students and a mostly young crowd raise their
glasses and voices above the din at Cafebar Belushi. ✉ *Montfortstr. 3*
☎ *07541/32531* ⊕ *www.cafe-bar-belushi.de.*

Graf-Zeppelin-Haus. Friedrichshafen's Graf-Zeppelin-Haus is a modern
convention center on the lakeside promenade, a seven-minute walk
from the train station. It's also a cultural center, where musicals, light
opera, and classical as well as pop-rock concerts take place several
times a week. The Graf-Zeppelin-Haus has a good modern restaurant
with a big terrace overlooking the harbor. ✉ *Olgastr. 20* ☎ *07541/2880.*

SHOPPING

Ebe. The gift shop Ebe sells handmade candles, toys, stationery, and
postcards, alongside some clothing and accessories. ✉ *Buchhornpl. 5*
☎ *07541/388–430.*

Weber & Weiss. Excellent chocolates are sold at Weber & Weiss.
■ TIP➔ Look for the special zeppelin airship–shape chocolates and candies. ✉ *Charlottenstr. 11* ☎ *07541/21771* ⊕ *www.weber-weiss.de.*

MEERSBURG

18 km (11 mi) west of Friedrichshafen.

Meersburg is one of the most romantic old towns on the German shore of the lake. Seen from the water on a summer afternoon with the sun slanting low, the steeply terraced town looks like a stage set, with its bold castles, severe patrician dwellings, and a gaggle of half-timber houses arranged around narrow streets. It's no wonder that cars have been banned from the center: the crowds of people who come to visit the sights on weekends fill up the streets. The town is divided into the Unterstadt (Lower Town) and Oberstadt (Upper Town), connected by several steep streets and stairs.

ESSENTIALS

Visitor Information Meersburg ⊠ *Tourism Meersburg, Kirchstr. 4*
☎ *07532/440–400* ⊕ *www.meersburg.de.*

EXPLORING

Fodor's Choice ★ **Altes Schloss** (*Old Castle; Burg Meersburg*). Majestically guarding the town is the Altes Schloss, the original Meersburg ("sea castle"). It's Germany's oldest inhabited castle, founded in 628 by Dagobert, king of the Franks. The massive central tower, with walls 10 feet thick, is named after him. The bishops of Konstanz used it as a summer residence until 1526, at which point they moved in permanently. They remained until the mid-18th century, when they built themselves what they felt to be a more suitable residence—the baroque Neues Schloss. Plans to tear down the Altes Schloss in the early 19th century were shelved when it was taken over by Baron Joseph von Lassberg, a man much intrigued by the castle's medieval romance. He turned it into a home for like-minded poets and artists, among them the Grimm brothers and his sister-in-law, Annette von Droste-Hülshoff (1797–1848), one of Germany's most famous poets. The Altes Schloss is still private property, but much of it can be visited, including the richly furnished rooms where Droste-Hülshoff lived and the chamber where she died, as well as the imposing knights' hall, the minstrels' gallery, and the sinister dungeons. The **Altes Schloss Museum** (Old Castle Museum) contains a fascinating collection of weapons and armor, including a rare set of medieval jousting equipment. ⊠ *Schlosspl. 10* ☎ *07532/80000* ⊕ *www.burg-meersburg.de* 🎫 *€8.50* ⊙ *Mar.–Oct., daily 9–6:30; Nov.–Feb., daily 10–6.*

Droste Museum. An idyllic retreat almost hidden among the vineyards, the Fürstenhäusle was built in 1640 by a local vintner and later used as a holiday home by poet Annette von Droste-Hülshoff. It's now the Droste Museum, containing many of her personal possessions and giving a vivid sense of Meersburg in her time. ⊠ *Stettenerstr. 11, east of Obertor, the town's north gate* ☎ *07532/6088* 🎫 *€4.90* ⊙ *Apr.–Oct., Tues.–Sat. 10–12:30 and 2–6, Sun. 2–6.*

Neues Schloss (*New Castle*). Set to reopen in spring 2012 following renovations, the spacious and elegant Neues Schloss is directly across from its predecessor. Designed by Christoph Gessinger at the beginning of the 18th century, it took nearly 50 years to complete. The grand double staircase, with its intricate grillwork and heroic statues, was the work of Balthasar Neumann. The interior's other standout is the glittering **Spiegelsaal** (Hall of Mirrors). In an unlikely combination of 18th-century grace and 20th-century technology, the first floor of the palace houses the **Dornier Museum.** Three rooms are devoted to Claude Dornier, the pioneer airplane builder, and his flying machines. ☏ *07532/440–4900* ≋*€4* ⊙ *Apr.–Oct., daily 10–1.*

Stadtmuseum. Right next to the Meersburg Tourist Office is the Stadtmuseum, or City Museum, in a former Dominican priory. You can see an overview of the town's history that celebrates some of its famous residents, such as Franz Anton Mesmer, who developed the theory of "animal magnetism." (His name gave rise to the verb "mesmerize.") ⊠ *Kirchstr. 4* ☏ *07532/440–4801* ≋*€2* ⊙ *Apr.–Oct., Wed., Thurs., and Sat. 2–6.*

Weinbau Museum (*Vineyard Museum*). Sunbathed, south-facing Meersburg and the neighboring towns have been the center of the Bodensee wine trade for centuries. You can pay your respects to the noble profession in the Weinbau Museum. A barrel capable of holding 50,000 liters (about the same number of quarts) and an immense winepress dating from 1607 are highlights of the collection. ⊠ *Vorburgg. 11* ☏ *07532/440–400* ≋*€2* ⊙ *Apr.–Oct., Tues., Fri., and Sun. 2–6.*

WHERE TO EAT

$$
GERMAN
★

✗ **Winzerstube zum Becher.** Fresh fish from the lake is a specialty at this traditional restaurant, which has been in the Benz family for three generations. You can pair the day's catch with white wine from their own vineyard. A popular meat entrée is *badische Ente* (duck with bacon and apples in a wine-kirsch sauce). The restaurant is near the New Castle, and reservations are recommended. ⊠ *Höllg. 4* ☏ *07532/9009* ⊕ *www.winzerstube-zum-becher.de* ⊙ *Lunch 11:30–2, dinner 5–10.* ⊙ *Closed Jan. and Mon.*

WHERE TO STAY

For expanded hotel reviews, visit Fodors.com.

$ ⌂ **Gästehaus am Hafen.** This family-run, half-timber pension is in the middle of the Old Town, near the harbor. **Pros:** close to the harbor; in the center of the Lower Town; good value. **Cons:** small rooms; no credit cards; parking is five minutes away on foot. ⊠ *Spitalg. 3–4* ☏ *07532/7069* ⊕ *www.amhafen.eu* ⇝ *7 rooms* ⌂ *In-room: no a/c. In-hotel: restaurant, parking, some pets allowed* ⊟ *No credit cards* ⊙ *Restaurant closed Tues., and Nov.–Mar.* ⓘ⊙*Breakfast.*

$ ⌂ **Hotel Weinstube Löwen.** Rooms at this local landmark—a centuries-old, ivy-clad tavern on Meersburg's market square—feature their

6

The Altes Schloss in Meersburg is a true Medieval castle and the museum includes armor and jousting equipment.

own corner sitting areas, some with genuine Biedermeier furniture. **Pros:** center of town; pleasant rooms; good food in a cozy restaurant. **Cons:** lots of daytime noise from tourists; no elevator. ⊠ *Marktpl. 2* ☎ *07532/43040* ⊕ *www.hotel-loewen-meersburg.de* ⤳ *20 rooms* ⚐ *In-room: no a/c, Wi-Fi. In-hotel: restaurant, bar, business center, parking, some pets allowed* ⊗ *Restaurant closed Wed. Nov.–Mar.* ⦿ *Breakfast.*

$$ 🏨 **Romantik Hotel Residenz am See.** This tastefully modern hotel overlook-
★ ing the lake features two restaurants, including the Michelin-starred Casala, and Residenz Restaurant, which specializes in regional fare. **Pros:** good food; pleasant rooms with lake view; quiet rooms toward the vineyards. **Cons:** not in center of town; only no-smoking rooms. ⊠ *Ufer-promenade 11* ☎ *07532/80040* ⊕ *www.hotel-residenz-meersburg.com* ⤳ *25 rooms* ⚐ *In-room: no a/c, Wi-Fi. In-hotel: restaurant, bar, laundry facilities, parking, some pets allowed* ⊗ *Restaurant Casala closed Mon. and Tues.* ⦿ *Multiple meal plans.*

$$ 🏨 **See Hotel Off.** Nearly all rooms at this bright and airy hotel just a
★ few steps from the shore offer balconies with views across the lake or vineyards. **Pros:** close to the lake; individually decorated rooms; away from center of town. **Cons:** not in center of town. ⊠ *Uferpromenade 51* ☎ *07532/44740* ⊕ *www.seehotel-off.de* ⤳ *22 rooms, 1 suite* ⚐ *In-room: no a/c, Wi-Fi. In-hotel: restaurant, bar, spa, parking, some pets allowed* ⊗ *Closed Jan.* ⦿ *Multiple meal plans.*

$ 🏨 **Zum Bären.** Individually furnished rooms lend character to this his-
toric hotel, whose ivy-covered facade, with its characteristic steeple, hasn't changed much over the centuries. **Pros:** center of town; historic building; good value. **Cons:** no elevator; some rooms are small; no

credit cards. ⊠ *Marktpl. 11* ☎ *07532/43220* ⊕ *www.baeren-meersburg. de* ⤳ *20 rooms* ⚹ *In-room: no a/c. In-hotel: restaurant, parking* ═ *No credit cards* ⊘ *Closed Dec.–Mar.* ��⧉ *Breakfast.*

SPORTS AND THE OUTDOORS

⟳ **Meersburg Therme.** The lakeside Meersburg Therme (Meersburg Spa) hot spring–fed pool complex east of the harbor has three outdoor pools, an indoor "adventure" pool, an indoor-outdoor thermal bath (34°C [93.2°F]), a sauna, and a volleyball court. ⊠ *Uferpromenade 12* ☎ *07532/440–2850* ⊕ *www.meersburg-therme.de* ⤶ *Bathing and sauna (3 hrs) €16.50, full day €18.50* ⊘ *Mon.–Sat. 10–10, Sun. 9–10.*

SHOPPING

⟳ **Omas Kaufhaus.** If you can't find something at this incredible gift shop (toys, enamelware, books, dolls, model cars, and much more), then at least you should see the exhibition of toy trains and tin boats on the first floor, the latter in a long canal filled with real water. ⊠ *Steigstr. 2* ☎ *07532/433–9611* ⊕ *www.omas-kaufhaus.de* ⊘ *Daily 10–6:30.*

EN ROUTE

Pfahlbauten (*"pile dwellings"*). As you proceed northwest along the lake's shore, a settlement of Pfahlbauten—a reconstructed village of Stone Age and Bronze Age dwellings built on stilts—sticks out of the lake. This is how the original lake dwellers lived, surviving off the fish that swam outside their humble huts. Real dwellers in authentic garb give you an accurate picture of prehistoric lifestyles. The on-site **Pfahlbauten Freilichtmuseum** (Open-Air Museum of German Prehistory) contains actual finds excavated in the area. Admission includes an obligatory 45-minute tour. ⊠ *Strandpromenade 6, Unteruhldingen* ☎ *07556/928–900* ⊕ *www.pfahlbauten.de* ⤶ *€7.50* ⊘ *Apr.–Sept., daily 9–7; Oct., daily 9–5; Nov.–Mar., hrs vary.*

ÜBERLINGEN

13 km (8 mi) west of Meersburg, 24 km (15 mi) west of Friedrichshafen.

This Bodensee resort has an attractive waterfront and an almost Mediterranean flair. It's midway along the north shore of the Überlingersee, a narrow finger of the Bodensee that points to the northwest. Überlingen is ancient—it's first mentioned in records dating back to 770. In the 14th century it earned the title of Free Imperial City and was known for its wines. No fewer than seven of its original city gates and towers remain from those grand days, as well as substantial portions of the old city walls. What was once the moat is now a grassy walkway, with the walls of the Old Town towering on one side and the Stadtpark stretching away on the other. The **Stadtgarten** (city garden), which opened in 1875, cultivates exotic plants and has a famous collection of cacti, a fuchsia garden, and a small deer corral. The heart of the city is the Münsterplatz.

ESSENTIALS

Visitor Information Überlingen ⊠ *Tourist-Information, Landungspl. 5* ☎ *07551/947–1522* ⊕ *www.ueberlingen.de.*

EXPLORING

Altes Rathaus (*Old Town Hall*). Inside the late-Gothic Altes Rathaus is a high point of Gothic decoration, the **Rathaussaal,** or council chamber, which is still in use today. Its most striking feature amid the riot of carving is the series of figures, created between 1492 and 1494, representing the states of the Holy Roman Empire. To visit the interior, you'll need to take the hour-long guided tour. Tours are free; simply show up shortly before the set start time. ⊠ *Münsterstr. 15* ⊡ *Free* ⊙ *Tours: May–Sept., Mon.–Thurs. 11 and 2, Fri. 11; Oct.–Apr., Wed. 11, Tues. and Thurs. 2.*

★ **Münster St. Nikolaus** (*Church of St. Nicholas*). The huge Münster St. Nikolaus was built between 1512 and 1563 on the site of at least two previous churches. The interior is all Gothic solemnity and massiveness, with a lofty stone-vaulted ceiling and high, pointed arches lining the nave. The single most remarkable feature is not Gothic at all but opulently Renaissance—the massive high altar, carved by Jörg Zürn from lime wood that almost looks like ivory. The focus of the altar is the Christmas story. ⊠ *Münsterpl.*

⊙ **Schloss Salem** (*Salem Castle*). Schloss Salem is in the tiny inland village
Fodor's Choice of Salem, 10 km (6 mi) north of Überlingen. This huge castle began
★ its existence as a convent and large church. After many architectural permutations, it was transformed into a palace for the Baden princes, though traces of its religious past can still be seen. You can view the royally furnished rooms of the abbots and princes, a library, stables, and the church. The castle also houses an interesting array of museums, workshops, and activities, including a museum of firefighting, a potter, a musical instrument builder, a goldsmith shop, a glassblowing shop, pony farms, a golf driving range, and a fantasy garden for children. There is a great path that leads from the southwestern part of the grounds through woods and meadows to the pilgrimage church of Birnau. The route was created by the monks centuries ago and is still called the Prälatenweg (path of the prelates) today. It's an 8-km (5-mi) walk (no cars permitted). ⊠ *Salem* ☎ *07553/916–5336* ⊕ *www.salem. de* ⊡ *€7* ⊙ *Apr.–Nov., Mon.–Sat. 9:30–6, Sun. 10:30–6.*

Städtisches Museum (*City Museum*). The Städtisches Museum is in the Reichlin-von-Meldegg house, 1462, one of the earliest Renaissance dwellings in Germany. It displays exhibits tracing Bodensee history and a vast collection of antique dollhouses. ⊠ *Krummebergstr. 30* ☎ *07551/991–079* ⊕ *www.museum-ueberlingen.de* ⊡ *€5* ⊙ *Apr.–Oct., Tues.–Sat. 9–12:30 and 2–5, Sun. 10–3.*

Fodor's Choice **Wallfahrtskirche Birnau** (*Pilgrimage Church; Basilika Birnau*). Just north-
★ west of Unteruhldingen, the Wallfahrtskirche Birnau is nestled among vineyards overlooking the lake. The church was built by the master architect Peter Thumb between 1746 and 1750. Its exterior consists of pink-and-white plaster and a tapering clock-tower spire above the main entrance. The interior is overwhelmingly rich, full of movement, light, and color. It's hard to single out highlights from such a profusion of ornament, but seek out the *Honigschlecker* ("honey sucker"), a gold-and-white cherub beside the altar, dedicated to St. Bernard of Clairvaux, "whose words are sweet as honey" (it's the last altar on the

Near Überlingen, Schloss Salem was constructed as a convent and then transformed into a palace. Leading from the palace grounds is a 5-mi path to Wallfahrtskirche Birnau (Pilgrimage Church).

right as you face the high altar). The cherub is sucking honey from his finger, which he's just pulled out of a beehive. The fanciful spirit of this dainty play on words is continued in the small squares of glass set into the pink screen that rises high above the main altar; the gilt dripping from the walls; the swaying, swooning statues; and the swooping figures on the ceiling. ⌧ *Birnau, Uhldingen-Mühlhofen* ⌖ *www.birnau.de* ⊙ *May.–Sep., daily 7:30–7; Oct.–Apr., daily 7:30–5:30.*

WHERE TO STAY

For expanded hotel reviews, visit Fodors.com.

$$ 🏨 **Bad Hotel mit Villa Seeburg.** This stately hotel with a charming 19th-century villa annex is both on the lake and in town, with spare modern rooms done in crisp white and cream. **Pros:** on the lake; in the center of town; quiet. **Cons:** rooms in the main building on the busy street can be noisy; parking is two minutes away on foot. ⌧ *Christophstr. 2* ☎ *07551/8370* ⌖ *www.bad-hotel-ueberlingen.de* 🛏 *65 rooms* ⌂ *In-room: no a/c, Wi-Fi. In-hotel: restaurant, bar, parking* ⊙ *Bar and restaurant closed Nov.–Mar. except briefly in Dec. (call for times)* ⃝ *Multiple meal plans.*

$ 🏨 **Landgasthof zum Adler.** This unpretentious, rustic country inn in a village a few miles north of Überlingen has a blue-and-white half-timber facade, scrubbed wooden floors, maple-wood tables, and thick down comforters on the beds. **Pros:** good food in old wooden restaurant; modern rooms in annex; family-friendly. **Cons:** rooms on the street side can be noisy; a bit far from Überlingen; family-oriented. ⌧ *Hauptstr. 44, Lippertsreute* ☎ *07553/82550* ⌖ *www.adler-lippertsreute.de* 🛏 *17 rooms* ⌂ *In-room: no a/c, kitchen. In-hotel: restaurant, parking, some pets allowed* ⃝ *Breakfast.*

$$ ⊡ **Romantik Hotel Johanniter Kreuz.** Parts of this half-timber hotel—which is in a small, peaceful village 3 km (2 mi) north of Überlingen—date from the 17th century, setting a romantic tone that's further enhanced by the huge fireplace in the center of the restaurant. **Pros:** choice of very different rooms; spacious; modern, and yet welcoming lobby; family run; cozy restaurant; golf course close by. **Cons:** not in center of town; long corridors from historic part of hotel to reach elevator in new part of the hotel. ⊠ *Johanniterweg 11, Andelshofen* ☎ *07551/937–060* ⊕ *www.johanniter-kreuz.de* ⟋ *29 rooms* ⌂ *In-room: no a/c, Internet, Wi-Fi. In-hotel: restaurant, gym, spa, business center, parking, some pets allowed* ⊗ *Restaurant closed Mon. No lunch Tues.* ⦿ *Breakfast.*

$$ ⊡ **Schäpfle.** The charm of this ivy-covered hotel in the center of town has been preserved and supplemented through time—in the hallways you'll find quaint furniture and even an old Singer sewing machine painted with flowers. **Pros:** center of town; local atmosphere in restaurant; annex with lake view. **Cons:** no elevator; no credit cards; no lobby. ⊠ *Jakob-Kessenringstr. 14* ☎ *07551/63494* ⊕ *www.schaepfle.de* ⟋ *32 rooms in 2 houses* ⌂ *In-room: no a/c. In-hotel: restaurant, some pets allowed* ⊟ *No credit cards* ⦿ *Multiple meal plans.*

SHOPPING

The beauty and charm of Überlingen apparently attract artists to come, work, and live here, as there are more than 20 ateliers and artists' shops in town where you can browse and buy at reasonable prices. ■ TIP→ **Ask at the tourist office for the brochure listing all the galleries.**

Holzer. Holzer is the studio of a master craftsman of gold jewelry. ⊠ *Turmg. 8* ☎ *07551/61525.*

THE UPPER SWABIAN BAROQUE ROAD

From Friedrichshafen, B-30 leads north along the valley of the little River Schussen and links up with one of Germany's less-known but most attractive scenic routes. The Oberschwäbische Barockstrasse (Upper Swabian Baroque Road) follows a rich series of baroque churches and abbeys, including Germany's largest baroque church, the basilica in Weingarten.

RAVENSBURG

20 km (12 mi) north of Friedrichshafen.

The Free Imperial City of Ravensburg once competed with Augsburg and Nürnberg for economic supremacy in southern Germany. The Thirty Years' War put an end to the city's hopes by reducing it to little more than a medieval backwater. The city's loss proved fortuitous only in that many of its original features have remained much as they were built (in the 19th century, medieval towns usually tore down their medieval walls and towers, which were considered ungainly and constraining). Fourteen of Ravensburg's town gates and towers survive, and the Altstadt is among the best preserved in Germany.

GETTING HERE AND AROUND

Consider taking an official tour of the city, which grants you access to some of the towers for a splendid view of Ravensburg and the surrounding countryside. Tours are available at the tourist office.

ESSENTIALS

Visitor Information Ravensburg ✉ *Tourist-Information, Kirchstr. 16* ☎ *0751/82800* ⊕ *www.ravensburg.de.*

EXPLORING

TOP ATTRACTIONS

Defensive Towers. Ravensburg is home to a remarkable collection of well-preserved medieval towers and city gates. Highlights include the **Grüner Turm** (Green Tower), so called for its green tiles, many of which are 14th-century originals. Another stout defense tower is the massive **Obertor** (Upper Tower), the oldest gate in the city walls. The curiously named **Mehlsack** (Flour Sack) tower—so called because of its rounded shape and whitewash exterior—stands 170 feet high and sits upon the highest point of the city. From April to October, visitors can climb to the top of the Mehlsack or the equally tall **Blaserturm** (Trumpeter's Tower) for rooftop views over the city. ☎ *0751/82800* ☉ *Mehlsack: Apr.–Oct., weekends 10–3. Blaserturm: Apr.–Oct., weekdays 2–5, Sat. 10–3.*

Marienplatz. Many of Ravensburg's monuments that recall the town's wealthy past are concentrated on this central square. To the west is the 14th-century **Kornhaus** (Granary); once the corn exchange for all of Upper Swabia, it now houses the public library. The late-Gothic **Rathaus** is a staid, red building with a Renaissance bay window and imposing late-Gothic rooms inside. Next to it stands the 15th-century **Waaghaus** (Weighing House), the town's weigh station and central warehouse. Its tower, the **Blaserturm** (Trumpeter's Tower), which served as the watchman's abode, was rebuilt in 1556 after a fire and now bears a pretty Renaissance helmet. Finally there's the colorfully frescoed **Lederhaus,** once the headquarters of the city's leather workers, now home to a café.

■ TIP➔ On Saturday morning the square comes alive with a large market.

WORTH NOTING

Evangelische Stadtkirche (*Protestant Church*). That ecclesiastical and commercial life were never entirely separate in medieval towns is evident in this church, once part of a 14th-century monastery. The stairs on the west side of the church's chancel lead to the meeting room of the Ravensburger Gesellschaft (Ravensburg Society), an organization of linen merchants established in 1400. After the Reformation, Catholics and Protestants shared the church, but in 1810 the Protestants were given the entire building. The neo-Gothic stained-glass windows on the west side, depicting important figures of the Reformation such as Martin Luther and Ulrich Zwingli, were sponsored by wealthy burghers. ✉ *Marienpl. 5.*

Kirche St. Peter und Paul. Just to the southwest of Ravensburg in the village of Weissenau stands this old church, which was part of a 12th-century Premonstratensian monastery and now boasts a high baroque facade. The interior is a stupendous baroque masterpiece, with ceiling paintings by Joseph Hafner that create the illusion of cupolas,

6

DID YOU KNOW?

The Weingarten Basilica's altar is said to hold a vial of Christ's blood. On the day after Ascension Thursday, a huge procession of pilgrims makes its way to the basilica.

and vivacious stuccowork by Johannes Schmuzer, one of the famous stucco artists from Wessobrunn. ⊠ *Abteistr. 2–3, Weissenau* ⊕ *www. pfarrgemeinde-weissenau.de* ⊙ *Daily 9–6.*

Liebfrauenkirche (*Church of Our Lady*). Ravensburg's true parish church, the Gothic 14th-century Liebfrauenkirche, is elegantly simple on the outside but almost entirely rebuilt inside, having reopened in early 2011 following major renovations. Among the finest treasures within are the 15th-century stained-glass windows in the choir and the heavily gilt altar. In a side altar is a copy of a carved Madonna, the *Schutzmantelfrau*; the late-14th-century original is in Berlin's Dahlem Museum. ⊠ *Kirchstr. 18* ⊙ *Daily 7–7.*

☾ **Museum Ravensburger.** Ravensburg is a familiar name to all jigsaw-puzzle fans, because its eponymous Ravensburg publishing house produces the world's largest selection of puzzles, in addition to many other children's games. Here you can explore the history of the company, founded in 1883 by Otto Robert Maier. Be sure to try out new and classic games via the interactive game stations in the games lounge on the top floor. ⊠ *Marktstr. 26* ☎ *07542/400–110* ⊕ *www.museum-ravensburger.de* ⊠ *€5* ⊙ *Apr.–Oct., Tues.–Sun. 10–6; Nov.–Mar., Tues.–Sun. 11–6.*

6

WHERE TO EAT AND STAY
For expanded hotel reviews, visit Fodors.com.

$ | CAFÉ | ╳ **Café Gelateria Firenze.** This bustling multilevel café opens early and closes late and offers a mind-boggling array of ice-cream dishes and other sweet treats, such as waffles and crepes. If you're more in the mood for a savory bite, consider the tasty breakfast fare, sandwiches, and German- and Italian-influenced items. ⊠ *Marienpl. 47, Ravensburg* ☎ *0751/24665* ▭ *No credit cards.*

$ | ECLECTIC | ╳ **Café-Restaurant Central.** This popular place, with two floors and a large terrace on Marienplatz, has an international range of dishes, from kebabs and curries to pastas and local specialties. You can also enjoy coffee, cakes, or an aperitif. ⊠ *Marienpl. 48* ☎ *0751/32533* ⊕ *www. cafebar-central.de.*

$$$ | GERMAN | Fodor'sChoice ★ | ╳ **Rebleutehaus.** Follow a small alley off the Marienplatz to this warm, relaxed restaurant set in an old guildhall with a beautiful *Tonnendecke* (barrel ceiling). The restaurant shares a kitchen with the Restaurant Waldhorn; the quality is the same, but the prices at Rebleutehaus are easier on the wallet. Try fish from the Bodensee in season. Reservations are advisable for dinner. ⊠ *Schulg. 15* ☎ *0751/36120* ⊕ *www.waldhorn. de* ⊙ *Closed Sun.*

$ | ☷ **Gasthof Ochsen.** The Ochsen is a typical, family-owned Swabian inn, and the personable Kimpfler family extends a warm welcome. **Pros:** warm atmosphere in the cozy restaurant; very good Swabian food. **Cons:** no elevator; rooms simply furnished. ⊠ *Eichelstr. 17, just off Marienpl.* ☎ *0751/25480* ⊕ *www.ochsen-rv.de* ↻ *13 rooms* ⌂ *In-room: no a/c, Wi-Fi. In-hotel: restaurant, some pets allowed* ⊙ *Restaurant closed to public Sun.* ⫿○⫾ *Breakfast.*

$$ | ★ | ☷ **Romantikhotel Waldhorn.** This historic hostelry in the heart of Ravensburg has been in the Dressel-Bouley family for more than 150 years. **Pros:** family-run historic institution; very warm relaxed atmosphere in

the restaurant; excellent food; innovative dishes. **Cons:** some wooden floors on the first floor need renovations; main restaurant is very elegant but stuffy. ⊠ *Marienpl. 15* ☎ *0751/36120* ⊕ *www.waldhorn.de* ⤶ *30 rooms, 3 suites, 7 apartments* ⌂ *In-room: no a/c, Wi-Fi. In-hotel: restaurant, parking, some pets allowed* ⊘ *Restaurant closed Sun. and Mon. No lunch Tues.* ⏺ *Breakfast.*

WEINGARTEN

5 km (3 mi) north of Ravensburg.

Weingarten is famous throughout Germany for its huge and hugely impressive basilica, which you can see up on a hill from miles away, long before you get to the town. The city has grown during the last century as several small and midsize industries settled here and is now an interesting mixture, its historic old town surrounded by a small, prosperous industrial city.

ESSENTIALS

Visitor Information Weingarten ⊠ *Amt für Kultur- und Tourismus, Münsterpl. 1* ☎ *0751/405–232* ⊕ *www.weingarten-online.de.*

EXPLORING

Alemannenmuseum. If you want to learn about early Germans—residents from the 6th, 7th, and 8th centuries whose graves are just outside town—visit the Alemannenmuseum in the Kornhaus, at one time a granary. Archaeologists discovered the hundreds of Alemannic graves in the 1950s. ⊠ *Karlstr. 28* ☎ *0751/405–125* ⊡ *€2* ⊘ *Tues.–Sun. 2–5.*

★ **Weingarten Basilica.** At 220 feet high and more than 300 feet long, Weingarten Basilica is the largest baroque church in Germany. It was built as the church of one of the oldest and most venerable convents in the country, founded in 1056 by the wife of Guelph IV. The Guelph dynasty ruled large areas of Upper Swabia, and generations of family members lie buried in the church. The majestic edifice was renowned because of its little vial said to contain drops of Christ's blood. First mentioned by Charlemagne, the vial passed to the convent in 1094, entrusted to its safekeeping by the Guelph queen Juditha, sister-in-law of William the Conqueror. At a stroke Weingarten became one of Germany's foremost pilgrimage sites. ■ TIP➜ **To this day, on the day after Ascension Thursday, the anniversary of the day the vial of Christ's blood was entrusted to the convent, a huge procession of pilgrims wends its way to the basilica. It's well worth seeing the procession, which is headed by nearly 3,000 horsemen (many local farmers breed horses just for this occasion).** The basilica was decorated by leading early-18th-century German and Austrian artists: stuccowork by Franz Schmuzer, ceiling frescoes by Cosmas Damian Asam, and a Donato Frisoni altar—one of the most breathtakingly ornate in Europe, with nearly 80-foot-high towers on either side. The organ, installed by Josef Gabler between 1737 and 1750, is among the largest in the country. ⊠ *Kirchpl. 6* ⊕ *www.st-martin-weingarten. de* ⊘ *Daily 8–6.*

Around the Bodanrück
Peninsula

AROUND THE BODANRÜCK PENINSULA

The immense Bodensee owes its name to a small, insignificant town, Bodman, on the Bodanrück Peninsula, at the northwestern edge of the lake. ■TIP➔ The peninsula's most popular destinations, Konstanz and Mainau, are reachable by ferry from Meersburg—by far the most romantic way to get to the area. The other option is to take the road (B-31, then B-34, and finally B-33) that skirts the western arm of the Bodensee and ends its German journey at Konstanz.

KONSTANZ

A ½-hr ferry ride from Meersburg.

The university town of Konstanz is the largest on the Bodensee; it straddles the Rhine as it flows out of the lake, placing itself both on the Bodanrück Peninsula and the Switzerland side of the lake, where it adjoins the Swiss town of Kreuzlingen. Konstanz is among the best-preserved medieval towns in Germany; during the war the Allies were unwilling to risk inadvertently bombing neutral Switzerland. On the peninsula side of the town, east of the main bridge connecting Konstanz's two halves, runs **Seestrasse,** a stately promenade of neoclassical mansions with views of the Bodensee. The Old Town center is a labyrinth of narrow streets lined with restored half-timber houses and dignified merchant dwellings. This is where you'll find eateries, hotels, pubs, and much of the nightlife.

It's claimed that Konstanz was founded in the 3rd century by Emperor Constantine Chlorus, father of Constantine the Great. The story is probably untrue, though it's certain there was a Roman garrison here. In the late 6th century Konstanz was made a bishopric; in 1192 it became a Free Imperial City. What put it on the map was the Council of Constance, held between 1414 and 1418 to settle the Great Schism (1378–1417), the rift in the church caused by two separate lines of popes, one ruling from Rome, the other from Avignon. The Council resolved the problem in 1417 by electing Martin V as the true, and only, pope. The church had also agreed to restore the Holy Roman emperor's (Sigismund's) role in electing the pope, but only if Sigismund silenced the rebel theologian Jan Hus of Bohemia. Even though Sigismund had allowed Hus safe passage to Konstanz for the Council, he won the church's favor by having Hus burned at the stake in July 1415. In a historic satire, French author Honoré de Balzac created a character called Imperia, a courtesan of great beauty and cleverness, who raised the blood pressure of both religious and secular VIPs during the council. No one visiting the harbor today can miss the 28-foot statue of **Imperia** standing out on the breakwater. Dressed in a revealing and alluring style, in her hands she holds two dejected figures: the emperor and the pope. This hallmark of Konstanz, created by Peter Lenk, caused controversy when it was unveiled in April 1993.

Most people enjoy Konstanz for its worldly pleasures—the elegant Altstadt, trips on the lake, walks along the promenade, elegant shops, the restaurants, the views. The heart of the city is the **Marktstätte** (Marketplace), near the harbor, with the simple bulk of the Konzilgebäude looming behind it. Erected in 1388 as a warehouse, the **Konzilgebäude** (Council Hall) is now a concert hall. Beside the Konzilgebäude are statues of Jan Hus and native son Count Ferdinand von Zeppelin (1838–1917). The Dominican monastery where Hus was held before his execution is still here, doing duty as a luxurious hotel, the Steigenberger Insel-Hotel.

GETTING HERE AND AROUND

Konstanz is in many ways the center of the lake area. You can reach Zürich airport by direct train in about an hour and Frankfurt in 4½ hours. Swiss autobahn access to Zürich is about 10 minutes away, and you can reach the autobahn access to Stuttgart in about the same time. To reach the island of Mainau, you can take a bus, but a much more pleasant way to get there is by boat via Meersburg. You can take another boat downriver to Schaffhausen in Switzerland, or east to the northern shore towns as well as Bregenz in Austria. The Old Town is manageable on foot.

ESSENTIALS

Visitor Information Konstanz ✉ *Tourist-Information, Konstanz, Bahnhofpl. 43*
☎ *07531/133032* ⊕ *www.konstanz-tourismus.de.*

EXPLORING

Altes Rathaus (*Old Town Hall*). The Altes Rathaus was built during the Renaissance and painted with vivid frescoes—swags of flowers and fruits, shields, and sturdy knights wielding immense swords. Walk into the courtyard to admire its Renaissance restraint. ✉ *Kanzleistr. 13.*

Münster (*Kirche Zu Unserer Lieben Frau*). Konstanz's cathedral, the **Münster**, was the center of one of Germany's largest bishoprics until 1827, when the seat was moved to Freiburg. Construction on the cathedral continued from the 10th through the 19th century, resulting in an interesting coexistence of architectural styles: the twin-tower facade is sturdily Romanesque; the elegant and airy chapels along the aisles are full-blown 15th-century Gothic; the complex nave vaulting is Renaissance; and the choir is severely neoclassical. The Mauritius Chapel

For views of the Bodensee from Konstanz, head to the Seestrasse promenade.

behind the altar is a 13th-century Gothic structure, 12 feet high, with some of its original vivid coloring and gilding. It's studded with statues of the Apostles and figures depicting the childhood of Jesus. ■ TIP→ Climb the Münsterturm (Münster Tower) for views over the city and lake. ⊠ *Münsterpl. 4* ⊙ *Daily 8–6. Tower: Mon.–Sat. 10–5:30 and Sun. 12:30–5.*

Niederburg. The Niederburg, the oldest part of Konstanz, is a tangle of twisting streets leading to the Rhine. From the river take a look at two of the city's old towers: the **Rheintorturm** (Rhine Tower), the one nearer the lake, and the aptly named **Pulverturm** (Powder Tower), the former city arsenal. ⊠ *Niederburg.*

Rosgartenmuseum (*Rose Garden Museum*). Within the medieval guildhall of the city's butchers, the Rosgartenmuseum has a rich collection of art and artifacts from the Bodensee region. Highlights include exhibits of the life and work of the people around the Bodensee, from the Bronze Age through the Middle Ages and beyond. There's also a collection of sculpture and altar paintings from the Middle Ages. ⊠ *Rosgartenstr. 3–5* ☎ *07531/900–246* ⊕ *www.rosgartenmuseum-konstanz.de* ⊠ *€3* ⊙ *Tues.–Fri. 10–6, weekends 10–5* ⊙ *Mon.*

ⓒ **Sealife.** The huge aquarium Sealife has gathered all the fish species that inhabit the Rhine and Lake Constance, from the river's beginnings in the Swiss Alps to its end in Rotterdam and the North Sea. If you're pressed for time, or the aquarium is crowded with schoolchildren, visit the **Bodensee Naturmuseum** at the side entrance, which gives a comprehensive overview of the geological history of the Bodensee and its fauna and flora right down to the microscopic creatures of the region. ⊠ *Hafenstr. 9* ☎ *07531/128–270* ⊕ *www.sealife.de* ⊠ *€15* ⊙ *Daily 10–5.*

WHERE TO EAT

$
GERMAN

✕**Brauhaus Joh. Albrecht.** This small brewery with shiny copper cauldrons serves simple dishes as well as regional specialties and vegetarian food on large wooden tables. Tuesday is schnitzel day, with half a dozen varieties on the menu, all of them filling—and all costing €8.99. ⊠ *Konradig. 2* ☏ *07531/25045* ⊕ *www.brauhaus-joh-albrecht.de.*

$$
ECLECTIC

✕**Hafenhalle.** Enjoy eclectic cooking—including Italian, Bavarian, and Swabian fare—at this warm-weather spot on the harbor. Sit outside on the terrace and watch the busy harbor traffic, or enjoy the beer garden with sandbox for children and big TV screen for watching sports. The restaurant presents sporting, culinary, and live music events frequently. ⊠ *Hafenstr. 10* ☏ *07531/21126* ⊕ *www.hafenhalle.com.*

WHERE TO STAY

For expanded hotel reviews, visit Fodors.com.

$$

🏨 **ABC Hotel.** This hotel offers large, comfortable, individually furnished rooms, all with kitchen facilities; book the unusual Turmsuite (Tower Suite) for an especially memorable stay among exposed beams and steeply sloping walls—and with private access to the top of the tower. **Pros:** warm welcome; large airy rooms; quiet location; enough parking space; free Wi-Fi. **Cons:** not in the center of town; no elevator. ⊠ *Steinstr. 19* ☏ *07531/8900* ⊕ *www.abc-hotel.de* ↰ *29 rooms* ⌂ *In-room: no a/c, kitchen, Internet, Wi-Fi. In-hotel: laundry facilities, business center, parking, some pets allowed* ¶⊘ *Breakfast.*

$

🏨 **Barbarossa.** This historic hotel in the heart of Old Town has been modernized inside, but such original elements as wooden support beams lend a romantic, authentic feel. **Pros:** historic building; cozy restaurant with good food; hotel-wide Wi-Fi. **Cons:** some rooms sparsely furnished; parking available but a third of a mile walk away. ⊠ *Obermarkt 8* ☏ *07531/128–990* ⊕ *www.hotelbarbarossa.de* ↰ *53 rooms* ⌂ *In-room: no a/c, Internet, Wi-Fi. In-hotel: restaurant, laundry facilities, business center, parking, some pets allowed* ¶⊘ *Breakfast.*

$$

🏨 **Stadthotel.** It's a five-minute walk to the lake from this friendly hotel, where rooms are modern, airy, and decorated in bright colors. **Pros:** center of town; quiet location with little traffic. **Cons:** no restaurant; parking garage five minutes away on foot. ⊠ *Bruderturmg. 12* ☏ *07531/90460* ⊕ *www.stadthotel-konstanz.com* ↰ *24 rooms* ⌂ *In-room: no a/c, Wi-Fi. In-hotel: parking, some pets allowed* ¶⊘ *Breakfast.*

$$$
Fodor'sChoice
★

🏨 **Steigenberger Insel-Hotel.** With its original cloisters intact, this former 16th-century monastery is now the most luxurious lodging in town. **Pros:** wonderful lake views; luxurious; good restaurants. **Cons:** a few rooms look out on railroad tracks; some others need refurnishing. ⊠ *Auf der Insel 1* ☏ *07531/1250* ⊕ *www.konstanz.steigenberger.com* ↰ *100 rooms, 2 suites* ⌂ *In-room: no a/c, Wi-Fi. In-hotel: restaurant, bar, gym, beach, business center, parking, some pets allowed* ¶⊘ *Breakfast.*

NIGHTLIFE AND THE ARTS

Casino. The Bodensee nightlife scene is concentrated in Konstanz. The casino is open daily 2 pm–2 am. ⊠ *Seestr. 21* ☏ *07531/81570* ▦ *€3.*

K 9 (*Kommunales Kunst-und Kulturzentrum K9*). K 9 draws all ages with its music and dance club, theater, comedy, and cabaret in the former Church of St. Paul. ⊠ *Hieronymusgasse 3* ☎ *07531/16713* ⊕ *www. k9-kulturzentrum.de.*

Kulturladen (*Kula*). Concerts and variously themed DJ nights are held at Kulturladen. ⊠ *Joseph Belli Weg 5* ☎ *07531/52954* ⊕ *www. kulturladen.de.*

Rock am See. This annual late-summer rock music festival has been drawing rock fans to the Bodensee for over 25 years. Held at Bodensee-Stadion in Konstanz, the festival features both German and international acts. ⊠ *Bodensee-Stadion, Eichhornstr. 89, Konstanz* ☎ *07531/908–844 ticket service* ⊕ *www.rock-am-see.de.*

Seekuh. An absolute must is the cozy and crowded Seekuh, which opens at 6 and features the occasional live jazz night. ⊠ *Konzilstr. 1* ☎ *07531/27232* ⊕ *www.seekuh.de.*

Seenachtfest (*Lake Night Festival*). Seenachtfest is a one-day city festival Konstanz shares with neighboring Kreuzlingen in Switzerland annually in mid-August, with street events, music, clowns, and magicians, and ending with fireworks over the lake. ⊕ *www.seenachtfest.de.*

Stadttheater. The Stadttheater, Germany's oldest active theater, has staged plays since 1609 and has its own repertory company. ⊠ *Konzilstr. 11* ☎ *07531/900–150.*

SPORTS AND THE OUTDOORS

BIKING Bike rentals generally cost €13 per day.

Kultur-Rädle. Kultur-Rädle rents bikes at the main train station. The longer you rent the bike, the cheaper the daily rate. ⊠ *Bahnhofpl., 29* ☎ *07531/27310* ⊕ *www.kultur-raedle.de.*

BOATING **Yachtcharter Konstanz.** Sail and motor yachts are available at Yachtcharter Konstanz. ⊠ *Hafenstr. 7b* ☎ *07531/363–3970* ⊕ *www.yachtcharter-konstanz.de.*

Bodensee Segelschule Konstanz/Wallhausen. Small sailboats can be chartered here. ⊠ *Wittmoosstr. 10, Wallhausen* ☎ *07533/4780* ⊕ *www. segelschule-konstanz-wallhausen.de.*

SHOPPING

It's worthwhile to roam the streets of the old part of town where there are several gold- and silversmiths and jewelers.

Modehaus Fischer. Elegant Modehaus Fischer has enough style for a city 10 times the size of Konstanz. The store gets most of its business from wealthy Swiss who come to Konstanz for what they consider bargain prices. Modehaus Fischer deals in well-known names such as Rena Lange and Celine and has some Italian lines such as Cavalli. Accessories from Prada, Armani, and others include handbags and exquisite shoes. Find the men's branch of this store a few blocks away at Obermarkt 1. ⊠ *Hussenstr. 29 and Obermarkt. 1* ☎ *07531/22990* ⊕ *www. modefischer.de.*

6

Mainau Island, on the Bodensee, is covered with flowering gardens.

MAINAU

Fodor'sChoice ★ *7 km (4½ mi) north of Konstanz by road; by ferry, 50 mins from Konstanz, 20 mins from Meersburg.*

One of the most unusual sights in Germany, Mainau is a tiny island given over to the cultivation of rare plants and splashy displays of more than a million tulips, hyacinths, and narcissi. Rhododendrons and roses bloom from May to July; dahlias dominate the late summer. A greenhouse nurtures palms and tropical plants.

The island was originally the property of the Teutonic Knights, who settled here during the 13th century. In the 19th century Mainau passed to Grand Duke Friedrich I of Baden, a man with a passion for botany. He laid out most of the gardens and introduced many of the island's more exotic specimens. His daughter Victoria, later queen of Sweden, gave the island to her son, Prince Wilhelm, and it has remained Swedish ever since. Today it's owned by the family of Prince Wilhelm's son, Count Lennart Bernadotte. In the former main reception hall in the castle are changing art exhibitions.

GETTING HERE AND AROUND

Ferries to the island from Meersburg and Konstanz depart from April to October approximately every 1½ hours between 9 and 5. You must purchase a ticket to enter the island, which is open year-round from dawn until dusk. There's a small bridge to the island. At night you can use it to drive up to the restaurants.

ESSENTIALS

Visitor Information **Mainau** ⊠ *Insel Mainau* ☎ *07531/3030* ⊕ *www.mainau.de* ☜ *€15.90, ½ price late Oct.–late March* ☾ *Dawn–dusk.*

EXPLORING

Das Schmetterlinghaus. Beyond the flora, the island's other colorful extravagance is Das Schmetterlinghaus, Germany's largest butterfly conservatory. On a circular walk through a semitropical landscape with water cascading through rare vegetation, you'll see hundreds of butterflies flying, feeding, and mating. The exhibition in the foyer explains the butterflies' life cycle, habitats, and ecological connections. Like the park, this oasis is open year-round.

Gärtnerturm. In the island's information center in the Gärtnerturm (Gardener's Tower) in the middle of the island, several films on Mainau and the Bodensee are shown.

WHERE TO EAT

There are seven restaurants and cafés on the island, but no lodgings.

\$\$
SCANDINAVIAN

✕ **Schwedenschenke.** The lunchtime crowd gets what it needs here—fast and good service. At dinnertime candlelight adds some extra style. The resident Bernadotte family is Swedish, and so are the specialties of the chef. Have your mainland hotel reserve a table for you. ■ TIP➔ In the evening your reservation will be checked at the gate, and you can drive onto the island without having to pay the admission fee. ⊠ *Insel Mainau* ☎ *07531/303–156* ⊕ *www.mainau.de/schwedenschenke.html* ☖ *Reservations essential* ☾ *Late Mar.–early Nov., daily 11–11; early Nov.–Dec., daily 11:30–3* ☾ *Closed end Dec.–late Mar.*

REICHENAU

10 km (6 mi) northwest of Konstanz, 50 mins by ferry from Konstanz.

Reichenau is an island rich in vegetation, but unlike Mainau, it features vegetables, not flowers. In fact, 15% of its area (the island is 5 km [3 mi] long and 1½ km [1 mi] wide) is covered by greenhouses and crops of one kind or another. ■ TIP➔ Though it seems unlikely amid the cabbage, cauliflower, lettuce, and potatoes, Reichenau has three of Europe's most beautiful Romanesque churches. This legacy of Reichenau's past as a monastic center in the early Middle Ages, and its warm microclimate, have earned the island a place on UNESCO's World and Nature Heritage list. Connected to the Bodanrück Peninsula by just a narrow causeway, Reichenau was secure from marauding tribesmen on its fertile island, and the monastic community blossomed from the 8th through the 12th century. Reichenau developed into a major center of learning and the arts. The churches are in each of the island's villages—**Oberzell, Mittelzell,** and **Niederzell,** which are separated by only 1 km (½ mi). Along the shore are pleasant pathways for walking or biking.

ESSENTIALS

Visitor Information **Reichenau** ⊠ *Tourist-Information, Pirminstr. 145* ☎ *07534/92070* ⊕ *www.reichenau.de.*

EXPLORING

Münster of St. Maria and St. Markus. Begun in 816, the Münster of St. Maria and St. Markus, the monastery's church, is the largest and most important of the island's trio of Romanesque churches. Perhaps its most striking architectural feature is the roof, whose beams and ties are open for all to see. The monastery was founded in 725 by St. Pirmin and became one of the most important cultural centers of the Carolingian Empire. It reached its zenith around 1000, when 700 monks lived here. It was then probably the most important center of book illumination in Germany. The building is simple but by no means crude. Visit the **Schatzkammer** (Treasury) to see some of its more important holdings. They include a 5th-century ivory goblet with two carefully incised scenes of Christ's miracles and some priceless stained glass that is almost 1,000 years old. ⊠ *Münsterpl. 3, Mittelzell* ☎ *07534/92070* ⊗ *Apr.–Oct., weekdays 10–noon and 3–5.*

Museum Reichenau. This museum of local history, in the Old Town Hall of Mittelzell, lends interesting insights into life on the island over the centuries. ⊠ *Ergat 1–3, Mittelzell* ☎ *07534/920–720* ⊕ *www.museumreichenau.de* ☎ *€3* ⊗ *Apr.–Oct., Tues.–Sun. 10:30–4:30; Nov.–Mar., weekends 2–5.*

Stiftskirche St. Georg (*Collegiate Church of St. George*). The Stiftskirche St. Georg, in Oberzell, was built around 900; now cabbages grow in ranks up to its rough plaster walls. Small round-head windows, a simple square tower, and massive buttresses signal the church's Romanesque origin from the outside. The interior is covered with frescoes painted by the monks in around 1000. They depict the eight miracles of Christ. Above the entrance is a depiction of the Resurrection.

Stiftskirche St. Peter und Paul (*St. Peter and Paul Parish Church*). The Stiftskirche St. Peter und Paul, at Niederzell, was revamped around 1750. The faded Romanesque frescoes in the apse contrast with bold rococo paintings on the ceiling and flowery stucco. ⊠ *Seestr.*

WHERE TO EAT AND STAY

For expanded hotel reviews, visit Fodors.com.

$ ✕ **Kiosk am Yachthafen.** This kiosk-style restaurant at Reichenau's yacht
GERMAN   harbor provides an ideal lunch, drink, or snack stop when wandering the island. In good weather, sit outside and watch the boats come and go. It's also a perfect place to try the Bodensee specialty *Zanderknusperle* (crispy battered zander fish bites)—fresh out of the lake. ⊠ *Yacht Harbor, Hermannus-Contractus-Str. 30, Reichenau* ☎ *07534/999–655* ⊕ *www.sbrestaurant-reichenau.de* ▭ *No credit cards* ⊗ *Closed Nov.–Mar.*

$$ 🏨 **Strandhotel Löchnerhaus.** The Strandhotel (Beach Hotel) stands commandingly on the water's edge and about 80 yards from its own boat pier. **Pros:** nice location; views over the lake into Switzerland; quiet. **Cons:** closed in winter; some rooms expensive. ⊠ *An der Schiffslände 12* ☎ *07534/8030* ⊕ *www.loechnerhaus.de* ↵ *41 rooms* ⌂ *In-room: no a/c, Wi-Fi. In-hotel: restaurant, gym, beach, business center, parking* ⊗ *Closed Nov.–Feb.* ❯○❮ *Breakfast.*

The Black Forest

WORD OF MOUTH

"The Black Forest is a pretty huge area. Baden-Baden would make a good gateway to the Northern half of the Black Forest, while Freiburg or even Basel are good gateways to the Southern half. Visiting the Black Forest is not 'done' by going to one specific village or town, you may want two days to do a bit of exploring."
—Cowboy 1968

WELCOME TO THE BLACK FOREST

TOP REASONS TO GO

★ **Extraordinary regional specialties:** Dig into Black Forest cake, Schwarzwald ham (only authentic if smoked over pinecones), and the incredible Tannen-Zäpfle Pilsner from the Rothaus Brewery.

★ **Freiburg Münster:** One of the most beautiful sandstone churches in southern Germany, the Cathedral of Freiburg survived the war unscathed. The view from the bell tower is stunning.

★ **Going cuckoo:** Look for a cuckoo clock from Triberg (or a nice watch from Pforzheim).

★ **Healing waters:** More than 30 spas with a wide range of treatments await to make visitors feel whole again, but nothing beats the 3½-hour session at the Friedrichsbad in Baden-Baden.

★ **Libations at Kaiserstuhl:** Enjoy a local wine in the wine-maker's yard or cellar with Black Forest ham and dark bread. It's especially nice when the grapes are being harvested.

1 The Northern Black Forest. The gem of the northern Black Forest is the genteel spa town of Baden-Baden, full of quiet charm and dripping with elegance.

2 The Central Black Forest. The central Black Forest typifies the region as a whole. Alpirsbach's half-timber houses, Triberg's cuckoo clocks, and the nation's highest waterfalls all nestle among a series of steep-sided valleys.

3 The Southern Black Forest. In the south, Freiburg is one of the country's most historic cities, and even the hordes of summer visitors can't quell the natural beauty of the Titisee Lake.

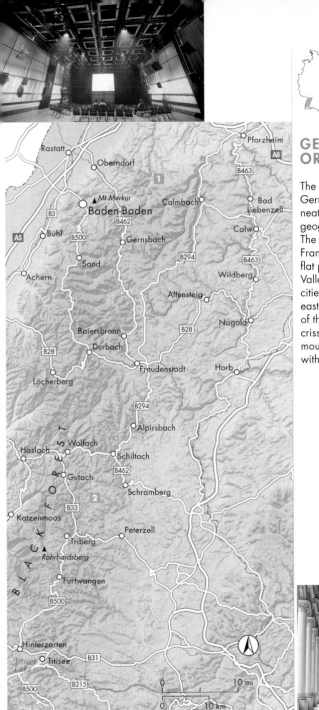

GETTING ORIENTED

The southwest corner of Germany divides itself neatly into two distinct geographical regions. The western half borders France and lies in the wide flat plains of the Rhine Valley, where all the larger cities are located. To the east tower the rugged hills of the Black Forest itself, crisscrossed by winding mountain roads and dotted with picturesque villages.

7

SPAS

The restorative powers of a good soak in a hot pool or sweating it out in a 190-degree sauna are well understood in Germany, where the concepts of wellness and relaxation, both physical and mental, are taken seriously.

(above and lower right) Relax in the warm thermal pools of the Black Forest's spas. (upper right) Waterfall at the Caracalla Therme in Baden-Baden.

Endowed with mountain air, salty coastlines, and natural thermal springs, Germany has long enjoyed a spa tradition. Seeking relief from the pains of battle, the Romans erected baths here almost two thousand years ago, and the 19th century saw spa towns across the country flourish as Europe's upper classes began to appreciate the soothing effects of fresh air and mineral waters. These days there are hundreds of facilities throughout the country ranging from huge, sophisticated resorts offering precious stone massages and chocolate baths to smaller "wellness" hotels with not much more than a sauna and a relaxation room. There are also plenty of public spas, where a day's bathing won't set you back much more than the price of a movie ticket.

—Jeff Kavanagh

DRINKING IT IN

Taking the waters in a spa town often involves imbibing some as well. Bad Mergentheim and Baden-Baden are renowned for their drinking water springs and the healing properties of the mineral waters that spill from them. Used for everything from the stimulation of the pancreas to curing a sore throat, they are drunk by thousands of visitors every year.

SPA ETIQUETTE

NUDITY

While sitting naked in a dimly lit, scorching hot room or floating au naturel in a thermal pool among a group of strangers may not be everyone's idea of relaxation, most Germans don't see it as much to get worked up about. Saunas and steam rooms are almost always *Frei Körper Kultur* (Free Body Culture) areas, as are some hot pools. They're also all mainly mixed sex. This can be a bit of a shock for the uninitiated, but the logic is that the body needs to be unencumbered to enjoy the full curative effects of the heat and water. You'll also be expected to strip down if you've booked a massage, although a towel will be provided to preserve a modicum of modesty. If you're not sure what to take off and what to leave on, don't be afraid to ask; you're almost certain not to offend anyone.

BATHROBES, TOWELS, AND SANDALS

More upmarket wellness locations will provide you with all three, while public spas will expect you to at least bring your own towel. Bathrobes and sandals should be worn in relaxation areas and left outside saunas and steam baths, and towels laid beneath you in the sauna to absorb excess sweat.

SHOWERING

A quick shower before first jumping in a pool or entering a sauna is expected, and certainly required between transferring yourself from a sweaty sauna to a plunge pool. A refreshing rinse between each sauna session is also advisable, not just for hygienic reasons but also for its therapeutic effects.

TALKING

Given that spas are designed to be oases of wellness and relaxation, loud conversation in "adult" areas of the facility, particularly in saunas, steam rooms and relaxation areas, will be met with sighs of disapproval and, in severe cases, a telling-off by fellow spa-enthusiasts.

SPA GLOSSARY

Algae and mud therapy: Applied as packs or full body bath treatments to nourish the skin and draw out toxins.

Aromatherapy baths: Oils such as bergamot, cypress, and sandalwood are added to hot baths in order to lift the spirits and reduce anxiety.

Ayurveda: Refers to Indian techniques including massage, oils, herbs and diet to encourage perfect body balance.

Jet massage: Involves standing upright and being sprayed with high-pressure water jets that follow the direction of your blood flow, thereby stimulating circulation.

Liquid sound therapy: A relaxation technique that entails lying in body temperature saltwater and listening to classical or electronic music being played through the water while a kaleidoscope of colors illuminates your surroundings.

Reflexology: Massage on the pressure points of feet, hands, and ears.

Thalasso therapy: A spa treatment employing sea air, water, and mud to heal the body.

7

Updated by
Lee A. Evans

The name conjures up images of a wild, isolated place where time passes slowly. The dense woodland of the Black Forest—Schwarzwald in German—stretches away to the horizon, but this southwest corner of Baden-Württemberg (in the larger region known as Swabia) is neither inaccessible nor dull.

The Black Forest is known the world over for cuckoo clocks; the women's native costume with huge red or black hat pom-poms; and the wild, almost pagan way the Carnival season is celebrated. Swabians are the butt of endless jokes about their frugality and supposedly simplistic nature. The first travelers checked in here 19 centuries ago, when the Roman emperor Caracalla and his army rested and soothed their battle wounds in the natural-spring waters at what later became Baden-Baden.

Europe's upper-crust society discovered Baden-Baden when it convened nearby for the Congress of Rastatt from 1797 to 1799, which attempted to end the wars of the French Revolution. In the 19th century kings, queens, emperors, princes, princesses, members of Napoléon's family, and the Russian nobility, along with actors, writers, and composers, flocked to the little spa town. Turgenev, Dostoyevsky, and Tolstoy were among the Russian contingent. Victor Hugo was a frequent visitor. Brahms composed lilting melodies in this calm setting. Queen Victoria spent her vacations here. Mark Twain put the Black Forest on the map for Americans by stating, "Here [. . .] you lose track of time in ten minutes and the world in twenty," in his 1880 book *A Tramp Abroad*. Today it's a favorite getaway for movie stars and millionaires. The spa is the great social equalizer where you can "take the waters," just as the Romans first did 2,000 years ago. The Black Forest sporting scene caters particularly to the German enthusiasm for hiking. The Schwarzwald-Verein, an outdoor association in the region, maintains no fewer than 30,000 km (18,000 mi) of hiking trails. In winter the terrain is ideally suited for cross-country skiing.

PLANNING

WHEN TO GO

The Black Forest is one of the most heavily visited mountain regions in Europe, so make reservations well in advance for the better-known spas and hotels. In summer the area around Titisee is particularly crowded. In early fall and late spring, the Black Forest is less crowded (except during the Easter holidays) but just as beautiful. Some spa hotels close for winter.

GETTING HERE AND AROUND

AIR TRAVEL

The closest major international airports in Germany are Stuttgart and Frankfurt. Strasbourg, in neighboring French Alsace, and the Swiss border city of Basel, the latter just 70 km (43 mi) from Freiburg, are also reasonably close. An up-and-coming airport is the Baden-Airpark, now known more commonly as Karlsruhe-Baden, near Baden-Baden. It is used by European budget carriers including Ryanair (⊕ *www.ryanair. com*) and Air Berlin (⊕ *www.airberlin.com*), serving short-haul international destinations such as London, Dublin, and Barcelona.

Airport Information **Aeroport International de Strasbourg** ☏ *00333/8864– 6767* ⊕ *www.strasbourg.aeroport.fr.* **EuroAirport Basel-Mulhouse-Freiburg** ☏ *0389/903–111 in France* ⊕ *www.euroairport.com.* **Flughafen Frankfurt Main** ☏ *01805/372–4636* ⊕ *www.frankfurt-airport.de.* **Flughafen Stuttgart** ☏ *01805/948–444* ⊕ *www.flughafen-stuttgart.de.* **Karlsruhe-Baden** ☏ *07229/662–000* ⊕ *www.badenairpark.de.*

BUS TRAVEL

The bus system is partially owned by and coordinated with the German Railways, so it's easy to reach every corner of the Black Forest by bus and train. Bus stations are usually at or near the train station. For more information, contact the Regionalbusverkehr Südwest (Regional Bus Lines) in Karlsruhe.

Bus Information **Regionalbusverkehr Südwest** (*Regional Bus Lines*). ✉ *Karlsruhe* ☏ *0721/84060* ⊕ *www.suedwestbus.de.*

CAR TRAVEL

The main autobahns are the A-5 (Frankfurt–Karlsruhe–Basel), which runs through the Rhine Valley along the western length of the Black Forest; A-81 (Stuttgart–Bodensee) in the east; and A-8 (Karlsruhe–Stuttgart) in the north. Good two-lane highways crisscross the entire region. B-3 runs parallel to A-5 and follows the Baden Wine Road. Traffic jams on weekends and holidays are not uncommon. Taking the side roads might not save time, but they are a lot more interesting. The Schwarzwald-Hochstrasse is one of the area's most scenic (but also most trafficked) routes, running from Freudenstadt to Baden-Baden. The region's tourist office has mapped out thematic driving routes: the Valley Road, the Spa Road, the Baden Wine Road, the Asparagus Road, and the Clock Road. Most points along these routes can also be reached by train or bus.

Freiburg, the region's major city, is 275 km (170 mi) south of Frankfurt and 410 km (254 mi) west of Munich.

TRAIN TRAVEL

Karlsruhe, Baden-Baden, and Freiburg are served by fast ICE trains zipping between Frankfurt-am-Main and Basel in Switzerland. Regional express trains also link these hubs with many other places locally, including Freudenstadt, Titisee, and, in particular, the spectacular climb from Baden-Baden to Triberg, one of the highest railways in Germany.

Local lines connect most of the smaller towns. Two east–west routes—the Schwarzwaldbahn (Black Forest Railway) and the Höllental Railway—are among the most spectacular in the country. Details are available from Deutsche Bahn.

Train Information Deutsche Bahn ☎ *11861* ⊕ *www.bahn.de.*

RESTAURANTS

Restaurants in the Black Forest range from award-winning dining rooms to simple country inns. Old *Kachelöfen* (tile stoves) are still in use in many area restaurants; try to sit near one if it's cold outside.

HOTELS

Accommodations in the Black Forest are varied and plentiful, from simple rooms in farmhouses to five-star luxury. Some properties have been passed down in the same family for generations. *Gasthöfe* offer low prices and local color. Keep in mind that most hotels in the region do not offer air-conditioning.

WHAT IT COSTS IN EUROS

	¢	$	$$	$$$	$$$$
Restaurants	under €9	€9–€15	€16–€20	€21–€25	over €25
Hotels	under €50	€50–€100	€101–€175	€176–€225	over €225

Restaurant prices are per person for a main course at dinner. Hotel prices are for two people in a standard double room, including tax and service.

PLANNING YOUR TIME

The lively, student-driven city of Freiburg, Germany's "greenest" town, is the obvious base from which to explore the Black Forest. Don't miss "taking the water" at a spa in Baden-Baden, a charming place with all facilities on tap. Bear in mind that driving times and distances push the farthest points in the Black Forest out of reach of easy day trips from these cities. The winding, often steep Black Forest highways can make for slow driving, so you may want to consider adding overnight stays at other locations. Freudenstadt's vast market square lends it a uniquely pleasant atmosphere, and Triberg's mountain location is popular, but it remains picturesque.

VISITOR INFORMATION

Schwarzwald Tourismus GmbH ✉ *Ludwigstr. 23, Freiburg* ☎ *0761/896–460* ⊕ *www.schwarzwald-tourismus.info.*

THE NORTHERN BLACK FOREST

This region is densely wooded, and dotted with little lakes such as the Mummelsee and the Wildsee. The Black Forest Spa Route (270 km [167 mi]) links many of the spas in the region, from Baden-Baden (the best known) to Bad Wildbad. Other regional treasures are the lovely Nagold River; ancient towns such as Hirsau; and the magnificent abbey at Maulbronn, near Pforzheim.

PFORZHEIM

35 km (22 mi) southeast of Karlsruhe, just off the A-8 autobahn, the main Munich–Karlsruhe route.

Pforzheim is not exactly the attractive place the Romans found at the junction of three rivers, the Nagold, the Enz, and the Würm. Nevertheless the town is considered the "gateway to the Black Forest." World War II almost completely destroyed the city center, and postwar reconstruction is hardly inspired. Pforzheim still owes its prosperity to its role in Europe's jewelry trade and its wristwatch industry. To get a sense of the "Gold City," explore the jewelry shops on streets around Leopoldplatz and the pedestrian area.

ESSENTIALS

Visitor Information Pforzheim ⊠ *Tourist-Information, Marktpl. 1* ☎ *07231/393–700* ⊕ *www.pforzheim.de.*

EXPLORING

★ **Kloster Maulbronn** (*Maulbronn Monastery*). Kloster Maulbronn, in the little town of Maulbronn, 18 km (11 mi) northeast of Pforzheim, is the best-preserved medieval monastery north of the Alps, with an entire complex of 30 buildings on UNESCO's World Heritage list. The name Maulbronn (Mule Fountain) derives from a legend. Monks seeking a suitably watered site for their monastery considered it a sign from God when one of their mules discovered and drank at a spring. The Kloster is also known for inventing the Maultasche, a kind of ravioli. The monks thought that by coloring the meat filling green by adding parsley and wrapping it inside a pasta pocket, they could hide it from God on fasting days. Today the Maultasche is the cornerstone of Swabian cuisine. ■TIP→ An audio guide in English is available. ⊠ *Off B-35* ☎ *07043/926–610* ⊕ *www.maulbronn.de* ☏ *€6* ☉ *Mar.–Oct., daily 9–5:30; Nov.–Feb., Tues.–Sun. 9:30–5; guided tour daily at 11:15 and 3.*

St. Michael. The restored church of St. Michael, near the train station, is the final resting place of Baden royalty. The original mixture of 13th- and 15th-century styles has been faithfully reproduced; compare the airy Gothic choir with the church's sturdy Romanesque entrance. ⊠ *Schlossberg 10* ☉ *Oct.–Apr., weekdays 3–6; May–Sept., Mon. and Wed.–Fri. 3–6.*

Schmuckmuseum (*Jewelry Museum*). The Reuchlinhaus, the city cultural center, houses the Schmuckmuseum. Its collection of jewelry from 5 millennia is one of the finest in the world. The museum nearly doubled in size in 2006, adding pocket watches and ethnographic jewelry to its

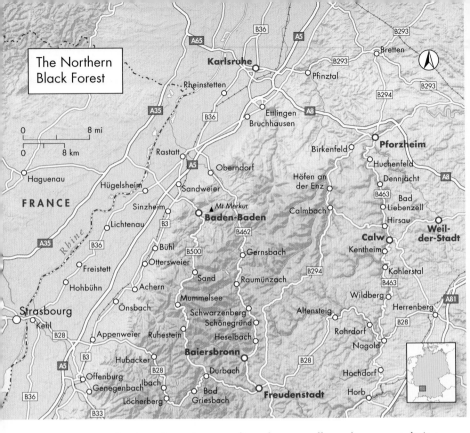

The Northern Black Forest

0   8 mi
0   8 km

B36 · A65 · A5 · B293

Karlsruhe

Bretten

Rheinstetten

Pfinztal

B293

Ettlingen
Bruchhausen

B36 · A35 · A8 · B294 · B293

Rastatt

Oberndorf

Birkenfeld

Pforzheim

Huchenfeld

Haguenau

Hügelsheim

Sandweier

Höfen an
der Enz

Dennjächt

A8

FRANCE

Sinzheim

Mt Merkur

Calmbach

B463 · Bad
Liebenzell

Lichtenau

B3

Baden-Baden

Hirsau

Calw

Weil-
der-Stadt

Rhine

B36

Bühl

B462

B500

Gernsbach

Kentheim

Kohlerstal

Freistett

Ottersweier

Sand

Raumünzach

B294

B463

Hohbühn

Achern

Mummelsee

Schwarzenberg

Wildberg

Herrenberg

Strasbourg

Önsbach

Schönegründ

Altensteig

B28

A81

Kehl

Ruhestein

Heselbach

Rohrdorf

B28

Appenweier

Baiersbronn

Nagold

Hubacker

Durbach

B28

Hochdorf

Offenburg

B28

Genegenbach

Ibach

Bad
Griesbach

Freudenstadt

Horb

B36

Löcherberg

B33

collection, plus a shop, a café, and a gem gallery where young designers exhibit and sell their work. Guided tours in English are available on request. ⊠ *Jahnstr. 42* ☎ *07231/392–126* ⊕ *www.schmuckmuseum-pforzheim.de* ⊠ *€3* ☉ *Tues.–Sun. 10–5.*

Technisches Museum (*Technical Museum*). Pforzheim has long been known as a center of the German clock-making industry. In the Technisches Museum, one of the country's leading museums devoted to the craft, you can see makers of watches and clocks at work; there's also a reconstructed 18th-century clock factory. ⊠ *Bleichstr. 81* ☎ *07231/392–869* ⊕ *www.technisches-museum.de* ⊠ *Free* ☉ *Wed. 9–noon and 3–6, 2nd and 4th Sun. of month 10–5.*

WHERE TO EAT

$$

FRENCH

✕ **Chez Gilbert.** The Alsatian owners of this cozy restaurant serve classic French-inspired cuisine, using the freshest local seasonal ingredients. The menu and wine lists are relatively small, but from the moment that you're greeted by Frau Nosser until the time you leave, you'll get the feeling that everything was planned just for you. The best bet is one of Chef Gilbert Noesser's seasonal four-course menus for €57. If you must dine a la carte, try the handmade goose bratwurst or the foie gras with peaches. ⊠ *Altstädter Kirchenweg 3* ☎ *07231/441–159* ⊕ *www.chez-gilbert.de/* ☉ *Closed 2 wks in Aug. No lunch Sat. No dinner Sun.*

EN ROUTE

Weil der Stadt. Weil der Stadt, a former imperial city, is in the hills 17 km (10 mi) southeast of Pforzheim. This small, sleepy town of turrets and gables has only its well-preserved city walls and fortifications to remind you of its onetime importance.

Kepler Museum. The astronomer Johannes Kepler, born here in 1571, was the first man to track and accurately explain the orbits of the planets, although most experts agree that Kepler stole his calculations from, and then quite possibly murdered, Tycho de Brahe. And, appropriately, the town now has a planetarium to graphically show you what he learned. The little half-timber house in which he was born is now the Kepler Museum in the town center. It's devoted to his writings and discoveries. ⊠ *Keplerg. 2* ☎ *07033/6586* ⊕ *www.kepler-museum. de* ⊠ *€2* ⊘ *Thurs. and Fri. 10–noon and 2–4, Sat. 11–noon and 2–4, Sun. 11–noon and 2–5* ⊕ *www.weil-der-stadt.de.*

CALW

24 km (14 mi) south of Pforzheim on B-463.

Calw, one of the Black Forest's prettiest towns, is the birthplace of Nobel Prize–winning novelist Hermann Hesse (1877–1962). The town's market square, with its two sparkling fountains surrounded by 18th-century half-timber houses whose sharp gables pierce the sky, is an ideal spot for relaxing, picnicking, or people-watching, especially when it's market time.

ESSENTIALS

Visitor Information Calw ⊠ *Stadtinformation Calw, Marktbrücke 1* ☎ *07051/167–399* ⊕ *www.calw.de.*

EXPLORING

Hermann Hesse Museum. The Hermann Hesse Museum recounts the life of the Nobel Prize–winning writer, author of *Steppenwolf* and *The Glass Bead Game,* who rebelled against his middle-class German upbringing to become a pacifist and the darling of the Beat Generation. The story of his life is told in personal belongings, photographs, manuscripts, and other documents. ■ TIP→ An audioguide in English is available. ⊠ *Markt-tpl. 30* ☎ *07051/7522* ⊕ *www.hermann-hesse.com* ⊠ *€5* ⊘ *Apr.–Oct., Tues.–Sun. 11–5; Nov.–Mar., Tues.–Sun. 2–5.*

Hirsau. Hirsau, 3 km (2 mi) north of Calw, has ruins of a 9th-century monastery, now the setting for the Klostersummer (open-air theater performances) in July and August.

Calw tourist office. Buy advance tickets for the Klostersummer here. ⊠ *Marktbrücke 1* ☎ *07051/968–810* ⊕ *www.kloster-hirsau.de.*

WHERE TO STAY

For expanded hotel reviews, visit Fodors.com.

$$ 🏨 **Hotel Kloster Hirsau.** This hotel, a model of comfort and gracious hospitality, is in Hirsau, 3 km (2 mi) from Calw. **Pros:** quiet location; homey atmosphere. **Cons:** located a bit far out of town. ⊠ *Wildbaderstr. 2, Calw-Hirsau* ☎ *07051/96740* ⊕ *www.hotel-kloster-hirsau.de* 📶 *42 rooms* ⌂ *In-room: no a/c, Internet, Wi-Fi. In-hotel: restaurant, pool,*

7

tennis court, some pets allowed ❖*Breakfast.*

$ ⊞ **Ratsstube.** Most of the original features, including 16th-century beams and brickwork, are preserved at this historic house in the center of Calw. **Pros:** great location overlooks historical market square; beautiful old half-timber building. **Cons:** parking around the corner; some rooms quite small; historic building means no elevator. ✉ *Marktpl. 12* ☎ *07051/92050* ⊕ *www.hotel-ratsstube-calw.de* ⤶*13 rooms* ♿ *In-room: no a/c. In-hotel: restaurant, some pets allowed* ❖*Breakfast.*

FREUDENSTADT

65 km (35 mi) south of Calw, 22 km (14 mi) southwest of Altensteig.

At an altitude of 2,415 feet, Freudenstadt claims to be the sunniest German resort. The town was flattened by the French in April 1945, and it has since been painstakingly rebuilt. Refugees and silver miners founded the "city of joy" in 1599 after escaping religious persecution in the Austrian province of Carinthia. The expansive central square, more than 650 feet long and edged with arcaded shops, is Germany's largest marketplace. The square still awaits the palace that was supposed to be built here for the city's founder, Prince Frederick I of Württemberg, who died before work could begin. It is difficult to admire its vastness, since a busy, four-lane street cuts it nearly in half. ■TIP➜ When the fountains all spout on this square, it can be quite a sight, and a refreshing one as well.

GETTING HERE AND AROUND
Freudenstadt is served by regular trains from both Karlsruhe and Stuttgart. The huge main square makes the city feel larger than it actually is. The central zone can easily be covered on foot.

ESSENTIALS
Visitor Information Freudenstadt ✉ *Kongresse-Touristik-Kur, Marktpl. 64* ☎ *07441/8640* ⊕ *www.freudenstadt.de.*

EXPLORING
Stadtkirche. Don't miss Freudenstadt's Protestant Stadtkirche, just off the square. Its lofty nave is L-shaped, a rare architectural liberty in the early 17th century. It was constructed in this way so the sexes would be separated and unable to see each other during services.

WHERE TO EAT
$ ✗ **Ratskeller.** Though there's a cellar, this restaurant with pine furnishings is more a modern bistro than traditional Ratskeller. Meatless Black
GERMAN   Forest dishes, served in frying pans, are huge and filling. Also offered are such Swabian dishes as *Zwiebelrostbraten* (steak and fried onions),

served with sauerkraut, and pork fillet with wild-mushroom sauce. A special menu for senior citizens has smaller portions. ⊠ *Marktpl. 8* ☎ *07441/952–805.*

$ ✕ **Turmbräu.** Lots of wood paneling, exposed beams, and a sprinkling
GERMAN of old sleds and hay wagons give this place, right on the main square, its rustic atmosphere. So do the large brass kettle and the symphony of pipes that produce the establishment's own beer. The restaurant serves hearty solid local fare, including the pizzalike Alsatian *Flammkuchen*, and a kebab of various types of meat marinated in wheat beer. Fondue is offered on Wednesday. Part of the restaurant turns into a disco on weekends. ⊠ *Marktpl. 64* ☎ *07441/905–121.*

$$$ ✕ **Warteck.** The leaded windows with stained glass, vases of flowers,
GERMAN and beautifully upholstered banquettes create a bright setting in the
★ two dining rooms. Chef Werner Glässel uses only organic products and spotlights individual ingredients. The variety of seasonal menus (€40) are always a good choice. Top off the meal with one of the many varieties of schnapps. ⊠ *Stuttgarterstr. 14* ☎ *07441/91920* ⊕ *www.warteck-freudenstadt.de* ⊗ *Closed Tues.*

WHERE TO STAY

For expanded hotel reviews, visit Fodors.com.

$ ⊞ **Bären.** The Montigels have owned this sturdy old hotel and restaurant, just two minutes from the marketplace, since 1878. **Pros:** great central location; friendly atmosphere. **Cons:** some rooms on the small side. ⊠ *Langestr. 33* ☎ *07441/2729* ⊕ *www.hotel-baeren-freudenstadt.de* ↪ *33 rooms* ⅏ *In-room: no a/c, Internet, Wi-Fi. In-hotel: restaurant* ⊗ *Restaurant closed Fri. No lunch Mon.–Sat.* ¹⊙¹ *Breakfast.*

$ ⊞ **Hotel Adler.** This simple hotel sits between the main square and the train station. **Pros:** friendly; informal; centrally located. **Cons:** some rooms small; furnishings from 1970s quite modest. ⊠ *Forststr. 15–17* ☎ *07441/91520* ⊕ *www.adler-fds.de* ↪ *16 rooms* ⅏ *In-room: no a/c, Wi-Fi. In-hotel: restaurant, business center* ⊗ *Restaurant closed Wed.* ¹⊙¹ *Breakfast.*

$$ ⊞ **Zum Schwanen.** This bright, white building just a few steps from the main square has a guest room with a water bed for those with allergies. **Pros:** great location; excellent-value restaurant. **Cons:** no elevator in historic building. ⊠ *Forststr. 6* ☎ *07441/91550* ⊕ *www.schwanen-freudenstadt.de* ↪ *17 rooms, 1 apartment* ⅏ *In-room: no a/c, Wi-Fi. In-hotel: restaurant, some pets allowed* ¹⊙¹ *Breakfast.*

EATING WELL IN THE BLACK FOREST

Don't pass up the chance to try *Schwarzwälder Schinken* (pinecone-smoked ham) and *Schwarzwälder Kirschtorte* (kirsch-soaked layers of chocolate cake with sour cherry and whipped-cream filling). *Kirschwasser,* locally called *Chriesewässerle* (from the French *cerise,* meaning "cherry"), is cherry brandy, the most famous of the region's excellent schnapps varieties. If traveling from May to June, keep an eye out for the "king of vegetables," white asparagus. Most restaurants develop special menus that feature this locally grown delicacy.

7

SHOPPING

Germans prize Black Forest ham (Schwarzwaldschinken) as an aromatic souvenir. You can buy one at any butcher shop in the region, but it's more fun to visit a *Schinkenräucherei* (smokehouse), where the ham is actually cured in a stone chamber.

Hermann Wein. Hermann Wein, in the village of Musbach, near Freudenstadt, has one of the leading smokehouses in the area. If you have a group of people, call ahead to find out if the staff can show you around. ■TIP➔ If you are looking for Black Forest ham, this is the place to go. ✉ *Dornstetterstr. 29, Musbach* ☎ *07443/2450* ⊕ *www.schinkenwein.de.*

BAIERSBRONN

7 km (4½ mi) northwest of Freudenstadt.

The mountain resort of Baiersbronn has an incredible collection of hotels and bed-and-breakfasts providing rest and relaxation in beautiful surroundings. Most people come here to walk, ski, golf, and ride horseback. ■TIP➔ You may want to walk through the streets to preview the many restaurants.

ESSENTIALS

Visitor Information Baiersbronn ✉ *Baiersbronn Touristik, Rosenpl. 3* ☎ *07442/84140* ⊕ *www.baiersbronn.de.*

EXPLORING

Hauffs Märchenmuseum (*Fairy-Tale Museum*). Near the town hall and church in the upper part of town is the little Hauffs Märchenmuseum, devoted to the crafts and life around Baiersbronn and the fairy-tale author Wilhelm Hauff (1802–27). ✉ *Alte Reichenbacherstr. 1* ☎ *07442/84100* ☞ *€1.50* ⊙ *Wed. and weekends 2–5.*

WHERE TO STAY

For expanded hotel reviews, visit Fodors.com.

$$$ 🏨 **Hotel-Café Sackmann.** This imposing cluster of white houses, set in the narrow Murg Valley north of Baiersbronn, has broad appeal. **Pros:** good for families; beautiful location. **Cons:** far from the sights. ✉ *Murgtalstr. 602, Schwarzenberg/Baiersbronn* ☎ *07447/2980* ⊕ *www.hotel-sackmann.de* ⬎ *65 rooms* ⌂ *In-room: no a/c, Internet. In-hotel: restaurant, bar, pool, children's programs* ⦙⊙⦙ *Breakfast.*

$$ 🏨 **Hotel Lamm.** The steep-roof exterior of this 200-year-old typical Black Forest building presents a clear picture of the hotel within. **Pros:** beautiful traditional building; friendly staff. **Cons:** can feel remote in winter. ✉ *Ellbacherstr. 4, Mitteltal/Baiersbronn* ☎ *07442/4980* ⊕ *www.lamm-mitteltal.de* ⬎ *33 rooms, 13 apartments* ⌂ *In-room: no a/c. In-hotel: restaurant, pool, some pets allowed* ⦙⊙⦙ *Breakfast.*

$$$$ 🏨 **Traube Tonbach.** This luxurious hotel has four fine restaurants. **Pros:**
Fodor'sChoice   beautiful countryside setting; friendly and efficient staff; good choice of
★   dining. **Cons:** expensive; credit cards only accepted in the restaurants, not in the hotel. ✉ *Tonbachstr. 237* ☎ *07442/4920* ⊕ *www.traube-tonbach.de* ⬎ *135 rooms, 23 apartments, 12 suites* ⌂ *In-room: no a/c, Internet. In-hotel: restaurant, bar, pool, tennis court, gym* ⦙⊙⦙ *Breakfast.*

Baden-Baden's Festspielhaus (Festival Hall) hosts concerts, operas, and ballets throughout the year; outside is a sculpture by Henry Moore.

BADEN-BADEN

51 km (32 mi) north of Freudenstadt, 24 km (15 mi) north of Mummelsee.

★ Baden-Baden, the famous and fashionable spa town, is downhill all the way north on B-500 from the Mummelsee. The town rests in a wooded valley and is atop the extensive underground hot springs that gave the city its name. Roman legions of the emperor Caracalla discovered the springs and named the area Aquae Aureliae. The leisure classes of the 19th century rediscovered the bubbling waters, establishing Baden-Baden as the unofficial summer residence of many European royal families. The town's fortunes also rose and fell with gaming: gambling began in the mid-18th century but was banned by the Kaiser between 1872 and 1933. Palatial homes and stately villas grace the tree-lined avenues, and the spa tradition continues at the ornate casino and two thermal baths, one historic and luxurious, the other modern and well used by families. Since Baden-Baden is only two hours from Frankfurt Airport by train, the spa makes a nice last stop on the way.

Though some Germans come here for two- to three-week doctor-prescribed treatments (German health insurance pays for a weeklong Kur [cure] once every five years), the spa concept also embraces facilities for those just looking for pampering. Shops line several pedestrian streets that eventually climb up toward the old marketplace. Two theaters present frequent ballet performances, plays, and concerts (by the excellent Southwest German Radio Symphony Orchestra).

GETTING HERE AND AROUND

High-speed ICE trains stop at Baden-Baden en route between Frankfurt and Basel. However, the station is some 4 km (2½ mi) northwest of the center. To get downtown, take one of the many buses that leave from outside the station. Once in the center, Baden-Baden is manageable on foot, but there is a range of alternatives available if you get tired, including a tourist train and horse-drawn carriages.

ESSENTIALS

Visitor Information Baden-Baden ⊠ *Baden-Baden Kur- und Tourismus GmbH, Solmsstr. 1* ☎ *07221/275–266* ⊕ *www.baden-baden.de.*

EXPLORING

Abtei Lichtenthal. The Lichtentaler Allee ends at Abtei Lichtenthal, a medieval Cistercian abbey surrounded by stout defensive walls. The small royal chapel next to the church was built in 1288 and was used from the late 14th century onward as a final resting place for the Baden dynasty princes. Call ahead if your group wants a tour. ⊠ *Hauptstr. 40* ☎ *07221/504–910* ⊕ *www.abtei-lichtenthal.de* 🎫 *Tours €3* ⊗ *Tours Wed. and weekends at 3.*

Casino. Baden-Baden is quite proud of its casino, Germany's oldest, opened in 1855 after Parisian interior decorators and artists had polished the last chandelier. Its concession to the times is that you may wear your jeans amid all the frescoes, stucco, and porcelain (but why would you?). Gentlemen must wear a jacket and tie with their jeans, but whatever you do, leave your sneakers at the hotel. It was in 1853 that a Parisian, Jacques Bénazet, persuaded the sleepy little Black Forest spa to build gambling rooms to enliven its evenings. The result was a series of richly decorated gaming rooms in which even an emperor could feel at home—and did. Kaiser Wilhelm I was a regular visitor, as was his chancellor, Bismarck. The Russian novelist Dostoyevsky, the Aga Khan, and Marlene Dietrich all patronized the place. The minimum stake is €2; maximum, €7,000. Passports are necessary as proof of identity. Guided tours (25 minutes) are offered in English, on request. ⊠ *Kaiserallee 1* ☎ *07221/30240* ⊕ *www.casino-baden-baden.de* 🎫 *€5, tour €5* ⊗ *Sun.–Thurs. 2 pm–2 am, Fri. and Sat. 2 pm–3 am. Tours Apr.–Sept., daily 9:30–11:30 am; Oct.–Mar., daily 10–11:30 am.*

Lichtentaler Allee. Bordering the slender Oos River, which runs through town, the Lichtentaler Allee is a groomed park with two museums and an extensive rose garden, the **Gönneranlage**, which contains more than 300 types of roses.

Museum Frieder Burda. The Museum Frieder Burda occupies a modern structure by acclaimed New York architect Richard Meier. Construction of this institution contributed greatly to pulling Baden-Baden out of its slumber. The private collection focuses on classic modern and contemporary art. Highlights are works of Picasso, German expressionists, the New York School, and American abstract expressionists. ⊠ *Lichtentaler Allee 8b* ☎ *07221/398–980* ⊕ *www.museum-frieder-burda.de* 🎫 *€10* ⊗ *Tues.–Sun. 11–6.*

Nägelsförster Hof vineyard. The region's wines, especially the dry Baden whites and delicate reds, are highly valued in Germany. ■ **TIP →** **Buy them directly from any vintner on the Baden Wine Road.** At Yburg, outside

The Baden-Baden Spa Experience

The history of "taking the waters" in Baden-Baden dates back to AD 75, when the Roman army established the city of Aquæ Aureliæ. The legions under Emporer Caracalla soon discovered that the regions' salty underground hot springs were just the thing for aching joints.

Römische Badruinen. The remains of the Roman settlement can be seen at the Römische Badruinen. ⊠ *Römerstr. 11* 🎫 *€2* 🕙 *Mar.–Nov., daily 11–1 and 2–5.*

The remains of the Roman bathhouse are explained with a computer animation that virtually reconstructs the entire area.

In a modern sense, bathing became popular within the upper-class elite when Friedrich I banned gambling in 1872. Everyone from Queen Victoria to Karl Marx dangled their feet in the pool and sang the curative praises of the salty warm water bubbling from the ground.

Friedrichsbad. In a city with many spa options, the Friedrichsbad, also known as the Roman-Irish Baths, is the most noble and elegant choice. If you choose to take the waters, the Friedrichsbad's ornate copper and terra-cotta temple is the best place to do it, though keep in mind that you'll have to bathe in the buff, as swimsuits aren't allowed. The spa treatment offers everything from a soap and brush massage to thermal steam baths. Spend at least a half hour in the relaxation area afterward to ease the transition back into the real world. Note children under 14 are not allowed. ⊠ *Römerpl. 1* 🎫 *07221/275–920* 🌐 *www.carasana.de* 🎫 *€31 for 3½ hrs all-inclusive, €21 with no massage.* 🕙 *Daily 9–10. Tues., Wed., Fri., and Sun. mixed bathing. Mon., Thurs., and Sat. gender-separate bathing.*

Caracalla Therme. If you are a bit modest and prefer to wear a swimsuit in the water, head to the more modern Caracalla Therme, named in honor of the Roman emperor who brought bathing to Baden-Baden. The indoor-outdoor pool area has three separate baths, with temperatures between 18°C and 38°C (64°F–100°F). Supplement the soaking experience with whirlpools, Jacuzzis, and waterfalls. Children under 7 are not allowed in the spa and children under 14 must be accompanied by an adult. ⊠ *Römerpl. 1* 🎫 *07221/275–940* 🌐 *www.carasana.de* 🎫 *€17 for 3 hrs* 🕙 *Daily 8–10.*

Baden-Baden, the 400-year-old Nägelsförster Hof vineyard has a shop where you can buy the product and sample what you buy (weekdays 9–6, Saturday 10–4). ⊠ *Nägelsförsterstr. 1* 🎫 *07221/398–980.*

Russian church. Close by, on the corner of Robert Kochstrasse and Lichtentalerstrasse, is the Russian church, identifiable by its golden onion dome. 🎫 *€1* 🕙 *Feb.–Nov., daily 10–6.*

WHERE TO EAT

$$$$
FRENCH
★

✕ **Der Kleine Prinz.** This gourmet hotel restaurant (⇨ *see the hotel review below*) is a local favorite in Baden-Baden. The cheery fireplace, lighted in winter, and candlelit dining provide an elegant atmosphere that complements the finest French-inspired dishes. The extensive wine list includes some excellent local offerings. As in the hotel, all the decor—designed by the owner's wife—right down to the dinner plates, reflect the children's tale from which the restaurant takes its name. ⊠ *Lichtentalerstr. 36* ☏ *07221/346–600.*

$$$$
FRENCH
✕ **Le Jardin de France.** This clean, crisp little French restaurant, whose owners are actually French, emphasizes elegant, imaginative dining in a modern setting. The restaurant sits in a quiet courtyard away from the main street, offering the possibility of alfresco dining in summer. The milk-fed suckling pig is well worth the visit. It also runs a school for budding chefs. ⊠ *Lichtentalerstr. 13* ☏ *07221/300–7860* ☾ *Closed Sun. and Mon.*

$
GERMAN
✕ **Weinstube im Baldreit.** This lively little wine bar enchants you with its lovely terraces and courtyard. It's nestled in the middle of the Old Town, making the garden and terrace the perfect place to meet friends over a dry Riesling. Enjoy some of the best *Maultaschen* (ravioli) in the huge barrel-vaulted cellar near the fireplace. ⊠ *Küferstr. 3* ☏ *07221/23136* ☾ *Closed Sun. No lunch weekdays Nov.–Mar.*

WHERE TO STAY

For expanded hotel reviews, visit Fodors.com.

$
🏨 **Am Markt.** This 250-plus-year-old building houses a modest inn run for more than 50 years by the Bogner family. **Pros:** quiet location; some rooms have great views. **Cons:** a stiff climb up from the main sights. ⊠ *Marktpl. 17–18* ☏ *07221/27040* ⊕ *www.hotel-am-markt-baden.de* ⇆ *25 rooms, 17 with bath* ⚘ *In-room: no a/c, no TV. In-hotel: some pets allowed* ⦿|*Breakfast.*

$$$$
🏨 **Brenner's Park Hotel & Spa.** With some justification, this stately hotel set in a private park claims to be one of the best in the world. **Pros:** elegant rooms; good location; quiet. **Cons:** professional staff sometimes lack personal touch. ⊠ *Schillerstr. 6* ☏ *07221/9000* ⊕ *www.brenners-park. com* ⇆ *70 rooms, 30 suites* ⚘ *In-room: Internet. In-hotel: restaurant, bar, pool, gym, spa, some pets allowed.*

$$$
Fodor's Choice
★
🏨 **Der Kleine Prinz.** Owner Norbert Rademacher, a veteran of New York's Waldorf-Astoria, and his interior-designer wife Edeltraud have skillfully combined two elegant city mansions into a unique, antiques-filled lodging. **Pros:** friendly and welcoming; some rooms have wood-burning fireplaces; most bathrooms have whirlpool tubs. **Cons:** rooms in one of the hotel's two buildings are only accessible via stairs. ⊠ *Lichtentalerstr. 36* ☏ *07221/346–600* ⊕ *www.derkleineprinz.de* ⇆ *26 rooms, 15 suites* ⚘ *In-room: Internet. In-hotel: restaurant, bar, parking, some pets allowed* ⦿|*Breakfast.*

$
🏨 **Deutscher Kaiser.** This centrally located hotel provides homey and individually styled rooms at prices that are easy on the wallet. **Pros:** some rooms have balconies; central location. **Cons:** some rooms quite small; down side street so views not great. ⊠ *Merkurstr. 9* ☏ *07221/2700* ⊕ *www.deutscher-kaiser-baden-baden.de* ⇆ *28 rooms* ⚘ *In-room: no a/c, Wi-Fi. In-hotel: some pets allowed* ⦿|*Breakfast.*

$$$
★
🏨 **Hotel Belle Epoque.** The sister hotel to Der Kleine Prinz is in a building formerly occupied by the army. **Pros:** beautiful gardens; room price includes afternoon tea; personal and friendly service. **Cons:** only the newer wing has an elevator. ⊠ *Maria-Viktoriastr. 2c* ☏ *07221/300–660* ⊕ *www.hotel-belle-epoque.de* ⇆ *20 rooms* ⚘ *In-room: a/c, Wi-Fi. In-hotel: parking, some pets allowed* ⦿|*Breakfast.*

WORD OF MOUTH

"On a recent trip to Germany, friends told us about the [Friedrichsbad] spa at Baden-Baden. You go through 17 different stations involving water, heat, and cold. Men on one side and women on another. In the middle, men and women meet in the thermal therapy pool. On certain days, men and women share all the facilities, on others the sexes are separated. On holidays, it is coed. Why must you know this? Because the spa is not a clothing-optional zone. Clothing is not allowed. . . . Nudity here is no big thing. In the summer people in the parks of Munich sunbathe topless and no one bats an eye. Going to a spa is just part of life here and it's considered therapeutic. . . . You change into your birthday suit, and take from your locker a sheet, which turns out is your towel. At each station, there are instructions on the wall, in English, telling you how long to stay in that particular room. After a good dousing, you go to the 'warm air bath'. It's then you discover that the sheet is not for covering you up, but to lay upon on the very hot wood tables in the sauna where the temperature is a balmy 129 degrees. Next, it's the 'hot air bath' and you ask yourself, what did I just have. Then you find out what hot is. 154 degrees for 5 minutes, I think. . . . Next you get to shower again before heading to the steam baths, 113 and 118 degrees, after which you start to cool down in the thermal whirlpool and therapy pools. The latter is under a huge domed room done in the Roman style. Next it's another shower before the cold water immersion bath at 64 degrees, which after what you just experienced feels like 30 degrees. Next you get a warm towel to dry off before going to the cream service room, where if you choose, you can rub various lotions on your body. Hey, I paid for it, I'm doing it. Lastly the relaxation room for 30 minutes. Here you lay on a table and the attendant wraps you in a warm sheet and blanket. The whole thing takes about 2.5 hours and you never have felt so relaxed and clean. . . . Was it worth it? You bet. Did I feel uncomfortable? Only for the first 5 minutes when I didn't know what to do with the sheet. Would I do it again? Why not?"

—dgassa

$$$$
★ 🏨 **Schlosshotel Bühlerhöhe.** This "castle-hotel" stands majestically on its own extensive grounds 10 km (6 mi) from Baden-Baden, with spectacular views over the heights of the Black Forest. **Pros:** quiet location; great for hikers. **Cons:** a long way from downtown. ✉ *Schwarzwaldhochstr. 1, Bühl* ☎ *07226/550* ⊕ *www.buehlerhoehe.de* ↵ *77 rooms, 13 suites* ⚒ *In-room: no a/c, Wi-Fi. In-hotel: restaurant, bar, pool, tennis court, business center, some pets allowed.*

NIGHTLIFE AND THE ARTS

Nightlife revolves around Baden-Baden's elegant **casino**, but there are cultural attractions as well.

Festspielhaus. The Festspielhaus is a state-of-the-art concert hall superbly fitted onto the old train station. ✉ *Beim Alten Bahnhof 2* ☎ *07221/301–3101* ⊕ *www.festspielhaus.de.*

Kurhaus. The Kurhaus adjoining the casino hosts concerts year-round. ✉ *Kaiserallee 1* ☏ *07221/353–202* ⊕ *www.kurhaus-baden-baden.de.*

Living Room. The Hotel Merkur has a small nightclub called the Living Room. ✉ *Merkurstr. 8* ☏ *07221/303–366.*

Oleander Bar. For a subdued evening, stop by the Oleander Bar. ✉ *Schillerstr. 6* ☏ *07221/9000.*

Theater. Baden-Baden has one of Germany's most beautiful performance halls, the Theater, a late-baroque jewel built in 1860–62 in the style of the Paris Opéra. It opened with the world premiere of Berlioz's opera *Beatrice et Benedict.* Today the theater presents a regular series of dramas, operas, and ballets. ✉ *Goethepl.* ☏ *07221/932–700* ⊕ *www.theater.baden-baden.de.*

Trinkhalle. Baden-Baden attracts a rather mature crowd, but the deep leather seats of the Trinkhalle make a hip lounge for those under age 40. At night this daytime bistro also takes over the portion of the hall where the tourist office has a counter, turning it into a dance floor. ✉ *Kaiserallee 3.*

SPORTS AND THE OUTDOORS

GOLF **Golf Club.** The 18-hole Baden-Baden course is considered one of Europe's finest. Contact the Golf Club. ✉ *Fremersbergstr. 127* ☏ *07221/23579* ⊕ *www.golf-club-baden-baden.de* ⌑ *€65 for 18 holes.*

HORSEBACK RIDING **Iffezheim.** The racetrack at nearby Iffezheim harks back to the days when Baden-Baden was a magnet for royalty and aristocrats. Its tradition originated in 1858; now annual international meets take place in late May, late August, early September, and October. ☏ *07229/1870.*

Reitzentrum Balg. Those wishing to ride can rent horses and get instruction at the Reitzentrum Balg. ✉ *Buchenweg 42* ☏ *07221/55920.*

KARLSRUHE

10 km (6 mi) north of Ettlingen.

Karlsruhe, founded at the beginning of the 18th century, is a young upstart, but what it lacks in years it makes up for in industrial and administrative importance, sitting as it does astride a vital autobahn and rail crossroads. It's best known as the seat of Germany's Supreme Court, and has a high concentration of legal practitioners.

GETTING HERE AND AROUND

The Autobahn A-5 connects Freiburg, Baden-Baden, and Karlsruhe. Karlsruhe's train station is an easy 15-minute walk from the city center and trains run frequently throughout the region; south to baden Baden (15 minutes) and Freiburg (1 hour), and east to Pforzheim (25 minutes) and Frankfurt (1 hour).

ESSENTIALS

Visitor Information Karlsruhe ✉ *Tourist-Information, Bahnhofpl. 6* ☏ *0721/3720–5383* ⊕ *www.karlsruhe.de.*

At the Zentrum für Kunst und Medientechnologie (Center for Art and Media Technology), known simply as the ZKM, you can view contemporary art or interact with media.

EXPLORING

Badisches Landesmuseum (*Baden State Museum*). The Badisches Landesmuseum, in the palace, has a large number of Greek and Roman antiquities and trophies that Ludwig the Turk brought back from campaigns in Turkey in the 17th century. Most of the other exhibits are devoted to local history. ⊠ *Schloss* ☎ *0721/926–6514* ⊕ *www.landesmuseum. de* ⤳ *€4* ⊘ *Tues.–Thurs. 10–5, Fri.–Sun. 10–6.*

Schloss. The town quite literally grew up around the former Schloss of the Margrave Karl Wilhelm, which was begun in 1715. Thirty-two avenues radiate from the palace, 23 leading into the extensive grounds, and the remaining 9 forming the grid of the Old Town.

Staatliche Kunsthalle (*State Art Gallery*). One of the most important collections of paintings in the Black Forest region hangs in the Staatliche Kunsthalle. Look for masterpieces by Grünewald, Holbein, Rembrandt, and Monet, and also for work by the Black Forest painter Hans Thoma. In the **Kunsthalle Orangerie,** next door, is work by such modern artists as Braque and Beckmann. ⊠ *Hans-Thoma-Str. 2–6* ☎ *0721/926–3359* ⊕ *www.kunsthalle-karlsruhe.de* ⤳ *Both museums €6* ⊘ *Tues.–Fri. 10–5, weekends 10–6.*

☺ **Zentrum für Kunst und Medientechnologie** (*Center for Art and Media Tech-*
★ *nology*). In a former munitions factory, the vast Zentrum für Kunst und Medientechnologie, or simply ZKM, is an all-day adventure consisting of two separate museums. At the **Medienmuseum** (Media Museum) you can watch movies, listen to music, try out video games, flirt with a virtual partner, or sit on a real bicycle and pedal through a virtual New York City. ■TIP➔ Take Tram 6 to ZKM to get here.

Museum für Neue Kunst (*Museum of Modern Art*). The Museum für Neue Kunst is a top-notch collection of media art in all genres from the end of the 20th century ☎ *0721/81000* ✉ *Lorenzstr. 19* ☎ *0721/81000* ⊕ *www.zkm.de* ▣ *Either museum €5, combined ticket €8, free after 2 on Fri.* ☉ *Wed.–Fri. 10–6, weekends 11–6.*

WHERE TO EAT AND STAY

For expanded hotel reviews, visit Fodors.com.

$$$
GERMAN
✕ **Buchmanns.** Elke and Günter Buchmann run a "linen tablecloth and real silver" establishment, with a beer garden and a bar. The various suggested courses are grouped in fancy handwriting on the menu, along with the fancy price of each dish. You can, of course, just order one of the courses, but be prepared for a disapproving look. The proprietors are Austrian, and the specialties of their country, such as *Tafelspitz* (boiled beef with horseradish applesauce) and *Kaiserschmarrn* (torn-up fluffy egg pancakes with apples, raisins, cinnamon, and jam), are recommended, but the Wiener schnitzel is divine. If you have trouble with the extensive wine list, the waitstaff is ready and willing to help. ✉ *Mathystr. 22–24* ☎ *0721/820–3730* ☉ *Closed Sun. No lunch Sat.*

$$
🏨 **Schlosshotel.** A few steps from the main station, this hotel looks, and sometimes behaves, like a palace. **Pros:** elegant hotel; friendly service; advanced online booking saves €50. **Cons:** on a noisy street; modern rooms don't live up to the historic feel of the hotel. ✉ *Bahnhofpl. 2* ☎ *0721/38320* ⊕ *www.schlosshotel-karlsruhe.de* ⤵ *93 rooms, 3 suites* ⌂ *In-room: no a/c, Internet. In-hotel: restaurant, bar, gym, business center, parking, some pets allowed.*

THE ARTS

Badisches Staatstheater. One of the best opera houses in the region is Karlsruhe's Badisches Staatstheater. ✉ *Baumeisterstr. 11* ☎ *0721/35570* ⊕ *www.staatstheater.karlsruhe.de.*

THE CENTRAL BLACK FOREST

The Central Black Forest takes in the Simonswald, Elz, and Glotter valleys as well as Triberg and Furtwangen, with their clock museums. The area around the Triberg Falls—the highest falls in Germany—is also renowned for pom-pom hats, thatch-roof farmhouses, and mountain railways. The Schwarzwaldbahn (Black Forest Railway; Offenburg–Villingen line), which passes through Triberg, is one of the most scenic in all of Europe.

ALPIRSBACH

16 km (10 mi) south of Freudenstadt.

The hamlet of Alpirsbach was founded in 1035 and developed around the Benedictine monastery Kloster Alpirsbach. Although the wages of the reformation forced the abbey to close its doors in 1535, the tradition of brewing is still going strong—it's well worth making a pilgrimage to the Alpirsbacher Klosterbräu (brewery). The village maintains a preserved historic core with a fine collection of half-timber houses.

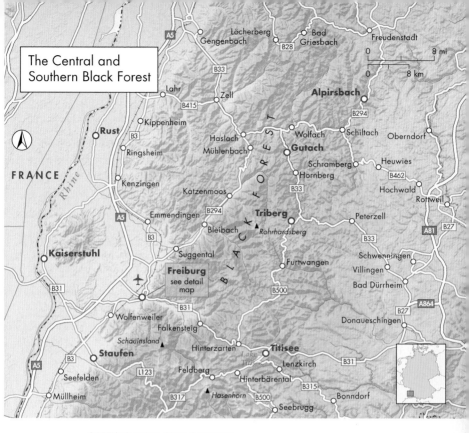

The Central and Southern Black Forest

GETTING HERE AND AROUND

Alpirsbach is on the direct train line between Freudenstadt and Offenburg. Alpirsbach is a great day trip by train from Freiburg (2 hours with a change in Offenburg)

ESSENTIALS

Visitor Information Alpirsbach ✉ *Tourist-Information, Hauptstr. 20* ☎ *07444/951–6281* ⊕ *www.alpirsbach.de.*

EXPLORING

Brauerei (*brewery*). The Brauerei was once part of the monastery, and has brewed beer since the Middle Ages. The unusually soft water gives the beer a flavor that is widely acclaimed. There are guided tours of the brewery museum daily at 2:30. ✉ *Marktpl. 1* ☎ *07444/67149* ⊕ *www. alpirsbacher-brauwelt.de* 🎫 *Tour €6.90* ⊗ *Mar.–Oct., weekdays 9:30–4:30, weekends 11–3; Nov.–Feb., daily 11–3.*

WHERE TO EAT

$ ✕ **Zwickel & Kaps.** The name is a highly sophisticated brewing term,
GERMAN describing the means by which the brewmaster samples the fermenting product. Sit down at one of the simple beech-wood tables and order a satisfying Swabian lentil stew with dumplings and sausages, or something more Mediterranean, such as salmon with pesto. ✉ *Marktstr. 3* ☎ *07444/51727* ⊗ *Closed Mon.*

GUTACH

17 km (11 mi) north of Triberg.

Gutach lies in Gutachtal, a valley famous for the traditional costume, complete with pom-pom hats, worn by women on feast days and holidays. Married women wear black pom-poms, unmarried women red ones. The village is one of the few places in the Black Forest where you can still see thatch roofs. However, escalating costs caused by a decline in skilled thatchers, and soaring fire-insurance premiums, make for fewer thatch roofs than there were 20 years ago.

GETTING HERE AND AROUND

Schwarzwälder Freilichtmuseum Vogtsbauernhof (*Black Forest Open-Air Museum*). Near Gutach is one of the most appealing museums in the Black Forest, the Schwarzwälder Freilichtmuseum Vogtsbauernhof. Farmhouses and other rural buildings from all parts of the region have been transported here from their original locations and reassembled, complete with traditional furniture, to create a living museum of Black Forest building types through the centuries. Demonstrations ranging from traditional dances to woodworking capture life as it was in centuries past. ✉ *B-33* ☎ *07831/93560* ⊕ *www.vogtsbauernhof.org* 🖃 *€7* ⊗ *Apr.–Oct., daily 9–6 (July and Aug. until 7).*

OFF THE BEATEN PATH

Schwarzwalder Trachtenmuseum. Regional traditional costumes can be seen at this museum in a former monastery in the village of Haslach, 10 km (6 mi) northwest of Gutach. The village is quaint, with a fine collection of half-timber houses. Pom-pom-topped straw hats, bejeweled headdresses, embroidered velvet vests, and *Fasnet* (Carnival) regalia of all parts of the forest are on display. ✉ *Klosterstr. 1* ☎ *07832/706–172* ⊕ *www.trachtenmuseum-haslach.de.vu* 🖃 *€2* ⊗ *Apr.–mid-Oct., Tues.– Sat. 9–5, Sun. 10–5; mid-Oct.–Dec., Feb.–Mar., Tues.–Fri. 9–noon and 1–5; Jan. by appointment.*

TRIBERG

16 km (10 mi) south of Gutach.

★ The cuckoo clock, that symbol of the Black Forest, is at home in the Triberg area. It was invented here, it's made and sold here, it's featured in two museums, and there are two house-size cuckoo clocks here.

GETTING HERE AND AROUND

Triberg is accessible via one of the prettiest train rides in Germany, with direct services to Lake Constance and Karlsruhe. The train station is at the lower end of the long main street, and the waterfalls are a stiff uphill walk away. You can take a bus up the hill from the train station to the entrance to the waterfalls, relieving most of the uphill struggle.

ESSENTIALS

Visitor Information Triberg ✉ *Tourist-Information, Wahlfahrtstr. 4* ☎ *07722/866–490* ⊕ *www.triberg.de.*

Cuckoo for Cuckoo Clocks

"In Switzerland they had brotherly love—they had 500 years of democracy and peace, and what did that produce? The cuckoo clock."

So says Harry Lime, played by Orson Welles in the classic 1949 film *The Third Man.* He misspoke in two ways. First, the Swiss are an industrious, technologically advanced people. And second, they didn't invent the cuckoo clock. That was the work of the Germans living in the adjacent Black Forest.

The first Kuckucksuhr was designed and built in 1750 by Franz Anton Ketterer in Schönwald near Triberg. He cleverly produced the cuckoo sound with a pair of wooden whistles, each attached to a bellows activated by the clock's mechanism.

The making of carved wooden clocks developed rapidly in the Black Forest. The people on the farms needed ways to profitably occupy their time during the long snowbound winters, and the carving of clocks was the answer. Wood was abundant, and the early clocks were entirely of wood, even the works.

Come spring one of the sons would don a traditional smock and hat, mount the family's winter output on a big rack, hoist it to his back, and set off into the world to sell the clocks. In 1808 there were 688 clock makers

and 582 clock peddlers in the districts of Triberg and Neustadt. The *Uhrenträger* (clock carrier) is an important part of the Black Forest tradition. Guides often wear the traditional costume.

The traditional cuckoo clock is made with brown stained wood with a gabled roof and some sort of woodland motif carved into it, such as a deer's head or a cluster of leaves. The works are usually activated by cast-iron weights, in the form of pinecones, on chains.

Today's clocks can be much more elaborate. Dancing couples in traditional dress automatically move to the sound of a music box, a mill wheel turns on the hour, a farmer chops wood on the hour, the Uhrenträger even makes his rounds. The cuckoo itself moves its wings and beak and rocks back and forth when calling.

The day is long past when the clocks were made entirely of wood. The works are of metal and therefore more reliable and accurate. Other parts of the clock, such as the whistles, the face, and the hands, are usually of plastic now, but hand-carved wood is still the rule for the case. The industry is still centered in Triberg. There are two museums in the area with sections dedicated to it, and clocks are sold everywhere, even in kiosks.

EXPLORING

Eble Uhren-Park. You can buy a cuckoo clock, or just about any other souvenir, at the huge Eble Uhren-Park, about 3 km (2 mi) from the town center in the district of Schonachbach. It's also the location of one of the house-size cuckoo clocks. You can enter it for €1.50 and examine the works. ⊠ *On Hwy. B-33 between Triberg and Hornberg* ☎ *07722/96220* ⊕ *www.eble-uhren-park.de* ☉ *Apr.–Oct., Mon.–Sat. 9–6, Sun. 10–6; Nov.–Mar., Mon.–Sat. 9–6, Sun. 11–4:30.*

Haus der 1000 Uhren (*House of 1,000 Clocks*). The Haus der 1000 Uhren has a shop right at the waterfall. The main store, just off B-33 toward Offenburg in the suburb of Gremmelsbach, boasts another of the town's giant cuckoo clocks. Both stores offer a rich variety of clocks, some costing as much as €3,000. ✉ *Hauptstr. 79–81* ☎ *07722/96300* ⊕ *www. houseof1000clocks.de* ⊗ *Mon.–Sat. 11–5, Sun. 11–4.*

Hubert Herr. Hubert Herr is the only factory that continues to make nearly all of its own components for its cuckoo clocks. The present proprietors are the fifth generation from Andreas and Christian Herr, who began making the clocks more than 150 years ago. The company produces a great variety of clocks, including one that, at 5¼ inches high, is claimed to be "the world's smallest." ✉ *Hauptstr. 8* ☎ *07722/4268* ⊕ *www.hubertherr.de* ⊗ *Weekdays 9–noon and 1:30–4.*

Schwarzwaldbahn (*Black Forest Railway*). The Hornberg–Triberg–St. Georgen segment of the Schwarzwaldbahn is one of Germany's most scenic train rides. The 149-km (93-mi) Schwarzwaldbahn, built from 1866 to 1873, runs from Offenburg to Lake Constance via Triberg. It has no fewer than 39 tunnels, and at one point climbs 656 yards in just 11 km (6½ mi). It's now part of the German Railway, and you can make inquiries at any station. ☎ *11861* ⊕ *www.bahn.de.*

Schwarzwaldmuseum (*Black Forest Museum*). Triberg's famous Schwarzwaldmuseum is a treasure trove of the region's traditional arts: wood carving, costumes, and handicrafts. The Schwarzwaldbahn is described, with historical displays and a working model. The Black Forest was also a center of mechanical music, and, among many other things, the museum has an "Orchestrion"—a cabinet full of mechanical instruments playing like an orchestra. ✉ *Wallfahrtstr. 4* ☎ *07722/4434* ⊕ *www.schwarzwaldmuseum.de* 🎟 *€5* ⊗ *Daily 10–5.*

Waterfall. At the head of the Gutach Valley, the Gutach River plunges more than 500 feet over seven huge granite cascades at Triberg's waterfall, Germany's highest. The pleasant 45-minute walk from the center of town is well signposted. A longer walk goes by a small pilgrimage church and the old Mesnerhäuschen, the sacristan's house. 🎟 *Waterfall €3.50.*

WHERE TO STAY

For expanded hotel reviews, visit Fodors.com.

$ 🏨 **Hotel-Restaurant-Pfaff.** Rooms at this restaurant-hotel are very comfortable. **Pros:** friendly service; close to waterfall. **Cons:** some rooms quite small; no elevator. ✉ *Hauptstr. 85* ☎ *07722/4479* ⊕ *www.hotelpfaff.com* ⇥ *10 rooms* ⌂ *In-room: no a/c. In-hotel: restaurant, some pets allowed* ⫴○⫴ *Breakfast.*

$$ 🏨 **Parkhotel Wehrle.** The wisteria-covered facade and steep eaves of this large mansion dominate the town center. **Pros:** elegant rooms; friendly service. **Cons:** main street outside can be noisy. ✉ *Gartenstr. 24* ☎ *07722/86020* ⊕ *www.parkhotel-wehrle.de* ⇥ *50 rooms, 1 suite* ⌂ *In-room: no a/c, Internet, Wi-Fi. In-hotel: restaurant, pool, gym, parking, some pets allowed* ⫴○⫴ *Breakfast.*

OFF THE BEATEN PATH

Stadtmuseum. Rottweil, 26 km (16 mi) east of Triberg, has the best of the Black Forest's Fasnet celebrations. Outside the Black Forest, the celebrations are good-natured and sophisticated, but here and in adjacent areas of Switzerland they're pagan and fierce. In the days just before Ash Wednesday, usually in February, witches and devils roam the streets wearing ugly wooden masks and making fantastic gyrations as they crack whips and ring bells. If you can't make it to Rottweil during the Carnival season, you can still catch the spirit of Fasnet. There's an exhibit on it at the Stadtmuseum, and tours are organized to the shops where they carve the masks and make the costumes and bells. The name "*Rottweil*" may be more familiar to you as the name for a breed of dog. The area used to be a center of meat production, and the Rottweiler was bred to herd the cattle.

EN ROUTE

Uhren Museum (*Clock Museum*). In the center of Furtwangen, 16 km (10 mi) south of Triberg, drop in on the Uhren Museum, the largest such museum in Germany. It charts the development of Black Forest clocks and exhibits all types of timepieces, from cuckoo clocks, church clock mechanisms, kinetic wristwatches, and old decorative desktop clocks to punch clocks and digital blinking objects. The most elaborate piece is the "art clock" by local artisan August Noll, built from 1880 to 1885 and featuring the time in Calcutta, New York, Melbourne, and London, among other places. It emits the sound of a crowing rooster in the morning, and other chimes mark yearly events. It's occasionally demonstrated during tours. You can set your own watch to the sundial built into the concrete of the square in front of the museum. This remarkable creation nearly ticks off the seconds. ⊠ *Robert-Gerwig-Pl. 1* ☎ *07723/920–2800* ⊕ *www.deutsches-uhrenmuseum.de* ⊠ *€6* ⊙ *Apr.– Oct., daily 9–6; Nov.–Mar., daily 10–5.*

THE SOUTHERN BLACK FOREST

In the south you'll find the most spectacular mountain scenery in the area, culminating in the Feldberg—at 4,899 feet the highest mountain in the Black Forest. The region also has two large lakes, the Titisee and the Schluchsee. Freiburg is a romantic university city with vineyards and a superb Gothic cathedral.

TITISEE

37 km (23 mi) south of Furtwangen.

Beautiful Titisee, carved by a glacier in the last ice age, is the most scenic lake in the Black Forest. The landscape is heavily wooded and ideal for long bike tours, which can be organized through the Titisee tourist office. The lake measures 2½ km (1½ mi) long and is invariably crowded in summer. Stop by one of the many lakeside cafés to enjoy some of the region's best Black Forest cherry cake with an unparalleled waterside view. ■TIP➔ Boats and Windsurfers can be rented at several points along the shore.

ESSENTIALS

Visitor Information Titlee-Neustadt ⊠ *Tourist-Information, Strandbadstr. 4* ☎ *07651/98040* ⊕ *www.titisee.de.*

WHERE TO STAY

For expanded hotel reviews, visit Fodors.com.

¢ 🔲 **Gasthaus Sonnenmatte.** There are countless hotels and restaurants clustered around the lakeshore, but for a quieter time and to escape the crowds in summer, it's worth heading farther from the lake. **Pros:** quiet rural location; friendly service; away from the Titisee crowds. **Cons:** away from the Titisee views; some rooms quite small. ⊠ *Spriegelsbach 5, Titisee-Neustadt* ☎ *07651/8277* ⊕ *www.sonnenmatte.de* ➽ *30 rooms* ⌂ *In-room: no a/c, Wi-Fi. In-hotel: restaurant, bar, pool, gym, some pets allowed* ⦿⊙ *Breakfast.*

EN ROUTE
To get to Freiburg, the largest city in the southern Black Forest, you have to brave the curves of the winding road through the **Höllental** (Hell Valley). In 1770 Empress Maria Theresa's 15-year-old daughter—the future queen Marie Antoinette—made her way along what was then a coach road on her way from Vienna to Paris. She traveled with an entourage of 250 officials and servants in some 50 horse-drawn carriages. The first stop at the end of the valley is a little village called **Himmelreich,** or Kingdom of Heaven. Railroad engineers are said to have given the village its name in the 19th century, grateful as they were to finally have laid a line through Hell Valley. At the entrance to Höllental is a deep gorge, the **Ravennaschlucht.** It's worth scrambling through to reach the tiny 12th-century chapel of **St. Oswald,** the oldest parish church in the Black Forest (there are parking spots off the road). Look for a bronze statue of a deer high on a roadside cliff, 5 km (3 mi) farther on. It commemorates the legend of a deer that amazed hunters by leaping the deep gorge at this point. Another 16 km (10 mi) will bring you to Freiburg.

FREIBURG

25 km (15½ mi) northwest of Hinterzarten.

Freiburg im Breisgau was founded in the 12th century. World War II left extensive damage, but skillful restoration helped re-create the original and compelling medieval atmosphere of one of the loveliest historic towns in Germany. The 16th-century geographer Martin Waldseemüller was born here; in 1507 he was the first to put the name *"America"* on a map.

For an intimate view of Freiburg, wander through the car-free streets around the Münster or follow the main shopping artery of Kaiser-Joseph-Strasse. After you pass the city gate (Martinstor), follow Gerberau off to the left. You'll come to quaint shops along the banks of one of the city's larger canals, which continues past the former Augustinian cloister to the equally picturesque area around the *Insel* (island). This canal is a larger version of the *Bächle* (brooklets) running through many streets in Freiburg's Old Town. The Bächle, so narrow you can step across them, were created in the 13th century to bring freshwater into the town. Legend

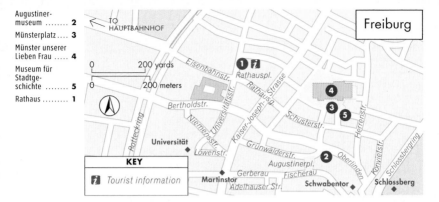

has it that if you accidentally step into one of them—and it does happen to travelers looking at the sights—you will marry a person from Freiburg. The tourist office sponsors English walking tours daily at 10:30, with additional tours on Friday and Saturday at 10. The two-hour tour costs €8.

GETTING HERE AND AROUND

Freiburg is on the main railway line between Frankfurt and Basel, and regular ICE express trains stop here. The railway station is a short walk from the city center. Although Freiburg is a bustling metropolis, the city center is compact. In fact, the bulk of the Old Town is closed to traffic, so walking is by far the most practical and pleasurable option. The Old Town is ringed with parking garages for those who arrive by car.

ESSENTIALS

Visitor Information Freiburg ⊠ *Tourist-Information, Rathauspl. 2–4* ☎ *0761/388–1880* ⊕ *www.freiburg.de.*

EXPLORING

Augustinermuseum. A visit to Freiburg's cathedral is not really complete without also exploring the Augustinermuseum, in the former Augustinian cloister. Original sculpture from the cathedral is on display, as well as gold and silver reliquaries. The collection of stained-glass windows, dating from the Middle Ages to today, is one of the most important in Germany. ⊠ *Am Augustinerpl.* ☎ *0761/201–2531* ⊕ *www.museen. freiburg.de* ⊠ *€6* ⊗ *Tues.–Sun. 10–5.*

Fodor's Choice ★ **Münster unserer Lieben Frau** (*Cathedral of Our Dear Lady*). The Münster unserer Lieben Frau, Freiburg's most famous landmark, towers over the medieval streets. The cathedral took three centuries to build, from around 1200 to 1515. You can easily trace the progress of generations of builders through the changing architectural styles, from the fat columns and solid, rounded arches of the Romanesque period to the lofty Gothic windows and airy interior of the choir. The delicately perforated 380-foot spire has been called the finest in Europe. ■TIP➔ If you can summon the energy, climb the tower. In addition to a magnificent view, you'll get a closer look at the 16 bells, including the 1258 "Hosanna," one of Germany's oldest functioning bells. ⊠ *Münsterpl.* ☎ *0761/388–101* ⊠ *Bell tower €1.50* ⊗ *Mon.–Sat. 9:30–5, Sun. 1–5.*

Visitors light candles at the Münster unserer Lieben Frau (Cathedral of Our Dear Lady).

Münsterplatz. The Münsterplatz, the square around Freiburg's cathedral, which once served as a cemetery, holds a market Monday to Saturday. You can stock up on local specialties, from wood-oven-baked bread to hams, wines, vinegars, fruits, and *Kirschwasser* (cherry brandy). The southern side, in front of the Renaissance **Kaufhaus** (Market House), is traditionally used by merchants. On the northern side of the square are farmers with their produce. This is where you can sample some local sausages served with a white roll and heaps of onions. The square is also lined with traditional taverns.

Museum für Stadtgeschichte (*Museum of City History*). The former home of painter, sculptor, and architect Johann Christian Wentzinger (1710–97) houses the Museum für Stadtgeschichte. It contains fascinating exhibits on the history of the city, including the poignant remains of a typewriter recovered from a bombed-out bank. The ceiling fresco in the stairway, painted by Wentzinger himself, is the museum's pride and joy. ⊠ *Münsterpl. 30* ☎ *0761/201–2515* ⊕ *www.museen.freiburg.de* ☞ *€3* ☉ *Tues.–Sun. 10–5.*

Rathaus. Freiburg's famous Rathaus (Town Hall) is constructed from two 16th-century patrician houses joined together. Among its attractive Renaissance features is an oriel, or bay window, clinging to a corner and bearing a bas-relief of the romantic medieval legend of the Maiden and the Unicorn. ⊠ *Rathauspl. 2–4* ☉ *Mon.–Thurs. 8–5:30, Fri. 8–4.*

WHERE TO EAT

$ ⨯ **Der Goldene Engel.** Oak beams festooned with plaster casts of cher-
GERMAN ubs, and angelic paintings on the walls, combine to create a charmingly kitsch atmosphere in "the golden angel." Local dishes are the

specialty here, and the Flammkuchen in particular are a good choice. Try the Schwarzwälder Kirschsteak, a wonderful pork chop with cherries. ⊠ *Münsterpl. 14* ☎ *0761/37933.*

$ ✕ **Kühler Krug.** Fresh fish and wild game are the specialties at this elegant
GERMAN yet homey restaurant around 2 km (1½ mi) south of the Old Town. Interesting dishes include rabbit in hazelnut sauce with baby vegetables, as well as salmon in saffron foam with a Riesling risotto. ⊠ *Torpl. 1, Freiburg-Günterstal* ☎ *0761/29103* ☽ *Closed Wed.*

WHERE TO STAY
For expanded hotel reviews, visit Fodors.com.

$$ ⊞ **Best Western Premier Hotel Victoria.** Despite its traditional appearance and comfort, this is a very eco-friendly hotel. **Pros:** eco-friendly; free city bus tickets available to guests. **Cons:** outside the medieval center. ⊠ *Eisenbahnstr. 54* ☎ *0761/207–340* ⊕ *www.victoria.bestwestern.de* ⊷ *63 rooms* ☖ *In-room: no a/c, Internet, Wi-Fi. In-hotel: bar, parking, some pets allowed.*

$$$$ ⊞ **Colombi.** Freiburg's most luxurious hotel is one of the few where
Fodor's Choice the owners are there to make sure your stay is perfect. **Pros:** friendly
★ service; quiet location; comfortable rooms. **Cons:** business hotel; often fully booked by conference visitors. ⊠ *Rotteckring 16* ☎ *0761/21060* ⊕ *www.colombi.de* ⊷ *111 rooms, 5 suites* ☖ *In-room: Internet, Wi-Fi. In-hotel: restaurant, bar, pool, gym, business center, parking, some pets allowed.*

$ ⊞ **Gasthaus zur Sonne.** The downside: the bathroom is down the hall for some rooms, there are no eggs at breakfast, the bedside lamps may or may not work, and it's a long way from the center of town. **Pros:** clean; friendly; good value. **Cons:** some shared bathrooms; far from the sights. ⊠ *Hochdorfstr. 1* ☎ *07665/2650* ⊕ *www.sonne-hochdorf.de* ⊷ *15 rooms, 7 with bath* ☖ *In-room: no a/c. In-hotel: restaurant, bar, parking, some pets allowed* ▭ *No credit cards* ⏀ *Breakfast.*

$ ⊞ **Hotel Schwarzwälder Hof.** Part of this hotel occupies a former mint, complete with graceful cast-iron railings on the spiral staircase and, unfortunately, paper-thin walls. ⊠ *Herrenstr. 43* ☎ *0761/38030* ⊕ *www.shof.de* ⊷ *42 rooms, 3 suites* ☖ *In-room: no a/c, Internet. In-hotel: restaurant, business center, parking, some pets allowed* ⏀ *Breakfast.*

$$ ⊞ **Oberkirchs Weinstube.** Across from the cathedral, this wine cellar, restaurant, and hotel is a bastion of tradition and *Gemütlichkeit* (comfort and conviviality). **Pros:** great central location. **Cons:** difficult parking access. ⊠ *Münsterpl. 22* ☎ *0761/202–6868* ⊕ *www.hotel-oberkirch.de* ⊷ *26 rooms* ☖ *In-room: no a/c, Wi-Fi. In-hotel: restaurant, some pets allowed* ☽ *Restaurant closed Sun. and 2 wks in Jan.* ⏀ *Breakfast.*

$$ ⊞ **Park Hotel Post Meier.** This century-old building near the train station has a copper dome and stone balconies overlooking a park. **Pros:** friendly; some rooms have park views. **Cons:** outside the medieval center. ⊠ *Eisenbahnstr. 35–37* ☎ *0761/385–480* ⊕ *www.park-hotel-post.de* ⊷ *43 rooms, 2 apartments* ☖ *In-room: no a/c, Wi-Fi* ⏀ *Breakfast.*

$$ ⊞ **Rappen.** This hotel's brightly painted rooms are on the sunny side of the cobblestone cathedral square and marketplace. **Pros:** central location; friendly service; clean rooms. **Cons:** difficult to access by car; located in pedestrian zone. ⊠ *Münsterpl. 13* ☎ *0761/31353* ⊕ *www.*

7

hotelrappen.de 🗗 *24 rooms* ⬧ *In-room: no a/c, Internet, Wi-Fi. In-hotel: restaurant, some pets allowed* ❙⦾❙ *Breakfast.*

$$ 🖼 **Zum Roten Bären.** Like several other hotels, the "Red Bear" claims to ★ be the "oldest in Germany," but this one has authenticated documentation going back 700 years to prove its heritage. **Pros:** dripping with history; great location. **Cons:** some rooms quite small. ⊠ *Oberlinden 12* ☎ *0761/387–870* ⊕ *www.roter-baeren.de* 🗗 *22 rooms, 3 suites* ⬧ *In-room: no a/c, Internet. In-hotel: restaurant, parking, some pets allowed* ⊘ *Restaurant closed Sun.* ❙⦾❙ *Breakfast.*

NIGHTLIFE AND THE ARTS

Cocktailbar Hemingway. Plenty of people take their nightcap in the Best Western Premier Hotel Victoria at the Cocktailbar Hemingway, which stays open until 2 am on weekends. ⊠ *Eisenbahnstr. 54* ☎ *0761/207–340.*

Jazzhaus. Jazzhaus sometimes has live music and draws big acts and serious up-and-coming artists to its brick cellar. ⊠ *Schnewlinstr. 1* ☎ *0761/34973* ⊕ *www.jazzhaus.de.*

Kagan. A very mixed crowd meets daily and nightly at Kagan on the 18th floor of the skyscraper over the train station, with an incomparable view of the Old Town. The club is open Wednesday through Saturday from 10 pm until the wee hours. The café is open Tuesday through Sunday. ⊠ *Bismarckallee 9* ☎ *0761/767–2766* ⊡ *€6.*

Stühlinger. Nightlife in Freiburg takes place in the city's *Kneipen* (pubs), wine bars, and wine cellars, which are plentiful on the streets around the cathedral. For student pubs, wander around Stühlinger, the neighborhood immediately south of the train station.

STAUFEN

20 km (12 mi) south of Freiburg via B-31.

Once you've braved Hell Valley to get to Freiburg, visit the nearby town of Staufen, where Dr. Faustus is reputed to have made his pact with the devil. The Faustus legend is remembered today chiefly because of Goethe's *Faust* (published in two parts, 1808–32). In this account, Faust sells his soul to the devil in return for eternal youth and knowledge. The historical Faustus was actually an alchemist whose pact was not with the devil but with a local baron who convinced him that he could make his fortune by converting base metal into gold. The explosion leading to his death at Gasthaus zum Löwen produced so much noise and sulfurous stink that the townspeople were convinced the devil had carried him off.

GETTING HERE AND AROUND

To reach Staufen, take the twice-hourly train from Freiburg and change at Bad Krozingen. The train station is a 15-minute walk northwest of the town center. The B-31 highway connects Staufen with Freiburg and the A-5 motorway.

Gasthaus zum Löwen. You can visit the ancient Gasthaus zum Löwen, where Faustus lived, allegedly in room No. 5, and died. Guests can stay overnight in the room, which has been decked out in period furniture

For a break from cathedrals and historic sites, take the kids to Europa Park in Rust.

and had all-modern conveniences removed (including the telephone) to enhance the effect. The inn is right on the central square of Staufen, a town with a visible inclination toward modern art in ancient settings. ⊠ *Rathausg. 8* ☎ *07633/908–9390* ⊕ *www.fauststube-im-loewen.de.*

WHERE TO STAY
For expanded hotel reviews, visit Fodors.com.

$ ☷ **Landgasthaus zur Linde.** Guests have been welcomed here for more than 350 years, but the comforts inside the inn's old walls are contemporary. **Pros:** friendly; quiet; good restaurant. **Cons:** remote; no elevator. ⊠ *Krumlinden 13, 14 km (9 mi) southeast of Staufen, Münstertal* ☎ *07636/447* ⊕ *www.landgasthaus.de* ⊃ *11 rooms, 3 suites* ☐ *In-room: no a/c. In-hotel: restaurant, some pets allowed* ⊗ *Restaurant closed Mon.* ⦿| *Breakfast.*

KAISERSTUHL

20 km (12 mi) northwest of Freiburg on B–31.

One of the unusual sights of the Black Forest is the Kaiserstuhl (Emperor's Chair), a volcanic outcrop clothed in vineyards that produce some of Baden's best wines—reds from the Spätburgunder grape and whites that have an uncanny depth. A third of Baden's wines are produced in this single area, which has the warmest climate in Germany. ■ TIP→ The especially dry and warm microclimate has given rise to tropical vegetation, including sequoias and a wide variety of orchids.

Weinmuseum (*Wine Museum*). The fine little Weinmuseum is in a renovated barn in the village center. A small vineyard out front displays the various types of grapes used to make wine in the Kaiserstuhl region. ⊠ *Schlossbergstr., Vogtsburg-Achkarren* ☎ *07662/81263* ⊡ *€2* ⊙ *Apr.–Oct., Tues.–Fri. 2–5, weekends 11–5.*

WHERE TO STAY

For expanded hotel reviews, visit Fodors.com.

$$ 🏨 **Hotel Krone.** You could spend an entire afternoon and evening here even if you don't stay overnight in the comfortable guest rooms. **Pros:** friendly; quiet. **Cons:** can feel remote. ⊠ *Schlossbergstr. 15, Vogtsburg-Achkarren* ☎ *07662/93130* ⊕ *www.Hotel-Krone-Achkarren.de* ⤵ *23 rooms* ⌂ *In-room: no a/c, Internet. In-hotel: restaurant, tennis court, some pets allowed* ⊙ *Restaurant closed Wed., and Thurs. in winter* ⍾ *Breakfast.*

$ 🏨 **Posthotel Kreuz-Post.** Set right in the middle of the Kaiserstuhl vineyards, this establishment has been in the hands of the Gehr family since its construction in 1809. **Pros:** quiet; in the middle of nowhere. **Cons:** quiet; in the middle of nowhere. ⊠ *Landstr. 1, Vogtsburg-Burkheim* ☎ *07662/90910* ⊕ *www.kreuz-post.de* ⤵ *35 rooms* ⌂ *In-room: no a/c. In-hotel: restaurant, some pets allowed* ⍾ *Breakfast.*

RUST

35 km (22 mi) north of Freiburg.

The town of Rust, on the Rhine almost halfway from Freiburg to Strasbourg, boasts a castle dating from 1577 and painstakingly restored half-timber houses. But its big claim to fame is Germany's biggest amusement park, with its own autobahn exit.

Ⓒ **Europa Park.** On an area of 160 acres, Europa Park draws more than **Fodor's Choice** 3 million visitors a year with its variety of shows, rides, dining, and ★ shops. Among many other things, it has the "Eurosat" to take you on a virtual journey past clusters of meteors and falling stars; the "Silver Star," Europe's highest roller coaster; a Spanish jousting tournament; and even a "4-D" movie in which you might get damp in the rain or be rocked by an earthquake. ⊠ *Europa-Park-Str. 2* ☎ *01805/776–688* ⊕ *www.europapark.de* ⊡ *€36* ⊙ *Apr.–Oct., daily 9–6.*

Heidelberg and the Neckar Valley

WORD OF MOUTH

"The Castle Road from Heidelberg to Rothenburg is really romantic—winding thru cute small towns and lovely countryside in the
Neckar River Valley."

—Palenque

WELCOME TO HEIDELBERG AND THE NECKAR VALLEY

TOP REASONS TO GO

★ **Heidelberg Castle:** The architectural highlight of the region's most beautiful castle is the Renaissance courtyard—harmonious, graceful, and ornate.

★ **Heidelberg's Alte Brücke:** After a walk under the twin towers that were part of medieval Heidelberg's fortifications, you have the best view of the city and the castle.

★ **Burg Hornberg:** With its oldest parts dating from the 12th century, this is one of the best of more than a dozen castles between Heidelberg and Stuttgart.

★ **Stuttgart's museums:** Top art galleries like the Staatsgalerie or the Kunstmuseum contrast with the Mercedes and Porsche museums, where the history of the *auto mobil* is illustrated by classic cars, from posh limousines to sleek racing cars.

★ **Tübingen Altstadt:** With its half-timber houses, winding alleyways, and hilltop setting overlooking the Neckar, Tübingen is the quintessential German experience.

1 Heidelberg. The natural beauty of Heidelberg is created by the embrace of mountains, forests, vineyards, and the Neckar River—all crowned by the famous ruined castle. The Neckar and the Rhine meet at nearby Mannheim, the biggest train hub for the superfast ICE (Intercity Express) trains of Germany, a major industrial center, and the second-largest river port in Europe.

2 The Burgenstrasse (Castle Road). If you or your kids like castles, this is the place to go. Of course you can always visit the crowded Heidelberg Castle, but the real fun starts when you venture up the Neckar River. There seems to be a castle on every hilltop in the valley. Burg Hornberg, offers lodging and a good restaurant.

3 Swabian Cities. Stuttgart, the state capital, has elegant streets, shops, hotels, and museums, as well as some of Germany's top industries, among them Mercedes and Porsche. Ludwigsburg, with its huge baroque castles and baroque flower gardens, is worth a visit. The most charmingly "Swabian" of all these cities is the old half-timber university town of Tübingen.

GETTING ORIENTED

Although not as well known as the Rhine, the Neckar River has a wonderful charm of its own. After Heidelberg it winds its way through a small valley guarded by castles. It then flows on, bordered by vineyards on its northern slopes, passing the interesting and industrious city of Stuttgart, before it climbs toward the Swabian Hills. You follow the Neckar until the old half-timber university town of Tübingen. The river continues toward the eastern slopes of the Black Forest, where it originates less than 80 km (50 mi) from the source of the Danube.

8

Updated by
Sarah Harman
and David
Levitz

Heidelberg remains one of the best-known—and most visited—cities in Germany, identifiable by its graceful baroque towers and the majestic ruins of its red sandstone castle. From this grand city, the narrow and quiet Neckar Valley makes its way eastward, then turns to the south, taking you past charming villages where the streets are lined with half-timber houses. Most are guarded by their own castle, sometimes in ruins but often revived as a museum or hotel. This part of Germany is aptly named the *Burgenstrasse* (Castle Road).

As the valley widens it opens up into one of the most industrious areas of Germany, with Stuttgart at its center. In this wealthy city, world-class art museums like the Staatsgalerie or the Kunstmuseum in the center of town contrast with the new and striking Mercedes and Porsche museums in the suburbs.

A bit farther south, the rolling Swabian Hills cradle the university town of Tübingen, a center of learning in a beautiful historic setting on the banks of the Neckar River. Overlooking the town is—of course—a mighty castle.

PLANNING

WHEN TO GO

If you plan to visit Heidelberg in summer, make reservations well in advance and expect to pay top rates. To get away from the crowds, consider staying out of town and driving or taking the bus or train into the city. Hotels and restaurants are much cheaper just a little upriver. A visit in late fall, when the vines turn a faded gold, or early spring, with the first green shoots of the year, can be captivating. In the depths of winter, river mists creep through the narrow streets of Heidelberg's Old Town and awaken the ghosts of a romantic past.

GETTING HERE AND AROUND

AIR TRAVEL

From the Frankfurt and Stuttgart airports, there's fast and easy access, by car and train, to all major centers along the Neckar.

BUS AND SHUTTLE TRAVEL

From Frankfurt Airport to Heidelberg, hop aboard the Lufthansa Airport Bus, which takes about an hour and is not restricted to Lufthansa passengers. Buses depart 11 times a day between 7 am and 10:30 pm from Arrivals Hall B of Terminal 1. Airport-bound buses leave the Crowne Plaza Heidelberg between 5:30 am and 8 pm. One-way tickets are €22 per person, or €20 with a Lufthansa flight ticket. With advance reservations you can also get to downtown Heidelberg via the shuttle service TLS. The trip costs €34 per person.

Bus Information **Lufthansa Airport Bus** ☎ *06152/976–9099* ⊕ *www. transcontinental-group.com/en/frankfurt-airport-shuttles.* **TLS** ☎ *06221/770–077* ⊕ *www.tls-heidelberg.de.*

CAR TRAVEL

Heidelberg is a 15-minute drive (10 km [6 mi]) on A-656 from Mannheim, a major junction of the autobahn system. The Burgenstrasse (Route B-37) follows the north bank of the Neckar River from Heidelberg to Mosbach, from which it continues south to Heilbronn as B-27, the road parallel to and predating the autobahn (A-81). B-27 still leads to Stuttgart and Tübingen.

TRAIN TRAVEL

Heidelberg is 17 minutes from Mannheim, by S-bahn regional train, or 11 minutes on hourly InterCity Express (ICE) trains. These sleek, super-high-speed trains reach 280 kph (174 mph), so travel time between Frankfurt Airport and Mannheim is a half hour. From Heidelberg to Stuttgart, direct InterCity (IC) trains take 40 minutes. Local services link many of the smaller towns.

RESTAURANTS

Mittagessen (lunch) in this region is generally served from noon until 2 or 2:30, *Abendessen* (dinner) from 6 until 9:30 or 10. *Durchgehend warme Küche* means that hot meals are also served between lunch and dinner. Slowly but surely, credit cards have gained acceptance, but this is by no means universal, and many restaurants will accept only cash or debit cards issued by a German bank. Casual attire is typically acceptable at restaurants here, and reservations are generally not needed.

HOTELS

This area is full of castle-hotels and charming country inns that range in comfort from upscale rustic to luxurious. For a riverside view, ask for a *Zimmer* (room) or *Tisch* (table) *mit Neckarblick* (with a view of the Neckar). The Neckar Valley offers idyllic alternatives to the cost and crowds of Heidelberg. Driving or riding the train from Neckargemünd, for example, takes 20 minutes.

8

WHAT IT COSTS IN EUROS				
¢	$	$$	$$$	$$$$
Restaurants	under €9	€9–€15	€16–€20	€21–€25	over €25
Hotels	under €50	€50–€100	€101–€175	€176–€225	over €225

Restaurant prices are per person for a main course at dinner. Hotel prices are for two people in a standard double room, including tax and service.

PLANNING YOUR TIME

To fully appreciate Heidelberg, try to be up and about before the tour buses arrive. After the day-trippers have gone and many shops have closed, the good restaurants and the nightspots open up. Visit the castles on the Burgenstrasse at your leisure, maybe even staying overnight. Leaving the valley toward the south, you'll drive into wine country. Even if you are not a car enthusiast, the museums of Mercedes and Porsche in Stuttgart are worth a visit. Try to get to Tübingen during the week to avoid the crowds of Swabians coming in for their *Kaffee und Kuchen* (coffee and cake). During the week, try to get a room and spend a leisurely evening in this half-timber university town.

DISCOUNTS AND DEALS

If you are staying more than one day in Heidelberg, do inquire about the HeidelbergCard with several reductions at your hotel or at the tourist-information office. The same goes for Stuttgart.

VISITOR INFORMATION

State Tourist Board Baden-Württemberg ⊠ *Esslingerstr. 8, Stuttgart* ☎ *0711/238–580* ⊕ *www.tourismus-bw.de.* **Die Burgenstrasse** ⊠ *Allee 28, Heilbronn* ☎ *07131/564–028* ⊕ *www.burgenstrasse.de.*

HEIDELBERG

57 km (35 mi) northeast of Karlsruhe.

If any city in Germany encapsulates the spirit of the country, it is Heidelberg. Scores of poets and composers—virtually the entire 19th-century German Romantic movement—have sung its praises. Goethe and Mark Twain both fell in love here: the German writer with a beautiful young woman, the American author with the city itself. Sigmund Romberg set his operetta *The Student Prince* in the city; Carl Maria von Weber wrote his lushly Romantic opera *Der Freischütz* here. Composer Robert Schumann was a student at the university. The campaign these artists waged on behalf of the town has been astoundingly successful. Heidelberg's fame is out of all proportion to its size (population 140,000); more than 3½ million visitors crowd its streets every year.

Heidelberg was the political center of the Lower Palatinate. At the end of the Thirty Years' War (1618–48), the elector Carl Ludwig married his daughter to the brother of Louis XIV in the hope of bringing peace to the Rhineland. But when the elector's son died without an heir, Louis XIV used the marriage alliance as an excuse to claim Heidelberg, and in 1689 the town was sacked and laid to waste. Four years later he sacked the town again. From its ashes arose what you see today: a baroque town built on Gothic foundations, with narrow, twisting streets and alleyways.

Above all, Heidelberg is a university town, with students making up a large part of its population. And a youthful spirit is felt in the lively restaurants and pubs of the Altstadt (Old Town). In 1930 the university was expanded, and its buildings now dot the entire landscape of Heidelberg and its neighboring suburbs. Modern Heidelberg changed as U.S. Army barracks and industrial development stretched into the suburbs, but the old heart of the city remains intact, exuding the spirit of romantic Germany.

GETTING HERE AND AROUND

Heidelberg is 15 minutes away from Mannheim, where four ICE trains and five Autobahn routes meet. Everything in town may be reached on foot. A funicular takes you up to the castle and Heidelberg's Königstuhl Mountain, and a streetcar takes you from the center of the city to the main station. From April through October there are daily walking tours of Heidelberg in German (Friday and Saturday also in English) at 10:30 am; from November through March, tours are in German only, Friday at 2:30 and Saturday at 10:30; the cost is €7. They depart from the main entrance to the Rathaus (Town Hall). Bilingual bus tours run April through October on Thursday and Friday at 1:30 and on Saturday at 1:30 and 3. From November through March, bus tours depart Saturday at 1:30. They cost €17 and depart from Universitätsplatz.

DISCOUNTS AND DEALS

The two-day HeidelbergCARD, which costs €13 per person or €28 for a family of up to five people, includes free or reduced admission to most tourist attractions as well as free use of all public transportation (including the Bergbahn [funicular] to the castle) and other extras, such as free guided walking tours, discounts on bus tours, and a city guidebook. It can be purchased at the tourist-information office at the main train station or the Rathaus, and at many local hotels.

TIMING

Walking the length of Heidelberg's Hauptstrasse (main street) will take an hour—longer if you are easily sidetracked by the shopping opportunities. Strolling through the Old Town and across the bridge to look at the castle will take you at least another half hour, not counting the time you spend visiting the sites.

ESSENTIALS

Visitor Information

Heidelberg Tourist Information ✉ *Tourist-Information im Rathaus, Marktpl., Heidelberg* ☎ *06221/19433* ⊕ *www.heidelberg-marketing.de.* **Heidelberg Tourist Information** ✉ *Tourist-Information am Hauptbahnhof, Willy-Brandt-Pl. 1* ☎ *06221/19433* ⊕ *www.heidelberg-marketing.de.*

EXPLORING

TOP ATTRACTIONS

Alte Brücke (*Old Bridge*). Framed by two *Spitzhelm* towers (so called for their resemblance to old German helmets), this bridge was part of medieval Heidelberg's fortifications. In the west tower are three dank dungeons that once held common criminals. Above the portcullis you'll see a memorial plaque that pays warm tribute to the Austrian forces that helped Heidelberg beat back a French attempt to capture the bridge in 1799. The bridge itself is one of many to be built on this spot; ice floes and floods destroyed its predecessors. The elector Carl Theodor, who built it in 1786–88, must have been confident that this one would last: he had a statue of himself erected on it, upon a plinth decorated with river gods and goddesses (symbolic of the Neckar, Rhine, Danube, and Mosel rivers). As you enter the bridge from the Old Town, you'll also notice a statue of an animal that appears somewhat catlike. It's actually a monkey holding a mirror. Legend has it the statue was erected to symbolize the need for both city-dwellers and those who lived on the other side of the bridge to take a look over their shoulders as they cross—that neither group was more elite than the other. The bridge is at the end of Steingasse, not far from the Marktplatz. ⊠ *End of Steingasse.*

Alte Universität (*Old University*). The three-story baroque structure was built between 1712 and 1735 at the behest of the elector Johann Wilhelm, although Heidelberg's Ruprecht Karl University was originally founded in 1386. Today it houses the **University Museum**, with exhibits that chronicle the history of Germany's oldest university. The present-day Universitätsplatz (University Square) was built over the remains of an Augustinian monastery that was destroyed by the French in 1693. ⊠ *Grabeng. 1–3* ☎ *06221/542–152* ⌨ *€3* ⏲ *Apr.–Sept., Tues.–Sun. 10–6; Oct., Tues.–Sun. 10–4, Nov.–Mar., Tues.–Sat. 10–4.*

Friedrich-Ebert-Gedenkstätte (*Friedrich Ebert Memorial*). The humble rooms of a tiny backstreet apartment were the birthplace of Friedrich Ebert, Germany's first democratically elected president (in 1919) and leader of the ill-fated Weimar Republic. The display tells the story of the tailor's son who took charge of a nation accustomed to being ruled by a kaiser. ⊠ *Pfaffeng. 18* ☎ *06221/91070* ⊕ *www.ebert-gedenkstaette. de* ⌨ *Free* ⏲ *Tues., Wed., and Fri.–Sun. 10–6; Thurs. 10–8.*

Heiliggeistkirche (*Church of the Holy Ghost*). The foundation stone of the building was laid in 1398, but it was not actually finished until 1544. Unlike that of most other Gothic churches, the facade of the Heiliggeistkirche is uniform—you cannot discern the choir or naves

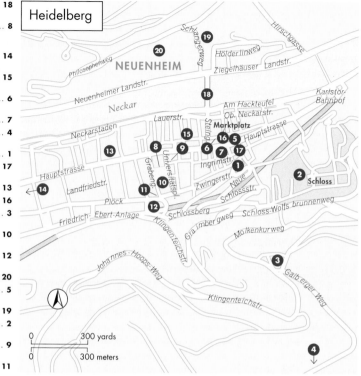

from the outside. The gargoyles looking down on the south side (where Hauptstrasse crosses Marktplatz) are remarkable for their sheer ugliness. The church fell victim to the plundering General Tilly, leader of the Catholic League during the Thirty Years' War. Tilly loaded the church's greatest treasure—the Bibliotheca Palatina, at the time the largest library in Germany—onto 500 carts and trundled it off to Rome, where he presented it to the pope. Few volumes found their way back. At the end of the 17th century, French troops plundered the church again, destroying the tombs; only the 15th-century tomb of Elector Ruprecht III and his wife, Elisabeth von Hohenzollern, remains today. ✉ *Marktpl.* ☎ *06221/21117* ⊕ *www.heiliggeistkirche.de* ☉ *Late Mar.– Oct., Mon.–Sat. 11–5, Sun. 12:30–5; Nov.–mid-Mar., Fri. and Sat. 11–3, Sun. 12:30–3.*

Hotel zum Ritter. The hotel's name refers to the statue of a Roman knight (Ritter) atop one of the many gables. Its French builder, Charles Bélier, had the Latin inscription "Persta Invicta Venus" added to the facade in gold letters—"Venus, Remain Unconquerable." It appears this injunction was effective, as this was the city's only Renaissance building to be spared the attentions of the invading French in 1689 and 1693. Between 1695 and 1705 it was used as Heidelberg's town hall; later it became an inn, and it's still a hotel today. ✉ *Hauptstr. 178* ☎ *06221/1350* ⊕ *www.ritter-heidelberg.de.*

Königstuhl (*King's Throne*). The second-highest hill in the Odenwald range—1,800 feet above Heidelberg—is only a hop, skip, and funicular ride from Heidelberg. On a clear day you can see as far as the Black Forest to the south and west to the Vosges Mountains of France. The hill is at the center of a close-knit network of hiking trails. Signs and colored arrows from the top lead hikers through the woods of the Odenwald.

WORD OF MOUTH

"We love the Heidelberg area! You won't run out of things to do. Though others dismiss the city as only deserving of a day, there are several wonderful museums and a very active cultural life. The Heiliggeist Kirche and the Jesuit Kirche have regular free organ recitals and other concerts as well." —klondike

Königstuhl Bergbahn (*funicular*). The funicular hoists visitors to the summit of the Königstuhl in 17 minutes. On the way it stops at the ruined Heidelberg Schloss and Molkenkur. A modern funicular usually leaves every 10 minutes, and a historical train comes every 20 minutes. The funicular will be temporarily replaced by bus service February–March 2012. ✉ *Kornmarkt* ⊕ *www.bergbahn-heidelberg.de* 🎫 *Round-trip to Königstuhl €12, round-trip to Schloss, including entrance to the castle courtyard, €5* ⊗ *Mid-Apr.–mid-Oct., daily 9–8:25; mid-Oct.–mid-Apr., daily 9–5:45.*

Kurpfälzisches Museum (*Palatinate Museum*). This baroque palace was built as a residence for a university professor in 1712. It's a pleasure just to wander around, which is more or less unavoidable, since the museum's layout is so confusing. Among the exhibits are two standouts. One is a replica of the jaw of Heidelberg Man, a key link in the evolutionary chain thought to date from a half-million years ago; the original was unearthed near the city in 1907. The larger attraction is the *Windsheimer Zwölfbotenaltar (Twelve Apostles Altarpiece)*, one of the largest and finest works of early Renaissance sculptor Tilman Riemenschneider. Its exquisite detailing and technical sophistication are evident in the simple faith that radiates from the faces of the Apostles. On the top floor of the museum there's a rich range of 19th-century German paintings and drawings, many depicting Heidelberg. ∎TIP→ The restaurant in the museum's quiet courtyard is a good place for a break. ✉ *Hauptstr. 97* ☎ *06221/583–4020* ⊕ *www.museum-heidelberg.de* 🎫 *€3* ⊗ *Tues.–Sun. 10–6.*

Marktplatz (*Market Square*). Heidelberg's main square, with the Rathaus on one side and the Heiliggeistkirche on the other, has been its focal point since the Middle Ages. Public courts of justice were held here in earlier centuries, and people accused of witchcraft and heresy were burned at the stake. The baroque fountain in the middle, the *Herkulesbrunnen* (Hercules Fountain), is the work of 18th-century artist H. Charrasky. Until 1740 a rotating, hanging cage stood next to it. For minor crimes, people were imprisoned in it and exposed to the abuse of their fellow citizens. ■TIP→ Today the Marktplatz hosts outdoor markets every Wednesday and Saturday.

Molkenkur. The next stop after the castle on the Königstuhl funicular, Molkenkur was the site of Heidelberg's second castle. Lightning struck it in 1537, and it was never rebuilt. Today it's occupied by a restaurant—which bears the creative name Molkenkur Restaurant—with magnificent views of the Odenwald and the Rhine plain.

Philosophenweg (*Philosophers' Path*). You can reach this trail high above the river in one of two ways—either from Neuenheim or by taking the Schlangenweg (Snake Path). Both are steep climbs, but you'll be rewarded with spectacular views of the Old Town and castle. From Neuenheim, turn right after crossing the bridge and follow signs to a small alleyway.

Rathaus (*Town Hall*). Work began on the town hall in 1701, a few years after the French destroyed the city. The massive coat of arms above the balcony is the work of Heinrich Charrasky, who also created the statue of Hercules atop the fountain in the middle of the square. ⊠ *Marktpl.*

Schlangenweg (*Snake Path*). This walkway starts just above the Alte Brücke opposite the Old Town and cuts steeply through terraced vineyards until it reaches the woods, where it crosses the Philosophenweg (Philosophers' Path).

Fodor's Choice ★ **Schloss** (*Castle*). What's most striking is the architectural variety of this great complex. The oldest parts still standing date from the 15th century, though most of the castle was built in the Renaissance and baroque styles of the 16th and 17th centuries, when the castle was the seat of the Palatinate electors. There's even an "English wing," built in 1612 by the elector Friedrich V for his teenage Scottish bride, Elizabeth Stuart; its plain, square-window facade is positively foreign compared to the castle's more opulent styles. (The enamored Friedrich also had a charming garden laid out for his young bride; its imposing arched entryway, the Elisabethentor, was put up overnight as a surprise for her 19th birthday.) The architectural highlight remains the Renaissance courtyard—harmonious, graceful, and ornate.

Even if you have to wait, you should make a point of seeing the *Grosses Fass* (Great Cask), an enormous wine barrel in the cellar, made from 130 oak trees and capable of holding 58,500 gallons. It was used to hold wines paid as taxes by wine growers in the Palatinate.

The Student Prince often figure prominently. The castle may be reached by taking the Königstuhl Bergbahn. Generations of earlier visitors hiked up to it on the Burgweg, a winding road.

LOCAL LEGEND

During the rule of the elector Carl Philip, the Great Cask in the Schloss was guarded by the court jester, a Tyrolean dwarf called Perkeo. When offered wine, he always answered, "*Perche no?*" ("Why not?"), hence his nickname. Legend has it that he could consume frighteningly large quantities of wine and that he died when he drank a glass of water by mistake. A statue of Perkeo stands next to the two-story-high barrel.

8

Heidelberg's Alte Brücke (Old Bridge) was part of the city's medieval fortifications and is a top site.

Deutsches Apotheken–Museum (*German Apothecary Museum*). The castle includes the Deutsches Apotheken–Museum. This museum, on the lower floor of the Ottheinrichsbau (Otto Heinrich Building), is filled with ancient flagons and receptacles (each with a carefully painted enamel label), beautifully made scales, little drawers, shelves, dried beetles and toads, and marvelous reconstructions of six apothecary shops from the 17th through the 20th centuries. The museum also offers young visitors the chance to smell various herbs and mix their own teas. ☎ *06221/25880* ⊕ *www.deutsches-apotheken-museum.de* ⊙ *Apr.–Oct., 10–6, Nov.–Mar., 10–5:30* ✉ *Schlosshof* ☎ *06221/538–431* ⊕ *www.heidelberg-schloss.de* 🎫 *€5 including funicular; €4 audio-guide* ⊙ *Jan.–mid-Dec., 8–5:30; tours in English daily 11–4, when demand is sufficient.*

WORTH NOTING

Deutsches Verpackungs-Museum (*German Packaging Museum*). A former church was innovatively converted to house this fascinating documentation of packaging and package design of brand-name products. Representing the years 1800 to the present, historic logos and slogans are a trip down memory lane. The entrance is in a courtyard reached via an alley. ✉ *Hauptstr. 22* ☎ *06221/21361* ⊕ *www.verpackungsmuseum.de* 🎫 *€3.50* ⊙ *Wed.–Fri. 1–6, weekends and public holidays 11–6.*

Kornmarkt (*Grain Market*). A baroque statue of the Virgin Mary is in the center of this old Heidelberg square, which has a view of the castle ruins.

Neue Universität (*New University*). The plain building on the south side of Universitätsplatz was erected between 1930 and 1932 through funds raised by the U.S. ambassador to Germany, J. G. Schurman, who had been a student at the university. The only decoration on the building's three wings is a statue of Athena, the Greek goddess of wisdom, above the entrance. The inner courtyard contains a medieval tower from 1380, the **Hexenturm** (Witches' Tower). Suspected witches were locked up there in the Middle Ages. It later became a memorial to former students killed in World War I. ⊠ *Grabeng.*

OFF THE
BEATEN
PATH

Neuenheim. To escape the crowds of Heidelberg, walk across the Theodor Heuss Bridge to the suburb of Neuenheim. At the turn of the 20th century this old fishing village developed into a residential area full of posh art nouveau villas. North of the Brückenkopf (bridgehead) you'll find antiques and designer shops, boutiques, and cafés on Brückenstrasse, Bergstrasse (one block east), and Ladenburger Strasse (parallel to the river). To savor the neighborhood spirit, visit the charming farmers' market on Wednesday or Saturday morning at the corner of Ladenburger and Luther streets.

Peterskirche (*St. Peter's Church*). Many famous Heidelberg citizens' tombstones, some more than 500 years old, line the outer walls of the city's oldest parish church (1485–1500). The church is open during the week for visits from April to October. ⊠ *Plöck 70.*

Studentenkarzer (*Student Prison*). University officials locked students up here from 1778 to 1914—mostly for minor offenses. They could be held for up to 14 days and were left to subsist on bread and water for the first 3 days; thereafter, they were allowed to attend lectures, receive guests, and have food brought in from the outside. ■ TIP→ There's bravado, even poetic flair, to be deciphered from two centuries of graffiti that cover the walls and ceilings of the narrow cells. ⊠ *Augustinerg.* 2 ☎ *06221/543–554* 🖾 *€3* ⊙ *Apr.–Sept. daily 10–6; Oct.–Apr., Mon.–Sat. 10–4.*

Universitätsbibliothek (*University Library*). Its 2½ million volumes include the 14th-century *Manesse Codex,* a unique collection of medieval songs and poetry once performed in the courts of Germany by the *Minnesänger* (troubadors). The original is too fragile to be exhibited, so a copy is on display. ⊠ *Plöck 107–109* ☎ *06221/542–380* ⊕ *www. ub.uni-heidelberg.de* 🖾 *Free* ⊙ *Mon.–Sat. 10–6.*

WHERE TO EAT

¢
CAFÉ

✕ **Café Knösel.** Heidelberg's oldest (1863) coffeehouse has always been a popular meeting place for students and professors. It's still producing café founder Fridolin Knösel's *Heidelberger Studentenkuss.* This "student kiss" is a chocolate wrapped in paper showing two sets of touching lips—an acceptable way for 19th-century students to "exchange kisses" in public. They are now being sold exclusively in a small, charming shop down the street. ⊠ *Haspelg.* 20 ☎ *06221/727–2754* ⊕ *www. cafek-hd.de.*

$
GERMAN
★

✕ **Schnitzelbank.** Little more than a hole in the wall, this former cooper's workshop has been transformed into a candlelit pub. No matter when you go, it seems to be filled with people seated around the wooden tables. If you are interested, ask to look at the old guest books and sign the newest. The menu features specialties from Baden and the Pfalz, such as *Schäufele* (pickled and slightly smoked pork shoulder); or a

EATING WELL IN THE NECKAR VALLEY

Fish and *Wild* (game) from the streams and woods lining the Neckar Valley, as well as seasonal favorites—*Spargel* (asparagus), *Pilze* (mushrooms), *Morcheln* (morels), *Pfifferlinge* (chanterelles), and *Steinpilze* (porcini)—are regulars on menus in this area. Pfälzer specialties are also common, but the penchant for potatoes yields to *Knödel* (dumplings) and pasta farther south. The latter includes the Swabian and Baden staples *Maultaschen* (stuffed "pockets" of pasta) and Spätzle (roundish egg noodles), as well as *Schupfnudeln* (finger-size noodles of potato dough), also called *Buwespitzle*. Look for *Linsen* (lentils) and sauerkraut in soups or as sides. *Schwäbischer Rostbraten* (beefsteak topped with fried onions) and *Schäufele* (pickled and slightly smoked pork shoulder) are popular meat dishes.

Considerable quantities of red wine are produced along the Neckar Valley. Crisp, light Trollinger is often served in the traditional *Viertele,* a round, quarter-liter (8-ounce) glass with a handle. Deeper-color, more-substantial reds include Spätburgunder (Pinot Noir) and its mutation Schwarzriesling (Pinot Meunier), Lemberger, and Dornfelder. Riesling, Kerner, and Müller-Thurgau (synonymous with Rivaner), as well as Grauburgunder (Pinot Gris) and Weissburgunder (Pinot Blanc), are the typical white wines. A birch broom or wreath over the doorway of a vintner's home signifies a *Besenwirtschaft* ("broomstick inn"), a rustic pub where you can enjoy wines with snacks and simple fare. Many vintners offer economical B&Bs. These places are ideal spots to try out your newly learned German phrases; you'll be surprised how well you speak German after the third glass of German wine.

hearty platter of bratwurst, *Leberknödel* (liver dumplings), and slices of *Saumagen* (a spicy meat-and-potato mixture encased in a sow's stomach). ⊠ *Bauamtsg. 7* ☎ *06221/21189* ⊕ *www.schnitzelbank-heidelberg. de* ⊙ *No lunch Apr.–Aug. No lunch weekdays Sept.–Mar.*

$

GERMAN

✕ **Schnookeloch.** This lively old tavern dates from 1703 and is inextricably linked with Heidelberg's history and university. Young and old alike crowd around the wooden tables in the wood-panel room, and piano music adds to the din Wednesday through Saturday nights. From salads and pasta to hearty roasts and steaks, there's a broad selection of food. Upstairs are modern, pleasantly furnished guest rooms. ⊠ *Haspelg. 8* ☎ *06221/138–080* ⊕ *www.schnookeloch.de.*

$$$$

ECLECTIC

★

✕ **Schwarz Das Restaurant.** Sleek, contemporary furnishings, soft lighting, stunning panoramic views, and Manfred Schwarz's creative cuisine make for unforgettable dining in this 12th-floor restaurant, complete with an aperitif bar and cigar lounge. The five- to seven-course gourmet menu of the month varies from Asiatic to Mediterranean to French. On the menu you may find sautéed goose liver on truffled polenta with raspberry vinegar sauce or gratinéed scallops with chive sauce and caviar. ⊠ *Kurfürsten-Anlage 60, opposite train station* ☎ *06221/757–030* ⊕ *www.schwarzdasrestaurant.com* ⊙ *Closed Sun., Mon., and 1st wk of Jan. No lunch.*

$$$
MEDITERRANEAN
★
× **Simplicissimus.** Olive oil and herbs of Provence accentuate many of chef Johann Lummer's culinary delights. Saddle of lamb and sautéed liver in honey-pepper sauce are specialties; the *Dessertteller,* a sweet sampler, is a crowning finish to any meal. The wine list focuses on old-world estates, particularly clarets. The elegant art nouveau interior is done in shades of red with dark-wood accents, and a quiet courtyard offers alfresco dining in summer. ⊠ *Ingrimstr. 16* ☎ *06221/183–336* ⊕ *www.restaurant-simplicissimus.de* ⊘ *Closed Sun., Mon., and 2 wks in Aug. and Sept. No lunch.*

$
ITALIAN
× **Trattoria Toscana.** You can choose from antipasti platters, pasta dishes, pizzas, and special daily offerings, all served in generous portions. If you sit at a table inside the restaurant you can enjoy good Italian food while you watch the crowds push by. ⊠ *Marktpl. 1* ☎ *06221/28619.*

$
GERMAN
× **Zum Roten Ochsen.** Many of the rough-hewn oak tables here have initials carved into them, a legacy of the thousands who have visited Heidelberg's most famous old tavern. Mark Twain, Marilyn Monroe, and John Wayne may have left their mark—they all ate here. You can wash down simple fare, such as goulash soup and bratwurst, or heartier dishes, such as *Tellerfleisch* (boiled beef) and sauerbraten, with German wines or Heidelberg beer. The "Red Ox" has been run by the Spengel family for 170 years. Come early to get a good seat. ⊠ *Hauptstr. 217* ☎ *06221/20977* ⊕ *www.roterochsen.de* ⊘ *Closed Sun. and mid-Dec.–mid-Jan. No lunch Nov.–Mar.*

$$$
CONTINENTAL
★
× **Zur Herrenmühle.** A 17th-century grain mill has been transformed into this romantic restaurant. The old beams add to the warm atmosphere. In summer, try to arrive early to get a table in the idyllic courtyard. Fish, lamb, and homemade pasta are specialties. The prix-fixe menu offers an especially good value. ⊠ *Hauptstr. 239, near Karlstor* ☎ *06221/602–909* ⊕ *www.herrenmuehle-heidelberg.de* ⊘ *Closed Sun. No lunch.*

WHERE TO STAY

For expanded hotel reviews, visit Fodors.com.

$$
⌂ **Crowne Plaza Heidelberg.** This grand hotel has a spacious lobby, stylish furnishings, soaring ceilings, and an enviable location—it's a five-minute walk from Old Town. **Pros:** parking garage; pool. **Cons:** chain hotel feel. ⊠ *Kurfürsten-Anlage 1* ☎ *06221/9170* ⊕ *www.crowneplaza.com* ⊟ *232 rooms, 4 suites* ⌂ *In-room: a/c, Wi-Fi. In-hotel: restaurant, bar, pool, gym, spa, business center, parking, some pets allowed.*

$$
Fodor's Choice
★
⌂ **Der Europäische Hof–Hotel Europa.** On secluded grounds next to the Old Town, this most luxurious of Heidelberg hotels boasts many public parlors outfitted with stunning turn-of-the-last-century furnishings. **Pros:** warm welcome; castle views from the two-story fitness and spa center. **Cons:** restaurant closed in July and August. ⊠ *Friedrich-Ebert-Anlage 1* ☎ *06221/5150* ⊕ *www.europaeischerhof.com* ⊟ *100 rooms, 15 suites, 3 apartments, 1 penthouse* ⌂ *In-room: a/c, Internet, Wi-Fi. In-hotel: restaurant, bar, pool, gym, spa, business center, parking, some pets allowed.*

$$
⌂ **Gasthaus Backmulde.** This traditional Gasthaus in the heart of Heidelberg has very nice new rooms at—for Heidelberg—affordable prices. **Pros:** quiet rooms; nice restaurant. **Cons:** difficult parking; restaurant closed Sunday. ⊠ *Schiffg. 11* ☎ *06221/53660* ⊕ *www.*

8

gasthaus-backmulde.de ⇱*25 rooms* ⚄ *In-room: a/c, Wi-Fi. In-hotel: restaurant, business center, parking, some pets allowed* ☾ *Restaurant closed Sun. No lunch Mon.* ¶◯| *Breakfast.*

$$ 🏨 **Holländer Hof.** The pink-and-white-painted facade of this ornate 19th-century building opposite the Alte Brücke stands out in its row fronting the Neckar River. **Pros:** nice view of river and beyond; comfortable accommodations; some rooms are handicap accessible. **Cons:** noisy at times; no restaurant or bar. ⊠ *Neckarstaden 66* ☎ *06221/60500* ⊕ *www.hollaender-hof.de* ⇱*38 rooms, 1 suite* ⚄ *In-room: a/c, Internet, Wi-Fi. In-hotel: business center, some pets allowed.*

$$$ 🏨 **Hotel Die Hirschgasse.** A stunning castle view marks this historic inn
Fodor's Choice   (1472), located across the river opposite Karlstor. **Pros:** terrific view;
★   very good food in both restaurants. **Cons:** limited parking; 15-minute walk to Old Town. ⊠ *Hirschg. 3* ☎ *06221/4540* ⊕ *www.hirschgasse.de* ⇱*20 suites* ⚄ *In-room: no a/c, Wi-Fi. In-hotel: restaurants, bar, business center, parking, some pets allowed* ☾ *Le Gourmet closed 2 wks in early Jan., 2 wks in early Aug., and Sun. and Mon.; Mensurstube restaurant closed Sun. No lunch at either restaurant.*

$$ 🏨 **KulturBrauerei Heidelberg.** Rooms with warm, sunny colors and modern decor are brilliantly incorporated into this old brewery in the heart of Old Town. **Pros:** stylish rooms; lively restaurant; beer garden. **Cons:** noisy in summer; Wi-Fi only in restaurant; difficult parking. ⊠ *Leyerg. 6* ☎ *06221/502–980* ⊕ *www.heidelberger-kulturbrauerei.de* ⇱*32 rooms, 2 suites* ⚄ *In-room: no a/c, Wi-Fi. In-hotel: restaurant, parking, some pets allowed* ¶◯| *Breakfast.*

$$ 🏨 **NH Heidelberg.** The glass-covered entrance hall of this primarily busi-
★   ness hotel is spacious—not surprising, as it was the courtyard of a former brewery. **Pros:** good food; reasonably priced. **Cons:** lacks charm; located about 1 km (½ mi) from the Old Town. ⊠ *Bergheimerstr. 91* ☎ *06221/13270* ⊕ *www.nh-hotels.com* ⇱*156 rooms, 18 suites* ⚄ *In-room: a/c, Internet, Wi-Fi. In-hotel: restaurant, bar, gym, spa, business center, parking, some pets allowed* ¶◯| *Breakfast.*

$$ 🏨 **Romantik Hotel zum Ritter St. Georg.** If this is your first visit to Germany,
★   try to stay here—it's the only Renaissance building in Heidelberg (1592) and has an unbeatable location opposite the market square in the heart of Old Town. **Pros:** charm and elegance; nice views; spacious rooms. **Cons:** off-site parking. ⊠ *Hauptstr. 178* ☎ *06221/1350* ⊕ *www.ritter-heidelberg.de* ⇱*36 rooms, 1 suite* ⚄ *In-room: no a/c, Internet, Wi-Fi. In-hotel: restaurant, some pets allowed.*

$$ 🏨 **Weisser Bock.** Exposed beams, stucco ceilings, warm wood furnishings, and individually decorated, comfortable rooms are all part of this hotel's charm. **Pros:** nicely decorated rooms; exceptional food; no smoking. **Cons:** parking difficult to find. ⊠ *Grosse Mantelg. 24* ☎ *06221/90000* ⊕ *www.weisserbock.de* ⇱*21 rooms, 2 suites* ⚄ *In-room: no a/c, Wi-Fi. In-hotel: restaurant, bar, some pets allowed.*

NIGHTLIFE AND THE ARTS

Information on all upcoming events is given in the monthly *Heidelberg aktuell*, free and available from the tourist office or on the Internet (⊕ *www.heidelberg-aktuell.de*).

heidelbergTicket. Theater tickets may be purchased at heidelbergTicket. ⊠ *Theaterstr. 4* ☎ *06221/582-0000* ⊕ *www.theaterheidelberg.de.*

THE ARTS

Heidelberg has a thriving theater scene.

Kulturhaus Karlstorbahnhof. This 19th-century train station has been repurposed as a theater and concert venue. ⊠ *Am Karlstor 1* ☎ *06221/978–911* ⊕ *www.karlstorbahnhof.de.*

Zimmertheater. Avant-garde theater productions are shown here. ⊠ *Hauptstr. 118* ☎ *06221/21069* ⊕ *www.zimmertheaterhd.de.*

Schlossfestspiele. Theatrical and musical performances are held at the Heidelberg castle during this annual festival from late June through July. ☎ *06221/582–0000* ⊕ *www.schlossfestspiele-heidelberg.de.*

NIGHTLIFE

Heidelberg nightlife is concentrated in the area around the Heiliggeistkirche (Church of the Holy Ghost), in the Old Town. Don't miss a visit to one of the old student taverns that have been in business for ages.

Schnookeloch. Heidelberg being a college town, this tavern has long been patronized by *Burschenschaften*, or dueling fraternities. ⊠ *Haspelg. 8* ☎ *06221/138–080* ⊕ *www.schnookeloch.de.*

Zum Roten Ochsen. Mark Twain rubbed elbows with students here during his 1878 stay in Heidelberg. ⊠ *Hauptstr. 217* ☎ *06221/20977.*

Today's students, however, are more likely to hang out in one of the dozen or more bars on **Untere Strasse**, which runs parallel to and between Hauptstrasse and the Neckar River, starting from the market square.

Billy Blues (im Ziegler). This restaurant, bar, and disco, has live music on Thursday. ⊠ *Bergheimer Str. 1b* ☎ *06221/25333* ⊕ *www.billyblues.de.*

Destille. The club plays rock music until 2 am on weekdays and 3 am on weekends, and the young crowd that packs the place is always having a good time. A tree in the middle of this club is decorated according to season. ⊠ *Untere Str. 16* ☎ *06221/22808* ⊕ *www.destilleonline.de.*

Nachtschicht. In the Landfried complex near the main train station, this is Heidelberg's biggest disco. The club is open until 4 am Thursday through Saturday. ⊠ *Bergheimer Str. 147* ☎ *06221/438–550* ⊕ *www. nachtschicht.com.*

Print media lounge. Facing the main train station is the chic, modern print media lounge, where you can dine all day or dance till the wee hours. It's open Monday–Saturday, with DJs Friday and Saturday and live bands on Monday. ⊠ *Kurfürsten–Anlage 60* ☎ *06221/653–949* ⊕ *www. printmedialounge.de* ☉ *Closed Sun. No lunch Sat.*

Schwimmbad Musikclub. Near the zoo, this is a fixture of Heidelberg's club scene. It occupies what was once a swimming pool, hence the name. It's open Thursday to Saturday. ⊠ *Tiergartenstr. 13* ☎ *06221/470–201* ⊕ *www.schwimmbad-club.de.*

SKYlounge Der Turm. For a nice view of the town, a menu of 120 cocktails, and relaxing music, head for the glass-walled SKYlounge. Choose between the dark-red walls on the seventh floor or the deep-blue shades

8

on the eighth floor. ⊠ *Alte Glockengiesserei* 9 ☏ *06221/434–967* ⊕ *www.skylounge-heidelberg.de.*

Vetters Alt-Heidelberger Brauhaus. It's worth elbowing your way into this bar for the brewed-on-the-premises beer. ⊠ *Steing.* 9 ☏ *06221/165–850* ⊕ *www.brauhaus-vetter.de.*

SPORTS AND THE OUTDOORS

The riverside path is an ideal route for walking, jogging, and bicycling, since it's traffic-free and offers excellent views of the area. If you access the paved pathway in the center of town, you can follow it for many kilometers in either direction.

SHOPPING

Heidelberg's **Hauptstrasse**, or Main Street, is a pedestrian zone lined

FESTIVALS

The **Schlossfestspiele** occurs on the castle grounds in Schwetzingen (May), Heidelberg (July and August), Zwingenberg (late August), and Ludwigsburg (June to mid-September). Since 1818 thousands have flocked to the Stuttgart suburb of Cannstatt in early October for the annual **Volksfest** (folk festival), which kicks off with a colorful parade of folk-dance groups and horse-drawn brewery wagons. Two wine festivals of particular note are the **Stuttgarter Weindorf**, from late August to early September, and the **Heilbronner Weindorf** in mid-September.

with shops, sights, and restaurants that stretches more than 1 km (½ mi) through the heart of town. But don't spend your money before exploring the shops on such side streets as **Plöck**, **Ingrimstrasse**, and **Untere Strasse**, where there are candy stores, bookstores, and antiques shops on the ground floors of baroque buildings. If your budget allows, the city can be a good place to find reasonably priced German antiques, and the Neckar Valley region produces fine glass and crystal.

Farmers' Markets. Heidelberg has open-air farmers' markets on Wednesday and Saturday mornings on Marktplatz and Tuesday and Friday mornings, as well as Thursday afternoons, on Friedrich-Ebert-Platz.

Aurum & Argentum. The finely executed, modern gold and silver pieces here are impeccably crafted. Prices start at €150. ⊠ *Brückenstr. 22* ☏ *06221/473–453* ⊙ *Tues.–Fri. 2:30–6:30, Sat. 10–2.*

Heidelberger Zuckerladen. The old glass display cases here are full of lollipops and "penny" candy. If you're looking for an unusual gift, the shop fashions colorful, unique items out of sugary ingredients such as marshmallow and sweetened gum. ⊠ *Plöck 52* ☏ *06221/24365* ⊙ *Weekdays noon–7, Sat. 11:15–3.*

OFF THE BEATEN PATH

A rare pleasure awaits you if you're in **Schwetzingen** in April, May, or June: the town is Germany's asparagus center, and nearly every local restaurant has a *Spargelkarte* (a special menu featuring fresh white asparagus dishes).

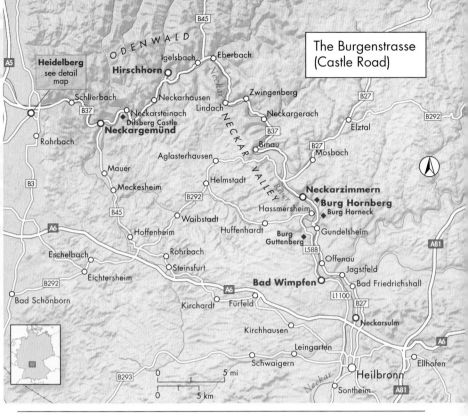

The Burgenstrasse
(Castle Road)

THE BURGENSTRASSE (CASTLE ROAD)

Upstream from Heidelberg, the Neckar Valley narrows, presenting a landscape of orchards, vineyards, and wooded hills crowned with castles rising above the gently flowing stream. It's one of the most impressive stretches of the Burgenstrasse. Along the B-37 are small valleys—locals call them *Klingen*—that cut north into the Odenwald and are off-the-beaten-track territory. One of the most atmospheric is the Wolfsschlucht, which starts below the castle at Zwingenberg. The dank, shadowy little gorge inspired Carl Maria von Weber's opera *Der Freischütz* (The Marksman).

NECKARGEMÜND

11 km (7 mi) upstream from Heidelberg.

Coming from the hustle and bustle of Heidelberg, you'll be pleased to discover that the hamlet of Neckargemünd is a quiet place where you can relax by the Neckar River and watch the ships go by. The town makes a good base from which to visit Heidelberg. Leave the car here and enjoy the 10-minute ride by bus or train.

WHERE TO STAY

For expanded hotel reviews, visit Fodors.com.

$ ⬚ **Art Hotel.** Spacious rooms, each individually decorated, make you feel welcome. **Pros:** rooms decorated with care; reasonable rates. **Cons:** on a busy street; no elevator. ⊠ *Hauptstr. 40* ☎ *06223/862–768* ⊕ *www. art-hotel-neckar.de* ⤵ *13 rooms* ⑂ *In-room: no a/c, Wi-Fi* ⑂*Breakfast.*

$ ⬚ **Gasthaus Reber.** If you're looking for a clean, simple room, this small inn may be just the place for you. **Pros:** unbeatable rates; close to public transportation. **Cons:** on busy street; restrooms down the hall. ⊠ *Bahnhofstr. 52* ☎ *06223/8779* ⊕ *www.gasthaus-reber.de* ⑂ *In-room: no a/c, Wi-Fi. In-hotel: restaurant, some pets allowed* ═ *No credit cards* ⊗ *Restaurant closed Wed. No lunch weekdays* ⑂*Breakfast.*

For expanded hotel reviews, visit Fodors.com.

EN
ROUTE

Schloss Zwingenberg. About 53 km (33 mi) from Heidelberg a castle stands above the village of Zwingenberg, its medieval towers thrusting through the dark woodland. Some say it's the most romantic of all the castles along the Neckar (except for Heidelberg, of course).

Schlossfestspiele Zwingenberg. The annual castle festival, which features theater and concert performances, takes place within the ancient walls of the Zwingenberg in August. ☎ *06263/771* ⊕ *www. schlossfestspiele-zwingenberg.de* ☎ *6263/411–010.*

Mosbach. The little town of Mosbach, 78 km (48 mi) southeast of Heidelberg, is one of the most charming towns on the Neckar. Its main street is pure half-timber, and its ancient market square contains one of Germany's most exquisite half-timber buildings—the early-17th-century Palm'sches Haus (Palm House), its upper stories laced with intricate timbering. The Rathaus, built 50 years earlier, is a modest affair by comparison.

NECKARZIMMERN

83 km (52 mi) from Heidelberg.

EXPLORING

Fodor'sChoice
★
Burg Hornberg. The massive, circular bulk of Burg Hornberg rises above the woods that drop to the riverbank and the town of Neckarzimmern. The road to the castle leads through vineyards that have been providing dry white wines for centuries. Today the castle is part hotel and part museum. In the 16th century it was home to the larger-than-life Götz von Berlichingen (1480–1562). When the knight lost his right arm fighting in a petty squabble, he had a blacksmith fashion an iron replacement. The original designs for this fearsome artificial limb are on view in the castle, as is his suit of armor. For most Germans, the rambunctious knight is best remembered for a remark that was faithfully reproduced in Goethe's play *Götz von Berlichingen*. Responding to an official reprimand, von Berlichingen told his critic, more or less, to "kiss my ass" (the original German is substantially more earthy). To this day the polite version of this insult is known as a *Götz von Berlichingen*. Inquire at the hotel reception about visiting the castle.

You can tour Burg Hornberg or spend the night at this spectacular castle.

WHERE TO STAY

For expanded hotel reviews, visit Fodors.com.

$$ ★ **Burg Hornberg Hotel.** Your host at this hotel with comfortable, modern rooms is the present baron of the castle. **Pros:** historic setting; nice restaurant; on-site wine shop. **Cons:** no elevator; restaurant can be crowded in season on weekends; not enough parking. ⊠ *Marucs Freiherr von Gemmingen* ☎ *06261/92460* ⊕ *www.castle-hotel-hornberg. com* ⌑ *22 rooms, 2 suites* ⌂ *In-room: no a/c, Internet. In-hotel: restaurant, some pets allowed* ⊙ *Closed late Dec.–late Jan.* ⫶○⫶ *Breakfast.*

EN
ROUTE

Burg Guttenberg. One of the best-preserved Neckar castles is the 15th-century Burg Guttenberg. Within its stone walls are a museum and a restaurant (closed January, February, and Monday) with views of the river valley. The castle is also home to Europe's leading center for the study and protection of birds of prey. Demonstration flights are given from the castle walls from April through October, daily at 11 and 3. ⊠ *6 km (4 mi) west of Gundelsheim, Neckarmühlbach* ☎ *06266/388* ⊕ *www.burg-guttenberg.de* ⫶ *Castle €4, castle and flight demonstration €11* ⊙ *Apr.–Oct., daily 10–6.*

BAD WIMPFEN

8 km (5 mi) south of Neckarzimmern.

Fodor's Choice
★   At the confluence of the Neckar and Jagst rivers, Bad Wimpfen is one of the most stunning towns of the Neckar Valley. The Romans built a fortress and a bridge here, on the riverbank site of an ancient Celtic settlement, in the 1st century AD. A millennium later, the Staufen emperor

Barbarossa chose this town as the site of his largest Pfalz *(residence).* The ruins of this palace still overshadow the town and are well worth a stroll.

TOURS

Medieval Bad Wimpfen offers a town walk year-round, Sunday at 2 (€2), departing from the visitor center inside the old train station. Private group tours may also be arranged for other days by calling the visitor center in advance.

DISCOUNTS AND DEALS

On arrival, ask your hotel for a free *Bad Wimpfen à la card* for reduced or free admission to historic sights and museums.

ESSENTIALS

Visitor Information Bad Wimpfen ⊠ *Tourist-Information, Bad Wimpfen–Gundelsheim, Carl-Ulrich-Str. 1* ☎ *07063/97200* ⊕ *www.badwimpfen.de.*

EXPLORING

Ritterstiftskirche St. Peter. Wimpfen im Tal (Wimpfen in the Valley), the oldest part of town, is home to the Benedictine monastery Gruessau and its church, Ritterstiftskirche St. Peter, which dates from the 10th and 13th centuries. The cloisters are delightful, an example of German Gothic at its most uncluttered. ⊠ *Lindenpl.*

Stadtkirche (*city church*). The 13th-century stained glass, wall paintings, medieval altars, and the stone pietà in the Gothic Stadtkirche are worth seeing, as are the Crucifixion sculptures (1515) by the Rhenish master Hans Backoffen on Kirchplatz, behind the church. ⊠ *Kirchsteige 8.*

Steinhaus. Germany's largest Romanesque living quarters and once the imperial apartments reserved for women, is now a history museum. Next to the Steinhaus are the remains of the northern facade of the palace, an arcade of superbly carved Romanesque pillars that flanked the imperial hall in its heyday. The imperial chapel, next to the Red Tower, holds a collection of ecclesiastical artworks (closed Monday). ⊠ *Kaiserpfalz.* ☎ *07063/97200* 🎟 *€2* ⊙ *Apr. 15–Oct. 1, Tues.–Sat. 10–noon, 2–4:30.*

Zunftmarkt. On the last weekend in August, the Old Town's medieval past comes alive during the Zunftmarkt, a historical market dedicated to the *Zünfte* (guilds). "Artisans" in period costumes demonstrate the old trades and open the festivities with a colorful parade on horseback. ⊕ *www.zunftmarkt.de.*

WHERE TO EAT AND STAY

For expanded hotel reviews, visit Fodors.com.

$ ✕**Weinstube Feyerabend.** Here you can have a glass of good Swabian
GERMAN wine with a snack. Or let yourself be tempted by the good-looking cakes from their own bakery. ⊠ *Hauptstr. 74* ☎ *07063/950–566* ⊕ *www.friedrich-feyerabend.de* ▬ *No credit cards* ⊙ *Closed Mon.*

$ 🏨 **Hotel Neckarblick.** You get a good *Neckarblick* (Neckar view) from the terrace, the dining room, and most guest rooms of this pleasant lodging. **Pros:** terrific view; personal touch. **Cons:** no restaurant or bar; not enough parking. ⊠ *Erich-Sailer-Str. 48* ☎ *07063/961–620* ⊕ *www.*

neckarblick.de ⤶ *14 rooms* ⌂ *In-room: no a/c, Wi-Fi. In-hotel: some pets allowed* ⦿ *Breakfast.*

OFF THE
BEATEN
PATH

Deutsches Zweirad–Museum (*German Motorcycle Museum*). Motorbike fans won't want to miss the town of Neckarsulm 10 km (6 mi) south of Bad Wimpfen. It's a busy industrial center, home of the German automobile manufacturer Audi and the Deutsches Zweirad–Museum. Among its 300 exhibits are the world's first mass-produced motorcycles (the Hildebrand and Wolfmüller); a number of famous racing machines; and a rare Daimler machine, the first made by that legendary name. All are arranged over five floors in a handsome 400-year-old castle that belonged to the Teutonic Knights until 1806. ⊠ *Urbanstr. 11* ☎ *07132/35271* ⊕ *www.zweirad-museum.de* ⊠ *€4.50* ⊙ *Tues.–Sun. 9–5.*

SWABIAN CITIES

Ludwigsburg, Stuttgart, and Tübingen are all part of the ancient province of Swabia, a region strongly influenced by Protestantism and Calvinism. The inhabitants speak the Swabian dialect of German. Ludwigsburg is known for its two splendid castles. Stuttgart, the capital of the state of Baden-Württemberg and one of Germany's leading industrial cities, is surrounded by hills on three sides, with the fourth side opening up toward its river harbor. The medieval town of Tübingen clings to steep slopes and hilltops above the Neckar.

LUDWIGSBURG

8

15 km (9 mi) north of Stuttgart.

Residenzschloss Ludwigsburg. Ludwigsburg merits a stop to visit Germany's largest baroque palace, Residenzschloss Ludwigsburg. The main palace is also home to the **Keramikmuseum,** a collection of historical treasures from the porcelain manufactories in Meissen, Nymphenburg, Berlin, Vienna, and Ludwigsburg, as well as an exhibit of contemporary ceramics. The **Barockgalerie** is a collection of German and Italian baroque paintings from the 17th and 18th centuries. The **Modemuseum** showcases three centuries of fashion, particularly royal clothing of the 18th century. In another part of the palace you'll find the **Porzellan-Manufaktur Ludwigsburg** (⊕ *www.ludwigsburger-porzellan.de*); you can tour the porcelain factory where each piece is handmade and hand-painted. The castle is surrounded by the fragrant, colorful 74-acre park **Blühendes Barock** (Blooming Baroque), filled with thousands and thousands of tulips, huge masses of rhododendrons, and fragrant roses. A Märchengarten (fairy-tale garden) delights visitors of all ages. In the midst of it all, you can take a break in the cafeteria in the Rose Garden. ⊠ *Schloss Str. 30* ☎ *07141/182–004* ⊕ *www.schloesser-und-gaerten.de* ⊠ *Palace €6.50, park €8, museums with audioguide €3.50, museum tour with audio €6.50, guide combination ticket €16* ⊙ *Park daily 7:30 am–8:30 pm, palace and museums daily 10–5.*

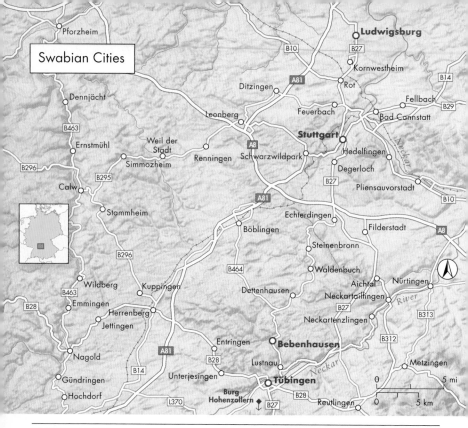

STUTTGART

50 km (31 mi) south on B-27 from Heilbronn.

Stuttgart is a place of extreme contradictions. It has been called, among other things, "Germany's biggest small town" and "the city where work is a pleasure." For centuries Stuttgart, whose name derives from *Stutengarten,* or "stud farm," remained a pastoral backwater along the Neckar. Then the Industrial Revolution propelled the city into the machine age. Leveled in World War II, Stuttgart has regained its position as one of Germany's top industrial centers.

This is Germany's can-do city, whose natives have turned out Mercedes-Benz and Porsche cars, Bosch electrical equipment, and a host of other products exported worldwide. Yet Stuttgart is also a city of culture and the arts, with world-class museums, opera, and a ballet company. Moreover, it's the domain of fine local wines; the vineyards actually approach the city center in a rim of green hills. Forests, vineyards, meadows, and orchards compose more than half the city, which is enclosed on three sides by woods.

An ideal introduction to the contrasts of Stuttgart is a guided city bus tour. Included is a visit to the needle-nose TV tower, high on a mountaintop above the city, affording stupendous views. Built in 1956, it was the first of its kind in the world. The tourist office also offers superb walking tours. On your own, the best place to begin exploring Stuttgart is the Hauptbahnhof (main train station); from there walk down the pedestrian street Königstrasse to Schillerplatz, a small, charming square named after the 18th-century poet and playwright Friedrich Schiller, who was born in nearby Marbach. It's surrounded by historic buildings, many of them rebuilt after the war.

GETTING HERE AND AROUND

Stuttgart is the major hub for the railway system in southwestern Germany, and two autobahns cross here. It's about 2½ hours away from Munich and a bit more than an hour from Frankfurt. The downtown museums and the main shopping streets are doable on foot. For the outlying attractions and to get to the airport, there is a very efficient S-bahn and subway system.

TOURS

The tourist office is the meeting point for city walking tours in German (year-round, Saturday at 10) for €8. There are daily bilingual walks April–October at 11 am for €18. Bilingual bus tours costing €8 depart from the bus stop around the corner from the tourist office, in front of Hotel am Schlossgarten (April–October, daily at 1:30; November–March, Friday–Sunday at 1:30). All tours last from 1½ to 2½ hours. Stuttgart Tourist-Information offers altogether 12 different special-interest tours. Call for details.

DISCOUNTS AND DEALS

The three-day **StuttCard** (€9) offers discounts to museums and attractions, with or without a free public transport pass. (€22 includes a transit card valid in the whole city or €18 for a transit card for the city center). All the cards are available from the Stuttgart tourist office opposite the main train station.

ESSENTIALS

Visitor Information Stuttgart ✉ *Touristik-Information i-Punkt, Königstr. 1A* ☎ *0711/222–8246* ∰ *www.stuttgart-tourist.de.*

EXPLORING

TOP ATTRACTIONS

Kunstmuseum Stuttgart (*Stuttgart Art Museum*). This sleek structure encased in a glass facade is a work of art in its own right. It features artwork of the 19th and 20th centuries and the world's largest Otto Dix collection (including the *Grossstadt* [*Metropolis*] triptych, which captures the essence of 1920s Germany). ■TIP→ The bistro-café on the rooftop terrace affords great views; the foyer houses a café and the museum shop. ✉ *Kleiner Schlosspl.1* ☎ *0711/216–2188* ∰ *www.kunstmuseum-stuttgart.de* 🖾 *€5, €8 special exhibition, €2.50 guided tours* ✆ *Tues.–Sun. 10–6.*

★ **Mercedes-Benz Museum.** Most visitors come to see the 160 vehicles on display, but quite a few are interested in the building's stunning futuristic architecture. When you enter, you are taken to the top floor, then wander down following your interests—following the history of automobiles, or looking at how racing cars are developed. Don't miss the special exhibitions like super sports cars or the 75th anniversary of the Silver Arrows. The bistro and the café stay open after the museum has closed its doors. ⌂ *Mercedesstr. 100, Stuttgart-Untertürkheim* ☎ *0711/173–0000* ⊕ *www.museum-mercedes-benz.com* ⌷ *€8* ⊙ *Tues.– Sun. 9–4.30.*

★ **Porsche Museum.** In the center of the Porsche factory in the northern suburb of Zuffenhausen an aluminum-clad structure seems to hover in space, yet it's actually resting on three concrete support columns. This daring building houses the Porsche Museum, a vast collection of legendary Porsche racing cars that delights fans from all over the world. There are also more than 200 exhibits on Porsche engineering. ■TIP➔ Across from the museum's main entrance is a shop selling watches, clothes, sunglasses, and other items with the Porsche logo. If you have been looking for a gift for a car fan, this is the place. ⌂ *Porschepl. 1, Stuttgart-Zuffenhausen* ☎ *0711/9112–0911* ⊕ *www.porsche.com/museum* ⌷ *€8* ⊙ *Tues.–Sun. 9–6.*

Schlossplatz (*Palace Square*). A huge area enclosed by royal palaces, the square has elegant arcades branching off to other stately plazas. The magnificent baroque **Neues Schloss** (New Palace), now occupied by Baden-Württemberg state government offices, dominates the square. ⌂ *Corner of Koenigstrasse and Planie, Mitte.*

Fodor'sChoice
★
Staatsgalerie (*State Gallery*). This not-to-be-missed museum displays one of the finest art collections in Germany. The old part of the complex, dating from 1843, has paintings from the Middle Ages through the 19th century, including works by Cranach, Holbein, Hals, Memling, Rubens, Rembrandt, Cézanne, Courbet, and Manet. Connected to the original building is the **Neue Staatsgalerie** (New State Gallery), designed by British architect James Stirling in 1984 as a melding of classical and modern, sometimes jarring, elements (such as chartreuse window mullions). Considered one of the most successful postmodern buildings, it houses works by such 20th-century artists as Braque, Chagall, de Chirico, Dalí, Kandinsky, Klee, Mondrian, and Picasso. ⌂ *Konrad-Adenauer-Str. 30–32, Mitte* ☎ *0711/470–400* ⊕ *www.staatsgalerie.de* ⌷ *€5.50 permanent collection, €10.00 special exhibitions. Free admission to the permanent collection Wed. and Sat.* ⊙ *Wed., Fri.–Sun. 10–6; Tues., Thurs. 10–8.*

WORTH NOTING

Altes Schloss (*Old Castle*). Across the street from the Neues Schloss stands this former residence of the counts and dukes of Württemberg, which was originally built as a moated castle around 1320. Wings were added in the mid-15th century, creating a Renaissance palace. The palace now houses the **Württembergisches Landesmuseum** (Württemberg State Museum), with imaginative exhibits tracing the development of the area from the Stone Age to modern times. ■TIP➔ Due to the replanning and new layout of the permanent exhibition, major sections of the Altes Schloss are currently closed for renovation. For this reason, the Württemberg State Museum will offer visitors free admission for one year beginning April 1, 2011. ⌂ *Schillerpl. 6, Mitte* ☎ *0711/279–3498* ⊕ *www. landesmuseum-stuttgart.de* ⌷ *Free until Apr. 2012* ⊙ *Tues.–Sun. 10–5.*

The fountain in Schlossplatz (Palace Square) is a great place to sit and contemplate the surrounding architecture.

Haus der Geschichte Baden-Württemberg (*Museum of the History of Baden-Württemberg*). In late 2002, Stuttgart's "cultural mile" was enriched with this postmodern masterpiece by architect James Stirling. It chronicles the state's history during the 19th and 20th centuries. Multimedia presentations enable you to interact with the thousands of fascinating objects on display. ⌧ *Konrad-Adenauer-Str. 16, Mitte* ☎ *0711/212–3989* ⊕ *www.hdgbw.de* ✆ *€3 permanent collection, €2.50 special exhibits, €4.50 combination ticket* ☉ *Tues., Wed., and Fri.–Sun. 10–6; Thurs. 10–9.*

Schlossgarten (*Palace Garden*). This huge city park borders the Schlossplatz and extends northeast across Schillerstrasse all the way to Bad Cannstatt on the Neckar River. The park is graced by an exhibition hall, planetarium, lakes, sculptures, and the hot-spring mineral baths Leuze and Berg.

Stiftskirche (*Collegiate Church of the Holy Cross*). Just off Schillerplatz, this is Stuttgart's most familiar sight, with its two oddly matched towers. Built in the 12th century, it was later rebuilt in a late-Gothic style. The choir has a famous series of Renaissance figures of the counts of Württemberg sculpted by Simon Schlör (1576–1608). ⌧ *Stiftstr. 12, Mitte.*

Wilhelma Zoologische-Botanische Garten (*Wilhelma Zoological and Botanical Garden*). Adjacent to Rosenstein Park, this park was originally intended as a garden for King Wilhelm I. The Moorish style buildings led it to be called the "Alhambra on the Neckar." Today it is a wildlife park and zoological garden. ⌧ *Neckartalstr., Wilhelma* ☎ *0711/54020*

The postmodern Neue Staatsgalerie (New State Gallery) is where you'll find 20th-century masterpieces by artists including Picasso and Chagall.

⊕ *www.wilhelma.de* ⊠ *€12; €8 Nov.–Feb. and in summer after 4 pm* ⊙ *May–Aug., daily 8:15–6; Sept.–Apr., daily 8:15–4.*

WHERE TO EAT

$$$$
CONTINENTAL
★

✕ **Wielandshöhe.** One of Germany's top chefs, Vincent Klink, and his wife Elisabeth are very down-to-earth, cordial hosts. Her floral arrangements add a baroque touch to the otherwise quiet decor, but your vision—and palate—will ultimately focus on the artfully presented cuisine. To the extent possible, all ingredients are grown locally. House specialties, such as saddle of lamb with a potato gratin and green beans or the Breton lobster with basil potato salad, are recommended. The wine list is exemplary. ⊠ *Alte Weinsteige 71, Degerloch* ☎ *0711/640–8848* ⊕ *www.wielandshoehe.de* 🍴 *Reservations essential* ⊙ *Closed Sun. and Mon.*

WHERE TO STAY

For expanded hotel reviews, visit Fodors.com.

$$$$
★

🏨 **Am Schlossgarten.** Stuttgart's top accommodation is a modern structure set in spacious gardens, a stone's throw from many of the top sights and opposite the main station. **Pros:** views of the park; welcoming lobby; ample parking. **Cons:** not all rooms face the park; rates are on the high end. ⊠ *Schillerstr. 23, Mitte* ☎ *0711/20260* ⊕ *www. hotelschlossgarten.com* 🛏 *106 rooms, 10 suites* △ *In-room: a/c, Wi-Fi. In-hotel: restaurants, bar, business center, some pets allowed* ⊙ *Zirbelstube closed 1st 2 wks in Jan., 3 wks Aug., Sun., and Mon. Schlossgarten closed Fri. and Sat. Vinothek closed Sun. and Mon.*

$$$$
★ ⚏ **Der Zauberlehrling.** The "Sorcerer's Apprentice" is aptly named as Karen and Axel Heldmann have conjured up a lovely luxury hotel with each room's decor based on a theme (Asian, Mediterranean, country manor). **Pros:** fabulous rooms with lots of surprises; enjoyable restaurant. **Cons:** minuscule lobby; no elevator. ⊠ *Rosenstr. 38, Bohnenviertel* ☎ *0711/237–7770* ⊕ *www.zauberlehrling.de* ⇥ *17 rooms* ⚒ *In-room: no a/c, Wi-Fi. In-hotel: restaurant, bar, business center* ☾ *No lunch weekends* ¡◎¡ *Breakfast.*

$$$
⚏ **Mövenpick Hotel Stuttgart Airport.** Across the street from Stuttgart Airport, the doors of this hotel open leading you into a completely soundproof glass palace. **Pros:** spacious; modern yet welcoming. **Cons:** swells with business travelers. ⊠ *Flughafenstr. 50, Flughafen* ☎ *0711/553–440* ⊕ *www.moevenpick-stuttgart-airport.com* ⇥ *326 rooms, 12 junior suites* ⚒ *In-room: a/c, Internet, Wi-Fi. In-hotel: restaurant, bar, gym, spa, business center, parking, some pets allowed.*

$$
⚏ **Wörtz zur Weinsteige.** As you wander through this hotel's small garden, its easy to forget that you are in the middle of a big city. **Pros:** welcoming atmosphere; underground garage; cozy restaurant with good food and terrific wine list. **Cons:** kitschy gold decorations; older rooms are noisy; no elevator in main building. ⊠ *Hohenheimerstr. 28, Mitte* ☎ *0711/236–7000* ⊕ *www.hotel-woertz.de* ⇥ *30 rooms* ⚒ *In-room: no a/c, Wi-Fi. In-hotel: restaurant, bar, parking* ☾ *Restaurant closed Sun. and Mon., 2 wks in Jan., and 2 wks in Aug.* ¡◎¡ *Breakfast.*

NIGHTLIFE AND THE ARTS

i-Punkt tourist office. Check out the i-Punkt for a current calendar of events and to buy tickets via phone weekdays 8:30–6; or in the office weekdays 9–8, Saturday 9–6, and Sunday 10–6 (May–October) or 1–6 (November–April). ⊠ *Königstr. 1A, Mitte* ☎ *0711/22280* ⊕ *www. stuttgart-tourist.de.*

THE ARTS

SI-Erlebnis-Centrum. This entertainment complex containing hotels, bars, restaurants, a casino, wellness center, cinemas, shops, and theaters was built to showcase big-budget musicals such as *42nd Street.* A calendar of events can be found on its Web site. ⊠ *Plieninger Str. 100, Stuttgart-Möhringen* ⊕ *www.si-centrum.de.*

Staatstheater. Stuttgart's internationally renowned ballet company performs at this theater. The ballet season runs from September through July and alternates with the highly respected State Opera. For program details, contact the Stuttgart tourist office. The box office is open weekdays 10–8, Saturday 10–2. ⊠ *Oberer Schlossgarten 6, Mitte* ☎ *0711/20320* ⊕ *www.staatstheater.stuttgart.de.*

NIGHTLIFE

There's no shortage of rustic beer gardens, wine pubs, or sophisticated cocktail bars in and around Stuttgart. Night owls should head for the **Schwabenzentrum** on Eberhardstrasse; the **Bohnenviertel**, or "Bean Quarter" (Charlotten-, Olga-, and Pfarrstrasse); the "party mile" along **Theodor-Heuss-Strasse; Calwer Strasse;** and **Wilhelmsplatz.**

8

Café Stella. If you enjoy live music, visit this trendy restaurant and bar, perfect for an evening of dinner and drinks. ⊠ *Hauptstätterstr. 57, Mitte* ☎ *0711/640–2583* ⊕ *www.cafe-stella.de.*

SPORTS AND THE OUTDOORS

BOAT TRIPS

Neckar-Käpt'n. From the pier opposite the entrance to the zoo, Neckar-Käpt'n offers a wide range of boat trips, as far north as scenic Besigheim. ☎ *0711/5499–7060* ⊕ *www.neckar-kaeptn.de.*

HIKING

Stuttgart has a 53-km (33-mi) network of marked hiking trails in the nearby hills; follow the signs with the city's emblem: a horse set in a yellow ring.

SWIMMING AND SPAS

Mineralbad Cannstatt. Bad Cannstatt's mineral springs are more than 2,000 years old and, with a daily output of about 5.8 million gallons, the second most productive (after Budapest) in Europe. The Mineralbad Cannstatt has indoor and outdoor mineral pools, hot tubs, a sauna, a steam room, and spa facilities. ⊠ *Sulzerrainstr. 2* ☎ *0711/216–9240.*

Mineralbad Berg. Take the waters in the indoor and outdoor pools and sauna; there are also therapeutic water treatments. ⊠ *Am Schwanenpl. 9* ☎ *0711/216–7090.*

Mineralbad Leuze. On the banks of the Neckar near the König-Karl Bridge is the Mineralbad Leuze, with eight pools indoors and out and an open-air mineral-water sauna. ⊠ *Am Leuzebad 2–6* ☎ *0711/216–4210.*

SHOPPING

Stuttgart is a shopper's paradise, from the department stores on the Königstrasse to the boutiques in the Old Town's elegant passages and the factory outlet stores.

Bohnenviertel (*Bean Quarter*). Some of Stuttgart's more unique shops are found in this older quarter. A stroll through the neighborhood's smaller streets reveals many tucked-away shops specializing in fashion, jewelry, artwork, and gifts.

Breuninger. This leading regional department-store chain has glass elevators that rise and fall under the dome of the central arcade. ⊠ *Marktstr. 1–3, Mitte* ☎ *0711/2110.*

Calwer Passage. Calwer Strasse is home to this glitzy chrome-and-glass arcade. Shops here carry everything from local women's fashion (Beate Mössinger) to furniture.

Markthalle. Don't miss the beautiful art nouveau Markthalle on Dorotheenstrasse. One of Germany's finest market halls, it's an architectural gem brimming with exotic fruits and spices, meats, and flowers.

Günter Krauss. The shop itself—walls of white Italian marble with gilt fixtures and mirrors—has won many design awards; it specializes in designer jewelry. ⊠ *Kronprinzstr. 21, Mitte* ☎ *0711/297–395* ⊕ *guenterkrauss.de* ⊙ *Closed Mon.*

BEBENHAUSEN

6 km (4 mi) north of Tübingen, on west side of B-27/464.

Between Stuttgart and Tübingen lies this small hamlet consisting of a few houses, a monastery, and the Waldhorn, an excellent and well-known restaurant. The monastery was founded in the 12th century by the count of Tübingen. Today it belongs to the state.

Fodor'sChoice ★ **Zisterzienzerkloster** (*Cistercian Monastery*). The Zisterzienzerkloster is a rare example of an almost perfectly preserved medieval monastery dating from the late 12th century. Owing to the secularization of 1806, the abbot's abode was rebuilt as a hunting castle for King Frederick of Württemberg. Expansion and restoration continued as long as the palace and monastery continued to be a royal residence. Visits to the palace are with guided tours only. ☎ *07071/602–802* ⊕ *www.bebenhausen.de* 🎫 *Monastery €4, palace €4.50* ⊗ *Nov.–Mar., Tues.–Sun. 10–noon and 1–5; Apr.–Oct. daily 9–6.*

WHERE TO EAT

$$$$
CONTINENTAL
Fodor'sChoice
★

× **Waldhorn.** Old favorites such as the *Vorspeisenvariation* (a medley of appetizers) are what keep people coming back to this eatery. The wine list features a well-chosen selection of international and top Baden and Württemberg wines. Garden tables have a castle view. A meal here is a perfect start or finale to the concerts held on the monastery-castle grounds in the summer. ⊠ *Schönbuchstr. 49* ☎ *07071/61270* ⊕ *www. waldhorn-bebenhausen.de* ⌕ *Reservations essential* ▭ *No credit cards* ⊗ *Closed Mon. and Tues.*

TÜBINGEN

40 km (25 mi) south of Stuttgart on B-27 on the Neckar River.

With its half-timber houses, winding alleyways, and hilltop setting overlooking the Neckar, Tübingen provides the quintessential German experience. The medieval flavor is quite authentic, as the town was untouched by wartime bombings. Dating to the 11th century, Tübingen flourished as a trade center; its weights and measures and currency were the standard through much of the area. The town declined in importance after the 14th century, when it was taken over by the counts of Württemberg. Between the 14th and the 19th century, its size hardly changed as it became a university and residential town, its castle the only symbol of ruling power.

Yet Tübingen hasn't been sheltered from the world. It resonates with a youthful air. Even more than Heidelberg, Tübingen is virtually synonymous with its university, a leading center of learning since it was founded in 1477. The best way to see and appreciate Tübingen is simply to stroll around, soaking up its age-old atmosphere of quiet erudition.

GETTING HERE AND AROUND

By regional train or by car on the autobahn, Tübingen is an hour south of Stuttgart. In the Old Town you reach everything on foot.

8

DID YOU KNOW?

You can pick up bread, cheese, flowers, and more in Tübingen's Marktplatz (Market Square) three days a week at the open-air farmers' market. It's a pleasant and atmospheric location any day of the week, with half-timber houses and sidewalk cafés.

TOURS

The Tübingen tourist office runs guided city tours year-round at 2:30. From March through October there are also tours that take place daily and cost €90. From November through February, tours are on weekends only. Tours start at the Rathaus on the market square.

DISCOUNTS AND DEALS

Overnight guests receive a free Tourist-Regio-Card from their hotel (ask for it) for reduced admission fees to museums, concerts, theaters, and sports facilities.

TIMING

A leisurely walk around the old part of town will take you about two hours, if you include the castle on the hill and Platanenallee looking at the Old Town from the other side of the river.

ESSENTIALS

Visitor Information Tübingen ⊠ *Verkehrsverein Tübingen, An der Neckarbrücke* ☏ *07071/91360* ⊕ *www.tuebingen-info.de.*

EXPLORING
TOP ATTRACTIONS

★ **Marktplatz** (*Market Square*). Houses of prominent burghers of centuries gone by surround this square. At the open-air market on Monday, Wednesday, and Friday you can buy flowers, bread, pastries, poultry, sausage, and cheese.

★ **Rathaus** (*Town Hall*). Begun in 1433, this building slowly expanded over the next 150 years. Its ornate Renaissance facade is bright with colorful murals and a marvelous astronomical clock dating from 1511. The halls and reception rooms are adorned with half-timber and paintings from the late 19th century. ⊠ *Marktpl.*

Stiftskirche (*Collegiate Church*). The late-Gothic church has been well preserved; its original features include the stained-glass windows, the choir stalls, the ornate baptismal font, and the elaborate stone pulpit. The windows are famous for their colors and were much admired by Goethe. The dukes of Württemberg, from the 15th through the 17th century, are interred in the choir. ⊠ *Holzmarkt.* 🗐 *Bell tower €1* ⊙ *Daily 9–4.*

WORTH NOTING

Alte Aula (*Old Auditorium*). Erected in 1547, the half-timber university building was significantly altered in 1777, when it acquired an Italian roof, a symmetrical facade, and a balcony decorated with two crossed scepters, symbolizing the town's center of learning. In earlier times grain was stored under the roof as part of the professors' salaries. ⊠ *Münzg.*

Bursa (*Student Dormitory*). The word *bursa* meant "purse" in the Middle Ages and later came to refer to student lodgings such as this former student dormitory. Despite its classical facade, which it acquired in the early 19th century, the building actually dates back to 1477. Medieval students had to master a broad curriculum that included the *septem artes liberales* (seven liberal arts) of grammar, dialectic, rhetoric, arithmetic, geometry, astronomy, and music. ⊠ *Bursag. 4.*

Hölderlinturm (*Hölderlin's Tower*). Friedrich Hölderlin, a visionary poet who succumbed to madness in his early thirties, lived here until his death in 1843, in the care of the master cabinetmaker Zimmer and his daughter. ☒ *Bursag. 6* ☎ *07071/22040* ⊕ *www. hoelderlin-gesellschaft.de* ☒ *€2.50* ⊙ *Tues.–Fri. 10–noon and 3–5.*

Kornhaus (*Grain House*). During the Middle Ages, townspeople stored and sold grain on the first floor of this structure built in 1453; social events took place on the second floor. It now houses the City Museum. ☒ *Kornhausstr. 10* ☎ *07071/204–1711* ☒ *€2.50* ⊙ *Tues.–Sun. 11–5.*

OFF THE BEATEN PATH

Kunsthalle (*Art Gallery*). An art gallery north of the Neckar, the Kunsthalle has become a leading exhibition venue and generates a special kind of "art tourism," making it difficult to find lodging if a popular exhibition is shown. ☒ *Philosophenweg 76* ☎ *07071/96910* ⊕ *www. kunsthalle-tuebingen.de* ☒ *€7* ⊙ *Tues. 11-7, Wed.–Sun. 11–6.*

Schloss Hohentübingen. The original castle of the counts of Tübingen (1078) was significantly enlarged and altered by Duke Ulrich during the 16th century. Particularly noteworthy is the elaborate Renaissance portal patterned after a Roman triumphal arch. The coat of arms of the duchy of Württemberg depicted in the center is framed by the emblems of various orders, including the Order of the Garter. Today the castle's main attraction is its magnificent view over the river and town.

Studentenkarzer (*Student Prison*). The oldest surviving university prison in Germany consists of just two small rooms. For more than three centuries (1515–1845) students were locked up here for such offenses as swearing, failing to attend sermons, wearing clothing considered lewd, or playing dice. The figures on the walls are not graffiti but scenes from biblical history that were supposed to contribute to the moral improvement of the incarcerated students. You can enter the prison on a guided tour organized by the Tübingen tourist board. ☒ *Münzg. 20* ☎ *07071/91360* ☒ *€1* ⊙ *Tour weekends at 2.*

WHERE TO EAT AND STAY
For expanded hotel reviews, visit Fodors.com.

$$
GERMAN

✕ **Forelle.** Beautiful ceilings painted with vine motifs, exposed beams, and an old tile stove make for a *gemütlich* (cozy) atmosphere. This small restaurant fills up fast, not least because of the Swabian cooking. The chef makes sure the ingredients are from the region, including the inn's namesake, trout. ☒ *Kronenstr. 8* ☎ *07071/24094* ⊕ *www. weinstube-forelle.de.*

8

$ ✗ **Wurstküche.** For more than 200 years, all sorts of people have come
GERMAN here: students, because many of the dishes are filling yet inexpensive;
locals, because the food is the typical Swabian fare their mothers made;
and out-of-town visitors, who love the old-fashioned atmosphere. In
summer you may get a seat at one of the tables on the sidewalk in
front of the restaurant. ⊠ *Am Lustnauer Tor 8* ☎ *07071/92750* ⊕ *www.
wurstkueche.com.*

$$ ⊡ **Hotel Am Schloss.** Close to the castle that towers over the town you'll
★ find this charming hotel. **Pros:** very nice views; valet parking. **Cons:** no
elevator. ⊠ *Burgsteige 18* ☎ *07071/92940* ⊕ *www.hotelamschloss.de*
↴ *37 rooms* ⚮ *In-room: no a/c, Wi-Fi. In-hotel: restaurant, business
center, some pets allowed* ⎮○⎮ *Breakfast.*

$$ ⊡ **Hotel Hospiz.** This modern, family-run hotel provides friendly service,
comfortable rooms, and a convenient Altstadt location near the castle.
Pros: some old beams; convenient location. **Cons:** many stairs in spite of
elevator; rooms simply furnished; no bar or restaurant. ⊠ *Neckarhalde
2* ☎ *07071/9240* ⊕ *www.hotel-hospiz.de* ↴ *50 rooms* ⚮ *In-room: no
a/c, Internet. In-hotel: some pets allowed* ⎮○⎮ *Breakfast.*

NIGHTLIFE AND THE ARTS

Die Kelter. You'll find jazz, light fare, and a wine shop here. ⊠ *Schmied-
torstr. 17* ☎ *07071/254–690* ⊕ *www.diekelter.de.*

Jazzkeller. Like dozens of other Old Town student pubs, Jazzkeller
attracts a lively crowd after 9. ⊠ *Haagg. 15/2* ☎ *07071/550–906.*

Tangente-Jour. From 9 am until past midnight there's action at this bistro
next to the Stiftskirche. ⊠ *Münzg. 17* ☎ *07071/24572.*

SPORTS AND THE OUTDOORS

The Tübingen tourist office has maps with hiking routes around the
town, including historical and geological *Lehrpfade,* or educational
walks. A classic Tübingen walk goes from the castle down to the little chapel called the **Wurmlinger Kapelle,** taking about two hours. On
the way you can stop off at the restaurant Schwärzlocher Hof (closed
Monday and Tuesday) for a glass of *Most* (apple wine), bread, and
sausages—all are homemade.

OFF THE
BEATEN
PATH

Burg Hohenzollern. The majestic silhouette of this castle is visible from miles
away. The Hohenzollern House of Prussia was the most powerful family
in German history. It lost its throne when Kaiser William II abdicated after
Germany's defeat in World War I. The Swabian branch of the family owns
one-third of the castle, the Prussian branch two-thirds. Today's neo-Gothic
structure, perched high on a conical wooded hill, is a successor of a castle
dating from the 11th century. On the fascinating castle tour you'll see the
Prussian royal crown and beautiful period rooms—splendid from floor to
ceiling, with playful details, such as door handles carved to resemble peacocks and dogs. The restaurant on the castle grounds, Burgschänke (closed
January and Monday in February and March) serves regional food. From
the castle parking lot (€2) it's a 20-minute walk to the entrance, or in
summer take the shuttle bus (€2.90 round-trip, €1.90 one-way). ⊠ *25 km
(15 mi) south of Tübingen on B-27, Hechingen* ☎ *07471/2428* ⊕ *www.
burg-hohenzollern.com* ⊠ *€10* ⊙ *Castle and shuttle bus mid-Mar.–Oct.,
daily 9–5:30; Nov.–mid-Mar., daily 10–4.*

Frankfurt

WORD OF MOUTH

"See the Alte Oper, the Jörg Rathgeb frescos in the Karmeliterkloster, the Jewish Holocaust Memorial Wall, the Jewish Ghetto Wall, the Kaiserdom, St. Leonhard, Alte Nikolaikirche, Eschenheimer Turm, the Bull and Bear, or visit Bornheim where there is a Farmers' Market and tons of little stores and cafés. Dinner is best over in Sachsenhausen's Apple wine pub district . . ."

—Mainhattengirl

WELCOME TO FRANKFURT

TOP REASONS TO GO

★ **Sachsenhausen:** Frankfurt's "South Bank"— with gourmet restaurants, fast food joints, live music establishments, and bars—is one big outdoor party in summer.

★ **Paleontology paradise:** Beyond a huge dinosaur skeleton, the Senckenberg Natural History Museum has exhibits of many other extinct animals and plants, plus dioramas of animals in their habitat.

★ **Enjoy the outdoors:** The parks and riverbanks are popular with locals and tourists for strolls, sunbathing, and picnics.

★ **Get some wheels:** Hop on and tour the city sites from your rented bike; you'll be in good company alongside locals.

★ **Exotic experience:** Go to the Frankfurt Zoo's exotarium where coral, fish, snakes, alligators, amphibians, insects, and spiders are on display.

1 City Center and Westend. Downtown Frankfurt includes the Altstadt (Old City), parts of which have been carefully restored after wartime destruction: the Zeil, allegedly Germany's number one "shop 'til you drop" mile: the Fressgass or "Gorge Street," and the bank district. The Westend is a mix of the villas of the prewar rich, a skyscraper extension of the business district and a popular place to live for the city's elite.

2 Sachsenhausen. Just across the river from downtown, Sachsenhausen is distinguished by the *Apfelwein* (apple wine) district and the Museumufer (Museum Riverbank). The apple wine district, now with every sort of restaurant and tavern, is one big party, especially in summer when the tables spill out onto the traffic-free streets. The Museum Riverbank has seven riverbank museums, practically next door to one another.

KEY

S	S-Bahn
i	Tourist information
U	U-Bahn

GETTING ORIENTED

Legend has it that the Frankish Emperor Charlemagne was chasing a deer on the Main's south bank when the animal plunged into the river and, to the emperor's amazement, crossed it with its head always above water. A stone ridge had made the river shallow at that point. That supposedly was the origin of Frankfurt (literally "Frankish Ford") as an important river crossing. Commerce flourished from then on and to this day Frankfurt is an important center of business and finance.

9

GERMAN SAUSAGES

The one thing you're guaranteed to find wherever your travels in Germany take you: sausages. Encased meats are a serious business here, and you could spend a lifetime working your way through 1,500 varieties of German sausages.

(above) Landjäger sausage; (lower right) Thüringer Rostbratwurst; (upper right) Frankfurter.

The tradition of making sausages goes back centuries. Not only was it a method to preserve food long before refrigeration, it was also the best way to use every last piece of precious meat. Sausage recipes go back for generations, and just like most German cooking, sausage types vary from region to region. There's also an abundance of ways to serve a sausage—grilled sausages are served up in a small roll, essentially just a sausage "holder," *Weisswurst* come to the table after a gentle bath in warm water, cured sausages are often served sliced, while other cooked sausages are dished up with sauerkraut. Germans don't mess around when it comes to their love for sausage, eating about 62 pounds of sausage per person each year.

—Tania Ralli

WEISSWURST ETIQUETTE

Bavarians are sticklers when it comes to eating Weisswurst, a delicate white sausage made with veal, bacon, lemon, and parsley. The casing is never eaten; to nosh it like a native, you want to *zuzeln* (suck) out the meat. Make a slit at the top, dunk it in sweet mustard, and suck out the insides. It's all right to slit and peel it as well.

FRANKFURTER

Once upon a time, the hotdog aspired to be a Frankfurter. In Germany this is no bland sausage to be doused in condiments like a ballpark frank—instead you'll immediately notice the snap of the Frankfurter's skin and a delicious smoky taste. Frankfurters are narrow by design, specifically to absorb as much flavor as possible during cold smoking. They're always served in a pair, and you should eat Frankfurters with your fingers, dipped in mustard.

THÜRINGER ROSTBRATWURST

This bratwurst dates back to 1613 and it's clear why it has stood the test of time: it's one of Germany's most delicious sausages. The *Rostbratwurst* is a mix of lean pork belly, veal, and beef, seasoned with herbs and spices. Most families closely guard their recipes, but they're known to add garlic, caraway, or nutmeg. You'll smell the scent of grilled *Thüringer* wafting through the streets because they're popular at street markets and festivals.

LANDJÄGER

This small, narrow and dense sausage is also sold in pairs. It's cured by air-drying, so it resembles a dry salami in color and texture. *Landjäger* are made of beef, sometimes with pork, and red wine and spices. Historically, fieldworkers and wine grape harvesters liked to eat these salty sausages. Landjäger keep

well, so they're a great snack to tuck in your backpack when you head out for a day of hiking in the mountains.

BLUTWURST

Sometimes called *Rotwurst* (red sausage), *Blutwurst* is a combination of ground pork, spices, and—the key ingredient—blood, fresh from the slaughter. After it's been cooked and smoked, the blood congeals, and the sausage takes on a dark hue and looks almost black. Depending on the region, it can be studded with bacon, pickled ox tongue, or potatoes. For most of its history Blutwurst has been considered a luxury item.

BOCKWURST

The sausage got its name when hungry students ordered it with a round of *Bockbier*, a style of beer, in Berlin in 1889. The sausage came from a nearby Jewish butcher, who made it with veal and beef. Bockwurst is a thick sausage seasoned with salt, white pepper, and paprika, in a natural casing. It's usually boiled and served hot, but it can also be grilled. It's one of Germany's most popular sausages, so you'll find it on menus all over the country.

9

Updated by
Dominika
Polatin

It's no wonder Frankfurt is Europe's financial center. The city's stock exchange, one of the half dozen most important in the world, was established in 1585, and the Rothschild family opened their first bank here in 1798. Although many consider Frankfurt more or less a gateway to their Europe travels, the city's rich culture and history, dining, and amusement options might just surprise you.

Standing in the center of the Römerberg (medieval town square), you'll see the city's striking contrasts at once. Re-creations of neo-Gothic houses and government buildings enfold the square, while just beyond them modern skyscrapers pierce the sky. The city cheekily nicknamed itself "Mainhattan," using the name of the Main River that flows through it to suggest that other famous metropolis across the Atlantic. Although modest in size (fifth among German cities, with a population of 688,492), Frankfurt is Germany's financial powerhouse. Not only is the German Central Bank (Bundesbank) here, but also the European Central Bank (ECB), which manages the euro. Some 300 credit institutions (more than half of them foreign banks) have offices in Frankfurt, including the headquarters of five of Germany's largest banks. You can see how the city acquired its other nickname, "Bankfurt am Main."

The long history of trade might help explain the temperament of many Frankfurters—competitive but open-minded. It's also one of the reasons Frankfurt has become Germany's most international city. Close to a quarter of its residents are foreign, including a large number of Turks, Italians, Eastern Europeans, and others who relocated here for business.

Because of its commercialism, Frankfurt has a reputation for being crass, cold, and boring. But people who know the city think this characterization is unfair. The district of Sachsenhausen is as *gemütlich* (fun, friendly, and cozy) as you will find anywhere. The city has world-class ballet, opera, theater, and art exhibitions; an important piece of Germany's publishing industry; a large university (35,000 students); and two of the three most important daily newspapers in Germany. There may not be that much here to remind you of the Old World, but there's a great deal that explains the success story of postwar Germany.

PLANNING

WHEN TO GO

The weather in Frankfurt is moderate throughout the year, though rather wet. Summers are mild with the occasional hot day and it rarely gets very cold in winter and hardly ever snows. As Frankfurt is one of the biggest trade fair cities in all of Europe, high season at all hotels is considered to be during trade shows throughout the year. Be sure to check dates to avoid paying premium price for a room or even finding a place to stay.

GETTING HERE AND AROUND

AIR TRAVEL

There are two airports with the name "Frankfurt": Flughafen Frankfurt Main (FRA), which receives direct flights from many U.S. cities and from all major European cities, and Frankfurt-Hahn (HHN), a former U.S. air base 112 km (70 mi) west of Frankfurt that handles some supercheap flights, mainly to and from secondary European airports.

Airport Contacts Flughafen Frankfurt Main ☎ *0800/234–5679* ⊕ *www. frankfurt-airport.de.* **Frankfurt-Hahn** ☎ *06543/509–113,* ⊕ *www.hahn-airport.de.*

AIRPORT TRANSFERS

Flughafen Frankfurt Main is 10 km (6 mi) southwest of the downtown area by the A5 autobahn and has its own railway station for the high-speed InterCity (IC) and InterCity Express (ICE) trains. Getting into Frankfurt from the airport is easy. S-bahn lines 8 and 9 run from the airport to downtown. Most travelers get off at the Hauptbahnhof (main train station) or at Hauptwache, in the heart of Frankfurt. Trains run at least every 15 minutes, and the trip takes about 15 minutes. The one-way fare is €3.80. A taxi from the airport into the City Center normally takes around 25 minutes (double that during rush hours). The fare is around €35. If driving a rental car from the airport, take the main road out of the airport and follow the signs reading "Stadt-mitte" (downtown).

Bohr Busreisen offers a regular bus service to and from Frankfurt-Hahn Airport. It leaves every hour to every 1½ hours, 3 am to 8 pm, from the south side of the Frankfurt Hauptbahnhof, with a stop 15 minutes later at the Terminal 1 bus station at Flughafen Frankfurt Main. The trip to Frankfurt-Hahn takes an hour and 45 minutes, and costs €13.

BUS AND SUBWAY TRAVEL

Frankfurt's smooth-running, well-integrated public transportation system (called RMV) consists of the U-bahn (subway), S-bahn (suburban railway), Strassenbahn (streetcars), and buses. Fares for the entire system, which includes an extensive surrounding area, are uniform, though they are based on a complex zone system. Within the time that your ticket is valid (one hour for most inner-city destinations), you can transfer from one part of the system to another.

Tickets may be purchased from automatic vending machines, which are at all U-bahn and S-bahn stations. Weekly and monthly tickets are sold at central ticket offices and newsstands. A basic one-way ticket for a ride in the inner zone costs €2.40 during the peak hours of 6 am–9 am and 4 pm–6:30 pm weekdays (€2.30 the rest of the time). There's also a reduced *Kurzstrecke* ("short stretch") fare of €1.50 the whole day. A day ticket for unlimited travel in the inner zones costs €6. If you're caught without a ticket, there's a fine of €40.

Some 200 European cities have bus links with Frankfurt, largely through Deutsche Touring. Buses arrive at and depart from the south side of the Hauptbahnhof and terminal 1 at the Frankfurt Main airport.

Bus Contacts Bohr Busreisen ☎ *0654/350190* ⊕ *www.omnibusse.bohr.de.* Deutsche Touring ✉ *Mannheimerstr. 15, City Center* ☎ *069/46092780* ⊕ *www. touring.de.* Verkehrsgesellschaft Frankfurt am Main (*Municipal Transit Authority*). ☎ *069/19449* ⊕ *www.vgf-ffm.de.*

CAR TRAVEL

Frankfurt is the meeting point of a number of major autobahns. The most important are A-3, running south from Köln and then on east to Würzburg and Nürnberg, and A-5, running south from Giessen and then on toward Heidelberg and Basel.

In Frankfurt, speeders are caught with hidden cameras, so be sure to stick to the speed limit. Tow trucks cruise the streets in search of illegal parkers. There are many reasonably priced parking garages around the downtown area and a well-developed "park-and-ride" system with the suburban train lines. The transit map shows nearly a hundred outlying stations with a blue "P" symbol beside them, meaning there is convenient parking there.

TAXI TRAVEL

Cabs are not always easy to hail from the sidewalk; some stop, whereas others will pick up only from the city's numerous taxi stands or outside hotels or the train station. You can always order a cab. Fares start at €2.75 (€3.25 in the evening) and increase by a per-kilometer (½ mi) charge of €1.65 (€1.35 after 10 km). Frankfurt also has Velotaxis, covered tricycles seating two passengers and a driver for sightseeing or getting to places on the traffic-free downtown streets. They charge €2.50 for the first kilometer, €1 for every additional kilometer.

Taxi Contacts Taxis ☎ *069/230–001.* Velotaxi ☎ *0700/8356–8294.*

TRAIN TRAVEL

EuroCity, InterCity, and InterCity Express trains connect Frankfurt with all German cities and many major European ones. The InterCity Express line links Frankfurt with Berlin, Hamburg, Munich, and a number of other major hubs. All long-distance trains arrive at and depart from the Hauptbahnhof, and many also stop at the long-distance train station at the airport.

Train Contacts Deutsche Bahn (*German Railways*) ☎ *01805/996–633* ⊕ *www. bahn.de.*

DID YOU KNOW?

The Main River is lined with paths on both sides that are popular places for recreation and relaxing. The paths even allow biking.

VISITOR INFORMATION

For advance information, write to the Tourismus und Congress GmbH Frankfurt–Main. The main tourist office is at Römerberg 27 in the heart of the Old Town. It's open weekdays 9:30–5:30 and weekends 10–4.

The airport's information office is on the first floor of Arrivals Hall B and open daily 6 am–10 pm. Another information office in the main hall of the railroad station is open weekdays 8 am–9 pm, weekends 9–6. Both can help you find accommodations.

Visitor Information **Tourismus und Congress GmbH Frankfurt/Main**
⊠ *Römerberg 27, Altstadt* ☎ *069/2123–8800* ⊕ *www.frankfurt-tourismus.de.*

DISCOUNTS AND DEALS

The Frankfurt tourist office offers a one- or two-day ticket—the Frankfurt Card (€8.90 for one day, €12.90 for two days)—allowing unlimited travel on public transportation in the inner zone, and to the airport. It also includes a 50% reduction on admission to 24 museums, the zoo, and the Palmengarten, and price reductions at some restaurants and stores.

TOURS

APPLE WINE EXPRESS TOUR

The one-hour Apple Wine Express (Ebbelwei Express) tour in a vintage streetcar is offered hourly weekends and some holidays. It gives you a quick look at the city's neighborhoods, a bit of Frankfurt history, and a chance to sample Apfelwein (a bottle, along with pretzels, is included in the €6 fare).

Contacts **Ebbelwei Express** ☎ *069/2132–2425* ⊕ *www.ebbelwei-express.com.*

BOAT TRIPS

Day trips on the Main River and Rhine excursions run from April through October and leave from the Frankfurt Mainkai am Eiserner Steg, just south of the Römer complex. ■ TIP→ The boats are available for private parties, too.

Contacts **Frankfurt Personenschiffahrt Primus-Linie** ⊠ *Mainkai 36, Altstadt* ☎ *069/133–8370* ⊕ *www.primus-linie.de.*

BUS TOURS

Two-hour city bus tours with English-speaking guides are offered by the Frankfurt Tourist Office throughout the year.

EXCURSION TOURS

On some Sundays, the Historische Eisenbahn Frankfurt runs a vintage steam train with a buffet car along the banks of the Main. The train runs from the Eiserner Steg bridge west to Frankfurt-Griesham and east to Frankfurt-Mainkur. The fare is €12.

Historische Eisenbahn Frankfurt ⊠ *Eiserner Steg, Altstadt* ☎ *069/436–093* ⊕ *www.frankfurt-historischeeisenbahn.*

WALKING TOURS

The tourist office's walking tours cover a variety of topics, including Goethe, Jewish history, apple wine, architecture, and banking. Tours can also be tailored to your interests. For an English-speaking guide, the group tour cost is €117.60 for up to two hours and prices vary depending on the type of tour.

Tour Contacts Tourismus und Congress GmbH Frankfurt/Main ☎ *069/2123–8800* ⊕ *www.frankfurt-tourismus.de.*

EXPLORING FRANKFURT

The Hauptbahnhof (main train station) area and adjoining Westend district are mostly devoted to business, as evidenced by the banks towering overhead. You'll find the department stores of the Hauptwache and Zeil a half-mile east of the station, and you'll want to avoid the drug-ridden red-light district southwest of the station. The city's past can be found in the Old Town's restored medieval quarter and in Sachsenhausen, across the river, where pubs and museums greatly outnumber banks.

CITY CENTER AND WESTEND

Frankfurt was rebuilt after World War II with little attention paid to the past. Nevertheless, important historical monuments can still be found among the modern architecture. The city is very walkable; its growth hasn't encroached on its parks, gardens, pedestrian arcades, or outdoor cafés. The riverbank paths make for great strolls or bike rides.

TOP ATTRACTIONS

Alte Oper (*Old Opera House*). Kaiser Wilhelm I traveled from Berlin for the gala opening of the opera house in 1880. Gutted in World War II, the house remained a hollow shell for 40 years while controversy raged over its reconstruction. The exterior and lobby are faithful to the original, though the remainder of the building is more like a modern multipurpose hall. ⊠ *Opernplatz 1, City Center* ☎ *069/13400* ⊕ *www. alteoper.de* Ⓜ *Alte Oper (U-bahn).*

OFF THE
BEATEN
PATH

Alter Jüdischer Friedhof (*Old Jewish Cemetery*). The old Jewish quarter is east of Börneplatz, a short walk south of the Konstablerwache, or east of the Römer U-bahn station. Partly vandalized in the Nazi era, the cemetery was in use between the 13th and 19th centuries and is one of the few reminders of prewar Jewish life in Frankfurt. A newer Jewish cemetery is part of the cemetery at Eckenheimer Landstrasse 238 (about 2½ km [1½ mi] north). ⊠ *Battonnstrasse 2, City Center* ☎ *069/2124–0000* 🖭 *Free* ⊙ *Sun.–Fri. 8:30–4:30* Ⓜ *Konstablerwache (U-bahn and S-bahn).*

Fressgass (*"Pig-Out Alley"*). Grosse Bockenheimer Strasse is the proper name of this pedestrian street, for which Frankfurters have given this nickname because of its amazing choice of delicatessens, wine merchants, cafés, and restaurants, offering everything from crumbly cheeses and smoked fish to vintage wines and chocolate creams. Ⓜ *Hauptwache (U-bahn and S-bahn), Alte Oper (U-bahn).*

★ **Goethehaus und Goethemuseum** (*Goethe's Residence and Museum*). The house where Germany's most famous poet was born in 1749 is furnished with many original pieces that belonged to his family, including manuscripts in his own hand. The original house was destroyed by

9

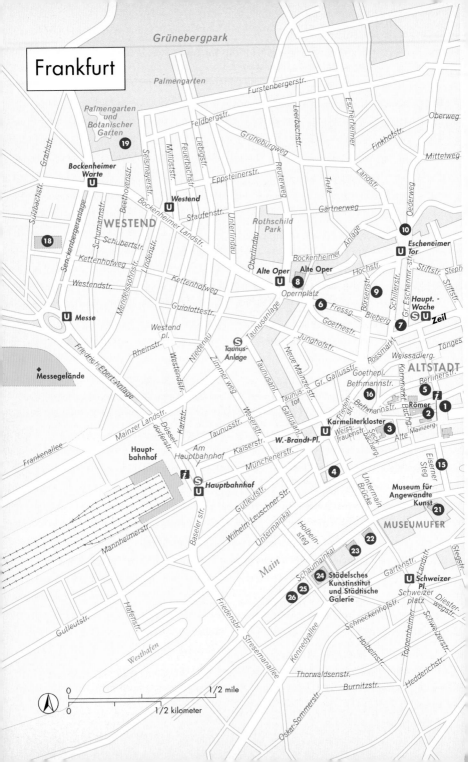

9

KEY

Ⓢ *S-Bahn*

🛈 *Tourist information*

Ⓤ *U-Bahn*

Geothe's House and Museum is filled with the manuscripts and paintings of Germany's best-loved poet.

Allied bombing and has been carefully rebuilt and restored in every detail.

Johann Wolfgang von Goethe studied law and became a member of the bar in Frankfurt. He was quickly drawn to writing, however, and in this house he eventually wrote the first version of his masterpiece, *Faust*. The adjoining museum contains works of art that inspired Goethe (he was an amateur painter) and works associated with his literary contemporaries. ⊠ *Grosser Hirschgraben 23–25, Altstadt* ☎ *069/138–800* ⊕ *www.goethehaus-frankfurt.de* 🎟 *€5* ⊙ *Mon.–Sat. 10–6, Sun. and holidays 10–5:30* Ⓜ *Hauptwache and Willy-Brandt-Platz (U-bahn and S-bahn).*

Jüdisches Museum (*Jewish Museum*). The story of Frankfurt's Jewish quarter is told in the former Rothschild Palais. Prior to the Holocaust, the community was the second largest in Germany. The museum contains a library of 5,000 books, a large photographic collection, and a documentation center.

   Museum Judengasse. This branch of the Jewish museum is built around the foundations of mostly 18th-century buildings, which once made up the Jewish quarter. The branch is also near the Alter Jüdischer Friedhof. ⊠ *Kurt-Schumacher-Str. 10, City Center* ☎ *069/297–7419* 🎟 *€2* ⊙ *Tues. and Thurs.–Sun. 10–5, Wed. 10–8* Ⓜ *Konstablerwache (U-bahn)* ⊠ *Untermainkai 14/15, Altstadt* ☎ *069/2123–5000* ⊕ *www.juedischesmuseum.de* 🎟 *€4* ⊙ *Tues. and Thurs.–Sun. 10–5, Wed. 10–8* Ⓜ *Willy-Brandt-Platz (U-bahn).*

★ **Kaiserdom.** Because the Holy Roman emperors were chosen and crowned here from the 16th to the 18th century, the church is known as the Kaiserdom (Imperial Cathedral), even though it isn't the seat of a bishop. Officially the Church of St. Bartholomew, it was built largely between the 13th and 15th century and survived World War II with the majority of its treasures intact. The most impressive exterior feature is the tall, red-sandstone tower (almost 300 feet high), which was added between 1415 and 1514. Climb it for a good view. The **Dommuseum** (Cathedral Museum) occupies the former Gothic cloister. ✉ *Domplatz 1, Altstadt* ☎ *069/1337–6184* ⊕ *www.dom-frankfurt.de* ✉ *Dommuseum €3* ⊘ *Church Mon.–Thurs. and Sat. 9–noon and 2:30–6, Fri. and Sun. 2:30–6. Dommuseum Tues.–Fri. 10–5, weekends 11–5* Ⓜ *Römer (U-bahn).*

Museum für Moderne Kunst (*Museum of Modern Art*). Austrian architect Hans Hollein designed this distinctive triangular building, shaped like a wedge of cake. The collection features works by artists such as Andy Warhol and Joseph Beuys. ✉ *Domstr. 10, City Center* ☎ *069/2123– 0447* ⊕ *www.mmk-frankfurt.de* ✉ *€8* ⊘ *Tues. and Thurs.–Sun. 10–6, Wed. 10–8* Ⓜ *Römer (U-bahn).*

☯ **Naturkundemuseum Senckenberg** (*Natural History Museum*). An impor-
★ tant collection of fossils, animals, plants, and geological exhibits is upstaged by the permanent dinosaur exhibit that is the most extensive of its kind in all of Germany and includes the famous diplodocus dinosaur, imported from New York—the only complete specimen of its kind in Europe. ■TIP➔ Many of the exhibits of prehistoric animals have been designed with children in mind, including a series of dioramas featuring stuffed animals. ✉ *Senckenberganlage 25, Bockenheim* ☎ *069/75420* ⊕ *www.senckenberg.de* ✉ *€6* ⊘ *Mon., Tues., Thurs., and Fri. 9–5, Wed. 9–8, weekends 9–6* Ⓜ *Bockenheimer Warte (U-bahn).*

☯ **Palmengarten und Botanischer Garten** (*Tropical Garden and Botanical Gardens*). A splendid cluster of tropical and semitropical greenhouses contains a wide variety of flora, including cacti, orchids, and palms. The surrounding park, which can be surveyed from a miniature train, has many recreational facilities, including a small lake where you can rent rowboats, a play area for children, and a wading pool. ■TIP➔ The Palmengarten offers free tours on a variety of topics on Sunday. In summer there's also an extensive concert program that takes place in an outdoor pavilion. ✉ *Siesmayerstr. 63, Westend* ☎ *069/2123–3939* ⊕ *palmengarten.frankfurt.de* ✉ *€5* ⊘ *Feb.–Oct., daily 9–6; Nov.–Jan., daily 9–4* Ⓜ *Westend (U-bahn).*

Paulskirche (*St. Paul's Church*). The first all-German parliament was held here in 1848. The parliament lasted only a year, having achieved little more than offering the Prussian king the crown of Germany. Today the church, which has been extensively restored, remains a symbol of German democracy and is used mainly for ceremonies. The most striking feature of the interior is a giant, completely circular mural showing an "endless" procession of the people's representatives into the Paulskirche. The work of Johannes Grützke, completed in 1991, it also shows such symbols as a mother and child, a smith to represent the common people, and a rejected crown. The plenary chamber upstairs is flanked by the flags of Germany, the 16 states, and the city of Frankfurt.

9

⊠ *Paulsplatz 11, Altstadt* ☎ *069/2123–8934* ⊙ *Daily 10–5* Ⓜ *Römer (U-bahn).*

Römerberg. This square north of the Main River, lovingly restored after wartime bomb damage, is the historical focal point of the city. The Römer, the Nikolaikirche, and the half-timber Ostzeile houses are all found here. The 16th-century Fountain of Justitia (Justice), which flows with wine on special occasions, stands in the center of the Römerberg. The square is also the site of many public festivals throughout the year, including the Christmas market in December. ⊠ *Between Braubachstr. and Main River, Altstadt* Ⓜ *Römer (U-bahn).*

Zeil. The heart of Frankfurt's shopping district is this bustling pedestrian street running east from Hauptwache Square. With mass consumerism in mind, it's lined with department stores, a few smaller boutiques, drugstores, cell-phone franchises, electronics shops, fast-food eateries, restaurants, and more. ■**TIP**→ **Stop in at the outdoor farmers' market every Thursday and Saturday for a freshly grilled Bratwurst and a beer.** Ⓜ *Hauptwache, Konstablerwache (U-bahn and S-bahn).*

Ⓒ **Zoologischer Garten** (*Zoological Garden*). Founded in 1858, this is one of
★ the most important and attractive zoos in Europe. Its remarkable collection includes some 4,500 animals of 500 different species, an exotarium (aquarium plus reptiles), a large ape house, and an aviary, reputedly the largest in Europe. Nocturnal creatures move about in a special section. ⊠ *Bernhard-Grzimek-Allee 1, Ostend* ☎ *069/2123–3735* ⊕ *www.zoo-frankfurt.de* 🎟 *€8* ⊙ *Nov.–Mar., daily 9–5; Apr.–Oct., daily 9–7* Ⓜ *Zoo (U-bahn).*

WORTH NOTING

Börse (*Stock Exchange*). This is the center of Germany's stock and money market. The Börse was founded in 1585, but the present domed building dates from the 1870s. These days computerized networks and international telephone systems have removed some of the drama from the dealers' floor, but it's still fun to visit the visitor gallery and watch the hectic activity. You must reserve your visit 24 hours in advance. ⊠ *Börsenplatz 4, City Center* ☎ *069/2110* ⊕ *www.boerse-frankfurt.de* 🎟 *Free* ⊙ *Visitor gallery weekdays 10–8* Ⓜ *Hauptwache (U-bahn and S-bahn).*

Eiserner Steg (*Iron Bridge*). A pedestrian walkway and the first suspension bridge in Europe, the Eiserner Steg connects the city center with Sachsenhausen and offers great views of the Frankfurt skyline. Excursions by boat and an old steam train leave from here. ⊠ *Mainkai, Frankfurt am Main.*

Eschenheimer Turm (*Eschenheim Tower*). Built in the early 15th century, this tower, a block north of the Hauptwache, remains the finest example of the city's original 42 towers. It now contains a restaurant–bar. ⊠ *Eschenheimer Tor, City Center* Ⓜ *Eschenheimer Tor (U-bahn).*

Hauptwache. The attractive baroque building with a steeply sloping roof is the actual Hauptwache (Main Guardhouse), from which the square takes its name. The 1729 building, which had been tastelessly added to over the years, was partly demolished to permit excavation for a

Climb to the top of Kaiserdom, officially called the Church St. Bartholomew, for a fantastic view of the city.

vast underground shopping mall. The building was then restored to its original appearance and is now considered the heart of the Frankfurt pedestrian shopping area. ■**TIP**→ The outdoor patio of the building's restaurant/café is a popular "people-watching" spot on the Zeil. ⊠ *An der Hauptwache 15, Frankfurt am Main* Ⓜ *Hauptwache (U-bahn and S-bahn).*

Karmeliterkloster (*Carmelite Monastery*). Secularized in 1803, the church contains the **Archaeologisches Museum** (Archaeological Museum), while the adjacent buildings house the city's Institut für Stadtgeschichte (Institute of History). The basement, titled "Die Schmiere" (The Grease), is a satirical theater.

Main cloister. The main cloister displays the largest religious fresco north of the Alps, a 16th-century representation of Christ's birth and death by Jörg Ratgeb. 🔄 *Free* ⊠ *Karmelitergasse 1, Altstadt* ☎ *069/2123–5896* ⊕ *www.archaeologisches-museum.frankfurt.de* 🔄 *Museum €6, free last Sat. of month* ⊙ *Tues.–Sun. 10 am–5 pm, Wed. 10–8. Closed Mon.* Ⓜ *Willy-Brandt-Platz (U-bahn).*

Römer (*City Hall*). Three individual patrician buildings make up the Römer, Frankfurt's town hall. The mercantile-minded Frankfurt burghers used the complex not only for political and ceremonial purposes but also for trade fairs and other commercial ventures. Its gabled facade with an ornate balcony is widely known as the city's official emblem.

The most important events to take place in the Römer were the festivities celebrating the coronations of the Holy Roman emperors. The first was in 1562 in the glittering **Kaisersaal** (Imperial Hall), which was last used in 1792 to celebrate the election of the emperor Francis II, who would later be forced by Napoléon to abdicate. Unless official business is being conducted you can see the impressive, full-length 19th-century portraits of the 52 emperors of the Holy Roman Empire, which line the walls of the reconstructed banquet hall. ⊠ *West side of Römerberg, Römerberg 27, Altstadt* ☎ *069/2123–4814* ✉ *€2* ⊘ *Daily 10–1 and 2–5; often closed for events, so check opening hrs before going* Ⓜ *Römer (U-bahn).*

Schirn Kunsthalle (*Schirn Art Gallery*). One of Frankfurt's most modern museums is devoted exclusively to changing exhibits of modern art and photography. The gallery is right beside the Kaiserdom and has a restaurant. ⊠ *Römerberg, Altstadt* ☎ *069/299–8820* ⊕ *www.schirn.de/* ✉ *Admission varies from €7 to €9 depending on exhibit.* ⊘ *Tues. and Fri.–Sun. 10–7, Wed. and Thurs. 10–10* Ⓜ *Römer (U-bahn).*

SACHSENHAUSEN

★ The old quarter of Sachsenhausen, on the south bank of the Main River, has been sensitively preserved, and its cobblestone streets, half-timber houses, and beer gardens make it a popular area to stroll. Sachsenhausen's two big attractions are the **Museumufer** (Museum Riverbank), which has nine museums almost next door to one another and offers beautiful views of the Frankfurt skyline, as well as the famous Apfelwein (apple wine or cider) taverns around the Rittergasse pedestrian area. You can eat well—and quite reasonably so—in these small establishments.

TOP ATTRACTIONS

☺ **Deutsches Filmmuseum** (*German Film Museum*). Germany's first museum of cinematography opened its doors again after a long renovation in the summer of 2011. Set in a historical villa on the river Main, the museum offers visitors a glimpse at the history of film with many clips, posters, and a little theater presenting the first filmed train ride and a "trip to the moon." Interactive exhibits show how films are photographed, given sound, and edited. A theater in the basement screens every imaginable type of film, from historical to avant-garde. ⊠ *Schaumainkai 41, Sachsenhausen* ☎ *069/9612–20220* ⊕ *www.deutschesfilmmuseum.de* ✉ *€2.50* ⊘ *Tues., Thurs., and Fri. 10–5, Sun. and Wed. 10–7, Sat. 2–7* Ⓜ *Schweizer Platz (U-bahn).*

Ikonen-Museum. The museum was opened in 1990 and is one of very few museums in the world to exhibit a wide spectrum of the Christian Orthodox world of images. The art and ritual of icons from the 15th to the 20th century are on display here and the collection has been expanded to more than 1,000 exhibits over the years. ⊠ *Brückenstrasse 3–7, Sachsenhausen, Frankfurt* ☎ *069/2123–6262* ✉ *€4* ⊘ *Tues.–Sun. 10–5, Wed. 10–8.*

Museum Giersch. This museum, set in a beautiful neoclassical villa along the strip of museums in Sachsenhausen, focuses on paintings from the 19th century and early 20th century of artists from the Rhine-Main region to showcase the area's diverse cultural landscape. ⊠ *Schaumainkai 83, Sachsenhausen, Frankfurt* ☎ *069/6314–8724* ✉ *€5* ⊘ *Tues.–Thurs. noon–7, Fri. noon–5, weekends 11–5.*

Sachsenhausen comes alive at night with a lively restaurant and bar scene.

★ **Städelsches Kunstinstitut und Städtische Galerie** (*Städel Art Institute and Municipal Gallery*). You'll find one of Germany's most important art collections at this museum, with paintings by Dürer, Vermeer, Rembrandt, Rubens, Monet, Renoir, and other masters. Opening in February 2012 is an addition to the museum, which will feature a large collection of works from contemporary artists. ■TIP→ The section on German Expressionism is particularly strong, with representative works by Frankfurt artist Max Beckmann. ⊠ *Schaumainkai 63, Sachsenhausen* ☎ *069/605–0980* ⊕ *www.staedelmuseum.de* ☒ *€14* ☉ *Tues. and Fri.–Sun. 10–6, Wed. and Thurs. 10–9* Ⓜ *Schweizer Platz (U-bahn).*

WORTH NOTING

Deutsches Architekturmuseum (*German Architecture Museum*). The Deutsche Architekturmuseum is housed in a late 19th-century villa, which was converted in the early 1980s to a design by Cologne-based architect Oswald Mathias Ungers. He created five levels from the simple basement space with its visible load-bearing structure to the walled complex of the ground floor and the complete house within a house on the third floor. The museum harbors a wealth of documents pertaining to the history of architecture and conducts contemporary debates on the future of the built environment. Each year, several major and numerous smaller exhibitions highlight issues in architectural history and current topics in architecture and urban design. A recently opened permanent exhibit features the most comprehensive collection of model panoramas in the history of German architecture. ⊠ *Schaumainkai 43, Sachsenhausen* ☎ *069/2123–8844* ⊕ *www.dam-online.de* ☒ *€7* ☉ *Tues. and Thurs.–Sat. 11–6, Sun, 11–7, Wed. 11–8* Ⓜ *Schweizer Platz (U-bahn).*

9

Museum für Angewandte Kunst (*Museum of Applied Arts*). More than 30,000 decorative objects are exhibited in this modern white building set back in grassy grounds. Chairs and furnishings and medieval craftwork are some of the thematic sections you'll find on the same floor. The exhibits come mainly from Europe and Asia. ✉ *Schaumainkai 17, Sachsenhausen* ☎ *069/2123–4037* ⊕ *www.museumfuerangewandtekunst. frankfurt.de* 🎫 *€8, free last Sat. of month* ⊙ *Tues. and Thurs.–Sun. 10–5, Wed. 10–9* Ⓜ *Schweizer Platz (U-bahn).*

Städtische Galerie Liebieghaus (*Liebig Municipal Museum of Sculpture*). The sculpture collection in this museum, from 5,000 years of civilizations and epochs, is considered one of the most important in Europe. Antiquity, the Middle Ages, the Renaissance, classicism, and the baroque are all represented. Some pieces are exhibited in the lovely gardens surrounding the house. ■TIP➜ Don't miss out on the freshly baked German cakes in the museum's café. ✉ *Schaumainkai 71, Sachsenhausen* ☎ *069/650–0490* ⊕ *www.liebieghaus.de* 🎫 *€9* ⊙ *Tues. and Fri.–Sun. 10–6, Wed. and Thurs. 10–9* Ⓜ *Schweizer Platz (U-bahn).*

WHERE TO EAT

Many international cuisines are represented in the financial hub of Europe. For vegetarians there's usually at least one meatless dish on a German menu, and substantial salads are popular, too (though often served with bacon). The city's most famous contribution to the world's diet is the *Frankfurter Würstchen*—a thin smoked pork sausage—better known to Americans as the hot dog. *Grüne Sosse* is a thin cream sauce of herbs served with potatoes and hard-boiled eggs. The oddly named *Handkäs mit Musik* (literally, "hand cheese with music") consists of slices of cheese covered with raw onions, oil, and vinegar, served with bread and butter (an acquired taste for many). There is the *Rippchen* or cured pork chop, served on a mound of sauerkraut, and the *Schlachtplatte*, an assortment of sausages and smoked meats. All these things are served with Frankfurt's distinctive drink, *Apfelwein* (apple wine, or hard cider).

Smoking is prohibited inside Frankfurt's bars and restaurants, but allowed in most beer gardens.

Use the coordinate (✥ C3) at the end of each listing to locate a site on the corresponding map.

WHAT IT COSTS IN EUROS				
¢	$	$$	$$$	$$$$
AT DINNER	under €9	€9–€15	€16–€20	€21–€25	over €25

Restaurant prices are per person for a main course at dinner.

BEST BETS FOR FRANKFURT DINING

With hundreds of restaurants to choose from, how will you decide where to eat? Fodor's writers and editors have selected their favorite restaurants by price, cuisine, and experience in the Best Bets lists here. In the first column, Fodor's Choice properties represent the "best of the best" in every price category. You can also search by neighborhood for excellent eats—just peruse our reviews on the following pages.

Zum Gemalten Haus, ¢, p. 390

BEST BEER GARDEN

Altes Zollhaus, $$, p. 390

Gerbermühle, $$, p. 391

GREAT VIEW

Frankfurter Botschaft, $$$, p. 384

Maintower, $$$$, p. 385

COCKTAILS

Eatdrinkmanwoman, ¢, p. 386

Maintower, $$$$, p. 385

Zenzakan, $$$$, p. 389

BRUNCH

El Pacifico, $, p. 386

Frankfurter Botschaft, $$$, p. 384

9

Fodor's Choice★

Erno's Bistro, $$$$, p. 387

Gargantua, $$$, p. 387

Maingau Stuben, $$$, p. 390

Surf'n Turf, $$$$, p. 389

By Price

¢

Pizza Pasta Factory, p. 390

Souper, p. 386

$

Adolf Wagner, p. 389

Omonia, p. 388

$$

Gerbermühle, p. 391

Holbeins, p. 390

$$$

Frankfurter Botschaft, p. 384

Maingau Stuben, p. 390

$$$$

Erno's Bistro, p. 387

Osteria Enoteca, p. 391

M Steakhouse, p. 388

Surf'n Turf, p. 389

Zenzakan, p. 389

By Cuisine

GERMAN

Steinernes Haus, $, p. 386

Zwölf Apostel, $, p. 386

FRENCH

Erno's Bistro, $$$$, p. 387

Gargantua, $$$, p. 387

ITALIAN

Osteria Enoteca, $$$$, p. 391

Pizza Pasta Factory, ¢, p. 390

CAFÉ

Café Laumer, ¢, p. 387

Neues Café Schneider, ¢, p. 385

ECLECTIC

Grössenwahn, $, p. 386

Long Island City Lounge, $$, p. 385

By Experience

BUSINESS DINING

Embassy, $, p. 384

Erno's Bistro, $$$$, p. 387

Surf'n Turf, $$$$, p. 389

APFELWEIN

Adolf Wagner, $, p. 389

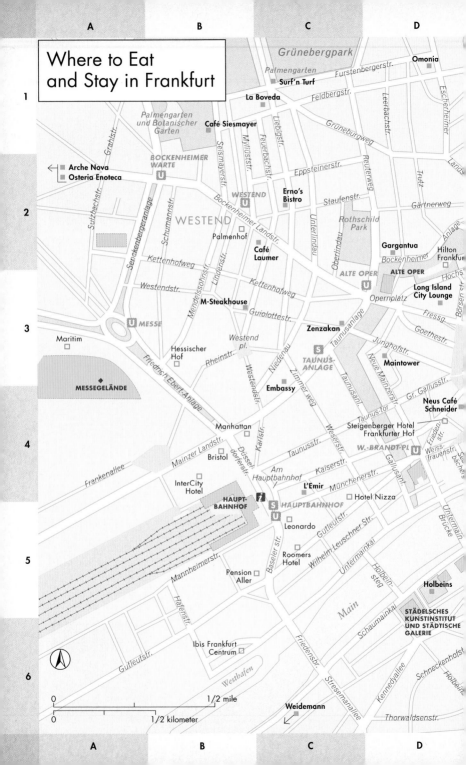

Where to Eat and Stay in Frankfurt

A **B** **C** **D**

1

Grünebergpark

Omonia

Palmengarten

Surf'n Turf

Furstenbergerstr.

Feldbergstr.

Eschenheimer

La Boveda

Palmengarten und Botanischer Garten

Café Siesmayer

Grüneburgweg

Leerbachstr.

Reuterweg

Landst

Trutz

← Arche Nova

Osteria Enoteca

Gratlstr.

BOCKENHEIMER WARTE

Seismayerstr.

Mylüsstr.

Lieblgstr.

Feuerbachstr.

Eppsteinerstr.

Grathstr.

2

Sulzbachstr.

Bockenheimer Landstr.

WESTEND

Erno's Bistro

Staufenstr.

Gärtnerweg

Anlage

WESTEND

Palmenhof

Unterlindau

Rothschild Park

Gargantua

Hilton Frankfur

Schumannstr.

Café Laumer

Oberlindau

Bockenheimer

Hochs

Kettenhofweg

ALTE OPER

ALTE OPER

Borsen str.

Westendstr.

Lindenstr.

Kettenhofweg

Long Island City Lounge

3

Mendelssohnstr.

M-Steakhouse

Guiolettstr.

Opernplatz

Fressg.

Maritim

MESSE

Hessischer Hof

Westend pl.

Zenzakan

Taunusanlage

Junghofstr.

Goethestr.

Rheinstr.

Niedenau

S

TAUNUS-ANLAGE

Neue Mainzer

Maintower

MESSEGELÄNDE

Friedrich-Ebert-Anlage

Westendstr.

Zimmerweg

Taunusanl.

Gr. Gallusstr.

4

Frankenallee

Mainzer Landstr.

Bristol

Karlstr.

Düsseldorfstr.

Embassy

Taunusstr.

Taunustor

Taunusstr.

Weserstr.

Steigenberger Hotel Frankfurter Hof

W.-BRANDT-PL

Neus Café Schneider

Friedens str.

Weissfrauenstr.

U

Manhattan

Am Hauptbahnhof

Kaiserstr.

L'Emir

Münchenerstr.

Hotel Nizza

Weiss

bächen

InterCity Hotel

HAUPT-BAHNHOF

i

S

HAUPTBAHNHOF

Untermain Brücke

5

Mannheimerstr.

Baseler str.

Leonardo

Gutleutstr.

Wilhelm Leuschner Str.

Untermainkai

Holbein

steg

Holbeins

Roomers Hotel

Pension Aller

Hafenstr.

Main

Schaumainkai

STÄDELSCHES KUNSTINSTITUT UND STÄDTISCHE GALERIE

Schneckenhofst

Holbein

6

Gutleutstr.

Ibis Frankfurt Centrum

Westhafen

Friedensbr.

Stresemannallee

Kennedyallee

Thorwaldsenstr.

0   1/2 mile

0   1/2 kilometer

Weidemann

A **B** **C** **D**

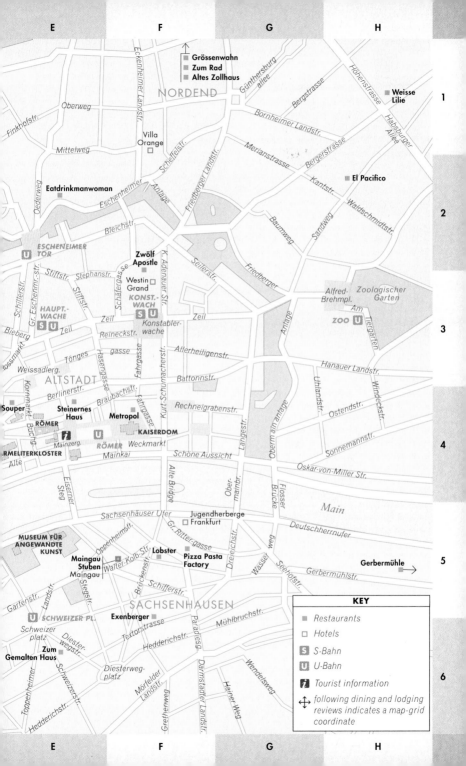

Don't leave Frankfurt without sampling a tall glass of Apfelwein (apple wine).

CITY CENTER

$
ECLECTIC
✕**Embassy.** Its location near many of the city's largest banks makes it a venue for business lunches, but it's also a popular spot for socializing. This modern restaurant, bar, and lounge attracts many young professionals for dinner and drinks. The moderately priced menu offers contemporary dishes, including pizzas, pastas, salads, steaks, duck, and a long list of appetizers. ⊠ *Zimmerweg 1(corner of Mainzer Landstr.), City Center* ☎ *069/7409–0844* ⊕ *www.embassy-frankfurt.de* ⊘ *Closed weekends* Ⓜ *Taunusanlage (S-bahn)* ✛ *C3.*

$$$
ECLECTIC
✕**Frankfurter Botschaft.** Frankfurt's Westhafen (West Harbor), once busy and commercial, has been transformed into a posh neighborhood of upscale apartments, a yacht club, and waterfront restaurants. One of the chicest is Frankfurter Botschaft, with a glass facade and a big terrace overlooking the Main River. Frankfurt's elite descend here for business lunches, a cocktail on the terrace at sunset, or the Sunday brunch. There is also a sandy beach area with folding chairs and umbrellas. The international food is mainly organic, and even the dinnerware is of a prize-winning design. ⊠ *Westhafenpl. 6–8, City Center* ☎ *069/2400–4899* ⊕ *www.frankfurter-botschaft.de* Ⓜ *Hauptbahnhof* ✛ *C6.*

$$
MIDDLE EASTERN
✕**L'Emir.** Near the main train station, L'Emir is about as authentically Lebanese as a place that serves alcohol can be. The atmosphere is right out of *One Thousand and One Nights*, with belly dancers performing every Friday and Saturday night urging patrons to join in. Those who are so inclined can retire to the lounge and smoke flavored tobacco from a water pipe. The exotic menu is largely vegetarian and heavy on garlic, olive oil, and lemon juice. The falafel is made from crushed beans and

Apfelwein

Cider it isn't. *Apfelwein* (apple wine), the quintessential Frankfurt drink, is more sour than sweet. To produce Apfelwein, the juice of pressed apples is fermented for approximately eight weeks. Its alcohol content of 5%–7% makes it a touch stronger than beer. Straight up, it is light and fizzy. You can also try it carbonated with seltzer (*Sauergespritzer*), or sweetened with lemonade (*Süssgespritzer*).

Apfelwein is drunk from a lattice-patterned glass called a *Gerippte*.

When among friends, it is poured from blue stoneware pitchers called *Bembels*, which range in size from big (a liter) to enormous (4 liters and up).

Popular throughout the state of Hesse, locals drink Apfelwein with pride. The largest concentration of Frankfurt's Apfelwein establishments is in the old neighborhood of Sachsenhausen. Look for establishments with a pine wreath hanging over the door; this signifies that Apfelwein is sold.

chickpeas, leeks, onions, parsley, coriander, peppermint, and more than 15 spices. ✉ *Ramada Hotel, Weserstr. 17, City Center* ☎ *069/2400–8686* ⊕ *www.lemir.de* ⚒ *Reservations essential* Ⓜ *Hauptbahnhof* ✚ *C4.*

$$ ✕ **Long Island City Lounge.** From Thursday to Saturday the bar here is
ECLECTIC just as popular as the restaurant, making this a prime spot for people-watching. The menu has a bit of everything: pasta, salads, seafood, vegetarian dishes, and German fare. ■TIP→ **Not far from the Alte Oper (Old Opera), this is an excellent choice for postconcert dining.** ✉ *Kaiserhofstr. 12, City Center* ☎ *069/9139–6146* ⊙ *Closed Sun.* Ⓜ *Hauptwache (U-bahn)* ✚ *D3.*

$$$$ ✕ **Maintower.** Atop the skyscraper that houses the Helaba Landesbank
GERMAN Hessen-Thüringen, this popular cocktail bar and gourmet restaurant
★ captures an unbeatable view. Through 25-foot floor-to-ceiling windows, you can take in all of "Mainhattan." The cuisine is part global, part regional. Dinner is a three- or five-course affair starting at €65 per person, not counting drinks or the €5 fee for the elevator. ✉ *Neue Mainzerstr. 52–58, City Center* ☎ *069/3650–4770* ⊕ *www.maintowerrestaurant.de* ⚒ *Reservations essential* ⊙ *Closed Mon.* Ⓜ *Alte Oper (U-Bahn) oder (S-Bahn) Taunusanlage* ✚ *D3.*

$ ✕ **Metropol.** Breakfast is the main attraction at this café near the Römer-
CAFÉ berg and Dom. The dining room is large, and in the warmer months it's extended to include seating on a garden patio. In addition to the daily selection of tantalizing cakes and pastries, the menu features salads, pastas, and a few traditional German dishes. If you're up late, remember the kitchen serves until 11 pm. ✉ *Weckmarkt 13–15, City Center* ☎ *069/288–287* ⊕ *www.metropolcafe.de* ⊟ *No credit cards* ⊙ *Closed Mon.* Ⓜ *Römer (U-bahn)* ✚ *F4.*

¢ ✕ **Neues Café Schneider.** Though it is no longer in the hands of the fam-
CAFÉ ily that had made it a Frankfurt fixture since 1906, Café Schneider's new owners are carrying on the tradition of cakes made in this beloved bakery. The bakery's output, which still includes chocolate creams, remains impressive, and they roast their own coffee. Soups, salads, and

9

mushroom toast are some of the lunch meals offered. ⊠ *Kaiserstr. 12, City Center* ☎ *069/281–447* ⊕ *www.wieners.de* ◷ *No dinner* Ⓜ *Willy-Brandt-Platz (U-bahn)* ✛ *D4.*

¢ ✗**Souper.** Hearty soups seem to be the favorite light lunch in Frank-
FAST FOOD furt these days. Although the bowls seem small for the price, the best selection can be found in this place near the Hauptwache. The daily selection may include such creations as Thai-style coconut chicken or lentil with sausage. Eat at the counter or take your soup and sandwich to go. ⊠ *Weissadlergasse 3, Altstadt* ☎ *069/2972–4545* ⊕ *www.souper.de* ▭ *No credit cards* ◷ *Closed Sun.* Ⓜ *Hauptwache (U-bahn and S-bahn)* ✛ *E4.*

$ ✗**Steinernes Haus.** Diners share long wooden tables beneath traditional
GERMAN clothing mounted on the walls. The house specialty is an uncooked steak brought to the table with a heated rock tablet on which it is prepared. The beef broth is the perfect antidote to cold weather. The menu has other old German standards along with daily specials. If you don't specify a *Kleines*, or small glass of beer, you'll automatically get a liter mug. ⊠ *Braubachstr. 35, Altstadt* ☎ *069/283–491* ⊕ *www.steinernes-haus.de* ⌂ *Reservations essential* Ⓜ *Römer (U-bahn)* ✛ *E4.*

$ ✗**Zwölf Apostel.** There are few inner-city restaurants that brew their
GERMAN own beer, and the Twelve Apostles is one of the pleasant exceptions. Enjoy homemade pilsners in the dimly lighted, cavernous cellar, and sample traditional international and Croatian dishes. Servings are large, prices are reasonable, and you can have a small portion at half price. ⊠ *Rosenbergerstr. 1, City Center* ☎ *069/288–668* ⊕ *www.12apostel.net* Ⓜ *Konstablerwache (U-bahn and S-bahn)* ✛ *F2.*

NORDEND/BORNHEIM

¢ ✗**Eatdrinkmanwoman.** The odd name comes from a film by acclaimed
ASIAN director Ang Lee that deals with relationships against a background of Chinese gourmet cooking. The big thing here is what might be called Asian tapas. Enjoy one of these small Pan-Asian dishes as a snack or combine three or four to a meal. The list of tapas is extensive, including chicken breast with orange-ginger sauce, salmon with mushrooms and curry sauce, and roast beef with pineapple. There's also a list of 150 cocktails. What purports to be the biggest aquarium in the city lines the walls. ⊠ *Jahnstr. 1, Nordend* ☎ *069/512–822* ⊕ *www.edmw.com* Ⓜ *Musterschule (U-bahn)* ✛ *E2.*

$ ✗**El Pacifico.** Some of Frankfurt's best Mexican cuisine is found in this
MEXICAN festive little place. Warm and colorful, this restaurant serves a variety of fruit-flavor margaritas and is well known for its hearty chicken-wings appetizer. The dimly lighted dining room is fairly small; reservations are recommended on weekends. It offers a good brunch on Sunday, but otherwise serves no lunch. ⊠ *Sandweg 79, Bornheim* ☎ *069/446–988* ⊕ *www.elpacifico.info* ◷ *No lunch* Ⓜ *Merianplatz (U-bahn)* ✛ *H2.*

$ ✗**Grössenwahn.** The Nordend is noted for its "scene" establishments,
ECLECTIC and this corner locale, which is often crowded, is one of the best. The name translates as "megalomania," which says it all. The menu is creative, with German, Greek, Italian, and French elements. ⊠ *Le-*

naustr. 97, Nordend ☎ *069/599–356* ⊕ *www.cafe-groessenwahn.de* ♣ *Reservations essential* Ⓜ *Glauburgstrasse (U-bahn)* ✤ *F1.*

¢ ✕**Weisse Lilie.** Come to this Bornheim favorite for the delicious tapas,
SPANISH paella, and other Spanish specialties, not to mention the reasonably
priced red wines. The dark interior has wooden tables brightened by
fresh-cut flowers and candles, making it a good spot for an intimate
dinner. In summer you can dine outside, German style, at long tables.
✉ *Berger Strasse 275, Bornheim* ☎ *069/453–860* ⊕ *www.weisse-lilie.*
com ♣ *Reservations essential* ⊗ *No lunch* Ⓜ *Bornheim Mitte (U-bahn)*
✤ *H1.*

WESTEND

¢ ✕**Café Laumer.** The ambience of an old-time Viennese café pervades
CAFÉ this popular spot, with a lovely summertime garden. It owes its literary tradition to Theodor Adorno, a philosopher and sociologist of the
Frankfurt School who dined here frequently, and serves some of the
city's best freshly baked cakes. The café is open for breakfast, lunch,
and afternoon coffee, but closes at 7 pm. ✉ *Bockenheimer Landstr. 67,*
Westend ☎ *069/727–912* ⊕ *www.cafe-laumer.de* ⊗ *No dinner* Ⓜ *West-*
end (U-bahn) ✤ *C2.*

$ ✕**Cafe Siesmayer.** This sleek establishment is at the Palmengarten, acces-
GERMAN sible either from the beloved botanical garden or from the street. It has
a terrace where you can enjoy your coffee and cake with a splendid
garden view. It is also a popular breakfast spot among locals and tourists alike, offering a full range of main courses; note the restaurant
closes at 7. ✉ *Siesmayerstr. 59, Westend* ☎ *069/9002–9200* ⊕ *www.*
palmengarten-gastronomie.de Ⓜ *Westend (U-bahn)* ✤ *B1.*

$$$$ ✕**Erno's Bistro.** This tiny, unpretentious place in a quiet Westend neigh-
FRENCH borhood seems an unlikely candidate for the best restaurant in Ger-
Fodor's Choice many. Yet that's what one French critic called it. The bistro's specialty,
★ fish, is often flown in from France. It's closed weekends, during the
Christmas and Easter seasons, and during much of summer—in other
words, when its patrons, well-heeled business executives, are unlikely
to be in town. ✉ *Liebigstr. 15, Westend* ☎ *069/721–997* ⊕ *www.*
ernosbistro.de ♣ *Reservations essential* ⊗ *Closed weekends and for 6*
wks during Hesse's summer school vacation Ⓜ *Westend (U-bahn)* ✤ *C2.*

$$$ ✕**Gargantua.** One of Frankfurt's most creative chefs, Klaus Trebes, who
FRENCH doubles as a food columnist, serves up modern versions of German
Fodor's Choice classics and French-accented dishes. His specialties include angel cod-
★ fish served with cabbage and a champagne-mustard butter, and stuffed
oxtail with mushrooms, onions, and a potato-celery puree. ■TIP➔One
corner of the restaurant is reserved for those who only want to sample
the outstanding wine list. ✉ *Park Gallery, An der Welle 3, Westend*
☎ *069/720–718* ⊕ *www.gargantua.de* ⊗ *Closed Sun. Open Sat. for*
private functions only. Ⓜ *Westend (U-bahn)* ✤ *D2.*

$$ ✕**La Boveda.** This quaint but somewhat expensive restaurant is tucked
SPANISH inside the dimly lighted basement of a Westend residential building.
(Appropriate, as the name means "wine cellar.") In addition to the
smaller plates of tapas, the menu features a long list of entrées. Especially interesting are the creative seafood combinations. And true to its

9

Riesling: Try It Dry

Germany's mild, wet climate and a wine-making tradition that dates back 2,000 years combine to produce some of the world's finest white wines.

The king of German varietals is Riesling. Grown on the banks of Germany's many rivers, most notably the Rhine, the grape produces wines of stunning variety and quality. Rieslings are noted for their strong acidity, sometimes-flowery aroma, and often mineral-tasting notes—stemming from the grape's susceptibility to influences from the soil. Riesling made its name throughout the world through sweet (*lieblich*) wines, but many Germans prefer them dry (*trocken*). Importers, especially in the United States, don't bring over many dry German Rieslings, so take the opportunity to sample some while in Frankfurt.

SIP IT HERE
The **Bockenheimer Weinkontor** (⌧ *Schlossstr. 92* ☎ *069/702-031* ⊕ *www.bockenheimer-weinkontor.de* Ⓜ *Bockenheimer Warte [U-bahn]*) is nearby the Messegelände (Exhibition Center), in the Bockenheim area. Through a courtyard and down a set of stairs, the cozy bar offers 15–20 reasonably priced local wines by the glass. The trellis-covered back garden is a treat.

For prestige wines, head to Piccolo (⌧ *Bornheimer Landstr. 56* ☎ *069/9441-1277* ⊕ *www.weinbar-piccolo.de* Ⓜ *Merianplatz [U-bahn]*), where the bilingual staff make solid recommendations. Try a glass from the Markus Molitor or Alexander Freimuth wineries. Along with wine, they serve a range of snacks and main courses. The space is small, so make reservations if you plan to dine here.

name, La Boveda offers an extensive wine menu. Reservations are recommended on weekends. ⌧ *Feldbergstr. 10, Westend* ☎ *069/723-220* ⊕ *www.la-boveda.de* ☾ *No lunch weekends* Ⓜ *Westend (U-bahn)* ✛ *C1.*

$$$$
STEAKHOUSE

✗ **M Steakhouse.** Set in the basement of an unsuspecting residential property in the Westend, many say the M-Steakhouse serves the best steak in Germany. A set of steps leads down into the restaurant's beautifully lighted outdoor patio, which is the perfect setting for a private romantic dinner. The main dining room inside is warm, welcoming, and offers an intimate setting for an unforgettable meal. The restaurant doesn't serve any seafood main courses, but why should it? The beef, imported from the United States, does not disappoint. The prices are quite reasonable for the quality of meat, and the sides complement the dishes perfectly. Although it opened back in 1998, the restaurant remains one of the most popular in Frankfurt. ▪TIP→ Be sure to make reservations and ask for a table on the patio in nice weather. ⌧ *Feuerbachstr. 11a, Westend, Frankfurt* ☎ *069/7103-4050* ☖ *Reservations essential* ☾ *Mon.–Fri. 12–3 pm and 6 pm–12 am; Sat. 6 pm–12 am* ✛ *C3.*

$
GREEK

✗ **Omonia.** This cozy cellar serves the city's best Greek cuisine. If you have a big appetite, try the Omonia Platter, with lamb cooked several ways and accompanied by Greek-style pasta. Vegetarians go for the *mestos sestos*, a plate of lightly breaded grilled vegetables served in a rich tomato-feta sauce. This family-owned place is popular, so make a reservation for one of the few tables. ✉ *Vogtstr. 43, Westend* ☎ *069/593–314* ⊕ *www.restaurant-omonia.de* ⌃ *Reservations essential* ⊘ *No lunch weekends* Ⓜ *Holzhausenstrasse (U-bahn)* ✛ *D1.*

$$$$
STEAKHOUSE
Fodor's Choice
★

✕ **Surf'n Turf.** The Mook Group's Surf'n Turf restaurant is a staple among businesspeople and steak connoisseurs alike. Set in a residential area near the Grüneburgpark, the restaurant's intimate and warm atmosphere is created by dark leather and wood paneling, as well as by the small tables scattered throughout the main dining room. Similar to the restaurant group's other steakhouse, the M Steakhouse, the beef is imported from Nebraska and each cut of meat is presented to guests before taking their orders. The waitstaff is knowledgeable, helpful, and friendly, making this a great place for a romantic dinner for two or for a casual business lunch. Highlights on the menu are the "tremendous truffle U.S. beef carpaccio" and the "yellowfin tuna tartare with wasabi guacamole." ✉ *Grüneburgweg 95, Westend, Frankfurt* ☎ *069/722–122* ⌃ *Reservations essential* ✛ *C1.*

$$$$
JAPANESE
★

✕ **Zenzakan.** Hailed as a Pan-Asian Supperclub, this large restaurant is as much a bar scene as a restaurant that is worth a visit. Buddha heads and Asian design–influences enhance the dining experience and create an exclusive ambience. The concept is unique and the food—especially the sushi—is exceptional. The sushi chef creates innovative maki such as the "Sexy Freak Wave Sake Roll" and is always on the search for something to add to the menu that will set it apart from others. One example is the rare and exclusive Mizubasho Sparkling Sake that he offers guests. The cocktails at the bar are equally innovative and include the Lemograss Martini and the Balsamic Touch. ✉ *Taunusanlage 15, Westend, Frankfurt* ☎ *069/9708–6908* ⌃ *Reservations essential* ⊘ *Closed for lunch and on Sun.* ✛ *C3.*

SACHSENHAUSEN

$
GERMAN

✕ **Adolf Wagner.** With sepia-tone murals of merrymaking, this Apfelwein classic succeeds in being touristy and traditional all at once. The kitchen produces the same hearty German dishes as other apple-cider taverns, only better. Try the schnitzel or the *Tafelspitz mit Frankfurter Grüner Sosse* (stewed beef with a sauce of green herbs), or come on Friday for fresh fish. Cider is served in large quantity in the noisy, crowded dining room. Warning: it serves no beer! ✉ *Schweizerstr. 71, Sachsenhausen* ☎ *069/612–565* ⊕ *www.apfelwein-wagner.com* Ⓜ *Schweizer Platz (U-bahn)* ✛ *E6.*

¢
FAST FOOD

✕ **Exenberger.** In many ways this place is typical of Old Sachsenhausen: apple wine and sauerkraut are served, there's no menu, and old sayings are written on the walls. But the interior is modern and the Frankfurt specialties are a cut above the rest. As proprietor Kay Exenberger puts it: "We're nearly as fast as a fast-food restaurant, but as gemütlich (quaint) as an apple wine locale must be." You order your food at the counter or by calling ahead, and everything can be wrapped up to go. It's so popular that reservations are advisable even at lunch. Many rave about the chocolate pudding with vanilla sauce. ✉ *Bruchstr. 14, Sachsenhausen* ☎ *069/6339–0790* ⊕ *www.exenberger-frankfurt.de* ⊟ *No credit cards* ⊘ *Closed Sun.* Ⓜ *Südbahnhof (U-bahn and S-bahn)* ✛ *F5.*

9

$$ ✕**Holbeins.** Portions are not large at this restaurant in the Städel
ECLECTIC   museum, but selections on the international menu are creative. Choose
from a variety of pastas, fish, steak, and even a few traditional German
dishes. Live piano (and sometimes jazz) is performed every evening
except Sundays. ⊠ *Holbeinstr. 1, Sachsenhausen* ☎ *069/6605–6666*
⊕ *www.holbeins.de* ⚿ *Reservations essential* ☉ *No lunch* Ⓜ *Schweizer
Platz (U-bahn)* ✛ *D5.*

$$ ✕**Lobster.** This small restaurant is a favorite of locals and visitors alike.
SEAFOOD   The menu, dramatically different from those of its neighbors, includes
mostly seafood. Fish and shellfish are prepared in a variety of styles,
but the strongest influence is French. ■**TIP➔** Contrary to the restaurant's
name, lobster does not appear on the menu, but is occasionally offered as a
special. Reservations are strongly recommended on weekends. ⊠ *Wall-
str. 21, Sachsenhausen* ☎ *069/612–920* ⊕ *www.lobster-weinbistrot.de*
☉ *Closed Sun. No lunch* Ⓜ *Schweizer Platz (U-bahn)* ✛ *F5.*

$$$ ✕**Maingau Stuben.** Chef Jörg Döpfner greets you himself and lights your
GERMAN   candle at this excellent restaurant. A polished clientele is drawn by the
Fodor's Choice   linen tablecloths, subdued lighting, and such nearly forgotten prac-
★   tices as carving the meat at your table. The menu includes asparagus
salad with homemade wild-boar ham and braised veal cheek with wild-
garlic risotto. The place also has a cellar full of rare German wines.
⊠ *Schifferstr. 38–40, Sachsenhausen* ☎ *069/610–752* ⊕ *maingau.de/de/
restaurant* ☉ *Closed Mon. No lunch Sat., no dinner Sun.* Ⓜ *Schweizer
Platz (U-bahn)* ✛ *F5.*

¢   ✕**Pizza Pasta Factory.** This restaurant started off with a theory: if you
ITALIAN   offer your food cheaply enough, you can make up the difference by sell-
ing a lot of it. So between 11:30 am and 4 pm and after 10 pm, this place
sells its pizzas and pastas (except lasagna) for only €3.80. There are 37
possible toppings, including some unlikely ones like pineapple, corn,
and eggs. ⊠ *Paradiesg. 67, Sachsenhausen* ☎ *069/6199–5004* ⊕ *www.
pizzapastafactory.de* ═ *No credit cards* Ⓜ *Lokalbahnhof (S-bahn)* ✛ *F5.*

¢   ✕**Zum Gemalten Haus.** There aren't many classic Apfelwein locales left,
GERMAN   but this is one of them. It's just as it has been since the end of the 19th
century: giant stoneware pitchers called *Bembels*, glasses that are ribbed
to give greasy hands traction, long tables that can seat 12 people in
kamaraderei, schmaltzy music, hearty food, and, as is traditional, no
beer. Try this one if you want to truly capture the spirit of Old Sach-
senhausen. ⊠ *Schweizerstr. 67, Sachsenhausen* ☎ *069/614–559* ⊕ *www.
zumgemaltenhaus.de* Ⓜ *Schweizer Platz (U-bahn)* ✛ *E6.*

OUTER FRANKFURT

$$ ✕**Altes Zollhaus.** Excellent versions of traditional German and interna-
GERMAN   tional specialties are served in this 230-year-old half-timber house on
the edge of town. If you're here in season, try a game dish. In summer
you can eat in the beautiful garden. To get here, take Bus 30 from
Konstablerwache to Heiligenstock, or drive out on Bundesstrasse 521
in the direction of Bad Vilbel. ⊠ *Friedberger Landstr. 531, Seckbach*
☎ *069/472–707* ⊕ *www.altes-zollhaus-frankfurt.de* ☉ *Closed Mon. No
lunch Tues.–Sat.* ✛ *F1.*

In summer, riverside bars and DJs spinning music are all part of the local scene.

$ **VEGETARIAN** ✕ **Arche Nova.** This sunny establishment is a feature of Frankfurt's Öko-haus, which was built according to environmental principles (solar panels, catching rainwater, etc.). It's more or less vegetarian, with such dishes as a vegetable platter with feta cheese or curry soup with grated coconut and banana. Much of what's served, even some of the beer, is organic. ✉ *Kasselerstr. 1a, Bockenheim* ☎ *069/707–5859* ⊕ *www.arche-nova.de* ▭ *No credit cards* Ⓜ *Westbahnhof (S-bahn)* ✛ *A2.*

$$ **GERMAN** ✕ **Gerbermühle.** So beautiful that it inspired works by Goethe, Frankfurt's favorite son and a frequent visitor, this beloved destination has come back to life after having closed for a time. Entrepreneurs have restored the 14th-century building and the century-long-plus tradition of hiking or biking to the chestnut-tree-shaded, riverside beer garden has returned. The garden is as nice as ever, and there's an indoor restaurant, hotel rooms, an attractive bar with the original stone walls, and even a bust of Goethe. An hour eastward down the Main's south bank, the place is so remote it is difficult to reach with public transportation. ✉ *Gerbermühlestr. 105, Oberrad* ☎ *069/6897–7790* ⊕ *www.gerbermuehle.de* ⊗ *Open daily 11:30 am–11 pm* ✛ *H5.*

$$$$ **ITALIAN** ✕ **Osteria Enoteca.** You don't have to go to Italy to enjoy the best of *haute cuisine alla italiana*. This place is small, crowded, and some even say stuffy, but it draws well-heeled gourmets from far and wide. The Sicilian chef, Carmelo Greco, has won a galaxy of stars from the critics for his Italian classics. The first dish he created, a Parmesan flan, remains his favorite. The wine cellar and vast choice of cheeses are renowned. ✉ *Arnoldshainerstr. 2, Rödelheim* ☎ *069/789–2216* ⊕ *www.osteria-enoteca.de* ⟿ *Reservations essential* Ⓜ *Rödelheim (S-bahn)* ✛ *A2.*

9

$$$$ ✕ **Weidemann.** In a half-timber farmhouse dating from the 19th century,
CONTINENTAL   the Weidemann is set in a quiet neighborhood across the river from
downtown. It's little wonder that business executives and gourmets have
discovered this inviting place with a chestnut-tree-shaded beer garden
and a glassed-in winter garden. Customers are cordially greeted by proprietor Angelo Vega, a Spaniard who has set out to prove to Germans
that there's a lot more to his country's cuisine than tapas and gazpacho.
He has won a steady clientele with imaginative versions of Spanish,
French, Italian, and other Mediterranean dishes. ⊠ *Kelsterbacher Str.
66, Niederrad* ☎ *069/675–996* ⊕ *www.weidemann-online.de* ☉ *Closed
Sun.* Ⓜ *Odenwaldstr. (streetcar)* ✚ *C6.*

$ ✕ **Zum Rad.** Named for the huge *Rad* (wagon wheel) that serves as
GERMAN   a centerpiece, this is one of the few Apfelwein taverns in Frankfurt
that makes its own apple wine. It's located in the villagelike district
of Seckbach, on the northeastern edge of the city. Outside tables are
shaded by chestnut trees in an extensive courtyard. The typically Hessian cuisine, with giant portions, includes such dishes as *Ochsenbrust*
(brisket of beef) with the ubiquitous herb sauce. Take the U-4 subway
to Seckbacher Landstrasse, then Bus 43 to Draisbornstrasse. ⊠ *Leon-
hardsg. 2, Seckbach* ☎ *069/479–128* ⊕ *www.zum-rad.de* ▭ *No credit
cards* ☉ *Closed Tues. No dinner Sun. and holidays* ✚ *F1.*

WHERE TO STAY

For expanded hotel reviews, visit Fodors.com.

Businesspeople descend on Frankfurt year-round, so most hotels in the
city are frequently booked up well in advance and are expensive (though
many offer significant reductions on weekends). Many hotels add as
much as a 50% surcharge during trade fairs (*Messen*), of which there
are about 30 a year. The majority of the larger hotels are close to the
main train station, fairgrounds, and business district (Bankenviertel).
The area around the station has a reputation as a red-light district, but
is well policed. More atmosphere is found at smaller hotels and pensions in the suburbs; the efficient public transportation network makes
them easy to reach.

*Use the coordinate (✚ C3) at the end of each listing to locate a site on
the corresponding map.*

WHAT IT COSTS IN EUROS				
¢	$	$$	$$$	$$$$
FOR TWO PEOPLE	under €50	€50–€100	€101–€175	€176–€225	over €225

Hotel prices are for two people in a standard double room, including tax and
service.

BEST BETS FOR FRANKFURT LODGING

Fodor's offers a selective listing of quality lodging experiences in every price range, from the city's best budget beds to its most sophisticated luxury hotels. Here, we've compiled our top recommendations by price and experience. The very best properties—in other words, those that provide a particularly remarkable experience in their price range—are designated in the listings with the Fodor's Choice logo.

Fodor's Choice★

Hilton Frankfurt, $$$$, p. 394
InterCity Hotel, $, p. 394
Steigenberger Hotel Frankfurter Hof, $$$$, p. 396
Roomers Hotel, $$$, p. 396

By Price

¢

Jugendherberge Frankfurt, p. 397
Pension Aller, p. 396

$

Ibis Frankfurt Centrum, p. 394

InterCity Hotel, p. 394

$$

Hotel Nizza, p. 394
Maritim, p. 396

$$$

Palmenhof, p. 396
Roomers Hotel, p. 396
Westin Grand, p. 397

$$$$

Hilton Frankfurt, p. 394
Steigenberger Hotel Frankfurter Hof, p. 396

By Experience

BEST INTERIOR DESIGN

Hessischer Hof, $$$$, p. 394
Hotel Nizza, $$, p. 394
Roomers Hotel, $$$, p. 396

BEST FOR BUSINESS TRAVEL

Hilton Frankfurt, $$$$, p. 394
InterCity Hotel, $, p. 394
Lindner Congress Hotel, $, p. 408
Roomers Hotel, $$$, p. 396

BEST OLD WORLD ELEGANCE

Palmenhof, $$$, p. 396
Steigenberger Hotel Frankfurter Hof, $$$$, p. 396

BEST ANTIQUE FURNISHINGS

Hessischer Hof, $$$$, p. 394
Hotel Nizza, $$, p. 394

BEST VIEW

Maritim, $$, p. 396

QUIETEST LOCATION

Ibis Frankfurt Centrum, $, p. 394
Villa Orange, $$, p. 396

BEST HOTEL BARS

Hessischer Hof, $$$$, p. 394

BEST ALL-NIGHT BARS

Bristol, $$, p. 394
Ibis Frankfurt Centrum, $, p. 394
Roomers Hotel, $$$, p. 396

BEST NEAR TRAIN STATION

Bristol, $$, p. 394
InterCity Hotel, $, p. 394

BEST NEAR SACHSENHAUSEN

Jugendherberge Frankfurt, ¢, p. 397
Maingau, $, p. 397

9

CITY CENTER, NORDEND, AND WESTEND

$$ ⊡ **Bristol.** You'll notice that great attention is paid to making you comfortable at the Bristol, one of the nicest hotels in the neighborhood around the main train station. **Pros:** bar is open 24 hours; beautiful garden patio. **Cons:** the neighborhood isn't appealing; small rooms. ⊠ *Ludwigstr. 15, City Center* ☎ *069/242–390* ⊕ *www.bristol-hotel.de* ⌨ *145 rooms* ⚙ *In-room: no a/c, Internet, Wi-Fi. In-hotel: bar, parking* ¶⊙¶ *Breakfast* Ⓜ *Hauptbahnhof (U-bahn and S-bahn)* ⊹ *B4.*

$$$$ ⊡ **Hessischer Hof.** This is the choice of many businesspeople, not just for its location across from the convention center but also for the air of class that pervades its handsome interior. **Pros:** close to the convention center and public transportation; site of Jimmy's, one of the town's cult bars. **Cons:** far from the stores and theaters; lobby can be crowded. ⊠ *Friedrich-Ebert-Anlage 40, Messe* ☎ *069/75400* ⊕ *www.hessischer-hof.de* ⌨ *110 rooms, 7 suites* ⚙ *In-room: a/c, Internet. In-hotel: restaurant, bar, parking, some pets allowed* Ⓜ *Messe (S-bahn)* ⊹ *B3.*

$$$$ ⊡ **Hilton Frankfurt.** This international chain's downtown Frankfurt out-
Fodor's Choice post has all the perks the business traveler wants, from secretarial ser-
★ vices to video conferencing facilities. **Pros:** child-friendly facilities and a large terrace overlooking a park. **Cons:** expensive rates; small bathrooms. ⊠ *Hochstr. 4, City Center* ☎ *069/133–8000* ⊕ *www.frankfurt.hilton.com* ⌨ *342 rooms* ⚙ *In-room: a/c, Internet, Wi-Fi. In-hotel: restaurant, bar, pool, gym, business center, parking, some pets allowed* Ⓜ *Eschenheimer Tor (U-bahn)* ⊹ *D2.*

$$ ⊡ **Hotel Nizza.** This beautiful Victorian building, a five-minute walk from
★ the main train station, is filled with antiques. **Pros:** antique furnishings; roof garden with shrubbery and a view of the skyline. **Cons:** the hotel is in the Bahnhof district, which can be a bit seedy at night. ⊠ *Elbestr. 10, City Center* ☎ *069/242–5380* ⊕ *www.hotelnizza.de* ⌨ *26 rooms* ⚙ *In-room: no a/c, Wi-Fi. In-hotel: bar, some pets allowed* ¶⊙¶ *Breakfast* Ⓜ *Willy-Brandt-Platz (U-bahn and S-bahn) or Hauptbahnhof (U-bahn and S-bahn)* ⊹ *C4.*

$ ⊡ **Ibis Frankfurt Centrum.** The Ibis is a reliable budget hotel that underwent a complete renovation at the end 2010 and offers simple, clean rooms on a quiet street near the river. **Pros:** short walk from the station and museums; 24-hour bar. **Cons:** far from stores and theaters. ⊠ *Speicherstr. 4, City Center* ☎ *069/273–030* ⊕ *www.ibishotel.com* ⌨ *233 rooms* ⚙ *In-room: a/c, Internet, Wi-Fi. In-hotel: bar, parking* Ⓜ *Hauptbahnhof (U-bahn and S-bahn)* ⊹ *B6.*

$ ⊡ **InterCity Hotel.** If there ever was a hotel at the vortex of arrivals and
Fodor's Choice departures, it's this centrally located one in an elegant Old World build-
★ ing across the street from the main train station. **Pros:** free passes for local transportation. **Cons:** overlooks a cargo facility. ⊠ *Poststr. 8, Bahnhof* ☎ *069/273–910* ⊕ *www.intercityhotel.com* ⌨ *384 rooms, 2 suites* ⚙ *In-room: a/c, Internet, Wi-Fi. In-hotel: restaurant, bar, gym, business center, some pets allowed* ¶⊙¶ *Breakfast* Ⓜ *Hauptbahnhof (U-bahn and S-bahn)* ⊹ *B4.*

$ ⊡ **Leonardo.** Across the street from the main train station, this modern, sparkling-clean hotel has its own underground garage. **Pros:** underground garage; quiet summer garden. **Cons:** on a busy street; in the

Hilton Frankfurt;

Steigenberger Hotel Frankfurter Hof

red-light district. ✉ *Münchenerstr. 59, City Center* ☎ *069/242–320* ⊕ *www.leonardo-hotels.com* ⤺ *106 rooms* ⚫ *In-room: no a/c, Wi-Fi. In-hotel: business center, parking* ⍾◉⍽ *Breakfast* Ⓜ *Hauptbahnhof (U-bahn and S-bahn)* ✛ *C5.*

$ ⚏ **Manhattan.** Get to all parts of town quickly from this centrally located hotel. **Pros:** opposite the main train station. **Cons:** no restaurant; in the red-light district. ✉ *Düsseldorferstr. 10, City Center* ☎ *069/269–5970* ⊕ *www.manhattan-hotel.com* ⤺ *60 rooms* ⚫ *In-room: no a/c. In-hotel: bar, business center* ⍾◉⍽ *Breakfast* Ⓜ *Hauptbahnhof (U-bahn and S-bahn)* ✛ *B4.*

$$ ⚏ **Maritim.** It's so close to the Messegelände (Exhibition Center) that you can reach the exhibition halls, as this top-notch business hotel puts it, "with dry feet." **Pros:** direct access to the convention center. **Cons:** expensive rates; hectic during fairs. ✉ *Theodor-Heuss-Allee 3, Messe* ☎ *069/75780* ⊕ *www.maritim.de* ⤺ *519 rooms, 24 suites* ⚫ *In-room: a/c, Internet, Wi-Fi. In-hotel: restaurant, bar, pool, gym, spa, laundry facilities, business center, parking, some pets allowed* Ⓜ *Messe (S-bahn)* ✛ *A3.*

$$$ ⚏ **Palmenhof.** This luxuriously modern hotel, in the same family for three generations, occupies a renovated art nouveau building dating from 1890. **Pros:** near the Palmengarten; less expensive than similar hotels. **Cons:** no restaurant; top floor can get very hot. ✉ *Bockenheimer Landstr. 89–91, Westend* ☎ *069/753–0060* ⊕ *www.palmenhof.com* ⤺ *45 rooms, 37 apartments, 1 suite* ⚫ *In-room: no a/c, Internet. In-hotel: parking, some pets allowed* ⍾◉⍽ *Breakfast* Ⓜ *Westend (U-bahn)* ✛ *B2.*

¢   ⚏ **Pension Aller.** Quiet, solid comforts come with a modest price and friendly welcome at this pension near the river. **Pros:** economical; near the station. **Cons:** need to reserve well in advance. ✉ *Gutleutstr. 94, City Center* ☎ *069/252–596* ⊕ *www.pension-aller.de* ⤺ *10 rooms* ⚫ *In-room: no a/c, Internet. In-hotel: some pets allowed* ▭ *No credit cards* ⍾◉⍽ *Breakfast* Ⓜ *Hauptbahnhof (U-bahn and S-bahn)* ✛ *B5.*

$$$ ⚏ **Roomers Hotel.** This lively and exclusive designer hotel conceptual-
Fodor'sChoice   ized by architect Oana Rosen features modern and sleek, yet eclectic
★   designs everywhere you look. ■TIP→ Grab a cocktail in the hotel bar between 5 and 9 pm and you'll receive a variety of complimentary appetizers for each drink order. ✉ *Gutleutstr. 85, Gutleutviertel, Frankfurt* ☎ *069/271–3420* ⤺ *116 rooms* ⚫ *In-room: a/c, Wi-Fi. In-hotel: restaurant, bar, gym* ✛ *C5.*

$$$$ ⚏ **Steigenberger Hotel Frankfurter Hof.** The neo-Gothic Frankfurter Hof
Fodor'sChoice   is the first lady of Frankfurt hotellerie, the choice of visiting heads
★   of state and business moguls. **Pros:** old-fashioned elegance; burnished wood floors; fresh flowers; thick carpeting. **Cons:** expensive rates. ✉ *Am Kaiserplatz, City Center* ☎ *069/21502* ⊕ *www.frankfurter-hof. steigenberger.de* ⤺ *280 rooms, 41 suites* ⚫ *In-room: a/c, Internet, Wi-Fi. In-hotel: restaurant, bar, business center, parking, some pets allowed* Ⓜ *Willy-Brandt-Platz (U-bahn)* ✛ *D4.*

$$ ⚏ **Villa Orange.** The moderately priced rooms at this bright, charm-ing hotel include canopy beds and spacious bathrooms. **Pros:** centrally located; on a quiet residential street; all rooms are smoke-free. **Cons:**

hard beds. ⊠ *Hebelstr. 1, Nordend* ☎ *069/405–840* ⊕ *www.villa-orange.de* ⤳ *38 rooms* ⚒ *In-room: Internet. In-hotel: bar, parking* ⏽◯⏽ *Breakfast* Ⓜ *Musterschule (U-bahn)* ✛ *F1.*

$$$ ▦ **Westin Grand.** Those who like downtown Frankfurt will appreciate the Westin's location, just steps from the famous Zeil shopping street. **Pros:** every luxury; handy to downtown. **Cons:** on a noisy street. ⊠ *Konrad Adenauer Str. 7, City Center* ☎ *069/29810* ⊕ *www.westingrandfrankfurt.com* ⤳ *371 rooms* ⚒ *In-room: a/c, Internet. In-hotel: restaurant, bar, pool, gym, spa, business center, parking, some pets allowed* Ⓜ *Konstablerwache (U-bahn and S-bahn)* ✛ *F3.*

SACHSENHAUSEN

¢   ▦ **Jugendherberge Frankfurt.** This combination youth hostel and family hotel offers clean, inexpensive, and very central accommodations in what is usually a pricey city. **Pros:** inexpensive; private rooms available; no smoking. **Cons:** basic rooms. ⊠ *Deutschherrnufer 12, Sachsenhausen* ☎ *069/610–0150* ⊕ *www.jugendherberge-frankfurt.de* ⤳ *110 rooms* ⚒ *In-room: no a/c, no TV. In-hotel: restaurant* ⏽◯⏽ *Breakfast* Ⓜ *Lokalbahnhof (S-bahn)* ✛ *F5.*

$ ▦ **Maingau.** You'll find this pleasant hotel and restaurant in the middle of the lively Sachsenhausen quarter. **Pros:** handy to Sachsenhausen nightlife; fantastic restaurant. **Cons:** on a busy street. ⊠ *Schifferstr. 38–40, Sachsenhausen* ☎ *069/609–140* ⊕ *www.maingau.de* ⤳ *78 rooms* ⚒ *In-room: no a/c. In-hotel: restaurant, some pets allowed* ⏽◯⏽ *Breakfast* Ⓜ *Schweizer Platz (U-bahn)* ✛ *F5.*

NIGHTLIFE AND THE ARTS

THE ARTS

The Städtische Bühnen—municipal theaters, including the city's opera company—are the prime venues for Frankfurt's cultural affairs. The city has what is probably the most lavish theater in the country, the Alte Oper, a magnificently ornate 19th-century opera house. (The building is no longer used for opera, which is presented at the Städtische Bühnen.) It's now a multipurpose hall for pop and classical concerts, and dances.

Best Tickets. Theater tickets can be purchased from Best Tickets downtown in the Zeilgalerie. ⊠ *Zeil 112–114, City Center* ☎ *069/9139–7621* ⊕ *www.journal-ticketshop.de* ⊗ *Mon.–Sat. 10–8.*

Frankfurt Ticket. Frankfurt Ticket sells theater, concert, and sports event tickets. ⊠ *Hauptwache Passage, City Center* ☎ *069/134–0400* ⊕ *www.frankfurtticket.de.*

BALLET, CONCERTS, AND OPERA

Alte Oper. The most glamorous venue for classical-music concerts is the Alte Oper; tickets to performances can range from €20 to nearly €150. ⊠ *Opernpl., City Center* ⊗ *Weekdays 10–2.*

Frankfurt Opera. The Frankfurt Opera has made a name for itself as a company for dramatic artistry. Richard Wagner and Richard Strauss

The elegant illumination of the Alte Oper (Old Opera House) and fountain make for magical nighttime viewing.

both oversaw their own productions here. ⊠ *Städtische Bühnen, Unter-mainanlage 11, City Center* ☎ *069/2124–9494.*

Bockenheimer Depot. A slimmed-down version of Frankfurt's once-acclaimed ballet company still performs in the Bockenheimer Depot, a former trolley barn also used for other theatrical performances and music events. ⊠ *Carlo-Schmidt-Pl. 1, Bockenheim.*

Festhalle. The Festhalle, on the fairgrounds, is the scene of many rock concerts, horse shows, ice shows, sporting events, and other large-scale spectaculars. Tickets are available through Frankfurt Ticket. ⊠ *Ludwig-Erhard-Anlage 1, Messe* ☎ *069/9200–9213.*

Kammermusiksaal. The city is also the home of the Radio-Sinfonie-Orchester Frankfurt, part of Hessischer Rundfunk. Considered one of Europe's best orchestras, it performs regularly in the 850-seat Kammer-musiksaal, part of that broadcasting operation's campuslike facilities. ⊠ *Bertramstr. 8, Dornbusch* ☎ *069/155–2000.*

THEATER

Theatrical productions in Frankfurt are usually in German.

Die Schmiere. For a zany theatrical experience, try Die Schmiere, which offers trenchant satire and also disarmingly calls itself "the worst the-ater in the world." The theater is closed in summer for a "creative break." ⊠ *Seckbächergasse 4, City Center* ☎ *069/281–066* ⊕ *www.die-schmiere.de.*

English Theatre. For English-language productions, try the English The-ater, continental Europe's largest English-speaking theater, which offers an array of musicals, thrillers, dramas, and comedy with British or

American casts. ☒ *Gallusanlage 7, City Center* ☎ *069/2423–1620* ⊕ *www.English-theatre.org.*

Internationales Theater Frankfurt. The Internationales Theater Frankfurt bills itself as presenting "the art of the world on the Main." It also has regular performances in English, as well as in German, French, Spanish, Italian, Romanian, and Russian. ☒ *Hanauer Landstr. 7, Ostend* ☎ *069/499–0980* ⊕ *www.internationales-theater.de.*

Künstlerhaus Mousonturm. The Künstlerhaus Mousonturm is a cultural center that hosts a regular series of concerts of all kinds, as well as plays, dance performances, and exhibits. ☒ *Waldschmidtstr. 4, Nordend* ☎ *069/4058–9520* ⊕ *www.mousonturm.de.*

Schauspielhaus. The municipally owned Schauspielhaus has a repertoire including works by Sophocles, Goethe, Shakespeare, Brecht, and Beckett. ☒ *Willy-Brandt-Pl., Neue Mainzer Strasse 17, City Center* ☎ *069/2124–9494* ⊕ *www.schauspielfrankfurt.de.*

NIGHTLIFE

Sachsenhausen (Frankfurt's "Left Bank") is a good place to start for bars, clubs, and Apfelwein taverns. The ever-more-fashionable Nordend has an almost equal number of bars and clubs but fewer tourists. Frankfurt was a real pioneer in the German jazz scene, and also has done much for the development of techno music. Jazz musicians make the rounds from smoky backstreet cafés all the way to the Old Opera House, and the local broadcaster Hessischer Rundfunk sponsors the German Jazz Festival in fall. The Frankfurter Jazzkeller has been the most noted venue for German jazz fans for decades.

Most bars close between 2 am and 4 am. Most dance and nightclubs charge entrance fees ranging from €5 to €20. In addition, some trendy nightclubs, such as King Kamehameha, enforce dress codes—usually no jeans, sneakers, or khaki pants admitted.

BARS AND LIVE MUSIC VENUES

Balalaika. The spacious Balalaika has an intimate feel, as candles are just about the only source of light. The proprietor is Anita Honis, an American singer hailing from Harlem, who likes to get out her acoustic guitar and perform on occasion. Everyone is invited to sing or play on the piano that is set up for impromptu and scheduled performances. ☒ *Schifferstr. 3, Sachsenhausen* ☎ *069/612–226* ☉ *Closed Sun.*

Cafe Extrablatt. In good weather the tables at this popular restaurant/café chain are scattered around the pleasant plaza in front of the medieval Eschenheimer Tower or at the Bockenheimer Warte, another Frankfurt location. During Wednesday's "Jumbo Hour," which runs from 7 to midnight, you get a supersize cocktail when you order an ordinary one. Cocktails are €4.95 during happy hours, Monday, Tuesday, and Thursday after 7, and weekends after 10 pm. ☒ *Grosse Eschenheimer Str. 45* ☎ *069/2199–4899.*

Champion's Bar. Like the rest of the Marriott Hotel, the Champion's Bar is designed to make Americans feel at home. The wall is lined with team jerseys, autographed helmets, and photographs of professional athletes.

9

Beer Bitte

The lager style that most of the world has come to know as "beer" originated in Germany. However, Germans don't just produce one beverage called beer; they brew more than 5,000 varieties in about 1,300 breweries. The hallmark of the country's dedication to beer is the Purity Law, *das Reinheitsgebot,* unchanged since Duke Wilhelm IV introduced it in Bavaria in 1516. The law decrees that only malted barley, hops, yeast, and water may be used to make beer, except for the specialty Weiss or Weizenbier (wheat beers). Although the law has been repealed, many breweries continue to follow its precepts.

The beer preferred in most of Germany is *Pils* (Pilsner), which has a rich yellow hue, hoppy flavor, and an alcohol content of about 5%. Frankfurt's local Pils brands are Binding and Henninger, but Licher, from the village of Lich nearby, is especially well balanced and crisp. The area is also home to Schöfferhofer, who brew Germany's number two style, *Hefeweizen* (wheat beer), which is cloudy, yeasty, and a bit sweet.

Few German bars offer more than one type of Pils or Weizen on tap, so you'll need to hit a few bars to sample a good variety. Not a bad proposition.

QUAFF IT HERE

Begin a night at **Klosterhof** (⊠ *Weissfrauenstr. 3* ☎ *069/9139–9000* ⊕ *www.klosterhof-frankfurt.de* Ⓜ *Willy-Brandt-Platz [U-bahn]*), a traditional restaurant and beer garden in Center City, where you can try Hessian favorites like *Handkäs mit Musik* (literally, hand cheese with music, a soft cheese served with chopped onions, oil, and vinegar), as well as their custom-brewed *Naturtrüb,* an unfiltered (and thus naturally cloudy) lager.

Eckhaus (⊠ *Bornheimer Landstr. 45* ☎ *069/491–197* Ⓜ *Merianplatz [U-bahn]*) is the perfect neighborhood bar to down a cold Binding or two. The restaurant, in a great location just off the Berger Strasse strip in leafy Nordend, offers a solidly executed menu of standards like schnitzel and roast chicken, along with a few creative specials.

The 23 TV monitors can be tuned to the American Forces Network, which carries the full range of American sports. The food leans toward buffalo wings, hamburgers, and brownies. ⊠ *Hamburger Allee 2, Messe* ☎ *069/7955–8305.*

Dreikönigskeller. Occupying a cellar in Sachsenhausen, the tiny but intimate Dreikönigskeller has live music throughout the week—mostly rock, jazz, blues, and other types aimed at a slightly older crowd. ⊠ *Färberstr. 71, Sachsenhausen* ☎ *069/6612–9804.*

EuroDeli. The after-work crowd gathers at EuroDeli. Because it's near many of the city's major banks, its happy hour is weekdays from 5 to 7. There's a DJ on Tuesday. ⊠ *Neue Mainzerstr. 60–66, City Center* ☎ *069/2980–1950* ⊗ *Closed weekends and holidays.*

Fox and Hound. Frankfurt is teeming with Irish pubs, but there is an occasional English pub, too. A good example is the Fox and Hound. Its patrons, mainly British, come to watch the latest football (soccer to

Americans), rugby, and cricket matches. Enjoy the authentic pub grub and the basket of chips. ☒ *Niedenau 2, Westend* ☏ *069/9720–2009* 🕐 *10 am–1 am.*

★ **Jimmy's Bar.** Jimmy's Bar, the meeting place of business executives since 1951, is classy and expensive—just like the Hessischer Hof Hotel in which it's located. There is live piano music every day from 10 pm to 3 am, and on every first Sunday of the month, you can watch renowned jazz artist Tom Schlüter perform. ■TIP➔ You must ring the doorbell to get in, although regulars have their own keys. ☒ *Friedrich-Ebert-Anlage 40, Messe* ☏ *069/7540–2461* 🕐 *8 pm–4 am daily.*

King Kamehameha Club. King Kamehameha Club is the king of the clubs in Frankfurt, occupying several floors and offering a steadily changing music program. There's a concert area and DJs who spin everything from soul to salsa. Starting in May, the King Kamehameha Beach Club opens and offers sun, music, food, and drinks. Did we mention there's also a swimming pool? ☒ *Hanauer Landstr. 192, Ostend* ☏ *069/4800–9610.*

Stereobar. University students and young professionals frequent Stereobar, found in a cellar beneath a narrow Sachsenhausen alleyway. DJs usually spin the music, although there are occasional live acts. There's a tiny dance floor if you feel like showing off your moves. ☒ *Abstgässchen 7, Sachsenhausen* ☏ *069/617–116.*

DANCE AND NIGHTCLUBS

Cocoon Club. One of Germany's most revered electro-techno DJs, Sven Väth, spins regularly at Cocoon Club. This ultramodern nightclub has several spacious dance floors that play different types of music, three bars, and two restaurants serving Asian–European cuisine. Comfort is a priority throughout the expansive club filled with reclining chairs and couches, some of which are built into the walls. Techno is the presiding music genre and draws a mostly young crowd; the club is open Friday and Saturday only. ■TIP➔ A night out here will take a toll on your wallet: a taxi is required to reach its location on the eastern edge of town, cover charges average €15, and cocktails are pricey. ☒ *Carl-Benz-Str. 21, Fechenheim* ☏ *069/900–200.*

Living XXL. Living XXL, one of the biggest restaurant-bars in Germany, is as hyped as the Eurotower, where it happens to be located. The Wednesday after-work parties are popular. The DJ spins hip-hop and soul on Friday and a mix of R&B, soul, and house on Saturday. The spacious, terraced interior has drawn praise from architects. ☒ *Kaiserstr. 29, City Center* ☏ *069/242–9370.*

Odeon. The type of crowd at Odeon depends on the night. The large club hosts student nights on Thursday, a "27 Up Club" on Friday (exclusively for guests 27 or older), disco nights on Saturday, as well as "Black Mondays"—a night of soul, hip-hop, and R&B music. It's housed in a beautiful white building that looks like a museum. ☒ *Seilerstr. 34, City Center* ☏ *069/285–055.*

Tigerpalast. There's not much that doesn't take place at Frankfurt's international variety theater, the Tigerpalast. Guests are entertained by international cabaret performers and the *Palast*'s own variety orchestra.

There's an excellent French restaurant that has been awarded a Michelin star, and the cozy Palastbar, under the basement arches, looks like an American bar from the 1920s. Shows often sell out, so book tickets as far in advance as possible. It's closed Monday. ⊠ *Heiligkreuzg. 16–20, City Center* ☏ *069/920–0220.*

U60311. The techno-heavy U60311, which bills itself as the center of the underground movement, couldn't be more underground. It's in a subway station, and gets its name (and telephone number) from its postal code. Its low ceilings make the music deafening. ⊠ *Rossmarkt 1, City Center* ☏ *069/2970–60311.*

JAZZ

Brotfabrik. An important address for jazz, rock, and disco is the Brotfabrik. Set in a former bakery, the building houses two stages, a concert hall, two restaurants, three not-for-profit projects, an ad agency, and a gallery. ⊠ *Bachmannstr. 2–4, Hausen* ☏ *069/2479–0800.*

Der Frankfurter Jazzkeller. The oldest jazz cellar in Germany, Der Frankfurter Jazzkeller was founded by legendary trumpeter Carlo Bohländer. The club, which has hosted such luminaries as Louis Armstrong, offers hot, modern jazz, at a cover of €5 to €25, depending on the stature of the performers. There are jam sessions on Wednesday and "Latin-funky" dances on Friday. It's closed Sunday to Tuesday. ⊠ *Kleine Bockenheimerstr. 18, City Center* ☏ *069/284–927.*

Jazzlokal Mampf. With posters of Chairman Mao on the walls, time seems to have stood still at the Jazzlokal Mampf. It looks straight out of the 1970s, but with live music to match, many don't think that's so bad. ⊠ *Sandweg 64, Ostend* ☏ *069/448–674* ⊕ *www.mampf-jazz.de.*

Sinkkasten. Sinkkasten, a Frankfurt musical institution, is a class act—a great place for blues, jazz, pop, and rock, with live groups, often up-and-coming ones, frequently replacing the DJ. ⊠ *Brönnerstr. 5, City Center* ☏ *069/280–385.*

SPORTS AND THE OUTDOORS

Despite summer's ever-present smog, Frankfurt is full of parks and other green oases where you can breathe easier.

Stadtwald. South of the city in Sachsenhausen, the huge, 4,000-acre Stadtwald (city forest) makes Frankfurt one of Germany's greenest metropoles. ■TIP→ The forest has innumerable paths and trails, bird sanctuaries, impressive sports stadiums, and a good restaurant. The Oberschweinstiege stop on streetcar Line 14 is right in the middle of the park.

BIKING

There are numerous biking paths within the city limits. The Stadtwald in the southern part of the city is crisscrossed with well-tended paths that are nice and flat. The city's riverbanks are, for the most part, lined with paths bikers can use. These are not only on both sides of the Main but also on the banks of the little Nidda River, which flows through Heddernheim, Eschersheim, Hausen, and Rödelheim before joining the

The Eiserner Steg (Iron Bridge) was Europe's very first suspension bridge, and a walk across promises great photo ops of Frankfurt's skyline.

Main at Höchst. Some bikers also like the Taunus Hills, but note that word "Hills."

SHOPPING

SHOPPING DISTRICTS

Frankfurt, and the rest of Germany, is finally free of the restrictive laws that kept the stores closed evenings and Saturday afternoons—the very times working people might want to shop. Stores now can stay open until 10 pm, but pretty much everything is closed on Sunday except for restaurants and bakeries. The tree-shaded pedestrian zone of the **Zeil** is said to be one of the richest shopping strips in Germany. There's no doubt that the Zeil, between Hauptwache and Konstablerwache, is incredible for its variety of department and specialty stores.

The Zeil is only the centerpiece of the downtown shopping area. The subway station below the Hauptwache also doubles as a vast underground mall, albeit a rather droll one. West of the Hauptwache are two parallel streets highly regarded by shoppers. One is the luxurious **Goethestrasse**, lined with trendy boutiques, art galleries, jewelry stores, and antiques shops. The other is **Grosse Bockenheimer Strasse**, better known as the Fressgass (Gorge Alley). Cafés, restaurants, and pricey food stores line the street.

For a total shopping blitz, head to the Zeil, where you'll find some of Germany's most upscale shops.

Schillerpassage. The Schillerpassage is strong on men's and women's fashion boutiques, particularly small and exclusive ones. ⊠ *Rahmhof-str. 2, City Center.*

Zeilgallerie. The moderately priced Zeilgallerie, which recently received a facelist, has 56 shops and an outstanding view from the rooftop terrace. ⊠ *Zeil 112–114, City Center* ⊘ *Mon.–Sat. 10–8.*

DEPARTMENT STORES

There are two department stores on the Zeil, offering much in the way of clothing, furnishings, electronics, food, and other items.

Galeria Kaufhof. The Galeria Kaufhof is one of Germany's biggest and most popular chain department stores and offers everything from clothing, jewelry, and sports equipment to cosmetics and toys. The Frankfurt store has a gourmet market on the bottom floor, and a restaurant on the top floor, which has a striking view of the city. ⊠ *Zeil 116–126, City Center* ☏ *069/21910.*

Karstadt. Karstadt is one of Germany's biggest department stores and is known for its splendid international gourmet food department, with plenty of opportunity to try the food and drink on the spot. ■ TIP➔ The store itself makes for a great shopping spot on the Zeil. ⊠ *Zeil 90, City Center* ☏ *069/929–050.*

GIFT IDEAS

Höchster Porzellan Manufaktur. The one real gift item that Frankfurt produces is fine porcelain. The Höchster Porzellan Manufaktur draws on a tradition dating back 200 years. The handmade products can be purchased at the workshop. ⊠ *Palleskestr. 32, Höchst* ☎ *069/300–9020.*

There are a number of not-so-elegant gift items that you might consider. One thing typical of the city is the Apfelwein. You can get a bottle of it at any grocery store, but more enduring souvenirs would be the Bembel pitchers and ribbed glasses that are equally a part of the Apfelwein tradition. Then there is the sausage. You can get the "original hot dog" in cans at any grocery store.

SPECIALTY STORES

CLOTHING STORES

★ **Peek & Cloppenburg.** Peek & Cloppenburg is a huge clothing store where men and women can find what they need for the office, gym, and nightclub. Clothes range from easily affordable items to pricier designer labels. ⊠ *Zeil 71–75, City Center* ☎ *069/298–950.*

Pfüller Modehaus. Pfüller Modehaus is mostly known as "the" designer clothing store for children of all ages. It offers a wide range of choices on three floors for women as well, from classic to trendy, from lingerie to overcoats, and from hats to stockings. The children's clothes designers showcase their most exclusive designs here and you'll find items and labels that you have not seen before. ⊠ *Goethestr. 12, City Center* ☎ *069/1337–8070.*

FOOD AND DRINK

Café Laumer. The pastry shop at Café Laumer has local delicacies such as *Bethmännchen und Brenten* (marzipan cookies) and *Frankfurter Kranz* (a kind of creamy cake). ⊠ *Bockenheimer Landstr. 67, Westend* ☎ *069/727–912.*

Café Mozart. This café is nostalgic of a traditional coffeehouse and offers all types of sweets and pastries, along with breakfast, lunch, and dinner just steps from the main shopping area on a quiet, tucked-away street. ⊠ *Töngesgasse 23, City Center* ☎ *069/291–954.*

Kleinmarkthalle. The Kleinmarkthalle is a treasure trove of stands selling spices, herbs, teas, exotic fruits, cut flowers, and live fish flown in from the Atlantic. And it offers all kinds of snacks in case you need a break while shopping. ⊠ *Haseng. 5–7, City Center* ☎ *069/2123–3696* ☺ *Weekdays 8-6, Sat. 8–4.*

Weinhandlung Dr. Teufel. Weinhandlung Dr. Teufel is as good a place as any for the popular wines, and the best place in town for diversity. There are also chocolate and cigars, a complete line of glasses, carafes, corkscrews, and other accessories, and books on all aspects of viticulture. The store has two locations, one in the city center, and one in the Westend. ⊠ *Kleiner Hirschgraben 4, City Center* ☎ *069/448–989.*

9

FLEA MARKET

Sachsenhausen's weekend **flea market** takes place on Saturday from 9 to 2 on the riverbank between Dürerstrasse and the Eiserner Steg. Purveyors of the cheap have taken over, and there's lots of discussion as to whether it is a good use for the elegant, museum-lined riverbank. ■TIP→ Get there early for the bargains, as the better-quality stuff gets snapped up quickly. Shopping success or no, the market can be fun for browsing.

SIDE TRIPS FROM FRANKFURT

Destinations reachable by the local transportation system include Höchst and the Taunus Hills, which include Bad Homburg and Kronberg. Just to the northwest and west of Frankfurt, the Taunus Hills are an area of mixed pine and hardwood forest, medieval castles, and photogenic towns that many Frankfurters regard as their own backyard. It's home to Frankfurt's wealthy bankers and business executives, and on weekends you can see them enjoying their playground: hiking through the hills, climbing the Grosse Feldberg, taking the waters at Bad Homburg's health-enhancing mineral springs, or just lazing in elegant stretches of parkland.

BAD HOMBURG

12 km (7 mi) north of Frankfurt.

Emperor Wilhelm II, the infamous "Kaiser" of World War I, spent a month each year at Bad Homburg, the principal city of the Taunus Hills. Another frequent visitor to Bad Homburg was Britain's Prince of Wales, later King Edward VII, who made the name *Homburg* world famous by associating it with a hat.

GETTING HERE AND AROUND

Bad Homburg is easily reached by the S-bahn from Hauptwache, the main station, and other points in downtown Frankfurt. The S5 goes to Bad Homburg. There's also a Taunusbahn (from the main station only) that stops in Bad Homburg and then continues into the far Taunus, including the Römerkastell-Saalburg and Wehrheim, with bus connections to Hessenpark. Bad Homburg is about a 30- to 45-minute drive north of Frankfurt on A-5.

The Bad Homburg tourist office is open until 6:30 pm weekdays, 2 pm Saturday, and is closed Sunday.

ESSENTIALS

Visitor Information **Kur- und Kongress GmbH Bad Homburg** ⊠ *Louisenstr. 58* ☎ *06172/178–110* ⊕ *www.bad-homburg.de.*

EXPLORING

Casino Bad Homburg. Adjacent to the Kurpark, the casino boasts with some justice that it is the "Mother of Monte Carlo." The first casino in Bad Homburg, and one of the first in the world, was established in 1841, but closed down in 1866 because Prussian law forbade gambling.

The proprietor, François Blanc, then established the famous Monte Carlo casino on the French Riviera, and the Bad Homburg casino wasn't reopened until 1949. A bus from south side of Frankfurt's Hauptbahnhof leaves every hour to every hour and a half between 2 pm and 1 am. Buses back to Frankfurt run every 1–2 hours from 4:30 pm to 4 am. The €6 fare will be refunded after the casino's full entry fee has been deducted. You must show a passport or other identification to gain admission. ⊠ *Kisseleffstr. 35* ☏ *06172/17010* ▨ *Slot-machine area free, gaming area €2.50* ⊙ *Slot machines noon–4 am, gaming area 2:30 pm–3 am, and until 4 am Thurs.–Sat.*

Freilichtmuseum Hessenpark. About an hour's walk through the woods along a well-marked path from the Römerkastell-Saalburg is an open-air museum at Hessenpark, near Neu-Anspach. The museum presents a clear picture of the world in which 18th- and 19th-century Hessians lived, using 135 acres of rebuilt villages with houses, schools, and farms typical of the time. The park, 15 km (9 mi) outside Bad Homburg in the direction of Usingen, can also be reached by public transportation. Take the Taunusbahn from the Frankfurt main station to Wehrheim; then transfer to Bus 514. ⊠ *Laubweg 5, Neu-Anspach* ☏ *06081/5880* ⊕ *www.hessenpark.de* ▨ *€6* ⊙ *Mar.–Oct., daily 9–6; Nov., daily 10–5.*

Grosser Feldberg. Just a short, convenient bus ride from Bad Homburg is the highest mountain in the Taunus, the 2,850-foot, eminently hikable Grosser Feldberg.

Kurpark (*spa*). Bad Homburg's greatest attraction has been the Kurpark, in the heart of the Old Town, with more than 31 fountains. Romans first used the springs, which were rediscovered and made famous in the 19th century. In the park you'll find not only the popular, highly saline Elisabethenbrunnen spring, but also a Siamese temple and a Russian chapel, mementos left by royal guests—King Chulalongkorn of Siam and Czar Nicholas II.

Römerkastell-Saalburg (*Saalburg Roman Fort*). Only 6½ km (4 mi) from Bad Homburg, and accessible by direct bus service, is the Römerkastell-Saalburg. Built in AD 120, the fort could accommodate a cohort (500 men) and was part of the fortifications along the Limes Wall, which ran from the Danube to the Rhine and was meant to protect the Roman Empire from barbarian invasion. The fort was restored more than a century ago. The site, which includes a museum of Roman artifacts, is north of Bad Homburg on Route 456 in the direction of Usingen. ⊠ *Archäologischer Park, Saalburg 1* ☏ *06175/93740* ▨ *€5* ⊙ *Mar.–Oct., daily 9–6; Nov.–Feb., Tues.–Sun. 9–4.*

Schloss Homburg. The most historically noteworthy sight in Bad Homburg is the 17th-century Schloss, where the kaiser stayed when he was in residence. The state apartments are exquisitely furnished, and the Spiegelkabinett (Hall of Mirrors) is especially worthy of a visit. In the surrounding park look for two venerable cedars from Lebanon, both now about 200 years old. ⊠ *Schloss, Bad Homburg vor der Höhe* ☏ *06172/926–2148* ▨ *€4* ⊙ *Tues.–Sun. 10–5.*

WHERE TO EAT AND STAY
For expanded hotel reviews, visit Fodors.com.

9

$ ✕**Kartoffelküche.** This simple restaurant serves traditional dishes accom-
GERMAN panied by potatoes cooked every way imaginable. The potato and broc-
coli gratin and the potato pizza are excellent. For dessert, try potato
strudel with vanilla sauce. ⊠ *Audenstr. 4* ☎ *06172/21500* ⊕ *www.
restaurant-kartoffelkueche.de.*

$$$ **Steigenberger Bad Homburg.** Renowned for catering to Europe's
★ royalty in its pre–World War I heyday, this building has been a hotel
since 1883. **Pros:** Old World elegance; handy to the Kurpark. **Cons:**
expensive; parking is difficult. ⊠ *Kaiser-Friedrich-Promenade 69–75*
☎ *06172/1810* ⊕ *www.bad-homburg.steigenberger.de* ⤴ *152 rooms,
17 suites* ⌂ *In-room: Internet, Wi-Fi. In-hotel: restaurant, bar, gym.*

HÖCHST

*Take S1 or S2 suburban train from Frankfurt's main train station,
Hauptwache, or Konstablerwache.*

Höchst, a town with a castle and an Altstadt (Old Town) right out of
a picture book, is now part of Frankfurt. It wasn't devastated by war-
time bombing, so its castle and the market square, with its half-timber
houses, are well preserved. It's a romantic place for outdoor dining and
drinking. For a week in July the whole Alstadt is hung with lanterns
for the Schlossfest, one of Frankfurt's more popular outdoor festivals.

Höchster Porzellan Manufaktur. Höchst was once a porcelain-manufac-
turing town to rival Dresden and Vienna. Production ceased in the late
18th century, but was revived by an enterprising businessman in 1965.
The Höchster Porzellan Manufaktur produces exquisite and expensive
tableware, but the intriguing part of its output is its accessories. There
are replicas of 18th-century items, including vases, cuff links, and bottle
stoppers. You can tour the workshop and shop at the store. ⊠ *Pallesk-
estr. 32* ☎ *069/300–9020* 🎫 *€5* ⊙ *Shop: weekdays 9:30–6, Sat. 9:30–2;
tours: Tues. at 10 and 3.*

Justinuskirche. Höchst's most interesting attraction is the Justinuskirche,
Frankfurt's oldest building and famous for its organ concerts. Dating
from the 7th century, the church is part early Romanesque and part
15th-century Gothic. The view from the top of the hill is well worth
the walk. ⊠ *Justinuspl. at Bolongerostr.* ⊙ *Apr.–Oct., Tues.–Sun. 2–5;
Nov.–Mar., weekends 2–4.*

WHERE TO STAY

For expanded hotel reviews, visit Fodors.com.

$ **Lindner Congress Hotel.** A 15-minute drive from the airport, Americans
like this hotel, if not for the American food it proudly offers, then for
the sports bar and its big-screen TV. **Pros:** perfect for the business trav-
eler; in a pleasant district. **Cons:** removed from downtown. ⊠ *Bolonga-
rostr. 100* ☎ *069/330–0200* ⊕ *www.lindner.de/de/LCH* ⤴ *285 rooms,
18 apartments* ⌂ *In-room: no a/c, kitchen, Internet, Wi-Fi. In-hotel:
restaurant, bar, gym, spa, laundry facilities, business center, parking,
some pets allowed.*

The Pfalz and Rhine Terrace

WORD OF MOUTH

"I have traveled that route [the German Wine Road] many times, always without any hotel reservations. There are lots of gasthauses in your price range, including rooms at a winery (Weingut) surrounded by vineyards. If you don't find something in one village, there will be something just a couple of kms down the road. . ."

—wanderfrau

WELCOME TO THE PFALZ AND RHINE TERRACE

TOP REASONS TO GO

★ **Wine:** German Rieslings are some of the most versatile white wines in the world—on their own or with food. For many, discovering Germany's drier-style wines is a revelation.

★ **Festivals:** Wine is a great excuse for merrymaking, and there are scores of wine festivals throughout the region. The biggest and best is the Bad Dürkheimer Wurstmarkt in the town of Bad Dürkheim, which features a wine barrel the size of a building.

★ **Pfälzerwald:** The Palatinate Forest is a paradise for hiking and cycling. Even a brief walk under the beautiful pine and chestnut trees is relaxing and refreshing.

★ **Castles:** Burg Trifels and Schloss Villa Ludwigshöhe are a contrast in style, inside and out. Both are wonderful settings for concerts.

★ **Cathedrals:** The cathedrals in Speyer, Worms, and Mainz are the finest examples of grand-scale Rhenish Romanesque architecture in Germany.

1 The German Wine Road. The picturesque Deutsche Weinstrasse (German Wine Road) weaves through the valleys and among the lower slopes of the Haardt Mountains. Along its length are a string of pretty half-timber wine-producing villages, each more inviting than the last.

2 The Rhine Terrace. Rheinhessen or "Rhine Terrace" is a broad fertile river valley, where grapes are but one of many crops. Here the medieval cities of Mainz, Worms, and Speyer all bear testament to the great power and wealth brought by the important trading route created by the mighty Rhine itself.

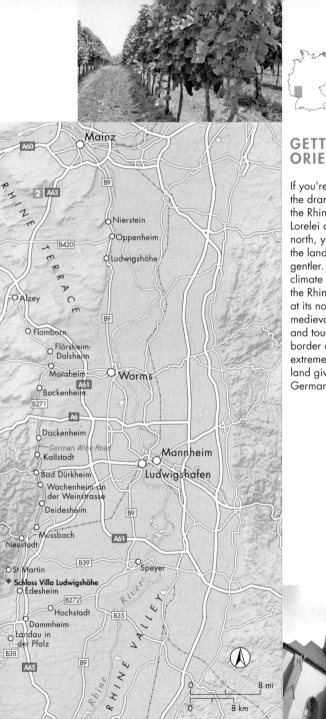

GETTING ORIENTED

If you're arriving from the dramatic stretch of the Rhine centered on the Lorelei and Koblenz to the north, you'll notice how the landscape here is far gentler. So, too, is the climate in this region of the Rhine Valley, guarded at its northern edge by the medieval city of Mainz and touching the French border at its southern extreme. This helps the land give birth to some of Germany's greatest wines.

10

Map labels

Mainz

A60

RHINE TERRACE

2 A63

B9

Nierstein
Oppenheim
Ludwigshöhe

B420

Alzey

B9

Flomborn

Flörsheim-Dalsheim

Monsheim

Worms

A61

Bockenheim

B271

A6

Dackenheim

German Wine Road

Kallstadt

Mannheim

Bad Dürkheim

Ludwigshafen

Wachenheim an der Weinstrasse

Deidesheim

B9

Mussbach

Neustadt

A61

St Martin

B39

Speyer

◆ Schloss Villa Ludwigshöhe

Edesheim

B272

Rhine River

Hochstadt

B35

Dammheim

Landau in der Pfalz

B38

B9

RHINE VALLEY

A65

Rhine

0   8 mi

0   8 km

DRIVING THE GERMAN WINE ROAD

Due to its sunny skies, warm weather, and fertile fields, many Germans consider the Pfalz their version of Tuscany. In addition to vineyards, the mild climate fosters fig, lemon, and chestnut trees.

(above) Autumn is a gorgeous time of year to tour the region. (upper right) Vineyards in Pfalz. (lower right) Winery-hopping by bike is a nice alternative to driving.

The best time for a drive is early spring, when the path is awash in pink and white almond blossoms or early fall when you can sample sweet, young wines. The Deutsche Weinstrasse begins in Schweigen-Rechtenbach and runs alongside the *Bundesstrassen* (highways) B-38 and B-271. Yellow signs depicting a cluster of grapes guide visitors along a picturesque path of villages and vineyards north, to the end of the route at the "House of the German Wine Road" in Bockenheim. The entire road is just a little more than 50 mi and can be driven in a few hours. However, if you take time to stop at roadside stands to savor seasonal produce and local wines, it can easily turn into a two-day drive. Get an early start and allow yourself to get lost in the charming villages along the way.

—Sarah Harman

DRINKING AND DRIVING

Germany has strict laws against driving (and biking) under the influence, so if you're planning to take advantage of the numerous *Weinprobe* (wine samples) offered along the route, make sure you have a designated driver. Alternatively, just let the vintner know what you like, and he can help you pick a bottle to enjoy when you reach your final destination.

The entire route is scenic, but if you're short on time, the stretch between Gleiszellen and Bad Dürkheim is particularly rich with castles, vineyards, and vistas. If you opt to start at Schweigen-Rechtenbach on the French border, the southernmost point of the route, you can begin by snapping a photo in front of the *Deutsches Weintor* (German Wine Gate). Otherwise, pick up the route in **Gleiszellen**, where you should stop to savor a glass of the hard-to-find Muskakeller wine, with its distinctly sweet aroma. **Weinstube Wissing** has a homey atmosphere and offers Muskateller in red, yellow, and rosé varieties.

Depending on the time of year, your trip may coincide with a local wine or produce festival—as you drive, keep your eyes peeled for signs advertising "Weinfest." Summer is the best time for festivals, but roadside stands offering fresh seasonal produce are present year-round. When you arrive in Edenkoben, stretch your legs at the Pompeian-style palace **Schloss Villa Ludwigshöhe**, then continue uphill via the Rietburgbahn chairlift to the vantage point at the **Rietburg Castle Ruins**. Evening is the perfect time for the journey, when the pathway is illuminated by Chinese lanterns (the chairlift is open until midnight in summer). If you plan to split the drive into two days, the neighboring village of **St. Martin** is an ideal place to overnight because it's about halfway through the drive. Spend the next morning exploring the winding streets of this charming village on foot.

Continue north, driving leisurely through the vineyards of **Deidesheim** and **Forst**, and stopping off at the imposing ruins of **Burgruine Hardenburg** (Hardenburg Fortress). End your day with a visit to the world's biggest wine barrel in **Bad Dürkheim**.

QUICK BITES

Alter Kastanienhof. Stop here for a delicious rendition of the regional specialty *Saumagen* (sow's stomach). The restaurant has a charming interior courtyard and sunny south-facing terrace, and a small but excellent selection of local wines. ⊠ *Theresienstr. 79, Rhodt u. Rietburg* ☎ *06323/81752* ▭ *No credit cards.*

Consulat des Weines. Oenophiles won't want to miss this vinothek in the charming village of St. Martin. It offers more than 80 varieties of wine from its vineyards in St. Martin and nearby Edenkoben. The sheer variety makes it easy to overindulge— good thing there's a hotel and restaurant on-site. ⊠ *Maikammerer Str. 44, St. Martin* ☎ *06323/8040* ▭ *No credit cards.*

Wochenmarkt. If you're in Bad Dürkheim on a Wednesday or a Sunday, head to this farmers' market for flowers, bread, wine, meats, cheeses, and vinegars. ⊠ *Am Obermarkt, Bad Dürkheim* ☎ *06323/8040* ⊘ *Apr.– Oct., Wed., and Sat. 6:30 am–1 pm.*

10

Updated by
Sarah Harman

Pfalz and wine go hand in hand. This region of vineyards and picturesque villages is the home of the German Wine Road and the country's greatest wine festival at Bad Dürkheim. No fewer than 6 of Germany's 13 wine-growing regions, including the two largest, are located in the area.

The Pfalz has a mild, sunny climate and an ambience to match. Vines carpet the foothills of the thickly forested Haardt Mountains, an extension of the Alsatian Vosges. The Pfälzerwald (Palatinate Forest) with its pine and chestnut trees is the region's other natural attraction. Hiking and cycling trails lead through the vineyards, the woods, and up to castles on the heights.

The border between the Pfalz and Rheinhessen is invisible, but a few miles after crossing it you begin to get a sense of Rheinhessen's character. It's a region of gentle, rolling hills and expansive farmland, where grapes are but one of many crops; vineyards are often scattered miles apart. The slopes overlooking the Rhine between Worms and Mainz—the so-called Rhine Terrace—are a notable exception, with a nearly uninterrupted ribbon of vines including the famous vineyards of Oppenheim, Nierstein, and Nackenheim on the outskirts of Mainz.

PLANNING

WHEN TO GO
The wine-festival season begins in March with the *Mandelblüten* (blossoming of the almond trees) along the Wine Road and continues through October. By May the vines' tender shoots and leaves appear. As the wine harvest progresses in September and October, foliage takes on reddish-golden hues.

GETTING HERE AND AROUND
AIR TRAVEL
Frankfurt is the closest major international airport for the entire Rhineland. International airports in Stuttgart and France's Strasbourg are closer to the southern end of the German Wine Road. If you're traveling

from within Europe, the oft-disparaged Ryanair hub in the Frankfurt suburb of Hahn is actually a convenient jumping-off point for a tour of the region, with bus service to Koblenz, Heidelberg, and Karlsruhe.

BIKE TRAVEL

There's no charge for transporting bicycles on local trains throughout Rheinland-Pfalz weekdays after 9 am and anytime weekends and holidays. For maps, suggested routes, bike-rental locations, and details on *Pauschal-Angebote* (package deals) or *Gepäcktransport* (luggage-forwarding service), contact Pfalz.Touristik or Rheinhessen-Information.

CAR TRAVEL

It's 162 km (100 mi) between Schweigen-Rechtenbach and Mainz, the southernmost and northernmost points of this region. The main route is the Deutsche Weinstrasse, which is a *Bundesstrasse* (two-lane highway), abbreviated "B," as in B-38, B-48, and B-271. The route from Worms to Mainz is B-9.

TRAIN TRAVEL

Mainz is on the high-speed ICE (InterCity Express) train route linking Wiesbaden, Frankfurt, and Dresden, and so forms a convenient gateway to the region. An excellent network of public transportation called **Rheinland-Pfalz-Takt** operates throughout the region with well-coordinated **RegioLinie** (buses) and **Nahverkehrszüge** (local trains). Regional trains link Mainz with other towns along the Rhine Terrace, including Worms and Speyer, while local branch lines serve key hubs along the Wine Road such as Neustadt and Bad Dürkheim. Smaller towns and villages connect with these hubs by an excellent network of local buses.

■ TIP→ The Rheinland-Pfalz Ticket is a great value if you plan to travel on the train. The ticket costs €21 for the first person and €3 for each additional person, up to five people. It's valid for a whole day, beginning at 9 am on weekdays and midnight on weekends and holidays. It can be used on all regional trains and buses, but not the high-speed ICE trains.

RESTAURANTS

Lunch in this region is generally served from noon until 2 or 2:30, dinner from 6 until 9:30 or 10. Credit cards have gained a foothold, but many restaurants will accept only cash or debit cards issued by a German bank. Casual attire is typically acceptable at restaurants here, and reservations are generally not needed.

HOTELS

Accommodations in all price categories are plentiful, but book in advance if your visit coincides with a large festival. Bed-and-breakfasts abound. Look for signs reading "Fremdenzimmer" or "Zimmer frei" (rooms available). A *Ferienwohnung* (holiday apartment), abbreviated FeWo in tourist brochures, is an economical option if you plan to stay in one location for several nights.

10

WHAT IT COSTS IN EUROS				
	¢	$	$$	$$$	$$$$
Restaurants	under €9	€9–€15	€16–€20	€21–€25	over €25
Hotels	under €50	€50–€100	€101–€175	€176–€225	over €225

Restaurant prices are per person for a main course at dinner. Hotel prices are for two people in a standard double room, including tax and service.

PLANNING YOUR TIME

Central hubs such as Bad Dürkheim or Neustadt make good bases for exploring the region, although the cities along the Rhine are livelier, particularly Mainz. Driving the Wine Road takes longer than you might expect, and will probably involve spur-of-the-moment stops, so you may want to consider a stopover in one of the many country inns en route.

When traveling with children, Neustadt and Worms are convenient bases from which to explore nearby Holiday Park.

DISCOUNTS AND DEALS

The **Freizeit Card** (€14 for one day, €41.50 for three days, €66 for six days) offers free or reduced admission to 168 museums, castles, and other sights, as well as city tours and boat trips throughout Rheinland-Pfalz and Saarland. The days you use the three- and six-day cards needn't be consecutive, as long as they're in the same season. The six-day card also includes admission to the Holiday Park in Hassloch. The Web site ⊕ *www.rlpcard.de* lists all of the sites you can visit with the card, and also gives you the opportunity to order it online. You can also buy it at all the community tourist offices in the region.

VISITOR INFORMATION

Contacts Deutsche Weinstrasse ⊠ *Martin-Luther-Str. 69, Neustadt a.d. Wein-strasse* ☎ *06321/912–333* ⊕ *www.deutsche-weinstrasse.de.* **Pfalz.Touristik** ⊠ *Martin-Luther-Str. 69, Neustadt a.d. Weinstrasse* ☎ *06321/39160* ⊕ *www. pfalz-touristik.de.* **Pfalzwein** ⊠ *Martin-Luther-Str. 69, Neustadt a.d. Wein-strasse* ☎ *06321/912–328* ⊕ *www.pfalzwein.de.* **Rheinhessen-Information** ⊠ *Wilhelm-Leuschner-Str. 44, Ingelheim* ☎ *06132/44170* ⊕ *www.rheinhessen. info.* **Rheinland-Pfalz Tourismus** ⊠ *Löhrstr. 103–105, Koblenz* ☎ *0621/915–200* ⊕ *www.rlp-info.de.*

THE GERMAN WINE ROAD

The Wine Road spans the length of the Pfalz wine region. You can travel from north to south or vice versa. Given its central location, the Pfalz is convenient to visit before or after a trip to the Black Forest, Heidelberg, or the northern Rhineland.

CLOSE UP

The Wines of Rheinland-Pfalz

The Romans planted the first Rhineland vineyards 2,000 years ago, finding the mild, wet climate hospitable to grape growing. By the Middle Ages viticulture was flourishing and a bustling wine trade had developed. Wine making and splendid Romanesque cathedrals are the legacies of the bishops and emperors of Speyer, Worms, and Mainz. This region, now the state of Rheinland-Pfalz (Rhineland Palatinate), is home to 6 of Germany's 13 designated wine-growing districts, including the two largest, Rheinhessen and the Pfalz.

In the Pfalz, you can follow the Deutsche Weinstrasse (German Wine Road) as it winds its way north from the French border. Idyllic wine villages beckon with flower-draped facades and courtyards full of palms, oleanders, and fig trees. "Weinverkauf" (wine for sale) and "Weinprobe" (wine-tasting) signs are posted everywhere—an invitation to stop in to sample the wines.

Most of the wines from both Pfalz and Rheinhessen are white, and the ones from Rheinhessen are often sweet, fragrant, and less dry than their counterparts from the Pfalz. Many are sold as *offene Weine* (wines by the glass). The classic white varieties are Riesling, Silvaner, Müller-Thurgau (also called Rivaner), Grauburgunder (Pinot Gris), and Weissburgunder (Pinot Blanc). Spätburgunder (Pinot Noir), Dornfelder, and Portugieser are the most popular red wines. The word *Weissherbst*, after the grape variety, indicates a rosé wine.

Riesling is the king of German grapes. It produces wines that range widely in quality and character; Rieslings are noted for their strong acidity, sometimes-flowery aroma, and often mineral-tasting notes—all reflections of the soil in which they're grown. Riesling made its name throughout the world as a sweet (lieblich) wine, but many Germans prefer dry (trocken) versions. Importers, especially in the United States, don't bring over many dry Rieslings, so take the opportunity to sample some while in Germany.

SCHWEIGEN-RECHTENBACH

21 km (13 mi) southwest of Landau on B-38.

The southernmost wine village of the Pfalz lies on the French border. During the economically depressed 1930s, local vintners established a route through the vineyards to promote tourism. The German Wine Road was inaugurated in 1935; a year later the massive stone Deutsches Weintor (German Wine Gate) was erected to add visual impact to the marketing concept. Halfway up the gateway is a platform that offers a fine view of the vineyards—to the south, French, to the north, German. Schweigen's 1-km (½-mi) Weinlehrpfad (educational wine path) wanders through the vineyards and, with signs and exhibits, explains the history of viticulture from Roman times to the present.

10

Some wineries offer seasonal outdoor seating areas where guests can enjoy samples.

BAD BERGZABERN

10 km (6 mi) north of Schweigen-Rechtenbach on B-38.

The landmark of this little spa town is the baroque **Schloss** (palace) of the dukes of Zweibrücken. The Gasthaus Zum Engel (⊠ *Königstr. 45*) is an impressive Renaissance house with elaborate scrolled gables and decorative oriels. ■**TIP**→ Visit Café Herzog (⊠ *Marktstr. 48*) for scrumptious, homemade chocolates, cakes, and ice creams made with unexpected ingredients, such as wine, pepper, cardamom, curry, thyme, or Feigenessig (fig vinegar). The café is closed Monday and Tuesday.

GETTING HERE AND AROUND

From Landau, you can take the regional train to Bad Bergzabern, which takes about an hour and requires a change in Winden (Pfalz). The Bus 543 also connects Bad Bergzabern along the Wine Road to Schweigen, over the French border to Wissembourg. The Rheinland-Pfalz ticket is valid on the train and the bus until the French border.

WHERE TO STAY

For expanded hotel reviews, visit Fodors.com.

$$

Fodor'sChoice ★

Hotel–Restaurant Zur Krone. A simple facade belies an upscale inn, which offers modern facilities, tasteful decor, and, above all, a warm welcome from the Kuntz family. **Pros:** quiet location; friendly atmosphere; great food. **Cons:** a big detour off the Wine Road, in-room Internet costs extra. ⊠ *Hauptstr. 62–64, Herxheim-Hayna* 🕾 *07276/5080* ⊕ *www.hotelkrone.de* ⤳ *42 rooms, 7 suites* ⚙ *In-room: no a/c, Internet, Wi-Fi. In-hotel: restaurant, bar, pool, tennis court, business center,* *some pets allowed ⊘ Restaurant Zur Krone closed Mon. and Tues., 1st 2 wks in Jan., and 3 wks in Aug. No lunch* ⍥Breakfast.

GLEISZELLEN

4 km (2½ mi) north of Bad Bergzabern on B-48.

Gleiszellen's **Winzergasse** (Vintners' Lane) is a little vine-canopied street lined with a beautiful ensemble of half-timber houses. Try a glass of the town's specialty: spicy, aromatic Muskateller wine, a rarity seldom found elsewhere in Germany.

GETTING HERE AND AROUND

Gleiszellen is on the 543 bus line that runs from Landau to the French border town of Wissembourg. The bus runs hourly.

WHERE TO EAT AND STAY

For expanded hotel reviews, visit Fodors.com.

$$ ✕**Weinstube Wissing.** Friendly service and a homey atmosphere awaits guests at Weinstube Wissing. Wines, fine spirits, and regional delicacies are offered in the former premises of the family-owned distillery. There are also rooms available for rent. ■TIP➔ Pick up a bottle of fresh Pfälzer Traubensaft (grape juice) for a tasty souvenir. ⊠ *Winzerg. 34, Gleiszellen* ☎ *06343/4711* ⊕ *www.weingut-wissing.de* ▭ *No credit cards.*

$$$ ⍟**Gasthof Zum Lam.** Flowers cascade from the windowsills of this half-timber inn in the heart of town. **Pros:** quiet location; charming courtyard; beautiful old building. **Cons:** no elevator. ⊠ *Winzerg. 37* ☎ *06343/939-212* ⊕ *www.zum-lam.de* ⇗ *11 rooms, 1 apartment* ♿ *In-room: no a/c. In-hotel: restaurant, bar, some pets allowed* ⊘ *Restaurant closed Wed. No lunch Nov.–Mar.* ⍥Breakfast.

OFF THE
BEATEN
PATH

★**Burg Trifels.** Burg Trifels perches on the highest of three sandstone bluffs overlooking Annweiler, which is 15 km (9 mi) northwest of Gleiszellen. Celts, Romans, and Salians had all made settlements on this site, but it was under the Hohenstaufen emperors (12th and 13th centuries) that Trifels was built on a grand scale. It housed the crown jewels from 1125 to 1274 (replicas are on display today). It was also an imperial prison, perhaps where Richard the Lion-Hearted was held captive in 1193–94.

Although it was never conquered, the fortress was severely damaged by lightning in 1602. Reconstruction began in 1938, shaped by visions of grandeur to create a national shrine of the imperial past. Accordingly, the monumental proportions of some parts of today's castle bear no resemblance to those of the original Romanesque structure. The imperial hall is a grand setting for the *Serenaden* (concerts) held in summer.

Arriving on foot: From the main train station in Annweiler, follow the local signs for Burg Trifels. The hike is about an hour. **Arriving by car:** Follow the A-65 direction Karl-Ludwigshafen, take exit Landau-Sued, then B-10 to Annweiler West. From there follow the local signs. Parking is at the foot of the fortress, a 20-minute walk from the top. ☎ *06346/8470* ⊕ *www.trifelsland.de* ⊠ *€3* ⊘ *Apr.–Sept., daily 9–6; Oct., Nov., and Jan.–Mar., daily 9–5.*

10

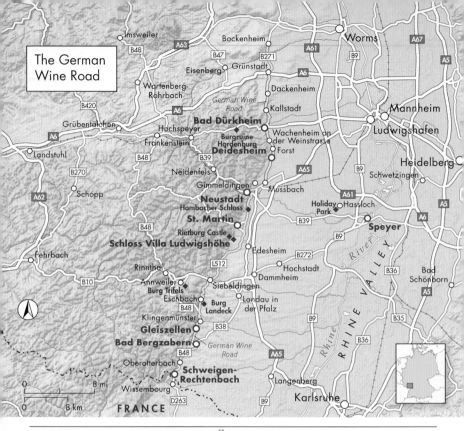

SCHLOSS VILLA LUDWIGSHÖHE

★ *24 km (15 mi) north of Annweiler, slightly west of Edenkoben on the Wine Rd.*

Schloss Villa Ludwigshöhe. Bavaria's King Ludwig I built a summer residence on the slopes overlooking Edenkoben, in what he called "the most beautiful square mile of my realm." The layout and decor of the palace—Pompeian-style murals, splendid parquet floors, and Biedermeier and Empire furnishings—provide quite a contrast to those of medieval castles elsewhere in the Pfalz. An extensive collection of paintings and prints by the leading German impressionist Max Slevogt (1868–1932) is on display. The rooms can be visited only on a guided tour, which must be scheduled in advance by phone.

You can reach the neoclassical Schloss Villa Ludwigshöhe by car, bus, or walking. The 506 Palatina bus goes directly from Edenkoen on Sunday and holidays. If you opt to walk, the *Weinlehrpfad* (educational trailpath) takes about 45 minutes. Historical winepresses and vintners' tools are displayed at intervals along the path, which starts at the corner of Landauer Strasse and Villa Strasse in Edenkoben. ☎ 06323/93016 ⊕ *www.burgen-rlp.de* 🖾 €4 🕙 *Apr.–Sept., Tues.–Sun. 9–6; Oct., Nov., and Jan.–Mar., Tues.–Sun. 9–5.*

EATING WELL IN THE PFALZ

Wine has a big influence on the cuisine here. Not only must the food taste good with a glass of wine, but it's often used as an ingredient. The *Weinkraut* is sauerkraut braised in wine; *Dippe-Has* is hare and pork baked in red wine; and *Backes Grumbeere* is scalloped potatoes cooked with bacon, sour cream, white wine, and a layer of pork. During the grape harvest, from September through November, there is *Federweisser*—fermenting grape juice. Among the regional dishes well suited to wine is the *Pfälzer Teller*—a platter of bratwurst (grilled sausage), *Leberknödel* (liver dumplings), and slices of *Saumagen* (a spicy meat-and-potato mixture cooked in a sow's stomach), with *Kartoffelpüree* (mashed potatoes) on the side. *Spargel* (asparagus), *Wild* (game), chestnuts, *Zwiebelkuchen* (onion quiche), and mushrooms, particularly *Pfifferlinge* (chanterelles), are seasonal favorites.

WHERE TO STAY
For expanded hotel reviews, visit Fodors.com.

$$$ 🏨 **Alte Rebschule.** Sonja Schaefer's hotel on the edge of the forest was once an old *Rebschule* (vine nursery). **Pros:** beautiful vineyard views; quiet; good restaurant. **Cons:** remote; far from the sights. ⊠ *3 km (2 mi) west of Schloss Villa Ludwigshöhe, Theresienstr. 200, Rhodt u. Rietburg* ☎ *06323/70440* ⊕ *www.alte-rebschule.de* ⤳ *29 rooms, 1 suite* ⌂ *In-room: no a/c, Internet. In-hotel: restaurant, bar, spa, business center* ⧈ *Some meals.*

ST. MARTIN

★ *26 km (16 mi) north of Annweiler, slightly west of the Wine Rd. Turn left at the northern edge of Edenkoben.*

This is one of the most charming wine villages of the Pfalz. The entire **Altstadt** (Old Town) is under historical preservation protection. For 350 years the Knights of Dalberg lived in the castle **Kropsburg**, the romantic ruins of which overlook the town. Renaissance tombstones are among the many artworks in the late-Gothic **Church of St. Martin.**

GETTING HERE AND AROUND
The easiest way to reach St. Martin is by car. There's no train station, but Bus 501 connects St. Martin with Neustadt and Edenkoben. The trip takes about 20 minutes, and the buses run approximately every half hour.

WHERE TO STAY
For expanded hotel reviews, visit Fodors.com.

$ 🏨 **Landhaus Christmann.** This bright, modern house in the midst of the vineyards has stylish rooms decorated with both antiques and modern furnishings. **Pros:** excellent value rooms; quiet location. **Cons:** remote. ⊠ *Riedweg 1* ☎ *06323/94270* ⊕ *www.landhaus-christmann.de* ⤳ *6 rooms, 3 apartments* ⌂ *In-room: no a/c, kitchen. In-hotel: business center, some pets allowed* ⧉ *No credit cards* ⊘ *Closed 4 wks in Jan. and Feb. and 2 wks in July and Aug.* ⧈ *Breakfast.*

10

$ St. Martiner Castell. The Mücke family transformed a simple vintner's house into a fine hotel and restaurant, retaining many of the original features, such as exposed beams and an old winepress. **Pros:** beautiful old home; central location. **Cons:** can be noisy. ⊠ *Maikammerer Str. 2* ☎ *06323/9510* ⊕ *www.hotelcastell.de* ⬦ *26 rooms* ᐟ *In-room: no a/c, Internet. In-hotel: restaurant, business center, some pets allowed* ⊙ *Hotel and restaurant closed Feb. Restaurant closed Tues.* ❢ *Breakfast.*

THE ARTS

Schloss Villa Ludwigshöhe, Kloster Heilsbruck (a former Cistercian convent near Edenkoben), and **Schloss Edesheim** are backdrops for concerts and theater in summer. For a calendar of events, contact the Südliche Weinstrasse regional tourist office in Landau (☎ *06341/940–407* ⊕ *www. suedlicheweinstrasse.de*).

SHOPPING

Doktorenhof. Artist Georg Wiedemann is responsible for both content and design of the exquisite products of Germany's premier wine-vinegar estate, Doktorenhof in Venningen, 2 km (1 mi) east of Edenkoben. Make an appointment for a unique vinegar tasting and tour of the cellars or pick up a gift at his shop (cash only). ⊠ *Raiffeisenstr. 5* ☎ *06323/5505* ⊕ *www.doktorenhof.de* ⊙ *Weekdays 8–4, Wed. 8–6, and Sat. 9–2.*

EN ROUTE Leave St. Martin via the Totenkopf-Höhenstrasse, a scenic road through the forest. Turn right at the intersection with Kalmitstrasse and proceed to the vantage point atop the **Kalmit**, the region's highest peak (2,200 feet). The view is second to none.

Hambacher Schloss. On the Wine Road, it's a brief drive to the Neustadt suburb of Hambach. The sturdy block of Hambacher Schloss is considered the "cradle of German democracy." It was here, on May 27, 1832, that 30,000 patriots demonstrated for German unity, raising the German colors for the first time. Inside there are exhibits about the uprising and the history of the castle. The French destroyed the 11th-century imperial fortress in 1688. Reconstruction finally began after World War II, in neo-Gothic style, and the castle is now an impressive setting for theater and concerts. On a clear day you can see the spire of Strasbourg Cathedral and the northern fringe of the Black Forest from the terrace restaurant.

Tours take about 45 minutes and begin at 11 am, noon, 2 pm, 3 pm, and 4 pm from April to October, and at 11 am, noon, and 2 pm from November to March. ⊠ *Hambach* ☎ *06321/30881* ⊕ *www.hambacher-schloss.de* ⬦ *€8* ⊙ *Mar.–Nov., daily 10–6.*

NEUSTADT

8 km (5 mi) north of St. Martin, 5 km (3 mi) north of Hambach on the Wine Rd.

Neustadt and its nine wine suburbs are at the midpoint of the Wine Road and the edge of the district known as Deutsche Weinstrasse–Mittelhaardt. With around 5,000 acres of vines, they jointly make up Germany's largest wine-growing community.

Pink and white almond blossoms line the roads of the region in spring.

GETTING HERE AND AROUND

Regular trains connect Neustadt with Ludwigshafen (connecting to Worms and Mainz). Coming from Speyer, change in Schifferstadt. Local buses connect Neustadt to other towns along the Wine Road. Once in Neustadt, the best way to get around is on foot. Neustadt tours cost €4 and take place April through October, Wednesday and Saturday at 10:30.

ESSENTIALS

Visitor Information **Neustadt-an-der-Weinstrasse** ⊠ *Tourist-Information, Hetzelpl. 1* ☎ *06321/926–892* ⊕ *www.neustadt.pfalz.com.*

EXPLORING

Eisenbahn Museum. Thirty historic train engines and railway cars are on display at the Eisenbahn Museum, behind the main train station. Take a ride through the Palatinate Forest on one of the museum's historic steam trains, the *Kuckucksbähnel* (€14), which departs from Track 5 around 10:30 am every other Sunday between Easter and mid-October. It takes a little over an hour to cover the 13-km (8-mi) stretch from Neustadt to Elmstein. ⊠ *Neustadt train station, Schillerstr. entrance* ☎ *06321/30390* ⊕ *www.eisenbahnmuseum-neustadt.de* ⊠ *€3* ☉ *Tues.– Fri. 10–1, weekends 10–4.*

Haus des Weines (*House of Wine*). At the Haus des Weines, opposite the town hall, you can sample some 30 of the 100 Neustadt wines sold. The Gothic house from 1276 is bordered by a splendid Renaissance court-yard, the Kuby'scher Hof. ⊠ *Rathausstr. 6* ☎ *06321/355–871* ⊕ *www. haus-des-weines.com* ☉ *Closed Sun. and Mon.*

BIKING, HIKING, AND WALKING

Country roads and traffic-free vineyard paths are a cyclist's paradise. There are also well-marked cycling trails, such as the **Radwanderweg Deutsche Weinstrasse**, which runs parallel to its namesake from the French border to Bockenheim, and the **Radweg** (cycling trail) along the Rhine between Worms and Mainz. The Palatinate Forest, Germany's largest single tract of woods, has more than 10,000 km (6,200 mi) of paths.

The **Wanderweg Deutsche Weinstrasse**, a walking route that traverses vineyards, woods, and wine villages, covers the length of the Pfalz. It connects with many trails in the Palatinate Forest that lead to Celtic and Roman landmarks and dozens of castles dating primarily from the 11th to 13th century. In Rheinhessen you can hike along two marked trails parallel to the Rhine: the **Rheinterrassenwanderweg** and the **Rheinhöhenweg** along the heights.

Marktplatz (*market square*). The Marktplatz is the focal point of the Old Town and a beehive of activity on Tuesday, Thursday, and Saturday, when farmers come to sell their wares. The square itself is ringed by baroque and Renaissance buildings (Nos. 1, 4, 8, and 11) and the Gothic **Stiftskirche** (Collegiate Church), built as a burial church for the Palatinate counts. In summer, concerts take place in the church (Saturday 11:30–noon). Afterward, you can ascend the southern tower (187 feet) for a bird's-eye view of the town. The world's largest cast-iron bell—weighing more than 17 tons—hangs in the northern tower. Indoors, see the elaborate tombstones near the choir and the fanciful grotesque figures carved into the baldachins and corbels.

QUICK BITES

Café Sixt. For the best "coffee and cake" or handcrafted pralines in town, head to Café Sixt. The *Pfälzer Kirschtorte* (cherry torte) is a favorite. ⊠ *Hauptstr. 3* ⊕ *www.cafesixt.de.*

Otto Dill Museum. The impressionist painter Otto Dill (1884–1957), a native of Neustadt, is known for powerful animal portraits (especially lions, tigers, and horses) and vivid landscapes. The Otto Dill Museum displays some 100 oil paintings and 50 drawings and watercolors from the Manfred Vetter collection. ⊠ *Rathausstr. 12, at Bachgängel 8* ☎ *06321/398–321* ⊕ *www.otto-dill-museum.de* ⏱*€2.50* ◷ *Wed. and Fri. 2–5, weekends 11–5.*

WHERE TO EAT

$$
GERMAN

✗ **Altstadtkeller bei Jürgen.** Tucked behind a wooden portal, this vaulted sandstone "cellar" (it's actually on the ground floor) is a cozy setting. Equally inviting is the terrace, with its citrus, olive, palm, and fig trees. The regular menu includes a number of salads and a good selection of fish and steaks. Owner Jürgen Reis is a wine enthusiast, and his well-chosen list shows it. ⊠ *Kunigundenstr. 2* ☎ *06321/32320* ⊕ *www.altstadtkeller-neustadt.de* ◷ *Closed Mon. No dinner Sun.*

$$$
GERMAN

✗ **Nett's Restaurant-Weinbar.** Susanne and Daniel Nett operate a chic wine restaurant-bar in a 16th-century vaulted stone cellar at Weingut A.

The Marktplatz in Neustad is your best bet for a meal alfresco.

Christmann, a top wine estate. Upscale versions of Pfälzer specialties as well as light cuisine with a Mediterranean touch are offered with about 200 Pfälzer wines and other top German reds and whites. Dining alfresco in the intimate courtyard is a romantic option in summer. The Netts also offer seven unique rooms ($$) for overnight guests, each with hardwood floors and Wi-Fi. ⊠ *Meerspinnstr. 46, Neustadt-Gimmeldingen* ☎ *06321/60175* ⊕ *www.nettsrestaurant.de* ⊟ *No credit cards* ⊘ *Closed Mon. and Tues. No lunch except summer Sun. and some holidays.*

$ ✕ **Weinstube Eselsburg.** The *Esel* (donkey) lends its name to Mussbach's
GERMAN   best-known vineyard, Eselshaut (donkey's hide); this wine pub; and one of its specialties, *Eselssuppe*, a hearty soup of pork, beef, and vegetables. Always packed with regulars, the season dictactes the menu. In spring, you can enjoy locally produced goat's cheese. In summer, savor top Pfälzer wines in the flower-filled courtyard, or in the warmth of an open hearth in winter. From October to April, try the *Schlachtfest* (meat and sausages from freshly slaughtered pigs) the first Tuesday of the month. ⊠ *Kurpfalzstr. 62, Neustadt-Mussbach* ☎ *06321/66984* ⊕ *www.eselsburg.de* ⊘ *Closed Sun. and Mon., and 3 wks in Aug. No lunch except during Schlachtfest.*

WHERE TO STAY

For expanded hotel reviews, visit Fodors.com.

$ ⊡ **Gästehaus Rebstöckel.** Enjoy vintner's hospitality in the Schlau and Moseler family's 17th-century stone guesthouse, with its beautiful cobblestone courtyard and magnificent fig tree. **Pros:** quiet; friendly; rustic location. **Cons:** no Internet; light from street lamp may bother light sleepers. ⊠ *Kreuzstr. 11, Neustadt-Diedesfeld* ☎ *06321/484–060* ⊕ *www.gaestehaus-rebstoeckel-pfalz.de/en* ↩ *5 rooms* ⚘ *In-room: no a/c, kitchen* ⊟ No credit cards ¦⊙¦ *Breakfast.*

$ ★ 🍴 **Mithras-Stuben/Weinstube Kommerzienrat.** In the picturesque village of Gimmeldingen, convivial proprietor and wine devotee Bernd Hagedorn rents four spacious apartments with contemporary furnishings, Oriental rugs, and modern baths. **Pros:** spacious; perfect for longer stays. **Cons:** no elevator. ⊠ *Loblocherstr. 34, Neustadt-Gimmeldingen* ☎ *06321/679–0335, 06321/68200* ⊕ *www.weinstube-kommerzienrat. de* ↩ *4 apartments* ⚘ *In-room: no a/c, kitchen, Internet. In-hotel: restaurant, some pets allowed* ⊟ No credit cards ⊙ *Hotel and restaurant closed 2 wks late Apr. Restaurant closed Thurs. No lunch.*

$ 🍴 **Steinhäuser Hof.** This architectural gem in the heart of the Old Town dates back to 1276 and is one of the oldest preserved stone mansions in Rhineland-Palatinate. **Pros:** beautiful old building; central location; friendly staff. **Cons:** no elevator. ⊠ *Rathausstr. 6* ☎ *06321/489–060* ⊕ *www.steinhaeuserhof.de* ↩ *6 rooms* ⚘ *In-room: no a/c. In-hotel: restaurant, bar, some pets allowed* ⊙ *Restaurant closed Mon.* ¦⊙¦ *Breakfast.*

NIGHTLIFE AND THE ARTS

Saalbau. The Saalbau, opposite the train station, is Neustadt's convention center and main venue for concerts, theater, and events. ⊠ *Bahnhofstr. 1* ☎ *06321/926–812.*

Villa Böhm. In summer there's open-air theater at Villa Böhm, which also houses the city's history museum. ⊠ *Maximilianstr. 25.*

SHOPPING

Keramik-Atelier Ingrid Zinkgraf. After seeing the water-spewing Elwetritschen fountain in action, you might want to take one home. The pottery store Keramik-Atelier Ingrid Zinkgraf has amusing ceramic renditions of the mythical birds, as well as modern and traditional pottery and sculptures. ⊠ *Weinstr. 1, Am Klemmhof* ☎ *06345/06345* ⊕ *www. keramikatelier-zinkgraf.de.*

EN ROUTE

↻ **Holiday Park.** The Holiday Park, in Hassloch, 10 km (6 mi) east of Neustadt, is one of Europe's largest amusement parks. The admission fee covers all attractions, shows including the Waterski Stuntshow, special events, and the children's world. The free-fall tower, hell barrels, and Thunder River rafting are standing favorites, and *Expedition GeForce* has the steepest drop (82 degrees) of any roller coaster in Europe. For a great panoramic view of the surroundings, whirl through the air on Lighthouse-Tower, Germany's tallest carousel (265 feet). On Friday and Saturday in summer, the "Summer Nights" spectacular features live music and an outdoor laser light show. ⊠ *Holiday Parkstr. 1–5* ☎ *06324/59930* ⊕ *www.holidaypark.de* 🎟 *€25* ⊙ *Mid-Apr.–Oct., daily 10–6.*

SPEYER

25 km (15 mi) east of Neustadt via B-39, 22 km (14 mi) south of Mannheim via B-9 and B-44.

Speyer was one of the great cities of the Holy Roman Empire, founded in pre-Celtic times, taken over by the Romans, and expanded in the 11th century by the Salian emperors. Between 1294, when it was declared a Free Imperial City, and 1570, no fewer than 50 imperial Diets were convened here. The term "Protestant" derives from the Diet of 1529, referring to those who protested when the religious freedom granted to evangelicals at the Diet of 1526 was revoked and a return to Catholicism was decreed. The neo-Gothic **Gedächtniskirche** on Bartolomäus-Weltz-Platz commemorates those 16th-century Protestants.

GETTING HERE AND AROUND

Speyer is a little ways off the German Wine Road. It is served by regular trains from Mannheim and Mainz. Buses ply the main street, but the center is compact enough that getting around on foot is not a problem. Tours (€5) are at 11 and 2 Saturday and 11 Sunday year-round.

ESSENTIALS

Visitor Information Speyer ⊠ *Tourist-Information, Maximilianstr. 13* ☎ *06232/142–392* ⊕ *www.speyer.de.*

EXPLORING

Altpörtel. Ascend the Altpörtel, the impressive town gate, for a grand view of Maximilianstrasse, the street that led kings and emperors straight to the cathedral. ⊠ *Rossmarktstr. 1* ☎ *€1* ⊙ *Apr.–Oct., week-days 10–noon, weekends 10–5.*

★ **Historisches Museum der Pfalz** (*Palatinate Historical Museum*). Opposite the cathedral, the museum houses the **Domschatz** (Cathedral Treasury). Other collections chronicle the art and cultural history of Speyer and the Pfalz from the Stone Age to modern times. Don't miss the "Golden Hat of Schifferstadt," a Bronze Age headdress used in religious ceremonies dating back to approximately 1300 BC. The **Wine Museum** houses the world's oldest bottle of wine, which is still liquid and dates to circa AD 300. The giant 35-foot-long wooden winepress from 1727 is also worth a look. ⊠ *Dompl. 4* ☎ *06232/13250* ⊕ *www.museum.speyer.de* ☎ *€8, special exhibitions €12* ⊙ *Tues.–Sun. 10–6.*

Fodor's Choice ★ **Kaiserdom** (*Imperial Cathedral*). The Kaiserdom, one of the finest Romanesque cathedrals in the world and a UNESCO World Heritage site, conveys the pomp and majesty of the early Holy Roman Emperors. It was built between 1030 and 1061 by the emperors Konrad II, Henry III, and Henry IV. The last replaced the flat ceiling with groin vaults in the late 11th century, an innovative feat in its day. A restoration pro-gram in the 1950s returned the building to almost exactly its original condition. ■ TIP→ There's a fine view of the east end of the structure from

10

A splendid example of Romanesque architecture, the Kaiserdom (Imperial Cathedral) has the largest crypt in Germany.

the park by the Rhine. Much of the architectural detail, including the dwarf galleries and ornamental capitals, was inspired and executed by stonemasons from Lombardy, which belonged to the German Empire at the time. The four towers symbolize the four seasons and the idea that the power of the empire extends in all four directions. Look up as you enter the nearly 100-foot-high portal. It's richly carved with mythical creatures. In contrast to Gothic cathedrals, whose walls are supported externally by flying buttresses, allowing for a minimum of masonry and a maximum of light, at Speyer the columns supporting the roof are massive. The **Krypta** (crypt) lies beneath the chancel. It's the largest crypt in Germany and is strikingly beautiful in its simplicity. Four emperors, four kings, and three empresses are buried here. ⊠ *Edith-Stein-Pl.* 🖾 *Donation requested* ⊗ *Apr.–Oct., daily 9–7; Nov.–Mar., daily 9–5; closed during services.*

Jewish quarter. Speyer was an important medieval Jewish cultural center. In the Jewish quarter, behind the Palatinate Historical Museum, you can see synagogue remains from 1104 and Germany's oldest (circa 1126) ritual baths, the 33-foot-deep *Mikwe.* Note: Although the official address is Judengasse, the entrance is around the corner at Kleine Pfaffengasse 21. ⊠ *Entrance around the corner at Kleine Pfaffeng. 21, Judeng.* 🕿 *06232/291–971* 🖾 *€3* ⊗ *Apr.–Oct., daily 10–5.*

🖑 **Sea Life.** If you're traveling with kids or just need some indoor entertainment on a rainy day, Sea Life, in Speyer's old harbor, has aquariums that offer a look at marine life in the Rhine as well as the world's oceans. ◼ TIP→ Save money on the entrance fee by booking your tickets online in advance. ⊠ *Im Hafenbecken 5, 15-min walk from large parking lot on*

THE ALTRHEIN

From April to October, take a brief river cruise to the north or south of Speyer to discover the idyllic landscape of the ancient, forested islands along the *Altrhein* (original course of the Rhine). The islands are home to rare flora, fauna, and many birds. There are grand views of the cathedral from the boat.

Fahrgastschifffahrt Speyer. In the summer months, boat tours depart from just outside the Sea Life Aquarium at noon, 2, and 4. The trip lasts about 1½ hours and offers a unique look at Speyer's old harbor.

⊠ *Hafenstr. 22* ⊕ *www.ms-sealife. de* ✉ *€9.*

Pfälzerland Fahrgastschiff. Enjoy a peaceful tour of the Speyer harbor on a ship built for 200 passengers. Homemade cakes and drinks are available on board. On Tuesday through Friday, 1½-hour tours depart at 1 and 3. On Saturday there's a two-hour tour at 3. The pick-up and drop-off point is on the Leinpfad. ⊠ *Dock: Leinpfad (via Rheinallee), on the Rhine riverbank, Rheinalle 2* ✑ *www.personenschifffahrt-streib. de* ✉ *€9.*

Festpl. ☎ *06232/69780* ⊕ *www.sealife.de* ✉ *€13.95* ☉ *Nov.–Mar, daily 10–4; Apr.–June, Sept., and Oct., weekdays 10–4, weekends 10–5; July and Aug., daily 10–6.*

☾ **Technik-Museum** (*Technology Museum*). A turn-of-the-20th-century factory hall houses the Technik-Museum, an impressive and vast collection of locomotives, aircraft, old automobiles, and fire engines. Automatic musical instruments, historical dolls and toys, and 19th-century fashion are displayed in the Wilhelmsbau. Highlights of the complex are the 420-ton U-boat (you can go inside) and the massive 3-D IMAX cinemas. There is also an exhibition hall devoted to outer space. ■TIP→ Allow at least three hours to visit this extensive museum, which covers several large buildings. ⊠ *Geibstr. 2* ☎ *06232/67080* ⊕ *www.technik-museum. de* ✉ *Museum €13, IMAX €10, combined ticket €18* ☉ *Weekdays 9–6, weekends 9–7.*

WHERE TO EAT AND STAY
For expanded hotel reviews, visit Fodors.com.

$$ ✕ **Kutscherhaus.** Charming rustic decor and a profusion of flowers have
GERMAN replaced the *Kutschen* (coaches) in this turn-of-the-20th-century coachman's house. The menu offers *Flammkuchen* (similar to pizza but baked on a wafer-thin crust) as well as creative fish, vegetarian, and pasta dishes. *Ochsenbrust mit Meerrettichsauce* (beef brisket with horseradish sauce) is a favorite. In summer you can sit beneath the old plane trees in the beer garden and select from a sumptuous buffet. ⊠ *Fischmarkt 5a* ☎ *06232/70592* ⊕ *www.kutscherhaus-speyer.de* ☉ *Closed Wed. Beer garden open daily all summer.*

$ ✕ **Rabennest.** It's small and often packed with local families, but the rus-
GERMAN tic cooking in this cozy restaurant is worth the wait. Hearty portions of regional specialties will delight both your mouth and your wallet. The *Leberknoedel* (liver dumplings) and *Rumpsteak* (round steak) are both excellent, and those in need of respite from meat and potatoes will be

happy to discover the selection of fresh salads. In the summer months, the patio seating is great for people-watching. ⊠ *Korngasse 5, Speyer* ☎ *06232/623–857* ▤ *No credit cards* ☾ *Closed Sun.*

$ ✕**Ratskeller.** Friendly service and fresh seasonal dishes make for an
GERMAN enjoyable dining experience in the town hall's vaulted cellar (1578). The frequently changing menu offers creative soups (pretzel soup, Tuscan bread soup) and entrées, such as *Sauerbraten nach Grossmutters Art* (grandmother's marinated pot roast) or *Bachsaibling* (brook char in a red-wine-butter sauce). Wines from the Pfalz predominate, with 18 available by the glass. Small plates and drinks are served in the courtyard May through September. ⊠ *Maximilianstr. 12* ☎ *06232/78612* ⊕ *www.ratskeller-speyer.de* ☾ *Closed Mon. and 2–3 wks in Feb. No dinner Sun.*

$ ✕**Wirtschaft Zum Alten Engel.** This 200-year-old vaulted brick cellar has
GERMAN rustic wood furnishings and cozy niches. Seasonal dishes supplement the large selection of Pfälzer and Alsatian specialties, such as *Ochsenfetzen* (slices of beef in garlic sauce), *Fleeschknepp* (spicy meatball in horseradish sauce), or a hearty *Pfälzer Platte* (a platter of bratwurst, Saumagen, and Leberknödel with sauerkraut and home-fried potatoes). The wine list features about 180 Pfälzer, European, and New World wines. ⊠ *Mühlturmstr. 7* ☎ *06232/70914* ⊕ *www.zumaltenengel.de* ☾ *No lunch.*

$$ ⌂**Hotel Goldener Engel.** A scant two blocks west of the Altpörtel is the "Golden Angel," a friendly, family-run hotel furnished with antiques and innovative metal-and-wood designer furniture. **Pros:** friendly; good location. **Cons:** some rooms are a little small. ⊠ *Mühlturmstr. 5–7* ☎ *06232/13260* ⊕ *www.goldener-engel-speyer.de* ⤴*44 rooms, 2 suites* ⌂ *In-room: no a/c, Internet. In-hotel: restaurant, some pets allowed* ¶⃝*Breakfast.*

NIGHTLIFE AND THE ARTS

Highlights for music lovers are **Orgelfrühling**, the organ concerts in the Gedächtniskirche (Memorial Church) in spring, the jazz festival in mid-August, and the concerts in the cathedral during September's **Internationale Musiktage.** Call the Speyer tourist office for program details and tickets.

Kulturhof Flachsgasse. Walk into the town-hall courtyard to enter the Kulturhof Flachsgasse, home of the city's art collection and special exhibitions. ⊠ *Flachsg.* ☎ *06232/142–399* ▱ *Free* ☾ *Tues.–Sun. 11–6.*

DEIDESHEIM

8 km (5 mi) north of Neustadt via the Wine Rd., B-271.

Deidesheim is the first of a trio of villages on the Wine Road renowned for their vineyards and the wine estates known as the Three Bs of the Pfalz—Bassermann, Buhl, and Bürklin.

The half-timber houses and historical facades framing Deidesheim's **Marktplatz** form a picturesque group, including the **Church of St. Ulrich,** a Gothic gem inside and out.

TOURS

The Deidesheim visitor center conducts tours May through October on Saturday at 10:30 (€5).

ESSENTIALS

Visitor Information Deidesheim
⊠ *Tourist-Information, Bahnhofstr. 5* ☎ *06326/96770* ⊕ *www.deidesheim.de.*

EXPLORING

Rathaus (*Town Hall*). The old Rathaus, whose doorway is crowned by a baldachin and baroque dome, is on the Marktplatz. The attractive open staircase leading up to the entrance is the site of the festive *Geissbock-Versteigerung* (billy-goat auction) every Pentecost Tuesday, followed by a parade and folk dancing. The goat is the tribute neighboring Lambrecht has paid Deidesheim since 1404 for grazing rights. Inside, see the richly appointed Ratssaal (council chamber) and the museum of wine culture. ⊠ *Marktpl.* ⊠ *Donation requested* ⊘ *Mar.– Dec., Wed.–Sun. 3–6.*

Schloss Deidesheim. Vines, flowers, and *Feigenbäume* (fig trees) cloak the houses behind St. Ulrich on Heumarktstrasse and its extension, Deichelgasse (nicknamed Feigengasse). ■ TIP→ To see the workshops and ateliers of about a dozen local artists and goldsmiths, follow the *Künstler-Rundweg*, a signposted trail (black on yellow signs). The tourist office has a brochure with a map and opening hours. Cross the Wine Road to reach the grounds of Schloss Deidesheim, now a wine estate and pub (November–March closed weekdays; no lunch weekdays). The bishops of Speyer built a moated castle on the site in the 13th century. Twice destroyed and rebuilt, the present castle dates from 1817, and the moats have been converted into gardens. ⊠ *Schlossstr. 4.*

WHERE TO EAT AND STAY

For expanded hotel reviews, visit Fodors.com.

$$$$
GERMAN
✕ **Restaurant Freundstück im Ketschauer Hof.** An 18th-century complex in a beautiful park has long been home to the Bassermann-Jordan wine estate. Inside the stunningly elegant restaurant and bistrolike wine bar elements of the original structures harmonize with modern, minimalist decor. The chef prepares gourmet fare in the restaurant and upscale regional dishes in the wine bar. The excellent wine list includes every vintage of Bassermann-Jordan since 1870. ⊠ *Ketschauerhofstr. 1* ☎ *06326/70000* ⊕ *www.ketschauer-hof.com* ⊘ *Closed 3 wks in Jan. Restaurant closed Sun. and Mon. No lunch Sat.*

$$
GERMAN
✕ **Restaurant St. Urban.** Named after St. Urban, the vintners' patron saint, this upscale wine restaurant offers traditional Palatinate cuisine and wines from more than 50 local wineries. If the weather is nice, enjoy an *Aperol Sprizz* (an apertif of sparkling wine, Aperol, and soda) on the terrace before sampling one of the hearty regional dishes. The restaurant is part of the Hotel Deidesheimer Hof. ⊠ *Am Marktpl. 1* ☎ *06326/96870* ⊕ *www.deidesheimerhof.de* ⊘ *Closed 2nd wk of Jan.*

SWEET SOUVENIRS

Josef Biffar & Co. The Biffar family not only runs a first-class wine estate but also manufactures very exclusive candied fruits and ginger that make delicious souvenirs. ⊠ *Niederkircher Str. 15* ☎ *06326/96760* ⊕ *www.biffar.com* ⊘ *Weekdays 9–noon and 1–5:30, Sat. 10–noon and 1:30–3:30.*

10

$$ GERMAN ✕ **Weinschmecker.** The restaurant and vinothek of Herbert Nikola, an expert on Pfälzer wines and festivals, is on the eastern edge of town. Italian tiles and whitewashed walls give it a light, airy Mediterranean look—much on the menu reflects the same culture. The focus, however, is on top-quality Pfälzer specialties and wines, 200 of which (from about 40 estates) are featured; 120 are available by the glass. ✉ *Steing. 2* ☎ *06326/980–460* 🌐 *www.weinschmecker-deidesheim.de* ▭ *No credit cards* ⊙ *Closed Sun. and Mon. No lunch.*

$$$ Fodor's Choice ★ **Hotel Deidesheimer Hof.** Despite the glamour of its clientele—the heads of state, entertainers, and sports stars line the guest book—this hotel retains its country charm and friendly service. **Pros:** some rooms have whirlpool baths; friendly staff; central location on the Marktplatz. **Cons:** rates don't include breakfast. ✉ *Am Marktpl. 1* ☎ *06326/96870* 🌐 *www.deidesheimerhof.de* *24 rooms, 4 suites* *In-room: Internet, Wi-Fi. In-hotel: restaurant, bar, business center, some pets allowed* ⊙ *Hotel closed 2nd wk of Jan. Restaurant closed Sun. and Mon., Jan., and 4 wks in July and Aug. No lunch.*

$ **Landhotel Lucashof.** The beautifully decorated, modern guest rooms are named after famous vineyards in Forst, and four have balconies—the room called Pechstein is particularly nice. **Pros:** quiet location; friendly; good value. **Cons:** far from the sights; difficult to reach without a car. ✉ *Wiesenweg 1a, Forst* ☎ *06326/336* 🌐 *www.lucashof.de* *7 rooms* *In-room: no a/c, Internet. In-hotel: business center, some pets allowed* ▭ *No credit cards* ⊙ *Closed mid-Dec.–Jan.* *Breakfast.*

EN ROUTE

Forst and **Wachenheim,** both a few minutes' drive north of Deidesheim, complete the trio of famous wine villages. As you approach Forst, depart briefly from B-271 (take the left fork in the road) to see the Old Town with its vine- and ivy-clad sandstone and half-timber vintners' mansions. Peek through the large portals to see the lush courtyards. Many estates on this lane have pubs, as does the town's *Winzerverein* (cooperative winery). Wachenheim is another 2 km (1 mi) down the road. Its cooperative, Wachtenburg Winzer (with a good restaurant), is on the left at the entrance to town. Head for the Wachtenburg (castle) ruins up on the hill for a glass of wine. The Burgschänke (castle pub) is open if the flag is flying.

BAD DÜRKHEIM

6 km (4 mi) north of Deidesheim on B-271.

This pretty spa-town is nestled into the hills at the edge of the Palatinate Forest and ringed by vineyards. The saline springs discovered here in 1338 are the source of today's drinking and bathing cures, and at harvest time there's a detoxifying *Traubenkur* (grape-juice cure). The town is the site of the Dürkheimer Wurstmarkt, the world's largest wine festival, held in mid-September. Legendary quantities of *Weck, Worscht, un Woi* (dialect for rolls, sausage, and wine) are consumed at the fair, including half a million *Schoppen,* the region's traditional pint-size glasses of wine. The festival grounds are also the site of the world's largest wine cask, the **Dürkheimer Riesenfass,** with a capacity of

WINE FESTIVALS

Attending a wine festival is fun and a memorable part of any vacation in wine country. You can sample local food and wine inexpensively and meet winegrowers without making an appointment. Wine and *Sekt* (sparkling wine) flow freely from March through October at festivals that include parades, fireworks, and rides. The Pfalz is home to the world's largest wine festival, in mid-September, the **Dürkheimer Wurst-markt** (Sausage Market, so named because of the 400,000 pounds of sausage consumed during eight days of merrymaking). In Neustadt, the German Wine Queen is crowned during the 10-day **Deutsches Weinlesefest** (German Wine Harvest Festival) in October. The **Mainzer Johannisnacht** (in honor of Johannes Gutenberg) in late June, the **Wormser Backfischfest** (fried-fish festival) in late August, and the **Brezelfest** (pretzel festival) in Speyer on the second weekend in July are the major wine and folk festivals along this part of the Rhine. See ⊕ *www.germanwines.de* for an events calendar with an up-to-date overview of many smaller, local wine festivals that take place in virtually every village.

450,000 gallons. Built in 1934 by an ambitious cooper, the cask is now a restaurant that can seat well more than 450 people.

GETTING HERE AND AROUND

Regional trains link Bad Dürkheim with Freinsheim and Neustadt. Once in town, all the hotels and restaurants are within easy walking distance. Bad Dürkheim has tours (€3) May through October, departing Monday and Saturday at 10:30 at the sign marked "Treffpunkt Führungen," near the entrance to the train station. You can check with Tourist-Information for a number of other interesting programs, including a Wine Road tour, wine tastings, and visits to the cure facilities.

ESSENTIALS

Visitor Information Bad Dürkheim ⊠ *Tourist-Information, Kurbrunnenstr. 14* ☎ *06322/956–6250* 🖶 *06322/956–6259* ⊕ *www.bad-duerkheim.com.*

10

EXPLORING

Burgruine Hardenburg (*Hardenburg Fortress*). The massive ruins of 13th-century Hardenburg Castle lie 3 km (2 mi) west (via B-37) of Kloster Limburg. In its heyday, it was inhabited by more than 200 people. It succumbed to fire in 1794. ⊠ *B-37* 🎟 *€3* ☉ *Apr.–Sept., Tues.–Sun. 9–1 and 1:30–6; Jan.–Mar., Oct., and Nov., Tues.–Sun. 9–1 and 1:30–5.*

Heidenmauer (*literally, "heathen wall"*). One kilometer northwest of town lies the Heidenmauer, the remains of an ancient Celtic ring wall more than 2 km (1 mi) in circumference and up to 20 feet thick in parts. The remnants are on the Kastanienberg, above the quarry. Nearby are the rock drawings at **Kriemhildenstuhl,** an old Roman quarry where the legionnaires of Mainz excavated sandstone.

Kloster Limburg (*Limburg Monastery*). Overlooking the suburb of Grethen are the ruins of Kloster Limburg. Emperor Konrad II laid the cornerstone in 1030, supposedly on the same day that he laid the cornerstone of the Kaiserdom in Speyer. The monastery was never completely rebuilt after a fire in 1504, but it's a majestic backdrop for open-air performances in summer. From the tree-shaded terrace of the Klosterschänke restaurant ($–$$), adjacent to the ruins, you can combine good food and wine with a great view (closed Monday). ✉ *Luitpoldweg 1.*

WHERE TO EAT

$$ ✕**Dürkheimer Riesenfass.** It's a bit of a tourist trap, but then again, how
GERMAN often do you get the chance to eat in the world's biggest wine barrel? The two-story "giant cask" is divided into various rooms and niches with rustic wood furnishings. Ask to see the impressive *Festsaal mit Empore* (banquet hall with gallery) upstairs. Regional wines, Pfälzer specialties, and international dishes are served year-round. ✉ *St. Michael Allee 1* ☎ *06322/2143* ⊕ *www.duerkheimer-fass.de.*

$ ✕**Petersilie.** Römerplatz abounds with cafés and eateries, but behind a
GERMAN group of lush, potted plants and a sign on the pink-and-white house reading "bier- und weinstube tenne" is Petersilie, a gem for homemade Pfälzer cuisine and wine. Patio seating is great for people-watching; indoors is warm and cozy, with rustic wooden tables and pillow-lined benches. The weekly changing, three-course Sunday menu ($) is a great value. ✉ *Römerpl. 12* ☎ *06322/4394* ⊕ *www.weinstube-petersilie.de* ⊟ *No credit cards* ⊗ *No lunch Wed.*

$$ ✕**Philip's Brasserie.** Römerplatz is Bad Dürkheim's culinary hub and
MEDITERRANEAN the location of this classy restaurant. Paintings by contemporary local artists—including those of the hosts—line the terra-cotta–color walls. Aromatic and flavorful seasonal cuisine starts with homemade bread and dip. The wine list is a showcase of great wines from the Pfalz, with a selection of international wines as well. ■**TIP→ On Monday, Thursday, and Friday, there's a lunch special for €9.50.** ✉ *Römerpl. 3* ☎ *06322/68808* ⊕ *www.philips-brasserie.de* ⊟ *No credit cards* ⊗ *Closed Tues., Wed., 1 wk in Jan., and 2 wks in mid-Sept. No lunch on weekends.*

WHERE TO STAY

For expanded hotel reviews, visit Fodors.com.

$$ 🏨**Kurparkhotel.** Part of the Kurhaus complex, the Kurparkhotel is the
★ place to be pampered from head to toe. **Pros:** good location; some balconies overlook park. **Cons:** on-site spa means slight smell of chlorine. ✉ *Schlosspl. 1–4* ☎ *06322/7970* ⊕ *www.kurpark-hotel.de* ⤶ *113 rooms* ♿ *In-room: no a/c, Internet. In-hotel: restaurant, bar, pool, gym, spa, business center, some pets allowed* ❡⊘❘ *Breakfast.*

$ 🏨**Weingut Fitz-Ritter.** The centuries-old stone cottage sleeps up to four people and has a private pool on the parklike grounds of the Fitz-Ritter wine estate, which dates to 1785. **Pros:** quiet location amid the vines; friendly staff. **Cons:** far from the sights. ✉ *Weinstr. Nord 51* ☎ *06322/5389* ⊕ *www.fitz-ritter.de* ⤶ *1 cottage, 4 rooms* ♿ *In-room: no a/c, Internet. In-hotel: pool.*

$ 🏨**Weingut und Gästehaus Ernst Karst und Sohn.** This cheerful guesthouse is adjacent to the Karst family's wine estate, in the midst of the vineyards. **Pros:** quiet location amid the vines; friendly staff. **Cons:** far from the sights. ✉ *In den Almen 15* ☎ *06322/2862* ⊕ *www.weingut-karst.de* ⤶ *3* *rooms, 6 apartments* ⚏ *In-room: no a/c, Wi-Fi. In-hotel: bar, business center* ▭ *No credit cards* ⊘ *Closed Nov.–Feb.* ⦿ *Breakfast.*

NIGHTLIFE AND THE ARTS

Kloster Limburg (*Limburg Monastery*). Concerts and theater take place at Kloster Limburg. Contact the local tourist office for program details.

Spielbank (*Casino*). On the grounds of the Kurparkhotel, this casino is open daily after 2 pm; jacket and tie are no longer required, but tennis shoes, T-shirts, and shorts are not allowed. Be certain to bring your passport for identification; the minimum age is 18. ✉ *Schlosspl. 6* ⛟ *€3.50.*

SHOPPING

Weindom. Several hundred wines from Bad Dürkheim and vicinity can be sampled and purchased at the Weindom next to the Dürkheimer Riesenfass (giant cask) on St. Michael Allee. The shop also sells other grape products and accessories. ✉ *St.-Michaels-Allee 10* ⊘ *Daily 10–6.*

SPORTS AND THE OUTDOORS

Kurhaus Staatsbad. The Kurhaus Staatsbad houses all kinds of bathing facilities for leisure and wellness, including thermal baths, herbal steam baths, a sauna, and a hammam (Turkish bath). ✉ *Kurbrunnenstr. 14* ☎ *06322/9640* ⊕ *www.kurzentrum-bad-duerkheim.de* ⊘ *Weekdays 9–8, Sat. 9–5, Sun. 9–2:30.*

EN ROUTE **Neuleiningen** is 4 km (2½ mi) west of the Wine Road town Kirchheim. **Bockenheim**, 10 km (6 mi) north, is dominated by an imposing gateway. There's a panoramic view of the Pfalz's "sea of vineyards" from the viewing platform. Like its counterpart in Schweigen-Rechtenbach, the **Haus der Deutschen Weinstrasse** marks the end (or start) of its namesake, the German Wine Road.

THE RHINE TERRACE

Like Speyer, the cities of Worms and Mainz were Free Imperial Cities and major centers of Christian and Jewish culture in the Middle Ages. Germany's first synagogue and Europe's oldest surviving Jewish cemetery, both from the 11th century, are in Worms. The imperial diets of Worms and Speyer in 1521 and 1529 stormed around Martin Luther (1483–1546) and the rise of Protestantism. In 1455 Johannes Gutenberg (1400–68), the inventor of movable type, printed the first Gutenberg Bible in Mainz.

10

WORMS

15 km (9 mi) east of Bockenheim via B-47 from Monsheim, 45 km (28 mi) south of Mainz on B-9.

Although devastated in World War II, Worms (pronounced *vawrms*) is among the most ancient cities of Germany, with a history going back some 6,000 years. Once settled by the Romans, Worms later became one of the imperial cities of the Holy Roman Empire. More than 100 imperial diets were held here, including the 1521 meeting where Martin

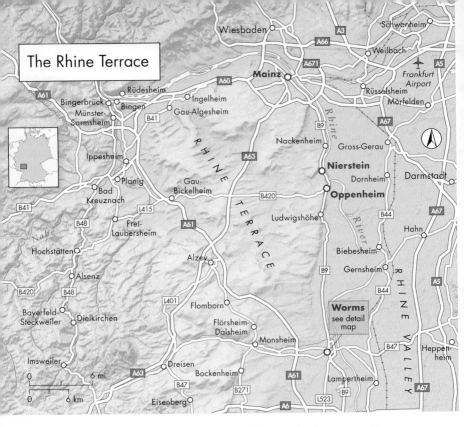

The Rhine Terrace

Luther pleaded his cause. In addition to having a great Romanesque cathedral, Worms is a center of the wine trade.

Worms developed into an important garrison town under the Romans, but it's better known for its greatest legend, the *Nibelungenlied,* derived from the short-lived kingdom established by Gunther and his Burgundian tribe in the early 5th century. The complex and sprawling story was given its final shape in the 12th century and tells of love, betrayal, greed, war, and death. It ends when Attila the Hun defeats the Nibelungen (Burgundians), who find their court destroyed, their treasure lost, and their heroes dead. One of the most famous incidents tells how Hagen, treacherous and scheming, hurls the court riches into the Rhine. Near the Nibelungen Bridge there's a bronze statue of him caught in the act. The Nibelungenlied may be legend, but the story is based on fact. A Queen Brunhilda, for example, is said to have lived here. It's also known that a Burgundian tribe was defeated in 436 by Attila the Hun in what is present-day Hungary.

Not until Charlemagne resettled Worms almost 400 years later, making it one of the major cities of his empire, did the city prosper again. Worms was more than an administrative and commercial center—it was a great ecclesiastical city as well. The first expression of this religious importance was the original cathedral, consecrated in 1018. Between

1130 and 1181 it was rebuilt in three phases into the church you see today.

GETTING HERE AND AROUND

Worms can be reached by direct trains from both Mannheim and Mainz (approximately 30 minutes from each). The city center is quite compact and negotiable on foot. Worms begins its tours at the southern portal (main entrance) of the cathedral on Saturday at 10:30 and Sunday at 2 from March through October. The cost is €4.

ESSENTIALS

Visitor Information Worms
✉ *Tourist-Information, Neumarkt 14* ☎ *06241/8530* ⊕ *www.worms.de.*

EXPLORING

TOP ATTRACTIONS

Heylshofgarten. An imperial palace once stood in this park just north of the cathedral. It was the site of the fateful meeting between Luther and Emperor Charles V in April 1521 that ultimately led to the Reformation. Luther refused to recant his theses demanding Church reforms and went into exile in Eisenach, where he translated the New Testament in 1521 and 1522. ✉ *Marktpl.*

Judenfriedhof Heiliger Sand (*Holy Sand Cemetery*). This is the oldest Jewish cemetery in Europe and one of the most atmospheric and picturesque. The oldest of some 2,000 tombstones date from 1076. Entry is via the gate on Willy-Brandt-Ring. ✉ *Andreasstr. and Willy-Brandt-Ring* ☉ *Daily 8 am–sunset or 8 pm.*

★ **Kunsthaus Heylshof** (*Heylshof Art Gallery*). Located in the Heylshofgarten, this is one of the leading art museums of the region. It has an exquisite collection of German, Dutch, and French paintings as well as stained glass, glassware, porcelain, and ceramics dating from the 15th to the 19th century. ✉ *Stephansg. 9* ☎ *06241/22000* ⊕ *www.museumheylshof.de* 💶 *€3.50* ☉ *May–Sept., Tues.–Sun. 11–5; Oct.–Dec. and mid-Feb.–Apr., Tues.–Sat. 2–5, Sun. 11–5.*

Liebfrauenkirche (*Church of Our Lady*). This twin-towered Gothic church is set amid vineyards on the northern outskirts of Worms. It's the namesake of the popular, mild white wine Liebfraumilch, literally, the "Milk of Our Lady." The wine was originally made from the grapes of the small vineyard surrounding the church, but today it's produced throughout Rheinhessen, the Pfalz, the Nahe, and the Rheingau wine regions. ✉ *Liebfrauenring 21.*

Lutherdenkmal. This monument commemorates Luther's appearance at the Diet of Worms. He ended his speech with the words: "Here I stand. I have no choice. God help me. Amen." The 19th-century

10

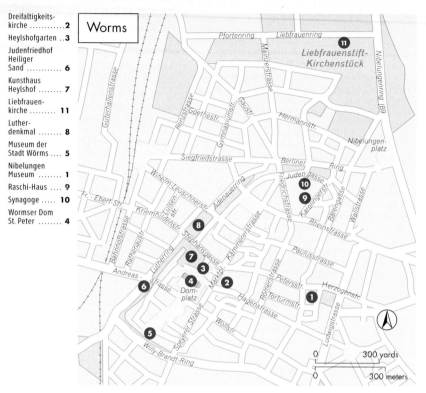

monument includes a large statue of Luther ringed by other figures from the Reformation. It's set in a small park on the street named Luther-ring. ⊠ *Lutherpl.*

★   **Nibelungen Museum.** This stunning sight-and-sound exhibition is dedicated to the Song of the Nieblungs, an epic German poem dating to around 1200. Cleverly installed in two medieval towers and the portion of the Old Town wall between them, the exhibition brings to life the saga of the dragon slayer Siegfried. The architecture of the structure itself is also fascinating, and the rampart affords a wonderful view of the town. Language is no problem: the tour script (via headphones and printed matter) is offered in English. ■ TIP→ Allow 1½ hours for a thorough visit. ⊠ *Fischerpförtchen 10* ☎ *06241/202–120* ⊕ *www. nibelungen-museum.de* ☎ *€5.50* ☉ *Tues.–Fri. 10–5, weekends 10–6.*

Synagogue. This first synagogue in Worms was built in 1034, rebuilt in 1175, and expanded in 1213 with a building for women. Destroyed in 1938, it was rebuilt in 1961 using as much of the original masonry as had survived. It is located in the Jewish quarter, which is along the town wall between Martinspforte and Friesenspitze and between Judengasse and Hintere Judengasse. ⊠ *Hintere Judeng.* ☉ *Apr.–Oct., daily 10–12:30 and 1:30–5; Nov.–Mar., daily 10–noon and 2–4; closed during services.*

One of the focal points of the Gothic Wormser Dom St. Peter (Worms Cathedral of St. Peter) is the gilded altar.

★ **Wormser Dom St. Peter.** If you've seen Speyer Cathedral, you'll quickly notice that the Worms Cathedral of St. Peter, in contrast, contains many Gothic elements. In part this is simply a matter of chronology. Speyer Cathedral was completed nearly 70 years before the one in Worms was even begun, long before the lighter, more vertical lines of the Gothic style evolved. Furthermore, once built, Speyer Cathedral was left largely untouched, whereas the Worms Cathedral was remodeled frequently as new architectural styles and new values developed. The Gothic influence can be seen both inside and out, from the elaborate tympanum with biblical scenes over the southern portal (today's entrance) to the great rose window in the west choir to the five sculptures in the north aisle recounting the life of Christ. The cathedral was completely gutted by fire in 1689 in the War of the Palatinate Succession. For this reason many of the furnishings are baroque, including the magnificent gilt high altar from 1742, designed by the master architect Balthasar Neumann (1687–1753). The choir stalls are no less decorative. They were built between 1755 and 1759 in rococo style. Walk around the building to see the artistic detail of the exterior. ⊠ *Lutherring 9* ☎ *06241/6115* ◸ *Donation requested* ◷ *Apr.–Oct., daily 9–5:45; Nov.–Mar., daily 9–4:45; closed during services.*

WORTH NOTING

Dreifaltigkeitskirche (*Church of the Holy Trinity*). This Lutheran church is just across the square from the Heylshofgarten. Remodeling during the 19th and 20th centuries produced today's austere interior, although the facade and tower are still joyfully baroque. ⊠ *Marktpl.* ◷ *Apr.–Sept., daily 9–5; Oct.–Mar., daily 10–4.*

Museum der Stadt Worms (*Municipal Museum*). To bone up on the history of Worms, visit this museum, housed in the cloisters of a Romanesque church in the Andreasstift. ⊠ *Weckerlingpl. 7* ☎ *06241/946–390* 🎫 *€2* ⏰ *Tues.–Sun. 10–5.*

Raschi-Haus. Next door to the synagogue, this former study hall, dance hall, and Jewish home for the elderly now houses the city archives and the **Jewish Museum.** The well-written illustrated booklet *Jewish Worms* chronicles a millennium of Jewish history in Worms. Rashi (Rabbi Solomon ben Isaac of Troyes [1040–1105]) studied at the Worms Talmud academy circa 1060. ⊠ *Hintere Judeng. 6* ☎ *06241/853–4707* 🎫 *€1.50* ⏰ *Tues.–Sun. 10–12:30 and 1:30–5.*

WHERE TO EAT

$
GERMAN
✕ **Gasthaus Hagenbräu.** Located a little to the west of the center, by the banks of the Rhine, this house brewery serves a good range of classic German dishes and regional specialties such as Saumagen to soak up the beers that are produced on the premises. Service and decor are bright and cheery, and you will be surrounded by copper vats and oak barrels as you dine. The summer terrace by the river is a chance to enjoy a brew with a view. ⊠ *Am Rhein 3* ☎ *06241/921–100* ⊕ *www.hagenbraeu.de* ⏰ *Closed Mon.*

$$$$
GERMAN
★
✕ **Rôtisserie Dubs.** A pioneer of the Rheinhessen restaurant scene, Wolfgang Dubs focused on creative regional cuisine and seasonal specialties long before it was in vogue. Fish, fowl, meat, and game are all expertly prepared and garnished—often with an Asian or Mediterranean accent. ■TIP➔ For a more casual meal, try his cozy Gasthaus Zum Schiff ($–$$), next door, where the daily specials are a very good value. A wine enthusiast, Dubs offers his own wines, top German and French estates, and a few New World wines, such as Opus One. Rheindürkheim is 9 km (5½ mi) north of Worms via B–9. The restaurant is near the *Kirche* (church), not far from the riverbank. ⊠ *Kirchstr. 6, Worms-Rheindürkheim* ☎ *06242/2023* ⊕ *www.dubs.de* ⏰ *Closed Tues. and 2 wks in Jan. No lunch Sat.*

WHERE TO STAY

For expanded hotel reviews, visit Fodors.com.

$$
🏨 **Dom-Hotel.** The appeal of this hotel with modern, comfortable rooms lies in its friendly staff and its terrific location in the heart of the pedestrian zone (a parking garage is available). **Pros:** central location. **Cons:** modern building design doesn't have much charm. ⊠ *Obermarkt 10* ☎ *06241/9070* ⊕ *www.dom-hotel.de* 🛏 *54 rooms, 2 suites* ⌂ *In-room: no a/c, Internet, Wi-Fi. In-hotel: some pets allowed* ⏶⏷ *Breakfast.*

$
🏨 **Land- und Winzerhotel Bechtel.** The friendly Bechtel family, winegrowers and proud parents of a former German Wine Queen, offer very pleasant accommodations on the grounds of their wine estate in the suburb of Heppenheim, about 10 km (6 mi) west of Worms (leave Worms on Speyerer Strasse, an extension of Valckenbergstrasse, which runs parallel to the east side of the Dom). **Pros:** quiet location; excellent value; rooms have balconies. **Cons:** far from the sights. ⊠ *Pfälzer Waldstr. 100, Worms-Heppenheim* ☎ *06241/36536* ⊕ *www.landhotel-*

bechtel.de ↩ *11 rooms* ⚿ *In-room: Internet. In-hotel: restaurant, bar, gym, business center, some pets allowed* ⚑| *Breakfast.*

$ ⚐ **Landhotel Zum Schwanen.** Bärbel Berkes runs this lovingly restored country inn in Osthofen, 10 km (6 mi) northwest of Worms. **Pros:** quiet location; friendly staff. **Cons:** far from the sights, no elevator. ✉ *Friedrich-Ebert-Str. 40, west of B–9, Osthofen* ☎ *06242/9140* ⊕ *www.zum-schwanen-osthofen.de* ↩ *30 rooms, 3 suites* ⚿ *In-room: no a/c, Internet. In-hotel: restaurant, business center, some pets allowed* ⊙ *No lunch Sun.* ⚑| *Breakfast.*

NIGHTLIFE AND THE ARTS

Concerts are also held in the Municipal Museum, in the Andreasstift, and at the 19th-century palace Schloss Herrnsheim, in the northern suburb of Herrnsheim.

SHOPPING

Der Weinladen. For tasteful wine accessories and other grape products, drop by this shop near the Municipal Museum, opposite the cathedral. ✉ *Weckerlingpl. 1* ☎ *06241/911–180* ⊟ *No credit cards* ⊙ *Closed Sun. and Mon.*

Star Region. In a historic building a short walk from the synagogue, Star Region offers products exclusively from Rheinhessen, Odenwald, and Pfalz. There's an excellent lunch buffet ($) featuring local specialties like creamed sauerkraut and *Spätburgundergulasch* (red wine gulasch) and a shop where you can pick up culinary souvenirs and wine. ✉ *Kammerstr., 60, Worms* ☎ *06241/269–796* ⊙ *Closed Sun.*

OPPENHEIM

26 km (16 mi) north of Worms, 23 km (16 mi) south of Mainz on B-9.

Oppenheim is slightly off the beaten path, making it an ideal destination if you're looking to avoid the hordes of tourists that often descend on the Wine Road in mid-summer.

The Katharinenkirche is the obvious crown of Oppenheim, but the picturesque Altstadt also hides a mysterious gem: the **Oppenheimer Kellerlabyrinth**, a 40-km, five-level deep underground passageway system. Tours cost €6; contact the **Oppenheim Tourist Office** for tickets.

GETTING HERE AND AROUND

An excellent network of regional trains connect Oppenheim with Mainz and Worms. In each case the journey takes about 15–20 minutes and trains depart about every half hour. Nearby Nierstein is just one stop away on the same regional train.

ESSENTIALS

Oppenheim Tourist Office ✉ *Merianstr. 4, Oppenheim* ☎ *06133/490–919.*

EXPLORING

Deutsches Weinbaumuseum (*German Viticultural Museum*). Oppenheim and its neighbors to the north, Nierstein and Nackenheim, are home to Rheinhessen's best-known, top vineyards. The Deutsches Weinbaumuseum has wine-related artifacts that chronicle the region's 2,000-year-old wine-making tradition, not to mention the world's largest collection

10

of mousetraps and more than 2,000 corkscrews. ✉ *Wormser Str. 49* ☎ *06133/2544* ⊕ *www.dwb-museum.de* 🖃 *€3* ⊘ *Apr.–Oct., Tues.–Fri. 2–5, weekends 10–5.*

★ **Katharinenkirche** (*St. Katharine's Church*). En route to Oppenheim, the vine-covered hills parallel to the Rhine gradually steepen. Then, unexpectedly, the spires of Oppenheim's Gothic Katharinenkirche come into view. The contrast of its pink sandstone facade against a bright blue sky is striking. Built between 1220 and 1439, it's the most important Gothic church between Strasbourg and Köln. The interior affords a rare opportunity to admire original 14th-century stained-glass windows and two magnificent rose windows, the Lily Window and the Rose of Oppenheim. The church houses masterfully carved tombstones, while the chapel behind it has a *Beinhaus* (charnel house) that contains the bones of 20,000 citizens and soldiers from the 15th to 18th century. ✉ *Katharinenstr. at Merianstr., just north of market sq.* ☎ *06133/2381* ⊘ *Apr.–Oct., daily 8–6; Nov.–Mar., daily 9–5.*

NIGHTLIFE AND THE ARTS

Burgruine Landskrone. Concerts are held in St. Katharine's, and open-air theater takes place in the Burgruine Landskrone, the 12th-century imperial fortress ruins. ■ TIP➜ From here there's a wonderful view of the town and the vineyards, extending all the way to Worms on a clear day. The castle ruins are northwest of the church. Follow the Dalbergerstrasse north; from there it's a short walk up to the ruins. For tickets to the open-air theater performances contact the Oppenheim tourist office.

NIERSTEIN

3 km (2 mi) north of Oppenheim on B-9.

Surrounded by 2,700 acres of vines, Nierstein is the largest wine-growing community on the Rhine and boasts Germany's oldest documented **vineyard** (AD 742), Glöck, surrounding St. Kilian's Church.

GETTING HERE AND AROUND

An excellent network of regional trains connect Neirstein with Mainz and Worms. In each case the journey takes about 25 minutes and trains depart approximately every half hour. Nearby Oppenheim is just one stop away on the same regional train line.

Winzergenossenschaft (*Cooperative winery*). You can sample wines at the Winzergenossenschaft, which is the starting point of an easy hike or drive to the vineyard heights and the vantage point at the *Wartturm* (watchtower). Tasting stands are set up along the route, providing delightful wine presentations in the vineyards *am roten Hang* (referring to the steep sites of red soils of slate, clay, and sand) in mid-June. ✉ *Karolingerstr. 6* ☎ *06133/97070.*

WHERE TO STAY

For expanded hotel reviews, visit Fodors.com.

$$ 🖫 **Best Western Wein & Parkhotel.** Spacious, light rooms decorated in
★   warm shades of ocher, chic bathrooms, and an inviting lounge and terrace make for comfortable, relaxing quarters. **Pros:** friendly; quiet location. **Cons:** a chain hotel offering few surprises. ✉ *An der Kaiserlinde*

1 ☎ 06133/5080 ⊕ *www.weinhotel.bestwestern.de* ⌐⊃ *55 rooms* ⌂ *In-room: Internet. In-hotel: restaurant, bar, pool, gym, business center* ⏺○⏺ *Breakfast.*

$$ ⊞ **Jordan's Untermühle.** The spacious grounds of an old mill are home

★ to a country inn, a restaurant, and a Vinothek. **Pros:** beautiful build-ings; great value; very quiet. **Cons:** a long way from anywhere; difficult to reach without your own transport. ⊠ *Ausserhalb 1, Köngernheim* ✛ *west of B-9, at Nierstein turn left on B-420 (toward Wörrstadt), drive through Köngernheim and turn right toward Selzen* ☎ 06737/71000 ⊕ *www.jordans-untermuehle.de* ⌐⊃ *25 rooms, 1 suite* ⌂ *In-room: no a/c, Internet, Wi-Fi. In-hotel: restaurant, some pets allowed* ⊙ *No lunch except Sun.* ⏺○⏺ *Breakfast.*

MAINZ

14 km (9 mi) north of Nackenheim, 45 km (28 mi) north of Worms on B-9, and 42 km (26 mi) west of Frankfurt on A-3.

Mainz is the capital of the state of Rheinland-Pfalz. Today's city was built on the site of a Roman citadel dating to 38 BC. Given its central location at the confluence of the Main and Rhine rivers, it's not surpris-ing that Mainz has always been an important trading center, rebuilt time and again in the wake of wars.

GETTING HERE AND AROUND

As the regional hub, Mainz is well served by trains, with fast connec-tions to Frankfurt (40 minutes) and Cologne (1 hour, 40 minutes). The station is a short walk west of the center. A comprehensive network of local buses makes getting around the city a breeze (route maps and timetables are posted at bus stops), while the upper areas of town are also served by trams. Although fairly spread out, those with a little energy will find all the sights are quite manageable on foot.

TOURS

Mainz has year-round tours departing Saturday at 2 (€5) from the Touristik Centrale. The office is one story above street level on the foot-bridge over Rheinstrasse. There are additional tours from May through October, on Sunday, Monday, Wednesday, and Friday at 2.

DISCOUNTS AND DEALS

■ TIP→ To see the sights, head for the Touristik Centrale (tourist office) to pick up a MainzCard, a two-day pass, for about €10. It covers a basic walk-ing tour, unlimited use of public transportation (including travel to and from Frankfurt Airport), and free entry to museums and the casino, as well as a reduction in price on some KD cruises and theater tickets. The card can also be bought from the station, some hotel receptions, and participating museums.

ESSENTIALS

Visitor Information Mainz ⊠ *Touristik Centrale, Brückenturm am Rathaus* ☎ 06131/286-210 🖷 06131/286–2155 ⊕ *www.info-mainz.de/tourist.*

10

In addition to Bibles printed circa 1455, the Gutenberg Museum has artifacts that tell the story of the printed word, including ancient manuscripts and presses.

EXPLORING
TOP ATTRACTIONS

★ **Dom** (*Cathedral of St. Martin and St. Stephan*). The entrance to the cathedral is on the south side of the market square, midway between the eastern and western chancels, which symbolize the worldly empire and the priestly realm, respectively. Emperor Otto II began building the oldest of the Rhineland's trio of grand Romanesque cathedrals in 975, the year in which he named Willigis archbishop and chancellor of the empire. Henry II, the last Saxon emperor of the Holy Roman Empire, was crowned here in 1002, as was his successor, Konrad II, the first Salian emperor, in 1024. In 1009, on the very day of its consecration, the cathedral burned to the ground. It was the first of seven fires the Dom has endured in the course of its millennium. Today's cathedral dates mostly from the 11th to 13th century. During the Gothic period, remodeling diluted the Romanesque identity of the original; an imposing baroque spire was added in the 18th century. Nevertheless, the building remains essentially Romanesque, and its floor plan demonstrates a clear link to the cathedrals in Speyer and Worms. The interior is a virtual sculpture gallery of elaborate monuments and tombstones of archbishops, bishops, and canons, many of which are significant artworks from the 13th to 19th century. ⊠ *Domstr. 3(Markt)* ☎ *06131/253–412* ⊕ *www.mainz-dom.de* ✉ *Donations requested* ☉ *Mar.–Oct., weekdays 9–6:30, Sat. 9–4, Sun. 1–2:45 and 4–6:30; Nov.–Feb., weekdays 9–5, Sat. 9–4, Sun. 1–2:45 and 4–5; closed during services.*

Dom und Diözesanmuseum. From the Middle Ages until secularization in the early 19th century, the archbishops of Mainz, who numbered among the imperial electors, were extremely influential politicians and property owners. The wealth of religious art treasures they left behind can be viewed in the cathedral cloisters. ✉ *Domstr. 3* ☎ *06131/253–344* ⊕ *www.dommuseum-mainz.de* 💶 *€3.50, Schatzkammer (treasure chamber) €3, combination ticket €5* ⊗ *Tues.–Sun. 10–5.*

★ **Gutenberg Museum.** Opposite the east end of the cathedral (closest to the Rhine), this fascinating museum is devoted to the history of writing and printing, from Babylonian and Egyptian times to the present. Exhibits include historical printing presses, incunabula (books printed in Europe before 1501), and medieval manuscripts with illuminated letters, as well as three precious 42-line Gutenberg bibles printed circa 1455. A replica workshop demonstrates how Gutenberg implemented his invention of movable type. ✉ *Liebfrauenpl. 5* ☎ *06131/122–640* ⊕ *www.gutenberg-museum.de* 💶 *€5* ⊗ *Tues.–Sat. 9–5, Sun. 11–3.*

Kupferberg Sektkellerei (*sparkling wine cellars*). These hillside cellars were built in 1850 on a site where the Romans had cultivated vines and cellared wine. The Kupferberg family expanded, creating 60 seven-story-deep vaulted cellars—the deepest in the world. The winery has a splendid collection of glassware; posters from the belle epoque period (1898–1914); richly carved casks from the 18th and 19th centuries; and the **Traubensaal** (Grape Hall), a tremendous example of the art nouveau style. Tours lasting from 1½ to 2 hours are offered most Saturdays in summer, and include several glasses of sparkling wines and champagne. Reservations are required. ✉ *Kupferbergterrasse 17–19* ☎ *06131/9230* ⊕ *www.kupferberg.de* 💶 *€14 1½-hr tour, €20.50 2-hr tour* ⊗ *Shop Mon.–Sat. 10–6.*

Landesmuseum (*Museum of the State of Rheinland-Pfalz*). The various collections of the museum are in the former electors' stables, easily recognized by the statue of a golden stallion over the entrance. Exhibits range from the Middle Ages to the 20th century. Among the highlights are paintings by Dutch masters, artworks from the baroque to art nouveau period, and collections of porcelain and faience. ✉ *Grosse Bleiche 49–51* ☎ *06131/28570* ⊕ *www.landesmuseum-mainz.de* 💶 *€5* ⊗ *Tues. 10–8, Wed.–Sun. 10–5.*

★ **Römisch-Germanisches Zentralmuseum.** A wonderful collection of original artifacts and copies of items that chronicle cultural developments in the area up to the early Middle Ages is housed in the Kurfürstliches Schloss (Electoral Palace). One of the highlights is a tiny Celtic glass dog from the 1st or 2nd century BC. The museum entrance is around the back, on the river (east) side of the building. ✉ *Ernst-Ludwig-Str. 2* ☎ *06131/91240* ⊕ *www.rgzm.de* 💶 *Free* ⊗ *Tues.–Sun. 10–6.*

★ **St. Stephanskirche** (*St. Stephen's Church*). It's just a short walk up Gaustrasse from Schillerplatz to the church, which affords a hilltop view of the city. Nearly 200,000 people make the trip each year to see the six blue stained-glass windows designed by the Russian-born artist Marc Chagall. ✉ *Kleine Weissg. 12, via Gaustr.* ☎ *06131/231–640* ⊗ *Mar.–Oct., Mon.–Sat. 10–5, Sun. noon–4:30; Nov.–Feb., Mon.–Sat. 10–4:30, Sun. noon–4:30.*

10

CLOSE UP

Gutenberg: The Father of Modern Printing

His invention—printing with movable type—transformed the art of communication, yet much about the life and work of Johannes Gutenberg is undocumented, starting with his year of birth. It's estimated that he was born in Mainz circa 1400 into a patrician family that supplied the city mint with metal to be coined. Gutenberg's later accomplishments attest to his own skill in working with metals. Details about his education are unclear, but he probably helped finance his studies by copying manuscripts in a monastic scriptorium. He moved to Strasbourg circa 1434, where he was a goldsmith by day and an inventor by night. It was here that he worked—in great secrecy—to create movable type and develop a press suitable for printing by adapting the conventional screw press used for wine making. By 1448 Gutenberg had returned to Mainz. Loans from a wealthy businessman enabled him to set up a printer's workshop and print the famous 42-line Bible. The lines of text are in black ink, yet each of the original 180 Bibles printed from 1452 to 1455 is unique, thanks to the artistry of the hand-painted illuminated letters.

Despite its significance, Gutenberg's invention was not a financial success. His quest for perfection rather than profit led to a legal battle during which his creditor was awarded the workshop and the Bible type. Gutenberg's attempts to set up another print shop in Mainz failed, but from 1465 until his death in 1468 he received an allowance for service to the archbishop of Mainz, which spared the "father of modern printing" from dying in poverty.

WORTH NOTING

Marktplatz. The area around the cathedral and the *Höfchen* (little courtyard) are the focal points of the town. ■ TIP→ Both are especially colorful on Tuesday, Friday, and Saturday, when farmers set up their stands to sell produce and flowers. ⊠ *Marktplatz.*

Schillerplatz. This square, ringed by beautiful baroque palaces, is the site of the ebullient **Fastnachtsbrunnen** (Carnival Fountain), with 200 figures related to Mainz's "fifth season" of the year. ⊠ *Schillerpl.*

WHERE TO EAT

$$
GERMAN
✕ **Eisgrub-Bräu.** It's loud, it's lively, and the beer is brewed in the vaulted cellars on-site. An Eisgrub brew is just the ticket to wash down a hearty plate of *Schweinehaxen* (pork knuckle) or *Meterwurst* (yard-long, rolled bratwurst), *Bratkartoffeln* (home fries), and sauerkraut. On the weekends, the breakfast buffet—which includes unlimited coffee—is a steal for just €6.90. During the week, there's a lunch special for €5.90. Brewery tours are free, but make reservations in advance. It's open daily 9 am–midnight, on Friday and Saturday until 1 am. ⊠ *Weisslilieng. 1a* ☎ *06131/221–104* ⊕ *www.eisgrub.de.*

$$$
GERMAN
★
✕ **Gebert's Weinstuben.** Gebert's traditional wine restaurant serves refined versions of regional favorites. In summer, the fresh asparagus dishes are popular. The *geeister Kaffee* (coffee ice cream and chocolate praline in a cup of coffee) uses delicious, handmade chocolate pralines.

German wines, especially Rheinhessen, dominate the excellent wine list. Dining alfresco is possible in the smartly renovated courtyard. ⊠ *Frauenlobstr. 94, near Rhine* ☎ *06131/611–619* ⊕ *www.gebertsweinstuben.de* ⊘ *Closed Mon. and 3 wks in July or Aug. No lunch Sat.*

$ ✕ **Haus des Deutschen Weines.** Late
GERMAN hours and luncheon specials are among the crowd-pleasers here, and the menu is broad enough to encompass both snacks and full-course meals, with huge salads and game year-round. Mainz specialties include *Spundekäs* (cheese whipped with cream and onions) or *Handkäse mit Musik* (pungent, semihard cheese served with diced onions in vinaigrette). As the name suggests, there's a great selection of German wines. ⊠ *Gutenbergpl. 3–5* ☎ *06131/221–300* ⊕ *www.hdw-gaststaetten.de.*

$ ✕ **Heiliggeist.** This lively café-bistro-bar serves breakfast, lunch, and din-
MEDITERRANEAN ner on weekends and dinner until midnight during the week. Modern, minimal decor provides an interesting contrast to the historic vaulted ceilings in this former almshouse and hospital church dating from 1236. In summer the beer garden is always packed. The compact menu includes elaborate salad platters as well as creatively spiced and sauced fish and meat dishes. One house specialty worth trying is the *Croustarte,* an upscale version of pizza. There's an extensive drink list. ⊠ *Mailandsg. 11* ☎ *06131/225–757* ⊕ *www.heiliggeist-mainz.de* ⚱ *Reservations not accepted* ▭ *No credit cards* ⊘ *No lunch weekdays.*

WHERE TO STAY

For expanded hotel reviews, visit Fodors.com.

$$ ⊡ **FAVORITE parkhotel.** Mainz's city park is a lush setting for the Barth
★ family's hotel, restaurants, and beer garden with a Rhine view; it's a 10-minute downhill walk through the park to the Old Town. **Pros:** quiet location; friendly staff; good views. **Cons:** a bit far from the sights. ⊠ *Karl-Weiser-Str. 1* ☎ *06131/80150* ⊕ *www.favorite-mainz.de* ⇗ *115 rooms, 7 suites* ⚲ *In-room: no a/c, Internet. In-hotel: restaurant, bar, pool, gym, business center, some pets allowed* ⊘ *Stadtpark closed Sun. evening and Mon.* ⍟ *Breakfast.*

$ ⊡ **Hotel Ibis.** Here you'll find modern, functional rooms and a great location on the edge of the Old Town. **Pros:** central location; good online deals often available. **Cons:** chain hotel lacking in character. ⊠ *Holzhofstr. 2, at Rheinstr.* ☎ *06131/2470* ⊕ *www.ibishotel.com* ⇗ *144 rooms* ⚲ *In-room: Internet, Wi-Fi. In-hotel: bar, business center, some pets allowed* ⍟ *Breakfast.*

$$$$ ⊡ **Hyatt Regency Mainz.** The blend of contemporary art and architecture with the old stone walls of historical Fort Malakoff on the Rhine is visually stunning. **Pros:** grand public spaces; friendly; riverside location. **Cons:** top-end rooms are expensive; breakfast costs extra.

CARNIVAL IN MAINZ

Carnival season runs from November 11 at 11:11 am to Ash Wednesday. There are dozens of costume balls, parties, and political cabaret sessions, but most of the heavy celebrating doesn't start until Weiberfastnacht, the Thursday preceding Ash Wednesday. The season culminates in a huge parade of colorful floats and marching bands through downtown on the Monday before Lent.

10

✉ *Malakoff-Terrasse 1* ☎ *06131/731–234* ⊕ *www.mainz.regency.hyatt. com* ⟿ *265 rooms, 3 suites* ⌂ *In-room: Internet. In-hotel: restaurant, bar, pool, gym, business center.*

NIGHTLIFE AND THE ARTS

Mainz supports a broad spectrum of cultural events—music (from classical to avant-garde), dance, opera, and theater performances—at many venues throughout the city. Music lovers can attend concerts in venues ranging from the cathedral, the Kurfürstliches Schloss, and the Kupferberg sparkling wine cellars to the Rathaus, market square, and historic churches.

Nightlife centers around the numerous wine pubs. Rustic and cozy, they're packed with locals who come to enjoy a meal or snack with a glass (or more) of local wine. Most are on the Old Town's main street, Augustinerstrasse, and its side streets (Grebenstrasse, Kirschgarten, Kartäuserstrasse, Jakobsbergstrasse), or around the Gutenberg Museum, on Liebfrauenplatz.

Wilhelmi. This wood-panel pub is a favorite with the poststudent crowd. ✉ *Rheinstr. 53* ☎ *06131/224–949.*

Schreiner. An old Mainz favorite, Schreiner attracts a mixed, jovial clientele. ✉ *Rheinstr. 38* ☎ *06131/225–720.*

SHOPPING

The Old Town is full of boutiques, and the major department stores (Karstadt and Kaufhof-Galeria) sell everything imaginable, including gourmet foods in their lower levels. The shopping district lies basically between the Grosse Bleiche and the Old Town and includes the **Am Brand Zentrum,** an ancient marketplace that is now a pedestrian zone brimming with shops.

Gutenberg-Shop. The Gutenberg-Shop in the building of the local newspaper, *Allgemeine Zeitung Mainz,* has splendid souvenirs and gifts—including pages from the Bible, books, posters, pens, and stationery. The friendly staff will also arrange to ship your purchases outside the country. There's a similar selection at the shop in the Gutenberg Museum. ✉ *Markt 17* ⊕ *www.gutenberg-shop.de* ⊗ *Closed Sun.*

Krempelmarkt. Antiques and perhaps a few hidden treasures await the patient shopper at Krempelmarkt. The flea market is on the banks of the Rhine (Rheinufer) between the Hilton hotel and Kaiserstrasse. At the Theodor Heuss Bridge you can find the children's flea market, where the youngest sellers offer clothes, toys, and books. ✉ *Rheinufer* ⊗ *Apr.–Oct., 1st and 3rd Sat. of month 7–1; Nov.–Mar., 3rd Sat. 7–1.*

Römerpassage. This city-center shopping mall offers 100,000 square feet of stores and restaurants. It also houses the remains of a Roman temple (AD 1) discovered in 1999 during construction of the mall. The temple, which is dedicated to the goddess Isis and Magna Mater, is in the basement of the building. ✉ *Lotharstr., near Grosse Bleiche.*

The Rhineland

"Cochem is indeed my favorite town in the region and has very good train connections, and I think for five days, it would be a good base town for you if you plan to visit Trier. If you plan to spend the bulk of your time on the Rhine . . . then Boppard or St. Goar are better located for Rhine outings."

—Russ

WELCOME TO THE RHINELAND

TOP REASONS TO GO

★ **Drachenfels:** This dramatic castle in Königswintur crowns a high hill overlooking the Rhine.

★ **Fastnacht:** Germany's Fastnacht (Carnival festivities) culminate with huge parades, round-the-clock music, and dancing in Düsseldorf, Köln, and Mainz the week before Ash Wednesday.

★ **Rhine in flames:** These massive displays of fireworks take place the first Saturday in May in Linz–Bonn; the first Saturday in July in Bingen–Rüdesheim; the second Saturday in August in Koblenz; the second Saturday in September in Oberwesel; and the third Saturday in September in St. Goar.

★ **The romance of the Rhine:** From cruises to Rhine-view rooms, castles to terraced vineyards, the Rhine does not disappoint.

★ **Spectacular wine:** The light white wines of the Rhine and Mosel are distinctive, and a whole culinary tradition has grown up around them.

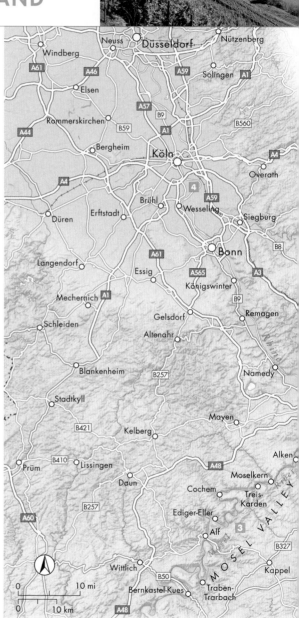

1 The Rheingau. Though the course of the Rhine is generally south to north, it bends sharply at Wiesbaden and flows east to west for 31 km (19 mi) to Rüdesheim. This means that the steep hills on its right bank have a southern exposure, and that vineyards there produce superb wines.

2 The Mittelrhein. The romance of the Rhine is most apparent in the Middle Rhine, from Bingen to Koblenz. The 65-km (40-mi) stretch of the Upper Middle Rhine Valley was designated a UNESCO World Heritage Site in 2002 with its concentration of awesome castles, medieval towns, and the vineyards of the Rhine Gorge.

3 The Mosel Valley. Koblenz and Trier aren't very far apart as the crow flies, but the driving distance along the incredible twists and turns of the Mosel River is 201 km (125 mi). The journey is worth it, though. The region is unspoiled, the towns gemlike, the scenery a medley of vineyards and forests, and there's a wealth of Roman artifacts, medieval churches, and castle ruins to admire.

4 Bonn and the Köln (Cologne) lowlands. North of Koblenz, the Rhine is less picturesque, but it does shoulder the cosmopolitan cities Köln and Düsseldorf, as well as the former capital city of Bonn.

GETTING ORIENTED

The most spectacular stretch of the Rhineland is along the Middle Rhine, between Mainz and Koblenz, which takes in the awesome castles and vineyards of the Rhine Gorge. Highways hug the river on each bank (B-42 on the north and eastern sides, and B-9 on the south and western sides), and car ferries crisscross the Rhine at many points. Cruises depart from many cities and towns, including as far south as Frankfurt. Trains service all the towns, and the Mainz–Bonn route provides river views all the way.

Willroth
A3
Neuwied — A48
B9
Koblenz
Winningen
Braubach — Pohl
A61 — Boppard
B260 — B54
B9 — St. Goar
Kemel
2
Oberwesel — Kaub
A3
Bucharach
Wiesbaden
B50
B9 — Eltville
A61 — Rüdesheim — A60 — Mainz
Bingen — Büdesheim
A63
Laubenheim

CRUISING THE RHINE AND MOSEL RIVERS

Lined by some of Europe's oldest, steepest vineyards, the Rhine and Mosel rivers boast breathtaking scenery punctuated by storybook castles and half-timber villages. A river cruise is a must-do.

(above) Bernkastel-Kues is one of the beautiful towns that line the Mosel. (upper right) Medieval Burg Eltz broods above the Mosel. (lower right) Cruising by Cochem.

Today, the Rhine and Mosel rivers are best known for their Riesling wines and the formidable medieval castles once used by robber barons to extort tolls from passing ships. But the rivers' history goes back even further to the Romans, who first established the region's viniculture.

Although the fastest way to get around the rivers is by car or train (and there are some gorgeous train routes directly on the Rhine), the rivers have been navigated by ship for thousands of years, and this option remains the most scenic, and the safest for visitors looking to drink in a little history. The Rhine is the more popular of the two rivers, but many find its little sister, the Mosel, even more beautiful with its narrow, twisting landscapes.

—David Levitz

WHEN TO GO

Day cruises on the Rhine and Mosel generally start around Easter and run through October. In summer, the hills are at their greenest and crowds gather to celebrate the Rhein in Flammen fireworks festivals. However, most wine festivals don't take place until August or September. Some multiday cruises also make extra trips in November and December to stop at Christmas markets.

A DAY ON THE RHINE AND MOSEL RIVERS

Day-trippers don't generally need advance reservations and the tourist offices in any major Rhine or Mosel town can give you information about short round-trip cruises (*Rundfahrten*) or waterbuses (*Linienfahrten*), which allow you to hop on or off the boat, and generally run on the Rhine daily from Easter to late October and on the Mosel from June through September. Although there are many boat trips available from Köln and Düsseldorf, the Rhine doesn't truly turn scenic until south of Bonn. The most popular starting point is Koblenz, where the two rivers converge. The area between Koblenz and Bingen, the Rhine Gorge, offers the shortest cruises with the highest concentration of castles.

From **Koblenz**, you can take a water taxi run by one of the biggest operators on the Rhine, **Köln-Düsseldorfer Deutsche Rheinschiffahrt** (*KD Rhine Line* ☎ *0221/208–8318* ⊕ *www.k-d.de*), which has many special offers, such as free travel on your birthday; half price for seniors on Monday and Friday; and free travel for up to three children for every adult on Wednesday. One good place to disembark and stretch your legs is **Boppard.** Take some time to sample the local wine, Bopparder Hamm. This route provides not only fantastic white wines, but also views of the legendary **Loreley** cliff and the **Marksburg,** the only Rhine castle never laid to ruin.

Personenschiffahrt Merkelbach (☎ *0261 /76810* ⊕ *www.merkelbach-personen-schiffe.de*) also does round-trip "castle cruises" on the Rhine from **Koblenz** to **Schloss Stolzenfels** (one hour) or the **Marksburg** (two hours).

Meanwhile, the Mosel's stunning, medieval **Burg Eltz** castle, and the towns of **Cochem** and **Bernkastel-Kues** between Koblenz and Trier, rival any sights along the Rhine. **Mosel-Schiffstouristic Hans Michels** of Bernkastel-Kues (☎ *06531/ 8222* ⊕ *www.mosel-personenschiff-fahrt.de*), goes from Bernkastel to Traben-Trarbach. **Personenschiffahrt Kolb** of Briedern (☎ *02651/26666* ⊕ *www. moselfahrplan.de*), runs a fleet of boats that cruise shorter stretches between Koblenz and Trier.

MULTIDAY CRUISES

Viking River Cruises (☎ *0221/25860, 877/ 668–4546 in U.S.* ⊕ *www.vikingrivers. com*) offers various multiday cruises on cabin ships between Amsterdam and Basel. The luxury **Uniworld** cruise line (☎ *800/733–7820 in U.S.* ⊕ *www. uniworld.com*) offers a two-week cruise of both rivers.

Updated by
David Levitz

The banks of the Rhine are crowned by magnificent castle after castle and by breathtaking, vine-terraced hills that
provide the livelihood for many of the villages hugging the
shores. In the words of French poet Victor Hugo, "The Rhine
combines everything. The Rhine is swift as the Rhône, wide
as the Loire, winding as the Seine . . . royal as the Danube
and covered with fables and phantoms like a river in Asia."

The importance of the Rhine can hardly be overestimated. Although not
the longest river in Europe (the Danube is more than twice its length),
the Rhine has been the main river-trade artery between the heart of the
continent and the North Sea (and Atlantic Ocean) throughout recorded
history. The Rhine runs 1,230 km (765 mi) from the Bodensee (Lake
Constance) west to Basel, then north through Germany, and, finally,
west through the Netherlands to Rotterdam.

Vineyards, a legacy of the Romans, are an inherent part of the Rhine
landscape from Wiesbaden to Bonn. The Rhine tempers the climate
sufficiently for grapes to ripen this far north, and the world's finest
Rieslings come from the Rheingau and from the Rhine's most important
tributary, the Mosel. Thanks to the river, these wines were shipped far
beyond the borders of Germany, giving rise to the wine trade that shaped
the fortune of many riverside towns. Rüdesheim, Bingen, Koblenz, and
Köln (Cologne) remain important commercial wine centers to this day.

The river is steeped in legend and myth. The Loreley, a jutting sheer
slate cliff, was once believed to be the home of a beautiful and bewitch-
ing maiden who lured boatmen to a watery end in the swift currents.
Heinrich Heine's poem *Song of Loreley* (1827), inspired by Clemens
Brentano's *Legend of Loreley* (1812) and set to music in 1837 by Friedrich Silcher, has been the theme song of the landmark ever since. The
Nibelungen, a legendary Burgundian people said to have lived on the
banks of the Rhine, serve as subjects for Wagner's epic opera cycle *Der
Ring des Nibelungen* (1852–72).

11

William Turner captured misty Rhine sunsets on canvas. Famous literary works, such as Goethe's *Sanct Rochus-Fest zu Bingen* (*The Feast of St. Roch*; 1814), Lord Byron's *Childe Harold's Pilgrimage* (1816), and Mark Twain's *A Tramp Abroad* (1880), captured the spirit of Rhine Romanticism on paper, encouraging others to follow in their footsteps.

PLANNING

WHEN TO GO

The peak season for cultural, food, and wine festivals is March–mid-November, followed by colorful Christmas markets in December. The season for many hotels, restaurants, riverboats, cable cars, and sights is from Easter through October, particularly in smaller towns. Opening hours at many castles, churches, and small museums are shorter in winter. Orchards blossom in March, and the vineyards are verdant from May until late September, when the vines turn a shimmering gold.

GETTING HERE AND AROUND

AIR TRAVEL

The Rhineland is served by three international airports: Frankfurt, Düsseldorf, and Köln-Bonn. Bus and rail lines connect each airport with its respective downtown area and provide rapid access to the rest of the region. There are direct trains from the Frankfurt airport to downtown Köln and Düsseldorf.

No-frills carriers that fly within Europe are based at smaller Frankfurt-Hahn Airport in Lautzenhausen, between the Rhine and Mosel valleys (a 1-hour drive from Wiesbaden or Trier; a 1½-hour bus ride from Frankfurt Airport). The Luxembourg Findel International Airport (a 30-minute drive from Trier) is close to the upper Mosel River valley.

Airport Contacts Flughafen Düsseldorf ☎ *0211/4210* ⊕ *www.duesseldorf-international.de.* **Flughafen Frankfurt** ☎ *01805/372–4636* ⊕ *www.frankfurt-airport.de.* **Flughafen Frankfurt-Hahn** ☎ *06543/509–200* ⊕ *www.hahn-airport.de.* **Flughafen Köln/Bonn** ☎ *02203/404–001* ⊕ *www.koeln-bonn-airport.de.* **Luxembourg Findel International Airport** ☎ *00352/24640* ⊕ *www.luxairport.lu.*

TRAIN TRAVEL

InterCity and EuroCity expresses connect all the cities and towns of the area. Hourly InterCity routes run between Düsseldorf, Köln, Bonn, and Mainz, with most services extending as far south as Munich and as far north as Hamburg. The city transportation networks of Bonn, Köln, and Düsseldorf are linked by S-bahn, regional and local trains (for information contact the KVB).

Train Contacts Deutsche Bahn ☎ *0180/599-6633* ⊕ *www.bahn.de.* **Kölner Verkehrs-Betriebe** (*KVB*). ☎ *01803/504–030* ⊕ *www.kbv-koeln.de.*

RESTAURANTS

Although Düsseldorf, Köln, and Wiesbaden are home to many talented chefs, some of Germany's most creative classic and contemporary cooking is found in smaller towns or country inns.

EATING WELL IN THE RHINELAND

The Rhineland's regional cuisine features fresh fish and *Wild* (game), as well as sauces and soups based on the local Riesling and Spätburgunder (pinot noir) wines. Boiled beef, formerly known in the region as *Tellerfleisch* (dish meat) or *Ochsenbrust* (brisket) is nowadays called by the more familiar Austrian name *Tafelspitz*. *Rheinischer Sauerbraten* (Rhenish marinated pot roast in a sweet-and-sour raisin gravy) is another traditional favorite. The *Kartoffel* (potato) is prominent in soups, *Reibekuchen* and *Rösti* (potato pancakes), and *Dibbe-* or *Dippekuchen* (dialect: *Döppekoche*), a casserole baked in a cast-iron pot and served with apple compote. *Himmel und Erde,* literally "heaven and earth," is a mixture of mashed potatoes and chunky applesauce, topped with panfried slices of blood sausage and onions.

The region is known for its wines: Riesling is the predominant white grape, and Spätburgunder (pinot noir) the most important red variety in the Rheingau, Mittelrhein, and Mosel wine regions *covered in this chapter.* Three abutting wine regions—Rheinhessen and the Nahe, near Bingen, and the Ahr, southwest of Bonn—add to the variety of wines available along the route.

Wines of Germany and the German Wine Institute provide background information and brochures about all German wine-growing regions. Tips on wine-related events and package offers are available from regional wine-information offices and any visitor information center along the Rhine and Mosel will put you in touch with local winegrowers.

WINE INFORMATION
German Wine Institute ⊕ *www. germanwines.de.*

Wines of Germany ✉ *950 3rd Ave., 7th Fl, New York, New York, USA* ☎ *212/994-7523* 🖷 *212/994-7596* ⊕ *www.germanwineusa.org.*

HOTELS

The most romantic places to lay your head are the old riverside inns and castle hotels. Ask for a *Rheinblick* (Rhine-view) room. Hotels are often booked well in advance, especially for festivals and when there are trade fairs in Köln, Düsseldorf, or Frankfurt, making rooms even in Wiesbaden and the Rheingau scarce and expensive. Many hotels close for winter.

WHAT IT COSTS IN EUROS					
	¢	$	$$	$$$	$$$$
Restaurants	under €9	€9–€15	€16–€20	€21–€25	over €25
Hotels	under €50	€50–€100	€101–€175	€176–€225	over €225

Restaurant prices are per person for a main course at dinner. Hotel prices are for two people in a standard double room, including tax and service.

PLANNING YOUR TIME

A good approach to a Rhineland tour depends on the sort of person you are. Those seeking "Rhine romance" should visit the quaint southern part of it, particularly the Rhine Gorge, with its castles, vineyards, and the Loreley. If nightlife and culture are your preferences, you'll like the cathedral city of Köln and cosmopolitan Düsseldorf; you can still take a day cruise along the Rhine from Köln.

DISCOUNTS AND DEALS

The **Rheinland-Pfalz and Saarland Card** (€14 for one day, €41 for three days, €66 for six days) offers free or reduced admission to museums, castles, and other sights, as well as city tours and boat trips throughout the two states. The three-day and six-day cards also include admission to the Holiday Park in Hassloch in the Pfalz. It's available at tourist offices in Rheinland-Pfalz and the Saarland.

VISITOR INFORMATION

Rheingau–Taunus Kultur & Tourismus ✉ *An der Basilika 11a, Oestrich-Winkel* ☎ *06723/99550* ⊕ *www.rheingau-taunus-info.de.*

Rheinland-Pfalz Tourismus ✉ *Löhrstr. 103–105, Koblenz* ☎ *0261/915–200* 📠 *0261/915–2040* ⊕ *www.romantic-germany.info.*

THE RHEINGAU

The heart of the region begins in Wiesbaden, where the Rhine makes a sharp bend and flows east to west for some 30 km (19 mi) before resuming its south to north course at Rüdesheim. Wiesbaden is a good starting point for touring any of the well-marked cycling, hiking, and driving routes through the Rheingau's villages and vineyards. ■ TIP→ Nearly every Rheingau village has an outdoor Weinprobierstand (wine-tasting stand), usually near the riverbank. It is staffed and stocked by a different wine estate every weekend in summer.

WIESBADEN

40 km (25 mi) west of Frankfurt via A-66.

Wiesbaden, the capital of the state of Hesse, is a small city of tree-lined avenues with elegant shops and handsome facades. Its hot mineral springs have been a drawing card since the days when it was known as Aquis Mattiacis ("the waters of the Mattiaci")—the words boldly inscribed on the portal of the Kurhaus—and Wisibada ("the bath in the meadow"). Bilingual walking tours of Wiesbaden depart from the Kurhaus, April–October, Saturday at 10 (November–March, the second and fourth Saturday).

In the 1st century AD the Romans built thermal baths here, a site then inhabited by a Germanic tribe, the Mattiaci. Modern Wiesbaden dates from the 19th century, when the dukes of Nassau and, later, the Prussian aristocracy commissioned the grand public buildings and parks that shape the city's profile today. Wiesbaden developed into a fashionable spa that attracted the rich and the famous. Their ornate villas on the Neroberg and turn-of-the-20th-century town houses are part of the city's flair.

For a one-hour ride through the city, board the little train **THermine**. The one-day ticket (€6.50) enables you to get on and off as often as you'd like to explore the sights. From mid-April to October it departs seven times daily (10–4:30) from Café Lumen (behind the Marktkirche) and stops at the Bowling Green, Greek Chapel, and Neroberg railway station. In winter, it operates only on weekends.

ESSENTIALS

Visitor Information Wiesbaden ⊠ *Tourist-Information, Marktpl. 1* ☎ *0611/172–9930* 🖶 *0611/172-9798* ⊕ *www.wiesbaden.de.*

EXPLORING

Altstadt (*Old Town*). The Altstadt is just behind the Stadtschloss (a former duke's palace, now the seat of state parliament, the Hessischer Landtag) on Grabenstrasse, Wagemannstrasse, and Goldgasse.

Kaiser-Friedrich-Therme. Today you can "take the waters" in an ambience reminiscent of Roman times in the **Kaiser-Friedrich-Therme**, a superb art nouveau bathhouse from 1913. ⊠ *Langg. 38–40* ☎ *0611/317–060.*

Kochbrunnen Fountain. Fifteen of Wiesbaden's 26 springs converge at the steaming Kochbrunnen Fountain, where the healthful (and sulfurous) waters are there for the tasting. ⊠ *Kochbrunnenpl.*

★ **Kurhaus.** Built in 1907, the neoclassical Kurhaus is the cultural center of town. It houses the casino and the Thiersch-Saal, a splendid setting for concerts. The Staatstheater (1894), opulently appointed in baroque and rococo revival styles, and two beautifully landscaped parks flank the Kurhaus. ⊠ *Kurhauspl.* ⊕ *www.wiesbaden.de/kurhaus.*

Marktplatz (*Market Square*). Historic buildings ring the Schlossplatz (Palace Square) and the adjoining Marktplatz, site of the annual wine festival (mid-August) and Christmas market (December). The farmers' market (Wednesday and Saturday) takes place behind the neo-Gothic brick Marktkirche (Market Church). ⊠ *Marktpl.*

Museum Wiesbaden. Nature and culture come together under one roof at the Museum Wiesbaden. The museum's natural history section exhibits a wealth of geological finds and preserved animals, while its art collection ranges from 12th-century polychromes to present-day installations. The museum is best known for its expressionist paintings, particularly the works of Russian artist Alexej Jawlensky. ⊠ *Friedrich-Ebert-Allee 2* ☎ *0611/335–2250* ⊕ *www.museum-wiesbaden.de* 🎟 *€5* 🕑 *Tues. 10–8, Wed.–Sun. 10–5.*

WHERE TO EAT

$$$$
ECLECTIC

✕ **Käfer's Bistro.** This popular bistro with striking art nouveau decor, a grand piano (live music nightly), and a good-size bar attracts an upscale clientele. Book a table for two in one of the window alcoves (Nos. 7, 12, 25, and 29) at least four weeks in advance for some privacy among the otherwise close-set tables. *Lachstatar* (salmon tartare) and *Bauernente* (farmer's duck) are standard favorites. A few champagnes are available by the glass and bottle. Käfer's also caters the beer garden behind the Kurhaus and the Bowling Green's terrace with concerts in summer. ⊠ *Kurhauspl. 1* ☎ *0611/536–200* ⊕ *www.kurhaus-gastronomie. de* 🍽 *Reservations essential.*

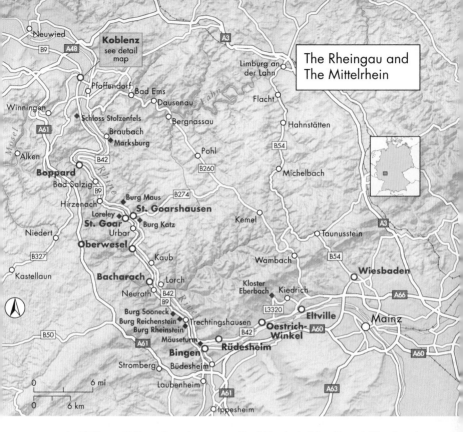

The Rheingau and The Mittelrhein

$ ✕ **Sherry & Port.** Austrian expat Gerd Royko's friendly neighborhood
ECLECTIC   bistro hosts live music on Friday and Saturday from October through
March. During warm months, dine at outdoor tables surrounding a
fountain on tree-lined Adolfsallee. In addition to the fantastic number of sherries and ports (60), there are more than 20 malt whiskies
served by the glass. There is also a good selection of beers and wines
to accompany everything from tapas and salads to steaks and popularly priced daily specials (€6.80). ⊠ *Adolfsallee 11* ☎ *0611/373–632*
⊕ *www.sherry-und-port.de* ▭ *No credit cards.*

WHERE TO STAY
For expanded hotel reviews, visit Fodors.com.

$$ 🏨 **Hotel de France.** Behind this 1880 facade is a lovingly restored hotel
and a restaurant that's an upscale culinary gem; both have sleek, modern
furnishings and lots of fresh flowers. **Pros:** centrally located. **Cons:** on
a busy street; small rooms. ⊠ *Taunusstr. 49* ☎ *0611/959–730* ⊕ *www.
hoteldefrance.de* ⤶ *34 rooms, 3 suites* ⌂ *In-room: no a/c, Internet,
Wi-Fi. In-hotel: restaurant, bar, some pets allowed* ⦿ *Breakfast.*

$ 🏨 **ibis.** This modern hotel, renovated in 2009, opposite the Kochbrunn-
nen on Kranzplatz offers excellent value and a location within walk-
ing distance of the shop-filled pedestrian zone, the Old Town, and all
sights. **Pros:** bar stays open 24 hours; four wheelchair-accessible rooms.

Cons: small rooms; breakfast not included. ✉ *Georg-August-Zinn-Str. 2* ☎ *0611/36140* ⊕ *www.ibishotel.com* ⇱ *131 rooms* ♿ *In-room: a/c, Internet, Wi-Fi. In-hotel: bar, parking, some pets allowed.*

$$$ ☆ **Hotel Nassauer Hof.** Wiesbaden's premier address for well over a cen-
★ tury boasts luxuriously appointed rooms, top-flight service, and three restaurants—and a guest list ranging from Dostoyevsky to the Dalai Lama. **Pros:** nice location opposite the Kurhaus; warm spring-fed pool. **Cons:** expensive. ✉ *Kaiser-Friedrich-Pl. 3–4* ☎ *0611/1330* ⊕ *www. nassauer-hof.de* ⇱ *136 rooms, 23 suites* ♿ *In-room: a/c, kitchen, Inter-net, Wi-Fi. In-hotel: restaurant, bar, pool, gym, spa, business center.*

$ ☆ **Town Hotel.** The Gerbers' modern, new hotel is a five-minute walk
★ from the Kurhaus, Old Town, and shopping district. **Pros:** new and inexpensive; free telephone calls to North America and most of Europe. **Cons:** often full during the week. ✉ *Spiegelg. 5* ☎ *0611/360–160* ⊕ *www.townhotel.de* ⇱ *24 rooms* ♿ *In-room: a/c, Internet, Wi-Fi. In-hotel: business center, parking, some pets allowed.*

NIGHTLIFE AND THE ARTS

In addition to the casino, restaurants, bars, and beer garden at the Kurhaus, nightlife is centered on the many bistros and pubs on Tau-nusstrasse and in the Old Town. The tourist office provides schedules and sells tickets for most venues listed here.

Caligari Filmbühne. Classics and avant-garde films are specialties here. ✉ *Marktpl. 9, behind Marktkirche* ☎ *0611/315–050* ⊕ *www.wiesbaden. de/caligari.*

Henkell & Co. The sparkling-wine cellars of Henkell & Co. host a series of concerts by young classical musicians from October to March in their splendid foyer. ✉ *Biebricher Allee 142* ☎ *0611/630* ⊕ *www.henkell-sektkellerei.com.*

Hessisches Staatstheater. The Hessisches Staatstheater presents classical and contemporary opera, theater, ballet, and musicals on four stages: Grosses Haus, Kleines Haus, Studio, and Wartburg. ✉ *Chr.-Zais-Str. 3* ☎ *0611/132–325* ⊕ *www.staatstheater-wiesbaden.de.*

Kurhaus. The Hessian State Orchestra performs eight programs a year at the Kurhaus. ✉ *Kurhauspl. 1* ☎ *0611/17290.*

Marktkirche. Many churches offer concerts, including the free organ concerts Saturday at 11:30 am in the Marktkirche. ✉ *Schlosspl. 4* ☎ *0611/900–1611* ⊕ *www.marktkirche-wiesbaden.de.*

Pariser Hoftheater. Smaller dramatic productions and cabaret are per-formed at this intimate theater. ✉ *Spiegelg. 9* ☎ *0611/300–607* ⊕ *www. pariserhoftheater.de.*

Rhein-Main-Hallen. Concerts and musicals are staged at this civic center. ✉ *Rheinstr. 20* ☎ *0611/1440* ⊕ *www.rhein-main-hallen.de.*

Spielbank (*casino*). The Klassische Spiel (roulette, blackjack) in the Kurhaus is lively from 3 pm to 3 am, while the Automatenspiel (slots and poker) in the neighboring Kolonnade is hopping from noon to 3 am. The former is one of Europe's grand casinos, where a jacket is required and tie recommended. However, you can be less formal at

SAUNA KNOW-HOW

Visiting one of Germany's fabulous saunas and bathhouses can be the perfect way to unwind from a busy travel itinerary, and it generally costs no more than a decent meal. But be aware: These day spas are enjoyed in the buff, and contrary to rumors of Germany's "casual" attitudes toward nudity, rules do apply. Although bathing suits are required at German swimming pools, you can expect a stern talking to for wearing one in a textile-free "Wellness" area, as the Germans call their saunas and steam rooms. Hygiene is also a big concern: in steam rooms, find the hose to rinse off your seat before sitting down. In a dry sauna, bring a large towel and make sure to place it underneath you, especially under your feet, to avoid sweat getting on the wood. Those who like it really hot should check for an *Aufguss* schedule in front of dry saunas. The event, which literally means "onpouring," gets visitors packed elbow to elbow for a good sweat as the *Saunameister* pours scented water over the sauna's coals. He or she might also distribute melted honey to rub into your skin, or a healthy snack at the end. After each time in the sauna, Germans take a cold shower to cool down. Note that saunas are generally mixed-gender, except on special women's days.

the Automatenspiel. The minimum age is 18 (bring your passport). ⊠ *Kurhauspl. 1* ☎ *0611/536–100* ⊕ *www.spielbank-wiesbaden.de.*

Thalhaus. Here you'll find a lively multiarts venue featuring an art gallery, theater and music performances, cabaret revues (sometimes performed in drag), and the occasional dance party. ⊠ *Nerotal 18* ☎ *0611/185–1267* ⊕ *www.thalhaus.de.*

Walhalla Studio Theater. Live concerts (jazz, blues, rock, and pop), often accompanied by theater, are held here. ⊠ *Mauritiusstr. 3a (use entrance of movie theater Bambi Kino)* ☎ *0611/910–3743* ⊕ *www.walhalla-studio.de.*

THERMAL SPRINGS, SPAS, AND POOLS

Kaiser-Friedrich-Therme. Pamper yourself with the thermal spring and cold-water pools, various steam baths and saunas, two solaria, and a score of health- and wellness treatments in elegant art nouveau surroundings. Towels and robes can be rented on-site, but come prepared for "textile-free" bathing. Children under 16 are not admitted. On Tuesday the facility is for women only. ⊠ *Langg. 38–40* ☎ *0611/317–060* 🖂 *May–Aug. €3.50 an hr, Sept.–Apr. €5 an hr* ☽ *Sept.–Apr., Mon.–Thurs. 10–10, Fri. and Sat. 10 am–midnight; May–Aug., daily 10–10.*

Thermalbad Aukammtal. There's year-round swimming indoors and out thanks to the thermal springs (32°C [90°F]) that feed the pools here. The facility includes seven saunas, a whirlpool, massage, and balneological treatments. ⊠ *Leibnizstr. 7, Bus 18 from Wilhelmstr. to Aukamm Valley* ☎ *0611/317–080* 🖂 *Pools €8.50, saunas €15, combined ticket €20* ☽ *Sun.–Thurs. 8 am–10 pm, Fri. and Sat. 8 am–midnight.*

Kloster Eberbach, a former Cistercian monastery, is worth a stop for its well-preserved architecture and its winery.

SHOPPING

Broad, tree-lined Wilhelmstrasse, with designer boutiques housed in its fin de siècle buildings, is one of Germany's most elegant shopping streets. Wiesbaden is also known as one of the best places in the country to find antiques; Taunusstrasse and Nerostrasse have excellent antiques shops. The Altstadt is full of upscale boutiques; Kirchgasse and its extension, Langgasse, are the heart of the shops-filled pedestrian zone.

ELTVILLE

14 km (9 mi) west of Wiesbaden via A-66 and B-42.

Kiedrich. For a good look at the central Rheingau, make a brief circular tour from Eltville. Drive 3 km (2 mi) north via the Kiedricher Strasse to the Gothic village of Kiedrich. In the distance you can see the tower of Scharfenstein Castle (1215) and the spires of St. Valentine's Basilica and St. Michael's Chapel, both from the 15th century. ■ TIP→ If you attend the basilica's 9:30 am Mass on Sunday, you can admire the splendid Gothic furnishings and star vaulting to the sounds of Gregorian chants and one of Germany's oldest organs. The chapel next door, once a charnel house, has a unique chandelier sculpted around a nearly life-size, two-sided Madonna.

   Weingut Robert Weil. Today Sutton's beautiful villa south of St. Valentine's Church is home to one of Germany's leading wine estates, Weingut Robert Weil. Its famed Kiedricher Gräfenberg Riesling wines can be sampled in the ultramodern tasting room. ⊠ *Mühlberg 5* ☏ *06123/2308* ⊕ *www. weingut-robert-weil.com* ☉ *Weekdays 8–5:30, Sat. 10–5, Sun. 11–5.*

11

Kloster Eberbach. The former Cistercian monastery Kloster Eberbach is idyllically set in a secluded forest clearing 3 km (2 mi) west of Kiedrich. ■TIP→ Its Romanesque and Gothic buildings (12th–14th century) look untouched by time—one reason why the film of Umberto Eco's medieval murder mystery, *The Name of the Rose*, starring Sean Connery, was filmed here. The monastery's impressive collection of old wine-presses bears witness to a viticultural tradition that spans nearly nine centuries. The wines can be sampled year-round in the **Vinothek** or restaurant on the grounds. The church, with its excellent acoustics, and the large medieval dormitories are the settings for concerts, wine auctions, and festive wine events. ⊠ *Stiftung Kloster Eberbach* ☎ 06723/917–8115 ⊕ *www.klostereberbach.de* €5.50 ⊗ *Apr.–Oct., daily 10–6; Nov.–Mar., daily 11–5.*

> ### HESSIAN STATE WINE DOMAINS
>
> *Sekt* (sparkling wine) production in the Rheingau is concentrated in Eltville, Wiesbaden, and Rüdesheim. The tree-lined Rhine promenade in Eltville hosts the annual Sekt festival during the first weekend of July. The administrative headquarters and main cellars of the Hessian State Wine Domains, Germany's largest wine estate, are in town. The estate owns nearly 500 acres of vineyards throughout the Rheingau and in the Hessische Bergstrasse wine region south of Frankfurt. Its shops—in the early Gothic hospital at Kloster Eberbach—offer a comprehensive regional selection.

Kurfürstliche Burg (*Electors' Castle*). Eltville flourished as a favorite residence of the archbishops of Mainz in the 14th and 15th centuries, and it was during this time that the castle was built. More than 300 varieties of roses grow in the castle's courtyard garden, on the wall, and along the Rhine promenade. During "Rose Days" (the first weekend in June) the flower is celebrated in shops and restaurants (as an ingredient in recipes) throughout town. ⊠ *Burgstr. 1* ☎ 06123/909–840 ⊕ *www.eltville.de* Tower €2, rose garden free ⊗ *Tower Apr.–mid-Oct., Fri. 2–6 and weekends 11–6; rose garden Easter–mid-Oct., daily 9:30–7; mid-Oct.–Easter, daily 10:30–5.*

Sts. Peter und Paul. The parish church of Saints Peter and Paul has late-Gothic frescoes, Renaissance tombstones, and a carved baptismal likely created by the Rhenish sculptor Hans Backoffen. ⊠ *Roseng.*

Steinberg. From Eberbach, take the road toward Hattenheim, stopping at the first right-hand turnoff to admire the monastery's premier vineyard, Steinberg. It's encircled by a 3-km-long (2-mi-long) stone wall (13th–18th century). In warmer months you can enjoy its vintages outdoors, overlooking the vines. ⊠ *Domäne Steinberg* ⊗ *May–Sept., weekends 11–7.*

WHERE TO EAT

$$ ✕ **Gutsausschank im Baiken.** This restaurant is on a hilltop amid the famed
GERMAN Rauenthaler Baiken vineyard. The magnificent panorama from the vine-canopied terrace, the fresh regional cooking, and superb wines—from the Hessian State Wine Domains—make for a "Rheingau Riesling" experience par excellence. ⊠ *Wiesweg 86, via Eltville* ☎ 06123/900–345 ⊕ *www.baiken.de* ⊗ *Closed Feb., Mon. and Tues. in Apr.–Oct.; Mon.–Wed. in Nov.–Mar. No lunch Mon.–Sat.*

$ ✕ **Klosterschänke und Gästehaus Kloster Eberbach.** Beneath the vaulted ceil-
GERMAN   ing of the Klosterschänke you can sample the wines of the Hessian State
Wine Domains with regional cuisine. Try the *Weinfleisch* (pork goulash
in Riesling sauce) or *Zisterzienser Brot,* which translates to "Cistercian
bread" (minced meat in a plum-and-bacon dressing with boiled potatoes). ⊠ *Kloster Eberbach, via Kiedrich or Hattenheim* ☎ *06723/993–
299* ⊕ *www.klostereberbach.de* ⊟ *No credit cards.*

$$$$ ✕ **Kronenschlösschen.** The atmosphere of this stylish art nouveau house
FRENCH   (1894) is intimate. Chef Patrik Kimpel, president of the German Young
Fodor'sChoice   Restaurateurs, oversees both the gourmet restaurant Kronenschlöss-
★   chen and the more casual bistro. The wine list focuses on the finest
Rheingau estates for whites and old- and new-world estates for reds.
In warmer months, you can also enjoy sensational fish creations in
the parklike garden. ⊠ *Rheinallee, Eltville-Hattenheim* ☎ *06723/640*
⊕ *www.kronenschloesschen.de.*

$$$$ ✕ **Schloss Reinhartshausen.** A palace in every sense of the word, this hotel
GERMAN   and wine estate overlooks the Rhine and beautifully landscaped gar-
★   dens. Antiques and artwork fill the house. You can enjoy breakfast,
lunch, and afternoon tea with *Rieslingtorte* in the airy, glass-lined Wintergarten. Upscale dinners are served in the elegant Prinzess von Erbach.
The economical Schloss Schänke, located in the old press house, offers
light fare and hearty snacks. The estate's wines are also sold daily in
the Vinothek. ⊠ *Hauptstr. 41, Eltville-Erbach* ☎ *06123/6760* ⊕ *www.
kempinski.com/en/eltville.*

$$$ ✕ **Zum Krug.** Winegrower Josef Laufer more than lives up to the hospi-
GERMAN   tality promised by the wreath and *Krug* (earthenware pitcher) hanging
above the front door. The wood-panel restaurant, with its old tiled stove
is cozy. The German fare includes wild duck, goose, game, or sauer-
braten served in rich, flavorful gravies. The wine list is legendary for its
scope (600 Rheingau wines) and selection of older vintages. ⊠ *Haupt-
str. 34, Eltville-Hattenheim* ☎ *06723/99680* ⊕ *www.hotel-zum-krug.de*
☼ *Closed 4 wks in Dec. and Jan. and 2 wks in July and Aug.*

WHERE TO STAY

For expanded hotel reviews, visit Fodors.com.

$ ▦ **Maximilianhof.** For generations the von Oetinger family has shared its
home, its wines, and its simple, hearty cooking (¢–$), with guests from
near and far, inviting them in with a warm art nouveau parlor and a
pretty summer terrace. **Pros:** art nouveau parlor; terrace. **Cons:** removed
from Eltville center. ⊠ *Rheinallee 2, Eltville-Erbach* ☎ *06123/92240*
⊕ *www.maximilianshof.de* ⇱ *9 rooms* ⚐ *In-room: no a/c, Wi-Fi. In-
hotel: restaurant, parking, some pets allowed* ⍟⊙⍟ *Breakfast.*

OESTRICH-WINKEL

21 km (13 mi) west of Wiesbaden, 7 km (4½ mi) west of Eltville on B-42.

Oestrich's vineyard area is the largest in the Rheingau. ■TIP→ Lenchen
and Doosberg are the most important vineyards. You can sample the wines
at the outdoor wine-tasting stand, opposite the 18th-century wine-loading
crane on the riverbank of Oestrich (nearly opposite Hotel Schwan).

The village of Winkel (pronounced *vin*-kle) lies west of Oestrich. A Winkeler Hasensprung wine from the fabulous 1811 vintage was Goethe's wine of choice during his stay here with the Brentano family in 1814.

Brentanohaus. The Goethe Zimmer (Goethe Room) in the Brentanohaus, with mementos and furnishings from Goethe's time, may be visited during a few visitors' days each year, or by appointment. ☒ *Am Lindenpl. 2* ☎ *06723/2068* ⊕ *www.brentano.de.*

★ **Schloss Johannisberg.** The origins of this grand wine estate date from 1100, when Benedictine monks built a monastery and planted vines on the slopes below. The palace and remarkable cellars (tours by appointment) were built in the early 18th century. There are tastings at the estate's restaurant. To get here from Winkel's main street, drive north on Schillerstrasse and proceed all the way uphill. After the road curves to the left, watch for the left turn to the castle. ☒ *Weinbaudomäne Schloss Johannisberg, Geisenheim-Johannisberg* ☎ *06722/70090* ⊕ *www.schloss-johannisberg.de* ☉ *Vinothek year-round weekdays 10–1 and 2–6; Mar.–May and Oct., weekends 11–6, May–Sept. and Nov.–Feb., weekends 11–7.*

★ **Schloss Vollrads.** Built in 1211 Schloss Vollrads is the oldest of Germany's great private wine estates. The moat-surrounded tower (1330) was the Greiffenclau residence for 350 years until the present palace was built in the 17th century. There is a Vinothek, and the period rooms are open during concerts, festivals, and wine tastings. It lies 3 km (2 mi) north of town. ☒ *Vollradser Allee* ⊹ *North on Kirchstrasse, continue on Vollradser Allee* ☎ *06723/6626* ⊕ *www.schlossvollrads.com* ☉ *Easter–Oct., weekdays 9–6, weekends 11–7; Nov.–Easter, weekdays 9–5, weekends noon–5.*

WHERE TO EAT

$
GERMAN
✕ **Die Wirtschaft.** Beate and Florian Kreller provide you with a warm welcome to their historic building on Winkel's Hauptstrasse (main street). Fresh flowers and candles top the tables set in a labyrinth of cozy niches with exposed beams and old stone walls. No less inviting is the pretty courtyard. Special emphasis is placed on fresh, local ingredients in season. Their lunch at €9.50 for two and €11 for three courses is an excellent value. ☒ *Hauptstr. 70, Winkel* ☎ *06723/7426* ⊕ *www.die-wirtschaft.net* ⊟ *No credit cards* ☉ *Closed Mon. and 2 wks in July and Aug. Sun. no dinner.*

$$
MEDITERRANEAN
✕ **Gutsrestaurant Schloss Vollrads.** Chef Alexander Ehrgott's seasonal German and light Mediterranean dishes are served with the estate's wines in the cavalier house (1650) or on the flower-lined terrace facing the garden. ☒ *Schloss Vollrads, Vollradser Allee, north of Winkel* ☎ *06723/660* ⊕ *www.gutsrestaurant-schlossvollrads.de* ☉ *Closed Mon. and Tues in Mar. and Apr; closed late Dec.–Feb.*

$$
GERMAN
★
✕ **Gutsschänke Schloss Johannisberg.** The glassed-in terrace affords a spectacular view of the Rhine and the vineyards from which the wine in your glass originated. Rheingau Riesling soup and *Bauernente* (farmer's duck) are among the house specialties. ☒ *Schloss Johannisberg, Geisenheim-Johannisberg* ☎ *06722/96090* ⊕ *www.schloss-johannisberg.de* ⌕ *Reservations essential.*

WHERE TO STAY

For expanded hotel reviews, visit Fodors.com.

$$ **Hotel Schwan.** Owned by the Wenckstern family since it was built in 1628, this green-and-white half-timber inn offers considerable comfort, though the rooms in the guesthouse are simpler than in the historic main building. **Pros:** right at the 18th-century crane; outdoor wine stands. **Cons:** rooms in the guesthouse lack charm. ⊠ *Rheinallee 5, in Oestrich* ☎ *06723/8090* ⊕ *www.hotel-schwan.de* ⊑ *52 rooms, 3 suites* ⚴ *In-room: no a/c, Wi-Fi. In-hotel: restaurant, bar, parking, some pets allowed* ⅠⓄⅠ *Breakfast.*

Fodor's Choice ★

RÜDESHEIM

30 km (19 mi) west of Wiesbaden, 9 km (5½ mi) west of Oestrich-Winkel on B-42.

Tourism and wine are the heart and soul of Rüdesheim. With south-facing slopes reaching down to the riverbanks, wine growing has thrived here for 1,000 years. Since being discovered by English and German romanticists in the early 19th century for its picturesque solitude, Rüdesheim has long lost its quiet innocence, as the narrow, medieval alleys fill with boatloads of cheerful visitors from all over the world.

ESSENTIALS

Visitor Information Rüdesheim ⊠ *Tourist-Information, Geisenheimer Str. 22* ☎ *06722/906–150* 🖷 *06722/3485* ⊕ *www.ruedesheim.de.*

EXPLORING

Drosselgasse (*Thrush Alley*). Less than 500 feet long, Drosselgasse is a narrow, pub-lined lane, which is abuzz with music and merrymaking from noon until well past midnight every day from Easter through October. ⊠ *Between Rheinstr. and Oberstr.*

Luftsport-Club Rheingau. With the wings of a glider you can silently soar over the Rhine Valley. At the Luftsport-Club Rheingau you can catch a 30- to 60-minute *Segelflug* (glider flight) on a glider plane between Rüdesheim and the Loreley; allow 1½ hours for pre- and postflight preparations. ⊠ *Eibinger Forstwiesen, 3 km (2 mi) north of Niederwald-Denkmal and Landgut Ebenthal* ☎ *06722/2979* ⊕ *www.lsc-rheingau.de* ⊑ *1st 5 mins €15, each additional min €0.50; 1st 15 mins in glider with motor €30, each additional min €2* ◷ *Apr.–Oct., weekends 10–7.*

Niederwald-Denkmal (*Niederwald Monument*). High above Rüdesheim and visible for miles stands Germania, a colossal female statue crowning the Niederwald-Denkmal. This tribute to German nationalism, which

Take the Seilbahn (cable car) over picturesque vineyards to the Niederwald-Denkmal monument above Rüdesheim.

will be under renovation for part of 2012, was built between 1877 and 1883 to commemorate the rebirth of the German Empire after the Franco-Prussian War (1870–71). Germania faces across the Rhine toward the eternal enemy, France. At her base are the words to a stirring patriotic song: "Dear Fatherland rest peacefully! Fast and true stands the watch, the watch on the Rhine!" There are splendid panoramic views from the monument and from other vantage points on the edge of the forested plateau. You can reach the monument on foot, by car (via Grabenstrasse), or over the vineyards in the *Seilbahn* (cable car). There's also a *Sessellift* (chairlift) to and from Assmannshausen, a red-wine enclave, on the other side of the hill. ⊠ *Oberstr. 37* ☎ *06722/2402* ⊕ *www.seilbahn-ruedesheim.de* ✉ *One-way €4.50, round-trip €6.50 or combined ticket for cable car and chairlift €7* ⊗ *Mid-Mar.–Apr. and Oct., daily 9:30–5; May and Nov., daily 9:30–4; June and Sept., daily 9:30–6; weekends in May, June, and Sept. 9:30–7; July and Aug., daily 9–7, late Nov.–mid Dec., weekdays 11–6, weekends 11–7.*

Weinmuseum Brömserburg (*Brömserburg Wine Museum*). Housed in one of the oldest castles on the Rhine (circa AD 1000), the museum displays wine-related artifacts and drinking vessels dating from Roman times. ■ TIP➔ There are great views from the roof and the terrace, where there are occasionally wine tastings (ask at the desk). ⊠ *Rheinstr. 2* ☎ *06722/2348* ⊕ *www.rheingauer-weinmuseum.de* ✉ *€5* ⊗ *Mar.–Oct., daily 10–6.*

WHERE TO STAY

For expanded hotel reviews, visit Fodors.com.

$$ 🖼 **Breuer's Rüdesheimer Schloss.** Vineyard views grace most of the rooms
★ at this stylish, historic hotel where guests are welcomed with a drink

from the family's Rheingau wine estate. **Pros:** right off the Drosselgasse; if you stay a week you only pay for six days. **Cons:** noisy tourist area. ✉ *Steing. 10* ☎ *06722/90500* 🌐 *www.ruedesheimer-schloss.com* *23 rooms, 3 suites* *In-room: no a/c, Wi-Fi. In-hotel: restaurant, bar, business center, parking, some pets allowed* ⏲ *Closed late Dec.–early Jan.* *Breakfast.*

$$ Fodor's Choice ★ **Hotel Krone Assmannshausen.** From its humble beginnings in 1541 as an inn for sailors and ferrymen, the Krone evolved into an elegant, antique-filled hotel with a restaurant ($$$$) that offers first-class service and fine wining and dining. **Pros:** lovely views of vineyards and the Rhine. **Cons:** right on a main rail line; rooms at the back have a less than spectacular view. ✉ *Rheinuferstr. 10, Rüdesheim-Assmannshausen* ☎ *06722/4030* 🌐 *www.hotel-krone.com* *52 rooms, 13 suites, 1 apartment* *In-room: no a/c, Wi-Fi. In-hotel: restaurant, bar, pool, parking* *Breakfast.*

THE MITTELRHEIN

Bingen, like Rüdesheim, is a gateway to the Mittelrhein. From here to Koblenz lies the greatest concentration of Rhine castles. Most date from the 12th and 13th centuries, but were destroyed after the invention of gunpowder, mainly during invasions by the French. It's primarily thanks to the Prussian royal family and its penchant for historical preservation that numerous Rhine castles were rebuilt or restored in the 19th and early 20th centuries.

Two roads run parallel to the Rhine: B-42 (east side) and B-9 (west side). The spectacular views from the heights can best be enjoyed via the routes known as the Loreley-Burgenstrasse (east side), from Kaub to the Loreley to Kamp-Bornhofen; or the Rheingoldstrasse (west side), from Rheindiebach to Rhens.

BINGEN

35 km (22 mi) west of Wiesbaden via Mainz and A-60; ferry from wharf opposite Rüdesheim's train station.

Bingen overlooks the Nahe-Rhine conflux near a treacherous stretch of shallows and rapids known as the Binger Loch (Bingen Hole). Early on, Bingen developed into an important commercial center, for it was here—as in Rüdesheim on the opposite shore—that goods were moved from ship to shore to circumvent the unnavigable waters. Bingen was also the crossroads of Roman trade routes between Mainz, Koblenz, and Trier. Thanks to this central location, it grew into a major center of the wine trade and remains so today. Wine is celebrated during 11 days of merrymaking in early September at the annual **Winzerfest.**

ESSENTIALS

Visitor Information Bingen ✉ *Tourist-Information, Rheinkai 21* ☎ *06721/184–205* 🌐 *www.bingen.de.*

EXPLORING

Basilika St. Martin. Not far from the thousand-year-old Drususbrücke, a stone bridge over the Nahe, is the late-Gothic Basilika St. Martin. It was built on the site of a Roman temple and first mentioned in 793. The 11th-century crypt and Gothic and baroque furnishings merit a visit. ⊠ *Basilikastr. 1.*

Burg Klopp. Bingen was destroyed repeatedly by wars and fires; thus there are many ancient foundations but few visible architectural remains of the past. Since Celtic times the Kloppberg (Klopp Hill), in the center of town, has been the site of a succession of citadels, all named Burg Klopp, since 1282. Here you'll find a terrace with good views of the Rhine, the Nahe, and the surrounding hills. ⊠ *Maria-Hilf-Str. 10.*

> **TAKE A HIKE!**
>
> The Rheinhöhenweg (Rhine Heights Path) affords hikers splendid views and descents into the villages en route. These marked trails run between Oppenheim on the Rhine Terrace and Bonn for 240 km (149 mi) and between Wiesbaden and Bonn-Beuel for 272 km (169 mi). The most extensive hiking trail is the Rheinsteig, from Wiesbaden to Bonn on the right side of the Rhine. It comprises 320 km (199 mi) of well-marked paths that offer everything from easy walks to challenging stretches on a par with Alpine routes.

★ **Historisches Museum am Strom** (*History Museum*). Here you can see the most intact set of Roman surgical tools ever discovered (2nd century), period rooms from the Rhine Romantic era, and displays about Abbess St. Hildegard von Bingen (1098–1179), one of the most remarkable women of the Middle Ages. An outspoken critic of papal and imperial machinations, she was a highly respected scholar, naturopath, and artist whose mystic writings and music are much in vogue today. An excellent illustrated booklet in English on Rhine Romanticism, *The Romantic Rhine*, is sold at the museum shop. The museum is housed in a former power station (1898) on the riverbank. ⊠ *Museumsstr. 3* ☎ *06721/184–350, 06721/184–353* ⊕ *www.bingen.de* ☞ *€3* ⊙ *Tues.–Sun. 10–5.*

Rochuskapelle (*St. Roch Chapel*). The forested plateau of the Rochusberg (St. Roch Hill) is the pretty setting of the Rochuskapelle. Originally built in 1666 to celebrate the end of the plague, it has been rebuilt twice. On August 16, 1814, Goethe attended the consecration festivities, the forerunner of today's Rochusfest, a weeklong folk festival in mid-August. The chapel (open during Sunday services at 8 and 10) contains an altar dedicated to St. Hildegard and relics and furnishings from the convents she founded on the Ruppertsberg (in the suburb of Bingerbrück) and in Eibingen (east of Rüdesheim).

Hildegard Forum. The Hildegard Forum, near the chapel, has exhibits related to St. Hildegard, a medieval herb garden, and a restaurant serving tasty, wholesome foods—many based on Hildegard's nutritional teachings. The lunch buffets (Tuesday–Saturday €9.9, Sunday €17.5) are a good value. ⊠ *Rochusberg 1* ☎ *06721/181–000* ⊕ *www.hildegard-forum.de* ⊙ *Tues.–Sun. 11–6* ⊠ *Rochusberg 3* ☎ *06721/14225.*

WHERE TO EAT

$$$$

CONTINENTAL

Fodor'sChoice

★

✕ **Johann Lafer's Stromburg.** It's a pretty 15-minute drive through the Binger Wald (Bingen Forest) to this luxurious castle hotel and restaurant overlooking Stromberg. Johann Lafer is a prolific chef who pioneered cooking shows in Germany. In the elegant Val d'Or the *Variationen* (medley) of foie gras and the *Dessert–Impressionen* are classics. The less formal Bistro d'Or offers tasty regional dishes. The wine list features some 200 top Nahe wines and several hundred Old and New World wines, with a particularly fine collection from Bordeaux and Burgundy. ⊠ *Am Schlossberg 1, 12 km (7½ mi) west of Bingerbrück via Weiler and Waldalgesheim, Stromberg* ☎ *06724/93100* ⊕ *www.johannlafer. de/stromburg* ⚍ *Reservations essential* ⊗ *Le Val d'Or closed Mon. and Tues. No lunch weekdays.*

$

GERMAN

✕ **Weinstube Kruger-Rumpf.** It's well worth the 10-minute drive from Bingen (just across the Nahe River) to enjoy Cornelia Rumpf's refined country cooking with Stefan Rumpf's exquisite Nahe wines (Riesling, Weissburgunder [Pinot Blanc], and Silvaner are especially fine). Seasonal house specialties include *geschmorte Schweinebacken* (braised pork jowls) with kohlrabi, boiled beef with green herb sauce, and *Winzer-schmaus* (casserole of potatoes, sauerkraut, bacon, cheese, and herbs). The house dates from 1790; the wisteria-draped garden beckons in summer. ⊠ *Rheinstr. 47, 4 km (2½ mi) southwest of Bingen, Münster-Sarmsheim* ☎ *06721/43859* ⊕ *www.kruger-rumpf.com* ⚍ *Reservations essential* ⊗ *Closed Mon. and 2 wks in Jan. No lunch weekdays.*

EN
ROUTE

Mäuseturm (*Mouse Tower*). On the 5-km (3-mi) drive on B-9 to Trechtingshausen you will pass by Bingen's landmark, the Mäuseturm, perched on a rocky island near the Binger Loch. The name derives from a gruesome legend. One version tells that during a famine in 969 the miserly Archbishop Hatto hoarded grain and sought refuge in the tower to escape the peasants' pleas for food. The stockpile attracted scads of mice to the tower, where they devoured everything in sight, including Hatto. In fact, the tower was built by the archbishops of Mainz in the 13th and 14th centuries as a *Mautturm* (watch tower and toll station) for their fortress, Ehrenfels, on the opposite shore (now a ruin). It was restored in neo-Gothic style by the king of Prussia in 1855, who also rebuilt Burg Sooneck. ⊠ *Mäuseturminsel.*

The three castles open for visits near Trechtingshausen (turnoffs are signposted on B-9) will fascinate lovers of history and art. As you enter each castle's gateway, consider what a feat of engineering it was to have built such a massive Burg (fortress or castle) on the stony cliffs overlooking the Rhine. They have all lain in ruin once or more during their turbulent histories. Their outer walls and period rooms still evoke memories of Germany's medieval past as well as the 19th-century era of Rhine Romanticism.

Fodor'sChoice
★

Burg Rheinstein. This castle was the home of Rudolf von Habsburg from 1282 to 1286. To establish law and order on the Rhine, he destroyed the neighboring castles of Burg Reichenstein and Burg Sooneck and hanged their notorious robber barons from the oak trees around the Clemens Church, a late-Romanesque basilica near Trechtingshausen. The Gobelin tapestries, 15th-century stained glass, wall and ceiling

11

frescoes, a floor of royal apartments, and antique furniture—including a rare "giraffe spinet," which Kaiser Wilhelm I is said to have played—are well worth seeing. All of this is illuminated by candlelight on some summer Fridays. Rheinstein was the first of many a Rhine ruin to be rebuilt by a royal Prussian family in the 19th century. ✉ *From the A-61, take exit AS Bingen center. Continue on the B-9 heading toward Bingerbrück, driving through Bingerbrück; the castle is between Bingerbrück and Trechtingshausen; parking is below the castle, at B-9, Trechtingshausen* ☎ *06721/6348* ⊕ *www.burg-rheinstein.de* 🎫 *€4.30* ⊙ *Mid-Mar.–mid-Nov., daily 9:30–6; mid-Nov.–mid-Mar., weekends only 10–5 (weather permitting; call to inquire). Closed late Dec.–Feb.*

Burg Reichenstein. This castle has collections of decorative cast-iron slabs (from ovens and historical room-heating devices), hunting weapons and armor, period rooms, and paintings. It's the only one of the area's three castles directly accessible by car. ✉ *Burgweg 7, Trechtingshausen* ☎ *06721/6117* ⊕ *www.burg-reichenstein.de* 🎫 *€4.30* ⊙ *Mar.–Nov., Tues.–Sun. 9–6; Dec.–Feb. by reservation only.*

Burg Sooneck. On the edge of the Soon (pronounced *zone*) Forest, this castle houses a valuable collection of Empire, Biedermeier, and neo-Gothic furnishings, medieval weapons, and paintings from the Rhine Romantic era. ✉ *Sooneckstr. 1, Niederheimbach* ☎ *06743/6064* ⊕ *www.burgen-rlp.de* 🎫 *€4* ⊙ *Apr.–Sept., Tues.–Sun. 9–6; Oct., Nov., and Jan.–Mar., Tues.–Sun. 9–5.*

BACHARACH

16 km (10 mi) north of Bingen, ferry 3 km (2 mi) north of town, to Kaub.

Bacharach, a derivative of the Latin *Bacchi ara* (altar of Bacchus), has long been associated with wine. Like Rüdesheim, Bingen, and Kaub, it was a shipping station where barrels would interrupt their Rhine journey for land transport. Riesling wine from the town's most famous vineyard, the Bacharacher Hahn, is served on the KD Rhine steamers, and Riesling is used in local cooking for marinades and sauces; you can even find Riesling ice cream. In late June you can sample wines at the Weinblütenfest (Vine Blossom Festival) in the side-valley suburb of Steeg and, in late August, at Kulinarische Sommernacht in Bacharach proper (⊕ *www.kulinarische-sommernacht.de*).

Park on the riverbank and enter the town through one of its medieval gateways. You can ascend the 14th-century town wall for a walk along the ramparts around the town, then stroll along the main street (one street but three names: Koblenzer Strasse, Oberstrasse, and Mainzer Strasse) for a look at patrician manors, typically built around a *Hof* (courtyard), and half-timber houses. Haus Sickingen, Posthof, Zollhof, Rathaus (Town Hall), and Altes Haus are fine examples.

ESSENTIALS

Visitor Information Bacharach ✉ *Tourist-Information, Oberstr. 45* ☎ *06743/919–303* ⊕ *www.rhein-nahe-touristik.de.*

EXPLORING

St. Peter. The massive tower in the center of town belongs to the parish church of St. Peter. A good example of the transition from Romanesque to Gothic styles, it has an impressive four-story nave. ⊠ *Blücherstr. 1.*

Wernerkapelle. From the parish church a set of stone steps (signposted) leads to Bacharach's landmark, the sandstone ruins of the Gothic Wernerkapelle, highly admired for its filigree tracery. The chapel's roof succumbed to falling rocks in 1689, when the French blew up Burg Stahleck. Originally a Staufen fortress (11th century), the castle lay dormant until 1925, when a youth hostel was built on the foundations. The sweeping views Stahleck affords are worth the 10-minute walk.

WHERE TO EAT AND STAY

For expanded hotel reviews, visit Fodors.com.

$ ✕ **Gutsausschank Zum Grünen Baum.** The Bastian family runs this cozy
GERMAN tavern in a half-timber house dating from 1421. They are the sole owners of the vineyard Insel Heyles'en Werth, on the island opposite Bacharach. The "wine carousel" is a great way to sample a full range of wine flavors and styles (15 wines). Snacks are served (from 1 pm), including delicious *Wildsülze* (game in aspic) with home fries, sausages, and cheese. Reservations recommended on summer weekends. ⊠ *Oberstr. 63* ☎ *06743/1208* ⊕ *www.weingut-bastian-bacharach.de* ⊗ *Closed Thurs. and Jan.–mid-Mar.*

$ ✕ **Weinhaus-Restaurant Altes Haus.** This charming medieval half-timber
GERMAN house (1389) is a favorite setting for films and photos. The cheerful
★ proprietor, Reni Weber, uses the freshest ingredients possible and buys her meat and game from local butchers and hunters. *Rieslingrahmsuppe* (Riesling cream soup), *Reibekuchen* (potato pancakes), and a refined version of boiled beef with horseradish sauce, *Tafelspitz mit Wasabi*, are favorites, in addition to the seasonal specialties. There is also a good selection of local wines. ⊠ *Oberstr. 61* ☎ *06743/1209* ⊗ *Closed Wed. and Dec.–Easter; closed weekdays in Apr. and Nov.*

$ ☷ **Altkölnischer Hof.** Flowers line the windows of country-style rooms in this pretty half-timber hotel near the market square. **Pros:** half-timber romance. **Cons:** noisy tourist area; 10-minute walk from the station. ⊠ *Blücherstr. 2* ☎ *06743/1339* ⊕ *www.altkoelnischer-hof.de* ⤺ *18 rooms, 2 suites, 4 apartments* ⚭ *In-room: no a/c, Internet, Wi-Fi. In-hotel: restaurant, bar* ⊗ *Closed Nov.–Mar.* ☷ *Breakfast.*

OBERWESEL

8 km (5 mi) north of Bacharach.

Oberwesel retains its medieval silhouette. Sixteen of the original 21 towers and much of the town wall still stand in the shadow of Schönburg Castle. The "town of towers" is also renowned for its Riesling wines, celebrated at a lively wine festival held the first half of September. Both Gothic churches on opposite ends of town are worth visiting.

ESSENTIALS

Visitor Information Oberwesel ⊠ *Tourist-Information, Rathausstr. 3* ☎ *06744/710–624* ⊕ *www.oberwesel.de.*

EXPLORING

Liebfrauenkirche (*Church of Our Lady*). Popularly known as the "red church" because of its brightly colored exterior, it has superb sculptures, tombstones, and paintings, and one of Germany's oldest altars (1331).

St. Martin. Set on a hill, the so-called white church with a fortresslike tower, has beautifully painted vaulting and a magnificent baroque altar.

WHERE TO EAT AND STAY

For expanded hotel reviews, visit Fodors.com.

$ | GERMAN | ✕ **Historische Weinwirtschaft.** Tables in the flower-laden garden in front of this lovingly restored half-timber house are at a premium in summer, yet seats in the nooks and crannies indoors are just as inviting. Dark beams, exposed stone walls, and antique furniture set the mood on the ground and first floors, and the vaulted cellar houses contemporary-art exhibitions. Ask Iris Marx, the ebullient proprietor, for an English menu if you're stumbling over the words in local dialect. She offers country cooking at its best. The excellent wine list features 32 wines by the glass. ⊠ *Liebfrauenstr. 17* ☎ *06744/8186* ⊕ *www.historische-weinwirtschaft. de* ⊗ *Closed Tues. and Jan. No lunch Mon.–Sat.*

$$ | GERMAN | ✕ **Hotel Römerkrug.** Rooms with exposed beams, pretty floral prints, and historic furnishings are tucked behind the half-timber facade (1458) of Elke Matzner's small inn on the market square. Fish (such as fresh trout from the Wisper Valley) and game are house specialties, but Marc Matzner also prepares Rhine specialties, such as *Himmel und Erde* (mashed apples and potatoes with bacon and onions). There's a well-chosen selection of Mittelrhein wines that can be purchased for takeout. ⊠ *Marktpl. 1* ☎ *06744/7091* ⊕ *www.hotel-roemerkrug.rhinecastles. com* ⊗ *Closed Wed. and 3 wks in Nov. and Feb.*

$$ | Fodor's Choice ★ | ☒ **Burghotel "Auf Schönburg."** Antique furnishings and historic rooms (library, chapel, prison tower) make for an unforgettable stay at this lovingly restored romantic hotel and restaurant in the 12th-century Schönburg Castle complex. **Pros:** castle right out of a storybook. **Cons:** lots of climbing; parking lot 100 yards downhill; train tracks nearby. ⊠ *Oberwesel* ☎ *06744/93930* ⊕ *www.hotel-schoenburg.com* ⇆ *19 rooms, 3 suites* ⌂ *In-room: no a/c, Internet. In-hotel: restaurant, business center, parking* ⊗ *Closed mid-Jan.–mid-Mar.* ⦿ *Breakfast.*

> ### BIKE THE MIDDLE RHINE
>
> There is a 132-km (82-mi) cycle path (Rheinradweg) through the Middle Rhine Valley running parallel to the road and the railway tracks from Bingen to Bonn. It's an ideal way of combining sightseeing with not-so-strenuous exercise, unless you attempt to reach the castles on the hills. Watch out for strolling pedestrians and racing rollerbladers!

ST. GOAR

7 km (4½ mi) north of Oberwesel, ferry to St. Goarshausen.

St. Goar and St. Goarshausen, its counterpoint on the opposite shore, are named after a Celtic missionary who settled here in the 6th century. He became the patron saint of innkeepers—an auspicious sign for both towns, which now live off tourism and wine. September is especially

DID YOU KNOW?

The gothic Liebfrauenkirche (Church of Our Lady), which dominates Oberwesel's skyline, is worth a look inside for its gilt altar, intricate carvings, and paintings.

busy, with Weinforum Mittelrhein (a major wine-and-food presentation in Burg Rheinfels) on the first weekend every other year and the annual wine festivals and the splendid fireworks display "Rhine in Flames" on the third weekend.

ESSENTIALS

St. Goar Tourist Information ⊠ *Heerstr. 86, St. Goar* 🕾 *06741/383* ⊕ *www. st-goar.de.*

EXPLORING

☾ **Burg Rheinfels.** The castle ruins overlooking the town bear witness to the fact that St. Goar was once the best-fortified town in the Mittelrhein. From its beginnings in 1245, it was repeatedly enlarged by the counts of Katzenelnbogen, a powerful local dynasty, and their successors, the Landgraviate of Hesse. Although it repelled Louis IV's troops in 1689, Rheinfels was blasted by the French in 1797. Take time for a walk through the impressive ruins and the museum, which has an exquisite model of how the fortress looked in its heyday. To avoid the steep ascent on foot, buy a round-trip ticket (€3) for the Burgexpress, which departs from the bus stop on Heerstrasse, opposite the riverside parking lot for tour buses. ⊠ *Off Schlossberg Str.* 🕾 *06741/7753* ⊕ *www. burg-rheinfels.com* 🖼 *€4* ⊘ *Mid-Mar.–Oct., daily 9–6; Nov.–mid-Mar., weekends 11–5.*

Stiftskirche. St. Goar's tomb once rested in this 15th-century collegiate church built over a Romanesque crypt, reminiscent of churches in Speyer and Köln. ⊠ *Marktpl.* ⊘ *Apr.–Oct., daily 10–6; Nov.–Mar., daily 11–6.*

WHERE TO EAT AND STAY

For expanded hotel reviews, visit Fodors.com.

$ ✕ **Flair Hotel Landsknecht.** Members of the Nickenig family make every-
GERMAN one feel at home in their riverside restaurant ($–$$) and newly reno-
vated hotel north of St. Goar. Daughter Martina, a former wine queen, and her winemaker husband, Joachim Lorenz, operate the Vinothek, where you can sample his delicious Bopparder Hamm wines. These go well with the restaurant's hearty local dishes, such as Rhine-style sau-erbraten or seasonal specialties (asparagus, game). ■ TIP→ The hotel is an official Rheinsteig and Rhein-Burgen trail partner—perfect for hikers. ⊠ *Rheinuferstr. B–9, St. Goar–Fellen* 🕾 *06741/2011* ⊕ *www.hotel-landsknecht.de.*

$$ ▦ **Romantik Hotel Schloss Rheinfels.** Directly opposite Burg Rheinfels, this
★ hotel offers modern comfort and expansive views from rooms taste-fully furnished in country manor style. **Pros:** marvelous views of the Rhine and the town. **Cons:** villa section with one of the suites and all three of the apartments is well removed from the hotel and lack-ing charm. ⊠ *Schlossberg 47* ⊕ *www.schloss-rheinfels.de* ➴ *56 rooms, 3 apartments, 4 suites* ⊘ *In-room: no a/c, Internet. In-hotel: restau-rant, bar, pool, gym, spa, business center, parking, some pets allowed* ⑩ *Breakfast.*

ST. GOARSHAUSEN

29 km (18 mi) north of Rüdesheim, ferry from St. Goar.

Katz and Maus Castles. St. Goarshausen lies at the foot of two 14th-century castles whose names, Katz (Cat) and Maus (Mouse), reflect but one of the many power plays on the Rhine in the Middle Ages. Territorial supremacy and the concomitant privilege of collecting tolls fueled the fires of rivalry. In response to the construction of Burg Rheinfels, the archbishop of Trier erected a small castle north of St. Goarshausen to protect his interests. In turn, the masters of Rheinfels, the counts of Katzenelnbogen, built a bigger castle directly above the town. Its name was shortened to Katz, and its smaller neighbor was scornfully referred to as Maus. Both castles are closed to the public.

Liebenstein and Sterrenberg. Some 10 km (6 mi) north of the Maus castle, near Kamp-Bornhofen, is a castle duo separated by a "quarrel wall": Liebenstein and Sterrenberg, known as the *Feindliche Brüder* (rival brothers). Both impressive ruins have terrace cafés that afford good views. ⊠ *Kamp-Bornhofen.*

Loreley. One of the Rhineland's main attractions lies 4 km (2½ mi) south of St. Goarshausen: the steep (430-foot-high) slate cliff named after the beautiful blond nymph Loreley. Here she supposedly sat, singing songs so lovely that sailors and fishermen were lured to the treacherous rapids—and their demise. The rapids really were treacherous, the Rhine is at its narrowest here and the current the swiftest. The Loreley nymph was invented in 1801 by author Clemens Brentano, who drew his inspiration from the sirens of Greek legend. Her tale was retold as a ballad by Heinrich Heine and set to music by Friedrich Silcher at the height of Rhine Romanticism in the 19th century. The haunting melody is played on the PA systems of the Rhine boats whenever the Loreley is approached. ⊠ *Lorely Visitor Center, Auf der Loreley 7.*

OFF THE BEATEN PATH

Loreley Besucherzentrum. The 3-D, 20-minute film and hands-on exhibits at this visitor center are entertaining ways to learn about the region's flora and fauna, geology, wine, shipping, and, above all, the myth of the Loreley. You can stock up on souvenirs in the shop and have a snack at the bistro before heading for the nearby vantage point at the cliff's summit. The center is on the Rheinsteig trail, and other hiking trails are signposted in the landscaped park. There is hourly bus service to and from the KD steamer landing in St. Goarshausen (Easter to October). ⊠ *Auf der Loreley 7* 🖀 *06771/599–093* ⊕ *www.loreley-besucherzentrum.de* 💳 *€2.50* ⊙ *Mar., daily 10–5; Apr.–Oct., daily 10–6; Nov.–Feb., weekends 11–4.*

BOPPARD

17 km (11 mi) north of St. Goar, ferry to Filsen.

Boppard is a pleasant little resort that evolved from a Celtic settlement into a Roman fortress, Frankish royal court, and Free Imperial City. Boppard's tourist office conducts free walking tours mid-April to mid-October, Saturday at 11, starting at the office on the market square.

ESSENTIALS

Visitor Information Boppard ⊠ *Tourist-Information, Marktpl. 17* ☎ *06742/3888* ☏ *06742/81402* ⊕ *www.boppard-tourismus.de.*

EXPLORING

Karmeliterkirche (*Carmelite Church*). Two baroque altars dominate the interior of the Gothic Karmeliterkirche on Karmeliterstrasse, near the Rhine. It houses intricately carved choir stalls and tombstones and several beautiful Madonnas. Winegrowers still observe the old custom of laying the first-picked *Trauben* (grapes) at the foot of the Traubenmadonna (1330) to ensure a good harvest. The annual wine festival takes place in late September, just before the Riesling harvest.

Severuskirche (*Church of St. Severus; 1236*). Excavations in the 1960s revealed ancient Roman baths beneath the twin-tower, Romanesque Severuskirche on the market square. The large triumphal crucifix over the main altar and a lovely statue of a smiling Madonna date from the 13th century. ⊠ *Untere Marktstr. 7.*

Vierseenblick. From the Mühltal station, let the *Sesselbahn* (chairlift) whisk you a half-mile uphill to the Vierseenblick, a vantage point from which the Rhine looks like a chain of lakes. ☎ *06742/2510* ⊕ *www. sesselbahn-boppard.de* ⧖ *Round-trip €6.50* ☉ *Mid-Apr.–mid-Oct., daily 10–6; 1st 2 wks of Apr. and last 1 wks of Oct., 10–5.*

WHERE TO EAT AND STAY

For expanded hotel reviews, visit Fodors.com.

¢ ✕**Weinhaus Heilig Grab.** This wine estate's tavern, Boppard's oldest, is
GERMAN full of smiling faces: the wines are excellent, the fare is simple but hearty, and the welcome is warm. Old chestnut trees shade tables in the courtyard. If you'd like to visit the cellars or vineyards, ask your friendly hosts, Rudolf and Susanne Schoeneberger. ⊠ *Zelkesg. 12* ☎ *06742/2371* ⊕ *www.heiliggrab.de* ☉ *Closed Tues. and 3 wks late Dec.–early Jan. No lunch.*

$$ ⊞ **Best Western Bellevue Rheinhotel.** You can enjoy a Rhine view from many of the rooms in this traditional hotel or from the terrace next to the waterfront promenade. **Pros:** marvelous view. **Cons:** parking is a problem; breakfast costs €11 extra. ⊠ *Rheinallee 41* ☎ *06742/1020* ⊕ *www.bellevue-boppard.de* ⧖ *93 rooms, 1 suite* ☖ *In-room: a/c, no a/c, Wi-Fi. In-hotel: restaurant, bar, pool, gym, spa, parking, some pets allowed.*

SPORTS AND THE OUTDOORS

Mittelrhein Klettersteig. For those with Alpine hiking ambitions, there is this climbing path, a *via ferrata,* complete with cables, steps, and ladders. It's an alternate route of the Rhein-Burgen-Wanderweg (hiking trail from Koblenz to Bingen). The trail starts at St.-Remigius-Platz, about 1 km (½ mi) from Boppard Hauptbahnhof. Allow two to three hours for the climb, though there are several possibilities to return to the "normal" path in-between climbs. Rent the necessary gear at the Aral gas station on Koblenzer Strasse in Boppard (☎ *06742/2447*). ⊠ *St.-Remigius-Pl., Boppard.*

Weinwanderweg (*Wine Hiking Trail*). The 10-km (6-mi) hiking trail from Boppard to Spay begins north of town on Peternacher Weg. Many other marked trails in the vicinity are outlined on maps and in brochures available from the tourist office.

EN
ROUTE

Marksburg. On the eastern shore overlooking the town of Braubach is the Marksburg. Built in the 13th century to protect the silver and lead mines in the area, it's the only land-based castle on the Rhine to have survived the centuries intact. Within its massive walls are a collection of weapons and manuscripts, a medieval botanical garden, and a self-service restaurant. Try to get a table on the terrace to enjoy the stunning view. ☎ *02627/206* ⊕ *www.marksburg.de* ⊒ *€6* ☉ *Easter–Oct., daily 10–5; Nov.–Easter, daily 11–4; restaurant daily.*

Schloss Stolzenfels. On the outskirts of Koblenz, the neo-Gothic towers of Schloss Stolzenfels come into view. The castle's origins date to the mid-13th century, when the archbishop of Trier sought to counter the influence (and toll rights) of the archbishop of Mainz, who had just built Burg Lahneck, a castle at the confluence of the Lahn and Rhine rivers. Its superbly furnished period rooms and beautiful gardens are well worth a visit. At this writing, the castle was closed for renovations. From B-9 (curbside parking) it's about a 15-minute walk to the castle entrance. ☎ *0261/51656* ⊕ *stolzenfels.gdke.webseiten.cc* ⊒ *€4* ☉ *Apr.–Sept., Tues.–Sun. 10–7; Oct., Nov., and Jan.–Mar., Tues.–Sun. 10–5.*

KOBLENZ

20 km (12 mi) north of Boppard.

The ancient city of Koblenz is at a geographic nexus known as the **Deutsches Eck** (German Corner) in the heart of the Mittelrhein region. Rivers and mountains converge here: the Mosel flows into the Rhine on one side; the Lahn flows in on the other a few miles south; and three mountain ridges intersect.

Founded by the Romans in AD 9, the city was first called Castrum ad Confluentes (Fort at the Confluence). It became a powerful city in the Middle Ages, when it controlled trade on both the Rhine and the Mosel. Air raids during World War II destroyed 85% of the city, but extensive restoration has done much to recreate its former atmosphere.

GETTING HERE AND AROUND

You can get here speedily by autobahn or via a leisurely scenic drive along the Rhine (or even more mellow, by cruise boat). The Europa-bus also serves the city. The Koblenz tourist office has guided English-language tours on Saturday at 3 from May to October. Tours are €3 and depart from the Historisches Rathaus on Jesuitenplatz.

ESSENTIALS

Visitor Information Koblenz ⊠ *Tourist-Information, Jesuitenpl. 2–4* ☎ *0261/130–920* ⊕ *www.koblenz-touristik.de.*

EXPLORING
TOP ATTRACTIONS

Deutsches Eck (*German Corner*). This pointed bit of land jutting into the river like the prow of an early ironclad warship is found at the sharp intersection of the Rhine and Mosel rivers. One of the more effusive manifestations of German nationalism—an 1897 equestrian statue of Kaiser Wilhelm I, first emperor of the newly united Germany—was erected here. It was destroyed at the end of World War II and replaced in 1953 with a ponderous monument to Germany's unity. After German reunification a new statue of Wilhelm was placed atop this monument in 1993. Pieces of the Berlin Wall stand on the Mosel side—a memorial to those who died as a result of the partitioning of the country.

Festung Ehrenbreitstein. Europe's largest fortress, towering 400 feet above the left bank of the Rhine, offers a magnificent view over Koblenz and where the Mosel and the Rhine rivers meet. The earliest buildings date from about 1100, but the bulk of the fortress was constructed in the 16th century. In 1801 it was partially destroyed by Napoléon, and the French occupied Koblenz for the next 18 years. For an introduction to the fortress and its history, head for the *Besucherdienst* (visitor center). English tours are for groups only, but you can often join a group that is registered for a tour.

Landesmuseum Koblenz (*State Museum*). As for the fortress's 16th-century Vogel Greif cannon, the French absconded with it in 1794, the Germans took it back in 1940, and the French commandeered it again in 1945. The 15-ton cannon was peaceably returned by French president François Mitterrand in 1984 and is now part of the exhibit on the history of local technologies, from wine growing to industry, in the fortress's Landesmuseum ☎ *0261/66750* ⊕ *www.landesmuseum-koblenz. de* ☜ *€4* ☽ *Mid-Mar.–mid-Nov., daily 9:30–5 (price and opening hrs may change for 2012).*

Ferry. To reach the fortress on the east bank of the Rhine, take Bus 9 or 10 from the train station or the ferry from the Pegelhaus on the Koblenz riverbank (near Rheinstrasse). There is also a direct bus from the station to the fortress Sunday afternoons April–October. ☜ *€2.60 round-trip* ☽ *Apr. and Nov., daily 8:30–6; May–Oct., daily 8–7.*

Seilbahn. Take the Sesselbahn to ascend to the fortress. ☎ *0261/6675– 4000* ⊕ *www.diefestungehrenbreitstein.de* ☜ *Grounds €1.10, tour €2.10, combined ticket €4 (price and hrs may change in 2012)* ☽ *Mid-Mar.–mid-Nov., daily 10–5.*

Ludwig Museum. Just behind the Deutsches Eck, housed in the spic-and-span Deutschherrenhaus, is this restored 13th-century building. Industrialist Peter Ludwig, one of Germany's leading contemporary-art collectors, has filled this museum with part of his huge collection. ✉ *Danziger Freiheit 1* ☎ *0261/304–040* ⊕ *www.ludwigmuseum.org* ☜ *€4, €5 with Mittelrhein Museum* ☽ *Tues.–Sat. 10:30–5, Sun. 11–6.*

Mittelrhein Museum. This museum houses the city's art collection in a lovely 16th-century building near the Old Town's central square, Am Plan. It has an extensive collection of landscapes focusing on the Rhine. It also has a notable collection of secular medieval art and works by regional artists. ✉ *Florinsmarkt 15* ☎ *0261/129–2520* ⊕ *www. mittelrhein-museum.de* 🎫 *€2.50, €5 with Ludwig Museum* ⊙ *Tues.– Sat. 10:30–5, Sun. 11–6.*

★ **St. Kastor Basilika** (*St. Castor Basilica*). It was in this sturdy Romanesque basilica consecrated in 836 that in 842 plans were drawn for the Treaty of Verdun, formalizing the division of Charlemagne's great empire and leading to the creation of Germany and France as separate states. Inside, compare the squat Romanesque columns in the nave with the intricate fan vaulting of the Gothic sections. The **St. Kastor Fountain** outside the church is an intriguing piece of historical one-upmanship. It was built by the occupying French to mark the beginning of Napoléon's ultimately disastrous Russian campaign of 1812. ✉ *Kastorhof* ⊕ *www. sankt-kastor-koblenz.de* ⊙ *Daily 9–6.*

WORTH NOTING

Kurfürstliches Schloss. Strolling along the promenade toward town, you'll pass this gracious castle. It was built in the late 18th century by Prince-Elector Clemens Wenzeslaus as an elegant escape from the grim Ehren-breitstein fortress. The palace itself is open to the public the first Sunday in May for *Wein im Schloss,* a large presentation of Lower Mosel, Nahe, Mittelrhein, and Ahr wines. In the garden behind the palace, don't miss the handsome statue of Father Rhine and Mother Mosel.

Liebfrauenkirche (*Church of Our Lady*). War damage is evidenced by the blend of old buildings and modern store blocks on and around Am Plan. The church stands on Roman foundations at the Old Town's highest point. The bulk of the church is of Romanesque design, but its choir is one of the Rhineland's finest examples of 15th-century Gothic architecture, and the west front is graced with two 17th-century baroque towers. ✉ *Am Plan* ⊙ *Mon.–Sat. 8–6, Sun. 9–8.*

Pfaffendorf Brücke (*Pfaffendorf Bridge*). This bridge marks the beginning of the Old Town.

Rheinanlagen (*Rhine Gardens*). This 10-km (6-mi) promenade runs along the riverbank past the Weindorf.

Rheinkran (*Rhine Crane*). The squat form of this crane, built in 1611, is one of Koblenz's landmarks. Marks on the side of the building indicate the heights reached by floodwaters of bygone years. In the mid-19th century a pontoon bridge consisting of a row of barges spanned the Rhine here; when ships approached, two or three barges were simply towed out of the way to let them through.

Weindorf. Just off the Pfaffendorf Bridge, between the modern blocks of the Rhein-Mosel-Halle and the Hotel Mercure, is the Weindorf, a wine "village" constructed for a mammoth exhibition of German wines in 1925, which is now a restaurant. ⊕ *www.weindorf-koblenz.de.*

WHERE TO EAT

$
ECLECTIC   ✗ **Café Einstein.** Portraits of Einstein line the walls of this lively restaurant where locals gather to watch live soccer matches on a projection screen. The friendly Tayhus family serves tasty fare daily, from a hearty breakfast buffet (brunch on Sunday—reservations recommended) to

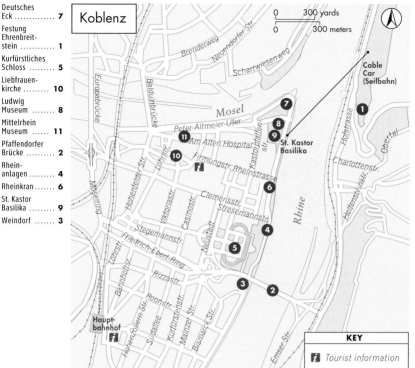

Koblenz

| 0 | 300 yards |
| 0 | 300 meters |

Cable
Car
(Seilbahn)

Mosel

St. Kastor
Basilika

Rhine

Haupt-
bahnhof

KEY

i Tourist information

late-night finger food. Fish specials are served year-round. ✉ *Firmungstr. 30* ☎ *0261/914–4999* ⊕ *www.einstein-koblenz.de.*

$$
MEDITERRANEAN
★

✕ **Da Vinci.** Noble and creative are the decor and fare at this smart restaurant in the heart of the Old Town. Da Vinci reproductions, including an original-size rendition of *The Last Supper,* adorn the walls. Leather upholstery, an elegant bar, and soft lighting round out the ambience. Rotating specialties such as suckling pig come and go, but Angus beef, grilled jumbo shrimp, and fresh fish stay on the menu year-round. The wine list contains more than 200 bottles, with a focus on fine Italian wines. ✉ *Firmungstr. 32b* ☎ *0261/921–5444* ⊕ *www.davinci-koblenz.de.*

$
GERMAN

✕ **Weindorf-Koblenz.** The Bastian family has upgraded the food and wine selection at this reconstructed "wine village" of half-timber houses grouped around a tree-shaded courtyard with an adjacent vineyard. Fresh renditions of traditional Rhine and Mosel specialties, a good selection of local wines, and a fabulous Sunday brunch (reservation recommended)—wine, beer, and nonalcoholic beverages are included in the price (€25)—make this a popular spot. ✉ *Julius-Wegeler-Str. 2* ☎ *0261/133–7190* ⊕ *www.weindorf-koblenz.de* ⊙ *No lunch Nov.–Mar.*

$
GERMAN

✕ **Weinhaus Hubertus.** Hunting scenes and trophies line the wood-panel walls of this cozy wine restaurant named after the patron saint of hunters. The decorations also include 100-year-old murals. Karin and Dieter Spahl serve hearty portions of fresh, traditional fare. ✉ *Florinsmarkt 6* ☎ *0261/*

31177   ⊕ *weinhaus-hubertus.de*
⊘ *Closed Tues. No lunch Nov.–Apr.*
and weekdays May–Oct.

$$
GERMAN
★

✕**Zum Weissen Schwanen.** Guests have found a warm welcome in this half-timber inn and mill since 1693, a tradition carried on by the Kunz family. It's located next to the 13th-century town gateway of Braubach, just below the Marksburg. This is a charming place to overnight or enjoy well-prepared, contemporary German cuisine with regional specialties. Brasserie Brentano ($) serves lighter fare and Sunday brunch. The hotel is an official Rheinsteig trail partner. ✉ *Brunnenstr. 4, 12 km (7½ mi) south of Koblenz via B-42, Braubach* ☎ *02627/9820* ⊕ *www.zumweissen-schwanen.de.*

WHERE TO STAY
For expanded hotel reviews, visit Fodors.com.

$ ⊞ **Hotel Kleiner Riesen.** You can literally watch the Rhine flowing by from the four front rooms of this friendly, family-operated hotel about a 10-minute walk from the station. **Pros:** quiet; on the river; close to piers. **Cons:** 20-minute walk from city center. ✉ *Januarius-Zick Str. 11, on the Rhine promenade* ☎ *0261/303–460* ⊕ *www.kleiner-riesen. de* ⤙ *19 rooms, 3 Suites* ⊘ *In-room: no a/c, Wi-Fi. In-hotel: business center, parking, some pets allowed* ⊙ *Breakfast.*

NIGHTLIFE AND THE ARTS

Café Hahn. Café Hahn, in the suburb of Güls, features everything from cabaret and stand-up comedians to popular musicians and bands. ✉ *Neustr. 15* ☎ *0261/42302* ⊕ *www.cafehahn.de.*

Circus Maximus. You'll find disco sounds, live music, and theme parties practically every evening here. On a balmy night, visit their Statt Strand beach bar on Universitätsstr on the banks of the Mosel near the university. ✉ *Stegemannstr. 30, at Viktoriastr* ☎ *0261/300–2357* ⊕ *www. circus-maximus.org; www.strand-koblenz.de.*

Enchilada. For Latin American music and good cocktails, head here. ✉ *Gerichtsstr. 2* ☎ *0261/100–4666* ⊕ *www.enchilada.de.*

Staatsorchester Rheinische Philharmonie (*Rhenish Philharmonic Orchestra*). The Philharmonic plays regularly at different concert venues around town. ✉ *Eltzerhofstr. 6a* ☎ *0261/301–2272* ⊕ *www.rheinische-philharmonie.de.*

Theater Koblenz. Built in 1787, this gracious neoclassic theater is still in regular use. ✉ *Clemensstr. 1–5* ☎ *0261/129–2870* ⊕ *www.theater-koblenz.de.*

Stroll through Koblenz's Old Town, stopping for a bite at a sidewalk café along one of the squares, such as Jesuitenplatz.

SHOPPING

Koblenz's most pleasant shopping is in the Old Town streets around the market square Am Plan.

Löhr Center. This modern, American-style, windowless mall has some 130 shops and restaurants. ⊠ *Hohenfelder Str. 22* ⊕ *www.loehr-center.de.*

THE MOSEL VALLEY

The Mosel is one of the most hauntingly beautiful river valleys on Earth. Here, as in the Rhine Valley, forests and vines carpet steep hillsides; castles and church spires dot the landscape; and medieval wine hamlets line the riverbanks. The Mosel landscape is no less majestic, but narrower and more peaceful than that of the Rhine Gorge; the river's countless bends and loops slow its pace and lend the region a special charm.

WINNINGEN

11 km (7 mi) southwest of Koblenz on B-416.

Winningen is a gateway to the Terrassenmosel (Terraced Mosel), the portion of the river characterized by steep, terraced vineyards. Winches help haul miniature monorails with the winegrowers and their tools aboard up the steep incline, but tending and harvesting the vines are all done by hand. ■ TIP→ For a bird's-eye view of the valley, drive up Fährstrasse to Am Rosenhang, the start of a pleasant walk along the Weinlehrpfad (Educational Wine Path).

As you head upstream toward Kobern-Gondorf, you'll pass the renowned vineyard site Uhlen. In Kobern the Oberburg (upper castle) and the St. Matthias Kapelle, a 12th-century chapel, are good vantage points. Half-timber houses reflecting the architectural styles of three centuries ring the town's pretty market square.

WHERE TO EAT AND STAY

For expanded hotel reviews, visit Fodors.com.

$$$
GERMAN
★

✕ **Alte Mühle Thomas Höreth.** Thomas and Gudrun Höreth's enchanting country inn is a labyrinth of little rooms and cellars grouped around oleander-lined courtyards. They have restored this former mill, originally dating to 1026, and furnished it with thoughtful details and authentic materials. Highlights of the menu include homemade cheeses, terrines, pâtés, and *Entensülze* (goose in aspic), served with the Höreths' own wines. For those who want to get away from the river, the Höreths have an award-winning hotel in the forest, Höreth im Wald ($$$). ✉ *Mühlental 17, via B-416, Kobern-Gondorf* ☎ *02607/6474* ⊕ *www. thomas-hoereth.de* ◔ *No lunch weekdays.*

$$$
GERMAN

✕ **Halferschenke.** This *Schenke* (inn) was once an overnight stop for *Halfer*, who with their horses towed cargo-laden boats upstream. Today the stone inn (1832) is run by a friendly young couple, Thomas and Eva Balmes. In the dining room dark wood, antiques, and lots of candles and flowers provide a lovely setting for the artfully prepared seasonal food. An excellent selection of Terrassenmosel wines is available. ✉ *Haupt-str. 63, via B-49, opposite Kobern, Dieblich* ☎ *02607/1008* ⊕ *www. halferschenke.de* ◔ *Closed Mon. No lunch Tues.–Sat.*

$

🛏 **Hotel Simonis.** Alexandra de Bruin and Paul Vollmer, a Dutch couple, run this traditional hotel on Kobern-Gondorf's market square, which includes two suites across the courtyard in what is allegedly Germany's oldest half-timber house (1321). **Pros:** half-timber setting. **Cons:** no elevator. ✉ *Marktpl. 4, Kobern-Gondorf* ☎ *02607/203* ⊕ *www. hotelsimonis.com* ⇌ *13 rooms, 2 suites* ⚙ *In-room: no a/c, Wi-Fi. In-hotel: restaurant, bar, some pets allowed* ◔ *Closed Jan. and Feb.* ⏇ *Breakfast.*

ALKEN

22 km (13½ mi) southwest of Koblenz.

Burg Thurant. This 12th-century castle towers over the village and the Burgberg (castle hill) vineyard. Wine and snacks are served in the courtyard; castle tours take in the chapel, cellar, tower, and a weapons display. Allow a good half hour for the climb from the riverbank. Call ahead in winter to make sure it is open. ☎ *02605/2004* ⊕ *www.thurant. de* 🎟 *€3.50* ◔ *Mar. and Apr., daily 10–5; May–Oct., daily 10–6; Nov.–Feb., weekends 10–4.*

WHERE TO EAT

EN
ROUTE

Burg Eltz (*Eltz Castle*). One of Germany's most picturesque, genuinely medieval castles (12th–16th century), Burg Eltz merits as much attention as King Ludwig's trio of castles in Bavaria. For the 40-minute English-language tour, given when enough English speakers gather, inquire at the souvenir shop. It guides you through the period rooms and massive kitchen. There's also a popular treasure vault filled with gold and silver. To get here, exit B-416 at Hatzenport (opposite and southwest of Alken), proceed to Münstermaifeld, and follow signs to the parking lot near the Antoniuskapelle. From here it's a 15-minute walk, or take the shuttle bus (€1.50). Hikers can reach the castle from Moselkern in 40 minutes. ⊠ *Burg Eltz, Münstermaifeld* ☏ *02672/950–500* ⊕ *www.burg-eltz.de* ⊡ *Tour and treasure vault €8* ⊙ *Apr.–Oct., daily 9:30–5:30.*

COCHEM

51 km (31½ mi) southwest of Koblenz on B-49, approximately 93 km (58 mi) from Trier.

Cochem is one of the most attractive towns of the Mosel Valley, with a riverside promenade to rival any along the Rhine. It's especially lively during the wine festivals in June and late August. If time permits, savor the landscape from the deck of a boat—many excursions are available, lasting from one hour to an entire day. The tourist office on Endertplatz has an excellent English-language outline for a walking tour of the town. From the **Enderttor** (Endert Town Gate) you can see the entrance to Germany's longest railway tunnel, the Kaiser-Wilhelm, an astonishing example of 19th-century engineering. The 4-km-long (2½-mi-long) tunnel saves travelers a 21-km (13-mi) detour along one of the Mosel's great loops.

ESSENTIALS

Visitor Information Cochem ⊠ *Tourist-Information, Endertpl. 1* ☏ *02671/60040* ⊕ *www.cochem.de.*

EXPLORING

Historische Senfmühle. At this 200-year-old mustard mill, Wolfgang Steffens conducts daily tours at 11, 2, 3, and 4, showing how he produces his gourmet mustard. Garlic, cayenne, honey, curry, and even Riesling wine are among the types you can sample and purchase in the shop. From the Old Town, walk across the bridge toward Cond. The mill is to the left of the bridgehead. ⊠ *Stadionstr. 1* ☏ *02671/607–665* ⊕ *www. senfmuehle.net* ⊡ *Tours €2.50* ⊙ *Daily 10–6.*

Reichsburg (*Imperial Fortress*). The 15-minute walk to the 1,000-year-old castle overlooking the town, will reward you with great views of the area. ■TIP→ Flight demonstrations (eagles and falcons) take place from Good Friday through October, Tuesday to Sunday at 11, 1, 2:30, and 4. With advance reservations, you can get a taste of the Middle Ages at a medieval banquet, complete with costumes, music, and entertainment. Banquets take place on Friday (7 pm) and Saturday (6 pm) and last four hours; the price (€45) includes a castle tour. During the *Burgfest* (castle festival) the first weekend of August, there's a medieval market and colorful tournaments. ☏ *02671/255* ⊕ *www.reichsburg-cochem. de* ⊡ *€5, including 40-min tour; flight demonstration €3.50* ⊙ *Mid-Mar.–early Nov., daily 9–5.*

WHERE TO EAT

¢ ╳ **Alte Gutsschänke.** Locals and tourists mingle naturally here near the
GERMAN open fireplace and antique wine-making paraphernalia. The food is
local and fortifying: sausages, cheeses, ham, and homemade soups
served with the wines from host Arthur Schmitz's, own estate. As the
night progresses, locals might unpack their musical instruments and
start playing. Note that this place doesn't serve beer. ⊠ *Schlossstr. 6,
on the way up to the castle* ☎ *02671/8950* ⊟ *No credit cards* ⊗ *No
lunch weekdays.*

$$$$ ╳ **Lohspeicher–l'Auberge du Vin.** In times past, oak bark for leather tan-
FRENCH ners was dried and stored in this building (1834). This house near the
market square is now a charming inn run by a vivacious young couple,
Ingo and Birgit Beth. His French-German delicacies are a pleasure for
the palate and the eye. At least one saltwater and one freshwater fish
are featured daily. Don't miss the dessert *Variation* (medley). Some 20
French and Italian wines supplement the family's own estate-bottled
wines. Nine rooms, four with a view of the castle, enhance the Beths'
hospitality. ⊠ *Oberg. 1, at Marktpl.* ☎ *02671/3976* ⊕ *www.lohspeicher.
de* ⊗ *Closed Wed. and Feb.*

$$$$ ╳ **Moselromantik Hotel Weissmühle.** This rustic family inn is set amid the
GERMAN forested hills of the Enderttal (Endert Valley) on the site of a historic
☾ mill that belonged to the current proprietor's great-grandfather. Lined
with photos and memorabilia from the original mill, it's an oasis from
traffic and crowds yet only 2½ km (1½ mi) from Cochem. Beneath the
exposed beams and painted ceiling of the restaurant, food from the
hotel's own trout farm will grace your table. German and French wines
are served. ∎TIP➔ The inn's underground bar, originally built to become a
swimming pool, opens around 9 pm and is a bastion of unintentional retro
flair. ⊠ *Wilde Endert 2* ☎ *02671/8955* ⊕ *www.hotel-weissmuehle.de.*

EDIGER-ELLER

61 km (38 mi) southwest of Koblenz on B-49.

Ediger-Eller, formerly two independent hamlets, is another photogenic
wine village with well-preserved houses and remnants of a medieval
town wall. It's particularly romantic at night when the narrow alleys
and half-timber buildings are illuminated by historic streetlights.

Martinskirche (*St. Martin's Church*). The church is a remarkable amalga-
mation of art and architectural styles, inside and out. Take a moment
to admire the 117 carved bosses in the star-vaulted ceiling of the nave.
Among the many fine sculptures throughout the church and the chapel
is the town's treasure: a Renaissance stone relief, *Christ in the Wine
Press.* ⊠ *Kirchstr.*

WHERE TO STAY

For expanded hotel reviews, visit Fodors.com.

$ ⊺ **Zum Löwen.** This simply furnished hotel, run by the Saffenreuther
family, boasts friendly service and a splendid terrace overlooking the
Mosel. **Pros:** fine view of the Mosel. **Cons:** on a busy street; no elevator. ⊠ *Moselweinstr. 23* ☎ *02675/208* ⊕ *www.mosel-hotel-loewen.de*
⇝ *19 rooms, 2 suites* ⊘ *In-room: no a/c, Wi-Fi. In-hotel: restaurant,*

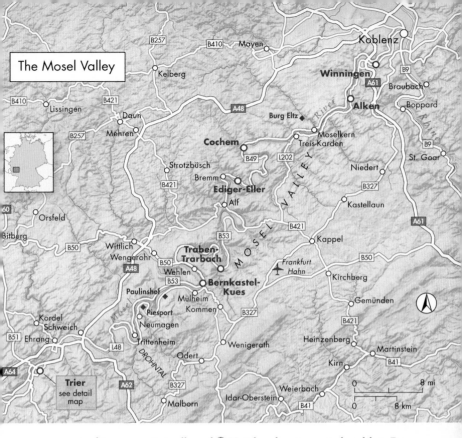

The Mosel Valley

parking, some pets allowed ☉ *Hotel and restaurant closed late Dec.–Mar.* ⊠ *Breakfast.*

EN ROUTE

Calmont. As you continue along the winding course of the Mosel, you'll pass Europe's steepest vineyard site, Calmont, opposite the romantic ruins of a 12th-century Augustinian convent and before the loop at Bremm.

Zell. This popular village is full of pubs and wineshops that ply the crowds with Zeller Schwarze Katz, "Black Cat" wine, a commercially successful product and the focal point of a large wine festival in late June. Some 6 million vines hug the slopes around Zell, making it one of Germany's largest wine-growing communities. The area between Zell and Schweich (near Trier), known as the Middle Mosel, is home to some of the world's finest Riesling wines.

TRABEN-TRARBACH

30 km (19 mi) south of Cochem.

The Mosel divides Traben-Trarbach, which has pleasant promenades on both sides of the river. Its wine festivals are held the second and last weekends in July. Traben's art nouveau buildings are worth seeing (Hotel Bellevue, the gateway on the Mosel bridge, the post office, the train station, and town hall).

Continued on page 494

In the heart of the Mosel Valley lies the Mittelmosel (Middle Mosel), where vineyards tumble down steep slate slopes to riverside villages full of half-timbered, baroque, and belle époque architecture. Famed for its warm climate and 2,000-year-old winemaking tradition, it produces some of the best Rieslings in the world. The Middle Mosel's many wineries and tasting rooms are concentrated along a meandering 75-mile stretch of lush river valley, picturesque towns, and rural estates between the ancient town of Trier and the village of Zell, allowing for multiple sips in a short amount of time.

By Jeff Kavanagh

Above, Dr Pauly-Bergweiler bottle.
Left, Vineyards in the Mosel Valley.

Wine Tasting
in the
Mosel Valley

Traben-Trarbach

TWO DAYS IN THE MIDDLE MOSEL

DAY 1

Small, family-run wineries that have been producing high-quality wines for generations dominate the Middle Mosel. Starting in Trier, just across the border from Luxembourg, the tour follows the B-53 and the Mosel River as it flows northwest through a succession of pretty wine villages and steep-sloped estates.

[Map of the Mosel Valley showing: Alf, Rebenhof, Schmitges, Kröv, Enkirch, Rachtig-Zeltingen, Weingut Martin M, Wengerohr, B50, Kerpen, Jugendstilh, Weinromantik Richtershof Hotel, Wehlen, Bellevue, Weingut Bauer, Traben-Trarb, Weingut Karp-Schreiber, Der Ratskeller, Bernkastel-Kues, Brauneberg, Mülheim, Dr. Pauly-Bergweiler, Piesport, Monzelfeld, Kommen, Weingut Lehnert-Veit, Klüsserath, Neumagen, Kordel, Schweich, MOSEL VALLEY, Moselle, Sektgut St. Laurentius, Dhrontal, Ehrang, Leiwen, Kenn, Mehring, Fell, Weinstube Kesselstatt, Episcopal Wine Estates, Trier, A48, B53, L48]

Episcopal Wine Estates
Drop down into a labyrinth of cellars beneath Trier's streets or visit the estate's elegant *vinothek* (wine store) to sample fine Rieslings built upon almost two millennia of priestly tradition. Try: fruity and elegant Scharzhofberger Riesling.
✉ Gervasiusstrasse 1, Trier
☎ 0651/145760
⊕ www.bwgtrier.de

Sektgut St. Laurentius
Whether in the spacious tasting room, on the outdoor terrace, or in the modern little wine bar near the river, there are plenty of places to taste this winery's *sekt* (sparkling wine), considered some of the best in the region. Try: fruity, creamy, and yeasty Cremant.
✉ Euchariusstrasse 15, Leiwen
☎ 06507/939055
⊕ www.st-laurentius-sekt.de

Weingut Lehnert-Veit
In addition to Riesling, visitors can sample Merlot, Pinot Noir, and Chardonnay in this winery's Mediterranean-style garden on the banks of the Mosel. Try: delicately flinty, well-balanced Falkenberg Riesling Mineral Kabinett Feinherb.
✉ In der Dur 10, Piesport
☎ 06507/2123
⊕ www.weingut-lv.net

Weingut Karp-Schreiber
This welcoming winery's varietals include Riesling, Weissburgunder, and Regent; and it also produces a nice Rotling, a *cuvée* (blend) of all three. When the sun's shining, the best place to taste them is on the winery's little trellised veranda. Try: fresh, elegant "my karp" Riesling.
✉ Moselweinstrasse 186, Brauneberg
☎ 06534/236
⊕ www.karp-schreiber.de

Weingut Bauer
An extension of the family home, where four generations reside beneath the same roof, the Bauer's simple, modern tasting room is a good place to sample award-winning still and sparkling white wines presented with old-fashioned hospitality. Try: fruity, refreshing Winzersekt Riesling Brut.
✉ Moselstrasse 3, 54486 Mülheim
☎ 06534/571
⊕ www.weingut-bauer.de

Mosel grape harvest

Wine barrels at Kerpen   Weingut Karp-Schreiber   Vineyards in the Mosel Valley

DAY 2

From the quiet village of Mül-heim, the Mosel makes a couple of sweeping loops up the val-ley, passing through the towns of Bernkastel-Kues and Traben-Trabach as it winds along.

Dr. Pauly-Bergweiler
This winery's presence in the Mosel includes vineyards in seven different villages and a grand villa in the center of Bernkastel, where its cozy vinothek finds space within the mansion's vaulted cellars. Try: racy, flinty Alte Badstube am Doktorberg Riesling.
✉ Gestade 15, Bernkastel
☎ 06531/3002
🌐 www.pauly-bergweiler.com

Kerpen
A friendly husband-and-wife-run winery, Kerpen has eight generations of winemaking tra-dition, a special collection of Rieslings with labels designed by visiting artists, and an un-pretentious tasting room within a stone's throw of the river. Try: dry Graacher Himmelreich Riesling Kabinett Feinherb.
✉ Werallee 6, Bernkastel-Wehlen
☎ 06531/6868
🌐 www.weingut-kerpen.de

Rebenhof
You'll find only Rieslings in Rebenhof's stylish, contempo-rary tasting room, which shares space with stainless-steel fermentation tanks. Try: flinty,

old-vine Ürziger Würtgarten Riesling Spätlese.
✉ Hüwel 2-3, Ürzig
☎ 06532/4546
🌐 www.rebenhof.de

Schmitges
Located on an unassuming village lane, Schmitges spe-cializes in the production of high-quality dry whites that, along with the modern, wine-bar style of their vinothek, distinguishes them from many other local establishments. Try: light, summery Rivaner.
✉ Im Unterdorf 12, Erden
☎ 06532/2743
🌐 www.schmitges-weine.de

Weingut Martin Müllen
Established in 1991, this winery is a mere infant com-pared to many others here, but its success has its roots in modern and traditional winemaking principles, and one of the best *Grand Cru* (great growth) vineyards in the region. Try: light but com-plex Trarbacher Hühnerberg Riesling Spätlese.
✉ Alte Marktstrasse 2, Traben-Trarbach
☎ 06541/9470
🌐 www.muellen.de

STOP FOR A BITE

✕ Weinstube Kesselstatt
Sitting beneath vines in the shadow of the Liebfrauen-kirche and the Trier Dom you can sip Kesselstatt estate wines and snack on wild boar and locally produced cheese.

✉ Liebfrauenstrasse 10, Trier
☎ 0651/41178
🌐 weinstube-kesselstatt.de

✕ Weinromantik Richters-hof Hotel
An ideal place for lovers of the grape, this stately hotel has a bistro that serves seasonal dishes such as white asparagus and ham, a gourmet restaurant offering contemporary cuisine, and a wine list that runs to 350 bottles, 150 of which are from the Mosel.
✉ Hauptstrasse 81-83, Mül-heim
☎ 06534/9480
🌐 www.weinromantikhotel.de

✕ Der Ratskeller
Just off Bernkastel's main square, Der Ratskeller's un-complicated regional fare can be enjoyed at an outside table with a view of the action or inside cozily sur-rounded by dark wood and leadlight windows.
✉ Markt 30, Bernkastel-Kues
☎ 06531/7474

✕ Jugendstilhotel Bellevue
Traben-Trarbach's premier hotel has a first-class repu-tation that derives from its belle époque architecture, fine cuisine, professional, knowledgeable staff, and su-perb wine list.
✉ An der Mosel 11, Traben-Trarbach
☎ 06541/7030
🌐 www.bellevue-hotel.de

WINE TOURING AND TASTING

WHEN TO GO

The best time to visit the region is between May and September, when a lightly chilled glass or two of wine is the perfect complement to a sunny spring day or a warm summer evening. This coincides with high season in the valley, when roads and cycle paths swell with tourists, particularly in the warmer months, and in September during the wine harvest. Fortunately, the next wine village is never far along the Mosel River. If you arrive and find a tasting room that's too busy, there's invariably another just around the corner.

IN THE TASTING ROOM

While varietals such as Müller-Thurgau, Weissburgunder, and Pinot Noir are produced in the Middle Mosel, the staple of most estates is Riesling. Given that the wineries are predominantly small, family-owned operations, there tends to be an emphasis on the production of high-quality, low-quantity wines. Their tasting rooms, when not part of the winery itself, are frequently extensions of family homes, affording visitors intimate contact with the winemakers. Naturally, German is the dominant language spoken by local tourists and many of the Dutch, Belgians, and Luxembourgers who pop across the border for a visit, but most winemakers speak English at least well enough to describe their wines. Opening hours vary, and although you can drop into most tasting rooms outside of these times, there may not always be someone around to serve you. To avoid disappointment it's worth checking websites for opening times first.

BOTTLE PRICES AND TASTING FEES

Once the most expensive wines in the world, Mosel Valley Rieslings have come down significantly in price since their heyday in the early 20th century, yet they remain world class. The average price for a quality bottle of Riesling is about €7–€10; each winery's price list is generally detailed in brochures found in its tasting room. Most wineries won't charge to taste a couple of their wines, but will expect you to purchase a bottle or two if you try more. Those that do have tasting fees, which are commonly between €5 and €15, will often waive them if you purchase a bottle.

Left, Romantic wine village on the Mosel River. Right, Bottle display from Mosel-Weinmuseum in Bernkastel-Kues

WINE TASTING PRIMER

Ordering and tasting wine—whether at a winery, bar, or restaurant—is easy once you master a few simple steps.

LOOK AND NOTE

Hold your glass by the stem and look at the wine in the glass. Note its color, depth, and clarity.

For whites, is it greenish, yellow, or gold? For reds, is it purplish, ruby, or garnet? Is the wine's color pale or deep? Is the liquid clear or cloudy?

SWIRL AND SNIFF

Swirl the wine gently in the glass to intensify the scents, then sniff over the rim of the glass. What do you smell? Try to identify aromas like:

- **Fruits**—citrus, peaches, berries, figs, melon
- **Flowers**—orange blossoms, honey, perfume
- **Spices**—baking spices, pungent, herbal notes
- **Vegetables**—fresh or cooked, herbal notes

- **Minerals**—earth, steely notes, wet stones
- **Dairy**—butter, cream, cheese, yogurt
- **Oak**—toast, vanilla, coconut, tobacco
- **Animal**—leathery, meaty notes

Are there any unpleasant notes, like mildew or wet dog, that might indicate that the wine is "off?"

SIP AND SAVOR

Prime your palate with a sip, swishing the wine in your mouth. Then spit in a bucket or swallow.

Take another sip and think about the wine's attributes. Sweetness is detected on the tip of the tongue, acidity on the sides of the tongue, and tannins (a mouth-drying sensation) on the gums. Consider the body—does the wine feel light in the mouth, or is there a rich sensation? Are the flavors consistent with the aromas? If you like the wine, try to pinpoint what you like about it, and vice versa if you don't like it.

Take time to savor the wine as you're sipping it— the tasting experience may seem a bit scientific, but the end goal is your enjoyment.

Mittelmosel Museum. For a look at fine period rooms and exhibits on the historical development of the area, visit the Mittelmosel Museum, in the Haus Böcking (1750). ⊠ *Casino Str. 2* ☎ *06541/9480* 🖅 *€2.50* 🕙 *Easter–Oct., Tues.–Sun. 10–5.*

EN ROUTE   During the next 24 km (15 mi) of your drive down the Mosel you'll pass by world-famous vineyards, such as Erdener Treppchen, Ürziger Würzgarten, the *Sonnenuhr* (sundial) sites of Zeltingen and Wehlen, and Graacher Himmelreich, before reaching Bernkastel-Kues.

BERNKASTEL-KUES

22 km (14 mi) southwest of Traben-Trarbach, 100 km (62 mi) southwest of Koblenz on B-53.

Bernkastel and Kues straddle the Mosel, on the east and west banks, respectively.

ESSENTIALS

Visitor Information Bernkastel-Kues ⊠ *Tourist-Information, Gestade 6* ☎ *06531/500–190* 🖷 *06531/500–1919* ⊕ *www.bernkastel.de.*

EXPLORING

Market square. Elaborately carved half-timber houses (16th–17th centuries) and a Renaissance town hall (1608) frame St. Michael's Fountain (1606) on Bernkastel's photogenic market square. In early September the square and riverbank are lined with wine stands for one of the region's largest wine festivals, the Weinfest der Mittelmosel.

Burg Landshut. From the hilltop ruins of the 13th-century castle, Burg Landshut, there are splendid views. It was here that Trier's Archbishop Boemund II is said to have recovered from an illness after drinking the local wine. This legendary vineyard, still known as "the Doctor," soars up from Hinterm Graben street near the town gate, Graacher Tor. You can purchase these exquisite wines at some of the wine dealers in town .

Jewish cemetery. Bernkastel's former Jewish population was well assimilated into town society until the Nazis took power. You can ask the tourist center to borrow a key to the town's Jewish cemetery, reachable by a scenic half-hour hike through the vineyards in the direction of Traben-Trarbach. Opened in the mid-19th century, it contains a few headstones from the destroyed 17th-century graveyard. ⊠ *Bernkastel-Kues.*

St.-Nikolaus-Hospital. The philosopher and theologian Nikolaus Cusanus (1401–64) was born in Kues. The St.-Nikolaus-Hospital is a charitable *Stiftung* (foundation) he established in 1458, and it still operates a home for the elderly and a wine estate.

Mosel-Weinmuseum (*Wine museum*). Within the hospital is a wine museum as well as a bistro and a wineshop. ⊕ *www.moselweinmuseum. de* 🖅 *€5* 🕙 *Mid-Apr.–Oct., daily 10–6; Nov.–mid-Apr., daily 2–5.*

Vinothek. You can sample more than 100 wines from the entire Mosel-Saar-Ruwer region in the Vinothek in the vaulted cellar. ⊕ *www. moselweinmuseum.de* 🖅 *€15 for admission and wine tasting* 🕙 *Mid-Apr.– Oct., daily 10–5; Nov.–mid-Apr., daily 2–5* ⊠ *Cusanusstr. 2* ☎ *06531/2260* ⊕ *www.cusanus.de* 🖅 *Tours €6 Tues. at 10:30 and Fri. at 3.*

11

WHERE TO EAT

$ ✕**Rotisserie Royale.** In one of Burgstrasse's picturesque half-timber
GERMAN houses, the Rotisserie Royale may look unassuming, but its fish menu,
its vegetarian selection, and the Busshoff family's fancy twists on traditional and regional dishes set it apart from the crowd. ⊠*Burgstr.*
19, Bernkastel-Kues ☎*06531/6572* ⊕*www.rotisserie-royale.de* ▭*No*
credit cards ⊘*Closed Wed.*

$$$$ ✕**Waldhotel Sonnora.** At their elegant country inn set in the forested
FRENCH Eifel Hills, Helmut and Ulrike Thieltges offer guests one of Germany's
Fodor'sChoice absolute finest dining experiences. Helmut is an extraordinary chef,
★ renowned for transforming truffles, foie gras, and Persian caviar into
culinary masterpieces. Challans duck in an orange-ginger sauce is his
specialty. The wine list is equally superb. The dining room, with gilded
and white-wood furnishings and plush red carpets, has a Parisian look.
Pretty gardens add to a memorable visit. ■TIP➜ Sonnora can prepare a
vegetarian menu if you call ahead of your visit. ⊠*Auf'm Eichelfeld, 8 km*
(5 mi) southwest of Wittlich, which is 18 km (11 mi) west of Kues
via B-50; from A-1, exit Salmtal, Dreis ☎*06578/98220* ⊕*www.hotel-*
sonnora.de ⌂*Reservations essential* ⊘*Restaurant and hotel closed*
Mon. and Tues., Jan., and 1st 2 wks in July.

$$ ✕**Weinhotel St. Stephanus.** Rita and Hermann Saxler operate a comfort-
CONTINENTAL able, modern hotel and upscale restaurant in a 19th-century manor
house on the *Ufer* (riverbank) at Zeltingen. Whether you opt for the
handsome dining room or the terrace overlooking the Mosel, Saxler's
Restaurant is a good destination for fine food. Herr Saxler accentuates
refined regional cooking with a Mediterranean touch. The spa offers
vinotherapy—treatments using grape-based products, such as grape-
seed oil. ⊠*Uferallee 9, Zeltingen-Rachtig* ☎*06532/680* ⊕*www.hotel-*
stephanus.de ⊘*No lunch Mon. Thurs. in Jan. Mar.*

WHERE TO STAY

For expanded hotel reviews, visit Fodors.com.

$ ☷**Gästehaus Erika Prüm.** The traditional wine estate S. A. Prüm has
★ state-of-the-art cellars and a tastefully designed Vinothek offering
cellar tours and tastings, as well as a stunning dining room and an
idyllic patio facing the Mosel and the Prüms' vineyards. **Pros:** spa-
cious rooms and baths; some rooms have vineyard and Mosel views.
Cons: no elevator. ⊠*Uferallee 25, north of Kues, Bernkastel-Wehlen*
☎*06531/3110* ⊕*www.sapruem.com* ⇴*8 rooms, 1 self-catering apart-*
ment ⌂*In-room: no a/c, Internet, Wi-Fi. In-hotel: parking* ⊘*Closed*
mid-Dec.–Feb. ◥*Breakfast.*

$$ ☷**Weinromantikhotel Richtershof.** This renovated 17th-century manor in
★ a shady park offers comfortable rooms and first-class friendly service.
Pros: garden terrace; wheelchair-accessible rooms; 24-hour room service. **Cons:** thin walls. ⊠*Hauptstr. 81–83, 5 km (3 mi) south of Ber-*
nkastel via B-53, Mülheim ☎*06534/9480* ⊕*www.weinromantikhotel.*
de ⇴*38 rooms, 5 suites* ⌂*In-room: no a/c. In-hotel: restaurants, bar,*
gym, spa, business center, parking, some pets allowed ◥*Breakfast.*

$$ ☷**Hotel zur Post.** The Rössling family makes you feel welcome at their
comfortable hotel dating from 1827. **Pros:** near the market square.
Cons: on a busy street. ⊠*Gestade 17* ☎*06531/96700* ⊕*www.*

hotel-zur-post-bernkastel.de ⟿ *42 rooms, 1 suite* ⟲ *In-room: no a/c. In-hotel: restaurant, bar, some pets allowed* ⊙ *Closed Jan. and Feb.* ⎟⊘⎟ *Breakfast.*

EN ROUTE

Paulinshof. The 55-km (34-mi) drive from Bernkastel to Trier takes in another series of outstanding hillside vineyards, including the Brauneberg, 10 km (6 mi) upstream from Bernkastel. On the opposite side of the river is the Paulinshof, where Thomas Jefferson was enchanted by a 1783 Brauneberger Kammer Auslese during his visit here in 1788. You can sample contemporary vintages of this wine in the beautiful chapel on the estate grounds. ⊠ *Paulinsstr. 14, Kesten* ☎ *06535/544* ⊕ *www. paulinshof.de* ⊙ *Weekdays 8–6, Sat. 9–4.*

Piesport. On a magnificent loop 12 km (7½ mi) southwest of Brauneberg is the famous village of Piesport, whose steep, slate cliff is known as the Loreley of the Mosel. The village puts a fireworks display for its Loreleyfest the first weekend in July. Wines from its 35 vineyards are collectively known as Piesporter Michelsberg; however, the finest individual vineyard site, and one of Germany's very best, is the Goldtröpfchen ("little droplets of gold").

TRIER

55 km (34 mi) southwest of Bernkastel-Kues via B-53, 150 km (93 mi) southwest of Koblenz; 30 mins by car from Luxemburg airport.

By 400 BC a Celtic tribe, the Treveri, had settled the Trier Valley. Eventually Julius Caesar's legions arrived at this strategic point on the river, and Augusta Treverorum (the town of Emperor Augustus in the land of the Treveri) was founded in 16 BC. It was described as a most opulent city, as beautiful as any outside Rome.

Around AD 275 an Alemannic tribe stormed Augusta Treverorum and reduced it to rubble. But it was rebuilt in even grander style and renamed Treveris. Eventually it evolved into one of the leading cities of the empire, and was promoted to "Roma secunda" (a second Rome) north of the Alps. As a powerful administrative capital it was adorned with all the noble civic buildings of a major Roman settlement, as well as public baths, palaces, barracks, an amphitheater, and temples. The Roman emperors Diocletian (who made it one of the four joint capitals of the empire) and Constantine both lived in Trier for years at a time.

Trier survived the collapse of Rome and became an important center of Christianity and, ultimately, one of the most powerful archbishoprics in the Holy Roman Empire. The city thrived throughout the Renaissance and baroque periods, taking full advantage of its location at the meeting point of major east–west and north–south trade routes and growing fat on the commerce that passed through.

GETTING HERE AND AROUND

The area is excellent for biking. The train station in Trier rents bikes; call the Deutsche Bahn bicycle hotline to reserve. Cyclists can follow the marked route of the *Radroute Nahe-Hunsrück-Mosel* from Trier to Bingen.

TOURS

You can circumnavigate the town with the narrated tours of the Römer-Express trolley or a tourist office bus. Both cost €7 and depart from Porta Nigra, near the tourist office. There is also a "hop on, hop off" bus. A 24-hour ticket on it costs €10.

There are also toga tours every Saturday at 12:30 May through October, in which actors dressed in Roman costume bring the history of the amphitheater, the Kaiserthermen, and the old town gate to life. A tour lasts two hours and costs €9. Reservations are essential. If you don't speak German, speak up! The tour guide and/or someone else in the group probably speak some English and will translate the basic points. The tourist office sells tickets for all tours and also leads various walks. A tour in English (€7.50) departs Saturday, May through October, at 1:30.

TIMING

To do justice to Trier, consider staying for at least two full days. A walk around Trier will take a good two hours, and you will need extra time to climb the tower of the Porta Nigra, walk through the vast interior of the Dom and its treasury, visit the underground passageways of the Kaiserthermen, and examine the cellars of the Amphitheater. Allow at least another half hour each for the Bischöfliches Museum and Viehmarktthermen, as well as an additional hour for the Rheinisches Landesmuseum.

DISCOUNTS AND DEALS

The **Trier Card,** available on the visitor center Web site or at the center in Porta Nigra, entitles the holder to free public transportation and discounts on tours and admission fees to Roman sights, museums, and sports and cultural venues. It costs €9 and is valid for three successive days.

ESSENTIALS

Tour Information **Deutsche Bahn bicycle hotline** ☎ *01805/151–415.*

Visitor Information **Trier** ✉ *Tourist-Information, An der Porta Nigra* ☎ *0651/978–080* ⊕ *www.trier.de.*

EXPLORING
TOP ATTRACTIONS

★ **Amphitheater.** The sheer size of Trier's oldest Roman structure (circa AD 100) is impressive; in its heyday it seated 20,000 spectators. You can climb down to the cellars beneath the arena—animals were kept in cells here before being unleashed to do battle with gladiators. During Brot & Spiele (Bread & Circus) in early August, there are live gladiator games in the arena, complete with horses (but not lions). ✉ *Olewiger Str.* ⌨ *€3, Brot & Spiele €22.50* ☉ *Apr.–Sept., daily 9–6; Oct. and Mar., daily 9–5; Nov.–Feb., daily 9–4.*

★ **Dom** (*Cathedral*). The oldest Christian church north of the Alps, the Dom stands on the site of the Palace of Helen. Constantine tore the palace down in AD 330 and put up a large church in its place. The church burned down in 336, and a second, even larger one was built. Parts of the foundations of this third building can be seen in the east end of the present structure (begun in about 1035). The cathedral you see today is a weighty and sturdy edifice with small round-head windows, rough stonework, and asymmetrical towers, as much a fortress as a church. Inside, Gothic styles predominate—the result of remodeling in the 13th century—although there are also many baroque tombs, altars, and confessionals.

Domschatzkammer (*Cathedral Treasure Chamber*). The highlight of this museum is the 10th-century Andreas Tragaltar (St. Andrew's Portable Altar), constructed of oak and covered with gold leaf, enamel, and ivory by local craftsmen. It's a reliquary for the soles of St. Andrew's sandals, symbolized by the gilded, life-size foot on the top of the altar ⌨ *€1.50; combined ticket with Bischöfliches Museum €4* ⊙ *Apr.–Oct. and Dec., Mon.–Sat. 10–5, Sun. 12:30–5; Nov. and Jan.–Mar., Mon.–Sat. 11–4, Sun. 12:30–4* ⊠ *Domfreihof* ☎ *0651/979–0790* ⊕ *www.dominformation.de* ⌨ *Tours €3.50* ⊙ *Apr.–Oct., daily 6:30–6; Nov.–Mar., daily 6:30–5:30.*

★ **Kaiserthermen** (*Imperial Baths*). This enormous 4th-century bathing palace once housed cold- and hot-water baths and a sports field. Although only the masonry of the Calderium (hot baths) and the vast basements remain, they are enough to give a fair idea of the original splendor and size of the complex. Originally 98 feet high, the walls you see today are just 62 feet high. During Brot & Spiele in early September there is a reconstructed Roman village on the sports field, with Roman arts-and-crafts workshops, and a sound-and-light show in the basements. ⊠ *At Weimarer-Allee and Kaiserstr.* ☎ *0651/436–2550* ⌨ *€3* ⊙ *Apr.–Sept., daily 9–6; Oct. and Mar., daily 9–5; Nov.–Feb., daily 9–4.*

★ **Porta Nigra** (*Black Gate*). The best-preserved Roman structure in Trier was originally a city gate, built in the 2nd century (look for holes left by the iron clamps that held the structure together). The gate served as part of Trier's defenses and was proof of the sophistication of Roman military might and its ruthlessness. Attackers were often lured into the two innocent-looking arches of the Porta Nigra, only to find themselves enclosed in a courtyard. In the 11th century the upper stories were converted into two churches, in use until the 18th century. The tourist office is next door. ⊠ *Porta-Nigra-Pl.* ☎ *0651/718–2451* ⌨ *€3* ⊙ *Apr.–Sept., daily 9–6; Oct. and Mar., daily 9–5; Nov.–Feb., daily 9–4.*

★ **Rheinisches Landesmuseum** (*Rhenish State Museum*). The largest collection of Roman antiquities in Germany is housed here. The highlight is the 4th-century stone relief of a Roman ship transporting barrels of wine up the river. This tombstone of a Roman wine merchant was discovered in 1874, when Constantine's citadel in Neumagen was excavated. Have a look at the 108-square-foot model of the city as it looked in the 4th century—it provides a sense of perspective to many of the sights you can still visit today. ⊠ *Weimarer-Allee 1* ☎ *0651/97740* ⊕ *www.landesmuseum-trier.de* ⌨ *€6* ⊙ *Tues.–Sun. 10–5.*

WORTH NOTING

Hauptmarkt. The main market square of Old Trier—lined with gabled houses from several ages—is easily reached via Simeonstrasse. The market cross (958) and richly ornate St. Peter's Fountain (1595), dedicated to the town's patron saint, stand in the square. ■ TIP➔ There is a flower and vegetable market held here every weekday, while a farmers' market can be found at Viehmarktplatz on Tuesday and Friday 8–2.

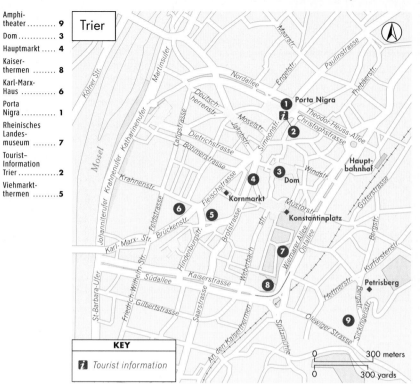

Trier

KEY

🇮 *Tourist information*

0   300 meters

0   300 yards

Karl-Marx-Haus. Marx was born on May 5, 1818, in this bourgeois house built in 1727. Visitors with a serious interest in social history will be fascinated by its small museum. Some of Marx's personal effects, as well as first-edition manifestos are on display. Audio guides are available in English, and English-language tours can be arranged on request. ✉ *Brückenstr. 10* ☎ *0651/970–680* ⊕ *www.fes.de/karl-marx-haus* 💶 *€3* ⊙ *Apr.–Oct., daily 10–6; Nov.–Mar., Mon. 2–5, Tues.–Sun. 11–5.*

OFF THE
BEATEN
PATH

Roscheider Hof. For a look at 19th- and 20th-century rural life in the Mosel-Saar area, visit this hilltop Freilichtmuseum (open-air museum) near Konz-Saar (10 km [6 mi] southwest of Trier via B–51). Numerous farmhouses and typical village buildings in the region were saved from the wrecking ball by being dismantled and brought to the Roscheider Hof, where they were rebuilt and refurnished as they appeared decades ago. Old schoolrooms, a barbershop and beauty salon, a tavern, a shoemaker's workshop, a pharmacy, a grocery, and a dentist's office have been set up in the rooms of the museum proper, along with period rooms and exhibitions on local trades and household work, such as the history of laundry. In 2005 a large collection of tin figures was added. A Biedermeier rose garden, museum shop, and restaurant with a beer garden (closed Monday, no credit cards) are also on the grounds. ✉ *Roscheiderhof 1, Konz* ☎ *06501/92710* ⊕ *www.roscheiderhof.de*

Trier's Porta Nigra (Black Gate), a city gate dating from the 2nd century, is the largest Roman structure north of the Alps.

✉ *€4 ⊙ Apr.–Oct., Tues.–Fri. 9–6, weekends 10–6; Nov.–Mar. only indoor facilities, Tues.–Fri. 9–5, weekends 10–5.*

Tourist-Information Trier. In addition to dispensing city information, this tourist office sells regional wines and souvenirs, from Trier mouse pads and replicas of Roman artifacts to Porta Nigra pasta. ✉ *An der Porta Nigra* ☎ *0651/978–080* ⊕ *www.trier.de* ⊙ *Jan. and Feb., Mon.–Sat. 10–5, Sun. 10–1; Mar., Apr., Nov., and Dec., Mon.–Sat. 9–6, Sun. 10–3; May–Oct., Mon.–Sat. 9–6, Sun. 10–5.*

Viehmarktthermen. Trier's third Roman bath (early 1st century) was discovered beneath Viehmarktplatz when ground was broken for a parking garage. Finds of the excavations from 1987 to 1994 are now beneath a protective glass structure. You can visit the baths and see the cellar of a baroque Capuchin monastery. ✉ *Viehmarktpl.* ☎ *0651/994–1057* ✉ *€3 ⊙ Tues.–Sun. 9–5.*

WHERE TO EAT

$$$$

GERMAN

★

✗ **Becker's Hotel.** This wine estate in the peaceful suburb of Olewig features a gourmet restaurant with prix-fixe menus, a second restaurant serving regional cuisine, and a casual Weinstube. Dining alfresco is a nice option in summer. Bordeaux and Burgundy wines are available in addition to the estate's own wines—and wine tastings, cellar visits, and guided tours on the wine path can be arranged. ✉ *Olewiger Str. 206, Trier-Olewig* ☎ *0651/938–080* ⊕ *www.beckers-trier.de* ⊙ *Gourmet restaurant closed Sun. and Mon.*

$$$$

FRENCH

✗ **Pfeffermühle.** For three decades chef Siegbert Walde has offered guests classic cuisine in elegant surroundings. The 18th-century house on the northern edge of town has two stories of cozy niches, with beautiful table settings in shades of pink; the terrace directly overlooks the Mosel. Foie gras is a favorite ingredient, served in a terrine or in Eisweinaspik (ice wine aspic). White wines from the Mosel's finest producers and top red Bordeaux wines make up the excellent wine list. ⊠ *Zurlaubener Ufer 76* ☎ *0651/26133* ⊕ *www.pfeffermuehle-trier.de* ⌲ *Reservations essential* ⊗ *Closed Sun. and Mon.*

$$$$
GERMAN

✕ **Schlemmereule.** The name means "gourmet owl," and, indeed, chef Peter Schmalen caters to gourmets in the 19th-century Palais Walderdorff complex opposite the cathedral. Lots of windows lend a light, airy look, and a replica of one of Michelangelo's Sistine Chapel paintings graces the ceiling. There's courtyard seating in summer. Truffles are a specialty, and the fish is always excellent. Wines from top German estates, particularly from the Mosel, and an extensive selection of red wines are offered. ⊠ *Palais Walderdorff, Domfreihof 1B* ☎ *0651/73616* ⊕ *www.schlemmereule.de* ⌲ *Reservations essential* ⊗ *Closed Sun.*

$
GERMAN

✕ **Weinstube Kesselstatt.** The interior has exposed beams and polished wood tables; the shady terrace is popular in summer. Two soups daily, hearty fare, and fresh, regional cuisine are served with wines from the Reichsgraf von Kesselstatt estate. The *Tagesgericht* (daily special) and *Aktionsmenü* (prix-fixe menu) are always a good bet. Das Beste der Region (the region's best) is an ample selection of local hams, cheeses, fish, and breads, served on a wooden board for two. ⊠ *Liebfrauenstr. 10* ☎ *0651/41178* ⊕ *www.weinstube-kesselstatt.de.*

$
GERMAN

✕ **Zum Domstein.** Whether you dine inside or out, don't miss the collection of Roman artifacts displayed in the cellar. In addition to the German dishes on the regular menu, you can order à la carte or prix-fixe menus based on the recipes of Roman gourmet Marcus Gavius Apicius in the evening. ⊠ *Am Hauptmarkt 5* ☎ *0651/74490* ⊕ *www. domstein.de.*

WHERE TO STAY

For expanded hotel reviews, visit Fodors.com.

$

🛏 **Hotel Ambiente.** Modern flair marks the style and decor that Markus and Monika Stemper—a passionate cook and a gracious hostess—offer in their country inn near the Luxembourg border. **Pros:** country atmosphere; legendary garden. **Cons:** removed from city center. ⊠ *In der Acht 1–2, 7 km (4½ mi) southwest of Trier via B-49, Trier-Zewen* ☎ *0651/827–280* ⊕ *www.ambiente-trier.de* ⟿ *12 rooms* ⌂ *In-room: no a/c, Wi-Fi. In-hotel: restaurant, bar, parking, some pets allowed* ⊗ *Restaurant closed Sun. and Thurs.* ⟟❘ *Breakfast.*

$

🛏 **Hotel Petrisberg.** The Pantenburgs' friendly, family-run hotel is high on Petrisberg hill overlooking Trier, not far from the amphitheater and a 20-minute walk to the Old Town. **Pros:** fine view of Trier. **Cons:** somewhat removed from the city center. ⊠ *Sickingenstr. 11–13* ☎ *0651/4640* ⊕ *www.hotelpetrisberg.de* ⟿ *31 rooms, 4 apartments* ⌂ *In-room: no a/c, Wi-Fi. In-hotel: bar, pool, business center, parking* ⟟❘ *Breakfast.*

$

🛏 **Römischer Kaiser.** Centrally located near the Porta Nigra, this handsome patrician manor from 1885 offers well-appointed rooms with handsome baths. **Pros:** near the Porta Nigra; free Wi-Fi. **Cons:** some rooms are dark due to a neighboring building. ⊠ *Am Porta-Nigra-Pl. 6* ☎ *0651/977–0100* ⊕ *www.friedrich-hotels.de* ⟿ *43 rooms* ⌂ *In-room:*

no a/c, Internet, Wi-Fi. In-hotel: restaurant, bar, parking, some pets allowed ✝○✝ *Breakfast.*

FESTIVALS

The **Europa-Volksfest** (European Folk Festival), in May or early June, features wine and food specialties from several European countries, in addition to rides and entertainment. In late June the entire Old Town is the scene of the **Altstadtfest.** The **Moselfest,** with wine, sparkling wine, beer, and fireworks, takes place in July along the riverbank in Zurlauben, followed by a large **Weinfest** (Wine Festival) in Olewig in early August, and Germany's largest Roman festival, **Brot & Spiele** (Bread & Circus), in early September. From late November until December 22, the annual **Weihnachtsmarkt** (Christmas market) takes place on the market square and in front of the cathedral.

NIGHTLIFE AND THE ARTS

■ TIP➔ For absolutely up-to-the-minute information on performances, concerts, and events all over town, visit the Web site ⊕ www.trier-today.de. Pop-up maps show exactly where everything is.

Theater Trier. The theater puts on opera, theater, and ballet performances as well as concerts. ⊠ *Am Augustinerhof* ☎ *0651/718–1818* ⊕ *www. theater-trier.de.*

TUFA–Tuchfabrik. Concerts, theater, and cultural events are staged here. ⊠ *Wechselstr. 4, at Weberstr.* ☎ *0651/718–2412.*

Pubs and cafés are centered on Viehmarktplatz and Stockplatz in the Old Town.

FORUM. This discotheque features international DJs, theme parties, and live music. ⊠ *Hindenburgstr. 4* ☎ *0651/710–3780–00* ⊕ *www.forum-trier.net.*

Walderdorff's. In the Palais Walderdorff, this bar has trendy DJ nights, early after-work parties, and occasional live bands. ⊠ *Domfreihof 1A* ☎ *0651/994–4412.*

BONN AND THE KÖLN (COLOGNE) LOWLANDS

Bonn, the former capital of West Germany, and reunified Germany until 1999, is the next major stop after Koblenz on the Rhine. It's close to the legendary Siebengebirge (Seven Hills), a national park and site of western Germany's northernmost vineyards. According to German mythology, Siegfried (hero of the Nibelungen saga) killed a dragon here and bathed in its blood to make himself invincible. The lowland, a region of gently rolling hills north of Bonn, lacks the drama of the Rhine Gorge upstream but offers the urban pleasures of Köln (Cologne), an ancient cathedral town, and Düsseldorf, an elegant city of art and fashion. Although not geographically in the Rhineland proper, Aachen is an important side trip for anyone visiting the region. Its stunning cathedral and treasury are the greatest storehouses of Carolingian art and architecture in Europe.

BONN

61 km (38 mi) north of Koblenz, 28 km (17 mi) south of Köln.

Bonn was the postwar seat of the federal government and parliament until the capital completed its return to Berlin in 1999. Aptly described by the title of John le Carré's spy novel *A Small Town in Germany,* the quiet university town was chosen as a stopgap measure to prevent such weightier contenders as Frankfurt from becoming the capital, a move that would have lessened Berlin's chances of regaining its former status. With the exodus of the government from Bonn, the city has lost some of its international flair. Still, Bonn thrives as the headquarters of two of Germany's largest multinational corporations (Deutsche Telekom and Deutsche Post/DHL), and the UN is expanding its presence in the city as well. The fine museums and other cultural institutions that once served the diplomatic elite are still here to be enjoyed.

GETTING HERE AND AROUND

The town center is a car-free zone; an inner ring road circles it with parking garages on the perimeter. A convenient parking lot is just across from the railway station and within 50 yards of the tourist office, which is on Windeckstrasse near the Hauptbahnhof. Bonn has extensive bike paths downtown; these are designated paths (often demarcated with blue-and-white bicycle symbols) on the edges of roads or sidewalks. ■ TIP→ Pedestrians, beware: anyone walking on a bike path risks getting mowed down. Bicyclists are expected to follow the same traffic rules as cars. In Bonn the Radstation, at the main train station, will not only rent you a bike and provide maps, but will fill your water bottle and check the pressure in your tires for free.

Bilingual bus tours of Bonn cost €15 and start from the tourist office. They're conducted daily at 2 from Easter to October, and Saturday only November to March. Walking tours are also available for €8; from April to October they are offered at 11 am.

DISCOUNTS AND DEALS

Bonn's tourism office sells the **Bonn Regio Welcome Card,** which offers an array of reductions, plus free entry into most museums, in combination with low- or no-cost transportation; the card costs €9 per 24-hour period.

ESSENTIALS

Visitor Information Bonn ⊠ *Bonn Information, Windeckstr. 1* ☎ *0228/775–000* ⊕ *www.bonn.de.*

Bicycle Contact Radstation ⊠ *Quantiusstr. 26* ☎ *0228/981–4636.*

EXPLORING

TOP ATTRACTIONS

Beethoven-Haus (*Beethoven House*). Beethoven was born in Bonn in 1770 and, except for a short stay in Vienna, lived here until the age of 22. You'll find scores, paintings, a grand piano (his last, in fact), and an ear trumpet or two. Thanks to the modern age, there's now a "Stage for Music Visualization," an interactive exhibit involving 3-D glasses that shows Beethoven's best-loved works. The attached museum shop carries

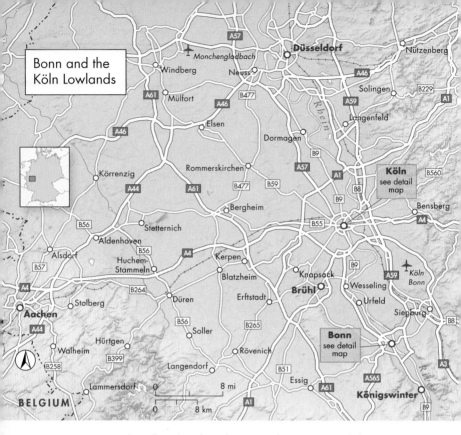

Bonn and the Köln Lowlands

everything from kitsch to elegant Beethoven memorabilia. ⊠ *Bonng. 20* ☏ *0228/981–7525* ⊕ *www.beethoven-haus-bonn.de* ⊠ *€5* ⊙ *Apr.–Oct., Mon.–Sat. 10–6, Sun. 11–6; Nov.–Mar., Mon.–Sat. 10–5, Sun. 11–5.*

Bundesviertel (*Federal Government District*). Walking through the amiable former government district is like taking a trip back in time to an era when Bonn was still the sleepy capital of West Germany. Bordered by Adenauerallee, Kaiser-Friedrich-Strasse, Franz-Josef-Strasse, and the Rhine, the quarter boasts sights such as the **Bundeshaus** with the Plenarsaal. This building, designed to serve as the new federal parliament, was completed only seven years before the capital was relocated to Berlin in 1999. A few steps away, you'll find the historic **Villa Hammerschmidt,** the German equivalent of the White House. This stylish neoclassical mansion began serving as the federal president's permanent residence in 1950, and is still his home when he stays in Bonn. Equally impressive is the **Palais Schaumburg,** another fine example of the Rhein Riveria estates that once housed the Federal Chancellery (1949–76). It became the center of cold war politics during the Adenauer administration. Tours of the quarter, including a visit to the Villa Hammerschmidt, are offered by the Bonn Tourist Office. ⊠ *U-Bahn Heussallee.*

Kunstmuseum Bonn (*Art Museum*). Devoted to contemporary art, this large museum focuses on Rhenish expressionists and German art since

1945 (Beuys, Baselitz, and Kiefer, for example). Changing exhibits are generally excellent, and help maintain a link to the international art scene. The museum's airy and inexpensive café is preferable to the stuffier version across the plaza at the Kunst- und Ausstellungshalle. ✉ *Friedrich-Ebert-Allee 2* ☎ *0228/776–260* ⊕ *www.kunstmuseum-bonn.de* 🎫 *€7* ⊘ *Tues.–Sun. 11–6 (Wed. 11–9)*.

Kurfürstliches Schloss (*Prince-Electors' Palace*). Built in the 18th century by the prince-electors of Köln, this grand palace now houses Bonn's university. If the weather is good, stroll through Hofgarten park in front of it. In Bonn's days as capital, this patch of grass drew tens of thousands to antinuclear demonstrations. Today it's mostly used for games of pickup soccer and ultimate Frisbee. ✉ *Am Hofgarten.*

Münster (*Minster*). The 900-year-old church is vintage late Romanesque, with a massive octagonal main tower and a soaring spire. It stands on a site where two Roman soldiers were executed in the 3rd century for having Christian beliefs. It saw the coronations of two Holy Roman Emperors (in 1314 and 1346) and was one of the Rhineland's most important ecclesiastical centers in the Middle Ages. The 17th-century bronze figure of St. Helen and the ornate rococo pulpit are highlights of the interior; outside you'll find two giant stone heads: those of Cassius and Florentius, the pious soldiers. ✉ *Münsterpl.* ☎ *0228/985–880* 🎫 *Free* ⊘ *Daily 7–7.*

WORTH NOTING

Altes Rathaus (*Old Town Hall*). This 18th-century rococo town hall, renovated in 2010, looks somewhat like a pink dollhouse. Its elegant steps and stair entry have seen a great many historic figures, including French president Charles de Gaulle and U.S. president John F. Kennedy. ✉ *Am Markt* ☎ *0228/774–288* 🎫 *Free* ⊘ *By tour only (call the visitor center).*

Arithmeum. Technophiles and technophobes alike enjoy this university-run museum, where even the abstract theme of discrete mathematics is made comprehensible. Its stated aim is to show "the interface of art and technology," and the core of the exhibit is a 1,200-piece collection of historical mechanical-calculating machines, which became obsolete with the advent of computers. The art comes in the form of a collection of constructivist paintings that resemble enlarged, colorful computer-chip designs. ✉ *Lennéstr. 2* ☎ *0228/738–790* ⊕ *www.arithmeum.uni-bonn.de* 🎫 *€3* ⊘ *Tues.–Sun. 11–6.*

Haus der Geschichte (*House of History*). German history since World War II is the subject of this museum, which begins with "hour zero," as the Germans call the unconditional surrender of 1945. The museum displays an overwhelming amount of documentary material organized on five levels and engages various types of media. It's not all heavy either—temporary exhibits have featured political cartoonists, cold war–era sporting contests pitting East Germany versus West Germany, and an in-depth examination of the song *Lili Marleen,* sung by troops of every nation during World War II. ✉ *Willy-Brandt-Allee 14* ☎ *0228/91650* ⊕ *www.hdg.de* 🎫 *Free* ⊘ *Tues.–Fri. 9–7; weekends 10–6.*

Kunst- und Ausstellungshalle der Bundesrepublik Deutschland (*Art and Exhibition Hall of the German Federal Republic*). This is one of the

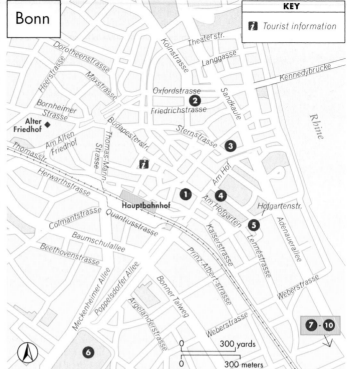

Rhineland's most important venues for major temporary exhibitions about art, culture, and archaeology. Its modern design, by Viennese architect Gustave Peichl, is as interesting as anything on exhibit in the museum. It employs three enormous blue cones situated on a lawnlike rooftop garden. ⊠ *Friedrich-Ebert-Allee 4* ☎ *0228/91710* ⊕ *www.kah-bonn.de* ⊠ *€8* ☾ *Tues. and Wed. 10–9, Thurs.–Sun. 10–7.*

Poppelsdorfer Schloss (*Poppelsdorf Palace*). This former electors' palace was built in the baroque style between 1715 and 1753, and now houses the university's mineralogical collection. Its botanical gardens exhibit 8,000 species, among the largest variety in Germany. ⊠ *Meckenheimer Allee 171* ☎ *0228/732–764* ⊠ *Mineralogical collection €2.50; botanical garden free during week, Sun. €2* ☾ *Mineralogical collection: Mon., Fri. 3–5; Sun. 10–5. Botanical garden: Apr.–Oct., Sun.–Fri. 10–6; Nov.–Mar., weekdays 10–4.*

OFF THE BEATEN PATH

Alter Friedhof (*Old Cemetery*). This ornate, leafy cemetery is the resting place of many of the country's most celebrated sons and daughters. Look for the tomb of composer Robert Schumann (1810–56) and his wife Clara, also a composer and accomplished pianist. To reach the cemetery from the main train station, follow Quantiusstrasse west, parallel to the tracks until it becomes Herwarthstrasse; before the street curves to the left, turning into Endenich-erstrasse, take the underpass below the railroad line. You'll then be on Thomastrasse, which borders the cemetery. ⊠ *Bornheimerstr.* ⊗ *Jan., daily 8–5; Feb., daily 8–6; Mar.–Aug., daily 7:15 am–8 pm; Sept., daily 8–8; Oct., daily 8–7; Nov. and Dec., daily 8–5.*

CLASSICAL MUSIC

Few regions in Europe rival the quality of classical music performances and venues on the Rhine. Beethoven was born in Bonn, and the city hosts a Beethoven festival every year in mid- to late September. Düsseldorf, once home to Mendelssohn, Schumann, and Brahms, has the finest concert hall in Germany after Berlin's Philharmonie: the Tonhalle, in a former planetarium. Köln also has one of Germany's best concert halls, and its opera company is known for exciting classical and contemporary productions. The cathedrals of Aachen, Köln, and Trier are magnificent settings for concerts and organ recitals.

WHERE TO EAT

$
SPANISH
✕ **Amadeo.** The popularity of this neighborhood restaurant is partly due to Germans' affinity for all things Spanish, but also to its food—12 to 20 seasonally changing tapas, for starters—which rarely miss the mark. The kitchen is especially proud of its Spanish cheese platter, featuring the beloved Manchego. ⊠ *Mozartstr. 1* ☎ *0228/635–534* ⊕ *www.amadeo-bonn.de* ⊟ *No credit cards* ⊗ *No lunch.*

$
GERMAN
✕ **Em Höttche.** Beethoven was a regular at this tavern, which has been around since the late 14th century. Today it offers one of the best-value lunches in town, and the kitchen stays open until 1 am. The interior is rustic, the food stout and hearty. ⊠ *Markt 4* ☎ *0228/690–009* ⊕ *www.em-hoettche.de* ⊟ *No credit cards.*

$$
ITALIAN
★
✕ **Ristorante Sassella.** When the Bundestag was still in town, this Bonn institution used to be cited in the press as frequently for its backroom political dealings as for its Lombardy-influenced food. Locals, prominent and otherwise, still flock to the restaurant, in an 18th-century house in the suburb of Kessenich. The style is pure Italian farmhouse, with stone walls and exposed beams, but the handmade pastas made by Giorgio and Francesco Tartero often stray from the typical—note the salmon-filled black-and-white pasta pockets in shrimp sauce. ⊠ *Karthäuserpl. 21* ☎ *0228/530–815* ⊕ *www.ristorante-sassella.de* ⌂ *Reservations essential* ⊗ *Closed Mon. No lunch Sat., no dinner Sun.*

$$$
CONTINENTAL
★
✕ **Strandhaus.** On a quiet residential street, and hidden from view in summer by an ivy-covered patio, this restaurant feels like a true escape—befitting its laid-back name ("beach house"). Chef Astrid Kuth insists on local produce, and presents her delicate, innovatively spiced food with flair, but no fuss. A carefully compiled wine list long on Geman bottles, along with a frequently changing menu, means locals come here frequently. ⊠ *Georgstr. 28, Altstadt* ☎ *0228/369–4949* ⊕ *www.strandhaus-bonn.de* ⊗ *Closed Sun. and Mon. No lunch.*

WHERE TO STAY

For expanded hotel reviews, visit Fodors.com.

$$$$ **Best Western Domicil.** A group of buildings around a quiet, central courtyard has been converted into a charming and comfortable hotel, with rooms individually furnished and decorated in styles ranging from fin de siècle romantic to Italian modern. **Pros:** quiet courtyard; handy to the train station. **Cons:** plain exterior. ⊠ *Thomas-Mann-Str. 24–26* ☎ *0228/729–090* ⊕ *domicil-bonn.bestwestern.de* ➪ *43 rooms, 1 apartment* △ *In-room: no a/c, Wi-Fi. In-hotel: restaurant, parking, some pets allowed* � ¶ *Breakfast.*

BIER AM RHEIN

When it's warm out, most Germans like nothing better than to sit outside with a beer in hand. In Bonn, the best beer gardens are right on the River Rhine, which runs through the city. On the Bonn city center side, there's the **Alter Zoll** (⊠ *Konviktstr. 11*) and **Schänzchen** (⊠ *Rosental 105*). Across the Kennedy Bridge in Beuel, however, is where the late afternoon sun shines best. On either side of the bridge are **Rheinlust** (⊠ *Rheinaustr. 134*) and **Bahnhöfchen** (⊠ *Rheinaustr. 116*).

$ **Hotel Mozart.** Elegant on the outside and simple on the inside, this small, attractive hotel is often recommended to friends by Bonn residents. **Pros:** quiet tree-lined street; close to the train station. **Cons:** thin walls. ⊠ *Mozartstr. 1* ☎ *0228/659–071* ⊕ *www.hotel-mozart-bonn.com* ➪ *37 rooms, 1 suite* △ *In-room: no a/c, Wi-Fi. In-hotel: parking, some pets allowed* ¶ *Breakfast.*

$$ **Sternhotel.** For solid comfort and a picturesque, central location, the Sternhotel is tops—and their weekend rates are a bargain. **Pros:** directly in the center of town; partnership with gym across the square, allowing guests free entry. **Cons:** some rooms are a bit old-fashioned; market square location can be noisy in the morning. ⊠ *Markt 8* ☎ *0228/72670* ⊕ *www.sternhotel-bonn.de* ➪ *80 rooms* △ *In-room: no a/c, Wi-Fi. In-hotel: some pets allowed* ¶ *Breakfast.*

THE ARTS

MUSIC   **Beethovenhalle.** The Bonn Symphony Orchestra opens its season in grand style every year in late summer with a concert on the market square, in front of town hall. Otherwise, concerts are held in the Beethovenhalle. ⊠ *Wachsbleiche 16* ☎ *0228/72220* ⊕ *www.beethovenhalle.de.*

Beethoven-Festival. Indoor and outdoor concerts are held at numerous venues during September's Beethoven-Festival. ☎ *0228/201–0345* ⊕ *www.beethovenfest.de.*

Beethoven-Haus. In the Beethoven-Haus, intimate recitals are sometimes given on a 19th-century grand piano, and concerts take place regularly in the chamber music hall. ⊠ *Bonngasse 20* ☎ *0228/981–750.*

Pantheon Theater. This is a prime venue for comedy and cabaret. ⊠ *Bundeskanzlerpl. 2–10* ☎ *0228/212–521* ⊕ *www.pantheon.de.*

Schumannhaus. Chamber-music concerts are given regularly at the Schumannhaus, where composer Robert Schumann spent his final years. ⊠ *Sebastianstr. 182* ☎ *0228/773–656* ⊕ *www.schumannhaus-bonn.de.*

Bonn is the city of Beethoven: he was born here, you can tour his home, there is a concert hall named after him, and a monument to him on Münsterplatz.

Theater Bonn. Operas are staged regularly at the Theater Bonn, which also hosts performances by world-renowned dance companies. ✉ *Am Boeselagerhof 1* ☎ *0228/778–000* ⊕ *www.theater-bonn.de.*

THEATER AND DANCE

Musicals and ballet are performed at the **Theater Bonn.**

Bonner Sommer. From May through September, the Bonner Sommer festival offers folklore, music, and street theater, much of it outdoors and most of it free. Information is available at the tourist office. ✉ *Tourist office, Windeckstr. 1* ☎ *0228/775–000.*

SHOPPING

There are plenty of department stores and boutiques in the pedestrian shopping zone around the Markt and the Münster.

Flohmarkt (*Flea Market*). Bargain hunters search for secondhand goods and knickknacks at the city's renowned—and huge—flea market held in Rheinaue south of the Konrad-Adenauer-Brücke on the third Saturday of each month from April through October.

Wochenmarkt (*Weekly Market*). Bonn's Wochenmarkt is open daily except Sunday, filling the Markt with vendors of produce and various edibles. Things get really busy in springtime when the locals flock to find the best asparagus and strawberries.

KÖNIGSWINTER

12 km (7 mi) southeast of Bonn.

Fodor's Choice ★

Drachenfels. The town of Königswinter has one of the most-visited castles on the Rhine, the Drachenfels. Its ruins crown one of the highest hills in the Siebengebirge, Germany's oldest nature reserve, with a spectacular view of the Rhine. The reserve has more than 100 km (62 mi) of hiking trails. The castle was built in the 12th century by the archbishop of Köln. Its name commemorates a dragon said to have lived in a nearby cave. As legend has it, the dragon was slain by Siegfried, hero of the epic *Nibelungenlied.*

Drachenfelsbahn. If hiking to Drachenfels isn't for you, you can also reach the castle ruins by taking the Drachenfelsbahn, a steep, narrow-gauge train that makes trips to the summit every half hour March through October and hourly in winter. ⊠ *Drachenfelsstr. 53* ☎ *02223/92090* ⊕ *www.drachenfelsbahn-koenigswinter.de* 🎫 *€9 round-trip* ⊙ *Mar. and Oct., daily 10–6; Apr., daily 10–7; May–Sept., daily 9–7; Nov.–Feb., weekdays noon–5, weekends 11–6.*

☾ **Sea Life.** Königswinter's huge aquarium features 3,000 creatures from the sea. The biggest pool has a glass tunnel that enables you to walk on the "bottom of the sea." ⊠ *Rheinallee 8* ☎ *0180/5666–90101* ⊕ *www. visitsealife.com* 🎫 *€14.50* ⊙ *Daily 10–6.*

WHERE TO EAT

$$ ✕ **Gasthaus Sutorius.** Across from the church of St. Margaretha, this wine
GERMAN   tavern serves refined variations on German cuisine with a nice selection of local wines. In summer, food is served outdoors beneath the linden trees. ⊠ *Oelinghovener Str. 7* ☎ *02244/912–240* ⊕ *www.sutorius.de* ⊙ *Closed Mon. No dinner Sun. No lunch Tues.–Sat.*

BRÜHL

20 km (12 mi) northwest of Bonn.

In the heart of Brühl you'll discover the Rhineland's most important baroque palace.

Schloss Augustusburg. This castle and the magnificent pleasure park that surrounds it were created in the time of Prince Clemens August, between 1725 and 1768. The palace contains one of the most famous achievements of rococo architecture, a staircase by Balthasar Neumann. The castle can be visited only on guided tours, which leave the reception area every hour or so. An English-language recorded tour is available. ⊠ *Max-Ernst-Allee* ☎ *02232/44000* ⊕ *www.schlossbruehl.de* 🎫 *€5* ⊙ *Feb.–Nov., Tues.–Fri. 9–noon and 1:30–4, weekends 10–5.*

KÖLN (COLOGNE)

28 km (17 mi) north of Bonn, 47 km (29 mi) south of Düsseldorf, 70 km (43 mi) southeast of Aachen.

Köln (Cologne in English) is the largest city on the Rhine (the fourth largest in Germany) and one of the most interesting. Although not as old as Trier, it has been a dominant power in the Rhineland since Roman times. Known throughout the world for its "scented water," Eau de Cologne (first produced here in 1709 from an Italian formula), Köln is today a major commercial, intellectual, and ecclesiastical center. The city is vibrant and bustling, with a light and jolly flair that is typical of the Rhineland. At its heart is tradition, manifested in the abundance of bars and brew houses serving the local Kölsch beer and old Rhine cuisine. These are good meeting places to start a night on the town. Tradition, however, is mixed with the contemporary, found in a host of elegant shops, sophisticated restaurants, modern bars and dance clubs, and an important contemporary-art scene (which is now hanging on for dear life against unstoppable competition from Berlin).

Köln was first settled by the Romans in 38 BC. For nearly a century it grew slowly, in the shadow of imperial Trier, until a locally born noble-woman, Julia Agrippina, daughter of the Roman general Germanicus, married the Roman emperor Claudius. Her hometown was elevated to the rank of a Roman city and given the name Colonia Claudia Ara Agrippinensium (Claudius Colony at the Altar of Agrippina). For the next 300 years Colonia (hence Cologne, or Köln) flourished. Evidence of the Roman city's wealth resides in the Römisch-Germanisches Museum. In the 9th century Charlemagne, the towering figure who united the sprawling German lands (and ruled much of present-day France) as the first Holy Roman Emperor, restored Köln's fortunes and elevated it to its preeminent role in the Rhineland by appointing the first archbishop of Köln. The city's ecclesiastical heritage is one of its most striking features; it has a full dozen Romanesque churches and one of the world's largest and finest Gothic cathedrals. In the Middle Ages it was a member of the powerful Hanseatic League, occupying a position of greater importance in European commerce than either London or Paris.

Köln was a thriving modern city until World War II, when bombings destroyed 90% of it. Only the cathedral remained relatively unscathed. But like many other German cities that rebounded during the "Economic Miracle" of the 1950s, Köln is a mishmash of old and new, sometimes awkwardly juxtaposed. A good part of the former Old Town along the Hohe Strasse (old Roman High Road) was turned into a remarkably charmless pedestrian shopping mall. The ensemble is framed by six-lane expressways winding along the rim of the city center—barely yards from the cathedral—perfectly illustrating the problems of postwar reconstruction. However, much of the Altstadt (Old Town), ringed by streets that follow the line of the medieval city walls, is closed to traffic. Most major sights are within this area and are easily reached on foot. Here, too, you'll find the best shops.

GETTING HERE AND AROUND

City bus tours leave from the tourist office and from Trankgasse, beside the cathedral twice per hour (and three times an hour on Friday and Saturday) from 10 am, year-round. The 90-minute tours cost €11–€15 and are conducted in English and German. Walking tours in English are often available by arrangement with the tourist office. Bus trips into the countryside (to the Eifel Hills, the Ahr Valley, and the Westerwald) are organized by several city travel agencies.

In Köln, Rent-a-Bike offers bike rental by the day (€10) from April through October as well as three-hour guided bike tours of the city (€15), departing daily at 1:30.

DISCOUNTS AND DEALS

Most central hotels sell the **Köln-Tourismus Card** (€9 for one day, €14 for two days, and €19 for three days), which entitles you to discounts on sightseeing tours, admissions to all the city's museums, free city bus and tram travel, and other reductions.

ESSENTIALS

Bicycle Contacts Rent-a-Bike ✉ *Markmannsg. next to the Deutzer Brücke (bridge)* ☎ *0171/629–8796* ⊕ *www.koelnerfahrradverleih.de.*

EXPLORING

TOP ATTRACTIONS

Fodor's Choice
★

Dom (*Cathedral*). Köln's landmark embodies one of the purest expressions of the Gothic spirit in Europe. The cathedral, meant to be a tangible expression of God's kingdom on Earth, was conceived with such immense dimensions that construction, begun in 1248, was not completed until 1880, after the original plan was rediscovered. At 515 feet high, the two west towers of the cathedral were briefly the tallest structures in the world when they were finished (before being eclipsed by the Washington Monument). The cathedral was built to house what are believed to be the relics of the Magi, the three kings who paid homage to the infant Jesus (the trade in holy mementos was big business in the Middle Ages—and not always scrupulous). The size of the building was not simply an example of self-aggrandizement on the part of the people of Köln, however; it was a response to the vast numbers of pilgrims who arrived to see the relics. The ambulatory, the passage that curves around the back of the altar, is unusually large, allowing cathedral authorities to funnel large numbers of visitors up to the crossing (where the nave and transepts meet and where the relics were originally displayed), around the back of the altar, and out again.

Today the relics are kept just behind the altar, in the original, enormous gold-and-silver **reliquary.** The other great treasure of the cathedral, in the last chapel on the left as you face the altar, is the **Gero Cross,** a monumental oak crucifix dating from 971. The Altar of the City Patrons (1440), a triptych by Stephan Lochner, Köln's most famous medieval painter, is to the right. Other highlights are the stained-glass windows, some dating from the 13th century and another, designed by Gerhard Richter with help from a computer program, from the 21st; the 15th-century altarpiece; and the early-14th-century high altar, with its glistening white figures and intricate choir screens. If you're up to it, climb to the top of the bell tower to get the complete vertical experience (but

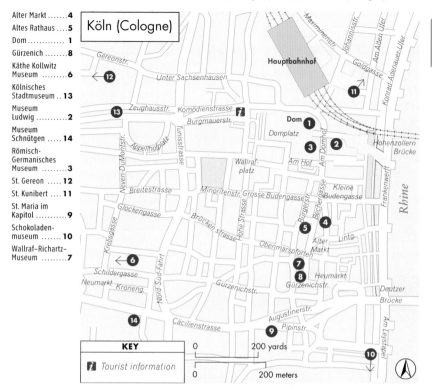

Köln (Cologne)

11

be aware that viewing Köln from the Dom itself removes the skyline's most interesting feature). Allow at least an hour for the whole tour of the interior, treasury, and tower climb.

Domschatzkammer (*Cathedral Treasury*). The treasury includes the silver shrine of Archbishop Engelbert, who was stabbed to death in 1225. ☎€5 ☉ *Daily 10–6* ⌧ *Dompl., Altstadt* ☎ *0221/9258–4730* ⊕ *www.koelner-dom.de* ☎ *Tower €3, cathedral treasury €5* ☉ *Daily 6 am–7:30 pm (May–Oct. 6–9 pm); tower and stairwell Nov.–Feb., daily 9–4; Mar., Apr., and Oct., daily 9–5; May–Sept., daily 9–6; treasury daily 10–6; guided tours in English Mon.–Sat. at 10:30 and 2:30, Sun. at 2:30.*

Museum Ludwig. This museum is dedicated to art from the beginning of the 20th century to the present day. ■TIP→ Its American pop-art collection (including Andy Warhol, Jasper Johns, Robert Rauschenberg, Claes Oldenburg, and Roy Lichtenstein) rivals that of most American museums. ⌧ *Heinrich-Böll-Pl., Innenstadt* ☎ *0221/2212–6165* ⊕ *www.museum-ludwig.de* ☎€10 ☉ *Tues.–Sun. 10–6; 1st Thurs. of every month 10–10. Closed 1 wk in mid-Feb.*

★ **Römisch-Germanisches Museum** (*Roman-Germanic Museum*). This cultural landmark was built in the early 1970s around the famous Dionysius mosaic discovered here during the construction of an air-raid shelter in 1941. The huge mosaic, more than 800 square feet, once formed the dining-room floor of a wealthy Roman trader's villa. Its millions of tiny earthenware and glass tiles depict some of the adventures of Dionysius, the Greek god of wine and, to the Romans, the object of a widespread and sinister religious cult. The pillared 1st-century tomb of Lucius Publicius (a prominent Roman officer), some stone Roman coffins, and everyday objects of Roman life are among the museum's other exhibits. Bordering the museum on the south is a restored 90-yard stretch of the old Roman harbor road. ✉ *Roncallipl. 4, Altstadt* ☎ *0221/2212–4438* ⊕ *www. museenkoeln.de* ☞ *€6* ⊘ *Tues.– Sun. 10–5.*

> ## EAU DE COLOGNE
>
> As Frankfurt was a sausage to many people before it was a city, Cologne was first a fragrance. Eau de Cologne is made from a secret formula and aged in oak barrels. The most famous cologne is 4711, which derives its name from the firm's address at 4711 Glockengasse. The building itself is equipped with a carillon, a museum, and a shop where Eau de Cologne can be purchased. The scent is not to everyone's taste, but it comes in an elegant bottle with a turquoise-and-gilt label, and makes a delightful souvenir.

Wallraf-Richartz-Museum. This museum contains paintings spanning the years 1300 to 1900. The Dutch and Flemish schools are particularly well represented, as is the 15th- to 16th-century Köln school of German painting. Its two most famous artists are the Master of the St. Veronica (whose actual name is unknown) and Stefan Lochner, represented by two luminous works, *The Last Judgment* and *The Madonna in the Rose Bower.* Large canvases by Rubens, who spent his youth in Köln, hang prominently on the second floor. There are also outstanding works by Rembrandt, Van Dyck, and Frans Hals. ✉ *Obenmarspforten, Altstadt* ☎ *0221/2212–1119* ⊕ *www.museenkoeln.de* ☞ *€9* ⊘ *Tues. and Wed. 10–6, Thurs. 10–9, Fri.–Sun. 10–6.*

WORTH NOTING

Alter Markt (*Old Market*). The square has an eclectic assembly of buildings, most of them postwar; two 16th-century houses survived the war intact—Nos. 20 and 22, which are today a Kölsch brewpub. The oldest structure dates from 1135. ✉ *Altstadt.*

Altes Rathaus (*Old Town Hall*). The Rathaus is worth a look, even from the outside. (Tours of the interior must be booked at the tourist office.) It's the oldest town hall in Germany, with elements remaining from the 14th century. The famous bell tower rings its bells daily at 9 am, noon, 3 pm, and 6 pm. Standing on pedestals at one end of the town hall are figures of prophets made in the early 15th century. Ranging along the south wall are nine additional statues, the so-called *Nine Good Heroes,* carved in 1360. Charlemagne, Alexander the Great, and King David are among them. Some 20th-century heroes have recently been added. Beneath a small glass pyramid near the south corner of the Rathaus is the **mikveh,** a 12th-century ritual bath from the then-surrounding medieval Jewish quarter. ✉ *Rathauspl., Altstadt* ☎ *0221/2212–3332.*

DID YOU KNOW?

The 515-foot-high west towers of Köln's Dom (Cathedral) were the tallest structures in the world until they were eclipsed by the Washington Monument.

KARNEVAL IN KÖLN

As the biggest city in the traditionally Catholic Rhineland, Köln puts on Germany's most exciting and rowdy carnival. The Kölsch starts flowing on November 11 at 11:11 am with screams of the famous motto *Kölle alaaf!* ("Köln is alive"). Karneval then calms down for a few months, only to reach a fever pitch in February for the last five days before Lent. On Fat Thursday, known as *Weiberfastnacht*, women roam the streets with scissors and exercise merciless precision in cutting off the ties of any men foolish enough to wear them. Starting then, bands, parades, and parties go all night, and people of all ages don silly costumes, including the customary red clown nose. It's a good time to meet new people; in fact, it is practically impossible not to, as kissing strangers is considered par for the course. ■TIP→ **During this time, visitors who may be claustrophobic or not like having beer spilled on them should especially avoid the Heumarkt area in the Old Town, and if possible the whole city.** The festivities come to an end Tuesday at midnight with the ritual burning of the "Nubbel"—a dummy that acts as the scapegoat for everyone's drunken, embarrassing behavior. Note: Many museums are closed during Karneval.

Gürzenich. This Gothic structure, located at the south end of Martinsviertel, was all but demolished in World War II, but carefully reconstructed afterward. It's named after a medieval knight from whom the city acquired valuable real estate in 1437. The official reception and festival hall here has played a central role in civic life through the centuries. At one end of the complex are the remains of the 10th-century Gothic church of **St. Alban,** which were left ruined after the war as a memorial. On what's left of the church floor you can see a sculpture of a couple kneeling in prayer, *Mourning Parents*, by Käthe Kollwitz, a fitting memorial to the ravages of war. ⊠ *Martinstr. 29–37, Altstadt.*

Käthe Kollwitz Museum. The works of Käthe Kollwitz (1867–1945), the most important German female artist of the 20th century, focus on social themes like the plight of the poor and the atrocities of war. This is the larger of the country's two Kollwitz collections and comprises all of her woodcuts, as well as paintings, etchings, lithographs, and sculptures. There are also changing exhibits of other modern artists. ⊠ *Neumarkt 18–24, in Neumarkt Passage, Innenstadt* ☎ *0221/227–2899* ⊕ *www.kollwitz.de* 🖃 *€3* ☉ *Tues.–Fri. 10–6, weekends 11–6.*

Kölnisches Stadtmuseum (*Köln City History Museum*). The triumphs and tragedies of Köln's rich past are packed into this museum at the historic *Zeughaus,* the city's former arsenal. Here you'll find an in-depth chronicle of Köln's history—including information about the lives of ordinary people and high-profile politicians, the industrial revolution (car manufacturer Henry Ford headquartered his European operations here), and the destruction incurred during World War II. For those who've always wanted to be privy to the inside stories surrounding local words such as *Klüngel, Kölsch,* and *Karneval,* the answers are waiting to be discovered within the museum's walls. ⊠ *Zeughausstr. 1–3, Altstadt* ☎ *0221/2212–5789* ⊕ *www.museenkoeln.de* 🖃 *€5* ☉ *Wed.–Sun. 10–5, Tues. 10–8.*

11

Museum Schnütgen. A treasure house of medieval art from the Rhine region, the museum has an ideal setting in a 12th-century basilica. Don't miss the crucifix from the St. Georg Kirche or original stained-glass windows and carved figures from the Dom. Other exhibits include intricately carved ivory book covers, rock-crystal reliquaries, and illuminated manuscripts. ⊠ *Cäcilienstr. 29, Innenstadt* ☎ *0221/2212–2310* ⊕ *www.museenkoeln.de* 🎫 *€5* ☉ *Tues.–Fri. 10–5, weekends 11–5.*

QUICK BITES

Café Stanton. Köln's main pedestrian shopping street is practical but utterly uninspiring—some even say ugly. This café is an airy, artsy oasis with outdoor terrace seating and a view of the 14th-century Antonite church. The food is international with an emphasis on the Mediterranean; the selection of cakes is divinely German, and there is a jazz dinner every Saturday. Three enormous, surprisingly delicate chandeliers, made entirely of plastic waste, provide lighting. ⊠ *Schilderg. 57, behind Antoniterkirche* ☎ *0221/271–0710* ⊕ *www.cafe-stanton.de.*

St. Gereon. Experts regard St. Gereon as one of the most noteworthy medieval structures in existence. This exquisite Romanesque basilica stands on the site of an old Roman burial ground six blocks west of the train station. An enormous dome rests on walls that were once clad in gold mosaics. Roman masonry forms part of the structure, which is believed to have been built over the grave of its namesake, the 4th-century martyr and Köln's patron. ⊠ *Gereonskloster 2–4* ☎ *0221/134– 922* 🎫 *Free* ☉ *Mon.–Fri. 10–6, Sat. 10–5:30, Sun. 12:30–6.*

St. Kunibert. The most lavish of the churches from the late-Romanesque period is by the Rhine, three blocks north of the train station. The apse's precious stained-glass windows have filtered light for more than 750 years (they were saved in protective storage during World War II). Consecrated in 1247, the church contains an unusual room, concealed under the altar, which gives access to a pre-Christian well once believed to promote fertility in women. ⊠ *Kunibertsklosterg. 6, Altstadt-Nord* ☎ *0221/121–214* ⊕ *www.basilika-st-kunibert.de* 🎫 *Free* ☉ *Mon.–Sat. 10–1 and 3–6, Sun. 3–6.*

St. Maria im Kapitol. Built in the 11th and 12th centuries on the site of a Roman temple, St. Maria is best known for its two beautifully carved 16-foot-high doors and its enormous crypt, the second-largest in Germany. The powerful organ shakes the building. ⊠ *Marienpl. 17–19, Altstadt* ☎ *0221/214–615* 🎫 *Free* ☉ *Daily 9–6, except during services.*

☺ **Schokoladenmuseum** (*Chocolate Museum*). This riverside museum south of the cathedral is a real hit, and so crowded on weekends that it can be unpleasant. It recounts 3,000 years of civilization's production and delectation of chocolate, from the Central American Maya to the colonizing and industrializing Europeans. It's also a real factory, with lava flows of chocolate and a conveyer belt jostling thousands of truffles. The museum shop, with a huge variety of chocolate items, does a brisk business, and the riverside panorama café offers some of the best cake in town. ⊠ *Am Schockoladenmuseum 1a, Rheinufer* ☎ *0221/931–8880* ⊕ *www.schokoladenmuseum.de* 🎫 *€7.50* ☉ *Tues.– Fri. 10–6, weekends 11–7.*

WHERE TO EAT

$$
FRENCH
Fodor's Choice
★

× **Capricorn i Aries.** This corner brasserie—part neighborhood bistro, part gourmet restaurant—serves the staples of French rural cuisine with a Rhineland twist. Co-owner Judith Kräber will make you feel at home while her husband, Martin Kräber, cooks you a simple soup or a five-course dinner. The couple's award-winning, four-table restaurant across the street is also available for special events. Those aiming to improve their own skills can participate in a Sunday cooking class, in which students get to prepare—and eat—four courses. ⊠ *Alteburger Str. 31, Neustadt Süd* ☎ *0221/397–5710* ⊕ *www.capricorniaries.com* 🍴 *Reservations essential* ▭ *No credit cards* ⊘ *Closed Sun. No lunch Sat.*

$$$
ITALIAN
★

× **Casa di Biase.** This romantic eatery serves sophisticated Italian cuisine in a warm, elegant setting. The seasonally changing menu focuses on fish and game, and the wine list is interesting and extensive—although sometimes pricey. Just next door is Casa di Biase's smaller and more casual sister, the Teca di Biasi. This cozy, wood-panel wine bar serves antipasti, salads, and main dishes for €15 or less. ⊠ *Eifelpl. 4, Südstadt* ☎ *0221/322–433* ⊕ *www.casadibiase.de* ⊘ *Closed Sun. No lunch Sat.*

¢
EUROPEAN

× **Café Elefant.** For three decades, writers and artists from Köln's elegant Agnesviertel neighborhood have been meeting at this cosy locale on a quiet, tree-lined street. Inside, the ambience—like a little corner of Montmartre—is just right for thinking deep thoughts, or simply chatting over a slice of chocolate cake. Even when the cake's all gone, night owls can enjoy the café's delicious Camembert and lingonberry blintzes. ⊠ *Weissenburgstr. 50, Köln* ☎ *0221/734–520* ▭ *No credit cards.*

$
GERMAN

× **Früh am Dom.** For real down-home cooking, there are few places that compare with this time-honored former brewery in the shadow of the Dom. It's often crowded, but the spirit is fantastic. Bold frescoes on the vaulted ceilings establish the mood, and the authentically Teutonic experience is completed by such dishes as *Hämmchen* (pork knuckle). The beer garden is delightful for summer dining. ⊠ *Am Hof 12–18, Altstadt* ☎ *0221/261–3211* ⊕ *www.frueh.de* ▭ *No credit cards.*

$$$
ECLECTIC

× **Heising & Adelmann.** A young crowd gathers here to do what people along the Rhine have done for centuries—talk, drink, and enjoy good company. There's a party every Friday and Saturday with a DJ. Consistently voted one of the best deals in town, this restaurant offers good German beer, tangy cocktails, and a creative mixture of German and French food. ⊠ *Friesenstr. 58–60, Neustadt-Nord* ☎ *0221/130–9424* ⊕ *www.heising-und-adelmann.de* ⊘ *Closed Sun. and Mon. No lunch.*

$
GERMAN

× **Päffgen.** There's no better *Bräuhaus* in Köln in which to imbibe Kölsch, the city's home brew. You won't sit long in front of an empty glass before a blue-aproned waiter sweeps by and places another one before you. With its worn wooden decor, colorful clientele, and typical Rhenish fare (sauerbraten, Hämmchen, and Reibekuchen), Päffgen sums up local tradition (making it hard to believe the brewery is the family business of the late singer-actress Nico, née Christa Päffgen, who became famous in the '60s through her collaborations with Andy Warhol and the Velvet Underground). ⊠ *Friesenstr. 64–66, Friesenviertel* ☎ *0221/135–461* ⊕ *www.paeffgen-koelsch.de* ▭ *No credit cards.*

WHERE TO STAY

For expanded hotel reviews, visit Fodors.com.

The tourist office, across from the cathedral, can make hotel bookings for you for the same night, at a cost of €10 per room. If you plan to be in town for the Karneval, be sure to reserve a room well in advance.

$$$$ 🏨 **Excelsior Hotel Ernst.** Old master paintings, including a Van Dyck, grace this 1863 hotel's sumptuous Empire-style lobby, while Gobelin tapestries hang in the ballroom of the same name. **Pros:** Van Dyck paintings and Gobelins. **Cons:** expensive. ✉ *Domplatz, Trankg. 1, Altstadt* ☎ *0221/2701* ⊕ *www. excelsiorhotelernst.de* 🛏 *108 rooms, 34 suites* ⚐ *In-room: no a/c, Internet, Wi-Fi. In-hotel: restaurant, bar, gym, business center, parking, some pets allowed.*

$$ 🏨 **Hopper Hotel et cetera.** The rooms in this former monastery are spare but not spartan, although a startlingly realistic sculpture of a bishop, sitting in the reception area, serves as a constant reminder of the building's ecclesiastic origins. **Pros:** chicly renovated; attractive neighborhood. **Cons:** not centrally located, showers tricky for older guests. ✉ *Brüsselerstr. 26, Belgisches Viertel* ☎ *0221/924–400* ⊕ *www.hopper.de* 🛏 *48 rooms, 2 suites* ⚐ *In-room: no a/c, Wi-Fi. In-hotel: restaurant, gym, business center, parking, some pets allowed* ⚏ *Breakfast.*

$ 🏨 **Hotel Chelsea.** This designer hotel with classic modern furnishings has a strong following among artists and art dealers, as well as with the musicians who come to play at the nearby Stadtgarten jazz club. **Pros:** an artsy clientele and neighborhood. **Cons:** some rooms need freshening up. ✉ *Jülicherstr. 1, Belgisches Viertel* ☎ *0221/207–150* ⊕ *www.hotel-chelsea.de* 🛏 *35 rooms (3 without bath), 3 suites, 1 apartment* ⚐ *In-room: no a/c, Wi-Fi. In-hotel: restaurant, parking, some pets allowed.*

$$ 🏨 **Hotel im Kupferkessel.** The best things about this small, unassuming, family-run hotel are its immaculate housekeeping—the very model of German fastidiousness—and the price (small single rooms with shared bath can be had for as low as €38). **Pros:** inexpensive. **Cons:** no elevator. ✉ *Probsteig. 6, Alstadt-Nord* ☎ *0221/270–7960* ⊕ *www. im-kupferkessel.de* 🛏 *12 rooms total, 5 without bath* ⚐ *In-room: no a/c, Internet, Wi-Fi. In-hotel: parking* ⚏ *Breakfast.*

$$$ 🏨 **Hotel im Wasserturm.** What used to be Europe's tallest water tower ★ is now an independent, 11-story luxury hotel-in-the-round that's welcomed guests like Brad Pitt and fashion mogul Wolfgang Joop. **Pros:** modern luxury at its finest. **Cons:** expensive. ✉ *Kayg. 2, Altstadt* ☎ *0221/20080* ⊕ *www.hotel-im-wasserturm.de* 🛏 *45 rooms, 33 suites*

♿ *In-room: Wi-Fi. In-hotel: restaurant, bar, gym, spa, business center, parking, some pets allowed.*

$$$ 🏨 **Savoy Hotel.** Glitz and sumptuous shag carpeting shove aside conventional notions of good taste at this campy luxury hotel with theme suites ranging from the daring red "Paris" rooms to the bachelor-pad-brown "New York" digs. **Pros:** excellent air-conditioning, great rooftop view. **Cons:** on a busy street; not for young children. ✉ *Turinerstr. 9, Eigelsteinviertel, Köln* 🕾 *0221/1623–200* ⊕ *www.savoy.de* ⤵ *58 rooms, 40 suites* ♿ *In-room: a/c, Internet, Wi-Fi. In-hotel: restaurant, bar, spa, parking* ⦿⟊ *Breakfast.*

NIGHTLIFE AND THE ARTS

Kölnticket. Tickets to most arts events can be purchased through Kölnticket. 🕾 *0221/2801* ⊕ *www.koelnticket.de.*

THE ARTS

Antoniterkirche. Organ recitals and chamber concerts are presented in many of the Romanesque churches and in the Antoniterkirche. ✉ *Schilderg. 57, Innenstadt* 🕾 *0221/925–8460* ⊕ *www.antonitercitykirche.de.*

Oper der Stadt Köln. Köln's opera company is known for exciting classical and contemporary productions, including collaborative efforts with French designer Christian Lacroix. ✉ *Offenbachpl., Innenstadt* 🕾 *0221/2212–8400* ⊕ *www.operkoeln.de.*

Philharmonie. Köln's Westdeutsche Rundfunk (WDR) Orchestra performs regularly in the city's excellent concert hall, the Philharmonie. ✉ *Bischofsgartenstr. 1, Altstadt* 🕾 *0221/204–080* ⊕ *www.koelnerphilharmonie.de.*

Schauspielhaus. Köln's principal theater is the Schauspielhaus, home to the 20 or so private theater companies in the city. ✉ *Offenbachpl. 1, Innenstadt* 🕾 *0221/2212–8400* ⊕ *www.schauspielkoeln.de.*

NIGHTLIFE

Köln's nightlife is centered on three distinct areas: along the river in the Old Town, which seems to be one big party on weekends; on Zulpicherstrasse near the university; and around the Friesenplatz U-bahn station. Many streets off the Hohenzollernring and Hohenstaufenring, particularly Roonstrasse and Aachenerstrasse, also provide a broad range of nightlife. In summer the Martinsviertel, a part of the Altstadt around the Gross St. Martin church, which is full of restaurants, brew houses, and *Kneipen* (pubs), is a good place to go around sunset.

Alter Wartesaal. For a true disco experience, make for the Alter Wartesaal in the Hauptbahnhof on Friday or Saturday night. The old train-station waiting room has been turned into a concert hall and disco,

> ### GO BELGIAN
>
> Among Köln's most enticing areas for a drink or light meal is the leafy and attractive Belgian quarter. German soap stars and media power brokers flock to eateries like **Pepe** (✉ *Antwerpenerstr. 63*), while they're joined by a more hipster crowd at cafés like **Hallmackenreuther** (✉ *Brüsselerpl. 9*) and **Salon Schmitz** (✉ *Aachenerstr. 30*)—the place to see and be seen, located at the nexus of the city's hippest bars.

where dancers swivel on ancient polished parquet and check their style in original mahogany-frame mirrors. ⊠ *Am Hauptbahnhof, Johannisstr. 11, Altstadt* ☎ *0221/912–8850* ⊕ *www.wartesaal.de.*

Papa Joe's Biersalon. This classic Altstadt bar is a bit kitschy but it offers oldies from Piaf to Porter. ⊠ *Alter Markt 50–52, Altstadt* ☎ *0221/ 258–2132.*

Papa Joe's Jazzlokale. For live jazz, head to the tiny Papa Joe's Jazzlokale, where there's never a cover charge. ⊠ *Buttermarkt 37, Altstadt* ☎ *0221/257–7931.*

Stadtgarten. In summer, head straight for the Stadtgarten and sit in the Biergarten for some good outdoor *Gemütlichkeit* (coziness). At other times of the year it's still worth a visit for its excellent jazz club. ■TIP→ Stadtgarten also runs a beer garden with cheap, tasty eats in the shaded Rathenauplatz park by Köln's synagogue. ⊠ *Venloerstr. 40* ☎ *0221/952–9940* ⊕ *www.stadtgarten.de.*

SHOPPING

A good shopping loop begins at the **Neumarkt Galerie**. From there, head down the charmless but practical pedestrian shopping zone of the Schildergasse. From Schildergasse, go north on Herzogstrasse to arrive at **Glockengasse**. A block north is Breite Strasse, another pedestrian shopping street. At the end of Breite Strasse is Ehrenstrasse, where the young and young-at-heart can shop for hip fashions and trendy housewares. After a poke around here, explore the small boutiques on Benesisstrasse, which will lead you to Mittelstrasse, best known for high-tone German fashions and luxury goods. Follow Mittelstrasse to the end to return to the Neumarkt.

Glockengasse. Köln's most celebrated product, Eau de Cologne No. 4711, was first concocted here by the 18th-century Italian chemist Johann Maria Farina. At the company's flagship store there's a small exhibition of historical 4711 bottles, as well as a perfume fountain you can dip your fingers in. ⊠ *No. 4711 Glockengasee, Innenstadt* ☎ *0221/2709–9910* ⊕ *www.glockengasse.de.*

Heubel. On Breite Strasse, a pedestrian shopping street, Heubel carries unusual, beautiful, and often inexpensive imported antiques, housewares, and jewelry. ⊠ *Breite Str. 118–120, Innenstadt* ☎ *0221/257– 6013* ⊕ *www.heubel.de.*

Neumarkt Galerie. This bright, modern indoor shopping arcade has a web of shops and cafés surrounding an airy atrium. Just look for the huge sculpture of an upside-down ice cream cone above the entrance. ⊠ *Richmodstr. 8.*

Peek & Cloppenburg. This big clothing store is a highlight of Shildergasse. The Renzo Piano–designed building looks like a spaceship, and its selection of fashions—for men and women, from budget to couture—is out of this world. ⊠ *Schilderg. 65–67, Innenstadt* ☎ *0221/453–900.*

AACHEN

70 km (43 mi) west of Köln.

At the center of Aachen, the characteristic *drei-Fenster* facades, three windows wide, give way to buildings dating from the days when Charlemagne made Aix-la-Chapelle (as it was then called) the great center of the Holy Roman Empire. Thirty-two German emperors were crowned here, gracing Aachen with the proud nickname "Kaiserstadt" (Emperors' City). Roman legions had been drawn here for the healing properties of the sulfur springs emanating from the nearby Eifel Mountains. (The name "Aachen," based on an old Frankish word for "water," takes note of this.) Charlemagne's father, Pepin the Short, also settled here to enjoy the waters, and to this day the city is also known as Bad Aachen, drawing visitors in search of a cure. One-and-a-half-hour walking tours depart from the tourist office throughout the year at 11 on weekends, as well as at 2 on weekdays from April to December. The Saturday tours are conducted in English as well as German.

ESSENTIALS

Visitor Information Aachen ⊠ *Aachen Tourist-Information, Friedrich-Wilhelm-Pl.* ☎ *0241/180–2960* ⊕ *www.aachen.de* ⊗ *Weekdays 9–6, Sat. 9–2.*

EXPLORING

TOP ATTRACTIONS

★ **Dom** (*Cathedral*). Aachen's stunning cathedral, the "Chapelle" of the town's earlier name, remains the single greatest storehouse of Carolingian architecture in Europe, and it was the first place in Germany to be named a UNESCO World Heritage Site. Though it was built over the course of 1,000 years and reflects architectural styles from the Middle Ages to the 19th century, its commanding image is the magnificent octagonal royal chapel, rising up two arched stories to end in the cap of the dome. It was this section, the heart of the church, that Charlemagne saw completed in AD 800. His bones now lie in the Gothic choir, in a golden shrine surrounded by wonderful carvings of saints. Another treasure is his marble throne. Charlemagne had to journey all the way to Rome for his coronation, but the next 32 Holy Roman emperors were crowned here in Aachen, and each marked the occasion by presenting a lavish gift to the cathedral. In the 12th century Emperor Frederick I (nicknamed "Barbarossa" by the Italians for his red beard) donated the great chandelier now hanging in the center of the Palatine chapel; his grandson, Friedrich II, donated Charlemagne's shrine. Emperor Karl IV journeyed from Prague in the late 14th century for the sole purpose of commissioning a bust of Charlemagne for the cathedral; now on view in the treasury, the bust incorporates a piece of Charlemagne's skull. ⊠ *Münsterpl.* ☎ *0241/477–090* ⊕ *www.aachendom.de* ⊠ *Free* ⊗ *Apr.–Dec., daily 7–7; Jan.–Mar., daily 7–6.*

Domschatzkammer (*The Cathedral Treasury*). The cathedral houses sacred art from late antiquity and the Carolingian, Ottonian, and Hohenstaufen eras; highlights include the Cross of Lothair, the Bust of Charlemagne, and the Persephone Sarcophagus. ☒ *Klosterpl. 2* ☎ *0241/4770–9127* ☜ *€5* ⊙ *Jan.–Mar., Mon. 10–1, Tues.–Sun. 10–5; Apr.–Dec., Mon. 10–1, Tues.–Sun. 10–6.*

Elisenbrunnen (*Elisa Fountain*). Southeast of the cathedral and the site of the city's tourist-information center, is an arcaded, neoclassical structure built in 1822. The central pavilion contains two fountains with thermal water—the hottest north of the Alps—that is reputed to help cure a wide range of ailments in those who drink it. If you can brave a gulp of the sulfurous water, you'll be emulating the likes of Dürer, Frederick the Great, and Charlemagne, who drank it before you.

Rathaus (*Town Hall*). Aachen's town hall sits behind the Dom, across Katschhof Square. It was built in the early 14th century on the site of the *Aula Regia,* or "great hall," of Charlemagne's palace. Its first major official function was the coronation banquet of Emperor Karl IV in 1349, held in the great Gothic hall you can still see today (though this was largely rebuilt after World War II). On the north wall of the building are statues of 50 emperors of the Holy Roman Empire. The greatest of them all, Charlemagne, stands in bronze atop the Karlsbrunnen in the center of the market square. ☒ *Marktpl.* ☎ *0241/432–7310* ☜ *€2.50* ⊙ *Daily 10–6.*

WORTH NOTING

Carolus-Thermen Bad Aachen. If you're a steam-lover, try this high-tech spa with a venerable history. In Dürer's time there were regular crackdowns on the orgiastic goings-on at the baths. Today taking the waters is done with a bathing suit on, but be aware—the sauna area is declared a "textile-free zone." ☒ *Passstr. 79* ☎ *0241/182–740* ⊕ *www.carolus-thermen.de* ☜ *€11, €22 with sauna for up to 2½ hrs; €14/€28 for full day* ⊙ *Daily 9 am–11 pm.*

Ludwig Forum für Internationale Kunst. Aachen has a modern side as well. One of the world's most important art collectors, chocolate magnate Peter Ludwig, endowed two museums in the town he called home. The Forum, the larger of the two, holds a portion of Ludwig's truly enormous collection of contemporary art and hosts traveling exhibits. ☒ *Jülicher Str. 97–109* ☎ *0241/180–7104* ⊕ *www.ludwigforum.de* ☜ *€5* ⊙ *Tues., Wed., and Fri. noon–6, Thurs. noon–10, weekends 11–6.*

Suermondt-Ludwig Museum. The smaller of the two Ludwig art institutions in town (Ludwig Forum is the larger institution), the collection here consists mainly of paintings, spanning the 12th to the early 20th century. ☒ *Wilhelmstr. 18* ☎ *0241/479–80* ⊕ *www.suermondt-ludwig-museum.de* ☜ *€7* ⊙ *Tues., Thurs., and Fri. noon–6, Wed. 11–8, weekends 11–6.*

WHERE TO EAT

$

GERMAN

✕ **Am Knipp.** At this Bierstube dating from 1698, run by three generations of the Ramrath family, guests dig into their regional dishes at low wooden tables next to the tile stove. Pewter plates and beer mugs

line the walls. ✉ *Bergdriesch 3* ☎ *0241/33168* ⊕ *www.amknipp.de*
⊘ *Closed Tues., Dec. 24–Jan. 2, and 2 wks in Apr. and Oct. No lunch.*

$
GERMAN
★
✕ **Der Postwagen.** This annex of the more upscale Ratskeller is worth a
stop for the building alone, a half-timber medieval edifice at one corner
of the old Rathaus. You'll be impressed by the food as well, which also
comes from the kitchen of Ratskeller chef Maurice de Boer. Sitting at
one of the low wooden tables, surveying the marketplace through the
wavy old glass, you can dine very respectably on solid German fare.
If you really want to go local, try Himmel und Erde. ✉ *Am Markt 40*
☎ *0241/35001* ⊕ *www.ratskeller-aachen.de.*

$$$$
FRENCH
★
✕ **La Becasse.** Chef Christof Lang's sophisticated French nouvelle cuisine and attentive staff are a hit among Aachen's discriminating diners.
The restaurant has been in operation just outside the Old Town by the
Westpark for three decades. Try the distinctively light calf's kidney or
the stingray lasagna. The five-course lunch menu (around €35) changes
daily. ✉ *Hanbrucherstr. 1* ☎ *0241/74444* ⊕ *www.labecasse.de* ⌂ *Reser-*
vations essential ⊘ *Closed Sun. No lunch Sat. or Mon.*

WHERE TO STAY
For expanded hotel reviews, visit Fodors.com.

$
▦ **All Seasons Aachen City.** A 15-minute walk from the Dom, this colorfully furnished modern budget hotel offers a good value, especially
for families with children. **Pros:** kids under 16 get their own room at
half price. **Cons:** on a busy street somewhat removed from the center.
✉ *Jülicherstr. 10–12, Aachen* ☎ *0241/51060* ⊕ *www.all-seasons-hotels.*
com ↴ *102* ⌂ *In-room: a/c, Wi-Fi. In-hotel: bar, parking, some pets*
allowed ⦿l *Breakfast.*

$$
▦ **Hotel Brülls am Dom.** In the historic heart of the city, this quaint, fam-
ily-run hotel offers tradition, convenience, and considerable comfort a
stone's throw away from nearly all the major attractions. **Pros:** central
location; warm breakfast served personally by the hostess. **Cons:** no ele-
vator; no Internet; no credit cards. ✉ *Hühnermarkt 2–3* ☎ *0241/31704*
↴ *10 rooms* ⌂ *In-room: no a/c. In-hotel: parking* ▭ No *credit cards*
⦿l *Breakfast.*

$$$
▦ **Pullmann Aachen Quellenhof.** One of Europe's *grandes dames*, this old-
style hostelry features rooms with high ceilings, a Roman-style spa
area and an inviting pool. **Pros:** spacious; elegant; formal. **Cons:** on a
busy street; expensive. ✉ *Monheimsallee 52* ☎ *0241/91320* ⊕ *www.*
accorhotels.com ↴ *185 rooms, 2 suites* ⌂ *In-room: a/c, Internet, Wi-Fi.*
In-hotel: restaurant, bar, pool, gym, business center, parking, some pets
allowed ⦿l *Breakfast.*

NIGHTLIFE AND THE ARTS
Most activity in town is concentrated around the market square and
Pontstrasse, a pedestrian street that radiates off the square.

Domkeller. Start out at Aachen's most popular bar, the Domkeller, to
mingle with locals of all ages at old wooden tables, enjoying an impressive selection of Belgian beers. There are free concerts every Monday.
✉ *Hof 1* ☎ *0241/34265* ⊕ *www.domkeller.de.*

Wild Rover. This Irish pub serves Murphy's Stout on tap to live music most nights starting at 8:30. It's closed Monday. ⊠ *Hirschgraben 13* ☎ *0241/35453.*

SHOPPING

■**TIP→** Don't leave Aachen without stocking up on the traditional local gingerbread, *Aachener Printen.* Each bakery in town offers its own varieties (topped with whole or crushed nuts, milk or dark chocolate, etc.), and guards its recipe like a state secret.

Alt Aachener Kaffeestuben. This café is also known as the Café Van den Daele. Some of the best *Aachener Printen* (gingerbread) can be found here. Another tasty Aachen specialty to try here is *Reisfladen,* a sort of tart filled with milk rice and often topped with fruit—especially pears, apricots, or cherries. The store-café is worth a visit for its atmosphere and tempting aromas, whether you intend to buy anything. It also ships goods. ⊠ *Büchel 18* ☎ *0241/35724* ⊕ *www.van-den-daele.de.*

DÜSSELDORF

47 km (29 mi) north of Köln.

Düsseldorf, the state capital of North Rhine–Westphalia, may suffer by comparison to Köln's remarkable skyline, but the elegant city has more than enough charm—and money—to boost its confidence. By contrast to Cologne's boisterous, working-class charm, Düsseldorf is known as one of the country's richest cities, with an extravagant lifestyle that epitomizes the economic success of postwar Germany. Since 80% of Düsseldorf was destroyed in World War II, the city has since been more or less rebuilt from the ground up—in part rebuilding landmarks of long ago and restoring a medieval riverside quarter.

At the confluence of the Rhine and Düssel rivers, this dynamic city started as a small fishing town. The name means "village on the Düssel," but obviously this Dorf is a village no more. Raised expressways speed traffic past towering glass-and-steel structures; within them, glass-enclosed shopping malls showcase the finest clothes, furs, jewelry, and other goods that money can buy.

GETTING HERE AND AROUND

Bus tours of Düsseldorf in summer leave daily at 11 and 2:30 (in winter on Saturday only at 2:30). Departures are from the corner of Steinstrasse and Königsallee. Tickets (€16.50) can be purchased on the bus, at the information center, or through Adorf Reisebüro. A walking tour of the Old Town is offered daily from April to October, and on Saturday the rest of the year at 2:30 pm for €10. The tour leaves from the Altstadt tourist-info center (Marktstrasse/Rheinstrasse corner).

DISCOUNTS AND DEALS

The **Düsseldorf WelcomeCard** costs €9 for 24 hours, €14 for 48 hours, and €19 for 72 hours, and allows free public transportation and reduced admission to museums, theaters, and even boat tours on the Rhine.

ESSENTIALS

Visitor Information Düsseldorf ⊠ *Marktstr. 6* ☎ *0211/172–020* ⊕ *www. duesseldorf-tourismus.de.*

Düsseldorf's elegant high-end malls are great for window shopping.

EXPLORING

TOP ATTRACTIONS

Altstadt (*Old Town*). This party-hearty district has been dubbed "the longest bar in the world" by locals. Narrow alleys thread their way to some 300 restaurants and taverns offering a wide range of cuisines. All crowd into the 1-square-km (½-square-mi) area between the Rhine and Heinrich-Heine-Allee. When the weather cooperates, the area seems like one big sidewalk café.

Königsallee. This is Düsseldorf's main shopping avenue and the epitome of the city's affluence; it's lined with the crème de la crème of designer boutiques and stores. Known as the Kö, this wide, double boulevard is divided by an ornamental waterway that is fed by the River Düssel. Rows of chestnut trees line the Kö, shading a string of sidewalk cafés. Beyond the Triton Fountain, at the street's north end, begins a series of parks and gardens. In these patches of green you can sense a joie de vivre hardly expected in a city devoted to big business.

Kunstsammlung Nordrhein-Westfalen (*Art Collection of North Rhine–Westphalia*). The museum, which was renovated and reopened in summer 2010, is split into two parts—plus an installation space. Behind the sleek, polished black stone facade of **K20**, is a treasure trove of art (*Kunst*, hence the *K*) of the 20th century, including works from masters like Picasso, Klee, and Richter. Within the more conservative 19th-century architecture of **K21** is edgier fare—international art since about 1980, including the works of Thomas Ruff and Nam June Paik. Rounding things off is the quirky, modern **Schmela Haus** (1967), a former commercial gallery, which the museum reopened in 2011 as a space for experimental art. ✉ *K20:, Grabbepl. 5* ☎ *0211/838–1130* ⊕ *www.kunstsammlung.de* ✉ *K20: €10; K21: €8. Both: €15 (prices vary); free entry 1st Wed. of month, 6–10; Schmela Haus free of charge.* ☉ *Tues.–Fri. 10–6, weekends 11–6; 1st Wed. of each month 10–10.* ✉ *K21, Ständehausstr. 1* ✉ *Schmela Haus, Mutter-Ey-Str. 3*

Neanderthal Museum. Just outside Düsseldorf, the Düssel River forms a valley, called the Neanderthal, where the bones of a Stone Age ancestor of modern man were found. A prize-winning museum, built at the site of discovery in the suburb of Mettmann, includes models of the original discovery, replicas of cave drawings, and life-size models of Neanderthal Man. Many scientists think he was a different species of human; short, stocky, and with a sloping forehead. The bones were found in 1856 by workers quarrying the limestone cliffs to get flux for blast furnaces. ✉ *Talstr. 300, Mettmann* ☎ *02104/97970* ⊕ *www.neanderthal.de* ✉ *€8* ☉ *Tues.–Sun. 10–6.*

Rhine Promenade. Traffic is routed away from the river and underneath this pedestrian strip, which is lined by chic shopping arcades and cafés. Joggers, rollerbladers, punks, and folks out for a stroll make much use of the promenade as well.

WORTH NOTING

Burgplatz (*Castle Square*). The traffic-free cobblestone streets of the Old Town lead to Castle Square.

Heinrich-Heine-Institut. This museum and archive houses significant manuscripts from the German poet and man of letters, Heinrich Heine. Part of the complex was once the residence of the composer Robert Schumann. ✉ *Bilkerstr. 12–14* ☎ *0211/899–2902* ⊕ *www.duesseldorf. de/heineinstitut* ✉ *€3* ☉ *Tues.–Fri. and Sun. 11–5, Sat. 1–5.*

Hofgarten Park. Once the garden of the elector's palace, the oldest remaining parts of the Hofgarten date back to 1769, when it was transformed into Germany's first public park. The promenade leading to the palace, Schloss Jägerhof, was all the rage in late 18th-century Düsseldorf before the park was largely destroyed by Napoléon's troops. Today it's an oasis of greenery at the heart of downtown.

MedienHafen. This stylish, revamped district is an eclectic mixture of late-19th-century warehouses and ultramodern restaurants, bars, and shops, and one of Europe's masterpieces in urban redevelopment. Surrounding the historic commercial harbor, now occupied by yachts and leisure boats, many media companies have made this area their home. On the riverbank you'll find Frank Gehry's **Neuer Zollhof,** a particularly striking ensemble of three organic-looking high-rises. The best way to tackle the buzzing architecture is to take a stroll down the promenade.

Museum Kunst Palast. This newly reopened art museum lies at the northern extremity of the Hofgarten, close to the Rhine. Its excellent German Expressionist collection (Beckmann, Kirchner, Nolde, Macke, etc.) makes it worth a trip, as does its collection of glass art—among the largest in Europe. ✉ *Ehrenhof 5* ☎ *0211/899–2460* ⊕ *www.smkp.de* ✉ *€7 for permanent collection, special exhibition prices vary* ☉ *Tues.–Sun. 11–6 (until 9 pm on Thurs.).*

St. Lambertus. This Gothic church is near the palace tower on Burgplatz. Its spire became distorted because unseasoned wood was used in its construction. The Vatican elevated the 14th-century brick church to a basilica minor (small cathedral) in 1974 in recognition of its role in church history. Built in the 13th century, with additions from 1394, St. Lambertus contains the tomb of William the Rich and a graceful late-Gothic tabernacle. ⊠ *Stiftspl. 7.*

Schloss Jägerhof. At the far-east edge of the Hofgarten, this baroque structure is more a combination town house and country lodge than a palace. It houses the **Goethe-Museum,** featuring original manuscripts, first editions, personal correspondence, and other memorabilia of Germany's greatest writer. There's also a museum housing a collection of Meissen porcelain. ⊠ *Jacobistr. 2* ☎ *0211/899–6262* ⊕ *www.goethe-museum.com* ⊠ *€3* ⊙ *Tues.–Fri. and Sun. 11–5, Sat. 1–5.*

Schlossturm (*Palace Tower*). A squat tower is all that remains of the palace built by the Berg family, which ruled Düsseldorf for more than five centuries. The tower also houses the **SchifffahrtMuseum,** which charts 2,000 years of Rhine boatbuilding and navigation. ⊠ *Burgpl. 30* ☎ *0211/899–4195* ⊠ *€3* ⊙ *Tues.–Sun. 11–6.*

WHERE TO EAT

$$$$ ✕ **Berens am Kai.** This sleek restaurant is the gourmet playground of
FRENCH   the young business elite of this affluent city. Set in the once derelict but
★   now modernized Düsseldorf harbor, the glass-and-steel building with its ceiling-to-floor windows looks more like a modern office complex than a restaurant. The steep prices are warranted by chef Holger Berens' exquisite cuisine, the refined service, and the great setting with magnificent views of the harbor and Düsseldorf, particularly stunning at night. Dishes include creative French recipes, a wine list with vintages from around the world, and tempting desserts—a must-visit if you are tired of old-style German cooking. ⊠ *Kaistr. 16* ☎ *0211/300–6750* ⊕ *www.berensamkai.de* ⌕ *Reservations essential* ⊙ *Closed Sun. No lunch Sat.*

¢   ✕ **Bistro Zicke.** Weekend brunch
FRENCH   (served until 4 pm) can be a busy affair at this French-inspired artists' café tucked away on a quiet square, one block from the riverfront. Otherwise, the bistro—with its big windows and walls plastered with old movie and museum posters—is an oasis from the hustle and bustle of the busy Altstadt. The word *Zicke* ("nanny goat") is a commonly used insult for a moody woman, yet the bistro is a friendly place to stop in for a drink or to try the simple

FLINGERN DISTRICT: ON THE RISE

The rapidly gentrifying Flingern district proves that even strait-laced Düsseldorf knows how to get funky. Cool indie cafés, galleries, and local designer shops line Ackerstrasse between Hermannstrasse and Birken-strasse. At night, youngsters flock to Trinkhalle (⊠ *Ackerstr.144*), a popular watering hole offering live music and DJ sets. But the neighborhood's not all hipster yet; there's still a neat mix of people and businesses, as evidenced by places like Okra (⊠ *Ackerstr. 119*), a simple Ethiopian restaurant with a retired bowling alley in its basement.

French-Italian cooking. ⊠ *Bäckerstr. 5a* ☎ *0211/327–800* ⊕ *www. bistro-zicke.de* ⊟ *No credit cards.*

$
GERMAN

✕ **Brauerei Zur Uel.** A nontraditional brew house, the Uel is the popular hangout for Düsseldorf's students. The basic menu consists of soups, salads, and pastas; the ingredients are fresh and the portions are generous. What seems like every cultural and political event in the city is advertised in the entry hall. ⊠ *Ratingerstr. 16* ☎ *0211/325–369* ⊟ *No credit cards.*

$$$$
FRENCH
★

✕ **Im Schiffchen.** Although it's out of the way, a meal at one of Germany's best restaurants makes it worth a trip. This is grande luxe, with cooking, under chef Jean-Claude Bourgueil, that's a fine art. The restaurant Jean-Claude's, on the ground floor, features lighter Continental fare created by the same chef but at lower prices. There are more than 1,100 wines in the cellar, many available by the glass. ⊠ *Kaiserswerther Markt 9* ☎ *0211/401–050* ⊕ *www.im-schiffchen.de* ⚐ *Reservations essential* ⊙ *Closed Sun. and Mon. No lunch.*

$$$$
GERMAN

✕ **Weinhaus Tante Anna.** This charming restaurant, six generations in the same family, is furnished with antiques. The cuisine presents modern versions of German classics, demonstrating that there's a lot more to the country's cooking than wurst and sauerkraut—a specialty is a hearty rump steak baked with mustard and onions. The restaurant also offers a full vegetarian prix-fixe menu. ⊠ *Andreasstr. 2* ☎ *0211/131–163* ⊕ *www.tanteanna.de* ⊙ *Closed Sun. No lunch.*

¢
GERMAN

✕ **Zum Uerige.** Among beer buffs, Düsseldorf is famous for its *Altbier,* so called because of the old-fashioned brewing method. The mellow and malty copper-color brew is produced by eight breweries in town. This tavern, which brews its own beer, provides the perfect atmosphere for drinking it. The beer is poured straight out of polished oak barrels and served with hearty local food by busy waiters in long blue aprons. The food offered is mainly snacks, with a small selection of entrées. After dinner, try the bar's award-winning house liquor, called "Stickum"—an unusual (but tasty) sort of beer brandy. ⊠ *Bergerstr. 1* ☎ *0211/866–990* ⊕ *www.uerige.de* ⊟ *No credit cards.*

WHERE TO STAY

For expanded hotel reviews, visit Fodors.com.

$$$$

▦ **Breidenbacher Hof.** The owners razed the original, two-centuries-old hotel of the same name to the ground to open this opulent, high-tech establishment in 2008. **Pros:** luxury; fun gadgets; great location on the Kö. **Cons:** expensive; somewhat charmless. ⊠ *Königsallee 11* ☎ *0211/1609–0909* ⊕ *www.capellahotels.com/dusseldorf* ⤺ *71 rooms, 16 suites* ⚘ *In-room: a/c, Internet, Wi-Fi. In-hotel: restaurant, bar, gym, spa, business center, parking, some pets allowed.*

$$

▦ **carathotel Düsseldorf.** Besides bright, good-size rooms, the true strength of this modern hotel is its location, near the market in the Altstadt. **Pros:** right in the Altstadt; free Wi-Fi. **Cons:** inappropriately modern exterior. ⊠ *Benratherstr. 7a* ☎ *0211/13050* ⊕ *www.carat-hotel-duesseldorf. de* ⤺ *72 rooms, 1 suite* ⚘ *In-room: a/c, Wi-Fi. In-hotel: bar, business center, parking, some pets allowed* ❙◎❙ *Breakfast.*

$$
★

▦ **Hotel Orangerie.** Steps away from Altstadt action and the Rhine, this small hotel on a cobblestone road offers simple comfort and a surprising amount of quiet. **Pros:** unbeatable location; free Wi-Fi. **Cons:** small rooms; no parking at the hotel; caters to business travelers. ⊠ *Bäckerg. 1* ☎ *0211/866–800* ⊕ *www.hotel-orangerie-mcs.de* ↩ *27* ⚲ *In-room: no a/c, Wi-Fi* ⫟⊙⫠ *Breakfast.*

NIGHTLIFE AND THE ARTS

The **Altstadt** is a landscape of pubs, dance clubs, ancient brewery houses, and jazz clubs in the vicinity of the Marktplatz and along cobblestone streets named Bolker, Kurze, Flinger, and Mühlen. These places may be crowded, but some are very atmospheric. The local favorite for nightlife is the **Hafen** neighborhood. Its restaurants and bars cater to the hip thirtysomething crowd that works and parties there.

Deutsche Oper am Rhein. Deutsche Oper am Rhein showcases the city's highly regarded opera company and ballet troupe. ⊠ *Heinrich-Heine-Allee 16a* ☎ *0211/892–5210* ⊕ *www.rheinoper.de.*

Robert-Schumann-Saal. The Robert-Schumann-Saal has classical and pop concerts, symposia, film, and international theater. ⊠ *Ehrenhof 4* ☎ *0211/899–2450* ⊕ *www.museum-kunst-palast.de.*

Roncalli's Apollo Varieté. One of Germany's finest variety and artistic shows is presented nightly at the Roncalli's Apollo Varieté. ⊠ *Apollo-Pl. 1* ☎ *0211/828–9090* ⊕ *www.apollo-variete.com.*

Tonhalle. Düsseldorf, once home to Mendelssohn, Schumann, and Brahms, has the finest concert hall in Germany after Berlin's Philharmonie—the Tonhalle, a former planetarium on the edge of the Hofgarten. It's the home of the Düsseldorfer Symphoniker, which plays from September to June. ⊠ *Ehrenhof 1* ☎ *0211/899–6123* ⊕ *www.tonhalle-duesseldorf.de.*

SHOPPING

For antiques, go to the area around Hohe Strasse. The east side of the **Königsallee** is lined with some of Germany's trendiest boutiques, grandest jewelers, and most extravagant furriers.

Kö Center. This shopping arcade houses clothing stores like Eickhoff, a Düsseldorf institution that offers more than 10,000 square feet of ultra-high-end goods, many straight from the runways of Paris and Milan. ⊠ *Königsallee 28–30.*

Kö Galerie. High-end boutiques and half a dozen restaurants line this luxurious two-story mall. ⊠ *Königsallee 60* ⊕ *www.koe-galerie.com.*

Schadow Arkaden. This mall caters to normal budgets, with stores such as H&M and Habitat. ⊠ *Schadowstr. 11, at end of Kö Galerie* ⊕ *www.schadow-arkaden.com.*

The Fairy-Tale Road

WORD OF MOUTH

"The Fairy-Tale Road is quite long. In general, this is more like a road trip, and you don't have to navigate big cities, so you could actually go from town to town and sleep in a different place every night. On your way, you can sleep in a 'fairy-tale castle,' near Sababurg. Or stay in a half-timber hotel in Hameln."

—Cowboy1968

WELCOME TO THE FAIRY-TALE ROAD

TOP REASONS TO GO

★ **Weser Valley Road:** Drive or bike the scenic highway between Hannoversch-Münden and Hameln: a landscape of green hills, Weser Renaissance towns, and inviting riverside taverns.

★ **Marburg:** Staircase streets and university students climb the steep hillsides of this half-timber town; sit outdoors and soak up the atmosphere.

★ **Bremen:** Browse the shops and galleries lining the picturesque Böttcherstrasse and Schnoorviertel, then savor the city's rich coffee tradition.

★ **Dornröschenschloss Sababurg:** The supposed inspiration for Sleeping Beauty's castle, Dornröschenschloss's spiral staircases, imposing turrets, and fairy-tale setting will delight lovers of the tale.

★ **Schlosspark Wilhelmshöhe:** Home to a stunning, crescent-moon palace and a fairy-tale castle, the park's trees, ponds, and wide-open spaces offer a dramatic contrast to the urbanity below.

12

1 **Hesse.** With Wiesbaden as its capital, Hesse ranks eighth in area among Germany's 16 states and fifth in population. Its northern part is a place of forests, castles, and inspiration for the tales transcribed by the Grimm brothers.

2 **Lower Saxony.** Germany's second-largest state after Bavaria and fourth-most populous, Lower Saxony (Niedersachsen) has a diverse landscape, including the Weser River, which forms a picturesque part of the Fairy-Tale Road, and the Lüneburg Heath. Its capital and largest city is Hannover.

GETTING ORIENTED

The Fairy-Tale Road begins 20 minutes east of Frankfurt in the city of Hanau, and from there wends its way north 700 km (about 430 mi) to the North Sea port of Bremerhaven, through the states of Hesse and Lower Saxony, following the Fulda and Weser rivers and traversing countryside as beguiling as any other in northern Europe. It may not have the glamour of the Romantic Road or the cosmopolitan flair of Germany's great cities, but neither does it have the crowds and commercialism.

DRIVING THE FAIRY-TALE ROAD

(above) Hannover's impressive Altes Rathaus illuminates a foggy night. (upper right) A kayaker paddles the flat Weser River.

Weaving its way through rolling hills and a gentle river valley, between whispering woods and past stone castles, this drive along the Fairy-Tale Road connects Göttingen, a vibrant university town, with tranquil riverside villages and the modern state capital of Hannover along the way.

Beginning in the south of Lower Saxony and ending in the heart of the state, with a brief excursion into Hesse, this two-day drive is best enjoyed in early spring when cherry and apple blossoms dot the countryside. Late summer is another good time to go—the weather is at its best and the roads are no longer cluttered with peak-season traffic. Avoiding the high-speed stress of the autobahns, the drive keeps mainly to country roads allowing time to take in the surroundings between stops. Gazing out at the landscape, it's not difficult to conjure images of wicked witches lurking among the trees, kind woodsmen, and fair maidens trapped in distant towers.

—Jeff Kavanagh

PADDLE THE WESER

Flowing placidly between Hannoversch Münden and Hameln, and on to the North Sea, the Weser passes through many towns offering equipment for rent. If time and weather permit, swap the car for a canoe and paddle the river's glassy waters. Check out ⊕ *www.weserbergland-tourismus.de* for details on canoe operators.

12

A hearty German breakfast at **Bullerjahn** in the lively town square in front of **Göttingen's** Altes Rathaus is a great way to start your trip. Once sated, jump in the car and drive 29 km (18 mi) west through the **Hannoversch-Münden** nature reserve to the town itself. Here, you can stroll among its delightful Renaissance architecture and watch the Fulda and Werra rivers amicably converge to form the Weser River. Half an hour up the road is the town of **Sababurg**, and perhaps the Fairy-Tale Road's most famous landmark, the **Dornröschenschloss**, Sleeping Beauty's castle. Spend some time wandering the castle's rose gardens and contemplating the princess's enchanted 100-year slumber. From the castle it's an easy 20-minute drive across the border to Hesse and the baroque spa town of **Bad Karlshafen**, where you can soothe whatever ails you with a long soak in a thermal, saltwater spring at **Weser-Therme**. Suitably relaxed, head to the peaceful riverside town of **Bodenweder,** which lies just more than 50 km (31 mi) to the north along winding country roads. Stay overnight here, and visit the small but fun **Münchhausen Museum** in the morning and enjoy the gentle murmur of the Weser as it flows its way past. Before lunch, travel 25 minutes north to **Hameln** and the home of the *Rattenfänger*, the Pied Piper, where you can experience "rat-theme" dining at the **Rattenfängerhaus**. Afterward, drive the 47 km (29 mi) up to **Hannover** for an afternoon of culture in one of the city's impressive museums and a predinner drink on the terrace of the stunning **Neues Rathaus**.

QUICK BITES

Bullerjahn. For a hearty breakfast, order the enormous "Gebrüder Grimm Frühstück," which consists of bread rolls, jams, honey, gouda, cold cuts, salmon, tomato and mozzarella, cream cheese, yogurt and fruit, orange juice, coffee, sparkling wine, and a boiled egg. ⊠ *Markt 9, undefined, Göttingen* ☎ *0551/307–0100* ⊕ *wwww.bullerjahn.info* ▭ *No credit cards.*

Museums Café. Afternoon coffee and cake is as strong a culinary tradition in Germany as tea and scones in England and this elegant café in Hameln has gateau and tortes that'll have you embracing the custom like a local in no time. ⊠ *Osterstr. 8, undefined, Hameln* ☎ *05151/21553.*

Back und Naschwerk. The delicious breads baked here use only natural, organic ingredients and real butter. Their maple syrup and walnut or poppy seed and nougat muffins are worth a visit alone. ⊠ *Kramerstr. 14, undefined, Hannover* ☎ *0511/7003–5221* ⊕ *www.back-und-naschwerk.de.*

Updated by
Jeff Kavanagh

With a name evocative of magic and adventure, the Fairy-Tale Road (Märchenstrasse) takes its travelers on a path through the land of the Brothers Grimm and a rolling countryside of farmland and forests that inspired tales of sleeping princesses, hungry wolves, and gingerbread houses. Flowing through the heart of western Germany to its North Sea coast, the Märchenstrasse stops along the way to visit the towns and villages where the brothers spent much of their lives two centuries ago.

It was here among medieval castles and witch towers that the brothers, first as young boys, and then later as students and academics, listened to legends told by local storytellers, and adapted them into the fairy tales that continue to be read around the world today; enchanted and frequently dark tales with names like *Sleeping Beauty*, *Little Red Riding Hood*, and *Hansel and Gretel*.

Following the Grimms' footsteps through a landscape of river valleys and wide-open skies, or down cobblestone streets flanked by half-timbered houses and baroque palaces, it's possible to imagine things haven't changed hugely since the brothers' time. Traditional taverns serving strong German beers and thick slabs of beef and pork dot the way, and storytelling continues to be a major attraction along the Fairy-Tale Road, though nowadays more commonly in the form of guided tours and interactive museum displays.

The Fairy-Tale Road, of course, is also a modern route, and its wide, smooth roads pass through larger urban areas, such as Kassel and Bremen, full of contemporary hotels, eateries, and stores. Like large parts of the rest of the country, many of these towns and cities were greatly damaged during World War II and their hurried reconstruction often favored functionality over form, so that many buildings now sit in stark contrast with the architecture they replaced. This contrast, however, often only serves to emphasize the beauty of what remained.

Not every town on the road can lay claim to a connection to the Brothers Grimm or the inspiration for a specific tale, but many continue to celebrate the region's fairy-tale heritage with theme museums, summer festivals, and outdoor plays.

It's this heritage, the natural appeal of the countryside, and the tradition and culture found in its towns and cities that attract travelers along the Märchenstrasse; that, mixed with the promise of adventure and the opportunity to create some tales of their own.

12

PLANNING

WHEN TO GO

Summer is the ideal time to travel through this varied landscape, although in spring you'll find the river valleys carpeted in the season's first flowers, and in fall the sleepy current of the Weser is often blanketed in mist. Keep in mind that retail stores and shops in the smaller towns in this area often close for two to three hours at lunchtime.

GETTING HERE AND AROUND

AIR TRAVEL

The closest international airports to this region are in Frankfurt, Hannover, and Hamburg. Frankfurt is less than a half hour from Hanau, and Hamburg is less than an hour from Bremen.

Airport Information Langenhagen Airport ⊠ *Flughafenstr 4, Hannover* ☎ *0511/9770.*

BIKE TRAVEL

The Fulda and Werra rivers have 190 km (118 mi) of bike paths, and you can cycle the whole length of the Weser River from Hannoversch-Münden to the outskirts of Bremen without making too many detours from the river valley. Five- and seven-day cycle tours of the Fulda and Werra river valleys are possible, including bike rentals, overnight accommodations, and luggage transport between stops.

Bike Tours SRJ GästeService ⊠ *Gneisenaustr. 10, Minden* ☎ *0571/889–1900* ⊕ *www.srj.de.*

BOAT TRAVEL

The eight boats of Flotte Weser operate short summer excursions along a considerable stretch of the Weser River between Bremen and Bad Karlshafen. The trip between Corvey and Bad Karlshafen, for example, takes slightly less than three hours and costs €14.

Rehbein-Linie Kassel operates a service from Kassel to Bad Karlshafen. It also prides itself on the only "three-river tour" in the area. In a single trip you travel on the Fulda and Werra rivers and also on the river formed when these two meet at the tour's starting point of Hannoversch-Münden, the Weser. One of the company's three boats, the *Deutschland,* has a bowling alley aboard. Personenschifffahrt K. & K. Söllner has two excursion boats plying between Kassel and Hannoversch-Münden.

Boat Tours Flotte Weser ⊠ *Am Stockhof 2, Hameln* ☎ *05151/939–999* ⊕ *www.flotte-weser.de.* **Personenschifffahrt K. & K. Söllner** ⊠ *Die Schlagd,*

Kassel ☎ *0561/774–670* ⊕ *www.personenschiffahrt.com/kassel/route.html.*
Rehbein-Linie Kassel ✉ *Ostpreusenstr. 8, Fuldatal* ☎ *0561/18505* ⊕ *www.fahrgastschiffahrt.com.*

BUS TRAVEL

Bremen, Kassel, Göttingen, Fulda, and Hanau are all reachable via
Deutsche Touring's Europabus. A local bus serves the scenic Weser Valley Road stretch (B-80 and B-83), between Hannoversch-Münden and
Hameln; total distance is approximately 103 km (64 mi).

Year-round tours of the region are offered by Herter-Reisen.

Bus Tours Deutsche Touring ☎ *069/7903-501* ⊕ *www.touring.de.* **Herter-Reisen** ✉ *Hildesheimer Str. 6, Hameln/Afferde* ☎ *05159/969–244* ⊕ *www.herter-reisen.de.*

CAR TRAVEL

The best way to travel is by car. The autobahn network serves Hanau,
Fulda, Kassel, Göttingen, and Bremen directly, but you can't savor the
fairy-tale country from this high-speed superhighway. Bremen is 60 km
(35 mi) northwest of Hannover.

The Fairy-Tale Road incorporates one of Germany's loveliest scenic
drives, the Wesertalstrasse, or Weser Valley Road (B-80 and B-83),
between Hannoversch-Münden and Hameln; total mileage is approximately 103 km (64 mi).

TRAIN TRAVEL

Hanau, Fulda, Kassel, Göttingen, Hannover, and Bremen are reachable via InterCity Express (ICE) trains from Frankfurt and Hamburg.
Rail service, but not ICE service, is available to Hannoversch-Münden,
Marburg, and Hameln.

Train Information Deutsche Bahn ☎ *0800/150–7090* ⊕ *www.bahn.de.*

RESTAURANTS

In this largely rural area many restaurants serve hot meals only between
11:30 am and 2 pm, and 6 pm and 9 pm. You rarely need a reservation
here, and casual clothing is generally acceptable.

HOTELS

Make hotel reservations in advance if you plan to visit in summer.
Though it's one of the less-traveled tourist routes in Germany, the main
destinations on the Fairy-Tale Road are popular. Hannover is particularly busy during trade-fair times.

WHAT IT COSTS IN EUROS				
	¢	$	$$	$$$	$$$$
Restaurants	under €9	€9–€15	€16–€20	€21–€25	over €25
Hotels	under €50	€50–€100	€101–€175	€176–€225	over €225

Restaurant prices are per person for a main course at dinner. Hotel prices are for
two people in a standard double room, including tax and service.

PLANNING YOUR TIME

The Fairy-Tale Road isn't really for the traveler in a hurry. If you only have a day or two to savor it, concentrate on a short stretch of it. A good suggestion is the Weser River route between Hannoversch-Münden and Hameln. The landscape is lovely and the towns are romantic. If you have more time, but not enough to travel the whole route, focus on the southern half of the road. It's more in character with the fairy tales.

DISCOUNTS AND DEALS

Free summer weekend performances along the Fairy-Tale Road include Münchhausen plays in Bodenwerder, the Dr. Eisenbart reenactments in Hannoversch-Münden, the Town Musicians shows in Bremen, and especially the Pied Piper spectacle at Hameln. Kassel, Hannover, and Bremen also sell visitor cards that let you ride free on public transportation, grant reduced admissions at museums, and give other perks.

VISITOR INFORMATION

Deutsche Märchenstrasse ⊠ *Kurfürstenstr. 9, Kassel* ☎ *0561/9204–7911* ⊕ *www.deutsche-maerchenstrasse.de.*

HESSE

The first portion of the Fairy-Tale Road, from Hanau to Bad Karl-shafen, lies within the state of Hesse. Since much of the Hessian population is concentrated in the south, in such cities as Frankfurt, Darmstadt, and Wiesbaden, the northern part is quite rural, hilly, forested, and very pretty. Here you'll find Steinau, the almost vertical city of Marburg, and Kassel, all of which have associations with the Grimm brothers.

HANAU

16 km (10 mi) east of Frankfurt.

The Fairy-Tale Road begins in once-upon-a-time fashion at Hanau, the town where the Brothers Grimm were born. Although Grimm fans will want to start their pilgrimage here, Hanau is now a traffic-congested suburb of Frankfurt, with post–World War II buildings that are not particularly attractive.

ESSENTIALS

Visitor Information **Hanau** ⊠ *Tourist-Information Hanau, Am Markt 14–18* ☎ *06181/295–950* ⊕ *www.hanau.de.*

GETTING HERE AND AROUND

Less than a 50-minute S-bahn (S9) journey from Frankfurt Airport, Hanau is also reachable by high-speed ICE trains from Berlin and Munich, or a combination of ICE and regional trains from Hannover, Bremen, and Hamburg.

EXPLORING

Nationaldenkmal Brüder Grimm (*Brothers Grimm Memorial*). Hanau's main attraction can be reached only on foot—the Nationaldenkmal Brüder Grimm in the Marktplatz. The bronze memorial, erected in

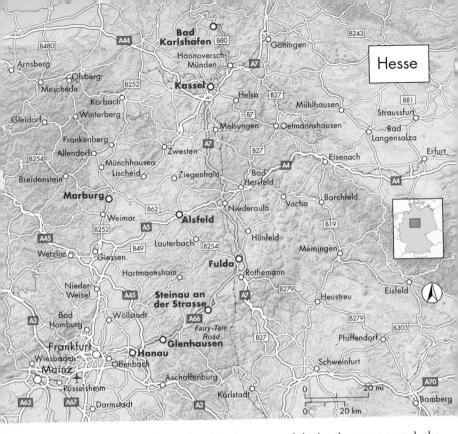

1898, is a larger-than-life-size statue of the brothers, one seated, the other leaning on his chair, the two of them pondering an open book.

Schloss Phillipsruhe. There is also a small Grimm exhibit, featuring clothing, artifacts, and writings, at Schloss Phillipsruhe, on the bank of the Main in the suburb of Kesselstadt (Bus 5 will take you there in 10 minutes). ■ TIP→ Historical Hanau treasures, including a priceless collection of faience, are also on display in the palace museum. ⊠ *Phillipsruher Allée 45* ☏ *06181/295–564* ⊕ *www.museen-hanau.de* .

Rathaus (*Town Hall*). The solid bulk of Hanau's 18th-century Rathaus stands behind the Grimm brothers' statue. Every day at noon its bells play tribute to another of the city's famous sons, the composer Paul Hindemith (1895–1963), by chiming out one of his canons. ⊠ *Marktpl. 14.*

GELNHAUSEN

20 km (12 mi) northeast of Hanau, 35 km (21 mi) northeast of Frankfurt.

Perched elegantly on the side of a hill above the Kinzig River, Gelnhausen's picturesque Altstadt (Old Town) offers the first taste of the half-timber houses and cobblestone streets that lie in abundance farther north. In spring and summer tours of school children dressed in traditional garb are guided down its winding streets and through lively little squares flanked by ice cream parlors and outdoor cafés, and listen to tales of Red Beard, and the fate of those poor townswomen suspected of being witches.

GETTING HERE AND AROUND

If you're flying into Frankfurt, Gelnhausen is an ideal spot for your first night on the Fairy-Tale Road. It's smaller and more charming than Hanau, and is still less than an hour's drive from Frankfurt's main airport. Trains to Gelnhausen leave from Frankfurt's main station every half hour and take approximately 35 minutes, and there are frequent connections from Hanau. Once here, the historic Old Town is hilly, but small enough to walk around, and, April through October, a walking tour leaves from the town hall at 2 on Sunday.

ESSENTIALS

Visitor Information Gelnhausen ⊠ *Tourist-Information, Obermarkt 7* ☎ *06051/830–300* ⊕ *www.gelnhausen.de.*

EXPLORING

Hexenturm (*Witches' Tower*). The Hexenturm, a grim prison, remains from the time when Gelnhausen was the center of a paranoiac witch hunt in the late 16th century. Dozens of women were burned at the stake or thrown—bound hand and foot—into the Kinzig River. Suspects were held in the Hexenturm of the town battlements. Today it houses a bloodcurdling collection of medieval torture instruments. Tours of the tower, in German only, are offered on Sunday afternoon from May through October. English-language tours for groups of up to 30 persons can be booked in advance for €57. ⊠ *Am Fratzenstein* ☎ *06051/830–300* ⊙ *May–Oct., tour Sun. at 2.*

Kaiserpfalz. On an island in the gentle little Kinzig River you'll find the remains of the Kaiserpfalz. Emperor Friedrich I—known as Barbarossa, or Red Beard—built the castle in this idyllic spot in the 12th century; in 1180 it was the scene of the first all-German Imperial Diet, a gathering of princes and ecclesiastical leaders. Today only parts of the russet walls and colonnaded entrance remain. Still, stroll beneath the castle's ruined ramparts on its water site, and you'll get a tangible impression of the medieval importance of the court of Barbarossa. ⊠ *Burgstr. 14* ☎ *06051/3805* ☑ *€3.50* ⊙ *Mar.–Oct., Tues.–Sun. 10–5; Nov. and Dec., Tues.–Sun. 10–4.*

WHERE TO STAY

For expanded hotel reviews, visit Fodors.com.

$$ 🏨 **Romantisches Hotel Burg Mühle.** *Mühle* means "mill," and this peaceful hotel, a few steps from the Kaiserpfalz and within an easy walk of the Altstadt, was once the castle's mill and sawmill. **Pros:** large rooms (many with balconies); spotlessly clean. **Con:** showing a little wear. ⊠ *Burgstr. 2* ☎ *06051/82050* ⊕ *www.burgmuehle.de* ⇄ *40 rooms* ⌂ *In-room: no a/c. In-hotel: restaurant, bar, business center* 🍽 *Breakfast.*

To begin your tour of the Grimm Brothers' fairytale landscape, head to the Nationaldenkmal Brüder Grimm (Brother's Grimm Memorial) in Hanau.

STEINAU AN DER STRASSE

30 km (18 mi) northeast of Gelnhausen, 65 km (40 mi) northeast of Frankfurt.

The little town of Steinau—full name Steinau an der Strasse (Steinau "on the road," referring to an old trade route between Frankfurt and Leipzig)—had a formative influence on the Brothers Grimm. They were preschoolers on arrival and under age 12 when they left after their father's untimely death.

Steinau dates from the 13th century, and is typical of villages in the region. Marvelously preserved half-timber houses are set along cobblestone streets; an imposing castle bristles with towers and turrets. In its woodsy surroundings you can well imagine encountering Little Red Riding Hood, Snow White, or Hansel and Gretel. A major street is named after the brothers; the building where they lived is now known as the Brothers Grimm House.

GETTING HERE AND AROUND

Regional trains leave hourly from Gelnhausen and take about 15 minutes to reach Steinau an der Strasse. The train station is just more than a kilometer from the Old Town's center and, should the walk be too far, the MKK90 bus into the town leaves hourly; get off at Ringstrasse. A city walking tour takes place April to October, the first Sunday of the month, leaving at 2 from the Märchenbrunnen (fountain).

ESSENTIALS

Visitor Information Steinau an der Strasse ⊠ *Verkehrsbüro, Brüder-Grimm-Str. 70* ☎ *06663/96310* ⊕ *www.steinau.eu.*

The Brothers Grimm

12

The Grimm fairy tales originated in the southern part of the Märchenstrasse. This area, mainly in the state of Hesse, was the home region of the brothers Jacob (1785–1863) and Wilhelm (1786–1859) Grimm. They didn't conceive the stories for which they are famous. Their feat was to mine the great folklore tradition that was already deeply ingrained in local culture.

For generations, eager children had been gathering at dusk around the village storyteller to hear wondrous tales of fairies, witches, and gnomes, tales passed down from storytellers who had gone before. The Grimms sought out these storytellers and recorded their tales.

The result was the two volumes of their work *Kinder- und Hausmärchen* (*Children's and Household Tales*), published in 1812 and 1814 and revised and expanded six times during their lifetimes. The last edition, published in 1857, is the basis for the stories we know today. Earlier versions contained more violence and cruelty than was deemed suitable for children.

That is how the world got the stories of Cinderella, Sleeping Beauty, Hansel and Gretel, Little Red Riding Hood, Snow White and the Seven Dwarfs, Rumpelstiltskin, Puss-in-Boots, Mother Holle, Rapunzel, and some 200 others, most of which remain unfamiliar.

Both Jacob and Wilhelm Grimm had distinguished careers as librarians and scholars, and probably would be unhappy to know that they are best remembered for the fairy tales. Among other things, they began what would become the most comprehensive dictionary of the German language and produced an analysis of German grammar.

The brothers were born in Hanau, near Frankfurt, which has a statue memorializing them and a Grimm exhibit at Schloss Phillipsruhe. They spent their childhood in Steinau, 30 km (18 mi) to the north, where their father was magistrate. There are two Grimm museums there, one in their home. On their father's untimely death they moved to their mother's home city of Kassel. It, too, has an important Grimm museum. They attended the university at Marburg from 1802 to 1805, then worked as librarians in Kassel. It was in the Kassel area that they found the best of their stories. They later worked as librarians and professors in the university town of Göttingen, and spent their last years as academics in Berlin.

EXPLORING

★ **Brüder Grimm Haus and Museum Steinau.** Occupying the house where the Brothers Grimm lived for much of their preadolescent lives and the house's old barn, respectively, the Brüder Grimm Haus and Museum Steinau are fun and engaging, modern little museums. Featuring a reconstruction of the family's old kitchen, the brothers' former house also displays old personal posessions such as letters and reading glasses, and has an upper floor divided into 10 rooms with interactive displays that celebrate the Grimms' stories and other fairy tales from around Europe. Across a small courtyard, the town's museum documents what life was like on the old trade route that ran through Steinau, incorporating into its exhibits a coach, inn signs, milestones, and the type of pistols travelers used to defend themselves from bandits. ✉ *Brüder-Grimm-Str. 80* ☎ *06663/7605* ⊕ *www.museum-steinau.de* ✑ *€3* ⊘ *Daily noon–5; closed 2 wks in late Dec.*

★ **Schloss Steinau** (*Steinau Castle*). Schloss Steinau is straight out of a Grimm fairy tale. It stands at the top of the town, with a "Fairy-tale Fountain" in front of it. Originally an early-medieval fortress, it was rebuilt in Renaissance style between 1525 and 1558 and first used by the counts of Hanau as their summer residence. Later it was used to guard the increasingly important trade route between Frankfurt and Leipzig. It's not difficult to imagine the young Grimm boys playing in the shadow of its great gray walls or venturing into the encircling dry moat.

The castle houses a **Grimm Museum,** one of two in Steinau, as well as an exhibition of marionettes from the marionette theater. The Grimm Museum exhibits the family's personal effects, including portraits of the Grimm relatives, the family Bible, an original copy of the Grimms' dictionary (the German equivalent of the Oxford English Dictionary), and all sorts of mundane things such as spoons and drinking glasses. Climb the tower for a breathtaking view of Steinau and the countryside. ☎ *06663/6843* ✑ *Museum €2.50, tower €1, tour of castle and museum €4* ⊘ *Mar.–Oct., Tues.–Thurs. and weekends 10–5; Nov.–mid-Dec., Tues.–Thurs. and weekends 10–4.*

☾ **Steinauer Marionettentheater** (*Steinau Marionette Theater*). The Steinauer Marionettentheater is in the castle's former stables and portrays Grimm fairy tales and other children's classics. Performances are held most weekends at 3. ✉ *Am Kumpen 4* ☎ *06663/245* ⊕ *www.die-holzkoeppe. de* ✑ *€6.50.*

WHERE TO EAT AND STAY

For expanded hotel reviews, visit Fodors.com.

$

GERMAN

✕ **Brathähnchenfarm.** This cheery hotel-restaurant is a long, long way from the center of Steinau, uphill all the way. But it's worth it. As your nose will tell you immediately, just about everything on the menu is charcoal-grilled. The name *"Brathähnchenfarm"* (Roast Chicken Farm) sets the theme, though other grilled meats are available. It is, in addition, a place of peace and quiet. ✉ *Im Ohl 1* ☎ *06663/228* ⊕ *www. brathaehnchenfarm.de* ▭ *No credit cards* ⊘ *Closed Mon. and late Dec.–mid-Feb.*

$ ⌂ **Burgmannenhaus.** Previously a 16th-century customs house, sitting on 1,000-year old foundations and a secret tunnel that runs to the nearby Schloss and church, this friendly travelers' inn is the type of place made for history buffs. **Pros:** in the middle of Steinau; tasty regional beer on tap. **Cons:** restaurant ($) serves solid, if unspectacular German food; Wi-Fi signal sometimes hard to pick up in guest rooms. ✉ *Brüder Grimm Str. 49, Steinau an der Strasse* ☎ *06663/912–436* ⊕ *www.burgmannenhaus-steinau.de* ⇗ *5* ⌂ *In-room: no a/c, Wi-Fi. In-hotel: restaurant, parking.*

FULDA

32 km (20 mi) northeast of Steinau an der Strasse, 100 km (62 mi) northeast of Frankfurt.

The Episcopal city of Fulda is well worth a detour off the Fairy-Tale Road. There are two distinct parts to its downtown area. One is a stunning display of baroque architecture, replete with cathedral, orangerie, and formal garden, which grew up around the palace. The other is the Old Town, where the incredibly narrow and twisty streets are lined with boutiques, bistros, and a medieval tower. ■TIP→ You'll find Kanalstrasse and Karlstrasse in the Old Town lined with good but inexpensive cafés and restaurants, ranging from German to Mediterranean.

GETTING HERE AND AROUND

Intercity Express trains connect Fulda with Frankfurt, Hannover and Hamburg, while regional trains link the city with many other Fairy-Tale Road destinations. Within Fulda itself, the Old Town and the city's other main attractions are all in walking distance of each other. Fulda's walking tours offer a recording with earphones, enabling you to follow the German tours in English. These start at the tourist office on Bonifatiusplatz, daily at 11:30 and 3.

ESSENTIALS

Visitor Information **Fulda** ⊠ *Tourismus- und Kongressmanagement, Bonifatiuspl. 1* ☎ *0661/102–1813* ⊕ *www.tourismus-fulda.de.*

EXPLORING

Dom. The Dom, Fulda's 18th-century cathedral with tall twin spires, stands on the other side of the broad boulevard that borders the palace park. The basilica accommodated the ever-growing number of pilgrims who converged on Fulda to pray at the grave of the martyred St. Boniface, the "Apostle of the Germans." A black alabaster bas-relief depicting his death marks the martyr's grave in the crypt.

Cathedral Museum. The Cathedral Museum contains a document bearing St. Boniface's writing, along with several other treasures, including Lucas Cranach the Elder's fine 16th-century painting *Christ and the Adulteress.* ☎ *0661/87207* ⊠ *€2.10* ⊗ *Apr.–Oct., Tues.–Sat. 10–5:30, Sun. 12:30–5:30; Nov., Dec., and mid-Feb.–Mar., Tues.–Sat. 10–12:30 and 1:30–4, Sun. 12:30–4* ⊠ *Eduard Schick Pl. 1–3* ⊗ *Apr.–Oct., daily 10–6; Nov.–Mar., daily 10–5.*

☻ **Kinder-Akademie-Fulda.** It's called Germany's first children's museum, with interactive objects from science and technology, including a "walkthrough heart." ⊠ *Mehlerstr. 4* ☎ *0661/902–730* ⊕ *www.kaf.de* ⊠ *€6* ⊗ *Weekdays 10–5:30, Sun. 1–5:30, and Apr.–Oct., Sat. 1–5.30.*

Stadtschloss (*City Palace*). The city's grandest example of baroque design is the immense Stadtschloss, formerly the residence of the prince-bishops. The **Fürstensaal** (Princes' Hall), on the second floor, provides a breathtaking display of baroque decorative artistry, with ceiling paintings by the 18th-century Bavarian artist Melchior Steidl, and fabric-clad walls. The palace also has permanent displays of the faience for which Fulda was once famous, as well as some fine Fulda porcelain.

Also worth seeing is the **Spiegelsaal,** with its many tastefully arranged mirrors. Pause at the windows of the Grünes Zimmer (Green Chamber) to take in the view across the palace park to the **Orangerie,** a large garden with summer-flowering shrubs and plants. ⊠ *Schlossstr. 1* ☎ *0661/102–1813* ⊡ *€3.50* ⊗ *Sat.–Thurs. 10–5, Fri. 2–5.*

⊛ **Vonderau Museum.** The Vonderau Museum is housed in a former Jesuit seminary. Its exhibits chart the cultural and natural history of Fulda and eastern Hesse. A popular section of the museum is its **planetarium,** with a variety of shows, including one for children. Since it has only 35 seats, an early reservation is advisable. Shows take place Friday at 7, Saturday and Sunday at 2, 3, and 4. ⊠ *Jesuitenpl. 2* ☎ *0661/928–350* ⊡ *Museum €3.50; planetarium €4.00* ⊗ *Tues.–Sun. 10–5.*

WHERE TO EAT AND STAY
For expanded hotel reviews, visit Fodors.com.

¢   ╳ **La Gondola.** The faded interior of this popular Italian restaurant in
ITALIAN   the Altstadt pedestrian zone may be at odds with the gold lettering and elegant window frames adorning its façade, but it's cozy and welcoming nonetheless. A local favorite for more than a quarter century, La Gondola serves homemade pasta, pizza (also family size), and salad; and the health-conscious can even enjoy a whole-wheat pizza. ⊠ *Karlstr. 29* ☎ *0661/71711.*

$ ╳ **Zum Stiftskämmerer.** This former episcopal treasurer's home, some-
GERMAN   what removed from the center of town, is now a charming tavern-restaurant, its menu packed with local fare prepared with imagination. A four-course menu priced around €30 is an excellent value, although à la carte dishes can be ordered for as little as €4.80. Try the *Schlemmertöpfchen,* a delicious (and very filling) combination of pork, chicken breast, and venison. ⊠ *Kämmerzeller Str. 10* ☎ *0661/52369* ⊕ *www.stiftskaemmerer.de* ⊗ *Lunch 11:30-2, Dinner 6 onward* ⊗ *Closed Tues.*

$$ ⊡ **Maritim Hotel am Schlossgarten.** At the luxurious showpiece of the Maritim chain, guests can breakfast beneath frescoed ceilings and enormous chandeliers in a stunning 18th-century orangerie overlooking Fulda Palace Park. **Pros:** large, comfortable rooms; lovely terrace with views of park and nearby cathedral. **Cons:** no air-conditioning; breakfast not included. ⊠ *Pauluspromenade 2* ☎ *0661/2820* ⊕ *www.maritim.de* ⊷ *111 rooms, 1 suite* ⊘ *In-room: no a/c, Internet. In-hotel: restaurant, bar, pool, some pets allowed* ⊠⊙ *No meals.*

$$ ⊡ **Romantik Hotel Goldener Karpfen.** An institution in Fulda for more than
★   a hundred years, the Goldener Karpfen has remained family-owned and -run, with its elegant disposition and engaging hosts attracting singers, actors, and archbishops through its doors. **Pros:** luxury lodging; a short stroll to the town's major attractions; excellent breakfast buffet. **Cons:** expensive; public spaces can feel cluttered with knickknacks. ⊠ *Simpliziusbrunnen 1* ☎ *0661/86800* ⊕ *www.hotel-goldener-karpfen.de* ⊷ *46 rooms, 4 suites* ⊘ *In-room: no a/c, Internet, Wi-Fi. In-hotel: restaurant, bar, some pets allowed* ⊠⊙ *Breakfast.*

EN ROUTE Marburg is the next major stop on the road. Take B-254 to **Alsfeld** (34 km [21 mi] northwest of Fulda), where you can make a short stop to admire its half-timber houses and narrow streets; then take B-62 into Marburg.

EATING WELL ON THE FAIRY-TALE ROAD

A specialty of northern Hesse is sausages with *Beulches,* made from potato balls, leeks, and black pudding. *Weck,* which is local dialect for "heavily spiced pork," appears either as *Musterweck,* served on a roll, or as *Weckewerk,* a frying-pan concoction with white bread. Heading north into Lower Saxony, you'll encounter the ever-popular *Speck-kuchen,* a heavy and filling onion tart. Another favorite main course is *Pfefferpothast,* a sort of heavily browned goulash with lots of pepper. Trout and eels are common in the rivers and streams around Hameln, and by the time you reach Bremen, North German cuisine has taken over the menu. *Aalsuppe grün,* eel soup seasoned with dozens of herbs, is a must in summer, and the hearty *Grünkohl mit Pinkel,* a cabbage dish with sausage, bacon, and cured pork, appears in winter. Be sure to try the coffee. Fifty percent of the coffee served in Germany comes from beans roasted in Bremen. The city has been producing the stuff since 1673, and knows just how to serve it in pleasantly cozy or, as locals say, *gemütlich* surroundings.

Alsfeld's **Altes Rathaus** (Old Town Hall) was built in 1512. Its facade—combining a ground floor of stone arcades; half-timber upper reaches; and a dizzyingly steep, top-heavy slate roof punctuated by two pointed towers shaped like witches' hats—would look right at home in Walt Disney World.

MARBURG

60 km (35 mi) northwest of Fulda.

Fodor's Choice ★

"I think there are more steps in the streets than in the houses." That is how Jacob Grimm described the half-timber hillside town of Marburg, which rises steeply from the Lahn River to the spectacular castle that crowns the hill. Many of the winding, crooked "streets" are indeed stone staircases, and several of the hillside houses have back doors five stories above the front doors. The town's famous university and its students are the main influence on its social life, which pulses through the many cafés, restaurants, and student hangouts around the marketplace. The Grimms themselves studied here from 1802 to 1805.

Many of the streets are closed to traffic, and are filled with outdoor tables when the weather cooperates. There is a free elevator near the tourist-information office on Pilgrimstein that can transport you from the level of the river to the Old Town.

GETTING HERE AND AROUND

Two hours away from Fulda by train, the cheapest way to get here is by taking a regional train to the town of Giessen, and changing there; and every two hours a regional train runs between Marburg and Kassel. By car, take the B-254 and then B-62 from Fulda.

ESSENTIALS

Visitor Information Marburg ⊠ *Tourismus und Marketing, Pilgrimstein 26* ☎ *06421/99120* ⊕ *www.marburg.de.*

Many of Marburg's cobblestone streets are pedestrian-only zones, perfect for strolling and people-watching.

EXPLORING

Elisabethkirche (*St. Elizabeth Church*). Marburg's most important building is the Elisabethkirche, which marks the burial site of St. Elizabeth (1207–31), the town's favorite daughter. She was a Hungarian princess, betrothed at age 4 and married at 14 to a member of the nobility, Ludwig IV of Thuringia. In 1228, when her husband fell in one of the Crusades, she gave up all worldly pursuits. She moved to Marburg, founded a hospital, gave her wealth to the poor, and spent the rest of her very short life (she died at the age of 24) in poverty, caring for the sick and the aged. She is largely responsible for what Marburg became. Because of her selflessness she was made a saint only four years after her death. The Teutonic Knights built the Elisabethkirche, which quickly became the goal of pilgrimages, enabling the city to prosper. You can visit the shrine in the sacristy that once contained her bones, a masterpiece of the goldsmith's art. The church is a veritable museum of religious art, full of statues and frescoes. Walking tours of Marburg begin at the church on Saturday at 3, year-round. ⊠ *Elisabethstr. 1.*

WHERE TO EAT AND STAY

For expanded hotel reviews, visit Fodors.com.

¢ ✕ **Cafe Vetter.** This café has the most spectacular view in town—and
GERMAN Marburg is famous for its panoramas. Both an outdoor terrace and a glassed-in terrace take full advantage of the site. The ambience of this institution, four generations in the same family, is "Viennese coffeehouse traditional," and the homemade cakes and chocolate creams are hard to resist. They also have piano music on weekend afternoons and

jazz on the occasional Friday evening. ✉ *Reitgasse 4* ☎ *06421/25888* 🌐 *www.cafe-vetter-marburg.de* ▭ *No credit cards* ⏲ *No dinner.*

¢ GERMAN ✕ **Weinlädele.** If you've tired of the big glasses of beer and plates of enormous schnitzel on offer in many of Marburg's traditional eating establishments, this half-timbered wine bar's fine selection of German wines, and light, crispy *Flammkuchen* (Tarte Flambe) is a welcome respite. Just up the street from the Old Town's main marketplace, it specializes in wines produced outside of Hesse, and is popular with patrons of all ages. When the weather is good, get there early, grab a table on its little terrace for a view down the hill, order a cheese platter and glass of white, and watch the world idle by. ✉ *Schlosstreppe 1, Marburg* ☎ *06421/14244* 🌐 *www.weinlaedele.com.*

$$ **Welcome Hotel am Schlossberg.** While the plain facade of this large, modern hotel may suffer in comparison with much of Marburg's traditional architecture, its generous rooms, comfy beds and excellent breakfast buffet are certain to draw guests back. **Pros:** across from the elevator to the Altstadt. **Cons:** no real views from many of the rooms. ✉ *Pilgrimstein 29* ☎ *06421/9180* 🌐 *www.schlossberg-marburg.de* *147 rooms, 3 suites* *In-room: Internet, Wi-Fi. In-hotel: restaurant, bar, parking, some pets allowed* *Breakfast.*

KASSEL

100 km (62 mi) northeast of Marburg.

The Brothers Grimm lived in Kassel, their mother's hometown, as teenagers, and also worked there as librarians at the court of the king of Westphalia, Jerome Bonaparte (Napoléon's youngest brother), and for the elector of Kassel. In their researching of stories and legends, their best source was not books but storyteller Dorothea Viehmann, who was born in the Knallhütte tavern, which is still in business in nearby Baunatal.

Much of Kassel was destroyed in World War II, and the city was rebuilt with little regard for its architectural history. The city's museums and the beautiful Schloss Wilhelmshöhe and Schlosspark, however, are well worth a day or two of exploration.

GETTING HERE AND AROUND

On a main Intercity Express line between Munich and Hamburg, you can also travel to Kassel-Wilhelmshöhe from Hannover and Bremen by high-speed train. By car, travel northeast from Marburg on the B-3 to Borken, then take autobahn A-49 into Kassel.

TOURS

Guided bus tours of Kassel set off from the Stadttheater on Saturday at 2.

DISCOUNTS AND DEALS

When you arrive, you may want to purchase a **Kassel Card.** This entitles you to a reduced rate for the city bus tour, free travel on the local transportation system, and reduced admission to the museums and the casino. It's available at the tourist office for €13 for one day and €16 for three days.

ESSENTIALS

Visitor Information Kassel ✉ *Marketing GmbH, Obere Königstr. 15* ☎ *0561/707–707* ⊕ *www.kassel.de.*

EXPLORING

Fodor's Choice ★ **Schloss und Schlosspark Wilhelmshöhe** (*Wilhelmshöhe Palace and Palace Park*). The magnificent grounds of the 18th-century Schloss und Schlosspark Wilhelmshöhe, at the western edge of Kassel, are said to be Europe's largest hill park. If you have time, plan to spend an entire day here exploring the various gardens, museums, and wooded pathways. Wear good walking shoes and bring some water if you want to hike all the way up to the giant statue of Hercules that crowns the hilltop.

The Wilhelmshöher Park was laid out as a baroque park in the early 18th century, its elegant lawns separating the city from the thick woods of the Habichtswald (Hawk Forest). Schloss Wilhelmshöhe was added between 1786 and 1798. The great palace stands at the end of the 5-km-long (3-mi-long) Wilhelmshöher Allée, an avenue that runs straight as an arrow from one side of the city to the other.

Staatliche Museen. Its esteemed collection includes 11 Rembrandts, as well as outstanding works by Rubens, Hals, Jordaens, Van Dyck, Dürer, Altdorfer, Cranach, and Baldung Grien.

Löwenburg (*Lion Fortress*). Amid the thick trees of the Wilhelmshöher Park, it comes as something of a surprise to see the turrets of a romantic medieval castle, the Löwenburg, breaking the harmony. There are more surprises, for this is no true medieval castle but a fanciful, stylized copy of a Scottish castle, built 70 years after the Hercules statue that towers above it. The Löwenburg contains a collection of medieval armor and weapons, tapestries, and furniture. ☎ *0561/3168–0244* 🎟 *€4 including tour* ⊗ *Mar.–Oct., Tues.–Sun. 10–5; Nov.–Feb., Tues.–Sun. 10–4.*

Statue of Hercules. The giant 18th-century statue of Hercules that crowns the Wilhelmshöhe heights is an astonishing sight. You can climb the stairs of the statue's castlelike base—and the statue itself—for a rewarding look over the entire city. At 2:30 pm on Sunday and Wednesday from mid-May through September, water gushes from a fountain beneath the statue, rushes down a series of cascades to the foot of the hill, and ends its precipitous journey in a 175-foot-high jet of water. A café lies a short walk from the statue. ✉ *Schlosspark 3* ☎ *0561/312–456* 🎟 *€3* ⊗ *Mar.–Oct., Tues.–Sun. 10–5* ✉ *Schloss Wilhelmshöhe* ☎ *0561/316–800* ⊕ *www.wilhelmshoehe.de* 🎟 *Schloss €6* ⊗ *Tues., Wed., and Fri.–Sun. 10–5; Thurs. 10–8.*

WHERE TO EAT AND STAY

For expanded hotel reviews, visit Fodors.com.

$ | ✕ **Brauhaus Knallhütte.** This brewery-cum-inn, established in 1752, was
GERMAN | the home of village storyteller Dorothea Viehmann. The Grimms got the best of their stories from her, including "Little Red Riding Hood," "Hansel and Gretel," and "Rumpelstiltskin." To this day "Dorothea" tells her stories here (unfortunately only in German) every Saturday at 5:30. The Knallhütte was once a wayside inn on the road to Frankfurt. That road is now the autobahn, making the tavern a superhighway rest

Climb to the top of the Schloss und Schlosspark Wilhelmshöhe where a giant statue of Hercules and a fantastic view of Kassel await.

stop. You'll find it on autobahn A-49 between the Baunatal Nord and Baunatal Mitte exits. You can dine at the restaurant at any time. With prior notice, you can tour the brewery and sample the beer and food for €15.90. ⊠ *Knallhütte. 1, Baunatal-Rengershausen* ☎ *0561/492–076* ⊕ *www.knallhuette.de.*

$$ ★ 🏨 **Hotel Gude.** It may be 10 minutes by tram away from the city center, but this modern, friendly hotel's spacious rooms, sauna, pool, and Pfeffermühle restaurant ($$$) justify the journey. **Pros:** close to the autobahn; easy parking; comfortable beds. **Cons:** removed from the city center; on a busy street. ⊠ *Frankfurter Str. 299* ☎ *0561/48050* ⊕ *www. hotel-gude.de* ↪ *84 rooms, 1 suite* ⌂ *In-room: no a/c, Internet. In-hotel: restaurant, bar, pool, parking, some pets allowed* ❏ *Breakfast.*

$$ 🏨 **Schlosshotel Wilhelmshöhe.** This hotel sits right beside the baroque gardens and woodland paths of the hilltop Wilhelmshöhe Park. **Pros:** tranquil atmosphere; historic setting. **Cons:** contemporary hotel, despite its romantic name. ⊠ *Am Schlosspark 8* ☎ *0561/30880* ⊕ *www. schlosshotel-kassel.de* ↪ *98 rooms, 3 suites* ⌂ *In-room: no a/c, Wi-Fi. In-hotel: restaurant, bar, some pets allowed.*

BAD KARLSHAFEN

50 km (31 mi) north of Kassel.

Popular with holidaymakers in mobile homes and caravans, who park up on the banks of the Weser directly across from its historic center, Bad Karlshafen's a pretty little spa town whose baroque architecture, while impressive, is showing some signs of wear and tear. Best viewed from the campsite side of the river, the town is surrounded by hills covered in dense forest and has for some time also found favor as a health resort. Its elevation and rural location provide fresh air, and there are salt springs that the locals believe can cure whatever ails you.

GETTING HERE AND AROUND

Regional trains run here from Göttingen, but infrequently so check train timetables well ahead of any visit.

ESSENTIALS

Visitor Information **Bad Karlshafen** ⊠ *Kur- und Touristik-Information, Hafenpl. 8* ☎ *05672/999–922* ⊕ *www.bad-karlshafen.de.*

EXPLORING

Rathaus. Bad Karlshafen's baroque beauty stands in surprising contrast to the abundance of half-timber architecture found along the rest of the Weser, and its stately Rathaus is the town's best example. A walking tour leaves from here on Sunday at 3, May through October. ⊠ *Hafenpl. 8.*

Weser-Therme. The Weser-Therme is a huge spa facility with whirlpools, sauna and steam baths, thermal saltwater pools, and an outdoor pool that supposedly is as salty as the Dead Sea. Sitting on the banks of the Weser River, the spa's waters are famed for their therapeutic benefits, and a couple of hours bathing in them is sure to help relieve aches and stress. Massages are available to further aid the relaxation process. ⊠ *Kurpromenade 1, Bad Karlshafen* ☎ *05672/92110* ⊕ *www. wesertherme.de* 🖃 *€9.50 just pools, €13 for pools and sauna for 3 hrs* ⊗ *Daily 9 am–10 pm, Fri. and Sat. 9 am–11 pm.*

WHERE TO STAY

For expanded hotel reviews, visit Fodors.com.

$ 🖵 **Hotel zum Weserdampfschiff.** From the snug riverside rooms of this popular hotel-tavern, guests can watch passengers step directly off Weser pleasurecraft and into the hotel's welcoming beer garden below. **Pros:** river view; inexpensive rates; near spa facilities. **Cons:** on a busy street; rooms a bit small. ⊠ *Weserstr. 25* ☎ *05672/2425* ⊕ *www. weserdampfschiff.de* 🛏 *14 rooms* ♿ *In-room: no a/c, Wi-Fi. In-hotel: restaurant, some pets allowed* ☰ *No credit cards* ¶◯¶ *Breakfast.*

$ 🖵 **Hessischer Hof.** In the heart of town, this inn started as a tavern and now includes several comfortably furnished bedrooms, plus an apartment suitable for larger families and the numerous cycling groups that visit. **Pros:** centrally located; reasonable rates; friendly staff. **Cons:** no elevator; décor dated in places. ⊠ *Carlstr. 13–15* ☎ *05672/1059* ⊕ *www.hess-hof.de* 🛏 *20 rooms* ♿ *In-room: no a/c, Wi-Fi. In-hotel: restaurant, bar, some pets allowed* ¶◯¶ *Breakfast.*

EN ROUTE

Fürstenberg Porcelain factory. Germany's second-oldest porcelain factory is at Fürstenberg, 8 km (5 mi) south of Höxter, in a baroque castle high above the Weser River. The crowned Gothic letter *F*, which serves as its trademark, is world famous. You'll find Fürstenberg porcelain in Bad Karlshafen and Höxter, but it's more fun to journey to the 18th-century castle where production first began in 1747, and buy directly from the manufacturer. Fürstenberg and most dealers will take care of shipping arrangements and any tax refunds. Tours of the factory in English are possible with advance notice. There's also a sales outlet, museum, and café. ■TIP→ The view from the castle is a pastoral idyll, with the Weser snaking through the immaculately tended fields and woods. You can also spot cyclists on the riverside paths. ⊠ *Schloss Fürstenberg* ☎ *05271/401–161* ⊕ *www.fuerstenberg-porzellan.com* 🖼 *Museum €5* ⊙ *Museum: Apr.–Oct., Tues.–Sun. 10–5; Nov.–Mar., weekends 10–5. Shop: mid-Jan.–Oct., Tues.–Sun. 10–6.*

LOWER SAXONY

Lower Saxony (Niedersachsen) was formed from an amalgamation of smaller states in 1946. Its picturesque landscape includes one of Germany's most haunting river roads, along the Weser River between Hannoversch-Münden and Hameln. This road, part of the Fairy-Tale Road, follows green banks that hardly show where the water ends and the land begins. Standing sentinel are superb little towns whose half-timber architecture gave rise to the expression "Weser Renaissance." The Lower Saxon landscape also includes the juniper bushes and flowering heather of the Lüneburg Heath.

HANNOVERSCH-MÜNDEN

24 km (15 mi) north of Kassel, 150 km (93 mi) south of Hannover.

★ This delightful town, seemingly untouched by the modern age, shouldn't be missed. You'll have to travel a long way through Germany to find a grouping of half-timber houses (700 of them) as harmonious as these. The town is surrounded by forests and the Fulda and Werra rivers, which join here and flow northward as the Weser River.

Much is made of the fact that the quack doctor to end all quacks died here. Dr. Johann Andreas Eisenbart (1663–1727) would be forgotten today if a ribald 19th-century drinking song ("*Ich bin der Doktor Eisenbart, widda, widda, wit, boom! boom!*") hadn't had him shooting out aching teeth with a pistol, anesthetizing with a sledgehammer, and removing boulders from the kidneys. He was, as the song has it, a man who could make "the blind walk and the lame see." This is terribly exaggerated, of course, but the town takes advantage of it.

GETTING HERE AND AROUND

Regional trains linking Hannoversch Münden to both Kassel and Göttingen run every hour. A walking tour of town takes place May to October, leaving daily at 10 and 2 from the town hall.

ESSENTIALS

Visitor Information **Hannoversch-Münden** ⊠ *Touristik Naturpark Münden, Lotzestr. 2* ☎ *05541/75313* ⊕ *www.hann.muenden.de.*

EXPLORING

City Tourist Office. Hannoversch-Münden stages Eisenbart plays 11:15 am on Sunday May to August. The doctor also has "office hours" in the town hall at 1:30 on Saturday from mid-May through October; and a glockenspiel on the town hall depicts Eisenbart's feats, to the tune of the Eisenbart song, daily throughout the year at noon, 3 pm, and 5 pm. There's a statue of the doctor in front of his home at Langestrasse 79, and his grave is outside the St. Ägidien Church. For information on the Dr. Eisenbart plays, contact the City Tourist Office. ☎ *05541/75313* ⊕ *www.hann.muenden.de.*

GÖTTINGEN

30 km (19 mi) northeast of Hannoversch-Münden, 110 km (68 mi) south of Hannover.

Distinguished by its famous university, where the Brothers Grimm served as professors and librarians between 1830 and 1837, the fetching town of Göttingen's streets buzz with student life. Young people on bikes zip past bookshops and secondhand boutiques while evenings see the town's cozy bars and cafés swell with students making the most of the drinks specials and free Wi-Fi on offer. Full of elegant, gable-roofed architecture, it's also a large and modern place and boasts the shiny stores, chain coffee shops, and other trappings you'd expect of a 21st-century German town. Though not strictly on the Fairy-Tale Road, despite its association with the Grimms, Göttingen is still well worth visiting.

GETTING HERE AND AROUND

Göttingen is a stop on the same Intercity Express line between Munich and Hamburg as Kassel-Wilhelmshöhe, and is also easily reached from Bremen.

TOURS

Göttingen offers walking tours in English on the first and third Saturday of the month, April to October at 11 from the Old Town Hall.

ESSENTIALS

Visitor Information **Göttingen** ⊠ *Tourist-Information, Altes Rathaus, Markt 9* ☎ *0551/499–800* ⊕ *www.goettingen-tourismus.de.*

EXPLORING

Altes Rathaus (*Old Town Hall*). Behind the Gänseliesel statue is the Altes Rathaus, begun in the 13th century but basically a part-medieval, part-Renaissance building. The tourist-information office is located on the first floor. ⊠ *Markt 9* ☎ *0551/499–800* ⊕ *www.goettingen.de* 🖼 *Free* ☉ *Weekdays 9:30–6, weekends 10–4.*

Gänseliesel. The statue of Gänseliesel, the little Goose Girl of German folklore, stands in the central market square, symbolizing the strong link between the students and their university city. The girl, according to the story, was a princess who was forced to trade places with a peasant, and the statue shows her carrying her geese and smiling shyly into the waters of a fountain. The students of Göttingen gave her a ceremonial role: traditionally, graduates who earn a doctorate bestow a kiss of thanks upon Gänseliesel. Göttingen's citizens say she's the most kissed girl in the world.

WHERE TO EAT AND STAY
For expanded hotel reviews, visit Fodors.com.

$$ ╳ **Gaudi.** In a town rich with cozy taverns and hearty local food, this

MEDITERRANEAN Mediterranean restaurant, with its terra-cotta and blue color scheme,

arty chandeliers, and light, airy spaces, is as eclectic as its cuisine. Right in the middle of Göttingen's historic Börner Viertel, the restaurant is a favorite with staff from the university who feast on its fine consommés, tapas, pasta, and fish and meat dishes. It may not be the cheapest place in town, but the food and excellent service are worth the extra euros. ⊠ *Rote Str. 16* ☎ *0551/531–3001* ⊕ *www.restaurant-gaudi.de.*

$　✕ **Landgasthaus Lockemann.** If you like to walk and hike, consider this
GERMAN　half-timber lodge at the edge of the Stadtwald (city forest). Locals descend on the friendly, country-style restaurant for hearty German cooking ($). Take Bus 10 from the Busbahnhof, direction Herbershausen, to the last stop; then walk left on Im Beeke. The trip will take 20 minutes. ⊠ *Im Beeke 1* ☎ *0551/209–020* ⊕ *www.landgasthaus-lockemann.de* ▭ *No credit cards* ⊗ *Closed Mon.*

$　✕ **Zum Schwarzen Bären.** The "Black Bear" is one of Göttingen's old-
GERMAN　est tavern-restaurants, a 16th-century half-timber house that breathes
★　history and hospitality. Its specialties are *Bärenpfanne,* a generous mixture of beef, pork, and lamb (but no bear meat), and its wide selection of fried-potato dishes. ⊠ *Kurzestr. 12* ☎ *0551/58284* ⊗ *No lunch Mon.–Thur.*

$$$　🏨 **Romantik Hotel Gebhards.** This family-run hotel stands aloof and unflurried on its own grounds, a modernized 18th-century building that's something of a local landmark. **Pros:** across from the train station.

The virgin forests of Sababurg where Sleeping Beauty lay asleep for 100 years are still wild and dense.

Cons: on a busy street. ⊠ *Goethe-Allée 22–23* ☏ *0551/49680* ⊕ *www.gebhardshotel.de* ⇆ *45 rooms, 5 suites* ⚇ *In-room: no a/c. In-hotel: restaurant, some pets allowed* ⑩ *Breakfast.*

NIGHTLIFE

Among the delights of Göttingen are the ancient taverns where generations of students have lifted their steins. Among the best known are the Kleiner Ratskeller and Trou. Don't be shy about stepping into either of these taverns or any of the others that catch your eye; the food and drink are inexpensive, and the welcome is invariably warm and friendly.

EN ROUTE To pick up the Fairy-Tale Road where it joins the scenic Weser Valley Road, return to Hannoversch-Münden and head north on B-80. In the village of Veckerhagen take a left turn to the signposted Sababurg.

SABABURG

60 km (36 mi) west of Göttingen, 100 km (62 mi) south of Hannover.

GETTING HERE AND AROUND

Removed from the main highway, and with no rail connection to Sababurg, visits to Dornröschenschloss are best made by car.

★ **Dornröschenschloss** (*Sleeping Beauty's Castle*). Sababurg is home to the Dornröschenschloss. It stands just as the Grimm fairy tale tells us it did, in the depths of the densely wooded Reinhardswald, still inhabited by deer and wild boar. Today it's a fairly fancy hotel. Even if you don't stay the night, a drive to the castle is scenic. There's a nominal fee to tour the grounds, which include a rose garden and ruins.

🐾 **Tierpark Sababurg.** The Tierpark Sababurg is one of Europe's oldest wildlife refuges. Bison, red deer, wild horses, and all sorts of waterfowl populate the park. There's also a petting zoo for children. ✉ *Sababurg 1* ☎ *05671/766–4990* ⊕ *www.tierpark-sababurg.de* ☜ *€6* ⊙ *Apr.–Sept., daily 8–7; Oct., daily 9–6; Nov.–Feb., daily 10–4; Mar., daily 9–5.*

WHERE TO STAY

For expanded hotel reviews, visit Fodors.com.

$$ 🏰 **Dornröschenschloss Sababurg.** The medieval fortress thought to have inspired "Sleeping Beauty" is now a small luxury hotel, surrounded by a forest of oaks, a bit to the northeast of Hofgeismar. **Pros:** incredibly romantic. **Cons:** ordinary rooms; takes some effort to find the place. ✉ *Im Reinhardswald, Hofgeismar* ☎ *05671/8080* ⊕ *www.sababurg.de* 🛏 *18 rooms* ⚲ *In-room: no a/c. In-hotel: restaurant, some pets allowed* ⌖ *No meals.*

EN ROUTE

Trendelburg. A short distance away is another hilltop castle-hotel, Trendelburg, which also has a fairy-tale association. Legend has it that its tower is the one in which a wicked witch imprisoned Rapunzel. It's near the town of the same name on Route 83 between Hofgeismar and Bad Karlshafen. From Trendelburg follow Route 83 north to Bad Karlshafen. ✉ *Steinweg 1* ☎ *05675/9090.*

> ### HIKING AND WALKING
>
> Two protected nature parks—the Weserergland and the Lüneburg Heath—are in or near the Fairy-Tale Road. You can hike the banks of the Weser, stopping at ancient waterside inns, from Hannoversch-Münden, in the south, to Porta-Westfalica, where the Weser River breaks through the last range of North German hills and into the plain of Lower Saxony. The Lüneburg Heath is flat, and hiking is particularly pleasant in late summer, when the heather is in bloom. The tourist offices can tell you where to find nearby trails.

HÖXTER

24 km (14 mi) north of Bad Karlshafen, 100 km (62 mi) south of Hannover.

Overshadowed by Sababurg's claim to Sleeping Beauty's castle and Bodenwerder's Baron von Münchhausen, Höxter's connection to a fairy tale is limited to a small Hansel and Gretel fountain in the middle of town. One of the bigger towns in the Weser valley, its appeal instead lies in its Rathaus, a perfect example of the Weser Renaissance style, and proximity to the impressive Reichsabtei Corvey, which lies a short drive away.

GETTING HERE AND AROUND

Every couple of hours buses and regional trains run from Bad Karlshafen to Höxter Rathaus and take about 45 minutes, or you can take a combination of regional trains from Göttingen that take from 90 minutes to 2½ hours.

Between April and October, a town walking tour leaves from the Rathaus at 10 on Wednesday and Saturday.

ESSENTIALS

Visitor Information Höxter ⊠ *Touristik- und Kulturinformation, Historisches Rathaus, Westerbachstr. 45* ☎ *05271/963–431* ⊕ *www.hoexter.de.*

EXPLORING

Reichsabtei Corvey (*Imperial Abbey of Corvey*). The Reichsabtei Corvey, or Schloss Corvey, is idyllically set between the wooded heights of the Solling region and the Weser River. During its 1,200-year history it has provided lodging for several Holy Roman emperors. Heinrich Hoffmann von Fallersleben (1798–1874), author of the poem "Deutschland, Deutschland über Alles," worked as librarian here in the 1820s. The poem, set to music by Joseph Haydn, became the German national anthem in 1922. A music festival is held in the church and great hall, the Kaisersaal, in May and June. Corvey, also the name of the village, is reached on an unnumbered road heading east from Höxter (3 km [2 mi]) toward the Weser. There are signposts to "Schloss Corvey." ☎ *05271/68120* ⊕ *www.schloss-corvey.de* 🎫*€5, abbey church €0.60* ⊗ *Apr.–Oct., daily 10–6; Apr. and Oct., closed Mondays.*

WHERE TO EAT

$ ✕ **Schlossrestaurant.** In summer you can dine under centuries-old trees
GERMAN   at the Reichsabtei Corvey's excellent restaurant. ◾TIP➔ With advance
★   notice, a *Fürstenbankett*, or princely banquet, can be arranged for groups in the vaulted cellars. ⊠ *Reichsabtei Corvey* ☎ *05271/8323* ⊗ *Apr.–Oct., Tues.–Sat. 11–6, Sun. 9.30–6; May and Oct., closed Tuesdays.*

BODENWERDER

34 km (21 mi) north of Höxter, 70 km (43 mi) south of Hannover.

The charming Weser town of Bodenwerder is the home of the Lügenbaron (Lying Baron) von Münchhausen (1720–97), who was known as a teller of whoppers and whose fantastical tales included a story about riding a cannonball toward an enemy fortress but then, having second thoughts, returning to where he started by leaping onto a cannonball heading the other way. Stretched out along a peaceful valley, the nicest part of the town is around the Baron's old home, now the town hall, its half-timbered architecture set against a backdrop of the river and surrounding hills. A regular stop for cyclists on the Wesertal route, the town also attracts canoeists, and anglers who can tell their own whoppers about the one that got away.

ESSENTIALS

Visitor Information Bodenwerder ⊠ *Tourist-Information, Münchhausenpl. 3* ☎ *05533/40542* ⊕ *www.muenchhausenland.de.*

GETTING HERE AND AROUND

Reachable from Höxter by a combination of bus and regional train, or by bus from Hameln, changes are required along the way and any visits requiring public transport should be planned in advance.

12

EXPLORING

Münchhausen Museum. Housed in an old, renovated farm building right next to the imposing family home in which Baron von Münchhausen grew up (now the Rathaus), the Münchhausen Museum is crammed with mementos of his adventurous life, including his cannonball. A fountain in front of the house represents another story. The baron, it seems, was puzzled when his horse kept drinking insatiably at a trough. Investigating, he discovered that the horse had been cut in two by a closing castle gate and that the water ran out as fast as the horse drank. The water in the fountain, of course, flows from the rear of a half-horse. On the first Sunday of the month from May through October, townspeople retell von Münchhausen's life story with performances in front of the Rathaus. ⊠ *Münchhausenpl. 1* ☎ *05533/409–147* 🖃 *Museum €2* ⊙ *Apr.–Oct., daily 10–5.*

WHERE TO STAY

For expanded hotel reviews, visit Fodors.com.

$ 🖥 **Hotel Goldener Anker.** A friendly husband and wife run this hotel on the banks of the Weser. **Pros:** directly beside the river; friendly staff. **Cons:** standard rooms are very simple; close to the town's main bridge. ■TIP→ Pay the extra few euros and upgrade to a deluxe room with a river view, it's well worth the money spent. ⊠ *Brückenstr. 5, Bodenwerder* ☎ *05533/400–730* ⊕ *www.bodenwerder-hotel.de* 🛏 *12 rooms* ⏃ *In-room: Wi-Fi. In-hotel: restaurant, some pets allowed* ⏹ *Breakfast.*

$ 🖥 **Parkhotel Deutsches Haus.** Clean, comfortable, and friendly, this country hotel combines a traditional half-timber facade with an uncomplicated, if a little dated, interior styling. **Pros:** elevator; rooms get plenty of natural light. **Cons:** on a busy street; next to a large parking lot. ⊠ *Münchhausenpl. 4* ☎ *05533/3925* ⊕ *www.parkhotel-bodenwerder. de* 🛏 *39 rooms* ⏃ *In-room: no a/c, Internet, Wi-Fi. In-hotel: restaurant, bar, some pets allowed* ⏹ *Breakfast.*

HAMELN

24 km (15 mi) north of Bodenwerder, 47 km (29 mi) southwest of Hannover.

★   Given their relationship with one of the most famous fairy-tale characters of all time, it's unsurprising, but perhaps a little risky if legend is to be believed, that Hameln's townsfolk continue to take advantage of the Pied Piper. Known locally as the *Rattenfänger*, or "rat-catcher," these days he tends to be celebrated more than exploited (even if his name does adorn everything from coffee mugs to restaurants), and regular costumed tours through the town relive his deeds, while a bronze statue of him stands proudly in the town's lovely pedestrian zone. Not as exciting as Hannover to the north or as relaxing as Bodenwerder to the south, Hameln's fairy-tale legacy, elegantly painted and inscribed half-timber buildings, and laid-back atmosphere will, nonetheless, please plenty of its visitors.

GETTING HERE AND AROUND

45 minutes away from Hannover by S-bahn (S5), Hameln is within easy reach of the Lower Saxon capital.

TOURS

Walking tours of Hameln are held year-round, leaving from the tourist office (April to October, Monday to Saturday at 2:30 and Sunday at 10:15 and 2:30; November to March, Saturday at 2:30, Sunday at 10:15).

ESSENTIALS

Visitor Information Hameln ⊠ *Hameln Marketing und Tourismus, Deisterallee 1* ☎ *05151/957–823* ⊕ *www.hameln.de.*

EXPLORING

Hochzeitshaus (*Wedding House*). On central Osterstrasse you'll see several beautiful half-timber houses, including the Rattenfängerhaus (Rat-Catcher's House) and the Hochzeitshaus, a 17th-century Weser Renaissance building now containing city offices. From mid-May to mid-September the Hochzeitshaus terrace is the scene of two free open-air events commemorating the legend. Local actors and children present a half-hour reenactment each Sunday at noon, and there is now also a 40-minute musical, *Rats*, each Wednesday at 4:30. The carillon of the Hochzeitshaus plays tunes every day at 9:35 and 11:35, and mechanical figures enact the piper story on the west gable of the building at 1:05, 3:35, and 5:35.

WHERE TO EAT AND STAY

For expanded hotel reviews, visit Fodors.com.

$
GERMAN
★
✗ **Rattenfängerhaus.** This brilliant example of Weser Renaissance architecture is Hameln's most famous building, reputedly where the Pied Piper stayed during his rat-extermination assignment (actually, it wasn't built until centuries after his supposed exploits). A plaque in front of it fixes the date of the incident at June 26, 1284. "Rats" are all over the menu, from the "rat-killer liqueur" to a "rat-tail flambé." But don't be put off by the names: the traditional dishes are excellent. ⊠ *Osterstr. 28* ☎ *05151/3888* ⊕ *www.rattenfaengerhaus.de.*

$
☷ **Hotel zur Börse.** A few paces off Hameln's picturesque pedestrian and shopping zone, this pleasant, modern hotel is also within easy walking distance of the rest of the town's main attractions. **Pros:** in the pedestrian zone; flat-screen TVs. **Cons:** modern look that's out of place; bathrooms on the small side. ⊠ *Osterstr. 41a, entrance on Kopmanshof* ☎ *05151/7080* ⊕ *www.hotel-zur-boerse.de* ⤶ *31 rooms* ⌂ *In-room: no a/c. In-hotel: restaurant, bar, some pets allowed* ⊙ *Breakfast.*

$
★
☷ **Hotel zur Krone.** On the Old Town's pedestrian zone, Hotel zur Krone has a terrace that lets you watch locals coming and going, and afternoon coffee here is a summer delight. **Pros:** a half-timber marvel; lovely terrace. **Cons:** modern annex lacks charm; new guest rooms a little small. ⊠ *Osterstr. 30* ☎ *05151/9070* ⊕ *www.hotelzurkrone.de* ⤶ *32 rooms* ⌂ *In-room: no a/c, Wi-Fi. In-hotel: restaurant, some pets allowed* ⊙ *Breakfast.*

HANNOVER

47 km (29 mi) northeast of Hameln.

A little off the Fairy-Tale Road, and probably better known internationally as a trade-fair center than a tourist destination, the Lower Saxon capital's attractive mix of culture, arts, and nature justifies a visit here all the same. Home to leading museums, an opera house of international repute, and the finest baroque park in the country, it's a place that packs a surprising amount into a city of only half a million people. Conveniently centered between the city's main train station and its pleasant inner city lake, most of Hannover's major attractions, including its fine New and Old Town Halls, are within an easy walk of one another. In spring and summer the city's parks fill with picnicking families, while fall and winter are celebrated with the second biggest Oktoberfest in the world and cheery Christmas markets respectively.

GETTING HERE AND AROUND

Travel northeast from Hameln on autobahn A-33 to Hannover. There is also frequent direct rail service from Hameln. Hannover has an airport, and is served by the InterCity Express (ICE) trains and the Europabus. From April to October, city bus tours of Hannover leave daily at 11 from the tourist office.

DISCOUNTS AND DEALS

A **Hannover Card** entitles you to free travel on local transportation, reduced admission to seven museums, and discounts on certain sightseeing events and performances at the theater and opera. It's available through the tourist office for €9.50 per day (€16 for three days).

ESSENTIALS

Visitor Information **Hannover** ⊠ *Hannover Tourismus, Ernst-August-Pl. 8* ☎ *0511/1684–9700* ⊕ *www.hannover.de.*

EXPLORING

TOP ATTRACTIONS

Altes Rathaus (*Old Town Hall*). It took nearly 100 years, starting in 1410, to build this gabled brick edifice that once contained a merchants' hall and an apothecary. In 1844 it was restored to the style of about 1500. The facade's fired-clay frieze depicts coats of arms and representations of princes, and a medieval game somewhat comparable to arm wrestling. Inside is a modern interior with boutiques and a restaurant. ⊠ *Köbelingerstr. 2.*

Herrenhausen. The gardens of the former Hannoverian royal summer residence are the city's showpiece (the 17th-century palace was never rebuilt after wartime bombing). The baroque park is unmatched in Germany for its formal precision, with patterned walks, gardens, hedges, and chestnut trees framed by a placid moat. There is a fig garden with a collapsible shelter to protect it in winter and dining facilities behind a grotto. From Easter until October there are fireworks displays and fountains play for a few hours daily (weekdays 11–noon and 3–5, weekends 11–noon and 2–5). Herrenhausen is outside the city, a short ride on Tramline 4 or 5. ⊠ *Herrenhauserstr. 5* ☎ *0511/1684–4543* ⊕ *www.*

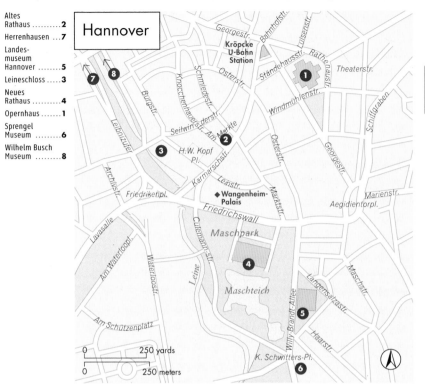

Hannover

hannover.de/herrenhausen €5 ☉ *Mar., Apr., and Sept., daily 9–7; May–Aug., daily 9–8; Oct., daily 9–6; Nov.–Feb., daily 9–4:30.*

Leineschloss. The former Hannoverian royal palace—whose members sat on the British throne from 1714 to 1837 as kings George I–IV—stands grandly beside the River Leine, and is now home to the Lower Saxony State Parliament. Although the interior of the palace is largely closed to the public, its imposing Corinthian columns and river setting provide some excellent photo opportunities. ⊠ *Hinrich-Wilhelm-Kopf-Pl. 1.*

Landesmuseum Hannover. The priceless art collection of this prestigious museum includes works by Tilman Riemenschneider, Veit Stoss, Hans Holbein the Younger, Claude Monet, and Lucas Cranach. There are also historical and natural history sections. ⊠ *Willy-Brandt-Allée 5* ☎ *0511/980–7686* ⊕ *www.nlmh.de* €4 ☉ *Tues., Wed., and Fri.–Sun. 10–5, Thurs. 10–7.*

Sprengel Museum. An important museum of modern art, the Sprengel holds major works by Max Beckmann, Max Ernst, Paul Klee, Emil Nolde, Oscar Schlemmer, Hans Arp, and Pablo Picasso. The street where it's located is named after Kurt Schwitters, a native son and prominent Dadaist, whose works are also exhibited. ⊠ *Kurt-Schwitters-Pl. 1* ☎ *0511/1684–3875* ⊕ *www.sprengel-museum.de* €7 ☉ *Tues. 10–8, Wed.–Sun. 10–6.*

WORTH NOTING

Neues Rathaus. The massive New Town Hall was built at the start of the 20th century in Wilhelmine style (for Kaiser Wilhelm), at a time when pomp and circumstance were important ingredients of heavy German bureaucracy. Four scale models on the ground floor depict Hannover in various stages of development and destruction: as a medieval walled city, in the years before World War II, immediately following World War II, and in its present-day form. An elevator rises diagonally to the dome for a splendid view. ⊠ *Trammpl. 2* ☎ *0511/1684–5333* 🎟 *Dome €2.50* ⊙ *Mar.–Oct., weekdays 9:30–6:30, weekends 10–6.30.*

TOURING TIPS

Scenic spot: The formal park and gardens at Herrenhausen, complete with moat and fountains, are a great photo op.

Red thread: Hannover's points of interest lie along a tourist trail marked by a red line on the sidewalk. It starts at the tourist office.

Opernhaus. Hannover's neoclassical opera house, completed in 1852, has two large wings and a covered, colonnaded portico adorned with statues of great composers and poets. The building originally served as the court theater, but now is used almost exclusively for opera. It was gutted by fire in a 1943 air raid and restored in 1948. ■TIP→ Unless you have tickets to a performance, the only part of the interior you can visit is the foyer with ticket windows. ⊠ *Opernpl. 1* ☎ *0511/9999–1111* ⊕ *www.staatstheater-hannover.de/oper.*

OFF THE BEATEN PATH

Wilhelm Busch Museum. This section of the Georgenpalais, near Herrenhausen, is devoted to the works of cartoonists and caricaturists through the centuries. Emphasis is on Wilhelm Busch, the "godfather of the comic strip," whose original drawings and effects are on display. More than a century ago, Busch (1832–1908) wrote and illustrated a very popular children's book, still in print, called *Max und Moritz*. The story tells of two boys who mixed gunpowder in the village tailor's pipe tobacco and, with fishing lines down the chimney, filched roasting chickens off the fire. The first American comic strip, *The Katzenjammer Kids* (1897), drew not only on Busch's naughty boys (they even spoke with a German accent) but also on his loose cartoon style. ⊠ *Georgengarten 1* ☎ *0511/1699–9916* ⊕ *www.karikatur-museum.de* 🎟 *€4.50* ⊙ *Tues.–Sun. 11–6.*

WHERE TO EAT

$$$
ECLECTIC
★

✕ **Basil.** Constructed in 1867 as a riding hall for the Royal Prussian military, this upmarket restaurant's home is as striking as the menu. Cast-iron pillars support the vaulted brick ceiling, and two-story drapes hang in the huge windows. The menu changes every few weeks and includes eclectic dishes from the Mediterranean to Asia. Game and white *Spargel* (asparagus) are served in season. ⊠ *Dragonerstr. 30* ☎ *0511/622–636* ⊕ *www.basil.de* ⊙ *Closed Sun. No lunch.*

$
GERMAN

✕ **Brauhaus Ernst August.** This brewery has so much artificial greenery that you could imagine yourself in a beer garden. Hannoverian pilsner is brewed on the premises, and regional specialties are the menu's focus. You can collect souvenirs there. Besides beer paraphernalia such as mugs and coasters, you can purchase, empty or full, a huge old-fashioned beer bottle with a wired porcelain stopper. There's live music on weekends and a DJ other nights. ✉ *Schmiedstr. 13* ☎ *0511/365–950* ⊕ *www.brauhaus.net.*

$

GERMAN

✕ **Grapenkieker.** An ancient pot steams in the aromatic, farmhouse-style kitchen, and simple, hearty fare prevails. Proprietor Karl-Heinz Wolf is locally famous for his culinary prowess and the warm welcome he gives his guests. The half-timber restaurant is 5 km (3 mi) from the city center, in the Isernhagen District, but it's well worth seeking out. ✉ *Hauptstr. 56* ☎ *05139/88068* ⊕ *www.grapenkieker.de* ⊟ *No credit cards* ⊙ *Closed Mon.*

WHERE TO STAY

For expanded hotel reviews, visit Fodors.com.

$$

⊞ **Concorde Hotel am Leineschloss.** Within touching distance of the elegant Altes Rathaus and the stately Leineschloss, and only a leisurely stroll removed from the Neues Rathaus, Opernhaus, and the city's main museums, this simple, modern hotel is easily one of the best situated in city. **Pros:** In the middle of the shopping district; close to the U-bahn (U-3 and U-7); every double room has a bath. **Cons:** No restaurant; not much character. ✉ *Am Markte 12, Hannover* ☎ *0511/357–910* ⤶ *81 rooms* ⌂ *In-room: no a/c, Wi-Fi. In-hotel: bar, parking, some pets allowed* ⦿ *Breakfast.*

$$

★

⊞ **Kastens Hotel Luisenhof.** Antiques are everywhere in this elegant hotel, which is traditional both in appearance and service; tapestries adorn the lobby walls, oil paintings hang in the foyer, and copper engravings enliven the bar. **Pros:** near the train station; helpful staff; old-world elegance. **Cons:** expensive; on a narrow, ordinary street. ✉ *Luisenstr.1–3* ☎ *0511/30440* ⊕ *www.kastens-luisenhof.de* ⤶ *143 rooms, 7 suites* ⌂ *In-room: no a/c, Wi-Fi. In-hotel: restaurant, bar, gym, spa, some pets allowed* ⦿ *No meals.*

NIGHTLIFE AND THE ARTS

Casino. Hannover's elegant casino is open daily noon to 3 am. ✉ *Osterstr. 40* ☎ *0511/980–660.*

Opera company. Hannover's nightlife is centered on the Bahnhof and the Steintor red-light district. The opera company of Hannover is internationally known, with productions staged in one of Germany's finest 19th-century classical opera houses. Call for program details and tickets. ☎ *0511/9999–1111.*

SHOPPING

Hannover is one of northern Germany's most fashionable cities, and its central pedestrian zone has international shops and boutiques, as well as the very best of German-made articles, from stylish clothes to handmade jewelry.

Galerie Luise. In the glassed-over Galerie Luise, accessible from an underground garage, you can spend a couple of hours browsing, with a leisurely lunch or afternoon tea at one of the restaurants and cafés. ✉ *Luisenstr. 5* ⊕ *www.galerie-luise.de.*

**EN
ROUTE**

The Fairy-Tale Road continues north of Hannover as far as Bremen, though any connection to the Grimm brothers is faint here. You can reach Bremen in less than an hour by taking autobahn A-7 to the Walsrode interchange and then continuing on autobahn A-27. An alternative is to return to Hameln and follow the Weser as it breaks free of the Wesergebirge upland at Porta Westfalica. The meandering route runs through the German plains to the sea and Bremen. You can also take a quick side trip to the northeast, to the Lüneburg Heath and Bergen-Belsen.

BERGEN-BELSEN

58 km (36 mi) northeast of Hannover.

GETTING HERE AND AROUND

Although it's possible to get to Bergen-Belsen on public transport, it requires traveling first to the town of Celle by train, and then taking an hour-long bus journey. Buses run every two hours and require multiple changes. By car, take autobahn exits Mellendorf or Solltau Süd and follow the signposts to the memorial.

Gedenkstätte Bergen-Belsen (*Bergen-Belsen Memorial*). At the site of the infamous concentration camp on the Lüneburg Heath, the Gedenkstätte Bergen-Belsen pays tribute to the victims of the Holocaust. Diarist Anne Frank was among the more than 80,000 persons who died here.

Only the gruesome photographs on display will tell what the camp looked like. There's nothing left of it. The British liberators found thousands and thousands of unburied corpses all over the camp, so as a precaution against disease, all structures were burned to the ground. Volunteer youth groups have unearthed the foundations of the barracks.

Those who venture onto the site of the camp may be surprised at its pleasant, parklike appearance. Reminders of the horrors that once happened here include numerous burial mounds, mostly overgrown with heather and stones with such inscriptions as "here lie 1,000 dead." Anne Frank probably lies in one of them. The SS officers had hoped to have the dead buried and out of sight before the British forces arrived, but the starving prisoners were too weak for the job. Under the direction of the British, the graves you see were dug and filled by the SS officers themselves. The British tried and executed the camp's SS commandant, Josef Kramer, the "Beast of Belsen."

Monuments and shrines include a Jewish memorial dating to 1946, with a commemorative stone dedicated by the Israeli president in 1987; an obelisk and memorial wall erected by the British; a wooden cross dating from only weeks after the liberation; and a commemorative stone from the German government. The main feature of the memorial is a permanent exhibition on the history of the camp and the Nazi persecution system. It's now located in a splendid building that includes a library and research facilities.

■ TIP→ Though all signs are in German, there are supplementary guides in English and eight other languages. There are also regular showings of a movie on the camp in English, German, and French. Children under

The "House of Silence" sculpture by Ingema Reuter and Gerd Winner in the Bergen-Belsen Memorial is a place for silent prayer and meditation.

12 are not admitted to the showings, and it's said that one of the British photographers who made the footage couldn't bear to look at his work in later years. ✉ *Just off unnumbered hwy. connecting Bergen and Winsen* ☎ *05051/6011* ⊕ *www.bergenbelsen.de* ✈ *Free* ☉ *Apr.–Sept., daily 10–6; Oct.–Mar., daily 10–5.*

BREMEN

110 km (68 mi) northwest of Hannover.

Germany's smallest city-state, Bremen, is also Germany's oldest and second-largest port (only Hamburg is larger). Together with Hamburg and Lübeck, Bremen was an early member of the merchant-run Hanseatic League, and its rivalry with the larger port on the Elbe River is still tangible. Though Hamburg may still claim its title as Germany's "door to the world," Bremen likes to boast: "But we have the key." Bremen's symbol is, in fact, a golden key, which you will see displayed on flags and signs throughout the city.

GETTING HERE AND AROUND
Bremen's international airport is a gate to many European destinations, and Intercity (IC) trains connect the city with much of the rest of Germany.

TOURS
Bremen offers both bus and walking tours in English. The bus tours depart Tuesday through Sunday at 10:30 from the central bus station on Breiteweg, the walking tours daily at 2 from the Tourist-Information Center on Oberstrasse.

DID YOU KNOW?

Schnoorviertel is Bremen's oldest quarter, dating from the 15th and 16th centuries. Today, it is filled with crafts-people's studios, boutiques, cafés, and souvenir shops.

ESSENTIALS
Visitor Information Bremen
✉ *Touristik-Zentrale, Findorffstr. 105*
☎ *01805/101–030* ⊕ *www.bremen-tourism.de.*

DISCOUNTS AND DEALS
Bremen has an ErlebnisCARD, which lets you ride free on the public transportation, gets you into museums and other cultural facilities at half price, and gets you a reduction on tours. It costs €8.90 for one day and €10.90 for two days and you can purchase it at the tourist information centers.

EXPLORING
TOP ATTRACTIONS
Böttcherstrasse (*Barrel Maker's Street*). Don't leave Bremen's Altstadt without strolling down this street, at one time inhabited by coopers. Between 1924 and 1931 the houses were torn down and reconstructed, in a style at once historically sensitive and modern, by Bremen coffee millionaire Ludwig Roselius. (He was the inventor of decaffeinated coffee, and held the patent for decades.) Many of the restored houses are used as galleries for local artists.

Marktplatz. Bremen's impressive market square sits in the charming Altstadt. It's bordered by the St. Petri Dom, an imposing 900-year-old Gothic cathedral; an ancient Rathaus; a 16th-century guildhall; and a modern glass-and-steel state parliament building, with gabled town houses finishing the panorama. Alongside the northwest corner of the Rathaus is the famous bronze statue of the four **Bremen Town Musicians,** one atop the other in a sort of pyramid. Their feats are reenacted in a free, open-air play at the Neptune Fountain near the cathedral, at noon each Sunday, from May to September. Another well-known figure on the square is the stone statue of **Roland,** a knight in service to Charlemagne, erected in 1404. Three times larger than life, the statue serves as Bremen's good-luck piece and a symbol of freedom and independence. It is said that as long as Roland stands, Bremen will remain a free and independent state.

★ **Schnoorviertel.** Stroll through the narrow streets of this idyllic district, a jumble of houses, taverns, and shops. This is Bremen's oldest district, dating back to the 15th and 16th centuries. The neighborhood is fashionable among artists and craftspeople, who have restored the tiny cottages to serve as galleries and workshops. Other buildings have been converted into popular antiques shops, cafés, and pubs.

WORTH NOTING
Rathaus. A 15th-century statue of Charlemagne, together with seven princes, adorns the Gothic town hall. It was he who established a diocese here in the 9th century. The Rathaus acquired a Weser Renaissance facade during the early 17th century. Tours, given when no official

ANIMAL MUSICIANS?

Bremen is central to the fable of the Bremer Stadtmusikanten, or Bremen Town Musicians. A donkey, dog, cat, and rooster ran away because they had become old and their masters were going to dispose of them. In order to support themselves they went to Bremen and tried to hire themselves out as musicians. Their music and singing were so awful that they caused a band of robbers to flee in terror. Statues of this group are in various parts of the city.

12

functions are taking place, are in German and English. ⊠ *Am Markt 21* 🚃 *Tour €5* ⊙ *Tours Mon.–Sat. at 11, noon, 3, and 4; Sun. at 11 and noon.*

Roselius-Haus. This 14th-century building, now a museum, stands at one end of Böttcherstrasse. It showcases German and Dutch art, notably the paintings of Paula Modersohn-Becker, a noted early expressionist of the Worpswede art colony. Notice also the arch of Meissen bells at the rooftop. ■TIP➔ Except when freezing weather makes them danger-ously brittle, the bells chime daily on the hour from noon to 6 (only at noon, 3, and 6 January–April). ⊠ *Böttcherstr. 6–10* 🕿 *0421/336–5077* 🚃 *€5* ⊙ *Tues.–Sun. 11–6.*

St. Petri Dom (*St. Peter's Cathedral*). Construction of the cathedral began in the mid-11th century. Its two prominent towers, one of which can be climbed, are Gothic, but in the late 1800s the cathedral was restored in the Romanesque style. It served as the seat of an archbishop until the Reformation turned the cathedral Protestant. It has a museum and five functioning organs. ⊠ *Sandstr. 10–12* 🚃 *Free* ⊙ *Apr–Oct., weekdays 10–5, Sat. 10–2, Sun. 2–5; Nov.–Mar., weekdays 11–4.*

WHERE TO EAT AND STAY
For expanded hotel reviews, visit Fodors.com.

$$$$
FRENCH
★

✕ **Grashoffs Bistro.** An enthusiastic crowd, willing to put up with incred-ibly cramped conditions, descends at lunchtime on this gourmet restau-rant-cum-deli. The room is so small that there's no room between the square tables; a table has to be pulled out for anyone who has a seat next to the wall. The menu has a French touch, with an emphasis on fresh fish from the Bremerhaven market. The deli has a whole wall of teas, another of cheeses, and a huge assortment of wines. ⊠ *Contres-carpe 80* 🕿 *0421/14740* ⊕ *www.grashoff.de* ⊙ *Closed Sun. No dinner.*

$
GERMAN
★

✕ **Ratskeller.** This cavernous cellar, with a three-story-high vaulted ceil-ing, is said to be Germany's oldest and most renowned town-hall restau-rant—it's been here for 600 years. Serving solid, typical North German fare, its walls are lined with wine casks, and there are intimate alcoves with doors, once shut tight by merchants as they closed their deals. ■TIP➔ By long tradition only German wines are served here, and the only beer you can get is Beck's and Franziskaner from the barrel. ⊠ *Am Markt 1* 🕿 *0421/321–676* ⊕ *www.ratskeller-bremen.de.*

¢

🛏 **Hotel Pension Weidmann.** There are only five rooms in this small and friendly family-run pension in one of the brick buildings so character-istic of Bremen. **Pros:** English-speaking staff; welcomes dogs (even large ones). **Cons:** no restaurant. ⊠ *Am Schwarzen Meer 35* 🕿 *0421/498–4455* ⊕ *www.pension-weidmann.de* 🛏 *5 rooms* 🛁 *In-room: no a/c, Wi-Fi. In-hotel: parking, some pets allowed* ▬ *No credit cards.*

$$$$
Fodor's Choice
★

🛏 **Park Hotel Bremen.** A palatial hotel between a lake on one side, and an extensive area of park and forest on the other sides, its heated outdoor pool and a fireplace in the lounge will tempt you to linger in the public spaces, no matter what the season. **Pros:** traditional luxury; on a lake. **Cons:** expensive; outside the city. ⊠ *Im Bürgerpark* 🕿 *0421/340–800* ⊕ *www.parkhotel-bremen.de* 🛏 *166 rooms, 11 suites* 🛁 *In-room: a/c, Wi-Fi. In-hotel: restaurant, bar, pool, some pets allowed* 🍽 *No meals.*

The Deutsches Auswandererhaus (German Emigration Center) in Bremerhaven is on the spot where 7 million Europeans set sail for the New World.

NIGHTLIFE AND THE ARTS

Bremen may be Germany's oldest seaport, but it can't match Hamburg for racy nightlife. Nevertheless, the streets around the central Markt-platz and in the historic Schnoor District are filled with all sorts of taverns and cafés. The Bremen coffee tradition will be evident when you have your coffee and cake at a café in a charming old building with plush sofas, huge mirrors, and chandeliers.

Bremen casino. Try your luck at American roulette, poker, slot machines, and blackjack at the Bremen casino, open daily noon–3 am. ⊠ *An der Schlachte 26* ☎ *0421/329–000.*

SHOPPING

Schnoorviertel. Bremen's Schnoorviertel is the place to go for souvenirs. Its stores are incredibly specialized, selling porcelain dolls, teddy bears, African jewelry, and smoking pipes among many other things.

BREMERHAVEN

66 km (41 mi) north of Bremen.

This busy port city, where the Weser empties into the North Sea, is part of Bremen, about an hour to the south. You can take in the enormity of the port from a promenade, which runs its length. In addition to being a major port for merchant ships, it is the biggest fishery pier in Europe, which means that the promenade is lined with excellent sea-food restaurants.

GETTING HERE AND AROUND

Regional trains run every two hours from Bremen to this North Sea port, and take 35 minutes to get here. Reederei HaRuFa offers a one-hour trip around the Bremerhaven harbor for €9. If you're in a hurry to see the stark, red cliff island of Helgoland, there's a daily round-trip flight for €157 per person with OLT.

ESSENTIALS

Visitor and Tour Information Bremerhaven ⊠ *Bremerhaven Touristik, H.-H.-Meierstr. 6* ☎ *0471/946–4610* ⊕ *www.bremerhaven-touristik.de.* **OLT Airlines** ⊠ *Flughafen, Am Luneort 15* ☎ *0471/77188* ⊕ *www.olt.de.* **Reederei HaRuFa** ⊠ *H.-H.-Meierstr. 4* ☎ *0471/415–850.*

EXPLORING

Deutsches Auswandererhaus (*German Emigration Center*). The award-winning Deutsches Auswandererhaus is made to order for those wanting to trace their German ancestry. The museum's Forum Immigration has a room full of computers to access the museum's archive and link to more than a dozen others, including an extensive collection of Bremen passenger lists. The museum is at the spot where 7 million Europeans set sail for the New World. Movie-set makers were called in to build authentic reconstructions of a big, dingy waiting hall and part of a historic steamship. The waiting room is crowded with mannequins in 19th-century costumes and piles of luggage. The "ship" is boarded across a swaying gangway, and once aboard, you can see how miserable life was during the voyage from the cabins and communal sleeping rooms. A theater screens an English-language film about six emigrant generations. ⊠ *Columbusstr. 65* ☎ *0471/902–200* ⊕ *www.dah-bremerhaven.de* ☎ *€11.20* ☼ *Mar.–Oct., daily 10–6; Nov.–Feb., daily 10–5.*

Deutsches Schifffahrtsmuseum (*German Maritime Museum*). The country's largest and most fascinating maritime museum, the Deutsches Schifffahrtsmuseum, is fun to explore. Part of the museum consists of a harbor, open from April through October, sheltering seven old trading ships. ⊠ *Hans-Scharoun-Pl. 1, from Bremen take A-27 to exit for Bremerhaven-Mitte* ☎ *0471/482–070* ⊕ *www.dsm.national.museum* ☎ *€6* ☼ *Daily 10–6.*

WHERE TO STAY

For expanded hotel reviews, visit Fodors.com.

$$ ⊞ **Hotel Haverkamp.** This hotel sits near the new harbor, and features the König City Bar, a restaurant with excellent seafood; a sauna; and the only indoor pool in Bremerhaven. **Pros:** convenient location. **Cons:** plain exterior; pool is very small. ⊠ *Prager Str. 34* ☎ *0471/48330* ⊕ *www.hotel-haverkamp.de* ⤴ *85 rooms* ⚴ *In-room: no a/c, Wi-Fi. In-hotel: restaurant, bar, pool, parking* ⫴ *Breakfast.*

Hamburg

WORD OF MOUTH

"I could feel the economy in high gear in Hamburg. From the swank shops near Neuer Wall (Hermes—oo la la—you have to go there just to look at the china) to the continuous traffic at the port, the place oozes mercantile power. I loved it."

—jahlie

WELCOME TO HAMBURG

TOP REASONS TO GO

★ **Alster cruises:** Marvel at the diversity of villas gracing the shores of the Alster lakes, relax and sip *glühwein* (warm, mulled wine) while listening to the major and minor details about the city.

★ **Historic harbor district:** Travel back in time and walk the quaint cobblestone alleys around Deichstrasse and the Kontorhausviertel.

★ **Hamburger Kunsthalle and the Deichtorhallen:** Spend an afternoon browsing through the fantastic art collections at two of Germany's leading galleries of modern art.

★ **Retail therapy:** Indulge your inner shopper as you weave your way through the streets behind the elegant Jungfernstieg, move up and down Mönckebergstrasse, stroll through Eppendorf and Schanzeviertel and end the afternoon at a charming Downtown café.

★ **Sin City:** Stroll down Reeperbahn, browse in the quirky sex shops, and dive into the bizarre nightlife of Europe's biggest party district.

1 Downtown Hamburg. Hamburg's downtown area is centered on two long boulevards, the Jungfernstieg and Mönckebergstrasse, which also are the most elegant shopping boulevards in town, pulsating with life.

2 The Harbor and Historic Hamburg. Hamburg's older sections are a fascinating patchwork of historic periods, where meticulously restored buildings hold their ground next to sleek high-rises. Along the waterfront, late-medieval and 19th-century warehouses contrast with the modern HafenCity development.

KEY

S	*S-Bahn*
i	*Tourist information*
U	*U-Bahn*

GETTING ORIENTED

13

The second-largest city in Germany after Berlin, Hamburg sits on northern Germany's fertile lowlands. Despite heavy destruction during World War II, Hamburg is surprisingly green and architecturally beautiful. With 1.8 million inhabitants on 295 square mi (764 square km), it is the least densely populated million-person metropolis in the world. Hamburg is spread out around an upscale, historic Downtown area of St. Georg, Neustadt, and Rotherbaum, but also contains village-like neighborhoods, like Bergstedt, and funky neighborhoods, like Altona and Sternschanze, or Schanzeviertel. Eimsbüttel is a neighborhood full of young families, cool cafés and interesting boutiques. Eppendorf is an upscale area famous for its beauty; plentiful and unique shopping; and thriving restaurant scene. Hamburgers are eagerly awaiting the completion of HafenCity, one of the world's largest urban-planning projects in 2025.

3 St. Pauli and the Reeperbahn. The Reeperbahn is Hamburg's infamous red-light district, but there is more here than just sex shows; dozens of pubs, bars, and dance clubs draw the crowds. St. Pauli is a hip district full of cool restaurants and bars.

COFFEE AND CAKE

When the afternoon rolls around, it's time for *Kaffe und Kuchen*, one of Germany's most beloved traditions. In villages and cities alike, patrons stroll into their favorite *Konditorei* (pastry shop) for a leisurely cup of coffee and slice of cake.

(above) Cake is serious business in Germany and you'll have your pick of many at any Konditorei worth their salt. (upper right) Mohnkuchen (poppy seed cake); (lower right) Gugelhupf.

The tradition stretches back hundreds of years, when coffee beans were first imported to Germany in the 17th century. Coffee quickly became the preferred hot drink of the aristocracy, who paired it with cake, their other favorite indulgence. Within time, the afternoon practice trickled down to the bourgeoisie, and was heartily embraced. Now everyone can partake in the tradition.

There are hundreds of German cakes, many of which are regional and seasonal with an emphasis on fresh fruits in summer, and spiced cakes in winter. Due to modern work schedules, not as many Germans take a daily coffee and cake break anymore. Families will have theirs at home on the weekend, and it's routinely an occasion for a starched tablecloth, the best china, and candles.

—Tania Ralli

VISITING THE KONDITOREI

Seek out the most old-fashioned shops, as these will invariably have the best cakes. Check out what's in the glass case, since most Konditorein don't have printed menus. Don't worry about a language barrier, when it comes time to order just point to the cake of your choice.

BEST CAKES TO TRY

FRANKFURTER KRANZ

The *Frankfurter Kranz,* or Frankfurt wreath, comes from—you guessed it—Frankfurt. Flavored with lemon zest and a touch of rum, this butter cake is then split into three layers and spread with fillings of buttercream and red preserves. The cake's exterior is generously coated with crunchy cookie crumbs or toasted nuts, and each slice is graced with a swirl of buttercream frosting and a bright red cherry.

GUGELHUPF

Of all cakes, the *Gugelhupf* has the most distinctive shape, one that you'll likely recognize as a bunt cake. It tends to be more popular in southern Germany. Gugelhupf had its start as a bready yeast cake, studded with raisins and citrus peel, but today you're just as likely to have it as a marble cake. During the Biedermeier period, in the early 19th century, the wealthy middle class regarded the Gugelhupf as a status symbol.

HERRENTORTE

A layer cake of dark chocolate, *Herrentorte* means "gentleman's cake." It's not as sweet or creamy as most layer cakes, and thus meant to appeal to a man's palate. A *Torte* refers to a fancier layered cake, as opposed to the more humble *Kuchen*, which is a more rustic cake. The Herrentorte has a rich and

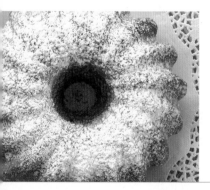

refined taste—in Germany, all chocolate is required to have a higher cocoa content, improving its overall taste and texture.

MOHNKUCHEN

Mohnkuchen is a poppy seed cake, but forget the poppy seed cake you know—this is a cake so completely brimming with poppy seeds you could mistake it for a piece of chocolate cake. You'll come across it as a tall wedge, sprinkled with powdered sugar, or a fat square glazed with a lick of icing. The poppy seeds are mixed with sugar, butter, and sometimes milk. Lightly crushed they make for a very moist filling.

STREUSELKUCHEN

This cake became especially popular in the 19th century, in Prussia. Owing to its versatility, you'll find it today all over Germany. The cake's selling point is its sugary, crunchy topping of pebbled *Streusel* that can stand on its own, or be combined with seasonal fruits like rhubarb, apricots, cherries, or apples. The Streusel tops a simple, buttery yeast cake. *Streuselkuchen* is baked on large sheet pans and cut into generous squares.

Updated
by Monica
McCollum

In Germany, Hamburg is known for its beauty and riches, and those traits' frequent companion—a cool attitude. Water plays a defining role in Hamburg, and the distinguishing feature of Downtown is the Alster (Alster lakes).

From its prominent spot on the Elbe River, which narrows and flows for about 298 km (185 mi) to the North Sea, the old city made its mark as a leader of the medieval Hanseatic League, the medieval union of northern German merchant cities that dominated shipping in the Baltic and North seas. Pride in this trade history can be seen in the *HH* (Hansestadt Hamburg) that is stamped on everything—from the official license plates to T-shirts. For all its pride in the past, however, Hamburg is forward looking. Today Hamburg boasts Europe's second-busiest port and the artificial Alster lakes are major draws.

Once an insignificant tributary, the Alster was dammed in the 13th century. Four hundred years later, the lake was divided into two bodies—the Binnenalster (Inner Alster) and the Aussenalster (Outer Alster). A pair of iconic bridges, the Lombardsbrücke and Kennedybrücke, marks the divide between the two lakes. The Inner Alster is lined with stately hotels, department stores, fine shops, and cafés; the Outer Alster is framed by parks and gardens against a backdrop of private mansions.

Fifteen of the 20 top-selling magazines in Germany are edited in Hamburg. The city is home to several influential publications, such as *Die Zeit, Der Spiegel,* and *Stern.* The home of international publishing giant Bauer sits in Downtown Hamburg. Hamburg is also the center of a new media boom. Not surprisingly, the city of movers and shakers is also the city with most of Germany's millionaires.

But for many Europeans, the port city invariably triggers thoughts of the Reeperbahn, the strip of sex shows and prostitution that helped earn Hamburg its reputation as "Sin City." Today the infamous red-light district is just as much a hip meeting place for young Hamburgers and tourist crowds, who flirt with the bright lights and chic haunts of the not-so-sinful Reeperbahn, especially on warm summer nights.

Hamburg, or "Hammaburg," was founded in 811. For centuries it was a walled city, its gigantic outer fortifications providing a tight little world relatively impervious to invasion.

Napoléon and the Thirty Years' War did not destroy the city but the interruption in commerce hurt Hamburg. Trade was so strong that the city reached the crest of its power by the middle of the 1800s, when the largest shipping fleets on the seas with some of the fastest ships afloat were based here. Its merchants traded with the far corners of the globe. During the four decades leading up to World War I, Hamburg became one of the world's richest cities. Its aura of wealth and power continued right up to the outbreak of World War II. These days, thousands of ships sail up the lower Elbe each year, carrying millions of tons of cargo—from petroleum and locomotives to grain and bananas.

What you see today is the "new" Hamburg. The Great Fire of 1842 all but obliterated the original city; a century later World War II bombing raids destroyed port facilities and leveled more than half of the city proper.

In spite of the 1940–45 raids, Hamburg now stands as a remarkably faithful replica of that glittering prewar city—a place of enormous style, verve, and elegance, with considerable architectural diversity, including *Jugendstil* buildings, Germany's version of art nouveau, erected at the turn of the 20th century. The Elbe and other waterways flow throughout the city. Hamburg also holds many parks and nature preserves within its borders. The northern Germany metropolis is, literally, a site to behold.

PLANNING

WHEN TO GO

In the often-rainy German north, Hamburg has weather that is actually better than its reputation. A pleasant spring arrives in late April and lasts until early June. One of the highlights is the Hafengeburtstag, or birthday of the harbor, in early May. The Elbe comes alive with a small regatta and outdoor food, concerts, and fireworks. Summer temperatures rarely exceed the mid-80s from mid-June through August, and the city has vibrant, blue skies from 5 am until almost 11 pm. Summer is a popular time to visit and boasts many festivals, such as the Alstervergnügen a four-day festival in August or September with sports, food, drinks, music, and performers from around the world. However, hotels and restaurants book up quickly and generally have higher prices and many attractions are crowded. From mid-June to mid-August, foodies get a treat: *Schlemmersommer* (Gourmet Summer). During this joyous time, more than 100 restaurants throughout the city, including award winners, create a four-course meal and charge €59 total for two people. September and October are usually good months to visit, even though rain or sleet will pick up in late October. Film buffs flock to the port city for Filmfest Hamburg, which runs for about 10 days from the end of September. The second-tier film festival attracts renowned artists from around the world to show off their work, which is usually in English or subtitled in English. Almost every neighborhood has a Christmas market, which draws people outdoors to shop and drink *glühwein* (mulled wine). Winter can be gloomy, however, with the sun rising after 7 and setting shortly after 4. Fortunately, Hamburg weather rarely dips below 35°F and snow is uncommon. Prices will be lower in this off-season. Many open-air activities, such as the zoo and boat cruises, continue operating in winter. In March, November, and July, the Hamburger Dom, a huge amusement park, opens in St. Pauli.

GETTING HERE AND AROUND

AIR TRAVEL

Hamburg Airport is 5 mi northwest of the city. The S1 line runs about every 10 minutes from the airport to Downtown Hamburg on its way to Altona. Including a small pause at Ohlsdorf station, where the train hitches up with another, it takes 25 minutes to get to central Hamburg. Tickets are €2.75. A taxi to the Downtown area will cost about €20. If you're driving a rental car from the airport, follow the signs to Centrum (Downtown). ■ TIP→ There is an Edeka supermarket on the arrivals level between Terminal 1 and 2. It's a bit smaller than a full-size German supermarket and the prices are a bit higher than they would be in town. However, it is a great place to pick up some snacks or drinks for your hotel room or a meal for an extended journey.

Airport Information **Hamburg Airport** ☎ *040/50750* ⊕ *www.airport.de.*

BUS AND SUBWAY TRAVEL

The HVV, Hamburg's public transportation system, includes the U-bahn (subway), the S-bahn (commuter train), ferries, buses, and express buses (which cost an additional €1.60). Distance determines fares; €2.80 covers the entire city and €1.30 pays for a ride Downtown. HVV offers passes that make travel even cheaper. With a Tageskarte, or day pass, an adult and three children under 15 can travel throughout Hamburg all day. The Tageskarte pass costs €6.80 when purchased before 9 am and €5.50 after that. The €9.60 Gruppenkarte is the best offer for traveling in a group. A group of five adults can use this card after 9 am on weekdays and all day on weekends. HVV has a three-day ticket for one person that costs €16.50. You can also order group passes at a reduced rate online. Tickets and passes are available on all buses and at automatic machines in every U- and S-bahn station. HVV is based on the honor system. You only need to show a ticket to the bus driver after 9 pm and all day on Sunday. You never show a ticket on a train. Inspectors randomly check for tickets and passes. Those who are caught without fare are fined €40 on the spot. The subway and commuter trains stop running around 12:30 am during the week. After that, night buses (Nos. 600–640) take over.

Information about the entire system is available in English at ⊕ *www. hvv.de/en.* The trip planner function gives the times, prices, walking directions, and maps for each journey. If you don't know the address of a site, you can simply use the name of the popular destination, such as "Hamburg airport." Prepared commuters can buy tickets (even the €1.30 ticket) and passes at the Web site and print them out.

Don't be afraid to take the bus. Buses have a dedicated special traffic lane; passengers use the back doors and do not bother the driver unless they need to pay; and there are not stops on each block, so travel is fast. You can excellent view of this beautiful city. Every bus is air conditioned, but not every subway is. Also, subway platforms are hot in the summer.

Hamburg's intercity bus station, the Zentral-Omnibus-Bahnhof (ZOB), is conveniently located diagonally across from the south exit of the main train station.

Bus Information HVV (*Hamburg Transportation Association*) ⊠ *Steindamm 94, Altstadt* ☎ *040/19449* ⊕ *www.hvv.de.* **Zentral-Omnibus-Bahnhof** (*ZOB*) ⊠ *Adenauerallee 78, St. Georg* ☎ *040/247–576.*

CAR TRAVEL

With its popular public transportation system, Hamburg is easier to handle by car than many other German cities, and traffic is relatively free-flowing. Of course, during rush hour there can be some gridlock. Several autobahns (A-1, A-7, A-23, A-24, and A-250) connect with Hamburg's three beltways, which then easily take you to the Downtown area. Follow the "Zentrum" signs.

TAXI TRAVEL

Taxi meters start at €2.70, then add €1.85 for the first 4 km; €1.75 for the next 6 km; and €1.28 after that. You can hail taxis on the street, outside subway and train stations, at popular locations (like along Mönckebergstrasse), or order one by phone or online.

Taxi Information Taxi ☎ *040/211–211* ⊕ *www.taxi211211.de.*

TRAIN TRAVEL

Hamburg Hauptbahnhof (Hamburg Central Station) is the source of trains to all of Europe. Trains from Hamburg-Altona link Hamburg with some parts of Germany.

Train Information Hauptbahnhof ⊠ *Hachmannplatz 16, Altstadt* ☎ *0180/5996–63361.*

VISITOR INFORMATION

Hamburg Tourismus (Hamburg Tourism Office) has several outlets around the city. The main office is in the Hauptbahnhof and is open Monday to Saturday 9 am–7 pm, Sunday 10–6. The airport branch is open from 6 am to 11 pm daily and sits on the departure level between Terminal 1 and 2. At the harbor there's an office at the St. Pauli Landungsbrücken, between Piers 4 and 5, open 9 am–6 pm Sunday to Wednesday and 9 am–7 pm, Thursday to Saturday. All tourist offices can help with accommodations, and there's a central call-in booking office for hotel and ticket reservations and general information, the Hamburg-Hotline. A €4.90 fee is charged for every room reserved.

Visitor Information Hamburg Hotline ☎ *040/3005–1300* ⊕ *www.hamburgtourism.de.* **Hamburg Tourismus.**

TOURS
BOAT TOURS
There are few better ways to get to know the city than by taking a trip on its waters. Alster Touristik operates a variety of picturesque boat trips around the Alster lakes and through the canals. Alster and canal tours leave from a small dock at the Jungfernstieg. The round-trip Alster cruise lasts one hour, costs €11, and leaves every half hour, April 1–October 7, daily 10–6; October 8–31, it leaves every half hour 11–6. The Winter Warmer Trip offers trips with hot chocolate and glüh-wein (additional charge) several times a day from November through March. Alster Touristik also offers sunset tours through the canals from Jungfernstieg to the bucolic Harvestehude neighborhood May through August and the waters around the historic warehouse district in September. Both tours start at 9:45 and run April through October, costs €14.50. A two-hour canal and Elbe tour costs €16.50 and runs April through October daily at 10:45, 1:45, and 4:45 and November through December daily only at 1:45 on Friday, Saturday, and Sunday. All tours offer commentary in English.

The HADAG line organizes tours of the lower Elbe to Stadersamd, a fruit-growing region outside Hamburg, lasting two hours each way. Visitors can get off at stops along the way (€5.30 to €8.30 each way). Throughout the year, the boats leave St. Pauli Landungsbrücken Pier 2 at 10 and 2:30 on weekends. Audio commentary is available in English.

Every day of the year, Kapitän Prüsse offers cruises around the Elbe harbor that last 60–90 minutes. The night cruise shows the city in a romantic glow. Cruises are €14 or €15. The boats leave throughout the day from Pier 3.

The Maritime Circle Line tours major attractions on the Elbe. Passengers embark at St Pauli Landungsbrücken's Pier 10 and can hop on and hop off at BallinStadt, Hamburg Harbour Museum, Speicherstadt/HafenCity, and the historic ship MV *Cap San Diego*. Tickets are €8 and include discounts at each venue. You can buy the ticket at the pier or online.

Boat Contacts Alster Touristik ☎ *040/357–4240* ⊕ *www.alstertouristik.de.* **HADAG** ☎ *040/311–7070* ⊕ *www.hadag.de.* **Kapitän Prüsse** ☎ *040/357–4240* ⊕ *www.kapitaen-pruesse.de.* **Maritime Circle Line** ✉ *Landungsbrücken 10, St. Pauli* ☎ *040/2849–3963* ⊕ *www.maritime-circle-line.de* ☉ *Apr.–Oct., daily 10–6; Nov.–Mar., Fri.–Sun. noon–4; boats run every 2 hrs.*

ORIENTATION TOURS
Sightseeing bus tours of the city, all with guides who rapidly narrate in both English and German, leave from Kirchenallee by the main train station. A bus tour lasting 1¾ hours sets off at varying times daily and costs €15. For €25, one of the bus tours can be combined with a one-hour boat trip on the harbor. Departure times for tours vary according to season.

Contacts Hamburger Stadtrundfahrt ☎ *040/792–8979* ⊕ *die-roten-doppeldecker.de.*

Take a relaxing boat cruise on the Alster Lakes and through the canals of the city.

WALKING TOURS

Several walking tours are available. Some are only offered April through November, while others run year-round. There are general guided tours of Downtown, the harbor district, and St. Pauli as well as theme excursions, such as the Beatles and Reeperbahn. Unfortunately, most tours are available only in German. To find an English tour, contact the Hamburg Tourism Office.

Contacts Hamburg Tourismus ⊠ *Steinstr. 7, Altstadt* ☎ *040/3005–1300* ⊕ *www.hamburg-tourism.de.*

PLANNING YOUR TIME

The Downtown area features most of Hamburg's must-see attractions, such as the grand, historic churches and most museums. Pride of place goes to the Rathaus (Town Hall), which is a good starting point for exploring the inner city, and the St. Michaelis Kirche, while other churches, notably St. Petri, St. Jakobi, and St. Katharinen, are a short 10- to 15-minute walk away from each other. Take a stroll along the two major boulevards in the area, the Jungfernstieg, to take in the Binnenalster, and Mönckebergstrasse, and venture out to the many side streets and canal-side walks. This can take up several hours, depending on how much of the area you want to explore. Some of the city's most important museums, such as the Kunsthalle with its superb collection of modern art, can be found near the Hauptbahnhof. Any visit to Hamburg should include a walk along the Reeperbahn in St. Pauli, as well as a closer inspection of the Altstadt with its 19th-century warehouses and cobblestone alleys. Each of these neighborhoods can easily take up half a day of exploring.

DISCOUNTS AND DEALS

Hamburg is one of Germany's most expensive cities, but the several citywide deals can make attractions more affordable.

The **Hamburg Card** allows unlimited travel on all public transportation (including express buses) within Hamburg and discounts on 160 museums, cruises, restaurants, and stores. The Hamburg Card is valid all day and costs €8.90 for one adult and up to three children under 15 and €20.90 for three days. The Hamburg Card *Gruppenkarte* costs €13.90 for one day and covers five people and €34.50 for three days. The Hamburg Card is available at tourist offices; HVV buses, vending machines, and service centers; many hotels; and the Web sites for HVV and Hamburg Tourism Office.

For €12, the new **Kombicard** allows entrance to Altonaer Museum, Archäologisches Museum Hamburg/Helms-Museum, Hafenmuseum Hamburg, Jenisch Haus, Krameramtswohnungen, Museum der Arbeit, Museum für Bergedorf und die Vierlande, Museum für Hamburgische Geschichte, Rieck Haus, and Speicherstadtmuseum over the course of two days. The pass is available at the participating museums or at ⊕ *www.museumsdienst-hamburg.de.*

EXPLORING HAMBURG

Hamburg's most important attractions stretch between the Alster lakes to the north and the harbor and Elbe River to the south. This area consists of four distinct quarters. St. Georg is the cultural district with a gay and lesbian presence around the Hamburger Hauptbahnhof (Central Station). The historic Altstadt (Old City) clusters near the harbor and surrounds the Rathaus (Town Hall). West of the Altstadt is Neustadt (New City). The shabby but thrilling neighborhood of St. Pauli includes the Reeperbahn, a strip of dance clubs, bars, and strip clubs.

DOWNTOWN HAMBURG

Downtown was heavily bombarded during World War II, so many of the buildings here were constructed after the war, but many red-brick historic 19th-century warehouses, city mansions, and historic landmarks have been restored to their old splendor and now house banks, insurance companies, and other big businesses. The city's heart is centered on two long boulevards, the Jungfernstieg and Mönckebergstrasse. Downtown may not be the most beautiful part of town, but its atmosphere is invigorating.

GETTING HERE AND AROUND

The best way to move through the Downtown area is to take the subway, the U-bahn or S-bahn, to Hamburger Hauptbahnhof. From the main railway station, just follow the shopping boulevard, Mönckebergstrasse, which will lead to you to most of the sights and is a good yardstick for orientation.

TIMING

If you plan four hours for visits to the museums and the Rathaus and two more hours for the delightful boat tour on the Alster lakes, you'll end up spending more than a full day Downtown.

TOP ATTRACTIONS

Fodor's Choice ★ **Alster** (*Alster lakes*). These twin lakes provide Downtown Hamburg with one of its most memorable vistas. The two lakes meet at the Lombardsbrücke and Kennedybrücke (Lombard and Kennedy bridges). The boat landing at the Jungfernstieg, below the Alsterpavillon, is the starting point for lake and canal cruises. Small sailboats and rowboats, hired from yards on the shores of the Alster, are very much a part of the summer scene.

13

Every Hamburger dreams of living within sight of the Alster, but only the wealthiest can afford it. Some lucky millionaires own the magnificent garden properties around the Alster's perimeter, known as the Millionaire's Coast. But you don't have to be a guest on one of these estates to enjoy the waterfront—the Alster shoreline has 6 km (4 mi) of tree-lined public pathways. ■TIP→ Popular among joggers, these trails are a lovely place for a stroll. Ⓜ *Jungfernstieg (U-bahn).*

★ **Hamburger Kunsthalle** (*Art Gallery*). One of the most important art museums in Germany, the Kunsthalle has 3,500 paintings, 650 sculptures, and a coin and medal collection that dates from the ancient Roman era. In the postmodern, cube-shaped building designed by Berlin architect O. M. Ungers, the **Galerie der Gegenwart** has housed a collection of international modern art since 1960, including works by Andy Warhol, Joseph Beuys, Georg Baselitz, and David Hockney. With 1,200 drawings and other visuals, graphic art is well represented, including works by Pablo Picasso and Horst Janssen, a Hamburg artist famous for his satirical worldview. In the other areas of the museum, you can view works by local artists dating from the 16th century. The outstanding collection of German Romantic paintings includes pieces by Caspar David Friedrich. Paintings by Holbein, Rembrandt, Van Dyck, Tiepolo, and Canaletto are also on view, while late-19th-century impressionism is represented by works by Leibl, Liebermann, Manet, Monet, and Renoir. ✉ *Glockengiesserwall, Altstadt* ☎ *040/4281–31200* ⊕ *www.hamburger-kunsthalle.de* 🎟 *Permanent exhibition €8.50* ⊙ *Tues., Wed., and Fri.–Sun. 10–6, Thurs. 10–9* Ⓜ *Hauptbahnhof (U-bahn and S-bahn).*

★ **Jungfernstieg.** This wide promenade looking out over the Alster lakes is the beginning of the city's premier shopping district. Laid out in 1665,

Hamburg

Moorweidenstr.

E. Siemers Allee

Theodor Heuss-pl.

seilerstr.

Dammtor Ⓢ

Mittelweg

Warburgstr.

Alsterufer

Aussenalster

Ⓤ 11

Ⓤ

Stephans-Platz

Dammtor Damm

Alsterglacis

Esplanade

Colonnaden

Dammtor Str.

Kennedybrücke

Lombardsbrücke

Holzdamm

An der Alster

Koppel

Lange Reihe

Kirchen Allee

❶

Ⓤ

Gänsemarkt Gänse-markt

Fuhlentwiete

Postr.

Grosse Bleichen

Hoheblerchen

Neuer Jungfernstieg

Binnenalster

❶

Ballindamm

Ferdinandstr.

Brandsende

Glockengiesser wall

Ernst. Merck-Str.

❷ Ⓤ Ⓢ

🛈 Hbf.-Nord

❸ Ⓢ Ⓤ

Hbf.-süd

Ⓤ Jungfern-Stieg

Ⓢ

Bergstr.

Schmeldstr.

Hermannstr.

Raboisen

Kurze Mühren

Gerh Hauptm Pl.

Lange Mühren

Adenauer allee

Steintor-wall

❹

Neuer Wall

Adolfstr.

Alter Wall

Petterstr.

Mönckebergstr.

❺

Johannis-Wall

Kurt-Schumacher-Allee

Klosterwall

❿

Ⓤ

Grosse Bleichen

Jungfernstieg

NEUSTADT

Stadthausbr.

Hofeblerchen

Bleichenbr.

Neuer Wall

❾ Rathaus

Ⓤ

❽

Gr. Johannisstr.

❼

Speer sort

❻

Burchardstr.

Steinstr.

Burchard-pl.

Steinstr. Ⓤ

Deichtor Pl.

Ⓢ Stadthaus-Brücke

Mönkedamm

Gr. Burstah

ALTSTADT

Domstrasse

Kl. Reichhenstr.

Ⓤ Rödingsmarkt

Burstah

Rödings Markt

Derch str.

❶⑯

Willy-Brandt-Strasse

Messberg Ⓤ

❷⓪ ❷①

❶⑮

Kajen

Neuen Krahn

aumwall

Binnenhafen

Zollkanal

B.D. Mühren

Kornhausbrücke

❶⑦ Zippelhaus

Neuer Wandrahm

Dovenfleet

Alter Wandrahm

❶⑧

Oberbaumbrücke

Deichtorstr.

Bankstr.

Brooktorkai

❶⑨

KEY

Ⓢ   *S-Bahn*

🛈   *Tourist information*

Ⓤ   *U-Bahn*

it used to be part of a muddy millrace that channeled water into the Elbe. Hidden from view behind the sedate facade of Jungfernstieg is a network of several small shopping centers that together account for almost a mile of shops selling everything from souvenirs to haute couture. Many of these passages have sprung up in the past two decades, but some have been here since the 19th century; the first glass-covered arcade, called Sillem's Bazaar, was built in 1845. ⊠ *Neustadt* Ⓜ *Jungfernstieg (U-bahn)*.

NEED A BREAK?

Alex im Alsterpavillon. Perhaps Hamburg's best-known café, the Alex im Alsterpavillon is sleek yet comfortable, with an ideal vantage point from which to observe the constant activity on the Binnenalster. ⊠ *Jungfernstieg 54, Neustadt* ☎ *040/350–1870.*

Mönckebergstrasse. This broad street of shops—Hamburg's major thoroughfare—cuts through both the historic and the new Downtown areas. It was built between 1908 and 1911 to connect the main train station to city hall. Because it's only open to taxis and buses, the street is a stroller's paradise. It's home to Karstadt and Galeria Kaufhof department stores, mega-electronics store Saturn, discount clothing store C & A, high-end women's fashion store AppelrathCüpper, modern fashions for both men and women at Peek & Cloppenburg, MAC cosmetics, Adidas, and other stores that sell a variety of products at every price point. ■ TIP→ The stores and shopping precincts on both sides of the street provide a wide selection of goods at more affordable prices than those on Jungfernstieg. ⊠ *Altstadt* Ⓜ *Mönckebergstrasse (U-bahn), Hauptbahnhof (U-bahn/S-bahn), Jungfernstieg (U-bahn).*

Fodor's Choice
★

Rathaus (*Town Hall*). To most Hamburgers this large building is the symbolic heart of the city. As a city-state—an independent city and simultaneously one of the 16 federal states of Germany—Hamburg maintains city and state governments, both of which have their administrative headquarters in the Rathaus. An ostentatious neo-Renaissance affair, the building dictates political decorum in the city. To this day, the mayor of Hamburg never welcomes VIPs at the foot of its staircase, but always awaits them at the very top—whether it's a president or the queen of England.

Both the Rathaus and the Rathausmarkt (Town Hall Market) lie on marshy land, a fact vividly brought to mind in 1962, when the entire area was flooded. The current city hall is the sixth one in Hamburg's history. The large square, with its surrounding arcades, was laid out after Hamburg's Great Fire of 1842. The Rathaus was begun in 1886, when 4,000 piles were sunk into the moist soil to support the structure. It was completed in 1897. Five years before, a cholera epidemic claimed the lives of 8,605 Hamburg residents in 71 days. The "Hygieia-fountain," a fountain and monument to that unhappy chapter in Hamburg's history sit in a rear courtyard of the Rathaus.

The immense neo-Renaissance building, with its 647 rooms and imposing central clock tower, is not the most graceful structure in the city, but the sheer opulence of its interior is astonishing. A 40-minute tour begins in the ground-floor Rathausdiele, a vast pillared hall. Although you can

Hamburg's neo-Renaissance Rathaus is worth a peek inside for its opulent interiors.

only view the state rooms, their tapestries, huge staircases, glittering chandeliers, coffered ceilings, and grand portraits give you a sense of the city's great wealth in the 19th century and its understandable civic pride.

For those with a political bent, you can view a session of Hamburg Parliament. To register for a ticket, call ☎ *040/42831–2409.* ✉ *Rathausmarkt, Altstadt* ☎ *040/42831–2064* ⊕ *www.hamburgische-buergerschaft.de* ⌨ *Tours €3* ⊘ *Tours weekdays, half-hourly 10:15–3:15; Sat., half-hourly 10:15–5:15; Sun., half-hourly 10:15–6:15; English tours weekdays 11:15, 1:15, and 3:15; Sat. 11:15, 1:15, 3:15, and 5:15; Sun. 11:15, 1:15, 3:15, and, if there is demand, 4:15* Ⓜ *Rathaus (U-bahn), Jungfernstieg (U-bahn/S-bahn).*

★ **St. Jacobi Kirche** (*St. James's Church*). This 15th-century church was almost completely destroyed during World War II. Only the interiors survived, and reconstruction was completed in 1963. The interior is not to be missed—it houses such treasures as a massive baroque organ and three Gothic altars from the 15th and 16th centuries. ✉ *Jacobikirchhof 22, at Steinstr., Altstadt* ☎ *040/303–7370* ✑ *info@jacobus.de* ⊕ *www.jacobus.de* ⊘ *Apr.–Sept., Mon.–Sat. 10–5, Sun. after service; Oct.–Mar., Mon.–Sat. 11–5, Sun. after service. German guided tours: 1st and 3rd Sat. at 2; 2nd Wed. at 11:30. English guided tours available on request at info@jacobus.de* Ⓜ *Rathaus (U-bahn), Jungfernstieg (U-bahn/S-bahn).*

St. Petri Kirche (*St. Peter's Church*). This church was created in 1195 and has been in continuous use since then. St. Petri is the only one of the five main churches in Hamburg that came out of World War II relatively undamaged. The current building was built in 1849, after the previous building burned down in the Great Fire of 1842. ■ TIP→ Every Wednesday at 5:15 pm you can listen to organ music in the Stunde der Kirchenmusik (Hour of Church Music). ✉ *Bei der Petrikirche 2, Altstadt* ☎ *040/325–7400* ⊕ *www.sankt-petri.de* ☉ *Weekdays 10–6:30, Sat. 10–5, Sun. 9–8. Tower Mon.–Sat., 10–4:30; Sun. after service until 4:30. Tours Thurs. at 3 and the 1st Sun. of month at 11:30* Ⓜ *Rathaus (U-bahn), Jungfernstieg (U-bahn/S-bahn).*

Ⓒ ★ **Tierpark Hagenbeck** (*Hagenbeck Zoo*). One of the country's oldest and most popular zoos is family-owned. Founded in 1907, it was the world's first zoo to let wild animals such as lions, elephants, chimpanzees, and others roam freely in vast, open-air corrals. In summer, you can ride a pony.

The Tropen-Aquarium sits on the same property as the zoo and a tour through it is like a trip around the world. Sea life, insects, curious reptiles, marvelous birds, and exotic mammals live in replicas of their natural habitat. Detailed re-creations of deserts, oceans, rain forests and jungles are home to birds, fish, mammals, insects, and reptiles from almost every continent, including a "Madagascar" village with black-tailed lemurs. ✉ *2 Lokstedter Str. at Hamburg-Stellingen, Stellingen* ☎ *040/530–0330* ⊕ *www.hagenbeck.de* ✇ *€17 for zoo, €14 for aquarium, €27 for zoo and aquarium* ☉ *Zoo: Mar.–June, Sept., and Oct., daily 9–6; July and Aug., daily 9–7; Nov.–Feb., daily 9–4:30. Aquarium: daily 9–6* Ⓜ *Hagenbecks Tierpark (U-bahn).*

WORTH NOTING

Bucerius Kunst Forum. This independent art gallery has staged four major exhibitions a year since 2002. Museum officials commission guest curators from around the world to create shows that cover every art period and style. ✉ *Rathausmarkt 2, Neustadt* ☎ *040/360–9960* ⊕ *www.buceriuskunstforum.de* ✇ *€7, €5 on Mon.* ☉ *Sun.–Wed. 11–7, Fri. and Sat. 11–7, Thurs. 11–9* Ⓜ *Rathaus (U-bahn).*

Hamburg Hauptbahnhof (*Main Train Station*). This central train station's cast-iron-and-glass architecture evokes the grandiose self-confidence of imperial Germany. The chief feature of the enormous 680-foot-long structure is its 446-foot-wide glazed roof. One of the largest structures of its kind in Europe, it's remarkably spacious and bright inside. Though completed in 1906 and having gone through many modernizations, it continues to have tremendous architectural impact. Today it sees a heavy volume of international, national, and suburban rail traffic. ✉ *Steintorpl., St. Georg* Ⓜ *Hauptbahnhof (U-bahn).*

Museum für Kunst und Gewerbe Hamburg (*Arts and Crafts Museum*). The museum houses a wide range of exhibits, from 15th- to 18th-century scientific instruments to an art nouveau interior complete with ornaments and furnishings. It was built in 1876 as a combination museum and school. Its founder, Justus Brinckmann, intended it to be a bastion of the applied arts that would counter what he saw as a decline in taste owing to industrial mass production. A keen collector, Brinckmann amassed a wealth of unusual objects, including a collection of ceramics from around the world. ⊠ *Steintorpl., Altstadt* ☎ *040/4281–34880* ⊕ *www.mkg-hamburg.de* 🎫 *€8; €5 Thurs. after 5* ⊙ *Tues., Wed., and Fri.–Sun. 11–6, Thurs. 11–9* Ⓜ *Hauptbahnhof (U-bahn/S-bahn).*

☾ **Planten un Blomen** (*Plants and Flowers Park*). In 1821, a botanist planted a sycamore tree in a park near Dammtor train station. From this tree, a sanctuary for birds and plants evolved and a botanical garden that resembles the current park opened in 1930. This 116-acre oasis features a grand Japanese garden, a mini-golf course, an outdoor roller-skating rink, trampolines, pony rides, and water features. The original sycamore tree still stands near an entrance. If you visit on a summer evening, you'll see the *Wasserlichtkonzerte*, the play of an illuminated fountain set to organ music. ■TIP➡ Make sure you get to the lake in plenty of time for the nightly show, which begins at 10 pm from May through August and at 9 pm in September. ⊠ *Stephanspl., Neustadt* ☎ *040/4285–44723* ⊕ *plantenunblomen.hamburg.de* 🎫 *Free* ⊙ *April daily 7 am–10 pm; May–Sept., daily 7 am–11 pm; Oct.–Mar., daily 7 am–8 pm* Ⓜ *Dammtor-Bahnhof (S-bahn), Messehallen (U-bahn), St. Pauli (S-bahn), Handwerkskammer (112 bus).*

THE HARBOR AND HISTORIC HAMBURG

Narrow cobblestone streets with richly decorated mansions lead to churches of various faiths, reflecting the diverse origins of the sailors and merchants drawn to the city. Small museums and old restaurants occupy buildings that once served as sailor taverns. Of note here are Hamburg's Free Port, the Gothic St. Michaeliskirche, the Warehouse district, and the ambitious HafenCity.

GETTING HERE AND AROUND

To reach the harbor area from the Messberg U-bahn station, walk down the busy Willy-Brandt-Strasse and turn down Brandstwiete. After crossing the bridge, the road turns into Bei St. Annen and quickly leads into the heart of the harbor area.

TOP ATTRACTIONS

★ **Deichstrasse.** The oldest residential area in the Old Town of Hamburg, which dates from the 14th century, now consists of lavishly restored houses from the 17th through the 19th century. Many of the original houses on Deichstrasse were destroyed in the Great Fire of 1842, which broke out in No. 38 and left approximately 20,000 people homeless; only a few of the early dwellings escaped its ravages. Today Deichstrasse and nearby Peterstrasse, which is steps away from the site of the former city wall, are of great historical interest. At No. 35–39 Peterstrasse, for example, is the replica of the baroque facade of the Beylingstift

Check out HafenCity for a look at the Hamburg of the future. It's an urban planner's dream, with offices, apartments, restaurants, museums, and entertainment spaces all in one neighborhood.

complex, built in 1751. Today, the Johannes Brahms Museum sits in No. 39, the composer's former home. All the buildings in the area have been painstakingly designed to look like the original buildings, thanks largely to nonprofit foundations. ✉ *Altstadt* Ⓜ *Rödingsmarkt (U-bahn).*

QUICK BITES

There are two good basement restaurants in this area.

Alt-Hamburger Aalspeicher. The Alt Hamburger Aalspeicher serves fresh-fish dishes, including Hamburg's famous *Aalsuppe* (officially, it is a clear broth with a variety of vegetables, seafood, and meat—everything that is leftover). However, because of the Hamburg accent, *alle* (German for everything) became mistaken for *aal* (German for eel), so some restaurants make eel the focus, while others create their own version of a light soup. ✉ *Deichstr. 43, Altstadt* ☎ *040/362–990.*

Das Kontor. This upscale historic Hamburg tavern offers some of the city's best fried potatoes and traditional desserts. ✉ *Deichstr. 32, Altstadt* ☎ *040/371–471.*

HafenCity (*Port City*). Opposite the historic Speicherstadt sits Europe's largest urban-development project, HafenCity. This new district will feature cultural, business, and residential areas spread over 388 acres. Once completed, the HafenCity will include a huge cruise ship terminal, a high-tech symphony hall (the Elbphilharmonie), hotels, stores, bars, restaurants, and a science center. Although the entire project is not scheduled to be completed until 2025, you can already see the difference. Apartment buildings with bold designs tower around the

Elbe's edge. Curious visitors have marveled at the vast collection of model ships at the International Maritime Museum since the summer of 2008. That same year Prototyp, a collection of prototypes of historic racing and sports cars opened. Since then several museums have opened, including tea museum Messner Momentum, Afghanisches Museum (Afghan Museum), and the HafenCity SustainabilityPavillon.

Architecture buffs can tour the construction of the symphony hall. Several restaurants have welcomed guests since 2009. Cruise ships have been sailing into two temporary terminals for years. You can see a model of the project in the visitor center in Speicherstadt's old power plant. Despite the construction, you can still take a contemplative stroll along the Elbe.

13

To accommodate the rise in activity at the waterfront, HVV is creating a new subway. The U-4, which will take riders from central Hamburg to HafenCity, should be completed by the end of 2012. ⊠ *Am Sandtorkai 30, HafenCity* ☎ *040/3690–1799* ⊕ *www.hafencity.com* ✉ *Free* ☉ *Visitor center: May–Sept., Tues., Wed., and Fri.–Sun. 10–6; Thurs. 10–8* Ⓜ *Messberg (U-bahn)*.

Fodor's Choice
★

St. Michaelis Kirche (*St. Michael's Church*). The Michel, as it's called locally, is Hamburg's principal church and northern Germany's finest baroque-style ecclesiastical building. Constructed between 1649 and 1661 (the tower followed in 1669), it was razed after lightning struck almost a century later. It was rebuilt between 1750 and 1786 in the decorative Nordic baroque style, but was gutted by a terrible fire in 1906. The replica, completed in 1912, was demolished during World War II. The present church is a reconstruction.

The distinctive 436-foot brick-and-iron tower bears the largest tower clock in Germany, 26 feet in diameter. Just above the clock is a viewing platform (accessible by elevator or stairs) that affords a magnificent panorama of the city, the Elbe River, and the Alster lakes. ■TIP→ Twice a day, at 10 am and 9 pm (Sunday at noon), a watchman plays a trumpet solo from the tower platform. In the crypt a 30-minute movie about the 1,000-year history of Hamburg and its churches is shown.

For a great view of Hamburg's skyline, head to the clock tower at night. In the evenings you can sip a complimentary soft drink while listening to classical music in a room just below the tower, usually held from 5:30 pm to 11:00 pm. Check ⊕ *www.nachtmichel.de* or call ☎ *040/2851–5791* to confirm times. ⊠ *Englische Planke 1, Neustadt* ☎ *040/376–780* ⊕ *www.st-michaelis.de* ✉ *Tower €4; crypt and movie €3; show, tower, and crypt €6* ☉ *May–Oct., daily 9–7:30; Nov.–Apr., daily 10–5:30* Ⓜ *Rödingsmarkt (U-bahn), Stadthausbrücke (S-bahn)*.

QUICK
BITES

Old Commercial Room. Just opposite the St. Michaelis Kirche is one of Hamburg's most traditional restaurants, the Old Commercial Room. Try one of the local specialties, such as Aal soup. If you don't make it to the restaurant, you can buy its dishes (precooked and canned) in department stores in both Hamburg and Berlin. ⊠ *Englische Planke 10, Neustadt* ☎ *040/366–319.*

⟲ **Speicherstadt** (*Warehouse District*). This imposing cluster of massive
Fodor's Choice brick buildings sits along canals near the Elbe and reveals yet another
★ aspect of Hamburg's extraordinary architectural diversity. Once home
to tons of cargo imported by Hamburg, today the area is a mix of
offices, restaurants, amusements, and warehouses. These warehouses
are still used to store and process every conceivable commodity, from
coffee and spices to raw silks and hand-woven Oriental carpets. An
entire residential area was torn down (including many Renaissance and
baroque buildings) to store the wares. Today, the area is home to Hamburg Dungeon, a haunted-house attraction; the Miniatur Wunderland,
the site of the largest model railway in the world; and a few museums
celebrating the area's shipping past.

Speicherstadtmuseum. Although you won't be able to tour the storage
spaces, the nonstop comings and goings will give you a good sense of a
port at work. If you want to learn about the history and architecture of
the old warehouses, detour to the Speicherstadtmuseum. ⊠ *St. Annen-
ufer 2, Speicherstadt* ☎ *040/321–191* ⊕ *www.speicherstadtmuseum.de*
🖃 *€3.50* ⊘ *Apr.–Oct., weekdays 10–5, weekends 10–6; Nov.–Mar.,
Tues.–Sun. 10–5* Ⓜ *Messberg (U-bahn)* ⊠ *Speicherstadt is bounded by
Am Sandtorkai and Brooktorkai and the Elbe River., Speicherstadt*
☎ *040/3690–1799* ⊕ *www.hafencity.com* 🖃 *Free* ⊘ *Visitor center:
May–Sept., Tues., Wed., and Fri.–Sun. 10–6, Thurs. 10–8* Ⓜ *Messberg
(U-bahn)*.

WORTH NOTING

Krameramtswohnungen (*Shopkeepers' Houses*). The shopkeepers' guild
built this tightly packed group of courtyard houses between 1620
and 1626 for members' widows. The houses became homes for the
elderly after 1866. The half-timber, two-story dwellings, with unusual
twisted chimneys and decorative brick facades, were restored in the
1970s. A visit inside gives you a sense of what life was like in these
17th-century dwellings. ⊠ *Historic
House C, Krayenkamp 10, Speicherstadt* ☎ *040/3750–1988* 🖃 *€2*
⊘ *Tues.–Sun. 10–5* Ⓜ *Rödingsmarkt (U-bahn), Stadtbahnstrasse
(S-bahn)*.

Mahnmal St. Nikolai (*St. Nicholas
Memorial*). Originally erected in
1195 and destroyed by fire in 1842,
the church was rebuilt in neo-Gothic
style, before it burned down again
during the air raids of World War
II. Today, the remains of the church
serve as a memorial for the victims
of war and persecution from 1933
to 1945. The memorial features an
exhibition on the air raids and the
destruction of Hamburg and other
European cities. A glass elevator
on the outside of the building takes

THE SPICE TRADE

Spicy's Gewürzmuseum. Hamburg's proud past as Europe's
gateway to the world comes to
life at the tiny but fascinating
Spicy's Gewürzmuseum in the
Speicherstadt, where you can
smell and touch more than 50
spices. More than 900 objects
chronicle five centuries of the
once-prosperous spice trade in
Hamburg. From November to June
the museum is open Tuesday–
Sunday 10–5; from July to October
it's open daily 10–5. ⊠ *Am Sandtorkai 32* ☎ *040/367–989* ⊕ *www.
spicys.de* 🖃 *€3.50.*

visitors 250 feet up to the steeple, which offers magnificent views of the surrounding historic streets. Lectures, film screenings, panel discussions, and concerts also take place at the memorial. ⊠ *Willy-Brandt-Str. 60, at Hopfenmarkt, Altstadt* ☎ *040/371–125* ⊕ *www.mahnmal-st-nikolai.de* 🎫 *€3.70* 𝕆 *Tours: Sat. at 2 (call to request an English tour); Oct.–Apr., daily 10–5; May–Sept., daily 10–8* Ⓜ *Rödingsmarkt (U-bahn).*

Ⓒ **Museum für Hamburgische Geschichte** (*Museum of Hamburg History*). The museum's vast and comprehensive collection of artifacts gives you an excellent overview of Hamburg's development, from its origins in the 9th century to the present. Pictures and models portray the history of the port and shipping between 1650 and the 20th century. ⊠ *Holstenwall 24, Neustadt* ☎ *040/42813–22380* ⊕ *www.hamburgmuseum.de* 🎫 *€8* 𝕆 *Tues.–Sat. 10–5, Sun. 10–6* Ⓜ *St. Pauli (U-bahn), Hamburger Museum (Bus 112).*

St. Katharinen Kirche (*St. Katharine's Church*). Founded in 1250 and completed in 1660, this house of worship was severely damaged during World War II, but has since been carefully reconstructed.

The interior was dotted with plaques honoring different people. Sadly, only two epitaphs remain from the original interior. Currently the church is closed because of major construction work and only tours of the tower are available. The church will open for the public again at Christmas 2011. Construction work will go on until the end of 2012. ⊠ *Katharinenkirchhof 1, near Speicherstadt, Altstadt* ☎ *040/3037–4730* ⊕ *www.katharinen-hamburg.de* 𝕆 *Tours of the tower only available on request (only German).* Ⓜ *Messberg (U-bahn), Brandstwiete (Bus 3, 4, and 6).*

ST. PAULI AND THE REEPERBAHN

The maritime district of St. Pauli is sometimes described as a "Babel of sin," but that's not really fair anymore. Hamburgers are proud they have one of the most famous red-light districts in the world. Prostitution is legal in Germany and its supporters could be found on the Reeperbahn, which is a major street and a neighborhood. There were also many sex shops and strip clubs. Although brothels and sex shops are still in operation in the area, today the Reeperbahn looks more like the French Quarter than Sodom and Gomorrah. At one end of the Reeperbahn sits the TUI Operettenhaus and at the other, lighted silhouettes of the Beatles, who perfected their skills at the Star Club, a major club that once roared on a side street.

Beyond this strip of pleasures, St. Pauli and Altona are two fun and hip areas bursting with cool restaurants, dive bars, and chic lounges.

GETTING HERE AND AROUND

The St. Pauli U-bahn station is at the beginning of the long, neon-lighted street that is the red-light Reeperbahn and the Reeperbahn S-bahn is at the other end.

TIMING

You can easily spend a full day and a long night, including an enjoyable boat trip through the harbor and a few hours in the theaters and bars along the Reeperbahn.

TOP ATTRACTIONS

Fischmarkt (*Fish Market*). A trip to the Altona Fischmarkt is worth getting out of bed early for—or staying up all night; it's only open from 5 to 9:30 (7 to 9:30 from November to March) in the morning. The pitch of fervent deal making is unmatched in Germany. Offering real bargains, the market's barkers are famous for their sometimes-rude but usually successful bids to shoppers. Sunday fish markets became a tradition in the 18th century, when fishermen sold their catch before church services. Today freshly caught fish are only a part of the scene. You can find almost anything here—from live parrots and palm trees to armloads of flowers and bananas, valuable antiques, and fourth-hand junk. ✉ *Grosse Elbestr. 9, St. Pauli* ☉ *Apr.–Oct., Sun. 5 am–9:30 am; Nov.–Mar. 7 am–9:30 am* Ⓜ *Landungsbrücken (U-bahn/S-Bahn), Fischmarkt (Bus 112).*

Landungsbrücken (*Piers*). A visit to the port is not complete without a tour of one of the most modern and efficient harbors in the world. ■ TIP→ There's usually a breeze in Germany's largest port, so dress accordingly. Barge tours of the harbor leave from the main passenger terminal, along with a whole range of ferries and barges heading to other destinations in the North Sea. Hamburgers and tourists flock to the area because of the port, the view, souvenir stores, and the variety of snack and ice cream shops.

Rickmer Rickmers. *Rickmer Rickmers*, an 1896 sailing ship that once traveled as far as Cape Town, is open to visitors and is docked at Pier 1. ✉ *St. Pauli Landungsbrücken Ponton 1a, St. Pauli* ☎ *040/319–5959* ⊕ *www.rickmer-rickmers.de* ✆ *Rickmer Rickmers €4* ☉ *Daily 10–6* Ⓜ *Landungsbrücken (U-bahn)*

Cap San Diego. Close to the *Rickmer Rickmers* sits the Cap San Diego, a seaworthy museum and hotel. Before it docked at Hamburg permanently, it regularly sailed to South America. ✉ *Überseebrücke, St. Pauli* ☎ *040/364–209* ⊕ *www.capsandiego.de* ✆ *Cap San Diego €7* ☉ *Daily 10–6* Ⓜ *Landungsbrücken U-bahn* ✉ *Bei den St. Pauli Landungsbrücken, St. Pauli* ☎ *040/3005–1300* Ⓜ *Landungsbrücken (U-bahn).*

Grosse Freiheit, a side street off the Reeperbahn, comes alive at night with crowds looking for a good time.

Reeperbahn. The hottest spots in town are concentrated in the St. Pauli Harbor area on the Reeperbahn thoroughfare and on a little side street known as the Grosse Freiheit (Great Liberty—and that's putting it mildly). In the early '60s a then obscure band called the Beatles polished their live act at the now-demolished Star Club.

The striptease shows are explicit, but a walk through this area is an experience in itself and costs nothing. There are crowds every night but it's especially busy on Thursday, Friday, and Saturday nights, when the area pulsates with people determined to have a good time.

There are quiet pubs, crazy bars, and booming dance clubs lining the street where rope makers once worked. On most nights of the week, people move from bar to bar in search of fun. (Although it is legal to drink alcohol in public in Germany, glass bottles are verboten on the Reeperbahn.) Many clubs have either no cover charge or €3 or €4 entrance fees.

Herbertstrasse, a small side street not far from Hans-Albers-Platz begins with a tall red wall warning women and children under 18 not to enter. This is the place to witness department-store-window prostitutes similar to those in Amsterdam or meet women offering their services as they walk down the street. Anyone can walk down any street in Germany but the reception for women and children on Herbertstrasse may not be very warm. Among the attractions in the St. Pauli area are theaters, clubs, music venues, discos, and all kinds of bizarre shops. ✉ *Millerntorndamm to Holstenstrasse and Simon-von-Utrecht-Strasse to Bernhard-Nocht-Strasse., Reeperbahn* Ⓜ *St. Pauli (U-bahn), Reeperbahn (S-bahn).*

QUICK BITES

Elbe beach. No Hanseatic summer would be complete without a visit to the Elbe beach, which becomes alive with activity come summertime. Chic bars, volleyball games, pulsating dance clubs, barbecue grills, and sunbathers appear on sand trucked onto the banks of the Elbe. ⊠ *Am Schulberg, Övelgönne* Ⓜ *Neumühlen/Övelgönne (Bus 112), Neumühlen (Ferry 62).*

WORTH NOTING

★ **BallinStadt.** This museum and family-research center tells the fascinating story of European emigration to the United States and elsewhere. The museum is on a peninsula where in the late 19th century the HAPAG shipping line began construction of a complex for passengers from across Europe who came to Hamburg to embark on trans-Atlantic ships; it was completed in 1907.

When they landed in the United States, immigrants were subjected to thorough physical examinations. Those who were deemed sick were quarantined for weeks or returned to their home country. To reduce the likelihood of trouble, HAPAG began examining passengers before they left Hamburg for new shores. During the first 34 years of the 20th century, about 1.7 million people passed through emigration halls. Processing this many people took a long time. Hamburg officials did not want foreigners roaming the city. To accommodate visitors for several days or months, the shipping company built a town, complete with a hospital, church, music hall, housing, and hotels. The emigrant experience comes to life with detailed reproductions of the buildings (all but one was demolished); firsthand accounts of oppression in Europe, life in the "city," conditions during the 60-day Atlantic crossing, and life in their new home; authentic artifacts; and interactive displays.

As compelling as the exhibits are, the main draw is the research booths, where you can search the complete passenger lists of all ships that left the harbor. ■TIP→ Research assistants are available to help locate and track your ancestors. From St. Pauli, the museum can be reached by S-bahn or Maritime Circle Line at St. Pauli Landungsbrücken No. 10. ⊠ *Veddeler Bogen 2, Veddel* ☎ *040/3197–9160* ⊕ *www.ballinstadt.de* ⊠*€12* ◷ *Apr.–Oct., 10–6; Nov.–Mar., 10–4:30* Ⓜ *Veddel (S-bahn).*

Blankenese. Blankenese is one of Hamburg's surprises—a quiet neighborhood west of Downtown with the feel of a quaint 19th-century fishing village. Some Germans like to compare it to the French and Italian rivieras; many consider it the most beautiful part of Hamburg. The most picturesque part of town is the steeply graded hillside, where paths and stairs barely separate closely placed homes. Ⓜ *Blankenese (S-bahn).*

HARBOR TOURS

A cruise of Germany's gateway to the world is a must. The energy from the continuous ebb and flow of huge cargo vessels and container ships, the harbor's prosperity, and its international flavor best symbolize the city's spirit. The surrounding older parts of town, with their narrow cobblestone streets and late-medieval warehouses, testify to Hamburg's powerful Hanseatic past.

Holsten Brauerei. Until the 20th century, German beer consumption was a regional thing. A thirsty German would walk in to a pub and say, "*Grosses Bier, bitte*" and a large beer simply appeared. There was no need to request a brand because there was one brand. Holsten and Astra had breweries in the heart of Hamburg. Holsten eventually bought its rival. Even though Carlsberg purchased Holsten in 2004, Holsten and Astra are still produced in Hamburg. After a short film about the company history and the beer-making process, you can tour the brewery. The brewery tour ends with a sample of two brews and snack of bold German ham and dark bread. ✉ *Holstenstr. 224, Altona-Nord* ☎ *040/3099–3098* ⊕ *www.carlsbergdeutschland.de* 💰 *€5* ⊗ *Call for tour times* Ⓜ *Holstenstrasse (S-bahn).*

13

Konzentrationslager Neuengamme (*Concentration Camp Neuengamme*). Hamburg is a city of great beauty and also tragedy. On the southeastern edge of the city, between 104,000 and 106,000 people were held at Neuengamme concentration camp. It was primarily a slave-labor camp, not an area focused on extermination, where bricks and weapons were the main products. German political prisoners and Europeans pushed into servitude composed most of the population. Neuengamme held gays, Roma (the preferred term for gypsies), Jewish people, and children. Jewish children were the subjects of cruel medical experiments; others worked with their parents or simply grew up in prison. To keep people in line, there were random acts of violence including executions, and atrocious living conditions. Officials estimate that as many as 50,000 people died at Neuengamme before it ceased operation in May 1945.

A memorial opened on the site in 2005. Where the dormitories, dining hall, and hospital once sat, there are low pens filled with large rocks. With so much open space, the camp has an eerie silence. There is still a gate at the entrance. The camp has several regions. The main area has exhibits describing working conditions in an actual factory as well as a museum. The museum has interactive displays describing the prisoner experience. Firsthand accounts, photographs from prisoners, furniture, clothing, and possessions make the experience even more affecting. ✉ *Jean-Dolidier-Weg 75, Neuengamme* ☎ *040/4281–31500* ⊕ *www.kz-gedenkstaette-neuengamme.de* 💰 *Free* ⊗ *The grounds are always accessible; exhibits are open Apr.–Sept., weekdays 9:30–4, weekends noon–7; Oct.–Mar., weekdays 9:30–4, weekends noon–5* Ⓜ *KZ-Gedenkstätte, Mahnmal (Bus 227 or 327 from Bergedorf station (S-bahn).*

WHERE TO EAT

Hamburg has plenty of chic restaurants to satisfy the fashion-conscious local professionals, as well as the authentic salty taverns typical of a harbor town. There's not much culinary diversity in Hamburg, but what's available is delicious.

Use the coordinate (✛ B2) at the end of each listing to locate a site on the corresponding map.

WHAT IT COSTS IN EUROS					
	¢	$	$$	$$$	$$$$
AT DINNER	under €9	€9–€15	€16–€20	€21–€25	over €25

Restaurant prices are per person for a main course at dinner.

DOWNTOWN AND HISTORIC HAMBURG

$$$ ✕ **Carl's an der Elbphilharmonie.** This extension of the Hotel Louis C.
FRENCH Jacob is a pleasure on many levels. The building, which sits at the edge of the Elbe and next to the site of the Elbphilharmonie, contains a casual restaurant (The Bistro), a more formal restaurant (The Brasserie), and a bar and a performance space (Kultur Salon). The Bistro has a relaxed atmosphere and offers quiche, tartine, and *petit bol*. The Brasserie looks like a typical Parisian brasserie and features a large bay window with excellent views of ships gliding up the Elbe. The French menu has touches of German flavors and local fish dishes. The service is warm and instructive. Below the two restaurants sit an elegant bar and the salon, with live classical music concerts and jazz performances. ⊠ *Am Kaiserkai 69, HafenCity* ☎ 40/3003–22400 ⊕ *www.carls-brasserie.de* ⌂ *Reservations essential* ✢ G6.

$$ ✕ **Das Feuerschiff.** This bright-red lightship served in the English Channel before it retired to the city harbor in 1989 and became a landmark restaurant, guesthouse, and pub. Fresh and tasty fish dishes are on the menu, as well as traditional seafood entrées from Scandinavia.
SEAFOOD ■TIP→ Jazz musicians take the stage on Monday and a variety of bands play a few times a month. ⊠ *Vorsetzen, City Sporthafen, Speicherstadt* ☎ 040/362–553 ⊕ *www.das-feuerschiff.de* Ⓜ *Baumwall (U-bahn)* ✢ D6.

$$$ ✕ **Deichgraf.** This small and elegant fish restaurant in the heart of the
GERMAN historic district is a Hamburg classic. It's one of the best places to get traditional dishes such as *Hamburger Pannfisch* (fried pieces of the day's catch prepared in a wine-and-mustard sauce) at a very reasonable price. The restaurant is in an old merchant house, and oil paintings in the dining room feature ships from the 19th century. Reservations are essential on weekends. ⊠ *Deichstr. 23, Altstadt* ☎ 040/364–208 ⊕ *www.deichgraf-hamburg.de* ۝ *Closed Sun. Open daily July and Aug. No lunch Sat.* Ⓜ *Rödingsmarkt (U-bahn)* ✢ E6.

$$$ ✕ **Die Bank.** The brasserie held onto the grand exterior of an 1897 bank.
FRENCH Brave visitors who open the restaurant's huge door are hit with a large
Fodor'sChoice room boasting a warren of small tables covered in white tablecloths, a
★ grand bar with seating for diners who were not lucky enough to get a reservation, a few feet from the bar black-clad tipplers talk the night away at a seating lining the wall, and three tall and long tables near the entrance for revelers. There's a lot going on here but everything is done well and with a twist. The snob factor has been replaced with a good sense of humor. Lightboxes highlight the image of Benjamin Franklin on the $100 bill. Observant visitors can catch the Renaissance man blinking. Lounge music is always moving above the din of the restaurant. On the weekends,

BEST BETS FOR HAMBURG DINING

13

a DJ brings the noise when the kitchen closes and diners become revelers. Despite the activity, Die Bank has not forgotten the food. The petite menu brings the flavors of Asia to French food. Nothing is what it seems. The menu says Breast and Thigh of Black Feather Chicken "Oriental Style" with shallots, couscous, and carrots. What arrives is a spoon and plate with chicken breast slices atop a small pool of pungent sauce next to carrot slices, a slightly mushy square of spicy couscous with vegetables, and a transparent glass with layers of mousselike concoctions of different colors. The spoon is used to dig through a layer of seasoned pureed lentils, a layer of carmelized shallots, and a chicken thigh shredded in an exotic sauce. Fun-loving foodies can spend an entire evening at Die Bank. ⊠ *Hohe Bleichen 17, Neustadt* ☎ *040/238–0030* ⊕ *www.diebank-brasserie.de* ⊙ *Closed Sun.* Ⓜ *Gänsemarkt (U-bahn)* ⊕ *E5.*

$$$ ✕**Fillet of Soul.** The art of fine dining is celebrated in the open show
GERMAN   kitchen of this hip yet casual restaurant set among modern art shows
★   of the Deichtorhallen. The chef prepares straightforward, light German nouvelle cuisine with an emphasis on fresh fish. The minimalist dining room, highlighted only by an orange wall, might not be to everyone's

Where to Eat and Stay in Hamburg

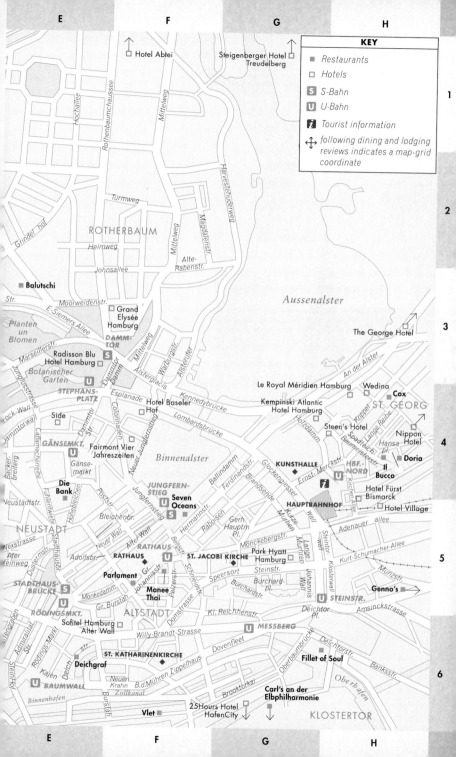

DID YOU KNOW?

You can get a great view of the Rathaus and a bite to eat at one of the cafés that line the Rathausmarkt.

CLOSE UP

Café Culture

The area around the Alster lakes and the canals are dotted with a variety of small restaurants with outside dining and an excellent selection of wine. Visitors can discover a refreshing *graubugunder* (pinot gris) while watching swans glide on the canal waters, sample classic French fare, or sip a perfect cup of coffee at one of the cafés sprinkled throughout central Hamburg. Here are a few places to start your café crawl:

Café Gnosa. Café Gnosa, a neighborhood favorite, has produced delicious desserts and the perfect breakfasts since 1987. It serves delicious comfort foods like pasta and schnitzel as well as salads. The friendly service and occasional drag performances attract many from inside and outside the gay and lesbian neighborhood. ⊠ *Lange Reihe 93, St. Georg* ☎ *040/243–034* ⊕ *www.gnosa.de.*

Café Paris. Across from the Rathaus, Café Paris offers excellent traditional French fare. The busy restaurant serves steak frites, beef tartar, croque monsieur, and other classics. Breakfasts here is a treat and a far cry from the traditional German bread-and-meat breakfast. The main dining room is crowded with tables. For a more intimate experience, reserve a table in the salon. Café Paris also has an excellent French wine list. ⊠ *Rathausstr. 4, Altstadt* ☎ *040/3252–7777* ⊕ *www.cafeparis. net.*

Saliba Alsterarkaden. This is one of the many restaurants that sit along a canal at Jungfernstieg. If the sun peeks out, the inside is empty, because everyone is perched at a waterside table. This café serves fine Syrian food and excellent German wine. In the afternoon, you can sip Gewürztraminer and watch swans glide across the water. At night, you can watch the stars ripple on the canal. ⊠ *Neuer Wall 13, Neustadt* ☎ *040/345–021* ⊕ *www.saliba.de.*

---

liking, but the buzzing atmosphere, artsy clientele, fragrant food, and great personal attention from the waitstaff make this the top choice. ⊠ *Deichtorstr. 2, Speicherstadt* ☎ *040/7070–5800* ⊕ *www.fillet-of-soul. de* ☉ *Closed Sun. and Mon.* Ⓜ *Steinstrasse (U-bahn)* ✥ *H6.*

$ ✕**Manee Thai.** Since 1992, this restaurant has delivered authentic and
THAI delicious Thai food in a charming atmosphere. Germans are not fans of spicy food, so many Asian restaurants here offer bland facsimiles of interesting dishes in overwhelming dining rooms decked out in reds, golds, and dragons. A few steps from Hamburg's Rathaus diners can sample tart Pad Thai and fiery red curry. The service is formal and some special requests are ignored but the chefs know best. There are also plenty of fish dishes. The international businesspeople who fill the tables at lunch and the locals and tourists who come at dinner are fans of the powerful flavors and the well-edited wine list. ⊠ *Schauenburgerstr. 59, 1st fl., Neustadt, Hamburg* ☎ *040/3339–5005* ⊕ *www.manee-thai.com* ⌕ *Reservations essential* ☉ *Closed Sun.* Ⓜ *Rathaus; Jungfernstieg* ✥ *F5.*

$ ✕**Parlament.** Set in what was once the Ratsweinkeller, the town hall's
GERMAN traditional pub, this restaurant is an almost ironic tribute to the basement's former occupant. With an eclectic mix of historic and modern

styles, Parlament is an intriguing version of a traditional Hamburg restaurant. On the menu are no-nonsense meat and fish meals with a light touch of German nouvelle cuisine. This grand restaurant creates amazing *flammkuchen*, Alsace's take on pizza. ⊠ *Rathausmarkt 1, Altstadt* ☎ *040/7038–3399* ⊕ *www.parlament-hamburg.de* ۞ *Closed Sun. Apr.–Oct.* Ⓜ *Rathaus (U-Bahn)* ✛ *F5.*

$$$
SEAFOOD
★

✕ **Seven Oceans.** Seven Oceans is an excellent new dining experience tucked into a downtown shopping mall. Try not to hold its location against it. Seven Oceans encompasses a cigar lounge, a sushi bar, a traditional bar, and a gourmet restaurant at the top of Europe Passage. One wall is lined in windows, so guests can watch passerbys on Binnenalster and Jungfernstieg. Service is formal in the gourmet restaurant but the food is an inspired twist on comfort food. A salmon appetizer arrives on a slate slab. The fish starter is a collage that includes fish wrapped in wontons, tartare with hints of dill, and a tartare accompanied by a square of mashed potato. Generous pieces of suckling pig have crackling skin and pearl onion and garlic tucked into them. A powerful kakao sauce provides excellent support for the meat. The restaurant has the excellent wine list that you would expect from this culinary powerhouse. You can choose from a gourmet dinner at the restaurant, sandwiches and appetizers at the Oceans Bar, and sake sashimi at the Sushi Bar. ⊠ *Europa Passage, Ballindamm 40; OG2, Neustadt, Hamburg* ☎ *40/3250–7944* ⊕ *www.se7en-oceans.de* ⌕ *Reservations essential* Ⓜ *Jungfernstieg (U-bahn/S-bahn)* ✛ *F5.*

$$
GERMAN

✕ **Vlet.** Inspired by its Speicherstadt location, the restaurant has the exposed brick and beams from the former warehouse that add a rustic charm to the sleek furniture and lighting in the large dining room. Like its architecture, the menu combines traditional German food with new techniques. Its Hamburger Aal Suppe is the traditional Hamburg staple with the twist of sweet apple. The kitchen offers diverse à la carte menus including the Elementar (classic) menu with traditional appetizers and entrées, and Elegant and Exquisit menus with more complex offerings and wine pairing. Although service is formal, the dining room is relaxed. ⊠ *Am Sandtorkai 23/24, entrance at Kibbelstegbrücke, Speicherstadt* ☎ *040/3347–53750* ⊕ *www.vlet.de* ۞ *Closed Sun. No lunch Sat.* ✛ *F6.*

ST. PAULI AND ALTONA

$$
ECLECTIC

✕ **Abendmahl.** Off the Reeperbahn, the small Abendmahl is a launching point for crowds getting ready for bars and clubs. The fresh dishes on the small menu change daily and focus on French, Asian, and northern German recipes. But the food plays second fiddle to the inexpensive and inventive drinks and the flirtatious atmosphere. ■ TIP→ The three-course dinner for just €25 is a great deal. ⊠ *Hein-Köllisch-Pl. 6, Reeperbahn* ☎ *040/312–758* ⊕ *www.restaurantabendmahl.de* ▭ No credit cards ۞ *No lunch* Ⓜ *Reeperbahn (S-bahn)* ✛ *B6.*

$$$ ✕**Au Quai.** The Au Quai is still the shining star among the row of
MEDITERRANEAN romantic restaurants nestled on the harbor's waterfront. In 2011, the
restaurant renovated its terrace, which draws many to the waterside
perch in the summer. The dining room, like the menu, is eclectic. An
Asian goddess statue looks over a koi pond and classic candelabras
illuminate contemporary tables and chairs when the sun stops shin-
ing through the wall of windows. A spring chicken filled with buffalo
mozzarella and sundried tomatoes sits on the same menu as a flavorful
soup boasting pureed yellow lentils, curry and cappuccino. ■ TIP➔ The
18.50 euro Business Lunch includes parking. ✉ *Grosse Elbstr. 145B–D,
Altona* ☎ *040/3803–7730* ⊕ *www.au-quai.com* ⌖ *Reservations essen-
tial* ♥ *Closed Sun. No lunch Sat.* Ⓜ *Königstrasse (S-bahn)* ⊹ *A6.*

$$$ ✕**Fischereihafen-Restaurant Hamburg.** For the best fish in Hamburg, book
GERMAN a table at this sprawling restaurant in Altona, just west of the downtown
area. The menu changes daily according to what's available in the fish
market that morning. The restaurant and its oyster bar are a favorite
with the city's beau monde. ■ TIP➔ In summer, try to get a table on the
sun terrace for a great view of the Elbe. ✉ *Grosse Elbstr. 143, Altona*
☎ *040/381–816* ⊕ *www.fischereihafenrestaurant.de* ⌖ *Reservations
essential* Ⓜ *Altona (S-bahn)* ⊹ *A6.*

$$$ ✕**Mess.** This is one of the most popular restaurants in the hip and
GERMAN upcoming Karolinenviertel (called "Karo-Viertel" by Hamburgers).
Fodor's Choice True to its worldly, young patrons, it dares to offer wild flavors like
★ *Thunfisch-Mangostapel mit Grüne Tomatenmarmelade, Pak Choi und
Jasminreis* (a tower of tuna and mango with green-tomato chutney
served with bok choi and jasmine rice) along with more traditional Ger-
man fare such as Wiener schnitzel and *Bratkartoffeln* (fried potatoes).
For lunch, order the two-course lunch menu (€19.80) or the daily pasta
special for just €7.90. ■ TIP➔ In summer, try to get a table in the small
garden under the pergola and sample vintages from the restaurant's own
specialty wine store. ✉ *Turnerstr. 9, St. Pauli* ☎ *040/4325–0152* ⊕ *www.
mess.de* ♥ *Closed Sun. No lunch Sat.* Ⓜ *Feldstrasse (U-bahn)* ⊹ *C4.*

$$$ ✕**Nil.** Media types—the intellectual and cultural elite of Hamburg—
GERMAN gather at this busy bistro. The kitchen serves seafood and modern Ger-
man cuisine in winter and lighter, Italian-oriented fare in summer. Nil
also offers inventive four-course meals that include a terrine of char with
fennel, dill, and lemon. ✉ *Neuer Pferdemarkt 5, St. Pauli* ☎ *040/439–
7823* ⊕ *www.restaurant-nil.de* ⌖ *Reservations essential* ▬ No *credit
cards* ♥ *Closed Tues. No lunch* Ⓜ *Feldstrasse (U-bahn)* ⊹ *C4.*

13

$$ **Rive.** This harborside oyster bar is known for both its German nou-
GERMAN velle cuisine and its classic local dishes. Choose between such dishes as hearty *Matjes mit dreierlei Saucen* (herring with three sauces) or *Dorade in der Salzkruste* (dorado cooked in salt crust). Media types come to this shiplike building for the fresh oysters, clams, and spectacular view. ✉ *Van-der-Smissen Str. 1, Kreuzfahrt-Center, Altona* ☎ *040/380–5919* ⊕ *www.rive.de* ⚓ *Reservations essential* Ⓜ *Königstrasse (S-bahn)* ✛ *A6.*

$ **River-Kasematten.** There is no other restaurant in town that better
ECLECTIC embodies Hamburg's international spirit and its lust for style, entertain-
★ ment, and good seafood. Once a legendary jazz club with performances by Ella Fitzgerald and the like, it now hosts a fascinating mix of hip guests. Sushi, spiced-up regional fish dishes, and exotic soups are the order of the day. The lunch buffet (weekdays noon–3) for just €9.90 is a steal; it's even better on the outside terrace. The ambience—black oak floors, leather seats, and redbrick walls—is elegant yet casual. ✉ *Fischmarkt 28–32, St. Pauli* ☎ *040/892–760* ⊕ *www.river-kasematten.de* ⚓ *Reservations essential* Ⓜ *Fischmarkt (Bus 112), Reeperbahn (S-bahn)* ✛ *B6.*

$$$ **Tafelhaus.** This airy gourmet restaurant has stunning views of the
ECLECTIC Hamburg harbor from its bay windows and serves some of the best food
★ in town. Chef Christian Rach creates innovative German cuisine with Italian and French touches; the menu has light "summer" standards (featured throughout the year, though) and a changing set of imagina-tive dishes, mostly seafood (pike, perch, salmon, oysters) and tradi-tional German meat dishes. ✉ *Neumühlen 17, Altona* ☎ *040/892–760* ⊕ *www.tafelhaus-hamburg.de* ⚓ *Reservations essential* ☾ *Closed Sun. No lunch Sat.* Ⓜ *Lawaetzhaus (Bus 112), Königstrasse (S-bahn)* ✛ *A6.*

ST. GEORG

$$ **Cox.** Cox has delighted guests with its nouvelle German cuisine for
GERMAN years. It remains one of the hippest places around yet waitstaff (and patrons, for that matter) won't give you any attitude. The dishes feature the careful use of fresh produce and spices from around the globe. The simple and cool interior with red-leather banquettes is reminiscent of a French brasserie. ✉ *Lange Reihe 68, at Greifswalder Str. 43, St. Georg* ☎ *040/249–422* ⊕ *www.restaurant-cox.de* ☾ *No lunch weekends* Ⓜ *Gurlittstrasse (Bus 6), Hauptbahnhof (U-bahn and S-Bahn)* ✛ *H4.*

$$ **Doria.** At the end of 2010, Doria started drawing foodies to a seedy
MODERN corner of St. Georg, called Hansaplatz. The restaurant is decorated
GERMAN with textured plaster walls, wood floors and large abstract artworks. Owner Hasko Sadrina calls the food modern European. The beef cheek braised for five hours and its accompanying sauce take two days to cre-ate. The dark and powerful sauce perfectly complements the delicate meat. Add to that, an expertly fried potato and a celery puree, and you have a perfect balance of flavors. Doria also offers steaks and chops. The wine list features accessible and interesting vintages from around the world. Best yet, the most expensive bottle costs €65 but most hover around €20. The laid-back service, creative cuisine and interesting din-ing room make dining at Doria a unique experience. ✉ *Hansaplatz 14, St. Georg, Hamburg* ☎ *3867–2848* ⊕ *www.doria14.de* ☾ *Closed Sun. and Mon.* Ⓜ *Hauptbahnhof (U-bahn)* ✛ *H4.*

HAMBURG'S CHAIN RESTAURANTS

After a long day of shopping or for a break between museums, stop for an economical but delicious bite at one of these chain restaurants.

Block House. Steak is not a common German entrée. Eugen Block opened the first Block House steak house in Hamburg in 1968 after falling in love with the concept in San Francisco. Today, there are 14 outlets in Hamburg and dozens more in the rest of Germany and Spain and Portugal. This steak house is reminiscent of its American forebears. Each steak comes with a baked potato, salad, and garlic bread. Unlike many German restaurants, servers ask you how you would like your steak prepared. ⊕ *www.block-house.de*.

Campus Suite. This northern German chain started on a university campus in Kiel. The restaurant, with 11 outposts in Hamburg, offers reasonably priced Asian and Italian pasta dishes, couscous, sandwiches, muffins, croissants, and coffee drinks. Thirsty guests can also have beer, wine, and champagne. ⊕ *www.campussuite.de*.

Schweinske. This is Germany's answer to T.G.I. Friday's. Crowds turn out for after-work drink specials and German comfort food, like schnitzel and curry wurst. This Hamburg creation has 32 outlets in the city and even more throughout the country. ⊕ *www.schweinske.com*.

Vapiano. This Italian restaurant was born in downtown Hamburg and there are three in central locations. To customize your dish, you first decide between pasta or pizza, then select the toppings, sauces, and ingredients for the dish. Italian wines and desserts finish off the meal. ⊕ *www.vapiano.com*.

$ ✕ **Il Buco.** This neighborhood favorite is easily missed. Il Buco sits on a
ITALIAN street off Hansaplatz and intrepid diners must then descend five steps and open a door to a warm and cozy dining room. The atmosphere is definitely more grandmother's living room than downtown trattoria. There's even a sofa-size painting of a cliff perched over water. In place of a menu, a server asks what you are in the mood for, describes the evening's options and makes recommendations. In a typical evening, a hearty saltimbocca follows a colorful antipasti plate. Even when dining alone, meals are comforting and filling. ⊠ *Zimmerpforte 5, St. Georg, Hamburg* ☎ *247–310* ⊙ *No lunch. Closed Sun.* Ⓜ *Hauptbahnhof (U-bahn/S-bahn)* ✛ *H4*.

ROTHERBAUM

$ ✕ **Balutschi.** A favorite among neighborhood students, Balutschi serves
INDIAN affordable and tasty Pakistani dishes, all prepared with organic products. The richly decorated dining room always seems to be crowded, and the smell of fresh spices and meat dishes, mostly lamb, hangs thick in the air. ■ TIP➔ On weekend nights a reservation is a must. ⊠ *Grindelallee 31, Rotherbaum* ☎ *040/452–479* ⊕ *www.balutschi.net* Ⓜ *Universität/Staatsbibliothek (Bus 5), Dammtor (S-bahn)* ✛ *E3*.

OTTENSEN, UHLENHORST, AND ELSEWHERE

$$
ITALIAN
★

✕**Genno's.** Genno's is far from the downtown district, in Hamburg-Hamm—a rundown residential area where you would hardly expect to find such a gem of high-quality dining. Chef Eugen Albrecht makes you feel at home with warm service and tasty dishes. The cuisine is a mixture of his personal preferences, including dishes such as *Lammfilet mit Rotweinsauce* (fillet of lamb with red wine sauce). ✉ *Hammer Steindamm 123, Hamm* ☎ *040/202–567* ⊕ *www.gennos.de* ⚓ *Reservations essential* ▭ *No credit cards* ⊙ *Closed Sun. No lunch* Ⓜ *Hasselbrook (S-bahn)* ✛ *H5.*

$$$$
GERMAN
Fodor's Choice
★

✕**Landhaus Scherrer.** Though this establishment is a 10-minute drive from downtown, its parklike setting seems worlds away from the high-rise hustle and bustle of the city. For 35 years, Landhaus Scherrer has been serving dynamic food for an international crowd. Wood-panel walls and soft lighting create a low-key mood in the building, which was originally a brewery. The restaurant recently started offering three menus: classic German food; cuisines that focuses on local ingredients; and a mixture of modern German dishes and flavors from around the world. The spectacular mingle with more down-to-earth local dishes. The wine list is exceptional. If the restaurant looks too highbrow to you, stick to the small bistro, where you get the same fare at lower prices. For delicious German comfort food (curry wurst and potato salad), sample the sister property, Ö1. ✉ *Elbchaussee 130, Ottensen* ☎ *040/880–1325* ⊕ *www.landhausscherrer.de* ⊙ *Closed Sun.* Ⓜ *Hohenzollernring (Bus 15, 36), Königstrasse (S-bahn)* ✛ *A6.*

$
ITALIAN

✕**Restaurant Eisenstein.** A longtime neighborhood favorite, Eisenstein serves fantastic food at affordable prices. The bubbly and mostly stylish crowd enjoys the Italian and international dishes. The Pizza Helsinki (made with crème fraîche, onions, and fresh gravlax) is truly delicious. The setting, a 19th-century industrial complex with high ceilings and dark brick walls, is very rustic. ✉ *Friedensallee 9, Ottensen* ☎ *040/390–4606* ⊕ *www.restaurant-eisenstein.de* ⚓ *Reservations essential* ▭ *No credit cards* Ⓜ *Altona (S-bahn)* ✛ *A5.*

$$$$
FRENCH

✕**Seven Seas.** A small hill in the countryside along the Elbe boasts one of the greatest views of the river you'll find anywhere and a sophisticated hotel and restaurant complex. The Seven Seas' award-winning French kitchen is run by one of Europe's premier chefs, Karlheinz Hauser, and features fish specialties served in four- to six-course dinners. ■TIP➔**If you don't want all the frills, try the bistro Süllbergterrrassen.** ✉ *Süllbergsterrasse 12, Blankenese* ☎ *040/8662–5212* ⊕ *www.suellberg-hamburg.de* ⚓ *Reservations essential* ⊙ *Closed Mon. and Tues. No lunch Wed.–Sat.* Ⓜ *Kahlkamp (Bus 48), Blankenese (S-bahn)* ✛ *A6.*

WHERE TO STAY

For expanded hotel reviews, visit Fodors.com.

Hamburg has a full range of hotels, from five-star, grande-dame luxury enterprises to simple pensions. Nearly year-round conference and convention business keeps most rooms booked well in advance, and the rates are high. But many of the more expensive hotels lower their rates on weekends, when businesspeople have gone home. The tourist office can help with reservations if you arrive with nowhere to stay. In Hamburg, independent hotels may not have coffeemakers or an information book in the guest rooms, but, in general, you will find generous-size rooms and staffs willing to answer questions about the hotel. Hotels without business centers will fax and copy for you. At hotels without concierges, front-desk staff will whip out a map and give recommendations. All accommodations offer no-smoking rooms. Although breakfast is not usually included, those who opt for the meal are usually greeted with an all-you-can-eat masterpiece with hot food options that sometimes includes an omelet station. Germans find the human body more natural than sexual. Be prepared to encounter nudity in coed saunas at most hotels. Also, most double beds are made of two single beds on a large platform and an individual blanket for each mattress.

Use the coordinate (✣ B3) at the end of each listing to locate a site on the corresponding map.

WHAT IT COSTS IN EUROS					
	¢	$	$$	$$$	$$$$
OR TWO EOPLE	under €50	€50–€100	€101–€175	€176–€225	over €225

Hotel prices are for two people in a standard double room, including tax and service.

DOWNTOWN AND HISTORIC HAMBURG

$$ **25Hours Hotel HafenCity.** Although the new 25hours Hotel HafenCity is a little more kitsch than thematic, it gives guests a fun trip back to Hamburg's maritime past. ⊠ *Überseeallee 5* ☎ *040/257–7770* ☎ *170* ☖ *In-room: a/c, Wi-Fi. In-hotel: bar, water sports, business center, parking* Ⓜ *Osakaallee (6 Bus); in 2012 Überseequartier U-bahn* ✣ *G6.*

$$$$ **Adina Apartment Hotel Hamburg Michel.** The Adina is less like a hotel and more like an apartment switch with some really cool friends. ■ TIP➔ The hotel is down the street from an Edeka supermarket. **Pros:** excellent location; huge guest rooms with many amenities; free Wi-Fi in public spaces. **Cons:** indoor pool area is small and can be rowdy; staff eager but not the most helpful; Wi-Fi fee in guest room. ⊠ *Neuer Steinweg 26, Altstadt, Hamburg* ☎ *040/226–3500* ⊕ *www.adina.eu/ adina-apartment-hotel-hamburg-michel* ☎ *128 rooms* ☖ *In-hotel: restaurant, bar, pool, gym, laundry facilities, parking* Ⓜ *Stadhausbrücke (S-bahn)* ✣ *D5.*

$$$$ **Fairmont Vier Jahreszeiten.** Some claim that this 19th-century town Fodor'sChoice   house on the edge of the Binnenalster is the best hotel in Germany. ★   **Pros:** luxury hotel with great view of Alster lakes; close to shopping on Jungfernstieg; charming, large rooms. **Cons:** formal service; high prices even in off-season; far away from new city quarters like Schanzen- and Katharinenviertel. ⊠ *Neuer Jungfernstieg 9–14, Neustadt* ☎ *040/34940* ⊕ *www.fairmont-hvj.de* ☎ *124 rooms, 32 suites* ☖ *In-room: a/c, Wi-Fi. In-hotel: restaurant, bar, gym, spa, parking* Ⓜ *Jungfernstieg (U-bahn)* ✣ *F4.*

13

BEST BETS FOR HAMBURG LODGING

Fodor's Choice★

Fairmont Vier Jahreszeiten, $$$$, p. 611

Hotel Louis C. Jacob, $$$$, p. 617

Le Royal Méridien Hamburg, $$$, p. 616

By Price

$

fritzhotel, p. 614

YoHo, p. 618

Hotel Village, p. 613

$$

Empire Riverside Hotel, p. 614

Linder Park-Hotel Hagenbeck, p. 617

Side, p. 613

$$$

Le Royal Méridien Hamburg, p. 616

$$$$

Adina Apartment Hotel Hamburg Michel, p. 611

Fairmont Vier Jahreszeiten, p. 611

Hotel Louis C. Jacob, p. 617

Sofitel Hamburg Alter Wall, p. 613

By Experience

BEST GRANDE DAMES

Fairmont Vier Jahreszeiten, $$$$, p. 611

Park Hyatt Hamburg, $$$, p. 613

Kempinski Atlantic Hotel Hamburg, $$$$, p. 616

BEST BEDS

Le Royal Méridien Hamburg, $$, p. 616

Radisson Blu Hotel, Hamburg, $$$, p. 613

BEST FOR KIDS

Lindner Park-Hotel Hagenbeck, $$, p. 617

Park Hyatt Hamburg, $$$, p. 613

BEST POOL

Le Royal Méridien Hamburg, $$$, p. 616

Kempinski Atlantic Hotel Hamburg, $$$$, p. 616

$$ **Grand Elysée Hamburg.** The "grand" at the Grand Elysée Hamburg refers to its size, from the near 11,000-square-foot wellness area and five restaurants to the guest rooms and extra-wide beds. **Pros:** large guestrooms; close to tourist sites; diverse artwork throughout hotel; free Wi-Fi. **Cons:** room decor is boring; staff can be unresponsive. ⊠ *Rothenbaumchaussee 10, Altstadt, Hamburg* ☎ *49040/414–120* ⊕ *www.grand-elysee.com* ⌂ *511* ⌂ *In-room: Wi-Fi. In-hotel: restaurants, bar, pool, gym, spa, parking* Ⓜ *Dammtor* ✛ *F3.*

$$ **Hotel Baseler Hof.** It's hard to find a fault in this central hotel near the Binnenalster and the opera house. **Pros:** quiet location near Binnenalster; upscale rooms and service for moderate prices; residential neighborhood. **Cons:** fee for Wi-Fi (free for one hour; small fee after); no air-conditioning in rooms but available in public areas; small rooms. ⊠ *Esplanade 11, Neustadt* ☎ *040/359–060* ⊕ *www.baselerhof. de* ⌂ *163 rooms, 4 suites* ⌂ *In-room: no a/c, Wi-Fi. In-hotel: restaurant, bar, gym, spa* ⏐◯⏐ *Breakfast* Ⓜ *Stephansplatz (U-bahn)* ✛ *F4.*

$ **Hotel Fürst Bismarck.** Despite its humble location on a busy street opposite the Hauptbahnhof, the Bismarck is a surprisingly attractive hotel, with a homey yet modern flair. **Pros:** centrally located; competitive prices; free pass for public transportation. **Cons:** neighborhood around the train station does not have much nightlife; small rooms; small fee for Wi-Fi. ⊠ *Kirchenallee 49, Altstadt* ☎ *040/280–1091* ⌂ *102 rooms*

♿ *In-room: no a/c, Wi-Fi. In-hotel: some pets allowed* Ⓜ *Hauptbahnhof (U-bahn and S-bahn)* ✚ *H5.*

$ ★ 🏨 **Hotel Village.** Once a thriving brothel nearby the central train station, this hotel still exudes lasciviousness. **Pros:** in the heart of downtown; cozy; individually designed rooms; fun decor; free coffee at reception. **Cons:** sometimes casual service; neighborhood lacks quality nightlife. ✉ *Steindamm 4, Altstadt* ☎ *040/480–6490* ⊕ *www.hotel-village.de* 🛏 *20 rooms, 3 suites, 4 apartments* ♿ *In-room: no a/c, Wi-Fi. In-hotel: bar, some pets allowed* Ⓜ *Hauptbahnhof (U-bahn and S-bahn)* ✚ *H5.*

$ 🏨 **Motel One Am Michel.** Part of the Motel One chain, this hotel is ideal for those looking for a trendy, design-minded, yet inexpensive base from which to explore Hamburg. **Pros:** close to activities; cool design; bar open 24 hours. **Cons:** no amenities; no telephones; no restaurant; small rooms; Wi-Fi available with purchase of breakfast. ✉ *Ludwig-Erhard-Strasse 26, Altstadt, Hamburg* ☎ *040/3571–8900* 🛏 *437* ♿ *In-room: a/c, Wi-Fi. In-hotel: bar, parking, some pets allowed* ✚ *D5.*

$$$ ★ 🏨 **Park Hyatt Hamburg.** This elegant hotel, one of the best in northern Germany, is filled with warm, brown colors and furnished with exquisite wooden floors and panels. **Pros:** close to shopping on Mönckebergstrasse and Jungfernstieg; close to museums; warm interior design; large, quiet rooms with all modern amenities; friendly and helpful service. **Cons:** fee for Wi-Fi (30 minutes free per day); far away from nightlife hot spots. ✉ *Bugenhagenstr. 8, Neustadt* ☎ *040/3332–1234* ⊕ *www.hamburg.park.hyatt.com* 🛏 *176 rooms, 21 suites, 31 apartments* ♿ *In-room: Wi-Fi. In-hotel: restaurant, bar, pool, gym, spa, parking, some pets allowed* Ⓜ *Mönckebergstrasse (U-bahn)* ✚ *G5.*

$$ 🏨 **Radisson Blu Hotel, Hamburg.** This hotel was famous for being the tallest building in Hamburg and for its outdated interiors. **Pros:** a chain hotel has familiar elements yet interesting style; connected to convention center; ladies-only sauna. **Cons:** small gym; sleeping area has a window into bathroom but the blinds are controlled from outside the bathroom; few good restaurants in area. ✉ *Marseiller Str. 2, Neustadt* ☎ *040/35020* ⊕ *www.radissonblu.de/hamburg* 🛏 *556 rooms, 9 suites* ♿ *In-room: a/c, Wi-Fi. In-hotel: restaurant, bar, gym, spa, parking* Ⓜ *Dammtor (S-bahn)* ✚ *E3.*

$$ ★ 🏨 **Side.** Deeming itself to be the design hotel of the 21st century, this ultrahip hotel is one of the most architecturally sophisticated places to stay in Germany. **Pros:** cool design; Nespresso pod coffeemakers in rooms; convenient downtown location yet quiet. **Cons:** somewhat sterile; Wi-Fi in guest rooms for three hours per stay; small rooms. ✉ *Drehbahn 49, Neustadt* ☎ *040/309–990* ⊕ *www.side-hamburg.de* 🛏 *168 rooms, 10 suites* ♿ *In-room: a/c, Wi-Fi. In-hotel: restaurant, bar, pool, gym, spa, parking, some pets allowed* Ⓜ *Gänsemarkt (U-bahn)* ✚ *E4.*

$$$$ 🏨 **Sofitel Hamburg Alter Wall.** Behind the facade of an administrative building for Deutsche Post, Germany's mail service, is one of the city's finest business hotels. **Pros:** in the historic downtown area; close to upscale shopping; large rooms. **Cons:** somewhat cold design; no real nightlife within walking distance. ✉ *Alter Wall 40, Altstadt* ☎ *040/369–500* ⊕ *www.sofitel.com* 🛏 *223 rooms, 18 suites* ♿ *In-room: a/c, Wi-Fi. In-hotel: restaurants, bar, pool, gym, parking, some pets allowed* Ⓜ *Rödingsmarkt (U-bahn)* ✚ *F6.*

13

ST. PAULI AND ALTONA

$$ ⊤ **25Hours Hotel Hamburg No. 1.** This hotel expertly packs fun and retro design in a relaxed package. **Pros:** cool design; lots of freebies for guests; relaxed atmosphere; free Wi-Fi in public spaces, near a shopping center. **Cons:** far from interesting sites and nightlife; some basics missing; no high-speed Internet in guest room, 12-minute walk to nearest subway. ⊠ *2 Paul-Dessau-Strasse, Bahrenfeld, Hamburg* ☎ *040/855-070* ⊕ *www.25hours-hotels.com/no1/* ☞ *128 rooms* ⟁ *In-room: no a/c, Wi-Fi. In-hotel: restaurant, bar, gym, laundry facilities, parking* Ⓜ *Bahrenfeld (S-bahn)* ✛ *A3.*

$$ ⊤ **The Boston.** Taking its cue from the funky Sternschanze neighborhood where it's located, The Boston is ultramodern and sleek. **Pros:** the design is chic but comfortable; staff is very helpful; close to hip bars and restaurants. **Cons:** no air-conditioning; the hotel has some fans for guests; windows open but noise from street traffic can be a problem. ⊠ *Missundestr. 2, Sternschanze* ☎ *040/5896–66700* ⊕ *www.boston-hamburg.de* ☞ *34 rooms, 12 suites* ⟁ *In-room: no a/c, Wi-Fi. In-hotel: restaurant, bar, parking* Ⓜ *Sternschanze (S-bahn)* ✛ *B3.*

$$ ⊤ **Empire Riverside Hotel.** The location near the Reeperbahn and the harbor, clever use of space and light, and a cool bar that attracts thousands every weekend make the Empire a favorite of locals and tourists. **Pros:** clever use of space; close to nightlife and leisure activities; excellent view of the city and river; bright rooms; free Wi-Fi in public areas. **Cons:** many steps or steep hill separate the hotel from the harbor; bar on the 20th floor is crowded after 9 pm on weekends; no information booklets in rooms. ⊠ *Bernhard-Nocht-Stra. 97, Reeperbahn* ☎ *040/311–190* ⊕ *www.empire-riverside.de* ☞ *315 rooms, 12 suites* ⟁ *In-room: a/c, Wi-Fi. In-hotel: restaurant, bar, gym, spa, parking* Ⓜ *Reeperbahn (S-bahn)* ✛ *B6.*

$ ⊤ **fritzhotel.** This intimate yet stylish hotel, squeezed into an old city apartment complex, has small but bright designer rooms complete with such amenities as wireless Internet access. **Pros:** clean rooms at budget prices; both S- and U-bahn nearby; free coffee, newspapers, fruits, and juices for guests. **Cons:** noisy due to close S-bahn tracks; away from major Hamburg sights; only limited facilities; high-speed Internet in rooms; no Wi-Fi in public areas. ⊠ *Schanzenstr. 101–103, Sternschanze* ☎ *040/8222–2830* ⊕ *www.fritzhotel.com* ☞ *15 rooms* ⟁ *In-room: no a/c. In-hotel: some pets allowed* Ⓜ *Sternschanze (S-bahn)* ✛ *C3.*

$$ ⊤ **Gastwerk Hotel Hamburg.** Proudly dubbing itself Hamburg's first design hotel, the Gastwerk, in an 1896 gas plant, is certainly the most stylish accommodation in town. **Pros:** large rooms; stunning interior design; large and well-equipped health club. **Cons:** far away from downtown area and any sightseeing; few restaurants nearby; public spaces like breakfast room and bar can get crowded. ⊠ *Beim Alten Gaswerk 3, Altona* ☎ *040/890–620* ⊕ *www.gastwerk.com* ☞ *127 rooms, 14 suites* ⟁ *In-room: a/c, Wi-Fi. In-hotel: restaurant, bar, gym, spa, parking, some pets allowed* Ⓜ *Bahrenfeld (S-bahn)* ✛ *A3.*

$$ ⊤ **Hotel Hafen Hamburg.** This harbor landmark, just across from the famous St. Pauli Landungsbrücken, is a good value considering its three-star status. **Pros:** top location for harbor and St. Pauli sightseeing; great

Fodor'sChoice ★

Hotel Louis C. Jacob

Le Royal Méridien Hamburg

Fairmont Vier Jahreszeiten

views; comfortable, fairly large rooms; free Wi-Fi in public areas. **Cons:** smoking allowed in Tower Bar; poor restaurant selection in neighborhood; must climb dozens of steps to reach hotel from the pier. ⊠ *Seewartenstr. 7–9, St. Pauli* ☎ *040/31113* ⊕ *www.hotel-hamburg.de* ⇆ *353 rooms* ☖ *In-room: no a/c, Internet. In-hotel: restaurant, bar, parking, some pets allowed* Ⓜ *Landungsbrücken (U-bahn)* ✛ *C6.*

$$ 〓 **Mövenpick Hotel Hamburg.** For its Hamburg outpost, Mövenpick turned a 19th-century landmark into a modern business-class hotel. **Pros:** very close to the convention center; free coffee drinks from machine in lobby; free newspaper available in English from reception and in restaurant; everything (signs on doors, etc.) is in English and German; excellent information book; free Wi-Fi in public areas. **Cons:** lackluster room design; paid Wi-Fi in some guest rooms; only a curtain separates washing area from sleeping area. ⊠ *Sternschanze 6, Sternschanze* ☎ *040/334–4110* ⊕ *www.moevenpick-hamburg.com* ⇆ *226 rooms, 10 suites* ☖ *In-room: a/c, Wi-Fi. In-hotel: restaurant, bar, gym, spa, parking* Ⓜ *Sternschanze (S-bahn)* ✛ *C3.*

ST. GEORG

$$$ 〓 **The George Hotel.** The George is a cool hotel in a groovy location that takes itself seriously. **Pros:** located near many good bars and restaurants; interesting design; nightlife in hotel; free Wi-Fi throughout hotel. **Cons:** can be noisy; some may find design unwelcoming; no business center. ⊠ *Barcastr. 3, St. Georg* ☎ *040/280–0300* ⊕ *www.thegeorge-hotel.de* ⇆ *118 rooms, 7 suites* ☖ *In-room: a/c, Wi-Fi. In-hotel: restaurant, bar, spa, parking* Ⓜ *Hauptbahnhof (U-bahn and S-bahn), AK St. Georg (Bus 6)* ✛ *H3.*

$$$$ 〓 **Kempinski Atlantic Hotel Hamburg.** There are few hotels in Germany
★ more sumptuous than this gracious Edwardian palace facing the Aussenalster, which draws celebrities and people searching for a lux retreat. **Pros:** large rooms; great views of lakeside skyline; impeccable service; historic flair; free Wi-Fi throughout the hotel. **Cons:** formal service; public areas can be crowded. ⊠ *An der Alster 72–79, St. Georg* ☎ *040/28880* ⊕ *www.kempinski.atlantic.de* ⇆ *167 rooms, 16 suites* ☖ *In-room: a/c, Wi-Fi. In-hotel: restaurant, bar, pool, gym, parking, some pets allowed* Ⓜ *Hauptbahnhof (U-bahn and S-bahn)* ✛ *G4.*

$$$ 〓 **Le Royal Méridien Hamburg.** This hotel offers you beauty inside and
Fodor'sChoice outside its walls. **Pros:** great location with views of the Alster; clean and
★ smartly designed, large rooms; outstanding pool area. **Cons:** no Wi-Fi in guest rooms; fee for Wi-Fi in public areas; top-floor bar and restaurant can be crowded. ⊠ *An der Alster 52–56, St. Georg* ☎ *040/21000* ⊕ *www.leroyalmeridienhamburg.com* ⇆ *265 rooms, 19 suites* ☖ *In-room: Internet. In-hotel: restaurant, bar, gym, parking* Ⓜ *Hauptbahnhof (U-bahn and S-bahn)* ✛ *H4.*

$ 〓 **Steen's Hotel.** This small, family-run hotel in a four-story town house near the central train station provides modest but congenial service. **Pros:** highly competitive prices; good breakfast; friendly service. **Cons:** some rooms are worn; few amenities and hotel services; limited restaurant selection nearby; fee for Wi-Fi. ⊠ *Holzdamm 43, St. Georg* ☎ *040/244–642* ⊕ *www.steens-hotel.com* ⇆ *15 rooms* ☖ *In-room: no* *a/c, Wi-Fi. In-hotel: parking* |○| *Breakfast* Ⓜ *Hauptbahnhof (U-bahn and S-bahn)* ✛ *H4.*

$$ ⊞ **Wedina.** This property brings a touch of Tuscany to central Hamburg. **Pros:** cozy flair and comfortable, quiet rooms; very accommodating; knowledgeable staff; inviting apartments; free Wi-Fi throughout hotel. **Cons:** hotel spread over several buildings; smallish rooms. ⊠ *Gurlittstr. 23, St. Georg* ☎ *040/280–8900* ⊕ *www.wedina.de* ⇱ *46 rooms, 13 apartments* ⌂ *In-room: no a/c, Internet. In-hotel: bar, parking, some pets allowed* |○| *Breakfast* Ⓜ *Hauptbahnhof (U-bahn and S-bahn), Gurlittstrasse (Bus 6)* ✛ *H4.*

13

LSEWHERE

$$$ ⊞ **Hotel Abtei.** On a quiet, tree-lined street about 3 km (2 mi) north of the downtown area, in Harvestehude, this elegant period hotel offers understated luxury and friendly, personal service. **Pros:** great historic flair; individually designed, upscale rooms; quiet location. **Cons:** very small and personal; away from many major sightseeing spots; very limited restaurant selection nearby. ⊠ *Abteistr. 14, Harvestehude* ☎ *040/442–905* ⊕ *www.abtei-hotel.de* ⇱ *8 rooms, 3 suites* ⌂ *In-room: no a/c. In-hotel: restaurant, bar, some pets allowed* Ⓜ *Klosterstern (U-bahn)* ✛ *F1.*

$$$$ ⊞ **Hotel Louis C. Jacob.** Would-be Hanseats frequent this small yet luxurious hotel nestled amid the older wharf dwellings along the banks of the Elbe. **Pros:** outstanding service with attention to personal requests; quiet, serene setting in the city's wealthiest neighborhood, with historic flair; extremely comfortable beds. **Cons:** rooms are surprisingly simple for luxury hotel; away from downtown area and most nightlife, restaurants, and shopping. ⊠ *Elbchaussee 401–403, Blankenese* ☎ *040/822–550* ⊕ *www.hotel-jacob.de* ⇱ *66 rooms, 19 suites* ⌂ *In-room: a/c, Wi-Fi. In-hotel: restaurant, bar, parking, some pets allowed* Ⓜ *Hochkamp (S-bahn)* ✛ *A6.*

Fodor'sChoice ★

$$ ⊞ **Lindner Park-Hotel Hagenbeck.** Everything at this hotel is aimed at transporting you from metropolitan Hamburg to the wilds of Asia and Africa. **Pros:** smartly designed Africa and Asia theme carried throughout hotel; friendly, helpful staff; quality dining options. **Cons:** no information book in guest rooms; fee for Wi-Fi; some design flaws. ⊠ *Hagenbeckstr. 150. 45, Stellingen* ☎ *040/8008–08100* ⊕ *www.lindner.de* ⇱ *151 rooms, 7 suites* ⌂ *In-room: a/c, Wi-Fi. In-hotel: restaurant, bar, gym, spa, parking* Ⓜ *Hagenbecks Tierpark (U-bahn)* ✛ *A1.*

$$ ⊞ **Nippon Hotel.** You'll be asked to remove your shoes before entering your room at the Nippon. **Pros:** Asian flair; inviting Japanese restaurant; quiet, residential neighborhood; free Wi-Fi throughout hotel. **Cons:** location away from all major sightseeing; very minimalist design. ⊠ *Hofweg 75, Uhlenhorst* ☎ *040/227–1140* ⊕ *www.nippon-hotel.de* ⇱ *41 rooms, 1 suite* ⌂ *In-room: a/c, Wi-Fi. In-hotel: restaurant, parking* Ⓜ *Mundsburg (U-bahn), Zimmerstrasse (Bus 6)* ✛ *H4.*

$$ ⊞ **Steigenberger Hotel Treudelberg.** People searching for calm or a few rounds of golf flock to this resort in Poppenbüttel, a residential area in northern Hamburg. **Pros:** large rooms; excellent wellness options; golf course; several restaurant options; relaxing surroundings. **Cons:** little to do near the hotel; sensors monitor the minibar; some rooms have

few amenities; no business center; fee for Wi-Fi available throughout hotel. ✉ *Lemsahler Landstr. 45, Poppenbüttel* ☎ *040/608–220* 🌐 *www.treudelberg.de* 🛏 *214 rooms, 10 suites* 🖒 *In-room: a/c, Wi-Fi. In-hotel: restaurant, bar, gym, spa, parking* Ⓜ *Treudelberg (Bus 176, 276 from Poppenbüttel [S-bahn])* ✣ *G1.*

$ ★ **YoHo.** Bargain hunters flock to this property for a comfortable yet minimalist escape. **Pros:** close to hip, artsy neighborhoods; historic flair; very good furnishings at budget prices; free Wi-Fi throughout hotel; free parking. **Cons:** limited breakfast; sometimes noisy due to young travelers; away from all major sightseeing. ✉ *Moorkamp 5, Eimsbüttel* ☎ *040/284–1910* 🌐 *www.yoho-hamburg.de* 🛏 *30 rooms* 🖒 *In-room: no a/c, Internet. In-hotel: restaurant, parking, some pets allowed* 🍽 *Breakfast* Ⓜ *Schlump (U-bahn)* ✣ *C2.*

NIGHTLIFE AND THE ARTS

THE ARTS

The arts flourish in this cosmopolitan city. Hamburg's ballet company is one of the finest in Europe, and the Hamburger Ballett-Tage, its annual festival, brings the best from around the world to Hamburg.

At the end of September, the city comes alive with film. The Hamburg Film Festival brings the best feature films, documentary, short films and children's movies to theaters around town. About 80% of the films are in English or have English subtitles. For two weeks, thousands of people watch mainstream and quirky films at this cinephile's dream.

Information on all major events are available on the Hamburg Tourism Office Web site. ■ **TIP→ The best way to order tickets for all major Hamburg theaters, musicals, and most cultural events is through the Hamburg-Hotline** (☎ *040/3005–1300*).

Funke Konzertkassen. Hamburg's largest ticket seller has box offices throughout Hamburg, including Dammtorbahnhof with English-speaking agents, and a Web site that is easy to navigate. A toll call connects culture vultures with representatives who can also speak English. The Web site also lists the direct-dial telephone number for each box office. ✉ *Dammtorbahnhof, Dag-Hammarskjöldplatz, Neustadt, Hamburg* ☎ *01805/663–661* 🌐 *www.funke-ticket.de.*

Kulturportal. This government Web site gives information about theater, dance, visual art, video, architecture, and film for all of Germany. The database is searchable by city, date, and medium. ☎ *030/2266–7748* 🌐 *kulturportal.de.*

Landungsbrücken. A number of agencies also sell tickets for plays, concerts, and the ballet. The Hamburg tourist office at the Landungsbrücken has a ticket office. ✉ *Between Brücke 4 and 5, St. Pauli* ☎ *040/3005–1300.*

BALLET AND OPERA

Hamburgische Staatsoper. One of the most beautiful theaters in the country, the Hamburgische Staatsoper is the leading northern German venue for opera and ballet. The Hamburg Ballet is directed by American John Neumeier. ⊠ *Grosse Theaterstr. 25, Neustadt* ☏ *040/356–868.*

TUI Operettenhaus. The TUI Operettenhaus stages productions of top musicals. *Sister Act* has called the theater home since December 2010. Inquiring minds can take a tour of the theater. ⊠ *Spielbudenpl. 1, St. Pauli* ☏ *01805/4444 tickets.*

CONCERTS

Laeiszhalle. Both the Philharmoniker Hamburg (Hamburg Philharmonic) and the Hamburger Symphoniker (Hamburg Symphony) appear regularly at the Laeiszhalle. Visiting orchestras from overseas are also presented. ⊠ *Johannes-Brahms-Pl., Neustadt* ☏ *040/3576–6666.*

FILM

Streits. Independent and mainstream English-language movies are shown at the grand Streits. ⊠ *Jungfernstieg 38, Neustadt* ☏ *040/346–051.*

Abaton. Artsy movies are shown at the Abaton. ⊠ *Allenpl. 3, Neustadt* ☏ *040/320–320.*

THEATER

Ticket and theater information is available at ⊕ *www.stage-entertainment.de* or ☏ *01805/4444.*

Deutsches Schauspielhaus. Deutsches Schauspielhaus, one of Germany's leading drama stages, is lavishly restored to its full 19th-century opulence and is the most important Hamburg venue for classical and modern theater. ⊠ *Kirchenallee 39, St. Georg* ☏ *040/248–710.*

English Theatre of Hamburg. The name says it all: the English Theatre, Hamburg's oldest professional house, is the city's premier theater for works in English. Actors from near and far bring contemporary and classic drama to life on the small stage of this historic building. ⊠ *Lerchenfeld 14, Uhlenhorst* ☏ *040/227–7089* ⊕ *www.englishtheatre.de.*

Neue Flora Theater. Tarzan flies across the stage of the Neue Flora Theater. ⊠ *Stresemannstr. 159a, at Alsenstr., Sternschanze* ☏ *01805/4444 tickets, 040/4316–5133 theater.*

Theater im Hamburger Hafen. Theater im Hamburger Hafen is staging *Der König der Löwen*, a German version of the Broadway musical hit *The Lion King.* You can reach the theater in the middle of the Elbe either by ferry from St. Pauli Landungsbrücken or driving across a bridge. ⊠ *Norderelbstr. 6, at Hamburger Hafen, follow signs to Schuppen 70, St. Pauli* ☏ *01805/4444.*

NIGHTLIFE

THE REEPERBAHN

Whether you think it sordid or sexy, the Reeperbahn, in the St. Pauli District, is as central to the Hamburg scene as the classy shops along Jungfernstieg. On nearby Grosse Freiheit you'll find a number of the better-known dance clubs. Hans-Elber-Platz has a cluster of bars, some with live music.

Schmidts Theater and Schmidts Tivoli. The quirky Schmidt Theater and Schmidts Tivoli has become Germany's most popular variety theater, presenting a classy repertoire of live music, vaudeville, chansons, and cabaret. ⊠ *Spielbudenpl. 24–28, St. Pauli* ☎ *040/3177–8899.*

BARS

COCKTAIL LOUNGES

Hamburg has a buzzing and upscale bar scene, with many spots that feature live music or DJs and dancing.

Christiansen's. Christiansen's Fine Drinks & Cocktails, near the Fischmarkt, is said to mix the best cocktails in town. ⊠ *Pinnasberg 60, St. Pauli* ☎ *040/317–2863.*

Mandalay. Mandalay is typical of the upscale, sleek bars catering to thirtysomethings that have sprung up recently in St. Pauli and Sternschanze. ⊠ *Neuer Pferdemarkt 13, Sternschanze* ☎ *040/4321–4922* ⊕ *www.mandalay.tv.*

HOTEL BARS

Like many cities, hotel bars in Hamburg have some of the hottest hangouts.

20 Up at the Empire Riverside Hotel. For a smooth cocktail, cool lounge music, and a chance for adventure, try 20 Up at the Empire Riverside Hotel. ⊠ *Bernhard-Nocht-Str. 97, Reeperbahn* ☎ *40/31119–70470.*

Bar DeCaio at the George Hotel. Bar DeCaio at the George Hotel has a black-on-black design. Despite its cool look, the bar has efficient service and endless drink options. ⊠ *Barcastrasse 3, St. Georg* ☎ *040/280–0300.*

Lounge No. 10 at the East Hotel. Lounge No. 10 at the East Hotel draws fashionable people of all ages. ⊠ *Simon-von-Utrecht-Strasse 31, Reeperbahn* ☎ *040/309–930.*

Tower Bar at Hotel Hafen Hamburg. The view from this bar on top of the riverside hotel attracts businesspeople and people looking for a relaxed place to hang. ⊠ *Seewartenstrasse 9, St. Pauli* ☎ *040/31113–70450.*

PUBS

The city also boasts plenty of homey pubs.

Brahmskeller. Hamburgers are renowned for their ability to go out but act like they are alone. Brahmskeller is a relaxed bar where guests can easily get caught up in friendly conversation. It's the kind of place where everyone is a regular, even newcomers. ⊠ *Grosse Bleichen 31, on the ground floor inside Kaufmannshaus, Neustadt* ☎ *040/353–306* ⊕ *www.brahmskeller.de.*

Gretel und Alfons. Germans are not known for mingling but at Gretel und Alfons you can strike up a conversation with the person sitting next to you at this small traditional German pub in the middle of the bustling Grosse Freiheit in the Reeperbahn area. Beware: After a few beers, patrons may begin singing old German folk songs and you will try to join in. ⊠ *Grosse Freiheit 29, Reeperbahn* ☎ *040/313–491* ⊕ *www.gretelundalfons.de/.*

HIP AND HAPPENING NIGHTLIFE

People flock to Hamburg for shopping but there is more to experience come nightfall. The city has several places where you can hop from bar to bar or lounge to lounge. Here are the hip and happening streets in Hamburg:

Reeperbahn, Grosse Freiheit, and the streets around Spielbudenplatz in St. Pauli: This sinful mile has everything—strip clubs, pubs, live music, dive bars, and nightclubs. It's loud and crazy and fun just to walk up and down the streets.

Grosse Elbstrasse in Altona: This is the home of the Altona Fischmarkt and a variety of restaurants and bars.

Schanzenstrasse in Sternschanze: Hipsters flock to this compact row of dive bars and laid-back lounges that pour onto the sidewalk when the weather is warm.

Grindelallee and side streets in Rotherbaum: With Universität der Hamburg in the area, students flock to the mix of small pubs and casual Asian restaurants.

Grossneumarkt: This square is packed with comfortable, relaxing pubs and German restaurants. In summer it's a popular meeting point for Hamburgers who want to sit outside and eat and drink in relaxed atmosphere.

13

DANCE CLUBS

China Lounge. The China Lounge, in a former Chinese restaurant, remains one of Hamburg's coolest lounges, mostly attracting hip and beautiful thirtysomethings. ⊠ *Nobistor 14, Reeperbahn* ☎ *040/3197–6622* ⊕ *www.china-hamburg.de.*

Golden Cut. At Golden Cut the DJs spin house, hip-hop, and electronic across from the main train station. ⊠ *Holzdamm 61, St. Georg* ☎ *040/8510–3532.*

Stage Club. One of the most appealing and entertaining clubs in Hamburg, Stage Club, on the first floor of the Theater Neue Flora, welcomes a mixed crowd to soul, funk, or jazz every night, followed by a DJ. ⊠ *Stresemannstr. 163, Sternschanze* ☎ *040/4316–5460.*

JAZZ AND LIVE MUSIC CLUBS

Birdland. Birdland is the best place in Hamburg to hear mainstream jazz, New Orleans sounds, swing, Latin, and modern jazz. ⊠ *Gärtnerstr. 122, Hoheluft* ☎ *040/405–277* ⊕ *www.jazzclub-birdland.de.*

Cotton Club. The Cotton Club, Hamburg's oldest jazz club, focuses on straightforward jazz. ⊠ *Alter Steinweg 10, Neustadt* ☎ *040/343–878* ⊕ *www.cotton-club.de.*

Docks. Docks has a stylish bar and is one of Hamburg's largest venues for live music. When the concert stage is empty, a hip-hop dance club takes over. ⊠ *Spielbudenpl. 19, Reeperbahn* ☎ *040/317–8830* ⊕ *www.docks.de.*

The HSH Nordbank Arena is home to the Hamburger SV football team.

SPORTS AND THE OUTDOORS

BIKING

Almost all sidewalks have a dark patch close to the street. This path is reserved for bicycles. Some of the major hotels will lend their guests bikes. With its StadtRAD program, Hamburg joined Paris and other major cities in offering rental bicycles in locations across the city. These red-framed bicycles can be found at the Hauptbahnhof, large subway stations, and popular tourist spots. Bikes are free for the first 30 minutes, and then rent for 4¢ a minute for the next 30. It's 8¢ per minute after that but the maximum daily rental is €12. When you're done with the bike, leave it at an authorized location. For more information and to register, visit ⊕ *www.stadtradhamburg.de*.

ADFC Hamburg. A complete list of bike rentals in Hamburg and the surrounding countryside can be obtained from the ADFC Hamburg. ✉ *Koppel 34–36, St. Georg* ☎ *040/390–3955* ⊕ *www.hamburg.adfc.de*.

JOGGING

The best places for jogging are the Planten un Blomen and Alter Botanischer Garten parks and along the leafy promenade around the Alster. The latter route is about 6 km (4 mi) long.

SAILING

You can rent rowboats and sailboats on the Alster in summer between 10 am and 9 pm. Rowboats cost around €10 to €12 an hour, sailboats around €16 an hour (usually accommodating two adults). The largest selection of boats is at the Gurlitt-Insel pier off An der Alster (on the east bank of the Aussenalster). Another rental outlet is at the very tip of the Alster, at the street Fernsicht.

SHOPPING

Although not as rich or sumptuous on first sight as Düsseldorf or Munich, Hamburg is nevertheless expensive, and ranks first among Germany's shopping experiences. Some of the country's premier designers, such as Karl Lagerfeld, Jil Sander, and Wolfgang Joop, are native Hamburgers, or at least worked here for quite some time. Hamburg has the greatest number of shopping malls in the country; mostly small but elegant Downtown arcades offering entertainment, fashion, and fine food.

All the big names—Chanel, Versace, Armani, Prada, Louis Vuitton, Cartier, Tiffany—are found in the warren of streets bounded by Jungfernstieg, the Rathaus, and Neues ABC Strasse. International chain stores, like Fossil, Adidas and MAC, and European chains, such as Görtz shoe stores, Zara clothing stores, and Christ jewelry stores, and German department stores mingle on Mönckebergstrasse. Independent boutiques sell primarily distinguished and somewhat conservative fashion; understatement is the style here. Eppendorf offers miles of unique shops for shoes, clothes, home design, and housewares with quaint cafés sprinkled among them. Sternschanze offers a funky mix of stores selling cool home accessories and fashion, with dive bars and small restaurants for pit stops.

SHOPPING DISTRICTS

Hamburg's shopping districts are among the most elegant on the continent, and the city has Europe's largest expanse of covered shopping arcades, most of them packed with small, exclusive boutiques. The streets **Grosse Bleichen** and **Neuer Wall**, which lead off Jungfernstieg, are a big-ticket zone. The Grosse Bleichen holds four malls with the most sought-after labels, several of these shopping centers are connected. The marble-clad **Galleria** is reminiscent of London's Burlington Arcade. Daylight streams through the immense glass ceilings of the **Hanse-Viertel**, an otherwise ordinary reddish-brown brick building. At 101, **Kaufmannshaus** is one of the oldest malls in Hamburg. Steps away from these retail giants are the fashionable **Hamburger Hof**, the historic Alte Post with a beautiful, waterfront promenade, the posh Bleichenhof, and the stunningly designed, larger Europa Passage.

In the fashionable Rotherbaum district, take a look at Milchstrasse and Mittelweg. Both are filled with small boutiques, restaurants, and cafés.

Walk down Susannenstrasse and Schanzestrasse in Sternschanze to find unique clothes, things for the home, and, even records. Eppendorfer Landstrasse and Eppendorfer Weg are brimming with stores that sell clothing in every flavor—designer labels, casual wear, sportswear, and German flair—and elegant and fun home decor.

Running from the main train station to Gerhard-Hauptmann-Platz, the boulevard Spitalerstrasse is a pedestrians-only street lined with stores.
■ TIP→ Prices here are noticeably lower than those on Jungfernstieg.

DEPARTMENT STORES

Alsterhaus. Alsterhaus is Hamburg's famous and high-end department store. A favorite with locals, it's a large and elegant landmark. For a treat, check out the gourmet food hall and the Champagne bar. ⊠ *Jungfernstieg 16–20, Neustadt* ☎ *040/3590–1218.*

Karstadt. Karstadt is Germany's leading department-store chain and offers the same goods as the Alsterhaus at similar prices. ■ TIP→ Hamburg's Downtown Karstadt Sports, which is up the street from the main store, is the city's best place to shop for sports clothing. ⊠ *Mönckebergstr. 16, Altstadt* ☎ *040/30940.*

Stilwerk. This stylish shopping center resembles a traditional mall but is a one-stop source for contemporary furniture and home-accessory shops. ⊠ *Grosse Elbstr. 68, Altona* ☎ *040/3062–1100.*

SPECIALTY STORES

ANTIQUES

Flohschanze. Germans in search of a great deal love a good "Flohmarkt" (Flea market). These markets unfold throughout Hamburg, but the most valuable is the weekly Flohschanze, a huge flea market that takes over a lot and indoor space in the Schanze Viertel. With acres of clothes, furniture, books, CDs, records, home accessories, jewelry, and art, the market attracts both collectors and bargain hunters every Saturday 8 am until 4 pm. ⊠ *Neuer Kamp 30, Sternschanze, Hamburg* ☎ *040/270–2766* ⊕ *www.marktkultur-hamburg.de/flohschanze.html.*

Kleidermarkt. Kleidermarkt (Dresses Market) is a seven-store German chain. Hamburg is blessed with two branches of this used-dress outlet. Both are massive and feature good specimens of the trends from the 1960s, '70s, and '80s. If the normal thrift-store prices were not enough, Kleidermarkts have reduced prices during Happy Hour. The Sternschanze outlet drops prices 20% every Tuesday between 11 am and 3 pm. The Altona branch is the largest secondhand store in Hamburg and offers shoppers a 30% discount from 11 am to 4 pm each Wednesday. ⊠ *Neuer Kamp 23, Hamburg* ☎ *040/433–717* ⊕ *www.kleidermarkt.de.*

St. Georg and Neustadt. ABC-Strasse is a happy-hunting ground for antiques lovers. Take a look at the shops in the St. Georg district behind the train station, especially those along Lange Reihe and Koppel. You'll find a mixture of genuine antiques (*Antiquitäten*) and junk (*Trödel*). You won't find many bargains, however.

FOOD MARKETS

Blankenese. This small but top-class food market in the heart of the Wochenmarkt manages to preserve the charm of a small village and sells only fresh produce from environmentally friendly farms. ⊠ *Bahnhofstr., Blankenese* ⊕ *www.hamburg.de/wochenmarkt-blankenese/* ☉ *Tues. 8–2, Fri. 8–6, Sat. 8–1* Ⓜ *Blankenese (S-bahn).*

Fischmarkt (⇨ *St. Pauli and the Reeperbahn in Exploring Hamburg*).

GIFT IDEAS

Baqu. Baqu fills two storefronts with wacky tchotchkes, useful home appliances, and modern decor. ✉ *Susannenstrasse 39, Sternschanze, Hamburg.*

Captain's Cabin. This Hamburg institution is an experience not to be missed. It's the best place for all of the city's specialty maritime goods. This souvenir emporium is open seven days a week. ✉ *Landungsbrücken 3, St. Pauli* ☎ *040/316–373* ⊕ *www.captains-cabin.de.*

Lille/Stor. Lille/Stor stocks an eclectic mix of casual clothes, shoes, colorful items for the home, and light jewelry. ✉ *Schanzenstrasse 97, Sternschanze, Hamburg* ☎ *040/343–741.*

Lizzart Living. Lizzart Living, the only source for Mariemekko in Hamburg, sells fun contemporary design and home accessories at every price point. ✉ *Lenhartzstrasse 1, Eppendorf, Hamburg* ☎ *040/484–104.*

Mimulus Naturkosmetik. Mimulus sells all-natural cosmetics and toiletries and offers an array of facial and body treatments at surprisingly reasonable prices. ✉ *Schanzenstrasse 39a, Sternschanze, Hamburg* ☎ *040/430–8037.*

Minipli: Altes & Neues. Minipli: Altes & Neues sells a quirky assortment of old and new shabby chic wares, like drinking glasses, knobs, handbags, and chandeliers. ✉ *Susannenstrasse 20, Sternschanze, Hamburg* ☎ *040/439–4114.*

WohnDesign Così. WohnDesign Così is bursting with the most interesting pieces of contemporary design from around the world. ✉ *Eppendorfer Landstrasse 48, Eppendorf, Hamburg* ☎ *040/470–670.*

JEWELRY

Wempe. Wempe is Germany's largest seller of fine jewelery. This is its flagship store (one of two Hamburg locations); the selection of watches here is particularly outstanding. ✉ *Jungfernstieg 8, Neustadt* ☎ *040/3344–8824.*

MEN'S CLOTHING

Feldenkirchen. One of Hamburg's hippest clothing shops is the quirky Feldenkirchen, which has a great selection of top international designer labels for men and women. ✉ *Poststrasse 51, Neustadt* ☎ *040/3571–0778.*

Thomas I-Punkt. The five-story Thomas I-Punkt, a Hamburg tradition and a must for the fashion-conscious traveler, sells hip designer clothes and suits of its own label. ✉ *Mönckebergstr. 21, Altstadt* ☎ *040/327–172.*

Wormland. The Hamburg outlet of the chain store is the city's largest store for men's clothes. Wormland offers both affordable no-name yet very fashionable clothes, as well as top designer wear. ✉ *Europa Passage, Ballindamm 40, Altstadt* ☎ *040/4689–92700.*

WOMEN'S CLOTHING

42 Plus. This secondhand store only sells clothes in European size 42 and higher (American size 14). The store only stocks high-quality clothing and shoes from traditional stores and designers. ✉ *Eppendorfer Weg 281, Eppendorf, Hamburg* ☎ *040/4677–4640.*

13

Anita Hass. Anita Hass, a Hamburg classic, sells both international brands and several German designers that focus on casual elegance. This impressive store covers several storefronts and has everything—the newest apparel, shoes, jewelry, handbags, and accessories, like iPhone covers. ⊠ *Eppendorfer Landstr. 60, Eppendorf* ☎ *040/465–909.*

Fräuleinwunder. This small emporium sells trendy sportswear, shoes, accessories, and jewelry for women. There's also a small selection of casualwear for men. ⊠ *Susannenstrasse 13, Sternschanze, Hamburg* ☎ *40/3619–3329.*

Hamburger Hof. The historic Hamburger Hof is one of the most beautiful, upscale shopping complexes—with a wide variety of designer clothing, jewelry, and gift stores—primarily catering to women. ⊠ *Jungfernstieg 26–30/Grosse Bleichen, Neustadt* ☎ *040/350–1680* ⊕ *www. hhof-passage.de.*

Jonas Ariaens Schuhe. This boutique sells a variety of women's shoes, including many styles with a focus on comfort. This store also has a good stock of shoes size 10 and larger. ⊠ *Eppendorfer Landstrasse 8, Neustadt, Hamburg* ☎ *040/4609–3248.*

Kaufrausch. The upscale shopping complex Kaufrausch has mostly clothing and accessories stores for women. ⊠ *Isestr. 74, Harvestehude* ⊕ *www.kaufrausch-hamburg.de.*

La Paloma. This small store features a well-edited collection of trendy clothes from casual labels from around the world with a focus on clothes from Danish designers. ⊠ *Susannenstrasse 5, Sternschanze, Hamburg* ☎ *040/4321–5333.*

Linette. A small but elegant store, Linette stocks only top designers. ⊠ *Hohe Bleichen 17, Neustadt* ☎ *040/346–411.*

Ono Koon. The German designer, Ono Koon, creates fun fashion in black and white. Hems are uneven, sleeves are long, and skirts balloon. Adventurous fashionistas in Hamburg only have one store to visit. ⊠ *Eppendorfer Landstrasse 13, Sternschanze, Hamburg* ☎ *040/4719–3403.*

Stiletto by Raffaele Riccardi. The understated German style stops at the door. This store is for women in search of bold leather shoes, boots, and sandals. The staff at the small, dark shop is helpful and friendly. ⊠ *Eppendorfer Weg 257, Neustadt, Hamburg* ☎ *040/4210–4549.*

Schleswig-Holstein and the Baltic Coast

WORD OF MOUTH

"[The] Baltic Sea coast [makes a good side trip from Hamburg]. The old beach resorts along Mecklenburg's coastline with their 1900 architecture, the Hanseatic cities like Lübeck, Wismar, Stralsund, Greifswald with their medieval brick architecture, the 19th century palace and town of Schwerin."

—quokka

WELCOME TO SCHLESWIG-HOLSTEIN AND THE BALTIC COAST

TOP REASONS TO GO

★ **Gothic architecture:** The historic towns of Lübeck, Wismar, and Stralsund have some of the finest redbrick Gothic architecture in northern Europe. A walk through medieval Stralsund, in particular, is like a trip into the proud past of the powerful Hanseatic League.

★ **Rügen:** One of the most secluded islands of northern Europe, Rügen is a dreamy Baltic oasis whose endless beaches, soaring chalk cliffs, and quiet pace of life have charmed painters, writers, and artists for centuries.

★ **Schwerin:** Nestled in a romantic landscape of lakes, rivers, forests, and marshland, the Mecklenburg state capital and its grand water palace make a great place to relax.

★ **Sylt:** Sylt is a windswept outpost in the rough North Sea. Throughout the year, Sylt is home to Germany's jet set, who come here for the tranquillity, the white beaches, the gourmet dining, and the superb hotels.

1 **Schleswig-Holstein.** Rural Schleswig-Holstein is accented by laid-back, medieval towns and villages famed for their fresh seafood and great local beers (such as Schleswig), and the bustling island of Sylt, a summer playground for wealthy Hamburgers.

2 **Western Mecklenburg.** Lakes, rivers, and seemingly endless fields of wheat and yellow rape characterize this rural landscape. Although the area is extremely popular with Germans, only a few western tourists or daytrippers from nearby Berlin venture here to visit beautiful Schwerin or enjoy the serenity. The area is famous for its many wellness and spa hotels, making it a year-round destination.

GETTING ORIENTED

The three major areas of interest are the western coastline of Schleswig-Holstein, the lakes inland in Western Mecklenburg, and Vorpommern's secluded, tundralike landscape of sandy heath and dunes. If you only have three days, slow down to the area's pace and focus on one area. In five days you could easily cross the region. Berlin is the natural approach from the east; Hamburg is a launching point from the west.

14

3 Vorpommern. Remote and sparsely populated, Vorpommern is one of Europe's quietest corners. Compared to the coast and islands in the West, sleepy Vorpommern sea resorts like Putbus, Baabe, and the Darss area have preserved a distinct, old-fashioned charm worth exploring.

BALTIC COAST BEACHES

Although Germany may not be the first place on your list of beach destinations, a shore vacation on the Baltic never disappoints. The coast here ranges from the remote bucolic shores of Usedom to the chic and inhibition-free beaches of Sylt.

(above) You can rent one of the colorful Strandkorb on Usedom Island's beaches.
(upper right) Stroll along Ahlbeck's beach and pier.
(lower right) The "it" crowd hangs out on Sylt.

Be sure to rent a *Strandkorb*, a kind of beach chair in a wicker basket, which gives you all of the sun, but protects you from the wind and flying sand. You can rent these chairs by the hour, half day, or day. There is usually an office near the chairs to help you; look for the kiosk that sells sundries and beach toys nearest the chair you want.

Look for the blue flag on the beach that indicates that the water is safe for swimming. But, be aware that water temperatures even in August rarely exceed 20°C (65°F). There's a *Kurtaxe* (entrance fee) of €1.50–€5 for most beaches; the fees on Sylt average €3 per entry.

Some beaches allow nude bathing. In German it's known as *Freikörperkultur* (literally "free body culture"), or FKK for short.

—Lee A. Evans

BALTIC AMBER

It is believed that a pine forest once grew in the area that is now the Baltic Sea about 40 million years ago. Fossilized resin from these trees, aka amber, lies beneath the surface. In fact, this area has the largest known amber deposit, at about 80% of the world's known accessible deposits. The best time for amber "fishing," dipping a net into the surf, is at low tide after a storm when pieces of amber dislodge from the sea floor.

BALTIC COAST BEST BEACHES

HIDDENSEE ISLAND

If you're looking for bucolic and tranquil, head to the car-free island of **Hiddensee**, Rügen's neighbor to the west. With a mere 1,300 inhabitants, Hiddensee is the perfect place to look for washed up amber.

RÜGEN ISLAND

Germany's largest island, Rügen is dotted with picture-perfect beaches, chalk cliffs, and pristine nature. It also served as the stomping ground for the likes of Albert Einstein, Christopher Isherwood, and Caspar David Friedrich. An easy day trip from Berlin, the town of **Binz** is the perfect Rügen getaway. Binz has a nice boardwalk, a pretty beach dotted with Strandkörbe, and fine mansions.

You'll find a wonderful white sand beach at **Prora** and a smattering of artist studios; the hulking abandoned resort here was designed by the Nazis to house 20,000 vacationers in the *Kraft durch Freude* (Strength Through Joy) program.

SYLT

Germany's northernmost island is the granddaddy of all beach resorts and by far the most popular seaside destination in Germany. Sylt is chic and trendy, but, despite being overrun by tourists, it is still possible to find your own romantic abandoned stretch of beach. **Westerland** is the most popular beach, with its long

promenade and sun-drenched sand. The "Fun-Beach Brandenburg" bursts at the seams with family-friendly activities, volleyball, and other sporting contests. Farther afield, the red cliffs of **Kampen** are the perfect backdrop for a little mellow sun and schmoozing with the locals. It's a lovely place for a walk along the shore and up the cliffs, where the view can't be beat. The best beach for families is at **Hörnum**, where a picture-perfect red-and-white lighthouse protects the entrance to the bay.

USEDOM ISLAND

The towns of **Ahlbeck** and **Herringsdorf** are the most popular on Usedom Island, with pristine 19th-century villas and mansions paired with long boardwalks extending into the sea. For the true and unspoiled experience, head west to **Ückeritz**, where the beach feels abandoned.

WARNEMÜNDE

A resort town popular with German tourists and local day-trippers from Rostock, the 20 km (12.4 mi) of windswept white-sand beach can't be beat. A fun beach promenade stretches the length of the beach and features daily music performances and restaurants ranging from fine dining to fish shacks where you can get a paper bag filled with fried mussels.

Updated by
Lee A. Evans

Germany's true north is a quiet and peaceful region that belies its past status as one of the most powerful trading centers in Europe. The salty air and lush, green landscape of marshlands, endless beaches, fishing villages, and lakes are the main pleasures here, not sightseeing. On foggy November evenings, or during the hard winter storms that sometimes strand islanders from the mainland, you can well imagine the fairy tales spun by the Vikings who lived here.

In Schleswig-Holstein, Germany's most northern state, the Danish-German heritage is the result of centuries of land disputes, flexible borders, and intermarriage between the two nations—you could call this area southern Scandinavia. Since the early 20th century its shores and islands have become popular weekend and summer retreats for the well-to-do from Hamburg. The island of Sylt, in particular, is known throughout Germany for its rich and beautiful sunbathers.

The rest of Schleswig-Holstein, though equally appealing in its green and mostly serene landscape, is far from rich and worldly. Most people farm or fish, and often speak Plattdütsch, or Low German, which is difficult for outsiders to understand. Cities such as Flensburg, Husum, Schleswig, Kiel (the state capital), and even Lübeck all exude a laid-back, small-town charm.

The neighboring state of Mecklenburg-Vorpommern includes the Baltic Coast and is even more rural. On the resort islands of Hiddensee and Usedom, the clock appears to have stopped before World War II. Though it has long been a popular summer destination for families, few foreign tourists venture here.

PLANNING

WHEN TO GO

The region's climate is at its best when the two states are most crowded with vacationers—in July and August. Winter can be harsh in this area, and even spring and fall are rather windy, chilly, and rainy. ■ TIP→ To avoid the crowds, schedule your trip for June or September. But don't expect tolerable water temperatures or hot days on the beach.

GETTING HERE AND AROUND

AIR TRAVEL

The international airport closest to Schleswig-Holstein is in Hamburg. For an eastern approach to the Baltic Coast tour, use Berlin's Tegel Airport.

BOAT AND FERRY TRAVEL

The Weisse Flotte (White Fleet) line operates ferries linking the Baltic ports, as well as short harbor and coastal cruises. Boats depart from Warnemünde, Zingst (to Hiddensee), Sassnitz, and Stralsund. In addition, ferries run from Stralsund and Sassnitz to destinations in Sweden, Denmark, Poland, and Finland.

Scandlines operates ferries between Sassnitz and the Danish island of Bornholm, as well as Sweden.

Contacts **Scandlines** ☎ 01805/116–688 ⊕ www.scandlines.de. **Weisse Flotte** ☎ 0180/321–2120 for Warnemünde and Stralsund, 0385/557–770 for Schwerin ⊕ www.weisseflotte.de.

BUS TRAVEL

Local buses link the main train stations with outlying towns and villages, especially the coastal resorts. Buses operate throughout Sylt, Rügen, and Usedom islands.

CAR TRAVEL

The two-lane roads (Bundesstrassen) along the coast can be full of traffic in summer. The ones leading to Usedom Island can be extremely log-jammed, as the causeway bridges have scheduled closings to let ships pass. Using the Bundesstrassen takes more time, but these often tree-lined roads are by far more scenic than the autobahn.

Sylt island is 196 km (122 mi) from Hamburg via Autobahn A-7 and Bundesstrasse B-199 and is ultimately reached via train. B-199 cuts through some nice countryside, and instead of A-7 or B-76 between Schleswig and Kiel you could take the slow route through the coastal hinterland (B-199, B-203, or B-503). Lübeck, the gateway to Mecklenburg-Vorpommern, is 56 km (35 mi) from Hamburg via A-1. B-105 leads to all sightseeing spots in Mecklenburg-Vorpommern. A faster route is the A-20, connecting Lübeck and Rostock. From Stralsund, Route 96 cuts straight across Rügen Island, a distance of 51 km (32 mi). From Berlin, take A-11 and head toward Prenzlau for B-109 all the way to Usedom Island, a distance of 162 km (100 mi). A causeway connects the mainland town of Anklam to the town of Peenemünde, on Usedom Island; coming from the west, use the causeway at Wolgast.

TRAIN TRAVEL

Train travel is much more convenient than bus travel in this area. Sylt, Kiel, Lübeck, Schwerin, and Rostock have InterCity train connections to either Hamburg or Berlin, or both.

A north–south train line links Schwerin and Rostock. An east–west route connects Kiel, Hamburg, Lübeck, and Rostock, and some trains continue through to Stralsund and Sassnitz, on Rügen Island.

TOURS

Although tourist offices and museums have worked to improve the English-language literature about this area, English-speaking tours are infrequent and must be requested ahead of time through the local tourist office. Because most tours are designed for groups, there's usually a flat fee of €20–€30. Towns currently offering tours are Lübeck, Stralsund, and Rostock. Schwerin has two-hour boat tours of its lakes. Many of the former fishermen in these towns give sunset tours of the harbors or shuttle visitors between neighboring towns. This is a unique opportunity to ride on an authentic fishing boat. In Kiel, Rostock, and on Sylt, cruise lines make short trips through the respective bays and/or islands off the coast, sailing even as far as Denmark and Sweden. Inquire at the local tourist office about companies and times, as well as about fishing-boat tours.

RESTAURANTS

Don't count on eating a meal at odd hours or after 10 pm in this largely rural area. Many restaurants serve hot meals only between 11:30 am and 2 pm, and 6 pm and 9 pm. You rarely need a reservation here, and casual clothing is generally acceptable.

HOTELS

In northern Germany you'll find both small *Hotelpensionen* and fully equipped large hotels; along the eastern Baltic Coast, some hotels are renovated high-rises dating from GDR (German Democratic Republic) times. Many of the small hotels and pensions in towns such as Kühlungsborn and Binz have been restored to the romantic, quaint splendor of German *Bäderarchitektur* (spa architecture) from the early 20th century. In high season all accommodations, especially on the islands, are in great demand. ■TIP→ If you can't book well in advance, inquire at the local tourist office, which will also have information on the 150 campsites along the Baltic Coast and on the islands.

WHAT IT COSTS IN EUROS				
¢	**$**	**$$**	**$$$**	**$$$$**
Restaurants	under €9	€9–€15	€16–€20	€21–€25	over €25
Hotels	under €50	€50–€100	€101–€175	€176–€225	over €225

Restaurant prices are per person for a median main course at dinner. Hotel prices are for two people in a standard double room, including tax and service.

PLANNING YOUR TIME

The bigger coastal Hanse cities make for a good start before exploring smaller towns. Lübeck is a natural base for exploring Schleswig-Holstein, particularly if you arrive from Hamburg. From here it's easy to venture out into the countryside or explore the coastline and towns such as Kiel, Flensburg, or Husum. The island of Sylt is a one- or two-day trip from Lübeck, though.

If you have more time, you can also travel east from Lübeck into Mecklenburg-Vorpommern: Some of the must-see destinations on an itinerary include Schwerin and the surrounding lakes, the island of Rügen, and the cities Wismar and Rostock.

DISCOUNTS AND DEALS

Larger cities such as Kiel, Lübeck, Wismar, Schwerin, and Rostock offer tourism "welcome" cards, which include sometimes-considerable discounts and special deals for attractions and tours as well as local public transport. Ask about these at the visitor information bureaus.

14

VISITOR INFORMATION

Tourismusverband Mecklenburg-Vorpommern ⊠ *Pl. der Freundschaft 1, Rostock* ☎ *0381/403–0500* ⊕ *www.tmv.de.*

SCHLESWIG-HOLSTEIN

This region once thrived, thanks to the Hanseatic League and the Salzstrasse (Salt Route), a merchant route connecting northern Germany's cities. The kings of Denmark warred with the dukes of Schleswig and, later, the German Empire over the prized northern territory of Schleswig-Holstein. The northernmost strip of land surrounding Flensburg became German in 1864. The quiet, contemplative spirit of the region's people, the marshland's special light, and the ever-changing face of the sea are inspiring. Today the world-famous Schleswig-Holstein-Musikfestival ushers in classical concerts to farmhouses, palaces, and churches.

HUSUM

158 km (98 mi) northwest of Hamburg.

The town of Husum is the epitome of northern German lifestyle and culture. Immortalized in a poem as the "gray city upon the sea" by its famous son, Theodor Storm, Husum is actually a popular vacation spot in summer.

The central **Marktplatz** (Market Square) is bordered by 17th- and 18th-century buildings, including the historic Rathaus (Town Hall), which houses the tourist-information office. The best impression of Husum's beginnings in the mid-13th century is found south of the Marktplatz, along **Krämerstrasse**; the **Wasserreihe**, a narrow and tortuous alley; and **Hafenstrasse**, right next to the narrow **Binnenhafen** (city harbor).

ESSENTIALS

Visitor Information Husum ⊠ *Grossstr. 27* ☎ *04841/89870* ⊕ *www.husum.de.*

EXPLORING

Schloss vor Husum (*Husum Castle*). Despite Husum's remoteness, surrounded by the stormy sea, wide marshes, and dunes, the city used to be a major seaport and administrative center. The Husum Castle, which was originally built as a Renaissance castle in the late 16th century, was transformed in 1752 by the dukes of Gottorf into a redbrick baroque country palace. ⊠ *Professor-Ferdinand-Tönnies-Allee* ☎ *04841/897-3130* 🎫 *€5* 🕐 *Mar.–Oct., Tues.–Sun. 11–5.*

Theodor-Storm-Haus. This is the most famous house on Wasserreihe, where writer Theodor Storm (1817–88) lived between 1866 and 1880. It's a must if you're interested in German literature or if you want to gain insight into the life of the few well-to-do people in this region during the 19th century. The small museum includes the poet's living room and a small *Poetenstübchen* (poets' parlor), where he wrote many of his novels. ⊠ *Wasserreihe 31* ☎ *04841/803–8630* ⊕ *www. storm-gesellschaft.de* 🎫 *€3* 🕐 *Apr.–Oct., Tues.–Fri. 10–5, Mon. and Sun. 2–5, Sat. 11–5; Nov.–Mar., Tues., Thurs., and Sat. 2–5.*

WHERE TO STAY

For expanded hotel reviews, visit Fodors.com.

$$ 🏨 **Geniesser Hotel Altes Gymnasium.** In a former redbrick high school
Fodor's Choice behind a pear orchard, you'll find a surprisingly elegant country-style
★

hotel. **Pros:** stylish and quiet setting; a perfect overnight stop on the way to Sylt. **Cons:** far from any other sights. ⊠ *Süderstr. 2–10* ☎ *04841/8330* ⊕ *www.altes-gymnasium.de* ⤳ *66 rooms, 6 suites* ♿ *In-room: no a/c, Wi-Fi. In-hotel: restaurant, bar, pool, gym, parking, some pets allowed* ❍ *Breakfast.*

SYLT

Fodor's Choice
★
44 km (27 mi) northwest of Husum, 196 km (122 mi) northwest of Hamburg.

Sylt (pronounced ts-oo-lt) is a long, narrow island (38 km [24 mi] by as little as 220 yards) of unspoiled beaches and marshland off the western coast of Schleswig-Holstein and Denmark. Famous for its clean air and white beaches, Sylt is the hideaway for Germany's jet set.

A popular activity here is *Wattwanderungen* (walking in the Watt, the shoreline tidelands), whether on self-guided or guided tours. The small villages with their thatch-roof houses, the beaches, and the nature conservation areas make Sylt one of the most enchanting German islands.

14

GETTING HERE AND AROUND

Trains are the *only* way to access Sylt (other than flying from Hamburg or Berlin). The island is connected to the mainland via the train causeway Hindenburgdamm. Deutsche Bahn will transport you and your car from central train stations at Dortmund, Düsseldorf, Hamburg, Stuttgart, and Frankfurt directly to the station Westerland on the island. In addition, a daily shuttle car train leaves Niebüll roughly every 30 minutes from 5:10 am to 10:10 pm (Friday and Sunday from 5:10 am to 9:40 pm). There are no reservations on this train.

ESSENTIALS

Visitor Information Kampen ⊠ *Tourismus-Service Kampen, Hauptstr. 12, Kampen* ☎ *04651/46980* ⊕ *www.kampen.de.* **Sylt** ⊠ *Sylt Marketing GmbH, Stephanstr. 6* ☎ *04651/82020* ⊕ *www.sylt.de.* **Westerland** ⊠ *Strandstr. 35* ☎ *04651/9988* ⊕ *www.westerland.de* ⊠ *Stephanstr. 6, Postfach 1260 .*

EXPLORING

TOP ATTRACTIONS

Kampen. The island's unofficial capital is the main destination for the wealthier crowd and lies 9 km (6 mi) northeast of Westerland. Redbrick buildings and shining white thatch-roof houses spread along the coastline. The real draw—apart from the fancy restaurants and chic nightclubs—is the beaches.

Rotes Kliff (*Red Cliff*). One of the island's best-known features is this dune cliff on the northern end of the Kampen beaches, which turns an eerie dark red when the sun sets.

WORTH NOTING

Altfriesisches Haus (*Old Frisian House*). For a glimpse of the rugged lives of 19th-century fishermen, visit the small village of **Keitum** to the south, and drop in on the Old Frisian House, which preserves an old-world peacefulness in a lush garden setting. The house also documents a time when most seamen thrived on extensive whale hunting. ⊠ *Am Kliff 13, Keitum* ☎ *04651/31101* ⊠ *€3.50* ⊗ *Easter–Oct., weekdays 10–5, weekends 11–5; Nov.–Easter, Tues.–Fri. 1–4.*

The Naturschutzgebiet Kampener Vogel-koje (*Birds' Nest Nature Conservation Area*). Built in the mid-17th century, this conservation area once served as a mass trap for wild geese. Today it serves as a nature preserve for wild birds. ⊠ *Lister Str., Kampen* ☎ *04651/871–077* 🖆 *€3* ⊙ *Apr.–Oct., weekdays 10–5, weekends 11–5.*

St. Severin Church. The 800-year-old church was built on the highest elevation in the region. Its tower once served the island's fishermen as a beacon. Strangely enough, the tower also served as a prison until 1806. Today the church is a popular site for weddings. ⊠ *Pröstwai 20, Keitum* ☎ *04651/31713* 🖆 *Free* ⊙ *Tours Apr.–Oct., Sun. at 10; Nov.–Mar. at 4.*

Sylter Heimatmuseum (*Sylt Island Museum*). This small museum tells the centuries-long history of the island's seafaring people. It presents traditional costumes, tools, and other gear from fishing boats and tells the stories of islanders who fought for Sylt's independence. ⊠ *Am Kliff 19, Keitum* ☎ *04651/31669* 🖆 *€3.50* ⊙ *Easter–Oct., weekdays 10–5, weekends 11–5; Nov.–Easter, Tues.–Fri. 1–4.*

Westerland. The island's major town is not quite as expensive as Kampen, but it's more crowded. An ugly assortment of modern hotels lines an undeniably clean and broad beach. Each September windsurfers meet for the Surf Cup competition off the **Brandenburger Strand,** the best surfing spot.

WHERE TO EAT

$$
GERMAN

✕ **Dorfkrug Rotes Kliff.** The Dorfkrug has fed the island's seafaring inhabitants since 1876. Enjoy meals such as *Steinbuttfilet* (halibut fillet) or *Gebratener Zander* (fried perch fillet) in a homey setting where the walls are covered in traditional blue-and-white Frisian tiles. The same owners run the Wiinkööv wine bar next door. Visitors to both venues can take advantage of their impressive wine knowledge and cellar. ⊠ *Braderuper Weg 3* ☎ *04651/43500* ⊙ *Closed Mon. in Jan.*

$$$$
SEAFOOD
Fodor'sChoice
★

✕ **Hotelrestaurant Jörg Müller.** Set in an old thatch-roof farmhouse, which doubles as a small hotel, chef and owner Jörg Müller is considered by many to be the island's leading chef, delivering haute cuisine served in a gracious and friendly setting. Of the two restaurants, the Pesel serves local fish dishes, whereas the formal Jörg Müller offers a high-quality blend of international cuisines, where any of the four- to six-course menus are a nice option. ⊠ *Süderstr. 8, Westerland* ☎ *04651/27788* ⊕ *www.hotel-joerg-mueller.de* ⌔ *Reservations essential.*

$$$$
ECLECTIC
★

✕ **Sansibar.** Sansibar is one of the island's most popular restaurants and a longtime favorite for a diverse clientele, who often make it a rambunctious night out by imbibing loads of drinks under the bar's maverick logo, crossed pirates' sabers. The cuisine includes seafood and fondue; more than 800 wines are on offer. The Sunday brunch is incredible. ■TIP→ To get a table even in the afternoon, you must reserve at least six weeks in advance. ⊠ *Strand, Rantum-Süd, Rantum* ☎ *04651/964–546* ⌔ *Reservations essential.*

The beach at Westerland on Sylt is clean and wide.

WHERE TO STAY

For expanded hotel reviews, visit Fodors.com.

$$$$
Fodor'sChoice
★

⛄ **Dorint Söl'ring Hof.** This luxurious resort is set *on* the dunes in a white, thatch-roof country house: the view from most of the rooms is magnificent—with some luck you may even spot frolicking harbor porpoises. **Pros:** one of the few luxury hotels on the island with perfect service and a top-notch restaurant; right on the beach. **Cons:** remote location; often fully booked; rooms tend to be small. ⊠ *Am Sandwall 1, Rantum/Sylt* ☎ *04651/836–200* ⊕ *www.soelring-hof.de* ⤴ *11 rooms, 4 suites* ⅃ *In-room: no a/c. In-hotel: restaurant, bar, gym, spa, beach, parking* ⎨◯⎬ *Breakfast.*

$$

⛄ **Ulenhof Wenningstedt.** The Ulenhof, one of Sylt's loveliest old thatch-roof apartment houses, is a quiet alternative to the busier main resorts in Kampen and Westerland. **Pros:** a great, but small, spa. **Cons:** off the beaten track and away from the main action in Kampen and Westerland. ⊠ *Friesenring 14, Wenningstedt* ☎ *04651/94540* ⊕ *www.ulenhof. de* ⤴ *35 apartments* ⅃ *In-room: no a/c. In-hotel: pool, gym, parking* ⎨⎬ *No credit cards* ⎨◯⎬ *Breakfast.*

NIGHTLIFE AND THE ARTS

Club Rotes Kliff. The nightspots in Kampen are generally more upscale and more expensive than the pubs and clubs of Westerland. One of the most classic clubs on Sylt is the Club Rotes Kliff, a bar and dance club that attracts a hip crowd of all ages. ⊠ *Braderuper Weg 3* ☎ *04651/43400.*

Compass. The Compass is not as trendy as the typical Sylt nightclub. The mostly young patrons, however, create a cheerful party atmosphere on weekend nights. ⊠ *Friedrichstr. 40, Westerland* ☎ *04651/23513.*

SCHLESWIG

82 km (51 mi) southeast of Sylt, 114 km (71 mi) north of Hamburg.

Schleswig-Holstein's oldest city is also one of its best-preserved examples of a typical north German town. Once the seat of the dukes of Schleswig-Holstein, it has not only their palace but also ruins left by the area's first rulers, the Vikings. Those legendary and fierce warriors from Scandinavia brought terror (but also commerce and a highly developed social structure) to northern Germany between 800 and 1100. Under a wide sky, Schleswig lies on the Schlei River in a landscape of freshwater marshland and lakes, making it a good departure point for bike or canoe tours.

GETTING HERE AND AROUND

Schleswig's train station is 3 km (2 mi) from the city center. It's easiest to take bus 1501, 1505, or 1506 into town. The buses leave from across the street from the front of the train station, and all stop at Schloss Gottorf.

EXPLORING

The Holm. The fishing village comes alive along the Holm, an old settlement with tiny and colorful houses. The windblown buildings give a good impression of what villages in northern Germany looked like 150 years ago.

Schloss Gottorf. The impressive baroque Schloss Gottorf, dating from 1703, once housed the ruling family. It has been transformed into the **Schleswig-Holsteinisches Landesmuseum** (State Museum of Schleswig-Holstein) and holds a collection of art and handicrafts of northern Germany from the Middle Ages to the present, including paintings by Lucas Cranach the Elder. ⊠ *Schloss Gottorf* ☎ *04621/8130* ⊕ *www.schloss-gottorf.de* ⊡ *€8* ⊘ *Apr.–Oct., daily 10–6; Nov.–Mar., Tues.–Fri. 10–4, weekends 10–5.*

☺ **Wikinger-Museum Haithabu** (*Haithabu Viking Museum*). The most thrilling museum in Schleswig is at the site of a Viking settlement. This was the Vikings' most important German port, and the boats, gold jewelry, and graves they left behind are displayed in the museum. Be sure to walk along the trail to the Viking village, to see how the Vikings really lived. The best way to get there is to take the ferry across the Schlei from the Schleswigs main fishing port. ⊠ *Haddeby* ☎ *04621/813–222* ⊕ *www.schloss-gottorf.de* ⊡ *€6* ⊘ *Apr.–Oct., daily 9–5; Nov.–Mar., Tues.–Sun. 10–4.*

WHERE TO EAT AND STAY

For expanded hotel reviews, visit Fodors.com.

$ ✕ **Asgaard Brauerei.** Taste the "Divine beer of the Vikings" at Schleswig's
GERMAN   only brewery. While the restaurant offers typical brewpub fare, it is the small Viking twists, like roast meat served only with a knife and horned glasses that make this place worth a visit. The Divine beer is a malty cold-fermented amber lager that can be highly addictive. ⊠ *Königstr. 27* ☎ *04621/29206.*

$ ✕ **Stadt Flensburg.** This small restaurant in a city mansion dating back to
SEAFOOD   1699 serves mostly fish from the Schlei River. The food is solid regional

EATING WELL IN SCHLESWIG-HOLSTEIN

The German coastline is known for fresh and superb seafood, particularly in summer. A few of the region's top restaurants are on Sylt and in Lübeck. Eating choices along the Baltic Coast tend to be more down-to-earth. However, restaurants in both coastal states serve mostly seafood such as *Scholle* (flounder) or North Sea *Krabben* (shrimp), often with fried potatoes, eggs, and bacon. Mecklenburg specialties to look for

are *Mecklenburger Griebenroller*, a custardy casserole of grated potatoes, eggs, herbs, and chopped bacon; *Mecklenburger Fischsuppe*, a hearty fish soup with vegetables, tomatoes, and sour cream; *Gefüllte Ente* (duck with bread stuffing); and *Pannfisch* (fish patty). A favorite local nightcap since the 17th century is *Grog*, a strong blend of rum, hot water, and local fruits.

14

fare such as *Zanderfilet* (perch fillets) or *Gebratene Ente* (roast duck). The familial, warm atmosphere and the local dark tap beers more than make up for the simplicity of the setting. Reservations are advised. ✉ *Lollfuss 102* ☎ *04621/23984* ☯ *Closed Wed.*

$$ 🏨 **Ringhotel Strandhalle Schleswig.** A modern hotel overlooking the small yacht harbor, this establishment has surprisingly low rates. **Pros:** hotel occupies central spot in the heart of Schleswig with great views. **Cons:** lack of flair; rather bland rooms. ✉ *Strandweg 2* ☎ *04621/9090* ⊕ *www. hotel-strandhalle.de* ⤳ *25 rooms* ⌂ *In-room: no a/c, Internet. In-hotel: restaurant, pool, parking, some pets allowed* ¶ *Breakfast.*

SHOPPING

Keramik-Stube. The tiny Keramik-Stube offers craft work and beautiful traditional handmade pottery. ✉ *Rathausmarkt 14* ☎ *04621/24757.*

Teekontor Hansen. Northern Germans are devout tea drinkers, and the best place to buy tea is Teekontor Hansen. Try the *Schliekieker*, a strong blend of different types, or the *Ostfriesenmischung*, the traditional daily tea. ✉ *Kornmarkt 3* ☎ *04621/23385.*

KIEL

53 km (33 mi) southeast of Schleswig, 130 km (81 mi) north of Hamburg.

The state capital, Kiel, is known throughout Europe for the annual Kieler Woche, a regatta that attracts hundreds of boats from around the world. Despite the many wharves and industries concentrated in Kiel, the **Kieler Föhrde** (Bay of Kiel) has remained mostly unspoiled. Unfortunately, this cannot be said about the city itself. Because of Kiel's strategic significance during World War II—it served as the main German submarine base—the historic city, founded more than 750 years ago, was completely destroyed. Sadly, due to the modern reconstruction of the city, there is no real reason to spend more than half a day in Kiel.

ESSENTIALS

Visitor Information Kiel ✉ *Andreas-Gayk-Str. 31* ☎ *0431/679–100* ⊕ *www.kiel.de.*

EXPLORING

Kieler Hafen (*Kiel Harbor*). At Germany's largest passenger-shipping harbor, you can always catch a glimpse of one of the many ferries leaving for Scandinavia from the **Oslokai** (Oslo Quay).

Kunsthalle zu Kiel (*Kiel Art Gallery*). One of northern Germany's best collections of modern art can be found here. Russian art of the 19th and early 20th centuries, German Expressionism, and contemporary international art are on display. ✉ *Düsternbrooker Weg 1* ☎ *0431/880–5756* ⊕ *www. kunsthalle-kiel.de* 🖭 *€7* ☉ *Tues. and Thurs.–Sun. 10–6, Wed. 10–8.*

U-Boot-Museum (*Submarine Museum*). A grim reminder of a different marine past is exhibited at this museum in Kiel-Laboe. The vessels of the much-feared German submarine fleet in World War I were mostly built and stationed in Kiel, before leaving for the Atlantic, where they attacked American and British supply convoys. Today the submarine U995 serves as a public-viewing model of a typical German submarine. The 280-foot-high **Marineehrenmal** (Marine Honor Memorial), in Laboe, was built in 1927–36. You can reach Laboe via ferry from the Kiel harbor or take B-502 north. ✉ *Strandstr. 92, Kiel-Laboe* ☎ *04343/42700* 🖭 *Memorial €3.50, museum €3.50* ☉ *Apr.–Oct., daily 9:30–6; Nov.–Mar., daily 9:30–4.*

WHERE TO EAT AND STAY

For expanded hotel reviews, visit Fodors.com.

$ ✕ **Kieler Brauerei.** The only historic brewery in town has produced beer
GERMAN   since the Middle Ages. You can try the *Naturtrübes Kieler* and other
★   north German beers in pitchers. ■TIP➔ You can also order a small barrel for your table and tap it yourself (other patrons will cheer you). The hearty food—mostly fish, pork, and potato dishes—does not earn awards, but it certainly helps get down just one more beer. ✉ *Alter Markt 9* ☎ *0431/906–290.*

$ ✕ **Quam.** Locals aren't looking for old-fashioned fish dishes—that's why
ECLECTIC   there isn't a traditional fish restaurant in town. They prefer preparations of fish from all over the world. The stylish Quam, its yellow walls and dimmed lights paying homage to Tuscany, serves specialties from Germany, Italy, France, and Japan to a mostly young, very chic crowd. ✉ *Düppelstr. 60* ☎ *0431/85195* 🖾 *Reservations essential* ☉ *Closed Sun. No lunch.*

$$$ 🛏 **Hotel Kieler Yachtclub.** This traditional hotel provides standard yet elegant, newly refurbished rooms in the main building and completely new, bright accommodations in the Villentrakt. **Pros:** central location in the heart of Kiel; nice views. **Cons:** service and attitude can feel a bit too formal at times. ✉ *Hindenburgufer 70* ☎ *0431/88130* ⊕ *www.*

hotel-kyc.de 🖙 *57 rooms, 4 suites* 🖒 *In-room: no a/c, Internet. In-hotel: restaurant, bar, parking, some pets allowed* ⎤⓪⎤*Breakfast.*

NIGHTLIFE AND THE ARTS

Hemingway. One of the many chic and hip bars is the Hemingway. ⊠ *Alter Markt 19* ☎ *0431/96812.*

Traumfabrik. A college crowd goes to Traumfabrik to eat pizza, watch a movie, or dance (Friday is best for dancing). ⊠ *Grasweg 19* ☎ *0431/ 544–450.*

LÜBECK

14

60 km (37 mi) southeast of Kiel, 56 km (35 mi) northeast of Hamburg.

Fodor'sChoice
★

The ancient core of Lübeck, dating from the 12th century, was a chief stronghold of the Hanseatic merchant princes. But it was the roving Heinrich der Löwe (King Henry the Lion) who established the town and, in 1173, laid the foundation stone of the redbrick Gothic cathedral. The town's famous landmark gate, the **Holstentor,** built between 1464 and 1478, is flanked by two round squat towers and serves as a solid symbol of Lübeck's prosperity as a trading center.

GETTING HERE AND AROUND

Lübeck is accessible from Hamburg in 45 minutes either by Intercity trains or by car via the A-24 and A-1, which almost takes you from one city center to the other. Lübeck is also well connected by autobahns and train service to Kiel, Flensburg, and the neighboring eastern coastline. The city, however, should be explored on foot or by bike, as the many tiny, medieval alleys in the center cannot be accessed by car. Tours of Old Lübeck depart daily from the tourist Welcome Center on Holstentorplatz (☉ *June–Aug., Sat. at 11:30* ⎙*€7).*

ESSENTIALS

Visitor Information Lübeck ⊠ *Holstentorpl. 1* ☎ *00451/889-9700* ⊕ *www. luebeck.de.*

EXPLORING

TOP ATTRACTIONS

Altstadt (*Old Town*). In the Altstadt, proof of Lübeck's former position as the golden queen of the Hanseatic League is found at every step. ■TIP➔ More 13th- to 15th-century buildings stand in Lübeck than in all other large northern German cities combined, which has earned the Altstadt a place on UNESCO's register of the world's greatest cultural and natural treasures.

Lübecker Dom (*Lübeck Cathedral*). Construction of this, the city's oldest building, began in 1173. ⊠ *Domkirchhof* ☎ *0451/74704* ☉ *Apr.–Oct., daily 10–6; Nov.–Mar., daily 10–4.*

Rathaus. Dating from 1240, the Rathaus is among the buildings lining the arcaded Marktplatz, one of Europe's most striking medieval market squares. ⊠ *Breitestr. 64* ☎ *0451/122–1005* ⎙ *Guided tour in German €4* ☉ *Tour weekdays at 11, noon, and 3; Sat. at 1:30.*

WORTH NOTING

Buddenbrookhaus. Two highly respectable-looking mansions are devoted to two of Germany's most prominent writers, Thomas Mann (1875–1955) and Günter Grass (born 1927). The older mansion is named after Mann's saga *Buddenbrooks*. Mann's family once lived here, and it's now home to the **Heinrich und Thomas Mann Zentrum**, a museum documenting the brothers' lives. A tour and video in English are offered. ⊠ *Mengstr. 4* ☎ *0451/122–4240* ⊕ *www.buddenbrookhaus.de* ⊡ *€10* ⊘ *Jan.–Mar., Tues.–Sun. 11–5; Apr.–Dec., daily 10–5.*

Günter Grass-Haus. Near the museum is the second mansion, which is devoted to Germany's most famous living writer and winner of the Nobel Prize for Literature (1999). ⊠ *Glockengiesserstr. 21* ☎ *0451/122–4230* ⊕ *die-luebecker-museen.de* ⊡ *€5* ⊘ *Jan.–Mar., Tues.–Sun. 11–5; Apr.–Dec., daily 10–5.*

Heilig-Geist-Hospital (*Hospital of the Holy Ghost*). Take a look inside the entrance hall of this Gothic building. It was built in the 14th century by the town's rich merchants and is still caring for the infirm. ⊠ *Am Koberg 11* ☎ *0451/790–7841* ⊡ *Free* ⊘ *Apr.–Sept., Tues.–Sun. 10–5; Oct.–Mar., Tues.–Sun. 10–4.*

Marienkirche (*St. Mary's Church*). The impressive redbrick Gothic structure, which has the highest brick nave in the world, looms behind the Rathaus. ⊠ *Marienkirchhof* ☎ *0451/397–700* ⊘ *Nov.–Feb., daily 10–4; Mar. and Oct., daily 10–5; Apr.–Sept., daily 10–6.*

WHERE TO EAT

$$
GERMAN
Fodor'sChoice
★

✕ **Schiffergesellschaft.** This dark, wood-paneled restaurant dating back to 1535 is the city's old Mariners' Society house, which was off-limits to women until 1870. Today locals and visitors alike enjoy freshly brewed beer and great seafood in church-style pews at long 400-year-old oak tables. Above are a bizarre collection of low-hanging old ship models. A good meal here is the *Ostseescholle* (plaice), fried with bacon and served with potatoes and cucumber salad. ⊠ *Breitestr. 2* ☎ *0451/76776.*

$$$$
GERMAN

✕ **Wullenwever.** This restaurant has set a new standard of dining sophistication for Lübeck. Committed to the city's maritime heritage, Wullenwever serves fish such as bass, halibut, plaice, pike, and trout, which is fried or sautéed according to local country cooking. It's certainly one of the most attractive establishments in town, with dark furniture, chandeliers, and oil paintings on pale pastel walls. In summer, tables fill a quiet flower-strewn courtyard. Don't order à la carte here. Instead choose one of the three- to seven-course menus, paired with wine. ⊠ *Beckergrube 71* ☎ *0451/704–333* ✍ *Reservations essential* ⊘ *Closed Sun. and Mon. No lunch.*

> **WORD OF MOUTH**
>
> "Lübeck is wonderful . . . Yes, do read *Buddenbrooks*. I read it with my book club while I lived in Stuttgart and it was great fun to visit the place where it all happened. We absolutely loved this little city and had a wonderful, memorable meal at the Schiffergesellschaft. If you enjoy history and food, this place is fantastic. You simply can't beat the medieval ambience." —hausfrau

14

WHERE TO STAY

For expanded hotel reviews, visit Fodors.com.

$ ★ **Hotel zur Alten Stadtmauer.** This historic town house in the heart of the city is Lübeck's most charming hotel. **Pros:** cozy hotel with personal, friendly service; great location. **Cons:** rather simply furnished rooms; if fully booked, the hotel feels cramped. ⊠ *An der Mauer 57* ☎ *0451/73702* ⊕ *www.hotelstadtmauer.de* ⊅ *22 rooms, most with bath* ⌂ *In-room: no a/c, Wi-Fi. In-hotel: parking* ⎮⊚⎮ *Breakfast.*

$$ ★ **Ringhotel Friederikenhof.** A lovely country hotel set in 19th-century, redbrick farmhouses 10 minutes outside Lübeck, the family-run Friederikenhof is a perfect hideaway with a soothing garden and great view of the city's skyline. **Pros:** charming, old-style farmhouse typical of the region; personal and very friendly service. **Cons:** distant location outside Lübeck. ⊠ *Langjohrd 15–19* ☎ *0451/800–880* ⊕ *www.friederikenhof. de* ⊅ *30 rooms* ⌂ *In-room: no a/c, Wi-Fi. In-hotel: restaurant, parking, some pets allowed* ⎮⊚⎮ *Breakfast.*

$ **Ringhotel Jensen.** Only a stone's throw from the Holstentor, this hotel is close to all the main attractions and faces the moat surrounding the Old Town. **Pros:** perfect location in the heart of Lübeck's downtown area; major sights are all within walking distance. **Cons:** small pensionlike hotel without many of the amenities of larger hotels; blandly decorated rooms. ⊠ *An der Obertrave 4–5* ☎ *0451/702–490* ⊕ *www. hotel-jensen.de* ⊅ *41 rooms, 1 suite* ⌂ *In-room: no a/c, Wi-Fi. In-hotel: restaurant, parking, some pets allowed* ⎮⊚⎮ *Breakfast.*

$$ **SAS Radisson Senator Hotel Lübeck.** Close to the famous Holstentor, this ultramodern hotel, with its daring architecture, still reveals a north German heritage: the redbrick building, with its oversize windows and generous, open lobby, mimics an old Lübeck warehouse. **Pros:** luxury hotel in a central location. **Cons:** lacks the historic charm typical of medieval Lübeck. ⊠ *Willy-Brandt-Allee 6* ☎ *0451/1420* ⊕ *www.senatorhotel.de* ⊅ *217 rooms, 7 suites* ⌂ *In-room: Wi-Fi. In-hotel: restaurant, bar, pool, spa, parking, some pets allowed.*

THE ARTS

Musik und Kongresshallen Lübeck. Contact the Musik und Kongresshallen Lübeck for schedules of the myriad concerts, operas, and theater performances in Lübeck. ⊠ *Willy-Brandt-Allee 10* ☎ *0451/79040.*

Schleswig-Holstein Music Festival. In summer, try to catch a few performances of the Schleswig-Holstein Music Festival (mid-July–late August), which features orchestras composed of young musicians from more than 25 countries. Some concerts are held in the Dom or the Marienkirche; some are staged in barns in small towns and villages.

Schleswig-Holstein Konzertorganisation. For exact dates and tickets to the Schleswig-Holstein Music Festival, contact Schleswig-Holstein Konzertorganisation. ⊠ *Kartenzentrale Kiel, Postfach 3840, Kiel* ☎ *0431/ 570–470* ⊕ *www.shfm.de.*

SHOPPING

Local legend has it that marzipan was invented in Lübeck during the great medieval famine. According to the story, a local baker ran out of grain for bread and, in his desperation, began experimenting with the only four ingredients he had: almonds, sugar, rosewater, and eggs. The result was a sweet almond paste known today as marzipan. The story is more fiction than fact; it is generally agreed that marzipan's true origins lie in the Middle East. ■TIP➔ Lübecker Marzipan, an appellation that has been trademarked, is now considered among the best in the world. Any Marzipan that uses the appellation Lübecker, must be made within the city limits.

Holstentor-Passage. The city's largest downtown mall, Holstentor-Passage, is next to the Holstentor and is filled with stores selling clothing or home accessories. ✉ *An der Untertrave 111* ☎ *0451/75292.*

Konditorei-Café Niederegger. Lübeck's most famous marzipan maker, Konditorei-Café Niederegger, sells the delicacy molded into a multitude of imaginative forms. ✉ *Breitestr. 89* ☎ *0451/530–1127.*

WESTERN MECKLENBURG

This long-forgotten Baltic Coast region, pinned between two sprawling urban areas—the state capital of Schwerin, in the west, and Rostock, in the east—is thriving again. Though the region is close to the sea, it's made up largely of seemingly endless fields of wheat and yellow rape and a dozen or so wonderful lakes. "When the Lord made the Earth, He started with Mecklenburg," wrote native novelist Fritz Reuter.

WISMAR

60 km (37 mi) east of Lübeck on Rte. 105.

★ The old city of Wismar was one of the original three sea-trading towns, along with Lübeck and Rostock, which banded together in 1259 to combat Baltic pirates. From this mutual defense pact grew the great and powerful private-trading bloc, the Hanseatic League, which dominated the Baltic for centuries. The wealth generated by the Hanseatic merchants can still be seen in Wismar's ornate architecture.

ESSENTIALS

Visitor Information Wismar ✉ *Stadthaus, Am Markt 11* ☎ *03841/19433* ⊕ *www.wismar.de.*

EXPLORING
TOP ATTRACTIONS

★ **Marktplatz** (*Market Square*). One of the largest and best-preserved squares in Germany is framed by patrician gabled houses. Their style ranges from redbrick late Gothic through Dutch Renaissance to 19th-century neoclassical. The square's **Wasserkunst,** the ornate pumping station done in Dutch Renaissance style, was built between 1580 and 1602 by the Dutch master Philipp Brandin.

St. Georgen zu Wismar (*St. George's Church*). This church, another victim of the war, stands next to the Fürstenhof. One of northern Germany's biggest Gothic churches, built between 1315 and 1404, it has been almost completely restored.

To'n Zägenkrog. If you have an hour to spare, wander among the jetties and quays of the port, a mix of the medieval and the modern. To'n Zägenkrog, a seamen's haven decorated with sharks' teeth, stuffed seagulls, and maritime gear, is a good pit stop along the harbor. ☒ *Ziegenmarkt 10* ☎ *03841/282–716.*

WORD OF MOUTH

"I loved Wismar. It is less spectacular [than Lübeck], but on the other hand less polished and less touristy than Lübeck. In the side streets you feel as if time stood still in the 1920s." —quokka

WORTH NOTING

Fürstenhof (*Princes' Court*). The home of the former dukes of Mecklenburg stands next to the Marienkirche. It's an early-16th-century Italian Renaissance structure with touches of late Gothic. The facade is a series of fussy friezes depicting scenes from the Trojan War.

Marienkirche (*St. Mary's Church*). The ruins of this church with its 250-foot tower, bombed in World War II, lie just behind the Marktplatz; the church is still undergoing restoration. ■TIP→ At noon, 3, and 5, listen for one of 14 hymns played on its carillon.

St. Nikolaikirche (*St. Nicholas's Church*). The late-Gothic church, with a 120-foot-high nave, was built between 1381 and 1487. A remnant of the town's long domination by Sweden is the additional altar built for Swedish sailors. ☒ *Marktpl.* ☎ *03841/210–143* ☉ *May–Sept., daily 8–8; Apr. and Oct., daily 10–6; Nov.–Mar., daily 11–4.*

WHERE TO EAT

$

GERMAN

★

✕ **Alter Schwede.** Regarded as one of the most attractive, authentic taverns on the Baltic—and correspondingly busy—this eatery focuses on Mecklenburg's game and poultry dishes, such as the traditional *Mecklenburger Ente* (Mecklenburg duck). This filling dish is filled with baked plums, apples, raisins, and served with red cabbage and potatoes. ☒ *Am Markt 19* ☎ *03841/283–552.*

$

GERMAN

★

✕ **Brauhaus am Lohberg.** Wismar's first brewery (1452) is the only place that still brews *Wismarer Mumme* a dark beer with enough alcohol to keep it fresh for export as far away as St. Petersburg. The restaurant serves up good-value typical pub food in an old half-timber house near the harbor. ☒ *Kleine Hohe Str. 15* ☎ *03841/250–238.*

WHERE TO STAY

For expanded hotel reviews, visit Fodors.com.

$$

▦ **Citypartner Hotel Alter Speicher.** This small and very personal family-owned hotel is behind the facade of an old merchant house in the downtown area. **Pros:** good location, as medieval parts of Wismar are within easy walking distance. **Cons:** rooms have outdated furnishings and ambience. ☒ *Bohrstr. 12–12a* ☎ *03841/211–746* ⊕ *www.hotel-alter-speicher.de* ⇆ *70 rooms, 3 suites, 2 apartments* ♨ *In-room: no a/c, Wi-Fi. In-hotel: restaurant, bar, gym, parking, some pets allowed* ℺ *Breakfast.*

The Baltic Coast

$$ 🏨 **Seehotel Neuklostersee.** Set at the dreamy Naun Lake, this country hotel is a hidden gem 15 km (9 mi) east of Wismar. **Pros:** great rural setting in quaint surroundings. **Cons:** outside Wismar; many day-trip visitors. ✉ *Seestr. 1, Nakenstorf* ☎ *038422/4570* ⊕ *www.seehotel-neuklostersee. de* ↪ *10 suites, 3 apartments* ⚷ *In-room: no a/c, Wi-Fi. In-hotel: restaurant, gym, beach, parking, some pets allowed* ⦿| *Breakfast.*

$ 🏨 **Steigenberger–Hotel Stadt Hamburg.** This first-class hotel hides behind a rigid gray facade dating back to the early 19th century. **Pros:** the only upscale hotel in town, with an appealing interior design; great package deals available. **Cons:** lacks atmosphere and personal touches. ✉ *Am Markt 24* ☎ *03841/2390* ⊕ *www.wismar.steigenberger.de* ↪ *102 rooms, 2 suites* ⚷ *In-room: no a/c, Wi-Fi. In-hotel: restaurant* ⦿| *Breakfast.*

SCHWERIN

32 km (20 mi) south of Wismar on Rte. 106.

★ Schwerin, the second-largest town in the region after Rostock and the capital of the state of Mecklenburg-Vorpommern, is worth a trip just to visit its giant island palace.

ESSENTIALS

Visitor Information Schwerin ⊠ *Am Markt 14* ☎ *0385/592–5212* ⊕ *www. schwerin.de.*

EXPLORING

⟳ **Alter Garten** (*Old Garden*). The town's showpiece square was the setting of military parades during the years of Communist rule. It's dominated by two buildings: the ornate neo-Renaissance state theater, constructed in 1883–86; and the **Kunstsammlungen Schwerin** (Schwerin Art Collection), which houses an interesting collection of paintings by Max Liebermann and Lovis Corinth. ⊠ *Alter Garten 3* ☎ *0385/595–8119* ⊕ *www.museum-schwerin.de* ⊠ *€8* ⊗ *Mid-Apr.–mid-Oct., Tues.–Sun. 10–6; mid-Oct.–mid-Apr., Tues.–Sun. 10–5.*

The Dom. This Gothic cathedral is the oldest building (built 1222–48) in the city. The bronze baptismal font is from the 14th century; the altar was built in 1440. Religious scenes painted on its walls date from the Middle Ages. Sweeping views of the Old Town and lake await those with the energy to climb the 219 steps to the top of the 320-foot-high cathedral tower. ⊠ *Am Dom 4* ☎ *0385/565–014* ⊗ *Tower and nave May–Oct., Mon.–Sat. 10–5, Sun. noon–5; Nov.–Apr., weekdays 11–4, Sat. 11–4, Sun. noon–4.*

Schlossmuseum. North of the main tower is the **Neue Lange Haus** (New Long House), built between 1553 and 1555 and now used as the Schlossmuseum. The Communist government restored and maintained the fantastic opulence of this rambling, 80-room reminder of an absolutist monarchy—and then used it to board kindergarten teachers in training. Antique furniture, objets d'art, silk tapestries, and paintings are sprinkled throughout the salons (the throne room is particularly extravagant), but of special interest are the ornately patterned and highly burnished inlaid wooden floors and wall panels. ⊠ *Lennéstr. 1* ☎ *0385/525–2920* ⊕ *www.museum-schwerin.de* ⊠ *€6* ⊗ *Mid-Apr.–mid-Oct., daily 10–6; mid-Oct.–mid-Apr., Tues.–Sun. 10–5.*

Schweriner Schloss. On the edge of Lake Schwerin, the meticulously restored palace once housed the Mecklenburg royal family. The original palace dates from 1018, but was enlarged by Henry the Lion when he founded Schwerin in 1160. Portions of it were later modeled on Chambord, in the Loire Valley. As it stands now, the palace is surmounted by 15 turrets, large and small, and is reminiscent of a French château. The portions that are neo-Renaissance in style are its many ducal staterooms, which date from between 1845 and 1857.

⟳ **Weisse Flotte.** The quintessential experience in Schwerin is one of the Weiss Flotte boat tours of the lakes—there are seven in the area. A trip to the island of Kaninchenwerder, a small sanctuary for more than 100 species of waterbirds, is an unforgettable experience. Boats for this 1½-hour standard tour depart from the pier adjacent to the Schweriner Schloss. ⊠ *Anlegestelle Schlosspier* ☎ *0385/557–770* ⊕ *www. weisseflotteschwerin.de* ⊠ *€9.50* ⊗ *Apr.–Oct., daily 10–5:30.*

If the weather if fine, take a stroll along Wismar's historic harbor.

WHERE TO EAT

$ ✕ **Alt-Schweriner Schankstuben.** A small, family-owned restaurant and
GERMAN hotel with 16 guest rooms, the Schankstuben emphasizes Mecklenburg
tradition. Its inviting restaurant is perfect for sampling local recipes
such as *Rullbraten von Spanferkel* (roast suckling pig) or *Maisscholle*
(corn-fed plaice). ⊠ *Schlachtermarkt 9–13* ☎ *0385/592–530* ⊕ *www.
alt-schweriner-schankstuben.de.*

$ ✕ **Weinhaus Krömer.** One of the most traditional and popular eateries
GERMAN in Schwerin, this restaurant has a long history of serving good wines
★ and dates back to 1740. The *Weinbistro* offers primarily German wine
tasting and a small menu (mostly cheese plates or soups such as lobster
cream soup). Regional and international specialties are served in the
modern restaurant, while in summer the Weingarten courtyard is one of
the city's most secluded spots to enjoy a good glass of wine. ⊠ *Grosser
Moor 56* ☎ *0385/562–956.*

$ ✕ **Zum Stadtkrug-Altstadtbrauhaus.** Don't be fooled by the prefab exterior,
GERMAN Schwerin's only brewery is an oasis of great beer and down-to-earth
regional and brauhaus specialties like the Malzsack (à la cordon bleu,
breaded with brewing malt) or Mecklenburger lamb. Wash it down
with the house brewed unfiltered light or dark beer. ⊠ *Wismarsche Str.
126* ☎ *0385/593–6693* ⊕ *www.altstadtbrauhaus.de.*

WHERE TO STAY

For expanded hotel reviews, visit Fodors.com.

$$ ▦ **Hotel Niederländischer Hof.** The city's most elegant hotel has a 4½-star
rating in view of its luxurious interior, decorated in a classic style; its
romantic, airy rooms; the impeccable service; and, of course, the fine

nouvelle cuisine à la Mecklenburg (mostly seafood dishes). **Pros:** interesting packages include tours, dinner, and more; great location right off a lake and within walking distance of the Schloss, boat docks, and downtown museums. **Cons:** formal atmosphere. ⊠ *Alexandrinenstr. 12–13* ☎ *0385/591–100* ⊕ *www.niederlaendischer-hof.de* ⤳ *27 rooms, 6 suites* ⚘ *In-room: no a/c. In-hotel: restaurant, parking, some pets allowed* ¶⊙¶ *Breakfast.*

$$ 🏨 **Sorat-Hotel Speicher am Ziegelsee.** Towering seven stories above the old harbor, the Speicher am Ziegelsee was once a wheat warehouse. **Pros:** unbeatable location on a lovely lake and lakeside dining; very friendly and professional service. **Cons:** old-style warehouse building, whose rooms may seem cramped for some travelers, a bit far from the action. ⊠ *Speicherstr. 11* ☎ *0385/50030* ⊕ *www.speicher-hotel.com* ⤳ *59 rooms, 20 apartments* ⚘ *In-room: no a/c, kitchen. In-hotel: restaurant, bar, parking, some pets allowed* ¶⊙¶ *Breakfast.*

NIGHTLIFE AND THE ARTS

Mecklenburgisches Staatstheater. The Mecklenburgisches Staatstheater stages German drama and opera. ⊠ *Am Alten Garten* ☎ *0385/53000.*

Schlossfestspiele. In June, check out the Schlossfestspiele for open-air drama or comedy performances.

Mexxclub. The Mexxclub is the city's hottest dance club, featuring house and soul DJs who attract a stylish young crowd every Saturday night. ⊠ *Klöresgang 2* ☎ *No phone.*

SHOPPING

■ TIP→ Antiques and bric-a-brac that have languished in cellars and attics since World War II are still surfacing throughout eastern Germany, and the occasional bargain can be found. The best places to look in Schwerin are on and around Schmiedestrasse, Schlossstrasse, and Mecklenburgstrasse.

BAD DOBERAN

60 km (37 mi) east of Wismar on Rte. 105, 90 km (56 mi) northeast of Schwerin.

Bad Doberan, mostly famous for its cathedral, is a quaint town with Germany's oldest sea resort, Heiligendamm. The city is a popular weekend and summer getaway for people from Rostock and Berlin, but has managed to maintain its laid-back charm.

ESSENTIALS

Visitor Information Bad Doberan ⊠ *Severinstr. 6* ☎ *038203/62154* ⊕ *www. bad-doberan.de.*

EXPLORING

★ **Doberaner Münster** (*monastery church*). Bad Doberan is home to the meticulously restored redbrick church, one of the finest of its kind in Germany. It was built by Cistercian monks between 1294 and 1368 in the northern German Gothic style, with a central nave and transept. The main altar dates from the early 14th century. ⊠ *Klosterstr.* ☎ *038203/62716* ⊕ *www.doberanermuenster.de* 🎟 *€2* ⊙ *May–Sept. Mon.–Sat. 9–6, Sun. 11–6; Mar., Apr., and Oct., Mon.–Sat. 10–5, Sun*

*11–5; Nov.–Feb., Mon.–Sat. 10–4, Sun. 11–4. Tours May–Oct., Mon.–
Sat. at noon and 3; Nov.–Apr., Mon.–Sat. at 11 and 1.*

🔁 **Molli.** No visit to this part of the country would be complete without a
ride on this steam train that has been chugging up and down a 16-km
(10-mi) narrow-gauge track between Bad Doberan and the nearby
beach resorts of **Heiligendamm** and **Kühlungsborn** since 1886. The train
was nicknamed after a little local dog that barked its approval every
time the smoking iron horse passed by. In summer *Molli* runs 13 times
daily between Bad Doberan and Kühlungsborn. ⊠ *Mecklenburgische
Bäderbahn Molli, Küstenbus GmbH* ☎ *038203/4150* ⊕ *www.molli-
bahn.de* ⊟ *Same-day round-trip €7.40–€11.40* ⊗ *From Bad Doberan:
May–Sept., daily 8:35–6:45; Oct.–Apr., daily 8:35–4:40.*

WHERE TO EAT AND STAY
For expanded hotel reviews, visit Fodors.com.

$
GERMAN

✕ **Weisser Pavillon.** Here's a mixed setting for you: a 19th-century
Chinese-pagoda-type structure in an English-style park. Come for lunch
or high tea; regional specialties are featured. In summer the café stays
open until 10 pm. ⊠ *Auf dem Kamp* ☎ *038203/62326* ⊟ *No credit
cards.*

$$$$
Fodor'sChoice
★

⊡ **Grand Hotel Heiligendamm.** The small beach resort of Heiligendamm
has regained its prewar reputation as a getaway for Berlin's up-and-
coming crowd. **Pros:** the only real first-class hotel on the Baltic Coast,
with a wide range of sports and activities. **Cons:** very large hotel spread
out in somewhat long distances; service is formal and stiff at times;
books up quickly in high season. ⊠ *Grand Hotel at Heiligendamm,
Prof.-Dr.-Vogel-Str. 16–18, Heiligendamm* ☎ *038203/7400* ⊕ *www.
grandhotel-heiligendamm.de* ⟿ *118 rooms, 107 suites* ⌂ *In-room:
Internet, Wi-Fi. In-hotel: restaurant, bar, pool, gym, spa, beach, busi-
ness center, parking, some pets allowed* †⊙| *Breakfast.*

ROSTOCK

14 km (9 mi) east of Bad Doberan on Rte. 105.

Rostock, the biggest port and shipbuilding center of the former East
Germany, was founded around 1200. Of all the Hanseatic cities, the
once-thriving Rostock suffered the most from the dissolution of the
League in 1669. The GDR (German Democratic Republic) reestab-
lished Rostock as a major port, but port work has been cut in half since
reunification, and though ferries come from Gedser (Denmark) and
Trelleborg (Sweden), there's little traffic. ■ TIP➔ **The biggest local annual
attraction is Hanse Sail, a week of yacht racing held in August.**

ESSENTIALS
Visitor Information Rostock ⊠ *Neuer Markt 3* ☎ *0381/32222* ⊕ *www.rostock.de.*

EXPLORING

TOP ATTRACTIONS
Kröpelinerstrasse. The pedestrians-only main street begins at the old
western gate, the Kröpeliner Tor. Here you'll find the finest examples
of late-Gothic and Renaissance houses of rich Hanse merchants.

14

St. Marienkirche (*St. Mary's Church*). This four-century-old church, the Gothic architectural prize of Rostock, boasts a bronze baptismal font from 1290 and some interesting baroque features, notably the oak altar (1720) and organ (1770). The huge astronomical clock, dating from 1472, has a calendar extending to 2017. The church is still open, but is being reconstructed and will be under scaffolding until at least 2020.
■ TIP➔ For a unique souvenir of the church, take some of the free medieval wood, copper fasteners, or nails from the bin near the information office. ⊠ *Am Ziegenmarkt 4* ☎ *0381/492–3396* ⊗ *Oct.–Apr., Mon.–Sat. 10–12:15 and 2–4, Sun. 11–12:15; May–Sept., Mon.–Sat. 10–6, Sun. 11:15–5.*

Universitätsplatz (*University Square*). The triangular University Square, commemorating the founding of northern Europe's first university here in 1419, is home to Rostock University's Italian Renaissance–style main building, finished in 1867.

WORTH NOTING

Neuer Markt (*Town Square*). Here, you'll immediately notice the architectural potpourri of the **Rathaus.** The pink baroque facade from the 18th century hides a wonderful 13th-century Gothic building underneath. The town hall spouts seven slender, decorative towers that look like candles on a peculiar birthday cake. Walk around back to see more of the Gothic elements. Historic gabled houses surround the rest of the square.

🕙 **Schifffahrtsmuseum** (*Maritime Museum*). Tracing the history of shipping on the Baltic, this museum displays models of ships, which especially intrigue children. It's just beyond the city wall, at the old city gateway, Steintor. ⊠ *August-Bebel-Str. 1* ☎ *0381/492–2697* ⊕ *www.schifffahrtsmuseum-rostock.de* ⊡ *€4* ⊗ *Tues.–Sun. 11–6.*

🕙 **Zoologischer Garten** (*Zoological Garden*). Here you'll find one of the largest collections of exotic animals and birds in northern Germany. This zoo is particularly noted for its polar bears, some of which were bred in Rostock. If you're traveling with children, a visit is a must. ⊠ *Rennbahnallee 21* ☎ *0381/20820* ⊕ *www.zoo-rostock.de* ⊡ *€11.50* ⊗ *Nov.–Mar., daily 9–5; Apr.–Oct., daily 9–7.*

WHERE TO EAT

$
GERMAN
✕ **Petrikeller.** Once you've crossed the threshold of the Petrikeller, you'll find yourself in the medieval world of Hanseatic merchants, seamen, and wild pirates such as Klaus Störtebecker. The restaurant's motto, "*Wer nicht liebt Wein, Weib und Gesang bleibt ein Narr sein Leben lang*" ("He who doth not love wine, woman, and song will be a fool his whole life long"), a quote from reformer Martin Luther no less, sets the right tone. ⊠ *Harte Str. 27* ☎ *0381/455–855* ⊕ *www.petrikeller.de* ⊟ *No credit cards* ⊗ *Closed Mon. No lunch.*

$$$
ASIAN
✕ **Restaurant & Bar Silo 4.** Rostock's latest culinary venture is proof that eastern Germany can do sleek and modern. At the top of a waterfront office tower, this innovative restaurant offers spectacular views of the river and a fun and interesting approach to Asian-fusion cuisine. The buffet consists of a list of ingredients and seasonings. Guests choose what they like and then leave it to the experts in the show kitchen to work their magic. ⊠ *Am Strande 3d* ☎ *0381/458–5800* ⊕ *www.silo4.de* ⊗ *Closed Mon. No lunch.*

$ ✕ **Zur Kogge.** Looking like the cabin of some ancient sailing vessel,
GERMAN   the oldest sailors' beer tavern in town serves mostly fish. Order the
★   *Mecklenburger Fischsuppe* (fish soup) if it's on the menu. The *Grosser Fischteller*, consisting of three kinds of fish—depending on the day's catch—served with vegetables, lobster and shrimp sauce, and potatoes, is also a popular choice. ⊠ *Wokrenterstr. 27* ☎ *0381/493–4493* ⌂ *Reservations essential.*

WHERE TO STAY

For expanded hotel reviews, visit Fodors.com.

$$ ⊡ **Pental Hotel.** A 19th-century mansion, this hotel is a genuine part of Rostock's historic Old Town. **Pros:** good location; very quiet backstreet. **Cons:** restaurant isn't very good; bland room design. ⊠ *Schwaansche Str. 6* ☎ *0381/49700* ⊕ *www.pentahotels.com* ⤴ *150 rooms, 2 suites* ⌂ *In-room: no a/c, Wi-Fi. In-hotel: restaurant, bar, gym, parking, some pets allowed* ❤️⃝ *Breakfast.*

$$ ⊡ **Steigenberger–Hotel zur Sonne Rostock.** With more than 200 years of
★   history behind it, the "Sun," located within the Old Town, is one of the nicest hotels in Rostock. **Pros:** nice view and near many sights; good restaurants, cafés, and bars nearby. **Cons:** rooms get direct sunlight in summer, and therefore are very warm; open setting of bed in the middle of the room may be unsettling for some. ⊠ *Neuer Markt 2* ☎ *0381/49730* ⊕ *www.rostock.steigenberger.de* ⤴ *90 rooms, 21 suites* ⌂ *In-room: no a/c, Wi-Fi. In-hotel: restaurant, bar, parking, some pets allowed* ❤️⃝ *Breakfast.*

NIGHTLIFE AND THE ARTS

The summer season brings with it a plethora of special concerts, sailing regattas, and parties on the beach.

Volkstheater. The Volkstheater presents plays and concerts. ⊠ *Patriotischer Weg 33* ☎ *0381/4600.*

SHOPPING

Echter Rostocker Doppel-Kümmel und -Korn, a kind of schnapps made from various grains and flavored with cumin, is a traditional liquor of the area around Rostock. Fishermen have numbed themselves to the cold for centuries with this 80-proof beverage; a bottle costs €8–€11.

WARNEMÜNDE

14 km (9 mi) north of Rostock on Rte. 103.

Warnemünde is a quaint seaside resort town with the best hotels and restaurants in the area, as well as 20 km (12 mi) of beautiful white-sand beach. It's been a popular summer getaway for families in eastern Germany for years.

There is little to do in Warnemünde except relax, and the town excels brilliantly at that. However, Warnemünde is a major cruise ship terminal. Whenever there is more than one ship at dock, the town explodes with a county fair–like atmosphere, where shops and restaurants stay open until the ships leave at midnight. The city celebrates the dreifache Anlauf, when three ships dock simultaneously, with fireworks.

14

GETTING HERE AND AROUND

Thanks to its close location to Rostock and the A-20, Warnemünde is easily accessible from any major city in the region. Traffic between the seaside district of Rostock and the downtown area can be heavy on summer weekends. The best way to explore the city is by riding a bike or walking.

EXPLORING

Alter Strom (*Old Stream*). Inland from the lighthouse is this yacht marina. Once the entry into the port of Warnemünde, it now has bars and shops. The fishing boats lining the Strom sell the day's catch, smoked fish, and bags of fried mussels.

Leuchtturm. Children enjoy climbing to the top of the town landmark, a 115-foot-high lighthouse, dating from 1898; on clear days it offers views of the coast and Rostock Harbor.

WHERE TO EAT AND STAY

For expanded hotel reviews, visit Fodors.com.

$ ✕ **Fischerklause.** Sailors have stopped in at this restaurant's bar since GERMAN the turn of the 20th century. The smoked fish sampler, served on a lazy Susan, is delicious, and the house specialty of fish soup is best washed down with some Rostocker Doppel-Kümmel schnapps. An accordionist entertains the crowd on weekends. ⊠ *Am Strom 123* ☎ *0381/52516* ⚞ *Reservations essential.*

$ 🏨 **Landhotel Ostseetraum.** This family-owned hotel, in a thatch-roof farmhouse outside Warnemünde, blends contemporary style with rural architecture. **Pros:** quiet; green setting not far away from the sea; friendly and personalized service; very private apartments. **Cons:** old-fashioned interior design in need of updating in some rooms and public areas; located outside Warnemünde proper. ⊠ *Stolteraerweg 34b, Warnemünde-Diedrichshagen* ☎☎ *0381/519–1848* ⊕ *www.ostseetraum.de* ⤴ *18 rooms* ⚲ *In-room: no a/c. In-hotel: restaurant, parking, some pets allowed* ⦿ *Breakfast.*

$$$ 🏨 **Yachthafenresidenz Hohe Düne.** The new star on the Baltic Coast is ★ this huge, modern resort comfortably residing on a peninsula between the yacht harbor, a sandy beach, and the port entrance. **Pros:** very well run; stylish hotel with a great ambience and all the amenities; impressive wellness and spa area. **Cons:** outside Warnemünde; accessible only by ferry from the town center and not along the central promenade; only a few attractions and restaurants in walking distance; pretentious staff. ⊠ *Hohe Düne, Am Yachthafen 1–8* ☎ *0381/5040* ⊕ *www.yhd.de* ⤴ *345 rooms, 23 suites* ⚲ *In-hotel: restaurant, bar, pool, gym, spa, beach, parking, some pets allowed* ⦿ *Breakfast.*

NIGHTLIFE

The pubs in the marina **Alter Strom** are fun gathering places.

Skybar. The Skybar is open Friday and Saturday until 3 am. ■ TIP➔ Roof access gives you the chance to sit under the stars and watch ship lights twinkle on the sea. ⊠ *Seestr. 19, 19th fl. of Neptun Hotel* ☎ *0381/7770.*

VORPOMMERN

The best description of this region is found in its name, which simply means "before Pomerania." This area, indeed, seems trapped between Mecklenburg and the authentic, old Pomerania farther east, now part of Poland. Its remoteness ensures an unforgettable view of unspoiled nature, primarily attracting families and younger travelers.

STRALSUND

68 km (42 mi) east of Rostock on Rte. 105.

This jewel of the Baltic has retained its historic city center and parts of its 13th-century defensive wall. The wall was built following an attack by the Lübeck fleet in 1249. In 1815 the Congress of Vienna awarded the city, which had been under Swedish control, to the Prussians.

14

GETTING HERE AND AROUND

Stralsund is well linked to both Rostock and Berlin by A-20 and A-19. The city is an ideal base for exploring the coast via the well-developed network of Bundesstrassen around it. Inside the city, walking or biking are better options, though, as the dense, historic downtown area makes it difficult to drive.

ESSENTIALS

Visitor Information Stralsund ⊠ *Alter Markt 9* ☎ *03831/24690* ⊕ *www. stralsund.de.*

EXPLORING

TOP ATTRACTIONS

Alter Markt (*Old Market Square*). The Alter Markt has the best local architecture, ranging from Gothic to Renaissance to baroque. Most buildings were rich merchants' homes, notably the late-Gothic **Wulflamhaus,** with 17 ornate, steeply stepped gables. Stralsund's architectural masterpiece, however, is the 14th-century **Rathaus,** considered by many to be the finest secular example of redbrick Gothic. The Rathaus is a mirror image of the a similar building in Lübeck, Stralsund's main rival in the Hanseatic League .

Deutsches Meeresmuseum (*German Sea Museum*). The Stralsund aquarium of Baltic Sea life is part of this three-floor museum, which also displays the skeletons of a giant whale and a hammerhead shark, and a 25-foot-high chunk of coral. ⊠ *Katharinenberg 14–20, entrance on Mönchstr.* ☎ *03831/265–021* ⊕ *www.meeresmuseum.de* ✆ *€7.50* ☉ *Oct.–May, daily 10–5; June–Sept., daily 10–6.*

St. Marienkirche (*St. Mary's Church*). This enormous church is the largest of Stralsund's three redbrick Gothic churches. With 4,000 pipes and intricate decorative figures, the magnificent 17th-century Stellwagen organ (played only during Sunday services) is a delight to see and hear. The view from the church tower of Stralsund's old city center is well worth climbing 349 steps. ⊠ *Neuer Markt, entrance at Bleistr.* ☎ *03831/293–529* ✆ *Tour of church tower €4* ☉ *May–Oct., weekdays 9–6, weekends 10–noon; Nov.–Apr., weekdays 10–noon and 2–6, weekends 10–noon.*

WORTH NOTING

Katherinenkloster (*St. Catherine's Monastery*). A former cloister, 40 of its rooms now house two museums: the famed Deutsches Meeresmuseum, and the Kulturhistorisches Museum.

Kulturhistorisches Museum (*Cultural History Museum*). This museum exhibits diverse artifacts from more than 10,000 years of this coastal region's history. Highlights include a toy collection and 10th-century Viking gold jewelry found on Hiddensee. You reach the museums by walking along Ossenreyerstrasse through the Apollonienmarkt on Mönchstrasse. ⊠ *Kulturhistorisches Museum, Mönchstr. 25–27* ☎ *03831/28790* ⛹ *€6* ⊙ *Tues.–Sun.10–5.*

St. Nikolaikirche (*St. Nicholas's Church*). The treasures of the 13th-century Gothic church include a 15-foot-high crucifix from the 14th century, an astronomical clock from 1394, and a famous baroque altar. ⊠ *Alter Markt* ☎ *03831/297–199* ⊙ *Apr.–Sept., Mon.–Sat. 10–6, Sun. 11–noon and 2–4; Oct.–Mar., Mon.–Sat. 10–noon and 2–4, Sun. 11–noon and 2–4.*

14

WHERE TO EAT AND STAY

For expanded hotel reviews, visit Fodors.com.

$ ✕ **Wulflamstuben.** This restaurant is on the ground floor of the Wulflam-
GERMAN haus, a 14th-century gabled house on the old market square. Steaks and fish are the specialties; in late spring or early summer, get the light and tasty *Ostseescholle* (grilled plaice), fresh from the Baltic Sea. In winter the hearty *Stralsunder Aalsuppe* (Stralsund eel soup) is a must. ⊠ *Alter Markt 5* ☎ *03831/291–533* ⟡ *Reservations essential.*

$ ✕ **Zum Alten Fritz.** It's worth the trip here just to see the rustic interior
GERMAN and copper brewing equipment. Since the restaurant is owned by the Stralsunder Brewery, all Stralsunder and Störtebecker beers are on tap, including the rare Störtebecker Roggen-Weizen, a wheat beer made with rye. In summer the beer garden gets somewhat rambunctious. ⊠ *Greifs-walder Chaussee 84–85, at B–96a* ☎ *03831/25550.*

$$ ▦ **Radisson Blu Hotel Stralsund.** This hotel, part of the Radisson brand, is
★ a modern property with winning amenities and great hospitality at an unbeatable price. **Pros:** top spa; solid and reliable services and amenities; long breakfast service (until 11 am). **Cons:** for Stralsund, this is a large, busy hotel, far away from city center (15 minutes). ⊠ *Grünhofer Bogen 18–20* ☎ *03831/37730* ⊕ *www.radissonblu.com/hotel-stralsund* ⟲ *109 rooms, 5 suites* ⟰ *In-room: Wi-Fi. In-hotel: restaurant, bar, pool, spa, business center, parking, some pets allowed* ⎮○⎮ *Breakfast.*

$$ ▦ **Hotel zur Post.** This redbrick hotel is a great deal for travelers looking for a homey yet first-class ambience. **Pros:** very good location in the heart of the historic downtown area; good deals offered on hotel Web site. **Cons:** very small rooms with too much furniture; some rooms in need of updating. ⊠ *Am Neuen Markt, Tribseerstr. 22* ☎ *03831/200–500* ⊕ *www.hotel-zur-post-stralsund.de* ⟲ *104 rooms, 2 suites, 8 apart-ments* ⟰ *In-room: no a/c, Wi-Fi. In-hotel: restaurant, bar, parking, some pets allowed* ⎮○⎮ *Breakfast.*

NIGHTLIFE

Bar Hemingway. Bar Hemingway lures a thirtysomething clientele with the best cocktails in town. ⊠ *Tribseerstr. 22* ☎ *03831/200–500.*

Fun und Lollipop. A young crowd dances at Fun und Lollipop. ⊠ *Grünhofer Bogen 11–14* ☎ *03834/399–039.*

Störtebeker-Keller. For a genuine old harbor *Kneipe* (tavern), head to the Störtebeker-Keller, named for an infamous pirate. ⊠ *Ossenreyerstr. 49* ☎ *03831/292–758.*

SHOPPING

Buddelschiffe (ships in a bottle) are a symbol of the magnificent sailing history of this region. They look easy to build, but they aren't, and they're quite delicate. Expect to pay more than €70 for a 1-liter bottle. Also look for *Fischerteppiche* (fisherman's carpets). Eleven square feet of these traditional carpets take 150 hours to create, which explains why they're meant only to be hung on the wall—and why they cost from €260 to €1,200. They're decorated with traditional symbols of the region, such as the mythical griffin.

RÜGEN ISLAND

4 km (2½ mi) northeast of Stralsund on Rte. 96.

Fodor's Choice
★

Rügen's diverse and breathtaking landscapes have inspired poets and painters for more than a century. Railways in the mid-19th century brought the first vacationers and many of the grand mansions and villas on the island date from this period. The island's main route runs between the **Grosser Jasmunder Bodden** (Big Jasmund Inlet), a giant sea inlet, and a smaller expanse of water, the **Kleiner Jasmunder Bodden** (Little Jasmund Inlet Lake), to the port of Sassnitz. You're best off staying at any of the island's four main vacation centers—Sassnitz, Binz, Sellin, and Göhren.

GETTING HERE AND AROUND

Rügen is an easy two-hour drive from Rostock and a 15-minute drive from Stralsund via the B-96. As there is only one bridge connecting the island to the mainland, the road can get clogged occasionally in summer. On the island, a car is highly recommended to reach the more-remote beaches, but watch out for island teenagers and their infatuation with muscle cars; give them a wide berth.

ESSENTIALS

Visitor Information Rügen Island ⊠ *Tourismusverband Rügen, Bahnhofstr. 15, Bergen* ☎ *03838/807–780* ⊕ *www.ruegen.de.* **Sassnitz** ⊠ *Bahnhofstr. 19a, Sassnitz* ☎ *038392/6490* ⊕ *www.insassnitz.de.*

EXPLORING

TOP ATTRACTIONS

Binz. The largest resort town on Rügen's east coast, it has white villas and a beach promenade. Four kilometers (2½ mi) north of Binz are five concrete quarters of **Bad Prora,** where the Nazis once planned to provide vacation quarters for up to 20,000 German workers. The complex was never used, except by the East German army. Museums and galleries here today include one that documents the history of the site. Standing on the highest point of East Rügen is the

Jagdschloss Granitz, a hunting lodge built in 1836. It offers a splendid view in all directions from its lookout tower and has an excellent hunting exhibit. ⊠ *2 km (1 mi) south of Binz* ☎ *038393/663–814* ⊕ *www.jagdschloss-granitz.de* ⊠ *€3* ⊗ *May–Sept., daily 9–6; Oct.–Apr., Tues.–Sun. 10–4*

Kap Arkona. Marking the northernmost point in eastern Germany

14

is the lighthouse at Kap Arkona, a nature lover's paradise filled with blustery sand dunes. The redbrick lighthouse was designed by Karl Friedrich Schinkel, the architect responsible for so many of today's landmarks in Berlin.

Sassnitz. This small fishing town is the island's harbor for ferries to Sweden. Sassnitz is surrounded by some of the most pristine nature to be found along the Baltic Coast. Ten kilometers (6 mi) north of Sassnitz are the twin chalk cliffs of Rügen's main attraction, the **Stubbenkammer** headland. From here you can best see the much-photographed white-chalk cliffs called the **Königstuhl**, rising 350 feet from the sea. A steep trail leads down to a beach.

Jasmund Nationalpark. From Sassnitz, walk to Jasmund Nationalpark to explore the marshes, lush pine forests, and towering chalk cliffs. ⊕ *www.nationalpark-jasmund.de.*

WORTH NOTING

Bergen. This small town is the island's administrative capital, founded as a Slavic settlement some 900 years ago. The **Marienkirche** (St. Mary's Church) has geometric murals dating back to the late 1100s and painted brick octagonal pillars. The pulpit and altar are baroque. Outside the front door and built into the church facade is a gravestone from the 1200s.

Putbus. The heart of this town, 28 km (17 mi) southwest of Binz, is the Circus, a round central plaza dating back to the early 19th century. The immaculate white buildings surrounding the Circus give the city its nickname, "Weisse Stadt" (White City). In summer the blooming roses in front of the houses (once a requirement by the ruling noble family of Putbus) are truly spectacular.

Rasender Roland (*Racing Roland*). From Putbus you can take a ride on the 90-year-old miniature steam train, which runs 24 km (16 mi) to Göhren, at the southeast corner of Rügen. Trains leave hourly from Göhren to Binz and every two hours from Binz to Putbus; the ride takes 70 minutes one way. ⊠ *Binzer Str. 12* ☎ *038301/8010* ⊕ *www.rasender-roland.de* ⊠ *€20 day ticket* ⊗ *Apr.–Oct., daily 7:48 am–7:46 pm with bi-hourly departures from Putbus. Nov.–Mar., daily 7:48 am–5:44 pm with departures every 2 hrs.*

OFF THE BEATEN PATH

Hiddensee. Off the northwest corner of Rügen is a smaller island called Hiddensee. The undisturbed solitude of this sticklike island has attracted such visitors as Albert Einstein, Thomas Mann, Rainer Maria Rilke, and Sigmund Freud. As Hiddensee is an auto-free zone, leave your car in Schaprode, 21 km (13 mi) west of Bergen, and take a ferry. Vacation cottages and restaurants are on the island.

WHERE TO EAT

$ ✕ **Panoramahotel Lohme.** Dinner at this restaurant dubbed "Rügen's balcony" offers some of the most beautiful views on the island. While enjoying fresh fish from local waters, prepared with a light Italian touch, you can watch the sunset over the cliffs of Kap Arkona. Chef Marcus Uhlich uses fresh produce from local farmers, and the superb vintages are from small private wineries. ■**TIP→** Make a reservation, and insist on a table in the *Fontane-Veranda* (in winter) or the *Arkonablick-Terrasse* (in summer). ⊠ *An der Steilküste 8, Lohme* ☎ *038302/9110* ▭ *No credit cards.*

GERMAN ★

WHERE TO STAY

For expanded hotel reviews, visit Fodors.com.

$ **Hotel Godewind.** This small hotel offers food and lodging at very reasonable prices. **Pros:** quiet setting; very cozy rooms with nice furniture. **Cons:** almost no amenities and services offered. ⊠ *Süderende 53, Vitte-Hiddensee* ☎ *038300/6600* ⊕ *www.hotelgodewind.de* ➫ *23 rooms, 19 cottages* ⌂ *In-room: no a/c. In-hotel: restaurant, some pets allowed* ▭ *No credit cards* ¶◯¶ *Breakfast.*

$ ★   **Hotel Villa Granitz.** The little town of Baabe claims to have Rügen's most beautiful beach. **Pros:** cozy hotel in the traditional architectural style of the area; very competitive prices for the size and comfort of rooms. **Cons:** off the beaten track at the outskirts of the city; a distance from the beach. ⊠ *Birkenallee 17, Baabe* ☎ *038303/1410* ⊕ *www.villa-granitz.de* ➫ *44 rooms, 6 suites, 8 apartments* ⌂ *In-room: no a/c. In-hotel: parking, some pets allowed* ▭ *No credit cards* ¶◯¶ *Breakfast.*

$$$$ ★   **Travel Charme Hotel Kurhaus Binz.** The grand old lady of the Baltic Sea, the neoclassical 19th-century Kurhaus Binz is reviving the splendor of times past, when Binz was called the Nice of the North. **Pros:** great breakfast buffet; extremely clean rooms and public areas; highly trained and friendly personnel; all the amenities. **Cons:** lacks the feel of a typical Rügen hotel; not very personal or intimate. ⊠ *Strandpromenade 27, Binz-Rügen* ☎ *038393/6650* ⊕ *www.travelcharme.com* ➫ *106 rooms, 20 suites* ⌂ *In-hotel: restaurants, bar, pool, gym, spa, beach, parking, some pets allowed* ¶◯¶ *Breakfast.*

$$ ★   **Vier Jahreszeiten.** This first-class beach resort in Binz is a sophisticated blend of historic seaside architecture and modern elegance. **Pros:** one of the area's few four-star hotels; varied cultural and entertainment programs; stylish spa with great massages. **Cons:** small rooms and bathrooms; many rooms with worn-out mattresses. ⊠ *Zeppelinstr. 8, Binz-Rügen* ☎ *038393/500* ⊕ *www.vier-jahreszeiten.de* ➫ *69 rooms, 7 suites, 50 apartments* ⌂ *In-room: Internet. In-hotel: restaurant, bar, pool, gym, spa, parking, some pets allowed* ¶◯¶ *Breakfast.*

Vacationers sunbathe in Strandkorb, or on a towel on Ahlbeck's beach.

USEDOM ISLAND

67 km (42 mi) to Wolgast bridge from Stralsund.

Usedom Island has almost 32 km (20 mi) of sandy shoreline and a string of resorts. Much of the island's untouched landscape is a nature preserve that provides refuge for a number of rare birds, including the giant sea eagle, which has a wingspan of up to 8 feet. Even in summer this island is more or less deserted, and is ready to be explored by bicycle.

GETTING HERE AND AROUND

From the west, Usedom is accessed via the causeway at **Wolgast**. The bridge closes to traffic at times to allow boats to pass through. From the south, the B-110 leads from Anklam to Usedom. In summer, particularly before and after weekends, traffic can be very heavy on both roads.

ESSENTIALS

Visitor Information Usedom Island ⊠ *Usedom Tourismus GmbH., Waldstr. 1, Seebad Bansin* ☎ *038378/47710* ⊕ *www.usedom.de.*

EXPLORING

Ahlbeck. The island's main town is also one of its best resorts. The tidy and elegant resort is one of the three *Kaiserbäder* (imperial baths)—the two others are Heringsdorf and Bansin—where the Emperor Wilhelm II liked to spend his summers in the early 20th century. Noble families and rich citizens followed the emperor, turning Ahlbeck into one of the prettiest villas on the Baltic Coast. Ahlbeck's landmark is the 19th-century wooden pier with four towers. Stroll the beach to the right of the pier and you'll arrive at the Polish border.

Peenemünde. At the northwest tip of Usedom, 16 km (10 mi) from land-side Wolgast, is the launch site of the world's first jet rockets, the V1 and V2, developed by Germany toward the end of World War II.

Das Historisch-Technische Museum Peenemünde (*Historical-Technical Museum Peenemünde*). You can view these rockets as well as models of early airplanes and ships at this extensive museum housed in the former factory power plant, one exhibit in particular covers the moral responsibility of scientists who develop new technology, by focusing on the secret plants where most of the rocket parts were assembled and where thousands of slave laborers died. Explanations of the exhibits in English are available ⊠ *Im Kraftwerk* 🕾 *038371/5050* ⊕ *www.peenemuende.de* 🖃 *€6* ⊗ *Apr.–Sept., daily 10–6; Oct.–Mar., daily 10–4; Nov.–Feb., Tues.–Sun. 10–4.*

WHERE TO STAY

For expanded hotel reviews, visit Fodors.com.

$$$
★
🏨 **Romantik Seehotel Ahlbecker Hof.** The first lady of Ahlbeck, this four-star hotel calls to mind the island's past as a getaway for Prussian nobility in the 19th century. **Pros:** has one of the area's best spas; two gourmet restaurants; near beach. **Cons:** no elevator. ⊠ *Dünenstr. 47, Seebad Ahlbeck* 🕾 *038378/620* ⊕ *www.seetel.de* 🛏 *70 rooms* 🛎 *In-room: safe. In-hotel: restaurant, bar, pool, gym, spa, beach, parking, some pets allowed* ⦿ *Breakfast.*

Berlin

WORD OF MOUTH

Berlin is a young, vibrant, artistic, and free city . . . I found so much to see in Berlin."

—danon

You can really get a feel of the city on the weekends. . . . People are friendly and international and it is hard NOT to meet people."

—quirrelman

Join, Ask, Share. www.fodors.com/community/

WELCOME TO BERLIN

TOP REASONS TO GO

★ **Affordability:** Of western and northern Europe's capitals, Berlin is by far the best bargain. Most museum prices remain less than €10, and hotel rooms and entertainment are relatively inexpensive.

★ **Long, creative nights:** The only European city without official closing hours, Berlin's young artists keep coming up with installations, performance events, and parties to keep you up all night.

★ **Museum Island:** The architectural monuments and art treasures here will take you from an ancient Greek altar to Egyptian busts and a Roman market town to 18th-century Berlin and back in a day.

★ **The Reichstag's cupola:** Reserve a coveted spot on a tour of Berlin's seat of parliament to admire the spectacular glass cupola, and to enjoy great views of central Berlin.

★ **Trace history's path:** The division of Berlin was an anomaly in urban history. Follow the cobblestone markers that remember the Wall's path.

1 Kurfürstendamm and Western Downtown. For many locals, Berlin's true heart still beats along Kurfürstendamm, or "Ku'damm"—the nickname for this boulevard that stretches for 3 km (2 mi) through the heart of the Western Downtown. The stately mansions in the posh side streets now house elegant boutiques, restaurants, bars, and galleries.

2 Potsdamer Platz and Kreuzberg. Once a no-man's-land in the shadow of the Wall, Potsdamer Platz reemerged as a shopping, office, and entertainment center in the 1990s. Hugging the square's backside is the Kulturforum, one of two major museums in the city. Hip and edgy Kreuzberg is right nearby.

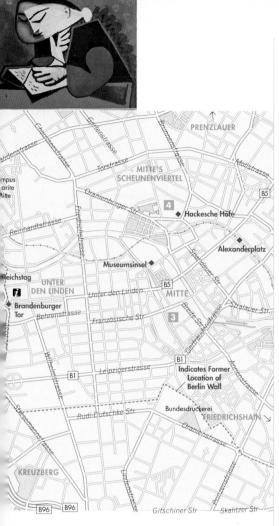

GETTING ORIENTED

In eastern Germany, almost halfway between Paris and Moscow, Berlin is laid out on an epic scale and, with nearly 3.5 million residents, is Germany's largest city. When the city-state of Berlin was incorporated in 1920, it swallowed towns and villages far beyond the downtown area around the two main rivers, the Spree and the Havel. Each of its boroughs has distinctive characteristics. Charlottenburg, Schöneberg, and Kreuzberg are popular areas in the west, and to the east, Prenzlauer Berg and Friedrichshain are favored residential and nightlife neighborhoods. Modern urban commercial centers such as Potsdamer Platz and Leipziger Platz still feel like odd insertions between the historically developed quarters surrounding them.

3 **Mitte.** Cutting through the historic core of Mitte, all the way from the Brandenburg Gate to Alexanderplatz, is the grand boulevard Unter den Linden. This area includes elegant shops along Friedrichstrasse.

4 **Mitte's Scheunenviertel, Prenzlauer Berg, and Friedrichshain.** Fashion, art, and trends are born in northern Mitte. The old working-class district of Prenzlauer Berg used to be one of the poorest sections of Berlin, but is now largely gentrified. Rough Friedrichshain attracts mostly students and artists from around the world.

BERLIN WALL WALK

The Berlin Wall (*Berliner Mauer*) came down more than 20 years ago, but it still manages to be a major tourist draw. How does a structure no longer standing affect the city even in its absence?

(above) Checkpoint Charlie. (upper right) Ampelmann crosswalk signs. (lower right) Mauer Park flea market.

When the Wall fell on November 9, 1989, it followed massive protests, an astonishing amount of community organizing, and the prayers of thousands in both west and east, all of whom couldn't quite believe such a momentous event was happening in their lifetimes. Many had felt the same way 28 years earlier, when the East German government, in an attempt to keep their beleaguered citizens from leaving, built the wall practically overnight. Now, except for a few sections left standing, all that remains of one of history's most notorious symbols of postwar oppression and imprisonment is a line of cobblestones wending its way through the streets of Berlin.

—Giulia Pines

FOLLOW THE COBBLESTONES

To get beyond the overly commercialized stretches of the former Wall, like East Side Gallery or Checkpoint Charlie, just look down. Follow the cobblestone line, marked every so often with a metal plaque bearing the words "Berliner Mauer 1961–1989." The path illuminates the effects of the Wall on the city: it cut through neighborhoods, bisected narrow streets, and sliced lives in half.

TWO BERLIN WALL WALKS

FRIEDRICHSHAIN TO TREPTOW VIA THE OBERBAUMBRÜCKE AND THE FLUTGRABEN

Starting at the **East Side Gallery**, cross the **Oberbaumbrücke**, a former border checkpoint, and turn left at **Schlesische Strasse**. There's no sign of the Wall here, but ubiquitous graffiti and crumbling buildings make it easy to imagine isolated Kreuzberg when it stood. At **Am Flutgraben**, you'll pick up the trail again, and up ahead is the **Grenzwachturm** (border watchtower). Stop at the nonprofit art collective **Flutgraben e.V.**, which hosts infrequent exhibitions. Turn right to follow the **Flutgraben** (small canal) south until you reach an overpass, part of an elevated railway that used to lead to the prewar train station Görlitzer Bahnhof. Now, the railway is a park connecting **Treptow** with **Görlitzer Park**, the site of the old station and a meeting point for anarchist groups and revolutionaries before the Wall fell.

BERNAUER STRASSE TO BORNHOLMER BRÜCKE VIA MAUER PARK

Behind **Nordbahnhof** (S-bahn), follow Bernauer Strasse to the **Gedenkstätte Berliner Mauer**, located in the former "death strip," where a church was blown up by the East because it was an obstruction to guards and an alleged hiding place for those trying to flee. Follow **Bernauer Strasse** until you reach the corner of Schwedter Strasse, then take the path that cuts through **Mauer Park**. Also in the former death strip, the park has one of the best flea markets in town. At the park's northern end, Schwedter Strasse turns into the **Schwedter Steg**, a footbridge over an impressive chasm of connecting train tracks and S-bahn lines. Turn around for a spectacular view of the TV tower. Head down steps on your left and continue along Norwegerstrasse. After going under the famous **Bornholmer Brücke**, take the flight of steps up to it. This is where East Berliners overwhelmed the Wall checkpoint and became the first to push through to West Berlin.

ICONIC EAST BERLIN

Many East Berlin designs have crept into daily life here, such as the figure that appears on the crosswalk traffic lights. The stocky East Berlin **Ampelmann** ("streetlight man") wears a wide-brim hat and walks with an animated gait. The Ampelmann has been adopted by all crosswalks in Berlin, not just those in the former east. He also adorns coffee cups and T-shirts, and there's even candy made in his image. Entire gift shops are dedicated to him, such as those found in the Hackesche Höfe in Mitte and the Arkaden mall at Potsdamer Platz.

The Brandenburg Gate may be the city symbol for Berlin tourism, but the soaring East German television tower, the **Berliner Fernsehturm,** is an enormously popular silhouette for Berlin-based companies' logos, nightclub flyers, and ads. You can buy T-shirts, messenger bags, and pillows emblazoned with the image, which was once referred to as the *Tele-spargel* (TV asparagus) for its spindly shape.

15

BERLIN STREET FOOD

Two dishes are emblematic of Berlin street food: the *Currywurst* and the *Döner Kebab*. Both are wildly popular, and the two could not be more different. Stands for currywurst and döner kebabs dot the city, so you're never far from your next snack.

(above) Locals line up for currywurst at Curry 36. (upper right) Currywurst is a sausage with curry ketchup. (lower right) Döner kebab is one of Berlin's favorite snacks.

The creative owner of a sausage stall named Herta Heuwer invented the currywurst in Berlin's lean postwar years. Legend has it she took some inspiration from the American and British troops stationed in Berlin after World War II. Herta deep-fried a pork sausage, then doused it in her own special version of tomato ketchup and sprinkled it with curry powder. An instant hit, it's still served the same way today. But in recent years, the döner kebab has outpaced the currywurst in popularity. First served by a Turkish immigrant in 1971, the sandwich resembles a Greek gyro. Grilled meat is shaved in razor-thin slivers from an upright rotating spit, and stuffed into grilled bread with dressing, then lettuce, tomato, cucumber, red onion, and shredded cabbage.

—Tania Ralli

BERLIN MARKETS

On Saturday, visit the sprawling **Winterfeldplatz market** in Schöneberg and try a *Bismarck Herring Brötchen*, a crusty roll with pickled herring. At Prenzlauer Berg's **Kollwitzplatz market**, also Saturday, try a falafel sandwich. Berlin's largest Turkish market is held on Tuesday and Friday on the **Maybachufer**. Snack on *gözleme*, a savory, flat Turkish pastry filled with meat, cheese, spinach, or potato.

BEST CURRYWURST AND DÖNER KEBAB IN BERLIN

Curry 36. This currywurst stand in Kreuzberg has a cult following. Stand beside cab drivers, students, and lawyers while you have your currywurst *mit oder ohne Darm* (with or without the skin). Most people order their sausage with a big pile of crispy fries served *rot-weiss* (red and white)—with ketchup and mayonnaise. ✉ *Mehringdamm 36, Kreuzberg* ☎ *251/7368* Ⓜ *Mehringdamm (U-bahn).*

Hisar. The lines here might be long, but they move fast and the combination of the seasoned, salty meat, with crunchy salad and warm bread is unbeatable. If you're just stopping for a quick döner kebab, line up outside on the sidewalk and order from the window. But if you prefer to eat at a more leisurely pace, enter the adjoining Turkish restaurant for the *Dönerteller* (döner plate), heaped with succulent meat, rice, potatoes, and salad. ✉ *Yorckstr. 49, Schöneberg* ☎ *216/5125* Ⓜ *Yorckstrasse (U-bahn and S-bahn).*

Konnopke's Imbiss. Sitting beneath the tracks of the elevated U2 subway line is Berlin's most beloved sausage stand for more than 70 years. Konnopke's is a family business, famous for its currywurst. It's served on a narrow paper tray with a plastic prong to spear the sauce-covered sausage slices. Line up

with young and old in the center of one of Berlin's trendiest neighborhoods and discover why Berliners love currywurst. ✉ *Schönhauser Allee 44b, Prenzlauer Berg* ☎ *442/7765* Ⓜ *Eberswalderstrasse (U-bahn).*

Mustafa's. For a twist on the traditional döner kebab, make a beeline for these mouthwatering vegetable kebabs. Toasted pita bread is stuffed full of roasted veggies—carrots, potatoes, zucchini—along with fresh tomato, lettuce, cucumber, and cabbage. The sandwich is napped with sauce, a generous squeeze of fresh lemon juice, and sprinkling of the creamiest, smoothest feta cheese. You'll lick your fingers and contemplate getting in line for another. ✉ *Mehringdamm 32, Kreuzberg* ☎ *283/2153* Ⓜ *Mehringdamm (U-bahn).*

Rosenthaler Grill und Schlemmerbuffet. Döner kebab aficionados love this restaurant, and not just because it's open 24 hours a day and in the middle of the city. Watch the friendly staff expertly carve paper-thin slices of crisped meat from the enormous, revolving spit. If you like heat, ask for the spicy red sauce. After eating your sandwich you'll better understand how Germans eat 400 tons of döner meat *each day*. Döner, which are wrapped in a paper sleeve are eaten fast, otherwise they fall apart. ✉ *Rosenthalerplatz 1, Mitte* ☎ *283/2153* Ⓜ *Rosenthaler Platz (U-bahn).*

15

SHOPPING IN MITTE

Berlin's near obsession with design is the city's calling card, touching everything from grand architectural projects to knickknack souvenirs sold at airport gift shops.

(above) Designs by Sabrina Dehoff. (lower right) A family enjoys a late afternoon brunch at a café near Zionskirche (Church of Zion).

The continually emerging fresh energy that local designers bring to the world of fashion spills out of their shops—many of which double as ateliers—into the streets of Berlin. The defining style is best described as pared-down modern mixed with a touch of avant-garde.

Most established local designers are found in Mitte, particularly on Mulackstrasse, and side streets clustered in between Rosenthaler Strasse in the west and Luxembourg Strasse in the east, south of Torstrasse. An edgier area with more of a hipster feel is around Volkspark am Weinberg, where leafy streets are lined with boutiques and cafés and a gorgeous church at the top of the hill. Head west on Torstrasse from Rosenthaler Strasse, for newer up-and-coming designers as well as galleries, bookshops, local greenmarkets, and gourmet stores.

—Rachel Klein

WHEN TO GO

Mitte is lively on the weekends but not overwhelmingly crowded, so it's possible to stroll along main streets and window-shop without being jostled. Restrictions on opening hours were lifted in Berlin a little more than five years ago, and most shops are open from 10 a.m. to as late as 8 p.m. Monday through Saturday. Sunday is a mixed bag, so if there's a specific store you're hoping to hit check hours in advance.

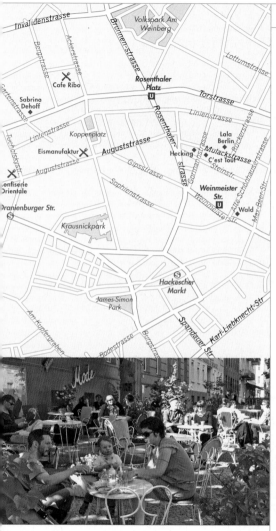

15

BEST FOR

CLOTHING

Lala Berlin. The pricey boutique has clothes and accessories with sophisticated prints on high-quality fabric. ✉ *Mulackstr. 7, Mitte* ☎ *03025/762–924* ◷ *Mon.–Fri. 11:30–7:30, Sat. 12–6.*

C'est Tout. Layering the neutral pieces here with a touch of sparkle create an *ooh-la-la* effect. ✉ *Mulackstr. 26, Mitte* ☎ *030275/95530* ◷ *Mon.– Sat. 12–7.*

Wald. A carefully curated mix of international designers' clothing hangs on racks at this posh boutique. ✉ *Mulackstr. 23, Mitte* ☎ *30754/42210.*

JEWELRY AND ACCESSORIES

Hecking. Find the city's best collection of scarves here at a wide range of price points. ✉ *Gormannstr. 8–9, entrance Mulackstr., Mitte* ☎ *0302404/8994* ◷ *Mon.–Fri., 1–7, Sat. 1–6, closed Tues..*

Sabrina Dehoff. This local designer balances bling and minimalism—bright crystals are paired with chunky metals. ✉ *Torstr. 175, Mitte* ☎ *030936/24680* ◷ *Mon.– Fri. and Sun. 12–7, Sat. 12–6.*

BEST SPOTS TO REFUEL

Cafe Ribo. Don't miss this café for simple, homemade, and inexpensive traditional German food on the lighter side. ✉ *Ackerstr. 157, Mitte* ☎ *76620–42369.*

Confiserie Orientale. Perk yourself up with a strong Turkish coffee or tea and authentic *lokum* (Turkish Delights) imported from Istanbul. ✉ *Linienstr. 113, Mitte* ☎ *03060/925–957.*

Eismanufaktur. You'll find the best gelato in the city here. ✉ *Auguststr. 63, Mitte* ⊕ *www.eismanufaktur-berlin.de.*

Updated by
Giulia Pines

Since the fall of the Iron Curtain, no other city in Europe has seen more change than the German capital. Two Berlins that had been separated for almost 30 years have become one, and in the scar of barren borderland between them cutting-edge architecture, culture, entertainment, nightlife and shopping make the city an überhip destination. After successfully uniting its own East and West, Berlin now plays a pivotal role in the European Union.

But even as the capital thinks and moves forward, history is always tugging at its sleeve. Between the wealth of neoclassical and 21st-century buildings there are constant reminders, both subtle and stark, of the events of the 20th century.

Berlin is quite young by European standards, beginning as two separate entities in 1237 on two islands in the Spree River, Cölln and Berlin. By the 1300s, the latter was prospering, thanks to its location at the intersection of important trade routes, and rose to power as the seat of the Hohenzollern dynasty. The Great Elector Friedrich Wilhelm, in the almost 50 years of his reign (1640–88), touched off a cultural renaissance. Later, Frederick the Great (1712–86) made Berlin and Potsdam his glorious centers of the enlightened yet autocratic Prussian monarchy.

In 1871 Prussia, ruled by the "Iron Chancellor" Count Otto von Bismarck, unified the many independent German states into the German Empire. Berlin maintained its status as capital for the duration of that Second Reich (1871–1918), through the post–World War I Weimar Republic (1919–33), and also through Hitler's so-called Third Reich (1933–45). The city's golden years were the Roaring '20s, when Berlin evolved as the energetic center for the era's cultural avant-garde. World-famous writers, painters, and artists met here while the impoverished bulk of its 4 million inhabitants lived in heavily overpopulated quarters. This "dance on the volcano," as those years of political and economic upheaval have been called, came to a grisly and bloody end after January 1933, when Adolf Hitler became chancellor. The Nazis made Berlin their capital but ultimately failed to remodel the city into a silent monument to their power. By World War II's end, 70% of the city lay in ruins, with more rubble than in all other German cities combined.

Along with the division of Germany after World War II, Berlin was partitioned into American, British, and French zones in the West and a Soviet zone in the East. The three western-occupied zones gradually merged, becoming West Berlin, while the Soviet-controlled eastern zone defiantly remained separate; in 1949 the Soviet Union established East Berlin as the capital of its new puppet state, the German Democratic Republic (GDR). The division of the city was cruelly finalized in concrete in August 1961, when the East German government erected the Berlin Wall, the only border fortification in history built to keep people from leaving rather than to protect them.

For nearly 30 years Berlin suffered under a terrible geographic and political situation, a city split in two by a concrete wall—its larger western half an island of capitalist democracy surrounded by an East Germany run by hard-line Communists. With the Wall relegated to the pile of history (most of it was recycled as street gravel), visitors can now appreciate the whole city and its anything-goes atmosphere.

15

PLANNING

WHEN TO GO

Berlin has a moderate, continental climate. However, due to its unprotected location in the northeastern lowlands of Germany, easterly winds often bring surprisingly harsh weather and storms in fall and winter. The perfect time to visit is May to early September, when temperatures usually hover around 70° to 80°F. Late July and early August, however, can be sizzling hot. Many open-air events are staged in summer, when the surprisingly green city is at its most beautiful. October and November can be overcast and rainy, but the city still sees its fair share of crisp blue autumn skies. Avoid the long winter months: despite the many cultural events, perpetually gray skies are marked by sleet, icy rain, strong winds, and freezing temperatures.

GETTING HERE AND AROUND

AIR TRAVEL

Major airlines will continue to serve western Berlin's Tegel Airport (TXL) after a first stop at a major European hub (such as Frankfurt or London) until some time in 2012, when eastern Berlin's Schönefeld Airport, about 24 km (15 mi) outside the center, will have been expanded into BBI "Willy Brandt"—the international airport of the capital region. Currently, Schönefeld is mostly used by charter and low-budget airlines. Massive Tempelhof Airport, an example of fascist architecture, is closed and has been transformed into a public park and event space. The two working Berlin airports share a central phone number.

AIRPORT TRANSFERS

Tegel Airport is 6 km (4 mi) from the downtown area. The express X9 airport bus runs at 10-minute intervals between Tegel and Bahnhof Zoologischer Garten (Zoo Station), the center of western Berlin. From here you can connect to bus, train, or subway. The trip takes 19 minutes; the fare is €2.30. The express bus TXL runs at 10-minute intervals between Tegel and Alexanderplatz via Hauptbahnhof and takes about 30 minutes. Alternatively, you can take Bus 128 to Kurt Schumacher Platz or Bus 109 to Jakob-Kaiser-Platz and change to the subway, where your bus ticket is also valid. Expect to pay about €15 for a taxi from the airport to the western downtown area. If you rent a car at the airport, follow the signs for the Stadtautobahn into Berlin. The exit to Kurfürstendamm is clearly marked. The system is a bit clumsy here. Look carefully for the DB office, which is upstairs to your right after you initially descend into the station. Buy an Einzelfahrt €3 ticket (ABC zone) from here or from an S-bahn platform vending machine (no credit cards) to get you into town. This ticket is good for both the S-bahn and the Airport Express train, which runs about every half hour from a track that has no vending machine. To take the Airport Express, look for a small dark-blue sign at the foot of the stairs leading to its platform. Bus 171 also leaves Schönefeld every 20 minutes for the Rudow subway station. A taxi ride from the Schönefeld Airport takes about 40 minutes and will cost around €35. By car, follow the signs for Stadtzentrum Berlin.

Airport Information **Central airport service** ☎ *0180/500–0186* ⊕ *www. berlin-airport.de.*

BUS TRAVEL

BerlinLinien Bus is the only intra-Germany company serving Berlin. Make reservations through ZOB-Reisebüro, or buy your ticket at its office at the central bus terminal, the Omnibusbahnhof. Public buses are the best way to reach the bus terminal, served by the lines X34, X49, 104, 139, 218, and 349. A more central place to buy bus tickets is Mitfahrzentrale, a tiny, busy office that also arranges car-ride shares. Only EC bank cards and cash are accepted.

Bus Information **Mitfahrzentrale** ⊠ *Joachimsthaler Str. 14, Western Downtown* ☎ *030/19444* ⊕ *www.mf24.de* ⊗ *Weekdays 9–6, weekends 10–2.* **ZOB-Reisebüro** ⊠ *Zentrale Omnibusbahnhof, Masurenallee 4–6, at Messedamm, Charlottenburg* ☎ *030/301–0380 for reservations* ⊕ *www.berlinlinienbus.de* ⊗ *Weekdays 6 am–9 pm, weekends 6 am–8 pm.*

CAR TRAVEL

Rush hour is relatively mild in Berlin, but the public transit system is so efficient here that it's best to leave your car at the hotel altogether. All cars entering downtown Berlin inside the S-bahn ring need to have an environmental certificate. All major rental cars will have these—if in doubt, ask the rental-car agent, as without one you can be fined €40. Daily parking fees at hotels can run up to €18 per day. Vending machines in the city center dispense timed tickets to display on your dashboard. Thirty minutes cost €0.50.

PUBLIC TRANSIT

The city has an efficient public-transportation system, a smoothly integrated network of subway (U-bahn) and suburban (S-bahn) train lines, buses, and trams (almost exclusively in eastern Berlin). Get a map from any information booth. ■ TIP➔ **Don't be afraid to try buses and trams—in addition to being well marked, they often cut the most direct path to your destination.**

From Sunday through Thursday, U-bahn trains stop around 12:45 am and S-bahn trains stop by 1:30 am. All-night bus and tram service operates seven nights a week (indicated by the letter *N* next to route numbers). On Friday and Saturday nights some S-bahn and all U-bahn lines except U4 run all night. Buses and trams marked with an *M* mostly serve destinations without an S-bahn or U-bahn link.

Most visitor destinations are in the broad reach of the fare zones A and B. The €2.30 ticket (fare zones A and B) and the €3 ticket (fare zones A, B, and C) allow you to make a one-way trip with an unlimited number of changes between trains, buses, and trams. There are reduced rates for children ages 6–13. Buy a Kurzstreckentarif ticket (€1.40) for short rides of up to six bus or tram stops or three U-bahn or S-bahn stops. The best deal if you plan to travel around the city extensively is the Tageskarte (day card for zones A and B), for €6.30, good on all transportation until 3 am. (It's €6.80 for A, B, and C zones.) A 7-Tage-Karte (seven-day ticket) costs €27.20 and allows unlimited travel for fare zones A and B; €33.50 buys all three fare zones.

15

The **Berlin WelcomeCard** (sold by EurAid, Berliner Verkehrsbetriebe offices, the tourist office, and some hotels) entitles one adult and three children up to age 6 to either two or three days of unlimited travel in the ABC zones for €18.90 or €24.90, respectively, and includes admission and tour discounts detailed in a booklet. The **CityTourCard,** good for two or three days of unlimited travel in the AB zones, costs €15.90 and €21.90, respectively, and details 50 discounts on a leaflet; up to three children under age 6 can accompany an adult.

Tickets are available from vending machines at U-bahn and S-bahn stations. After you purchase a ticket, you are responsible for validating it when you board the train or bus. Both Einzelfahrt and Kurzstreckentarif tickets are good for 120 minutes after validation. If you're caught without a ticket or with an unvalidated one, the fine is €40.

DISABILITIES AND ACCESSIBILITY. ■TIP➜ The BVG website (*www.bvg.de*) makes planning any trip on public transportation easier. Enter your origin and destination point into their "Journey Planner" to see a list of your best routes, and a schedule of the next three departure times. If you're not sure which station is your closest, simply type in your current address and the system will tell you (along with the time it takes to walk there).

All major S-bahn and U-bahn stations have elevators, and most buses have hydraulic lifts. Check the public transportation maps or call the Berliner Verkehrsbetriebe. The Deutscher Service-Ring-Berlin e.V. runs a special bus service for travelers with physical disabilities, and is a good information source on all travel necessities, that is, wheelchair rental and other issues.

Accessibility Information Berliner Verkehrsbetriebe ☎ *030/19449* ⊕ *www. bvg.de.* Deutscher Service-Ring-Berlin e.V. ☎ *030/859–4010.*

Public Transit Information Berliner Verkehrsbetriebe (*BVG*) ☎ *030/19449* ⊕ *www.bvg.de* ⊙ *Mon.–Thurs. 7–11, Fri. 7–12, weekends 24 hours.* S-Bahn Berlin GmbH ☎ *030/2974–3333* ⊕ *www.s-bahn-berlin.de.* VBB ✉ *Hardenbergpl. 2, Western Downtown* ☎ *030/2541–4141* ⊕ *www.vbbonline.de* ⊙ *Weekdays 8–8, weekends 9–6.*

TAXI TRAVEL

The base rate is €3.20, after which prices vary according to a complex tariff system. Figure on paying around €8–€10 for a ride the length of the Ku'damm. ■TIP➔ If you've hailed a cab on the street and are taking a short ride of up to 2 km (1 mi), ask the driver as soon as you start off for a special fare (€4) called *Kurzstreckentarif*. You can also get cabs at taxi stands or order one by calling; there's no additional fee if you call a cab by phone. U-bahn employees will call a taxi for passengers after 8 pm.

BikeTaxi, rickshawlike bicycle taxis, pedal along Kurfürstendamm, Friedrichstrasse, and Unter den Linden, and in Tiergarten. Just hail a cab on the street along the boulevards mentioned. The fare is €5 for up to 1 km (½ mi) and €3 for each additional kilometer, and €22.50 to €30 for longer tours. Velotaxis operate April–October, daily noon–7. ■TIP➔ Despite these fixed prices, make sure to negotiate the fare before starting the tour.

Taxi Information **Taxis** ☎ *030/210–101, 030/210–202, 030/443–322, 030/261–026.*

TRAIN TRAVEL

All long-distance trains stop at the huge and modern central station, Hauptbahnhof, which lies at the north edge of the government district in former West Berlin. Regional trains also stop at the two former "main" stations of the past years: Bahnhof Zoo (in the West) and Ostbahnhof (in the East). Regional trains also stop at the central eastern stations Friedrichstrasse and Alexanderplatz.

VISITOR INFORMATION

The main information office of Berlin Tourismus Marketing is in the Neues Kranzler Eck, a short walk from Zoo Station. There are branches in the south wing of the Brandenburg Gate, at Hauptbahnhof (Level 0), and in a pavilion opposite the Reichstag that are open daily 10–6. The tourist-information centers have longer hours April–October. The tourist office publishes the Berlin Kalender (€1.60) six times a year and Berlin Buchbar (free) two times a year. Both are written in German and English. The office and Berlin's larger transportation offices (BVG) sell the WelcomeCard (€21), which grants three days of free transportation and 25%–50% discounts at museums and theaters (it does not include the state museums). Some Staatliche (state) museums are closed Monday. A free audio guide is included at all state museums. The MD Infoline provides comprehensive information about all of Berlin's museums, exhibits, and themed tours.

Visitor Information **Berlin Tourismus Marketing** (*Berlin Tourist Info*). ✉ *Kurfürstendamm 22, Passage, Western Downtown* ☎ *030/250–025* ⊕ *www.visitberlin.de* ⊙ *Mon.–Sat. 10–8, Sun. 10–6.* **Museumsinformation Berlin** ☎ *030/2474–9888* ⊙ *Weekdays 9–4, weekends 9–1.* **Staatliche Museen zu Berlin** ☎ *030/2664–24242 operator* ⊕ *www.smb.museum.* **Tourist-Information Center in Prenzlauer Berg** ✉ *Kuturbrauerei closest entrance Schönhauser Allee 36, Prenzlauer Berg* ☎ *030/4435–2170* ⊕ *www.tic-berlin.de* ⊙ *Sun.–Mon. 12–6, Tues.–Sat. 12–8.*

A boat tour along the Spree River is a lovely way to take in the sights.

TOURS
BOAT TOURS

Tours of central Berlin's Spree and Landwehr canals give you up-close views of sights such as Charlottenburg Palace, the Reichstag, and the Berliner Dom. Tours usually depart twice a day from several bridges and piers in Berlin, such as Schlossbrücke in Charlottenburg; Hansa-brücke and Haus der Kulturen der Welt in Tiergarten; Friedrichstrasse, Museum Island, and Nikolaiviertel in Mitte; and near the Jannowit-zbrücke S-bahn and U-bahn station. Drinks, snacks, and wursts are available during the narrated trips. Reederei Riedel offers three inner-city trips that range from €8.50 to €18.

A tour of the Havel Lakes (which include Tegeler See and Wannsee) begins at the Wannsee, where you can sail on either the whale-shape vessel *Moby Dick* or the *Havel Queen*, a Mississippi-style boat, and cruise 28 km (17 mi) through the lakes and past forests (Stern- und Kreisschiffahrt). Tours can last from one to seven hours, and cost between €8 and €20. There are 20 operators.

Boat Tour Information Reederei Bruno Winkler ☏ *030/349–9595* ⊕ *www. reedereiwinkler.de.* **Reederei Riedel** ☏ *030/693–4646* ⊕ *www.reederei-riedel. de.* **Stern und Kreisschiffahrt** ☏ *030/536–3600* ⊕ *www.sternundkreis.de.*

BUS TOURS

Four companies (Berliner Bären Stadtrundfahrten, Berolina Berlin-Service, Bus Verkehr Berlin, and Severin & Kühn) jointly offer city tours on yellow, double-decker City Circle buses, which run every 15 or 30 minutes, depending on the season. The full circuit takes two hours, as does the recorded narration listened to through headphones. For €20 you can jump on and off at the 16 stops. The bus driver sells tickets. During the warmer months, the last circuit leaves at 6 pm from the corner of Fasanenstrasse and Kurfürstendamm. Most companies have tours to Potsdam. Severin & Kühn also runs all-day tours to Dresden.

The Stadtrundfahrtbüro Berlin offers a 2½-hour tour (€15) and 1¾-hour tour (€12) at 10:15, 10:45, 11, 11:30, 1 pm, and 1:30 pm, 3 pm, 3:30 pm, and 5 pm. A guide narrates in both German and English. The bus departs from Kurfürstendamm 236, at the corner of Rankestrasse.

Bus Tour Information **BBS Berliner Bären Stadtrundfahrt** (*BBS*) ✉ *Seeburgerstr. 19b, Spandau* ☎ *030/3519–5270* ⊕ *www.sightseeing.de.* **Berolina Berlin-Service** ✉ *Kurfürstendamm 220, at Meinekestr., Western Downtown* ☎ *030/8856–8030* ⊕ *www.berolina-berlin.com.* **Bus Verkehr Berlin** (*BVB*) ✉ *Kurfürstendamm 225, Western Downtown* ☎ *030/683–8910* ⊕ *www.bvb.net.* **Severin & Kühn** ✉ *Kurfürstendamm 216, Western Downtown* ☎ *030/880–4190* ⊕ *www.severin-kuehn-berlin.de.* **Stadtrundfahrtbüro Berlin** ✉ *Kurfürstendamm 236, Western Downtown* ☎ *030/261–2001* ⊕ *www.stadtrundfahrtbuero-berlin.de.*

WALKING AND BIKE TOURS

Getting oriented through a walking tour is a great way to start a Berlin visit. In addition to daily city highlight tours, companies have themed tours such as Third Reich Berlin, Potsdam, and pub crawls. Berlin Walks offers a Monday "Jewish Life" tour, a Potsdam tour on Thursday and Sunday, and visits to the Sachsenhausen concentration camp. Insider Tours has a "Cold War" Berlin tour about the Soviet era and a bike tour as well as a Cruise'n'Walk tour, a combination of boating and walking. Brit Terry Brewer's firsthand accounts of divided and reunified Berlin are a highlight of the all-day "Brewer's Best of Berlin" tour. Tours cost from €9 to €15. Printable discount coupons may be available on the tour operators' Web sites; some companies grant discounts to WelcomeCard and CityCard holders. Fat Tire Bike Tours rides through Berlin daily early March–November and has a Berlin Wall tour. The 4½-hour city tour costs €22, bike rental included.

Walking and Bike Tour Information **Original Berlin Walks** ☎ *030/301–9194* ⊕ *www.berlinwalks.com.* **Brewer's Berlin Tours** ☎ *0177/388–1537* ⊕ *www. brewersberlintours.com.* **Fat Tire Bike Tours** ✉ *Panoramastr. 1a, base of TV tower, Mitte* ☎ *030/2404–7991* ⊕ *www.fattirebiketoursberlin.com.* **Insider Tour** ✉ *Bahnhof Zoologischer Garten, outside McDonalds, Western Downtown* ☎ *030/692–3149* ⊕ *www.insidertour.com.*

PLANNING YOUR TIME

As one of Europe's biggest cities and top capitals with very distinctive individual neighborhoods and sights, Berlin is difficult to tackle in just one or two days. The Kurfürstendamm is the city's premier shopping boulevard. For culture buffs, great antique, medieval, Renaissance, and modern art can be found at the Kulturforum in the Tiergarten, and on Museum Island in Mitte—both cultural centers are a must, and either will occupy at least a half day. Most of the historic sights of German and Prussian history line the city's other grand boulevard, Unter den Linden, in eastern Berlin, which can be strolled in a leisurely two hours, with stops. Note that most shops are closed on Sunday, with the exception of those located in major train stations.

DISCOUNTS AND DEALS

Berlin remains a relatively inexpensive central European destination. The **Berlin WelcomeCard** (sold by EurAid, BVG offices, the tourist office, and some hotels) entitles one adult and three children under the age of 14 to either two or three days of unlimited travel in the ABC zones for €18.90 or €24.90, respectively, and includes admission and tour discounts detailed in a booklet. The CityTourCard, good for two or three days of unlimited travel in the AB zones costs €15.90 and €21.90, respectively, and details 50 discounts on a leaflet; up to three children under age 6 can accompany an adult.

Many of the 17 Staatliche Museen zu Berlin (state museums of Berlin) offer several ticket options (children up to 18 are welcomed free of charge). A single ticket ranges €4–€8. A three-day pass (*Tageskarte or SchauLust Museen Ticket*) to all state museums costs €19. This ticket allows entrance to all state museums plus many others for three consecutive days. State museums tend to cluster near one another, and usually a single entrance ticket grants admission to all museums in that area. These areas include Charlottenburg (€8), Dahlem (€6), the Kulturforum in Tiergarten (€8), Hamburger Bahnhof in Moabit (€12), and all museums on Museum Island (€14) in Mitte. All these entrance tickets are for the permanent exhibitions and include an audio guide; special exhibits cost extra.

EXPLORING BERLIN

Berlin is a large city with several downtown centers that evolved during the 30 years of separation. Of Berlin's twelve boroughs, the five of most interest to visitors are Charlottenburg-Wilmersdorf in the west; Tiergarten (a district of the Mitte borough) and Kreuzberg-Friedrichhain southeast of the center; Mitte, the historic core of the city in the central eastern part of town; and Prenzlauer Berg in the northeast. Southwest Berlin has lovely escapes in the secluded forests and lakes of the Grunewald area.

KURFÜRSTENDAMM AND WESTERN DOWNTOWN BERLIN

Shoppers are the life force of the boulevard Kurfürstendamm (Ku'damm), with enough energy and euros to support the local boutiques on the quieter side streets, too. Out-of-towners take it easy at Ku'damm's sidewalk tables as Berliners bustle by with a purpose.

TOP ATTRACTIONS

Kaiser-Wilhelm-Gedächtnis-Kirche (*Kaiser Wilhelm Memorial Church*). A dramatic reminder of World War II's destruction, the ruined bell tower is all that remains of this once massive church, which was completed in 1895 and dedicated to the emperor, Kaiser Wilhelm I. The Hohenzollern dynasty is depicted inside in a gilded mosaic, whose damage, like that of the building, will not be repaired. The exhibition revisits World War II's devastation throughout Europe. On the hour, the tower chimes out a melody composed by the last emperor's great-grandson, the late Prince Louis Ferdinand von Hohenzollern.

The modern sculpture on Breitscheidplatz frames the Kaiser-Wilhelm-Gedächtnis-Kirche in the background.

In stark contrast to the old bell tower (dubbed the "Hollow Tooth"), which is in sore need of restoration now, are the adjoining Memorial Church and Tower, designed by the noted German architect Egon Eiermann and finished in 1961. These ultramodern octagonal structures, with their myriad honeycomb windows, have nicknames as well: the "Lipstick" and the "Powder Box." Brilliant, blue stained glass designed by Gabriel Loire of Chartres, France, dominates the interiors. Church music and organ concerts are presented in the church regularly, which is slated for restoration in the near future. ⊠ *Breitscheidpl., Western Downtown* ☎ *030/218–5023* ⊕ *www.gedaechtniskirche-berlin.de* ⊠ *Free* ⊘ *Memorial Church daily 9–7* Ⓜ *Zoologischer Garten (U-bahn and S-bahn).*

Kaufhaus des Westens (*Department Store of the West*). The completely refurbished and modernized KaDeWe isn't just Berlin's classiest department store; it's also continental Europe's largest, a grand-scale emporium in modern guise and an historic landmark of Western capitalism for decades. Sold away from its Jewish owners during the Nazi era, nearly destroyed by an American airplane that crashed into it toward the end of the war, and then rebuilt in the years before the Wall went up, KaDeWe's history is Berlin's history in a nutshell. Today, its seven floors hold an enormous selection, but it is best known for the food and delicatessen counters, restaurants, champagne bars, and beer bars that occupy its two top floors, as well as for its crowning rooftop winter garden. ⊠ *Tauentzienstr. 21–24, Western Downtown* ☎ *030/21210* ⊕ *www.kadewe-berlin.de* ⊘ *Mon.–Thurs. 10–8, Fri. 10–9, Sat. 9:30–8* Ⓜ *Wittenbergplatz (U-bahn).*

Schleusenkrug. Forget the fast-food options at Zoo Station. Instead, follow the train tracks to the back of the taxi and bus queues, where you'll enter Tiergarten and within 100 yards come upon the best hideaway in the area: Schleusenkrug. In warmer weather you can order at the window and sit in the beer garden or on the back patio, watching pleasure ships go through the lock. Inside is a casual restaurant with a changing daily menu. Between November and mid-March the Krug closes at 7 pm. ⊠ *Tiergarten, Müller-Breslau-Str., Western Downtown* ☎ *030/313–9909* ⊕ *www.schleusenkrug. de/* ☉ *Daily 10–12 am.*

Kurfürstendamm. This busy thoroughfare began as a riding path in the 16th century. The elector Joachim II of Brandenburg used it to travel between his palace on the Spree River and his hunting lodge in the Grunewald. The Kurfürstendamm (Elector's Causeway) was transformed into a major route in the late 19th century, thanks to the initiative of Bismarck, Prussia's Iron Chancellor.

Even in the 1920s, the Ku'damm was still relatively new and by no means elegant; it was fairly far removed from the old heart of the city, Unter den Linden in Mitte. The Ku'damm's prewar fame was due mainly to its rowdy bars and dance halls, as well as the cafés where the cultural avant-garde of Europe gathered. Almost half of its 245 late-19th-century buildings were completely destroyed in the 1940s, and the remaining buildings were damaged to varying degrees. As in most of western Berlin, what you see today is either restored or newly constructed. Many of the 1950s buildings have been replaced by high-rises, in particular at the corner of Joachimstaler Strasse. Although Ku'damm is still known as the best shopping street in Berlin, its establishments have declined in elegance and prestige over the years. Nowadays you'll want to visit just to check it off your list, but few of the mostly down-market chain stores will impress you with their luxury.

Zoologischer Garten (*Zoological Gardens*). Even though Knut, the polar bear cub who captured the heart of the city, is sadly no longer with us, there are 14,000 other animals to see here, many of whom may be happy to have their time in the spotlight once again. There are 1,500 different species (more than any other zoo in Europe), including those rare and endangered, which the zoo has been successful at breeding. New arrivals in the past years include a baby rhinoceros. ■TIP→ **Check the feeding times posted to watch creatures such as seals, apes, hippos, crocodiles, and pelicans during their favorite time of day.** The animals' enclosures are designed to resemble their natural habitats, though some structures are ornate, such as the 1910 Arabian-style Zebra House. Pythons, frogs, turtles, invertebrates, Komodo dragons, and an amazing array of strange and colorful fish are part of the three-floor aquarium. ⊠ *Hardenbergpl. 8 and Budapester Str. 32, Western Downtown* ☎ *030/254–010* ⊕ *www.zoo-berlin.de* ⌑ *Zoo or aquarium €13, combined ticket €20* ☉ *Zoo: Oct.–mid-Mar., daily 9–5; mid-Mar.–Oct., daily 9–7. Aquarium: daily 9–6* Ⓜ *Zoologischer Garten (U-bahn and S-bahn).*

15

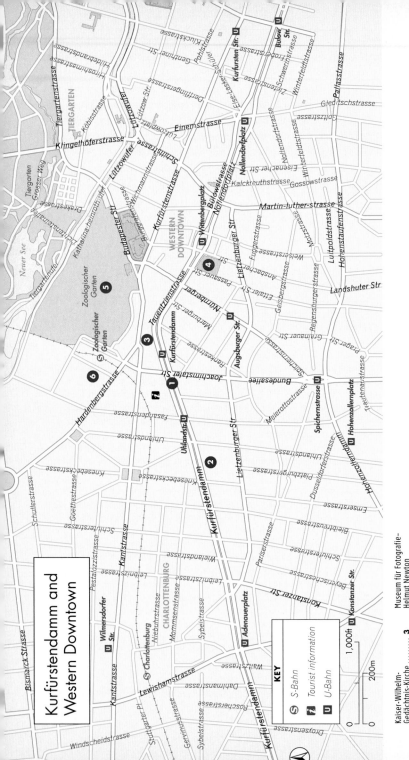

Kurfürstendamm and Western Downtown

KEY

S	S-Bahn
i	Tourist information
U	U-Bahn

0 — 200m
0 — 1,000ft

Kaiser-Wilhelm-
Gedächtnis-Kirche **3**
Kauthaus des Westens **4**
Kurfürstendamm **1**

Museum für Fotografie–
Helmut Newton
Stiftung **6**
The Story of Berlin **2**
Zoologischer Garten **5**

WORTH NOTING

Museum für Fotografie–Helmut Newton Stiftung. Native son Helmut Newton (1920–2004) pledged this collection of 1,000 photographs to Berlin months before his unexpected death. The man who defined fashion photography in the 1960s through 1980s was an apprentice to Yva, a Jewish fashion photographer in Berlin in the 1930s. Newton fled Berlin with his family in 1938, and his mentor was killed in a concentration camp. The photographs, now part of the state museum collection, are shown on a rotating basis in the huge Wilhelmine building behind the train station Zoologischer Garten. You'll see anything from racy portraits of models to serene landscapes. ⊠ *Jebenstr. 2, Western Downtown* ☎ *030/3186–4856* ⊕ *www.helmutnewton.com* ✉ *€8* ⊗ *Thurs.–Sun. 10–6 (Thurs. until 10)* Ⓜ *Zoologischer Garten (U-bahn and S-bahn).*

☾ **The Story of Berlin.** You can't miss this multimedia museum for the airplane wing exhibited outside. It was once part of a "Raisin bomber," a U.S. Air Force DC-3 that supplied Berlin during the Berlin Airlift in 1948 and 1949. Eight hundred years of the city's history, from the first settlers casting their fishing lines to Berliners heaving sledgehammers at the Wall, are conveyed through hands-on exhibits, film footage, and multimedia devices in this unusual venue. The sound of footsteps over broken glass follows your path through the exhibit on the *Kristallnacht* pogrom, and to pass through the section on the Nazis' book burning on Bebelplatz, you must walk over bookbindings. Many original artifacts are on display, such as the stretch Volvo that served as Erich Honnecker's state carriage in East Germany. ■TIP→ The eeriest relic is the 1974 nuclear shelter, which you can visit by guided tour on the hour. Museum placards are also in English. ⊠ *Ku'damm Karree, Kurfürstendamm 207–208, Western Downtown* ☎ *030/8872–0100* ⊕ *www.story-of-berlin.de* ✉ *€10* ⊗ *Daily 10–8; last entry at 6* Ⓜ *Uhlandstrasse (U-bahn).*

TIERGARTEN AND THE GOVERNMENT DISTRICT

The Tiergarten, a bucolic 630-acre park with lakes, meadows, and wide paths, is the "green heart" of Berlin. In the 17th century it served as the hunting grounds of the Great Elector (its name translates into "animal garden"). Now it's the Berliners' backyard for sunbathing and barbecuing. Berlin's most fertile grounds for modern architecture—the government district, Potsdamer Platz, and the embassy district—ring the park from its eastern to southern edges. Some of the embassies have exhibitions open to the public, and Germany's parliament convenes beneath the glass dome of the Reichstag. Bordering Tiergarten and the government district is the meticulously restored Brandenburger Tor, the unofficial symbol of the city, and the Memorial to the Murdered Jews of Europe, whose design and scope engendered many debates.

TIMING

A leisurely walk from Zoo Station through the Tiergarten to the Brandenburger Tor and the Reichstag will take at least 90 minutes, two to three hours if you want to spend more time photographing and visiting the Holocaust Memorial. You must reserve a spot on a tour in advance in order to visit the Reichstag, but don't let that stop you: the new rules have done a lot to dissipate the lines that used to snake around the building. The Hamburger Bahnhof, Museum für Gegenwart–Berlin is just down the street from Hauptbahnhof. A quick ride on Berlin's newest—and with only three stops, shortest—underground line, the U55, will get you there from the Brandenburg Gate or the Reichstag.

TOP ATTRACTIONS

Fodor's Choice
★
Brandenburger Tor (*Brandenburg Gate*). Once the pride of Prussian Berlin and the city's premier landmark, the Brandenburger Tor was left in a desolate no-man's-land when the Wall was built. Since the Wall's dismantling, the sandstone gateway has become the scene of the city's Unification Day and New Year's Eve parties. This is the sole remaining gate of 14 built by Carl Langhans in 1788–91, designed as a triumphal arch for King Frederick Wilhelm II. Its virile classical style pays tribute to Athens's Acropolis. The quadriga, a chariot drawn by four horses and driven by the Goddess of Victory, was added in 1794. Troops paraded through the gate after successful campaigns—the last time in 1945, when victorious Red Army troops took Berlin. The upper part of the gate, together with its chariot and Goddess of Victory, was destroyed in the war. In 1957 the original molds were discovered in West Berlin, and a new quadriga was cast in copper and presented as a gift to the people of East Berlin. A tourist-information center is in the south part of the gate.

The gate faces the historic square **Pariser Platz,** with bank headquarters, the ultramodern French embassy, and the offices of the federal parliament. On the southern side, Berlin's sleek Academy of Arts, integrating the ruins of its historic predecessor, and the DZ Bank, designed by star architect Frank Gehry, stand next to the new American embassy, rebuilt on its prewar location and reopened on July 4, 2008. The legendary Hotel Adlon (now the Adlon Kempinski) looks on from its historic home at the southeast edge of the square. ⊠ *Pariser Pl., Mitte* Ⓜ *Unter den Linden (S-bahn).*

Denkmal für die Ermordeten Juden Europas (*Memorial to the Murdered Jews of Europe*). An expansive and unusual memorial dedicated to the 6 million Jews who were killed in the Holocaust, the monument was designed by American architect Peter Eisenman. The stunning place of remembrance consists of a grid of more than 2,700 concrete stelae, planted into undulating ground. The abstract memorial can be entered from all sides and offers no prescribed path. ■TIP➔ An information center that goes into specifics about the Holocaust lies underground at the southeast corner. ⊠ *Cora-Berliner-Str. 1, Mitte* ☎ *030/2639–4336* ⊕ *www.stiftung-denkmal.de* ◻ *Free* ☉ *Daily 24 hrs; information center: Oct.–Mar., Tues.–Sun. 10–7; Apr.–Sept., Tues.–Sun. 10–8* Ⓜ *Unter den Linden (S-bahn).*

★ **Reichstag** (*Parliament Building*). After last meeting here in 1933, the Bundestag, Germany's federal parliament, returned to its traditional seat in the spring of 1999. British architect Sir Norman Foster lightened up the gray monolith with a glass dome, which quickly became a main attraction: you can circle up a gently rising ramp while taking in the rooftops of Berlin and the parliamentary chamber below. At the base of the dome is an exhibit on the Reichstag's history, in German and English. ■TIP➔ After terrorism warnings at the end of 2010, the Reichstag tightened its door policy, asking all visitors to register their names and birthdates in advance and reserve a place on a guided tour. Since then, the crowds that used to snake around the outside of the building have subsided, and a visit is worth the planning. As always, a reservation at the pricey rooftop Käfer restaurant (☎ 030/2262–9933) will also get you in. Those with reservations can use the doorway to the right of the Reichstag's main staircase. Completed in 1894, the Reichstag housed the imperial German parliament and later served a similar function during the ill-fated Weimar Republic. On the night of February 27, 1933, the Reichstag burned down in an act of arson, a pivotal event in Third Reich history. The fire led to state protection laws that gave the Nazis a pretext to arrest their political opponents. The Reichstag was rebuilt but again badly damaged in 1945. The graffiti of the victorious Russian soldiers can still be seen on some of the walls in the hallways. The building is surrounded by ultramodern federal government offices, such as the boxy, concrete **Bundeskanzleramt** (Federal Chancellery), which also has a nickname of course: the "Washing Machine." Built by Axel Schultes, it's one of the few new buildings in the government district by a Berlin architect. Participating in a guided tour of the Chancellery is possible if you apply in writing several weeks prior to a visit. A riverwalk with great views of the government buildings begins behind the Reichstag. ⊠ *Pl. der Republik 1, Tiergarten* ⊠ *Bundeskanzleramt, Besucherdienst* ☎ *030/2273–2152, 030/2273–5908 Reichstag* 🖷 *030/2273–0027 Reichstag, 030/4000–1881 Bundeskanzleramt* ⊕ *www.bundestag.de* 🖃 *Free* ☉ *Daily at 10:30, 1:30, 3:30, 6:30* Ⓜ *Unter den Linden (S-bahn).*

Tiergarten (*Animal Garden*). The quiet greenery of the 630-acre Tiergarten is a beloved oasis, with some 23 km (14 mi) of footpaths, meadows, and two beer gardens. The inner park's 6½ acres of lakes and ponds were landscaped by garden architect Joseph Peter Lenné in the mid-1800s.

Café am Neuen See. On the shore of the lake in the southwest corner of the park, you can relax at the Café am Neuen See, a café and beer garden. ⊠ *Lichtensteinallee 2, Tiergarten* ☎ *030/25449300* ⊕ *www. cafe-am-neuen-see.de/*

Haus der Kulturen der Welt. Off the Spree River and bordering the Kanzleramt (Chancellery) is the former congress hall, now serving as the Haus der Kulturen der Welt. It is fondly referred to as the "pregnant oyster" because the sweeping, 1950's design of its roof resembles a shellfish opening. Thematic exhibits, festivals, and concerts take place here, and it's also a boarding point for Spree River cruises. ⊠ *House of the World Cultures, John-Foster-Dulles Allee 10, Tiergarten* ☎ *030/397–870* ⊕ *www.hkw.de* ☉ *Daily 10–7.*

15

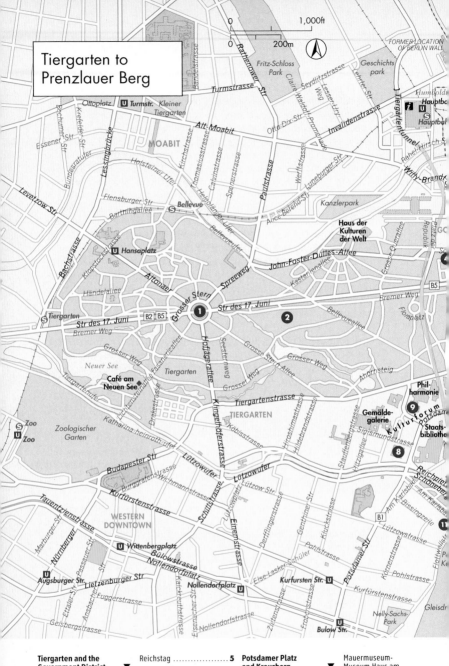

Tiergarten to Prenzlauer Berg

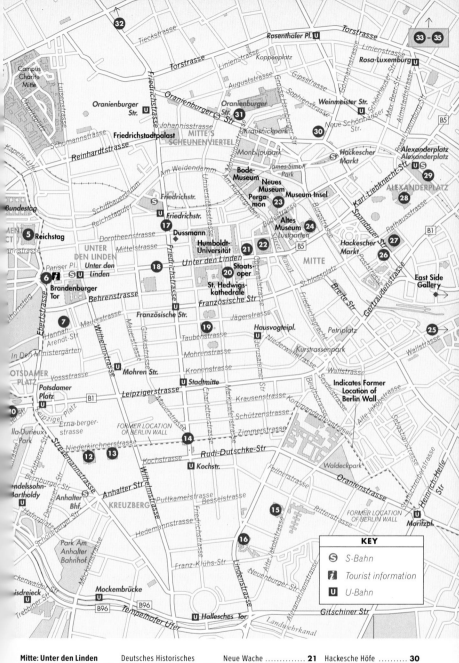

WORTH NOTING

Hamburger Bahnhof - Museum für Gegenwart - Berlin (*Museum of Contemporary Art*). This light-filled, remodeled train station is home to a rich survey of post-1960 Western art. The permanent collection includes installations by German artists Joseph Beuys and Anselm Kiefer, as well as paintings by Andy Warhol, Cy Twombly, Robert Rauschenberg, and Robert Morris. An annex presents the hotly debated Friedrich Christian Flick Collection, the largest and most valuable collection of the latest in the world's contemporary art. The 2,000 works rotate, but you're bound to see some by Bruce Naumann, Rodney Graham, and Pipilotti Rist. ✉ *Invalidenstr. 50–51, Tiergarten* ☎ *030/3978–3411* ⊕ *www.smb.museum* ✇ *€12* ⊙ *Tues.–Fri. 10–6, Sat. 11–8, Sun. 11–6* Ⓜ *Naturkundemuseum (U-bahn), Hauptbahnhof (S-bahn).*

Siegessäule (*Victory Column*). The 227-foot granite, sandstone, and bronze column is topped by a winged, golden goddess and has a splendid view of Berlin. It was erected in front of the Reichstag in 1873 to commemorate Prussia's military successes and then moved to the Tiergarten in 1938–39. You have to climb 270 steps up through the column to reach the observation platform, but the view is rewarding. The gold-tipped cannons surrounding the column are those the Prussians captured from the French in the Franco-Prussian War. ✉ *Strasse des 17. Juni/Am Grossen Stern, Tiergarten* ☎ *030/391–2961* ✇ *€2.20* ⊙ *Nov.–Mar., weekdays 10–5, weekends 10–5:30; Apr.–Oct., weekdays 9:30–6:30, weekends 9:30–7; last admission ½ hr before closing* Ⓜ *Tiergarten (S-bahn), Bellevue (S-bahn).*

Sowjetisches Ehrenmal (*Soviet Memorial*). Built immediately after World War II, this monument stands as a reminder of the Soviet victory over the shattered German army in Berlin in May 1945. The Battle of Berlin was one of the deadliest on the European front. A hulking bronze statue of a soldier stands atop a marble plinth taken from Hitler's former Reichkanzlei (headquarters). The memorial is flanked by what are said to be the first two T-34 tanks to have fought their way into the city. The Sowjetisches Ehrenmal in Treptower Park in the eastern Berlin district of Treptow might just take the hard-earned title of most impressively bombastic memorial in Berlin. The size of several city blocks, this memorial celebrates the Soviet victory with inscriptions in both Russian and German, accompanying a series of Socialist realist reliefs lining both sides of an elaborate plaza. At one end stands an enormous bronze of a Russian soldier cradling a child in one arm and wielding a sword with the other while stomping on a crumpled swastika. Well-placed text and photos educate on the history and importance of the monument in the former East, as well as explaining why it was preserved after the fall of the Wall. (S-bahn Treptower Park) ✉ *Str. des 17. Juni, Tiergarten* Ⓜ *Unter den Linden (S-bahn).*

POTSDAMER PLATZ AND KREUZBERG

The once-divided capital is rejoined on Potsdamer Platz, which was Berlin's inner-city center and Europe's busiest plaza before World War II. Bombings and the wall system left this area a sprawling, desolate lot, where tourists in West Berlin could climb a wooden platform to peek into

The Brandenburger Tor (Brandenburg Gate) is a must-see site in Berlin, especially at night.

East Berlin's death strip. After the Wall fell, various international companies made a rush to build their German headquarters on this prime real estate. In the mid-1990s Potsdamer Platz became Europe's largest construction site. Today's modern complexes of red sandstone, terra-cotta tiles, steel, and glass have made it a city within a city. The subtle reminder that this was an empty plot for nearly 50 years is a line of cobblestones that traces the path of the Wall on the west side of Stresemannstrasse.

A few narrow streets cut between the hulking modern architecture, which includes two high-rise office towers owned by Daimler, one of which was designed by star architect Renzo Piano. The round atrium of the Sony Center comes closest to rendering a traditional square used as a public meeting point. Farther down Potsdamer Strasse are the state museums and cultural institutes of the Kulturforum.

Kreuzberg held the American side of the border-crossing Checkpoint Charlie, and is a lively Berlin district. A largely Turkish population shares the residential streets with a variegated assortment of political radicals and bohemians of all nationalities. In the minds of most Berliners, it is split into two even smaller sections: Kreuzberg 61 has gone upscale in the last decade, and contains a variety of small and elegant shops and restaurants, while Kreuzberg 36 has stayed more true to its gritty character, symbolized by the garbage-strewn but much-beloved Görlitzer Park. Oranienstrasse, the spine of life in the Kreuzberg 36 district, has mellowed from hard-core to funky since reunification. When Kreuzberg literally had its back against the Wall, West German social outcasts, punks, and the radical left made this old working-class street their territory. Since the 1970s the population has become largely

DID YOU KNOW?

The Sony Center, with its colorful atrium, is Berlin's best example of how traditional squares were used—as a central meeting spot for locals.

Turkish, and many of yesterday's outsiders have turned into successful owners of shops and cafés. The vibrant stretch is between Skalitzer Strasse and Oranienplatz. Use Bus M29 or the Görlitzer Bahnhof or Kottbusser Tor U-bahn station to get here.

TIMING

The sights on this tour are close to one another until you set off for the Jüdisches Museum. In 30 minutes you can take in the architecture at Potsdamer Platz and reach the Kulturforum complex for a look from the outside. To retrace your steps and reach the Topographie des Terrors will take 20 minutes. Owing to its small size and popularity, you may experience a wait or slow line at the Checkpoint Charlie Museum. Monday is a popular day for it and for the Jüdisches Museum, since the state museums are closed that day.

TOP ATTRACTIONS

★ **Kulturforum** (*Cultural Forum*). This unique ensemble of museums, galleries, and the Philharmonic Hall was long in the making. The first designs were submitted in the 1960s and the last building completed in 1998. Now it forms a welcome modern counterpoint to the thoroughly restored Prussian splendor of Museum Island, although Berliners and tourists alike hold drastically differing opinions on the area's architectural aesthetics. Whatever your opinion, Kulturforum's artistic holdings are unparalleled and worth at least a day of your time, if not more.

Gemäldegalerie (*Picture Gallery*). The Gemäldegalerie reunites formerly separated collections from East and West Berlin. It's one of Germany's finest art galleries, and has an extensive selection of European paintings from the 13th to 18th century. Seven rooms are reserved for paintings by German masters, among them Dürer, Cranach the Elder, and Holbein. A special collection has works of the Italian masters—Botticelli, Titian, Giotto, Lippi, and Raphael—as well as paintings by Dutch and Flemish masters of the 15th and 16th centuries: Van Eyck, Bosch, Brueghel the Elder, and van der Weyden. The museum also holds the world's second-largest Rembrandt collection. ⊠ *Matthäikirchpl. 4, Tiergarten* ☎ *030/2664–24242* ⊕ *www.smb.museum* ✉ *€8* ☉ *Tues., Wed., and Fri.–Sun. 10–6; Thurs. 10–10* Ⓜ *Potsdamer Platz (U-bahn and S-bahn).*

Kunstbibliothek (*Art Library*). With more than 400,000 volumes on the history of European art, the Kunstbibliothek (art library) is one of Germany's most important institutions on the subject. It contains art posters and advertisements, examples of graphic design and book design, ornamental engravings, prints and drawings, and a costume library. Visitors can view items in the reading rooms, but many samples from the collections are also shown in rotating special exhibitions ⊠ *Matthäikirchpl. 4, Tiergarten* ☎ *030/2664–24242* ⊕ *www. smb.museum* ✉ *€8* ☉ *Tues.–Sun. 10–6, Thurs. 10–10; reading room weekdays 9–8.*

Kupferstichkabinett (*Drawings and Prints Collection*). The Kupferstichkabinett has occasional exhibits, which include European woodcuts, engravings, and illustrated books from the 15th century to the present (highlights of its holdings are pen-and-ink drawings by Dürer and drawings by Rembrandt). You can request to see one or two drawings in the study room. Another building displays paintings dating from the late Middle Ages to 1800 ⊠ *Matthäikirchpl. 4, Tiergarten* ☎ *030/2664–24242* ⊕ *www.smb.museum* 🖼 *€8* ⊙ *Tues.–Fri. 10–6, weekends 11–6.*

Kunstgewerbemuseum (*Museum of Decorative Arts*). Inside the Kunstgewerbemuseum are European arts and crafts from the Middle Ages to the present. Among the notable exhibits are the Welfenschatz (Welfen Treasure), a collection of 16th-century gold and silver plates from Nürnberg, as well as ceramics and porcelains. Another branch of the museum can be found at Schloss Köpenick, in the town of Köpenick east of Berlin ⊠ *Herbert-von-Karajan-Str. 10, Tiergarten* ☎ *030/266–2902* ⊕ *www.smb.museum* 🖼 *€8* ⊙ *Tues.–Fri. 10–6, weekends 11–6.*

Philharmonie. The mustard-yellow complex that resembles a great tent belongs to the Philharmonie, home to the renowned Berlin Philharmonic Orchestra since 1963. Despite a fire in 2008, the now renovated concert hall hasn't lost its heavenly, unique sound. The Philharmonie and the smaller Chamber Music Hall adjoining it were designed by Hans Scharoun. ■ TIP→ There's a €3 tour of the Philharmonie daily at 1 pm. ☎ *030/254–880.*

Musikinstrumenten-Museum (*Musical Instruments Museum*). Across the parking lot from the Philharmonie, the Musikinstrumenten-Museum has a fascinating collection of keyboard, string, wind, and percussion instruments. ■ TIP→ These are demonstrated during an 11 am tour on Saturday, which closes with a 20-minute Wurlitzer organ concert for an extra €2 ⊠ *Ben-Gurion-Str. 1, Tiergarten* ☎ *030/2548–1178* 🖼 *€4* ⊙ *Tues., Wed., and Fri. 9–5; Thurs. 9 am–10 pm; weekends 10–5.*

Staatsbibliothek (*National Library*). The Staatsbibliothek is one of the largest libraries in Europe, and was a setting in Wim Wenders's 1987 film *Wings of Desire* ⊠ *Potsdamer Str. 33* ☎ *030/2660* 🖼 *€10* ⊙ *Weekdays 9–9, Sat. 9–5.*

★ **Mauermuseum-Museum Haus am Checkpoint Charlie.** Just steps from the famous crossing point between the two Berlins, the Wall Museum–House at Checkpoint Charlie presents visitors with the story of the Wall and, even more riveting, the stories of those who escaped through, under, and over it. The homespun museum reviews the events leading up to the Wall's construction and, with original tools and devices, plus recordings and photographs, shows how East Germans escaped to the West (one ingenious contraption was a miniature submarine). Exhibits about human rights and paintings interpreting the Wall round out the experience. ■ TIP→ Come early or late in the day to avoid the multitudes dropped off by tour buses. (Monday can be particularly crowded.) ⊠ *Friedrichstr. 43–45, Kreuzberg* ☎ *030/253–7250* ⊕ *www.mauermuseum.com* 🖼 *€12.50* ⊙ *Daily 9 am–10 pm* Ⓜ *Kochstrasse (U-bahn).*

★ **Neue Nationalgalerie** (*New National Gallery*). Bauhaus member Mies van der Rohe originally designed this glass-box structure for Bacardi Rum in Cuba, but Berlin became the site of its realization in 1968. The main exhibits are below ground. Highlights of the collection of 20th-century paintings, sculptures, and drawings include works by expressionists Otto Dix, Ernst Ludwig Kirchner, and Georg Grosz. Special

CLOSE UP

Symbols and Shifts in East and West

The year 2009 marked the 20th anniversary of the fall of the Berlin Wall, and a year later, Berlin celebrated the 20th year of German unity. In fact, most of today's young Berliners, both from East and West, are *Einheitskinder*, children of German reunification, and have no recollection of the troubled days of division. But even though the Wall may be gone, its consequences are still keenly felt by both sides.

Ask Berliners old enough to remember the days of the Wall, and a certain percentage of them, mostly "Ossies" (East Germans), may admit that they prefer their GDR lifestyle, a yearning known as Ostalgie ("nostalgia for the East"). Many West Germans remain resentful of the tax money poured into Berlin postreunification in order to get it back on its feet economically.

Meanwhile, that economy is still fumbling. Nearly 30 years living with the constant threat of Soviet invasion certainly had an effect on West Berlin, while the same amount of time behind the Iron Curtain meant that East Berliners found themselves confronting a world that had moved on without them. Unresolved problems

such as high unemployment rates and overstretched city budgets are still worrying many, while wide-open spaces in the middle of the city serve as testaments to just how far Berlin's recovery still has to go.

In former times, Berlin may have protected the character of each *Kiez*, or neighborhood, but this had more to do with social reasons than East versus West. Now in many areas, such as Prenzlauer Berg and northern Mitte, two proud eastern districts, the former population has all but vanished: first affluent West Berlin families moved in, and then West German or foreign "invaders" took over leases. Today, luxury condos are popping up in popular residential areas in an effort to lure ever more wealthy buyers.

Still, the city embraces its future as an international center for avant-garde fashion, culture, art, and media, with a zeal rarely found in better-off cities. The next decade will see the German capital making some tough decisions: will it embrace its characterization as "poor but sexy," coined by flamboyant mayor Klaus Wowereit, or leave it squarely behind?

---

exhibits often take precedence over the permanent collection however. ✉ *Potsdamer Str. 50, Tiergarten* ☎ *030/2664–24242* ⊕ *www.smb. museum* 🎟 *€10* ⊙ *Tues., Wed., and Fri. 10–6; Thurs. 10–10; weekends 11–6* Ⓜ *Potsdamer Platz (U-bahn and S-bahn).*

Panoramapunkt. Located 300 feet above Potsdamer Platz at the top of one of its tallest towers, the new Panoramapunkt (Panoramic Viewing Point) not only features the world's highest-standing original piece of the Berlin wall, but also a fascinating, multimedia exhibit about the dramatic history of Berlin's former urban center. A café and a sun terrace facing west make this open-air viewing platform one of the city's most romantic. ✉ *Potsdamer Pl. 1, Tiergarten* ☎ *030/2593–7080* ⊕ *www. panoramapunkt.de* 🎟 *€5.50* ⊙ *Summer daily 10–8, Winter daily 10–5, last entrance 30 minutes before closing.*

Continued on page 702

Art Berlin Contemporary 2010 Opening

Paste-up street art

Capitain Petzel

East Side Gallery, Berlin Wall

Stencil by XOOOOX

Gallery Klosterfelde

Neue Nationalgalerie

Alexandre da Cunha, "Monolith," Sommer & Kohl Gallery

BERLIN'S EVOLVING ART SCENE

Berlin's contemporary art world is a perpetual work in progress. Hip galleries appear and then move on to bigger or trendier spaces almost before the paint is dry. The hottest players rotate with the seasons. But a few things always stay the same, like edgy ideas and constantly expanding frontiers in a city with a seemingly endless supply of spaces to reclaim. The art world here is unpretentious and easy to access—you might just meet Berlin's next art star along the way.

By Kimberly Bradley

THE ART SCENE: THEN AND NOW

The art scene has exploded in the past decade, evolving from a local community of dealers and artists to an international urban art center. Emerging artists of the 1990s, like Olafur Eliasson and Tacita Dean, remain in Berlin, despite having become international stars. And while a true "Berlin School" doesn't exist, the admittedly fragmented scene shows a strong tendency toward conceptual and performance art. Artist collectives also tap into the city's collaborative spirit.

EXPANDING FROM THE CENTER

In recent years the scene has evolved in ways no one could have predicted. What used to be two centralized art hubs—the edgy, experimental Mitte in the east and established, blue-chip Charlottenburg in the west—have multiplied throughout the city. Galleries have opened, often in clusters, far beyond Mitte's original main drag of Auguststrasse, to Heidestrasse behind the Hamburger Bahnhof museum, Lindenstrasse and the area around the Jewish Museum on Mitte's southern edge, and most recently Potsdamer Strasse near the New National Gallery.

ART FAIRS

Two recently founded events now bring in the well-heeled international crowd: **Gallery Weekend Berlin** (⊕ *www.gallery-weekend-berlin.de*) in April and **Art Berlin Contemporary** (⊕ *www.artberlincontemporary.com*), which began as a rogue sculpture exhibition in 2008 and is now the city's only large-scale fall art fair.

RECESSION AND REBOUND

Berlin's art scene has not been immune to global issues. There were about 500 galleries in Berlin before 2008's financial crash, and the number has gone down to a bit more than 400 since then as galleries are forced to close. Still, a few truly top-notch venues have since settled into architecturally interesting spaces: **Sprüth Magers** (⊕ *www.spruethmagers.com*) shows art stars in a vast gallery, **Capitain Petzel** (⊕ *www.capitainpetzel.de*) exhibits large-scale work in a modernist East German building that resembles a glass cube, and **Koch Oberhuber Wolff** (⊕ *www.kow-berlin.info*) takes up three floors of a striking new concrete building by local architect Arno Brandlhuber.

LOOKING FORWARD

Berlin being Berlin, the underground is never far away. Curators here throw innovative party-shows in garages and nightclubs around town, like **Tape** (⊕ *tapeberlin.de*) and **Autocenter** (⊕ *www.autocenterart.de*). Young artists are settling into the city's newest art neighborhood, Neukölln, in the southeast, and project spaces and new galleries can't be far behind.

ART OUTSIDE THE BOX

Left, The East Side Gallery, Berlin Wall. Right, stencil street art.

Museums and galleries are merely the tip of Berlin's art-world iceberg.

STREET ART

Street art abounds in the German capital. Tags (symbols identifying individual graffiti artists) adorn walls everywhere, but the areas around Köpernicker Strasse or Schlesiches Tor in Kreuzberg are especially thick with expertly executed paste-ups (posters) and stenciled art. Building-size murals can be seen around the Schlesiche Strasse area on the border between the Kreuzberg and Treptow districts, and in 2011, a sanctioned art project invited major international bombers (graffiti artists) to paint murals on blank firewalls in Berlin's Wedding district.

Take note of the **yellow bananas** marking gallery spaces; they are artist Thomas Baumgärtel's seal of approval, which he has been bestowing on worthy locations since 1986.

For curated exhibitions featuring works by artists with street-art backgrounds, head to **Circle Culture Gallery** (✉ *Gipsstrasse 11* ☎ *27581/7886* ⊕ *circleculture-gallery. de*) in Mitte. For online insight into the scene, see ⊕ *urbanartcore.eu*.

PRIVATE COLLECTIONS

Following in the footsteps of the **Sammlung Hoffmann** (✉ *Sophie-Gips-Höfe, Aufgang C, Sophienstr. 21* ☎ *2849/ 9120* ⊕ *www.sammlung-hoffmann.de* ☎ *€8*), several private collectors have opened their own mini-museums. Inside an ominous war bunker in Mitte is the **Boros Collection** (✉ *Reinhardtstrasse 20* ☎ *27594/065* ⊕ *sammlung-boros.de* ☎ *€10*), which highlights early work by some of Berlin's finest artists, like Olafur Eliasson. Christiane zu Salm's **About Change, Collection** (✉ *Am Kupfergraben 10* ⊕ *about-change-collection.de*) lies atop a sleek building designed by David Chipperfield, just off Museumsinsel. **Sammlung Haubrok** (✉ *Strausberger Platz 19* ☎ *172210/9525* ⊕ *sammlung-haubrok.de*) mounts exhibitions using the collection of Barbara and Axel Haubrok, who own more than 500 works by mostly European artists. And Thomas Olbricht's **me Collector's Room** (✉ *Auguststrasse 68* ☎ *86008/510* ⊕ *www.me-berlin.com* ☎ *€6*) displays his admittedly kitschy art and his collection of curiosities, like shrunken heads and ivory carvings.

TOURS

AlternativeBerlin (☎ *16281/98264 walternativeberlin.com*) offers workshops and tours of street art. For a customized art tour of the city, no one beats **Go Art!'s** (✉ *Potsdamer Str. 81B* ☎ *3087/3626* ⊕ *goart-berlin.de*) Miriam Bers, a Berlin art-world veteran.

GALLERY WALK:
POTSDAMER STRASSE

Berlin's galleries are notorious for playing musical chairs, and since 2009, a critical mass of excellent art venues have convened in—surprise!—former West Berlin, which represents a shift away from the hipper eastern district. The somewhat nondescript area on and around Potsdamer Strasse, not far from Potsdamer Platz, is now home to both Berlin stalwarts and highbrow newcomers. But you wouldn't necessarily see them from the street; most galleries here are in second-floor apartment-like spaces or tucked away in courtyards.

Galerie Giti Nourbakhsch

PLANNING

Two to three hours is plenty of time for a gallery overview, but you may want to spend more time looking at the art. If you only have an hour, limit your tour to these blue-chip best bets: Esther Schipper, Isabella Bortolozzi, Blain|Southern, Klosterfelde, and Helga Maria Klosterfelde Edition. Galleries are generally open Tuesday to Saturday, noon to 6. ■TIP→ For current exhibition information, download the EYEOUT Berlin app or pick up a copy of the *Index* gallery guide.

POTSDAMER STRASSE TO SCHÖNEBERGER UFER

Start at the **Neue Nationalgalerie** at Potsdamer Strasse 50. Architect Mies van der Rohe's impressive glass box—his only museum project—has been up for more than 50 years, and

it often mounts blockbuster shows by artists like Thomas Demand or Jenny Holzer.

Cross the canal, turn right, and walk along Schöneberger Ufer to see the **Galerie Verein Berliner Künstler** in a lovely townhouse at No. 55. Founded in 1841, this is Germany's oldest artist-run association, and the exhibition halls are dedicated to showing members' work.

At No. 61, **Galerie Isabella Bortolozzi** exhibits some of the city's edgiest artists, including brilliant Vietnamese artist Danh Vo, whose conceptual work explores the overlap between public and private life. The gallery has an unconventional interior with dark, wood-paneled rooms.

One of Berlin's top dealers, **Esther Schipper**, moved to her second-floor gallery and sleek courtyard at No. 65 in 2011. Her star-studded roster includes multitalented Young British Artists star Liam Gillick, Belgian artist Carsten Höller, who is famous for his audience-participation art, and Thomas Demand, whose still photographs subtly criticize modern society.

BISSINGZEILE TO KURFÜRSTENSTRASSE

Backtrack along the canal to Potsdamer Strasse and turn right. At No. 70 is **Nymphius Projekte**, a project space often featuring themed group shows, such as the art of the 1980s. Across the street at Nos. 77–87 is the impressive **Blain|Southern**, which opened in a vast space that was once the printing room of the *Tagesspiegel* daily newspaper, in spring 2011. Created by the original founders of international powergallery Haunch of Venison, Blain|Southern brings a formidable artist roster from its base in London. Other galleries have crept into spaces in the same courtyard, like the excellent **Nolan Judin Berlin** next door, which favors artists who are master draftspeople, like Danica Phelps, and **401 Contemporary** in the brick building across the yard. Berlin fashion pioneer **Andreas Murkudis** also moved his exclusive stores, with carefully curated women's and menswear, here in July 2011.

Poke into the huge, brick-lined back courtyard at No. 91 to the **Freies Museum Berlin** (Free Museum of Berlin), a 175-square-meter artist-run space that hosts conceptual shows and sponsors artistic research. The low-key **Walden** gallery is also on site.

Neue Nationalgalerie

Art Opening at Sprüth Magers

At No. 93, climb a set of curved stairs to **Klosterfelde**, whose interlocking rooms and ceiling moldings evoke the gilded age and are a far cry from the gallery's former big white box space. Owner Martin Klosterfelde's roster includes hot international artists like John Bock, whose messy installations and offbeat performances long ago earned him an *enfant-terrible* reputation. Downstairs, in a former stationary store with antique fixtures, is **Helga Maria Klosterfelde Edition** (No. 97). This smaller exhibition space featuring works on paper and prints is named after Martin's mother. A bit farther, past bakeries and second-hand clothing shops, is **Galerie Cinzia Friedlaender** (No. 105), which shows funky, sometimes lighthearted work by artists like Sunah Choi.

KURFÜRSTENSTRASSE TO BLUMENTHALSTRASSE

Continue to Kurfürstenstrasse and turn left. In the courtyard of No. 12 is **Galerie Giti Nourbakhsch**, an early supporter of some of Berlin's now best-known artists, like Anselm Reyle, whose large-scale sculptures and paintings are a riot of texture and color, as well as a cofounder of Gallery Weekend Berlin. Next door, the lovely **Sommer & Kohl** gallery (No. 13) represents some of the international art scene's most promising young talent in a for-

mer featherbed factory. Down the street at No. 5/5a, see what's on at **Reception**, a collaborative project between Zurich gallerist Victor Gisler and curator Christine Heidemann. Cross the street and make a quick detour onto the quiet tree-lined Blumenthalstrasse to check out a small, bright space belonging to **Galerie Sassa Trülzsch** (No. 8). Back on Kurfürstenstasse at No. 156, in a former corner pub, **Tanya Leighton**—who has curated at the Whitney Museum in New York—not only mounts fascinating conceptual exhibitions but also hosts lectures and events that explore art's wider meaning.

QUICK BITES

Head to **Joseph-Roth-Diele**, a cozy reading room-cum-restaurant at 75 Potsdamer Strasse, for German comfort food. Or, pop into the chic **Victoria Bar** at 102 Potsdamer Strasse for a cocktail.

Gallery Weekend Opening

Sony Center. This glass-and-steel construction wraps around a spectacular circular forum. Topping it off is a tentlike structure meant to emulate Mount Fuji. The architectural jewel, designed by German-American architect Helmut Jahn, is one of the most stunning public spaces of Berlin's new center, filled with restaurants, cafés, movie theaters, and apartments. A faint reminder of glorious days gone by is the old **Kaisersaal** (Emperor's Hall), held within a very modern glass enclosure, and today a pricey restaurant. The hall originally stood 75 yards away in the Grand Hotel Esplanade (built in 1907) but was moved here lock, stock, and barrel. Red-carpet glamour returns every February with the Berlinale Film Festival, which has screenings at the commercial cinema within the center.

Museum für Film und Fernsehen. Within the Sony Center is the small but fun Museum für Film und Fernsehen, which presents the groundbreaking history of German moviemaking with eye-catching displays. Descrptions are in English, and there's an audio guide as well. Memorabilia includes personal belongings of Marlene Dietrich and other German stars, while special exhibitions go into depth about outstanding directors, movements, and studios. A good selection of films, from the best classics to the virtually unknown art house finds, are shown in the theater on the lower level. During the Berlinale film festival in February, this place becomes one of the centers of the action. ⊠ *Potsdamer Str. 2, Tiergarten* ☎ *030/300–9030* ⊕ *www.deutsche-kinemathek.de* ⌷ *€6* ☉ *Tues., Wed., and Fri.–Sun. 10–6, Thurs. 10–8.*

Legoland Discovery Centre. A must-see when traveling with children is the Legoland Discovery Centre, the Danish toy company's only indoor park. Children can build their very own towers while their parents live out their urban development dreams, even testing if the miniature construction would survive an earthquake. In a special section, Berlin's landmarks are presented in a breathtaking miniature world made up of thousands of tiny Lego bricks. ⊠ *Potsdamer Str. 4, Tiergarten* ☎ *030/301–0400* ⊕ *www.legolanddiscoverycentre.de* ⌷ *€15.95, €7 online* ☉ *Daily 10–7; last admittance 5.*

WORTH NOTING

Berlinische Galerie. Talk about site-specific art: all the modern art, photography, and architecture models and plans here, created between 1870 and the present, were made in Berlin (or in the case of architecture competition models, intended for the city). Russians, secessionists, Dadaists, and expressionists all had their day in Berlin, and individual works by Otto Dix, George Grosz, and Georg Baselitz, as well as artists' archives such as the Dadaist Hannah Höch's, are highlights. ■TIP→ Bus M29 to Waldeckpark/Oranienstrasse is the closest transportation stop. ⊠ *Alte Jakobstr. 124–128, Kreuzberg* ☎ *030/7890–2600* ⊕ *www.berlinischegalerie.de* ⌷ *€6* ☉ *Wed.–Mon. 10–6* Ⓜ *Kochstrasse (U-bahn).*

Deutsches Technikmuseum (*German Museum of Technology*). A must if you're traveling with children, this musem will enchant anyone who's interested in technology or fascinated by trains, plains, and automobiles. Set in the remains of Anhalter Bahnhof's industrial yard and enhanced with a newer, glass-enclosed wing, the museum has several floors of machinery, including an airplane room on the upper floor crowned with a "Rosinenbomber," an airplane that delivered supplies to Tempelhof Airport during the Berlin Airlift of 1948. Don't miss the train shed, a three-dimensional, walkable timeline of trains throughout history, and the historical brewery, which has a great rooftop view of today's trains, U-bahn lines U-1 and U-2, converging at the neighboring Gleisdreieck station. ✉ *Trebbiner Str. 9, Kreuzberg, Berlin* ☎ *030/902–540* 🎫 *€4.50* ⊙ *Tues.–Fri. 9–5:30, weekends 10–6* Ⓜ *Gleisdreieck (U-bahn), Anhalter Bahnhof (S-bahn).*

Jüdisches Museum Berlin (*Jewish Museum*). The history of Germany's Jews from the Middle Ages through today is chronicled here, from prominent historical figures to the evolution of laws regarding Jews' participation in civil society. A few of the exhibits document the Holocaust itself, but this museum celebrates Jewish life and history far more than it focuses on the atrocities committed during WWII. An attraction in itself is the highly conceptual building, designed by Daniel Libeskind, who will also direct the construction of a new adjacent building holding a library and temporary exhibitions. Various physical "voids" in the oddly constructed and intensely personal modern wing of the building represent the idea that some things can and should never be exhibited when it comes to the Holocaust. ■TIP➡ Reserve at least three hours for the museum and devote more time to the second floor if you're already familiar with basic aspects of Judaica, which are the focus of the third floor. ✉ *Lindenstr. 9–14, Kreuzberg* ☎ *030/2599–3300* ⊕ *www.jmberlin.de* 🎫 *€5* ⊙ *Mon. 10–10, Tues.–Sun. 10–8* Ⓜ *Hallesches Tor (U-bahn).*

Martin-Gropius-Bau. This magnificent palazzo-like exhibition hall dates back to 1877, and once housed Berlin's Arts and Crafts Museum. Its architect, Martin Gropius, was the great-uncle of Walter Gropius, the Bauhaus architect who also worked in Berlin. The international, changing exhibits on art and culture have recently included Aztec sculptures, Henri Cartier-Bresson's photographs, and an expansive Frida Kahlo retrospective. ✉ *Niederkirchnerstr. 7, Kreuzberg* ☎ *030/254–860* ⊕ *www. gropiusbau.de* 🎫 *Varies with exhibit* ⊙ *Wed.–Mon. 10–8* Ⓜ *Kochstrasse (U-bahn), Potsdamer Platz (U-bahn and S-bahn).*

Topographie des Terrors (*Topography of Terror*). Before 2010, Topographie des Terrors was an open-air exhibit, fully exposed to the elements. Now, in a stunning new indoor exhibition center at the same location, you can view photos and documents explaining the secret state police and intelligence organizations that planned and executed Nazi crimes against humanity. The fates of both victims and perpatrators are given equal attention here. Free audio guides for the exhibit are available. The cellar remains of the Nazis' Reich Security Main Office (which was composed of the SS, SD, and Gestapo) where the main exhibit used to be, are still open to the public, and now contain a new exhibit: Berlin from 1933 to 1945. ✉ *Niederkirchnerstr. 8, Kreuzberg* ☎ *030/2545–0950* ⊕ *www.topographie.de* 🎫 *Free* ⊙ *Daily 10–8.*

15

CLOSE UP

Up-and-Coming Berlin

Berlin may be relatively cheap by international standards but that doesn't keep rents—especially in the center—from rising. As a consequence, neighborhoods that were once considered fringe have now moved to the forefront of young Berlin's consciousness, discovered as they often are first by (mainly Turkish) immigrants, next by artists, then by entrepreneurs, and finally by wealthier professionals who have the money to transform them, for better or worse.

Two former West Berlin neighborhoods fighting for their identities while on the cusp of gentrification are Neukölln, just southeast of Kreuzberg below the Landwehrkanal, and Wedding, north of Mitte-Tiergarten and west of Prenzlauer Berg. While these areas don't boast a wealth of tourist attractions, a leisurely walk through them turns up enough shops, cafés, parks, and local eateries to make visiting well worthwhile.

The Wedding Amtsgericht (local courthouse ⊠ Brunnenplatz ☎ 1030/901–560) is an imposing structure resembling a gothic castle that glows green at night, but during the day is the center point of a charming neighborhood full of newly renovated buildings and artist's ateliers that push up against a small canal just to the north. Leopoldplatz is the spiritual and commercial heart of Wedding, anchored by the complementary churches Neue Nazareth Kirche (⊠ Neue Nazareth-strasse 51 ☎ 0177/270–4385) and Alte Nazareth Kirche (designed by Schinkel) (Leopoldplatz), and bordered on one side by the main commercial street Müllerstrasse.

In Neukölln, the charming Rixdorf centers on Richardplatz, a perfectly-preserved example of an Old Berlin village within the big city, which hosts what many consider to be the city's best Christmas market on the first weekend in December. The beautifully kept and colorful Körnerpark is a welcome respite from such a bustling part of town and the refurbished Neuköllner Oper (opera house ⊠ Karl-Marx-Str. 131 ☎ 030/688–9070) is making its mark once again with alternative and surprising performances of long-forgotten operas as well as humorous musical productions.

MITTE: UNTER DEN LINDEN TO ALEXANDERPLATZ

The Mitte (Middle) district is where Berlin first began as two fishing villages separated by the Spree River. Throughout its 772-year-plus history it has served as a seat of government for Prussian kings, German emperors, the Weimar Republic, Hitler's Third Reich, the communist German Democratic Republic, and, since 1999, reunited Germany. Treasures once split between East and West Berlin museums are also reunited on Museum Island, a UNESCO World Heritage Site.

The historic boulevard Unter den Linden proudly rolls out Prussian architecture and world-class museums. Its major cross street is Friedrichstrasse, which was revitalized in the mid-1990s with car showrooms (including Bentley, Bugatti, and Volkswagen) and upscale malls. At its eastern end, Unter den Linden turns into Karl-Liebknecht-Strasse, which leads to vast Alexanderplatz, where eastern Berlin's handful of skyscrapers are dwarfed beneath the city's most visible landmark, the Berlin TV tower.

TIMING

If you don't look closely at any museums or highlights, you could ramble this route in two hours. To speed your way down Unter den Linden, you can hop one of the three bus lines that make stops between Wilhelmstrasse and Alexanderplatz. A few state museums in this area are closed Monday.

TOP ATTRACTIONS

Bebelplatz. After he became ruler in 1740, Frederick the Great personally planned the buildings surrounding this square (which has a huge parking garage cleverly hidden beneath the pavement). The area received the nickname "*Forum Fridericianum,*" or Frederick's Forum. On May 10, 1933, Joseph Goebbels, the Nazi minister for propaganda and "public enlightenment," organized one of the nationwide book-burnings here. The books, thrown on a pyre by Nazi officials and students, included works by Jews, pacifists, and Communists. In the center of Bebelplatz, a modern and subtle memorial (built underground but viewable through a window in the cobblestone) marks where 20,000 books went up in flames.

Staatsoper Unter den Linden (*State Opera*). A music lover, Frederick the Great had the Staatsoper Unter den Linden as his first priority. Berlin's lavish opera house was completed in 1743 by the same architect who built Sanssouci in Potsdam, Georg Wenzeslaus von Knobelsdorff. The house is currently undergoing a complete makeover, set to be completed in 2013, when the historic interior will be replaced with a modern design. The show goes on at the Schiller Theater across town, where maestro Daniel Barenboim continues to oversee a diverse repertoire. ⊠ *Unter den Linden 7, Mitte* ☎ *030/2035–4555* ⊕ *www. staatsoper-berlin.de* ☉ *Box office Mon.–Sat. 10–8, Sun. 12–8* Ⓜ *Französische Strasse (U-bahn).*

St. Hedwigskathedrale (*St. Hedwig's Cathedral*). The green-patina dome belongs to St. Hedwigskathedrale. Begun in 1747, it was modeled after the Pantheon in Rome, and was the first Catholic church built in resolutely Protestant Berlin since the 16th-century Reformation. It was Frederick the Great's effort to appease Prussia's Catholic population after his invasion of Catholic Silesia (then Poland). A treasury lies inside. ⊠ *Bebelpl., Mitte* ☎ *030/203–4810* ⊕ *www.hedwigs-kathedrale.de* ☉ *Weekdays 10–5, Sun. 1–5* Ⓜ *Französische Strasse (U-bahn)* ☞ *Tours (€1.50) available in English; call ahead.*

Humboldt-Universität. Running the length of the west side of Bebelplatz, the former royal library is now part of Humboldt-Universität, whose main campus is across the street on Unter den Linden. The university building was built between 1748 and 1766 as a palace for Prince Heinrich, the brother of Frederick the Great. With its founding in 1810, the university moved in. The fairy-tale-collecting Grimm brothers taught here, and political philosophers Karl Marx and Friedrich Engels studied within its hallowed halls. Albert Einstein taught physics from 1914 to 1929, when he left Berlin for the United States. ⊠ *Unter den Linden 6, Mitte.*

15

Opernpalais. The Opernpalais, next to the opera house and within the former Crown Princesses' Palace, is home to a café famous for its enormous selection of cakes and pies, plus other sweet treats. ⊠ *Unter den Linden 5, Mitte* ☎ *030/202–683* ⊕ *www.opernpalais.de.*

Berliner Dom (*Berlin Cathedral*). A church has stood here since 1536, but this enormous version dates from 1905, making it the largest 20th-century Protestant church in Germany. The royal Hohenzollerns worshipped here until 1918, when Kaiser Wilhelm II abdicated and left Berlin for Holland. The massive dome wasn't restored from World War II damage until 1982; the interior was completed in 1993. The climb to the dome's outer balcony is made easier by a wide stairwell, plenty of landings with historic photos and models, and even a couple of chairs. The 94 sarcophagi of Prussian royals in the crypt are significant, but to less-trained eyes can seem uniformly dull. All morning services include communion. ⊠ *Am Lustgarten 1, Mitte* ☎ *030/2026–9136* ⊕ *www.berlinerdom.de* ⊠ *€8 with audio guide, €5 without* ◔ *Mon.–Sat. 9–8, Sun. noon–8* Ⓜ *Hackescher Markt (S-bahn).*

♺ **Berliner Fernsehturm** (*Berlin TV Tower*). Finding Alexanderplatz is no problem: just head toward the 1,207-foot-high tower piercing the sky. Built in 1969 as a signal to the West (clearly visible over the Wall, no less) that the East German economy was thriving, it is deliberately higher than both western Berlin's broadcasting tower and the Eiffel Tower in Paris. You can get the best view of Berlin from within the tower's disco ball–like observation level; on a clear day you can see for 40 km (25 mi). One floor above, the city's highest restaurant rotates for your panoramic pleasure. ■ TIP→ During the summer season, order VIP tickets online to avoid a long wait. ⊠ *Panoramastr. 1a, Mitte* ☎ *030/247–5750* ⊕ *www.tr-turm.de* ⊠ *€10.50* ◔ *Nov.–Feb., daily 10 am–midnight; Mar.–Oct., daily 9 am–midnight; last admission ½ hr before closing* Ⓜ *Alexanderplatz (U-bahn and S-bahn).*

Deutsches Historisches Museum (*German History Museum*). The museum is composed of two buildings. The magnificent pink, baroque Prussian arsenal (Zeughaus) was constructed between 1695 and 1730, and is the oldest building on Unter den Linden. It also houses a theater, the Zeughaus Kino, which regularly presents a variety of films, both German and international, historic and modern. The new permanent exhibits, reopened after much debate in mid-2006, offer a modern and fascinating view of German history since the early Middle Ages. Behind the arsenal, the granite-and-glass Pei-Bau building by I. M. Pei holds often stunning and politically controversial changing exhibits, such as 2010's unprecedented blockbuster "Hitler und die Deutschen" ("Hitler and the Germans"), which explored the methods of propaganda used by Hitler and the Nazis to gain power. ⊠ *Unter den Linden 2, Mitte* ☎ *030/203–040* ⊕ *www.dhm.de* ⊠ *€5* ◔ *Daily 10–6.*

Friedrichstrasse. The once-bustling street of cafés and theaters of prewar Berlin has risen from the rubble of war and Communist neglect to reclaim the crowds with shopping emporiums.

Heading south from the Friedrichstrasse train station, you'll pass hotels and various stores (including the sprawling, comprehensive bookstore

Berliner Dom (Berlin's Cathedral) is one of the city's most impressive buildings, and a popular gathering spot in nice weather.

Dussmann and its large but cozy new English-language bookshop around the corner).

Galeries Lafayette. Standing at the corner of Französische Strasse (meaning "French Street" for the nearby French Huguenot cathedral) is the French department store Galeries Lafayette. French architect Jean Nouvel included an impressive steel-and-glass funnel at its center, which is surrounded by four floors of expensive clothing and luxuries as well as an excellent food department with counters offering French cuisine, and a market with some of the best produce in the area. ⊠ *Friedrichstr. 76–78* ☎ *030/209–480.*

Friedrichstadtpalast. The ugly Friedrichstadtpalast, Europe's largest variety theater, may be just a poor modern copy of its former glamorous past, but increasingly manages to stage spiced-up Las Vegas–style shows (despite dire finances). ⊠ *Friedrichstr. 107, Mitte* ☎ *030/2326–2326* ⊕ *www.friedrichstadtpalast.de.*

Admiralspalast. The meticulously restored Admiralspalast is the successful rebirth of a glittering Jazz Age entertainment temple. Reopened with a hotly debated production of Brecht's *Threepenny Opera*, it now houses two stages, a club, and an upscale but generic Italian restaurant. ⊠ *Friedrichstr. 101* ☎ *030/4799–7499.*

Gendarmenmarkt. This is without a doubt the most elegant square in former East Berlin. Anchored by the beautifully reconstructed 1818 **Konzerthaus** and the **Deutscher Dom** and **Französischer Dom** (German and French cathedrals) and lined with some of the city's best restaurants, it also hosts one of Berlin's classiest annual Christmas markets.

Hugenottenmuseum. The Französischer Dom, built by Kaiser Friedrich II for the Protestant Huguenots who fled France and settled in Berlin, contains the Hugenottenmuseum, with exhibits charting their history and art. The Huguenots were expelled from France at the end of the 17th century by King Louis XIV. Their energy and commercial expertise contributed much to Berlin. ⊠ *Gendarmenmarkt 5, Mitte* ☎ *030/229–1760* ✆ *€2* ☻ *Tues.–Sun. noon–5.*

Deutscher Dom. The Deutscher Dom holds an extensive exhibition on the emergence of the democratic parliamentary system in Germany since the late 1800s. The free museum is sponsored by the German parliament. Leadership and opposition in East Germany are also documented. ■ TIP➔ **An English-language audio guide covers a portion of the exhibits on the first three floors.** Floors four and five have temporary exhibitions with no English text or audio. ⊠ *Gendarmenmarkt 1, Mitte* ☎ *030/2273–0431* ✆ *Free* ☻ *Oct.–Apr., Tues.–Sun. 10–6; May–Sept., Tues.–Sun. 10–7.*

Fodor'sChoice ★ **Museumsinsel** (*Museum Island*). On the site of one of Berlin's two original settlements, this unique complex of four state museums, a UNESCO World Heritage Site, is an absolute must.

The **Alte Nationalgalerie** (Old National Gallery, entrance on Bodestrasse) houses an outstanding collection of 18th-, 19th-, and early-20th-century paintings and sculptures. Works by Cézanne, Rodin, Degas, and one of Germany's most famous portrait artists, Max Liebermann, are part of the permanent exhibition. Its Galerie der Romantik (Gallery of Romanticism) collection has masterpieces from such 19th-century German painters as Karl Friedrich Schinkel and Caspar David Friedrich, the leading members of the German Romantic school. The **Altes Museum** (Old Museum), a red-marble, neoclassical building abutting the green Lustgarten, was Prussia's first building purpose-built to serve as a museum. Designed by Karl Friedrich Schinkel, it was completed in 1830. The permanent collection of the Altes Museum consists of everyday utensils from ancient Greece as well as vases and sculptures from the 6th to 4th century BC. Etruscan art is its highlight, and there are a few examples of Roman art. Antique sculptures, clay figurines, and bronze art of the Antikensammlung (Antiquities Collection) are also housed here; the other part of the collection is in the Pergamonmuseum. At the northern tip of Museum Island is the **Bode-Museum,** a somber-looking gray edifice graced with elegant columns. The museum presents the state museums' stunning collection of German and Italian sculptures since the Middle Ages, the Museum of Byzantine Art, and a huge coin collection. Museum Island's new shining star, however, is the **Neues Museum** (New Museum), which reopened in 2009. Originally designed by Friedrich August Stüler in 1843–55, the building was badly damaged in World War II and only now has been elaborately redeveloped by British star architect David Chipperfield, who has been overseeing the complete restoration of Museum Island. Instead of completely restoring the Neues Museum, the architect decided to integrate modern elements into the historic landmark, while leaving many of its heavily bombed and dilapidated areas untouched. The result is a stunning experience. Home to the Egyptian Museum, including the famous bust of Nefertiti (who, after some 70 years, has returned to her first museum location in Berlin), it also features the Papyrus Collection and the Museum of Prehistory and Early History. Even if you think you aren't interested in the ancient world, make an exception for the **Pergamonmuseum** (entrance on Am Kupfergraben). The museum's name is derived from its principal display, the Pergamon Altar, a monumental Greek temple discovered in what is now Turkey and dating from 180 BC. The altar was shipped to Berlin in the late 19th century. Equally impressive are the gateway to the Roman town of Miletus and the Babylonian processional way. If you get tired of antiques and paintings, drop by any of the museums' cafés. ✉ *Entrance to Museumsinsel: Am Kupfergraben, Mitte* ☎ *030/2664–24242* ⊕ *www.smb.museum* ◷ *All Museum Island museums: €14* ⊘ *Pergamonmuseum: Fri.–Wed. 10–6, Thurs. 10–10. Alte Nationalgalerie: Tues., Wed., and Fri.–Sun. 10–6; Thurs. 10–10. Altes Museum: Fri-Wed. 10–6, Thurs. 10–10. Neues Museum: Sun.–Wed. 10–6, Thurs.–Sat. 10–8. Bode-Museum: Fri.–Wed. 10–6, Thurs. 10–10* Ⓜ *Hackescher Markt (S-bahn).*

Nikolaiviertel (*Nicholas Quarter*). Renovated in the 1980s and a tad concrete-heavy as a result, this tiny quarter grew up around Berlin's oldest parish church, the medieval, twin-spire **St. Nikolaikirche** (St. Nicholas's Church), now a museum, dating from 1230. The adjacent Fischerinsel (Fisherman's Island) area was the heart of Berlin 765 years ago, and retains a bit of its medieval character. At Breite Strasse you'll find two of Berlin's oldest buildings: No. 35 is the **Ribbeckhaus,** the city's only surviving Renaissance structure, dating from 1624, and No. 36 is the early baroque **Marstall,** built by Michael Matthais between 1666 and 1669. The area feels rather artificial, but draws tourists to its gift stores, cafés, and restaurants. ✉ *Church: Nikolaikirchpl., Mitte* ☎ *030/2400–2162* ⊕ *www.stadtmuseum.de* Ⓜ *Alexanderplatz (U-bahn and S-bahn).*

Unter den Linden. The name of this historic Berlin thoroughfare, between the Brandenburg Gate and Schlossplatz, means "under the linden trees," and it was indeed lined with fragrant and beloved lindens until the 1930's. Imagine Berliners' shock when Hitler decided to fell the trees in order to make the street more parade-friendly. The grand boulevard began as a riding path that the royals used to get from their palace to their hunting grounds (now the central Berlin park called Tiergarten). It is once again lined with linden trees planted after World War II.

WORTH NOTING

Alexanderplatz (*Alex*). This bleak square, bordered by the train station, the Galeria Kaufhof department store, and the 37-story Park Inn Berlin-Alexanderplatz hotel, once formed the hub of East Berlin and was originally named in 1805 for czar Alexander I. German writer Alfred Döblin dubbed it the "heart of a world metropolis" (text from his 1929 novel *Berlin Alexanderplatz* is written on a building across the northeastern side of the square). Today it's a basic center of commerce and the occasional demonstration. The unattractive modern buildings are a reminder not just of the results of Allied bombing but also of the ruthlessness practiced by East Germans when they demolished what remained. A famous meeting point in the south corner is the World Time Clock (1969), which even keeps tabs on Tijuana.

Berliner Rathaus (*Berlin Town Hall*). Nicknamed the *"Rotes Rathaus"* (Red Town Hall) for its redbrick design, the town hall was completed in 1869. Its most distinguishing features are its neo-Renaissance clock tower and frieze that depicts Berlin's history up to 1879 in 36 terra-cotta plaques, each 20 feet long. Climb the grand stairwell to view the coat-of-arms hall and a few exhibits. ■ TIP→ The Rathaus has a very inexpensive, cafeteria-style canteen offering budget lunches. The entrance is inside the inner courtyard. ⊠ *Rathausstr. 15, Mitte* ☎ *030/90260* 🖃 *Free* ⊙ *Weekdays 9–6* Ⓜ *Alexanderplatz (U-bahn and S-bahn).*

OFF THE
BEATEN
PATH

East Side Gallery. This 1-km (½-mi) stretch of concrete went from guarded border to open-air gallery within three months. East Berliners breached the Wall on November 9, 1989, and between February and June of 1990, 118 artists from around the globe created unique works of art on its longest-remaining section. Restoration in 2010 renewed the old images with a fresh coat of paint, but while the colors of the artworks now look like new, the gallery has lost a bit of its charm. One well-known work by Russian artist Dmitri Vrubel depicts Brezhnev and Honnecker (the former East German leader) kissing, with the caption "My God. Help me survive this deadly love." The stretch along the Spree Canal runs between the Warschauer Strasse S- and U-bahn station and Ostbahnhof. The redbrick Oberbaumbrücke (an 1896 bridge) at Warschauer Strasse makes that end more scenic. Just past the bridge there's also a man-made beach with a bar, restaurant, and club popular with the after-work crowd, called Strandgut (⊕ *www.strandgut-berlin. com*). ⊠ *Mühlenstr., Friedrichshain* Ⓜ *Warschauer Strasse (U-bahn and S-bahn), Ostbahnhof (S-bahn).*

Märkisches Museum (*Brandenburg Museum*). This redbrick attic includes exhibits on the city's theatrical past, its guilds, its newspapers, and the March 1848 revolution. Paintings capture the look of the city before it crumbled in World War II. ■ TIP→ The fascinating collection of mechanical musical instruments is demonstrated on Sunday at 3 pm. ⊠ *Am Köllnischen Park 5, Mitte* ☎ *030/2400–2162* ⊕ *www.stadtmuseum.de* 🖃 *€5* ⊙ *Tues., Thurs.–Sun. 10–6; Wed. noon–8* Ⓜ *Märkisches Museum (U-bahn).*

Neue Wache (*New Guardhouse*). One of many Berlin projects by the early-19th-century architect Karl Friedrich Schinkel, this building served as both the Royal Prussian War Memorial (honoring the dead of the Napoleonic Wars) and the royal guardhouse until the kaiser abdicated in 1918. In 1931 it became a memorial to those who fell in World War I. Badly damaged in World War II, it was restored in 1960 by the East German state and rededicated as a memorial for the victims of militarism and fascism. After unification it regained its Weimar Republic appearance and was inaugurated as Germany's central war memorial. Inside is a copy of Berlin sculptor Käthe Kollwitz's *Pietà*, showing a mother mourning over her dead son. The inscription in front of it reads, "to the victims of war and tyranny." ⊠ *Unter den Linden, Mitte* ⊙ *Daily 10–6.*

MITTE'S SCHEUNENVIERTEL AND PRENZLAUER BERG

The hip scene of Mitte, the historic core of Berlin, is best experienced in the narrow streets and courtyard mazes of the Scheunenviertel (Barn Quarter), which also encompasses the former Spandauer Vorstadt (Jewish Quarter), the streets around Oranienburger Strasse. Some streets are lined with edgy shops, bars, and eateries, while others look empty and forlorn. During the second half of the 17th century, artisans, small-business men, and Jews moved into this area at the encouragement of the Great Elector, who sought to improve his financial situation through their skills. As industrialization intensified, the quarter became poorer, and in the 1880s many East European Jews escaping pogroms settled here.

Northeast of Mitte, the old working-class district of Prenzlauer Berg used to be one of the poorest sections of Berlin. In socialist East Germany, the old and mostly run-down tenement houses attracted the artistic avant-garde, who transformed the area into a refuge for alternative lifestyles (think punk singer Nina Hagen, stepdaughter of a folk singer expelled by the East German government). The renovated 19th-century buildings with balconies and stuccowork tend to feature unwanted graffiti, but Prenzlauer Berg is now a trendy area full of young couples with babies in tow.

Though not full of sightseeing attractions, the two areas are great for wandering, shopping, and eating and drinking. Mitte's Scheunenviertel is popular with tourists, and you'll find a denser concentration of locals and settled-in expats in Prenzlauer Berg.

TOP ATTRACTIONS

★ **Hackesche Höfe** (*Hacke Courtyards*). Built in 1905–07, this series of eight connected courtyards is the finest example of art nouveau industrial architecture in Berlin. Most buildings are covered with glazed white tiles, and additional Moorish mosaic designs decorate the main courtyard off Rosenthaler Strasse. Shops (including one dedicated to Berlin's beloved street-crossing signal, the "Ampelmann"), restaurants, the variety theater Chamäleon Varieté, and a movie theater populate the spaces once occupied by ballrooms, a poets' society, and a Jewish girls' club. ⊠ *Rosenthaler Str. 40–41, and Sophienstr. 6, Mitte* ☎ *030/2809–8010* ⊕ *www.hackesche-hoefe.com* Ⓜ *Hackescher Markt (S-bahn).*

QUICK BITES

Anatre Feinkost. Within the first courtyard of Hackesche Höfe, Anatre Feinkost uses top-quality ingredients for its Mediterranean sandwiches and pastas. You can also just sit with a coffee or glass of wine. ⊠ *Rosenthaler Str. 40–41, Mitte* ☎ *030/2838–9915.*

Neue Synagoge (*New Synagogue*). This meticulously restored landmark, built between 1859 and 1866, is an exotic amalgam of styles, the whole faintly Middle Eastern. Its bulbous, gilded cupola stands out in the skyline. When its doors opened, it was the largest synagogue in Europe, with 3,200 seats. The synagogue was damaged on November 9, 1938 (*Kristallnacht*—Night of the Broken Glass), when Nazi looters rampaged across Germany, burning synagogues and smashing the few Jewish shops and homes left in the country. It was destroyed by

Allied bombing in 1943, and it wasn't until the mid-1980s that the East German government restored it. The effective exhibit on the history of the building and its congregants includes fragments of the original architecture and furnishings. ■**TIP→** Sabbath services are held in a modern addition. ⊠ *Oranienburger Str. 28–30, Mitte* ☎ *030/8802–8316* ⊕ *www.zentrumjudaicum.de* ☒ *€3.50* ◷ *Apr.–Sept., Sun.–Mon. 10–8, Tues.–Thurs. 10–6, Fri. 10–5; Nov.–Feb., Sun.–Thurs. 10–6, Fri. 10–2; Mar. and Oct., Sun.–Mon. 10–8, Tues.–Thurs. 10–6, Fri. 10–2. English/Hebrew audio guides €3* Ⓜ *Oranienburger Tor (U-bahn), Oranienburger Strasse (S-bahn).*

WORTH NOTING

Gedenkstätte Berliner Mauer (*Berlin Wall Memorial Site*). This site combines memorials and a museum and research center on the Berlin Wall. The division of Berlin was particularly heart-wrenching on Bernauer Strasse, where neighbors and families on opposite sides of the street were separated overnight. The Reconciliation Chapel, completed in 2000, replaced the community church dynamited by the Communists in 1985. The church had been walled into the "death strip," and was seen as a hindrance to patrolling it. A portion of the Wall remains on Bernauer Strasse, and an installation meant to serve as a memorial unfortunately only confuses those wondering what the border once looked like. For a wealth of images and information, head into the museum, where German-speakers can even hear radio broadcasts from the time the Wall was erected. ⊠ *Bernauer Str. 111, Wedding* ☎ *030/464–1030* ⊕ *www.berliner-mauer-gedenkstaette.de* ☒ *Free, tours €3* ◷ *Apr.–Oct., Tues.–Sun. 9:30–7; Nov.–Mar., Tues.–Sun. 9:30–6* Ⓜ *Bernauer Strasse (U-bahn), Nordbahnhof (S-bahn).*

Kollwitzplatz (*Kollwitz Square*). Named for the painter, sculptor, and political activist Käthe Kollwitz (1867–1945), who lived nearby, the square is the center of the old working-class district of Prenzlauer Berg. Kollwitz, who portrayed the hard times of area residents, is immortalized here in a sculpture based on a self-portrait. Ironically, this image of the artist now has a view of the upwardly mobile young families who have transformed the neighborhood since reunification. Bars and restaurants peal off from the square, and a great organic market takes over on weekends.

Jüdischer Friedhof (*Jewish Cemetery*). More than 150,000 graves make this peaceful retreat in Berlin's Weissensee district Europe's largest Jewish cemetery. The grounds and tombstones are in excellent condition—a seeming impossibility, given its location in the heart of the Third Reich. To reach the cemetery, take the M4 tram from Hackescher Markt to Albertinenstrasse and head south on Herbert-Baum-Strasse. At the gate you can get a map from the attendant. The guidebook is in German only. ⊠ *Grosse Hamburger Str. 26–27* ☎ *030/925–3330* ◷ *Summer, Mon.–Thurs. 7:30–5, Fri. 7:30–2:30, Sun. 8–5; Winter, Mon.–Thurs. 7:30–4, Fri. 7:30–2:30, Sun. 8–4.*

Kulturbrauerei (*Culture Brewery*). The redbrick buildings of the old Schultheiss brewery are typical of late-19th-century industrial architecture. Parts of the brewery were built in 1842, and at the turn of

Part of Museumsinsel (Museum Island), the Pergamonmuseum is where you'll find a wealth of artifacts from the ancient world.

the 20th century the complex expanded to include the main brewery of Berlin's famous Schultheiss beer, then the world's largest brewery. Today, the multicinema, pubs, clubs, and a concert venue that occupy it make up an arts and entertainment nexus (sadly, without a brewery). Pick up information at the Prenzlauer Berg tourist office here, and come Christmastime, visit the market, which includes children's rides. ⊠ *Schönhauser Allee 36–39, and Knaackstr. 97, Prenzlauer Berg* ☎ *030/4431–5152* ⊕ *www.kulturbrauerei-berlin.de* Ⓜ *Eberswalder Strasse (U-bahn).*

PALACES, MUSEUMS, AND NATURE IN OUTER BERLIN

In the city's outlying areas there are palaces, lakes, and museums set in lush greenery. Central to the former West Berlin but now a western district of the united city, Charlottenburg was once an independent and wealthy city, which became part of Berlin only in 1920. Here, the baroque Charlottenburg Palace and, across the street, a collection of Picassos in the Museum Berggruen can be found. The southwest part of Berlin holds the vast Grunewald (green forest), which borders the Havel River and Lake Wannsee. In good weather Berliners come out in force, swimming, sailing their boats, tramping through the woods, and riding horseback. A starting point for cruises plying the water is opposite the Wannsee stop on the S-bahn. The Wannsee Station is also the transfer point for buses to the Wannsee beach to the north; Bus 216 to Pfaueninsel (Peacock Island); and Bus 114 to the lakeside villa where the Holocaust was first planned. From Wannsee, Potsdam, the city of summer palaces, is just another three stops on the S-bahn.

CLOSE UP

Jewish Berlin Today

As the city continues to grapple with the past, important steps toward celebrating Jewish history and welcoming a new generation of Jews to Berlin are in the making.

Somber monuments have been built in memory of victims of the Holocaust and National Socialism. An especially poignant but soft-spoken tribute is the collection of **Stolpersteine** (stumbling blocks) found all over Berlin, imbedded into sidewalks in front of the Pre-Holocaust homes of Berlin Jews, commemorating former residents simply with names and dates. German artist Gunter Demnig has personally installed these tiny memorials in big cities and small towns across Germany and Austria.

The **Ronald S. Lauder Foundation** has gone a step further. Along with **Lauder Yeshurun**, Berlin's Jewish communities have been further strengthened by building housing for Jews in the city center, founding a Yeshiva, a Rabbinical school, and offering special services for returning Jews.

It's difficult to say how many Jews live in Berlin today, but an official estimate puts the number at 22,000–27,000. About 12,000 members of the Jewish community are practicing Jews, mostly from the former Soviet Union, who belong to one of several synagogues, in addition to about 10,000–15,000 Israeli Jews. These numbers don't include the secular and religious Jews who wish to remain anonymous in the German capital.

The government supports Jewish businesses and organizations with funding, keeps close ties with important members of the community, and, perhaps most visibly, provides 24-hour police protection in front of any Jewish establishment that requests it. Two recent events proved that Jewish Berlin is thriving once again. On November 4, 2010, three young rabbis were ordained at the Pestalozzi Strasse synagogue, the first ceremony of its kind to occur in Berlin since before the Holocaust. Also in 2010, Charlotte Knobloch, a Holocaust survivor and the president of the German Jewish Council, showed the ultimate faith in Germany's recovery and reparation efforts by declaring the country "once again a homeland for Jews."

TOP ATTRACTIONS

Bildungs- und Gedenkstätte Haus der Wannsee-Konferenz (*Wannsee Conference Memorial Site*). The lovely lakeside setting of this Berlin villa belies the unimaginable Holocaust atrocities planned here. This elegant edifice hosted the fateful conference held on January 20, 1942, at which Nazi leaders and German bureaucrats, under SS leader Reinhard Heydrich, planned the systematic deportation and mass extinction of Europe's Jewish population. Today this so-called *Endlösung der Judenfrage* ("final solution of the Jewish question") is illustrated with a chilling exhibition that documents the conference and, more extensively, the escalation of persecution against Jews and the Holocaust itself. A reference library offers source materials in English. ■TIP→ Allow at least two hours for a visit. ⊠ *Am Grossen Wannsee 56–58, from the Wannsee S-bahn station, take Bus 114, Zehlendorf* ☎ *030/805–0010* ⊕ *www.ghwk.de* 🔁 *Free, tour €2* ⊙ *Daily 10–6; library weekdays 10–6* Ⓜ *Wannsee (S-bahn).*

★ **Museum Berggruen.** This small modern-art museum holds works by Matisse, Klee, Giacometti, and Picasso, who is particularly well represented with more than 100 works. Heinz Berggruen (1914–2007), a businessman who left Berlin in the 1930s, collected the excellent paintings. He narrates portions of the free audio guide, sharing anecdotes about how he came to acquire pieces directly from the artists, as well as his opinions of the women portrayed in Picasso's portraits. ⊠ *Schlossstr. 1, Charlottenburg* 🕾 *030/3269–5815* ⊕ *www.smb.museum* 🎫 *€8* ☉ *Tues.–Sun. 10–6* Ⓜ *Sophie-Charlotte-Platz (U-bahn), Richard-Wagner-Platz (U-bahn).*

★ **Gedenkstätte und Museum Sachsenhausen** (*Sachsenhausen Memorial and Museum*). This concentration camp near the Third Reich capital was established in 1936, where 200,000 prisoners from every nation in Europe, including British officers, Joseph Stalin's son, and 12,000 Soviet prisoners of war were held, and it's estimated that 50,000 died here.

Between 1945 and 1950 the Soviets used the site as a prison, and malnutrition and disease claimed the lives of 20% of the inmates. The East German government made the site a concentration camp memorial in April 1961. A few original facilities remain; the barracks, which has exhibits, are reconstructions.

To reach Sachsenhausen, take the S-bahn 1 to Oranienburg, the last stop. The ride from the Friedrichstrasse Station will take 50 minutes. Alternatively, take the Regional 5 train, direction north, from one of Berlin's main stations. From the Oranienburg Station it's a 25-minute walk (follow signs), or you can take a taxi or Bus 804 (a 7-minute ride, but with infrequent service) in the direction of Malz. ■TIP➔ An ABC zone ticket will suffice for any type of train travel and bus transfer. Allow three hours at the memorial, whose exhibits and sites are spread apart. Oranienburg is 35 km (22 mi) north of Berlin. ⊠ *Str. der Nationen 22, Oranienburg* 🕾 *03301/200–200* ⊕ *www.stiftung-bg.de* 🎫 *Free, audio guide €3* ☉ *Mid-Mar.–mid-Oct., Tues.–Sun. 8:30–6; mid-Oct.–mid-Mar., Tues.–Sun. 8:30–4:30; last admission ½ hr before closing* Ⓜ *Oranienburg (S-bahn).*

Schloss Charlottenburg (*Charlottenburg Palace*). A grand reminder of imperial days, this showplace served as a city residence for the Prussian rulers. The gorgeous palace started as a modest royal summer residence in 1695, built on the orders of King Friedrich I for his wife, Sophie-Charlotte. In the 18th century Frederick the Great made a number of additions, such as the dome and several wings designed in the rococo style. By 1790 the complex had evolved into a massive royal domain that could take a whole day to explore. Behind heavy iron gates, the Court of Honor—the front courtyard—is dominated by a baroque statue of the Great Elector on horseback.

Altes Schloss (*Old Palace*). The Altes Schloss is the main building of the Schloss Charlottenburg complex, with the ground-floor suites of Friedrich I and Sophie-Charlotte. Paintings include royal portraits by Antoine Pesne, a noted court painter of the 18th century. A guided tour visits the Oak Gallery, the early-18th-century palace chapel, and the suites of Friedrich Wilhelm II and Friedrich Wilhelm III, furnished

15

in the Biedermeier style. Tours leave every hour on the hour from 9 to 5. The upper floor has the apartments of Friedrich Wilhelm IV, a silver treasury, and Berlin and Meissen porcelain and can be seen on its own ☎ *030/320–910* 🎫 *€12 with tour* ⊘ *Apr.–Oct., Tues.–Sun. 10–6; Nov.– Mar., Tues.–Sun. 10–5* Ⓜ *Richard-Wagner-Platz (U-bahn).*

Neuer Flügel (*New Wing*). The Neuer Flügel, where Frederick the Great once lived, was designed by Knobbelsdorff, who also built Sanssouci. The 138-foot-long Goldene Galerie (Golden Gallery) was the palace's ballroom. West of the staircase are Frederick's rooms, in which parts of his extravagant collection of works by Watteau, Chardin, and Pesne are displayed. An audio guide is included in the admission ☎ *030/320–910* 🎫 *€6* ⊘ *Nov.–Mar., Wed.–Mon. 10–5; Apr.–Oct., Wed.–Mon. 10–6.*

Schlosspark Charlottenburg. The park behind the Charlottenburg palace was laid out in the French baroque style beginning in 1697, and was transformed into an English garden in the early 19th century. In it stand the Neuer Pavillon by Karl Friedrich Schinkel and Carl Langhan's Belvedere Pavillon, which overlooks the lake and the Spree River and holds a collection of Berlin porcelain. ☎ *030/320–910* ⊕ *www.spsg. de* 🎫 *€3* ⊘ *Park open daily, Belvedere Apr.–Oct., Tues.–Sun. 10–6; Nov.–Mar. Weekends 10–5.* ✉ *Spandauer Damm 20–24, Charlottenburg* ☎ *030/320–911* ⊕ *www.spsg.de* 🎫 *A Tageskarte (day card) for €15 covers admission for all bldgs., excluding tour of Altes Schloss baroque apartments* Ⓜ *Richard-Wagner-Platz (U-bahn).*

WHERE TO EAT

Neighborhood stalwarts serve residents from morning to night with a mix of German and international cuisine. Berlin is known for curt or slow service, except at high-end restaurants. Note that many of the top restaurants are closed Sunday.

The most common food for meals on the go are *Wursts* (sausages). *Currywurst*, a pork sausage served with a mildly curried ketchup, is local to Berlin. Even more popular are Turkish *Döner* shops that sell pressed lamb or chicken in flat-bread pockets with a variety of sauces and salads.

Top-end restaurants can easily import fresh ingredients from other European countries, but some rely on farmers close to home. Surrounding the city is the rural state of Brandenburg, whose name often comes before *Ente* (duck) on a menu. In spring, *Spargel*, white asparagus from Beelitz, is all the rage, showing up in soups and side dishes. Berlin's most traditional four-part meal is *Eisbein* (pork knuckle), always served with sauerkraut, pureed peas, and boiled potatoes. Other old-fashioned Berlin dishes include *Rouladen* (rolled stuffed beef), *Spanferkel* (suckling pig), *Berliner Schüsselsülze* (potted meat in aspic), and *Hackepeter* (ground beef). Stands near subway stations sell spicy *Currywurst*, a chubby frankfurter served with tomato sauce made with curry and pepper. Turkish food is an integral part of the Berlin diet. On almost every street you'll find narrow storefronts selling *Döner* (grilled lamb or chicken served with salad in a flat-bread pocket).

Use the coordinates (✛ B3) at the end of each listing to locate a site on the corresponding map.

WHAT IT COSTS IN EUROS					
	¢	$	$$	$$$	$$$$
AT DINNER	under €9	€9–€15	€16–€20	€21–€25	over €25

Restaurant prices are per person for a main course at dinner.

CHARLOTTENBURG AND WESTERN DOWNTOWN

$$
ITALIAN

✕ **Adnan.** For the past three decades, Turkish owner, Adnan, has been an incredibly successful fixture in Berlin's restaurant scene, always a gracious host schmoozing with the rich and beautiful. His Italian restaurant serves tasty, thin-crust pizzas, traditional pasta, light seafood, and saucy meat creations. There can sometimes be a long wait for a table, so making a reservation would be wise, particularly in summer, if you want a coveted outside table. ⊠ *Schlüterstr. 33, Charlottenburg* ☎ *030/5471–0590* ⌂ *Jacket required* ⊘ *Closed Sun.* Ⓜ *Kurfürstendamm (U-bahn)* ✛ *1:C3.*

$$
AUSTRIAN
Fodor's Choice
★

✕ **Café Einstein Stammhaus.** The Einstein is a Berlin landmark and a leading coffeehouse in town. Set in the historic grand villa of silent movie star Henny Porten, it charmingly recalls the elegant days of the Austrian-Hungarian empire, complete with slightly snobbish waiters gliding across squeaking parquet floors. The Einstein's very own roasting facility produces some of Germany's best coffee, and the cakes are fabulous, particularly the fresh strawberry cake best enjoyed in the shady garden behind the villa in summer. The café also excels in preparing solid Austrian fare such as schnitzel or goulash for an artsy, highbrow clientele. ⊠ *Kurfürstenstr. 58, Schoeneberg* ☎ *030/2639–1918* ⊕ *www.cafeeinstein.com* Ⓜ *Kurfürstenstrasse (U-bahn)* ✛ *1:C5.*

$
ITALIAN

✕ **Casa Italiana.** An unassuming small spot off Ku'damm, this is one of western downtown's best-kept secrets. Run by three brothers from Macedonia, Casa is a popular neighborhood joint with an affordable lunch menu, serving exceptional food, primarily homemade pasta, fresh fish and seafood, as well as homemade classic desserts. While dishes are not overly imaginative, the quality of produce and the careful preparation, along with the extensive wine list, make this one of Berlin's top Italian restaurants. In summer, make sure to reserve an outside table under the leafy canopy. ⊠ *Damaschkestr. 17, Charlottenburg* ☎ *030/3199–7788* ☰ *No credit cards* ⊘ *Closed Sun.* Ⓜ *Adenauerplatz (U-bahn)* ✛ *1:C1.*

$$
GERMAN

✕ **Engelbecken.** The beer coasters are trading cards of the Wittelsbach dynasty in this relaxed but high-quality restaurant serving dishes from Bavaria and the Alps. Classics like Wiener schnitzel and grilled saddle steak are made of "bio" meat and vegetable products, meaning that even the veal, lamb, and beef are the tasty results of organic and humane

15

BEST BETS FOR BERLIN DINING

With hundreds of restaurants to choose from, how will you decide where to eat? Fodor's writers and editors have selected their favorite restaurants by price, cuisine, and experience in the Best Bets lists below. In the first column, Fodor's Choice properties represent the "best of the best" in every price category. You can also search by neighborhood for excellent eats—just peruse our reviews on the following pages.

Fodor'sChoice★

Café Einstein Stammhaus, $$, p. 717
Facil, $$$$, p. 727
Restaurant Reinstoff, $$$$, p. 726
Weinbar Rutz, $$$$, p. 727

Best by Price

¢
Maria Bonita, p. 730
Monsieur Vuong, p. 726

$
Casa Italiana, p. 717
Hot Spot, p. 719

Kuchi, p. 719
Lubitsch, p. 720

$$
Café Einstein Stammhaus, p. 717
Engelbecken, p. 717

$$$
Francucci's, p. 719
Lutter & Wegner, p. 723

$$$$
Facil, p. 727

Best By Cuisine

GERMAN
Florian, $$, p. 719
Renger-Patzsch, $$, p. 720
Restaurant Reinstoff, $$$$, p. 726

AUSTRIAN
Lutter & Wegner, $$$, p. 723
Ottenthal, $, p. 720

ITALIAN
Francucci's, $$$, p. 719

ASIAN
Hot Spot, $, p. 719
Kuchi, $, p. 719

FRENCH
Bandol sur Mer, p. 722

Best By Experience

BUSINESS DINING
Café Einstein Stammhaus, $$, p. 717
Lubitsch, $, p. 720

CHILD-FRIENDLY
Casa Italiana, $, p. 717
Engelbecken, $$, p. 717

LATE-NIGHT DINING
Habel Weinkultur, $$, p. 723
Lubitsch, $, p. 720
Lutter & Wegner, $$$, p. 723

HIDDEN HISTORY
Bandol sur Mer, $, p. 722
Paris-Moskau, $$$, p. 726
Zur Letzten Instanz, $, p. 727

MOST ROMANTIC
Facil, $$$$, p. 727
Hartmanns, $$$$, p. 729

QUIET MEAL
Defne, $, p. 728
Ottenthal, $, p. 720

upbringing. ■ TIP➜ In warm weather, try to get a sidewalk table. With its corner position facing a park bordering Lake Lietzensee, Engelbecken is a lovely open-air dining spot. ✉ *Witzlebenstr. 31, Charlottenburg* ☎ *030/615–2810* ⊕ *www.engelbecken.de* Ⓜ *Sophie-Charlotte-Platz (U-bahn)* ✛ *1:B1.*

$$ **✕ Florian.** The handwritten menu is just one page, but there's always a
GERMAN changing variety of fish, fowl, and meat dishes in this well-established restaurant in the heart of the buzzing nightlife scene around Savigny-platz. *Steinbeisser,* a white, flaky fish, might be served with a salsa of rhubarb, chili, coriander, and ginger, or you can opt for some Franco-nian comfort cuisine such as *Kirchweihbraten* (marinated pork with baked apples and plums) or their legendary *Nürnberger Rostbratwurst* (small pork sausages) served as late-night snacks. ■ TIP➜ The kitchen is open until 1 am, and smaller dishes are available until 2 am. ✉ *Grolmanstr. 52, Western Downtown* ☎ *030/313–9184* ⊕ *www.restaurant-florian.de* ♨ *Reservations essential* ◐ *No lunch* Ⓜ *Savignyplatz (S-bahn)* ✛ *1:B3.*

$$$ **✕ Francucci's.** This upscale restaurant on the far western end of
ITALIAN Kurfürstendamm is a best-kept Italian secret in Berlin. You won't find any tourists here: the posh neighborhood's residents pack the cheerful, rustic dining room. The high-quality, straightforward cooking yields incredibly fresh salads and appetizers (the bruschetta, for example, undoubtedly has the juiciest tomatoes in town), homemade breads, and exquisite pasta recipes. More-refined Tuscan and Umbrian cre-ations might utilize wild boar, but also encompass Mediterranean fish classics such as grilled *loup de mer* or dorade. ■ TIP➜ In warm weather, reserve a sidewalk table on Ku'damm to people-watch at Francucci's and on the boulevard. ✉ *Kurfürstendamm 90, Wilmersdorf* ☎ *030/323–3318* ⊕ *www.francucci.com* Ⓜ *Adenauerplatz (U-bahn)* ✛ *1:C1.*

$ **✕ Hot Spot.** In a sea of pseudo-Asian restaurants that serve bland, taste-
CHINESE less versions of curries, noodles, and rice dishes, this place really stands out for its daring and authenticity. The menu here features recipes from the provinces of Sichuan, Jiangsu, and Shanghai, and the freshest ingre-dients are guaranteed—no MSG. The mala (spicy) dishes are a specialty, and the (mostly cold) appetizers, like the beef in chili sauce cannot be found anywhere else in Berlin. Mr. and Mrs. Wu, who own the restaurant, have a love for German wines and offer a large selection. The atmosphere is comfortable, but certainly not luxurious. In sum-mer, make a reservation for an outside table on the sidewalk for some people-watching. ✉ *Eisenzahnstr. 66, Charlottenburg* ☎ *030/8900–6878* ⊕ *www.restaurant-hotspot.de* Ⓜ *Adenauerplatz (U-bahn)* ✛ *1:C1.*

$ **✕ Kuchi.** Sushi, sashimi, yakitori, and dunburi dishes, along with some
JAPANESE Thai, Chinese, and Korean recipes are served in this groovy landmark restaurant, one of the finest sushi places in town. Chefs work with an almost religious devotion to quality and imagination (they even wear shirts saying "sushi warrior"), and the knowledgeable Asian-German staff makes you feel at home. The spicy, fresh, and healthy ingredients and the laid-back vibe pack the restaurant in the evening, so reservations are a must. There is also a Hackescher Markt location, at Gipsstrasse 3. ✉ *Kantstr. 30, Western Downtown* ☎ *030/3150–7815* ⊕ *www.kuchi.de* ♨ *Reservations essential* Ⓜ *Savignyplatz (S-bahn)* ✛ *1:C1.*

15

$ ╳ **Lubitsch.** One of the few traditional, artsy restaurants left in bohe-
GERMAN mian Charlottenburg, the Lubitsch—named after the famous Berlin film
director Ernst Lubitsch and exuding a similar air of faded elegance—
serves hearty local and light international dishes that are hard to find
these days. Reminiscent of good old home cooking, dishes like *Königs-
berger Klopse* (cooked dumplings in a creamy caper sauce) or *Kassler
Nacken mit Sauerkraut* (salted, boiled pork knuckle) are devoured
mostly by locals, who don't mind the dingy seating or good-humored,
but sometimes cheeky service. In summer the outdoor tables make for
some great people-watching on one of Berlin's most beautiful streets.
Enjoy a three-course lunch for just €10. ⊠ *Bleibtreustr. 47, Western
Downtown* ☎ *030/882–3756* ⊕ *www.restaurant-lubitsch.de* Ⓜ *Savignyplatz (S-bahn)* ✣ *1:B3.*

$ ╳ **Ottenthal.** This intimate restaurant with white tablecloths is the city
AUSTRIAN cousin of the Austrian village of Ottenthal, which delivers up the
wines, pumpkinseed oil, and organic ingredients on the menu. Curious combinations might include pike, perch with lobster sauce, and
pepper-pine-nut risotto, or venison medallions with vegetable-potato-
strudel, red cabbage, and rowanberry sauce. The huge Wiener schnitzel
extends past the plate's rim, and the pastas and strudel are homemade.
■TIP➡ Offering a good meal for your money in Berlin, Ottenthal is a particularly good choice on Sunday evening, when many of Berlin's finer restaurants are closed. It's just around the corner from both the zoo and
the Ku'damm. ⊠ *Kantstr. 153, Western Downtown* ☎ *030/313–3162*
⊕ *www.ottenthal.com* ⊘ *No lunch* Ⓜ *Zoologischer Garten (U-bahn and
S-bahn)* ✣ *1:B4.*

$$ ╳ **Renger-Patzsch.** Black and white photographs from German landscape
ECLECTIC photographer Albert Renger-Patzsch, the restaurant's namesake, deco-
rate a darkwood-paneled dining room at this Schöneberg spot. In the
less than four years since opening, Renger-Patzsch has become a beloved
local gathering place. With a changing daily menu, chef Hannes Behr-
mann focuses on top-notch ingredients, respecting the classics while
also reinventing them. Juicy bits of quail sit atop a bed of celery puree,
and lamb comes braised in red wine and oranges with crisp polenta
dumplings. The attentive and good-humored service makes this a fine
place to relax, even on the busiest nights. ⊠ *Wartburgstr. 54, Schoene-
berg, Berlin* ☎ *030/784–2059* ⌲ *Reservations essential* ⊟ *No credit
cards* ✣ *1:D5.*

¢ ╳ **Vapiano.** This immensely successful self-service Italian restaurant in
ITALIAN the Hotel Concorde building off Ku'damm is the perfect spot for a
quick bite. The airy eating area is very large, but is often crowded,
so at times it can be difficult to find a place to sit. Though it is fun to
watch the chefs prepare dishes right in front of you, this is certainly not
gourmet quality; what counts here is speed, efficiency, and prices. One
of the draws, however, is the fact that you can create your own pasta
or salad dish. ⊠ *Augsburger Str. 43, Charlottenburg* ☎ *030/8871–4195*
⊕ *www.vapiano.com* ⌲ *Reservations not accepted* Ⓜ *Kurfürstendamm
(U-bahn)* ✣ *1:C4.*

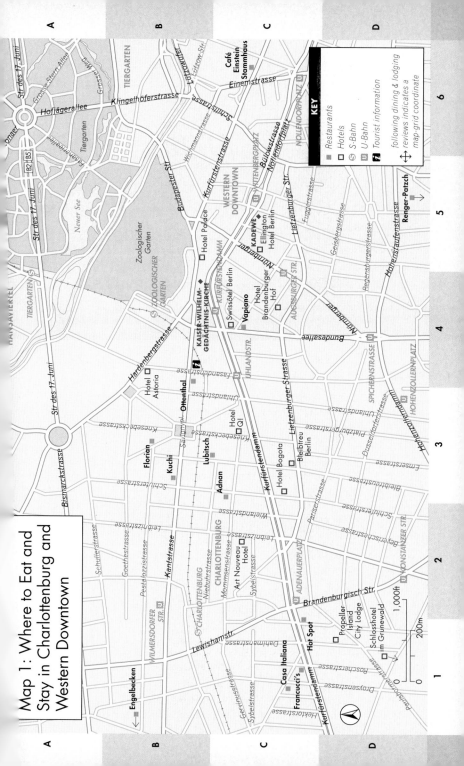

Map 1: Where to Eat and Stay in Charlottenburg and Western Downtown

KEY

- ■ Restaurants
- □ Hotels
- Ⓢ S-Bahn
- Ⓤ U-Bahn
- 𝒊 Tourist information

↔ following dining & lodging reviews indicates a map-grid coordinate

TIERGARTEN

HANSAVIERTEL

Str des 17. Juni

Grosse-Stern-Allee

Hofjägerallee

Klingelhöferstrasse

Neuer See

Zoologischer Garten

Ⓢ ZOOLOGISCHER GARTEN

Bismarckstrasse

Kaiserdamm

Kantstrasse

Schillerstrasse

Pestalozzistrasse

Goethestrasse

Leibnizstrasse

Schlüterstrasse

Knesebeckstrasse

Hardenbergstrasse

Fasanenstrasse

Uhlandstrasse

Budapester Str.

Kurfürstenstrasse

Lützowufer

Schillstrasse

Einemstrasse

Café Einstein Stammhaus

WESTERN DOWNTOWN

WITTENBERGPLATZ Ⓤ

Bülowstrasse

NOLLENDORFPLATZ Ⓤ

KAISER-WILHELM-GEDÄCHTNIS-KIRCHE ◆

KURFÜRSTENDAMM

Tauentzienstrasse

Nürnberger Str.

KADEWE

Vapiano

Ellington Hotel Berlin

Hotel Berlin

Hotel Brandenburger Hof

□ **Hotel Palace**

□ Swissôtel Berlin

𝒊

Ottenthal

□ Hotel Astoria

Florian

Kuchi

Lubitsch

Adnan

□ Hotel Q!

□ Hotel Bogota

Bleibtreu Berlin

Art Nouveau Hotel

CHARLOTTENBURG

Niebuhrstrasse

Mommsenstrasse

Sybelstrasse

Wielandstrasse

Bleibtreustrasse

Schlüterstrasse

Leibnizstrasse

Wilmersdorfer Str.

Lietzenburger Strasse

ADENAUERPLATZ Ⓤ

Brandenburgisch Str.

Hot Spot

Casa Italiana

Francucci's

Kurfürstendamm

Hektorstrasse

Gervinusstrasse

Sybelstrasse

Dahlmannstrasse

Lewishamstrasse

Droysenstrasse

Roscherstrasse

Paulsbornerstrasse

□ Propeller Island City Lodge

□ Schlosshotel im Grunewald →

Nürnberger Str.

ADALBERTSTR. Ⓤ

SPICHERNSTRASSE Ⓤ

HOHENZOLLERNPLATZ Ⓤ

KONSTANZER STR. Ⓤ

Uhlandstrasse

Düsseldorfer Strasse

Pariserstrasse

Emserstrasse

Regensburger Strasse

Geisbergstrasse

Augsburger Str.

Fuggerstrasse

Hohenstaufenstrasse

Renger-Patzch →

Hohenzollerndamm

Platzburgerstrasse

Bleibtreustrasse

Beyerischestrasse

WILMERSDORFER STR. Ⓤ

CHARLOTTENBURG Ⓢ

Savignyplatz Ⓢ

SAVIGNYPLATZ

Krummestrasse

Wichmannstrasse

TIERGARTEN Ⓢ

Str des 17. Juni

Engelbecken →

0   200m

0   1,000ft

A   B   C   D

1   2   3   4   5   6

Berliners anxiously await the first warm day of the year to sunbathe in deck chairs on the banks of the Spree River.

MITTE

¢ ✕ **Altes Europa.** By day, this is a quiet café reminiscent of the classic
GERMAN Viennese coffeehouses, shabby but trendy, with fashionable Mitte-ites
chatting in one corner while middle-aged intellectuals page through
newspapers and magazines. At night, it turns into a comfortable and
bustling neighborhood pub, just crowded enough to look like a scene,
but never too packed. Somewhere in between, Altes Europa ("old
Europe") manages to construct a daily menu of six or seven tasty dishes
like classic German *knödel* (dumplings) baked with mushrooms and
spinach or *tafelspitz* (boiled beef) with potatoes. All are inventively
prepared, described well by the attentive staff, and served in record
time. ✉ *Gipsstr. 11, Mitte, Berlin* ☎ *303/2809–3840* ▭ *No credit cards*
✛ *2:A6.*

$ ✕ **Bandol sur Mer.** This tiny, 20-seat French eatery offers French classics;
FRENCH the foie gras and entrecôte are must-haves. The restaurant has a good
wine selection, comfortable atmosphere, and friendly service. Ever since
Brad Pitt paid Bandol a visit, getting a table has gotten much more dif-
ficult. ✉ *Torstr. 167, Mitte* ☎ *030/6730–2051* ✍ *Reservations essential*
▭ *No credit cards* ۞ *Closed Sun. No lunch weekdays* Ⓜ *Rosenthaler
Platz (U-bahn)* ✛ *2:F1.*

¢ ✕ **Chén Chè.** This sister restaurant to Chi Sing is located right across the
ASIAN street but half-hidden, tucked into a courtyard behind the B-flat Jazz
Club. ✉ *Rosenthaler Str. 13, Mitte, Berlin* ☎ *030/2888–4282* ⊕ *www.
chenche-berlin.de* ▭ *No credit cards* ۞ *Open for lunch daily* ✛ *2:A6.*

¢ ✕ **Chi Sing.** This elegant Hackescher Markt area restaurant offers a new
ASIAN and refreshing take on Asian cuisine in Berlin. On the corner of Mitte's

charming Mulackstrasse, Chi Sing focuses on fresh ingredients, expert cooking methods, and an extensive exotic tea list. Although the usual suspects are all here, like fresh summer rolls and skewered meats with peanut sauce, a bit of daring when ordering will yield some true originals, like black rice balls or pickled Vietnamese eggplant. ⊠ *Rosenthaler Str. 62, Mitte, Berlin* ☎ *030/2008–9284* ⊕ *www.chising-berlin.de* ⊟ *No credit cards* ☉ *Open for lunch daily* ✛ *2:E3.*

$$
VEGETARIAN

⤫ **Cookies Cream.** With three restaurants, a club, and a bar to his name, Berlin nightlife "mogul" Cookie is a fixture on the Mitte scene. Cookies Cream, the vegetarian fine-dining establishment above the club Cookies, is his crowning achievement. The semi-underground restaurant is accessible only via a dingy alleyway between the Westin Grand Hotel and the Komische Oper next door, and its hidden entrance seems designed to deter would-be visitors. Once you're through the door, service is friendly and casual. Its young chef Stephan Hentschel has pledged never to serve pasta- or rice-based dishes (that would be too easy in a vegetarian restaurant), focusing instead on fresh produce. Whipping up thrilling concoctions with vegetables that might have seemed downright dreary on your childhood plate, such as kohlrabi turned into ravioliesque pockets with lentils, or barley as a savory pastry with asparagus and spinach jus, Hentschel converts even the most steadfast carnivores. ⊠ *Behrenstr. 55, Mitte, Berlin* ☎ *030/2749–2940* ⤳ *Reservations essential* ☉ *Tues.–Sun. from 7 pm* ✛ *2:E3.*

$$
GERMAN

⤫ **Habel Weinkultur.** Located under the arches of an S-bahn station, Habel Weinkultur seems unassuming from outside, but inside you'll find modest and faded elegance typical of Berlin. The no-nonsense waiters know the menu well, which includes local classics, like lamb, Wiener schnitzel, and weisser Spargel (asparagus). Ingredients for many of the main courses are bought locally at the weekly open-air markets. The restaurant offers small portions, a huge wine selection, and a jolly atmosphere. ⊠ *Luisenstr. 19, Mitte* ☎ *030/2809–8484* ⊕ *www.wein-habel.de* ☉ *Closed for dinner Sun.* Ⓜ *Kurfürstenstrasse (U-bahn)* ✛ *2:E3.*

$$
GERMAN

⤫ **Hackescher Hof.** This huge and yet cozy German restaurant is in the middle of the action at bustling Hackesche Höfe, and a great place to munch on internationally flavored German food while doing some fascinating people-watching. The Hackescher Hof—sporting the walking green man symbol from East Berlin's stoplights—is a mix of *Ostalgie* (nostalgia for the East), solid cooking (if available, go for the regional country dishes) and an intriguing clientele made up of tourists, intellectuals, artists, journalists, and writers, all coming together in a beautiful, wood-paneled but always smoky dining hall with some outside tables in the courtyard. The place is usually packed in the evening, so reservations are a must. ⊠ *Rosenthaler Str. 40–41, inside Hackesche Höfe, Mitte* ☎ *030/2835–293* Ⓜ *Hackescher Markt (S-bahn)* ✛ *2:A6.*

$$$
GERMAN

⤫ **Lutter & Wegner.** One of the city's oldest vintners (*Sekt*, German Champagne, was first conceived here in 1811 by actor Ludwig Devrient), Lutter & Wegner has returned to its historic location across from Gendarmenmarkt. The dark-wood-panel walls, parquet floor, and multitude of rooms take you back to 19th-century Vienna. The cuisine is mostly Austrian, with superb game dishes in winter and, of course, a Wiener

15

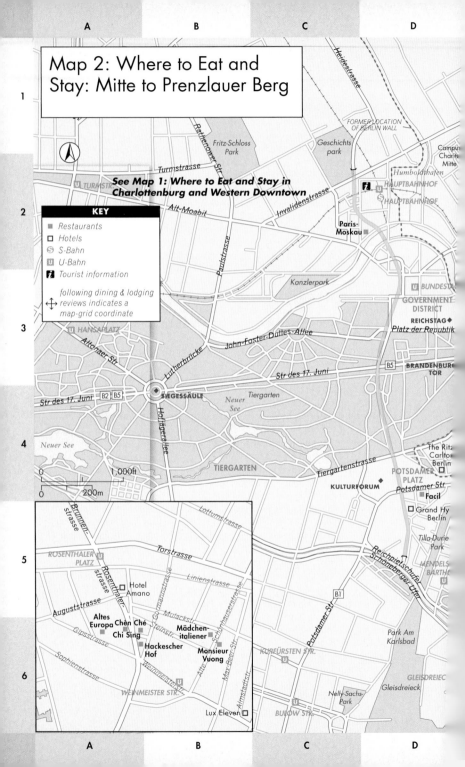

Map 2: Where to Eat and Stay: Mitte to Prenzlauer Berg

See Map 1: Where to Eat and Stay in
Charlottenburg and Western Downtown

KEY

- ■ Restaurants
- □ Hotels
- ⓢ S-Bahn
- Ⓤ U-Bahn
- 🛈 Tourist information

↔ following dining & lodging
reviews indicates a
map-grid coordinate

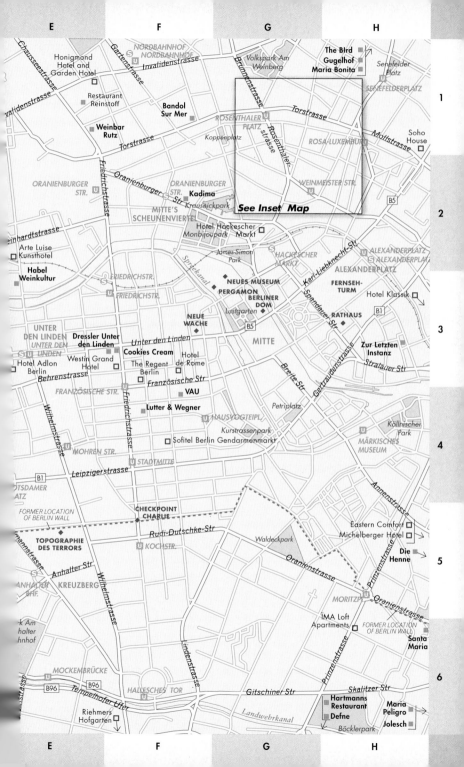

schnitzel with lukewarm potato salad. The sauerbraten (marinated pot roast) with red cabbage has been a national prizewinner. ■TIP→ **In the Weinstube, meat and cheese plates are served until 3 am.** ⊠ *Charlottenstr. 56, Mitte* ☎ *030/2029–5417* ⊕ *www.l-w-berlin.de* Ⓜ *Französische Strasse and Stadtmitte (U-bahn)* ✛ *2:F4.*

$ ✕ **Mädchenitaliener.** This cozy Mitte spot has two rooms: the bustling
ECLECTIC front room suitable for walk-ins, and a darker, more romantic back room for those who wish to linger with friends or simply brood in a corner over a glass of wine. A short but inspiring menu includes small and large antipasti plates with grilled vegetables, olives, cheeses, and meats, and unusual pasta combinations like tagliatelle with crawfish in lemon-mint sauce, or with pine nuts and balsamic-roasted figs. Chestnut-filled ravioli with pears is a favorite in winter. Make reservations on weekends. ⊠ *Alte Schönhauser Str. 12, Mitte, Berlin* ☎ *030/4004–1787* ▭ *No credit cards* ✛ *2:B6.*

¢ ✕ **Monsieur Vuong.** This hip Vietnamese eatery is a convenient place to
VIETNAMESE meet before hitting Mitte's galleries or clubs, or for slipping in just a few calories before wiggling into the wares of neighboring boutiques. Inevitably, the same steamy dishes and soups, such as *goi bo* (spicy beef salad) or *pho ga* (chicken noodle soup), land on each low table, as there are only five items and two specials on offer. But people keep coming back for their favorites, and for the teas and shakes served along with them. ⊠ *Alte Schönhauser Str. 46, Mitte* ☎ *030/9929-6924* ⊕ *www.monsieurvuong.de* ◬ *Reservations not accepted* Ⓜ *Rosenthaler Strasse (U-bahn)* ✛ *2:B6.*

$$$ ✕ **Paris-Moskau.** If you're looking to have a one-of-a-kind experience,
ECLECTIC train your sights on the barren stretch of land between Hauptbahnhof and the government quarter. Amidst a few vacant lots roped off for construction stands a single half-timbered house: the restaurant Paris-Moskau, first built more than 100 years ago as a pub and guesthouse along the Paris-Moscow railway. Today, it serves up dishes so intricately prepared they look like works of art, with refreshing flavor combinations such as ray with avocado and passion fruit, or guinea hen with beetroots and dates. In addition to the à la carte menu, the restaurant also offers an evening menu from which you can choose five to eight courses (or order à la carte). A well-edited wine list and extremely attentive service also make this restaurant a standout. ⊠ *Alt-Moabit 141, Mitte, Berlin* ☎ *030/394–2081* ⊕ *www.paris-moskau.de* ◬ *Reservations essential* ☽ *Lunch weekdays* ✛ *2:D2.*

$$$$ ✕ **Restaurant Reinstoff.** Considered a top newcomer of the past few years,
GERMAN this Michelin-starred Reinstoff is a delight to visit. The perfectly crafted
Fodor's Choice and creative haute cuisine, prepared by renowned chef Daniel Achilles,
★ focuses on traditional German recipes with a twist. The competent yet relaxed service and great atmosphere make this an enjoyable dining destination. Guests usually choose from three- to eight-course menus, carefully orchestrated to lead into each other and create an unforgettable dining experience. The varied wine selection is heavy on German and Spanish wines. ⊠ *Schlegelstr. 26c, Mitte* ☎ *030/3088–1214* ⊕ *www.reinstoff.eu* Ⓜ *Nordbahnhof (S-bahn)* ✛ *2:E1.*

$$$$ ✕ **VAU.** Trendsetter VAU defined hip in the Mitte district years ago and
GERMAN   remains a favorite even as it ages. The excellent German fish and game
dishes prepared by chef Kolja Kleeberg have earned him endless praise
and awards. Daring combinations include *Ente mit gezupftem Rot-
kohl, Quitten, und Maronen* (duck with selected red cabbage, quinces,
and sweet chestnuts) and *Steinbutt mit Kalbbries auf Rotweinscha-
lotten* (turbot with veal sweetbread on shallots in red wine). A four-
course menu costs €100; a six-course, €120. A lunch entrée is a bargain
at €18. The cool interior was designed by one of Germany's leading
industrial architects. ⊠ *Jägerstr. 54/55, Mitte* ☎ *030/202–9730* ⊕ *www.
vau-berlin.de* ⌦ *Reservations essential* ◷ *Closed Sun.* Ⓜ *Französische
Strasse (U-bahn), Stadtmitte (U-bahn)* ⊕ *2:F4.*

$$$$ ✕ **Weinbar Rutz.** The Rutz might be the most unassuming Michelin-
GERMAN   starred restaurant in the world. Its narrow facade is tucked away on a
Fodor's Choice   sleepy stretch of Chausseestrasse (the northern extension of Friedrich-
★   strasse), but its location belies its excellence. The victual creations of
chef Marco Mueller are small masterpieces. The elegant and enjoyable
ambience matches the quality of the food, with surprising combinations
like roe deer with stinging nettle puree, or monkfish with a ginger and
radish ragout. For a truly astonishing array of flavors, try the "Inspiration" tasting menus, which offer dual interpretations (labled "experiences") of luxury ingredients like goose liver or Wagyu beef. Sommelier
and owner, Billy Wagner, is there to recommend wines from a list of
more than one thousand vintages—the largest selection in all of Berlin. ⊠ *Chausseestr. 8, Mitte* ☎ *030/2462–8760* ⊕ *www.weinbar-rutz.de*
Ⓜ *Oranienburger Tor (S-bahn)* ⊕ *2:E1.*

$ ✕ **Zur Letzten Instanz.** Berlin's oldest restaurant (established in 1621)
GERMAN   lies half hidden in a forgotten nest of medieval streets. The small menu
focuses on some of Berlin's most traditional specialties, including *Eisbein* (pork knuckle), and takes its whimsical dish titles from classic
legal jargon. (The national courthouse is around the corner, and the
restaurant's name is a rought equivalent of the term "at the eleventh
hour.") The restaurant is cozy, and while the service is always friendly
it can sometimes feel a bit erratic. Napoléon is said to have sat alongside the tile stove, Mikhail Gorbachev sipped a beer here in 1989, and
Chancellor Gerhard Schröder treated French president Jacques Chirac
to a meal here in 2003. ⊠ *Waisenstr. 14–16, Mitte* ☎ *030/242–5528*
⊕ *www.zurletzteninstanz.de* ⌦ *Reservations essential* Ⓜ *Klosterstrasse
(U-bahn)* ⊕ *2:H3.*

ᵀIERGARTEN

$$$$ ✕ **Facil.** One of Germany's top restaurants, Facil is also the most afford-
ECLECTIC   able and relaxed in its class. The elegant, minimalist setting—with
Fodor's Choice   exquisite wall panels and a Giallo Reale patinato floor all set under a
★   glass roof that opens in summer—and the impeccable, personal service
highlight experiencing one of the six-course dinners. The inspiration
varies, but is now a careful combination of German classics with some
Asian inspiration. Seasonal dishes include goose liver with celery and
haselnuts, char with an elderflower emulsion sauce, or roasted regional
squab. Don't hesitate to ask sommelier Felix Voges for advice, as he

15

certainly ranks among the most knowledgeable in his art. ⊠ *Potsdamer Str. 3, at the Mandala Hotel, Tiergarten* ☎ *030/5900–51234* ⊕ *www. facil.de* ⊘ *Closed weekends* Ⓜ *Potsdamer Platz (U-bahn and S-bahn)* ✦ *2:D4.*

KREUZBERG AND PRENZLAUER BERG

$ ✕ **The Bird.** Yes it serves burgers, and yes it's run by Americans, but the

AMERICAN Bird, overlooking a corner of Mauer Park in Prenzlauer Berg, is more than just an expat burger joint. Burger spots have recenly been popping up everywhere, but Bird remains one of the best, and is practically the only place in town where the word "rare" actually means pink and juicy on the inside. Besides cheekily named burgers like the "Bronx Jon" (mushrooms and swiss cheese) and "Da Woiks" (everything, including guacamole if you ask for it), the Bird also serves up a mean steak frites suitable for two. Your best bet is to grab a seat at the bar, yell out the order, chow down, and be on your way unless you're with a large group, as the tables are packed in tight with crowds. ⊠ *Am Falkpl. 5, Prenzlauer Berg, Berlin* ☎ *030/5105–3283* ⊕ *www.thebirdinberlin.com* ⊟ *No credit cards* ⊘ *Lunch on weekends* ✦ *2:G1.*

$ ✕ **Defne.** Among the myriad of Turkish restaurants in the city, Defne

QUIET MEAL stands out for its exquisitely prepared food, friendly service, and pleasant setting. Beyond simple kebabs, the fresh and healthy menu here includes a great selection of hard-to-find fish dishes from the Bosphorus, such as *acili ahtapot* (spicy octopus served with mushrooms, olives, onions, garlic, and bell pepper in a white-wine-and-tomato sauce). Defne is near the Maybachufer, a well-visited bank of the Landwehrkanal that runs through Berlin, and its beloved Turkish market. ⊠ *Planufer 92c, Kreuzberg* ☎ *030/8179–7111* ⊕ *www.defne-restaurant.de* ⊟ *No credit cards* ⊘ *No lunch* Ⓜ *Kottbusser Tor (U-bahn)* ✦ *2:H6.*

¢ ✕ **Die Henne.** This 100-year-old Kreuzberg stalwart has survived a lot.

GERMAN After two world wars, it found itself quite literally with its back against the wall: the Berlin Wall was built right next to its front door, forcing it to close its front-yard beer garden. But Die Henne (which means "the hen") has managed to stick around thanks in part to its most fantastic dish, which is still just about all they serve: the crispy, buttermilk-coated, golden-fried half chicken. The menu is as short as one would expect, with little else aside from beers on tap, coleslaw and potato salad, and a pair of boulette (meat patties). Orders may take a while (the menu claims they need time to get the dish perfect for each customer) but once the food appears, the entire table will go silent, with murmurs of satisfaction and licking of fingers. The beer garden, reopened after 1989, is once again a lovely and lively place to sit in summer. ⊠ *Leuschnerdamm 25, Kreuzberg, Berlin* ☎ *030/614–7730* ⊿ *Reservations essential* ⊟ *No credit cards* ⊘ *Closed Mon.* ✦ *2:H5*

$ ✕ **Gugelhof.** Far from the Alsace-Lourraine region in France that inspires

ECLECTIC the hearty fare here, pop in to the busy but homey Kollwitzplatz eatery any night of the week and you'll be pleasantly surprised—and thoroughly stuffed. Classic Choucroute comes with Blutwurst (blood sausage) provided by an award-winning Berlin butcher. The raclette for two and "Pate d'Allemagne" are the best you're likely to get this side of the

Hackesche Höfe's eight connected courtyards are an always-buzzing, hip place to hang out in the city.

Rhine, and even the Tarte Flambée, a crispy crust topped with creamy cheese and grilled vegetables, manages to hold its own on a menu that is mainly meat. ⊠ *Knaackstr. 37, Kreuzberg, Berlin* ☎ *030/442–9229* ⊕ *www.gugelhof.de* ⚐ *Reservations essential* ✛ *2:G1.*

$$$$
GERMAN

✕ **Hartmanns Restaurant.** The romantic Hartmanns restaurant, named for the acclaimed young chef Stefan Hartmann, is located in the heart of Kreuzberg. The food is straightforward, with a focus on fresh produce and a subtle combination of tastes. The changing menu includes revived classic German dishes, with Mediterranean influences. Although it is possible to order à la carte, the real treat is the chef's three-to-seven course tasting menu, which can be served with or without wine pairings according to the diner's wishes. Each plate is like a work of art, and the service is impeccable and friendly. ⊠ *Fichtestr. 31, Kreuzberg* ☎ *030/6120–1003* ⊕ *www.hartmanns-restaurant.de* ⚐ *Reservations essential* ⏰ *Closed Sun.* Ⓜ *Südstern (U-bahn)* ✛ *2:H6.*

$
AUSTRIAN

✕ **Jolesch.** With a front bar area and a cozy, sage-painted dining room, Jolesch is enlivened with chattering locals and the occasional dog peeking out from under the table (pets are allowed in unexpected places in Berlin, including many restaurants). The house specialties include Viennese classics like Wiener schnitzel and apple strudel, but the surprises are in the seasonal daily menu, full of inspiring ingredients and unusual combinations like grilled octopus with saffron sorbet in spring, or a trio of duck, including silky foie gras, in fall. ■TIP➜ Come here during "Spargelzeit" in late April and May, when the entire country goes crazy for white asparagus, for a special menu devoted to the pale vegetable. ⊠ *Muskauer Str. 1, Kreuzberg, Berlin* ☎ *030/612–3581* ⊕ *www.jolesch. de* ⏰ *Open for lunch daily* ✛ *2:H6.*

Brunch the Berlin Way

Some Berliners can only be lured out of bed on a Sunday morning with the promise of a Sonntagsbrunch ("Sunday brunch") at one of the dozens of new hot spots that have cropped up. Most restaurants are pay-once, refill-the-plate-forever deals, and you can always sneak in and survey the spreads before you make your decision. Lingering for hours over a second, third, or fourth helping is encouraged.

Our top picks can be found near popular squares in less touristy neighborhoods. On warm days, patrons take over outdoor tables on Kollwitzplatz and Helmholtzplatz in Prenzlauer Berg, or around Oranienstrasse and Wrangelstrasse in Kreuzberg.

Frida Kahlo (✉ Lychener Str. 37 ☎ 030/445–7016) benefits from its prime spot at the southwest corner of Helmholtzplatz, as well as its huge selection of brunchtime goodies that just seem to keep on coming. Breakfast classics like eggs and sausage are served up alongside lunch savories such as honey-roasted chicken wings and grilled veggies, making this a perfect spot for a big group with varied tastes.

Within view (and earshot) of the elevated U1 line, **Morgenland** (✉ Skalitzer Str. 35 ☎ 030/611–3291)

devotes a whole room to its buffet, which means table space can be scarce on Sundays. Still, make reservations if you plan to show up with a group. Its Turkish-inspired dishes (an ode to the home country of many a Kreuzberg native) are the perfect alternative to more traditional brunches in town.

Pasternak (✉ Knaackstr. 22 ☎ 49030/441–3399) serves up one of the best brunches in the city, with Russian-inspired treats such as deviled eggs topped with salmon roe, blini with sour cream and dill, and pierogi. Tables are hard to come by and while at 12 Euro per person it isn't the cheapest option in town, the food is tasty and inventive. If you nab an outside table, you'll be eating within view of a Berlin oddity: a historic brick water tower that is now an apartment complex.

Restauration 1900 (✉ Husemannstr. 1 ☎ 030/442–2494) is a popular brunch spot on Kollwitzplatz, an upscale, family-friendly square busy on Sunday. (Don't miss the sprawling Saturday market here as well, with sellers offering fresh produce, cheeses, and meats.) The cozy wood-paneled interior and sumptuous spreads really do make you feel like you stumbled upon a gastronomic time capsule; a classic from old Berlin.

¢ ✕ **Maria Bonita.** This Mexican restaurant is an unassuming walk-in space
MEXICAN on Prenzlauer Berg's Danziger Strasse. The three young owners (hailing from Mexico, Texas, and Australia) came together with different ideas of what Mexican food could be, but shared one dream: to bring the authentic cuisine to a city that had survived too long on the Tex-Mex variety. Their popularity exploded overnight, and two more restaurants followed, providing a quick fix in another neighborhood as well. The food is authentic, fans will attest, and the hot sauce is satisfyingly hot in a country known for sensitive taste buds and blandly spiced dishes. But

what keeps them coming back is a welcoming sense of camaraderie: The restaurants host frequent parties (Cinco de Mayo is the most raucous, of course) and have done a lot to invite the neighborhood in. ⊠ *Danziger Str. 33, Prenzlauer Berg, Berlin* ☎ *030/2025–5338* ⊕ *www.lasmarias. de* ▭ *No credit cards* ☾ *Open for lunch daily* ⊹ *2:G1.*

¢ ✗ **Maria Peligro.** From the owners of Maria Bonita comes their second
MEXICAN restaurant, which offers more space, a full bar, and an expanded menu. It's located on Kreuzberg's Skalitzer Strasse. ⊠ *Skalitzer Str. 81, Kreuzberg, Berlin* ☎ *030/176–7012–7179* ⊕ *www.lasmarias.de* ▭ *No credit cards* ⊹ *2:H6.*

¢ ✗ **Santa Maria.** From the owners of Maria Peligro and Maria Bonita
MEXICAN comes this taco joint, located on Oranienstrasse. ⊠ *Oranienstr. 170, Kreuzberg, Berlin* ☎ *030/9221–0027* ⊕ *www.lasmarias.de* ▭ *No credit cards* ☾ *Open for lunch daily* ⊹ *2:H6.*

WHERE TO STAY

15

For expanded hotel reviews, visit Fodors.com.

Tourism is on the upswing in Berlin. Though prices in midrange to luxury hotels have increased, Berlin's first-class hotels still tend to be cheaper than their counterparts in Paris, London, or Rome. And compared to other European cities, most hotel rooms in Berlin are large, though many are part of chains that allow for less individual character.

Hotels listed here as $$$$ often come down to a $$ level on weekdays or when there is low demand. You often have the option to decline the inclusion of breakfast, which can save you anywhere from €8 to €30 per person per day.

■TIP→ The least expensive accommodations are in pensions, mostly in western districts such as Charlottenburg, Schöneberg, and Wilmersdorf. German and European travelers often use rooming agents, and Americans on a budget should consider this as well (apartments start at €350 per month). In Berlin, double rooms with shared bathrooms in private apartments begin around €33 per day.

WHAT IT COSTS IN EUROS				
	¢	$	$$	$$$	$$$$
FOR TWO PEOPLE	under €50	€50–€100	€101–€175	€176–€225	over €225

Hotel prices are for two people in a standard double room, including tax and service.

¢ ☷ **Wohn-Agentur Freiraum.** This English-speaking agency has its own guesthouse with rooms and apartments, as well as private room listings all over Berlin. ⊠ *Wiener Str. 14, Kreuzberg* ☎ *030/618–2008* ⊕ *www. frei-raum.com.*
Use the coordinate (⊹ 1:B3) at the end of each listing to locate a site on the corresponding map.

CHARLOTTENBURG

$$$ ⊡ **Art Nouveau Hotel.** The English-speaking owners' discerning taste in antiques, color combinations, and even televisions (designed by Philippe Starck) makes this B&B-like pension a great place to stay. **Pros:** stylish ambience; friendly and personal service; great B&B feeling; despite being a hotel. **Cons:** can be noisy due to heavy traffic on Leibnizstrasse; few amenities for a hotel of this price category; downtown location, yet longer walks to all major sights in the area. ⊠ *Leibnizstr. 59, Charlottenburg* ☎ *030/327–7440* ⊕ *www.hotelartnouveau.de* ⟿ *19 rooms, 3 suites* ⟡ *In-room: no a/c, Wi-Fi. In-hotel: bar* ⦿ *Breakfast* Ⓜ *Adenauerplatz (U-bahn)* ✛ *1:C2.*

$$ ⊡ **Propeller Island City Lodge.** At this wildly eccentric accommodation, you can choose from 31 Wonderlands (read the website carefully before picking which pill to pop). **Pros:** individually designed rooms; personal and friendly atmosphere; quiet location on Ku'damm side street. **Cons:** designer art rooms can be overwhelming; few amenities; slow service. ⊠ *Albrecht-Achilles-Str. 58, Charlottenburg* ☎ *030/891–9016 8 am–noon, 0163/256–5909 noon–8 pm, general info/inquiries* ⊕ *www.propeller-island.de* ⟿ *30 rooms, 26 with bath; 1 suite* ⟡ *In-room: no a/c, no TV, Wi-Fi. In-hotel: some pets allowed* Ⓜ *Adenauerplatz (U-bahn)* ✛ *1:D1.*

$$$$ ⊡ **Schlosshotel im Grunewald.** In the beautiful, verdant setting of residential Grunewald, the small but palatial hotel is full of classic style and lavish decor. **Pros:** quiet and green setting with lovely garden; large rooms in classic style; impeccable service. **Cons:** far away from any sights; sometimes stiff atmosphere; not for families. ⊠ *Brahmsstr. 10, Grunewald* ☎ *030/895–840* ⊕ *www.schlosshotelberlin.com* ⟿ *53 rooms (including 12 suites)* ⟡ *In-room: Wi-Fi. In-hotel: restaurant, bar, pool, gym, parking* Ⓜ *Grunewald (S-bahn)* ✛ *1:D1.*

WESTERN DOWNTOWN

$$$ ⊡ **Bleibtreu Berlin.** Opened in 1995, Berlin's first design hotel still feels fresh and light. **Pros:** warm, welcoming service; top location on one of Ku'damm's most beautiful side streets; international clientele. **Cons:** design somewhat dated; rooms not overly comfortable for price; few amenities. ⊠ *Bleibtreustr. 31, Western Downtown* ☎ *030/884–740* ⊕ *www.bleibtreu.com* ⟿ *60 rooms* ⟡ *In-room: no a/c, Wi-Fi. In-hotel: bar* Ⓜ *Uhlandstrasse (U-bahn)* ✛ *1:C3.*

$$
Fodor's Choice
★
⊡ **Ellington Hotel Berlin.** This new designer hotel is tucked away behind the beautiful, historic facade of a grand Bauhaus-style office building, just around the corner from KaDeWe and Kurfürstendamm. **Pros:** stylish interior design with alluring 1930s touches; perfect location off Tauentzienstrasse and great for shopping sprees; nice bar; great, green courtyard. **Cons:** very small rooms; no spa. ⊠ *Nürnberger Str. 50–55, Western Downtown* ☎ *030/683–150* ⊕ *www.ellington-hotel.com* ⟿ *285 rooms* ⟡ *In-room: Internet, Wi-Fi. In-hotel: restaurant, bar, parking* Ⓜ *Wittenbergplatz (U-bahn)* ✛ *1:C5.*

$$ ⊡ **Hotel Astoria at Kurfürstendamm.** Each simple room in this small building dating to 1898 is different, and the family owners are diligent about

BEST BETS FOR
BERLIN LODGING

Fodor's offers a selective listing of quality lodging in every price range, from the city's best budget beds to its most sophisticated luxury hotels. Here, we've compiled our top recommendations by price and experience. The best properties—those that provide a remarkable experience in their price range—are designated in the listings with the Fodor's Choice logo.

15

making renovations every year. **Pros:** some rooms are individually designed with Old World style; warm and very personal service; quiet location in central Ku'damm side street. **Cons:** furniture and rooms need update; many rooms on the smaller side; many rooms without air-conditioning. ✉ *Fasanenstr. 2, Western Downtown* 🕾 *030/312–4067* ⊕ *www.hotelastoria.de* 🛏 *31 rooms, 1 suite* ⌂ *In-room: no a/c, Wi-Fi. In-hotel: bar, laundry facilities, business center, parking, some pets allowed* Ⓜ *Uhlandstrasse (U-bahn), Zoologsicher Garten (U-bahn and S-bahn)* ✛ *1:B4.*

$ 🏨 **Hotel Bogota.** Fashion photography and hall lamps remind guests of the artists and designers who lived in this apartment house on an elegant Ku'damm side street beginning in 1911. **Pros:** historic ambience; on one of Ku'damm's most beautiful side streets; large, comfortable rooms. **Cons:** thin walls; some rooms with 1950s feeling; breakfast is nothing special. ✉ *Schlüterstr. 45, Western Downtown* 🕾 *030/881–5001* ⊕ *www.bogota.de* 🛏 *114 rooms, 70 with bath* ⌂ *In-room: no a/c, no TV, Wi-Fi* ⓘⓞⓘ *Breakfast* Ⓜ *Uhlandstrasse (U-bahn)* ✛ *1:C3.*

$$$$ 🏨 **Hotel Brandenburger Hof.** The foyer of this turn-of-the-20th-century mansion is breathtaking, with soaring white Doric columns, but once past these you'll find luxurious minimalism. **Pros:** great mansion; quiet location only steps away from the Ku'damm; large rooms. **Cons:** stuffy atmosphere; extras are expensive; no pool or fitness club on-site. ✉ *Eislebener Str. 14, Western Downtown* 🕾 *030/214–050* ⊕ *www.brandenburger-hof.com* 🛏 *58 rooms, 14 suites* ⌂ *In-room: no a/c, Wi-Fi. In-hotel: restaurant, bar, spa, business center, parking* Ⓜ *Augsburger Strasse (U-bahn)* ✛ *1:C4.*

$ 🏨 **Hotel Palace.** This is the only privately owned first-class hotel in the heart of western downtown, and its First Floor restaurant with a view over the zoo's greenery has made the hotel a favorite of gourmands. **Pros:** large rooms; quiet, central location; impeccable service. **Cons:** interior design outdated in some areas; nearby area of Europe-Center and Breitscheidplatz may be uninviting for some travelers. ✉ *Europa Center, Budapester Str. 45, Western Downtown* 🕾 *030/25020* ⊕ *www.palace.de* 🛏 *249 rooms, 33 suites* ⌂ *In-room: Wi-Fi. In-hotel: restaurant, bar, pool, spa, parking, some pets allowed* Ⓜ *Zoologsicher Garten (U-bahn and S-bahn)* ✛ *1:B5.*

$$ 🏨 **Hotel Q!.** The Q! has received several international design awards and it's easy to see how the gently sloping, sweeping interior of the hotel could charm any judge. **Pros:** beautiful design; affordable rates; great location for exploring Western downtown. **Cons:** not for families; nightlife at times makes the hotel noisy. ✉ *Knesebeckstr. 67, Charlottenburg* 🕾 *030/810-0660* ⊕ *www.loock-hotels.com* 🛏 *77 rooms, 10 suite* ⌂ *In-room: no a/c, Wi-Fi. In-hotel: restaurant, bar, spa* ⓘⓞⓘ *Breakfast* Ⓜ *Uhlandstrasse (U-bahn), Savignyplatz (S-bahn)* ✛ *1:C3.*

$$ 🏨 **Swissôtel Berlin.** At the bustling corner of Ku'damm and Joachimstahler Strasse, this hotel excels with its reputable Swiss hospitality—from accompanying guests to their floor after check-in to equipping each room with an iron, an umbrella, and a Nespresso espresso machine that preheats the cups. **Pros:** large, quiet rooms; unobtrusive yet perfect service; great location on western Berlin's busiest street crossings. **Cons**

Hotel Adlon Kempinski Berlin

Soho House

Arte Luise Kunsthotel

on top of shopping mall with lobby on higher floor; noisy when room windows are open; mostly for business travelers. ✉ *Augsburger Str. 44, Western Downtown* ☎ *030/220–100* ⊕ *www.swissotel.com* ⇙ *300 rooms, 18 suites* ⌂ *In-room: Internet, Wi-Fi. In-hotel: restaurant, bar, gym, business center, parking, some pets allowed* Ⓜ *Kurfürstendamm (U-bahn)* ✛ *1:C4.*

MITTE

$$
Fodor'sChoice
★

⊡ **Arte Luise Kunsthotel.** This hotel's name suggests a bohemian commune, but all the residents are paying guests. **Pros:** quiet location; historic flair; individually designed rooms. **Cons:** simple rooms with limited amenities and hotel facilities; no elevator. ✉ *Luisenstr. 19, Mitte* ☎ *030/284–480* ⊕ *www.luise-berlin.com* ⇙ *50 rooms, 34 with bath* ⌂ *In-room: no a/c, no TV, Wi-Fi. In-hotel: some pets allowed* Ⓜ *Friedrichstrasse (U-bahn and S-bahn)* ✛ *2:E2.*

$$$
Fodor'sChoice
★

⊡ **Grand Hyatt Berlin.** Europe's first Grand Hyatt is *the* address for entourages attending the Berlinale Film Festival in February. **Pros:** large and nicely appointed rooms; plus the city's best service; large, stylish spa and pool area. **Cons:** location can be very busy; architecture may be too minimalist for some travelers; not a hotel for families; in-room Wi-Fi is only free for the first 13 minutes. ✉ *Marlene-Dietrich-Pl. 2, Mitte* ☎ *030/2553–1234* ⊕ *www.berlin.grand.hyatt.de* ⇙ *326 rooms, 16 suites* ⌂ *In-room: Internet. In-hotel: restaurant, bar, pool, gym, spa, parking* Ⓜ *Potsdamer Platz (U-bahn and S-bahn)* ✛ *2:D5.*

$$

⊡ **Honigmond Hotel and Garden Hotel.** These two hotels are charming, quaint oases only a few steps away from the buzzing neighborhoods in Mitte. **Pros:** individually designed rooms; warm, welcoming service; quiet courtyard rooms. **Cons:** front rooms can be noisy due to busy street; restaurant is expensive relative to the area's budget choices. ✉ *Tieckstr. 12 and Invalidenstr. 122, Mitte* ☎ *030/284–4550* ⊕ *www. honigmond.de* ⇙ *90 rooms* ⌂ *In-room: Wi-Fi. In-hotel: restaurant, parking* Ⓜ *Nordbahnhof (S-bahn)* ✛ *2:E1.*

$$$$
Fodor'sChoice
★

⊡ **Hotel Adlon Kempinski Berlin.** Aside from its prime setting on Pariser Platz, the allure of the government's unofficial guesthouse is its almost mythical predecessor. **Pros:** top-notch luxury hotel; surprisingly large rooms; excellent in-house restaurants. **Cons:** sometimes stiff service with an attitude; rooms off the Linden are noisy with the windows open; inviting lobby often crowded. ✉ *Unter den Linden 77, Mitte* ☎ *030/22610* ⇙ *304 rooms, 78 suites* ⌂ *In-room: Wi-Fi. In-hotel: restaurants, bar, pool, gym, spa, parking, some pets allowed* Ⓜ *Unter den Linden (S-bahn)* ✛ *2:E3.*

$

⊡ **Hotel Amano.** A newcomer to the Mitte scene, Hotel Amano opened in 2009 with great expectations, and has lived up to its reputation as a "budget design hotel." **Pros:** Excellent location; good in-room amenities including air-conditioning, hair dryers, and safes. **Cons:** No room service; too trendy for some. ✉ *Auguststr. 43, Mitte, Berlin* ☎ *030/809– 4150* ⊕ *www.hotel-amano.com* ⇙ *163 rooms, including 46 apartments* ⌂ *In-room: a/c, kitchen, Wi-Fi. In-hotel: bar, business center* Ⓜ *Rosenthaler Platz (U-bahn)* ✛ *2:A5.*

$$$$ — **Fodor's Choice** ★

🏨 **Hotel de Rome.** Managing to retain a traditional feel, with natural wood walls and an ornate pink-lighted ballroom, the Hotel de Rome mostly surprises with eccentric design ideas such as oversize furniture. **Pros:** great location; large rooms. **Cons:** design may be over the top for some guests; quite expensive even for a five-star hotel; can be dark during the day due to low lighting. ⊠ *Behrenstr. 37, Mitte* ☎ *030/460–6090* ⊕ *www.hotelderome.com* ⌧ *146 rooms, 43 suites* ⚹ *In-room: a/c, Wi-Fi. In-hotel: restaurant, bar, spa, business center* ❢⊙❚ *Breakfast* Ⓜ *Französische Strasse (U-bahn)* ✛ *2:F3.*

$ — 🏨 **Hotel Hackescher Markt.** Amid the nightlife around Hackescher Markt, this hotel provides discreet and inexpensive top services. **Pros:** great location for shops, restaurants, and nightlife; large rooms. **Cons:** some rooms may be noisy due to tram stop; no air-conditioning. ⊠ *Grosse Präsidentenstr. 8, Mitte* ☎ *030/280–030* ⊕ *www.hotel-hackescher-markt.com* ⌧ *29 rooms, 3 suites* ⚹ *In-room: no a/c, Wi-Fi. In-hotel: bar, some pets allowed* Ⓜ *Hackescher Markt (S-bahn)* ✛ *2:G2.*

$$ — **Fodor's Choice** ★

🏨 **Lux Eleven.** This designer apartment hotel is coveted for its discreet service and great minimalist design. **Pros:** great location in northern Mitte; extremely stylish yet comfortable rooms; friendly, knowledgeable service. **Cons:** immediate neighborhood may be noisy; not a good choice for families. ⊠ *Rosa-Luxemburg-Str. 9–13, Mitte* ☎ *030/936–2800* ⊕ *www.lux-eleven.com* ⌧ *73 apartments* ⚹ *In-room: no a/c, Wi-Fi. In-hotel: restaurant* Ⓜ *Rosa-Luxemburg-Platz (U-bahn)* ✛ *2:B6.*

$$$$ — 🏨 **The Regent Berlin.** One of Germany's most esteemed hotels, the Regent pairs the opulence of gilt furniture, thick carpets, marble floors, tasseled settees, and crystal chandeliers with such modern conveniences as flat-screen TVs. **Pros:** Berlin's most hushed five-star hotel; unobtrusive service; very large rooms and top location off Gendarmenmarkt. **Cons:** some public areas in need of update; the only hotel restaurant specializes in fish only. ⊠ *Charlottenstr. 49, Mitte* ☎ *030/20338* ⊕ *www.regenthotels.com* ⌧ *156 rooms, 39 suites* ⚹ *In-room: Internet, Wi-Fi. In-hotel: restaurant, bar, gym, parking, some pets allowed* ✛ *2:F3.*

$$$$ — 🏨 **The Ritz-Carlton Berlin.** Judging from the outside of this gray, high-rise hotel that soars above Potsdamer Platz, you may never guess that inside it's all luxurious 19th-century grandeur. **Pros:** stylish and luxurious interior design; great views; elegant setting yet informal service. **Cons:** rooms surprisingly small for a newly built hotel; not family-friendly (business-oriented atmosphere). ⊠ *Potsdamer Pl. 3, Mitte* ☎ *030/337–777* ⊕ *www.ritzcarlton.com* ⌧ *263 rooms, 40 suites* ⚹ *In-room: Internet. In-hotel: restaurant, bar, pool, gym, spa, parking* Ⓜ *Potsdamer Platz (U-bahn and S-bahn)* ✛ *2:D4.*

$$ — 🏨 **Sofitel Berlin Gendarmenmarkt.** This luxurious place to stay has maximized the minimalist look of East Berlin before the Wall came down. **Pros:** great location off a beautiful square; sumptuous breakfast buffet; great Austrian restaurant, Aigner. **Cons:** only top floor has a good view; limited facilities for a luxury hotel; smallish rooms. ⊠ *Charlottenstr. 50–52, Mitte* ☎ *030/203–750* ⊕ *www.sofitel.com* ⌧ *70 rooms, 22 suites* ⚹ *In-room: Internet, Wi-Fi. In-hotel: restaurant, gym, spa* Ⓜ *Französische Strasse (U-bahn)* ✛ *2:F4.*

15

$$$ 🏨 **Soho House.** This brand-new hotel has a clubby atmosphere. **Pros:**
Fodor'sChoice   great staff; perfect location for club- and bar-hopping; rooftop pool.
★   **Cons:** can be too clubby and stylish. ✉ *Torstr. 1, Prenzlauer Berg*
☎ *030/405–0440* ⊕ *www.sohohouseberlin.com* 🛏 *40 rooms, 2 suites*
♿ *In-room: no a/c. In-hotel: restaurant, bar, pool, gym* ⓧ◎ *Breakfast*
Ⓜ *Rosa-Luxemburg-Platz (U-bahn)* ✛ *2:H1.*

$$ 🏨 **Westin Grand Hotel.** This large hotel in a renovated East German building has a great location at the corner of Friedrichstrasse and Unter den
Linden. **Pros:** impressive lobby; recently updated rooms; perfect location for historic sights and shopping. **Cons:** service often not on five-star
level; no great views; may feel street vibrations in lower rooms off Friedrichstrasse, as well as noise due to street construction. ✉ *Friedrichstr.*
158–164, Mitte ☎ *030/20270* ⊕ *www.westingrandberlin.com* 🛏 *357*
rooms, 43 suites ♿ *In-room: Internet, Wi-Fi. In-hotel: restaurant, bar,*
pool, spa, parking, some pets allowed Ⓜ *Friedrichstrasse (S-bahn and*
U-bahn) ✛ *2:F3.*

KREUZBERG

$ 🏨 **Eastern Comfort.** The Spree River is one of Berlin's best assets, and
you'll wake up on it in this moored, three-level ship with simple cabins.
Pros: unique accommodation on a boat; friendly staff; perfect location
for nightclubbing in Kreuzberg and Friedrichshain. **Cons:** insects may be
bothersome in summer; smallish rooms not pleasant in rainy or stormy
weather; lack of privacy. ✉ *Mühlenstr. 73–77, Kreuzberg* ☎ *030/6676–*
3806 ⊕ *www.eastern-comfort.com* 🛏 *26 cabins* ♿ *In-room: no a/c, no*
TV, Wi-Fi. In-hotel: bar, business center Ⓜ *Warschauer Strasse (U-bahn*
and S-bahn) ✛ *2:H5.*

$ 🏨 **Hotel Klassik.** One of the best things about the Hotel Klassik is its
central location, walking distance to Friedrichshain's countless eating,
drinking, and shopping hot spots. **Pros:** excellent location for neighborhood vibe and access to transportation; plentiful, fresh breakfast
buffet; friendly and helpful staff. **Cons:** located on a loud and busy
corner. ✉ *Revaler Str. 6* ☎ *30/319–8860* ⊕ *www.hotelklassik-berlin.*
com 🛏 *59 rooms* ♿ *In-room: kitchen, Wi-Fi. In-hotel: restaurant, bar,*
business center ✛ *2:H3.*

$ 🏨 **ÏMA Loft Apartments.** A comfortable cross between apartment rental
and hotel, ÏMA's aim is to throw its guests into the fray of Kreuzberg's
hectic, artistic, multicultural scene. **Pros:** maximum privacy (a separate
entrance insures that you never have to interact with hotel staff and
other guests unless you want to). **Cons:** minimal amenities and services. ✉ *Ritterstr. 12–14, Kreuzberg, Berlin* ☎ *030/6162-8913* ⊕ *www.*
imavillage.com 🛏 *22 rooms* ♿ *In-room: kitchen, Wi-Fi. In-hotel: res-*
taurant Ⓜ *Moritzplatz (U-bahn)* ✛ *2:H6.*

$ 🏨 **Michelberger Hotel.** Started by a group of young Berliners who
dreamed of a uniquely designed, artsy space, the Michelberger Hotel is
part budget hotel, part clubhouse, and part bar and restaurant. **Pros:**
located at the epicenter of eastern Berlin nightlife; great design and
fun atmosphere; affordable prices **Cons:** busy thoroughfare and transit
hub, so front rooms can be noisy; casual service without luxury amenities; no phone in rooms. ✉ *Warschauer Str. 39–40, Friedrichshain,*

Berlin ☎ *030/2977–8590* ⊕ *www.michelbergerhotel.com* ⤵ *119 rooms* ⌂ *In-room: no a/c, Wi-Fi. In-hotel: restaurant, bar* Ⓜ *Warschauer Str. (S-bahn)* ✛ *2:H5.*

$$ 🏨 **Riehmers Hofgarten.** The appeal of this late-19th-century apartment house with a leafy courtyard is its location in a lively neighborhood marked by the streets Mehringdamm and Bergmannstrasse. **Pros:** good location for exploring Kreuzberg; typical Berlin, high-ceiling, historic rooms; great on-site restaurant, E.T.A. Hoffmann. **Cons:** street-side rooms very noisy; breakfast not very special. ⊠ *Yorckstr. 83, Kreuzberg* ☎ *030/7809–8800* ⊕ *www.hotel-riehmers-hofgarten.de* ⤵ *22 rooms, 1 suite* ⌂ *In-room: no a/c, Internet, Wi-Fi. In-hotel: restaurant, bar, parking, some pets allowed* 🍽 *Breakfast* Ⓜ *Mehringdamm (U-bahn)* ✛ *2:F6.*

NIGHTLIFE AND THE ARTS

15

THE ARTS

Detailed information about events is covered in the *Berlin Programm*, a monthly tourist guide to Berlin arts, museums, and theaters. The magazines *Tip* and *Zitty*, which appear every two weeks, provide full arts listings (in German), although the free weekly *(030)* is the best source for club and music events. For listings in English, consult the monthly *Ex-Berliner*, or their Web site (⊕ *www.exberliner.com*), which is updated regularly.

Showtime Konzert- und Theaterkassen. If your hotel can't book a seat for you or you can't make it to a box office directly, go to a ticket agency. Surcharges are 18%–23% of the ticket price. Showtime Konzert- und Theaterkassen has offices within the major department stores. ⊠ *KaDeWe, Tauentzienstr. 21, Western Downtown* ☎ *030/217–7754* ⊕ *www.showtimetickets.de.*

Theaterkasse Centrum. There's a very informed and helpful staff at this agency. ⊠ *Meinekestr. 25, Western Downtown* ☎ *030/882–7611.*

Hekticket offices. The Hekticket offices offers discounted and last-minute tickets. ⊠ *Karl-Liebknecht-Str. 13, off Alexanderpl., Mitte* ✉ *Next to Zoo-Palast, Hardenbergstr. 29d, Western Downtown* ☎ *030/230–9930.*

BERLIN FESTIVAL WEEKS

Berliner Festspiele. This annual Berlin festival, held from late August through September or early October, unites all the major performance halls as well as some smaller venues for concerts, opera, ballet, theater, and art exhibitions. It also sponsors some smaller-scale events throughout the year. ⊠ *Ticket office, Schaperstr. 24* ☎ *030/2548–9100* ⊕ *www. berlinerfestspiele.de.*

CONCERTS

Konzerthaus Berlin. The beautifully restored hall at Konzerthaus Berlin is a prime venue for classical music concerts. Its box office is open from noon to curtain time. ⊠ *Gendarmenmarkt, Mitte* ☎ *030/2030–92101* ⊕ *www.konzerthaus.de* 🕙 *Mon.–Sat. noon–7 pm, Sun. noon–4 pm.*

Philharmonie mit Kammermusiksaal. Among the major symphony orchestras and orchestral ensembles in Berlin is the Berlin Philharmonic Orchestra, which resides at the Philharmonie mit Kammermusiksaal. The Kammermusiksaal is dedicated to chamber music. Tickets sell out in advance for the nights when Sir Simon Rattle or other star maestros conduct, but other orchestras and artists appear here as well. Tuesday's free Lunchtime Concerts fill the foyer with eager listeners of all ages at 1 pm. Daily guided tours (€3) also take place at 1 pm. ⊠ *Herbert-von-Karajan-Str. 1, Tiergarten* ☎ *030/254–880* ⊕ *www. berliner-philharmoniker.de.*

DANCE, MUSICALS, AND OPERA

Berlin's three opera houses also host guest productions and companies from around the world. Vladimir Malakhov, a principal guest dancer with New York's American Ballet Theatre, is a principal in the Staatsballett Berlin as well as its director. The company performs its classic and modern productions between the Deutsche Oper in the west and the Staatsoper in the east.

Deutsche Oper Berlin. Of the 17 composers represented in the repertoire of Deutsche Oper Berlin, Verdi and Wagner are the most frequently presented. ⊠ *Bismarckstr. 35, Charlottenburg* ☎ *030/343–8401* ⊕ *www. deutscheoperberlin.de.*

Hebbel am Ufer Theater (*HAU*). This theater consists of three houses (HAU 1, 2, 3) within a five-minute walk of one another. Fringe theater, international modern dance, and solo performers share its stages. ⊠ *Stresemannstr. 29, Kreuzberg* ☎ *030/2590–0427* ⊕ *www.hebbel-am-ufer.de.*

Komische Oper. Most of the operas are sung in German at the Komische Oper, however their lavish and at times over-the-top, kitschy staging and costumes make for a fun night even if you don't speak the language. ⊠ *Behrenstr. 55–57, Mitte* ☎ *030/4799–7400* ⊕ *www.komische-oper-berlin.de.*

Schaubühne am Lehniner Platz. This was once considered the city's most experimental stage, and while the lively actors have mellowed somewhat, they still give great performances. Their frequent, avant-garde stagings of well-known Shakespeare plays are a wonderful opportunity to enjoy German theater, even if you don't know a word of German. You can always brush up on the story beforehand and follow along with your own English text. ⊠ *Kurfürstendamm 153, Western Downtown* ☎ *030/890–023* ⊕ *www.schaubuehne.de.*

Tanzfabrik. The Tanzfabrik is still Berlin's best venue for young dance talents and the latest from Europe's avant-garde. ⊠ *Möckernstr. 68, Kreuzberg* ☎ *030/786–5861* ⊕ *www.tanzfabrik-berlin.de.*

Tempodrom. The white, tentlike Tempodrom, beyond the ruined facade of Anhalter Bahnhof, features international music, pop, and rock stars. ⊠ *Askanischer Pl. 4, Kreuzberg* ☎ *01805/554–111* ⊕ *www.tempodrom.de.*

Theater des Westens. The late-19th-century Theater des Westens, one of Germany's oldest musical theaters, features musicals such as *Dance of the Vampires* and recently, *We Will Rock You*, the over-the-top musical about the rock band Queen. ⊠ *Kantstr. 12, Western Downtown* ☎ *01805–4444* ⊕ *www.stage-entertainment.de.*

FILM

International and German movies are shown in the big theaters on Potsdamer Platz and around the Ku'damm. If a film isn't marked "OF" or "OV" (*Originalfassung*, or original version) or "OmU" (original with subtitles), it's dubbed. Many Berlin theaters let customers reserve seats in advance when purchasing tickets, so buy them early to nab those coveted center spots. ■ TIP→ Previews and commercials often run for 25 minutes, so don't worry if you walk in late.

Babylon. Partially hidden behind Kottbusser Tor, Babylon shows English-language films with German subtitles. You can reach it by cutting through a building overpass off Adalbertstrasse. ⊠ *Dresdener Str. 126, Kreuzberg* ☎ *030/6160–9693* ⊕ *www.yorck.de.*

CineStar im Sony Center. Mainstream U.S. and British productions are screened in their original versions at the CineStar im Sony Center. Tuesday is a discount evening. ⊠ *Potsdamer Str. 4, Tiergarten* ☎ *030/ 2606–6400.*

Freiluftkinos (*Free Air Cinemas*). When warm weather hits the city and Berliners come out of hibernation, they often head to the Freiluftkinos (free air cinemas). These outdoor viewing areas are in just about every park in town, offer food and drinks, and screen a good balance of German and international films, many of them new releases. Check the Web site for schedules from three of the city's best, in Volkspark Friedrichshain, Mariannenplatz Kreuzberg, and Volkspark Rehberge in Wedding. ⊕ *www.freiluftkino-berlin.de* ☎ €6.50.

Hackesche Höfe. Documentary films, international films in their original language, and German art-house films are shown at Hackesche Höfe. There's no elevator to this top-floor movie house, but you can recover on the wide banquettes in the lounge. Monday and Tuesday are discount evenings. ⊠ *Rosenthaler Str. 40–41, Mitte* ☎ *030/283–4603.*

Internationale Filmfestspiele (*Berlinale*). In February, numerous cinemas host the prestigious Internationale Filmfestspiele, or Berlinale, a 10-day international festival at which the Golden Bear award is bestowed on the best films, directors, and actors. Ticket counters open three days before the party begins, but individual tickets are also sold on each day of the festival, if you're willing to wait in line for what can be hours. ■ TIP→ Film buffs should purchase the season pass, or act quickly when tickets are sold online. ⊕ *www.berlinale.de.*

THEATER

Theater in Berlin is outstanding, but performances are usually in German. The exceptions are operettas and the (nonliterary) cabarets.

Deutsches Theater. The theater most renowned for both its modern and classical productions is the Deutsches Theater. ⊠ *Schumannstr. 13a, Mitte* ☎ *030/2844–1225* ⊕ *www.deutschestheater.de.*

Berliner Ensemble. The excellent Berliner Ensemble is dedicated to Brecht and works of other international playwrights. ⊠ *Bertolt Brecht-Pl. 1, off Friedrichstr., just north of train station, Mitte* ☎ *030/2840–8155* ⊕ *www.berliner-ensemble.de.*

15

English Theatre Berlin. In a black-box theater, the English Theatre presents dramas and comedies in English. ⊠ *Fidicinstr. 40, Kreuzberg* ☎ *030/691–1211* ⊕ *www.etberlin.de.*

Grips Theater. For children's theater, head for the world-famous Grips Theater, whose musical hit *Linie 1*, about life in Berlin viewed through the subway, is just as appealing for adults. ⊠ *Altonaer Str. 22, Tiergarten* ☎ *030/3974–740* ⊕ *www.grips-theater.de.*

Volksbühne am Rosa-Luxemburg-Platz. The Volksbühne am Rosa-Luxemburg-Platz is unsurpassed for its aggressively experimental style, and Berliners often fill its 750 seats. The unusual building was reconstructed in the 1950s using the original 1914 plans. It also houses two smaller performance spaces—the Roter Salon and the Grüner Salon—which host everything from retro Motown nights and salsa classes for all levels to touring independent pop and rock acts. ⊠ *Rosa-Luxemburg-Pl., Mitte* ☎ *030/2406–5777* ⊕ *www.volksbuehne-berlin.de.*

VARIETY SHOWS, COMEDY, AND CABARET

Berlin's variety shows can include magicians, circus performers, musicians, and classic cabaret stand-ups. Be aware that in order to understand and enjoy traditional cabaret, which involves a lot of political humor, your German has to be up to snuff.

Bar Jeder Vernunft. The intimate Bar Jeder Vernunft is housed within a glamorous tent and features solo entertainers. ■ TIP→ Somewhat set back from the street, this venue is not easy to find. Just to the left of Haus der Berliner Festspiele, look for a lighted path next to a parking lot and follow it until you reach the tent. ⊠ *Schaperstr. 24, Wilmersdorf* ☎ *030/883–1582* ⊕ *www.bar-jeder-vernunft.de.*

BKA–Berliner Kabarett Anstalt. Social and political satire has a long tradition in cabaret theaters. The BKA–Berliner Kabarett Anstalt features not only guest performances by Germany's leading young comedy talents but also chanson vocalists. ⊠ *Mehringdamm 34, Kreuzberg* ☎ *030/202–2007* ⊕ *www.bka-luftschloss.de.*

Chamäleon Varieté. Within the Hackesche Höfe, the Chamäleon Varieté is the most affordable and offbeat variety venue in town. German isn't required to enjoy most of the productions. ⊠ *Rosenthaler Str. 40–41, Mitte* ☎ *030/400–0590* ⊕ *www.chamaeleonberlin.com.*

Friedrichstadtpalast. Europe's largest variety show takes place at the Friedrichstadtpalast, a glossy showcase for revues, famous for its leggy female dancers. Most of the guests seem to arrive via bus tours and package hotel deals. ⊠ *Friedrichstr. 107, Mitte* ☎ *030/2326–2326* ⊕ *www.friedrichstadtpalast.de.*

Tipi das Zelt (*Tipi am Kanzleramt*). Tipi das Zelt is a tent venue between the Kanzleramt (Chancellor's Office) and Haus der Kulturen der Welt. Artists featured are well suited for an international audience, and you can opt to dine here before the show. Even the back-row seats are good. ⊠ *Grosse Queralle, Tiergarten* ☎ *030/3906–6550* ⊕ *www.tipi-am-kanzleramt.de.*

Wintergarten Varieté. The Wintergarten Varieté pays romantic homage to the old days of Berlin's original variety theater in the 1920s. ⊠ *Potsdamer Str. 96, Tiergarten* ☎ *030/588–433* ⊕ *www.wintergarten-variete.de.*

In hip Kreuzberg, you can sip drinks canal-side at Freischwimmer.

NIGHTLIFE

Berlin's nightspots are open to the wee hours of the morning, but if you stay out after 12:45 Monday–Thursday or Sunday, you'll have to find a night bus (designated by "N" before the number, which often corresponds to the subway line it is replacing) or catch the last S-bahn home. On Friday and Saturday nights all subway lines (except U4) run every 15 to 20 minutes throughout the night. Clubs often switch the music they play nightly, so their crowds and popularity can vary widely. Though club nights are driven by the DJ name, the music genres are written in English in listing magazines.

Clubs and bars in Western Downtown Berlin as well as in Mitte tend to be dressier and more conservative; the scene in Kreuzberg, Prenzlauer Berg, the Scheunenviertel, and Friedrichshain is laid-back and alternative. For the latest information on Berlin's house, electro, and hip-hop club scene, pick up *(030)*, a free weekly. Dance clubs don't get going until about 12:30 am, but parties labeled "after-work" start as early as 8 pm for professionals looking to socialize during the week.

BARS AND LOUNGES

In Germany the term *Kneipen* is used for down-to-earth bars that are comparable to English pubs. These places are pretty simple and laid-back; you probably shouldn't try to order a three-ingredient cocktail at one unless you spot a lengthy drink menu.

Elegant bars and lounges can be found in Western Downtown Berlin and in Berlin's five-star hotels, and new cocktail bars are cropping up in unexpected places, like Kreuzberg and Schöneberg.

Bar am Lützowplatz. The cocktail menu is the size of a small guidebook at Bar am Lützowplatz, where an attractive, professional crowd line the long blond-wood bar. ✉ *Am Lützowpl. 7, Tiergarten* ☎ *030/262–6807* ⊕ *www.baramluetzowplatz.com.*

Bellmann Bar. The candlelit, rough wood tables, water-stained walls, and frequent appearances by local musicians just dropping by for a few tunes gives this cozy cocktail bar a distinctly old-world, artistic feel. Lovingly nicknamed "the gramophone bar" for the old gramophone, complete with horn, that sits in its window, Bellmann's is a place to linger and chat over a glass of wine or a whiskey from their outstanding collection. ■TIP→ Although there's no U-bahn station nearby, take the reliable M29 bus to Glogauer Str. from Moritzplatz on the U8 or Görlitzer Bahnhof on the U1. ✉ *Reichenberger Str. 103, Kreuzberg, Berlin* ☎ *030/3117–3162.*

Freischwimmer. Sitting canal-side on a deck chair at Freischwimmer is perfect for warm nights, but heat lamps and an enclosed section make a cozy setting on cool ones, too. To get here, walk five minutes east of the Schlesisches Tor subway station and turn left down a path after the 1920s Aral gas station, the oldest in Berlin. ✉ *Vor dem Schlesischen Tor 2a, Kreuzberg* ☎ *030/6107–4309* ⊕ *www.freischwimmer-berlin.de.*

Green Door. A mature crowd focused on conversation and appreciating outstanding cocktails heads to Green Door, a Schöneberg classic with touches of 1960s retro style, like gingham walls and stand-alone lamps. ■TIP→ Although the expertly crafted drinks are not cheap by Berlin standards, you can always drop by at happy hour (6–9) to sample them at nearly half price. ✉ *Winterfeldstr. 50, Schöneberg* ☎ *030/215–2515* ⊕ *www.greendoor.de.*

Newton. Now the oldest posh bar in Mitte, marble-lined Newton flaunts Helmut Newton's larger-than-life photos of nude women across its walls. ✉ *Charlottenstr. 57, Mitte* ☎ *030/2029–5421* ⊕ *www.newton-bar.de.*

Solar. The laid-back, loungelike Solar is the playground for the city's younger party crowd. It's located on the top floor of a building in a part of Kreuzberg just south of Potsdamer Platz with a slightly abandoned feel. Go at sunset to take full advantage of the magnificent views. ✉ *Stresemannstr. 76, Kreuzberg* ☎ *0163/765–2700* ⊕ *www.solarberlin.de.*

Victoria Bar. The subdued and elegant Victoria Bar is an ironic homage to the '60s and '70s jet-set age, and ultimately stylish. It usually attracts a middle-aged, affluent, and artsy crowd. ✉ *Potsdamer Str. 102, Tiergarten* ☎ *030/2575–9977* ⊕ *www.victoriabar.de.*

Würgeengel. Named after a 1962 surrealist film from Luis Buñuel (*The Exterminating Angel* in English), this classy joint has offered an elaborate cocktail menu in a well-designed space off Kottbusser Tor since 1992—long before that part of Kreuzberg was hip, or even safe. Today, its loyal fans spill out onto the streets on busy nights, and an evening tapas menu comes from the neighboring restaurant **Gorgonzola Club.** ✉ *Dresdener Str. 122, Kreuzberg* ⟊ *Dresdener Str. is reachable through the passageway under the buildings at Kottbusser Tor, next to Adalbertstr.* ☎ *030/615–5560* ⊕ *www.wuergeengel.de* ☾ *Open 7–late.*

CLOSE UP

Berlin's Hot Spots

Here's a quick list of the city's best streets and squares.

- Savignyplatz in Charlottenburg: Great restaurants and shopping.

- Ludwigkirchplatz in Wilmersdorf: Charming cafés surrounding a beautiful church.

- Nollendorfplatz and Winterfeldplatz in Schöneberg: The cultural centers of Schöneberg; the latter hosts a fab weekly market.

- Oranienstrasse and Wiener Strasse as well as both riverbanks of the Spree in Kreuzberg and Friedrichshain to Treptow: The former is the lively center of Turkish Kreuzberg; the banks of the Spree have a number of large clubs in industrial spaces.

- Hackescher Markt and Oranienburgerstrasse as well as surrounding side streets in Mitte-Scheunenviertel: The center of historical and cultural Berlin, with the most mainstream and popular nightlife.

- Kastanienallee and Helmholzplatz in Prenzlauer Berg: A widely trafficked street and square in Berlin, full of both young expats and local families.

- Boxhagenerplatz and Boxhagener Strasse in Friedrichshain: Home to a weekly flea market, a busy area both day and night with cafés, bars, and restaurants.

- Hermannplatz in Neukölln: The jumping off point for a night out in one of Berlin's newly hip districts.

15

CLUBS

★ **Clärchen's Ballhaus.** A night out at Clärchen's Ballhaus (Little Clara's Ballroom) is like a trip back in time. Opened in 1913, the club is an impressive sight on Mitte's now-upscale Auguststrasse. On summer nights the front courtyard comes alive with patrons dining alfresco on brick-oven pizzas, and a line for the club stretches out the door. The main ballroom features a different style of music every night and offers dance lessons before the party starts. The upstairs Spiegelsaal ("mirror hall") holds intimate, salon-type concerts on Sunday. ⊠ *Auguststr. 24, Mitte, Berlin* ☎ *030/282–9295* ⊕ *www.ballhaus.de* ☼ *Lunch and dinner daily.*

Club der Visionaere. Club der Visionaere is little more than a series of wooden rafts and a few shoddily constructed shacks, but it remains a beloved outdoor venue in town. The place is packed at all hours, either with clubbers on their last stop of the evening before going home, or with students soaking up the sunshine on a Sunday morning. Since it shares a narrow canal with Freischwimmer, which hosts a massive brunch on Sunday, an easy hop across the water (by bridge, of course) will get you coffee and breakfast at dawn. ⊠ *Am Flutgraben, Treptow, Berlin* ♣ *Follow Schlesische Strasse east from the U-bahn station until you cross two small canals* ☎ *030/6951–8942* ☼ *Weekdays 2 pm–late, weekends noon–late* Ⓜ *Schlesisches Tor (U-bahn).*

Havanna Club. Berlin's mixed, multi-culti crowd frequents the Havanna Club, where you can dance to soul, R&B, or hip-hop on four different dance floors. The week's highlights are the wild salsa and merengue nights (Wednesday at 9 pm, Friday and Saturday at 10 pm). If your

Havana Club heats up on salsa and merengue nights.

Latin steps are weak, come an hour early for a lesson. ■TIP→ Fridays and Saturdays are "ladies free" nights until 11. ✉ *Hauptstr. 30, Schöneberg* ☎ *030/784–8565* ⊕ *www.havanna-berlin.de.*

Felix. The prestigious and over-the-top Felix greatly benefits from its location behind the famous Adlon Kempinski Hotel. Hollywood stars drop by when shooting in town, or during the frenzied weeks of the Berlinale. The door policy can be tough, but dress in your finest and hope for the best. ✉ *Behrenstr. 72, Mitte* ☎ *030/301–117–152* ⊕ *www. felix-clubrestaurant.de.*

Kaffeeburger. More of a neighborhood clubhouse than just a bar, Kaffeeburger always has something going on. The original home of writer Wladimir Kaminer's popular Russendisko ("Russian disco") nights, this spot has a cozy dance floor and a separate smoking room. On any given night, you might encounter electro, rock, funk, swing, or Balkan beats, and live bands play frequently. ✉ *Torstr. 60, Mitte, Berlin* ☎ *030/2804–6495* ⊕ *www.kaffeeburger.de.*

Klub der Republik (*KDR*). Although Klub der Republik takes its name from the late Palast der Republik, the magnificent work of Soviet architecture that used to stand just south of Alexanderplatz, it has little else to do with cold war–era Berlin. The decor includes a sampling of retro-kitsch furnishings taken from the Palast, but otherwise it's fashion-forward. Large glass panels overlook Prenzlauer Berg's Pappelallee from its second-floor room (accessible by a fire escape staircase in the back courtyard), and there's a rotating list of local DJ talent. ✉ *Pappelallee 81, Prenzlauer Berg, Berlin* ☎ *No phone.*

Sage Club. Sage Club is the most popular of Berlin's venues for young professionals who dance to house and some techno music. On some nights it can be tough getting past the man with the "by invitation only" list. Expect a line out the door, and very different crowds depending on the night of the week (check the program on the website). ⊠ *Köpenicker Str. 76, Mitte* ☎ *030/278–9830* ⊕ *www.sage-club.de.*

Watergate. Elegant Watergate sits languidly at the base of the Oberbaumbrücke on the Kreuzberg side. It has two dance floors with bars, and is a great chill-out spot with its terrace extending over the Spree River. Well designed with a comfortable, user-friendly layout, this is a club for people who usually don't like clubbing. In addition to hosting internationally renowned DJs, the club makes a beautiful and intimate setting for infrequent but popular classical music nights. ⊠ *Falckensteinstr. 49, Kreuzberg* ☎ *030/6128–0396* ⊕ *www.water-gate.de* Ⓜ *Schlesisches Tor (U-bahn); Warschauer Str. (U-bahn and S-bahn).*

GAY AND LESBIAN BARS

Berlin is unmistakably Germany's gay capital, and many Europeans come to partake in the diverse scene, which is concentrated in Schöneberg (around Nollendorfplatz) and Kreuzberg. Check out the magazines *Siegessäule, (030),* and *blu.*

Berghain. Berghain rose with a vengeance from the ashes of '90s techno club Ostgut. Located in an imposing power station in a barren stretch of land between Kreuzberg and Friedrichshain (hence the name, which borrows from both neighborhoods), Berghain has achieved international fame as the hedonistic heart of techno music. Although it's also a well-respected center of gay nightlife in Berlin, the club welcomes both genders. It's only open on weekends (but 48 hours from midnight on Friday to midnight on Sunday), and it has become something of a local tradition to arrive on Sunday morning and dance until closing time. ⊠ *Am Wriezener Bahnhof, Friedrichshain, Berlin* ⊹ *Exit north from Ostbahnhof and follow Strasse der Pariser Kommune, then make a right on the badly marked Am Wriezener Bahnhof and look for a line.* ☎ *030/2936–0210* Ⓜ *Ostbahnhof (S-bahn).*

Connection. Just south of Wittenbergplatz, the dance club Connection provides heavy house music and lots of dark corners. ⊠ *Fuggerstr. 33, Schöneberg* ☎ *030/218–1432* ⊕ *www.connection-berlin.de.*

Hafen. The decor and the energetic crowd at Hafen makes it ceaselessly popular and a favorite singles mixer. ⊠ *Motzstr. 19, Schöneberg* ☎ *030/211–4118* ⊕ *www.hafen-berlin.de.*

Roses. If you don't bump up against any eye candy at tiny Roses there are always the furry red walls and kitschy paraphernalia to admire. It opens at 10 pm. ⊠ *Oranienstr. 187, Kreuzberg* ☎ *030/615–6570.*

Schwuz. Schwuz consists of two dance floors underneath the laid-back café Melitta Sundström, which is located right next to the Schwules Museum, Berlin's very own gay museum. Eighties music and house are the normal fare. ⊠ *Mehringdamm 61, Kreuzberg* ☎ *030/629–0880* ⊕ *www.schwuz.de.*

15

Gay Berlin

The area around Nollendorfplatz is the heart and soul of gay Berlin, even though areas like Schönhauser Alle in Prenzlauer Berg, Schlesische Strasse in Kreuzberg, and various clubs in the Mitte-Scheunenviertel area are more popular with the younger crowd. However, in a city that historically has been a center of gay culture and one that has an openly gay mayor, Klaus Wowereit, the gay scene is not limited to these areas. Typical for Berlin is the integration of homosexuals of all walks of life throughout the city—from the politician and manager to the bus driver and waiter. The general attitude of most Berliners toward gays is tolerant and open-minded; however, openly gay couples should avoid outer areas such as Lichtenberg or towns in Brandenburg, the region surrounding Berlin. These areas are exceptions in a city that has an estimated 300,000 gays and lesbians in residence.

Large festivals such as the annual Christopher Street Day bring together hundreds of thousands of gays and lesbians each summer. Gay travelers are embraced by the city's tourist office: up-to-date information is provided in special brochures, such as "Out in Berlin" at the tourist info-stores.

Mann-o-Meter e.V. Detailed information on gay-friendly hotels and the clubbing and bar scene are provided by the city's largest gay community center, the Mann-o-Meter e.V. Talks are held in the café, which has a variety of books and magazines. ⊠ *Bülowstr. 106, Schöneberg* ☎ *030/216–8008* ⊕ *www.mann-o-meter.de* ☉ *Tues.–Fri. 4–10, Sat.–Sun. 4–8.*

JAZZ CLUBS

A-Trane. A-Trane in West Berlin has hosted countless greats throughout the years, like Herbie Hancock and Wynton Marsalis. Its weekly free jam nights on Saturday and numerous other free events make it a good place to see jazz on a budget. ⊠ *Bleibtreustr. 1, Charlottenburg, Berlin* ☎ *030/313–2550* ⊕ *www.a-trane.de* Ⓜ *Savignypl. (S-bahn).*

B-Flat. With no columns to obstruct your view, you can see young German artists almost every night at B-Flat. The well-known and well-attended Wednesday jam sessions focus on free and experimental jazz, and once a month on Thursdays the Berlin Big Band takes over the small stage with up to 17 players. Snacks are available. ⊠ *Rosenthaler Str. 13, Mitte* ☎ *030/283–3123* ⊕ *www.b-flat-berlin.de.*

Kunstfabrik Schlot. Schlot hosts Berlin jazz scenesters, aspiring musicians playing their Monday night free jazz sessions, and local heavy-hitters. It's a bit hard to find, located in the cellar of the Edison Höfe, which is a brick complex currently undergoing a lot of construction, but enter the courtyard via Schlegelstrasse and follow the music. ⊠ *Chaussestr. 18, Entrance at Schlegelstr. 26 due to construction, Mitte* ☎ *030/448–2160* Ⓜ *Nordbahnhof (S-bahn), Naturkundemuseum (U-bahn).*

Quasimodo. Descend a small staircase to the basement of the Theater des Westens for Quasimodo, the most established and popular jazz venue in the city. Despite its college-town pub feel, the club has hosted many

Berlin and international greats. Seats are few, but there's plenty of standing room in the front. ⊠ *Kantstr. 12a, Charlottenburg* ☎ *030/312–8086* ⊕ *www.quasimodo.de.*

SPORTS AND THE OUTDOORS

Olympic Stadium. Berlin's famous sports attraction is the 1936 Olympic Stadium, which received a thorough modernization in 2004. American sprinter Jesse Owens won his stunning four gold medals in 1936; these days, the Berlin Thunder, a mixed nationality team playing American football in the European league, and the local soccer team Hertha BSC are the stars in the arena. The stadium hosted the World Cup soccer final match in July 2006 and served as a spectacular backdrop to the Athletics World Championship in 2009. Different themed tours are offered throughout the year; one option is touring on your own with an audio guide (€4), but only a guided tour (€8) will show you the nonpublic areas. Tours in English are offered less frequently, so check the website or call ahead for the schedule. ⊠ *Olympischer Pl. 3, Charlottenburg* ☎ *030/2500–2322* ⊕ *www.olympiastadion-berlin.de* 🎟 *€4, tours €7–€10* ☉ *Daily general tour at 11, 1, 3, and 5 in summer months but open times vary on days before and after major sports events, so call ahead.* Ⓜ *Olympiastadion (U-bahn).*

BIKING

Bike paths are generally marked by red pavement or white markings on the sidewalks. Try to avoid walking on bike paths and be careful when crossing them. Look both ways, as cyclists are liable not to follow traffic patterns on these paths, even though Berlin bike etiquette dictates that they should. Many stores that rent or sell bikes carry the Berlin biker's atlas.

Fahrradstation. Fahrradstation rents bikes for €15 per day (12 hours) or €35 for three days. Bring ID and call for its other locations. ⊠ *Dorotheenstr. 30, Mitte* ☎ *0180/510–8000* ⊕ *www.fahrradstation.de.*

JOGGING

The Tiergarten is the best place for jogging in the downtown area. Run down the paths parallel to Strasse des 17. Juni and back, and you'll have covered 8 km (5 mi). Joggers can also take advantage of the grounds of Charlottenburg Palace, 3 km (2 mi) around, and a scenic route along much of the Spree River in Mitte. For longer runs, make for the Grunewald.

SOCCER

Hertha BSC. Tickets for the home games of Berlin's premier soccer team, Hertha BSC, held at the Olympic Stadium, can be booked via phone or online. ⊠ *Olympic Stadium, Olympischer Pl. 3, Charlottenburg* ☎ *01805/189–200* ⊕ *www.herthabsc.de* Ⓜ *Olympiastadion (U-bahn).*

SWIMMING

Public pools throughout the city cost €4 for a day pass. For full listings, ask at the tourist office or navigate (in German) ⊕ *www.berlinerbaederbetriebe.de.* The lakes Wannsee, Halensee, Müggelsee, and Plötzensee all have beaches.

15

The dome atop Reichstag is one of the city's top attractions, and a walk inside it offers superb views.

Arena Badeschiff. In summer, a trip to the Arena Badeschiff is a must. The outdoor pool is set on a boat anchored on the river Spree, offering great views of the Kreuzberg skyline. It's open May 1 to late August/September, daily 8–midnight. In winter (September–March) the pool is transformed into an indoor sauna. ⊠ *Eichenstr. 4, Kreuzberg/Treptow* ☎ *030/533–2030* ☽ *Daily 8–12* Ⓜ *Schlesisches Tor (U-bahn).*

Liquidrom. Germans love their thermal baths and saunas, and this is just about the classiest around. The dramatic main thermal pool lies under a vaulted ceiling, where glowing lights and soothing music that can be heard underwater enhance a feeling of calm. In addition to several saunas and a steam room, take advantage of the outdoor hot tub in the enclosed courtyard, best at night under stars. There's a bar and a healthy snack menu, just in case all that relaxation leaves you hungry. Full nudity is to be expected here, even in coed areas. ⊠ *Möckernstr. 10, Kreuzberg* ☎ *030/2580–0782–0* ⊕ *www.liquidrom-berlin.de* ☞ *€19.50 for 2 hrs, €24.50 for 4 hrs, €29.50 whole day* ☽ *Sun.–Thurs. 10 am–midnight, Fri. and Sat. 10 am–1 am* Ⓜ *Anhalter Bahnhof (S-bahn).*

Strandbad Wannsee. The huge Strandbad Wannsee attracts as many as 40,000 Berliners to its fine, sandy beach on summer weekends. ⊠ *Wannseebad-weg 25, Zehlendorf* ☎ *030/7071–3833.*

SHOPPING

What's fashionable in Berlin is creative, bohemian style, so designer labels have less appeal here than in Hamburg, Düsseldorf, or Munich. For the young and trendy, it is bad form to be seen wearing clothes that appear to have cost much more than a brötchen (bread roll), so most step out in vintage and secondhand threads.

SHOPPING DISTRICTS

CHARLOTTENBURG

Although Ku'damm is still touted as the shopping mile of Berlin, many shops are ho-hum retailers. The best stretch for exclusive fashions, such as Bruno Magli, Hermès, and Jil Sander, are the three blocks between Leibnizstrasse and Bleibtreustrasse. For home furnishings, gift items, and unusual clothing boutiques, follow this route off Ku'damm: Leibnizstrasse to Mommsenstrasse to Bleibtreustrasse, then on to the ring around Savignyplatz. Fasanenstrasse, Knesebeckstrasse, Schlüterstrasse, and Uhlandstrasse are also fun places to browse.

Ku'damm ends at Breitscheidplatz, but the door-to-door shopping continues along Tauentzienstrasse, which, in addition to international retail stores, offers continental Europe's largest department store, the upscale Kaufhaus des Westens, or KaDeWe.

MITTE

The finest shops in historic Berlin are along Friedrichstrasse, including the French department store Galeries Lafayette. Nearby, Unter den Linden has just a few souvenir shops and a Meissen ceramic showroom. Smaller clothing and specialty stores populate the Scheunenviertel. The area between Hackescher Markt, Weinmeister Strasse, and Rosa-Luxemburg-Platz alternates pricey independent designers with groovy secondhand shops, and a string of ultrahip flagship stores by the big sports and fashion designer brands. Neue Schönhauser Strasse meets up with Rosenthaler Strasse on one end and curves into Alte Schönhauser Strasse on the other. All three streets are full of stylish and original casual wear. Galleries along Gipsstrasse and Sophienstrasse round out the mix.

DEPARTMENT STORES

Department Store Quartier 206. The smallest and most luxurious department store in town, Department Store Quartier 206 offers primarily French women's and men's designer clothes, perfumes, and home accessories. ☒ *Friedrichstr. 71, Mitte* ☎ *030/2094–6240* ⊗ *Mon.–Fri. 10:30–7:30, Sat. 10–6.*

Galeria Kaufhof. Anchoring Alexanderplatz, Galeria Kaufhof is the most successful branch of the German chain, though the wares are fairly basic. ☒ *Alexanderpl. 9, Mitte* ☎ *030/247–430* ⊕ *www.kaufhof.de* ⊗ *Mon.–Wed. 9:30–8, Thurs.–Sat. 9:30–10.*

Galeries Lafayette. Intimate and elegant, Galeries Lafayette carries almost exclusively French products, including designer clothes, perfume, and housewares, as well as gourmet treats, bread, and pastries in its food hall. ⊠ *Friedrichstr. 76–78, Mitte* ☎ *030/209–480* ⊘ *Daily 10–8.*

Kaufhaus des Westens (*KaDeWe*). The largest department store in continental Europe, classy Kaufhaus des Westens (KaDeWe) has a grand selection of goods on seven floors, as well as food and deli counters, Champagne bars, beer bars, and a winter garden on its top floor. Its wealth of services includes fixing umbrellas and repairing leather and furs. ⊠ *Tauentzienstr. 21–24, Western Downtown* ☎ *030/21210* ⊕ *www.kadewe.de* ⊘ *Mon.–Thurs. 10–8, Sat. 10–9, Sun. 9:30–8.*

GIFT IDEAS

Harry Lehmann. If you want a taste—or rather, a smell—of old Berlin, head to Harry Lehmann on Kantstrasse in Charlottenburg. The shopkeeper will greet you in a white lab coat, helpfully explaining the origin and inspiration of the expertly mixed perfumes, which fill large apothecary jars along a mirrored wall. This shop has been around for a long time (they just celebrated their 85th year in business). Scents are fresh, simple, and clean, and a 30ml bottle (€15.50) makes for a reasonably priced gift or souvenir. ⊠ *Kantstr. 106, Charlottenburg, Berlin* ☎ *030/324–3582* ⊕ *www.parfum-individual.de* ⊘ *Weekdays 9–6:30, Sat. 9–2.*

Königliche Porzellan Manufaktur. Fine porcelain is still produced by Königliche Porzellan Manufaktur, the former Royal Prussian Porcelain Factory, also called KPM. You can buy this delicate handmade, hand-painted china at KPM's two stores, but it may be more fun to visit the factory salesroom, which also sells seconds at reduced prices. ⊠ *Wegelystr. 1, Tiergarten* ☎ *030/390–090* ⊠ *Kurfürstendamm 27, Western Downtown* ☎ *030/8862–7961.*

Puppenstube im Nikolaiviertel. This is the ultimate shop for any kind of (mostly handmade) dolls, including designer models as well as old-fashioned German dolls. It's for collectors, not kids. ⊠ *Propststr. 4, Mitte* ☎ *030/242–3967* ⊕ *www.puppen1.de* ⊘ *Mon.–Sat. 10–6:30, Sun. 11–6.*

s.wert. Products here are inspired by Berlin's facades (pillows), grafitti (scratched glasses), and civic symbols (on polo shirts). ⊠ *Brunnenstr. 191, Mitte* ☎ *030/4005–66555* ⊕ *www.s-wert-design.de* ⊘ *Mon.–Fri., 12–8, Sat. 11–6.*

Scenario. Tucked under the elevated train tracks, Scenario sells stationery articles, gifts of any kind, and a lot of leather wares and jewelry. The designs here are modern. ⊠ *Savignypl. 1, Western Downtown* ☎ *030/312–9199.*

Wohnart Berlin. In the homey setting of Wohnart Berlin you can imagine how the stylish European furnishings, lamps, house wares, or stationery items might suit your own pad. ⊠ *Uhlandstr. 179–180, Western Downtown* ☎ *030/882–5252* ⊘ *Mon.–Sat. 10–7, Sun. 11–5.*

SPECIALTY STORES

ANTIQUES

Not far from Wittenbergplatz lies Keithstrasse, a street full of antiques stores. Eisenacher Strasse, Fuggerstrasse, Kalckreuthstrasse, Motzstrasse, and Nollendorfstrasse—all close to Nollendorfplatz—have many antiques stores of varying quality. Another good street for antiques is Suarezstrasse, between Kantstrasse and Bismarckstrasse. Other antiques stores are found under the tracks from Friedrichstrasse Station east to Universitätsstrasse, open Monday and Wednesday–Sunday 11–6.

JEWELRY

Bucherer. Fine handcrafted jewelry, watches, and other stylish designer accessories can be found at Bucherer. ⊠ *Kurfürstendamm 45, Western Downtown* ☏ *030/880–4030* ⊕ *www.bucherer.com* ☉ *Weekdays 10–7, Sat. 10–6.*

Oliver Hofmann. German designers featured at Oliver Hofmann share a philosophy of sleek minimalism. Rubber and diamond rings and matte platinum and diamond pieces are conscious understatements at this jewelry showroom. ⊠ *Kurfürstendamm 197, Western Downtown* ☏ *030/8847–1790* ☉ *Weekdays 10–7, Sat. 10–6.*

MEN'S CLOTHING

Budapester Schuhe. Handmade and timeless shoes and brogues, mostly from England, Austria, and Hungary, are sold at Budapester Schuhe. ⊠ *Kurfürstendamm 43, Western Downtown* ☏ *030/8862–4206* ⊠ *Bleibtreustr. 24, Western Downtown* ☏ *030/8862–9500.*

Mientus. The gentlemen's outfitter Mientus stocks Armani, Versace Classic, and Boss and has an in-house tailor. The Wilmersdorfer Strasse location is their flagship, and offers free parking for customers. ⊠ *Wilmersdorfer Str. 73, Western Downtown* ☏ *030/323–9077* ⊠ *Kurfürstendamm 52, Western Downtown* ☏ *030/323–9077.*

WOMEN'S CLOTHING

Claudia Skoda. The creations of Berlin's top avant-garde designer, Claudia Skoda, are mostly for women, but there's also a selection of men's knitwear. ⊠ *Alte Schönhauser Str. 35, Mitte* ☏ *030/280–7211.*

Jil Sander. The flagship store of German designer Jil Sander carries her complete line of understated clothing. ⊠ *Kurfürstendamm 185, Western Downtown* ☏ *030/886–7020.*

Peek & Cloppenburg. Peek & Cloppenburg, or "P & C," stocks women's, men's, and children's clothes on five floors. Don't miss the designer shop-in-shop areas on the second and third floors and the international, young-designer department in the basement. ⊠ *Tauentzienstr. 19, Western Downtown* ☏ *030/212–900.*

15

Flea Market Finds

Along with brunch, flea markets are another perennial Sunday staple in Berlin, and this town has one of them to suit every disposition.

While the antique market on **Strasse des 17. Juni** holds down the high end of the spectrum, markets in former East Berlin districts are, unsurprisingly, perfect for unearthing both trash and treasures.

The flea market at **Mauer Park**, a favorite among hipsters and tourists, is absolutely packed on Sunday in nice weather, turning the intersection of Bernauer Strasse and Oderberger Strasse (where the unofficial market outside the market begins) into a veritable Times Square of fun- and sun-loving young people.

The flea market at **Treptower Park** (just in front of Arena and the Badeschiff on the Spree River) takes up several large halls of an old warehouse, but it's much more of a rummage sale and junkyard than a real flea market. Tables of kitchen ware and rows of old bikes and mechanical parts do obscure some real treasures here, so come prepared to spend some time digging.

Closest in purpose to **Strasse des 17. Juni**, the **Grosser Antikmarkt am Ostbahnhof** is made up almost entirely of treasures, with little effort but a bit more money required to find something truly special to take home. Pre-edited selections of antiquarian books, gramophones, jewelry, and kitschy East German items can be found here.

The market at **Boxhagner Platz** in Friedrichshain is another popular weekend meeting spot, surrounded by cafés that have capitalized on the Sunday crowds. It's a good place to find that one item of furniture your apartment is missing, or to get a souvenir from the many local artists who sell their works here.

SIDE TRIP TO POTSDAM

A trip to Berlin wouldn't be complete without paying a visit to Potsdam and its park, which surrounds the important Prussian palaces Neues Palais and Sanssouci. This separate city, the state capital of Brandenburg (the state surrounding Berlin), can be reached within a half hour from Berlin's Zoo Station and most major Berlin S-bahn stations.

Potsdam still retains the imperial character it earned during the many years it served as a royal residence and garrison quarters. The Alter Markt and Neuer Markt show off stately Prussian architecture, and both are easily reached from the main train station by any tram heading into the town center.

GETTING HERE AND AROUND
Potsdam is 20 km (12 mi) southwest of Berlin's center and a half-hour journey by car or bus. From Zoo Station to Potsdam's main train station, the regional train RE 1 takes 17 minutes, and the S-7 line of the S-bahn takes about 30 minutes; use an ABC zone ticket for either service. City traffic is heavy, so a train journey is recommended. Several Berlin tour operators have Potsdam trips.

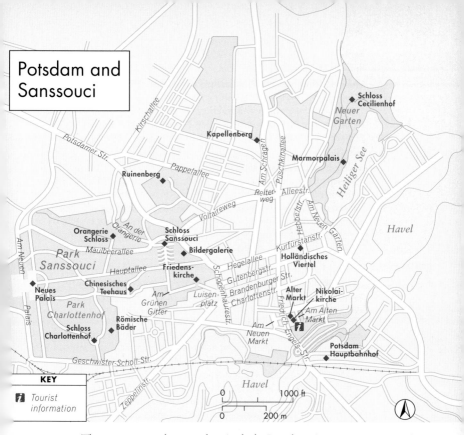

Potsdam and Sanssouci

KEY

🚩 Tourist information

0 — 1000 ft

0 — 200 m

There are several tours that include Potsdam (most are two or six hours). They leave from the landing across from Berlin's Wannsee S-bahn station between late March and early October. Depending on the various tours on offer, a round-trip ticket costs €7.50–€23.

ESSENTIALS

Visitor Information **Potsdam Tourist Office** ✉ *Touristenzentrum Potsdam, Brandenburger Str. 3, at Brandenburger Tor Potsdam* ☎ *0331/275–580* ⊕ *www. potsdamtourismus.de.*

EXPLORING

Alter Markt. Once dominated by the city's baroque palace, Alter Markt was heavily destroyed by Allied bombing in World War II and then blown up by the East German regime in 1960. Reminiscent of a similar debate in Berlin, Potsdam, too, has decided to rebuild its palace; the reconstructed structure will house the state parliament. Thanks to private donors, the first element, a magnificent replica of the **Fortunaportal,** now stands proudly on the square, while the palace's main sections are currently being built in a combination of modern and historic elements.

Nikolaikirche. Karl Friedrich Schinkel designed the Alter Markt's domed Nikolaikirche. In front of it stands an Egyptian obelisk erected by Schloss Sanssouci architect von Knobelsdorff.

Rathaus. A gilded figure of Atlas tops the tower of the old Rathaus, built in 1755.

Haus der Brandenburg-Preussischen Geschichte (*House of Brandenburg-Prussian History*). The region's history museum, the Haus der Brandenburg-Preussischen Geschichte, is in the royal stables in the square opposite the Nikolaikirche. ✉ *Am Neuen Markt 9* ☎ *0331/620–8550* ⊕ *www.hbpg.de* ⊠ *€4.50* ⊙ *Tues.–Thurs. 10–5, Fri. 10–7, weekends 10–6.*

Holländisches Viertel (*Dutch Quarter*). The center of the small Holländisches Viertel is an easy walk north along Friedrich-Ebert-Strasse to Mittelstrasse. Friedrich Wilhelm I built the settlement in 1742 to entice Dutch artisans who could support the city's rapid growth. Few Dutch came, and the gabled, mansard-roof brick houses were largely used to house staff. Stores and restaurants inhabit the buildings now, and the area is Potsdam's most visited.

QUICK BITES

Wiener Restaurant-Café. Fine coffee blends and rich cakes are offered at the Wiener Restaurant-Café, an old-style European coffeehouse on the way to the Grünes Gitter entrance to Sanssouci. ⊠ *Luisenpl. 4* ☎ *0331/6014–9904.*

Schloss Sanssouci. Prussia's most famous king, Friedrich II—Frederick the Great—spent more time at his summer residence, Schloss Sanssouci, than in the capital of Berlin. Its name means "without a care" in French, the language Frederick cultivated in his own private circle and within the court. Some experts believe that Frederick actually named the palace "Sans, Souci," which they translate as "with and without a care," a more apt name; its construction caused him a lot of trouble and expense, and sparked furious rows with his master builder, Georg Wenzeslaus von Knobelsdorff. His creation nevertheless became one of Germany's greatest tourist attractions. The palace lies on the edge of Park Sanssouci, which includes various buildings and palaces with separate admissions and hours. ■ TIP→ Be advised that during peak tourism times, timed tickets for Schloss Sanssouci tours can sell out before noon.

Neue Kammern (*New Chambers*). To the west of the palace are the Neue Kammern, which housed guests of the king's family after its beginnings as a greenhouse. ☎ *0331/969–4206* ⊠ *€3 guided tour only* ⊙ *Apr.–mid-May, weekends 10–5; May–Oct., Tues.–Sun. 10–5.*

Bildergalerie (*Picture Gallery*). Just east of Sanssouci Palace is the Bildergalerie, with expensive marble from Siena in the main cupola. The gallery displays Frederick II's collection of 17th-century Italian and Dutch paintings, including works by Caravaggio, Rubens, and Van Dyck. ☎ *0331/969–4181* ⊠ *€2* ⊙ *May–mid-Oct., Tues.–Sun. 10–5* ✉ *Park Sanssouci* ☎ *0331/969–4202* ⊕ *www.spsg.de* ⊠ *€12, Apr.–Oct., €8 Nov.–Mar.* ⊙ *Apr.–Oct., Tues.–Sun. 10–6; Nov.–Mar., Tues.–Sun. 10–5.*

Neues Palais (*New Palace*). The Neues Palais, a much larger and grander palace than Sanssouci, stands at the end of the long avenue that runs through Sanssouci Park. It was built after the Seven Years' War (1756–63), when Frederick loosened the purse strings. It's said he wanted to demonstrate that the state coffers hadn't been depleted too severely by the long conflict. Interiors that impress include the Grotto Hall with walls and columns set with shells, coral, and other aquatic decor. The royals' upper apartments have paintings by 17th-century Italian masters. You can opt to tour the palace yourself only on weekends between late April and mid-May. ⊠ *Str. am Neuen Palais, Sanssouci* ☎ *0331/969–4361* ⊕ *www.spsg.de* ☒ *Apr.–Oct., €5, €6 with tour; Nov.–Mar., €5 with tour* ☉ *Apr.–Oct. 9–5; Nov.–Mar., Wed.–Mon. 9–4, closed Fri.*.

Schloss Charlottenhof. Schloss Charlottenhof is in the southern part of Sanssouci Park, an expansive, landscaped promenade with fountains, streams, manicured gardents, and wide walkways as well as some hidden paths. After Frederick the Great died in 1786, the ambitious Sanssouci building program ground to a halt, and the park fell into neglect. It was 50 years before another Prussian king, Friedrich Wilhelm IV, restored Sanssouci's earlier glory. He engaged the great Berlin architect Karl Friedrich Schinkel to build this small palace for the crown prince. Schinkel's demure interiors are preserved, and the most fanciful room is the bedroom, decorated like a Roman tent, with its walls and ceiling draped in striped canvas. Between the Sanssouci palaces are later additions to the park.

Römische Bäder (*Roman Baths*). Friedrich Wilhelm IV built the Römische Bäder (Roman Baths), also designed by Schinkel, from 1829 to 1840. Like many of the other structures in Potsdam, this one is more romantic than authentic. Half Italian villa, half Greek temple, the structure is nevertheless a charming addition to the park. ☒ *€3 with exhibit* ☉ *May–Oct., Tues.–Sun. 10–5.*

Orangerieschloss und Turm. The Orangerieschloss und Turm was completed in 1864; its two massive towers linked by a colonnade evoke an Italian Renaissance palace. Today it houses 47 copies of paintings by Raphael. ☒ *Guided tour €3, tower only €2* ☉ *Palace and tower mid-May–mid-Oct., Tues.–Sun. 10–5; tower opens Apr., only weekends 10–5.*

Chinesisches Teehaus (*Chinese Teahouse*). The Chinesisches Teehaus was erected in 1757 in the Chinese style that was all the rage at the time. It houses porcelain from Meissen and Asia. ☒ *€1* ☉ *May–Oct., Tues.–Sun. 10–5.*

Friedenskirche (*Peace Church*). Completed in 1848, the Italianate Friedenskirche houses a 12th-century Byzantine mosaic taken from an island near Venice ☎ *0331/974–009* ☒ *Free* ☉ *Late Mar.–Apr. and 1st 2 wks in Oct., Mon.–Sat. 12–5, Sun. 11–5; May–Sept., Mon.–Sat. 12–6, Sun. 10–6* ☎ *0331/969–4200* ☒ *€4 with tour* ☉ *Easter wk and May–Oct., Tues.–Sun. 10–6.*

QUICK
BITES

Drachenhaus (*Dragon House*). Halfway up the hill leading to the Belvedere, past the Orangerie, stands the curious Drachenhaus, modeled in 1770 after the Pagoda at London's Kew Gardens and named for the gargoyles ornamenting the roof corners. It now houses a popular restaurant and café.

15

Schloss Cecilienhof (*Cecilienhof Palace*). Resembling a rambling, Tudor manor house, Schloss Cecilienhof was built for Crown Prince Wilhelm in 1913, on a newly laid-out stretch of park called the New Garden, which borders the Heiliger See. It was in this, the last palace to be built by the Hohenzollerns, that the Allied leaders Stalin, Truman, and Churchill (later Attlee) hammered out the fate of postwar Germany at the 1945 Potsdam Conference. ■TIP→ From Potsdam's main train station, take a tram to Reiterweg/Alleestrasse, and then transfer to Bus 692 to Am Neuer Garten. ☎ *0331/969–4200* ⊕ *www.spsg.de* ✉ *€6 with tour (Nov.–Mar. tour is mandatory), €4 tour of royal couple's private apartments* ☉ *Tues.–Sun. 10–6. Tours of royal couple's private apartments at 10, 12, 2, 4.*

WHERE TO EAT AND STAY

For expanded hotel reviews, visit Fodors.com.

$$ ✕ **Juliette.** In a city proud of its past French influences, the highly praised
FRENCH French cuisine here is delivered to your table by French waiters, no less. The intimate restaurant at the edge of the Dutch Quarter has old-fashioned brick walls and a fireplace. The menu offers small portions of dishes such as rack of lamb, wild-hare pie with hot peppered cherries, and a starter plate of four foie-gras preparations. Its wine list of 120 French vintages is unique in the Berlin area. ■TIP→ Company chief Ralph Junick has really cornered the market in Potsdam, with two other French restaurants, a tasty creperie, and a coffee shop. If you'll be in Potsdam for more than one meal, check Juliette's Web site to see what else is in town. ✉ *Jägerstr. 39* ☎ *0331/270–1791* ⊕ *www.restaurant-juliette.de.*

$$ ⌂ **Hotel am Luisenplatz.** Behind a somber-looking facade, this intimate hotel conceals a warm, upscale elegance and friendly, personal service. **Pros:** great central location near pedestrian zones of downtown Potsdam; personal flair; great views. **Cons:** tour buses stop for meals and restaurant crowded during these visits; no air-conditioning; sometimes-busy Luisenplatz right in front of rooms. ✉ *Luisenpl. 5* ☎ *0331/971–900* ⊕ *www.hotel-luisenplatz.de* ⇱ *38 rooms, 4 suites* ⌂ *In-room: no a/c, Wi-Fi. In-hotel: spa, parking, some pets allowed* ⎮◎⎮ *Breakfast.*

Saxony, Saxony-Anhalt, and Thuringia

WORD OF MOUTH

"[T]he Leipzig area [is very interesting]. [B]ase in a town like Weimar—and hop to Erfurt, Leipzig, Naumburg and Eisenach—home of Wartburg Castle where Martin Luther was hiding out and famously saw the Devil—the ink stains from the inkwell he flung at the Devil still standing witness to that on the walls."

—PalenQ

WELCOME TO SAXONY, SAXONY-ANHALT, AND THURINGIA

TOP REASONS TO GO

★ **Following Martin Luther:** Trace the path of the ultimate medieval rebel in Wittenberg, Eisenach, and the Wartburg and gain valuable insight into the mind and culture of a person whose ideas helped change the world.

★ **Frauenkirche in Dresden:** Rising like a majestic baroque phoenix, the church is a worthy symbol of a city destroyed and rebuilt from its ashes.

★ **Görlitz:** Balanced on the border between Germany and Poland, this architectural gem is relatively undiscovered; you'll feel as if you have the whole town to yourself.

★ **Weimar:** The history of Germany seems to revolve around this small town, whose past residents are a veritable who's who of the last 400 years, including Goethe, Schiller, Bach, Liszt, and Gropius.

★ **Wine tasting in the Salle-Unstrut:** The castle-topped, rolling hills covered in terraced vineyards are perfect for biking, hiking, and horseback riding.

1 Saxony. Saxony is the pearl of East Germany: the countryside is dotted with beautifully renovated castles and fortresses, and the people are charming and full of energy. (They also speak in an almost incomprehensible local dialect.) Dresden and Leipzig are cosmopolitan centers that combine the energy of the avant-garde with a distinct respect for tradition.

2 Saxony-Anhalt. Although long ignored by travelers, Saxony-Anhalt has more UNESCO World Heritage sites than any other region in Europe. The city of Naumburg is famed for its cathedral and for the wines produced in the surrounding vineyards.

GETTING ORIENTED

These three states cover the southeastern part of the former East Germany. You will still see old, dirty, and depressing industrial towns that recall the Communist past but some of Germany's most historic cities are here, too, and 20 years of reconstruction programs have slowly restored them. Dresden is promoting its reputation as "the Florence on the Elbe," and just downstream Meissen has undergone an impressive face-lift. Weimar, one of the continent's old cultural centers, and Leipzig, in particular, have washed off their grime and almost completely restored their historic city centers. Görlitz, Germany's easternmost city, benefited from an infusion of cash and is consistently lauded as one of the country's 10 most beautiful cities.

16

3 Thuringia. Of all the East German states, Thuringia has the best tourist infrastructure. Western visitors to the classical jewel of Weimar and those interested in outdoor sports in the lush Thuringian Forest have been vital sources of hard currency. This still holds true today: Thuringia offers unparalleled natural sights as well as classical culture at reasonable prices.

FOLLOWING MARTIN LUTHER

Saxony-Anhalt and Thuringia are currently celebrating the "Luther decade," preparing to mark the Protestant Reformation's 500th anniversary in 2017. A drive through *Lutherstadt* (Luther Country) allows for a deeper understanding of Martin Luther and the Reformation.

(above) Lutherhaus in Eisenach, where he lived as a student. (upper right) Martin Luther. (lower right) Memorial for Martin Luther in Eisleben.

Dissatisfaction was already brewing, but Martin Luther (1483–1546) was the first to speak out against the Catholic Church. He took issue with the sale of indulgences—letters from the Pope purchased by wealthy Christians to absolve them of sins. His 95 Theses, which he brashly nailed to a church door, called for a return to faith in the Bible's teachings over the Pope's decrees, and an end to the sale of indulgences. Despite such so-called heretical beginnings, Luther overcame condemnation by the Pope and several other governing bodies. He continued to preach, building a family with Katharina von Bora, a former nun he controversially married after "rescuing" her from a convent. After his death, Lutheranism spread across Europe as an accepted branch of Christianity.

—Giulia Pines

LUTHER QUOTES

"I am more afraid of my own heart than of the pope and all his cardinals. I have within me the great pope, Self."

"[When] the Devil . . . sees men use violence to propagate the gospel[, h]e . . . says with malignant looks and frightful grin: 'Ah, how wise these madmen are to play my game! Let them go on; I shall reap the benefit . . .'"

—Martin Luther

ON THE TRAIL OF MARTIN LUTHER

Start in the town of Wittenberg, the unofficial capital of *Lutherstadt*. The comprehensive **Lutherhaus** museum is in the Augustinian monastery where Luther lived twice, first as a monk and later with his family. This multilevel, bilingual museum will convince the skeptics that Luther is worth remembering. From the museum, it's a short walk down the main thoroughfare Collegienstrasse to two churches that felt the influence of his teachings. The first is **Stadtkirche St. Marien** (Parish Church of St. Mary), where Luther often preached. The second, **Schlosskirche** (Castle Church), is where Luther changed history by posting his 95 Theses. The original wooden doors were destroyed in a 1760 fire, now replaced by bronze doors with the Latin text of the 95 Theses. On the way from one church to the other, stop to admire the statues of Luther and his friend and collaborator Philipp Melanchthon—they are buried next to each other in Schlosskirche.

In the nearby town of Eisleben, the houses where Luther was born, the **Luthers Geburtshaus** (✉ *Lutherstr. 15* ☎ *03475/714–7814*), and died, **Luthers Sterbehaus** (✉ *Sangerhäuser Str. 46* ☎ *03475/67680*) lie 10 minutes from each other (the latter is closed for renovation until mid-2012). From there, it's easy to spot the steeples of two churches: **St. Petri-Pauli-Kirche** (*Church of Sts. Peter and Paul* ✉ *Petristr.* ☎ *03475/602–229*) and **St. Andreaskirche** (*St. Andrew's Church* ✉ *Andreaskirchpl.* ☎ *03475/602–229*). The first was Luther's place of baptism, while the second houses the pulpit where Luther gave his last four sermons. His funeral was also held here before his body was taken back to Wittenberg.

Continuing southwest the stunning medieval castle **Wartburg** is in the hills high above the town of Eisenach. Luther took refuge here after he was excommunicated by the Pope and outlawed by a general assembly called the Diet of Worms, famously translating the New Testament from the original Greek into German.

REFORMATION TIMELINE

1517: Martin Luther nails his 95 Theses to the door of Wittenberg's Schlosskirche.

1521: Luther is excommunicated after refusing to recant his works.

1525: Anabaptist movement is founded, rejecting conventional Christian symbolism and ritualism.

1537: Christian III of Denmark declares Lutheranism the state religion, encouraging its spread through Scandinavia.

1555: Charles V signs Peace of Augsburg treaty, effectively ending the battle between Catholicism and Lutheranism and granting the latter an official status as one of two main branches of Christianity.

1558: Queen Elizabeth I of England supports the establishment of the English Protestant Church.

1577: After Luther's death, the Formula of Concord puts an end to disputes between various sects, thereby strengthening and preserving Lutheranism.

1600s and beyond: Lutheran explorers and settlers bring their beliefs to the New World.

16

BAUHAUS IN WEIMAR

Begun in Weimar, the Bauhaus movement's futuristic design, "form from function" mentality, and revolutionary spirit has inspired artists worldwide.

(above) Bauhaus Museum in Weimar. (upper right) Bauhaus Building in Dessau.

Founded in 1919 by architect Walter Gropius, the Bauhaus movement had roots in the past but was also unabashedly modern. Based on the principles of William Morris and the Arts and Crafts movement, Bauhaus promoted the idea of creation as a service to society, holding practical objects such as a chair, teapot, or lamp to the same high standards as true works of art. Its style was art deco but less ornate, machine-age but not industrial, its goal to put both spaces and materials to their most natural and economical uses. Although the Bauhaus school was shut down by the Nazis in the early 1930s, many former Bauhaus students left Germany and went to work in other parts of the world. Today, their influence can even be seen as far away as Tel Aviv, where Jewish architects fleeing Europe came to build their vision of a modern city.
—Giulia Pines

BAUHAUS IN DESSAU

If you have an extra day, take the train to Dessau, Bauhaus's second city, to see the iconic **Bauhaus Building**, adorned on one side with vertical block lettering spelling out "Bauhaus." Still an architecture school, it now houses the Bauhaus Dessau Foundation, and a multilevel Bauhaus Museum. You can even stay in the monastic Bauhaus studio flats here.

A BAUHAUS WALK IN WEIMAR

Start with the **Bauhaus Museum** in Weimar's central Theaterplatz, which offers a film about the history of Bauhaus and rotating exhibitions covering much of what there is to see in Weimar. Head south along Schützengasse and continue down Amalienstrasse to catch a glimpse of the Henry van de Velde–designed main building of **Bauhaus University** (✉ *Geschwister-Scholl-Strasse 8* ☎ *03643/580* ⊕ *www. uni-weimar.de*), formerly the Grand Ducal School of Arts and Crafts. A faithful reconstruction of Gropius's office can be found here as well. The **Bauhaus Atelier** (✉ *Geschwister-Scholl-Strasse 6a* ☎ *03643/583–000*) at the university is a central meeting place for students. It contains a café and shop offering books about the movement as well as Bauhaus-designed souvenirs, and also marks the starting point for university-run Bauhaus walks. Head just south for the Gropius-designed **Monument to the March Dead** in Weimar's **Historischer Friedhof** (Historical Cemetery). This jagged expressionist structure, built in 1921, commemorates those who died in the Kapp Putsch, an attempt to overthrow the Weimar Republic a year earlier. Follow the signs for **Goethes Gartenhaus** (perhaps the most visited historical structure in Weimar) through the Park on the Ilm, and look just beyond it for the **Haus am Horn** (✉ *Am Horn 61* ☎ *03643/904–056*). This modest, cubical structure designed by Georg Muche for the 1923 Bauhaus exhibition was meant to be a model of Bauhaus's functional philosophy. It was fully restored in 1999 to mark the 80 anniversary of the founding of Bauhaus.

STYLE ELEMENTS

According to the standards of Bauhaus, good design should be accompanied by good engineering. That's why so many Bauhaus buildings still look so strikingly modern and even industrial, though they may have been designed as early as the 1920s. To spot Bauhaus or Bauhaus influence anywhere in the world, look for unadorned, **boxlike structures** with repeating parallel lines, **flat roofs**, and rectangular windowpanes. Furniture and household objects are characterized by strong lines and retro-futuristic shapes, as well as the abundant use of **metals**. Bauhaus designers were also instrumental in creating *The New Typography*, of which the sign on the Bauhaus Building in Dessau is a prime example: look for **clear, boxy typefaces**, often combined collagelike with photographs and **colorful graphics** and shapes to create bold messages.

Updated by
Lee A. Evans

Germany's traditional charm is most evident in the eastern states of Saxony, Saxony-Anhalt, and Thuringia. Since the former communist German Democratic Republic (commonly referred to by its German acronym—DDR or its English equivalent GDR) resolutely clung to its German heritage, an unspoiled German state of mind still survives here.

East Germans proudly preserved their connections with such national heroes as Luther, Goethe, Schiller, Bach, Handel, Wagner, and the Hungarian-born Liszt. Towns in the regions of the Thüringer Wald (Thuringian Forest) or the Harz Mountains—long considered the haunt of witches—are drenched in history and medieval legend. The area hides a fantastic collection of rural villages and castles unparalleled in other parts of the country.

Many cities, such as Erfurt, escaped World War II relatively unscathed, and the East Germans extensively rebuilt those towns that were damaged by bombing. The historical centers have been restored to their past splendor, but there are also eyesores of industrialization and stupendously bland housing projects. Famous palaces and cultural wonders— the rebuilt historical center of Dresden, the Wartburg at Eisenach, the Schiller and Goethe houses in Weimar, Luther's Wittenberg, as well as the wonderfully preserved city of Görlitz—are waiting to be discovered by Western visitors.

PLANNING

WHEN TO GO

Winters in this part of Germany can be cold, wet, and dismal, so unless you plan to ski in the Harz Mountains or the Thüringer Wald, visit in late spring, summer, or early autumn. Avoid Leipzig at trade-fair times, particularly in March and April. In summer every city, town, and village has a festival, with streets blocked and local culture spilling out into every open space.

GETTING HERE AND AROUND
AIR TRAVEL
It's easiest, and usually cheapest, to fly into Berlin or Frankfurt and rent a car from there. Dresden and Leipzig both have international airports that are primarily operated by budget carriers serving European destinations. Dresden Flughafen is about 10 km (6 mi) north of Dresden, and Leipzig's Flughafen Leipzig-Halle is 12 km (8 mi) northwest of the city.

Airport Contacts **Dresden Flughafen** ☎ *0351/881–3360* ⊕ *www.dresden-airport.de.* **Flughafen Leipzig-Halle** ☎ *0341/224–1155* ⊕ *www.leipzig-halle-airport.de.*

BUS TRAVEL
Long-distance buses travel to Dresden and Leipzig. Bus service within the area is infrequent and mainly connects with rail lines. Check schedules carefully at central train stations or call the service phone number of Deutsche Bahn (German Railway) at local railway stations.

CAR TRAVEL
Expressways connect Berlin with Dresden (A-13) and Leipzig (A-9). Both journeys take about two hours. The A-4 stretches east–west across the southern portion of Thuringia and Saxony.

A road-construction program in eastern Germany is ongoing, and you should expect traffic delays on any journey of more than 300 km (186 mi). The Bundesstrassen throughout eastern Germany are narrow, tree-lined country roads, often jammed with traffic. Roads in the western part of the Harz Mountains are better and wider.

Cars can be rented at the Dresden and Leipzig airports, at train stations, and through all major hotels. Be aware that you are not allowed to take rentals into Poland or the Czech Republic.

TRAIN TRAVEL
The fastest and least inexpensive way to explore the region is by train. East Germany's rail infrastructure is exceptional; trains serve even the most remote destinations with astonishing frequency. Slower S, RB, and RE trains link smaller towns, while Leipzig, Dresden, Weimar, Erfurt, Naumburg, and Wittenberg are all on major ICE lines. Some cities—Dresden and Meissen, for example—are linked by commuter trains.

From Dresden a round-trip ticket to Leipzig costs about €43 (a 1½-hour journey one-way); to Görlitz it's about €38 (a 1½-hour ride). Trains connect Leipzig with Halle (a 30-minute ride, €10), Erfurt (a 1-hour ride, €28), and Eisenach (a 1½-hour journey, €28). The train ride between Dresden and Eisenach (2½ hours) costs €56 one-way.

■ TIP→ Consider using a Länder-Ticket, a €29 regional day ticket from the German Railroad that covers local train travel in the respective state (for example, within Sachsen, Sachsen-Anhalt, or Thüringen).

TOURS
Viking K–D has two luxury cruise ships on the Elbe River. It operates a full program of cruises of up to eight days in length, from mid-April until late October, that go from Hamburg as far as Prague. All the historic cities of Saxony and Thuringia are ports of call—including Dres-

16

den, Meissen, Wittenberg, and Dessau. *For details see Cruise Travel in Travel Smart Germany.*

Weisse Flotte's historic paddle-steam tours depart from and stop in Dresden, Meissen, Pirna, Pillnitz, Königsstein, and Bad Schandau. Besides tours in the Dresden area, boats also go into the Czech Republic. For more information contact the Sächsische Dampfschiffahrt.

In Saxony two historic narrow-gauge trains still operate on a regular schedule. Both the *Lössnitzgrundbahn,* which connects Ost-Radebeul-Ost and Radeburg, as well as the *Weisseritzelbahn,* which operates between Freital-Hainsberg and Kurort Kipsdorf, are perfect for taking in some of Saxony's romantic countryside and the Fichtelberg Mountains. A round-trip ticket is between about €7 and €11, depending on the length of the ride. For schedule and information, contact Deutsche Bahn's regional Dresden office.

The famous steam locomotive *Harzquerbahn* connects Nordhausen-Nord with Wernigerode and Gernerode in the Harz Mountains. The most popular track of this line is the *Brockenbahn,* a special narrow-gauge train transporting tourists to the top of northern Germany's highest mountain. For schedule and further information, contact the Harzer Schmalspurbahnen GmbH.

Tour Contacts German Railroad (Deutsche Bahn) ☏ *0180/599/6633* ⊕ *www.bahn.de.* Harzer Schmalspurbahnen GmbH ☏ *03943/5580* ⊕ *www.hsb-wr.de.* Lössnitzgrundbahn ☏ *0351/46165–63684* ⊕ *www. loessnitzgrundbahn.de.* Sächsische Dampfschiffahrt ☏ *0351/866–090* ⊕ *www. saechsische-dampfschiffahrt.de.* Weisseritztalbahn ☏ *0351/641/2701* ⊕ *www. weisseritztalbahn.de.*

RESTAURANTS

Enterprising young managers and chefs have established themselves in the East, so look for new, usually small, restaurants. People in the region are extremely particular about their traditional food (rumor has it that one can be deported for roasting Mützbraten over anything other than birch), but some new chefs have successfully blended contemporary German with international influences. Medieval-theme restaurants and "experience dining," complete with entertainment, are all the rage in the East, and warrant at least one try. Brewpubs have sprouted up everywhere, and are a good bet for meeting locals.

HOTELS

Hotels in eastern Germany are up to international standards and, due to economic subsidies in the 1990s, often far outshine their West German counterparts. In the East it's quite normal to have a major international hotel in a 1,000-year-old house or restored mansion. Smaller and family-run hotels are more charming local options, and often include a good restaurant. Most big hotels offer special weekend or activity-oriented packages that aren't found in the western part of the country. All hotels include breakfast, unless indicated otherwise.

During the trade fairs and shows of the **Leipziger Messe,** particularly in March and April, most Leipzig hotels increase their prices.

WHAT IT COSTS IN EUROS

	¢	$	$$	$$$	$$$$
Restaurants	under €9	€9–€15	€16–€20	€21–€25	over €25
Hotels	under €50	€50–€100	€101–€175	€176–€225	over €225

Restaurant prices are per person for a main course at dinner. Hotel prices are for two people in a standard double room, including tax and service.

PLANNING YOUR TIME

Eastern Germany is a small, well-connected region that's well suited for day trips. Dresden and Leipzig are the largest cities with the most facilities, making them good bases from which to explore the surrounding countryside, either by car or train. Both are well connected with Berlin, Munich, and Frankfurt. Leipzig, Dresden, Lutherstadt-Wittenberg, and Dessau can be explored as day trips from Berlin. Any of the smaller towns offer a quieter, possibly more authentic look at the area. A trip into the Salle-Unstrut wine region is well worth the time, using Naumburg as a base.

DISCOUNTS AND DEALS

Most of the region's larger cities offer special tourist exploring cards, such as the **Dresdencard, Hallecard, Leipzigcard,** and **Weimarcard,** which include discounts at museums, concerts, hotels, and restaurants or special sightseeing packages for up to three days. For details, check with the local visitor information office.

> **THE FIVE KS**
>
> A long-standing joke is that the priorities of the people of Saxony, Saxony-Anhalt, and Thuringia can be summed up in five Ks: Kaffee, Kuchen, Klösse, Kartoffeln, and Kirche (coffee, cake, dumplings, potatoes, and church)—in that order.

SAXONY

The people of Saxony identify themselves more as Saxon than German. Their hardworking and rustic attitudes, their somewhat peripheral location on the border with the Czech Republic and Poland, and their almost incomprehensible dialect, are the targets of endless jokes and puns. However, Saxon pride rebuilt three cities magnificently: Dresden and Leipzig—the showcase cities of eastern Germany—and the smaller town of Görlitz, on the Neisse River.

LEIPZIG

184 km (114 mi) southwest of Berlin.

Leipzig is, in a word, cool—but not so cool as to be pretentious. With its world-renowned links to Bach, Schubert, Mendelssohn, Martin Luther, Goethe, Schiller, and the fantastic Neue-Leipziger-Schule art movement, Leipzig is one of the great German cultural centers. It has impressive art nouveau architecture, an incredibly clean city center, meandering narrow streets, and the temptations of coffee and cake on every corner. In *Faust*, Goethe describes Leipzig as "a little Paris"; in reality it's more reminiscent of Vienna, while remaining a distinctly energetic Saxon town.

Leipzig's musical past includes Johann Sebastian Bach (1685–1750), who was organist and choir director at Leipzeig's Thomaskirche, and the 19th-century composer Richard Wagner, who was born in the city in 1813. Today's Leipzig continues the cultural focus with extraordinary offerings of music, theater, and opera, not to mention fantastic nightlife.

Wartime bombs destroyed much of Leipzig's city center, but reconstruction efforts have uncovered one of Europe's most vibrant cities. Leipzig's art nouveau flair is best discovered by exploring the countless alleys, covered courtyards, and passageways. Many unattractive buildings from the postwar period remain, but only reinforce Leipzig's position on the line between modernity and antiquity.

With a population of about 523,000, Leipzig is the second-largest city in eastern Germany (after Berlin) and has long been a center of printing and bookselling. Astride major trade routes, it was an important market town in the Middle Ages, and it continues to be a trading center, thanks

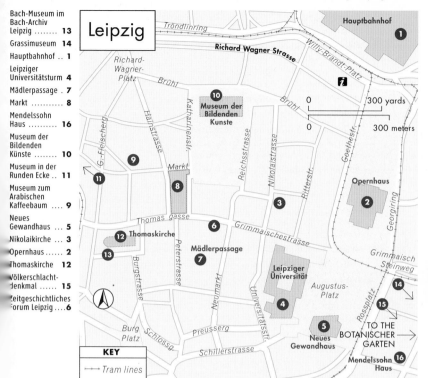

to the *Leipziger Messe* (trade and fair shows) throughout the year that bring together buyers from East and West.

Unfortunately, Leipzig has a tendency to underwhelm first-time visitors. If you take Leipzig slow and have some cake, its subtle, hidden charms may surprise you.

GETTING HERE AND AROUND

Leipzig is an hour from Berlin by train. Leipzig-Halle airport serves many European destinations, but no North American ones.

TIMING

Leipzig can easily be explored in one day; it's possible to walk around the downtown area in just about three hours. The churches can be inspected in less than 20 minutes each. But if you're interested in German history and art, plan for two full days, so you can spend one day just visiting the museums and go to the symphony. The Völkerschlachtdenkmal is perfect for a three-hour side trip.

ESSENTIALS

Visitor Information Leipzig Tourismus und Marketing e.V. ✉ *Richard-Wagner-Str. 1* ☎ *0341/710–4260* 🖷 *0341/710–4301* ⊕ *www.leipzig.de.*

EXPLORING
TOP ATTRACTIONS

Grassimuseum. British star architect David Chipperfield restored and modernized this fine example of German art deco in 2003–05. The building, dating to 1925–29, houses three important museums.

Museum für Angewandte Kunst (*Museum of Applied Art*). The Museum für Angewandte Kunst showcases 2,000 years of works from Leipzig's and eastern Germany's proud tradition of handicrafts, such as exquisite porcelain, fine tapestry art, and modern Bauhaus design. ☎ *0341/222–9100* ⊕ *www. grassimuseum.de* ✉ *€5* ☉ *Tues.–Sun. 10–6.*

Museum für Völkerkunde (*Ethnological Museum*). The Museum für Völkerkunde presents arts and crafts from all continents and various eras, including a thrilling collection of Southeast Asian antique art, and the world's only Kurile Ainu feather costume, in the Northeast Asia collection. ☎ *0341/973–1300* ⊕ *www.grassimuseum.de* ✉ *€6* ☉ *Tues.– Sun. 10–6.*

Museum für Musikinstrumente (*Musical Instruments Museum*). The Museum for Musical Instruments showcases musical instruments, mostly from the Renaissance, including the world's oldest clavichord, constructed in 1543 in Italy. There are also spinets, flutes, and lutes. Recordings of the instruments can be heard at the exhibits. ☎ *0341/ 973–0750* ⊕ *mfm.uni-leipzig.de* ✉ *€5* ☉ *Tues.–Sun. 10–6* ✉ *Johannispl. 5–11.*

Mädlerpassage (*Mädler Mall*). The ghost of Goethe's Faust lurks in every marble corner of Leipzig's finest shopping arcade. One of the scenes in *Faust* is set in the famous Auerbachs Keller restaurant, at No. 2. A bronze group of characters from the play, sculpted in 1913, beckons you down the stone staircase to the restaurant. ■TIP→ **Touching the statues' feet is said to bring good luck.** A few yards away is a delightful art nouveau bar called Mephisto. ✉ *Grimmaische Str.*

Markt. Leipzig's showpiece is its huge, old market square. One side is completely occupied by the Renaissance town hall, the **Altes Rathaus.**

Stadtgeschichtliches Museum. Inside the Altes Rathaus, this museum documents Leipzig's past. The entrance is behind the Rathaus. ✉ *Markt 1* ☎ *0341/965–130* ⊕ *www.stadtgeschichtliches-museum-leipzig.de* ✉ *€4* ☉ *Tues.–Sun. 10–6.*

★ **Museum der Bildenden Künste** (*Museum of Fine Arts*). The city's leading art gallery is minimalism incarnate, set in a huge concrete cube encased in green glass in the middle of Sachsenplatz Square. The museum's collection of more than 2,700 paintings and sculptures represents everything from the German Middle Ages to the modern Neue Leipziger

TOURING TIPS

Information: The friendly tourist-information office is at Richard-Wagner-Strasse 1. If you plan to visit any museums, consider the Leipzigcard.

People-watching: Take a seat upstairs—above the elephant heads—at the coffeehouse Riquet and watch the world go by.

Typically Leipzig: Drink a Gose and try the updated "Meadowlark" pastry.

Bach was choirmaster at the Thomaskirche and is buried here. Bach wrote cantatas for the boys' choir here, which you can still hear performed.

Schule. Especially notable are the collections focusing on Lucas Cranach the Elder and Caspar David Friedrich. ■TIP➔ Be sure to start at the top and work your way down. Don't miss Max Klinger's Beethoven as Zeus statue. ⊠ *Katharinenstr. 10* ☎ *0341/216–990* ⊕ *www.mdbk.de* ✉ *€5, €6 for special exhibits* ⊗ *Tues.–Sun. 10–6, Wed. noon–8.*

★ **Nikolaikirche** (*St. Nicholas Church*). This church with its undistinguished facade was center stage during the demonstrations that helped bring down the Communist regime. Every Monday for months before the government collapsed, thousands of citizens gathered in front of the church chanting "*Wir sind das Volk*" ("We are the people"). Inside are a soaring Gothic choir and nave. Note the unusual patterned ceiling supported by classical pillars that end in palm-tree-like flourishes. Martin Luther is said to have preached from the ornate 16th-century pulpit. ■TIP➔ The prayers for peace that began the revolution in 1989 are still held on Monday at 5 pm. ⊠ *Nikolaikirchhof* ☎ *0341/960–5270* ✉ *Free* ⊗ *Mon.–Sat. 10–6; Sun. services at 9:30, 11:15, and 5.*

★ **Thomaskirche** (*St. Thomas's Church*). Bach was choirmaster at this Gothic church for 27 years, and Martin Luther preached here on Whit-sunday 1539, signaling the arrival of Protestantism in Leipzig. Originally the center of a 13th-century monastery, the tall church (rebuilt in the 15th century) now stands by itself. Bach wrote most of his cantatas for the church's famous boys' choir, the Thomanerchor, which was founded in the 13th century; the church continues as the choir's home as well as a center of Bach tradition.

The great music Bach wrote during his Leipzig years commanded little attention in his lifetime, and when he died he was given a simple grave, without a headstone, in the city's Johannisfriedhof (St. John Cemetery). It wasn't until 1894 that an effort was made to find where the great composer lay buried, and after a thorough, macabre search, his coffin was removed to the Johanniskirche. That church was destroyed by Allied bombs in December 1943, and Bach subsequently found his final resting place in the church he would have selected: the Thomaskirche. ■TIP➔ You can listen to the famous boys' choir during the *Motette,* a service with a special emphasis on choral music.

Bach's 12 children and the infant Richard Wagner were baptized in the early-17th-century font; Karl Marx and Friedrich Engels also stood before this same font, godfathers to Karl Liebknecht, who grew up to be a revolutionary as well.

In front of the church is a rebuilt memorial for Felix Mendelssohn. The Nazis destroyed the original in front of the Gewandhaus, and the current memorial is a result of a Leipzig Citizens Initiative that collected donations and other funds to rebuild it. ⊠ *Thomaskirchhof off Grimmaische Str.* ☎ *0341/222–240* ⊕ *www.thomaskirche.org* ⊠ *Free, Motette €2* ☽ *Daily 9–6; Motette Fri. at 6 pm, Sat. at 3; no Motette during Saxony summer vacation (usually mid-July until the end of August).*

WORTH NOTING

Bach-Museum im Bach-Archiv Leipzig (*Bach Museum at the Bach Archives Leipzig*). The Bach family home, the old Bosehaus, stands opposite the Thomaskirche, and is now a museum devoted to the composer's life and work. The newly renovated museum offers several interactive displays; arranging the instrumental parts of Bach's hymns is by far the most entertaining. ⊠ *Thomaskirchhof 16* ☎ *0341/913–7200* ⊠ *€6* ☽ *Tues.–Sun. 10–6.*

Hauptbahnhof. With 26 platforms, Leipzig's main train station is Europe's largest railhead. It was built in 1915 and is now a protected monument, but modern commerce rules in its bi-level shopping mall (the Promenaden). The only thing the complex is missing is a pub. ■TIP➔ Many of the shops and restaurants stay open until 10 pm and are open on Sunday. Thanks to the historic backdrop, this is one of the most beautiful shopping experiences in East Germany. ⊠ *Willy-Brandt-Pl.* ☎ *0341/141–270 for mall, 0341/9968–3275 for train station.*

Leipziger Universitätsturm (*Leipzig University Tower*). Towering over Leipzig's city center is this 470-foot-high structure, which houses administrative offices and lecture rooms. Dubbed the "Jagged Tooth" by some University of Leipzig students, it supposedly represents an open book. Students were also largely responsible for changing the university's name, replacing its postwar title, Karl Marx University, with the original one. The **Augustusplatz** spreads out below the university tower like a space-age campus.

Mendelssohn Haus (*Mendelssohn House*). The only surviving residence of the composer Felix Mendelssohn-Bartholdy is now Germany's only museum dedicated to him. Mendelssohn's last residence and the place of his death has been preserved in its original 19th-century state. Concerts are held every Sunday at 11. ⊠ *Goldschmidtstr. 12* ☎ *0341/127–0294* ⊕ *www.mendelssohn-haus.de* ⊠ *€4.50* ☽ *Daily 10–6.*

Museum in der Runden Ecke (*Museum in the Round Corner*). This building once served as the headquarters of the city's secret police, the dreaded *Staatssicherheitsdienst*. The exhibition *Stasi—Macht und Banalität* (Stasi—Power and Banality) not only presents the offices and surveillance work of the Stasi but also shows hundreds of documents revealing the magnitude of its interests in citizens' private lives. The material is written in German, but the items and the atmosphere convey an impression of what life under such a regime might have been like. The exhibit about the death penalty in the GDR is particularly chilling. ⊠ *Dittrichring 24* ☎ *0341/961–2443* ⊕ *www.runde-ecke-leipzig.de* ☞ *Free; €3 with tour in English, by appointment only* ⊗ *Daily 10–6.*

Museum zum Arabischen Kaffeebaum (*Arabic Coffee Tree Museum*). This museum and café-restaurant tells the fascinating history of coffee culture in Europe, particularly in Saxony. The café is one of the oldest on the continent, and once proudly served coffee to such luminaries as Gotthold Lessing, Schumann, Goethe, and Liszt. The museum features many paintings, Arabian coffee vessels, and coffeehouse games. It also explains the basic principles of roasting coffee. The café is divided into traditional Viennese, French, and Arabian coffeehouses, but no coffee is served in the Arabian section, which is only a display. ■ TIP➔ The cake is better and the seating more comfortable in the Viennese part. ⊠ *Kleine Fleischerg. 4* ☎ *0341/960–2632* ⊕ *www.coffe-baum.de* ☞ *Free* ⊗ *Tues.–Sun. 11–5.*

Neues Gewandhaus (*New Orchestra Hall*). In the shadow of the Leipziger Universitätsturm is the glass-and-concrete home of the Leipzig Philharmonic Orchestra. Kurt Masur is a former director, and Michael Köhler is currently at the helm. Owing to the world-renowned acoustics of the concert hall, a tone resonates here for a full two seconds. ⊠ *Augustuspl. 8* ☎ *0341/127–0280.*

Opernhaus (*Opera House*). Leipzig's stage for operas was the first postwar theater to be built in Communist East Germany. Its solid, boxy style is the subject of ongoing local discussion. ⊠ *Opposite Gewandhaus, on north side of Augustuspl.*

Völkerschlachtdenkmal (*Memorial to the Battle of the Nations*). On the city's outskirts, Prussian, Austrian, Russian, and Swedish forces stood ground against Napoléon's troops in the Battle of the Nations of 1813, a prelude to the French general's defeat two years later at Waterloo. An enormous, 300-foot-high monument erected on the site in 1913 commemorates the battle. Despite its ugliness, the site is well worth a visit, if only to wonder at the lengths—and heights—to which the Prussians went to celebrate their military victories, and to take in the view from a windy platform (provided you can climb the 500 steps to get there). The Prussians did make one concession to Napoléon in designing the monument: a stone marks the spot where he stood during the three-day battle. An exhibition hall explains the history of the memorial. The memorial can be reached via Streetcar 15 or 21 (leave the tram at the Probstheida station). ⚠ Due to ongoing renovations, rotating sections of the museum and monument may be closed briefly until 2013. It is still worth a visit as the viewing platform at the top remains open. ⊠ *Prager Str.* ☎ *0341/878–0471* ☞ *€6* ⊗ *Nov.–Apr., daily 10–4; May–Oct., daily 10–6; tour Tues. at 5.*

16

Zeitgeschichtliches Forum Leipzig (*Museum of Contemporary History Leipzig*). This is an excellent museum of postwar German history. It focuses on issues surrounding the division and reunification of Germany after World War II. ⊠ *Grimmaische Str. 6* ☎ *0341/225–0500* ⊠ *Free* ⊙ *Tues.–Sun. 10–6.*

WHERE TO EAT

$ ✕ **Auerbachs Keller.** The most famous of Leipzig's restaurants consists
GERMAN   of an upscale, international gourmet restaurant and another restaurant
Fodor's Choice   specializing in hearty Saxon fare, mostly roasted meat recipes. There's
★   also a good wine list. ■TIP→ It has been around since 1530 (making it one of the oldest continually running restaurants on the continent), and Goethe immortalized one of the several vaulted historic rooms in his *Faust.* Bach was also a regular here because of the location halfway between the Thomaskirche and the Nikolaikirche. The rowdy beer cellar shares a space with an interesting gourmet restaurant—the five-course menus (€110) are worth a splurge. ⊠ *Mädlerpassage, Grimmaische Str. 2–4* ☎ *0341/216–100* △ *Reservations essential* ⊙ *Closed Mon.*

$ ✕ **Barthels Hof.** The English-language menu at this restaurant explains
GERMAN   not only the cuisine but the history of Leipzig. Waitresses wear traditional *Trachten* dresses, but the rooms are quite modern. With a prominent location on the Markt, the restaurant is popular with locals, especially for the incredible breakfast buffet. Barthels has managed to elevate the local *Leipziger Allerlei* (vegetables and crayfish in beef bouillon) to an art form. Enjoy a meal here with a fresh Bauer Gose. ⊠ *Hainstr. 1* ☎ *0341/141–310.*

$ ✕ **Gasthaus & Gosebrauerei Bayrischer Bahnhof.** Hidden on the far south-
GERMAN   east edge of the city center, the Bayrischer Bahnhof was the terminus of
★   the first rail link between Saxony and Bavaria. The brewery here is the heart of a cultural renaissance, and is the only place currently brewing Gose in Leipzig. The restaurant is well worth a visit for its solid Saxon and German cuisine. Brewery accents surface in dishes such as rump steak with black-beer sauce, and the onion rings can't be beat. If the Gose is too sour for your tastes, order it with one of the sweet syrups—raspberry is the best. Groups of four or more can try dinner prepared in a *Römertopf* (a terra-cotta baking dish; the first was brought to Germany by the Romans, centuries ago). ■TIP→ In summer the beer garden is a pleasant place to get away from the bustle of the city center. ⊠ *Bayrischer Pl. 1* ☎ *0341/124–5760* ⊕ *www.bayrischer-bahnhof.de* ⊟ *No credit cards.*

¢   ✕ **Kaffeehaus Riquet.** The restored art nouveau house dates from 1908.
CAFÉ   Riquet is a company that has had dealings in the coffee trade in Africa and East Asia since 1745, as is indicated by the large elephant heads adorning the facade of the building. The upstairs section houses a pleasant Viennese-style coffeehouse—the best views are had from up here—while downstairs is noisier and more active. ■TIP→ Afternoon coffee and cake are one of Leipzig's special pleasures (in a country with an obsession for coffee and cake), and Riquet is the best place in the city to satisfy the urge. ⊠ *Schulmachergässchen 1* ☎ *0341/961–0000* ⊕ *www. riquethaus.de* ⊟ No credit cards ⊙ *Closed Mon.*

$ **✕ Thüringer Hof.** One of Germany's
GERMAN oldest restaurants and pubs (dating back to 1454) served its hearty Thuringian and Saxon fare to Martin Luther and the like—who certainly had more than a mere pint of the beers on tap. The menu in the reconstructed, cavernous, and always buzzing dining hall doesn't exactly offer gourmet cuisine, but rather an impressively enormous variety of game, fish, and bratwurst dishes. The Thuringian sausages (served with either sauerkraut and boiled potatoes or onions and mashed potatoes) and the famous Thuringian sauerbraten (beef marinated in a sour essence) are musts. ✉ *Burgstr. 19* ☎ *0341/994–4999.*

$ **✕ Zill's Tunnel.** The "tunnel" refers
GERMAN to the barrel-ceiling ground-floor restaurant, where foaming glasses of excellent local beer are served with a smile. The friendly staff will also help you decipher the Old Saxon descriptions of the menu's traditional dishes. Upstairs there's a larger wine restaurant with an open fireplace. Try the pan-seared *maischolle,* a type of flatfish. ✉ *Barfussgässchen 9* ☎ *0341/960–2078.*

> **GOSE**
>
> Bismark once remarked that "Gose isn't a beer, it is a way of viewing the world." Gose, which originated in Goslar, is an obscure, top-fermented wheat beer flavored by adding coriander and salt to the wort. Gose came to Leipzig in 1738, and was so popular that by the end of the 1800s it was considered the local brewing style. It's extremely difficult to make, and after beer production stopped during the war (due to grain shortages), the tradition seemed lost. Today, through the efforts of Lothar Goldhahn at the Bayrischer Bahnhof, Gose production has returned to Leipzig.

16

WHERE TO STAY
For expanded hotel reviews, visit Fodors.com.

$$ **🛏 Hotel Fürstenhof Leipzig.** The city's grandest hotel—part of Starwood's
Fodor'sChoice Luxury Collection—is inside the renowned Löhr-Haus, a revered old
★ mansion 500 meters from the main train station on the ring road surrounding the city center. **Pros:** an elegant full-service hotel with stunning rooms; safes big enough for a laptop are a nice touch. **Cons:** the ring road can be noisy at night, especially on Friday and Saturday. ✉ *Tröndlinring 8* ☎ *0341/140–370* ⊕ *www.luxurycollection.com* ⤴ *80 rooms, 12 suites* ⚴ *In-room: Internet, Wi-Fi. In-hotel: restaurant, bar, pool, gym, spa, parking, some pets allowed.*

$ **🛏 Ringhotel Adagio Leipzig.** The quiet Adagio, tucked away behind the facade of a 19th-century city mansion, is centrally located between the Grassimuseum and the Neues Gewandhaus. **Pros:** large rooms with luxurious bathrooms; breakfast available all day. **Cons:** room decor is slightly bland; hotel not built to accommodate disabled guests. ✉ *Seeburgstr. 96* ☎ *0341/216–690* ⊕ *www.hotel-adagio.de* ⤴ *30 rooms, 2 suites, 1 apartment* ⚴ *In-room: no a/c, Internet. In-hotel: parking, some pets allowed* ⏌ *Breakfast.*

EATING WELL IN SAXONY

The cuisine of the region is hearty and seasonal, and almost every town has a unique specialty unavailable outside the immediate area. Look for *Gebratene Kalbsbrust* (roast veal breast), spicy *Thüringer Bratwurst* (sausage), *Schlesische Himmelreich* (ham and pork roast smothered in baked fruit and white sauce, served with dumplings), *Teichlmauke* (mashed potato in broth), *Blauer Karpfe* (blue carp, marinated in vinegar), and *Raacher Maad* (grated and boiled potatoes fried in butter and served with blueberries). Venison and wild boar are standards in forest and mountainous areas, and lamb from Saxony-Anhalt is particularly good. In Thuringia, *Klösse* (potato dumplings) are virtually a religion.

Eastern Germany is experiencing a Renaissance in the art of northern German brewing. The first stop for any beer lover should be the Bayrische Bahnhof in Leipzig, to give Gose a try. Dresden's Brauhaus Watzke, Quedlinburg's Lüddebräu, and even the Lansdkron brewery in Görlitz are bringing craft brewing back to a region inundated with mass-produced brew.

Saxony has cultivated vineyards for more than 800 years, and is known for its dry red and white wines, among them Müller-Thurgau, Weissburgunder, Ruländer, and the spicy Traminer. The Sächsische Weinstrasse (Saxon Wine Route) follows the course of the Elbe River from Diesbar-Seusslitz (north of Meissen) to Pirna (southeast of Dresden). Meissen, Radebeul, and Dresden have upscale wine restaurants, and wherever you see a green seal with the letter *S* and grapes depicted, good local wine is being served. One of the best kept secrets in German wine making is the Salle-Unstrut region, which produces spicy Silvaner and Rieslings.

NIGHTLIFE AND THE ARTS

THE ARTS

Krystallpalast. The variety theater Krystallpalast features a blend of circus, vaudeville, and comedy that is fairly accessible for non-German speakers. ⊠ *Magazing. 4* ☎ *0341/140–660* ⊕ *www.krystallpalast.de.*

Leipziger Pfeffermühle. One of Germany's most famous cabarets, the Leipziger Pfeffermühle, has a lively bar off a courtyard opposite the Thomaskirche. On pleasant evenings the courtyard fills with benches and tables, and the scene rivals the indoor performance for entertainment. ⊠ *Thomaskirchhof 16* ☎ *0341/960–3196.*

Music Days. Leipzig's annual music festival, Music Days, is in June.

Neues Gewandhaus. The Neues Gewandhaus, a controversial piece of architecture, is home to an undeniably splendid orchestra. Tickets to concerts are difficult to obtain unless you reserve well in advance. Sometimes spare tickets are available at the box office a half hour before the evening performance. ⊠ *Augustuspl. 8* ☎ *0341/127–0280* ⊕ *www. gewandhaus.de.*

NIGHTLIFE

With a vast assortment of restaurants, cafés, and clubs to match the city's exceptional musical and literary offerings, Leipzig is a fun city at night. The *Kneipenszene* (pub scene) is centered on the **Drallewatsch** (a Saxon slang word for "going out"), the small streets and alleys around Grosse and Kleine Fleischergasse and the Barfussgässchen.

Moritzbastei. A magnet for young people is the Moritzbastei, reputedly Europe's largest student club, with bars, a disco, a café, a theater, and a cinema. Nonstudents are welcome—if you're cool enough. ☒ *Universitätsstr. 9* ☎ *0341/702–590.*

Schauhaus. A favorite hangout among the city's business elite is the Schauhaus, a stylish bar serving great cocktails. ☒ *Bosestr. 1* ☎ *0341/960–0596.*

Spizz Keller. One of the city's top dance clubs is the hip Spizz Keller. ☒ *Markt 9* ☎ *0341/960–8043.*

Tanzpalast. The Tanzpalast, in the august setting of the *Schauspielhaus* (city theater), attracts a thirtysomething crowd. ☒ *Dittrichring* ☎ *0341/960–0596.*

Weinstock. The upscale bar, pub, and restaurant Weinstock is in a Renaissance building and offers a huge selection of good wines. ☒ *Markt 7* ☎ *0341/1406–0606.*

16

SHOPPING

Small streets leading off the Markt attest to Leipzig's rich trading past. Tucked in among them are glass-roof arcades of surprising beauty and elegance, including the wonderfully restored **Specks Hof, Barthels Hof, Jägerhof,** and the **Passage zum Sachsenplatz.** Invent a headache and step into the *Apotheke* (pharmacy) at Hainstrasse 9—it is spectacularly art nouveau, with finely etched and stained glass and rich mahogany. For more glimpses into the past, check out the antiquarian bookstores of the nearby **Neumarkt Passage.**

Hauptbahnhof. The Hauptbahnhof, Leipzig's main train station, has more than 150 shops, restaurants, and cafés, all open Monday through Saturday 9:30 am–10 pm; many are also open on Sunday, with the same hours. ☒ *Willy-Brandt-Pl.*

> **LEIPZIGER LERCHE**
>
> As far back as the 18th century, Leipzig was known for a bizarre culinary specialty: roast meadowlark in crust. The dish was so popular that Leipzig consumed more than 400,000 meadowlarks every month. When the king of Saxony banned lark hunting in 1876, Leipzig's industrious bakers came up with a substitute: a baked short-crust pastry filled with almonds, nuts, and strawberries. Today, the substitute Meadowlark, when prepared correctly, is a delicious treat—found only in Leipzig.

DRESDEN

25 km (16 mi) southeast of Meissen, 140 km (87 mi) southeast of Leipzig, 193 km (120 mi) south of Berlin.

Saxony's capital city sits in baroque splendor on a wide sweep of the Elbe River, and its proponents have worked with German thoroughness to recapture the city's old reputation as "the Florence on the Elbe." Its yellow and pale-green facades are enormously appealing, and their mere presence is even more overwhelming when you compare what you see today with photographs of Dresden from February 1945, after an Allied bombing raid destroyed the city overnight. Dresden was the capital of Saxony as early as the 15th century, although most of its architectural masterpieces date from the 18th century and the reigns of Augustus the Strong and his son, Frederick Augustus II.

Although some parts of the city center still look as if they're stuck halfway between demolition and construction, the present city is an enormous tribute to the Dresdeners' skills and dedication. The resemblance of today's riverside to Dresden cityscapes painted by Canaletto in the mid-1700s is remarkable. Unfortunately, the war-inflicted gaps in the urban landscape in other parts of the city are too big to be closed anytime soon.

GETTING HERE AND AROUND

Dresden is two hours from Berlin on the Hamburg-Berlin-Prague-Vienna train line. The city's international airport serves mostly European destinations with budget airlines. The newly completed Norman Foster train station is a short walk along the Prager Strasse from the city center. Streetcars are cheap and efficient.

Dresden bus tours (in German and English, run by the Dresdner Verkehrsbetriebe) leave from Postplatz daily at 10, 11:30, and 3; the Stadtrundfahrt Dresden bus tours (also in German and English) leave from Theaterplatz/Augustusbrücke (April–October, daily 9:30–5, every 30 minutes; November–March, daily 10–3, every hour) and stop at most sights.

TIMING

A long full day is sufficient for a quick tour of historic Dresden with a brief visit to one of the museums. The focus of your day should be a visit to the Grünes Gewölbe. If you plan to explore any of the museums at length, such as the Zwinger, or take a guided tour of the Semperoper, you'll need more time. One of the best ways to see Dresden is as a stop between Berlin and Prague.

ESSENTIALS

Tour Information Dresdner Verkehrsbetriebe AG ☎ *0351/857–2201* ⊕ *www.dvbag.de.* **Stadtrundfahrt Dresden** ☎ *0351/899–5650* ⊕ *www.stadtrundfahrt.com.*

Visitor Information Dresden Tourist ✉ *Dresden Tourist, Schlossstr. 1, inside the Kulturpalast* ☎ *0351/491–920* ⊕ *www.dresden.de.*

16

EXPLORING
TOP ATTRACTIONS

Fodor'sChoice
★

Frauenkirche (*Church of Our Lady*). Dresden's Church of Our Lady, completed in 1743, was one of the masterpieces of baroque church architecture. The huge dome set on a smaller square base, known as the Stone Bell, was the inspiration of George Bähr, who designed the church to be built "as if it was a single stone from the base to the top." On February 15, 1945, two days after the bombing of Dresden, the burned-out shell of the magnificent Stone Bell collapsed. For the following five decades the remains of the church, a pile of rubble, remained a gripping memorial to the horrors of war. In a move shocking to the East German authorities, who organized all public demonstrations, a group of young people spontaneously met here on February 13, 1982, for a candlelight vigil for peace.

Although the will to rebuild the church was strong, the political and economic situation in the GDR prevented it. It wasn't until the reunification of Germany that Dresden began to seriously consider reconstruction. In the early 1990s a citizens' initiative, joined by the Lutheran Church of Saxony and the city of Dresden, decided to rebuild the church using the original stones. The goal of completing the church by 2006, Dresden's 800th anniversary, seemed insurmountable. Money soon started pouring in from around the globe, however, and work began. The rubble was cleared away, and the size and shape of each stone were cataloged. Computer-imaging technology helped place each recovered stone in its original location.

During construction, guided tours and Frauenkirche concerts brought in donations. The biggest supporter of the project in the United Kingdom, the Dresden Trust, is centered in the city of Coventry, itself bombed mercilessly by the German *Luftwaffe* during the war. The Dresden Trust raised more than €600,000, and donated the gold pinnacle cross that now graces the church dome.

On Sunday, October 30, 2005 (almost a year ahead of schedule), Dresden's skyline became a little more complete with the consecration of the Frauenkirche. Leading the service was the Bishop of Coventry. Although the church is usually open to all, it closes frequently for concerts and other events. Check the English-language schedule next to entrance D. ✉ *An der Frauenkirche* ☎ *0351/498–1131* ⊕ *www.frauenkirche-dresden.org* 🎫 *Free; cupola and tower €8; audio guides in English €2.50* ⊙ *Weekdays 10–noon and 1–6, cupola and tower daily 10–6.*

Residenzschloss (*Royal Palace*). Restoration work is still under way behind the Renaissance facade of this former royal palace, much of which was built between 1709 and 1722. Some of the finished rooms in the **Georgenbau** (Count George Wing) hold historical exhibits, among them an excellent one on the reconstruction of the palace itself. The palace's main gateway, the Georgentor, has an enormous statue of the fully armed Saxon count George. ■TIP➔ From April through October, the palace's old Hausmannsturm (Hausmann Tower) offers a wonderful view of the city and the Elbe River.

The main attraction in the Royal Palace, though, is the world-famous **Grünes Gewölbe** (Green Vault). Named after a green room in the palace of Augustus the Strong, the collection is divided into two sections. No one should leave Dresden without seeing the Historic Green Vault, but tickets are hard to come by and are often sold out months in advance: 75% of the tickets are available for advance purchase, while 25% are held for sale at the door. ■TIP➔ Even if the advance tickets for the date of your visit are sold out, you should keep checking right up until you plan to visit the museum because it's common for reservations to be canceled. According to the museum, persistence is often rewarded.

Neues Grünes Gewölbe (*New Green Vault*). The Neues Grünes Gewölbe contains an exquisite collection of unique objets d'art fashioned from gold, silver, ivory, amber, and other precious and semiprecious materials. Among the crown jewels are the world's largest "green" diamond, 41 carats in weight, and a dazzling group of tiny gem-studded figures called *Hofstaat zu Delhi am Geburtstag des Grossmoguls Aureng-Zeb* (the Court at Delhi during the Birthday of the Great Mogul Aureng-Zeb). The unwieldy name gives a false idea of the size of the work, dating from 1708; some parts of the tableau are so small they can be admired only through a magnifying glass. Somewhat larger and less delicate is the drinking bowl of Ivan the Terrible, perhaps the most sensational artifact in this extraordinary museum ⊕ *www.skd.museum.*

The Frauenkirche was painstakingly rebuilt after it was reduced to rubble in the bombing of Dresden.

Historisches Grünes Gewölbe (*Historic Green Vault*). The Historisches Grünes Gewölbe is the section of the castle most reflective of Augustus the Strong's obsession with art as a symbol of power. The intricately restored baroque interior highlights the objects in the collection and is an integral part of the presentation itself. The last section of the museum houses the Jewel Room, displaying the ceremonial crown jewels of Augustus the Strong and his son. Access to the Historic Green Vault is limited to 100 visitors per hour and is by appointment only. Tickets can be reserved by phone or online ☎ *0351/4919–2285 for tours* ⊕ *www.skd.museum* ✉ *€12* ⊙ *By appointment only.*

The palace also houses the **Münzkabinett** (Coin Museum) and the **Kupferstichkabinett** (Museum of Prints and Drawings), with more than 500,000 pieces of art spanning several centuries. Changing exhibits at the Kupferstichkabinett have presented masterworks by Albrecht Dürer, Peter Paul Rubens, and Jan van Eyck, as well as 20th-century art by Otto Dix, Edvard Munch, and Ernst Ludwig Kirchner, as well as East European art and some Southeast Asian prints. Also in the palace is the new **Türckische Cammer** (Turkish Chamber), a huge collection of Ottoman artifacts collected by Saxon dukes over centuries. It's worth going just to see the six carved Arabian horses, bedecked with jeweled armor. ⊠ *Schlosspl.* ☎ *0351/491–4619* ✉ *All museums and collections at palace (except Historic Green Vault) €10; Historic Green Vault €12* ⊙ *Wed.–Mon. 10–6; Historic Green Vault by appointment only.*

★ **Semperoper** (*Semper Opera House*). One of Germany's best-known and most popular theaters, this magnificent opera house saw the premieres of Richard Wagner's *Rienzi, Der Fliegende Holländer,* and *Tannhäuser*

and Richard Strauss's *Salome, Elektra,* and *Der Rosenkavalier.* The Dresden architect Gottfried Semper built the house in 1838–41 in Italian Renaissance style, then saw his work destroyed in a fire caused by a careless lamplighter. Semper had to flee Dresden after participating in a democratic uprising but his son Manfred rebuilt the theater in the neo-Renaissance style you see today, though even Manfred Semper's version had to be rebuilt after the devastating bombing raid of February 1945. On the 40th anniversary of that raid—February 13, 1985—the Semperoper reopened with a performance of *Der Freischütz,* by Carl Maria von Weber, the last opera performed in the building before its destruction. There is a statue of Weber, another artist who did much to make Dresden a leading center of German music and culture, outside the opera house in the shadow of the Zwinger. Even if you're no opera buff, the Semper's lavish interior can't fail to impress. Velvet, brocade, and well-crafted imitation marble create an atmosphere of intimate luxury (it seats 1,323). Guided tours (must be reserved in advance) of the building are offered throughout the day, depending on the opera's rehearsal schedule. Check the Web site for schedules. Tours begin at the entrance to your right as you face the Elbe River. ✉ *Theaterpl. 2* ☎ *0351/491–1496* ⊕ *www.semperoper-erleben.de* 🎫 *Tour €8.*

16

Fodor's Choice **Zwinger** (*Bailey*). Dresden's magnificent baroque showpiece is entered by
★ way of the mighty Kronentor (Crown Gate), off Ostra-Allee. Augustus the Strong hired a small army of artists and artisans to create a "pleasure ground" worthy of the Saxon court on the site of the former bailey, part of the city fortifications. The artisans worked under the direction of the architect Matthäus Daniel Pöppelmann, who came reluctantly out of retirement to design what would be his greatest work, begun in 1707 and completed in 1728. Completely enclosing a central courtyard filled with lawns, pools, and fountains, the complex is made up of six linked pavilions, one of which boasts a carillon of Meissen bells, hence its name: Glockenspielpavillon.

The Zwinger is quite a scene—a riot of garlands, nymphs, and other baroque ornamentation and sculpture. Wide staircases beckon to galleried walks and to the romantic Nymphenbad, a coyly hidden courtyard where statues of nude women perch in alcoves to protect themselves from a fountain that spits unexpectedly. The Zwinger once had an open view of the riverbank, but the Semper Opera House now occupies that side. Stand in the center of this quiet oasis, where the city's roar is kept at bay by the outer wings of the structure, and imagine the court festivities once held here.

Gemäldegalerie Alte Meister (*Gallery of Old Masters*). The Gemäldegalerie Alte Meister, in the northwestern corner of the complex, was built to house portions of the royal art collections. Among the priceless paintings are works by Dürer, Holbein, Jan van Eyck, Rembrandt, Rubens, van Dyck, Hals, Vermeer, Raphael, Titian, Giorgione, Veronese, Velázquez, Murillo, Canaletto, and Watteau. On the wall of the entrance archway you'll see an inscription in Russian, one of the few amusing reminders of World War II in Dresden. It rhymes in Russian: "Museum checked. No mines. Chanutin did the checking." Chanutin, presumably, was the Russian soldier responsible for checking one of Germany's greatest art galleries for anything more explosive than a Rubens nude. The highlight of the collection is Raphael's *Sistine Madonna*, whose mournful look is slightly less famous than the two cherubs who were added by Raphael after the painting was completed, in order to fill an empty space at the bottom. ☎ *0351/491–4679* 🖾 *€10* 🕙 *Tues.–Sun. 10–6.*

Porzellansammlung (*Porcelain Collection*). The Zwinger's Porzellansammlung, stretching from the curved gallery that adjoins the Glockenspielpavillon to the long gallery on the east side, is considered one of the best of its kind in the world. The focus, naturally, is on Dresden and Meissen china, but there are also outstanding examples of Japanese, Chinese, and Korean porcelain. ☎ *0351/491–4619* 🖾 *€10* 🕙 *Tues.–Sun. 10–6.*

Rüstkammer (*Armory*). The Rüstkammer holds medieval and Renaissance suits of armor and weapons. Note that the Rustkammer is in two parts: the main exhibit in the Semperbau and the Türckisches Cammer in the Residenzschloss. ☎ *0351/491–4619* 🖾 *€3* 🕙 *Tues.–Sun. 10–6* ✉ *Zwinger entrance, Ostra–Allee* ⊕ *www.skd.museum.*

WORTH NOTING

★ **Albertinum.** The Albertinum is named after Saxony's King Albert, who between 1884 and 1887 converted a royal arsenal into a suitable setting for the treasures he and his forebears had collected. This massive, imperial-style building houses one of the world's great galleries featuring works from the romantic period to the modern. The Galerie Neue Meister (New Masters Gallery) has an extensive collection ranging from Caspar David Friedrich and Gauguin to Ernst Kirchner and Georg Baselitz. ✉ *Am Neumarkt, Brühlsche Terrasse* ☎ *0351/49849–14973* ⊕ *www.skd.museum* 🖾 *€8* 🕙 *Wed.–Mon. 10–6.*

Altmarkt (*Old Market Square*). Although dominated by the nearby, unappealing, Kulturpalast (Palace of Culture), the Altmarkt is a fascinating concrete leftover from the 1970s (check out the workers and peasants GDR mosaic); the broad square and its surrounding streets are the true center of Dresden. The colonnaded beauty (from the Stalinist-era architecture of the early 1950s) survived the efforts of city planners to turn it into a huge outdoor parking lot. The rebuilt **Rathaus** (Town Hall) is here (go around the front to see bullet holes in the statuary), as is the yellow-stucco, 18th-century Landhaus, which contains the Stadtmuseum Dresden im Landhaus. ⚠ Dresdners joke that you should never park your car here because the square is under almost constant construction and you might never find it again.

Augustusbrücke (*Augustus Bridge*). This bridge, which spans the river in front of the Katholische Hofkirche, is the reconstruction of a 17th-century baroque bridge blown up by the SS shortly before the end of World War II. It was restored and renamed for Georgi Dimitroff, the Bulgarian Communist accused by the Nazis of instigating the Reichstag fire; after the fall of Communism the original name, honoring Augustus the Strong, was reinstated.

Deutsches Hygiene-Museum Dresden. This unique (even in a country with a national tendency for excessive cleanliness) and unfortunately named museum relates the history of public health and science. The permanent exhibit offers lots of hands-on activities. The building itself housed the Nazi eugenics program, and the special exhibit on this period is not recommended for children under 12. ✉ *Lingnerpl. 1* ☎ *0351/48460* ⊕ *www.dhmd.de* 🎫 *€7, free on Friday after 3 pm* ☉ *Tues.–Sun. 10–6.*

Johanneum. At one time the royal stables, this 16th-century building now houses the **Verkehrsmuseum** (Transportation Museum), a collection of historic conveyances, including vintage automobiles and engines. The former **stable exercise yard,** behind the Johanneum and enclosed by elegant Renaissance arcades, was used during the 16th century as an open-air festival ground. A ramp leading up from the courtyard made it possible for royalty to reach the upper story to view the jousting below without having to dismount. More popular even than jousting in those days was *Ringelstechen*, a risky pursuit in which riders at full gallop had to catch small rings on their lances. Horses and riders often came to grief in the narrow confines of the stable yard.

■ TIP→ On the outside wall of the Johanneum is a remarkable example of porcelain art: a 336-foot-long Meissen tile mural of a royal procession. More than 100 members of the royal Saxon house of Wettin, half of them on horseback, are represented on the giant mosaic, known as the "Procession of Princes," which is made of 25,000 porcelain tiles, painted in 1904–07 after a design by Wilhelm Walther. The representations are in chronological order: at 1694, Augustus the Strong's horse is trampling a rose, the symbol of Martin Luther and the Protestant Reformation. The Johanneum is reached by steps leading down from the Brühlsche Terrasse. ✉ *Am Neumarkt at Augustusstr. 1* ☎ *0351/86440* ⊕ *www.verkehrsmuseum-dresden.de* 🎫 *€4.50* ☉ *Tues.–Sun. 10–5.*

Katholische Hofkirche (*Catholic Court Church*). The largest church in Saxony is also known as the Cathedral of St. Trinitatis. Frederick Augustus II (who reigned 1733–63) brought architects and builders from Italy to construct a Catholic church in a city that had been the first large center of Lutheran Protestantism (like his father, Frederick Augustus II had to convert to Catholicism to be eligible to wear the Polish crown). Inside, the treasures include a beautiful stone pulpit by the royal sculptor Balthasar Permoser and a painstakingly restored 250-year-old organ said to be one of the finest ever to come from the mountain workshops of the famous Silbermann family. In the cathedral's crypt are the tombs of 49 Saxon rulers and a reliquary containing the heart of Augustus the Strong, which is rumored to start beating if a beautiful woman comes near. ✉ *Schlosspl.* ☎ *0351/484–4712* 🎫 *Free* ☉ *Mon.–Thurs. 9–5, Fri. 1–5, Sat. 10–5, Sun. noon–4:30.*

Kreuzkirche (*Cross Church*). Soaring high above the Altmarkt, the richly decorated tower of the baroque Kreuzkirche dates back to 1792. The city's main Protestant church is still undergoing postwar restoration, but the tower and church hall are open to the public. A famous boys' choir, the Kreuzchor, performs here regularly (check Web site or call for times). ✉ *Altmarkt* ☎ *0351/439–390* ⊕ *www.dresdner-kreuzkirche.de* 🎫 *Tower €1.50* ☉ *Nov.–Mar., weekdays 10–4, Sun. 11–4; Apr.–Oct., daily 10–6.*

16

Pfund's Molkerei (*Pfund's Dairy Shop*). This decorative 19th-century shop has been a Dresden institution since 1880, and offers a wide assortment of cheese and other goods. The shop is renowned for its intricate tile mosaics on the floor and walls. Pfund's is also famous for introducing pasteurized milk to the industry; it invented milk soap and specially treated milk for infants as early as 1900. ⊠ *Bautzener Str. 79* ☎ *0351/808–080* ⊕ *www.pfunds.de* ⊗ *Mon.–Sat. 10–6, Sun. 10–3.*

OFF THE
BEATEN
PATH

Panometer Dresden. You can step back in time and get a sense of how Dresden looked in 1756 by viewing this 360-degree panorama portrait of the city. Artist Yadegar Asisi's monumental 105-by-27-meter painting locates the viewer on the tower of the Stadtschloss, with extremely detailed vistas in all directions. The painting is located in an old natural-gas store. To get here from Dresden Main Station, take S1 or S2 to the station Dresden-Reick (five minutes). From the Altmarkt take Tram 1 or 2 to the Liebstädterstrasse stop (15 minutes). ⊠ *Gasanstaltstr. 8b* ☎ *0351/860–3940* ⊕ *www.asisi.de* 🖃 *€10* ⊗ *Tues.–Fri. 9–7, weekends 10–8.*

Stadtmuseum Dresden im Landhaus (*Dresden City Museum at the Landhaus*). The city's small but fascinating municipal museum tells the ups and downs of Dresden's turbulent past—from the dark Middle Ages to the bombing of Dresden in February 1945. There are many peculiar exhibits on display, such as an American 250-kilogram bomb and a stove made from an Allied bomb casing. The building has the most interesting fire escape in the city. ⊠ *Wilsdruffer Str. 2* ☎ *0351/656–480* ⊕ *www.stmd.de* 🖃 *€4* ⊗ *Tues.–Sun. 10–6 (Fri. until 8).*

WHERE TO EAT

$$
GERMAN
★

✕ **Alte Meister.** Set in the historic mansion of the architect who rebuilt the Zwinger, and named after the school of medieval painters that includes Dürer, Holbein, and Rembrandt, the Alte Meister has a sophisticated old-world flair that charms locals and tourists alike. The food is very current, despite the decor, and the light German nouvelle cuisine with careful touches of Asian spices and ingredients has earned chef Dirk Wende critical praise. In summer this is one of the city's premier dining spots, offering a grand view of the Semperoper from a shaded terrace ⊠ *Braun'sches Atelier, Theaterpl. 1a* ☎ *0351/481–0426.*

$
GERMAN

✕ **Ball und Brauhaus Watzke.** One of the city's oldest microbreweries, the Watzke offers a great reprieve from Dresden's mass-produced Radeberger. Several different homemade beers are on tap—you can even help brew one. Tours of the brewery cost €5 with a tasting, or €12.50 with a meal, and you can get your beer to go in a 1- or 2-liter jug called a *siphon.* The food is hearty, contemporary Saxon. When the weather is nice, enjoy the fantastic panoramic view of Dresden from the beer garden. ⊠ *Koetzschenbroderstr. 1* ☎ *0351/852–920.*

$
GERMAN

✕ **Watzke Brauereiausschank am Goldenen Reiter.** Watzke microbrewery operates this smaller restaurant with the same beer and hearty menu as the Ball und Brauhaus Watzke directly across from the Goldene Reiter statue of Augustus the Strong. ⊠ *Hauptstrasse 11* ☎ *0351/810–6820.*

WHERE TO STAY
For expanded hotel reviews, visit Fodors.com.

$ ⊡ **artotel Dresden.** The artotel keeps the promise of its name. **Pros:** art elements make the hotel fun. **Cons:** bathrooms have a opaque window into the room; decor is not for everyone. ⊠ *Ostra-Allee 33* ☎ *0351/49220* ⊕ *www.parkplaza.com* ⤳ *155 rooms, 19 suites* ⟁ *In-room: Wi-Fi. In-hotel: restaurant, bar, gym, parking, some pets allowed* ⦿ *Breakfast.*

$$ ⊡ **Hotel Bülow-Residenz.** One of the most intimate first-class hotels in eastern Germany, the Bülow-Residenz is in a baroque palace built in 1730 by a wealthy Dresden city official. **Pros:** extremely helpful staff. **Cons:** air-conditioning can be noisy; hotel is located in Neustadt, a 10-minute walk across the river to the city center. ⊠ *Rähnitzg. 19* ☎ *0351/80030* ⊕ *www.buelow-residenz.de* ⤳ *25 rooms, 5 suites* ⟁ *In-room: no a/c, Wi-Fi. In-hotel: restaurant, bar, parking, some pets allowed.*

$ ⊡ **Hotel Elbflorenz.** This centrally located hotel bears Dresden's somewhat presumptuous nickname *Elbflorenz,* or "Florence on the Elbe." **Pros:** extraordinary breakfast buffet. **Cons:** in need of renovation; located at edge of city center. ⊠ *Rosenstr. 36* ☎ *0351/86400* ⊕ *www.hotel-elbflorenz.de* ⤳ *212 rooms, 15 suites* ⟁ *In-room: Internet. In-hotel: restaurant, bar, gym, children's programs, parking, some pets allowed* ⦿ *Breakfast.*

$$$ ⊡ **Kempinski Hotel Taschenbergpalais Dresden.** Destroyed in wartime
★ bombing but now rebuilt, the historic Taschenberg Palace—the work of Zwinger architect Matthäus Daniel Pöppelmann—is Dresden's premier address and the last word in luxury, as befits the former residence of the Saxon crown princes. **Pros:** ice-skating in the courtyard in winter; concierge knows absolutely everything about Dresden. **Cons:** expensive extra charges for breakfast and Internet. ⊠ *Taschenberg 3* ☎ *0351/49120* ⊕ *www.kempinski-dresden.de* ⤳ *188 rooms, 25 suites* ⟁ *In-room: Internet, Wi-Fi. In-hotel: restaurant, bar, pool, parking, some pets allowed.*

$ ⊡ **Rothenburger Hof.** One of Dresden's smallest and oldest luxury hotels, the historic Rothenburger Hof opened in 1865, and is only a few steps away from the city's sightseeing spots. **Pros:** nice garden and indoor pool. **Cons:** across the river in Neustadt, about 20 minutes from the city center; street can be noisy in summer. ⊠ *Rothenburger Str. 15–17* ☎ *0351/81260* ⊕ *www.dresden-hotel.de* ⤳ *26 rooms, 13 apartments* ⟁ *In-room: no a/c, Internet. In-hotel: bar, pool, gym, parking* ⦿ *Breakfast.*

NIGHTLIFE AND THE ARTS

THE ARTS

Filmnächte am Elbufer (*Elbe Riverside Film Nights*). In addition to the annual film festival in April, open-air Filmnächte am Elbufer takes place on the banks of the Elbe from late June to late August. ⊠ *Am Königsufer, next to State Ministry of Finance* ☎ *0351/899–320.*

Jazz. May brings an annual international Dixieland-style jazz festival, and the Jazz Autumn festival follows in October.

Philharmonie Dresden (*Philharmonic Orchestra Dresden*). Dresden's fine Philharmonie Dresden takes center stage in the city's annual music festival, from mid-May to early June. ⊠ *Kulturpalast am Altmarkt* ☎ *0351/486–6286.*

The Semperoper (Semper Opera House) saw the openings of some of Richard Wagner's and Richard Strauss's best-loved operas. Its plush interiors are rich with velvet and brocade.

Semper Opera House (*Sächsische Staatsoper Dresden*). The opera in Dresden holds an international reputation largely due to the Semper Opera House. Destroyed during the war, the building has been meticulously rebuilt and renovated. Tickets are reasonably priced but also hard to come by; they're often included in package tours. ■ TIP→ Try reserving tickets on the Web site, or stop by the box office about a half hour before the performance. If that doesn't work, take one of the operahouse tours. ⊠ *Theaterpl.* ⊕ *www.semperoper.de* ⊠ *Evening box office (Abendkasse), left of main entrance* ☎ *0351/491–1705.*

NIGHTLIFE

Dresdeners are known for their industriousness and efficient way of doing business, but they also know how to spend a night out. Most of Dresden's pubs, and *Kneipen* (bars) are in the **Äussere Neustadt** district and along the buzzing **Münzgasse** (between the Frauenkirche and the Brühlsche Terrasse).

Aqualounge. One of the best bars in town is the groovy and hip Aqualounge. ⊠ *Louisenstr. 56* ☎ *0351/810–6116.*

Bärenzwinger. Folk and rock music are regularly featured at Bärenzwinger. ⊠ *Brühlscher Garten* ☎ *0351/495–1409.*

Dance Factory. The hip club Dance Factory is in an old Stasi garrison. ⊠ *Bautzner Str. 118* ☎ *0351/802–0066.*

Motown Club. The Motown Club attracts a young and stylish crowd. ⊠ *St. Petersburger Str. 9* ☎ *0351/487–4150.*

Planwirtschaft. The name of the Planwirtschaft ironically refers to the socialist economic system; it attracts an alternative crowd. ⊠ *Louisenstr. 20* ☎ *0351/801–3187.*

Tonne Jazz Club. Jazz musicians perform most nights of the week at the friendly, laid-back Tonne Jazz Club. ⊠ *Waldschlösschen, Am Brauhaus 3* ☎ *0351/802–6017.*

MEISSEN

25 km (15 mi) northwest of Dresden.

This romantic city with its imposing castle looming over the Elbe River is known the world over for its porcelain, bearing the trademark crossed blue swords. The first European porcelain was made in this area in 1708, and in 1710 the Royal Porcelain Workshop was established in Meissen, close to the local raw materials.

The story of how porcelain came to be produced in Meissen reads like a German fairy tale: the Saxon elector Augustus the Strong, who ruled from 1694 to 1733, urged his court alchemists to find the secret of making gold, something he badly needed to refill a state treasury depleted by his extravagant lifestyle. The alchemists failed to produce gold, but one of them, Johann Friedrich Böttger, discovered a method for making something almost as precious: fine hard-paste porcelain. Already a rapacious collector of Oriental porcelains, Prince August put Böttger and a team of craftsmen up in a hilltop castle—Albrechtsburg—and set them to work.

16

GETTING HERE AND AROUND

Meissen is an easy 45-minute train ride from Dresden. On arrival, exit the station and walk to the left; as you turn the corner there is a beautiful view of Meissen across the river. Trains run about every 30 minutes.

ESSENTIALS

Visitor Information **Tourist-Information Meissen** ⊠ *Markt 3* ☎ *03521/41940* 🖷 *03521/419–419* ⊕ *www.touristinfo-meissen.de.*

EXPLORING

Albrechtsburg. The Albrechtsburg, where the story of Meissen porcelain began, sits high above Old Meissen, towering over the Elbe River far below. The 15th-century castle is Germany's first truly residential one, a complete break with the earlier style of fortified bastions. In the central *Schutzhof,* a typical Gothic courtyard protected on three sides by high rough-stone walls, is an exterior spiral staircase, the **Wendelstein,** a masterpiece of early masonry hewn in 1525 from a single massive stone block. The ceilings of the castle halls are richly decorated, although many date only from a restoration in 1870. Adjacent to the castle is an early Gothic cathedral. It's a bit of a climb up Burgstrasse and Amtsstrasse to the castle, but a bus runs regularly up the hill from the Marktplatz. ☎ *03521/47070* ⊕ *www.albrechtsburg-meissen.de* 🖭 *€8, €6 with tour* ⊗ *Mar.–Oct., daily 10–6; Nov.–Feb., daily 10–5.*

Alte Brauerei (*Old Brewery*). Near the Frauenkirche is the Alte Brauerei, which dates to 1569 and is graced by a Renaissance gable. It now houses city offices.

Franziskanerkirche (*St. Francis Church*). The city's medieval past is recounted in the museum of the Franziskanerkirche, a former monastery. ⊠ *Heinrichspl. 3* ☎ *03521/458–857* ⊑ *€3* ⊙ *Daily 11–5.*

Frauenkirche (*Church of Our Lady*). A set of porcelain bells at the late-Gothic Frauenkirche, on the central Marktplatz, was the first of its kind anywhere when installed in 1929.

Nikolaikirche (*St. Nicholas Church*). Near the porcelain works is the Nikolaikirche, which holds the largest set of porcelain figures ever crafted (8¼ feet tall) as well as the remains of early Gothic frescoes. ⊠ *Neumarkt 29.*

Staatliche Porzellan–Manufaktur Meissen (*Meissen Porcelain Works*). The Staatliche Porzellan–Manufaktur Meissen outgrew its castle workshop in the mid-19th century and today is on the southern outskirts of town. One of its buildings has a demonstration workshop and a museum whose Meissen collection rivals that of the Porcelain Museum in Dresden. ⊠ *Talstr. 9* ☎ *03521/468–208* ⊕ *www.meissen.de* ⊑ *€9 including workshop and museum* ⊙ *May–Oct., daily 9–6; Nov.–Apr., daily 9–5.*

WHERE TO EAT AND STAY
For expanded hotel reviews, visit Fodors.com.

$ ✕ **Domkeller.** Part of the centuries-old complex of buildings ringing the
GERMAN   town castle, this ancient and popular hostelry is a great place to enjoy fine wines and hearty German dishes. It's also worth a visit for the sensational view of the Elbe River valley from the large dining room and tree-shaded terrace. ⊠ *Dompl. 9* ☎ *03521/457–676.*

$ ✕ **Restaurant Vincenz Richter.** Tucked away in a yellow wooden-beam
GERMAN   house, this historic restaurant has been painstakingly maintained by
★   the Richter family since 1873. The dining room is adorned with rare antiques, documents, and medieval weapons, as well as copper and tin tableware. Guests can savor the exquisite dishes on the Saxon-German menu while sampling the restaurant's own personally produced white wine; a bottle of the Riesling is a real pleasure. Try the delicious wild rabbit with bacon-wrapped plums, paired with a glass of Kerner *Meissener Kapitelberg.* ⊠ *An der Frauenkirche 12* ☎ *03521/453–285* ⊙ *Closed Mon. No dinner Sun.*

$ ⌂ **Welcome Parkhotel Meissen.** This art nouveau villa on the bank of the Elbe sits across from the hilltop castle. **Pros:** gorgeous views; elegant rooms; fine dining. **Cons:** villa rooms are not as newly furnished; international chain hotel. ⊠ *Hafenstr. 27–31* ☎ *03521/72250* ⊕ *www.*

> ### THE ORIGINS OF THE MEISSEN FUMMEL
>
> At the beginning of the 18th century, the Great Elector of Saxony routinely sent proclamations by messenger to his subjects in Meissen. The messengers were known to chase women and behave poorly, often drinking so much of the famous Meissen wine that their horses were the only ones who remembered the way back to Dresden. To curb this behavior, the elector charged the bakers of Meissen with creating an extremely fragile cake, which the messengers would have to remain sober enough to deliver to the elector intact. Today, the Meissner Fummel remains a local specialty.

welcome-hotel-meissen.de ⌐ *92 rooms, 5 suites* ⟠ *In-room: no a/c, Internet. In-hotel: restaurant, bar, gym, parking, some pets allowed* †⊙† *Breakfast.*

THE ARTS

Concerts. Regular concerts are held at the Albrechtsburg castle, and in early September the *Burgfestspiele*—open-air evening performances—are staged in the castle's romantic courtyard. ☏ *03521/47070.*

Dom. Meissen's cathedral, the Dom, has a yearlong music program, with organ and choral concerts every Saturday in summer. ✉ *Dompl. 7* ☏ *03521/452–490.*

SHOPPING

Sächsische Winzergenossenschaft Meissen. To wine connoisseurs, the name "Meissen" is associated with vineyards producing top-quality white wines much in demand throughout Germany—try a bottle of Müller-Thurgau, Weissburgunder, or Goldriesling. You can buy them directly from the producer, Sächsische Winzergenossenschaft Meissen. ✉ *Bennoweg 9* ☏ *03521/780–970.*

Staatliche Porzellan–Manufaktur Meissen. You can purchase Meissen porcelain directly from the Staatliche Porzellan–Manufaktur Meissen and in every china and gift shop in town. ✉ *Talstr. 9* ☏ *03521/468–700.*

BAUTZEN/BUDYŠIN

53 km (33 mi) east of Dresden.

Bautzen has perched high above a deep granite valley formed by the River Spree for more than 1,000 years. Its almost-intact city walls hide a remarkably well-preserved city with wandering back alleyways and fountain-graced squares. Bautzen is definitely a German city, but it is also the administrative center of Germany's only indigenous ethnic minority, the Sorbs.

In the area, the Sorb language enjoys equal standing with German in government and education, and Sorbs are known for their colorful folk traditions. As in all Slavic cultures, Easter Sunday is the highlight of the calendar, when ornately decorated eggs are hung from trees and when the traditional *Osterreiten*, a procession of Catholic men on horseback who carry religious symbols and sing Sorbian hymns, takes place.

GETTING HERE AND AROUND

Bautzen is halfway between Dresden and Görlitz. Trains leave both cities once every hour; travel time is about an hour.

ESSENTIALS

Visitor Information Bautzen ✉ *Tourist-Information Bautzen-Budyšin, Hauptmarkt 1* ☏ *03591/42016* 🖷 *03591/327–629* ⊕ *www.bautzen.de.*

EXPLORING

Alte Wasserkunst (*Old Waterworks*). Erected in 1558, the Alte Wasserkunst served as part of the town's defensive fortifications, but its true purpose was to pump water from the Spree into 86 cisterns spread throughout the city. It proved so efficient that it provided the city's water supply until 1965. It is now a technical museum. ✉ *Wendischer*

Kirchhof 7 ☎ *03591/41588* 🎫 *€3* ⊙ *Daily 10–5.*

Dom St. Petri (*St. Peter's Cathedral*). Behind the Rathaus is one of Bautzen's most interesting sights: Dom St. Petri is Germany's only *Simultankirche*, or "simultaneous" church. In order to avoid the violence that often occurred during the Reformation, St. Peter's has a Protestant side and a Roman-Catholic side in the same church. A short fence, which once reached a height of 13 feet, separates the two congregations. The church was built in 1213 on the sight of a Milzener (the forerunners of the Sorbs) parish church. ✉ *An der Petrikirche 6* ☎ *03591/31180* ⊕ *www.dompfarrei-bautzen.de* 🎫 *Free* ⊙ *May–Oct., Mon.–Sat. 10–3, Sun. 1–4; Nov.–Apr., daily 11–noon.*

> **BAUTZEN CUTS THE MUSTARD**
>
> Bautzen is famous for mustard, which has been ground here since 1866. Mustard is Germany's favorite condiment, and East Germans consume an average of 5 pounds of the stuff annually. It's so deeply ingrained that here one "gives his mustard" in the same way English speakers would their "two cents." The most popular Bautzen mustard, Bautz'ner Senf, is one of the rare East German products that sells in the West. Available at almost every supermarket, a 200-milliliter tube costs approximately €0.30, making it a great present for those at home.

Hexenhäuser (*Witches' Houses*). Below the waterworks and outside the walls, look for three reddish houses. The Hexenhäuser were the only structures to survive all the city's fires—leading Bautzeners to conclude that they could only be occupied by witches.

Rathaus. Bautzen's main market square is actually two squares: the **Hauptmarkt** (Main Market) and the **Fleischmarkt** (Meat Market) are separated by the yellow, baroque Rathaus. The current town hall dates from 1705, but there has been a town hall in this location since 1213. Bautzen's friendly tourist-information is next door: stop here to pick up a great Bautzen-in-two-hours walking-tour map or to rent their MP3 guide to the city. ✉ *Fleischmarkt 1.*

Reichenturm (*Rich Tower*). Bautzen's city walls have a number of gates and towers. The most impressive tower is the Reichenturm, at the end of Reichenstrasse. Although the tower base dates from 1490, it was damaged in four city fires (in 1620, 1639, 1686, and 1747) and rebuilt, hence its baroque cupola. The reconstruction caused the tower to lean, however, and its foundation was further damaged in 1837. The "Leaning Tower of Bautzen" currently sits about 5 feet off center. ■TIP→ The view from the top is a spectacular vista of Bautzen and the surrounding countryside. ✉ *Reichenstr. 1* ☎ *03591/460–431* 🎫 *€1.50* ⊙ *Daily 10–5.*

WHERE TO EAT AND STAY

For expanded hotel reviews, visit Fodors.com.

$

EASTERN
EUROPEAN

★

✕ **Wjelbik.** The name of Bautzen's best Sorbian restaurant means "pantry." Very popular on Sorb holidays, Wjelbik uses exclusively regional produce in such offerings as the *Sorbisches Hochzeitsmenu* (Sorb wedding feast)—a vegetable and meatball soup followed by beef in creamed

Görlitz's Untermarkt contains the Rathaus and also building number 14, where all goods coming into the city were weighed and taxed.

horseradish. The restaurant is in a 600-year-old building near the cathedral. ⊠ *Kornstr. 7* ☎ *03591/42060.*

$ ★ 🏨 **Hotel Goldener Adler.** This pleasant hotel occupies a 450-year-old building on the main market square. **Pros:** a complete package: comfortable historical hotel, good restaurant, and yummy fondue. **Cons:** a little too modern for a historical town. ⊠ *Hauptmarkt 4* ☎ *03591/48660* ⊕ *www.goldeneradler.de* ⇗ *30 rooms* ⌂ *In-hotel: restaurant, bar, parking, some pets allowed.*

GÖRLITZ

48 km (30 mi) east of Bautzen, 60 km (38 mi) northeast of Dresden.

Tucked away in the country's easternmost corner (bordering Poland), Görlitz's quiet, narrow cobblestone alleys and exquisite architecture make it one of Germany's most beautiful cities. It emerged from the destruction of World War II relatively unscathed. As a result it has more than 4,000 historic houses in styles including Gothic, Renaissance, baroque, rococo, Wilhelminian, and art nouveau. Although the city has impressive museums, theater, and music, it's the ambience created by the casual dignity of these buildings, in their jumble of styles, that makes Görlitz so attractive. Notably absent are the typical socialist eyesores and the glass-and-steel modernism found in many eastern German towns.

The Gothic Dicker Turm (Fat Tower) guards the entrance to the city; it's the oldest tower in Görlitz, and its walls are 5 meters thick.

GETTING HERE AND AROUND

Görlitz can be reached by hourly trains from Dresden (1½ hours) and from Berlin (3 hours, with a change in Cottbus). Görlitz's train station (a wonderful neoclassical building with an art nouveau interior) is a short tram ride outside town.

ESSENTIALS

Visitor Information Görlitz ⊠ *Tourist-Information, Bruderstr. 1* ☎ *03581/47570* 🖷 *03581/475–727* ⊕ *www.goerlitz.de.*

EXPLORING

Biblical House. The Biblical House is interesting for its Renaissance facade decorated with sandstone reliefs depicting biblical stories. The Catholic Church banned religious depictions on secular buildings, but by the time the house was rebuilt after a fire in 1526, the Reformation had Görlitz firmly in its grip. ⊠ *Neissestr. 29.*

Dreifaltigkeitskirche (*Church of the Holy Trinity*). On the southeast side of the market lies the Dreifaltigkeitskirche, a pleasant Romanesque church with a Gothic interior, built in 1245. The interior of the church houses an impressive Gothic triptych altarpiece. The clock on the thin tower is set seven minutes fast in remembrance of a trick played by the city guards on the leaders of a rebellion. In 1527 the city's disenfranchised cloth makers secretly met to plan a rebellion against the city council and the powerful guilds. Their plans were uncovered, and by setting the clock ahead the guards fooled the rebels into thinking it was safe to sneak into the city. As a result they were caught and hanged.

Karstadt. The Karstadt, dating from 1912–13, was Germany's only original art nouveau department store and inside, the main hall has a colorful glass cupola and several stunning freestanding staircases. The store dominates the Marienplatz, a small square outside the city center that serves as Görlitz's transportation hub. Next to Karstadt is the 15th-century Frauenkirche, the parish church for the nearby hospital and the poor condemned to live outside the city walls. ⚠ **The department store is closed, but the city is looking for a way to keep it open to the public. You can still peek inside through the perfume shop.** ⊠ *An der Frauenkirche 5–7* ☎ *03581/4600.*

Kirche St. Peter und Paul (*St. Peter and Paul Church*). Perched high above the river is the Kirche St. Peter und Paul, one of Saxony's largest late-Gothic churches, dating to 1423. The real draw of the church is its famous one-of-a-kind organ, built in 1703 by Eugenio Casparini. The Sun Organ gets its name from the circularly arranged pipes and not from the golden sun at the center. Its full and deep sound, as well as its birdcalls, can be heard on Sunday and Wednesday afternoons. ⊠ *Bei der Peterkirche 5* ☎ *03581/409–590* 🖾 *Free* ⊙ *Mon.–Sat. 10:30–4, Sun. 11:30–4; guided tours Thurs. and Sun. at noon.*

OFF THE
BEATEN
PATH

The Landskron Brewery. The Landskron Brewery is Germany's easternmost Brauhaus and one of the few breweries left that gives tours. Founded in 1869, Landskron isn't very old by German standards, but it's unique in that it hasn't been gobbled up by a huge brewing conglomerate. *Görlitzer* are understandably proud of their own Premium Pilsner, but the brewery also produces good dark, Silesian, and winter beers. Landskron Hefeweizen is one of the best in the country. ☒ *An der Landskronbrauerei* ☎ *03581/465–121* ⊕ *www.landskron.de* ☐ *Tours €6.50–€9.50, by arrangement only* ☉ *Sun.–Thurs.*

Obermarkt (*Upper Market*). The richly decorated Renaissance homes and warehouses on the Obermarkt are a vivid legacy of the city's wealthy past. During the late Middle Ages the most common merchandise here was cloth, which was bought and sold from covered wagons and on the ground floors of many buildings. Napoléon addressed his troops from the balcony of the house at No. 29.

Schlesisches Museum (*Silesian Museum*). The Schlesisches Museum explores 900 years of Silesian culture, and is a meeting place for Silesians from Germany, Poland, and the Czech Republic. The museum is housed in the magnificent Schönhof building, one of Germany's oldest Renaissance *Patrizierhäuser* (grand mansions of the city's ruling business and political elite). ☒ *Brüderstr. 8* ☎ *03581/87910* ⊕ *www. schlesisches-museum.de* ☐ *€5* ☉ *Tues.–Sun. 10–5.*

Untermarkt (*Lower Market*). The Untermarkt is one of Europe's most impressive squares, and a testament to the prosperity brought by the cloth trade. The market is built up in the middle, and the most important building is No. 14, which formerly housed the city scales. The duty of the city scale masters, whose busts adorn the Renaissance facade of the Gothic building, was to weigh every ounce of merchandise entering the city and to determine the taxes due.

The square's most prominent building is the Rathaus. Its winding staircase is as peculiar as its statue of the goddess of justice, whose eyes—contrary to European tradition—are not covered. The corner house on the square, the Alte Ratsapotheke (Old Council Pharmacy), has two intricate sundials on the facade (painted in 1550).

Verrätergasse (*Traitors' Alley*). On Verrätergasse, across the square, is the **Peter-Liebig-Haus,** where the initials of the first four words of the rebels' meeting place, *Der verräterischen Rotte Tor* (the treacherous gang's gate), are inscribed above the door. The Obermarkt is dominated by the **Reichenbach Turm,** a tower built in the 13th century, with additions in 1485 and 1782. Until 1904 the tower housed the city watchmen and their families. The apartments and armory are now a museum. There are great views of the city from the tiny windows at the top. The massive **Kaisertrutz** (Emperor's Fortress) once protected the western city gates, and now houses late-Gothic and Renaissance art from the area around Görlitz, as well as some impressive historical models of the city. Both buildings are part

GÖRLITZ'S SECRET ADMIRER

After German unification, Görlitz was a run-down border town, but renovations costing upward of €400 million returned the city to much of its former splendor. In 1995 it got an additional boost when an anonymous philanthropist pledged to the city a yearly sum of 1 million marks. Every March, Görlitz celebrates the arrival in its coffers of the mysterious Altstadt-Million (albeit, with the change in currency, now €511,000).

16

of the Kulturhistorisches Museum. ⚠ The interior of the Emperor's Fortress will be closed until 2013. ⊠ *Kaisertrutz and Reichenbacher Turm, Pl. des 17. Junis* ☎ *03581/671–355* 🎫 *€3.50, tickets valid on day of purchase and following day* ⊙ *Tues.–Thurs. and weekends 10–5.*

WHERE TO EAT AND STAY
For expanded hotel reviews, visit Fodors.com.

$ ✕ **Die Destille.** This small family-run establishment overlooks the Niko-
GERMAN laiturm, one of the towers from the city's wall. The restaurant offers good solid Silesian fare and absolutely the best *Schlesische Himmelreich* (ham and pork roast smothered in baked fruit and white sauce, served with dumplings) in town. There are also eight inexpensive, spartan guest rooms where you can spend the night. ⊠ *Nikolaistr. 6* ☎ *03581/405–302* ▭ *No credit cards* ⊙ *Sometimes closed in Sept.*

$ 🏨 **Hotel Bon-Apart.** The name says it all: this hotel is a homage to Napoléon, whose troops occupied Görlitz, and it's a splendid departure from a "normal" hotel. **Pros:** large rooms with kitchens and artistically decorated bathrooms; huge breakfast buffet. **Cons:** eclectic design may not appeal to everyone; neighboring market can be noisy in the morning; no elevator. ⊠ *Elisabethstr. 41* ☎ *03581/48080* ⊕ *www.bon-apart. de* ⇱ *20 rooms* ♿ *In-room: no a/c, kitchen. In-hotel: restaurant, bar, parking, some pets allowed.*

SAXONY-ANHALT

The central state of Saxony-Anhalt is almost untouched by modern visitors and is a region rich in natural attractions. In the Altmark, on the edge of the Harz Mountains, fields of grain and sugar beets stretch to the horizon. In the mountains themselves are the deep gorge of the Bode River and the stalactite-filled caves of Rubeland. The songbirds of the Harz are renowned, and though pollution has taken its toll, both the flora and the fauna of the Harz National Park (which encompasses much of the region) are coming back. Atop the Brocken, the Harz's highest point, legend has it that witches convene on Walpurgis Night (the night between April 30 and May 1).

LUTHERSTADT-WITTENBERG

107 km (62 mi) southwest of Berlin, 67 km (40 mi) north of Leipzig.

Protestantism was born in the little town of Wittenberg (officially called Lutherstadt-Wittenberg). In 1508 the fervent, idealistic young Martin Luther, who had become a priest only a year earlier, arrived to study and teach at the new university founded by Elector Frederick the Wise. Nine years later, enraged that the Roman Catholic Church was pardoning sins through the sale of indulgences, Luther posted his 95 Theses attacking the policy on the door of the Castle Church.

Martin Luther is still the center of attention in Wittenberg, and sites associated with him are marked with plaques and signs. You can see virtually all of historic Wittenberg on a 2-km (1-mi) stretch of Col-

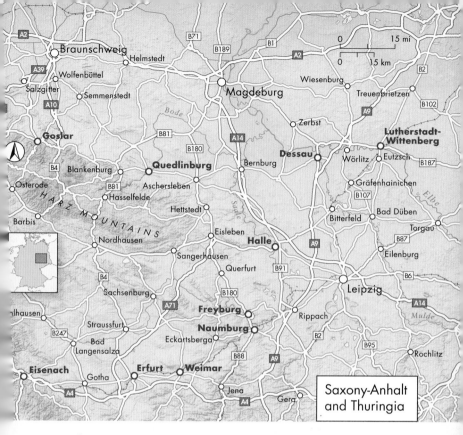

Saxony-Anhalt and Thuringia

legienstrasse and Schlossstrasse that begins at the railroad tracks and ends at the Schlosskirche (Castle Church).

Luthers Hochzeit (*Luther's Wedding*). The best time to visit Wittenberg is during Luthers Hochzeit, the city festival that commemorates (and reenacts) Martin Luther's marriage to Katharina von Bora. On the second weekend in June the city center goes back in time to 1525, with period costumes and entertainment. ⊕ *www.lutherhochzeit.de.*

GETTING HERE AND AROUND
Lutherstadt-Wittenberg is approximately halfway between Berlin and Leipzig, and is served by regional and ICE trains. The station is slightly outside the city center, a pleasant walking distance away.

ESSENTIALS
Visitor Information Wittenberg ⊠ *Tourist-Information, Schlosspl. 2* ☎ *03491/498–610* 🖷 *03491/498–611* ⊕ *www.wittenberg.de.* **Wittenberg District Rural Information Office** ⊠ *Neustr. 13* ☎ *03491/402–610* 🖷 *03491/405–857.*

EXPLORING
Cranachhaus. Renaissance man Lucas Cranach the Elder, probably the wealthiest man in Wittenberg in his day, lived in two different houses during his years in town. In a second Cranachhaus, near the

Schlosskirche (Castle Church), he not only lived and painted but also operated a print shop, which has been restored, and an apothecary. The courtyard, where it's thought he did much of his painting, remains much as it was in his day. Children attend the **Malschule** (drawing school) here. ⊠ *Schlossstr. 1* ☎ *03491/410–912* 🖾 *Free* ⊙ *Mon.–Thurs. 8–4, Fri. 8–3.*

Cranachhaus. The Cranachhaus is believed to have been the first home, in town, of Lucas Cranach the Elder, the court painter, printer, mayor, pharmacist, and friend of Luther. His son, the painter Lucas Cranach the Younger, was born here. Some of the interior has been restored to its 17th-century condition. It's now a gallery with exhibits about Cranach's life and work. Check out the goldsmith and potter that are occasionally on hand demonstrating their crafts in the courtyard. ⊠ *Markt 4* ☎ *03491/420–190* 🖾 *€3* ⊙ *Mon.–Sat. 10–5, Sun. 1–5.*

Haus der Geschichte. The museum Haus der Geschichte is a valiant attempt to evaluate the history of the GDR. It provides fascinating insight into the day-to-day culture of East Germans through the display of more than 20,000 objects, ranging from detergent packaging to kitchen appliances. There is a special section dealing with Germans and Russians in the Wittenberg region. ⊠ *Schlossstr. 6* ☎ *03491/409–004* ⊕ *www.pflug-ev.de* 🖾 *€5* ⊙ *Weekdays 10–5, weekends 11–6.*

Luther Melanchthon Gymnasium (*Luther Melanchthon High School*). In 1975 the city erected a typical East German prefab building to house the Luther Melanchthon Gymnasium, but in the early 1990s, art students contacted Friedensreich Hundertwasser, the famous Austrian architect and avant-garde artist who designed the Hundertwasserhaus in Vienna. Hundertwasser, who argued that there are no universal straight lines or completely flat surfaces in nature, agreed to transform the school, and renovations were completed in 1998. The school is one of only three Hundertwasser buildings in eastern Germany and an interesting contrast to the medieval architecture in the rest of the city. Although the building is a school, the students operate a small office that distributes information about the school and Hundertwasser's art. ⊠ *Str. der Völkerfreundschaft 130* ☎ *03491/881–131* ⊕ *www.hundertwasserschule.de* 🖾 *€2* ⊙ *Tues.–Fri. 2:30–4, weekends 10–4.*

Luthereiche (*Luther Oak*). In a small park where Weserstrasse meets Collegienstrasse, the Luthereiche marks the spot where, in 1520, Luther burned the papal bull excommunicating him for his criticism of the Church. The present oak was planted in the 19th century.

Fodor's Choice **Lutherhaus** (*Luther's House*). Within Lutherhaus is the Augustinian monastery where Martin Luther lived both as a teacher-monk and later, after the monastery was dissolved, as a married man. Today it's a museum dedicated to Luther and the Reformation. Visitors enter Lutherhaus through a garden and an elegant door with a carved stone frame; it was a gift to Luther from his wife, Katharina von Bora. Be sure to visit the monks' refectory, where works by the painter Lucas Cranach the Elder, Luther's contemporary, are displayed. The room that remains closest to the original is the dark, wood-panel Lutherstube. The Luthers and their six children used it as a living room, study, and meeting place

Martin Luther taught in the Lecture Hall within Lutherhaus, which is now a museum dedicated to Martin Luther and the Reformation.

for friends and students. Prints, engravings, paintings, manuscripts, coins, and medals relating to the Reformation and Luther's translation of the Bible into the German vernacular are displayed throughout the house. ⊠ *Collegienstr. 54* ☏ *03491/42030* ⊕ *www.martinluther.de* ▧ *€5* ⊘ *Apr.–Oct., daily 9–6; Nov.–Mar., Tues.–Sun. 10–5.*

Marktplatz (*Market Square*). Two statues are the centerpiece of the Marktplatz: an 1821 statue of Luther by Johann Gottfried Schadow, designer of the quadriga and Victory atop Berlin's Brandenburg Gate, and an 1866 statue of Melanchthon by Frederick Drake. Gabled Renaissance houses containing shops line part of the square.

Rathaus. The backdrop of the two statues on the Marktplatz is the handsome, white High Renaissance Rathaus. ⊠ *Markt 26* ☏ *03491/421–720* ⊘ *Daily 10–5* .

Melanchthonhaus (*Melanchthon House*). In the elegantly gabled Renaissance Melanchthonhaus, the humanist teacher and scholar Philipp Melanchthon corrected Luther's translation of the New Testament from Greek into German. Luther was hiding in the Wartburg in Eisenach at the time, and as each section of his manuscript was completed it was sent to Melanchthon for approval. (*Melanchthon* is a Greek translation of the man's real name, Schwarzerdt, which means "black earth"; humanists routinely adopted such classical pseudonyms.) The second-floor furnishings have been painstakingly re-created after period etchings. Due to much-needed reconstruction efforts, the Melanchthonhaus will be closed until late 2012. ⊠ *Collegienstr. 60* ☏ *03491/403–279* ⊕ *www.martinluther.de* ▧ *€2.50* ⊘ *Apr.–Oct., daily 10–6; Nov.–Mar., Tues.–Sun. 10–5.*

Fodor's Choice **Schlosskirche** (*Castle Church*). In 1517 the indignant Martin Luther
★ nailed his 95 Theses attacking the Roman Catholic Church's policy
of selling indulgences to the doors of the Schlosskirche. Written in
Latin, the theses might have gone unnoticed had not someone—without Luther's knowledge—translated them into German and distributed
them. In 1521 the Holy Roman Emperor Charles V summoned Luther
to Worms when Luther refused to retract his position. It was on the way
home from his confrontation with the emperor that Luther was "captured" by his protector, Elector Frederick the Wise, and hidden from
papal authorities in Eisenach for the better part of a year. The Theses
are hung on the original door in bronze. Inside the church, simple
bronze plaques mark the burial places of Luther and Melanchthon.
⊠ *Schlosspl.* ☎ *03491/402–585* 🖃 *Free, tower €2* ⊙ *May–Oct., Mon.–
Sat. 10–5, Sun. 11:30–5; Nov.–Apr., Mon.–Sat. 10–4, Sun. 11:30–4.*

Stadtkirche St. Marien (*Parish Church of St. Mary*). From 1514 until his
death in 1546, Martin Luther preached two sermons a week in the
twin-tower Stadtkirche St. Marien. He and Katharina von Bora were
married here (Luther broke with monasticism in 1525 and married the
former nun). The altar triptych by Lucas Cranach the Elder includes
a self-portrait, as well as portraits of Luther wearing the knight's disguise he adopted when hidden at the Wartburg; Luther preaching;
Luther's wife and one of his sons; Melanchthon; and Lucas Cranach
the Younger. Also notable is the 1457 bronze baptismal font by Herman Vischer the Elder. On the church's southeast corner you'll find a
discomforting juxtaposition of two Jewish-related **monuments**: a 1304
mocking caricature called the Jewish Pig, erected at the time of the
expulsion of the town's Jews, and, on the cobblestone pavement, a
contemporary memorial to the Jews who died at Auschwitz. ⊠ *Kirchpl.*
☎ *03491/404–415* 🖃 *€1.50, including tour* ⊙ *May–Oct., daily 10–5;
Nov.–Apr., daily 10–4.*

Wittenberg English Ministry. The Wittenberg English Ministry offers
English-speaking visitors the opportunity to worship in the churches
where Martin Luther conducted his ministry. During the summer months
the ministry brings English-speaking pastors from the United States and
provides Lutheran worship services in the Castle Church and in the
Parish Church. The services follow German Protestant tradition (albeit
in English) and conclude with singing Luther's "A Mighty Fortress Is
Our God," accompanied on the organ. The Ministry also offers tours
of Wittenberg and other Luther sites. ⊠ *Schlosspl. 2* ☎ *03491/498–
610* ⊕ *www.wittenberg-english-ministry.com* ⊙ *May–Oct., Sat. 5 at
Schlosskirche or Stadtkirche St. Marien. Other times by request.*

WHERE TO EAT

$ ✕ **Brauhaus Wittenberg.** This historic brewery-cum-restaurant is the perGERMAN fect stop for a cold beer after a long day of sightseeing. ■TIP➔ Set in
★ the Old Town's magnificent Beyerhof courtyard, the Brauhaus still produces
local beer such as Wittenberger Kuckucksbier. In the medieval restaurant
with its huge beer kettles, you can sample local and south German
cuisine; a specialty is the smoked fish—such as eel, trout, and halibut—from the Brauhaus smokery. In summer, try to get a table in the
courtyard. ⊠ *Markt 6* ☎ *03491/433–130.*

$ **✕Schlosskeller.** At the back of the Schlosskirche, this restaurant's four
GERMAN dining rooms are tucked away in a basement with 16th-century stone
walls and barrel-vaulted ceilings. The kitchen specializes in German
dishes, such as *Kümmelfleisch mit Senfgurken* (caraway beef with
mustard-seed pickles). ⊠ *Schlosspl. 1* ☎ *03491/480–805.*

DESSAU

35 km (22 mi) southwest of Wittenberg.

The name "Dessau" is known to students of modern architecture as
the epicenter of architect Walter Gropius' highly influential Bauhaus
school of design. During the 1920s, Gropius hoped to replace the dark
and inhumane tenement architecture of the 1800s with standardized
yet spacious and bright apartments. His ideas and methods were used
in building 316 villas in the city's Törten neighborhood in the 1920s.

GETTING HERE AND AROUND
Dessau makes an excellent day trip from Berlin. The Regional Express
train leaves Berlin every hour and the trip takes two hours with a
change in Rosslau.

ESSENTIALS
Visitor Information Dessau ⊠ *Tourist-Information Dessau, Zerbster Str. 2c*
☎ *0340/204–1442* 🖶 *0340/220–3003* ⊕ *www.dessau.de.*

EXPLORING
★ **Bauhaus Building.** Architectural styles that would influence the appearance of such cities as New York, Chicago, and San Francisco were
conceived in the Bauhaus Building. The architecture school is still operating, and the building can be visited. Other structures designed by
Gropius and the Bauhaus architects, among them the Meisterhäuser,
are open for inspection off Ebertallee and Elballee. ⊠ *Gropiusallee 38*
☎ *0340/650–8251* ⊕ *www.bauhaus-dessau.de* 🎟 *€6* ☉ *Daily 10–6.*
*Meisterhäuser: Nov.–mid-Feb., Tues.–Sun. 10–5; mid-Feb.–Oct., Tues.–
Sun. 10–6.*

Georgkirche (*St. George's Church*). For a contrast to the no-nonsense
Bauhaus architecture, look at downtown Dessau's older buildings,
including the Dutch-baroque Georgkirche, built in 1712. ⊠ *Georgen-
str. 15.*

Technikmuseum Hugo Junkers (*Hugo Junkers Technical Museum*). The
Bauhaus isn't the only show in town. Professor Hugo Junkers was one
of the most famous engineers-cum-inventors of the 20th century, and his
factories were at the forefront of innovation in aircraft and industrial
design until they were expropriated by the Nazis in 1933. The star of
the Technikmuseum Hugo Junkers is a completely restored JU-52/3—
the ubiquitous German passenger airplane transformed into military
transport. The museum also houses a fascinating collection of industrial
equipment, machinery, engines, and the original Junkers wind tunnel.
⊠ *Kühnauerstr. 161a* ☎ *0340/661–1982* ⊕ *www.technikmuseum-
dessau.de* 🎟 *€3* ☉ *Daily 10–5.*

16

HALLE

52 km (32 mi) south of Dessau.

Halle is a city that deserves a second look. The first impression of ever-under-construction train station and dismal tram ride into town hides a pretty 1,000-year-old city built on the salt trade. It straddles the River Saale, whose name is derived from the German word for salt; the name Halle comes from the Celtic word for salt. The city has suffered from the shortfalls of Communist urban planning, yet the Old Town has an unusual beauty, particularly in its spacious central marketplace, the **Markt**, with its five distinctive sharp-steepled towers.

GETTING HERE AND AROUND

Frequent S-bahn trains connect Halle with Leipzig (30 minutes) and with Naumburg (20 minutes).

ESSENTIALS

Visitor Information Halle ⊠ *Stadtmarketing Halle, Marktpl. 1360* ☎ *0345/122–9984* ⊕ *www.stadtmarketing-halle.de.*

EXPLORING

Dom (*Cathedral*). Halle's only early-Gothic church, the Dom stands about 200 yards southeast of the Moritzburg. Its nave and side aisles are of equal height, a common characteristic of Gothic church design in this part of Germany. ⊠ *Dompl. 3* ☎ *0345/202–1379* ☞ *Free* ☉ *June–Oct., Mon.–Sat. 2–4.*

OFF THE BEATEN PATH

Halloren Schokoladenfabrik. The Halloren Schokoladenfabrik, Germany's oldest chocolate factory, was founded in 1804 and has changed hands several times (including a brief period when it was used to manufacture airplane wings during the war). Its Schokoladenmuseum explores 200 years of chocolate production and is unique because of a 27-square-meter room made entirely from chocolate. Entrance to the museum also allows you entrance to the glass-enclosed production line, where you can watch almost all aspects of chocolate making. ■TIP➜ The factory is on the other side of the train station from the main town. To get here, take Tram 7 to Fiete-Schultze-Strasse and walk back 200 meters. ⊠ *Delitzscherstr. 70* ☎ *0345/5642–192* ⊕ *www.halloren.de* ☞ *€7, includes samples* ☉ *Mon.–Sat. 9–4.*

Händelhaus. Handel's birthplace, the Händelhaus, is now a museum devoted to the composer. The entrance hall displays glass harmonicas and curious musical instruments perfected by Benjamin Franklin in the 1760s. ■TIP➜ Be sure to look for the small courtyard where Handel played as a child. ⊠ *Grosse Nikolaistr. 5* ☎ *0345/500–900* ☞ *Free* ☉ *Tues.–Wed., and Fri.–Sun. 9:30–5:30; Thurs. 9:30–7.*

Marienkirche (*St. Mary's Church*). Of the four towers belonging to the late-Gothic Marienkirche, two are connected by a vertiginous catwalk bridge. Martin Luther preached in the church, and George Friedrich Handel (Händel in German), born in Halle in 1685, was baptized at its font. He went on to learn to play the organ beneath its high, vaulted ceiling.

Marktschlösschen (*Market Palace*). The Marktschlösschen, a late-Renaissance structure just off the market square, has an interesting collection of historical musical instruments, some of which could have been played by Handel and his contemporaries. ✉ *Marktpl. 13* ☎ *0345/202–9141* ⬛ *Free* ⊙ *Tues.– Fri. 10–7, weekends 10–6.*

Moritzburg (*Moritz Castle*). The Moritzburg was built in the late 15th century by the archbishop of Magdeburg after he claimed the city for his archdiocese. The typical late-Gothic fortress, with a dry moat and a sturdy round tower at each of its four corners, was a testament to Halle's early might, which vanished with the Thirty Years' War. Prior to World War II the castle contained a leading gallery of German Expressionist paintings, which were ripped from the walls by the Nazis and condemned as "degenerate." Some of the works are back in place at the **Staatliche Galerie Moritzburg,** together with some outstanding late-19th- and early-20th-century art. ■TIP→ You'll find Rodin's famous sculpture The Kiss here. ✉ *Friedemann-Bach-Pl. 5* ☎ *0345/212–590* ⊕ *www.moritzburg. halle.de* ⬛ *€4* ⊙ *Tues. 11–8:30, Wed.–Sun. 10–6.*

Neue Residenz (*New Residence*). The former archbishop's home, the 16th-century Neue Residenz, houses the **Geiseltalmuseum** and its world-famous collection of fossils dug from brown coal deposits in the Geisel Valley near Halle. ✉ *Dornstr. 5* ☎ *0345/552–6135* ⬛ *Free* ⊙ *Weekdays 9–noon and 1–5; every 2nd and 4th weekend 9–1.*

Roter Turm (*Red Tower*). The Markt's fifth tower is Halle's celebrated Roter Turm, built between 1418 and 1506 as an expression of the city's power and wealth. The carillon inside is played on special occasions. ✉ *Markt.*

ॐ **Technisches Halloren- und Salinemuseum** (*Technical Saline Extraction Museum*). The salt trade on which Halle built its prosperity is documented in the Technisches Halloren- und Salinemuseum. A replica brine mill shows the salt-extraction process, and the exquisite silver-goblet collection of the Salt Workers' Guild (the Halloren) is on display. The old method of evaporating brine from local springs is sometimes demonstrated. The museum is on the south side of the Saale River (cross the Schiefer Bridge to get there). ✉ *Mansfelderstr. 52* ☎ *0345/202–5034* ⬛ *€3.50* ⊙ *Tues.–Sun. 10–5.*

WHERE TO EAT AND STAY

Halle's café scene spreads out along the Kleine Ullrichstrasse. It's a good area for searching out an affordable meal and lively conversation.

For expanded hotel reviews, visit Fodors.com.

SALT AND CHOCOLATE

In Halle the salt trade was controlled by the *Halloren* (members of the brotherhood of salt workers), who cooked brine into salt on the banks of the Saale River. All that remains of the once incredibly powerful Halloren are the tasty *Halloren-Kügel,* a praline made by the Halloren Schokoladenfabrik, Germany's oldest chocolate factory. The candy is modeled after the silver buttons worn by the Halloren. Very popular in eastern Germany, the chocolates can be purchased just about anywhere in town—there is an outlet store in the train station.

16

DID YOU KNOW?

George Frideric Handel was baptized and learned to play the organ at Halle's Marienkirche.

$ ✕**Hallesches Brauhaus Kühler Brunnen.** Halle's first and best brewpub
GERMAN   serves traditional brewery fare in huge portions at reasonable prices.
The Brauhaus is most famous for its large selection of *Flammkuchen,*
a kind of thin-crust pizza originated in the Alsace region of France.
The best beer is the brewery's own Hallsch, an amber top-fermented
ale served in funky glasses. ⊠ *Grosse Nikolaistr. 2* ☎ *0345/212–570*
⊟ *No credit cards.*

$ ✕**Restaurant Mönchshof.** Hearty German fare in heartier portions is
GERMAN   served in high-ceiling, dark-wood surroundings. Lamb from Saxony-
☺   Anhalt's Wettin region and venison are specialties in season, but there
are always fish and crisp roast pork on the menu. The wine list is extensive, with international vintages. The restaurant is popular with locals,
and the staff are particularly accommodating with children. ⊠ *Talamt-
str. 6* ☎ *0345/202–1726.*

$$ ⊡ **Ankerhof Hotel.** The Ankerhof, in an old warehouse, is a unique
reflection on Halle's salt-strewn past. **Pros:** casual elegance worked
into a traditional setting. **Cons:** building creaks and groans when it is
windy; can be cold in winter. ⊠ *Ankerstr. 2a* ☎ *0345/232–3200* ⊕ *www.
ankerhofhotel.de* ⥂ *49 rooms, 1 suite* ⚿ *In-room: no a/c, Internet. In-
hotel: restaurant, gym, parking, some pets allowed* ⍩ *Breakfast.*

THE ARTS

The city of Handel's birth is, not surprisingly, an important music center.
Halle is famous for its opera productions, its orchestral concerts, and
particularly its choirs.

Opernhaus. For schedules, prices, and reservations of opera performances
staged at the city's renowned Opernhaus, call ☎ *0345/5110–0355.*

Philharmonisches Staatsorchester Halle (*State Philharmonic Orchestra*).
The city's main orchestra, the Philharmonisches Staatsorchester Halle,
performs at the Konzerthalle. ⊠ *Grosse Gosenstr. 12* ☎ *0345/523–3141
for concert information and tickets* ⊕ *www.staatskapelle.halle.de.*

Handel Festival. The annual Handel Festival takes place in the first half
of June, and two youth-choir festivals occur in May and October.
☎ *0345/5009–0222.*

16

NAUMBURG

60 km (65 mi) south of Halle.

Once a powerful trading and ecclesiastical city, 1,000-year-old Naum-
burg is the cultural center of the Salle-Unstrut. Although the city is most
famous for its Romanesque/Gothic cathedral, it hides a well-preserved
collection of patrician houses, winding back alleys, and a marketplace so
distinctive that it warrants the appellation "Naumburger Renaissance."

GETTING HERE AND AROUND

From the train station the fun way to get into the city is to take the
Naumburger Historical Tram, which runs every 30 minutes. A single
ride on Europe's smallest tramway, in antique streetcars, costs €1.50.

ESSENTIALS

Visitor Information Naumburg ⊠ *Tourist und Tagungsservice Naumburg, Markt 12* ☏ *03445/273-125* 🖶 *03445/273-128* ⊕ *www.naumburg-tourismus.de.*

EXPLORING

Dom St. Peter und Paul (*St. Peter and Paul Cathedral*). Perched high above the city and dominating the skyline stands the symbol of Naumburg: the Dom St. Peter und Paul. For the most part, the cathedral was constructed during the latter half of the 13th century, and it's considered one of the masterpieces of the late Romanesque period. What makes the cathedral unique, however, is the addition of a second choir in the Gothic style less than 100 years later. The Gothic choir is decorated with statues of the cathedral's benefactors from the workshop of the Naumburger Meister. The most famous statues are of Uta and Ekkehard, the city's most powerful patrons. Uta's tranquil face is everywhere, from postcards to city maps. ⊠ *Dompl. 16* ☏ *03445/23010* 🎫 *€4* ⊗ *Mon.– Sat. 10–4, Sun. noon–4; guided tours by appointment.*

Marientor. Naumburg was once ringed by a defensive city wall with five gates. The only remaining gate, the Marientor, is a rare surviving example of a dual-portal gate from the 14th century. The museum inside the gate provides a brief history of the city's defenses. ■ TIP➔ A pleasant walk along the remaining city walls from Marienplatz to the Weingarten is the easiest way to explore the last intact section of Naumburg's wall, moat, and defensive battlements. ⊠ *Marienpl.* 🎫 *€0.50* ⊗ *Daily 10–4:30.*

Marktplatz. Naumburg's historic Marktplatz lies strategically at the intersection of two medieval trade routes. Although the market burned in 1517, it was painstakingly rebuilt in Renaissance and baroque styles.

Rathaus. Naumburg's Rathaus was rebuilt in 1523, incorporating the remnants of the building destroyed by fire. ⊠ *Markt 1.*

Kaysersches Haus (*Imperial House*). The Kaysersches Haus is supported by seven Gothic gables and has a carved oak doorway from the Renaissance ⊠ *Markt 10.*

Schlösschen (*Little Castle*). The Schlösschen houses the offices of Naumburg's first and only Protestant bishop, Nikolaus von Amsdorf, who was consecrated by Martin Luther in 1542 ⊠ *Markt 2.*

Naumburger Wein und Sekt Manufaktur. The Naumburger Wein und Sekt Manufaktur produces fine still and sparkling wines on the bank of the Salle River. The 200-year-old monastery is a pleasant 2-km (1-mi) walk or bike ride from Naumburg's city center. Tours of the production rooms and the vaulted cellar, with wine tastings, take place whenever a group forms and last about an hour. The wine garden is a pleasant place to relax on the bank of the river and the restaurant serves small snacks. Larger appetites find relief across the street at the Gasthaus Henne. ⊠ *Blütengrund 35* ☏ *03445/202–042* ⊕ *www.naumburger.com* 🎫 *Tours €5* ⊗ *Daily 11–6; tours given Apr.–Oct.*

Nietzsche Haus Museum. The philosopher Friedrich Nietzsche's family lived in Naumburg from 1858 to 1897, in a small classical house in the Weingarten. The Nietzsche Haus Museum documents the life and times of one of Naumburg's most controversial residents. The exhibition does not delve into Nietzsche's philosophy, but focuses a great deal on his bizarre relationship with his sister and her manipulation of his manuscripts. ✉ *Weingarten 18* ☎ *03445/703–503* ⊕ *www. mv-naumburg.de* ✉ *€3* ☉ *Tues.– Fri. 2–5, weekends 10–4.*

St. Wenceslas. The southern end of the Markt is dominated by the parish church of St. Wenceslas. A church has stood on this spot since 1218, but the current incarnation dates from 1426, with interior renovations in 1726. The church is most famous for its huge Hildebrandt Organ, which was tested and tuned by J. S. Bach in 1746. Fans of Lucas Cranach the Elder get their due with two of his paintings, *Suffer the Little Children Come Unto Me* and the *Adoration of the Three Magi.* The 73-meter-tall tower belongs to the city, *not* the church, and was used as a watchtower for the city guards, who lived there until 1994. ✉ *Topfmarkt* ☎ *03445/208–401* ✉ *Free, tower €2* ☉ *Mon.–Sat. 10–noon and 2–5, tower daily 10–5.*

SALLE-UNSTRUT: WINE COUNTRY

The Salle-Unstrut is Europe's northernmost wine-growing region, and with more than 30 different grape varieties one of the most diverse. The region stretches from Halle to Eisleben, and has more than 700 vintners operating on a mere 1,600 acres. Grapes are grown on the terraced slopes of rolling hills, guarded by numerous castles and fortresses. The area is easy to explore by the regional train that meanders through the Unstrut Valley once every hour or the bicycle path that stretches along the banks of both rivers.

WHERE TO EAT AND STAY

For expanded hotel reviews, visit Fodors.com.

$ ✕ **Alt-Naumburg.** Enjoy simple but tasty regional specialties directly in
GERMAN front of the Marientor. The Alt-Naumburg beer garden is a good place to relax away from the action of the city center. The three-room pension is often booked far in advance. ✉ *Marienpl. 13* ☎ *03445/234–425* ☐ *No credit cards.*

$ ▦ **Hotel Stadt Aachen.** Many of the simply decorated rooms overlook the central market at this pleasant hotel in a medieval house. **Pros:** comfortable hotel in the middle of the action; helpful staff. **Cons:** location by the market is sometimes noisy. ✉ *Markt 11* ☎ *03445/2470* ⊕ *www. hotel-stadt-aachen.de* ⇆ *38 rooms* ⌂ *In-hotel: restaurant, parking, some pets allowed.*

REYBURG

10 km (6 mi) north of Naumburg.

Stepping off the train in the sleepy town of Freyburg, it is not difficult to see why locals call the area "the Tuscany of the North." With clean, wandering streets, whitewashed buildings, and a huge castle perched on a vine-terraced hill, Freyburg is a little out of place. The town owes its existence to Schloss Neuenburg, which was built by the same Thuringian count who built the Wartburg. Although most visitors head straight for the wine, the historic Old Town and castle certainly warrant a visit.

16

Freyburg is surrounded by a 1,200-meter-long almost completely intact city wall. The **Ekstädter Tor** was the most important gate into the city, and dates from the 14th century. The gate is dominated by one of the few remaining barbicans in central Germany.

ESSENTIALS

Visitor Information Freyburg ⊠ *Freyburger Fremdenverkehrsverein, Markt 2* ☎ *034464/27260* 🖷 *034464/273–760* ⊕ *wwwfreyburg-info.de.*

EXPLORING

Rotkäppchen Sektkellerei (*Little Red Riding Hood Sparkling Wine*). Freyburg is the home of one of Europe's largest producers of sparkling wine, Rotkäppchen Sektkellerei, a rarity in eastern Germany with significant market share in the West. Hour-long tours of the production facility, including the world's largest wooden wine barrel, take place daily at 11 and 2, with additional tours on Saturday and Sunday at 12:30 and 3:30. ⊠ *Sektkellereistr. 5* ☎ *034464/340* ⊕ *www.rotkaeppchen.de* 🎫 *€5* ☉ *Daily 10–6.*

St. Marien Kirche. In 1225 the Thuringian count Ludwig IV erected St. Marien Kirche as a triple-naved basilica and the only church within the city walls. The coquina limestone building, which resembles the cathedral in Naumburg, was renovated in the 15th century into its current form as a single-hall structure. The great carved altarpiece also dates from the 15th century and the baptistery from 1592. ⊠ *Markt 2.*

Schloss Neuenburg (*Neuenburg Castle*). Schloss Neuenburg has loomed protectively over Freyburg since its foundation was laid in 1090 by the Thuringian Ludwig I. The spacious residential area and huge towers date from the 13th century, when Neuenburg was a part of Thuringia's eastern defenses. The spartan Gothic double-vaulted chapel from 1190 is one of the few rooms that evokes an early medieval past, since most of the castle was renovated in the 15th century. ⊠ *Schloss 1* ☎ *34464/35530* 🎫 *€6* ☉ *Tues.–Sun. 10–5.*

Winzervereinigung-Freyburg. The best place to try Salle-Unstrut wine is at the Winzervereinigung-Freyburg (Freyburg Vintner's Association). Its 500 members produce some of Germany's finest wines, both white and red, mostly pure varietals, with some limited blends. (A wonderful light red from a hybrid of the Blauer Zweigelt and St. James grape, called Andre, may change how you think about German red wine.) Tastings and tours can be arranged in advance, or you can simply show up. Options range from the simple tour of one of Germany's largest barrel cellars (daily at 1 pm, €3) to the grand tasting (by arrangement, €10.20). The association goes out of its way to cater to the tastes of its guests, and bread, cheese, and water are always in plentiful supply. ⊠ *Querfurter Str. 10* ☎ *034464/30623* ⊕ *www.winzervereinigung-freyburg.de* ☉ *Mon.–Sat. 10–6, Sun. 10–4.*

WHERE TO EAT

$

GERMAN

✕ **The Küchenmeisterey.** Where better than a castle serenely overlooking the village of Freyburg for a medieval restaurant? Everything is prepared according to historical recipes with ingredients from the region. Try the roast chicken with honey or any of the grilled meats. Most menu items are available in the spacious beer garden. ⊠ *Schloss 1* ☎ *034464/66200* ⊘ *Closed Jan. No dinner Sun. and Mon.*

QUEDLINBURG

79 km (49 mi) northwest of Halle.

This medieval Harz town has more half-timber houses than any other town in Germany: more than 1,600 of them line the narrow cobblestone streets and squares. The town escaped destruction during World War II and was treasured in GDR days, though not very well preserved. Today the nicely restored town is a UNESCO World Heritage Site.

For nearly 200 years Quedlinburg was a favorite imperial residence and site of imperial diets, beginning with the election in 919 of Henry the Fowler (Henry I) as the first Saxon king of Germany. It became a major trading city and a member of the Hanseatic League, equal in stature to Köln.

ESSENTIALS

Visitor Information Quedlinburg ⊠ *Tourismus-Marketing GmbH, Markt 2* ☎ *03946/905–624* 🖷 *03946/905–629* ⊕ *www.quedlinburg.de.*

EXPLORING

Lyonel Feininger Gallery. Placed behind half-timber houses so as not to affect the town's medieval feel is the sophisticated, modern Lyonel Feininger Gallery. When the art of American-born painter Lyonel Feininger, a Bauhaus teacher in both Weimar and Dessau, was declared "decadent" by the Hitler regime in 1938, the artist returned to America. Left behind with a friend were engravings, lithographs, etchings, and paintings. The most comprehensive Feininger print collection in the world is displayed here. ⊠ *Finkenherd 5a* ☎ *03946/2238* ⊕ *www. feininger-galerie.de* 🎟 *€6* ⊘ *Apr.–Oct., Tues.–Sun. 10–6; Nov.–Mar., Tues.–Sun. 10–5.*

Marktplatz. The Altstadt (Old Town) is full of richly decorated half-timber houses, particularly along Mühlgraben, Schuhof, the Hölle, Breitestrasse, and Schmalstrasse. Notable on the Marktplatz are the Renaissance **Rathaus**, with a 14th-century statue of Roland signifying the town's independence, and the baroque 1701 Haus Grünhagen. Street and hiking maps and guidebooks (almost all in German) are available in the information office at the Rathaus. ⊠ *Markt 2* ☎ *03946/90550* 🎟 *Free* ⊘ *Mon.–Sat. 9–3.*

Schlossmuseum (*Castle Museum*). Quedlinburg's largely Renaissance castle buildings perch on top of the Schlossberg (Castle Hill), with a terrace overlooking woods and valley. The grounds include the Schlossmuseum, which has exhibits on the history of the town and castle, artifacts of the Bronze Age, and the wooden cage in which a captured 14th-century robber baron was put on public view. Restored 17th- and 18th-century rooms give an impression of castle life at that time. ⊠ *Schlossberg 1* ☎ *03946/2730* 🎟 *€4* ⊘ *Mar.–Oct., daily 10–6; Nov.– Feb., Sat.–Thurs. 10–4.*

16

Ständerbau Fachwerkmuseum. The oldest half-timber house in Quedlinburg, built about 1310, is the Ständerbau Fachwerkmuseum, now a museum. ⊠ *Wordg. 3* ☎ *03946/3828* 💷 *€3* ⊘ *Nov.–Mar., Fri.–Wed. 10–4; Apr.–Oct., Fri.–Wed. 10–5.*

Stiftskirche St. Servatius (*Collegiate Church of St. Servatius*). The simple, graceful Stiftskirche St. Servatius is one of the most important and best-preserved 12th-century Romanesque structures in Germany. Henry I and his wife Mathilde are buried in its crypt. The renowned Quedlinburg Treasure of 10th-, 11th-, and 12th-century gold and silver and bejeweled manuscripts is also kept here (what's left of it). In Nazi days SS leader Heinrich Himmler made the church into a shrine dedicated to the SS, insisting that it was only appropriate, since Henry I was the founder of the first German Reich. ⊠ *Schlossberg 1* ☎ *03946/709–900* 💷 *€4* ⊘ *May–Oct., Tues.–Fri. 10–6, Sat. 10–5, Sun. noon–6; Nov.–Apr., Tues.–Sat. 10–4, Sun. noon–4.*

WHERE TO EAT AND STAY

For expanded hotel reviews, visit Fodors.com.

$ ✕ **Lüdde Bräu.** Brewing *Braunbier* (a hoppy, top-fermented beer) has
GERMAN   been a Quedlinburg tradition for several centuries. The Lüdde brewery
★   traces its history back to 1807, when Braunbier breweries dotted the Harz Mountains, and it was the last surviving brewery when it closed its doors in 1966. After German reunification, Georg Lüdde's niece reopened the business, and it remains the only Braunbier brewery in Quedlinburg. Sampling the reemergence of an almost lost German tradition, as well as some incredible beer-based game dishes, makes the restaurant well worth a visit—the Braunbier is called *Pubarschknall.* ⊠ *Carl-Ritter-Str. 1* ☎ *03946/901–481* ⊕ *www.hotel-brauhaus-luedde. de.*

$ 🛏 **Hotel Zum Brauhaus.** The hotel is located in a beautifully restored
★   half-timber house. **Pros:** friendly staff; location next to Lüdde brewery. **Cons:** a little rough around the edges; upper rooms get hot in summer. ⊠ *Carl-Ritter-Str. 1* ☎ *03946/901–481* ⊕ *www.hotel-brauhaus-luedde. de* 🛏 *50 rooms, 1 suite* ☖ *In-room: no a/c. In-hotel: restaurant, parking, some pets allowed* ⼮ *Breakfast.*

$ 🛏 **Hotel Zur Goldenen Sonne.** Rooms in this baroque half-timber inn
★   are furnished in a pleasing, rustic fashion. **Pros:** beautiful half-timber house with modern conveniences; reasonable rates. **Cons:** the clock on the square strikes every 15 minutes; rooms in the renovated section not quite as nice as the ones in the half-timber house. ⊠ *Steinweg 11* ☎ *03946/96250* ⊕ *www.hotelzurgoldenensonne.de* 🛏 *27 rooms* ☖ *In-room: no a/c. In-hotel: restaurant, parking, some pets allowed* ⼮ *Breakfast.*

GOSLAR

48 km (30 mi) northwest of Quedlinburg.

Goslar, the lovely, unofficial capital of the Harz region, is one of Germany's oldest cities and is known for the medieval glamour expressed in the fine Romanesque architecture of the Kaiserpfalz, an imperial palace of the German Empire. Thanks to the deposits of ore close to

Adorable Quedlinburg has 1,600 half-timber houses—that's more than any other town in Germany.

the town, Goslar was one of the country's wealthiest hubs of trade during the Middle Ages. In this town of 46,000, time seems to have stood still among the hundreds of well-preserved (mostly typical northern German half-timber) houses built over the course of seven centuries. Despite Goslar's rapid decline after the breakup of the Holy Roman Empire, the city—thanks to its ore deposits—maintained all the luxury and worldliness born of economic success.

GETTING HERE AND AROUND

Hourly trains whisk travelers from Hanover to Goslar in about an hour.

ESSENTIALS

Visitor Information Goslar ⊠ *Tourist-Information, Markt 7* ☎ *05321/78060* 🖨 *05321/780–644* ⊕ *www.goslar.de.*

EXPLORING

Erzbergwerk Rammelsberg. The source of the town's riches is outside the city in the Erzbergwerk Rammelsberg, the world's only silver mine that was in continuous operation for more than 1,000 years. It stopped operating in 1988, but you can explore the many tunnels and shafts of the old mine. ⊠ *Bergtal 19* ☎ *05321/7500* ⊕ *www.rammelsberg.de* 🎟 *€12, including tour* ☉ *Daily 9–6; tours given as needed 9:30–4:30.*

★ **Kaiserpfalz.** The impressive Kaiserpfalz, set high above the historic downtown area, dates to the early Middle Ages. It once was the center of German imperial glory, when emperors held their regular diets here. Among the rulers who frequented Goslar were Heinrich III (1039–56) and his successor, Heinrich IV (1056–1106), who was also born in Goslar. You can visit an exhibit about the German medieval kaisers who stayed here, inspect the small chapel where the heart of Heinrich III is buried (the body is in Speyer), and view the beautiful ceiling murals in the Reichssaal (Imperial Hall). ☒ *Kaiserbleek 6* ☎ *05321/311–9693* 🖃 *€5* ☉ *Apr.–Oct., daily 10–5; Nov.–Mar., daily 10–4.*

Rathaus. The Rathaus with its magnificent **Huldigungssaal** (Hall of Honor) dates to 1450 and testifies to the wealth of Goslar's merchants. ☒ *Markt 7* ☎ *05321/78060* 🖃 *€3.50* ☉ *Daily 11–3.*

WHERE TO STAY

For expanded hotel reviews, visit Fodors.com.

$$ 🏨 **Kaiserworth-Hotel und Restaurant.** Hidden behind the reddish-brown walls of a 500-year-old house, the seat of medieval tailors and merchants, this hotel offers small but bright, pleasantly furnished rooms. ☒ *Markt 3* ☎ *05321/7090* ⊕ *www.kaiserworth.de* 🛏 *66 rooms* ⚠ *In-room: no a/c, Internet. In-hotel: restaurant, parking, some pets allowed* 🍴*Breakfast.*

THURINGIA

Unlike other eastern states, unassuming Thuringia was not taken from the Slavs by wandering Germanic tribes but has been German since before the Middle Ages. The hilly countryside is mostly rural and forested, and it preserves a rich cultural past in countless small villages, medieval cities, and country palaces. In the 14th century traders used the 168-km (104-mi) Rennsteig ("fast trail") through the dark depths of the Thuringian Forest, and cities such as Erfurt and Eisenach evolved as major commercial hubs. Today the forests and the Erzgebirge Mountains are a remote paradise for hiking and fishing. The city of Weimar is one of Europe's old cultural centers, where Germany attempted its first go at a true democracy in 1918. Thuringia is the land of Goethe and Schiller, but it is also tempered by the ominous presence of one of the Third Reich's most notorious concentration camps, at Buchenwald.

EISENACH

160 km (100 mi) south of Goslar, 95 km (59 mi) northeast of Fulda.

When you stand in Eisenach's ancient market square it's difficult to imagine this half-timber town as an important center of the East German automobile industry. Yet this is where Wartburgs (very tiny, noisy, and cheaply produced cars, which are now collector's items) were made. The cars were named after the Wartburg, the famous castle that broods over Eisenach from atop one of the foothills of the Thuringian Forest. Today West German automaker Opel continues the tradition by building one of Europe's most modern car-assembly lines on the outskirts of town.

GETTING HERE AND AROUND

Hourly trains connect Eisenach with Leipzig (two hours) and Dresden (three hours). There are frequent connections to Weimar and Erfurt.

ESSENTIALS

Visitor Information Eisenach ☒ *Eisenach-Information, Markt 24* ☎ *03691/79230* 🖷 *03691/792–320* ⊕ *www.eisenach.de.*

EXPLORING

Bachhaus. Johann Sebastian Bach was born in Eisenach in 1685. The Bachhaus has exhibits devoted to the entire lineage of the musical Bach family and includes a collection of historical musical instruments. It is the largest collection of Bach memorabilia in the world, and includes a bust of the composer built using forensic science from a cast of his skull. ⊠ *Frauenplan 21* ☎ *03691/79340* ⊕ *www.bachhaus.de* ✎ *€7.50* ⊙ *Daily 10–6.*

Lutherhaus. The Lutherhaus, in downtown Eisenach, has many fascinating exhibits illustrating the life of Martin Luther, who lived here as a student. ⊠ *Lutherpl. 8* ☎ *03691/29830* ⊕ *www.lutherhaus-eisenach.de* ✎ *€4.50* ⊙ *Daily 10–5.*

Narrowest house. At Johannesplatz 9, look for what is said to be the narrowest house in eastern Germany, built in 1890; its width is just over 6 feet, 8 inches; its height, 24½ feet; and its depth, 34 feet.

Reuter-Wagner-Museum. Composer Richard Wagner gets his due at the Reuter-Wagner-Museum, which has the most comprehensive exhibition on Wagner's life and work outside Bayreuth. Monthly concerts take place in the old **Teezimmer** (tearoom), a hall with wonderfully restored French wallpaper. The Erard piano, dating from the late 19th century, is occasionally rolled out. ⊠ *Reuterweg 2* ☎ *03691/743–293* ✎ *€4* ⊙ *Tues.–Wed., and Fri.–Sun. 11–5; Thurs. 3–8.*

FodorśChoice
★
Wartburg Castle. Begun in 1067 (and expanded through the centuries), the mighty Wartburg Castle has hosted a parade of German celebrities. Hermann I (1156–1217), count of Thuringia and count palatine of Saxony, was a patron of the poets Walther von der Vogelweide (1170–1230) and Wolfram von Eschenbach (1170–1220). Legend has it that this is where Walther von der Vogelweide, the greatest lyric poet of medieval Germany, prevailed in the celebrated *Minnesängerstreit* (minnesinger contest), which is featured in Richard Wagner's *Tannhäuser*.

Within the castle's stout walls, Frederick the Wise (1463–1525) shielded Martin Luther from papal proscription from May 1521 until March 1522, even though Frederick did not share the reformer's beliefs. Luther completed the first translation of the New Testament from Greek into German while in hiding, an act that paved the way for the Protestant Reformation. You can peek into the simple study in which Luther worked. ■ TIP➔ Be sure to check out the place where Luther saw the devil and threw an inkwell at him. Pilgrims have picked away at the spot for centuries, forcing the curators to "reapply" the ink.

Frederick was also a patron of the arts. Lucas Cranach the Elder's portraits of Luther and his wife are on view in the castle, as is a very moving sculpture, the *Leuchterengelpaar* (Candlestick Angel Group), by the great 15th-century artist Tilman Riemenschneider. The 13th-century great hall is breathtaking; it's here that the minstrels sang for courtly favors. ■ TIP➔ Don't leave without climbing the belvedere for a panoramic view of the Harz Mountains and the Thuringian Forest. ☎ *03691/2500* ⊕ *www.wartburg-eisenach.de* ✎ *€9, including guided tour* ⊙ *Nov.–Feb., daily 9–3:30; Mar.–Oct., daily 8:30–5.*

WHERE TO STAY

For expanded hotel reviews, visit Fodors.com.

$$$$ **Hotel auf der Wartburg.** In this castle hotel, where Martin Luther, Johann Sebastian Bach, and Richard Wagner were guests, you'll get a splendid view over the town and the countryside. **Pros:** medieval music and fireplaces in the lobby. **Cons:** it's a hike to and from the city center. ⊠ *Wartburg* ☎ *03691/7970* ⊕ *www.wartburghotel.de* ⌐ *35 rooms* ♧ *In-room: no a/c, Wi-Fi. In-hotel: restaurant, parking, some pets allowed* ⦿ *Breakfast.*

$ **Hotel Glockenhof.** At the base of Wartburg Castle, this former church-run hostel has blossomed into a handsome hotel, cleverly incorporating the original half-timber city mansion into a modern extension. **Pros:** out of the hustle and bustle of the downtown; plenty of parking; an incredible breakfast buffet. **Cons:** uphill walk from the station is strenuous; location is a bit far from the city center. ⊠ *Grimmelg. 4* ☎ *03691/2340* ⊕ *www.glockenhof.de* ⌐ *38 rooms, 2 suites* ♧ *In-room: no a/c, Internet. In-hotel: restaurant, parking, some pets allowed* ⦿ *Breakfast.*

ERFURT

55 km (34 mi) east of Eisenach.

The city of Erfurt emerged from World War II relatively unscathed, with most of its innumerable towers intact. Of all the cities in the region, Erfurt is the most evocative of its prewar self, and it's easy to imagine that many of the towns in northern Germany would look like this had they not been destroyed. The city's highly decorative and colorful facades are easy to admire on a walking tour. ■ TIP→ Downtown Erfurt is a photographer's delight, with narrow, busy, ancient streets dominated by a magnificent 14th-century Gothic cathedral, the Mariendom.

ESSENTIALS

Visitor Information Erfurt ⊠ *Tourist-Information, Benediktspl. 1* ☎ *0361/66400* 🖷 *0361/664–0290* ⊕ *www.erfurt-tourist-info.de.*

EXPLORING

Anger. Erfurt's main transportation hub and pedestrian zone, the Anger, developed as a result of urban expansion due to the growth of the railroad in Thuringia in the early 19th century. With some exceptions, the houses are all architecturally historicized, making them look much older than they really are. Look for the **Hauptpostgebäude,** which was erected in 1892 in a mock Gothic style. he **Bartholomäusturm** (Bartholomew Tower), the base of a 12th-century tower, holds a 60-bell carillon.

Domplatz (*Cathedral Square*). The Domplatz is bordered by houses dating from the 16th century.

Klein Venedig (*Little Venice*). The area around the bridge, crisscrossed with old streets lined with picturesque and often crumbling homes, is known as Klein Venedig because of the recurrent flooding it endures.

★   **Krämerbrücke** (*Merchant's Bridge*). Behind the predominantly neo-Gothic Rathaus you'll find Erfurt's most outstanding attraction spanning the Gera River, the Krämerbrücke. This Renaissance bridge, similar to the Ponte Vecchio in Florence, is the longest of its kind in Europe and the only one north of the Alps. Built in 1325 and restored in 1967–73, the bridge served for centuries as an important trading center. Today antiques shops fill the majority of the timber-frame houses built into the bridge, some dating from the 16th century. The bridge comes alive on the third weekend of June for the Krämerbrückenfest.

★ **Mariendom** (*St. Mary's Cathedral*). The Mariendom is reached by way of a broad staircase from the expansive Cathedral Square. Its Romanesque origins (foundations can be seen in the crypt) are best preserved in the choir's glorious stained-glass windows and beautifully carved stalls. The cathedral's biggest bell, the Gloriosa, is the largest free-swinging bell in the world. Cast in 1497, it took three years to install in the tallest of the three sharply pointed towers, painstakingly lifted inch by inch with wooden wedges. No chances are taken with this 2-ton treasure; its deep boom resonates only on special occasions, such as Christmas and New Year's. ✉ *Dompl.* ☎ *0361/646–1265* 🎫 *Tour €2.50* ⊘ *May–Oct., Mon.–Sat. 9–5, Sun. 1–4; Nov.–Apr., Mon.–Sat. 10–11:30 and 12:30–4, Sun. 1–4.*

St. Augustin Kloster (*St. Augustine Monastery*). The young Martin Luther studied the liberal arts as well as law and theology at Erfurt University from 1501 to 1505. After a personal revelation, Luther asked to become a monk in the St. Augustin Kloster on July 17, 1505. He became an ordained priest here in 1507, and remained at the Kloster until 1511. Today the Kloster is a seminary and retreat hotel. ✉ *Augustinerstr. 10* ☎ *0361/576–600* ⊕ *www.augustinerkloster.de* ⊘ *Mon.–Sat. 10–noon and 2–4, irregular Sun. hrs.*

St. Severus. The Gothic church of St. Severus has an extraordinary font, a masterpiece of intricately carved sandstone that reaches practically to the ceiling. It's linked to the cathedral by a 70-step open staircase.

Zum Stockfisch. Erfurt's interesting local-history museum is in a late-Renaissance house, Zum Stockfisch. ✉ *Johannesstr. 169* ☎ *0361/655–5644* 🎫 *Museum €4* ⊘ *Tues.–Sun. 10–6.*

WHERE TO EAT

$$$$
GERMAN
★
✕ **Alboth's.** This restaurant in the historic, elegant Kaisersaal edifice is the star in Erfurt's small gourmet sky. Chef Claus Alboth has worked in various top restaurants in Berlin, and now develops his own style and vision of a gourmet restaurant: a cozy, service-oriented oasis in which to enjoy delicious international dishes with a Thuringian accent. Alboth's serves delicious four- and five-course menus. Try the *Thüringenmenü*, a set four-course dinner with local specialties such as ravioli filled with Thuringian blood sausage. The wine list is one of the best in eastern Germany, offering more than 300 vintages from around the world. ✉ *Futterstr. 1, 15–16* ☎ *0361/568–8207* ⊕ *www.alboths.de* ⊘ *Closed Sun. and Mon. No lunch. Usually closed Jan. and/or Feb.*

$
GERMAN
✕ **Faustus Restaurant.** In the heart of historic Erfurt the stylish Faustus defines fine Thuringian dining. This restaurant is in an old mansion, with both an inviting summer terrace and a bright, airy dining room. An after-dinner drink at the superb bar is a must. ✉ *Wenigermarkt 5* ☎ *0361/540–0954* ▭ *No credit cards.*

16

$ ✕ **Luther Keller.** Head down the straw-covered stairs in front of Alboth's
GERMAN   restaurant, and you'll find yourself transported to the Middle Ages.
The Luther Keller offers simple but tasty medieval cuisine in a candlelit vaulted cellar. Magicians, minnesingers, jugglers, and other players round out the enjoyable experience. Sure, it's pure kitsch, but it
is entertaining, and the roast wild boar is delicious. ⊠ *Futterstr. 15*
☎ *0361/568–8205* ☾ *Closed Mon. and Sun. No lunch.*

$ ✕ **Zum Goldenen Schwan.** Beer lovers rejoice: in addition to the Braugold
GERMAN   brewery, Erfurt has six brewpubs, among which this is by far the best.
The house beer is a pleasant unfiltered *Kellerbier,* and other beers are
brewed according to the season. The constantly changing seasonal menu
is a step above normal brewpub fare and their sauerbraten defines how
the dish should be made. ⊠ *Michaelisstr. 9* ☎ *0361/262–3742* ☾ *Daily
11 am–1 am.*

WHERE TO STAY

For expanded hotel reviews, visit Fodors.com.

$$ ⊡ **Radisson Blu Hotel Erfurt.** Since the SAS group gave the ugly high-rise
Kosmos a face-lift, the socialist-realist look of the GDR years no longer
intrudes on Hotel Erfurt. **Pros:** a safe, clean option in the city center;
good restaurant. **Cons:** rather characterless business hotel. ⊠ *Juri-
Gagarin-Ring 127* ☎ *0361/55100* ⊕ *www.radissonblu.com* ⤢ *282
rooms, 3 suites* ⚐ *In-room: Wi-Fi. In-hotel: restaurant, bar, gym, spa,
parking, some pets allowed* ¶❍¶ *Breakfast.*

WEIMAR

21 km (13 mi) east of Erfurt.

Sitting prettily in the geographical center of Thuringia, Weimar occupies
a place in German political and cultural history completely dispropor-
tionate to its size (population 63,000). It's not even particularly old
by German standards, with a civic history that started as late as 1410.
Yet by the early 19th century the city had become one of Europe's
most important cultural centers, where poets Goethe and Schiller wrote,
Johann Sebastian Bach played the organ for his Saxon patrons, Carl
Maria von Weber composed some of his best music, and Franz Liszt was
director of music, presenting the first performance of *Lohengrin* here. In
1919 Walter Gropius founded his Staatliches Bauhaus here, and behind
the classical pillars of the National Theater the German National Assem-
bly drew up the constitution of the Weimar Republic, the first German
democracy. After the collapse of the Weimar government, Hitler chose
the little city as the site for the first national congress of his Nazi party.
On the outskirts of Weimar the Nazis built—or forced prisoners to build
for them—the infamous Buchenwald concentration camp.

GETTING HERE AND AROUND

Weimar is on the ICE line between Dresden/Leipzig and Frankfurt.
IC trains link the city with Berlin. Weimar has an efficient bus system,
but most sights are within walking distance in the compact city center.

ESSENTIALS

Visitor Information Weimar ✉ *Tourist-Information Weimar, Markt 10* ☎ *03643/7450* 🖷 *03643/745–420* ⊕ *www.weimar.de.*

EXPLORING

Bauhaus Museum. Walter Gropius founded the Staatliches Bauhaus, or Bauhaus design school in Weimar in 1919. It was Germany's most influential and avant-garde design school, and it ushered in the era of modern architecture and design just before the start of World War II. Although the school moved to Dessau in 1925, Weimar's Bauhaus Museum is a modest, yet superb collection of the works of Gropius, Johannes Itten, and Henry van de Velde. ✉ *Theaterpl.* ☎ *03643/545–961* ⊕ *www.klassik-stiftung.de* 🖃 *€4.50* ⊙ *Nov.–Mar., Tues.–Sun. 10–4; Apr.–Oct., Tues.–Sun. 10–6.*

OFF THE
BEATEN
PATH

Gedenkstätte Buchenwald. Just north of Weimar, amid the natural beauty of the Ettersberg hills that once served as Goethe's inspiration, sits the blight of Buchenwald, one of the most infamous Nazi concentration camps. Sixty-five thousand men, women, and children from 35 countries met their deaths here through forced labor, starvation, disease, and gruesome medical experiments. Each is commemorated by a small stone placed on the outlines of the barracks, which have long since disappeared from the site, and by a massive memorial tower. In an especially cruel twist of fate, many liberated inmates returned to the camp as political prisoners of the Soviet occupation; they are remembered in the exhibit Soviet Special Camp #2. Besides exhibits, tours are available. To reach Buchenwald by public transportation, take Bus 6 (in the direction of Buchenwald, not Ettersburg), which leaves every 10 minutes from Goetheplatz in downtown Weimar. The one-way fare is €1.25. ☎ *03643/4300* ⊕ *www.buchenwald.de* 🖃 *Free* ⊙ *May–Sept., Tues.–Sun. 10–5:30; Oct.–Apr., Tues.–Sun. 9–4:30.*

16

Fodor'sChoice ★ **Goethe Nationalmuseum** (*Goethe National Museum*). Goethe spent 57 years in Weimar, 47 of them in a house two blocks south of Theaterplatz that has since become a shrine attracting millions of visitors. The Goethe Nationalmuseum consists of several houses, including the **Goethehaus,** where Goethe lived. It shows an exhibit about life in Weimar around 1750 and contains writings that illustrate not only the great man's literary might but also his interest in the sciences, particularly medicine, and his administrative skills (and frustrations) as minister of state and Weimar's exchequer. You'll see the desk at which Goethe stood to write (he liked to work standing up) and the modest bed in which he died. The rooms are dark and often cramped, but an almost palpable intellectual intensity seems to illuminate them. ✉ *Frauenplan 1* ☎ *03643/545–320* ⊕ *www.weimar-klassik.de/english* 🖃 *€8.50* ⊙ *Nov.–Mar., Tues.–Fri., and Sun. 9–4, Sat. 9–7; Apr.–Oct., Tues.–Sun. 9–6.*

Goethes Gartenhaus (*Garden House*). Goethe's beloved Gartenhaus is a modest country cottage where he spent many happy hours, wrote much poetry, and began his masterly classical drama *Iphigenie*. The house is set amid meadowlike parkland on the bank of the River Ilm. Goethe is said to have felt very close to nature here, and you can soak up the same rural atmosphere on footpaths along the peaceful little river.

Take a carriage ride through Weimar to absorb the city's impressive history.

✉ *Im Park an der Ilm, Hans-Wahl-Str. 4* ☎ *03643/545–375* ⊕ *www. weimar-klassik.de/english* 🎟 *Cottage €4.50* ⊙ *Nov.–Mar., daily 10–4; Apr.–Oct., daily 9–6.*

Herderkirche. On the central town square, at the Herderkirche (two blocks east of Theaterplatz), you'll find the home of Lucas Cranach the Elder. Cranach lived here during his last years, 1552–53. Its wide, imposing facade is richly decorated and bears the coat of arms of the Cranach family. It now houses a modern art gallery. The Marktplatz's late-Gothic **Herderkirche** (Herder Church) has a large winged altar started by Lucas Cranach the Elder and finished by his son in 1555.

Historischer Friedhof (*Historic Cemetery*). Goethe and Schiller are buried in the Historischer Friedhof, a leafy cemetery where virtually every gravestone commemorates a famous citizen of Weimar. Their tombs are in the vault of the classical-style chapel. The cemetery is a short walk past Goethehaus and Wieland Platz. ✉ *Am Poseckschen Garten* ☎ *03643/545–400* 🎟 *Goethe-Schiller vault €2.50* ⊙ *Nov.–Mar., Wed.–Mon. 10–1 and 2–4; Apr.–Oct., Wed.–Mon. 9–1 and 2–6.*

Neues Museum Weimar (*New Museum Weimar*). The city is proud of the Neues Museum Weimar, eastern Germany's first museum exclusively devoted to contemporary art. The building, dating from 1869, was carefully restored and converted to hold collections of American minimalist and conceptual art and works by German installation-artist Anselm Kiefer and American painter Keith Haring. In addition, it regularly presents international modern-art exhibitions. ✉ *Weimarpl. 5* ☎ *03643/545–930* ⊕ *www.kunstsammlungen-weimar.de* 🎟 *€5.50* ⊙ *Apr.–Oct., Tues.–Sun. 11–6; Nov.–Mar., Tues.–Sun. 11–4.*

Schillerhaus. The Schillerhaus, a green-shuttered residence and part of the Goethe National Museum, is on a tree-shaded square not far from Goethe's house. Schiller and his family spent a happy, all-too-brief three years here (he died here in 1805). Schiller's study is tucked underneath the mansard roof, a cozy room dominated by his desk, where he probably completed *Wilhelm Tell*. Much of the remaining furniture and the collection of books were added later, although they all date from around Schiller's time. ⊠ *Schillerstr. 17* ☎ *03643/545–350* ⊕ *www.klassik-stiftung. de* ⊡ *€5* ⊘ *Nov.–Mar., Wed.–Mon. 9–4; Apr.–Oct., Wed.–Mon. 9–6.*

★ **Stadtschloss** (*City Castle*). Weimar's 16th-century Stadtschloss is around the corner from the Herderkirche. It has a finely restored classical staircase, a festival hall, and a falcon gallery. The tower on the southwest projection dates from the Middle Ages, but received its baroque overlay circa 1730. The **Kunstsammlung** (art collection) here includes several works by Cranach the Elder and many early-20th-century pieces by such artists as Böcklin, Liebermann, and Beckmann. ⊠ *Burgpl. 4* ☎ *03643/545–930* ⊕ *www.klassik-stiftung.de* ⊡ *€3* ⊘ *Apr.–Oct., Tues.–Sun. 10–6; Nov.–Mar., Tues.–Sun. 10–4.*

Theaterplatz. A statue on Theaterplatz, in front of the National Theater, shows Goethe placing a paternal hand on the shoulder of the younger Schiller.

16

Wittumspalais (*Wittum Mansion*). Much of Weimar's greatness is owed to its patron, the widowed countess Anna Amalia, whose home, the Wittumspalais, is surprisingly modest. In the late 18th century the countess went talent hunting for cultural figures to decorate the glittering court her Saxon forebears had established. Goethe was one of her finds, and he served the countess as a counselor, advising her on financial matters and town design. Schiller followed, and he and Goethe became valued visitors to the countess's home. Within this exquisite baroque house you can see the drawing room in which she held soirées, complete with the original cherrywood table at which the company sat. The east wing of the house contains a small museum that's a fascinating memorial to those cultural gatherings. ⊠ *Am Theaterpl.* ☎ *03643/545–377* ⊡ *€5* ⊘ *Nov.–Mar., Tues.–Sun. 10–4; Apr.–Oct., Tues.–Sun. 9–6.*

WHERE TO EAT

¢ ✕ **Felsenkeller.** When Ludwig Deinhard purchased the Weimar Stadt-
GERMAN brauerei in 1875, Felsenkeller was already 100 years old. Beer has been brewed here in small batches ever since. Although the brewpub is outside the city center, it's worth a trip to sample the brews and the inventive seasonal selections. The pub serves standard fare at reasonable prices. ⊠ *Humboldtstr. 37* ☎ *03643/414–741* ⊟ *No credit cards* ⊘ *Closed Mon.*

$ ✕ **Ratskeller.** This is one of the region's most authentic town hall–cellar
GERMAN restaurants. Its whitewashed, barrel-vaulted ceiling has witnessed centuries of tradition. At the side is a cozy bar, where you can enjoy a preprandial drink beneath a stunning art nouveau skylight. The delicious sauerbraten and the famous bratwurst (with sauerkraut and mashed potatoes) are the highlights of the Thuringian menu. If venison is in season, try it—likewise the wild duck or wild boar in red-wine sauce. ⊠ *Am Markt 10* ☎ *03643/850–573.*

$ ✕ **Scharfe Ecke.** If *klösse* (dumplings) are a religion, this restaurant is
GERMAN   their cathedral. Thuringia's traditional klösse are at their best here, but
🕑   be patient—they're made to order and can take 20 minutes. The klösse
★   come with just about every dish, from roast pork to venison stew, and
the wait is well worth it. The ideal accompaniment to anything on the
menu is one of the three locally brewed beers on tap or the fine selection of Salle-Unstrut wines. ⊠ *Eisfeld 2* ☎ *03643/202–430* ⊟ *No credit
cards* ⊗ *Closed Mon.*

$ ✕ **Sommer's Weinstuben und Restaurant.** The city's oldest pub and restau-
GERMAN   rant, a 130-year-old landmark in the center of Weimar, is still going
strong. The authentic Thuringian specialties and huge *Kartoffelpfan-
nen* (potato pans), with fried potatoes and various kinds of meat, are
prepared by the fifth generation of the Sommer family, and are as tasty
as ever. Add to that the superb wine list with some rare vintages from
local vineyards and the romantic courtyard, and your Weimar experience will be perfect. ⊠ *Humboldtstr. 2* ☎ *03643/400–691* ⊟ *No credit
cards* ⊗ *Closed Sun. No lunch.*

WHERE TO STAY
For expanded hotel reviews, visit Fodors.com.

$ 🏨 **Amalienhof VCH Hotel.** Book far ahead to secure a room at this friendly
little hotel central to Weimar's attractions. **Pros:** surprisingly good value;
rooms are often upgraded to the highest available category at check-in.
Cons: street noise can be bothersome. ⊠ *Amalienstr. 2* ☎ *03643/5490*
⊕ *www.amalienhof-weimar.de* ⤴ *23 rooms, 9 apartments* ⌂ *In-room:
no a/c. In-hotel: parking, some pets allowed* ⧙⧘ *Breakfast.*

$$ 🏨 **Grand Hotel Russischer Hof.** This historic, classical hotel, once the haunt
Fodor'sChoice   of European nobility and intellectual society, continues to be a luxuri-
★   ous gem in the heart of Weimar—it's one of eastern Germany's finest
hotels. **Pros:** a quiet hotel in the city center. **Cons:** rooms are on the
small side, with thin walls; some overlook an unsightly back courtyard.
⊠ *Goethepl. 2* ☎ *03643/7740* ⊕ *www.russischerhof.com* ⤴ *119 rooms,
6 suites* ⌂ *In-room: Internet. In-hotel: restaurant, bar, parking, some
pets allowed.*

$$ 🏨 **Hotel Elephant.** The historic Elephant, dating from 1696, has been
Fodor'sChoice   famous for its charm—even through the Communist years. **Pros:** a beau-
★   tiful historical building right in the city center. **Cons:** no air-conditioning;
rooms in the front are sometimes bothered by the town clock if windows
are open. ⊠ *Markt 19* ☎ *03643/8020* ⊕ *www.hotelelephantweimar.com*
⤴ *94 rooms, 5 suites* ⌂ *In-room: no a/c, Internet, Wi-Fi. In-hotel: restaurant, bar, parking, some pets allowed* ⧙⧘ *Breakfast.*